THE
CALIFORNIA
DOG LOVER'S
COMPANION

By Maria Goodavage

Foghorn
Press
BOOKS BUILDING COMMUNITY™

1-57354-046-3

Foghorn Outdoors' guidebooks are available wherever books are sold. To find a retailer near you or to order, call 1-800-FOGHORN (364-4676) or (707) 521-3300 or visit the Foghorn Press Web site at www.foghorn.com. Foghorn Press titles are available to the book trade through Publishers Group West (800-788-3123) as well as through wholesalers.

Library of Congress ISSN Data:
June 1998
The California Dog Lover's Companion:
The Inside Scoop on Where to Take Your Dog
Third Edition
ISSN: 1086-7856

CONTENTS

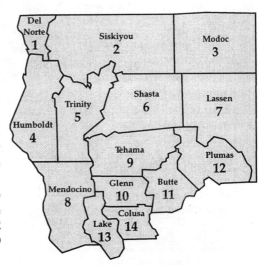

Bay Area/Delta Counties

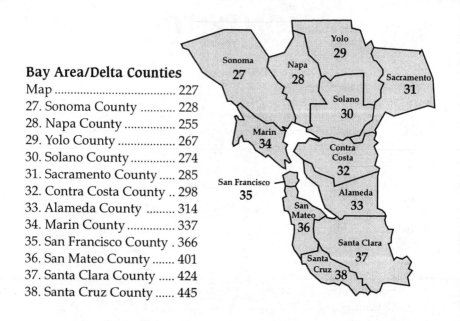

Central Area Counties

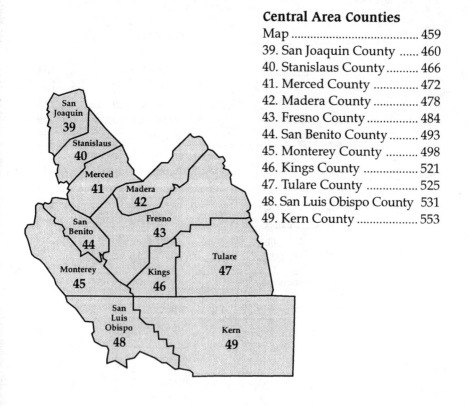

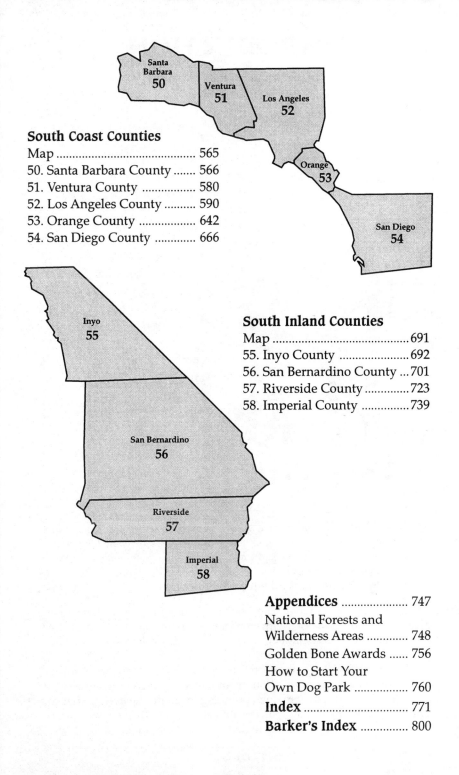

South Coast Counties

South Inland Counties

INTRODUCTION

"Now, Charley is a mind-reading dog. There have been many trips in his lifetime, and often he has to be left at home. He knows we are going long before the suitcases come out, and he paces and worries and whines and goes into a state of mild hysteria, old as he is."
From *Travels with Charley,* by John Steinbeck.

There was a time when dogs could go just about anywhere they pleased. Well-dressed dogs with embarrassing names attended afternoon teas, while their less-kempt counterparts sauntered into saloons without anyone blinking a bloodshot eye.

No one thought it strange to see a pug-nosed little snoochum-woochums of a dog snuggled on his mistress' lap on a long train journey. Equally accepted were dogs prancing through fine hotels, dogs at dining establishments, and dogs in almost any park they cared to visit.

But as the world gets more crowded and patience grows thinner, fewer and fewer places permit dogs. As deep as the human-dog bond goes, people seem to feel increasing pressure to leave their dogs behind when they take to the open road.

The guilt that stabs at you as you push your dog's struggling body back inside the house and tug the door shut can be so painful that sometimes you just can't look back. Even a trip to the grocery store can become a heart-wrenching tale of woe. A recent survey by the American Animal Hospital Association showed that 76 percent of pet owners feel guilty when leaving their pet at home, and that's including cat owners and even iguana owners! Without them, there's no telling how high the dog people guilt number would be.

Joe, my Airedale terrier, was born with an unparalleled gift for knowing how to make people feel guilty—and not your ordinary, run-of-the-mill guilt where you smart for a couple of hours after seeing your dog's moping eyes follow your car as you speed away. It's that deep-in-the-gut-for-days guilt, where the sight of that pouting snout, those drooping ears, and that tail lowered to half-mast hangs with you until you return home.

John Steinbeck's blue poodle, Charley, was a master of powerful pleas that were carefully designed to allow him to accompany his people on trips. Eventually, his hard work paid off and he won himself a seat in Steinbeck's brand-new truck/house on their epic journey across America. They sought and found the heart of this country in their adventures across 34 states.

Joe's guilt-inducing expertise won him a spot in my rusty, beat-up, hiccuping pickup truck in our sporadic little journeys throughout California. We sought and found thousands of dog-friendly places in our adventures and misadventures through California's 58 counties.

Joe and I were frequently joined by two other experts in the field of rating parks and sniffing out good dog attractions. Nisha, our old-lady springer spaniel, insisted on standing in the back of the truck, under the camper top, madly wagging her tail for hours on end as we drove and drove and drove. She was a real asset to have around when it came to checking out beaches, lakes, rivers, and ponds—any area with water. (Joe hates to get his paws wet, so he couldn't be impartial in his rating of watery attractions.)

Bill, a big, lovable galoot of a dog, was my other canine researcher. I found him partway through my travels. He was trembling in the middle of a Northern California road, with a big chain tight around his neck. He'd evidently broken loose, because the last link of the thick chain was mauled. I came to find out that his owner beat him regularly. Bill went back to San Francisco with me that afternoon.

During the months when I was looking for the perfect home for him, he became one of the friendliest, most outgoing dogs I've ever had the pleasure to meet. His presence during my journeys was invaluable. He lifted my spirits when I was tired, and his 85 pounds of muscle kept away bad spirits when we visited questionable areas. (Bill, by the way, found an incredible home. Actually, two. His wonderful people spend half their time at their large San Francisco home, which has a big redwood in the backyard, and half their time at their home on 200 acres of Sierra Nevada heaven. Lucky dog!)

You'll be meeting up with the three dogs throughout this book. I think you'll find them fine representatives of the 5.7 million dogs who live in California. (The dog population was derived by the American Veterinary Medical Association from the group's recent survey of 80,000 California households.)

Many of the areas we visited together had higher elevations than populations. Those were often our favorite places. "The remoter, the better" seems to be the creed of dogs everywhere. People in relaxed, out-of-the-way communities would sometimes call a leash a "leach." Or a "lease." No wonder dogs love the countryside.

These were some of the most polite folks I came across. Sometimes people I met in urban areas would immediately ask me why I was traveling alone with dogs—was I running away from something, or just trying to find myself? The more rural folks would smile at me, nod at the dogs, and ask no pointed questions. They'd feel around in an indirect manner ("You don't see that brand of dog much anymore. Did you travel far with him?"), but they'd rarely come right out with a heat-seeking missile of a question.

I spent a good deal of time in these less-populated areas, because during my research, I discovered an amazing statistic: Far from the reaches of most cities, 40 percent of California is open to dogs who are obedient enough to be off leash. Wowza—40 percent! I normally jump for joy to find two acres that permit off-leash pooches, but 40 million acres? The thought is enough to make a grown dog swoon. This amazing acreage is part of two federal entities—the Bureau of Land Management and the U.S. Department of Agriculture's Forest Service. I've described many of these parcels throughout the book. The national forests also have their own chapter here (see page 748). If you have a dog who longs to be a real off-leash explorer, take advantage of California's wealth of leash-free lands.

I've tried to find the very best of everything you can do with your dog in California, so you'll never again have to face the prospect of shutting the door on your dog's nose. This book is packed with descriptions of thousands of dog-friendly parks, restaurants with outdoor tables, and lodgings. The book also describes dozens of unusual adventures you and your dog can share in this crazy Golden State. You can ride on steam trains, ferries, and surreys. You can gaze at the stars with an astronomy club or sip sauvignon together at a winery whose logo is a dog. You can pan for gold, attend a San Francisco Giants game, march in pet parades, visit small museums, go to drive-in movies, and shop at high-fashion stores. You can even get married, with your dog serving as flower girl or best man.

This third edition of the book is the most fun-packed yet. We've added hundreds of new places to go with your dog, many of them discovered through readers whose dogs insist on writing to tell us about their favorite new park or a cool eatery or a pooch-loving hotel. We're so grateful to these dogs that, whenever possible, we acknowledge them under the new listing. (See page 20 for easy new ways to get in touch with us with your hot dog tips.)

We're also very excited about the launching of "The Golden Bone Awards" in this edition. These soon-to-be-coveted awards go to inns, stores, restaurants, and other special businesses that roll out the welcome rug for dogs in an especially delightful way. Recipients get a certificate suitable for framing, and the knowledge that they're putting smiles on the snouts of many a California canine. Please see page 756 for this edition's Golden Bone winners.

Other changes in the book include a new category called "Doggy Days" (for festivals and fun events revolving around dogs) and a brand-new chapter on how to start a dog park in your own community. More on that later, in the "To Leash or Not to Leash" section of the introduction.

In our travels for the new edition of the book, Joe and I came to find a more dog-friendly demeanor across the board than we found a few years ago. Even the dogs we ran into seemed happier. In many ways, California seems to be becoming even a better place to be a dog than it was before. Dogs are going to work more with their people, they're going on vacations, and they're assuming their rightful role as an integral part of the family. Tails are wagging so much these days in California that you can almost feel the breeze. And you thought it was El Niño.

THE PAWS SCALE

At some point, we've got to face the facts: Humans and dogs have different tastes. We like eating oranges and smelling lilacs and covering our bodies with soft clothes. They like eating roadkill and smelling each other's unmentionables and covering their bodies with horse manure.

The parks, beaches, and recreation areas in this book are rated with a dog in mind. Maybe your favorite park has lush gardens, a duck pond, a few acres of perfectly manicured lawns, and sweeping views of a nearby skyline. But unless your dog can run leash-free, swim in the pond, and roll in the grass, that park doesn't deserve a very high rating.

The very lowest rating you'll come across in this book is the fire hydrant symbol (🔥). When you see it, that means the park is merely "worth a squat." Visit one of these parks only if your dog just can't hold it any longer. These parks have virtually no other redeeming qualities for canines.

Beyond that, the paws scale starts at one paw (🐾) and goes up to four paws (🐾🐾🐾🐾), with increments of half a paw in between (such as 🐾🐾½). A one-paw park isn't a dog's idea of a great time. Maybe it's a tiny park with few trees and too many kids running around. Or perhaps it's a magnificent-for-people national park that bans dogs from every inch of land except paved roads and a few campsites. Four-paw parks, on the other hand, are places your dog will drag you to visit. Some of these areas come as close to dog heaven as you can get on this planet. Many have water for swimming or zillions of acres for hiking. Some are small, fenced-in areas where leash-free dogs can tear around without danger of running into the road. Just about all four-paw parks give you the option of letting your dog off leash (although most have restrictions, which I detail in the descriptions).

This book is not a comprehensive guide to all of the parks in California. If a book included all the parks, it would be larger than a multivolume set of *Encyclopedia Brittanica*. I tried to find the best, largest, and most convenient parks. Some counties have so many wonderful parks that I had to make some tough choices in deciding which to include and which to leave out. Other counties had such a limited supply of parks that, for the sake of dogs living and visiting there, I ended up listing parks that wouldn't otherwise be worth mentioning.

I've given very specific directions to the major parks and to parks located near highways. Other parks are listed by their cross streets. I highly recommend picking up detailed street maps from the California Automobile Association (they're free to members) before you and your dog set out on your adventures.

Note: I'll no longer be using the foot (◀●) symbol, which in previous editions indicated places humans would find interesting. I found this was such a subjective rating that it wasn't worth it. Some people think just about any park is wonderful, others need trees, others prefer perfectly manicured places, others long for historic parks, others only want to rough it on long trails, and on and on. So from now on, the only feet you'll see here are dog feet.

TO LEASH OR NOT TO LEASH

That is not a question that plagues dogs' minds. Ask just about any normal, red-blooded American dog if she'd prefer to visit a park and be on leash or off, and she'll say "Arf!" No question about it, most dogs would give their canine teeth to be able to frolic about without a cumbersome leash.

When you see the running dog symbol in this book (🐕), you'll know that under certain circumstances, your dog can run around in leash-free bliss. Fortunately, California is home to dozens of such parks. The rest of the parks demand leashes. I wish I could write about the parks where dogs get away with being scofflaws. Unfortunately, those would be the first parks the animal control patrols would hit. I don't advocate breaking the law, but if you're going to, please follow your conscience and use common sense.

And just because dogs are permitted off leash in certain areas doesn't necessarily mean you should let your dog run free. In national forests and large tracts of wild land, unless you're sure your dog will come back to you when you call or will never stray more than a few yards from your side, you should probably keep her leashed. An otherwise docile homebody can turn into a savage hunter if the right prey is near. Or your curious dog could perturb a rattlesnake or dig up a rodent whose fleas carry bubonic plague. In pursuit of a strange scent, your dog could easily get lost in an unfamiliar area. (Some forest rangers recommend having your dog wear a bright orange collar, vest, or backpack when you're out in the wilderness.) And there are many places where certain animals would love to have your dog for dinner—and not in a way Miss Manners would condone. Be careful out there.

If your dog really needs leash-free exercise but can't be trusted off leash in remote areas, she'll be happy to know that several beaches permit well-behaved, leashless pooches, as do a growing number of beautiful, fenced-in dog exercise areas. The San Francisco Bay Area is the best place to find such off-leash freedom, but many other parts of California are starting to follow suit.

Fenced-in dog parks are the fastest-growing types of parks for pooches. In fact, back when this book was in its first edition, there were only six fenced-in dog parks in the state. Now there are more than 30! And more are in the works. Dogs with a disdain for leashes are applauding wildly. Aroooo! If you're interested in starting a dog park in your own community, you'll want to check out the brand-new chapter called "How to Start Your Own Dog Park." (We don't beat around the bush.) It begins on page 760. If you succeed in starting one, please get in touch with me at the phone number or address listed at the end of the introduction and we'll check out your park for the next edition. Good luck!

THERE'S NO BUSINESS LIKE DOG BUSINESS

There's nothing appealing about bending down with a plastic bag or a piece of newspaper on a chilly morning and grabbing the steaming remnants of what your dog ate for dinner the night before. It's disgusting. Worse yet, you have to hang onto it until you can find a trash can. And how about when the newspaper doesn't endure before you can dispose of it? Yuk! It's enough to make you wish your dog could wear diapers. But as gross as it can be to scoop the poop, it's worse to step in it. It's really bad if a child falls in it, or—gasp!—starts eating it. And have you ever walked into a park where few people clean up after their dog? The stench could make a hog want to hibernate.

Unscooped poop is one of a dog's worst enemies. Public policies banning dogs from parks are enacted because of it. At present, a few good California parks and beaches that permit dogs are in danger of closing their gates to all canines because of the negligent behavior of a few owners. A worst-case scenario is already in place in several California communities—dogs are banned from all parks. Their only exercise is a leashed sidewalk stroll. That's no way to live.

Just be responsible and clean up after your dog everywhere you go. Stuff plastic bags in your jackets, your purse, your car, your pants pockets—anywhere you might be able to pull one out when needed. Or if plastic isn't your bag, newspapers do the trick. If it makes it more palatable, bring along a paper bag, too, and put the used newspaper or plastic bag in it. That way you don't have to walk around with dripping paper or a plastic bag whose contents are visible to the world. If you don't enjoy the squishy sensation, try one of those cardboard or plastic bag pooper-scoopers sold at pet stores. If you don't feel like bending down, buy a long-handled scooper. There's a scooper for every taste.

This is the only lecture you'll get on scooping in this entire book. To help keep parks alive, I should harp on it in every park description, but that would take another 100 pages, and you'd start to ignore it anyway. And if I mentioned it in some parks and not others, it might convey that you don't have to clean up after your dog in the descriptions where it's not mentioned.

A final note: Don't pretend not to see your dog while he's doing his bit. And don't pretend to look for it without success. And don't fake scooping it up when you're really just covering it with sand. I know these tricks because I've been guilty of them myself—but no more. I've seen the light. I've been saved. I've been delivered from the depths of dog-doo depravity.

ETIQUETTE REX: THE WELL-MANNERED MUTT

While cleaning up after your dog is your responsibility, a dog in a public place has his own responsibilities. Of course, it really boils down to your responsibility again, but the burden of action is on your dog. Etiquette for restaurants and hotels is covered in other sections of the introduction. What follows is some very basic dog etiquette. I'll go through it quickly, but if your dog's a slow reader, he can go over it again: No vicious dogs; no jumping on people; no incessant barking; dogs should come when they're called; dogs should stay on command; no leg lifts on surfboards, backpacks, human legs, or any other personal objects you'll find hanging around beaches and parks.

Joe Dog has managed to violate all but the first of these rules. Do your best to remedy any problems. It takes patience and it's not always easy. For instance, there was a time during Joe's youth when he seemed to think that human legs were tree trunks. Rather than pretending I didn't know the beast, I strongly reprimanded him, apologized to the victim from the depths of my heart, and offered money for dry cleaning. Joe learned his lesson—$25 later.

SAFETY FIRST

A few essentials will keep your traveling dog happy and healthy. For further reading on the subject, I recommend the book *The Portable Pet*, by Barbara Nicholas (1983, The Harvard Common Press, Boston). It's soon to be out of print and some of the information about state regulations is out of date, but the basics about car and air travel safety are valuable and still pertinent.

• **Heat:** If you must leave your dog alone in the car for a few minutes, do so only if it's cool out and if you can park in the shade. Never, ever, ever leave a dog in a car with the windows rolled up all the way. Even if it seems cool, the sun's heat passing through the window can kill a dog in a matter of minutes. Roll down the window enough so your dog gets air, but so that there's no danger of your dog getting out or someone breaking in. Make sure your dog has plenty of water.

You also have to watch out for heat exposure when your car is in motion. Certain cars, like hatchbacks, can make a dog in the backseat extra hot, even while you feel okay in the driver's seat.

Try to take your vacation so you don't visit a place when it's extremely warm. Dogs and heat don't get along, especially if the dog isn't used to heat. The opposite is also true. If a dog lives in a hot climate and you take him to a freezing place, it may not be a healthy shift. Check with your vet if you have any doubts. Spring and fall are usually the best times to travel.

• **Water:** Water your dog frequently. Dogs on the road may drink even more than they do at home. Take regular water breaks, or bring a heavy bowl (the thick clay ones do nicely) and set it on the floor so your dog always has access to water. I use a non-spill bowl, which comes in really handy on curvy roads. When hiking, be sure to carry enough for you and a thirsty dog.

• **Rest stops:** Stop and unwater your dog. There's nothing more miserable than being stuck in a car when you can't find a rest stop. No matter how tightly you cross your legs and try to think of the desert, you're certain you'll burst within the next minute. But think of how a dog feels when the urge strikes and he can't tell you the problem. There are plenty of rest stops along the major California freeways. I've delineated many parks close to freeways as well for dogs who need a good stretch with their bathroom break.

How frequently you stop depends on your dog's bladder. If your dog is constantly running out the doggy door at home to relieve himself, you may want to stop every hour. Others can go significantly longer without being uncomfortable. Watch for any signs of restlessness and gauge it for yourself.

• **Car safety:** Even the experts differ about how a dog should travel in a car. Some suggest doggy safety belts, available at pet supply stores. Others firmly believe in keeping a dog kenneled. They say it's safer for the dog if there's an accident, and it's safer for the driver because there's no dog underfoot. Still others say you should just let your dog hang out without straps and boxes. They believe that if there's an accident, at least the dog isn't trapped in a cage. They say that dogs enjoy this more anyway.

I'm a follower of the last school of thought. Joe loves sticking his snout out of the windows to smell the world go by. The danger is that if the car kicks up a pebble or ires a bee, his nose and eyes could be injured. So far he's okay, as has been every other dog who has explored the Golden State with us, but I've seen dogs who needed to be treated for bee stings to the nose because of this practice. If in doubt, try opening the window just enough so your dog can't stick out much snout.

Whatever way you choose, your pet will be more comfortable if he has his own blanket with him. A veterinarian acquaintance uses a faux-sheepskin blanket for his dogs. At night in the hotel, the sheepskin doubles as the dog's bed.

Planes: Air travel is even more controversial. Personally, unless my dogs could fly with me in the passenger section (which very tiny dogs are sometimes allowed to do), I'd rather find a way to drive the distance or leave them at home with a friend. I've heard too many horror stories of dogs suffocating in what was supposed to be a pressurized cargo section, and of dogs dying of heat exposure, and of dogs going to Miami while their people end up in Seattle. There's just something unappealing about the idea of a dog flying in the cargo hold, like he's nothing more than a piece of luggage. Of course, many dogs survive just fine, but I'm not willing to take the chance.

But if you need to transport your dog by plane, try to fly nonstop, and make sure you schedule takeoff and arrival times when the temperature is below 80 degrees (or not bitterly cold in winter). You'll want to consult the airline about regulations and required certificates. And check with your vet to make sure your pooch is healthy enough to fly.

The question of tranquilizing a dog for a plane journey is very controversial. Some vets think it's insane to give a dog a sedative before flying. They say a dog will be calmer and less fearful without taking a disorienting drug. Others think it's crazy not to afford your dog the little relaxation he might not otherwise get without a tranquilizer. Discuss the issue with your vet, who will take the trip's length and your dog's personality into account.

Many Web sites deal with air-bound pooches, as do some books on dog health. Check them out for further info on air travel with your dog.

THE ULTIMATE DOGGY BAG

Your dog can't pack his own bags, and even if he could, he'd probably fill them with dog biscuits and chew toys. It's important to stash some of those in your dog's vacation kit, but here are some other items to bring along: bowls, bedding, a brush, towels (for those muddy days), a first-aid kit, pooper-scoopers, water, food, prescription drugs, tags (see below), treats, toys, and, of course, this book.

Be sure your dog wears his license, identification tag, and rabies tag. On a long trip, you may even want to bring along your dog's rabies certificate. Some parks and campgrounds require rabies and licensing information. You never know how picky they'll be.

It's a good idea to snap one of those barrel-type IDs on your dog's collar, too, showing the name, address, and phone number of where you'll be vacationing, or of a friend who will be home to field calls. That way, if your dog should get lost, at least the finder won't be calling your empty house. My friend Gina Spadafori has a great suggestion in her wonderful book, *Dogs for Dummies*: If you're going to be stopping at a few different locations during your travels, buy a pack of those paper key chains at the hardware store. (They're very inexpensive, and usually come in little bags of 100.) Each day, you can use a new tag and write down the current info on where you'll be staying, even if it's just a campground site number. That way, if your dog finds herself missing, there will be an easy way to get in touch with you locally. You'd be surprised at how many people don't want to make a long-distance phone call.

Some people think dogs should drink only water brought from home, so their bodies don't have to get used to too many new things. I've never had a problem feeding my dogs tap water from other parts of the state, nor has anyone else I know. Most vets think your dog will be fine drinking tap water in most other U.S. cities.

"Think of it this way," says Pete Beeman, a longtime San Francisco veterinarian. "Your dog's probably going to eat poop if he can get hold of some, and even that's probably not going to harm him. I really don't think that drinking water that's okay for people is going to be bad for dogs."

DINING WITH DOG

In Europe, dogs enter restaurants and dine alongside their folks as if they were people, too. (Or at least they sit and watch and drool while their people dine.) Not so in America. Rightly or wrongly, dogs are considered a health threat. But health inspectors I've spoken with say they see no reason why clean, well-behaved dogs shouldn't be permitted inside a restaurant. "Aesthetically, it may not appeal to Americans," an environmental specialist with the state Department of Health told me. "But the truth is, there's no harm in this practice."

Ernest Hemingway made an expatriate of his dog, Black Dog (aka Blackie), partly because of America's restrictive views on dogs in dining establishments. In "The Christmas Gift," a story published in *Look* magazine in 1954, he describes how he made the decision to take Black Dog to Cuba, rather than leave him behind in Ketchum, Idaho.

"This was a town where a man was once not regarded as respectable unless he was accompanied by his dog. But a reform movement had set in, led by several local religionists, and gambling had been abolished and there was even a movement on foot to forbid a dog from entering a public eating place with his master. Blackie had always tugged me by the trouser leg as we passed a combination gambling and eating place called the Alpine where they served the finest sizzling steak in the West. Blackie wanted me to order the giant sizzling steak and it was difficult to pass the Alpine.... We decided to make a command decision and take Blackie to Cuba."

Fortunately, you don't have to take your dog to a foreign country in order to eat together at a restaurant. California is full of restaurants with outdoor tables, and hundreds of them welcome dogs to join their people for an alfresco experience. The law on patio-dining dogs is somewhat vague, and each county has differing versions of it. But in general, as long as your dog doesn't go inside a restaurant (even to get to outdoor tables in the back) and isn't near the food preparation areas, it's probably legal. The decision is then up to the restaurant proprietor.

The restaurants listed in this book have given us permission to tout them as dog-friendly eateries. But keep in mind that rules can change and restaurants can close, so I highly recommend phoning before you get your stomach set on a particular kind of cuisine. Since some of the restaurants close during colder months, phoning ahead is a doubly wise thing to do. (Of course, just assume that where there's snow or ultracold temperatures, the outdoor tables are indoors for a while.) If you can't call first, be sure to ask the manager of the restaurant for permission before you sit down with your sidekick. Remember, it's the restaurant owner, not you, who will be in trouble if someone complains.

Some basic restaurant etiquette: Dogs shouldn't beg other diners, no matter how delicious their steak looks. They should not attempt to get their snouts (or their entire bodies) up on the table. They should be clean, quiet, and as unobtrusive as possible. If your dog leaves a good impression with the management and other customers, it will help pave the way for all the other dogs who want to dine alongside their best friends in the future.

A ROOM AT THE INN

Good dogs make great hotel guests. They don't steal towels, and they don't get drunk and keep the neighbors up all night. California is full of lodgings whose owners welcome dogs. This book lists dog-friendly accommodations of all types, from motels to bed-and-breakfast inns to elegant hotels. But the basic dog etiquette rules are the same.

Dogs should never be left alone in your room. Leaving a dog alone in a strange place is inviting serious trouble. Scared, nervous dogs can tear apart drapes, carpeting, and furniture. They can even injure themselves. They can also bark nonstop and scare the daylights out of the housekeeper. Just don't do it.

Only bring a house-trained dog to a lodging. How would you like a houseguest to go to the bathroom in the middle of your bedroom?

It helps if you bring your dog's bed or his blanket. Your dog will feel more at home and won't be tempted to jump on the bed. If your dog sleeps on the bed with you at home, bring a sheet and put it on top of the bed so the hotel's bedspread won't get furry or dirty.

After a few days in a hotel, some dogs come to think of it as home. They get territorial. When another hotel guest walks by, it's "Bark! Bark!" When the housekeeper knocks, it's "Bark! Snarl! Bark! Gnash!" Keep your dog quiet or you'll both find yourselves looking for a new home away from home.

For some strange reason, many lodgings prefer small dogs as guests. All I can say is, "Yip! Yap!" It's really ridiculous. Large dogs are often much calmer and quieter than their tiny, high-energy cousins.

If you're in a location where you can't find a hotel that will accept you and your big brute, it's time to try a sell job. Let the manager know how good and quiet your dog is (if he is). Promise he won't eat the bathtub or run around and shake the hotel. Offer a deposit or sign a waiver, even if they're not required for small dogs. It helps if your sweet, soppy-eyed dog is at your side to convince the decision-maker.

I've sneaked dogs into hotels, but I don't recommend doing it. The lodging might have a good reason for its rules. Besides, you always feel as if you're going to be caught and thrown out on your petard. You race in and out of your room with your dog as if ducking sniper fire. It's better to avoid feeling like a criminal and move on to a more dog-friendly location. In these situations, it's helpful to know that just about every Motel 6 permits one small pooch per room. (I know of only one exception—the one at Los Angeles International Airport. But as Motel 6s undergo their face-lifts, there may be a few more.) Some have more lenient rules than others. Their nationwide reservation and information line is (800) 466-8356.

The lodgings described in this book are for dogs who obey all the rules. I list the range of a lodging's rates, for the least expensive room during low season to the priciest room during high season. Most of the rooms are doubles, so there's not usually a huge variation. But when you see a room get into the thousands of dollars, you know we're looking at royal suites here. Joe can only drool.

Some lodgings charge extra for your dog. If you see "Dogs are $5 (or whatever the amount is) extra," that means $5 extra per night. Some charge a fee for the length of a dog's stay, and others ask for a deposit. Those are also noted in the lodging's description. Many still ask for nothing more than your dog's promise that you'll be on your best behavior. So if no extra charge is mentioned in a listing, it means your dog can stay with you for free.

RUFFING IT TOGETHER

Whenever we go camping, Joe insists on sleeping in the tent. He sprawls out and won't budge. At the first hint of dawn, he tiptoes outside (sometimes right through the bug screen) as if he'd been standing vigil all night. He tries not to look shamefaced, but under all that curly hair lurks an embarrassed grin.

Actually, Joe might have the right idea. Some outdoor experts say it's dangerous to leave even a tethered dog outside your tent at night. The dog can escape or can become bait for some creature hungry for a late dinner.

All state parks require dogs to be kept in a tent or vehicle at night. Some county parks follow suit. Other policies are more lenient. Use good judgment.

If you're camping with your dog, chances are that you're also hiking with him. Even if you're not hiking for long, you have to watch out for your dog's paws, especially the paws of those who are fair of foot. Rough terrain can cause a dog's pads to become raw and painful, making it almost impossible to walk. Several types of dog boots are available for such feet. It's easier to carry the booties than to carry your dog home.

Be sure to bring plenty of water for you and your pooch. Stop frequently to wet your whistles. Some veterinarians recommend against letting your dog drink out of a stream, because of the chance of ingesting giardia and other internal parasites, but it's not always easy to stop a thirsty dog.

On any but the most strenuous hikes, most dogs can muscle a little of the load themselves, if given the right attire. Dog backpacks are becoming more widely available these days in pet stores and catalogs, as well as outdoor stores. They enable a pooch to carry dog food, maps, bowls, or just about any other essentials that aren't too heavy. They're also convenient if you bring your dog fishing. What dog wouldn't want to help you carry a bunch of worms? If you can't find a backpack in your neck of the woods, call Dog Togs at (800) DOG-TOGS. They've got some terrific backpacks, including one that comes with ethylene foam inserts that quickly convert the backpack into a buoyancy vest. Joe, who can't swim, finds he's a little more at ease around water with his "backpack" on. (And he doesn't have to tell his friends it's really a life jacket.)

NATURAL TROUBLES

Chances are that your adventuring will go without a hitch, but you should always be prepared to deal with trouble. Make sure you know the basics of animal first aid before you embark on a long journey with your dog.

The more common woes—ticks, foxtails, poison oak, and skunks—can make life with a traveling dog a somewhat trying experience.

Ticks are hard to avoid in Northern California. They can carry Lyme disease, so you should always check yourself and your dog all over after a day in tick country. Don't forget to check ears and between the toes. If you see one, just pull it straight out with tweezers, not your bare hands.

The tiny deer ticks that carry Lyme disease are difficult to find. Consult your veterinarian if your dog is lethargic for a few days, has a fever, loses her appetite, or becomes lame. These symptoms could indicate Lyme disease. Some vets recommend a new vaccine that is supposed to prevent the onset of the disease.

Foxtails—those arrow-shaped pieces of dry grass (see the illustration below) that attach to your socks, your sweater, and your dog—are an

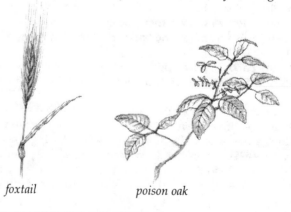

foxtail   *poison oak*

everyday annoyance. But in certain cases, they can be lethal. They can stick in your dog's eyes, nose, ears, or mouth and work their way in. Check every nook and cranny of your dog after a walk if you've been anywhere near dry grass. Despite my constant effort to find these things in Joe's curly fur, I've missed a few and they've beaten a path through his foot and into his leg. Be vigilant.

Poison oak (see the illustration on previous page) is also a common California menace. Get familiar with it through a friend who knows nature or through a guided nature walk. Dogs don't generally have reactions to poison oak, but they can easily pass its oils on to people. If you think your dog has made contact with some poison oak, avoid petting her until you can get home and bathe her (preferably with rubber gloves). If you do pet her before you can wash her, don't touch your eyes and wash your hands immediately.

If your dog loses a contest with a skunk (and she always will), rinse her eyes first with plain warm water, then bathe her with dog shampoo. Towel her off, then apply tomato juice. We once went through four gallons of the stuff before Joe started smelling less offensive. (And walking into the store to buy it was a real hoot. I had obviously absorbed some of the stench myself. Everyone was turning around and saying, "Whew! Do you smell a skunk?" as I wafted by.) If you can't get tomato juice, you can also use a solution of one pint of vinegar per gallon of water to decrease the stink.

HE, SHE, IT

In this book, whether neutered, spayed, or au naturel, dogs are never referred to as "it." They are either "he" or "she." I alternate pronouns so no dog reading this book will feel left out.

BEYOND THE BORDERS

There may be times when you and your dog actually find yourselves leaving California to visit other parts of the United States. Because *The California Dog Lover's Companion* has been so well received, Foghorn Press has launched a Dog Lover's series of books for different parts of the country, including Seattle, Boston, Atlanta, Washington, D.C., Florida, and Texas. All of the authors are experts in their areas and have adventurous dogs who help them explore and rate various attractions. If you can't find them in local bookstores, call Foghorn Press at (800) FOG-HORN (364-4676) to order yours.

Another fun way to keep up with dog travel news around the country is through a subscription to a doggone fine newsletter called *DogGone*. As its masthead states, *DogGone* is "about fun places to go and cool stuff to do with your dog." A subscription to this attractive, informative 12-page publication is $24 per year (six issues). For more information, or to subscribe, contact DogGone, P.O. Box 651155, Vero Beach, FL 32965; (888) 364-8728. You can also e-mail *DogGone* at doggonenl@aol.com.

Freedom-loving dogs now have a fun, informative Web site devoted to cool off-leash places to take a dog nationally. At press time, the Freedog site was just starting to branch out beyond the San Francisco Bay Area, but it's growing fast and shows great promise. The writing is wry, funny, and clever. Your dog will laugh out loud. You'll find the site at www.freedog.com.

A DOG IN NEED

If you don't currently have a dog but could provide a good home for one, I'd like to make a plea on behalf of all the unwanted dogs who will be euthanized tomorrow and the day after that and the day after that. Animal shelters and humane organizations are overflowing with dogs who would devote their lives to being your best buddy, your faithful traveling companion, and a dedicated listener to all your tales of bliss and woe.

Need a nudge? Remember the oft-quoted words of Samuel Butler: "The great pleasure of a dog is that you may make a fool of yourself with him and not only will he not scold you, but he will make a fool of himself, too."

KEEP IN TOUCH!

Our readers mean everything to us. We explore California so you and your dogs can spend true quality time together. Your input to this book is very important. In the last few years, we've heard from many wonderful dogs and their people about new dog-friendly places, or old dog-friendly places we didn't know about. We check out the tip and if it turns out to be a good one, include it in the next edition, giving a thank-you to the dog and/or person who sent in the suggestion.

Now we're making it easier than ever to get in touch with us. You can call the new California Dog Lover's Companion Hotline at (707) 773-4264 and leave your tip. When you call, be sure to leave your name, city, and your dog's name so we can give you credit in the book. It's our way of paying homage to you and your best friend. You can also write to Joe Dog and me at 340 Bodega Avenue, Petaluma, CA 94952. And you can e-mail us at foghorn@well.com.

POSTSCRIPT

Nisha, our dear, life-loving, ever-energetic springer spaniel, left our world in the autumn of 1997 at the age of 15. We miss her very, very much.

I will continue to include her in the book in places she explored with us, as long as the places still allow dogs. After all, her wagging tail helped me judge the dog-friendliness of many a park and restaurant. Besides, she's still with us, in a sense. A dog like Nisha gets deep into your soul and never leaves.

In fact, she's immortalized in yet another way. Since the last edition of this book, my husband and I had a human child, Laura. She's now 17 months old, and lives for dogs. Her first word, at nine months, was "doggy." She was just under a year when Nisha died. After Nisha's death, Laura took up barking a lot, and panting like Nisha panted. I've never seen a child (and I've rarely seen a dog) bark and pant as much as Laura does. She even routinely tries to eat from the dog food bowl, sneaking kibble from Joe, much as Nisha used to do. Joe and Laura, by the way, are now best friends. (I'd like to think it's that natural, beautiful animal-child bond, but frankly I think it's all the food she throws him from her high chair.)

Nisha lives on through this child and through this book.

For Mom, Dad, and Muttley, who made growing up
as much fun as walking in a lush redwood forest
with a dog who heeds every word you utter.

Note to all dog lovers:

While our information is as current as possible, changes to fees, regulations, parks, roads, and trails sometimes are made after we go to press. Businesses can close, change their ownership, or change their rules. Earthquakes, fires, rainstorms, and other natural phenomena can radically change the condition of parks, hiking trails, and wilderness areas. Before you and your dog begin your travels, please be certain to call the phone numbers for each listing for updated information.

Attention dogs of California:

If we've missed your favorite park, beach, outdoor restaurant, hotel, or dog-friendly activity, please let us know. You'll be helping countless other dogs get more enjoyment out of life in the Golden State. We always welcome your comments and suggestions about *The California Dog Lover's Companion*. Please write to the Publisher, Foghorn Press, 340 Bodega Avenue, Petaluma, CA 94952.

NORTHERN AREA COUNTIES

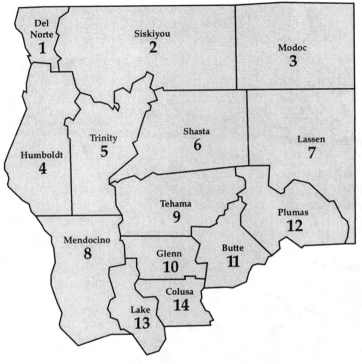

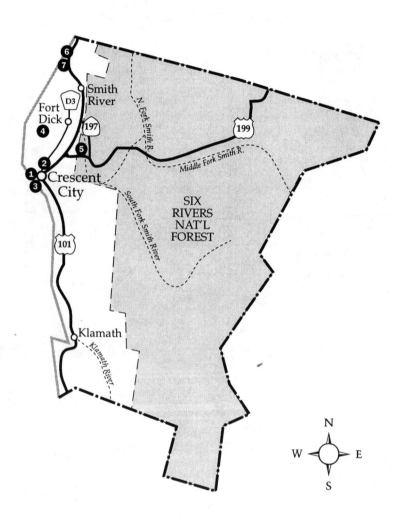

SIX RIVERS NAT'L FOREST

Smith River

Fort Dick

Crescent City

Klamath

N. Fork Smith R.

Middle Fork Smith R.

South Fork Smith River

Klamath River

D3

197

199

101

6
7
5
2
1
3
4

N
W E
S

1
DEL NORTE COUNTY

Don't call this beautiful coastal redwood empire "Del Nort-*ay*" County, as many Californians do because of all the Spanish influence in this state. It's as much of a giveaway that you're from out of town as pronouncing the next state north "Or-ih-*gohn*" instead of "Or-ih-*ghin*." Pronounce this county "Del Nort," even if it reminds you of something Ralph Kramden would say.

If you want a real coastal getaway, you couldn't ask for a more beautiful, remote area. Part of the reason so few Californians know the local pronunciation of this county is because it's so out of the way that we don't often hear about it.

As one of the state's best-kept secrets, it's a gem for people vacationing with a dog. While there are plenty of leash laws, there are also many places where civilization hasn't yet encroached sufficiently to make leashes a mandatory part of a dog's attire. The 305,000-acre Smith River National Recreation Area (see Six Rivers National Forest on page 754), which makes up the majority of this county, allows dogs off leash everywhere except in campgrounds!

The climate in Del Norte County is very mild, with coastal temperatures generally ranging from 65 to 75 degrees Fahrenheit. That's good news for dogs who don't like temperature extremes. But this region is also known for its rain. One hundred inches a year here is common, making outdoor cafes almost nonexistent. The forests are actually rain forests. They're lush and verdant. They're also often wet. Some dogs and people prefer this to the drought scenarios in other parts of the state. With a slicker, a dog towel, and a love of the outdoors, you and your dog could be very happy here.

NATIONAL FORESTS

See the National Forests and Wilderness Areas chapter starting on page 748 for important information and safety tips on visiting national forests with your dog.

• **Six Rivers National Forest** 🐾🐾🐾🐾 🐕

This county is green thanks in great part to the lush 305,000-acre Smith River National Recreation Area, which is part of Six Rivers National Forest. The U.S. Forest Service has been designated as the steward of this fairly new national recreation area, and that's fantastic for dogs. The Wild and Scenic River, the 65 miles of trails, and the seven distinct plant communities can all be enjoyed by off-leash dogs, as long as they're obedient. See page 754 for a more complete description of the forest.

CRESCENT CITY

This 1.25-square-mile coastal city was devastated by a giant tsunami in 1964. A series of waves about 12 feet high rushed inland as far as 1,600 feet, destroying 29 downtown blocks and killing 11 people. The city has since rebuilt, and the beach that the tsunami washed over is now awash with happy dogs (see Beachfront Park under Parks, Beaches, and Recreation Areas). Although the city itself has no leash law, it follows the county's leash law, so pooches must be appropriately attired.

PARKS, BEACHES, AND RECREATION AREAS

• **Beachfront Park** 🐾🐾🐾½ *See* ❶ *on page 24.*

Pooches are supposed to be leashed at this often empty 80-acre beach/grassy park, but that doesn't stop them from having a ball here. They run and roll and do some mighty fine beachcombing. They stretch out beside their people in the charming gazebo, and they even manage to do the dog paddle when the surf is down. (Watch out for Elk Creek, which empties into the harbor here. Occasionally it can be too swift for even the strongest canine swimmer.)

If dogs aren't the only people in your life, this is an especially fun park to visit. Children can check out the playground, while anglers can make the acquaintance of fish at the 850-foot public fishing pier.

From U.S. 101, go west on Front Street. The park is at Front Street between B and F Streets. (707) 464-9507.

• **Florence Keller Regional Park** 🐾🐾🐾 *See* ❷ *on page 24.*

This 30-acre county park is one big redwood grove with space carved out for trails, playing fields, and playgrounds. It's a good balance of wild and civilized, if you need that kind of balance. Dogs have to be leashed. Camping at any of the 31 sites here costs $10 a night. It can fill up in the summer, so reservations are recommended.

Exit U.S. 101 at Cunningham Lane and follow the signs to the park. (707) 464-7230.

• **Redwood National Park (north section)** 😺 😺 ½ *See* ❸ *on page 24.*
For a national park, this is a fairly unrestrictive place, both here and in its south half in Humboldt County. In national parks, dogs are usually permitted only on paved roads, in parking lots, and in the occasional campground. But here, leashed dogs are actually allowed on a trail and a beach.

The Enderts Beach Trail is a 1.2-mile walk on the bluffs behind Enderts Beach. Crescent Beach, just off Enderts Beach Road, is a good place for beachcombing dogs. Both are fine if you don't mind leashing your dog. But if you're not bent on being near the coast, the Smith River National Recreation Area can make a dog much happier. (See Six Rivers National Forest on page 754.)

As much as dogs enjoy walking around here, they seem to enjoy camping even more. It's a terrific place to spend the night with your dog. Canine camping is restricted to a few sites, but dogs don't seem to mind. Sites are $14 to $16. Call (800) 444-PARK for reservations.

Start your visit to Redwood National Park at the park's headquarters in Crescent City, at Second and K Streets. You can get maps, brochures, and trail updates that will make your visit a more enjoyable one. (707) 464-6101.

RESTAURANTS
Glen's Bakery: They make their own jam at this bakery. Add it to the fresh-baked bread, and you and your dog can feast. Try the clam chowder if you're in the mood for something hot. Dine with doggy at the outdoor bench. 723 Third Street; (707) 464-2914.

PLACES TO STAY
Days Inn: No big dogs are allowed. Rates are $29 to $89. 220 M Street, Crescent City, CA 95531; (707) 464-9553.

Del Norte Coast Redwoods State Park: Dogs aren't allowed on the trails here, but they can sleep in one of the 145 campsites under a grove of redwoods. Rates are $12 to $16. Dogs are $1 extra. The campground is about 10 miles southeast of Crescent City, just off U.S. 101. For reservations, call Parknet at (800) 444-PARK. For information on the park, phone (707) 464-6101.

Econo Lodge: Dogs are allowed at the manager's discretion, and in only two rooms. Rates are $55 to $70. Dogs are $5 extra. 119 L Street, Crescent City, CA 95531; (707) 464-2181.

Florence Keller Regional Park: See Florence Keller Regional Park on page 26 for camping information.

Pacific Motor Hotel: Good news for some dogs: No cats allowed! Bad news for some dogs: No cats allowed. Smallish dogs only, please. Rates are $39 to $65. Dogs are $5 extra. 440 U.S. 101 North, Crescent City, CA 95531; (707) 464-4141.

Redwood National Park: See Redwood National Park above for camping information.

Royal Inn: Rates are $35 to $75. There's a $5 fee for dogs. 102 L Street, Crescent City, CA 95531; (707) 464-4113.

Town House Motel: Rates are $26 to $50. There's a $20 dog deposit. They prefer smaller dogs, but if your big pooch is well groomed and well behaved, he'll probably be welcome. 444 U.S. 101 South, Crescent City, CA 95531; (707) 464-4176.

FORT DICK

PARKS, BEACHES, AND RECREATION AREAS

•**Lake Earl Wildlife Area** 🐾🐾 ⤫ *See* ❹ *on page 24.*

Dogs can cavort about unleashed at this 5,000-acre state wildlife area only if they're here to help when you shoot waterfowl (and we're not talking cameras here). During hunting seasons, working dogs and their gun-toting buddies can hunt the lake itself and 100 feet from the edge of the water.

If you and your dog aren't of the hunting persuasion, it's perfectly okay to roam around, but rangers ask that you leash up.

From Crescent City, take Lake Earl Drive north. Turn left at Old Mill Road. Proceed 1.5 miles to the wildlife area headquarters on the right. (707) 464-2523.

•**Ruby Van Deventer Park** 🐾🐾🐾 *See* ❺ *on page 24.*

What dog wouldn't enjoy a park that's beside a river and home to drippy redwood trees? Ruby Van Deventer Park covers only 10 acres, and it's usually devoted to people who camp here, but dogs don't care. The park is set on the north bank of the Smith River, so even if a dog has to camp here in order to hang out here, it's a treat. Dogs who like to swim, fish, or sleep by rivers really love this place.

There are 17 campsites. One site, appropriately named the Riverfront Site, is set right beside the river when the river is at its fullest. It's a very peaceful place to spend the night. Sites are $10. From U.S. 101, take the Highway 199 exit and drive four miles east to the park. (707) 464-7230.

PLACES TO STAY

Ruby Van Deventer Park: See Ruby Van Deventer Park above for camping information.

KLAMATH

DIVERSIONS

Meet a tall, wooden, handsome man (and his ox): A visit to the campy but fascinating Trees of Mystery will be a visit you and your canine buddy will never forget. First, a 50-foot-tall Paul Bunyan greets patrons in the parking lot. His ox doesn't speak, but Bunyan utters enough sentences to make even the most savvy dog stand in openmouthed awe. Then the nature trail takes you through some of the world's oldest and largest trees. But these are no ordinary trees: These are Trees of Mystery! We won't ruin the many surprises that await you, but let's just say you'll definitely want a camera with a wide-angle lens. The entry fee is $6.50 for adults and $4 for children ages 6 to 12. Dogs get in free. 15500 U.S. 101. (707) 482-5613 or (800) 638-3389.

Drive through a tree: We're not talking Casper tricks here. We're talking good old non-ghoulish fun. You and the dog of your dreams can drive right on through the base of a 700-year-old redwood tree, known as the Tour-Thru Tree. If any people or pooches in your party are prone to claustrophobia, don't hang out in the tree for too long. It's kind of tight. You can do all your lollygagging afterward, at a decent little picnic area near the tree's gift shop. Your dog can stretch his legs here, but try not to let him do leg lifts on the giant tree. It's insulting enough to the tree to have a hole the size of a Ford Explorer in its middle.

The fee is $2 per car or 50 cents if you prefer to walk through. (Dogs generally prefer walking.) From U.S. 101, take the Terwer Valley exit east about one-quarter of a mile to the tree. (707) 482-5971.

SMITH RIVER

PARKS, BEACHES, AND RECREATION AREAS

•**Pelican State Beach** 😺 😺 😺 *See* ❻ *on page 24.*

It's only five acres, but that's plenty of running room for a dog who's been cooped up in the car all day. Pelican State Beach is actually a few miles northwest of Smith River, the closest California city to the Oregon border. It seems to be a popular stop for folks who've just gone over or are about to go over to visit our northern neighbor. Dogs are supposed to be leashed, but they love sniffing around the beach for the driftwood that's so plentiful here.

The beach is just west of U.S. 101, five miles south of the Oregon border. (707) 464-6101.

•**Smith River County Park** 😺 😺 😺 *See* ❼ *on page 24.*

This is a beautiful park, right on the mouth of the Smith River, which is part of the state's Wild and Scenic River system. It's a great place to relax on the pebbly beach and take in the sights, or walk to Pyramid Point and do a little bird-watching with your leashed dog. It's also a popular backdrop for photographs. If your dog wants to be in pictures, this might be the place to snap away.

The park is at the end of Smith River Road. (707) 464-7230.

RESTAURANTS

Rubio's Mexican Restaurant: See Casa Rubio below.

PLACES TO STAY

Casa Rubio: This beach house is dog heaven—at least female dog heaven. Boy dogs are banned here. Owner Tony Rubio says too much of his exquisite landscaping has been ruined by male dogs exploring and marking the territory.

Joe is still trying to cheer up after hearing the news. This is his kind of place. Of the three units in this 1940s beach house, one allows girl dogs (Joe now wants to call them by their true name). It's roomy (sleeps up to six), with a private yard and a kitchen. And when you open the door, you're just a few steps from the sands of a wide, quiet beach!

Your beach house is stocked daily with fresh croissants or muffins, plus juice and coffee. Another bonus: When you stay here two nights or more, you'll get two free dinners at Rubio's, a yummy restaurant in Brookings,

Oregon, just up the road. The restaurant features tasty Mexican food and fresh seafood—and your dog can accompany you if you eat at the patio tables. The restaurant is at 1136 Chetco Avenue (U.S. 101). Ask the staff at Casa Rubio for directions.

Check out the hotel's Web page at members.aol.com/casarubio. Room rates are $68 to $98. 17285 Crissey Road, Smith River, CA 95567; (707) 487-4313 or (800) 357-6199.

Clifford Kamph Memorial Park: Camp at the ocean in one of eight sites at this two-acre county-run campground. One site is on the beach, a couple are on a bluff, and the rest are set just a bone's throw inland. Sites are a mere $5. The park is about halfway between the town of Smith River and Oregon, just west of U.S. 101. (707) 462-7230.

Ship Ashore Best Western: If yours is a teeny-weeny dog, she can stay here with you. The weight limit for pets is 10 pounds. Fortunately, there is no weight limit for human guests. But in case you need the exercise, there's a pooch path on the premises. Rates are $55 to $100. 12370 U.S. 101 North, Smith River, CA 95567; (707) 487-3141 or (800) 528-1234.

2
SISKIYOU COUNTY

Siskiyou County is home to some of the least creative names for parks that we've ever seen. Even Joe was yawning when we checked out four cities that had parks called "City Park." But fortunately, two of the four City Parks are really outstanding—as are many of the parks and recreation areas in this huge and wild county.

The visual highlight of Siskiyou County is towering Mount Shasta, but there's so much beauty here that almost anywhere you go, something's bound to impress your senses. Two national forests make up a big part of the county. As you travel on Highway 96, you'll find dozens of places to pull off and explore the Klamath River in the Klamath National Forest. If you stop at a wide river access point that's far from the road, your dog can trot around off leash while you fish or soak your weary legs. Be careful, though. The current can really whip in some spots.

Lava Beds National Monument on the eastern edge of the county is off-limits to dogs, unless they like walking on paved roads. It's a sore disappointment to many dogs and their drivers. You can drive through here with a dog, but this park is more of a stop-and-check-it-out place, where you should walk through gigantic lava tubes and experience other unusual adventures. Rangers say they've been getting more strict about dogs recently because they've noticed that dogs have been doing their doggy business in the caves, so if you think you're going to get away with sneaking your dog around here, you're probably wrong. There are plenty of other places to visit that welcome dogs, although they don't have lava tubes.

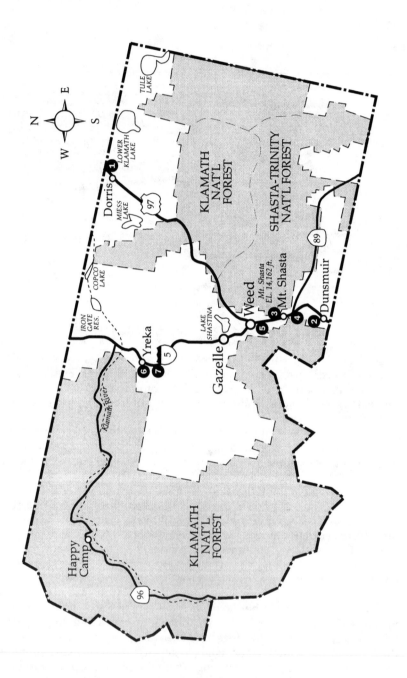

NATIONAL FORESTS

See the National Forests and Wilderness Areas chapter starting on page 748 for important information and safety tips on visiting national forests with your dog.

• **Klamath National Forest** 😊😊😊😊 🐕
See page 750.

• **Shasta-Trinity National Forest** 😊😊😊😊 🐕
See page 754.

DORRIS

PARKS, BEACHES, AND RECREATION AREAS

• **Lower Klamath National Wildlife Refuge** 😊😊😊½ 🐕
See ❶ on page 32.

This 54,000-acre waterfowl haven may be home to the largest wintering concentration of bald eagles in the lower 48 states. Dogs are allowed off leash only if they're helping you during waterfowl and pheasant hunting seasons. Otherwise, they have to be leashed at all times to protect this important nesting and migration area.

Lower Klamath Lake and the surrounding marshy area and uplands are a bird-watcher's paradise. During summer you'll see avocets, grebes, herons, white pelicans, black-necked stilts, and killdeers. Nearly one million waterfowl use this and nearby Tule Lake during fall migration. Keep those binoculars peeled.

The refuge has many entrances. From U.S. 97 at the Oregon border, head east on Highway 161. The refuge's entrances will be on your right in a few miles. Call (530) 667-2231 for information and directions to other areas of the refuge.

DUNSMUIR

When I first visited this old town on the Sacramento River, it was July of 1991 and I was covering the toxic metam sodium spill that wiped out river life and made residents ill. The sign at the town's entrance boasting "Dunsmuir—home of the best water on earth" was nothing but a sad irony and a good line for an article.

But these days, the river is clean and burgeoning with life again. The sign at the town's entrance is no longer incongruous. Check out the crystal-clear water from City Park (see below) while you and your leashed dog picnic along the river. It's so nice not to have bright green clouds of toxic pesticides floating by while you're trying to eat.

PARKS, BEACHES, AND RECREATION AREAS

• **City Park** 😊😊😊½ *See ❷ on page 32.*

This is not your typical, well-groomed city park. It's wild, woodsy, and full of trails winding up and down hills surrounding the Sacramento River. It's almost completely shaded here, keeping it cool during all but the hottest days of summer.

If it's a particularly sticky day, you and your panting pooch can dip your toes in the always-cool river. If your dog is a landlubber like Joe, he may want to hang out near the shaded picnic tables, so be sure to pack a little snack. "Make mine mignon," says Joe.

Take the Central Dunsmuir exit off Interstate 5 and go north on Dunsmuir Avenue. The park will be on your left. (530) 235-4822.

RESTAURANTS
Burger Barn: Dogs like to drool while you dine on a burger at this eatery's picnic tables. 5942 Dunsmuir Avenue; (530) 235-2140.

PLACES TO STAY
Dunsmuir Travelodge: Your dog is a mere quarter of a mile away from the city park here. Rates are $40 to $70. Dogs are $5 extra. 5400 Dunsmuir Avenue, Dunsmuir, CA 96025; (530) 235-4395 or (800) 578-7878.

Railroad Park Resort/Caboose Motel: Stay here in a caboose that was once an important part of any of several major rail lines, including the Santa Fe. These restored caboose cars are intriguing places to hang your leash with your good dog, who is welcome as long as you call ahead and get the okay. The owners prefer dogs to bring their own beds. Humans get comfy brass beds and cushy armchairs. If you stay in the deluxe boxcar, you'll get your own wet bar and your tub will have claw feet (dogs can relate). The rooms have no kitchens, but a terrific restaurant in the dining car makes up for this (no dogs, though). You can also stay at one of the resort's cabins.

The grounds of the resort are like a park, with plenty of places to walk a dog. Your pooch can even watch you fish at the resort's very own fishing pond. If you have no luck angling, don't worry: You'll at least be able to watch some happy fish at the resort's little carp pool. Pooches have to stay off landscaped areas. Rates are $60 to $85. Dogs are $7.50 extra. 100 Railroad Park Road, Dunsmuir, CA 96025; (530) 235-4440.

GAZELLE
PLACES TO STAY
Hollyhock Farm Bed and Breakfast: Dogs are sometimes welcome to stay at the private guest house adjacent to the inn's main Normandy-style stone farmhouse. The quiet, attractive guest house is perfect for a good night's sleep. Mount Shasta towers photogenically in the distance. The owner loves dogs. She also loves horses, but they have to stay outside. Actually, depending on the day, your dog may need to stay in the farmhouse's kennel, which comes with its own doghouse. Be sure to call first to check on poochy accommodations, because if your dog is anything like Joe, he'd rather stay home than in a strange kennel.

The rate for the guest house is $80, which includes a full country-style breakfast. Hollyhock is conveniently located off Interstate 5, at 18705 Old Highway 99, P.O. Box 152, Gazelle, CA 96034; (530) 435-2627.

HAPPY CAMP
PLACES TO STAY
Forest Lodge Motel: This is the only motel in town with phones in the

rooms. The managers stress that dogs have to be housebroken to stay here (as they must always be when you're taking them to a hotel). They've had some bad experiences with pets who weren't housebroken. Rates are $48 to $59. 63712 Highway 96, Happy Camp, CA 96039; (530) 493-5424.

MOUNT SHASTA

This small town sits under the watchful eye of the mighty mountain that goes by the same name. It can provide a quick highway rest stop for the weary or an enchanting place to unwind for days. Some who have come for a few days end up spending the rest of their lives here. Mount Shasta has the best of all worlds—it's remote and wildly natural, yet civilized to the point of being the area's cultural hub. Even dogs like the combination.

PARKS, BEACHES, AND RECREATION AREAS

• **City Park** 🐾🐾🐾 *See* ❸ *on page 32.*

We have to stop here every time we pass Mount Shasta. We bring a couple of empty water bottles and a big thirst, since this fairly small city park is actually home to the headwaters of the Sacramento River. The crystal-clear, cold water comes bubbling down the rocks of a couple of small streams that become the Sacramento. It's the best water we've ever tasted, and it's free! There are no rules yet on how much water people can take, but there may be in the future if people abuse the privilege. Don't be a glutton and you'll be able to dip your cup into eternity.

Dogs have to be leashed at this shady park, but they don't seem to mind. This is a relaxing place, where you have the chance to sit under a tree in a green meadow or under the gazebo and tune out the world for a while. Bring a picnic and toast your favorite dog with your favorite water at one of the riverside picnic tables. If your dog needs to stretch his legs more, there's a wide trail that starts in the area behind the stream. But do keep him out of the water. Dog hair doesn't go well with bottled water.

From Interstate 5, take the Mount Shasta Boulevard exit and head southeast. Turn right within a half mile at Nixon Road and bear right into the park. (530) 926-2494.

• **Lake Siskiyou** 🐾🐾🐾½ *See* ❹ *on page 32.*

This man-made reservoir, created solely for recreational use, sits in the morning shadow of awesome Mount Shasta. Trout fishing is one of the big draws—the lake is stocked with 20,000 trout each year! But you can also have a great vacation just camping and hiking in the area surrounding this 437-acre lake. Leashed dogs may go pretty much everywhere except the swimming beach.

Several trails wind through the ponderosa pines and cedars that encircle much of the lake. You can actually leave the campground and walk around the entire lake with your dog, as long as you don't mind hoofing it across a small section of the Sacramento River.

The day-use fee is $1 per human. Rangers here are so adamantly against people leaving dogs in their cars during the day that they'll flat out turn you back if they catch you. It's a good, lifesaving policy. Dogs don't pay anything during the day, but it costs $1 extra per night if your dog camps with you. There are 365 sites with fees ranging from $10 to $22. From Interstate 5, take the Central Mount Shasta exit, turn left at the stop sign, and follow the signs west on W. A. Barr Road to the lake. (530) 926-2610.

RESTAURANTS

Avalon Square Deli: Dogs love to watch you dine on salads and sandwiches at the many outdoor, umbrella-covered tables. 401 North Mount Shasta Boulevard; (530) 926-4998.

PLACES TO STAY

Econo Lodge: Rates are $45 to $90. There's a $20 deposit for dogs. 908 South Mount Shasta Boulevard, Mount Shasta, CA 96067; (530) 926-3145.

Lake Siskiyou: See Lake Siskiyou on page 35 for camping information.

Mountain Air Lodge: If your dog likes a little grass around his lodgings, he'll like a night or two here. Rates are $40 to $59. Dogs are $5 extra. 1121 South Mount Shasta Boulevard, Mount Shasta, CA 96067; (530) 926-3411.

Mount Shasta Ranch Bed & Breakfast: A stay at this elegant two-story ranch house puts you up close and personal with Mount Shasta. This historic inn offers spacious suites, a quaint vacation cottage, a large fireplace, an outdoor spa, and a tasty country-style breakfast. Dogs will enjoy the good dog-walking trails.

Your dog's requirement: He has to be flea-free to stay. Rooms are furnished with Oriental rugs and antiques, and a flea infestation would not be a good thing. Rates are $60 to $95. 1008 W. A. Barr Road, Mount Shasta, CA 96067; (530) 926-3870.

Swiss Holiday Lodge: Sleep here and watch the sun rise on Mount Shasta right from your window. Rates are $33 to $57. 2400 South Mount Shasta Boulevard, Mount Shasta, CA 96067; (530) 926-3448.

The Tree House Best Western: There's no tree house here, so please, no leg lifts on the nice cedar exterior. Some of the rooms have views of Mount Shasta. Dogs 25 pounds and under only, please. Rates are $56 to $160. 111 Morgan Way, Mount Shasta, CA 96067; (530) 926-3101.

WEED

At times, the name Weed has been a stumbling block in public relations, but it doesn't stop people from visiting this old town nestled in the western slopes of Mount Shasta. Today it's a sleepy place with breathtaking views of the mountain. But between the 1900s and the 1940s, it was considered to be the Sodom and Gomorrah of Siskiyou County. Because of its remote location, the law was barely enforced. Things sometimes would get so out of hand that train conductors would warn people not to disembark here.

PARKS, BEACHES, AND RECREATION AREAS

We were disappointed in Lake Shastina, the beautiful lake that was turned into a golf resort just outside town. It used to be much wilder, but now about the wildest areas the public can access are the sand traps. And since dogs aren't permitted on the courses, it's not much fun.

Fortunately, just to the east of Weed is the Shasta-Trinity National Forest's Shasta Wilderness Area, complete with magnificent 14,162-foot Mount

Shasta and even a few fairly nonstrenuous trails (see page 754 for a description of Shasta-Trinity National Forest).

•**City Park** 🐾1/2 *See* ❺ *on page 32.*
Much of this park is taken up by ball fields, but there's still some room for leashed dogs to roam and a few trees for them to mark. It's a convenient stop if your dog is crossing his legs while you're driving on Interstate 5. Exit at the College of Siskiyou turnoff and take South Weed Boulevard south one block, then go right on College Avenue. The park is on your left after three blocks. (530) 938-5020.

RESTAURANTS
Pizza Factory: Joe's favorite food here is the juicy calzone, which he enjoys smelling at a table under the awning. 132 North Weed Boulevard; (530) 938-3088.

PLACES TO STAY
Motel 6: Rates are $34 for the first adult, $6 for the second. The rule here is one small pooch per room. 466 North Weed Boulevard, Weed, CA 96094; (530) 938-4101.

YREKA
Yreka, Eureka, Ukiah, Arcata. Traveling in Northern California can be confusing, with cities whose names sound like bad Scrabble hands. But here's an easy way to have Yreka (pronounced "why-*reek*-uh") stick out in your mind: When you're here, just look south. See spectacular, snowy Mount Shasta in the distance? Yreka is an Indian word for "white mountain." The "Y" in Yreka sounds sort of like the "white" in white mountain. Got it?

This is the county seat of Siskiyou County, and it's an attractive, historic place on the eastern edge of a huge portion of the Klamath National Forest. (See page 750 for a description of the forest.) Dogs prefer to run around unleashed in the forest, but there's a city park in town where they can enjoy a more civilized walk. And if your dog is small, he can have a roaring good time aboard the Blue Goose Steam Train (see page 38).

PARKS, BEACHES, AND RECREATION AREAS
•**City Park** 🐾🐾 *See* ❻ *on page 32.*
This small city park is conveniently located near the historic district of Yreka. Dogs like it just fine, as long as they don't mind a leash. The grass is green and the shade trees are big. There's also a playground and a ball field so the kids can work off their energy while the dog explores.

From Highway 3, drive west about six blocks on West Miner Street. The park is on your left, at Gold and West Miner Streets. (530) 842-4386.

•**Greenhorn Park** 🐾1/2 *See* ❼ *on page 32.*
The park is indeed green. The only problem is that dogs aren't allowed on the vast, lush lawn areas. They're relegated to the trails, which aren't bad. You can walk next to Greenhorn Creek, which leads to Greenhorn Reservoir on the eastern end of the park. But no swimming is allowed for dogs or their people.

From Highway 3, drive west for one block on Payne Lane, then south on

Oregon Street until the road comes to a T. Then turn right on Greenhorn Road and drive about a half mile. The park entrance is on your left, just past the reservoir. (530) 842-4386.

PLACES TO STAY

Best Western Miner's Inn: Small- and medium-sized dogs are invited to sleep here. Rates are $49 to $95. 122 East Miner Street, Yreka, CA 96097; (530) 842-4355.

Thunderbird Lodge: There's plenty of land around here for a little romping with your pooch. Rates are $35 to $45. 526 South Main Street, Yreka, CA 96097; (530) 842-4404.

Wayside Inn: This bright inn has interesting knotty pine furniture. Rates are $30 to $65. Dogs are $3 extra. 1235 South Main Street, Yreka, CA 96097; (530) 842-4412.

DIVERSIONS

Choo choo with your poochoo: Put on your engineer caps and get ready to steam along a short-line railroad that's been in continuous operation since 1889. Dogs who fit on your lap are allowed to accompany you on the Blue Goose Steam Train for this magical three-hour tour from Yreka east through Shasta Valley. You'll pass lumber mills, cross the Shasta River, and chug along through beautiful cattle country—all with majestic Mount Shasta in the background.

The 1915 Baldwin steam engine stops at the old cattle town of Montague, where you can picnic in the park while listening to the entertainment that's been rustled up for you. You can visit the old-fashioned soda fountain in town or take a wagon ride set up for the train's guests.

Dogs who are small adore this ride. Dogs who are larger would love it, too, but unfortunately railway manager Larry Bacon says too many people gripe about anything larger than a lapdog. These complainers are a bunch of old poops, young poops, too, who'd moan about anything," says dog-loving Bacon.

Meanwhile, back on the train, teacup poodles, beagles, and their ilk will get to choose from an open car, two 1920s cars, and a couple of vintage 1948 passenger cars. Unless your dog doesn't like the wind in his face or the sound of steam bursting forth in Wizard of Oz fashion, the open cars are the best ones for canines. Just keep hold of that leash, in case Toto or some other interesting creature comes charging by.

The train runs from Memorial Day weekend through the end of October. Rates are $9 for adults, $4.50 for kids. Dogs who qualify size-wise go for free. If your dog is too big for your lap, you can either get a bigger lap or ask if he can stay in the manager's office while you ride without him. Bacon says he occasionally allows good doggies to stay with him, which is sure nice of him. Dogs take a liking to Bacon. With a name like that, they can't help themselves.

Exit Interstate 5 at the Central Yreka exit. The depot is just east of the freeway. (530) 842-4146.

3
MODOC COUNTY

Not too many people or dogs venture to the far northeast reaches of the state, but those who do find dog heaven. About 90 percent of this county is made up of Modoc National Forest and other public lands. That means years of off-leash walks for you and your pooch.

Many folks travel through here on U.S. 395 on the way from the Pacific Northwest to Reno. Alturas is a popular stopping point. But check out the numerous entrances to the eastern chunk of Modoc National Forest. Just north of Alturas you can follow Highway 299 east into the Cedar Mountain area, where there are a couple of primitive campgrounds. Closer to the town of Likely, you can head east and enter the South Warner Wilderness for access to numerous lakes, streams, and trails.

Alturas, the county seat and only town of notable size, has a population of 3,000. That should tell you all you need to know about this get-away-from-it-all county.

NATIONAL FORESTS

See the National Forests and Wilderness Areas chapter starting on page 748 for important information and safety tips on visiting national forests with your dog.

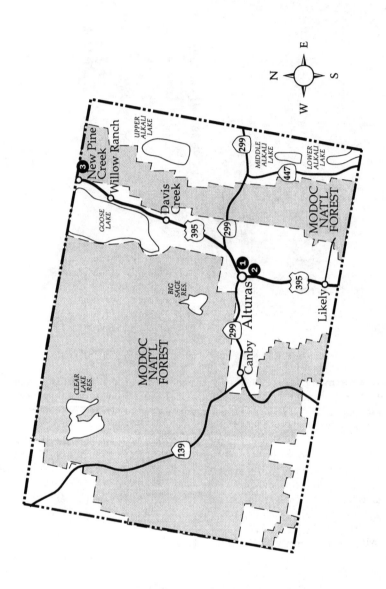

• **Modoc National Forest** 🐾🐾🐾🐾🐕

The South Warner Wilderness, located about 14 miles east of the town of Likely, is a serene place to visit. Clear little lakes abound, as do the creeks that feed them. See page 752 for more information on Modoc National Forest.

ALTURAS

Even though there's not much going on here for the dog in your life, if you visit Veteran's Memorial Park (see below), you can be entertained by the stories of Virgie Meyer, who's in her 90s and still works at the neighboring Alturas Chamber of Commerce. Meyer, a native of Alturas, makes the history of this area come alive through her colorful narratives.

PARKS, BEACHES, AND RECREATION AREAS

• **Modoc National Wildlife Refuge** 🐾🐾🐾🐕 See ❶ on page 40.

The only dogs who are allowed off leash here are bird hunters, and only during the appropriate seasons. Otherwise, dogs have to wear leashes in the Dorris Reservoir area of the refuge.

Sections of the reservoir are closed during nesting season, but you can usually take your leashed dog on a hike on the horse trail that goes across the top of the dam and down to the surrounding land. The bird-watching is excellent at the right time of year. Bring your binoculars and get up close and personal with tundra swans, Canada geese, and cinnamon teal. Earthbound residents include coyotes, antelope, and rabbits. It's hard to hold binoculars while your dog is tugging at the leash, but make sure your pooch doesn't get away.

From Alturas, drive about three miles east on Parker Creek Road. Call (530) 233-3572 for dates and restrictions.

• **Veteran's Memorial Park** 🐾🐾 See ❷ on page 40.

About the size of a city block, this park is chock full of trees on one side and covered with grass on the other. Picnic tables dot the grounds. Since there are no restaurants with outdoor tables for dogs and their people in Alturas, this is a good place to bring your lunch so you can break bread with your pooch. Dogs must be leashed.

The park is on County Road 56 and U.S. 395. (530) 233-2512.

PLACES TO STAY

It may seem as though Alturas has an incongruously high number of motels per capita, but when you consider how many people pass through here, it makes sense. The dogs sure appreciate the small-town hospitality.

Best Western Trailside Inn: Rates are $44 to $60. 343 North Main Street, Alturas, CA 96101; (530) 233-4111.

Drifters Inn: This one's on lots of property. Rates are $29 to $46. Dogs are $3 extra. 395 Lake View Road, Alturas, CA 96101; (530) 233-2428.

Essex Motel: Rates are $35 to $48. Small dogs only, please. 1216 North Main Street, Alturas, CA 96101; (530) 233-2821.

Frontier Motel: There's a big backyard behind the motel, and good dogs are allowed to check it out. Rates are $28 to $43. 1033 North Main Street, Alturas, CA 96101; (530) 233-3383.

Hacienda Motel: Rates are $27 to $45. 201 East 12th Street, Alturas, CA 96101; (530) 233-3459.

Wagon Wheel Motel: Rates are $29 to $39. 308 West 12th Street, Alturas, CA 96101; (530) 233-5866.

NEW PINE CREEK

PARKS, BEACHES, AND RECREATION AREAS

•**Cave Lake/Lily Lake** 🐾🐾🐾🐾 🐕 *See ❸ on page 40.*

You can't get much more remote than this in California. These small, trout-filled lakes are on the Oregon border, and it takes a six-mile drive up a fairly steep gravel road to get there. You probably won't find any people here, but you'll find all the peace you need. The world is truly hushed at this 6,600-foot elevation.

Dogs love it because they're allowed to hike leash-free. The campground at Cave Lake has six sites, each available on a first-come, first-served basis. Leash your dog if anyone else is camping here. The campground is free and is open from July to October.

From U.S. 395 in New Pine Creek, take unpaved Forest Service Road 2 east about six long, uphill miles. The campsites are just after the Lily Lake picnic area. (530) 233-5811.

PLACES TO STAY

Cave Lake/Lily Lake: See Cave Lake/Lily Lake above for camping information.

4
HUMBOLDT COUNTY

Bigfoot. Giant redwoods. Fog. Off-leash beaches. Humboldt County is home to the magical, mythical wonders of Northern California. Dogs love them all, with the possible exception of Bigfoot (see Willow Creek on page 53).

The coast here is one of the best in the state, as far as dogs are concerned. Several beaches and one 62,000-acre coastal park allow your dog to strip and go leashless.

Sun worshipers won't share a dog's excitement about the coast. If fog is a four-letter word to you, try another county, or at least drive inland a bit. The fog can be so thick in Arcata that you'll have a hard time seeing your dog on the beach. But then as you drive east on mountainous Highway 299, the fog gives way a little at a time. As you reach higher elevations, white mist swirls around the taller trees, and on the way downhill, it's suddenly gone. You're free to frolic in the sun, but your beaches will be far behind.

If you and your dog like fishing, the Eel, Trinity, and Klamath Rivers offer easy roadside access at hundreds of points throughout the county. Joe always gets excited when there's a fish at the end of the line. He'll sit and watch for hours for the pleasure of witnessing the moment of truth, and if we throw the fish back, he'll sit and stare at the water, awaiting its return.

No visit to Humboldt County is complete without a drive down the Avenue of the Giants. This world-famous 31-mile scenic drive between Redway and Pepperwood will take you past some of the biggest and most magnificent redwoods in the world. Just about all the adjectives for "really old" have been used to name the giants in this area. You can visit the Grandfather Tree, the Eternal Tree, and the Immortal Tree, to name a few of the

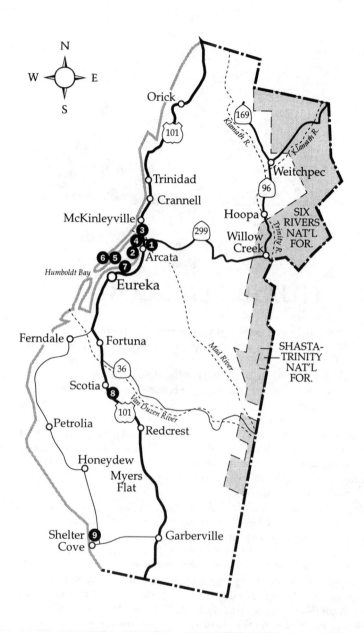

Orick

101

Trinidad

Crannell

McKinleyville

3
4 **1**
2

6 **5** **7**

Arcata

Humboldt Bay

Eureka

299

Hoopa

Willow
Creek

Weitchpec

169

96

Klamath R.

Klamath R.

Trinity R.

SIX
RIVERS
NAT'L
FOR.

Mad River

Ferndale

Fortuna

36

Scotia

8

101

Van Duzen River

Petrolia

Redcrest

Honeydew

Myers
Flat

SHASTA-
TRINITY
NAT'L
FOR.

Shelter
Cove

9

Garberville

elderly stars appearing on The Strip.

NATIONAL FORESTS

See the National Forests and Wilderness Areas chapter starting on page 748 for important information and safety tips on visiting national forests with your dog.

• **Shasta-Trinity National Forest** 🐾🐾🐾🐾 🐕
See page 754.

• **Six Rivers National Forest** 🐾🐾🐾🐾 🐕
See page 754.

ARCATA

For a university town, Arcata is a mellow place. But dogs who want to have a wild time have ample opportunity. Although canines are not permitted in the lush green park in the old town square, they're allowed off leash at a couple of really prime areas, and on leash in a few more magical spots. For added dog pleasure, it's usually cool and foggy here, so it's a wonderful place to visit when the rest of the state is broiling.

PARKS, BEACHES, AND RECREATION AREAS

• **Arcata Community Forest/Redwood Park** 🐾🐾🐾½
See ❶ on page 44.

Just a couple of minutes away from the quaint old downtown area of Arcata, this 575-acre park offers 17 trails with 10 miles of hiking for you and your leashed dog. Mornings are enchanting here. Songbirds come to life, and the earth and the redwoods smell fresh in the damp, foggy air.

From U.S. 101, exit at Samoa Boulevard and drive east. At Union Street, go north a few blocks and make a right onto 14th Street. Drive into the forest and park in the large lot. Several trailheads start here. (707) 822-7091.

• **Arcata Marsh and Wildlife Sanctuary** 🐾🐾🐾 *See ❷ on page 44.*

Formerly a sanitary landfill, this 174-acre model restoration project has three freshwater marshes, a brackish lake, and one saltwater marsh. Together, they attract some 200 species of birds, as well as critters like river otters and muskrats. To add to your dog's joy, treated wastewater helps in wetlands restoration here.

Dogs must be leashed, for obvious reasons. Bird-watchers come from all over the state to view a vast array of fine feathered friends, including Iceland gulls, old-squaws, bald eagles, and endangered brown pelicans. Despite Joe's exemplary behavior on a recent visit, he got the evil eye from a couple of people who were chirping to some birds hidden in a tree. I found that walking around with binoculars helps these avid folks realize you're just like them, except you have a dog who shares in the wonders of our winged friends. If you've got a yapper dog, take him somewhere else.

Exit U.S. 101 at Samoa Boulevard and drive west, following the coastal access signs. Turn left on I Street and drive about a mile. The parking lot is on your right. Once in the marsh area, bear right at the wood-chip trail for the best walk possible. You can get a map and guide to the area by calling (707) 822-7091.

• **Clam Beach County Park** 🐾🐾🐾🐾 🐕 *See* ❸ *on page 44.*

Not only can your dog run leash-free at this long ocean beach, you can actually get here very easily from U.S. 101! The combination is almost non-existent in Northern California.

The beach is a good clamming area, as even your dog might have guessed from the park's name. Some dogs like to help you dig for your bivalve supper, which you can cook at the campground here. There are 12 to 14 tent sites in sand dunes, available on a first-come, first-served basis. Sites are $8 to $10. Dogs are $1 extra.

From U.S. 101, about seven miles north of Arcata, take the Clam Beach Park exit west a couple of miles. (707) 445-7652.

• **Mad River County Park** 🐾🐾🐾🐾 🐕 *See* ❹ *on page 44.*

As you drive to this park past old barns and huge green fields full of grazing cows, you'll feel as though you're in the English countryside, especially if it's foggy. Dogs are delirious enough about the rural five-mile drive from Arcata. But when they behold the magnificent beach where they can run leashless, they're dumbstruck. Joe didn't talk the whole time we were here.

The beach is wide, long, and desolate. Beachcombing is fun and there's plenty of driftwood to keep your dog intrigued. The only other people we've ever seen here have been old men with metal detectors, hippies who sometimes spend the night, and dedicated dog owners willing to make the labyrinthine drive from town so their pooches can experience heaven on earth.

From U.S. 101, exit west on Giuntoli Lane and go right almost immediately onto Heindon Road. Follow the signs to the park. On the way, you'll pass one end of the Hammond Trail, a 2.2-mile hiking/biking coastal trail between Arcata and McKinleyville. It's an invigorating walk, but you have to keep your dog leashed. Once at the Mad River, you'll see a sign leading you to the right for fishing access. That's where you can launch your boat on the river, but chances are your dog would prefer to run on the beach, so keep going straight until you hit the small parking lot at the end of the road. (707) 445-7651.

RESTAURANTS

Hole in the Wall: This is a popular pooch hangout. The sandwiches and vegetarian dishes are very satisfying. 590 G Street; (707) 822-7407.

PLACES TO STAY

Best Western Arcata Inn: Rates are $52 to $83. Dogs are $5 extra and are allowed only in smoking rooms (hack, woof). 4827 Valley West Boulevard, Arcata, CA 95521; (707) 826-0313.

Clam Beach County Park: See Clam Beach County Park above for camping information.

Hotel Arcata: Dogs seem to sense the history at this refurbished 1915 hotel. When Joe visited, all he could do was stick his snout around the baseboards and snort in the scents. It's not a graceful technique, but apparently it's efficient. Rates are $55 to $150. Dogs are $5 extra. A $50 pooch deposit is required. 708 Ninth Street, Arcata, CA 95521; (707) 826-0217.

Motel 6: This one is right beside U.S. 101, and they'll often put dogs and their human companions in the rooms closest to the highway because there's a little on-leash dog-relief area there. The constant drone of cars can actually be soothing at 3 A.M. when your dog decides to start scratching himself. The rule here is one smallish pooch per room. Rates are $37 for the first adult, $6 for the second. 4755 Valley West Boulevard, Arcata, CA 95521; (707) 822-7061.

Quality Inn–Mad River: Medium-sized dogs are more than welcome. And there's a beach next door where leashed dogs like to roam. Rates are $45 to $83. Dogs are $5 extra. 3535 Janes Road, Arcata, CA 95521; (707) 822-0409.

EUREKA

This is the county seat of Humboldt, and it's a bustling small city. Fortunately, it also has some Victorian charm, as well as the ocean and Humboldt Bay, so it's not a typical center of commerce.

PARKS, BEACHES, AND RECREATION AREAS

Dogs aren't allowed in Eureka's best city park, Sequoia Park, but that's okay. We found a couple of areas that more than make up for the loss.

• **Samoa Boat Ramp County Park** 🐾🐾½ 🐕 *See ⑤ on page 44.*

If you own a boat and a dog, and you've got them both with you, you'll be glad to know about this small park. Not only is there a launch ramp into the south end of Humboldt Bay, there's also a small beach here so your dog can run around and stretch his legs before he becomes your crewmate during a cruise on the bay. Dogs are allowed off leash on this tiny beach, but somehow the privilege isn't as magnificent as it would be if the Samoa Dunes Recreation Area (see below) wasn't just across the street.

From Eureka, turn west on Highway 255 and cross the Samoa Bridge. Once on the Samoa Peninsula, turn left on New Navy Base Road. The park is about five miles south of the bridge, on the left side of the street. (707) 445-7651.

• **Samoa Dunes Recreation Area** 🐾🐾🐾🐾 🐕 *See ⑥ on page 44.*

Does your dog like sand, sand, and more sand? How does 300 acres of coastal dunes between the Pacific and Humboldt Bay sound? How about boundless, fairly calm ocean? Cool breezes year-round?

If your dog isn't salivating about this park yet, here's the clincher: Well-behaved dogs can run off leash everywhere except the established trails at this Bureau of Land Management park! While you cast for surfperch, hunt for driftwood, or just relax and listen to the foghorns and gulls, your dog is free to run around, as long as he'll come when you call.

We learned about the vital importance of voice control when we spotted an injured duck waddling along the shore. Another dog, a retriever type, scooped up the bird in her mouth and brought it back to her owner. Fortunately, Joe was well leashed by the time he decided he'd like to look into a duck dinner. And even more luckily, once the bird overcame its fear, it got up and continued waddling down the beach as if nothing had happened.

The retriever's owner was shocked that her dog had taken off. "She's so obedient. She always comes when I call," she explained after severely reprimanding her dog. It just goes to show that even the most obedient dogs can get out of hand in tempting situations, so even if you've got a voice-control champ, keep a close eye on him when he's off leash.

This area is actually for off-highway vehicles to peruse, but we didn't see any on either of our visits. The place was deserted, except for a few beachcombers, a couple of dogs, and a kayaker. But keep in mind that your peace might be shattered by the roar of engines. The drivers of these noisy vehicles may not always be aware of dogs, so make sure you and your dog are aware of them. Also be aware that cars are allowed on the beach, but they generally tend to drive very slowly. There's ample room for vehicles, people, and dogs.

From Eureka, turn west on Highway 255 and cross the Samoa Bridge. Once on the Samoa Peninsula, turn left on New Navy Base Road. The park is about five miles south of the bridge, on the right side of the street. There are also several small access points along the road, but it's best to start from the main lot here. (707) 825-2300.

• **South Eureka Coastal Access** 🐾 *See ❼ on page 44.*

The signs along U.S. 101 might beckon you to visit, but you'll be disappointed. The beach is tiny, narrow, and very close to the road. What's more, it's right next to the Elk River Sewage Treatment Plant. Dogs might like the odd odors that waft by, but they're not generally appealing to the human olfactory system. Dogs must be leashed.

Here are the directions, in case your dog can't hold it until you get to a decent park. From U.S. 101, go west on Hilfiker Lane and follow the road as it veers south. A small parking area is on the right. (707) 441-4186.

RESTAURANTS

This often foggy city does not exactly abound with outdoor eateries.

Fresh Freeze Drive-In: Like burgers and ice cream? Tell your dog to make sure you visit this decadent place. At Harris and F Streets; (707) 442-6967.

PLACES TO STAY

Eureka Inn: Dogs don't often get to stay in a national historic landmark, so take advantage of the dog-friendly attitude here. From the Tudor architecture and lobby with high beam ceilings and a fireplace, to the rooms with Queen Anne–style furnishings, the place exemplifies casual elegance. Dogs are asked to stay in the ground-floor rooms. It's usually cooler there in the summer, anyway. Rates are $110 to $240. 518 Seventh Street, Eureka, CA 95501; (707) 442-6441 or (800) 862-4906.

Red Lion Inn: Rates are $79 to $89. Dogs require a $50 deposit, and they're relegated to the first floor. Joe thinks the first floor is the best anyway—none of those pesky stairs to deal with. 1929 Fourth Street, Eureka, CA 95501; (707) 445-0844.

Travelodge: Rates are $50 to $65. Small pooches are preferred. 4 Fourth Street, Eureka, CA 95501; (707) 443-6345 or (800) 255-3050.

FERNDALE

This sweet Victorian town is so historically and architecturally authentic that the entire village is a state historic landmark. You and your dog can savor a walk down Main Street, where you're sure to pass at least a few other dogs with their people. It's so old and refined that it looks like it could be the model for Disneyland's Main Street. If you're hungry, try one of the eateries where dogs can dine at your side on this historic street.

RESTAURANTS
Ferndale is filled with great places to eat. Most of them didn't want to publicize that they allow dogs at their outdoor tables, but here are two that didn't mind:

No Brand Burger Stand: Their logo is a steer skull. The place is located right behind the Yancey Feed Company. Is there any connection here? Eat big burgers at the picnic table. 989 Milton Avenue; (707) 786-9474.

Red Front Store: This is a convenience store with a little bench where you and your dog can eat the little hot dogs they make inside. 577 Main Street; (707) 786-9611.

PLACES TO STAY
The Victorian Inn: Ahh, romance. It's not an impossible dream when you and your special someone are vacationing with your pet. You just have to find the right spot for it. A Motel 6 probably won't do the trick. But a stay at a place like the Victorian Inn will.

This 1890s inn, situated in the heart of sweet, downtown Ferndale, has been named the most beautiful building in Humboldt County. It's lovely on the outside and just as attractive inside. Each room is decorated with a Victorian theme and has real antiques, goosedown comforters, oversized towels, and period art. Our favorite, room 204, even has a fireplace. All have bathrooms, but only three of the rooms have phones, which makes the place feel even more Victorian and romantic. Who needs the phone ringing when you and your special someone are toasting to each other in your room's little turret sitting area, with your dog looking on and waiting for some bread and brie?

Breakfast comes with your room, as do evening hors d'oeuvres and piano music. You can also get a first-class lunch and dinner at the inn's restaurant, but poochies can't dine with you.

If you happen to be traveling with children, they'll delight in the after-dinner toys provided at the inn. The inn also offers knock-your-socks-off romantic packages, which include horse-and-carriage rides, champagne, sweet surprises, and even rose petals on your bed at evening turndown.

Room rates are $75 to $125. There's a $100 deposit for dogs. 400 Ocean Avenue, Ferndale, CA 95536; (707) 786-4949 or (800) 576-5949.

GARBERVILLE
This is a town where many weary travelers with dogs pull off the road for a restful night on their way to magnificent parks in the north, south, east, and west. Sadly, the magnificent Benbow Inn changed its dog-friendly policy since the last edition of this book, but there's still room at the Best Western Humboldt House Inn.

PLACES TO STAY

Benbow Lake State Recreation Area: Of the 975 acres here, dogs are relegated to the campground areas. We've seen some people fishing with their dogs down by the South Fork of the Eel River, but rangers differ about whether or not that's okay.

The park is just off U.S. 101, about two miles south of Garberville. Follow the signs. Campsites are $12 to $16. Dogs are $1 extra. To reserve one of the 75 sites, call Parknet at (800) 444-PARK.

Best Western Humboldt House Inn: Dogs are allowed in a few of the smoking rooms here. This is a decent place to stop if you're on a long road trip, and it's fairly earthquake resistant, if that's the kind of thing that concerns you. I stayed here one night when I was covering a big earthquake. A big old aftershock rattled everyone out of bed, but nothing fell on our heads and the front desk had plenty of flashlights to go around. Fortunately, Joe was back in safe, unshakable San Francisco, but one of the pooches who was a guest here went tearing out of his owner's room and hid until dawn.

Rates are $64 to $89. 701 Redwood Drive, Garberville, CA 95542; (707) 923-2771.

MYERS FLAT

DIVERSIONS

Give him the ultimate tree experience: Most dogs love to relax in the shade of trees or sniff at trees for hints of other dogs. But how many dogs know they can actually drive smack through the center of a tree? Few trees oblige such a fantasy, so the Shrine Drive-Thru Tree is a real find. Dogs seem to enjoy riding through the car-sized hole in the 275-foot-tall redwood's 21-foot-diameter base. But, to be honest, they seem to prefer the adjacent picnic area, where sticky droplets of ice cream sold at the tree's kitschy but fun gift shop hide in the grass.

The sign here says the tree is 5,000 years old, but the folks who take your money say that it's more like 2,000 years. It doesn't really matter. It's big and it's old and it's dog-friendly. "We get lots of dogs come through here. They like the whole tree thing I think," says a Shrine Drive-Thru Tree employee.

It costs $1.50 per person for folks over 11 years old. Dogs, regardless of age, go free, but they must be leashed. 13078 Avenue of the Giants; (707) 943-3154.

ORICK

PLACES TO STAY

Redwood National Park (south section): Dogs used to be allowed on a one-mile-long trail here, but alas, that exception to the stringent national park service rules is gone. Dogs can still camp at the undeveloped Freshwater Lagoon camping area.

From U.S. 101, follow the signs to the park's information center, where you can pick up literature and maps. You can also have a feast at the picnic area there with your leashed dog. Sites are $6 and available on a first-come, first-served basis. For more information, call (707) 464-6101, ext. 5064.

REDCREST

You want redwood gifts? This is your town. The few stores in this tiny community along the Avenue of the Giants carry every redwood gift imaginable, most of no practical value. From redwood burl wall clocks to giant redwood Indians, they've got it all.

RESTAURANTS

Eternal Tree Cafe: Dine on big old redwood tables under the shade of big old redwoods. (Is this like eating a hamburger in front of a cow?) Then visit the Eternal Tree House giant redwood tree, just behind the building (see below). 26510 Avenue of the Giants; (707) 722-4247.

PLACES TO STAY

Redcrest Motor Inn Resort: You and your dog can spend the night in a cabin, tent, or tepee amid the giant redwoods here. The tepee is a truly fun experience for pooches. "We've had one woman who keeps coming up to stay in the tepee with her dog because he loves it so much," says Jeanne, who recently bought the resort with her family and made it very dog-friendly.

The cabins now permit pooches, too, which is a real boon in the colder months. This great pooch policy was the brainchild of Mandy, one of the new owners. She's an affable golden retriever who will be so thrilled to see you that her tail might be in danger of wagging off. If you forget her name, just look at your brochure. She's listed right up there with the rest of the owners. By the way, they're just as dog-friendly. "We LOVE dogs!" exclaims Jeanne.

Cabins are $40 to $70, with kitchens available in some cabins for an additional $9. Tent sites are $14, RV sites are $16 to $20, and the tepees are $20. Dogs pay $5 extra in the cabins, $1 extra for the other places. 26459 Avenue of the Giants; (707) 722-4208.

DIVERSIONS

Survive the ultimate temptation: Your boy dog won't believe his eyes when he visits the Eternal Tree House, along the Avenue of the Giants. When Joe saw this 2,500-year-old giant redwood, he tugged on his leash incessantly so he could get a closer sniff and decide what part of this tree he wanted to claim. It took all my strength to convince him not to desecrate this natural wonder. It's just one of many reasons your dog should be leashed here. The tree (there's no actual "tree house") is at 26510 Avenue of the Giants; (707) 722-4262.

SCOTIA

This small mill town is actually owned by the Pacific Lumber Company. Scotia is home to the world's largest redwood sawmill, and you can tour it for free, but someone else has to wait outside with your pooch. Your dog is allowed to visit the demonstration forest just four miles south of town. It's much quieter than the sawmill, and the trees here are upright—the position that boy dogs prefer.

PARKS, BEACHES, AND RECREATION AREAS

• **Pacific Lumber Company Demonstration Forest** 🐾 🐾 🐾
  See ❽ on page 44.

This 50-acre forest just off the Avenue of the Giants is where you can learn all about native plants and trees. As you walk the two short trails here, signs explain what you see. You'll emerge from the forest enlightened and your dog will emerge refreshed.

Many dogs and people like to bring a snack and eat it at the shaded picnic tables. Don't forget to bring an empty water bottle: the creek has some of the best-tasting water in California.

Tempting as it may be, do not let your dog off leash. Darrell Jarman, who runs the place some summers, says an Akita recently bolted away after a deer. The dog's owners searched for hours, but never found him. There are a few roads around the perimeter of the forest, which makes it even more hazardous if your dog runs away.

The forest is open only in the summer. From U.S. 101, take the Jordan Creek exit (about five miles south of Scotia) and go left. You'll see a large billboard advertising the forest. Follow the signs. (707) 764-2222.

SHELTER COVE

This coastal community is located in the heart of the Lost Coast area of California. It's known for its pristine beauty and prime fishing. But dogs like it because it's surrounded by the King Range National Conservation Area (see Parks, Beaches, and Recreation Areas below). Three areas of this preplanned, privately owned community provide ocean access. We like the Little Black Sand Beach, just off Dolphin Drive.

PARKS, BEACHES, AND RECREATION AREAS

• **King Range National Conservation Area** 🐾🐾🐾🐾 🐕
   See ❾ on page 44.

We came upon this magnificent 62,000-acre coastal area by accident, and all Joe can do is thank the Great Dog in the Sky. This primitive region, which constitutes a good chunk of the Lost Coast, has everything a dog desires deep in his heart: ocean, grassy flats, sandy beaches, trees galore, and best of all, leash-free living.

In less than a three-mile stretch, the King Range rises from sea level to 4,087 feet. The topography is rugged, but far from impassable. Several trails take you across some of the most unspoiled coastal territory in California.

A few Indiana Jones–like dogs can handle the 35-mile wilderness trek along the Lost Coast Trail. Most of the trail is along the beach, and in the mornings you'll likely come to know one of the reasons this area is called the Lost Coast. The fog sometimes gets so thick that even the gulls are silent. But when it lifts, what spectacular sights you'll see! You and your dog will traverse green meadows, Douglas fir groves, and many streams. The terrain is fairly flat, so the real challenge is its length, if you should choose to hike the entire trail. Don't forget, there's always the walk back! Most people prefer to leave a car at one end to make the round-trip easier. You should also keep in mind that this trail can be tough on "house dog" paws. Rangers advise dog booties for parts of the trail.

Joe is the kind of soft-pawed pooch who prefers trails like the Lightning Trail. It's the shortest and shadiest route to King's Peak. Joe approves of the sparkling mountain streams, the shade from the firs, and the brushy meadowland where he can roll like a fool. He especially likes the trail's length—a mere 2.5 miles. The view from the top is hard to beat.

During your hikes, you may run into deer, cattle, sheep, horses, rattlesnakes, and poison oak, so if you let your dog off leash, do so only if she's under excellent voice control. And be sure to keep your pooch very far away from the marine mammals who clamber onto the beaches and rocks. This is a popular rookery, and dogs and sea critters do not mix.

You may camp anywhere you please for no fee, but you need a permit for campfires. Dogs must be leashed in designated campgrounds. It's a good idea to leash your dog at night anyway. Many dogs feel even safer in your tent.

Exit U.S. 101 at Redway and follow Briceland Thorne Road west to this Bureau of Land Management area. For more specific directions to your exact destination in this sprawling conservation area, contact the Bureau of Land Management, Arcata Resource Area, 1125 16th Street, P.O. Box 1112, Arcata, CA 95521; (707) 825-2300.

PLACES TO STAY

King Range National Conservation Area: See King Range National Conservation Area above for camping information.

TRINIDAD

This small coastal town, complete with its own white lighthouse and rocky outcroppings, is like a Mendocino that hasn't been taken over by tourists and artists. Visit before your dog spreads the word about this well-kept secret spot.

While you're here, be sure to stop at Katy's Smokehouse, at 740 Edwards Street, for some of the best doggone smoked salmon you've ever laid your tastebuds on. There's no dining area, so have a friend wait outside with your pooch while you pick up the goods.

PLACES TO STAY

Bishop Pine Lodge: Most of the rustic, wood-paneled cottages here have kitchens, but does your dog care? Not unless you happen to be cooking a burger with his name on it. Dogs care much more about what's outside the cozy cabins at this very dog-friendly lodge. And what's outside is sure to put a smile on even the most somber snout. The lodge is on eight acres of tree-studded land where well-behaved pooches may walk leash-free with you. Rates are $50 to $90. Dogs are $8 extra (think of it as $1 per acre). 1481 Patrick's Point, Trinidad, CA 95570; (707) 677-3314.

Trinidad Inn: At this small, pleasant motel, you and your dog can walk right outside your door and find a trail leading to the woods nearby. Rates are $45 to $105. Dogs are $5 extra and require a $20 deposit. 1170 Patrick's Point, Trinidad, CA 95570; (707) 677-3349.

WILLOW CREEK

Nestled along the banks of the Wild and Scenic Trinity River, this rustic community boasts that it's the gateway to Bigfoot Country. People in these parts frequently report seeing Bigfoot, aka Sasquatch—a manlike, 700-pound hairy creature who's seven to nine feet tall and reputedly has body odor.

I'm not sure what Joe would do if he came across Bigfoot, but since he slunk backwards with his tail between his legs when he saw the statue of Bigfoot in the center of town, it probably wouldn't be one of his prouder moments.

Willow Creek is surrounded by Six Rivers National Forest, where dogs can run around off leash. Stop at the Chamber of Commerce here and pick up maps of the forests and explanations of the available trails. Also see page 754 for more details on the forest. The town is at Highways 299 and 96, about an hour west of Arcata.

5
TRINITY COUNTY

Think about this place we call dog heaven. What are some of the ingredients your dog would desire in his elysian ideal? Besides having you at his side without a leash, he'd want lots of trees, that's for sure. Rivers. Lakes. The scents of nature and rich earth. And maybe some decaying woodland critter to roll on.

Trinity County has all a dog could ever want in heaven or on earth. Joe even managed to find a decaying woodland critter when we last visited, and he rolled all over it and then came running up to me to spread the good news all over my jeans. When I walked into a store to buy some supplies later that day, the clerk and all the customers started asking each other if they smelled a mighty bad stench. I joined them in wrinkling my nose and nodding my head, praying no one would figure out my guilt until I was long gone.

The county has a couple of charming old towns, but the real charm here for dogs and their people is that more than 90 percent of the land is part of the national forest system. When driving from just about any location to just about any other location in the county (other than the few main towns on the east side), there are countless places where you can pull your car over and take your obedient dog for a leash-free hike. As long as you're in a national forest and away from houses and developed areas, it's generally okay.

While here, you mustn't miss the magnificent Trinity Alps. You'll feel as if you're in Switzerland, only your dog won't have to be quarantined for six months! The only papers you'll need to hike the Trinity Alps Wilderness is a permit from the U.S. Forest Service. See Shasta-Trinity National Forest on page 754 for more information on this spectacular spot.

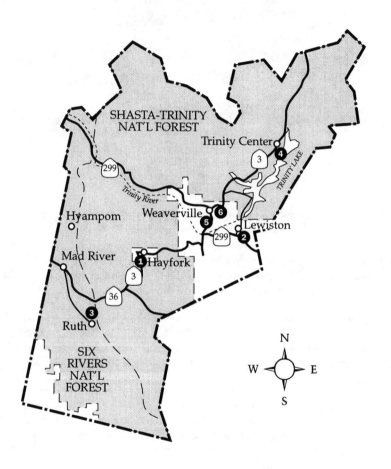

SHASTA-TRINITY
NAT'L FOREST

Trinity Center

299 4

TRINITY LAKE

299

Trinity River

Hyampom

Weaverville 6
5

Lewiston

299 2

Mad River

1 Hayfork

3

36

Ruth 3

SIX
RIVERS
NAT'L
FOREST

N
W E
S

NATIONAL FORESTS

See the National Forests and Wilderness Areas chapter starting on page 748 for important information and safety tips on visiting national forests with your dog.

- **Shasta-Trinity National Forest** 🐾 🐾 🐾 🐾 🐕
  See page 754.
- **Six Rivers National Forest** 🐾 🐾 🐾 🐾 🐕
  See page 754.

DOUGLAS CITY

PLACES TO STAY

Trinity Island Resort: If you've got a water dog who likes to hike and hankers for an extra-large site to park his RV or set up his pup tent, look no further. The Trinity Island Resort, located on the banks of the Trinity River, has just what he needs. For dogs and people who need to get away from it all, the resort offers some secluded spaces right on the river. But you'll never be far from the resort's activities, which include fly-fishing, gold panning, hiking, horseshoes, volleyball, and badminton. A small store sells groceries and fishing supplies, and boasts "free fishing advice, sometimes reliable, but improving."

The resort will soon be renting out "yurts." They're a kind of tent/cabin complete with bathroom, and they're good for visitors year-round. Dogs dig 'em because it's kind of like being in the great outdoors without having to really rough it.

Sites are $13 to $19. Dogs are $1 extra. The mailing address is P.O. Box 237, Douglas City, CA 96024. Call (530) 623-5798 for directions.

HAYFORK

This valley town in the Trinity Alps was at the heart of the state's logging culture for nearly a century. But overharvesting and environmental concerns pretty much put an end to logging here in the early 1990s. Times are tough. Businesses are closing at an alarming rate. But the town's main park (see Hayfork Park below) remains at the core of many a resident's and visiting dog's good times. (Okay, two of Hayfork's three bars still exist, but dogs, especially teetotaler dogs, prefer the park.)

PARKS, BEACHES, AND RECREATION AREAS

- **Hayfork Park** 🐾 🐾 ½
  See ❶ on page 56.
  The spreading oak trees are enough to make a grown dog quiver with joy. Human adults love to lounge in the shade of the trees' canopies or stroll across the park to visit the historic schoolhouse. Kids love the pool, the playground, and the tennis courts. Dogs like the grass, but they're not too fond of the leashes they must wear.

The park is at Community Drive and Highway 3. (530) 623-1319.

HYAMPOM

Don't worry if you're a native Californian and you've never heard of Hyampom: some folks in adjacent towns have never heard of it either. Hyampomeranians (that's not what they call themselves, but Joe Dog thinks it's an appropriate term considering the subject matter) identify their location by telling you they're "about 20 miles away from Hayfork." Well now, that certainly settles things. Dogs like it because there's plenty of national forestland around the area, and the people who live here (250 on a very good day) seem to have a big place in their hearts for dogs.

PLACES TO STAY

Ziegler's Trails End: The seven wooden housekeeping cabins at this little resort are charming and promise to become even better (wood-burning stoves and other improvements to come soon), but what really sets dogs' tails to wagging is the natural splendor outside the cabins. The resort is set on some beautifully landscaped land along the South Fork of the Trinity River. Apple, peach, and pear trees abound, as do brilliant flowers.

There's something for everyone. Water dogs and their soggy people can head for the relaxing beach and swimming area. (Well-behaved dogs can be leash-free on most of the property.) Anglers will drool over the great steelhead and trout fishing. Bird-watchers can take a gander at great blue herons, ospreys, and bald eagles. Folks who enjoy working the land can pick blackberries in season. And anyone who relishes wholesome country foods will love the fresh eggs (from Lee and Thora Ziegler's very own brood) and fresh-baked bread available here for a very reasonable rate.

Rates are $50 for up to two people. Each additional guest is $10. Dogs are free. Weekly rates are available. The resort is off Highway 3. The mailing address is P.O. Box 150, Hyampom, CA 96046; (800) 566-5266.

LEWISTON

This is a tiny, historic mining town that has so few tourists, you'll think you're in a time warp. What's really great about a visit to Lewiston is that there's plenty of access to the Trinity River. Just look around and it's there. The area off Rush Creek Road at Lewiston Road is a popular access point.

PARKS, BEACHES, AND RECREATION AREAS

• Community Park 🐾 *See* ❷ *on page 56.*

You may as well take your dog on a walking tour of this quaint town, because you'll definitely cover more land, and you'll surely see more grass, trees, and bushes than you will in this small park. It's a pretty spot for humans, but only about one of its two acres is accessible right now. Dogs may find it a little restricting, but if your leashed dog just needs to stretch her legs, it's not a bad place to set a spell.

Located on Lewiston Road at Viola Lane, the park is run entirely through volunteer efforts by the residents of this small community, so there's no phone number for it.

RESTAURANTS

The Hitchin' Post: Buy your night crawlers here and have a bite to eat at this charming old house, chock full of outdoor tables. Depending on how busy it is, your dog might have to be tied to the proverbial hitchin' post here, but he'll get a big bowl of water and a doggy bone regardless of where he reposes. The place doesn't serve food at all in the winter. At the Lewiston Turnpike and Deadwood Road, in historic Lewiston; (530) 778-3486.

PLACES TO STAY

Lakeview Terrace Resort: If you ever wanted a place to call your own right on fishable, swimmable Lewiston Lake, this is about as close as you'll come (unless you call the local real estate agent). You and the dog of your choice get to stay in your very own, very clean, air-conditioned housekeeping cabin. The owners of the cabins are sweet people who love dogs. Their German shepherd will vouch for them. They'll be happy to point you to some good on-leash walking areas around the grounds. Boat rentals are available.

Rates are $45 to $100. Dogs are $3 extra. RVs can stay here for $18. The resort is at Star Route Box 250, Lewiston, CA 96052; (530) 778-3803.

Old Lewiston Inn: Half of the people who visit this very charming, very romantic inn, located in the National Historic District of Lewiston, are fly-fishing enthusiasts, since an attractive catch-and-release section of the Trinity River is only 200 feet away. The inn offers fly-fishing packages, which include all meals (at nearby restaurants) and fishing instructions. Dogs who enjoy nosing around water and sniffing the mighty pines that tower above will love this aspect of the inn.

But the place is also renowned for its non-angling charm. Rooms have antiques from the mining era, but they aren't so antique that they don't have heating, air-conditioning, and cable TV. A hot tub, located beside the river in an enclosed room, offers privacy from other guests but an up-close-and-personal view of nature and a very starry sky.

The owners, Connor and Mary Nixon, owned and operated a jungle tour lodge at the headwaters of the Amazon River for 13 years, so they know how to make guests feel at home when they're far from their usual setting. Witness breakfast, for instance. It's a full, country-style feast. The Nixons welcome good dogs, saying that in six years, they've had only one problem with a guest's pet. ("And it wasn't really the pet's fault," says Connor.)

Rates are $75 to $95. Fly-fishing packages start at $140. Deadwood Road Historic Area (P.O. Box 688), Lewiston, CA 96052; (800) 286-4441.

RUTH

PARKS, BEACHES, AND RECREATION AREAS

•Ruth Lake 🐾 🐾 🐾 *See* ❸ *on page 56.*

Ruth Lake doesn't need to go on a diet—it's skinny enough. On a map or from the air, it looks like an eight-mile-long caterpillar. But seen in person, it's an attractive lake surrounded by alpine lands. Dogs have to be leashed here, but they have a good time following you around from the campsites to the lake. Plenty of dogs go fishing in their people's boats. Some anglers say their dogs bring them good luck. There are plenty of trout here and even some black bass.

The lake is actually a reservoir, created by the damming of the Mad River. In good times, it's about 1,200 surface acres. Six Rivers National Forest has hundreds of thousands of off-leash acreage not far from here. (See page 754 for more information on this forest.) Call the ranger district office at (707) 574-6233. Unfortunately, at the moment there are no trails close to the lake. But ranger Steve Pollard says he recently discovered a very run-down trail that was used by pioneers back in the late 1800s. If the U.S. Forest Service can clean it up and make it hikeable again, dogs will be allowed, but only on leash.

The trail would be accessible from both campgrounds here. Sites at the Bailey Canyon Campground are $6. That campground is about 13 miles southeast of the town of Mad River on Lower Mad River Road. The Fir Cove Campground is just 12 miles southeast of Mad River. Sites there are also $6. The campgrounds are open from May to early September. Call the ranger district at (707) 574-6233 for details.

PLACES TO STAY

Bailey Canyon Campground: See Ruth Lake above for camping information.

Fir Cove Campground: See Ruth Lake above for camping information.

TRINITY CENTER

This tiny community is the home, in spirit if nothing else, of the giant and breathtaking Trinity Lake. It's also quite close to the breathtaking Trinity Alps Wilderness, where dogs can hoof it off leash (see page 754).

PARKS, BEACHES, AND RECREATION AREAS

• **Trinity Lake** 🐾🐾🐾🐾 🐕 *See ❹ on page 56.*

Even the national forest staff here call this place dog heaven. One dog-friendly ranger told me, "You just take your boat, pull up to just about any bank, and say, 'Okay, Fido, let's get a little exercise. No leashes required!'"

And he's right. While the lake's 145 miles of shoreline have no real trails, there are still plenty of places where your dog can stretch his unleashed body. The lake is quite low of late and it's probably going to remain that way. The folks who decide such things have deemed that, to prevent floods, the lake should be 20 feet lower than the past norm. That means that except for some steep banks and developed areas, there's plenty of romping room for dogs.

Your best bet is to take your dog to the more remote parts of the lake. And the best way to get there is by boat. If you don't have one, why not rent one? And what better boat to rent than a houseboat? (See Diversions on page 61 for details on this great adventure.)

Mid-June to mid-July is the best time of year to come here. Snow still covers the peaks of the glorious Trinity Alps (which you can see in all their glory from almost anywhere on the lake), but the weather at the lake is great. So is the fishing. It's not nearly as crowded as Lake Shasta to the east, so you can fish without worrying about too many loud jet skiers or fast boats.

The south end of the lake is 14 miles north of Weaverville on Highway 3. Call the Shasta-Trinity National Forest District Office at (530) 623-2121 for more details and suggestions on which area would best suit your purposes.

PLACES TO STAY

There are campgrounds all around Trinity Lake. Most are concentrated on the lake's south side, but a couple of the more secluded ones are toward the north. Below we've listed one on each side of the lake. Call the Shasta-Cascade Wonderland Association at (800) 326-6944 for more information on cabins and other lakeside lodgings.

Cedar Stock Resort: This is a great place to enjoy a vacation at Trinity Lake. The cabins are rented by the week, with costs ranging from $375 to $950. Dogs are $35 a week extra. Just bring your own bedding and you'll be set. The kitchen and utensils are all part of the deal. And if you're in the mood for a nautical stay, see Diversions below for information on houseboat rentals. The resort is 15 miles north of Weaverville on Highway 3. The mailing address is HCR 1, Box 510, Lewiston, CA 96052; (530) 286-2225 or (800) 982-2279.

Clark Springs Campground: There are enough lakeside sites to make everyone happy. An added bonus for boaters is a boat ramp that's just a stick's throw away. Sites are $8, first come, first served. Dogs must be leashed. From Weaverville, drive 18 miles north on Highway 3. The campground is at Mule Creek Station. (530) 623-2121.

Jackass Springs Campground: This one's a rustic and fairly secluded campground with 21 sites on the northeast section of the lake. There's no fee, so you can buy your leashed pooch a bone with the money you save. All sites are first come, first served.

This is not the kind of place you want to visit for just one night. The ride itself may make you want to stay for the rest of your life or be airlifted out. From Highway 299, turn north on Trinity Mountain Road (west of Whiskeytown Lake) and drive about 12 miles to the Trinity Mountain Station. Turn right and drive about 12 miles on East Side Road—it's gravel, so be ready for some hopping around. At Delta Road (it's dirt), go left and drive about three more miles to the campground. It's actually worth the drive to get away from the more crowded southeast side. (530) 623-2121.

Ripple Creek Cabins: The Trinity River runs right by these cozy, homey cabins. You'll have no shortage of outdoor adventures to share with your dog here. Rates are $64 to $125. Dogs are charged a $10 onetime fee. P.O. Box 4020, Star Route 2, Trinity Center, CA 96091; (530) 266-3505 or (510) 531-5315.

DIVERSIONS

Float in a houseboat: Wow! This is one adventure your dog will never forget. Renting a houseboat is the ultimate way of staying with your dog on vacation. As long as you pull up to shore enough for her to get plenty of exercise and do her thing, she's going to be one happy pooch. Remember that the lake is pretty much surrounded by national forestland, where your dog can exercise leash-free. Make sure you keep an eye on her, though, and don't forget about her while you're inside making a soufflé.

Houseboats can be small and simple or large and fairly luxurious. (Okay,

okay, they usually do look like mobile homes, but they are comfortable.) Chances are pretty good that you don't already own your own houseboat, but fear not. There are plenty of places to rent them in the area.

One of the largest and most dog-friendly is the Cedar Stock Resort. "Dogs are just as much a part of the family as everyone else. They can't miss a vacation like this," says Steve, one of the resort's managers. Bringing a dog along will cost you $35 extra per week. The houseboats here run from $825 to $2,500 weekly, with big off-season discounts. You may want to invite some friends along to share the costs. The smaller ones fit up to six folks and the larger ones can stash all your relatives.

The Cedar Stock Resort's houseboat headquarters is 15 miles north of Weaverville on Highway 3. The mailing address is HCR 1, Box 510, Lewiston, CA 96052; (530) 286-2225 or (800) 982-2279. For other houseboat rental companies, call the Trinity County Chamber of Commerce at (530) 623-6101. Be sure to reserve early. Sometimes all the houseboats for the summer are booked by April! Houseboat "high season" is usually from April to November.

WEAVERVILLE

This is the gateway to the Trinity Alps, and what a gateway it is. It's a former boomtown with a Main Street that's almost unchanged from the 1850s, complete with spiral staircases and brick facades.

Some 2,500 Chinese immigrants were among the miners who came here during the Gold Rush. The Joss House State Historic Park contains the oldest active Chinese temple in California. Dogs aren't allowed inside, but as you're driving to the adjacent Lee Fong Park (see below) on Main Street, you can take a gander at it.

Work has started on an integrated trail around the periphery of Weaverville. When it's done, it will be an excellent way to explore the town with your leashed dog. Call the Trinity County Chamber of Commerce at (530) 623-6101 or the Shasta-Trinity National Forest ranger station at (530) 623-2121 for updates.

PARKS, BEACHES, AND RECREATION AREAS

• Lee Fong Park 🐾 🐾 🐾 ½ *See* ❺ *on page 56.*

Set on the land once owned and farmed by a prominent local Chinese family, this magnificent park still has the appeal of an old-time farm. It even has several apple and pear trees that still bear fruit—but don't steal from the branches. (We were told that it's okay to pick up a piece of fruit from the ground, though.)

The park is undeveloped and fairly large. It's far from the paved road, but leashes are the law here anyway. A dirt path will take you around the park's perimeter in about 10 minutes if you want a fast walk, but most people who come here like to stop and smell the fresh and fruity air. You can pretend it's your own orchard, and chances are good that no other park user will stop by and ruin your fantasy. For some reason, the place gets very little use.

Dogs seem to love this park. Joe and Bill had a field day sniffing the freshly fallen fruit and checking out what was lurking in the tall grass. Each walked away with a fairly mushy apple in his mouth.

The park is on Main Street/Highway 299 just south of the historic part of town. It will be on your right as you're driving south. Although a small sign points to the park, the bigger farmer's market sign is actually a better landmark. Turn right and drive a few hundred feet to the dirt parking lot. When you see the bathroom in front of you and the old ranch house on your left beyond some trees, you'll know you're in the right place. (530) 623-5925 or (530) 623-6101.

• **Lowden Park** 🐾 🐾 ½ See **6** on page 56.

Dogs who like big pine trees like Lowden Park. The park has playing fields, playgrounds, and an area where you don't have to do anything at all. Its edges are lined by pines and a tall fence. Dogs have to be leashed, but it's good to know that if they pull the leash from your hands, they'll still be pretty safe from traffic.

From Highway 3 in the north part of town, go south on Washington Street. The park will be on your left in about a block. (530) 623-1319.

RESTAURANTS

Alan's Oak Pit: Come and get just about anything that can possibly be barbecued. 1324 Nugget Lane; (530) 623-2182.

Miller's Drive-In: You can't sit at the outdoor area with your dog, but you and your pooch can pretend you're living back in the 1950s and get served in your car. Joe likes this idea, but I think he's just hoping to see a waitress in a poodle skirt. 796 Main Street; (530) 623-4585.

PLACES TO STAY

49er Motel: Rates are $32 to $55. 718 Main Street, Weaverville, CA 96093; (530) 623-4937.

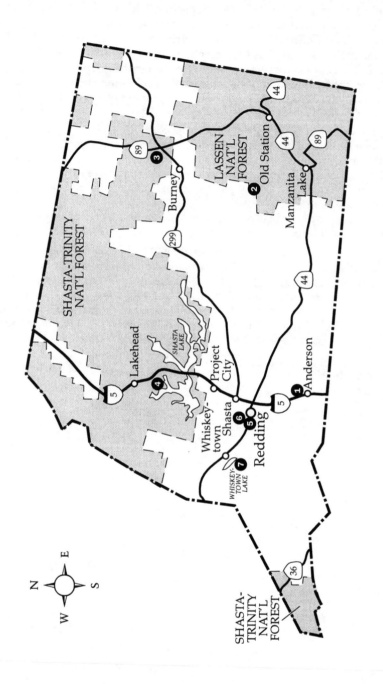

6
SHASTA COUNTY

If you and your dog are aching to get away from city life, have we got a county for you! See that leash draped over your banister? You'll have to bring it, but you won't have to use it much.

Between the national forests, a state forest, and even a small city park, your obedient pooch can get all the leash-free exercise she needs. She'll go home with a wide grin on her snout. Your snout will be smiling, too.

NATIONAL FORESTS

See the National Forests and Wilderness Areas chapter starting on page 748 for important information and safety tips on visiting national forests with your dog.

• **Lassen National Forest** 🐾🐾🐾🐾 🐕
See page 751.

• **Shasta-Trinity National Forest** 🐾🐾🐾🐾 🐕
The forest pretty much surrounds beautiful, fish-filled Shasta Lake (see page 68). If it's not too snowy before Christmas, you and your dog can pay $8 and go find yourselves a Christmas tree. Not many people have hundreds of thousands of acres of Christmas tree lots. See page 754 for more information on this forest.

NATIONAL PARKS

• **Lassen Volcanic National Park** 🚒
Dogs are barely allowed to set paw in this fascinating park. For more details on what you and your dog are not missing if you stay away from this national park, see the description on page 76 in the Lassen County chapter.

ANDERSON

PARKS, BEACHES, AND RECREATION AREAS

• **Anderson River Park** 🐾 🐾 🐾 1/2 *See* ❶ *on page 64.*

This 425-acre park has plenty of trees for boy dogs with bottomless bladders. Dogs seem to like the one-mile nature trail better than anything, except for the sweet little pond full of ducks. The ducks would like to remind you that dogs must be leashed here. For the humans in the crowd, the park has picnic tables and a playground.

The park is on Rupert Road at the Sacramento River. Driving south on Interstate 5, exit at the North Street off-ramp and follow North Street north a few blocks to Stingy Lane. Turn right and drive a few blocks to Rupert Road, then turn left. Drive to the end and you'll be at the park. (530) 378-6656.

PLACES TO STAY

Best Western Knights Inn: Rates are $46 to $60. Small dogs only, please. 2688 Gateway Drive, Anderson, CA 96007; (530) 365-2753.

BURNEY

This scenic mountain community is an excellent place to get away from urban life without getting carried away with the idea. There's enough civilization here to please even the primmest poodle.

I don't normally mention dog groomers in this book, unless they happen to offer something for pets and their people at the same time, like self-serve dog washes. But I have to put in a kind word for a place called The Pet Set. While we were visiting with 15-year-old Nisha one hot summer day, we could see the heat was really getting the poor old girl down and that there was no way she could spend the afternoon outdoors with us. So we called the only groomer in the Burney phone book, hoping she could spend the day somewhere cool and get a haircut to boot, and the kindly folks there rearranged their schedule to fit in Nisha on very short notice. They gave her extra tender care ("We love old dogs," says one of the owners), a comfy, air-conditioned setting, and a very short haircut. Nisha left looking and feeling like a million bucks, and the price was so reasonable that Nisha could have paid for it out of her own pocket. We'll always think of The Pet Set when we think of Burney. (In case you find yourself in a similar pickle, or if you just want the kindest cut, their phone number is 530-335-3761).

PARKS, BEACHES, AND RECREATION AREAS

You won't find many community-style parks in these parts. What you will find are forests everywhere—many thousands of acres. Much of the surrounding land is public land, and people and their pooches just have to pull off the road for a fun little hike. But make sure you're not treading on private property first. Just ask around town and you'll get so much help from the dog-friendly folks here that you'll have a hard time deciding which piece of dog heaven to visit.

For a great hiking experience in a place with well-defined dog rules (off leash!) and boundaries, take your dog to the Latour Demonstration State Forest.

• **Latour Demonstration State Forest** 🐾🐾🐾🐾 🐕
See ❷ on page 64.

This 9,033-acre forest provides sweeping vistas of the Cascade Range. The 67 miles of logging roads are open to people and their leash-free pooches. But don't take your dog off leash unless she's 101 percent obedient, since the park is home to bobcats and mountain lions and bears (oh my!). "Be careful, because dogs are real tasty tidbits to bears," says Dan Higgins, assistant manager of the forest.

Firs, pines, mountain shrubs, and delicate wildflowers abound. You don't have to stay on the logging roads to enjoy the forest. Because of the sustainable-yield forestry practiced here, it's not a dense forest. "You can just pick out a creek and follow it all day and have a magnificent time," says Higgins.

Camping is terrific and fairly primitive. Eight campsites, available on a first-come, first-served basis, are spread throughout the forest. Better yet, there's no fee. The forest is off-limits through the winter, unless your dog knows how to use a snowmobile.

From Highway 299 just west of Burney, drive south on Tamarack Road. In about 10 miles, Tamarack will fork. Take the road that keeps going straight, Jack's Backbone Road/Road 16. In about six more miles, you'll see a sign for the forest. Turn right and drive to the forest headquarters to pick up a map. The park is also accessible from Redding. Call (530) 225-2422 for directions or information.

• **McArthur–Burney Falls Memorial State Park** 🐾1/2
See ❸ on page 64.

This park is home to breathtaking 129-foot Burney Falls, which Theodore Roosevelt once dubbed "the eighth wonder of the world." Dogs can get a glimpse of this wonder from a point at the top of the falls, next to the parking lot. Since dogs can't go on any trails here, this is the only area where you and your dog can ooh and ahh at the falls. Don't be surprised if your pooch gets that "I gotta go to the bathroom" look while gazing at the falls. About 100 million gallons of icy water cascade down daily. It's enough to make a grown dog cross his legs.

You can camp at one of the park's 128 sites with your pooch. Rates are $12 to $16. Dogs are $1 extra. The day-use rate is $5 per car, plus $1 for dogs. From Burney, drive about five miles northeast on Highway 299, then go north on Highway 89 about another six miles to the park. Call Parknet at (800) 444-PARK for reservations. For park information, call (530) 335-2777.

RESTAURANTS

Alpine Drive-In: The beef is here. Eat a hamburger at the outdoor tables with your pooch. 37148 Main Street; (530) 335-2211.

Wiggy's: The food here isn't fancy, but that's just how dogs like it. They can dine with you at the outdoor tables. There's no real street address, but it's on Highway 299, right in town. (530) 335-2120.

PLACES TO STAY

Charm Motel: Rates are $46 to $75. Dogs are $5 extra. 37363 Main Street, Burney, CA 96013; (530) 335-2254.

Green Gables Motel: You won't find Anne (of Green Gables) around here, but you will find yourself feeling at home at this little motel nestled in pine-studded surroundings. It's conveniently located for fishing. All rooms come with coffeepots and refrigerators. Rates are $44 to $88. Dogs pay a $5 fee per visit. 37385 Main Street, Burney, CA 96013; (530) 335-2264.

Latour Demonstration State Forest: See the Latour Demonstration State Forest on page 67 for camping information.

McArthur–Burney Falls Memorial State Park: See McArthur–Burney Falls Memorial State Park on page 67 for camping information.

DOGGY DAYS

Is that a mask, or . . . ?: If your dog is so ugly that even Rodney Dangerfield would be speechless, enter him in the Ugly Dog Contest at the annual Burney Basin Days celebration. It's a howl. The contest is part of the weekend-long event around July 4. Call (530) 335-2111 for details.

FALL RIVER MILLS

PLACES TO STAY

Fall River Hotel: As long as dogs go in through the side door (there's a good, flea-free restaurant and bar in the front), they're very welcome at this historic, friendly 12-room hotel. Between the brass beds, antique furnishings (including quaint Victorian lampshades, for dogs who are Martha Stewart fans), and handmade quilts, a stay at this lodging, built in 1935, makes you feel like you've stepped back in time. So will the price. Rooms are $40 to $60. Some rooms have private baths, and one even has its own kitchen. The hotel also offers a "fun package," which includes a gourmet dinner and a terrific country breakfast.

The cost is $89 for two. The hotel is located near a PGA-rated golf course and some world-class fishing, and it's about halfway between Lassen Volcanic National Park and Mount Shasta. 24860 Main Street, P.O. Box 718, Fall River Mills, CA 96028; (530) 336-5550.

LAKEHEAD

PARKS, BEACHES, AND RECREATION AREAS

• **Shasta Lake** 🐾 🐾 🐾 🐾 🐕 *See ❹ on page 64.*

At 29,500 acres, this is California's largest man-made lake. If you and your dog fish, swim, or watch waterfowl, you'll be in heaven here. When full, it has 370 miles of shoreline—more than San Francisco Bay.

The lake is surrounded by national forestland. More than 30 miles of trails travel into the nearby forest, and once you're away from civilization and campsites, your dog can throw his leash to the wind. Depending on where you hike, you'll pass all kinds of natural wonders, from wooded flats and secluded creeks to rocky mountains and gushing waterfalls. Keep in mind that even though this is a northern lake location, it can still get mighty toasty in the summer, so try to bring your dog here at some cooler time of year.

The U.S. Forest Service manages 380 sites at 21 campgrounds. Some are very primitive, while others seem like mini-motels. Sites cost from $9 to $22. The lake is one of the few in California where you and your dog can camp along the shore. If your pooch has been extra good, he deserves to "ruff" it at one of these sites. About a quarter of the sites are available first come, first served. For reservations at the others, call (800) 280-2267.

A first visit to Shasta Lake can be a confusing experience. The lake has so many arms and so many trails that it's hard to know where to go. The trails at Jones Valley, Packers Bay, Bailey Cove, Shasta Dam, and Hirz Bay not only make for excellent woodland hiking, but provide good access to shoreline fishing. (The lake can get very crowded during the summer, so be prepared to sacrifice solitude for the sounds of water-skiers and jet skiers.)

There's also such a wide variety of campsites that it can make your head ache just thinking about the possibilities. And who needs that just before a four-paw vacation?

Here's a suggestion: Get a map or a brochure of the lake and a little advice from a ranger. The folks at the visitors center are very helpful, but you may find them insisting that your dog must be leashed everywhere in the forest. As of this printing, that's just not true. To get to the visitors center, take the Mountain Gate–Wonderland Boulevard exit off Interstate 5 about four miles south of the lake. Follow the signs. The phone number is (530) 275-1587. Call the Forest Service supervisor's office at (530) 246-5222 for the latest on the leash/leashless law.

PLACES TO STAY

The area has numerous places to park your pooch for the night. Around here, they're called resorts, but please don't start thinking of Beverly Hills spas and lush oceanside luxury suites. The resorts here are usually rustic, wooden lakeside cabins. They make wonderful retreats after a long day at the lake, and many are surrounded by great hiking land. We're listing just one here, but the Shasta–Cascade Wonderland Association can provide you with more. Call the dog-friendly folks there at (800) 326-6944.

O'Banion's Sugarloaf Cottages Resort: The comfortably furnished cottages are just a Frisbee's throw from the lake. We've really enjoyed our sojourns to these modern but cozy cabins. If you visit at the right time, you'll be stunned at the peace and quiet. We stayed here once in April, and boy was it ever quiet. Of course, it was freezing cold and pouring rain, so maybe that had something to do with it. But the comfy cabins were sure good to come home to after a long day of wet outdoor fun.

The folks who run this place have a wonderful dog of their own, and he has the run of the place. His name is Bailey, and he loves people and pooches. Don't be surprised to see his big, friendly face at your front door. He probably just wants you to accompany him on a stroll to the lakeshore.

Daily rates from Labor Day to Memorial Day are $59 to $122. During the rest of the year, the cabins must be rented by the week, and they cost from $660 to $1,400. 19667 Lakeshore Drive, Lakehead, CA 96051; (530) 238-2448.

Shasta Lake: See Shasta Lake on page 68 for camping information.

DIVERSIONS

Leave the doggone Dramamine behind: Life on the waters of Shasta Lake is bliss for anyone of the seasick persuasion. The best way to experience this calm, flat body of water is to rent a houseboat for a few days. The only thing that may make you nauseated is having to go home at the end of your floating vacation.

Most houseboats aren't terribly attractive on the outside (unless you have a predilection for the mobile-home look), and they're not fast or exciting, but they're so much fun that you may wish you could stay forever. Imagine waking up in a secluded cove in the morning, taking your dog off the boat for a lakeside hike and a brief swim, and then sitting down to a big breakfast cooked in your boat's well-equipped kitchen before setting off to cruise around the lake. (Joe, the landlubbing Airedale, says pass the bacon but forget about the swim.)

Several local houseboat outfitters permit pooches on their boats. Rates start at about $800 a week, or $200 nightly, but are generally considerably more. Although houseboats are meant to be shared with friends, you won't want to fill the boat to capacity if you're bringing your dog along. Two big people, one or two kids, and a dog on a boat that sleeps six gives you plenty of paw room.

Four dog-friendly houseboat renters are Seven Crown Resorts, (800) 752-9669; Antlers Resort, (530) 238-2553 or (800) 238-3924; Holiday Harbor, (800) 776-BOAT; and Jones Valley Resort, (530) 275-7950.

MILL CREEK

PLACES TO STAY

Mill Creek Resort: The nine housekeeping cabins here aren't terribly fancy, but the location is to drool for: The resort is located along Mill Creek, a catch-and-release trout stream in the Southern Cascades, near Lassen Volcanic National Park. (Sorry, no dogs are allowed at Lassen unless they want to walk along paved roads or camp.) The elevation is 4,800 feet, which means lots of fresh air and some cold mountain streams. Dogs enjoy the trees here, but keep them leashed, because chaseable creatures (deer, raccoons, squirrels) abound.

Rates are $40 to $70. Dogs are $1 extra. 1 Highway 172, Mill Creek, CA 96061; (530) 595-4449.

REDDING

It may be full of franchise motels and restaurant chains, but this city is the hub of the northern reaches of California. It's an excellent base for exploring the surrounding wildlands.

PARKS, BEACHES, AND RECREATION AREAS

Dogs have their own park here and they're allowed to hike on the Sacramento River Trail. Other than that, city parks are off-limits to pooches.

• **Benton Airpark Park** 🐾🐾🐾🐾 🐕 *See ❺ on page 64.*

Joe's eyes opened wide and he stood utterly still for a few moments when he first saw this park. Somehow, although there were no dogs in it at the time, it seemed he could tell that this was a place of great dog happiness.

He sniffed that joyous dog smell in the air, his tail started twitching, and he began pawing the gate to get in.

Once inside this large, completely fenced dog park, he rolled for several minutes. He rolled underneath the cold aluminum picnic table. He rolled on the mud around the water fountain. He rolled in the grass on the park's east side, and then in the grass on the west side. He stopped rolling only when another dog came in to share the park with him. They chased each other around like fiends for 30 seconds. Then he started rolling again, this time on the grass in the north side of the park. He was in heaven.

We've had mixed signals from parks department officials regarding the leash law here. Some have told us well-behaved dogs are free to tear around off leash. One told us pooches must be leashed except during organized dog-training sessions. The latest word from a park official is that no leash is okay. Eventually there may be signs that clarify the matter. Meanwhile, let your conscience be your guide.

Leashed or unleashed, dogs seem to really like it here. The fact that there are only a couple of small trees doesn't seem to bother them. If they want shade, they can go under the picnic tables. If they need to lift a leg, there's always a fence post.

From Interstate 5, exit at Highway 299 and go west for about two miles, following Highway 299 through a couple of turns in central Redding. At Walnut Street, turn left. Drive five blocks and turn right on Placer Street. You'll see the park in one block, at the corner of Placer Street and Airpark Drive, adjacent to the Benton Airpark (where the airplane activity provides amusement for bird dogs here). (530) 225-4095.

• **Sacramento River Trail** 🐾 🐾 🐾 ½ *See* ❻ *on page 64.*

This 5.7-mile paved trail follows the wide and wonderful Sacramento River, leading you and your leashed dog through riparian terrain and rolling hills. It's best to visit on weekdays or uncrowded weekends, because on some days your dog can get the feeling of being mighty squished with the masses who like to hike and bike through here.

Bill loves to take a dip in the water when we visit. He could lie in the Sacramento all day, but he hates the idea that he's missing out on sniffing the scents left by other dogs. When he's in the river, he's constantly looking to see who passes on the trail. When he's on the trail, he always keeps one eye on the beckoning river. It's a real doggy dilemma, but he manages.

From Market Street/Highway 273, go west on Riverside Drive (just south of the river). Head west to the parking area. There are many other access points. Call (530) 225-4095 for details. See Doggy Days on page 72 for a couple of the dog-oriented events that take place here every year.

RESTAURANTS

Between the Bun: You and your pooch are welcome on the veranda of this aptly named burger joint. 1718 Placer Street; (530) 243-2449.

Hamburger: Sit on the patio with your favorite dog and eat their classic burgers. The place has been here since 1938. 1320 Placer Street; (530) 241-0136.

Hill o' Beans: Eat good croissant sandwiches and wash them down with hot coffee at the outdoor patio. 1804 Park Marina Drive; (530) 246-8852.

PLACES TO STAY

Thanks to the very dog-friendly new manager of several motels around town, Redding has become an easy, convenient place to spend the night with your traveling pooch.

Americana Lodge: Rates are $25 to $45. Dogs require a $100 deposit. 1250 Pine Street, Redding, CA 96001; (530) 241-7020 or (800) 626-1900.

Best Western Hospitality House: Rates are $45 to $75. There's a $6 doggy charge and a $25 dog deposit. 532 North Market Street, Redding, CA 96003; (530) 241-6464.

Best Western Ponderosa Inn: Rates are $45 to $65. Dogs require a $100 deposit. 2220 Pine Street, Redding, CA 96001; (530) 241-6300 or (800) 626-1900.

Capri Motel: Rates are $25 to $45. Dogs require a $100 deposit. 4620 Highway 99 South, Redding, CA 96001; (530) 241-1156 or (800) 626-1900.

Comfort Inn: Rates are $45 to $70. Dogs require a $100 deposit. 2059 Hilltop Drive, Redding, CA 96002; (530) 221-6530 or (800) 626-1900.

Doubletree Hotel: As long as your dog isn't of the Great Dane/Saint Bernard size, she's welcome here. Rates are $79 to $160. 1830 Hilltop Drive, Redding, CA 96002; (530) 221-8700.

Motel Orleans: Rates are $35 to $55. Dogs require a $100 deposit. 2240 Hilltop Drive, Redding, CA 96002; (530) 221-5432 or (800) 626-1900.

Motel 6: One small pooch per room is permitted. Rates are $40 for the first adult, $6 for the second. 1640 Hilltop Drive, Redding, CA 96002; (530) 221-1800.

DOGGY DAYS

Jog your dog: Each April, the city sponsors a canine run along the Sacramento River Trail. Leashed dogs have a choice of running three miles or 5.7 miles. Most prefer the three-mile course. Water and treats are ample rewards for a jog well done. For entry information and exact dates, call (530) 225-4095.

Bless your dog, then take a hike: This terrific doggy day in early October starts with a nondenominational Blessing of the Animals, honoring St. Francis (your dog's patron saint). Then it's off for a one-mile strut or a three-mile stroll along the Sacramento River Trail. Your dog will get plenty of water along the way. Afterward, join the rest of the leashed pooches for a slew of post-walk activities, including fly-ball, obedience, and agility demonstrations. Call the Haven Humane Society at (530) 241-1653 for entry info and dates.

SHINGLETOWN

RESTAURANTS

The Shingle Shack: The town's name and the name of this little restaurant could well inspire thoughts of a certain rather miserable malady, but keep thinking to yourself, "They mean wooden shingles, they mean wooden shingles," and your appetite will soon return. The food here is unpretentious and reasonable. Dine with doggy at a large selection of outdoor tables. The address is simply Highway 144. You'll know it when you see it. (530) 474-5652.

WHISKEYTOWN

PARKS, BEACHES, AND RECREATION AREAS

•**Whiskeytown Lake** 🐾🐾🐾½ *See* ❼ *on page 64.*

Many miles of trails await you and your leashed, four-legged beast at this 42,500-acre segment of the Whiskeytown-Shasta-Trinity National Recreation unit. The lake has 36 miles of shoreline for great fishing and paw dipping, but most dogs seem to like to hang out here with all four feet planted on terra firma.

The short Shasta Divide Nature Trail, the three-mile Davis Gulch Trail, and many miles of unimproved backcountry trails beckon dogs who like to wake up and smell the earth. You can get a map and a little advice from a ranger about your hiking options.

For pooches who like to sleep in all day, the camping is divine. Sites are on a first-come, first-served basis from Labor Day to Memorial Day, but reservations are needed during the busy summer months. Call (800) 365-CAMP. Sites are $8 to $16. There's no day-use fee.

From Redding, drive about eight miles west on Highway 299. The information center and overlook is at Highway 299 and Kennedy Memorial Drive. It's not far from Dog Gulch, in case your dog was asking. (530) 246-1225.

PLACES TO STAY

Whiskeytown Lake: See Whiskeytown Lake above for camping information.

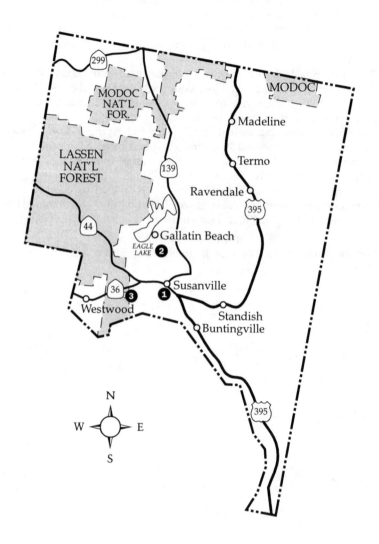

MODOC NAT'L FOR.

MODOC

LASSEN NAT'L FOREST

299

Madeline

Termo

139

Ravendale

395

44

Gallatin Beach

EAGLE LAKE ❷

Susanville

36 ❸ ❶

Westwood

Standish
Buntingville

395

N
W · E
S

395

7
LASSEN COUNTY

There's not much civilization around here, so you and your dog will have to be content with hiking, camping, spending quality time at an incredible ranch (see Spanish Springs Ranch on page 76), or cross-country skiing. Blue skies, crystal lakes, rugged mountains, and silent deserts await you, so it's not a bad fate—unless your teacup poodle is absolutely longing to visit a really nouvelle sushi joint.

NATIONAL FORESTS

See the National Forests and Wilderness Areas chapter starting on page 748 for important information and safety tips on visiting national forests with your dog.

• **Lassen National Forest** 🐾🐾🐾🐾 🐕
They're a little more sticky about off-leash dogs here than at most national forests. Dogs are allowed sans leash, but rangers say they're quick to bow to the county leash law if there's any complaint. This could be because the forest surrounds Lassen Volcanic National Park, which has extremely strict dog laws. See page 751 for more information on this forest.

• **Modoc National Forest** 🐾🐾🐾🐾 🐕
See page 752.

NATIONAL PARKS

• Lassen Volcanic National Park 🔥

Don't get your hopes up about enjoying this astounding national park with your dog. Pooches are all but banned from this geological wonderland. Here's the long and exciting list of places they're allowed to visit: parking lots, paved main roads, and campgrounds.

Since walking in a parking lot or along a heavily used road probably isn't your dog's idea of a good time, we'll just describe the camping. Dogs are permitted, on leash, at the four campgrounds that are accessible by car. There are a total of 357 campsites, all first come, first served. Sites are $6 to $8 and are located in both Shasta and Lassen Counties. Call (530) 595-4444 for directions to the campground most convenient to you.

MINERAL

This place is rock-solid, in Joe's opinion. (His sense of humor isn't.)

PLACES TO STAY

Lassen Mineral Lodge: Dogs are allowed in the older rooms in this motel, and they can camp with you at all the lodge's tent and RV sites. Some motel rooms have kitchens. There's a general store and a restaurant on the premises, and plenty of hiking nearby. Motel rates are $60 to $90. Campsites are $15 to $20. Dogs are $5 extra. The lodge is on Highway 36 East. The mailing address is P.O. Box 160, Mineral, CA 96063; (530) 595-4422.

RAVENDALE

PLACES TO STAY

Spanish Springs Ranch: A stay at this 5,000-acre ranch could be the vacation of a lifetime for you, your dog, and the other members of your family. Don't come here just to spend the night. Come here to experience ranch life on the high desert firsthand.

Spanish Springs offers such authentic ranch activities as branding and sorting cattle, cattle drives, and horse drives, plus archery, clay shooting, cross-country skiing (in winter), and horseback riding. Lodgings at the main ranch consist of several comfortable wooden suites/cabins. The big, cozy lodge has a huge fireplace in the main room. At Christmas, the tree in the lodge is decorated in a delightful Western motif. The lodge is also where you'll get your meals, which are out of this world.

Dogs need to be on leash when near the hub of the main ranch, but with 5,000 acres, there are plenty of trails where you can let them off leash. Co-owner Sharon Roberts will be happy to point you to some mighty fine spots. Spanish Springs is actually much bigger than 5,000 acres, but since other segments of the ranch are loaded with livestock, dogs are permitted only at the main ranch.

The rate here is $125 per adult. Children are a little more than half price. Dogs are free. The price includes a spacious two-room suite, all your meals, and all your activities. Spanish Springs is located just east of U.S. 395. The mailing address is P.O. Box 70, Ravendale, CA 96123; (530) 234-2050 or (800) 272-8282.

SUSANVILLE

Susanville is the second-oldest town in the western Great Basin, and a stroll through the historic uptown area with the city's free "Come Walk with Us" guide will fill you with all the historical knowledge you and your dog could ever need. But quite frankly, your dog will probably enjoy romping outdoors in this area much better than boning up on the local lore.

PARKS, BEACHES, AND RECREATION AREAS

• **Biz Johnson Rail Trail** 🐾🐾🐾🐾 🐕 *See* ❶ *on page 74.*

Whether your dog is a couch poochtato or a super athlete, this trail is bound to become a favorite. The wide trail winds more than 25 miles from Susanville to Mason Station and then follows existing roads another 4.5 miles into Westwood. You'll know you're there when you see the 25-foot carved redwood statue of Paul Bunyan and Babe the Blue Ox. (Boy dogs, have some respect for this folklore hero and fight the temptation to do leg lifts on him and his bovine buddy. This is his "birthplace," and they say his ghost doesn't take kindly to such indiscretions.)

With 11 bridges and two tunnels, the trail follows the Fernley and Lassen Railway line, which was built in 1914 to serve the world's largest pine mill. As you hike, you'll find signs marking the locations of a 300-man logging camp, freight and passenger stations, and logging spur lines. The place is popular in the warmer months. Obedient dogs are allowed off leash, but beware of fast mountain bikes. In winter, it's a cross-country skier's heaven. Leashless dogs love charging through the white powder at your side.

If your dog prefers his hikes or ski jaunts to be short, you can use any of six trailheads and flip around when he's looking bored or bedraggled. If he's a rugged outdoor kind of guy, you'll want to consider hiking longer portions of the trail and camping along the way. Primitive sites are open year-round along the very scenic Susan River, and there's no fee. It's advisable to pack your own water or treat the river water before you drink it.

From Susanville, follow Highway 36 to South Lassen Street at the western end of town. Go left on South Lassen Street for four blocks to the trail. Call the Bureau of Land Management's Eagle Lake Resource Area at (530) 257-0456 for directions to other trailheads and for pocket-sized trail guides and plant identification keys. Some of the land here is also under the management of Lassen National Forest. Call their headquarters at (530) 257-2151.

• **Eagle Lake** 🐾🐾🐾½ *See* ❷ *on page 74.*

Tired of all those look-alike man-made reservoirs and lakes? Here's a lake that's large and natural. In fact, at 42 square miles, Eagle Lake is the second-largest natural lake in California. Better yet, it's also one of the state's cleanest and least crowded lakes.

If you like trout fishing, you and your dog will enjoy angling for Eagle Lake trout, which are found nowhere else in the world. In the cold fall months, you can fish from the north shore and land some big ones. But don't forget that even though your dog is wearing a coat, he's going to freeze if you don't occasionally get up and walk around with him.

The northern end of this clear blue lake is characteristic of high desert country, with sage and juniper, rocky shoreline, and reed patches. There's plenty of open land where you and your dog can dillydally the day away. The land leading down to the south shore is a drastic contrast, with lush pine forests and mountains of green.

Dogs should be leashed, because critters ranging from deer and pronghorn antelope to bald eagles are quite common here.

The U.S. Forest Service runs four campgrounds here, with a total of 325 sites. Fees range from $9 to $12. Call (800) 280-CAMP for reservations. The Bureau of Land Management's North Eagle Lake Campground has some rugged sites on the north end of the lake. BLM sites are $6 per night, and they're available on a first-come, first-served basis. Call (530) 257-0456 for BLM camping information.

From Susanville, drive 2.5 miles west on Highway 44, then turn north at County Road A1. After about 16 miles, you'll reach the south shore campgrounds. Watch for signs. For more information, call Lassen National Forest at (530) 257-2151.

PLACES TO STAY

Biz Johnson Rail Trail: See Biz Johnson Rail Trail on page 77 for camping information.

Eagle Lake: See Eagle Lake on page 77 for camping information.

River Inn Motel: Rates are $40 to $56. Dogs are $5 extra. 1710 Main Street, Susanville, CA 96130; (530) 257-6051.

Super 8 Motel: Rates are $38 to $50. 2975 Johnstonville Road, Susanville, CA 96130; (530) 257-2782.

WESTWOOD

PARKS, BEACHES, AND RECREATION AREAS

•**Biz Johnson Rail Trail** 😺😺😺😺 ✕ *See ❸ on page 74.*

See page 77, under Susanville, for trail information. The Westwood section of the trail starts at Ash Street near Third Street and follows Ash Street and County Road A21 four miles to the Mason Station trailhead. That's where the main part of the trail begins.

8
MENDOCINO COUNTY

When people from out of town think of Mendocino County, they often think of quaint inns, sweeping seascapes, and perfect little coastal villages teeming with artists and tourists. But there's one vital image missing, that of a nosy dog sniffing about, exploring forests and fields, oceans and rivers, and some of the most dog-friendly inns in the state.

While the coast of Mendocino County attracts most visitors, dogs have much more freedom inland, where they're allowed to run off leash in three very large parcels of land. But there's still something magical about the Mendocino coast. Although it offers no leash-free areas, dogs thrive on the ever-cool climate and the salty air. Joe once perched himself on a Mendocino bluff top for a solid hour and sat utterly still, except for his flaring nostrils. For Mr. Mobility to have such patience and fascination, there must be magic in the air (or at least the smell of a few deceased fish).

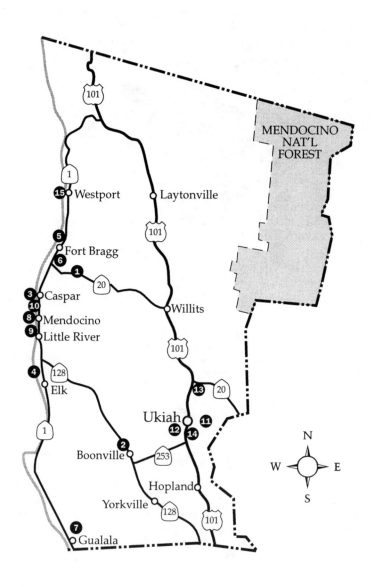

MENDOCINO
NAT'L
FOREST

101

1
15 Westport
Laytonville

101

5
Fort Bragg
6
1
20
3 Caspar
10
8 Mendocino
9 Little River

Willits

101

4
128
Elk

13
20

1

Ukiah
12
14
11

2
Boonville
253

Hopland
Yorkville
128
101

7
Gualala

N
W E
S

NATIONAL FORESTS

See the National Forests and Wilderness Areas chapter starting on page 748 for important information and safety tips on visiting national forests with your dog.

• **Mendocino National Forest** 🐾🐾🐾🐾 🐕

Only a tiny portion of this national forest rests in its namesake county. Some rangers prefer to have dogs off leash only in the two wilderness areas, neither of which is in Mendocino County. Others say it's okay for dogs to be leash-free everywhere but in camping areas. See page 752 for more information.

STATE FORESTS

• **Jackson State Forest** 🐾🐾🐾🐾 🐕 *See ❶ on page 80.*

What a treat! Almost all of this 50,000-acre park is available to dogs who don't want to be attached to a leash. This is a demonstration area for forest management practices, featuring self-guided educational nature trails and many miles of hiking available on old logging roads.

One of the more popular trails is the Tree Identification Trail, just off Highway 20, about 11 miles east of Highway 1. It's one of the few areas of the forest that's actually marked from the highway, and it's a great place for you and your dog to learn the difference between madrone, hemlock, redwood, fir, and any other varieties that confuse you (including the oft-ignored wax myrtle). Dogs probably already know all about these trees, since the males of the species have made intimate acquaintances with so many in their lives. But they won't mind going along for the walk.

Critters abound, so if you can't trust your dog 100 percent, it's a good idea to keep him leashed. We've run into only the occasional quail and salamander during our sojourns, but we hear there are black bears and mountain lions around as well.

Sadly, the budget for the state forests has been cut so drastically that some trails might become neglected and some campgrounds may have to close. Call the forest before you visit to find out the status and obtain maps. As of press time, the forest had 44 campsites, available at no fee. You'll need to bring your own water (and don't forget your dog's) because the sites don't runneth over with amenities. You'll also need a camping permit and a campground map. Call (707) 964-5674 or pick up maps and information in person at the Department of Forestry office at 802 Main Street in Fort Bragg.

The forest stretches along Highway 20 from just east of Mendocino and Fort Bragg to about nine miles west of Willits.

BOONVILLE

PARKS, BEACHES, AND RECREATION AREAS

• **Faulkner County Park** 🐾🐾½ *See ❷ on page 80.*

Since you and your dog probably each enjoy flowering shrubs for your own reasons, you'll have a pleasant stroll here. Of the two trails that wind through this 40-acre park, the Azalea Discovery Trail is the one nosy dogs like best. This is a 12-stop nature trail through a stand of azalea shrubs and redwoods. Difficult as it may be, try to prevent your dog from doing one-leg salutes to the azaleas.

The park also features a hiking trail to the top of the ridge. It's a short trail, but it gets the blood flowing after a long car trip. Kids enjoy the small playground near the entrance.

The park is on Mountain View Road, two miles west of Boonville. (707) 463-4267.

RESTAURANTS

Boont Berry Farm: The food at this quaint yet rustic restaurant is health-ful and delicious. Most of the produce is organic, and most of the deli food is vegetarian. Pick up goodies for a picnic or dine with your dog at one of two wooden benches outside the attractive storefront. 13981 Highway 128; (707) 895-3576.

CASPAR

PARKS, BEACHES, AND RECREATION AREAS

•**Caspar State Beach** 🐾🐾🐾 *See* ❸ *on page 80.*

The beach here is small, but it's a good place to walk your dog if you're between Mendocino and Fort Bragg and your dog starts getting that desper-ate look. You won't find many people here, but dogs still have to be leashed.

The beach is at Doyle Creek, off Point Cabrillo Drive (Old Highway 1). (707) 937-5804.

PLACES TO STAY

Caspar Beach RV Park: A mini-city, this RV park is for people who want to get away from civilization while not getting too far from it. About 25 tent sites are available, but you can feel lost among the mobile homes. In addi-tion to hiking with your on-leash dog at the adjacent beach, you can also rent a video or play your favorite game in the video arcade. It's not exactly roughing it, but some people and their dogs are in heaven here.

Rates are $18 to $25. Dogs are $1 extra. From Mendocino, drive three miles north and take the Point Cabrillo Drive exit to Russian Gulch State Park. Take Point Cabrillo Drive west to the campground. (707) 964-3306.

ELK

PARKS, BEACHES, AND RECREATION AREAS

•**Greenwood State Park** 🐾🐾🐾 *See* ❹ *on page 80.*

Leashed dogs enjoy a romp on the quarter-mile-long beach here just about as much as their people do. The sea stacks alone are worth checking out, but with 47 acres of park set along coastal bluffs, there's more to do than just gawk.

Admission is free. The park is conveniently located beside the divine Greenwood Pier Inn (see below). You'll see the signs for the park once you're in the area. (707) 937-5804.

RESTAURANTS

Greenwood Pier Cafe: Dogs and their guests can sit at the outdoor tables among lettuce, herbs, and other plants growing for the scrumptious salads served here. Fresh local seafood is the specialty, but the place will tickle your taste buds no matter what you choose. The cafe is a new addition to the four-paw Greenwood Pier Inn (see below). 5928 South Highway 1; (707) 877-9997 or (707) 877-3423.

PLACES TO STAY

Greenwood Pier Inn: Joe and I drool when we think of the Greenwood Pier Inn. It can't be helped. The place is a peaceful, spectacular work of art with one of the best locations of any inn we've ever come across. It's located at the top of a magnificent ocean bluff. The views of the ocean are amazing, there's easy beach access, and the food is to die for (see Greenwood Pier Cafe, above). There's even a big outdoor hot tub perched on a bluff. (Sorry, water dogs, but the tub is for humans only.) The inn's cozy rooms are adorned with fireplaces, handmade quilts, and original, unique artwork.

Rates are $110 to $120. Dogs and extra people (more than two) are an additional $12 each. 5928 South Highway 1, P.O. Box 336, Elk, CA 95432; (707) 877-9997 or (707) 877-3423.

FORT BRAGG

While Fort Bragg is now the commercial hub of the Mendocino coast, it once served as a fort built to maintain order for the Mendocino County Indian Reservation. The fort was abandoned in 1864, and it wasn't until 20 years later that Fort Bragg found its calling as a lumber town.

You and your dog can visit the Chamber of Commerce and pick up a walking-tour map of historic Fort Bragg. This won't substitute for a visit to the many wonderful beaches in the area, but it's a good way to learn about history while your dog puts his nose to the ground and learns who's been walking on the city's sidewalks.

Joe's favorite part of town is the Noyo fishing village. Fishing fleets come in here with their catches and unload them at restaurants and processing plants. This is the real thing, not a San Francisco Fisherman's Wharf facade where selling T-shirts has come to replace the real business of fishing. And mmmm, it smells so fishy. Dogs are exhilarated just breathing the air.

PARKS, BEACHES, AND RECREATION AREAS

• **MacKerricher State Park** 🐾 🐾 🐾 1/2 *See* ❺ *on page 80.*

This eight-mile beach encompasses a few smaller beaches, including the secluded Pudding Creek Beach at MacKerricher's southern end. Unfortunately, dogs are forbidden at the strip of beach near the main parking lot, but all you have to do is walk north or south a few hundred yards and miles of beach are all yours.

Joe adores this seaweed-strewn beach, although his species is supposed to be leashed. There's a little of everything here, from headlands to forests to a small lake. For dog exercise, it's best to stick to the beach. You'll run into fewer people and horses than you will in other park areas. Near the northern section of the beach, it gets so wide that you feel as though you and your dog are walking with Lawrence of Arabia. It may be tempting to walk on for what seems like eternity, but keep an eye on the time: It's tough walking back when it's dark.

Wildlife is everywhere. More than 100 species of birds inhabit the park. Tidepools are rich with life. And harbor seals bask and breed on secluded rock outcroppings, sometimes even in the beach areas. But don't go anywhere near them, with or without your dog! They're shy creatures and will balk at the slightest disturbance, sometimes diving for long periods of time to avoid the possible threat.

It's fun to camp with your dog here. The 142 campsites are roomy and often surrounded by trees. Sites are $12 to $14. Dogs are $1 extra. Phone Parknet at (800) 444-PARK for reservations.

The best place for doggy access to the beach is at the Ward Avenue entrance, about a half mile north of the main park entrance. This is also where the beach starts becoming an enormous sandy mass. But if you're camping in the main section, beach access is just a short walk north or south. If you're unsure of where you and the pooch can walk on the beach, ask a ranger. The areas are not clearly marked.

The main entrance is on the west side of Highway 1, about three miles north of Fort Bragg. It's marked by a large sign. You'll pass by a ranger kiosk, but there's no fee for day use. (707) 937-5804.

• **Noyo Beach** 🐾 🐾 🐾 *See* ➏ *on page 80.*

A better name would be Solitude Beach. We've never seen anyone here, although we've seen footprints, so someone else must know about this place. This small, sandy beach on the mouth of the Noyo River has a leash law, but dogs enjoy trekking around and watching the boats come in with the catch of the day. This is also a good place to pick up the Coastal Trail. For great views, follow it northwest to the entrance to Noyo Bay.

Heading north on Highway 1, go right on North Harbor Drive and loop around down to the beach. (707) 964-4719.

RESTAURANTS

Jenny's Giant Burger: Dogs love to smell the fries frying, the burgers grilling, the milk shakes shaking. It may not be healthy food, but it's good. Dine with doggy at the outdoor seating. 940 North Main Street; (707) 964-2235.

Thai Cafe: When we dined on the porch here, we were in the company of a huge black dog who sneaked some of his owner's pad thai dish when his back was turned. The owner has a dog and says this about dogs eating here: "We like 'em." Outdoor tables are shaded by umbrellas. 500 South Main Street; (707) 964-7931.

PLACES TO STAY

Beachcomber Motel: Dogs love this place just a pinecone's throw from the beach and MacKerricher State Park. Rates are $65 to $275. Dogs are $10 extra. 111 North Main Street, Fort Bragg, CA 95437; (707) 964-2402.

Coast Motel: Who needs a dog with this place around? The owner permits dogs to run leashless on five tree-filled acres of land behind the motel! It's pretty safe from traffic. Rates are $32 to $55. Dogs are $5 extra. 18661 Highway 1, Fort Bragg, CA 95437; (707) 964-2852.

Ebb Tide Lodge: Rates are $55 to $190. Small dogs only, please, and they're

$5 extra. 250 Main Street, Fort Bragg, CA 95437; (707) 964-5321.

MacKerricher State Park: See MacKerricher State Park on page 83 for camping information.

DOGGY DAYS

Looks aren't everything: Dogs not only get to witness four days of people showing off their strength and logging skills when they attend Paul Bunyan Days, they actually get to participate. They can't take part in the ax throwing or the power saw bucking. But if your dog is ugly—so ugly that cats laugh at him and babies scream when he walks by—he can enter in the annual Ugly Dog Contest. It usually takes place on the Saturday of this four-day Labor Day weekend event. There are also contests for the largest dog, the smallest dog, the smartest dog, and the Frisbee-est dog.

The dog part of the festival takes place at the middle school fields, at the corner of Harold and Laurel Streets. (707) 964-9446 or (707) 964-4465.

DIVERSIONS

Climb aboard the Skunk Train: Lapdogs and their people wag their tails furiously when they learn they're allowed to take this fun train from Fort Bragg to Willits (and back). The Skunk Train travels along the Noyo River, among mighty redwoods, and through a couple of tunnels—all of which give dogs a thrill. You may want to pack a lunch for you and the pooch, especially if you're going all the way to Willits. (You can disembark at a station at the halfway point and come back, which isn't a bad idea if you don't want to choo choo all day with your dog.) Either way, you're given ample opportunity at a couple of stops to get out and stretch all of your legs. Rates are $35 for a round-trip ticket, $25 for a one-way or half-way ticket. Dogs go for free, but keep in mind that they have to be small lapdogs, not lapdogs like 65-pound Joe.

You embark on your journey at the foot of Laurel Street. For more information or reservations (which are recommended, and often required), call (707) 964-6371.

GUALALA

Gualala is a funny-sounding name for a cute little seaside town. The southernmost coastal town in Mendocino County, Gualala is the perfect place to visit if you're staying in Sea Ranch, just down the road in Sonoma County (see page 249), and are getting tired of all that uninterrupted tranquillity.

PARKS, BEACHES, AND RECREATION AREAS

• **Gualala Point Regional Park** 🐾 🐾 🐾 *See ❼ on page 80.*

This is the pristine, driftwood-strewn beach you can see from the town of Gualala, just over the Mendocino/Sonoma County border. The small, friendly visitors center offers displays of shore life, Pomo Indian artifacts, and old machinery. Outside is a sandstone bull sea lion. From there, it's a half-mile walk to the beach on a smoothly paved trail, where you and your leashed dog will stroll through mixed grasses, ferns, berries, dunes, and rows of pines and cypresses. At the beach, you can take a trail through a marsh or along a coastal bluff. On the beach you'll find driftwood and piles of kelp bulbs, good for jumping on for their satisfying pop.

The day-use fee is $3. Campsites are $14 (for up to two vehicles), with overnight dogs costing $1. Mendocino County residents pay only $12 per site. There are 26 sites, available on a first-come, first-served basis only. From U.S. 101, turn just south of Gualala at the sign announcing the park and the Sea Ranch Golf Links. (707) 527-2041.

RESTAURANTS
Java Point: Dogs, take note: This is a very, very dog-friendly place. The folks who work here love dogs. So do the owners. So do the patrons, usually. They even give dog cookies to poochies who visit. They're pretty nice to humans, too, serving up extremely fresh soups and unique sandwiches, in addition to the usual coffees and yummy pastries. Dine at the outdoor tables with your happy dog. There's not really an address, but it's on the west side of Highway 1, partway through town, at the Seacliff Center. (707) 884-9020.

PLACES TO STAY
Gualala Point Regional Park: See Gualala Point Regional Park on page 85 for camping information.

HOPLAND
RESTAURANTS
Hopland Farms General Store: You and your dog can eat tasty deli food at any of three outdoor tables across the street from the Fetzer Winery. The employees here are very dog-friendly. 13501 U.S. 101 South; (707) 744-1298.

LAYTONVILLE
PLACES TO STAY
Gentle Valley Ranch and the Ranch Motel: These dog-friendly lodgings are completely separate. Dogs prefer the Gentle Valley Ranch cottages set on 260 acres of prime valley ranch land that, until recently, was a working cattle ranch. The new owners are letting the acreage return to a natural state, and the place is becoming a miniature wildlife preserve. A creek cuts through the northern portion of the Gentle Valley, and it helps attract plenty of wildlife, so keep your dog leashed!

Guests at the comfortable, homey motel, located in the heart of laid-back Laytonville, also have access to the ranch land. It's a good thing, too, because many a dog owner has come here thinking they could take advantage of the nearby Northern California Coast Range Preserve, which consists of more than 7,500 acres of old-growth forests and wildlife habitats run by the Nature Conservancy. But alas, dogs are banned, ixnay, verboten, and just plain old forbidden.

You may even be able to talk the owners into letting you camp on the ranch land. Motel rates are $26 to $45. Cottages at the ranch and in town are $50 and require a minimum three-night stay. The mailing address is P.O. Box 1535, Laytonville, CA 95454; (707) 984-8456.

LEGGETT

DIVERSIONS

Hang around a chandelier: The Chandelier Tree beckons all dogs and people who have ever stood with mouths agape at nature's awesome work. Sure, the 315-foot-high, 2,400-year-old tree has a painful-looking gaping hole in the center of its 21-foot-diameter base so cars can pass through. But of all the drive-through trees on California's north coast, this is the most spectacular: The thick limbs (some of which are eight feet in diameter) branch out about 100 feet above the ground in a most fascinating, chandelier-like way.

Dogs dig the tree, but they generally prefer the little nature trail that starts near the gift shop. It winds through a small portion of fern-carpeted redwood forest. The short hike hits the spot after a long car ride. At the trailhead, you'll be greeted by a sign with a sweet sentiment:

To be like trees, straight true and fine
To make our world, like theirs, a shrine
Sink down, oh traveler, on your knees
God stands before you in these trees.

If you care to continue the religious theme, down the road a bit is a roadside wooden-statue business called Carving for Christ. Dogs must not tempt the wrath of any higher powers by doing leg lifts on these life-sized statues.

The entry fee for the park is $3 per car. It's located just south of Leggett, near the junction of U.S. 101 and Highway 1. Follow the signs. (707) 925-6363.

LITTLE RIVER

PLACES TO STAY

S.S. Seafoam Lodge: If your dog is a water dog, she'll take to this place in a snap. Each room has a nautical motif, and some provide views of the shoreline in the distance. You'll even have access to a secluded little beach. The cottages and small buildings are set in big tree territory, just a few miles south of Mendocino.

With all this going for it, who could ask for anything more? Okay, since you asked: The owners of the S.S. Seafoam Lodge love dogs, so your pooch will be a most welcome guest here. Rates are $95 to $150. Special winter rates are available. Dogs are $10 extra. The lodge is located at 6751 North Highway 1 in Little River. The mailing address is P.O. Box 68, Mendocino, CA 95460; (707) 937-1827.

Sweetwater Inn: This is the cute little sibling of the terrific Sweetwater Inn in Mendocino (see page 90). The inn is set on a sunny hill above Buckhorn Cove. You and your leashed pooch can saunter on down to that sheltered cove for some fine dog ambles along the water.

Dogs are allowed in two of the six rooms here. Each has a fireplace and a fridge. The price is right, too. Rates are $55 to $75. Dogs are $15 extra. You'll have to write to or call Mendocino's Sweetwater (aka The Big Sister) for reservations and more information. You check in at the Mendocino inn and get directions to this one while you're there. The Mendocino Sweetwater is at 955 Ukiah Street, Mendocino, CA 95460; (707) 937-4076.

The Victorian Farmhouse Inn: The owners of this beautiful 1877 Victorian are really good, nice folks who allow good, nice pooches to run around the seven acres surrounding the inn. Dogs love romping around the redwoods and fir trees here, but they love the ocean being just across the street even more.

The inn has been completely renovated and is full of period antiques. All 10 guest rooms have private baths, and most have fireplaces. One of the many benefits of staying here is that you get breakfast served in your room. Yum! Rates are $130 to $150. 7001 North Highway 1, Little River, CA 95456; (707) 937-0697 or (800) 264-4723.

MENDOCINO

Take your dog to New England and never leave the Golden State! Visiting this quaint village, which stood in as Angela Lansbury's hometown in *Murder, She Wrote,* is like stepping across the country and back in time. (Dogs can actually stay in the inn that was supposed to be her home. See the Blair House Inn, page 89.)

Mendocino is no stranger to the limelight; it's been cast in many movies and TV shows (usually as a New England town). Credits include *East of Eden* (1955), *The Russians are Coming! The Russians are Coming!* (1966), and even *Humanoids from the Deep* (1980). Take a stroll with your dog and see if anything looks familiar. If you're a James Dean fan, stop at the corner of Main and Kasten to see where Dean brooded while sitting on a curb in the beginning of *East of Eden*. Dogs may not enjoy this part of your stay too much, because no *Lassie* or *Rin Tin Tin* episodes were shot here. But they don't mind going along for the exercise.

The art galleries that give Mendocino its flavor generally don't allow dogs. But at least you can window-shop with your favorite canine critic. If you see something you like, the artists and gallery owners tend to be very accommodating. One art collector we know ended up having tea and toast in a gallery where she was buying several small prints. Her mutt, Rosy, got her own piece of toast and was offered a pot of tea, which she couldn't drink because it was too warm. The artist obligingly found some ice.

PARKS, BEACHES, AND RECREATION AREAS

• **Friendship Park** 🐾🐾 *See* ❽ *on page 80.*

If your dog is bursting at the seams, this is a decent place to pull off Highway 1. Otherwise, the Mendocino Headlands (see below) are a much better deal for dogs.

The park is small, but friendly to leashed dogs. There's green grass, a playing field, and even some picnic tables in case your dog doesn't want to visit the local eateries after taking care of essential business here. Friendship Park is at Little Lake Road and School Street. (707) 937-4133.

• **Mendocino Headlands State Park/Big River Beach** 🐾🐾🐾½
See ❾ *on page 80.*

Mendocino's sculpted shoreline is a spectacular place for you and your dog to enjoy the sights, scents, and sounds of the Mendocino coast. Unlike most state parks, this one allows leashed dogs on the trails, which wind around the rocky bluffs and provide good views of wave tunnels and arched rocks. Fields extend along the cliff tops, so there's plenty of room for dogs who don't like to hover over the edge of promontories. It's cool year-round, so even malamutes can enjoy an August romp. A sandy beach at the mouth of the Big River near the southern headlands is a tempting place to let your dog off her leash, but watch out: The place can be heavily patrolled.

It's difficult to explore the tiny town of Mendocino without running into the headlands at every turn. Exit Highway 1 at Lansing Street and drive west. The park actually surrounds the little Mendocino peninsula, so just stop at any part that looks appealing. Parking won't be far away. To get to the sandy beach, exit Highway 1 at the sign for Mendocino Headlands State Park and Big River Beach. Follow the signs east. (707) 937-5804.

• **Russian Gulch State Park** 😃 😃 😃 *See* ⑩ *on page 80.*

Your dog will enjoy this small, wild park whose streams drain Russian Gulch. You must leash up, though, and stay off the trails here. But you can still enjoy exploring among the trees of the deciduous forest. And dogs of the leg-lifting persuasion like the fact that huge groves of willows line the gulch. In wet season, you'll have to wade across the gulch to reach the beach, a small one with cliffs at each end. The surf is ferocious; don't let your dog near it. Swimming in the fresh creeks is much more fun for her, anyway.

About two miles north of Mendocino, watch for a small brown sign marking the turnoff. There's a dirt parking lot at the entrance. (707) 937-5804.

RESTAURANTS

Mendocino Bakery: The food here is scrumptious and often even good for you. The bakery concentrates on vegetarian meals, and the pizza is out of this world. Dine with your dog at the many outdoor tables alongside the restaurant. 10483 Lansing Street; (707) 937-0836.

Mendocino Cafe: Dogs love coming here. They get treated beautifully, with a bowl of fresh water and lots of love (if it's not too busy). Reader Melissa Miller, and her German shepherd Lassy, wrote and told us that a waitress gave Lassy "a lovely plate of cooked beef chunks." Now that's one lucky Lassy! (Actually, Lassy lived the first part of her life in Hong Kong, and Miller says her life there was less than perfect, so she deserves this kind of beefy luck, doesn't she?)

Oh, the food for humans is good, too, with a wide range of choices, from light and healthful to sticky and sinful. Dine with your dog on the deck overlooking the water and a garden. 10451 Lansing Street; (707) 937-2422.

Patterson's Pub: You have a choice of 100 (yes, one hundred) beers here, as well as tasty and hearty pub food like fish-and-chips, burgers, and sandwiches. Sip a cold brew and get a hot meal with your pooch at the picnic tables in the enclosed grassy outdoor garden area. Lassy Dog and Melissa Miller turned us on to this great place, too, and we thank them for another terrific tip. 10485 Lansing Street; (707) 937-4782.

PLACES TO STAY

Blair House Inn: The Blair House is probably the most well-known house

---

in Mendocino. If this Victoria

it's probably because it starre

by Angela Lansbury) home i

thought she lived in Cabot C(

The house really does ma

There's a simple, clean elegan

ish and American antiques, o

since you're staying here wi

house itself. That's okay, tho

your very own carriage hous

than the main house, but it's s

a bathroom (with shower), a

The inn is a very short w

88.) Rates for the carriage h(

Little Lake Street, P.O. Box

(800) 699-9296.

The Stanford Inn by the
surroundings, and the ocean? Have we got a place for you.

The Stanford Inn by the Sea has plenty of all three. There's luxury: The beds are big, comfortable antiques, and the rooms all have fireplaces and French doors leading to private decks. There's rustic scenery: The redwood inn is nestled in a grove of pines, surrounded by 11 acres. There's water: On one side of the property is the Pacific, on the other is the Big River.

What more could you want? Red-carpet treatment for your dog? How's this: Dogs are provided with doggy sheets so they can relax anywhere in your room and not leave it covered with their dogginess. Not enough? Okay, we'll tell all: Dogs get the canine equivalent of a pillow chocolate—dog biscuits wrapped with ribbons. (And humans get the real gourmet deal.) There's also a VIP ("very important pet") photo album in the lobby, as well as a collection of dog books. That should get a wag or two out of your pooch.

Humans get the royal treatment at the inn, too. Guests all get to use plush white terry robes, swim in the beautiful greenhouse's heated pool, and partake of wine and tasty snacks at the end of a day of adventuring.

Rates are $190 to $325. Your dog's entire stay will cost him $25. Additional pooches are $7.50 each. The inn is at Comptche-Ukiah Road and Highway 1. The mailing address is P.O. Box 487, Mendocino, CA 95460; (707) 937-5615 or (800) 331-8884.

Sweetwater Spa & Inn: The Sweetwater is even more dog-friendly than it was in its former incarnation as the Sears House Inn. The new owner says dogs have been such great guests that he couldn't help but open up some new areas to them. Dogs are welcome to lounge around with you at the three small cottages (complete with fireplaces or Franklin stoves) that surround this Victorian inn in the heart of Mendocino. They're now even allowed in one room in the cozy inn. It's furnished with beautiful oak antiques from Belgium.

But Joe's top choice of places to stay is the smaller of the two water towers, where he can watch tourists and local cats stroll by in three directions.

The tower has a spiral staircase leading up to a wonderful loft-bedroom area. Downstairs is another bedroom and a skylighted sitting room with a Franklin fireplace. The cottages and water tower all come with yards, so if your dog feels the urge to visit the WC at 3 A.M., you don't have to trudge to the parks. Of course, don't forget to scoop the poop.

The Sweetwater also now includes beautiful ocean-view lodging in Little River. (See page 87.) Pooches are permitted in two rooms there.

The best part of the Sweetwater, in this human's opinion, is its spa. Yummy professional massages and an oh-so-relaxing atmosphere will melt the tension out of any visitor. Another feature that makes it an ideal place to stay is its proximity to the ocean and town—and especially its proximity to the terrific Cafe Beaujolais. Dogs aren't allowed there, but there's nothing wrong with take-out.

Rates are $100 to $115. Dogs are $15. 955 Ukiah Street, Mendocino, CA 95460; (707) 937-4076.

UKIAH

PARKS, BEACHES, AND RECREATION AREAS

• **Cow Mountain Recreation Area** 🐾🐾🐾🐾 🐕 *See* ⑪ *on page 80.*

How does 27,000 acres of leashless bliss sound? This rugged recreation area, run by the Bureau of Land Management, is heaven for dogs who need real, off-leash exercise. With elevations ranging from 800 to 4,000 feet, a good-sized portion of this land is probably off-limits for couch-potato dogs. But there are plenty of trails that even the most sedentary dog/human pair can enjoy.

Dogs can be off leash everywhere but in developed areas like the two small designated campgrounds. (Pitching a tent at one of the 12 designated, first-come, first-served sites won't cost you a cent.) Make sure that your dog is under voice control when he's off leash: Many mountain lions, deer, and bears call Cow Mountain their home, and you don't want your dog tangling with any of them.

If you like nature watching, you'll really enjoy it here. Quail, doves, rabbits, and feral pigs are common sights. Hunters also like it here for the same reasons. Anglers can fish the entire area, including the cold-water streams, which often brim with rainbow trout. Several of the small reservoirs have been stocked with sunfish.

The park is actually 50,000 acres, but 23,000 of those acres in the South Cow Mountain Recreation Area are devoted to off-highway vehicles. If you venture on that acreage with your dog, do keep him on leash. But why go there when you can stay to the north, where the only forms of transportation you have to watch out for are horses and bicycles?

Other than Jackson State Forest and little bits of Mendocino National Forest that sneak into this county, this is the only public land that allows dogs off leash in all of Mendocino County. Use it well, tread lightly, and pack out what you pack in.

Exit U.S. 101 at Talmage Road and drive east until you come to the City of

10,000 Buddhas, where the road ends. Make a right onto East Side Road, and in about a half mile, go left on Mill Creek Road. The entrance to Cow Mountain will be on your left. For information and maps, call (707) 468-4000.

•**Low Gap Regional County Park** 🐾🐾🐾½ *See* ⑫ *on page 80.*

Location isn't everything. This 80-acre park is set just west of the county jail and kitty-corner from the huge Ukiah Cemetery—not exactly ideal neighbors, but that's okay. The park is a great place to go to enjoy an afternoon romp with the dog. You won't even know that grave diggers and prisoners are just down the road.

The park's amenities include 6.5 miles of hiking trails, an 18-hole Frisbee golf course, an amphitheater, and ball fields. Just watch out that your dog doesn't become a bull's-eye for the archery range here. It's about the only possible danger; since no bikes are allowed, you and your leashed pooch won't be run over by speed demons. In summer, Joe likes the nature trail the best. It offers the most shade and is the most secluded.

Exit U.S. 101 at Perkins Street and drive west to State Street. Go north on State Street, then west on Brush Street/Low Gap Road. The entrance is on your left in about a mile. (707) 463-4267.

•**Mendocino Lake Recreation Area** 🐾🐾🐾½ *See* ⑬ *on page 80.*

Next time there's a full moon rising at sunset, this is the place to take your dog. He probably won't become a werewolf, or even a weredog, but there's something magical here when the moon rises over the mountains and lake. It starts its lunar journey as an enormous, orange disk on the horizon, almost as grand as the moon Mrs. Moore saw in *A Passage to India*. As it rises through the fading sky, its face stares into eternity and glows whiter with each degree it ascends. The white cuts a gossamer streak through the lake, and the chorus of serenading crickets becomes almost deafening. You'll want to stay all night, but this is when you should exit, because park gates close shortly after sunset. While the moon provides a wondrous show, it's not worth staying late and having to sleep in your car until the next day. Doggy morning breath can be atrocious.

For all those other days of the year when there's not a full moon rising at sunset, this huge area is still a fun place for a dog who doesn't mind a leash. A couple of trails wind around about half of the lake and frequently take you right down to the lake's edge. It's very quiet here, barring jet skiers. You can throw a line into the lake and come up with dinner in the form of bass or trout. Or just take time out from your hike to watch the deer and the buffleheads play.

From U.S. 101, take Lake Mendocino Drive and follow it east to the lake. You'll have to make a short jog north on North State Road, but you'll catch up with Lake Mendocino Drive in 30 seconds. Then veer east again. The best place to enter with your dog is at the Joe Riley Area, past the boat launching ramp. This is a grassy picnic area, perfect for lunch before a hike. The trailhead starts just beyond the picnic area. (707) 462-7581.

•**Mill Creek County Park** 🐾🐾🐾½ *See* ⑭ *on page 80.*

This 400-acre park directly across from Cow Mountain (see page 91) has everything dogs could want, except off-leash freedom. They can hike, splash in streams, picnic, relax in the shade of bay trees, and draw deep dog breaths on ridge tops.

Exit U.S. 101 at Talmage Road and drive east until you come to the City of 10,000 Buddhas, where the road ends. Make a right onto East Side Road, and in about a half mile, go left on Mill Creek Road. After you pass the pond, you'll see signs for the park. Go right almost immediately, into a group picnic/playground area. Your dog can frolic in the meadow or hike with you on the trail that starts on the west end of the group picnic area. That trail branches off into several different trails, including a nature trail that follows the creek and a trail that leads you to the top of the southernmost ridge where the views are unbeatable. Alternate entrances, in case the gate to the picnic area is shut, are available around the creek and pond, near the small, strategically located parking lots. (707) 463-4267.

PLACES TO STAY

Cow Mountain Recreation Area: See Cow Mountain Recreation Area on page 91 for camping information.

Motel 6: Rates are $30 for the first adult, $6 for the second. And 25 cents will get you 15 minutes of vibrating bed time. It's always relaxing after traveling with the dog. The rule here is one small pooch per room. 1208 South State Street, Ukiah, CA 95482; (707) 468-5404.

WESTPORT

Here's another New England look-alike. Westport is a tiny coastal town with a couple of inns and restaurants and a whole lot of charm. It's a wonderful place to visit if you like the appeal of Mendocino but prefer your sidewalks tourist-free and your beaches isolated.

PARKS, BEACHES, AND RECREATION AREAS

• **Westport-Union Landing State Beach** 🐾🐾🐾½ *See* ⓰ *on page 80.*

On one of the busiest weekends of the year, not a soul was using this beach. Only one of the 100 campsites was occupied. This is the kind of place you can pretend is your own almost year-round. You and your dog may well find yourself alone in the campgrounds and along the sandy beaches, but pooches are still supposed to be leashed.

One of the best times to visit is during the gray whale migration from January to April. There are several good spots on the bluff tops where you can whale watch in comfort. Just set up a lawn chair, sit back with your binoculars, and wait. Even if you don't see a leviathan, at least you and your dog will have spent some good outdoor hanging-out time together. To make it even better, have a picnic.

Campsites are $10 to $12 and are first come, first served. Dogs are $1 extra. The sites are all on the bluff tops, near the park road, and not far from Highway 1. There's no shade and no privacy unless you're the only camper (you camp just off the parking lots), but plenty of quiet. At night, it's easy to fall asleep to the gentle churning of the Pacific. The park has three entrances. We hear that the farther north you go, the better your chances of finding people. The beach is about 2.5 miles north of the town of Westport. You can't miss the empty parking lots, but if you do, you'll still see the signs. (707) 937-5804.

PLACES TO STAY

Howard Creek Ranch: This rustic and historic redwood inn, built in 1867, offers privacy, quiet, and 40 acres of coastal beauty. Each room at this working ranch is unique, with features so special it's hard to decide where to stay. Joe likes the old boat, which is now a miniature cabin, complete with wood-burning stoves and low wooden ceilings. He doesn't have to duck here like his human companions often do, and he seems to get a real kick out of hearing the thwack of a Homo sapien's head against a thick beam. The redwood cabin is in the woods next to a stream that runs through the property, and it's oh so private.

For a truly relaxing weekend, stay in a room with a hot tub or sauna. After your own personalized spa treatment, take your best bud for a romp at the ocean, which is only about 300 yards away.

Rooms are $55 to $145 a night. Dogs are $5 extra and are permitted only by prior arrangement. If you care to visit the Web site before you visit the ranch, the address is www.howardcreekranch.com. 40501 North Highway 1, Westport, CA 95488; (707) 964-6725.

Westport-Union Landing State Beach: See Westport-Union Landing State Beach on page 93 for camping information.

WILLITS

Although it's at the junction of U.S. 101 and Highway 20 (a main artery to Fort Bragg), there's precious little for dogs in the town of Willits. We couldn't even find a hotel that allows dogs, although once I did manage to sneak Joe into a motel here. But it got embarrassing when Joe literally ran right into the innkeeper on a midnight walk. In a panic I thought of telling Mr. Motel that I'd just found Joe on the side of the road, but I was honest, and Joe ended up spending the night in the car—at least until Mr. Motel was safely back in his room. This is not a good example of proper dog etiquette.

YORKVILLE

PLACES TO STAY

Sheep Dung Estates: People often ask about staying somewhere really dog-friendly. You won't find many better places than the four cottages and one guest house on 320 acres in this rustic haven near Boonville. (The place grew from two cottages and 160 acres since the last edition of this book. Dogs everywhere are applauding.) To attest to this, 80 percent of the visitors here bring dogs!

The place looks much better than its name implies. From the huge windows of the homey, airy cottages, you and your dog can enjoy sweeping vistas of the Anderson Valley and surrounding forests. The secluded cottages each have private roads, wood-burning stoves, down comforters, mini-kitchens stocked with breakfast fixings, and covered porches. The cottages are also stocked with some mighty handy items for dogs and their people, including water bowls, dog brushes, and some excellent doggy first-aid items (with many things for foxtail encounters). The newest cottage, the Hill House, actually has its own small guest house, called the Tree Top. It's ideal for couples traveling together. Owners Anne and Aaron Bennett ask that you bring a sheet if your dog insists on sleeping on the bed with you, because the luxurious bedding can't take the beating dogs give.

Your pooch need not look farther than his own front door for a place to run around and just be a dog, since voice-controlled dogs are free to run and explore the huge property. The Bennetts recently made a 1.5-mile trail that goes to the top of the ridge. "We call it Big Rock Trail," says charming, dog-adoring, and vivacious Anne Bennett. "But guests call it Cardiac Hill."

If you and your dog like your walks a little less sweaty, there's a gorgeous 40-acre area with gently rolling hills dotted with firs and oaks. Guests call that one Geriatric Park, but young-at-heart (and body) dogs and people love it. There's even a very large pond where water dogs can practice the dog paddle. Anne says many dogs have learned to swim here because they wanted to be with their swimming humans. Plus, it's nice and safe and quiet, with no jet skis, no waves, none of the stuff that dogs balk at in most areas where they can swim.

There's a two-night minimum stay. Rates for this magnificent chunk of dog heaven are $85 to $95 nightly during the week and $125 to $140 per night on weekends and holidays. The Hill House/Tree Top cottages are rented together and cost $175 on weekdays and $225 per night on weekends. Sheep Dung Estates is about 40 miles southeast of Mendocino, near Highway 128. The Bennetts will give you directions when you make your reservation. (Say, isn't that your dog behind you, handing you the phone?) The mailing address is P.O. Box 49, Yorkville, CA 95494; (707) 894-5322.

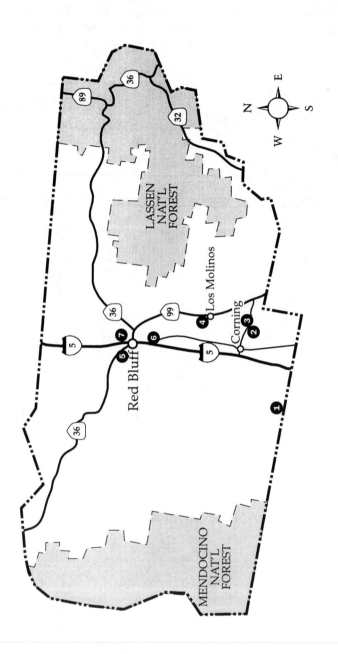

9
TEHAMA COUNTY

The county has a little bit of Lassen National Forest on one side, a touch of Mendocino National Forest on the other, and lots of farmland in between. If you feel like doing your dog a favor, stop in Red Bluff and visit lush and lovely Dog Island (see page 99). If it weren't for the leash thing, dogs would probably never want to go home.

NATIONAL FORESTS

See the National Forests and Wilderness Areas chapter starting on page 748 for important information and safety tips on visiting national forests with your dog.

• **Lassen National Forest** 🐾🐾🐾🐾 🐕
  See page 751.
• **Mendocino National Forest** 🐾🐾🐾🐾 🐕
  The forest is full of campgrounds in the southwest part of the county. See page 752.

CORNING

PARKS, BEACHES, AND RECREATION AREAS

• **Black Butte Lake** 🐾🐾🐾🐾 🐕 See ❶ on page 96.
  See page 103 in the Glenn County chapter.
• **Tehama County River Park** 🐾🐾🐾½ See ❷ on page 96.
  This park is almost directly across from the Woodson Bridge State Recreation Area (see page 98). While it's not as large as the state park, there's no fee to use it, which makes it a very attractive alternative.
  South Avenue bisects the park. The north side is grassy and fairly unde-

---

veloped, with great fishing access. When we visited, each of the three people fishing in the Sacramento had at least one dog. All the dogs were in and out of the river constantly, shaking on their masters and chasing each other back in again. We've rarely seen such happy, content pooches. Of course, if the ranger had stopped by, their owners may not have been so happy. They could have gotten slapped with a fine for allowing their dogs off leash. It's too bad there's a leash law here, because the area is quite safe from the road and other people.

The section to the south of South Avenue is more developed, with playgrounds, a little store, and a picnic area. You can go back and forth between the two sections via a very, very short tunnel under the road.

From Interstate 5, take the South Avenue exit and drive about eight miles east to the park. (530) 527-4630.

• **Woodson Bridge State Recreation Area** 🐾🐾🐾½
   See ❸ on page 96.

You're in the middle of giant oak country here—a fact that sends many dogs into fits of happiness. Between all the oaks (and poison oak, so watch it!), walnuts, cottonwoods, elderberries, and willows, your boy dog will hardly be able to contain himself.

Wildflowers are abundant in this 428-acre park. With its location, flanking both sides of the Sacramento River, there's plenty of beauty, especially in spring. Autumn is also a spectacular and colorful sight. Just get on the nature trail and hike your city woes away.

During your visit, some of your neighbors may include Columbian blacktailed deer, bats, muskrats, hares, river otters, and skunks. If you like to bird-watch, you'll love this place. If you're lucky, you may even spot the rare and endangered yellow-billed cuckoo. You'll know it when you see it.

The law requires that you keep your dog on a leash here. The day-use fee is $5. There are 46 campsites, ranging from $12 to $14 each. Dogs are $1 extra during the day or when camping. From Interstate 5, take the South Avenue exit and drive about eight miles east to the park. Call Parknet at (800) 444-PARK for campsite reservations or (530) 839-2112 for park info.

PLACES TO STAY

Days Inn: Rates are $30 to $60. Dogs are $5 extra and require a $25 deposit. 3475 Highway 99W, Corning, CA 96021; (530) 824-2735.

Olive Inn: There's a big area to walk your pooch here. Rates are $35 to $40. 2165 Solano Street, Corning, CA 96021; (530) 824-2468.

Shilo Inn: This is a quiet place, with a good continental breakfast and a relaxing steam room. (Sorry, dogs. No steam for you.) Rates are $59 to $69. Dogs are $7 extra. 3350 Sunrise Way, Corning, CA 96021; (530) 824-2940.

Woodson Bridge State Recreation Area: See Woodson Bridge State Recreation Area above for camping information.

LOS MOLINOS

PARKS, BEACHES, AND RECREATION AREAS
• **Mill Creek County Park** 🐾🐾½ *See ❹ on page 96.*

This park has great access to the Sacramento River for dogs who like to help you catch dinner or like to screw up your chances of catching it by wading in all the fishy water. Since dogs are supposed to be leashed, you can usually control the situation pretty well.

Landlubbing pooches prefer the shaded meadows and the fenced-in ball fields. All in all, this is a peaceful, relaxing place to come with a dog.

From Highway 99E, go west on Tehama & Vina Road. (If you find that you're in a spot where you can only go east, drive north a bit and you'll come to the right portion of the road.) In about a mile, you'll come to the Hidden Harbor fishing resort. Immediately after it is the gate to Mill Creek Park. (530) 384-1250.

PLACES TO STAY

Hidden Harbor RV Park and Fishing Resort: This is the closest an RV park can come to being a serene place to stay. It must have something to do with all the water around here. The park is located on the Sacramento River and bordered by Mill Creek, and has a harbor with slips for your boat. This is a great place to stay in the fall if you like to fish for salmon. Many folks use the park as their home salmon-fishing base. Pooches like it here because there's a nearby field for walks.

The rate for a site with a full hookup is $16.50. 24680 Hidden Harbor Drive, Los Molinos, CA 96055; (530) 384-1800.

RED BLUFF

PARKS, BEACHES, AND RECREATION AREAS

• **Dog Island Park/Samuel Ayer Park** 🐾🐾🐾½ *See* **5** *on page 96.*

Wow! A park named for the very creatures who most enjoy being here! Now if only dogs could legally run off leash, someone would have to change the name of this place to Dog Heaven Park.

This is a terrific place to take a dog. The park is lush, wild, and alive with riparian vegetation. You almost feel like somehow it's too verdant to be part of California. We hiked through here during a light rain once. It was incredibly relaxing. (All Joe could do was shake those evil raindrops off his coat, but he had a big smile plastered on his snout for the rest of the day once he was in the dry car.)

Numerous nature trails wind throughout the park. One of them leads to a footbridge that takes you over to Dog Island, a big chunk of land nestled securely in the crook of a Sacramento River bend. The island is just as enchanting as the mainland section of park. It's not super quiet in the island area, though. Interstate 5 crosses over the river a mere two-tenths of a mile to the north.

From Interstate 5, take the Red Bluff/Highway 36 exit west, cross the river, and turn right on Main Street. Follow Main Street to the sign for Dog Island Park, which will be on your right in a few blocks. (530) 527-2605.

• **Red Bluff Diversion Dam Recreation Area** 🐾🐾🐾
See **6** *on page 96.*

Don't be fooled. On a map, this area looks like it must be dog heaven. It's on the water (called Lake Red Bluff here, but it's actually just a wider, dammed section of the Sacramento River), it's fairly big, and it's got several campsites perched over the river. But in person, it looks more like something you'd find in Brooklyn. It's almost barren, slightly industrial, and can smell a little funky at times.

A couple of trails take you and your leashed dog short distances, but at least there's plenty of parking. You won't be excited about the fishing, but the fish watching can be interesting. There's a fish-viewing platform set up next to the dam.

Camping at the 30 sites is first come, first served and costs $10 per site. Each campsite has a pretty good tree next to it, so you'll be buffered from the hot summer afternoons a little. You can fish here, but the fishing isn't always so good these days, especially from shore.

Exit Interstate 5 at Highway 36 and head east. Take the first right turn, Sale Lane, and follow it to the end. That's where you'll find the camping and the visitors kiosk. Call the Corning Ranger District of Mendocino National Forest for the best times of year to watch the fish. (530) 824-5196.

•**William B. Ide Adobe State Historic Park** 🐾1/2 *See* ❼ *on page 96.*
This is a fun and historically interesting park to set paw in, but pooches can visit only under very restricted conditions—they're not allowed to visit the historic zone or the area where the animals hang out. (The chickens here are frequently mauled by marauding pooches, and the donkey was once attacked by three pit bulls, so the park's rangers are understandably protective.)

In fact, dogs are pretty much relegated to the picnic area overlooking the Sacramento River. But that's okay with most dogs, since it's more fun to sniff the ground for fallen macaroni salad than to stare blankly at the adobe memorial to a man who was president for 22 days during the infamous Bear Flag Revolt. As a human, you're allowed to peruse the historic grounds, but you'll have to leave the dog with another human friend in the picnic area while you sniff around the artifacts.

The entry fee is $3 per vehicle. From northbound Interstate 5, take the Antelope Boulevard exit and drive west a few blocks to Main Street. Turn right, drive about a mile to Adobe Road, and go right again. The park will be on your right in about one mile. (530) 529-8599.

PLACES TO STAY

Cinderella Riverview Motel: You really can see the river from here, and there are plenty of balconies to prove it. Rates are $32 to $48. Small pooches only, please, and they're $5 extra. 600 Rio Street, Red Bluff, CA 96080; (530) 527-5490.

Red Bluff Diversion Dam Recreation Area: See Red Bluff Diversion Dam Recreation Area on page 99 for camping information.

Sportsman's Lodge: This motel is so doggone animal friendly that someone's pet camel stayed here one fine night. If you're heading for a dog show at the fairgrounds, this is a close, convenient place to stay with your pooch. Rates are $30 to $65. Dogs are $3 extra. 768 Antelope Boulevard, Red Bluff, CA 96080; (530) 527-2888.

10
GLENN COUNTY

There's not much in Glenn County that people or dogs would drive hundreds of miles to see. But several big wildlife areas can provide you and your dog with many memorable nature-watching hikes. Don't come here if you're seeking the bohemian cafe society life.

NATIONAL FORESTS

See the National Forests and Wilderness Areas chapter starting on page 748 for important information and safety tips on visiting national forests with your dog.

• **Mendocino National Forest** 🐾🐾🐾🐾 🐕

You'll find many rugged, attractive camping areas in the northwest corner of the county, where the land is about a mile above sea level. See page 752 for more information on the forest.

HAMILTON CITY

PARKS, BEACHES, AND RECREATION AREAS

• **Bidwell Sacramento River State Recreation Area** 🐾🐾🐾

See ❶ on page 102.

Sacramento River access at this park is easy as one, two, wade. Fishing along the four miles of riverfront here is popular, but chances are you won't find too many people on the hiking trail. That's good news if you want to exercise your leashed dog before a day of angling together.

Dogs have limited access to this 180-acre state recreation area. They're not allowed at the Chico Creek Day-Use Area. Your best bet is to stop at the first section of park you come to, the Indian Fishery Day-Use Area, where there's a small picnic setting and an attractive wooded trail leading down to the river. It's usually really quiet here.

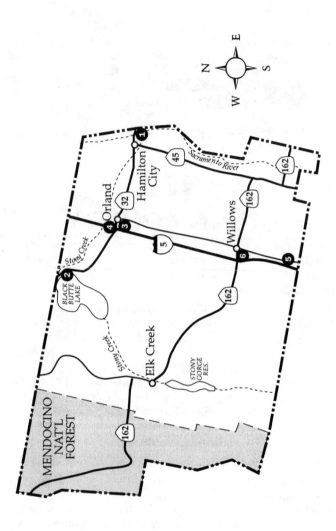

N
E
S
W

Orland
Hamilton City
① 45 Sacramento River 162
32
④ ③ 162
5 Willows 162
Stony Creek ⑥ 5
② 162
BLACK BUTTE LAKE
Stony Creek
Elk Creek
STONY GORGE RES.
MENDOCINO NAT'L FOREST
162

From Highway 32, go south on River Road. It's about 4.5 miles to the Indian Fishery Day-Use Area. (530) 342-5185.

ORLAND

PARKS, BEACHES, AND RECREATION AREAS

Great news for dogs in Orland: As with most other cities, there's an ordinance stating that pooches must be under their owner's control. But the similarities to most other cities stop there. That control can be via leash or via voice, which means freedom for obedient dogs at the city's four parks! The parks are not exactly Golden Gate Park in San Francisco, but you can't be choosy when it comes to leashless lolling.

The Black Butte Lake area isn't part of the city, but it also has its own off-leash potentials (see below).

•Black Butte Lake 🐾 🐾 🐾 🐾 🐕 *See ❷ on page 102.*

It's mighty secluded out here in the undeveloped parts of this big reservoir area run by the U.S. Army Corps of Engineers—so secluded, in fact, that you can hunt, if that's what you like to do. And if you hunt for birds, you can bring your dog along leash-free during the appropriate seasons.

Dogs don't have to be leashed in undeveloped areas, but they have to be under your control, even in the most remote acreage. The deer and rabbits appreciate it. If you're not going to be hunting, you might want to stay away from the very roughest land and enjoy any of three self-guided nature trails. You'll find nature at its best on these trails, without the brambles and burrs that take hours to pull out of your dog's coat. The Buckhorn Trail, an easy 1.5-hour walk, is at its freshest and most vibrant in the spring. You can pick up trail guides at the park headquarters or at the trailhead at the Buckhorn Campground.

The fishing at the lake is excellent in the spring and early summer. If some folks in your party aren't the angling types, they can hang out on land and picnic, visit the playground, or hike the nature trails. There are 40 miles of shoreline, and while dogs aren't allowed to swim at the Buckhorn Day-Use Beach, they can practice the dog paddle in most other places.

Camping with your dog is loads of fun, especially when the full moon slips over the lake and turns it a ghostly white. The 100 developed Class A campsites are $10 to $12, and they're available on a first-come, first-served basis. Dogs must be leashed in camping areas.

Exit Interstate 5 at the Highway 32/Black Butte Lake exit at Orland and drive west (the road will turn into Road 200) for about six miles. You'll come to a fork in the road. To get to the park headquarters, continue straight another couple of miles. That's also the way to the Buckhorn Recreation Area, with its nature trail and plenty of camping. To get to the other two nature trails, go left at the fork in the road, onto County Road 206. The Paul Thomas Trail is located in the Orland Buttes Recreation Area. The Big Oak Trail is located on County Road 200A, which continues on from County Road 206. (Definitely bring a map.)

The most remote area is Grizzly Flat, which is barely accessible by car. Drive around the southernmost point of the lake on County Road 200A and you'll soon come to a rough gravel road, and then no road at all. You'll know you're there when you're still bouncing even though your car has stopped. For more info, you can write or call: Park Manager, 19225 Newville Road, Orland, CA 95963-8901; (530) 865-4781.

• **Library Park** 🐾🐾🐾 🐕 *See* ❸ *on page 102.*

Library Park may occupy only one city block, but the landscapers have made the very best of that one block. The grass is more perfect than AstroTurf, and there are so many tall trees that the place is shaded during much of the day, making for a refreshing summertime outing for you and your hot dog.

The really good news is that dogs under voice control may be off leash here. Just make sure your dog is truly obedient, because with the small size of the park, there's not much room for error.

From Interstate 5, exit at Newville Road/County Road 200 and drive southeast one-third of a mile to County Road 200. The road then becomes Swift Street. Continue on Swift Street for three blocks, then turn right at Fourth Street. Drive two blocks south. The park is on the corner of Fourth and Mill Streets. (530) 277-6060.

• **Vinsonhaler Park** 🐾🐾½ 🐕 *See* ❹ *on page 102.*

This isn't a terribly attractive city park, but very obedient dogs are allowed off leash here, as they are at Orland's other parks. At four square blocks, it's the biggest of the city's parks. The only fenced area is the ball field, and it's not foolproof, so be careful if your dog is an escape artist.

There's enough grass for rolling on and enough trees for lots of leg lifts. Unfortunately, there are also enough people hanging out at picnic tables all day that your dog may just be in the way at times.

From Interstate 5, exit at Newville Road/County Road 200 and drive southeast one-third of a mile to County Road 200. The road then becomes Swift Street. Continue on Swift Street for seven blocks, then turn left at A Street. Drive three blocks north, and the park will be right in front of you, on Shasta Street. (530) 277-6060.

PLACES TO STAY

Amber Light Inn Motel: Small dogs are allowed, but only at the manager's discretion. Rates are $26 to $36. 828 Newville Road, Orland, CA 95963; (530) 865-7655.

Black Butte Lake: See Black Butte Lake on page 102 for camping information.

Orland Inn: Rates are $33 to $41. 1052 South Street, Orland, CA 95963; (530) 865-7632.

WILLOWS

PARKS, BEACHES, AND RECREATION AREAS

• **Sacramento National Wildlife Refuge** 🐾🐾🐾½ 🐕
See ❺ *on page 102.*

Only hunting dogs are allowed off leash here, and only in specified areas during hunting season. But plain old average everyday pooches are allowed to explore along the 10,700 acres of marshy waterfowl territory, as long as they're leashed and stay on the walking trails. Fortunately, the trails aren't muddy and mucky, so tell your dog not to feel too bad about being tethered.

More than 300 species of birds and mammals use the refuge throughout the year. It's a phenomenal place for wildlife observation. Bring your binoculars and a field guidebook, and you and your dog can learn all about the birds and the beasts here.

The refuge is open year-round. The entrance is about eight miles south of Willows. From Willows, take the Road 57 exit and drive south along the frontage road about six miles to the entrance. The refuge is off-limits during certain times of year. Call (530) 934-2801 for the schedule.

•**Sycamore Park** 🐾 🐾 1/2 *See* **6** *on page 102.*

This is a pretty big park for Willows. It's green, grassy, and groovy for dogs who like to roam around open fields wearing a leash. A paved path runs through the park and passes by medium-sized trees and several picnic tables.

The park is on the corner of Sycamore Street and Culver Avenue, right next to downtown Willows. (530) 934-7041.

PLACES TO STAY

Best Western Golden Pheasant: Springers and pointers drool at the name of this hotel. Small dogs are allowed and larger ones may be permitted if you call first. There's plenty of room on the hotel's grounds for your pooch to stretch her legs. Rates are $60 to $86. There's a $10 fee per pooch visit. 249 North Humboldt Avenue, Willows, CA 95988; (530) 934-4603 or (800) 528-1234.

Cross Roads West Inn: All you Saint Bernard owners, rejoice. They have absolutely no compunctions at all about the size of the dogs who stay here. They even had an elephant as a guest once! (Although he didn't stay in a room.) Dogs (and small elephants?) have to stay in smoking rooms. Rates are $34 to $61. 452 North Humboldt Avenue, Willows, CA 95988; (530) 934-7026.

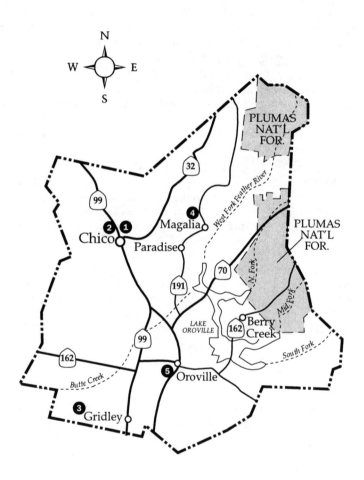

PLUMAS
NAT'L
FOR.

PLUMAS
NAT'L
FOR.

West Fork Feather River

32

99

2 1
Chico
Paradise

4
Magalia

70

N. Fork

191

Mid Fork

LAKE
OROVILLE

162 Berry
Creek

99

South Fork

162

Butte Creek

5
Oroville

3 Gridley

N
W E
S

11
BUTTE COUNTY

A couple of large off-leash parks, as well as the off-leash Plumas National Forest, make Butte County a fine place to take the four-footed beast in your life.

NATIONAL FORESTS

See the National Forests and Wilderness Areas chapter starting on page 748 for important information and safety tips on visiting national forests with your dog.

•**Plumas National Forest** 🐾🐾🐾🐾 🐕

A good-sized chunk of the northeast corner of the county is made up of this magical forest. See page 753 for more information.

BERRY CREEK

PLACES TO STAY

Lake Oroville Bed and Breakfast: This romantic, charming, cozy country inn is a treasure for pooches and their people. The six airy, antique-furnished bedrooms are so sweet that your dog's mouth might gape in awe that he's welcome here. Dogs are so welcome, in fact, that owners Ron and Cheryl Damberger provide tasty homemade dog biscuits wrapped in ribbon upon arrival of your pooch.

All the bedrooms come with private baths, and five have whirlpool tubs. Adding to the enchantment is an inviting parlor with a fireplace, a sunroom/reading room, a children's playroom, a warmly hued old-style billiard room, a wraparound porch, a barbecue area with great views, and a spectacular breakfast. Cheryl uses organically grown foods as much as possible, and can cater to people with special diets, such as vegans or diabetics.

Dogs think all this is just keen, but most care much more about what's outside the big white doors. The inn is set on 40 acres of private property in the rolling hills overlooking Lake Oroville. Birds, butterflies, and wildflowers abound. Well-behaved pooches are even allowed to go leashless (which is a real blessing, especially considering that the nearby town of Oroville doesn't even allow dogs in its parks). But if your dog might chase deer or skunks, keep him leashed for everyone's sake.

The resident cat, Chelsea, generally stays out of the way of visiting dogs. And the resident yellow Lab, Abby, is at least as enchanting as the inn itself. When we visited, we could have sworn she was smiling as she followed us around the grounds.

Rates are $95 to $135. Dogs are $10 extra. 240 Sunday Drive, Berry Creek, CA 95916; (530) 589-0700.

CHICO

The laid-back atmosphere of California State University Chico helps make this community a relaxed, dog-friendly place. There's even a sweeping section of a park near campus where dogs can run around off leash (see Bidwell Park, below).

PARKS, BEACHES, AND RECREATION AREAS

• **Bidwell Park** 🐾🐾🐾🐾 🐕 See **1** on page 106.

Some city brochures claim this is the third-largest municipal park in the United States. Others step the claim down a notch and call it the fourth largest. Dogs don't care about such distinctions. They just know this 3,670-acre park is a happening place for dogs to trot around, do leg lifts, and get back to nature.

Most dogs Joe knows prefer the rougher, untamed sections of the Upper Park segment. And guess what? That's exactly where they're allowed to run around off leash. The entire huge area north of Upper Park Road is a leash-free swath of dog heaven. You can explore the terrain via miles of trails that run through here or just kick up your heels in a grassy field. Only the lakes are off-limits.

If you want your dog to be leashless in a more developed area, you'll have to get up early. The large section of park west of Manzanita Avenue permits leashless dogs from half an hour before sunrise to 8:30 A.M. You have to stay away from playgrounds, picnic areas, and swimming holes, but your dog can still have a great run here. There are plenty of trails and wooded portions that are well protected from traffic.

A fun, recent addition to the park is a 37-acre parcel that was once a U.S. Forest Service tree nursery. A newly renovated half-mile trail, called the World of Trees Independence Trail, runs through the property. Dogs like the name, but they have to be leashed. In the 1890s, 16,000 trees from around the world were planted here to see which would do well in the climate. Many of those trees survived, and the trail has 20 "stops" where you can read about various trees. It's educational for humans and a good romp for dogs. It's even an excellent place for working companion and guide dogs, since the trail is accessible to the physically and visually challenged. Signs are in English and braille. The trail is off Cedar Grove Road, near East Eighth Street.

The park stretches 10 miles, from the university area all the way east to the rugged crags of Big Chico Creek Canyon. From Highway 99, exit at Highway 32 and head east to Bruce Road. Turn left on Bruce Road and drive north. The road will curve sharply to the right and become Chico Canyon Drive. Bear left at Manzanita Avenue and drive about a half mile to Upper Park Road. Turn right and you'll be in the park. Watch for signs for the dog area on your left. For the limited leash-free area, a good way to find a place with trails is to make a left turn from Manzanita Avenue onto Vallombrosa Avenue. Park on the road and walk in at any of several open areas in the wood fence. (530) 895-4972.

• **Chico City Plaza** 🐾 ½ *See* ❷ *on page 106.*

This is a sweet little park tucked in between municipal buildings in the center of town. Leashed dogs can hang out at the gazebo, on the lawn area, or under tall shady trees.

The park is in the heart of the old downtown area of Chico, so if you're going cafe hopping or window-shopping with your pooch, you'll have a green spot for resting all your weary bones.

Concerts are held here during the summer, and as long as your dog doesn't disturb the peace, she's welcome to accompany you.

The park is on Main Street between East Fourth and East Fifth Streets. (530) 895-4972.

RESTAURANTS

Oy Vey Cafe: Jennifer Fredericks and Asta Dog, of Sacramento, wrote to tell us about this terrific eatery in an attractive part of downtown Chico: "The waitress gave him (Asta) a bowl of water, but the clincher was a bag of doggy 'Bagel Bones' for $1. Asta loves gnawing on the hard, stale bagels!" And you'll love gnawing on the soft, fresh bagels at the beautiful covered outdoor area. Some egg dishes are available, but Oy Vey specializes in quicker foods and coffees. A waitress here brags that Oy Vey has the "second-best view in downtown Chico." We didn't ask what the best view is, because that's a little subjective; Joe thinks it's the yellow fire hydrant down the street. 146 Second Street; (530) 891-6710.

Shubert's Ice Cream: If your dog comes here at the right time, he'll be in for a snout-licking treat. Shubert's owners, Chuck and Kay Pullian, hate to see ice cream go to waste, and they love dogs, so when someone's ice cream falls off the cone and onto the floor here, the Pullians put it in a container, pop it in a special section of a freezer, and save it for the next dog customer. Same for ice cream that a customer licked but didn't like. These mishaps don't happen often, so you do have to be somewhat lucky to get one of these free dog delights. (Don't get the idea that this is a swell way to provide yourself with a free scoop of ice cream. A few bargain-hunting humans with little concern about pre-licked ice cream already tried this trick, and the Pullians now require you to show a dog when you get the free ice cream.)

If you don't luck out, your dog can still enjoy Shubert's delicious ice cream at the outdoor benches here. "Lots of people buy their dog their own cone," says Kay. "Some people even buy one and share it with their dog.

The person licks it, then their dog licks it, and they take turns. I don't know about that." Blech! I don't either, but Joe Dog says he's not so sure he wants to share a cone with me anyway.

Shubert's celebrated its 60th anniversary in 1998. It's been owned by the same family all these years, with the fourth generation now manning (and womanning) the scoops. That alone makes it worth a visit. 178 East Seventh Street; (530) 342-7163.

PLACES TO STAY

Chico Oxford Suites: Dogs like it here, but not necessarily because of the clean and pleasant nature of the lodging. More likely it's because of the nearby open field pooches can peruse. Rates are $63 to $109. Dogs are $15 extra. 2035 Business Lane, Chico, CA 95928; (530) 899-9090 or (800) 870-7848.

Holiday Inn of Chico: As long as your dog is "no bigger than a polar bear or a desk clerk," says the desk clerk, you and he (your dog, not the clerk) can cozy up together and watch satellite TV. Be sure to call ahead of time so they can set up you and your dog in a ground-level room. Rates are $69 to $79. There's a $25 pooch fee per visit. 685 Manzanita Court, Chico, CA 95926; (530) 345-2491.

Motel Orleans: Small dogs only, please (20 pounds is the limit). Rates are $35 to $39. A $100 dog deposit is required. (That's about $5 per pound for the biggest dog. Ouch!) 655 Manzanita Court, Chico, CA 95926; (530) 345-2533.

Motel 6: Rates are $33 for the first adult, $6 for the second. The rule here is one small pooch per room. 665 Manzanita Court, Chico, CA 95926; (530) 345-5500.

Safari Garden Motel: If you and your pooch stay here, you'll be only a mile from wonderful Bidwell Park (see page 108). Rates are $41 to $53. A $25 deposit is required for dogs. Management prefers smaller pooches, but will consider larger ones. 2352 Esplanade, Chico, CA 95926; (530) 343-3201.

Vagabond Inn: This is a convenient place to stop for a night with a pooch; it's not far from dog-lovin' Bidwell Park (see page 108), and one block from another city park. Dogs are allowed only in smoking rooms on the first floor. If your dogs smokes and doesn't like stairs, it's perfect. The pool here makes hot humans happy. Rates are $40 to $49. Dogs are $10 extra. 630 Main Street, Chico, CA 95928; (530) 895-1323 or (800) 522-1555.

GRIDLEY

PARKS, BEACHES, AND RECREATION AREAS

• **Grey Lodge State Wildlife Area** 🐾🐾🐾🐾 🐕 *See* ❸ *on page 106.*

Hunting dogs are the only ones who can be off leash in this spectacular wetland, and only during certain times of year. But this 8,400-acre wildlife area is a wonderful place to take well-behaved, leashed dogs the rest of the year. Barkers and yappers should be left at home, especially during waterfowl season. Many of the birds have flown thousands of miles, and if they're disturbed, it could be detrimental to their health.

For most of the year, you can walk around on about 25 miles of hiking trails and levees. During waterfowl and nesting seasons, the hiking is very limited. But you don't have to walk a marathon to see amazing wildlife. Among some of the critters you may run into are sandhill cranes, hawks, river otters, egrets, waterfowl, deer, beavers, orioles, and black-shouldered kites.

From Highway 99, turn west on Sycamore Road and go six miles to Pennington Road. Turn left and continue three miles to the entrance on the right. The main parking lot is two miles to the west. The California Department of Fish and Game provides a handy little brochure with a decent trail map. You may be able to pick one up at the wildlife area, or order one by calling (530) 846-5176.

MAGALIA

According to a recent article in a clever historical publication called the *Dogtown Territorial Quarterly*, Magalia used to be known as Dogtown back in the days when there were far more dogs here than people.

That was thanks to a woman named Mrs. Bassett, who had only a tent and three mutts when she arrived during the Gold Rush. She was in dire straits when one of her dogs had a big litter of pups. Realizing that most men who came to California back then came by themselves or with other men, she had the idea that the pups would provide good companionship for the fellows. She began selling dogs to local miners for one pinch of gold dust per pup.

According to the article, "Soon every cabin in the area had a canine companion. There were dogs in the stores, dogs in the saloons, dogs everywhere!" (Read that section out loud to your dog. They love that part.)

Unfortunately, Dogtown lost its name in 1862. It seems the women friends of these miners were starting to come out from the east and call Dogtown home—and there was something about calling Dogtown home that turned their stomachs. An item appeared in the local paper from one of the discontented wives, who wrote, "We should hate to live in a place called Dogtown, particularly if we had a large correspondence and had to write the name frequently."

The female residents of Dogtown subsequently demanded that the community be renamed Magalia. It's the Latin word for "cottages." (If your dog whimpers right about now, please try to understand why.)

You can find out more about Dogtown and the *Dogtown Territorial Quarterly* by writing to Bill Anderson at 6848-U Skyway, Paradise, CA 95969. The publication is working on gathering a list of the dozen or so Dogtowns that sprung up in California around the Gold Rush. It should make for interesting reading.

PARKS, BEACHES, AND RECREATION AREAS

• **Upper Ridge Nature Preserve** 🐾🐾🐾 1/2 *See* ❹ *on page 106.*

The soft dirt trails here are covered with pine needles, making this one of the cushiest parks around. Dogs enjoy winding along these nature trails while you stop at the numbered stations and learn all about this piece of pine and oak forest.

When you arrive at the preserve, go to the kiosk near the parking area, pick up a wonderfully detailed nature-trail map, and get your bearings. You can follow one of two mile-long trails. Both are lovely and will take you and your leashed pooch past streams, springs, and a whopping variety of trees. Joe prefers the trail across the street from the parking area. It's a little more secluded.

The 80-acre park is leased from the Bureau of Land Management by a group of energetic, wilderness-loving retired men and women. They created the trails so people could learn about the natural environment here. They're working on many more projects, including a wheelchair-accessible trail. Says Tom Rodgers, who helped get the group started in his mid-80s, "It's such a pleasure knowing that nature is a little better for what we've done, and that so are the people who nature helps educate."

From the Magalia area, follow Skyway to Ponderosa Way and turn left. Drive a little more than a mile and follow the signs to the preserve, which is just down the road on a gravel drive. The lessees have no phone number, but you can contact them by writing to Upper Ridge Wilderness Areas, P.O. Box 154, Magalia, CA 95945. The Bureau of Land Management may be able to help with questions. Call them at (530) 224-2100.

DOGGY DAYS

You can always go dogtown: The Dogtown Fair celebrates the usual July 4 stuff. But more important to pooches, it gives a nod to dogs and their contribution to this community (see page 111). A humorous dog show features pooches competing in categories such as "Best Smile" and "Waggliest Tail." There's even a talent show, so if your dog didn't make David Letterman's "Stupid Pet Tricks," he still has a shot at fame.

The festival is held on the grounds of the Magalia Community Church at 13700 Old Skyway. Call (530) 877-7963 for information.

OROVILLE

PARKS, BEACHES, AND RECREATION AREAS

Dogs are not allowed in any Oroville city parks, nor in any Feather River Recreation and Park District parks. Oh boy, party on, dogs! The saving grace is the Oroville State Wildlife Area/Thermalito Afterbay (see below).

•**Oroville State Wildlife Area/Thermalito Afterbay** 🐾🐾🐾🐾 🐕
See ❺ on page 106.

Unlike at many other wildlife areas, if your dog isn't a hunting companion, she can still be off leash here as long as she's under voice control. There are some 5,000 acres of grasslands, marshlands, and riparian forests for you and your dog to explore. Where it's too wet to walk, take a levee.

Be sure to bring your binoculars if you enjoy bird-watching. More than 140 songbirds have been seen here. As you wander through the forests of cottonwoods, willows, and valley oaks, you may also spot other interesting fauna. If you're not certain your dog will stay close by, do the animals a favor and leash her.

From Highway 162, go south on Larkin Road (just east of the Oroville

Airport). Follow the road a few miles to Vance Avenue and turn left. In three-quarters of a mile, you'll be at the wildlife area. Maps are usually available at the entry stations. (530) 538-2236.

PLACES TO STAY

Lake Oroville State Recreation Area: This is a state park and it's one of the strict ones. Although it's a 30,000-acre park with 20 miles of trails, dogs can't go on the trails or the picnic areas or far off a paved road. In essence, all they can really do here is hang out with you on your boat or go camping with you.

There are 300 sites available. Campsites are $10 to $20. Dogs are $1 extra. If you choose to stay on and around the paved roadways with your leashed pooch, you can enter the park for a $3 day-use fee, plus $1 for the dog. From Montgomery Street in the main part of Oroville, follow the green line down the road to the lake. For park information, call (530) 538-2200.

Motel 6: Rates are $30 for the first adult, $6 for the second. The rule here is one small pooch per room. 505 Montgomery Street, Oroville, CA 95965; (530) 532-9400.

PARADISE

As you enter town, a big wooden sign announces "PARADISE. To be all its name implies." Sorry, Paradise. You failed the dog test. The Happy Hunting Grounds you are not. Dogs are banned at all municipal parks, and that gets their fur standing on end. (Besides, if you're going to have a sign like that, maybe you should put it in a place where the next thing you see is not a sign advertising duplexes, and then a Burger King, and then a tire shop and a wig store. It kind of takes the oomph out of a heavenly idea.)

Fortunately, the beautiful Upper Ridge Nature Preserve (see page 111) just north of town in Magalia, has everything a leashed dog could want. And some of the scenery in the less-populated parts of Paradise really is beautiful. The town is surrounded by mountains, spectacular canyons, and tall pines.

RESTAURANTS

Brunch House: Your dog is welcome to join you for brunch until 3 P.M. on the combination patio/porch here. The restaurant even provides a small lot out back if your pooch needs to discreetly relieve herself. 6333 Skyway; (530) 877-7176.

Dolly O Donuts: The last name here may be "Donuts," but the middle name is "O," as in "O! My dog and I had no idea you also serve homemade soup and decent sandwiches." Dine at the outdoor benches. 591 Pearson Road; (530) 877-4331.

PLACES TO STAY

Palos Verdes Motel: Rates are $35 to $40. Dogs are $5 extra. 5423 Skyway, Paradise, CA 95969; (530) 877-2127.

Ponderosa Gardens Motel: Rates are $54 to $85. Dogs are $4 extra. 7010 Skyway, Paradise, CA 95969; (530) 872-9094.

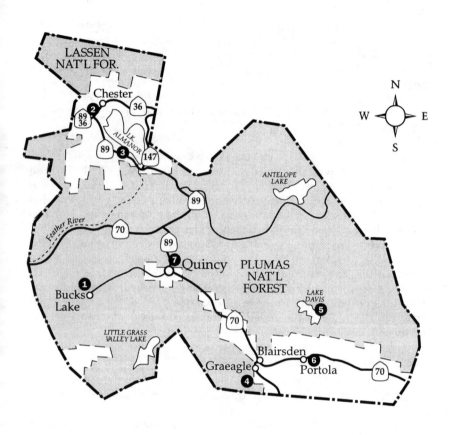

LASSEN
NAT'L FOR.

Chester

36

89
36

J.K.
ALMANOR

89

3

147

ANTELOPE
LAKE

89

Feather River

70

89

7 Quincy

PLUMAS
NAT'L
FOREST

1

Bucks
Lake

LAKE
DAVIS

5

70

LITTLE GRASS
VALLEY LAKE

Blairsden

Graeagle

6

Portola

70

4

N

W   E

S

12
PLUMAS COUNTY

Hidden between the ever-popular vacationlands of Shasta and Tahoe, Plumas County lives up to its publicity slogan, "California's Best Kept Secret." Even people in the next county asked, "Where's that?" when I told them where we'd just visited.

This county is 67 percent Plumas National Forest, which means there's natural beauty and off-leash dog heaven at almost every turn. It's Feather River Country here, with dozens of lakes and hundreds of miles of streams and rivers. That translates into endless good times hiking, fishing, swimming, wading, and cross-country skiing for you and your pooch.

Plumas is one of those counties so untouched by tourists that you can still find the best of rural life. The towns of Quincy and Portola have some of the most delicious country-style cooking we've ever tasted. And the country-style humor (like how all those yellow roadside deer warning signs have the deer sporting big red noses) isn't bad either.

NATIONAL FORESTS

See the National Forests and Wilderness Areas chapter starting on page 748 for important information and safety tips on visiting national forests with your dog.

• **Lassen National Forest** 🐾🐾🐾🐾 🐕
Only a tiny portion of this national forest falls in Plumas County. See page 751 for more on this magnificent forest.

• **Plumas National Forest** 🐾🐾🐾🐾 🐕
See page 753.

BLAIRSDEN

RESTAURANTS

Mohawk Deli, Cafe & Ice Cream Parlor: The coffees here are fresh and delicious, and the ice cream is the same. But for good, hearty cuisine, try the smoked chicken. You can get it to go and bring it along on a picnic in nearby Plumas National Forest. 1123 Johnsville Road; (530) 836-0901.

PLACES TO STAY

Gray Eagle Lodge: Pooch Paradise. Human Heaven. Glowing elysian comparisons are only natural when you stay at this extraordinary Sierra lodge, set in the middle of some of the best national forestland in the state. Reader Cynthia Harris says she and her new hubby brought their two basset hounds, Otis and Monroe, along on their honeymoon and had the time of their lives. "Our cabin had a deck that descended down to a stream, which was ideal for swimming bassets!" she writes. Joe Dog (aka Mr. "Water is to drink, not to swim in") would like to know how they wring all that water from their hush puppy ears. (He's just jealous that they can float and he can't.)

A dozen Plumas National Forest trailheads start at the property. Well-behaved pooches can go leash free on the trails, which lead to meadows, peaceful ponds, streams, and 40 alpine lakes where the fishing can be so good that the angler in you may never want to leave. If you catch a fish and clean it, the chef here will cook it up for your breakfast. But the brochure admonishes "Keep in mind, Chef's largest frying pan is ONLY 24 inches wide!" Those guests who tell a good fish story will be rewarded with a glass of champagne, so if you err on the side of exaggeration, this is your kind of place.

You can really get away from it all at the cozy TV-free and phone-free wood cabins. But don't leave your taste buds behind, because the gourmet meals here (full breakfast and a four-course dinner are included in the room price) are wonderful. Picnic lunches are available for an additional charge. Among the ever-changing dinner entrées: roasted duck with raspberry sauce, roasted half chicken in a garlic rosemary seasoning, tiger prawns sautéed in a lemon garlic butter sauce with linguine pasta, and grilled pork tenderloin in a honey-mustard glaze.

After a long day of exploring and eating, you and your dogs can relax by the big fireplace in the main lodge. The lodge is open May to October. Rates are $160 to $195 per couple and include the sumptuous meals. Dogs are $10 extra each, and you can't have more than two per room. The lodge is off Gold Lake Road in Blairsden, P.O. Box 38, Blairsden, CA 96103; (530) 836-2511 or (800) 635-8778.

BUCKS LAKE

PARKS, BEACHES, AND RECREATION AREAS

• Bucks Lake 😊 😊 😊 😊 🐕 *See ❶ on page 114.*

During warmer months, you and your dog can hike, swim, and fish till you drop. Campgrounds here are good places to drop, and the 49 sites in

Plumas National Forest are free. Twenty-nine of these sites are right along the lake's 14-mile shoreline, making for exquisite views. Sites are $12 to $14. All are first come, first served.

If trout fishing is your fancy, you'll have a hard time finding a much troutier lake. The lake is stocked annually with rainbow trout, so it's a great place to take young anglers and dogs who are entertained by fishing activity.

The lake is almost completely surrounded by Plumas National Forest, where dogs can run free in undeveloped areas. On the northeast side is the beautiful Bucks Lake Wilderness, where your obedient dog may also accompany you without a leash. From some of the peaks in this wilderness, you can see forever—or at least as far as Mount Lassen.

During winter, the Bucks Lake area is a great spot for cross-country skiing. Dogs love going along for a little exercise, as long as the snow isn't too high.

From Highway 70 in Quincy, take Bucks Lake Road west about 12 miles to the lake. For information on campgrounds and the lake, call (530) 283-0555.

PLACES TO STAY

Bucks Lake: See Bucks Lake above for camping information.

Bucks Lake Lodge: You and your pooch can stay at any of a dozen rustic housekeeping cabins at this lakeside resort. There's plenty of wilderness and open space around for you and your dog to explore. The lodge has a restaurant, bar, and small store, so you can stay here for a while and never have to get into your car.

The road to the lodge is closed in winter, so plan ahead. If you really want to stay here in the cold months, you have to use a snowmobile or cross-country skis. (And unless your dog is bipedal, the ski option just isn't going to cut it.) Rates are $54 to $95. Dogs are $5 extra. 16525 Bucks Lake Road, P.O. Box 236, Quincy, CA 95791; (530) 283-2262.

CHESTER/LAKE ALMANOR

PARKS, BEACHES, AND RECREATION AREAS

• **Collins-Almanor Forest** 🐾🐾🐾🐾 🐕 *See ❷ on page 114.*

"Dogs love trees, and we love dogs," says dog-loving forester Dan Howell. That's why the Collins Pine Company rolls out the pine needle carpet for pooches in its 91,000-acre mixed conifer forest. Leashes can be shoved in your backpack, and you and your dog can hike unattached throughout this glorious working forest.

This is one of the most environmentally correct timber companies in the country, so you won't be seeing clear-cut patches that make the landscape look like a dog with mange. The family-owned company has been logging this forest since 1941, but with such a commitment to long-term sustainable forestry that they even win accolades from environmentalists.

You'll love this place so much that you may want to spend a few days here. That means spending a few nights here. Many camping areas are available, and the ones near streams are the best. There's no fee for any of this.

You'll want to stop in at the Chester office to get additional information

---

about the best access routes for your level of hiking and to find out what areas of the forest are open. The office is at 500 Main Street. It's the one with the big green lawn (at least in the spring and summer). The phone number is (530) 258-2111.

• **Lake Almanor** 🐾 🐾 🐾 ½ *See* ❸ *on page 114.*

The azure waters of this idyllic lake make a beautiful centerpiece for an adventurous canine time. The lake is big (52 square miles), and sections of the surrounding areas are controlled by many different entities, both public and private. It can be confusing, and you can get yourself into trouble if you stumble onto the wrong land parcel with a dog.

Although parts of the lake are surrounded by both the Plumas and Lassen National Forests, neither of these areas is set up for hiking around the lake. They're geared more toward camping. Dogs should remain on leash in the portions of forest immediately around the lake. That will also keep them from bounding onto the privately owned land that weaves throughout the public lands here.

If you stay at the resorts along Lake Almanor, keep in mind that most have their own land, which you can explore with a leashed dog. Some even have views of magnificent snowcapped Mount Lassen rising in the distance.

A fun stop with your pooch comes just after the dam at the south end of the lake as you're driving north on Highway 89. You can pull off to the right, near the Canyon Dam Boat Launch, and trot along the flats near the lake. Bring your fishing equipment and make a few casts as you meander along. The lake, actually a reservoir, is known for its salmon, trout, and even smallmouth bass.

For general lake and camping information, contact the Almanor Ranger District of Lassen National Forest at (530) 258-2141. When in Chester, you can visit the ranger station and pick up maps and advice. It's at 900 East Highway 36. The Chester/Lake Almanor Chamber of Commerce can also provide you with good information. Call them at (530) 258-2426.

PLACES TO STAY

Cedar Lodge Motel: The owner here loves dogs, so you'll feel mighty welcome. Rates are $32 to $57. Some rooms have kitchens. Highway 36, Box 677, Chester, CA 96020; (530) 258-2904.

Collins-Almanor Forest: See Collins-Almanor Forest on page 117 for camping information.

Lake Almanor Resort: Cabins and a cozy lodge are available to you and your dog. The lodge is right on the lake and provides good views, while the cabins are set among the trees. The resort is open from May to mid-October. Rates are $47 to $90. Dogs are $5 extra. 2706 Big Springs Road, Lake Almanor, CA 96137; (530) 596-3337.

Lassen View Resort: The housekeeping cabins here range from $56 to $88. You'll get slapped with an extra charge if you don't pick up after your pooch, so, as you should everywhere, scoop the poop. The 94 campsites are $16. The resort is open from May to November. 7457 Eastshore Drive, Lake Almanor, CA 96137; (530) 596-3437.

Little Norway Resort: Dogs enjoy the lakeside housekeeping cabins almost as much as they dislike the loud jet skis the resort rents out. It usually is quiet here, though. The resort has enough land around it so dogs and their people can get some good exercise. Rates are $55 to $105. Pooches are $5 extra. 432 Peninsula Drive, Lake Almanor, CA 96137; (530) 596-3225.

Timber House: They say they don't want Shetland ponies or Saint Bernards at this motel, but just about any other size pooch is okay. Rates are $45 to $65. Dogs are $5 extra. Chester Park is nearby. First and Main Streets, P.O. Box 1010, Chester, CA 96020; (530) 258-2729.

GRAEAGLE

PARKS, BEACHES, AND RECREATION AREAS

• **Plumas-Eureka State Park** 🐾🐾🐾🐾 *See* ❹ *on page 114.*

Your dog isn't going to believe his pointy ears when you tell him the following news. (Before you tell him, make sure he's sitting.) Here it is: Dogs are actually allowed on a trail in this park. State parks pretty much ban pooches from trails, but because this is such a short trail and it leads to a very long and wonderful national forest trail, it's A-OK.

Dogs have to be leashed on the state park end of the trail. But it may be a wise idea to keep your dog leashed when you hit national forestland—even though leashes aren't mandatory—since there are bears in dem dar hills. We know this firsthand, because on our camping honeymoon, Mr. Bear visited our secluded campsite at Rock Lake. He hung out from midnight until about 3 A.M., when he probably realized he wasn't going to enjoy our dehydrated camping food any more than we did.

Back to state park grounds, dogs are very limited in their activities in the historic 5,000-acre park surrounding the old mining town of Johnsville. But one thing they can do is camp with you at one of the 67 sites here. Fees are $12 to $14 a night. Dogs are $1 extra. The campground can get crowded, and sites are first come, first served, so arrive early in the day during summer months.

If you want to skip the more heavily used part of the park and get right to the Jameson Creek Trail (which leads to several isolated, pristine lakes), look for a sign for the trail on the left, about one-eighth of a mile before the park entrance. Follow the dirt road to the trailhead. You can also pick up the trail from the main part of the park. Just ask a ranger where it starts.

From Highway 89, take County Road A14 west a few miles to the park. (530) 836-2380.

RESTAURANTS

Graeagle Outpost: Forget about the tasty coffees and snacky foods (hot dogs, pastries, etc.) you can eat with your dog at one of three outdoor tables here. What dogs love about this enchanting place is that it's set on 10 acres, complete with a pond with a one-mile trail around it. Dogs under voice control are allowed to walk off leash with you! The outpost even rents paddleboats, and your dog is allowed to go along for the ride. The Outpost is a wonderful place to stop, grab a bite, and stretch your legs. The restaurant is located on Highway 89 in "downtown" Graeagle. There's no street address, but you won't miss it. (530) 836-2414.

PLACES TO STAY

Plumas-Eureka State Park: See Plumas-Eureka State Park on page 119 for camping information.

PORTOLA

This old town is right on the Middle Fork Feather River, which is very accessible from many parts of town. Just bring your rod, reel, hiking shoes, and dog, and you can create a canine's dream day. Sadly, the wonderful Portola Railroad Museum no longer allows dogs on its trains.

PARKS, BEACHES, AND RECREATION AREAS

• **Lake Davis** 🐾🐾🐾 🐕 *See ❺ on page 114.*

This is the largest of the three Upper Feather River lakes, with 32 miles of shoreline, most of it in Plumas National Forest (see page 753). The hiking right at the lake is limited, but you can manage to get in some exercise on trails and dirt roads that extend into the national forest from the lake area.

It's the perfect spot if you're vacationing with an avid angler. The hiking is excellent and off leash once you're out of the campgrounds and adjacent state game refuge and into the undeveloped areas of the Plumas National Forest. And there's plenty of nature to watch: Waterfowl, bald eagles, and bats are easy to see at various times of year.

Leashed dogs can choose from a total of 165 campsites. About half are available on a first-come, first-served basis. You'll need a reservation for the rest. Call (800) 280-CAMP to reserve a site. Tent campsites are $6 to $13. Self-contained mobile homes stay for free. From Highway 70, take Grizzly Road or Lake Davis Road about seven miles north to the lake. For information on Lake Davis or to get maps of the forest near the other two Upper Feather River lakes, call (530) 836-2575.

• **Portola City Park** 🐾🐾🐾 🐕 *See ❻ on page 114.*

Much more space is devoted to human activities than dog activities here, but there's still a decent little field, some trees, and a gazebo that leashed dogs seem to enjoy. The great news is that if your dog is under voice control, he can be leash free here, as long as you keep him from the more developed spots. It's not far from the street, so think twice before you unleash. Either way, this is a nice little place to take a break with your dog.

From Highway 70, go south on South Gulling Street. The park will be on your left, across from City Hall, shortly after you cross over the bridge. (530) 832-4216.

RESTAURANTS

Good & Plenty Restaurant: This place doesn't have outdoor tables, but it has such delicious down-home cooking that Joe recommended I mention it anyway. You can always get your food to go and eat it beside the nearby Feather River with your dog drooling at your side. Better yet, take it to Portola City Park (see above). When it's cold out, the windows get steamy from the wholesome food cooking in the kitchen, and the railroad workers flock here. It's a little off the beaten path, so you'll be hard pressed to find a tourist. The place specializes in seafood these days, but you can still get hearty non-fish meals that really satisfy an empty tummy.

Another plus, for road-weary hungry travelers: This cozy eatery is open seven days a week, 24 hours a day. 241 Commercial Street; (530) 832-5795.

PLACES TO STAY

Lake Davis: See Lake Davis on page 120 for camping information.

Sleepy Pines Motel: The owners of this homey motel have their own dog, and they'll often allow dogs as guests, but they want "nothing huge or dangerous." The lodging is very close to the Feather River. The owners can point you to the best fishing spots. Rates are $40 to $70. 74631 Highway 70, Portola, CA 96122; (530) 832-4291.

QUINCY

This is a Main Street community with restored and preserved buildings dating back to the town's roots in the mid-1800s. If you whiz through town heading west, you'll barely get a glimpse of the downtown area, which is home to a couple of good, dog-friendly restaurants. Main Street only goes east and it's worth a gander.

PARKS, BEACHES, AND RECREATION AREAS

•**Gansner Park** 🐾🐾🐾 *See* ❼ *on page 114.*

Dogs enjoy bouncing around this long and luscious park. They're supposed to bounce around on leash, but if your dog happens to escape from your grasp, there's little danger: The park is almost entirely fenced. Generally, where there aren't fences, trees and brush are so thick that dogs would have a difficult time getting out. The grass is very green, the pines are very large, and the park generally is very uninhabited. You can picnic, barbecue, play tennis, or watch the kids at the park's small playground.

From Highway 70/89 just north of town, turn east on Gansner Park Road (there will be signs for the park). (530) 283-3278.

RESTAURANTS

The Bakery & Deli: Have you always wanted to see what your dog looks like on a cake? (Not in a cake, as was Billy Dog's style.) Bring in a picture of your pooch, and the bakers here will put his likeness in living color on your favorite kind of cake. You can do this with people portraits, too. If you're in the mood for something more substantial and less artistic, order some deli food and munch it at the outdoor tables. 411 West Main Street; (530) 283-2253.

Morning Thunder Cafe: "So long as your dog doesn't offend anyone," says a manager, she's welcome to join you and eat hearty food on the sweet, old wood porch shaded with latticework and grapevines. Joe didn't happen to offend anyone when we visited, so not only did he get to stay, he also got a free piece of bread from an unoffended dining neighbor. 557 Lawrence Street; (530) 283-1310.

Stoney's Country Burger: "Dogs? They're my favorite animals," says the kindly owner of this burger cafe. Try the Stoney burger. You'll love it, and if you don't, your dog will. 11 Lindan Avenue; (530) 283-3911.

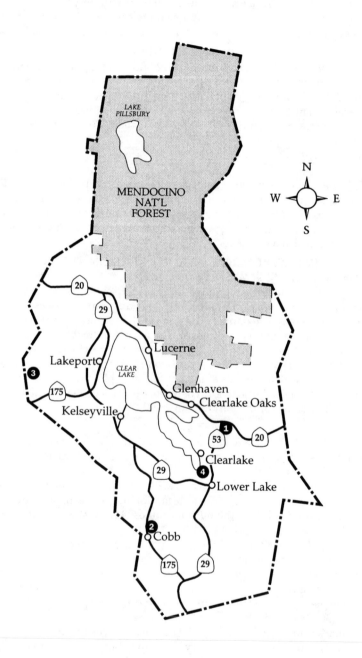

LAKE
PILLSBURY

MENDOCINO
NAT'L
FOREST

N
W E
S

20

29

Lucerne

Lakeport
CLEAR
LAKE

❸ 175

Kelseyville

Glenhaven
Clearlake Oaks

❶
53 20

29 Clearlake
❹
Lower Lake

❷ Cobb

175 29

13
LAKE COUNTY

This is a county with an attitude about dogs—a bad attitude. (For a major exception, please see the Edgewater Resort listing on page 126.) Dogs aren't allowed in any county parks. Since parks in the small towns are county parks, that's a double dose of bad news. The major cities (Clearlake and Lakeport) also ban dogs from their parks, and dogs aren't permitted at public beaches around Clear Lake.

Signs throughout the county shout that dogs must be licensed and leashed and will be shot if they're caught molesting farm critters. Even the trash barrels in county parks are painted with big white "No Dogs" warnings. Looks like you can't even walk your dog in a garbage can around here.

Welcome to Lake County, a major disappointment for our fine four-legged friends. The county slogan that occasionally pops up here is "Lake County: Dare to Explore." But that's a cruel joke for the canines in our midst. If they dare to explore too much, they're going to get socked with a big fine. And guess who has to pay?

What's a dog to do? She could start by thanking the Big Dog in the Sky for the national forests, the Bureau of Land Management, the California Department of Forestry, and (I never thought I'd say this) the state park system. If not for these, dogs would have to sneak around everywhere.

If your dog wants to hang out near the lake, you'll have to stay in one of the private resorts that has lakeside access. The Edgewater Resort, in the Kelseyville area (see page 126), is the best of these, at least from a dog's point of view. But there are plenty of others, should you follow the county's slogan and "Dare to Explore."

NATIONAL FORESTS

See the National Forests and Wilderness Areas chapter starting on page 748 for important information and safety tips on visiting national forests with your dog.

•**Mendocino National Forest** 🐾🐾🐾🐾🐕‍🦺

A huge portion of this forest is in Lake County. It's a relief to dogs who aren't even permitted to set paw in county parks. See page 752 for more information.

CLEARLAKE

Dogs aren't allowed in any Clearlake parks. The woman at the Chamber of Commerce is sorry about that, but it's not her fault. She wears a doggy charm bracelet and owns a toy poodle who's the star of the parties she attends. Her solution to the area's strict dog rules? "My dog is just like a person," she says. "She just walks around the neighborhood with me on a leash and we go home and eat."

PLACES TO STAY

Clearlake Travelodge: This motel is located in downtown Clearlake, one block from the lake. Rates are $42 to $58. Dogs are $10 extra. 4775 Old Highway 53, Box 5166, Clearlake, CA 95422; (707) 994-1499.

CLEARLAKE OAKS

PARKS, BEACHES, AND RECREATION AREAS

•**Cache Creek Recreation Area** 🐾🐾🐾🐾🐕‍🦺 *See ❶ on page 122.*

This 50,000-acre Bureau of Land Management area is a very welcome sight for dogs, who are banned from most parks in the county. Not only can they explore this huge and wild area, they can do so off leash, as long as they're obedient sorts. If you can't trust your dog not to wander away and get eaten, or not to wander away and eat another animal, then please keep him leashed.

Bring your binoculars, because you'll need them. You may see bald eagles, blue herons, tule elk, or even a black bear. A seven-mile trail (steep at times) provides you and the dog in your life with ample room to start an adventure. We like to visit in the spring, when the wildflowers open their blazing petals to a new year.

You can also camp here in primitive, fee-free sites. You'll need to get a campfire permit from the California Department of Forestry office. The entrance to this patch of dog heaven is about eight miles east of town, on the south side of Highway 20. You'll see the signs. (707) 468-4000.

PLACES TO STAY

Cache Creek Recreation Area: See Cache Creek Recreation Area above for camping information.

Lake Haven Motel: This motel located on a sheltered canal is owned by folks who love dogs and welcome leashed pooches to sniff out the surrounding area. Rates are $36 to $53. 100 Short Street, Clearlake Oaks, CA 95423; (707) 998-3908.

COBB MOUNTAIN

PARKS, BEACHES, AND RECREATION AREAS

• **Boggs Mountain Demonstration State Forest** 🐾🐾🐾🐾 🐕
See ❷ on page 122.

You and your blissfully leash-free dog can hike for days in a 3,500-acre forestry experiment. The forest is being studied as an example of how a forest that was nearly stripped by someone else can be brought back and managed for continuous forest production, public recreation, wildlife habitat, and a watershed.

It's working. You'll hike on miles of trails that wander through mixed conifer forests and grasslands. As long as your dog is obedient, you can let her off leash. But if she can't be trusted around deer and other critters of the woods, keep her leashed.

If you like it here so much that you want to stay, you can camp at one of 14 sites, and so far, it won't cost you a cent. The state is considering asking a small fee, but luckily nothing has changed yet. Dogs must be leashed at the campground.

From Highway 175 about a mile north of Cobb Mountain, watch for a blue and white sign for the state fire station. At the first intersection past it, go east for about a quarter of a mile to the park's entrance. (707) 928-4378.

PLACES TO STAY

Boggs Mountain Demonstration State Forest: See the Boggs Mountain Demonstration State Forest above for camping information.

Yogi Bear's Camp Resort: Hey, Boo Boo! You can stay with your dog in your own tent or RV, or try one of the resort's tepees for a unique experience. It won't be a deep wilderness experience (tent sites have their own sink, water, and electricity), but there's a pond with kayaks and canoes, and enough room to stretch your paws. Rates are $18 to $24. 14417 Bottle Rock Road, P.O. Box 49, Cobb Mountain, CA 95426; (707) 928-4322 or (800) 307-CAMP.

GLENHAVEN

PLACES TO STAY

Indian Beach Resort: Stay at any of nine cottages on the lake. All have kitchenettes. There's plenty of room to walk your leashed pooch. Rates are $40 to $100. 9945 East Highway 20, P.O. Box 648, Glenhaven, CA 95443; (707) 998-3760.

KELSEYVILLE

Kelseyville calls itself "a friendly little country town." (It also calls itself "pear capital of the world.") The Main Street area does, indeed, look a little like something out of *The Andy Griffith Show*—at least if you don't have your glasses on.

Dogs like this ambience. But more than that, they like the Edgewater Resort. If you love your dog, and you love Clear Lake, you're barking up the wrong tree if you don't pay a visit. See below for more information on this very dog-friendly place.

PLACES TO STAY

Clear Lake State Park: Dogs enjoy spending the night under the oaks at one of the 147 sites at this lakeside park. Since they're not permitted on trails or in the water, they can't do much else here anyway. Rates are $12 to $19. Dogs are $1 extra. From Highway 29, take the Kelseyville exit and turn north on Main Street. The road will turn into State Street, then Gaddy Lane. In about two miles, go right on Soda Bay Road. The park will be on your left in about a half mile. For reservations, phone Parknet at (800) 444-PARK. For park information, call (707) 279-4293.

Creekside Lodge: Rates are $34 to $55. You have to sign a waiver taking responsibility for dog damage, and there's a $25 dog deposit. 79901 Highway 29, Kelseyville, CA 95451; (707) 279-9258.

Edgewater Resort: Wanna make your dog happy? Come here. The Edgewater Resort is one of the most hot-diggety-doggone dog-friendly places we've run across. How dog friendly is it? (Warning: This will be like Rodney Dangerfield without the humor.) It's so dog-friendly that one of its brochures shows a big photo of a fluffy white dog inspecting a black bass caught by her human. It's so dog-friendly that another of its brochures beckons obedient dogs to run off leash on its beach. It's so dog-friendly that it offers an intoxicatingly fun weekend called Pet Club Med at least twice a year.

The Edgewater's dog rules are even written in dog-eze: "Dear People Owners," the rule list begins. "Thank you for bringing your people to visit the Edgewater Resort. Here are a few tips to help keep them in line!" It then delineates things like the leash rules and the off-leash rules, and tells where pooper-scoopers are located. We've rarely seen such a creative, kind way to let a dog's humans know what's expected of them.

The relatively new owners, Sandra West and Lora Tell, adore dogs, if you couldn't already figure that out. They'll greet your dog with loving hugs and a dog biscuit if they're here when you check in. You and poochface can stay in a cozy cabin by the lake, or camp in your tent or RV. The cabins aren't the Taj Mahal, but they have real wood paneling and kitchens, and they're surrounded by lawn and big old trees. You can fish off a 230-foot fishing pier here or swim at the beach (humans can swim at the pool). There's even a game room in the clubhouse.

If a weekend of unadulterated dog bliss appeals to you, call about the next Pet Club Med session. Groomers, vets, and a noted dog person or two will give workshops, and there will be plenty of fun activities for dogs. If the occasion warrants (i.e. if it's anywhere near the birthdays of your dog hostesses Stella or Dallas), there's a dog birthday party and barbecue, complete with hot dogs, burgers, and birthday cake. And in the late afternoon there's usually a Big Dog Frolic on the beach and a Small Dog Social on the lawn. Of course, if your small dog thinks he's big, or vice versa, the lines can be crossed. The Edgewater does not discriminate. Call for this year's dates and prices.

Rates at the resort are $25 for tent or RV camping and $65 to $85 for a cabin. The seventh night is free. Dogs are $2.50 extra in tents or RVs, and $5 extra in the cabins. 6420 Soda Bay Road, Kelseyville, CA 95451; (707) 279-0208 or (800) 396-6224.

Jim's Soda Bay Resort: Stay in an attractive housekeeping cottage on the lake. There's plenty of room for your leashed dog to walk around and dip her paws. (Be sure to bring your pooper-scooper on your jaunts.) The management here asks that you tell them how big your dog is when you make a reservation. They used to allow only relatively small dogs, but now they just don't want any surprises. If you have a Great Dane, tell them the truth, and you probably won't regret it. Rates are $52 to $62. 6380 Soda Bay Road, Kelseyville, CA 95451; (707) 279-4837.

LAKEPORT

PARKS, BEACHES, AND RECREATION AREAS

•**Cow Mountain Recreation Area** 🐾🐾🐾🐾 🐕 *See* ❸ *on page 122.*
This is a great place to visit with your dog, who can run leash-free in many areas. The main entrance is on the other side of the county border, near Ukiah. From Lake County, enter at Younce Road (Old Toll Road). See page 91 for more details.

RESTAURANTS

Park Place: The fresh-made pasta here is delightful. Wash it down with your favorite local wine while you and your dog relax at the outdoor tables. The restaurant is next to a lakeside park, but since dogs aren't permitted at the park, all they can do is watch the ducks go by. 50 Third Street; (707) 263-0444.

PLACES TO STAY

Chalet Motel: Some kitchenettes are available at this lakefront motel, located north of downtown. There's a little walking room for your dog here. Rates are $40 to $50. 2802 Lakeshore Boulevard, Lakeport, CA 95453; (707) 263-5040.

Rainbow Lodge Motel: Rates are $35 to $55. 2569 Lakeshore Boulevard, Lakeport, CA 95453; (707) 263-4309.

LOWER LAKE

PARKS, BEACHES, AND RECREATION AREAS

•**Anderson Marsh State Historic Park** 🐾🐾 *See* ❹ *on page 122.*
For humans without dogs, this 870-acre park is a terrific adventure. Several miles of trails lead to remote bird-watching areas far from any roads.

But if you're lucky enough to be traveling with a dog, this park is just a leg-stretching zone. Dogs are not permitted on trails, but they're allowed at the picnic area at the ranch house. This is a pleasant place to plop down for a while. They're also permitted in the open fields behind the old Anderson barn. Since only the area adjacent to the barn is mowed, there's not much room to roam. The tall grass beyond the lawn can be full of ticks. At least your leashed dog will get to sniff an old outhouse or sit patiently outside the portable toilet while you explore its inner realms.

The fee is $2 per car and $1 per dog. The ranger is usually in the form of an iron post with a box on it, so if you'll be here only a few minutes, you might not need to pay. But real human rangers can come out of the woodwork (and there's quite a lot of wood around the barn), so be careful.

From Highway 53 just north of Lower Lake, turn west at Anderson Ranch Parkway and make an immediate right into the park. (707) 994-0688 or (707) 279-2267.

UPPER LAKE

PLACES TO STAY

The Narrows Lodge Resort: Located on relatively serene Blue Lakes, the Narrows Lodge Resort is a great place to visit if you want to get away from the crowds that can descend on Clear Lake. Unfortunately, dogs are allowed only in tent and RV sites, not in the housekeeping cabins here. The manager says you can tie your dog to the porch at night if you rent a cabin, but Joe so firmly puts his paw down about this (he's no city fool—he knows about mountain lion danger, mosquitoes, etc.) that we're not even going to tell you about the cabins.

Boat rentals are available, and there's plenty of opportunity for walkies nearby. The Mendocino National Forest is very close.

Rates are $19 to $21. Dogs are $3 extra. 5690 Blue Lakes Road, Upper Lake, CA 95485; (707) 275-2718 or (800) 476-2776.

14
COLUSA COUNTY

This is a county of refuge. Actually, it's a county of a few refuges. Birds see the refuges on their little bird maps and flock here by the millions. It's an amazing sight to see with your leashed pooch during the winter months.

ARBUCKLE

PARKS, BEACHES, AND RECREATION AREAS

•**City Park** 🐾🐾 *See* ❶ *on page 130.*

We made an emergency rest stop for the dogs here one time and they were most grateful. The park has a big green field that's fairly far from the road (dogs must be leashed anyway), and a fenced-in ball field, a wooden playground, and many picnic tables. In addition, the park is edged with bushes—something boy dogs can appreciate.

From Interstate 5, take the Arbuckle exit, follow it south about a half mile to Hall Street, and turn right. The park will be on your right in a couple of blocks. There's no phone number to contact for information about the park.

COLUSA

PARKS, BEACHES, AND RECREATION AREAS

•**Colusa Levee Scenic Park** 🐾🐾🐾 *See* ❷ *on page 130.*

If you have a dog, you've got a great excuse to take a hike through the historic part of town. This park takes you on a wide and wonderful levee above the Sacramento River, on the edge of the sweet old River District,

---

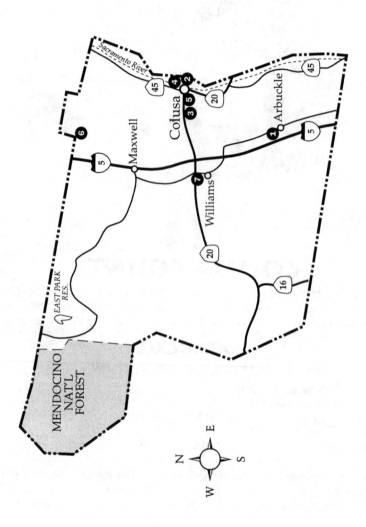

MENDOCINO NAT'L FOREST

EAST PARK RES.

Sacramento River

Maxwell

Colusa

Williams

Arbuckle

5

45

45

20

20

16

6

4

2

3 5

1

7

N E S W

which has a real genteel feel.

Our favorite entry point is between Sixth and Ninth Streets at Main Street (across from the brick River District Building). A couple of wooden staircases on Main Street take you up to the levee. (530) 458-5622.

• **Colusa National Wildlife Refuge** 🐾🐾🐾½ *See* ❸ *on page 130.*

Unless your dog is helping you hunt here, he has to follow the dress code and wear a leash. The 4,040-acre refuge has a self-guided auto tour and, better for dogs, a really good walking trail. Pick up a pamphlet or check out the interpretive panels at the kiosk. You won't believe all the waterfowl you'll see, especially if you visit in December or January. We're talking flocks bigger than even Alfred Hitchcock could have conjured. (If you're at all spookable, you may not want to rent the movie *The Birds* just before your visit.)

From Colusa, drive a half mile west on Highway 20 to the refuge entrance. The refuge is off-limits during certain times of the year. Call (530) 934-2801 for the schedule.

• **Colusa/Sacramento River State Recreation Area** 🐾🐾🐾½
See ❹ *on page 130.*

Primitive trails and mucky riverbeds are begging to be explored here. Dogs adore this place, but they're supposed to be leashed.

Our favorite trail starts right next to the boat launch area. If you ignore some of the smaller trails that branch off it, the main trail will take you down to the sandy/muddy "beach" area along the Sacramento River. Some folks like to fish here, so if you want to get away, just head left and walk down the riverbed. You'll likely see dozens of beasty footprints from the night's activities. Dogs love to sniff at raccoon, deer, and bird prints.

The day-use fee is $5. It costs $10 to $14 to camp at one of their 14 sites. Dogs are $1 extra when camping. Campsite reservations are accepted from the middle of April through September. Highway 20 will take you directly to the park. Coming from Interstate 5, Highway 20 changes its name to 10th Street once you enter Colusa. Follow 10th Street through town and into the park. For camping reservations, call Parknet at (800) 444-PARK. For park information, call (530) 458-4927

• **Memorial Park** 🐾🐾½ *See* ❺ *on page 130.*

The park is in a really beautiful old section of town. It fits in well here, with graceful palms, stately trees, ultra-green grass, and plenty of places to sit. It's only a square block in area, but leashed dogs get plenty of fulfillment. Humans also enjoy the posh and relaxing surroundings.

The park is located between Market and Jay Streets and Ninth and 10th Streets. (530) 458-5622.

RESTAURANTS

Rick's Burgers & Shakes: They like dogs at this place and will probably give your pooch some water if she's thirsty. 854 10th Street; (530) 458-2831.

PLACES TO STAY

Colusa–Sacramento River State Recreation Area: See the Colusa–Sacramento River State Recreation Area above for camping information.

MAXWELL

PARKS, BEACHES, AND RECREATION AREAS

The Delevan National Wildlife Refuge is not currently open to the public, but the Sacramento National Wildlife Refuge is quite a special place to visit with a dog.

• **Sacramento National Wildlife Refuge** 🐾🐾🐾½ 🐕
  See **6** on page 130.

The southern end of this magnificent refuge extends into northern Colusa County. See page 104 for a description.

WILLIAMS

Guys who wear cowboy hats for real hang out in Williams. So do oodles of people traveling on Interstate 5. The latter folks don't stop because of any tourist attraction. They stop for gas and food. Fortunately, this town has much more ambience than most pit stops on the interstate.

PARKS, BEACHES, AND RECREATION AREAS

• **City Park** 🐾½ See **7** on page 130.

If you're stopping in Williams for gas, you may as well come here and give your pooch a quick walk. A few trees and a bit of grass will be welcome sights to the dog in your life, and a tiny playground seems to please any tots tagging along.

Exit Interstate 5 at the main Williams exit, drive west to Ninth Street, and turn left. The park will be on your left in a couple of blocks. (530) 473-5389.

RESTAURANTS

A&W: Dine on good old-fashioned fast-food burgers and famous root beer at the half-dozen outdoor tables here. It's at the corner of Seventh and D Streets; (530) 473-5616.

Granzella's: The food here is mahhvelous. Joe drools like a fool when he sees anyone eating the special hot turkey and gravy sandwich. Best of all, the restaurant folks love dogs as much as dogs love the restaurant. "We're real animal lovers," says owner Linda Granzella. "We'll even go around the restaurant and find people who left their dogs in the cars with the windows rolled up." They're even happy to give your dog water. Eat at the wood picnic tables on the porch. 451 Sixth Street; (530) 473-5583.

La Fortuna Bakery: Eat fattening bakery food at two picnic tables. 669 F Street; (530) 473-2023.

PLACES TO STAY

Motel 6: Rates are $30 for the first adult, $6 for the second. This one allows one small pooch per room. 455 Fourth Street, Williams, CA 95987; (530) 473-5337.

Stage Stop Motel: There's a fridge in every room here. It's not quite like a chicken in every pot, but it's not bad. Rates are $28 to $39. Dogs are $3 extra. 330 Seventh Street, Williams, CA 95987; (530) 473-2281.

Woodcrest Inn: Rates are $45 to $54, and that includes a continental breakfast. Dogs are $5 extra. 400 C Street, Williams, CA 95987; (530) 473-2381.

SIERRA AREA COUNTIES

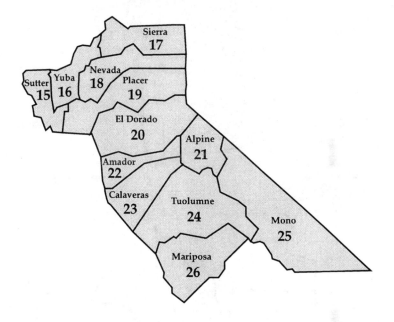

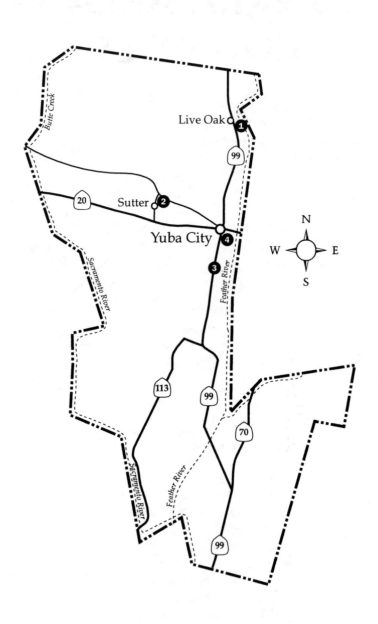

Live Oak

① 99

20 Sutter ②

Yuba City ④

③

Butte Creek

Sacramento River

Feather River

113 99

70

Feather River

Sacramento River

99

N
W ✦ E
S

15
SUTTER COUNTY

There's not much to do here with a dog, but where there's a full bladder, there's a way.

LIVE OAK

PARKS, BEACHES, AND RECREATION AREAS

• **Live Oak Recreation Park** 🐾🐾🐾 *See ❶ on page 134.*

This park doesn't have any big trails, but you and your leashed dog can hike around the dirt roads that wind through the park or just walk around the grassy fields. Feather River fans will appreciate the decent boat launch. People with pooches like to picnic under the oaks and willows before turning in for the night at the county's only campground. Small trails lead to the river, but it's a little rough at times and swimming is not allowed.

The day-use fee is $3 per car. Camping at one of the 25 sites is $7 a night. You might be able to drive in and get a site, but if you don't want to take a chance that they'll all be gone, call (530) 695-3823 for reservations. Exit Highway 99 at Penington Road and drive east about a mile to the end of the road, where you'll find the park. (530) 695-3823.

PLACES TO STAY

Live Oak Recreation Park: See Live Oak Recreation Park above for camping information.

SUTTER

PARKS, BEACHES, AND RECREATION AREAS

• **Vera Carroll Park** 🐾 *See ❷ on page 134.*

The huge orchard across from this tiny park may be tempting to visit

---

with your dog, but if you don't own it or work on it, you can't set foot on it.

The park has a fenced-in playing field, a few shaded picnic tables, and a swimming pool. As long as your dog is leashed and stays out of the pool, he'll be welcome here.

From Highway 20, go north on Acacia Avenue for about two miles. The park will be on your right, at College Avenue. It's run by the Sutter Youth Organization. (530) 673-2495.

YUBA CITY

PARKS, BEACHES, AND RECREATION AREAS

"Our parks are for the people, not for the animals. We'd rather not be put in that book," a parks department staffer told me. But since dogs are permitted at all city parks on an eight-foot leash, Joe thought it would be nice for dogs to know their rights.

• **Blackburn Talley Park** 🐾 🐾 ½ *See* ❸ *on page 134.*
The South Water Reclamation Plant is right next to this nine-acre park. There's always a high-pitched hum here, like a TV set gone bad, but dogs don't seem to mind. Something much better comes along with the reclamation plant—a slightly foul odor, which the dogs love. Their noses flutter with joy when the smell hits them broadside.

When we visited, there was an ugly, torn-up field on the Burns Drive side of the park. It's the best place to take a dog in this otherwise well-manicured, recreation-oriented park. We hear that field could soon be re-seeded and just as green as the rest of the park, but for dogs' sakes, we hope it's left as rough as can be.

From Highway 99, turn east on Lincoln Road and drive about a mile to Garden Highway, where you'll turn right. The park will be on your left in just under a half mile. Turn left onto Burns Drive and park in the lot or on the street. (530) 741-4601.

• **Sam Brannan Park** 🐾 🐾 ½ *See* ❹ *on page 134.*
The back area of this park is nicely fenced, so if your leashed dog makes a break for it, she'll be relatively safe. Otherwise, peruse the big grassy area, let your dog sniff the trees, or have a relaxing picnic at the many tables here.

From Highway 99, turn east on Bridge Street, drive a few blocks, and go left on Gray Avenue. The park is on your left in a few more blocks. (530) 741-4601.

RESTAURANTS

Izzy's Burger Spa: This place serves giant burgers to match its giant outdoor picnic area. 411 Colusa Avenue; (530) 674-9400.

Pizza Pizzazz: You and the pooch can share pizza, pasta, and sandwiches at this garden cafe. 1190 Bridge Street; (530) 671-2323.

PLACES TO STAY

Garden Court Inn: Rates are $29 to $32. There's a $5 fee per visit for pooches. 4228 South Highway 99, Yuba City, CA 95991; (530) 674-0201.

Motel 6: Rates are $32 for the first adult, $6 for the second. One small pooch per room is allowed. 700 North Palora Avenue, Yuba City, CA 95991; (530) 674-1710.

16
YUBA COUNTY

If you're just passing through with a dog, you're doing the right thing. With the exception of a small piece of national forestland, Yuba County isn't exactly dog heaven. Besides, if you want to spend the night, you'll have to either camp, knock on a friend's door, or find the one lodging in the entire county where dogs are allowed.

NATIONAL FORESTS

See the National Forests and Wilderness Areas chapter starting on page 748 for important information and safety tips on visiting national forests with your dog.

• **Tahoe National Forest** 🐾🐾🐾🐾 🐕
A tiny portion of this forest creeps into the eastern edge of Yuba County. See page 755 for details.

DOBBINS

PARKS, BEACHES, AND RECREATION AREAS

• **Bullard's Bar Reservoir** 🐾🐾🐾½ 🐕 *See ❶ on page 138.*
This 16-mile-long crystal-clear lake is heaven to anglers and paradise to pooches. "You betcha, the fishing's the best and we like well-behaved dogs

---

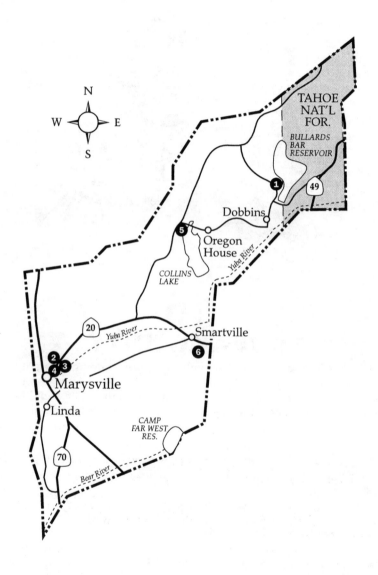

TAHOE
NAT'L
FOR.

*BULLARDS
BAR
RESERVOIR*

49

1

Dobbins

5

Oregon
House

Yuba River

*COLLINS
LAKE*

20

Yuba River

Smartville

6

2
3
4

Marysville

Linda

70

*CAMP
FAR WEST
RES.*

Bear River

a lot," says a manager of the Emerald Cove Resort and Marina, the full-service concession located at the southern tip of the lake.

While dogs must be leashed in campgrounds, developed areas, and at the Emerald Cove facilities, they're permitted to be leash-free in much of the land surrounding the eastern portion of the lake. That's because the land is part of the mighty dog-friendly Tahoe National Forest (see page 755). The Sierra foothills here are full of pine, manzanita, and oak. This makes boy dogs happy, and also makes for some good-looking scenery.

The lake has 60 miles of shoreline and contains such goodies as black bass, kokanee salmon, and rainbow trout. If you've got the urge to wet a line, Bullard's Bar is a wise choice. If you need a boat to tote you around, Emerald Cove rents all kinds of fun water vehicles (see Diversions below).

Camping is available at three main campgrounds, and there's even some shoreline camping. Sites are $14. A $5 reservation fee may be charged. The good news is that if you camp from October through March, you'll camp for free.

From Highway 20 about 12 miles east of Marysville, turn north on Marysville Road/County Road E21. Drive north about 15 miles on the narrow, winding road to Bullard's Bar Reservoir. When you pass by the tiny town of Dobbins (the closest town to the main resort area), you and your potentially carsick passengers will be glad to know you've got less than a mile to go. (530) 692-3200.

PLACES TO STAY

Bullard's Bar Reservoir: See Bullard's Bar Reservoir above for camping information.

DIVERSIONS

Get soggy with your doggy: So, you're visiting Bullard's Bar Reservoir (see above) and you're overcome with the urge to make like Captain Crunch and hang out at the helm of a boat? If the closest thing you have to a water vehicle is your set of water wings, fret not. You're in luck: Emerald Cove Resort and Marina rents just about any kind of lake boat you and your dog may desire. You can rent patio boats, houseboats, paddleboats, and even fishing boats for competitive prices. Call for a price list and brochure. (530) 692-3200.

MARYSVILLE

The historic district in Marysville is a real charmer—quite different from anything else you'll find in this sprawling, suburban-style county.

PARKS, BEACHES, AND RECREATION AREAS

• **Ellis Lake Park** 🐾🐾🐾 *See* ❷ *on page 138.*

Swans, ducks, and geese enjoy this quaint park at least as much as people and their dogs. Most of the park's 30 acres is taken up by a decent-sized lake, which was once a sprawling swamp. In 1924, John McLaren, designer of San Francisco's Golden Gate Park, presented a local women's civic group with plans for transforming the swamp to its present pleasant state.

An attractive path encircles the lake, but you and your leashed pooch can also spend time at an old stone footbridge, a gazebo, and picnic tables.

Dogs who like grass and dirt (and what dog doesn't?) enjoy lounging in the shade of the maples that dot the park.

Ellis Lake Park is between Ninth and 14th Streets and B and D Streets. You won't want to hang out at the B Street side, because that's where all the car shops and convenience stores are located. (530) 741-6666.

• **Plaza Park** 🐾½ *See* ❸ *on page 138.*

This park is very tiny, but it's green, close to the Yuba River, and in the historic district next to the Chinese Bok Kai Temple, home of Bok Kai, the river god of good fortune.

Joe likes to picnic at the little table here. It's a very peaceful setting and it's usually quite lush, unlike the neighboring Riverfront Park. Dogs must be leashed. The park is at the foot of D Street, at First Street. (530) 741-6666.

• **Riverfront Park** 🐾 🐾 *See* ❹ *on page 138.*

When you see this park on the map, you'll say "Wow! This place is almost half the size of Marysville itself! We must visit, Rex." (Or something like that.) But when you visit, you're apt to be more than a little disappointed. Two major roads straddle the park and the noise creates anything but a peaceful, parklike setting. About a third of the park is devoted to a British Motor Cross course. Much of the park is fenced off and out of commission. And there's a water treatment plant (peeeuw!) that occupies a nice-sized chunk of the southern area of the park.

So what's a dog to do at this 193-acre park? Well, there are some softball and soccer fields that are good for a leashed stroll when there's no one playing, and a few grassy areas where no one plays anything but footsie are always okay for a walk. Other than these sections, dogs don't think too highly of the place.

From the southern end of the historic district, go west on First Street, which turns into Bizz Johnson Drive once in the park. The first thing you'll notice may be the odor of the water treatment plant. No matter how much your dog begs you to stop at the stinky treatment plant, keep going until you get to the area that interests you. (530) 741-6666.

RESTAURANTS

Four Seasons Deli: Located right beside Ellis Lake, this is the place to go after you've become thirsty and tired from playing at the park there (see page 139). 423 B Street; (530) 743-8221.

Silver Dollar Saloon: This is a wonderful place with a big side patio for you and your dog. It's right next to Plaza Park's Chinese Bok Kai Temple. Just sit at the edge of the patio, near the gate, to keep your dog out of the bustle of this busy spot. The saloon has a pretty substantial menu, including steaks, sandwiches, and salads. 330 First Street; (530) 742-9020.

PLACES TO STAY

Marysville Motor Lodge: If you're in Yuba County and need a place to stay, you must check out this place, dahling. Literally, you must, because this is the only lodging in the entire county that allows dogs. Rates are $32 to $40. Dogs are $5 extra. 904 E Street, Marysville, CA 95901; (530) 743-1531.

OREGON HOUSE

PARKS, BEACHES, AND RECREATION AREAS

• **Collins Lake** 🐾🐾🐾🐾 🐕 *See* **⑤** *on page 138.*

Good dogs who won't chase deer, skunks, and other critters are welcome to strip off their leashes and trot naked around the 600 acres of oaks and pines that surround 1,000-acre Collins Lake. Dog paddling is a popular pastime with unleashed pooches, so if you have a water dog, you couldn't ask for a more dog-friendly swimming hole. Dogs can't go swimming at the official swim beach, but there are plenty of other places to dip a paw. The fishing is terrific, too. Make sure your dog is leashed when you go anywhere near anglers or the developed area of the lake.

The lake has one developed campground and one undeveloped one. The latter is dog heaven. There are no barbecues or tables, but you won't have any neighbors, either. You'll be surrounded by trees and plenty of land. It's a first-rate way to get away from noise, loud kids, radios, and just about everything that reminds you of civilization.

There are 155 sites here, with nightly fees ranging from $15 to $24. Reservations are recommended in spring and summer. Dogs are $1 extra. The park's day-use fee is $5 per vehicle. From Marysville, take Highway 20 east for 12 miles and turn north on Marysville Road. The lake entrance will be on your right in about 10 miles. (530) 692-1600.

PLACES TO STAY

Collins Lake: See Collins Lake above for camping information.

SMARTVILLE

When Smartville's new post office was built in 1968, all the paperwork had gone through before someone realized they'd added an extra "s" to Smartville's name. Since then, the town's name has gradually shifted to reflect the "Smartsville" error. But because the old-timers cringe when they hear "Smartsville," we'll refer to it as "Smartville," in their honor.

PARKS, BEACHES, AND RECREATION AREAS

• **Spenceville Wildlife and Recreation Area** 🐾🐾🐾🐾 🐕
See **⑥** *on page 138.*

First the bad news: If your dog isn't a hunting companion, she can't be off leash here. Now the better news: Non-hunting dogs are welcome at this 11,213-acre wildlife area year-round.

More than 20 miles of hiking trails await you, your dog, and your binoculars. Among the wildlife you may see are coyotes, mule deer, quail, and great blue herons (there's a great blue heron rookery here). If you have a hankering to do some angling, the fishing is fine at pure, cool Dry Creek. Don't miss its waterfall.

From Highway 20 in Smartville, take Smartville Road south. You'll find several entryways in the next several miles. Call about hunting seasons and off-limit areas. (530) 538-2236.

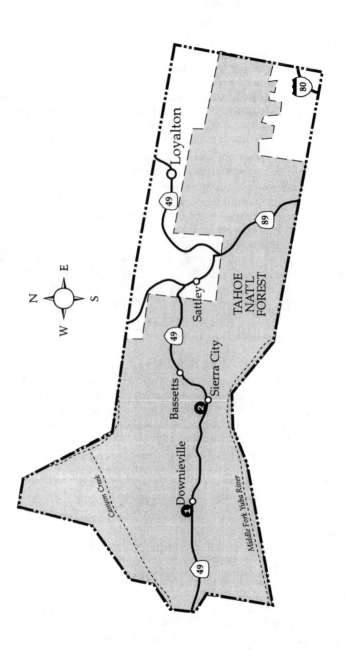

17
SIERRA COUNTY

Tahoe National Forest makes up a huge portion of this mountainous county, causing dogs to give almost the entire county a four-paw rating. Peaks stretch up to 9,000 feet above sea level and plunge down into gigantic, serene meadows carpeted with wildflowers in the spring and snow in the colder months.

The North Fork of the Yuba River cuts through big rocks and mountains of tall pines and oaks. In summer, you and your dog can pull off Highway 49 and swim, fish (the fly-fishing is exceptional here), or pan for gold in the river. In autumn, bask in bright colors as the water maples and aspens prepare for winter.

Campgrounds are plentiful along Highway 49. They can be good places to start hikes, but there are actually only a few trailheads that begin near the road. A portion of the Pacific Crest Trail passes between Bassetts Station and Sierra City. It's a great place to hike with an off-leash dog, because this section is on dog-friendly national forestland.

NATIONAL FORESTS

See the National Forests and Wilderness Areas chapter starting on page 748 for important information and safety tips on visiting national forests with your dog.

• **Tahoe National Forest** 🐾🐾🐾🐾 🐕
See page 755.

CALPINE

PLACES TO STAY

Sierra Valley Lodge: Dogs who like their vacations far from the hubbub of humans enjoy coming to the historic Sierra Valley Lodge. It's the only public-oriented business in this logging town of 200 people, and you won't get a TV or telephone in your room. A rustic lounge with a large rock fireplace adds to the peaceful flavor of this old-timey place—although on some weekends there's live music. If your dog's fur stands on end at the thought of this, please ask before booking a reservation. Dogs are allowed in two of the lodge's rooms. Rates are $45 to $48. 151 Main Street, Calpine, CA 96124; (530) 858-0322 or (800) 858-0322.

DOWNIEVILLE

While visiting this Old West gold town, you and your dog may feel as if some old miner might come running up behind you screaming he's hit the Mother Lode. It could happen. A couple of years ago, Joe and I ran into a prospector who was selling a chunk of gold big enough to pay his bills for two years. Granted, his bills were minimal since he lived out of a camper truck, but it was still impressive. He bought a drink for everyone within 100 feet and treated Joe to a piece of pizza.

Authentic is not the word for Downieville. Authentic implies that something has changed over time and then been restored to be more like the original. But Downieville has barely changed since its heyday in the 1850s. Wood planks still serve as sidewalks and many buildings still have walls made of thick stones. The streets are narrow and jagged, just wide enough for a few stagecoaches (although cars do manage here nowadays). Ghastly green gallows stand next to the county jail, a grim reminder of the town's rowdy past. And gold miners still gather at the local assay office at dusk to weigh and sell the gold flecks and chunks they find in the North Fork of the Yuba River.

Inspired by this gold, Joe and I bought a $4 gold pan and a little red book that tells you how to pan for the stuff. We drove west of town a few miles on Highway 49 and stopped when we found what looked like a lucky spot on the Yuba River in Tahoe National Forest (see page 755). We could feel our fortune in the air. We knew that after we spent a couple hours sifting gravel and dirt, we'd find something that would let us retire early, or at least buy a bag of dog food. It was one of those things you could just sense.

Two hours later, I was still trying to get Joe to stop digging holes and covering up my freshly shaken gold pan with his freshly dug river dirt. It was bad enough that we had to watch the little red instruction booklet float away, then sink, after Joe crashed into me and knocked me into the river in a fit of canine glee within minutes of getting to our spot.

We left with soggy coats and unfulfilled dreams. That night, we bought a lottery ticket, won $5, and felt much better.

PARKS, BEACHES, AND RECREATION AREAS

•Lion's Memorial Park 🐾 🐾 *See* ❶ *on page 142.*

If you like looking at old mining equipment, you'll enjoy this park. Several old, rusty gold mining relics are constantly on display here. The park is also a decent place to take a break from exploring town and relax on a bench with your dog.

The best part of this small, on-leash park is that it provides easy access to the Downie River, which runs right through town. Just watch out for the pair of geese who seem to run the place. Both times we visited, they honked us right off the beach. The park is just next to Courthouse Bridge. (530) 289-3201.

RESTAURANTS

Indian Valley Outpost: Step inside and order a good home-cooked meal. While you wait (with someone waiting by the picnic tables outside with your dog), shop the little store here for things like handmade earrings and other local crafts. It's a fun place to spend a few extra dollars. Highway 49, about 12 miles west of Downieville; (530) 289-3630.

River View Pizzeria: Dine at any of several rugged picnic tables in the front of the restaurant, or take your pizza out back to Lion's Memorial Park (see above) and eat at the picnic tables overlooking the Downie River. 103 Nevada Street; (530) 289-3540.

PLACES TO STAY

Camp Yuba: The three rustic cabins and five RV camp spaces here are nestled in Tahoe National Forest on the north fork of the Yuba River. The camp is located about five miles east of downtown Downieville, so there's plenty of space for walking around with your best buddy. RV spaces are $20 nightly. Cabins are available on a weekly basis for $560 to $595. The address is Highway 49, Downieville, CA 95936; (530) 289-0107.

Dewarts Riverside Inn: Stay here and stay at the confluence of the Yuba and Downie Rivers. Joe (aka "Mr. Don't Get Me Wet") could give a hoot, but it's truly a water dog's dream. The 1940s-style motel has knotty-pine rooms with balconies overlooking the water below. It's a peaceful place to snooze the night away, since the sounds of the river can cover up the sounds of your snoring dog. Rates are $55 to $100. Dogs are $5 extra. 206 Commercial Street, Downieville, CA 95936; (530) 289-1000.

Saundra Dyer's Resort: Dogs love this beautiful, dog-friendly Old West inn at least as much as their humans do. That's partly because owner Saundra Dyer adores dogs. She and her energetic Bouvier, Charlie, will even show good dogs a special, secret riverfront beach they can visit. Sadly, Dyer's beloved rottweiler, Baron, died recently. But if you listen very carefully and the wind is just right, you might still be able to hear him howling "Happy

Trails"—a trick that made him famous throughout the Gold Country during his too-short life.

Rates are $59 to $125. The inn is at 9 River Street, across the river and just west of the main part of town. The mailing address is P.O. Box 406, Downieville, CA 95936; (530) 289-3308 or (800) 696-3308.

LOYALTON

RESTAURANTS

Country Cookin' Restaurant and Inn: See the listing below, under Places to Stay.

PLACES TO STAY

Country Cookin' Restaurant and Inn: This little lodging has six units that share one common kitchen and three bathrooms. It's fun to stay here with your dog because it's kind of like home away from home. You can bring your own groceries and never worry about searching out a dog-friendly restaurant. But should you decide to search, you won't have to look much beyond your own front door. The inn's restaurant, Country Cookin', has an outdoor patio area that welcomes good dogs. And dogs and humans think the Old West, country-style cooking is the cat's meow. You want hearty? Try the biscuits and gravy or one of the special omelets they whip up here. The restaurant is open for breakfast and lunch.

Room rates are $45. 820 Main Street, Loyalton, CA 96118; (530) 993-1162.

Golden West Saloon: This inn's lobby and bar date back to about 100 years ago, but the room where you and your pooch are allowed to stay is merely a throwback to the 1970s. That's okay with Joe, who says any place that specializes in prime rib (served at the inn's restaurant, where the rule is no dogs) has got to be okay. The mailing address is just Highway 49 (Main Street), Loyalton, CA 96118; (530) 993-4467.

SATTLEY

PLACES TO STAY

Yuba Pass Campground: Stay here and your dog can brag to his buddies that he slept right on Yuba Pass, at an elevation of 6,708 feet. With only 20 campsites, it's fairly private and quiet. Dogs have to be leashed in the camping areas, but if you go on a hike in surrounding Tahoe National Forest, obedient dogs can go off leash.

Sites are $5, and they're available on a first-come, first-served basis. The campground is about seven miles west of Sattley, off Highway 49 at Yuba Pass; (530) 265-4531.

SIERRA CITY

PARKS, BEACHES, AND RECREATION AREAS

• **Sierra County Historical Park** 🐾🐾 ½ See ❷ on page 142.

A restored hard rock gold mine and stamp mill are the main attractions at this hilly, forested park a mile east of Sierra City. It's fascinating to learn about how gold ore is mined, crushed, and has its gold extracted. While dogs are not allowed in the museum, they are sometimes permitted to go on a guided tour of the Kentucky Mine with you. Or you can take your own tour, looking into a restored miner's cabin or down a deep hole into the mine.

Leashed dogs enjoy the paved paths that lead to the attractions and the amphitheater (see Diversions, below). But they seem to like the smaller, dirt paths above the amphitheater even more. If you continue on those paths, eventually you'll be in national forest jurisdiction. But it's best to start one of those magical off-leash romps at designated sites within the forest.

The park is just east of the main part of Sierra City, on Highway 49. It's open Memorial Day through October. Hours vary, so contact the park at P.O. Box 260, Sierra City, CA 96125, or call (530) 862-1310.

RESTAURANTS

Sierra Country Store: There's no street address, but it's on Highway 49, and you can't miss it. Eat grocery store cuisine with your dog at the outside benches. (530) 862-1181.

PLACES TO STAY

Buckhorn Lodge: Outdoorsy dogs will enjoy this lodge. It's located just off the Yuba River. The Pacific Crest Trail and some quiet lakes aren't too far away either. Some of the units in this attractive wood-shingled lodge have kitchens. Many have decks overlooking the Yuba. Rates are $40 to $125. 230 Main Street (Highway 49), Sierra City, CA 96125; (800) 991-1170.

Herrington's Sierra Pines Resort: This pretty, old resort is located on the Yuba River, which is great for a good night's sleep. But it's even better for a good day's walk with your best pal, because well-behaved dogs are allowed off leash at the river's edge. And better yet, obedient dogs are allowed leash free on the 55 acres of land surrounding the resort. It's one of the most dog-friendly lodgings this side of the Sierra.

For dogs whose people like to fish, there's a pond stocked with 3,000 rainbow trout. If the fish outwit you, you can enjoy a scrumptious meal at the resort's beautiful dining room, which has a cozy, log-cabin feel.

The rooms are mostly motel-style, with wood paneling, and there are a few housekeeping units. The resort is closed from Thanksgiving to March. Rates are $49 to $90. 101 Main Street (Highway 49), Sierra City, CA 96125; (530) 862-1151.

Shannon's Cabins: These rustic buildings are located in Tahoe National Forest, and just across the road is river access to the Yuba. Dogs dig it here because the land in the back of the cabins is great for doggy hikes and comes complete with fragrant pines and cedars. It also comes with bears, coyotes, foxes, and raccoons, so it's a good idea to keep your pooch leashed. Rates are $25 to $40. The address is just Highway 49, Sierra City, CA 96125; (530) 862-1287.

DIVERSIONS

Give your canine culture: The Kentucky Mine Concert Series, at Sierra County Historical Park (see page 146), provides a summer of musical entertainment for you and your extraordinarily well-behaved dog. The concerts feature a wide variety of music, from Broadway to Celtic to Old West. Dogs who promise not to bark, howl, or thump their foot while scratching are allowed to sit with you in the small, outdoor amphitheater.

An added requirement: Dogs must be able to remain calm when Willie, the resident cat, streaks across the stage with a mouse in his mouth. He does this during at least a couple of concerts each season. Tickets are $10 at the door, $8 in advance. For schedules and information, write P.O. Box 368, Sierra City, CA 96125, or call (530) 862-1310.

SIERRAVILLE

This charming old town is just down the road from the amazing Sierra Hot Springs (formerly Campbell Hot Springs). Dogs aren't allowed there, so we offer some good camping alternatives. At worst, you and a friend can take turns dogsitting and visiting the hot springs.

PLACES TO STAY

Cottonwood Creek Campground: Surrounded by big forests and set along Cottonwood Creek at an elevation of 5,600 feet, this campground with 48 sites is an enchanting one. It's not a typical remote national forest camp, but it's not exactly bustling either. Leashed dogs are welcome to peruse the area. They especially enjoy the three miles of trails that start at the main trailhead. Water dogs go gaga for the Fisherman's Trail, which runs alongside the creek.

Sites are $9. From Sierraville, take Highway 89 about four miles southeast. The campground will be on your left. For reservations, call (800) 280-CAMP. For more information, call (530) 994-3401.

Stampede Reservoir Campground: This is a huge and popular campground on the huge and popular Stampede Reservoir. The reservoir has 25 miles of shoreline. Fishing is great, and hiking is even better. When you get away from people, you can even let your dog off leash, since it's all part of Tahoe National Forest (see page 755).

You'll have your choice of 252 campsites on the south side of the reservoir. Sites are $12 to $18. From Interstate 80, take the Boca-Hirschdale/Stampede Meadows Road exit about eight miles north. At the reservoir's dam, turn left and drive a mile to the campground. Call (800) 280-CAMP for campsite reservations. For mo0re information, phone (530) 587-3558.

18
NEVADA COUNTY

Do you have a digging dog? Buy yourself a plot of land and start scooping that dirt. Locals boast that more than half the gold that came out of California during the Gold Rush was found in Nevada City, Grass Valley, and other foothill areas of this county. Your hot-diggedy dog probably won't come up with much, but it's always fun to dream.

If you want to see where the riches really were, your best bet is to visit the Empire Mine State Historic Park (see page 152), where hole-digging dogs can ooh and ahh at the mouth of the mine shaft that winds 5,000 feet below the surface.

Autumn in Nevada County is about as beautiful as autumn in New England. Pick up a map for a self-guided tour of Nevada City's fall colors from the city's Chamber of Commerce, at 132 Main Street, or phone them at (530) 265-2692.

Much of the county, especially Tahoe National Forest (see page 755) in the east, shows its true colors in the winter, when mountains are a crispy white. In Spanish, the very name *nevada* means "snow-covered." If you've always wanted a white Christmas, this is a spectacular place to watch the flurries fly.

NATIONAL FORESTS

See the National Forests and Wilderness Areas chapter starting on page 748 for important information and safety tips on visiting national forests with your dog.

•**Tahoe National Forest** 🐾🐾🐾🐾 🐕
See page 755.

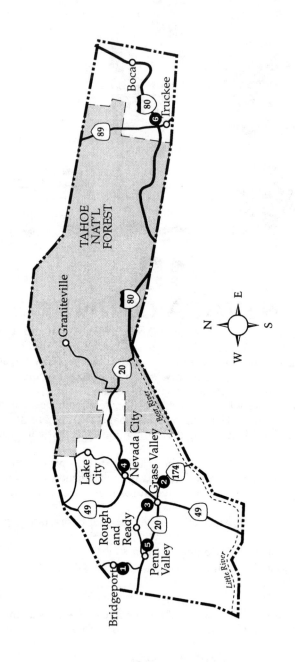

Boca

80
6 Truckee

89

TAHOE
NAT'L
FOREST

80

Graniteville

20

N
W — E
S

Bear River

Lake
City

Nevada City
4
Grass Valley
2 174
3
49
20

49

49

5

Rough
and
Ready

Penn
Valley

Little River

1 Bridgeport

BOCA

PLACES TO STAY

Boca Rest Campground: This is one of a few campgrounds along the striking Boca Reservoir. It's at an elevation of 5,700 feet and is surrounded by tall pines, low grassy areas, and steep bluffs. The Boca Rest Campground, with 25 sites, is the only one with piped water. Better yet, there's plenty of hiking available, and since it's in Tahoe National Forest (see page 755), it's okay to unleash your dog on the trails outside the campground.

The campground is open from May through October. Sites are $8. Take the Boca-Hirschdale/Stampede Meadows Road exit north from Interstate 80. The campground is on the northeast edge of the lake. For reservations, call (800) 280-CAMP. For more information, phone (530) 265-4531.

CHICAGO PARK

PLACES TO STAY

Rollins Lakeside Inn: The cozy, knotty pine-paneled cabins here include completely furnished kitchens and a barbecue, and sleep up to eight people (or dogs). For real privacy, try the attractive, secluded chalet. Rollins Lakeside Inn is kind of like a home away from home, especially if your home has a solar-heated swimming pool and all kinds of recreational opportunities, including horseshoes and volleyball. The inn is surrounded by plenty of tall pines, which boy dogs especially appreciate. It's just a couple of hundred feet from Rollins Lake, with good lake access. The view of the lake from the inn's large wooden deck and some of the cabins is to die for.

The owners love dogs, and even have a "Dog Wall of Fame," full of photos of dogs who have stayed here. Be sure to take a photo of your grinning pooch so she, too, can be immortalized here.

Rates are $70 to $175. Weekly rates are available. There's a two-night minimum stay from May through October. During winter, the cabins are rented by the month. 18145 Rollins View Drive, Chicago Park, CA 95712; (530) 273-0729.

GRANITEVILLE

PLACES TO STAY

Bowman Lake Campground: If you want to get away from all those city-like campgrounds, try this one. Since there are only seven campsites, you'll never feel the crunch of crowds. And if you're willing to do a little hiking, you can really escape civilization. The campground and surrounding areas are part of Tahoe National Forest (see page 755), so good dogs may go leash-free in forests outside the camping area. There is no fee. All sites are first come, first served. Keep in mind that the campground may not open until as late as June each year because of snow.

From Interstate 80 just east of Emigrant Gap, you can take Bowman Lake Road north to the lake. It's about 10 miles east of Graniteville. (530) 265-4531.

GRASS VALLEY

Like Nevada City a few miles up the road, Grass Valley is a classic Old West town, only older and wester.

PARKS, BEACHES, AND RECREATION AREAS

We had a major disappointment when we tried to visit Condon Park, a huge, hilly, wooded city park. A big sign, somewhat hidden behind a rapidly growing tree, announced "NO DOGS ALLOWED." If you find yourself in the park's vicinity just west of the historic downtown and your dog is getting that desperate look, your only alternative is Minnie Park (see below).

•**Empire Mine State Historic Park** 🐾🐾🐾 *See ❶ on page 150.*

At one time, miners descended in cagelike trains deep into the earth here and rumbled the ground searching for gold in 350 miles of tunnels. The place was alive 24 hours a day—dirty, dusty, and dancing with gold: Miners extracted more than six million ounces of the precious ore during the mine's century of use.

Now, it's a quiet, calm 800-acre park with lush gardens and green meadows. While the mine and surrounding buildings are inactive, they're still fascinating to inspect. On hot summer days, a dog's favorite place is the shaft viewing area. It's a few dozen feet below ground, and the earthy scents are almost as relaxing as the cool, damp air.

The fee for adults is $3. For kids and (leashed) dogs, it's $1. From Highway 49, drive east on Highway 20/Empire Street about 1.5 miles. The park is on the right. (530) 273-8522.

•**Minnie Park/Memorial Park** 🐾 **½** *See ❷ on page 150.*

Minnie Park, in comparison to the large, canine-banning Condon Park right next to it, seems like it should be called "Mini" Park. It's a relatively tiny, unremarkable park, but it does have shade, decent lawns, picnic tables, and a small playground. And it does allow your leashed pooch. It's on Cornwall Avenue and Brighton Street. (530) 274-4390.

RESTAURANTS

Cousin Jack's Pasties: British dogs go wild when they smell the Cornish pasties (yummy meat-and-potato pies) you can eat on the porch here. "Dogs are very welcome, and may even get an extra snack," says a dog-loving manager. 100 South Auburn Street; (530) 272-9230.

Subway Sandwiches & Salads: Dine on myriad subs at the outdoor tables. Joe recommends the foot-long meatball sub. If you see him here and you happen to drop a meatball, he'll be your lifelong friend. Drop two and he'll follow you home. 716 Freeman Lane; (530) 273-7789.

PLACES TO STAY

Alta Sierra Resort Motel: Your dog will like the views of the small lake you can see from your roomside deck. The lodging is on four acres, all of which have views of the lake or the golf course. Rates are $49 to $150. Dogs are $10 extra. 11858 Tammy Way, Grass Valley, CA 95949; (530) 273-9102 or (800) 992-5300.

Golden Chain Resort Motel: If it's hot, this is a cool place to stay—shady trees abound on the property. Rates are $42 to $78. Dogs are $6 extra. They like small dogs here. 13363 Highway 49, Grass Valley, CA 95949; (530) 273-7279.

Holiday Lodge: You and your leashed dog can go on gold-panning tours run by the hotel! And the hotel even has a little area for walking pooches. Unfortunately, only small dogs are allowed to stay here. Rates are $38 to $60. Dogs require a $20 deposit. 1221 East Main Street, Grass Valley, CA 95949; (530) 273-4406.

Swan-Levine House: This big, airy house was built in 1880 and soon after was transformed into a small hospital. Now it's a magical inn, complete with an art studio (where you can try your hand at printmaking), brightly colored rooms furnished with antiques, and cozy fireplaces. Dogs who stay here should like cats—there are plenty of these critters on the property. In fact, if you're planning to visit with your pooch, call first and tell the owner about any cat-munching idiosyncrasies your dog may or may not have. Pooches stay at the discretion of the owner, so you'll need to have a chat first anyway. Rates are $70 to $95. 328 South Church Street, Grass Valley, CA 95945; (530) 272-1873.

LAKE CITY

PLACES TO STAY

Malakoff Diggins State Historic Park: If only dogs could explore this fascinating park with you, they'd get to see what the world's richest and largest hydraulic gold mine was like in its heyday. Fortunately, dogs don't care about such things. But they do generally enjoy a good night of camping, and this park lets them stay overnight for $1. And while dogs aren't allowed on the trails or in the Blair Lake area, they are permitted to join you in certain spots in the park. In case you're interested in a very limited day excursion with your dog, the day-use fee is $5.

There are 30 campsites, ranging from $7 to $10. Take Highway 49 from Nevada City and go right at Tyler Foote Crossing Road. Drive 16 miles to the park on this sometimes paved, sometimes precipitous, gravelly road. For camping reservations, call Parknet at (800) 444-PARK. For park information, phone (530) 265-2740.

NEVADA CITY

Dogs are everywhere in this colorful Gold Rush town in the Sierra foothills. They dine with their owners, frolic off leash in Pioneer Park, and hang out with human friends on historic Broad Street. They sometimes even get to go shopping in some of the cutesy tourist-oriented stores.

The entire Old West/Victorian downtown is registered as a national historic landmark. On winter nights, when snow falls around the gaslit lamps in the narrow streets, it's classic Currier & Ives. Your dog trotting along will only add to the sweet scene.

PARKS, BEACHES, AND RECREATION AREAS

•**Pioneer Park** 🐾🐾🐾🐾 🐕 *See* ❸ *on page 150.*

The one exception to this historic city's leash law is at this fine, green park. Dogs who are under extremely good voice control can go leashless. The park has open fields for running. Dogs love the tall pines that edge the park. These trees provide both shade and places for dogs to do their thing. Ball fields, a playground, a pool, and a shed with old firewagons are the major human interests here.

From northbound Interstate 80, exit at Sacramento Street and go right immediately on Nile Street (at the sign for Pioneer Park). When the road comes to a T, go right. The park is on your left. You can either drive all the way in and park near the fountain, or park on Nimrod Street and walk down a paved road into the park's largest open field. (530) 265-2521.

RESTAURANTS

Walking Dog: The hot dogs at this stand are quite tasty, but the Walking Dog logo looks more like Mister Peanut on a bad hair day than an ambulatory wiener. Joe thinks it should look more like a walking canine, but the implications of that idea might make you think twice before biting that frankfurter. 408 Broad Street; there's no phone number.

PLACES TO STAY

The Marsh House: This famous three-acre estate with an 1873 Italianate mansion and four-bedroom carriage house is listed on the National Register of Historic Places. Can you believe your pooch can stay here? The owner likes dogs but has to know ahead of time if you're bringing one, since dogs are permitted in only one suite.

The grounds are as exquisite as the mansion. You and your dog will enjoy a stroll around the lawns and lush gardens. (The orchids are to die for.) The Marsh House is two blocks from historic downtown Nevada City. Rates are $135 to $225. A doggy deposit may be required. 254 Boulder Street, Nevada City, CA 95959; (530) 265-5709.

Nevada Street Cottages: The four attractive cottages here make dogs feel completely at home. "It's a nice place for a dog to spend the night," says one of the managers. The cottages are on the edge of Nevada City, in the historic part of town. Dogs are allowed to traverse the attractive, parklike grounds around the cottages. Rates are $70 to $110. 690 Nevada Street, Nevada City, CA 95959; (530) 265-8071.

DIVERSIONS

Get the drift of a draft horse: Dogs think being drawn along the historic streets of Nevada City in a carriage pulled by a hunky Percheron draft horse is one of the most riveting olfactory experiences ever. They thrill at the scent of horse heinie, their noses quivering perchance the horse does his horse business. And it's almost inevitable the horse will provide such canine entertainment: These big, calm beauties eat 20 pounds of grain and 30 pounds of hay daily. Fortunately for the carriage driver, no pooper-scooper is necessary.

The Nevada City Carriage Company offers terrific rides through historic downtown and the Victorian district. Rides are $20 to $80, depending on the length of the tour and the number of people in your party. Dave, the dog-friendly manager, also offers special rides in more elaborate horse-drawn vehicles. Hours for regular rides vary by season, but the horses are out there daily year-round, weather permitting.

You'll often find the carriages until 6 P.M. in front of the Buttonworks or the National Hotel downtown. In the evening, they'll be in front of Friar Tuck's Restaurant, at 111 North Pine Street. Look for the "Carriage for Hire" sign. For an information card, write 17790 Cooper Road, Nevada City, CA 95959, or call (530) 265-8778.

PENN VALLEY

PARKS, BEACHES, AND RECREATION AREAS

• **South Yuba River State Park** 🐾🐾🐾½ *See* ❹ *on page 150.*

This is one of the newest and most interesting units in the state park system. For now, at least, leashed dogs are allowed to peruse the place. This is great news for pooches who like nature at its finest. The park is a patchwork of lands spread over a 20-mile length along the South Yuba River Canyon, from the top of Englebright Lake at Bridgeport to Tahoe National Forest above Malakoff Diggins State Historic Park (see page 153).

There are many access points to the park, but our favorites are in the western section. For seclusion and serene beauty, try the westernmost access area. Driving north from Lake Wildwood on Pleasant Valley Road, you'll see a sign for the park and a small parking/pullout area on your left (there's space for only a few cars). If you're coming from Grass Valley or the town of Penn Valley, take Highway 20 west, turn right (north) on Pleasant Valley Road, and drive about six miles to the park.

As soon as you get out of the car, you and your leashed dog will hear the flowing river. Hike down the wide dirt path and when you come to a gravel section, go left. A few yards in, you'll come to one of the most beautiful sections of the South Yuba. The beach around it is sandy and the water in the river is a clear tropical blue (during non-rainy times of year). You'll want to stay forever.

If you're going to run into any people in this part of the park, it's going to be here. The maximum number of humans we've seen at one time at this beachy area has been two. If you want real privacy, you can always ford the river. If the river is high, the current is slow, and your dog's a swimmer, just do the dog paddle across. You're almost guaranteed that no one will be on the other side. Or if you're looking for exercise, continue along the first dirt trail and you can hike your heart out.

Just a few hundred feet up Pleasant Valley Road is the Bridgeport Recreation Area, a much more widely used part of the park with bigger parking lots. Here's where you and your leashed dog can walk across the longest (243 feet) single-span covered bridge in existence. It's been around since 1862! Back then, it cost a whopping $5.50 to get across, but the fee included you, a loaded wagon, and six mules, oxen, or horses. These days, it's free.

You can also relax and picnic at a riverside table, swim in the crystal-clear Yuba, or hike a number of trails. One of the most rugged and scenic trails starts to the left of the covered bridge as you cross from the parking lot. The narrow trail takes you to Englebright Lake, about a mile away. (530) 432-2546

•**Western Gateway Regional Park** 🐾🐾🐾 *See* ❺ *on page 150.*

One of the favorite summertime activities at this park is for kids to lie facedown on the big water pipes over the creek and watch the water gurgle by. Dogs love to watch the water, too, but it's best if they do it downstream a little. Just walk down the bank to a more secluded spot, where your splashing dog won't frighten or dampen kids.

The park has wide meadows, a mini-forest area with small dirt trails, and lots of shrubs for dogs. Leashed dogs love all that. For kids, the place is loaded with playgrounds, ball fields, and basketball courts. Dogs are banned from the playing fields, but they are free to walk on leash around the rest of the park.

From Highway 20, go south about a half block on Indian Springs Road, then turn left on Penn Valley Drive. The park is on the left. (530) 432-1990.

ROUGH AND READY

This tiny community was once a thriving little Gold Rush town that took its name from "Old Rough-and-Ready" Zachary Taylor. In 1850, about a year after the town was settled, the townfolk concluded that mining taxes were getting to be too much and voted to secede from the Union. But the Great Republic of Rough and Ready was not destined to last long. When the Fourth of July came along just three months after the secession, Old Glory went up the flagpole and the new Republic was down the tubes.

"It was the wonders of alcohol more than anything else," says Everett Burkhard, of the Rough and Ready Chamber of Commerce (an organization that serves the town's four businesses nicely). "They discovered it was too difficult to get it, so they rejoined. It was a good enough reason at the time."

DIVERSIONS

Take in some "R&R" with your pooch: Toast Rough and Ready's rough-and-tumble history as a Great Republic on the last Sunday of June. Every year, from morning till evening, Rough and Ready relives the glory days of its short-lived independence. Locals put on a spirited play reenacting the events leading up to and including the secession, but leashed dogs prefer to concentrate on more important matters—the pancake breakfast for one and the chili cook-off for another. There's entertainment all day long, crafts, games for kids, and even blacksmith shop demonstrations.

The celebration is held in the heart of downtown Rough and Ready, on Rough and Ready Highway (where else?). It's easy to miss downtown Rough and Ready, so if you have any questions, the Chamber of Commerce welcomes calls. (530) 272-4320.

TRUCKEE

If you want a preview of just what you're going to see when you visit this colorful old city, rent the silent Charlie Chaplin flick *The Gold Rush.* Some of the late-1800s architecture along Truckee's main street, Commercial Row, appears in the film. As rapidly as towns grow in California, you'll see that this enchanting old street hasn't changed much.

Your dog will enjoy the rough, Old West feel of the historic part of town, and you'll like the myriad enchanting shops and restaurants. But sadly for people with dogs, Commercial Row is so old-style that it doesn't have room for outdoor tables for human and doggy dining.

Truckee is home to Donner Lake, where many in the ill-fated Donner Party died in the winter of 1846 after running out of provisions during a "short cut" leg of their journey from the Midwest. The tragic tale of their starvation and resulting cannibalism is recounted at Donner Memorial State Park (see page 158).

A more upbeat way to experience Truckee's freshwater wonders is to go hiking or trout fishing at the Truckee River. One of the access points just outside downtown is described below. It's a great location if someone you're traveling with wants to shop while you and the dog get your paws wet.

PARKS, BEACHES, AND RECREATION AREAS

Truckee has a perfectly manicured regional park, but dogs don't feel welcome there. We prefer to drive another mile down the road and enjoy the wonders of the Martis Creek Lake. The recreation area surrounding the lake straddles two counties, and is described on page 164 in the Placer County chapter.

• **Truckee River (access outside downtown Truckee)** 🐾🐾🐾🐾 🐕
See ❻ on page 150.

This beautiful, trout-filled river beckons hikers and anglers and their adventurous canines. The really good news is that dogs are allowed off leash along the river, since it's in Tahoe National Forest! Your pup can frolic while you catch and release all day. Use artificial lures and barbless hooks only.

Once you get past the first couple of hundred feet along the riverbank, the trail can be narrow and rocky. If your dog is a klutz or has thin-skinned paws, you may not want to go any farther. She can still have plenty of fun sniffing around while you cast all day for the big one hiding behind the boulder.

From central Truckee, drive northeast on Highway 267 and go right on Glenshire Drive (it's about halfway between downtown and Interstate 80). After 4.5 miles, you'll come to the Glenshire Bridge. Make a sharp right onto a dirt road after the bridge, and park in the flat, dirt area near the river. When choosing a fishing spot, be sure to head to the left as you face the river. If you walk to the right, you'll be in very private fishing grounds very quickly.

The folks at Mountain Hardware can give you fishing tips and updated regulations. Call them at (530) 587-4844. The Truckee Ranger District of Tahoe National Forest wasn't as knowledgeable about this part of the river when we called, but they can be helpful with other information. (530) 587-3558.

RESTAURANTS

Gateway Deli: Eat tasty deli fare with your favorite dog at the outdoor tables here. 11012 Donner Pass Road; (530) 587-3106.

Sizzler Restaurant: This is one of few franchises in this chain with outdoor seating. You'll need to tie your dog near the deck if other folks are on it, but otherwise, good dogs are mighty welcome here. 11262 Donner Pass Road; (530) 587-1824.

PLACES TO STAY

Alpine Village: Last time we visited, a big sign in front of the motel advertised "PETS WELCOME." That's the kind of sign we like to see. The motel is conveniently located just off Interstate 80, near Donner Lake. Rates are $45 to $78. 12260 Deerfield Drive, Truckee, CA 96161; (530) 587-3801 or (800) 933-1787.

Donner Memorial State Park: Dogs aren't allowed on the trails or in the museum that tells the tragic story of the Donner Party, trapped here for the winter of 1846. But they can stay with you at any of the park's 150 campsites. And they can also accompany you to pay homage to the dozens of pioneers who perished here. There's a 22-foot-high monument on a stone base that's 16 feet high; 22 feet was the depth of the snow during that desperate winter. It's within doggy access.

Sites are $12 to $14. Dogs are $1 extra. The park is about two miles west of the town of Truckee, on Donner Pass Road. Phone Parknet at (800) 444-PARK for reservations, or call the park at (530) 582-7892 for more information.

19
PLACER COUNTY

If your dog likes fresh mountain air, world-class ski resorts, and rivers rushing over hidden gold, Placer County is her kind of place. The county has a little of everything, and dogs should experience its diversity.

Most dogs think the county gets better as they go from its more populated western end past the Mother Lode and into the magnificent mountains. Unless your dog likes to shop 'til she drops, the western valley region of Placer County probably won't be nearly as appealing to her as the high country.

Part of the appeal of the eastern half is that much of it is Tahoe National Forest land, where dogs can shed their leashes everywhere except in campgrounds and developed recreation areas. Keep in mind that the northwest corner of the Granite Chief Wilderness bans dogs from May 15 to July 15 because of deer fawning (see page 755).

The western half of the county is far from a suburban slumberland. In fact, a good part of it is heavily agricultural. You and your dog can experience the farming life firsthand by driving the 49er Fruit Trail. The trail passes

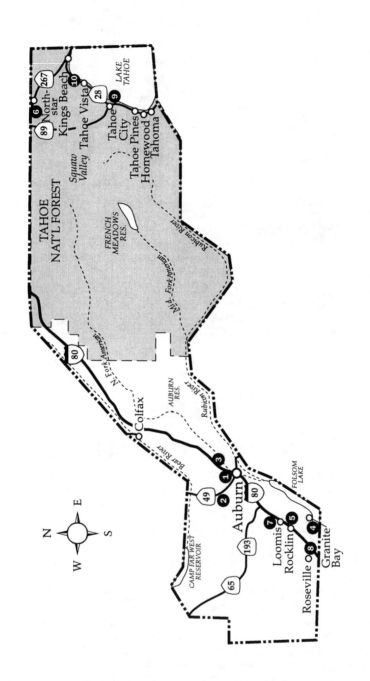

LAKE TAHOE

267

Northstar
Kings Beach

10

Tahoe Vista

28

89

6

9

Tahoe
City
Tahoe Pines
Homewood
Tahoma

Squaw
Valley

TAHOE
NAT'L FOREST

Rubicon River

FRENCH
MEADOWS
RES.

N.J. Fork American

80

N. Fork American

Colfax

AUBURN
RES.

Rubicon River

Bear River

3

1

49

Auburn

2

80

FOLSOM
LAKE

7

5

4

193

Loomis

Rocklin

8

CAMP FAR WEST
RESERVOIR

65

Roseville

Granite
Bay

N
E
S
W

by 100 farms, where you (and often your dog) can stop, look around, and buy very fresh farm goods—everything from apples to grapes to walnuts. There are even places to buy trout, sheep, and catfish! Before you let your dog out of the car, ask the farmer if it's okay. If it's not, and it's hot, continue on. Don't leave your dog in the car in warm weather even for a few minutes. For a map and list of all the farms, send a note and a stamped, self-addressed, legal-sized envelope to 49er Fruit Trail, P.O. Box 317, Newcastle, CA 95658.

Be aware, anyone stopping in Placer County with a female dog in heat: While she may be in the mood, you'll be in a bad mood if she gets caught seducing a guy dog. The fine for her "contact with male dogs" (that's county talk for "messing around") is $70.

NATIONAL FORESTS

See the National Forests and Wilderness Areas chapter starting on page 748 for important information and safety tips on visiting national forests with your dog.

• **Tahoe National Forest** 🐾🐾🐾🐾 🐕
See page 755.

AUBURN

While this city has sprawled in so many directions that it looks like a giant mall, there's still a fairly large, very historic downtown that's great for walking through with your dog. This is Joe's favorite Gold Country city. It looks like one big old valuable antique.

PARKS, BEACHES, AND RECREATION AREAS

• **Ashford Park** 🐾🐾 *See* ❶ *on page 160.*
This city park is convenient to Interstate 80 travelers whose leashed dogs like their rest room breaks nice and pretty. While the park is only seven acres, it has a little pond and is full of trees and picnic tables on well-manicured grass. Kids like the playground, so it's an ideal rest stop for your whole carload.

From Interstate 80, exit at Foresthill Road and go west for a couple of blocks. When you cross over railroad tracks, the entrance will be coming up on your left. Park on the street. (530) 885-8461.

• **Auburn District Regional Park** 🐾🐾½ *See* ❷ *on page 160.*
You can roll up your overalls and fish in the park's willow-shaded pond and feel remarkably like Tom Sawyer. Except for the sports fields and playground, this 62-acre park is a quiet one. Dogs may feel a little intimidated by the perfect green meadows, but if you look hard, there are a couple of scruffier sections around the edges. Leashes are a must.

Take the Dry Creek Road exit from Highway 49 and go west a few blocks to Richardson Drive. (530) 885-8461.

• **Auburn State Recreation Area** 🐾🐾🐾½ *See* ❸ *on page 160.*
This 30,000-acre park is located along 30 miles of the North and Middle Forks of the American River. A few of the activities (and inactivities) available include fishing, gold panning, rafting, swimming, hiking, biking, horse-

back riding, sunbathing, picnicking, and camping. Since dogs are supposed to stay out of the rivers and they don't ride bikes or horses, their selection is more limited.

On a quiet day when it's just you, your leashed dog, and the river, try to imagine 10,000 miners crowded into this area in hot pursuit of gold. It makes the occasional passerby seem less obtrusive.

If you and your dog have good hiking feet, 57 miles of trails await you. There are several trailheads. For an easy-to-find, quick hike to break up a long Interstate 80 trip, take the Foresthill Road exit off Interstate 80 and drive east. As soon as you pass over the Foresthill Bridge (it's the one that's 750 feet above the North Fork of the American River and a little more than a mile from the highway), pull over in the tiny off-road parking area to the right. Walk back toward the bridge and bear left when you see a little dirt area with signs that ban motorcycles from the trails.

Not only is this a superb area to view the lands around the north fork of the river, it's also the starting point for several trails that wind their way down toward the river. Some are very steep and attract mountain bikers. From the trailhead you can see which trails have a gentler grade—it's better for everyone if you choose one of the less precarious ones.

If you want a longer hike, a very popular starting point is behind the Auburn Fairgrounds, at Pleasant Avenue. Park in the large lot. If you're planning on hiking the whole trail, you'd better bring a few horses to carry your gear: The trail goes to the confluence of the Middle and North Forks of the American River, and then continues through national forests all the way to Squaw Valley.

Dogs are allowed at all areas and campsites in the Auburn State Recreation Area except around Lake Clementine and its campsites. Supervising Ranger Mike Van Hook says that area was closed to canines because inconsiderate owners didn't clean up after them and let them wreak general havoc. It's rare to find a state park that allows dogs on the trails, so let's be careful. You also have to watch out for mountain lions. This is the area where a woman was killed by a lion a few years ago. If you don't know how to handle a mountain lion encounter, contact the ranger. Chances are you'll never see one of these wild cats, but it's better to be on the safe side.

The recreation area has 78 campsites. They are first come, first served and cost $7 to $9 a night. Dogs are $1 extra. A favorite for people who like to get away from the crowds is the Ruck-A-Chucky Campground. It's a quiet, primitive campground next to the Ruck-A-Chucky rapids on the Middle Fork of the American River. Ruck-A-Chucky has only seven campsites, but it has a pleasant day-use area with picnic tables. (530) 885-4527.

RESTAURANTS

Awful Annie's: The name doesn't reflect the cuisine here, according to Reggie Dog, who stopped in with his folks, Denise and Kevin, and called to tell us about it. The food is good breakfast and lunch cuisine, with omelettes, soups, and salads. Vegetarians get to choose from a few dishes. Reggie Dog got a bowl of fresh water when he visited and was very impressed.

Dine with your dog on the attractive deck in Oldtown Auburn. 160 Sacramento Street; (530) 888-9857.

Country Naturals: Located in downtown Auburn, this is a good place to stop for a juice on a hot day. Swig it at the two outdoor tables. (You can also pick up your vitamins here, but make sure a friend is hanging out with your dog while you shop inside.) 346 Elm Avenue; (530) 823-1615.

Dairy Queen: Okay, so it's not Ben & Jerry's, but the ice cream hits the spot on a warm Sierra day. If you and the pooch want something more substantial, share a burger or hot dog while listening to the drone of Interstate 80 below. 13411 Lincoln Way; (530) 823-6257.

Ikeda's Tasty Burgers: "A lot of people bring dogs. They have good taste," says Steve, Ikeda's co-owner. A local sheriff's official tells us Ikeda's has the "best burgers for a long ways," and we believe him. You can see Ikeda's from Interstate 80, so it's a good place to come when you get the road-hungries. 13500 Lincoln Way; (530) 885-4243.

La Bou: Eat yummy baked goods, sip stimulating coffee. Do it all under the shade of La Bou's canopy. 2150 Grass Valley Highway; (530) 823-2303.

PLACES TO STAY

Auburn State Recreation Area: See Auburn State Recreation Area on page 161 for camping information.

Travelodge: Rates are $35 to $79. There's a $10 pooch fee per visit. 13480 Lincoln Way, Auburn, CA 95603; (530) 885-7025.

GRANITE BAY

PARKS, BEACHES, AND RECREATION AREAS

• **Folsom Lake State Recreation Area** 🐾 🐾 🐾 1/2 *See ❹ on page 160.*

An important entrance to this popular lake is in Granite Bay, just south of Folsom Road. Although most of this large park is in Placer County, we've listed it in Sacramento County, under its namesake, the town of Folsom. See page 289.

KINGS BEACH

A stinky new law has dogs bumming out here. Dogs are no longer allowed at Coon's Beach. Granted, it wasn't exactly poochy paradise, but it was good for a little paw stretching. The problem: poop. Or to be exact, the lack of scooping. You'd think dog people would learn . . .

RESTAURANTS

Char Pit: Usually, any restaurant with the word "pit" in it would make me balk, but this is a fun place to grab a bite with your dog. Munch on burgers, frosties, and ice cream at the outdoor tables. 8732 North Lake Boulevard; (530) 546-3171.

PLACES TO STAY

North Shore Lodge: Owner Jim is the first to tell you not to "expect the Ritz" when you visit. Along the same theme, reader Susan Kim (chauffeur of Maddie Dog) says, "It's not the Fairmont. But it's a great place if you want to feel cozy in the winter (it has that ski cabin effect)." Indeed, the cabins and even the motel rooms here are comfy and quiet. Better yet, the lodge sports a small, mostly fenced area dotted with pines. Dogs dig it. They also like the shaded picnic area in back of the lodge. Rates are $55 to $170. Dogs are $5 extra. 8755 North Lake Boulevard, Kings Beach, CA 96143; (530) 546-4833.

Stevenson's Inn: Innkeepers Rowland and Paulette Trent love dogs. They have a little pooch themselves, and that's part of the reason why if you're going to stay at this comfortable motel, you're going to have to sign a contract stating you won't leave your dog in the room by herself. "We believe people should treat their pet like they would treat a young child," says Rowland. "It's not fair to leave them locked in a strange room while you go gambling or skiing."

In addition to the Trents' concern for dogs is their concern for the rooms and for your neighbors. "Even if the dogs are great at home, they may bark all night. They go to the bathroom on the carpeting and tear up the furniture if they're alone," says Rowland. Your dog will pay the price if you disobey this common-sense house rule: The Trents reserve the right to call Animal Care and Control to pick up your dog.

If you're a good dog person, you'll have absolutely no trouble here. And you'll have an especially good, romantic time if you stay at one of the two-level suites that have wonderful wood-burning fireplaces. Room rates are $40 to $100. There's a $25 deposit for dogs, and they're $5 extra. 8742 North Lake Boulevard, Kings Beach, CA 96143; (530) 546-2269 or (800) 634-9141.

LOOMIS

PARKS, BEACHES, AND RECREATION AREAS

• **Loomis Basin Regional Park** 🐾🐾 *See* ❺ *on page 160.*

This park is divided into two sections—one for people, one for horses. Dogs can enjoy both, as long as they are leashed and as long as they stay off the baseball fields and the corral area when they're in use. That doesn't leave much room to romp, but it's a decent place to stop, especially if you have kids. The playground is a popular one.

The park is an easy stop off Interstate 80. Exit at Penryn Road, go south about a half mile, and turn right at Kings Road. Within a few blocks, the road bisects the park. (916) 652-1840.

NORTHSTAR

PARKS, BEACHES, AND RECREATION AREAS

• **Martis Creek Lake** 🐾🐾🐾½ *See* ❻ *on page 160.*

This is a prime wildlife viewing area, with great catch-and-release trout fishing and more than 1,400 acres of meadows, rolling sagebrush hills, and dense conifer forests. There's very little shade around the lake itself, so in hot weather don't plan to paddle around the lake all day while a friend and your dog watch from shore.

You and your leashed dog will have a chance to gawk at all kinds of wildlife, including red-tailed hawks, mule deer, and chickadees. In spring, you can lay back in the meadows full of alpine wildflowers and watch life unfold.

Dogs and their friends enjoy the lake's campground. It's set in a prime wildlife-viewing area and is fairly quiet. The 25 sites are often filled with early rising anglers or bird-watchers. Sites are $10. All sites but the two for campers with disabilities are available on a first-come, first-served basis.

The lake is halfway between Truckee and Northstar. From Northstar, travel about two miles northwest on Highway 267 to the park entrance. The campground is open from May through September. Call (530) 639-2342 for reservations for the sites for disabled campers or for more information on the lake.

PLACES TO STAY

Martis Creek Lake: See Martis Creek Lake above for camping information.

ROCKLIN

PARKS, BEACHES, AND RECREATION AREAS

• **Johnson-Springview Park** 🐾🐾🐾 *See* ❼ *on page 160.*

Dogs like picnicking here after walking on the park's well-maintained trails and working up an appetite. When we visited, a black Lab was sitting on his family's picnic table, right beside the fried chicken. This is fairly large for a community park, and there's plenty of shade under the big oaks.

It's an easy drive from Interstate 80. Take the Rocklin Road exit west for several blocks and go left on Fifth Street. The park is on your right. (916) 632-4100.

ROSEVILLE

PARKS, BEACHES, AND RECREATION AREAS

For many years, dogs were banned from all Roseville parks. They couldn't set paw in them, even on leash. Eventually, this led dogs to convince their people that something should be done, so their people did something. They talked the city into giving dogs a park of their very own! Dogs are still verboten in all city parks except this one, but that's okay with them. When you have a slice of poochy paradise, who needs a people park?

• **Marco Dog Park** 🐾🐾🐾½ 🐕 *See* ❽ *on page 160.*

Doggone it, this is one great place to be a dog. The park, which opened in 1996, is a tail-waggin', leash-free kind of place. It consists of three fenced acres, with hills, flatlands, lots of young trees (they manage to give some shade despite their tender age), a few big willows, a doggy/human water fountain, and benches.

The park is immensely popular with dogs and their folks. "People are going nuts about the park. It's a huge hit," says Renee St. Denis, who was the driving force behind the park's birth. (She was inspired by her dogs Euler and Jordie, who bristle when they see "No Dogs Allowed" signs.) It's so popular that the city is considering other sites for more dogs parks. "They came to us this time," says St. Denis.

Marco Dog Park would be a perfect park, except for one little problem: It was built on property that's used as flood control land during the rainy months. That means that during much of the winter, the flat area is under three or so feet of water. In winter, it's closed to dogs. But ducks love it, if that's any consolation. Thousands come to dip their little webbed toes and bob around for a bit. Duck Park is what locals call it then.

The park, like Petaluma's Rocky Memorial Dog Park (see page 242), was named after a police dog who was killed in the line of duty during a drug raid. Maybe Rocky and Marco are romping around together in Dog Heaven right now with big grins on their snouts, comparing the parks that bear their names.

For giving us the scoop on this park, we want to thank dogs Fulton, Mattie, Isaac, and Chelsea, and their humans Dave, Lisbeth, Robert, and Karen. Marco Dog Park is located at Sierra Gardens Drive just north of Douglas Boulevard. (916) 774-5242.

SQUAW VALLEY

RESTAURANTS

Mother Barclay's Cafe: Gorgeous golden retriever Miles and his people, Russ and Jean Glines, wrote to give us the heads-up about this wonderfully dog-friendly cafe. "The owners have two goldens and the walls are adorned with picture after picture of their beloved dogs (Barclay and Berger). This was a true find. They literally hovered over Miles, offering biscuits, water, and hugs," wrote Jean.

Turns out restaurant owners Jay and Pat love all dogs, not just goldens. Pooch customers really do feel welcomed by lots of attention and pats and hugs (when it's not too busy), and they also get free doggy biscuits. Even the cafe's logo is dog-loving—a dog (Barclay, we presume) in a chef's hat surrounded by mixing bowls and spoons. I frankly wouldn't feel comfortable with Joe Dog preparing my meal, but goldens are another matter all together. On the menu, in small print: "We accept Visa, MasterCard, and 50-Lb. bags of Eukanuba." You've gotta love this place, whether you're a human or a dog.

The food is delicious, hearty breakfast and lunch cuisine. The menu breaks it down into cute sections like "traditional stuff" and "not so traditional stuff." Several of the dishes have Barclay's name on them, including Barclay's Bad Boy Burrito, Famous Barclay Burger, and Barclay's Snow King Breakfast. There's something for everyone here. Health-conscious folks can order the Newport 9-Grain Cereal (served hot with brown sugar and raisins), and those in need of extra carbohydrates for the slopes can order Powder Day Potatoes or the KT-22 Carbo Load (all-you-can-eat linguine, available in winter only).

You and your pooch can dine in spring, summer, and fall at the outdoor, umbrella-topped tables. If you're visiting during ski season, you'll have to take your carbos to go. The cafe is located in Squaw Valley, USA. You'll know it when you see it. (530) 581-3251.

PLACES TO STAY

Squaw Valley itself doesn't allow dogs in lodgings. But there's a good campground up the road about three miles that welcomes pets.

Silver Creek Campground: This attractive summertime campground where Deer Creek meets the Truckee River is just the place for people and dogs who like to be near water. The fishing is good, the hiking along Deer Creek is great, and the 27-site campground isn't half bad either. Sites are $8. For reservations, call (800) 280-CAMP. The campground is about three miles north of Squaw Valley on Highway 89. For information, phone (530) 587-3558.

DIVERSIONS

Get high with your dog: During summer and autumn, you and the dog of your choice can be whisked halfway to the stars by cable cars normally used for skiers. You'll dangle high above the mountains on the way up, so if you've ever felt like James Stewart in *Vertigo,* here's some advice: Don't look down, not even at your dog, who will probably be smiling and sniffing everyone's feet anyway.

Once the cable car drops you off, you can hike down the mountain on any number of trails. Or if you're just visiting for the view, you can turn around and go back on the next cable car. Dogs and their people think the hike is the best way to go, especially in early summer when it's still cool and the wildflowers are blooming.

The Squaw Valley ski resort cable car ride costs $14 per adult. After 5 P.M., it's $5. Dogs go for free. Hours can vary but are usually around 9:30 A.M. to 9:30 P.M. Unless there's a full moon or a guide dog around, nighttime hikes down the mountain trails can be tricky. (530) 583-6985.

TAHOE CITY

Tahoe City is a fun and scenic place to go for a bite to eat with your dog. During summer, there are so many eateries with outdoor tables in this lakeside village that you and your dog will drool just making the choice. It's an ideal place to bring your appetites after a long day of hiking in nearby Tahoe National Forest (see page 755).

PARKS, BEACHES, AND RECREATION AREAS

•**William B. Layton Park** 🐾🐾 *See* **9** *on page 160.*

Dogs are banned from all Tahoe City parks and beaches except this one. While they have to stay out of the park's most interesting feature, the Gatekeeper's Cabin Museum, leashed dogs may stroll the 3.5 green acres of park on the shores of Lake Tahoe. Because of the park's picturesque gardens and ancient conifers, the place is often rented out for weddings and private parties. If your dog isn't invited, he has to stay away.

The park has picnic tables in the shade, but it's so close to many of the city's dog dining joints that you probably won't be hungry by the time you arrive here. The park is at 130 West Lake Boulevard. (530) 583-1762.

RESTAURANTS

Here's a sampling of the dog-friendly restaurants in Tahoe City:

Fiamma Cucina Rustica: This is a beautiful, romantic restaurant with some scrumptious pastas, chicken dishes, and pizzas. The smoked mozzarella and roasted eggplant pizza is out of this world. Dogs are allowed to dine with you at the lovely wooden tables outside, as long as it's not too busy. 521 North Lake Boulevard; (530) 581-1416.

Izzy's Burger Spa: Chicken, fries, onion rings, and beer are the staples. Dine at umbrella-covered tables. 100 West Lake Boulevard; (530) 583-4111.

Naughty Dawg: Attention all dogs! Come! Eat! Drink! Run up and down a doggy run (on leash)! Bring your picture and put it up on the Dog Wall of Fame! Dogs, this is your place! You're not in Tahoe, you're in heaven. The dog motif goes deep, thanks to co-owner Laurie-Jean Shaw and her dalmatian, Clyde Naughty Dawg, and his younger sister Bonnie. The bar is even a part of the dog theme, with entertaining beach-dog mosaics. If you still have time after checking out all the cool dog stuff, you can eat at one of the many patio tables outdoors. Pooches get free bowls of water, while people can choose from a mouthwatering variety of dishes, including Cajun shrimp tacos, steamed spinach salads, and big juicy burgers. The restaurant is in the heart of downtown Tahoe City, "a stick's throw from Lucky's," says Shaw. 255 North Lake Boulevard; (530) 581-DAWG.

Rosie's Cafe: Eat steaks, burgers, and pasta on the charming porch. 561 North Lake Boulevard; (530) 583-8504.

Sunnyside Market: It's not exactly the most elegant dining experience, but you and your pooch may eat on benches outside this little convenience store. 1780 West Lake Boulevard; (530) 583-7626.

PLACES TO STAY

Coldwell Banker Hauserman Real Estate's Rental Department: This is one of the most dog-friendly vacation rental agencies we've run across.

Rates for cabins and houses are $60 to $400, depending on the location and size of the rental, and there's a $15 cleaning fee for dogs. 475 North Lake Boulevard, Tahoe City, CA 96145; (800) 20-TAHOE.

DIVERSIONS

Send your dog to camp: Okay, so you're going on vacation, and you just can't take your dog with you. You don't want to leave him with friends or in a kennel. What to do? Well, if your pooch has a love of nature and you have some extra cash, you could consider sending him to Sierra Mountain Doggie Camp.

This intimate camp (no more than three doggy guests at a time) is blissville for dogs with a sense of adventure. If it makes you feel any better, it's probably way better than the camp you had to go to once upon a time. There are no arts and crafts classes, there's no greasy food, and best of all, there's no skit to perform at the end of the camp session. There's only the glorious outdoors, mixed with a cozy camp cabin the dogs share with the human director and counselor. Kennels and cages don't exist here.

Dogs get to go on custom-tailored hiking adventures, from one to 15 miles, in the nearby pristine environs. They get to swim in Lake Tahoe, unless they sink like a lead brick. (No, Joe, we're not mentioning any names here.) They go canoeing. They play catch, hide-and-seek, and other games that promote good dog skills and socialization. They eat terrific food, drink clean mountain water, and are never without a human buddy at their side.

The camp director, Suzy Scully, will take photos of your dog having fun and put them into an album for you and your dog to paw through later.

Dogs are kept so busy with fun activities that they may not have much time to be homesick, although Scully does recommend sending along a photo of yourself so she can put it near the bed your poochie chooses. (Joe says sending along something that smells like you would be a better idea. "After all, we're dogs, doggonit," he muttered when he heard about the photo suggestion. He was never one for separation.)

Before you start packing up your pooch, it's best to know some prices. For round-trip airfare on Reno Air (Scully says she'll greet your dog immediately upon arrival), door-to-door camp transportation, and all the food and fun your dog can handle, the cost ranges from $640 for three days to $1,500 for seven days. Subtract $200 if you'll be bringing your pet yourself. Discounts are available for dogs camping for more than seven days, or for more than one dog from the same family. The mailing address is P.O. Box 325, Tahoe City, CA 96145; (530) 581-0623. You can also visit the camp on the Web at www.sierradoggiecamp.com.

Say your nuptials while your pup chills: Calm, well-behaved, flea-free dogs are welcome to join you and your future spouse when you launch your lifetime of togetherness at A Chapel by the River. As the name implies, this cute little chapel is located adjacent to the Truckee River. You can say your wedding vows outside or inside the little barn-red wood building. And fear not: The interior of the chapel is not gauche. "There's nothing plastic, glitzy, or Elvis about it," says owner Beverly Bedard. In fact, with its wood beam ceiling, wood and wrought iron benches, and fresh green plants, the chapel is a charmer.

The basic wedding ceremony is $175, which includes your wedding license. For more information, write to 115 West Lake Boulevard, Tahoe City, CA 96154, or call (530) 581-2757.

TAHOE PINES

PLACES TO STAY

Kaspian Campground: This small summertime campground has room for only 10 tents, so you probably won't be encountering "The Camp Party from Hell." Sites are $8. Reservations may not be needed, but if you want to guarantee a spot, call (800) 280-CAMP. The campground is four miles south of Tahoe City, on Highway 89. Follow the signs when you get there. (530) 573-2600.

TAHOE VISTA

PARKS, BEACHES, AND RECREATION AREAS

Boo hoo! Dogs are no longer allowed on the National Avenue Beach, thanks to some folks who weren't scooping the poop. Well, at least they're still allowed in the regional park here . . . for now. Plus, Tahoe National Forest is right in your backyard.

• **North Tahoe Regional Park** 🐾🐾🐾 *See* ⑩ *on page 160.*

This kind of land is very rare in these parts. Leashed dogs are allowed everywhere except on the playing fields and bleachers in this 108-acre park. That means four miles of hiking trails are at their disposal. Better yet, some of those trails lead to Tahoe National Forest, where your dog can run untethered (see page 755). The regional park is even fun in the winter because of its popular snow-play hill.

If you're shopping around for a companion for your dog, stop in at the county animal shelter, just a Frisbee's throw from the park. You can't miss the signs for it. The shelter has many sweet dogs who would much rather be romping around in parks with you than caged up and worrying about their fate. They're at 875 National Avenue; call (530) 546-4269.

The park is at the corner of Donner Road and National Avenue. From Highway 28, drive inland a few blocks past the scenic cinderblock manufacturer and its neighboring mobile home park. Turn left at the sign for the park. (530) 546-7248.

PLACES TO STAY

Holiday House: The views of Lake Tahoe from the front decks of this lakeside lodging are picture perfect. Even pooches look pleased as they check out the sights and smells here, especially if the sights and smells involve a juicy steak on your deck's barbecue grill.

The suites are spacious and comfortable, with kitchenettes and hot tubs. The Holiday House even has mooring buoys, so you and your lake-faring dog can bring the boat with you and park it in the lake, just a bone's throw away. This is one of the most dog-friendly places around. That's thanks to owner Alvina Patterson. "I'm enjoying the dogs so much when they visit," she says.

Rates are $95 to $145. Weekly rates are available. There's a $25 dog fee for up to a five-day stay. The fee after five days is $5 daily. 7276 North Lake Boulevard, Tahoe Vista, CA 96148; (530) 546-2369 or (800) 2-WINDSURF.

Rustic Cottages: This resort has been dog-friendly since 1925! It recently changed hands (it was formerly Tatami Cottage Resort) and went through a major overhaul. It's now one of the most lovely places we've encountered for a poochy vacation, and with plans for further improvements (new kitchens in all cottages), it's going to be a doggone dynamite place. The new owners are very nice folks, but they did a lot of work on the place and they're a little wary about allowing dogs, so please let your dog inspire them to have confidence in their ilk.

The beds here are one of the biggest draws. One of the resort's new owners handcrafts wrought iron and brass beds for a living, so his talent was put to use in each of the 18 cottages here. The linens are also first-rate, so the owners ask you not to let your dog on the bed unless you bring your own sheet to cover up the bed first.

The cottages even have new TVs, which get a whopping 30 channels each, not that you want to be a couch tater when you're vacationing in Tahoe. But just in case, each TV has a VCR, so you can bring your own videos or borrow one of the hundred or so the resort loans out to guests. Reggie Dog, a boxer friend, told us he recently checked out the "Dog Babysitter" video here. He found it a bore, but one of his chauffeurs, Denise Selleck, was mesmerized. In the morning, you can pick up homemade muffins in the main cottage. (You can nab a homemade cookie there all day.) Joe likes that parenthetical sentence.

Better yet, though, is that the place is on two acres, with a small, semienclosed lot where your pooch can run leash-free if you stay with him and have a little faith that he won't escape. The lot isn't anything fancy, but dogs don't mind a little overgrown grass and a tree stump. In fact, most dogs prefer this decor to a perfectly manicured lawn. If you want quaint scenery, just look around the cottages. In the warmer months, fresh flowers adorn most cottage fronts. Lake Tahoe is across the street, but there's no beach access there for dogs. But some Tahoe National Forest land is behind the resort, and it's a four-paw adventure for dogs and their people. Reggie Dog and his people got rather lost on a trail here one day, but they eventually made it back to civilization.

Rates are $59 to $139. Dogs are $10 extra. 7449 North Lake Boulevard, Tahoe Vista, CA 96148; (530) 546-3523 or (888) 778-7842.

Woodvista Lodge: All rooms at this motel have a small fridge, and there's a pool and hot tub. Rates are $55 to $105. Dogs are $10 extra. 7699 North Lake Boulevard, Tahoe Vista, CA 96148; (530) 546-3839.

TAHOMA

RESTAURANTS

Norfolk Woods Inn: This inn has an excellent, dog-friendly restaurant. Please see Places to Stay, below, for details.

PLACES TO STAY

Norfolk Woods Inn: Dogs are "very welcome" to stay at the rustic cabins of this sweet bed-and-breakfast inn. "We love dogs," says manager Suzanne. The cabins have two bedrooms upstairs and a kitchen downstairs. Fireplaces make the cabins extra cozy in the winter. A heated pool makes for a refreshing dip during the warmer months.

The inn also has an award-winning restaurant, complete with a veranda for you and your dog. The country-style breakfasts are hearty and delicious, but Joe prefers dinner, where he can sniff at things like rack of lamb.

Rates for the cabins are $140 to $160. Dogs are $10 extra on each of the first two nights of your stay, then $5 per night. 6941 West Lake Boulevard, Tahoma, CA 96142; (530) 525-4411.

Tahoe Lake Cottages: Dogs think this place is tops, but not necessarily because of the cozy cottages with full kitchens, knotty pine interiors, and "old Tahoe" shingled exteriors. More likely it's because of the old-growth cedars and sugar pines that surround those cottages. "They get my leg a-twitchin'," says Joe Dog.

The owners, the Lafferty family, adore dogs and kids. They have a dog of their own. Brody's his name, but Mike Lafferty prefers to call him "Brody, the World-Famous Tree-Climbing Dog." You'll see why when you visit. He's 110 pounds of fun. The cottages also have a pool and a hot tub, but no dogs, please, lest their fur gunk up the works.

Rates for the cottages are $125 to $195. 7030 Highway 89, Tahoma, CA 96142; (530) 525-4411 or (800) 852-8246.

Tahoma Lodge: Boyce, who owns these cabins, puts it simply: "I've been allowing dogs here for 19 years. Let's say they're quite welcome." Cabins come with a wood stove or fireplace. There's a pool on the premises and a hot tub, but only for critters of the human persuasion. Rates are $45 to $120. 7018 West Lake Boulevard, Tahoma, CA 96142; (530) 525-7721.

20
EL DORADO COUNTY

From Lake Tahoe to the lands east of the Mother Lode vein, this county is as attractive to people as it is to their dogs. Unfortunately, El Dorado County doesn't exactly roll out the gold carpet for canines. The south edge of Lake Tahoe isn't very hospitable to dogs, and formerly wild and woolly Gold Rush towns like Placerville and Georgetown are doggone deficient in such canine creature comforts as parks.

If it weren't for Eldorado National Forest, which makes up more than half the land here, dogs might ask to visit another county. Dogs can run leashless in most of this mighty Sierra Nevada forest. Keep in mind that a huge stretch of the forest is recuperating from the devastating 1992 blaze that left thousands of acres of charred tree skeletons starting just west of Kyburz. Tread gently.

NATIONAL FORESTS

See the National Forests and Wilderness Areas chapter starting on page

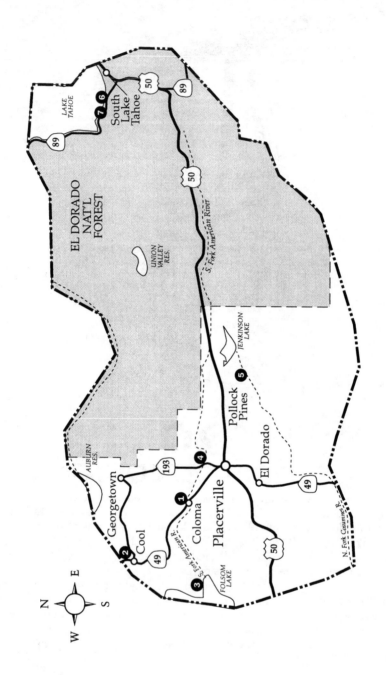

748 for important information and safety tips on visiting national forests with your dog.

• **Eldorado National Forest** 🐾🐾🐾🐾 🐕‍🦺
See page 750.

The major portion of Eldorado National Forest is located in its namesake county. An exception to the off-leash policy of the national forests is in the Desolation Wilderness, where dogs are supposed to be leashed at all times.

COLOMA

PARKS, BEACHES, AND RECREATION AREAS

• **Marshall Gold Discovery State Historic Park** 🐾🐾🐾
See ❶ on page 174.

James Marshall, whose discovery of gold in John Sutter's mill here started the Gold Rush, died a penniless recluse. But at least he had a dog-friendly state park dedicated to him.

Dogs are allowed in more places here than at most state parks. While they're banned from American River beaches and all trails, they can hang out with you at picnic areas and walk with you in the meadow behind the visitors center. They can stroll along Main Street and peer at historic buildings, including a replica of Sutter's Mill. Dogs are even permitted to accompany you to the Munroe Orchard, where you can pick a piece of fruit and sit under a tree to while away the afternoon while your friends pan for gold in the river.

Rates are $5 per car, with dogs costing $1 extra. The park is on Highway 49 between Placerville and Auburn. (530) 622-3470.

COOL

By virtue of its name alone, this town southeast of Auburn is worth a stop. Unfortunately, Cool doesn't have many amenities for pooches who are just visiting. For this reason, we think the town should be renamed Kinda Cool. So far, residents aren't buying the idea.

PARKS, BEACHES, AND RECREATION AREAS

• **Auburn State Recreation Area** 🐾🐾🐾½ *See ❷ on page 174.*

This 30,000-acre park is just a couple of miles up Highway 49 from the main part of Cool. Most of it is in Placer County, and it's described more fully in that chapter (see page 161). But there is a section you can hike with your dog that starts less than a half mile before the first bridge you come to after leaving Cool (going toward Auburn). The parking area and trailhead are unmarked, so be on the lookout for a dirt road that veers off sharply to the right. If you miss it, just turn around at the bridge and come back almost a half mile and you'll be there. (530) 885-4527.

EL DORADO

Upon entering this tiny town south of Placerville on Highway 49, a sign announces "Population: 26." For such a small place, El Dorado has a great deal of charm and one dog-friendly eatery.

RESTAURANTS
El Dorado Grocery and Deli: Eat at the shaded table outside this old-fashioned deli. 6203 Main Street; (530) 626-1015.

GEORGETOWN
On the way here on Highway 193, don't be surprised if you run into signs warning strongly against letting dogs run free near a couple of farms. The penalty: Your dog gets shot.

Fortunately, Georgetown is not known for its parks, so there's little danger of your dog escaping and running into an angry farmer.

PLACES TO STAY
American River Inn: If you want to bring a dog here, you'll have to prove to the owners that your dog will behave better than Miss Manners herself. If they say no, please don't hassle them. This bed-and-breakfast is full of antiques and expensive furnishings, and you should give them credit for even considering pooches. It's a huge old place with a beautiful New England–style backyard and sitting area.

Call first to make special arrangements if you're hoping to pack your pooch along. Rates are $85 to $115. The inn is located at Main and Orleans Streets. The mailing address is P.O. Box 43, Georgetown, CA 95643; (530) 333-4499.

PILOT HILL
PARKS, BEACHES, AND RECREATION AREAS
• **Folsom Lake State Recreation Area** 🐾🐾🐾½ *See ❸ on page 174.*
A big portion of this 12,000-acre lake is in El Dorado County, but it's listed under Folsom in Sacramento County. See page 289 for details.

PLACERVILLE
When this city was one of the great camps of Gold Country, it was first known as Dry Diggins. The name lasted about a year. In 1849, after a number of lynchings, the place became known as Hangtown.

People had it tough back then. But dogs may have it even tougher here today, since there are very few parks. Open la nd has been replaced by strip shopping centers and new housing. The name Placerville may have been good for welcoming suburbia, but dogs should be sorely disappointed at the changes the decades have brought to this city on the east side of the famous Mother Lode vein.

Still, the historic downtown is a fun place to stroll with your dog. And you can even learn something about the old Gold Rush days if you visit Hangtown's Gold Bug Park (see below).

PARKS, BEACHES, AND RECREATION AREAS
• **Hangtown's Gold Bug Park** 🐾🐾½ *See ❹ on page 174.*
Dogs dig it here. But it's not the gold they dig (lucrative as they may be, such terrier-like habits are discouraged). It's the park itself. Gold Bug is the

city's largest park. While dogs aren't allowed to run around without a leash, it's a great place to come to stretch their legs while they explore a park that was once home to 250 mines.

If you're traveling with another human, one of you can walk around the park's dirt paths with the dog or picnic in the shade of oaks and pines while the other visits the Gold Bug Mine, which bans dogs. The mine is an educational experience for anyone who ever wondered what it was like inside one of these places. Admission to the mine is $3 for adults. Half-pints are a buck. Quarter-pints (under 8) are free. An additional $1 will rent you a fascinating tape-guided tour.

The park is easily accessible from U.S. 50. Take the Bedford Avenue exit north for almost a mile and you're there. (530) 642-5232.

RESTAURANTS

Sweetie Pie's: The owners describe themselves as "major dog lovers," so your dog will feel right at home at the umbrella-topped tables here. The muffins, fresh fruit, sandwiches, quiche, and homemade soups taste extra good knowing you're not getting the evil eye from the management. 577 Main Street; (530) 642-0128.

Togo's Eatery: Dogs like to go to this Togo's because it has a few tables out front where they can sniff at the feet of passersby. 1390 Broadway; (530) 621-2050.

PLACES TO STAY

Gold Trail Motor Lodge: There's plenty of shade on the well-landscaped grounds of this motel, a real plus in the hot summer months. Rates are $36 to $51. Dogs are $5 extra. 1970 Broadway, Placerville, CA 95667; (530) 622-2906.

Mother Lode Motel: Rates are $36 to $58. Dogs are $5 extra. 1940 Broadway, Placerville, CA 95667; (530) 622-0895.

POLLOCK PINES

PARKS, BEACHES, AND RECREATION AREAS

•**Sly Park Recreation Area** 🐾 🐾 🐾 *See* ❺ *on page 174.*

Does your leashed dog like boating, hiking, and watching people ride by on horses? Does she like camping, but prefer to do it in a somewhat civilized fashion? If so, this Jenkinson Lake camping area is for her. There are 190 sites in this year-round campground, so she'll never feel alone.

Reservations are accepted May through September. Otherwise, sites are first come, first served. Sites are $15 a night. Dogs are an additional $1.50. From U.S. 50, go south on Sly Park Road for about five miles. (530) 644-2545.

RESTAURANTS

D's Burgers: The ice cream here tastes really good on warm summer afternoons. 6373 Pony Express Trail; (530) 676-5740.

Pioneer Kitchen: Dogs are welcome to join you on the sweet, awning-covered deck. They don't serve dinner, but breakfast and lunch are great. 6404 Pony Express Trail; (530) 644-2805.

Sly Park Recreation Area: See Sly Park Recreation Area on page 177 for camping information.

SOUTH LAKE TAHOE

South Lake Tahoe is paradise for people, but just so-so for dogs. Beaches that allow dogs are almost nil—a real slap in the snout to water dogs. Most lodgings also ban dogs, although we've managed to get the scoop on many that accept them. One of the reasons so many lodgings don't allow dogs is that they don't want them left alone in the room while their people sneak over the state line to gamble the night away. Do your pooch a favor: If you're going to do the night scene in Nevada, don't bring her to South Lake Tahoe unless someone will be at her side while you're gone. Or check out one of the rental homes, listed in the Places to Stay section on page 179. Even then, if your dog gets nervous when she's in a strange new environment, you shouldn't leave her by herself.

PARKS, BEACHES, AND RECREATION AREAS

South Lake Tahoe has very few places to walk with your dog. Pooches are banned from city beaches and even from those federal beaches and federal parks that charge entrance fees. State parks here allow dogs only in camping and picnic areas. But there are a couple of places (both run by the folks who run the national forests) that dogs will be as excited to visit as humans.

• **Kiva Beach** 🐾🐾🐾½ *See* ❻ *on page 174.*

The huge swath of scattered pine trees that greets you as you enter this area is just as enticing for your leashed dog as the beach itself. There's some sage undergrowth, but it's fairly easy to navigate.

If you want to go directly to the beach, just park and take the long dirt trail. The beach is large and sandy and provides a great panorama of Lake Tahoe. Apparently there have been some problems with off-leash dogs of late, so the pooch patrol is out in force. If you don't want a citation, don't forget to leash up.

If lounging around in the sand is boring your canine, take him on a hike up the Tallac Historic Trail, which starts near the east end of the beach. There he'll be shaded from the sun and inundated with fascinating tidbits about the area's past.

From the junction of U.S. 50 and Highway 89, take Highway 89 north about 2.5 miles. The entrance is on your right. There's talk of this beach being renamed Visitors Center Beach soon, so if you see signs for that, you're not lost. (530) 573-2600.

• **Lake Tahoe Visitors Center** 🐾🐾🐾½ *See* ❼ *on page 174.*

This is among the most fascinating and well-developed wildlife viewing areas in the state. You and your dog can spend the whole day here agog at Mother Nature while learning about this wet meadow area and the abundant life it supports.

A half-dozen trails with interpretive displays lead you over creeks, through aspen forests and grassy wetlands, and among wildlife you never dreamed you'd see so close to Harrah's and Caesars Tahoe. Among some of the critters you might spot are ospreys, beavers, Canada geese, kokanee salmon, trout, and, yes, hairy woodpeckers. There's even the possibility you'll see some deer and coyotes, so keep a tight hold of that leash.

The park may have the only aquarium in the world that welcomes dogs. It's not exactly the Monterey Bay Aquarium, but it is an underwater building where you can see native fish in their native stream.

The beach and undeveloped forestlands around the visitors center provide ample room to get away from the crowds that can get heavy in the summer. If you plan to make a day of it, pack a lunch to eat at the park's comfortable picnic areas.

From the junction of U.S. 50 and Highway 89, the park is about 3.5 miles north on Highway 89. The entrance is on your right. There's talk of this place being renamed Taylor Creek Visitors Center, so if you see signs for that, you're not lost. (530) 573-2600.

RESTAURANTS

Bayer's Bagel Bakery: Oy, the bagels here are great, but your dog will really drool when you slather the bagels with some of the bakery's fancy cream cheeses. Nosh with your pooch at the tables outside. 2701 Lake Tahoe Boulevard; (530) 541-7882.

Grass Roots Natural Foods: This is a great place to visit for healthful, wholesome food. It even tastes delicious! Your dog can join you at the benches outside the big old blue house/store. 2040 Dunlap Drive; (530) 541-7788.

Sprouts: As the name might imply, fresh natural foods, not greasy onion rings and shakes, are the forte here. Eat at the picnic tables with your pooch. 3125 Harrison Avenue; (530) 541-6969.

PLACES TO STAY

Please don't leave your dog alone in your room and go gamble across the state line! See the introduction to South Lake Tahoe on page 178 for more on this.

Alder Inn and Cottages: If you feel like hitting the slopes but your dog just doesn't have the urge to don her skis, the inn will supply you with a convenient pet-sitting service. It costs $6 per hour for one pooch. If you have more than one pooch, it will cost you a little extra. We've never used the service, but we've heard dogs get lots of tender loving care. Rates are $38 to $95. Dogs are $10 extra. 1072 Ski Run Boulevard, South Lake Tahoe, CA 96150; (530) 544-4485.

Beachside Inn & Suites: Pooches are permitted in the honeymoon suite here, so if your dog is along for your nuptials, he can join you here, too. The Beachside is also a quick walk to some nearby doggy areas the owner can tell you about, and a really quick walk to the beach. Rates are $30 to $80. Dogs are $5 extra. 930 Park Avenue, South Lake Tahoe, CA 96150; (530) 544-2400 or (800) 884-4920.

Best Western Lake Tahoe Inn: Rates are $49 to $135. A $100 doggy deposit is required. 4110 Lake Tahoe Boulevard, South Lake Tahoe, CA 96150; (530) 541-2010 or (800) 528-1234.

Big Lake Motel: Some rooms here have fridges, so if your dog likes his Pawrier water well chilled, you won't have to disappoint him. Rates are $35 to $70. Dogs are $10 extra. Medium-sized dogs and smaller pooches only, please. 1055 Ski Run Boulevard, South Lake Tahoe, CA 96150; (530) 541-2399.

Days Inn: Bosco, a Mill Valley dog of the half-beagle persuasion, heartily recommends this Days Inn. "It's a great place, for a Days Inn," he writes. Rates are $59 to $84. Pooches are $5 extra and require a $25 deposit. Be sure to let the staff know ahead of time that you're bringing a pooch; otherwise the pooch-designated rooms might be booked with non-dog people. 968 Park Avenue, South Lake Tahoe, CA 96157; (530) 541-4800.

Emerald Bay State Park: Camping is available only in the summer months. Although dogs are not allowed on the trails, it's worth it to camp here just to be in this park's splendor. Some 100 campsites are located on the south side of the tranquil bay.

Sites are $12 to $14. Dogs are $1 extra. The park is located on Highway 89, about eight miles north of the junction of Highway 89 and U.S. 50. Call park headquarters at (530) 525-7277 for information. For reservations, call Parknet at (800) 444-PARK.

Fallen Leaf Lake: This is a good place for dogs who enjoy socializing. In summer, chances are good that you'll be in close proximity to dozens of campers in this popular recreational lake area on U.S. Forest Service land. Anglers with dogs like to come here to take advantage of the hot bite the lake has in the summer months.

There are 205 campsites. Fees are $14 a night. From the junction of Highway 89 and U.S. 50, go north about two miles on Highway 89 to the Fallen Leaf Lake turnoff. Go left and drive 1.5 miles to the camping area. Call (530) 573-2600 for park information. For reservations, call (800) 280-CAMP.

If you prefer to be away from the madding crowd, the Desolation Wilderness is accessible from here. There you can camp in peace, except for the occasional twittering of songbirds. Camping here costs $5 per night for the first two nights. After that, there's no charge. You must have a permit. And unlike many other wilderness areas, dogs must be leashed.

Inn at Heavenly B&B: If you like mountains, trees, steam baths, saunas, and bed-and-breakfast inns, and if you really like your dog, come here! Dogs are welcome at this cozy B&B, which is surrounded by a lovely wooded park. Most rooms have attractive river-rock gas fireplaces, patchwork quilts, and even log furniture. And unlike many other bed-and-breakfasts, each of the 14 rooms has its own bathroom and cable TV. None of that business of sharing the WC with the neighbors while pining away for ESPN. Rooms also have their own mini-fridges and microwaves. An added bonus: Human guests get to use the spa room (hot tub, steam bath, and sauna) privately for one hour per day. Rates are $85 to $135. Dogs are $10 extra. 1261 Ski Run Boulevard, South Lake Tahoe, CA 96150; (530) 544-4244 or (800) 692-2246.

La Baer Inn: This decent lodging brags that it's "only steps" from the casinos, so it's a convenient place to stay if one human wants to go win big at the tables while the other checks out the sights with the pooch. Rates are $39 to $109. Dogs require a $10 deposit. 4133 Lake Tahoe Boulevard, South Lake Tahoe, CA 96150; (530) 544-2139 or (800) 544-5575.

Lakepark Lodge: Rates are $45 to $65. A $50 deposit is required for dogs, and you'll get $40 back if all's okay. To Joe that sounds like a $10 doggy fee, but he doesn't want to put words in anyone's mouth. 4081 Cedar Avenue, South Lake Tahoe, CA 96150; (530) 541-5004.

Motel 6: Rates are $34 to $45 for the first adult and $6 for the second. One small pooch per room is the rule here. 2375 Lake Tahoe Boulevard, South Lake Tahoe, CA 95731; (530) 542-1400.

Red Carpet Inn: They really roll out the red carpet for dogs here—at least the red carpet of friendliness. "We really love good dogs," one enthusiastic manager told us. Rates are $40 to $120. 4100 Lake Tahoe Boulevard, South Lake Tahoe, CA 96150; (530) 544-2261 or (800) 336-5553.

South Lake Tahoe Reservation Bureau: Tired of motel roulette? Sick of toilet bowls with banners bragging about their sanitary conditions? You and your dog should consider phoning this reputable vacation rental bureau, where you can choose from about 20 dog-friendly cabins, condos, and houses. Many of the rentals even come with fenced-in yards. Rentals range from studios to four-bedroom homes. Rates are $108 to $650. Dogs require a $100 deposit and a $25 cleaning fee, which covers the length of your stay. The agency works hand-in-hand with the Tahoe Keys Resort (see below), but these rentals are in areas other than the Keys. 599 Tahoe Keys Boulevard, South Lake Tahoe, CA 96151; (530) 544-5397 or (800) 462-5397.

Super 8 Motel: Rates at this Super 8 are $42 to $68. Dogs are $10 extra. 3600 Lake Tahoe Boulevard, South Lake Tahoe, CA 96150; (530) 544-3476 or (800) 237-8882.

Tahoe Keys Resort: Dogs who like to have a home away from home, as opposed to a motel room away from home, will drool for joy when you spend your vacation here. And if your dog is a water dog, get out the drool bucket: The resort is a 750-acre community laced with 11 miles of inland waterways, right on the southern edge of Lake Tahoe. Each house is a waterfront home, located on one of numerous lagoons. Rentals range from studio condos to four-bedroom homes. Pooches are permitted in a bunch of the homes. Rates are $95 to $1,700 per night. Dogs require a $100 deposit and a $25 cleaning fee, which covers the length of your stay. 599 Tahoe Keys Boulevard, South Lake Tahoe, CA 96151; (530) 544-5397 or (800) 462-5397.

Tahoe Marina Inn: Wow! An attractive, decent-sized hotel that's right on a 500-foot-wide swatch of beach, with mountains in the background! Rooms with views that will make your dog pant, and condos that feature fireplaces, fully equipped kitchens, and a sleeping loft! What could be better? Well, it would be better if dogs were allowed during a time of year where they don't need to don a down jacket. Unfortunately, dogs are permitted only from November to May, and not during any holidays. But it's not so bad if your dog doesn't mind his nose getting a little colder. In fact, if you have to stay up this way during the winter, this is a mighty cozy place, no matter what the season.

Rates are $69 to $99. 930 Bal Bijou Road, South Lake Tahoe, CA 95705; (530) 541-2180 or (800) 448-4577.

Tahoe Tropicana Lodge: You won't find Ricky Ricardo at this Tropicana, but at least your dog will be welcomed here. Rooms are $35 to $55. 4132 Cedar Avenue, South Lake Tahoe, CA 96150; (530) 541-3911.

Tahoe Valley Campground: This is an attractive campground for such a large one, with a total of 413 campsites and RV sites gracing the place. There's a rec room, a heated pool, laundry facilities, a tennis court, and a playground, to name a few of the amenities. There's even a free casino shuttle bus that will shuffle you off to the wonders on the other side of the state border. (No dogs allowed, but that's okay since most dogs don't understand crapshooting or blackjack.) The Truckee River is about a quarter of a mile from the park, and there are plenty of trees surrounding the campground.

It's open from April 15 to October 15. Rates are $21 to $29. Dogs are $2 extra. 1175 Melba Street, South Lake Tahoe, CA 96158; (530) 541-2222.

Tahoe Valley Lodge: Small pooches only, please. Rates are $85 to $150. Dogs are $10 extra. 2241 Lake Tahoe Boulevard, South Lake Tahoe, CA 96150; (530) 541-0353.

DIVERSIONS

Here comes the bride . . . and the groom . . . and the dog: They've seen it all at the Chapel of the Bells. Dogs have worn tuxedos to weddings. They've been the best man, the maid of honor, the ring bearer. They've given away the bride. "They've even cried," says manager Carolyn Lewis.

The chapel has both an indoor and an outdoor facility, located in the heart of a woodsy but suburban neighborhood. The basic wedding costs $120, including the license but excluding the donation for the minister. For that kind of price, you can afford to bring the dog along on the honeymoon.

If you're in the Tahoe area and want to get married fast but this chapel doesn't ring your bells, just pick up a phone book and look in the Yellow Pages under Weddings. You're sure to find something the bride, groom, and pooch will all remember happily ever after.

The Chapel of the Bells is at 2700 U.S. 50. Their mailing address is P.O. Box 18410, South Lake Tahoe, CA 96151. Call the chapel at (530) 544-1112 or (800) 247-4333.

21
ALPINE COUNTY

More people live in one Los Angeles high-rise than in this entire county! With a population of only 1,100, Alpine County has plenty of room for a few good dogs. More than 90 percent of the land is public, most of it in the form of very dog-friendly national forests.

You'll find trailheads into the Eldorado, Stanislaus, and Toiyabe National Forests along Highways 88, 89, and 4. You can just pull over into a safe zone and hike with your dog if you know it's national forestland. As soon as you're away from roads and campgrounds, your dog can go leashless in nearly 800 square miles of meadows, alpine forests, and rocky mountains. There's one exception to this, just east of the county line in the Mokelumne Wilderness of Eldorado National Forest off Highway 88 (see page 750).

A drive along Highway 4 can be exciting as well as very scenic. The street gets so narrow that eventually the stripes in the middle of the road disappear. It's steep and winding in parts, so tell your dog to look up if he's scared of heights. As you ascend to nearly 9,000 feet, the scenery becomes otherworldly. Huge rock formations are everywhere. They're rounded from the passage of time and some are stacked in impossible configurations.

Since the road is so winding, it's a good idea to make frequent stops, especially if your dog starts turning green. At Ebbett's Pass (elevation 8,730

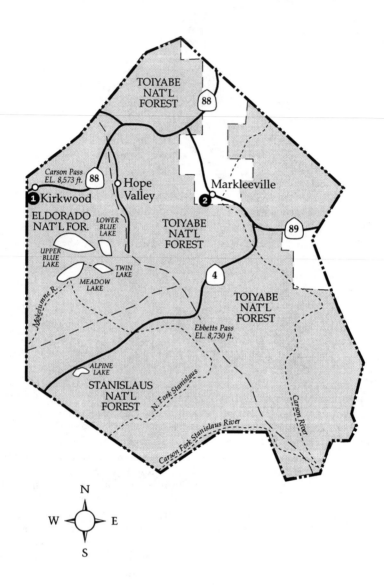

TOIYABE NAT'L FOREST

88

Carson Pass
EL. 8,573 ft. 88 ○ Hope
①Kirkwood   Valley

Markleeville
②

ELDORADO
NAT'L FOR.   LOWER
             BLUE
             LAKE

TOIYABE
NAT'L
FOREST

89

UPPER
BLUE
LAKE
             TWIN
             LAKE
    MEADOW
    LAKE

4

TOIYABE
NAT'L
FOREST

Mokelumne R.

Ebbetts Pass
EL. 8,730 ft.

ALPINE
LAKE

STANISLAUS
NAT'L
FOREST

N. Fork Stanislaus

Carson Fork Stanislaus River

Carson River

N
W ◆ E
S

feet), you can pull over and take the dog out to a large meadow on your left or to the rocky hill on your right. Because it's part of the Stanislaus National Forest, he can go leashless. There are several campgrounds and limitless backcountry camping in the national forests along the way, so there's no shortage of places to pitch a tent.

Dogs also like to visit Mosquito Lake and Lake Alpine. Since there can be many other visitors, dogs should be leashed in these areas. (See Stanislaus National Forest, page 755.)

The four seasons are magical in Alpine County. Springtime brings an incomparable carpet of wildflowers. Summer days rarely get too warm. When we last visited, it was mid-August. During the day, people were wearing sweaters. Dogs, even those sporting thick coats, weren't panting. In autumn, aspen and cottonwoods burst into magnificent oranges, yellows, and reds. Dogs who claim to have black-and-white vision may not appreciate it, but the seasonal change can be a bit of a thrill for their caretakers. During winter, Alpine County is a wonderland of white, but some of the mountain roads can be impassable. It's a good idea to call your destination to check road conditions before setting paw out of your front door.

NATIONAL FORESTS

Sections of the following three national forests are located in Alpine County. See the National Forests and Wilderness Areas chapter starting on page 748 for important information and safety tips on visiting national forests with your dog.

- **Eldorado National Forest** 🐾🐾🐾🐾 🐕
  See page 750.
- **Stanislaus National Forest** 🐾🐾🐾🐾 🐕
  See page 755.
- **Toiyabe National Forest** 🐾🐾🐾🐾 🐕
  See page 755.

HOPE VALLEY

PLACES TO STAY

Sorensen's Resort: Several trails that start around the Sorensen property are ideal for hiking or cross-country skiing. The three cabins that allow dogs are great places to stay if you want to take the dog on a cross-country ski vacation. One has a wood-burning stove and the others are warmed by conventional modern means.

Unfortunately, of the 28 cabins that make up the resort, the three that permit pooches are closest to the road. Highway 88 isn't exactly a superfreeway, but it's also not what you want to see out your window when you're trying to get away from civilization. Still, it's an enchanting place to spend a long winter's night.

Rates for the dog cabins vary seasonally, from $85 to $350. Since not many places around here take dogs, these cabins are in high demand, so reserve well in advance of your stay. 14255 Highway 88, Hope Valley, CA 96120; (530) 694-2203 or (800) 423-9949.

KIRKWOOD

Kirkwood, one of the best ski and summer recreation areas in California, is also quite accommodating to dogs. The town is split among three counties, but most people here consider Alpine County home.

PARKS, BEACHES, AND RECREATION AREAS

•Kirkwood Ski and Summer Resort 🐾 🐾 🐾½ *See* ❶ *on page 184.*

During summer, you can't help but see dog after dog romping around this serene high Sierra playground. Most of them have smiles on their slobbery faces because they're welcome to explore the resort's 12 miles of trails through meadows and up slopes and back bowl areas. They have to be on leash, but it's a small price for your dog to pay to be able to tell his friends he vacationed here.

The resort is about 60 miles northeast of Jackson, on Highway 88. You can't miss the signs for it. Once there, ask for a map of the trails from the general store/reservations desk. (209) 258-6000.

RESTAURANTS

Kirkwood Inn: This place has barely changed since it was built in 1864 by early settlers Zachary and Eliza Kirkwood. You'll still find bullet holes in the thick wood ceiling when you walk inside to order your down-home cooking, and the bar is the original one (except for a section a drunk woman crushed while dancing on it in the winter of 1992). Dogs like it here, but despite the place's wild and woolly past, they're relegated to the outdoor tables when they're not covered with snow. If you like burgers and steak, this is an excellent place to visit. The restaurant is at Highway 88, across from the entrance to Kirkwood Ski and Summer Resort (six miles west of Carson Pass); (209) 258-7304.

PLACES TO STAY

Kirkwood Accommodations: From June through September, lucky dogs are allowed to stay in some of the lodges and condominiums at the Kirkwood Ski and Summer Resort. They're located right across from the ski lifts, which won't matter to you in the summer. There's tons of hiking in the area, in addition to fishing, swimming, and general reposing in this peaceful Sierra setting. And three cheers for the owner of a lovely three-bedroom house in Kirkwood. He has a dog, and when he's not there, you and your dog can rent the place—year-round! That means winter fun is now within reach for you and your pooch. Rates for the condos are $60 to $160 a night. The house rents for $250. Weekly and monthly rates are available. Pooches require a $100 cash deposit. The resort is about 60 miles northeast of Jackson, on Highway 88. You can't miss the signs. P.O. Box 1, Kirkwood, CA 95646; (209) 258-8575.

MARKLEEVILLE

Jacob Marklee founded this Old West town in 1861 and spent the rest of his years—all three of them—here. In 1864, he was dead, the loser in a shootout with a fellow named H. W. Tuttle. Today, Markleeville has the distinction of being the county seat of the least-populous county in California.

PARKS, BEACHES, AND RECREATION AREAS

•**Grover Hot Springs State Park** 🐾🐾🐾½ *See* ❷ *on page 184.*

This is a rare bird for a state park—dogs are actually allowed to walk with you on trails. Leashed dogs can hike through ponderosa pine, incense cedars, and quaking aspen year-round. They're also allowed to camp with you in all four seasons. About the only thing they can't do is bask in the 105-degree Fahrenheit water in the pools or refresh themselves in the cold plunge area.

But that doesn't mean you have to deprive yourself of the possibly therapeutic effects of the waters. You and a friend can take turns. One can soak in the hot mineral water (it actually comes out of the ground at 148 degrees Fahrenheit!) while the other takes the dog for a walk or on a mini-fishing trip at the creeks and lakes here. Then switch. This way, everyone gets to enjoy the best this park has to offer.

It costs $4 per adult to enter the pool and $2 for children. Use of the picnic area is $2 for under an hour or $5 for the day. Sleeping at one of the 76 campsites costs $12 to $16 a night. Dogs cost $1 extra, for day use and camping. The park is three miles west of Markleeville, off Highway 88 on Hot Springs Road. Call (916) 694-2248 for information. For reservations, call Parknet at (800) 444-PARK.

RESTAURANTS

After a day at the hot springs, there's nothing like a good meal. In warmer weather, Markleeville has plenty of restaurants with outdoor tables where dogs are welcome.

Funny thing is, these places are not listed in the phone book or with directory assistance. In fact, they just recently got street addresses, and people there still don't use them. The best advice they have is to just come into town, look for the places with outdoor tables, check with the manager if it's okay to sit a spell with your dog, and enjoy. There are a few of them, and they're all along a very short strip of Highway 89, so you won't have any trouble finding them.

PLACES TO STAY

Grover Hot Springs State Park: See Grover Hot Springs State Park above for camping information.

Marklee Toll Station: Rates for this old downtown Markleeville hotel are $40 to $45. Dogs are $6 extra. It's a homey place to stay if you want to get the feel for old-style Markleeville. The hotel even has a restaurant with outdoor tables, where pooches are welcome to dine at your side. 14856 Highway 89, Markleeville, CA 96120; (530) 694-2507.

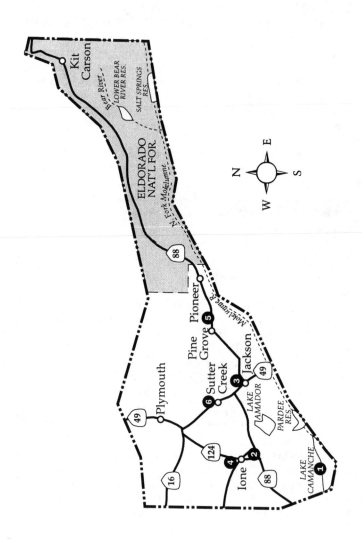

22
AMADOR COUNTY

Amador County is a place too many people drive through without stopping to take a look around. Highway 88 makes it easy to cruise through this narrow county on the way to another destination. But if you drive past here with blinders on, not only are you missing some quaint old Gold Rush towns, you're also bypassing some of the most unusual vista points in California.

Among the sights you should try to take in is the Devil's Garden vista point, along the eastern part of the county along Highway 88 in Eldorado National Forest. If a devil ever did have a garden, it would be here in this rocky terrain. Nearby are several trailheads leading into portions of this vast forest where dogs can usually prance about leashless. Eldorado National Forest is the only swath of public land in Amador County where dogs can experience this blissful freedom.

NATIONAL FORESTS

See the National Forests and Wilderness Areas chapter starting on page 748 for important information and safety tips on visiting national forests with your dog.

• **Eldorado National Forest** 🐾🐾🐾🐾 ✕
See page 750.

CAMANCHE VILLAGE

PARKS, BEACHES, AND RECREATION AREAS

• **Lake Camanche** 🐾🐾🐾 *See* ❶ *on page 188.*

See the Calaveras County listing for Lake Camanche on page 198 for details. Camanche Village is just north of the lake's north shore.

IONE

PARKS, BEACHES, AND RECREATION AREAS

• **Charles Howard Park** 🐾🐾½ *See* ❷ *on page 188.*

This is your basic community park. Nice trees, nice grass, nice cemetery. Keep in shape together by jogging on the track that goes around the park. It's at Brickyard Road and Church Street. (209) 274-2412.

RESTAURANTS

Erma's Diner: Burgers are the specialty of the house at Erma's. Eat lunch with your pooch at the two picnic tables out front. 4 Plymouth Highway; (209) 274-4116.

JACKSON

Jackson is one Old West town where there's still plenty of evidence of a rich and colorful heritage. The streets of downtown look like they were pulled from a Hollywood back lot. You can even hear lively piano music pouring out of the classic old National Hotel (no dogs allowed).

Dogs are welcome to stroll through the historic downtown district with you. A couple of stores that sell goods reminiscent of the Gold Rush era might allow you in with your dog. These shop owners asked Joe not to tell anyone he shopped there, so we can't divulge the names.

The city has only a couple of parks, but there's no shortage of restaurants that will let your dog dine outside with you during good weather.

PARKS, BEACHES, AND RECREATION AREAS

• **Detert Park** 🐾🐾½ *See* ❸ *on page 188.*

Does your pup like square dancing? Then dog-si-do on over to this pleasant community park's bandstand. Two local square dancing clubs practice here some enchanted evenings, and if you're lucky, you might get to watch (or take part in) some of the finest square dancing around.

If your dog prefers to stroll (on leash), the park has lush lawns and many shady trees. For the kids, there's a swimming pool and a very unique playground. The park is an ideal stop if you're visiting the historic part of town. It's just east of Highway 49/88, north of Hoffman Street. (209) 223-1646.

• **Kennedy Tailing Wheels Park** 🐾🐾 *See* ❹ *on page 188.*

This is the less lovely of the two larger city parks. Instead of grass, there's usually dirt underfoot. But there's plenty of shade from large oak trees, so your leashed dog will be comfortable as you walk around learning about the history of the gold mines from the kiosks and placards here. The park is famous for its huge tailing wheels, built to carry non-gold waste away to nearby ponds. (Boy dogs: Keep your legs down. These are antiques!)

Follow North Main Street to the northern part of the city, where the name of the street changes to Jackson Gate Road. Big signs mark the park on the east side of the street. (209) 223-1646.

RESTAURANTS

Mel & Faye's Diner: Dine on burgers, steak, and chicken while sitting out on the patio. 205 North Highway 49; (209) 223-0853.

PLACES TO STAY

Amador Motel: Dogs, if you want to feel mighty welcome, trot on over to this motel. "I'd rather have dogs here than children," says Mary, the owner. She'll even let pooches run free in the big backyard area here. All this made me realize Mary is a smart woman, but when she told me "your book is my favorite book," I realized she also has very good taste. Rates are $37 to $57. 12408 Kennedy Flat Road, Jackson, CA 95642; (209) 223-0970.

Jackson Holiday Lodge: Rates are $50 to $85. (The more expensive rate is for the cottages.) Dogs are $10 extra. 850 North Highway 49, Jackson, CA 95642; (209) 223-0486.

KIT CARSON

PLACES TO STAY

Kit Carson Campground: If you and your dog like trout fishing or peace and quiet, this high Sierra camp on the West Fork of the Carson River is a great spot to pitch a tent. Since there are only a dozen campsites, you won't have typical Tent City woes.

Campsites are $8 a night and are available only from spring to late summer. They're first come, first served. The campground is about six miles southeast of Kirkwood on Highway 88. (702) 882-2766.

PINE GROVE

PARKS, BEACHES, AND RECREATION AREAS

•**Indian Grinding Rock State Historic Park** 🐾🐾 *See* ❺ *on page 188.*

Dogs aren't permitted on trails here, but they are allowed to visit bits of the reconstructed Miwok village and sniff at the old grinding rock. Leashed dogs can even read some of the petroglyphs around the park if they're of the erudite ilk.

Day-use visits costs $5 per carload. There are 23 campsites, available on a first-come, first-served basis. Rates are $12 to $14 per night. Dogs are $1 extra, for day use and camping. The park is about halfway between Pine Grove and Volcano, on Pine Grove Volcano Road. Call (209) 296-7488 for park information.

PLACES TO STAY

Indian Grinding Rock State Historic Park: See Indian Grinding Rock State Historic Park above for camping information.

PIONEER

RESTAURANTS

Sierra Trading Post: Dogs like to dine at the picnic table outside this old-style convenience store on Highway 88. There are only a couple of businesses here, and you can's miss it. (209) 295-3725.

SUTTER CREEK

John Sutter, who owned the mill where gold was first discovered in the Mother Lode, also had his Midas-touch hand in a nearby creek. The creek was named after him, and the town came next.

PARKS, BEACHES, AND RECREATION AREAS

•**Minnie Provis Park** 🐾🐾 *See* ❻ *on page 188.*

How often does a dog get to visit a park named after a city clerk? Minnie Provis Park, set in the heart of historic Sutter Creek, may be the only one with such a namesake. Minnie was Sutter Creek's first city clerk. She must have been a good one.

This small, green park is ideally located if you and your leashed dog happen to be exploring the old downtown section of Sutter Creek. The park is located just behind City Hall. Exit Highway 49 at Church Street and go east a half block. Park on the street. (209) 267-5647.

23
CALAVERAS COUNTY

There's only one traffic light in this entire Mother Lode county, and it's very new. Only one town is incorporated. If you want to mall-hop, you have to drive at least 70 miles. And just about every pickup truck has a dog.

"This is where dogs are still dogs, and there may be more of them than of us people," says Pat Mulgrew, the resident caretaker of a park in the "town" of Murphys. "It's very old California. There's a leash law and it should be obeyed. But local dogs often choose to walk on their own, visit the park, and hang out with their friends. It's just that kind of place."

At least it's that way until the rest of the world moves in with all its ugly baggage. The folks at the Calaveras Lodging and Visitors Association boast that this is the fastest-growing county in California. They're trying to attract more and more companies so they can bring in more residents. The real estate business is booming. Visit while you can, before this historic land succumbs to suburban sprawl.

NATIONAL FORESTS

See the National Forests and Wilderness Areas chapter starting on page 748 for important information and safety tips on visiting national forests with your dog.

• Stanislaus National Forest 🐾🐾🐾🐾 🐕

About one-third of Calaveras County has the privilege of being part of Stanislaus National Forest. See page 755.

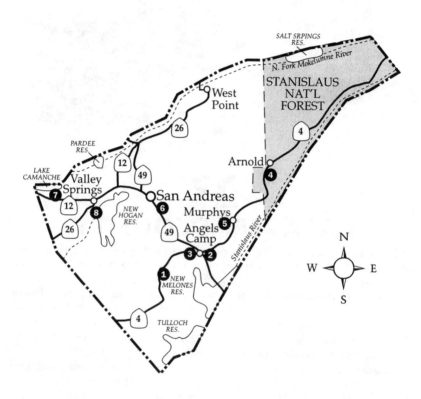

SALT SRPINGS
RES.

N. Fork Mokelumne River

STANISLAUS
NAT'L
FOREST

West
Point

26

PARDEE
RES.

LAKE
CAMANCHE

Valley
Springs

12

49

4

Arnold

4

7

San Andreas

12

8

NEW
HOGAN
RES.

6

Murphys

49

Angels
Camp

5

3 2

Stanislaus River

1

NEW
MELONES
RES.

4

TULLOCH
RES.

N
W E
S

ANGELS CAMP

You can still check out the saloon in the Angels Hotel, on Main Street, where a barkeep told 29-year-old Mark Twain the tale that inspired his first published short story, "The Notorious Jumping Frog of Calaveras County."

Since the story was set in this dog-friendly land, it wouldn't have been complete without an interlude about a dog. The one in Twain's story was named Andrew Jackson, and he was apparently a bulldog. Twain's narrative could easily have been called "The Notorious Fighting Dog of Calaveras County," but publishers may not have jumped at it.

Fighting dogs aren't welcome here, but jumping frogs have never been forgotten. Each year, the town hosts the world-famous Jumping Frog Jubilee. As you may have guessed, dogs are not particularly welcome.

PARKS, BEACHES, AND RECREATION AREAS

• **New Melones Reservoir** 🐾🐾🐾 *See* ❶ *on page 194.*

When the lake is full, the trail that meanders around part of it may actually come close to the shore. But usually you and your leashed dog will have to be content wandering around the rolling foothills, among small scrub oaks that provide little shade. In the summer, it's probably not worth the visit. But the rest of the year, the hiking is pleasant—and the scenery is quite breathtaking in the spring.

The lake's five-mile trail will become much longer if the U.S. Bureau of Reclamation can secure prison labor to continue to build it. That's about the only way it's going to happen, according to the folks who run the reservoir.

Fishing isn't the best in the area, but in the spring the bass bite isn't bad, especially at the lake's northern arms. Your dog is welcome to wet his paws while you fish from shore or to join you on your fishing boat.

There are 300 campsites. They cost $14 a night and are available on a first-come, first-served basis. There's no day-use fee. From Angels Camp, head south on Highway 49 and follow the signs to the lake's north end. (209) 536-9094.

• **Tryon Park** 🐾🐾 *See* ❷ *on page 194.*

You and your gold-digging canine can pan for gold at Angels Creek, which runs right through this small park. It's a good place to take a rest if you're traveling on Highway 4. The park is located on Highway 4 at Booster Way. (209) 736-2181.

• **Utica Park** 🐾🐾 *See* ❸ *on page 194*

Mark Twain's statue is here, and your leashed dog is welcome if he promises not to do leg lifts on it. (Twain may have been amused, but it's just not a respectful way to treat the memory of someone who wrote so much good stuff about dog beasts.)

The park only covers 2.63 acres (you can afford to measure land that's this small by the hundredth of an acre), but it seems a good deal bigger. There's plenty of grass for rolling on and plenty of trees for shading you on warmer days. During the summer, you and your dog can attend a few free concerts here (see Diversions on page 196). The park is conveniently located on Highway 49/Main Street at Sam's Way. (209) 736-2181.

RESTAURANTS

Mr. B's Frosty: Share a shake with your pooch on the patio of this fast-food eatery. 22 North Main Street; (209) 736-4312.

PLACES TO STAY

Angels Inn Motel: Rates are $60 to $70. 600 North Main Street, Angels Camp, CA 95221; (209) 736-4242.

New Melones Reservoir: See New Melones Reservoir on page 195 for camping information.

DIVERSIONS

Lend a pointy ear: Floppy ears, hairy ears, and ears that drag all the way down to the ground are welcome to enjoy the series of free summertime concerts at Utica Park. These Wednesday evening affairs feature a variety of musicians, from Gypsy violinists to bluegrass bands. "People are encouraged to bring a picnic and a well-behaved dog," says Rachel Martin of the Calaveras Lodging and Visitors Association. See page 195 for info on the park. Call (800) 225-3764 for a schedule of this year's concerts.

ARNOLD

PARKS, BEACHES, AND RECREATION AREAS

• **Calaveras Big Trees State Park** 🐾 🐾 🐾 *See* ❹ *on page 194.*

Dogs aren't permitted on the trails here, but nothing's stopping them from hiking along the fire roads. "You and your dog might see more wilderness on these fire roads than you would on the regular trails," says interpretive ranger Joe Von Herrman.

The giant sequoias aren't accessible from the fire roads, but you'll probably pass by some of the largest sugar pines in existence. Depending on which roads you take, you could hike close to the Stanislaus River, pass by a historic logging railroad, or walk through chaparral-covered slopes and fir-filled forests.

For $1 you can buy a map of the fire roads and trails at the entry kiosk. The day-use fee is $5. There are 129 campsites, with nightly rates ranging from $12 to $16. Dogs are $1 extra. The park is four miles northeast of Arnold, on Highway 4. Follow the signs. For camping reservations, call Parknet at (800) 444-PARK. For park information, phone (209) 795-2334.

RESTAURANTS

The Hungry Prospector: You and your pooch can dine together on the deck here. The place serves typical fast-food fare, including burgers, fried chicken, deli sandwiches, and fish. If you thought your dog gave up begging, just watch him when he smells your fresh-off-the-griddle cheeseburger. You can also get breakfast. 961 Highway 4; (209) 795-2128.

Just Delicious: Most of the food is as advertised. Dogs like to join you on the patio. 140 Highway 4; (209) 795-2805.

Tallahan's Cafe: Your dog can't be at your feet here, but he'll be grateful for that if you've just come back from a hard and sweaty hike. Dogs seem content to be tied within a few feet of your table at the outer edge of the deck. The food is an eclectic mix. 2224 Oak Circle; (209) 795-4005.

PLACES TO STAY

Calaveras Big Trees State Park: See Calaveras Big Trees State Park on page 196 for camping information.

Ebbett's Pass Lodge: Rates are $40 to $74. Dogs are $5 extra. 1173 Highway 4, Arnold, CA 95223; (209) 795-1563.

Meadowmont Lodge: Huge dogs can't stay here, but all others are welcome. Rates are $41 to $61. The location is Country Club Drive and Highway 4. The mailing address is P.O. Box E, Arnold, CA 95223; (209) 795-1394.

Sierra Vacation Rentals: Rent a cabin or mountain chalet to take your favorite canine companion and a few friends for an extra-special vacation getaway. All of the rentals have fireplaces or wood-burning stoves for those cold winter nights. Rates for up to six people and a dog are $130 to $170 for the first night and $70 to $90 for each additional night. Each extra person costs $10 per night. Dogs require a $150 deposit. P.O. Box 1080, Arnold, CA 95223; (209) 795-2422 or (800) 995-2422.

MURPHYS

PARKS, BEACHES, AND RECREATION AREAS

•**Murphys Park** 🐾 🐾 ½ *See* ❺ *on page 194.*

This is where the local dogs hang out. They like the shade, they enjoy the creek that flows through here year-round, and they appreciate each other's company. Many of them don't even wait for their owners to leash them up and walk them here. They head over by themselves. "It's breaking the rules, but they don't get themselves in trouble and they have real street smarts," says Pat Mulgrew, a park caretaker.

They also have good taste. The creek here is large, with a wood footbridge you can cross to walk on the shadier, more secluded side of the park. It's located at Main and South Algiers Streets. (209) 728-8726.

RESTAURANTS

If you and your dog are hungry, beware of being lured to Murphys Dog House. It may have a dog-oriented name, but my researchers and I were treated so rudely here that we tremble to think that any kindly dog owner might make the same mistake we did. (At press time, it was for sale, so maybe in the future it will have mended its ways.) Try Celeste's instead.

Celeste's: Eat homemade soup and rolls at the many outdoor tables here. Dogs don't mind if you order Celeste's tasty pizza with extra pepperoni. (Joe made me write that.) 409 Main Street; (209) 728-2875.

SAN ANDREAS

PARKS, BEACHES, AND RECREATION AREAS

•**Nielsen Park** 🐾 🐾 ½ *See* ❻ *on page 194.*

If you've just come from visiting the haunting Mokelumne Hill area (eight miles north), this park is an excellent place for a pit stop. It's not only grassy, shady, and set along the refreshing San Andreas Creek, it's also right along the way.

The park is on Main Street, just east of Highway 49 and close to the local visitors center. There's no official phone number.

PLACES TO STAY

Black Bart Inn and Motel: You and your dog won't have to sniff out a park if you stay here, since the Black Bart Inn comes complete with its own park. It even has a gazebo and a huge barbecue area. Rates are $43 to $50. 35 Main Street, San Andreas, CA 95249; (209) 754-3808.

The Courtyard Bed and Breakfast: This is a truly enchanting inn. Dogs, don't tell a soul about it. It's our little secret. One of the two rooms here is so romantic it could make a grown dog blush. It's the honeymoon suite, complete with a baby grand piano, private access, a private deck, and a fireplace. There's even a stained glass window over the bath, for those who like to watch Mr. Bubble in living color. The other room is also enchanting, with French blue highlights and oak and wicker furniture.

Hungry travelers like the fact that refreshments are served upon arrival. In the morning, fresh-brewed coffee is delivered to your room. Then you can amble down to the inn's cheery breakfast room, or in good weather, outside to the deck, where you can eat a big breakfast under the shade of a walnut tree. (Dogs prefer the latter option.) If your muscles are aching after a long drive, soak in the outdoor hot tub here. No dogs in the hot tub, though; they have to settle for a good back rub.

The rate for the magical suite is a mere $85. The other room is $65. There's a $25 fee (they call it a nonrefundable deposit) when you make your reservation, with or without dog. The folks here don't have doggy visitors very often, so they get a kick out of the occasional canine companion. 334 West Saint Charles Street, San Andreas, CA 95249; (209) 754-1518.

VALLEY SPRINGS

PARKS, BEACHES, AND RECREATION AREAS

• Lake Camanche 🐾 🐾 🐾 *See* ❼ *on page 194.*

Come here during the off-season, when it's not too hot or too inundated by water-skiers, and your dog will have a delightful visit. Pooches aren't allowed on trails here, but the land is very open, with scattered oaks on rolling hills and lakeside flats. Dogs can walk anywhere you do, as long as you stay off the trails.

Your dog can dip her paws in the water, but since she's supposed to be leashed, she can't pull an Esther Williams. The fishing is fantastic in the spring and early summer. If thoughts of catching bass, bluegill, or trout keep you awake at night, come here, fulfill your dreams, and rest easy.

There are 500 campsites, with rates of $15 a night. Dogs are $1 extra. Sites are open year-round on a first-come, first-served basis, although reservations are available for holiday weekends. The day-use fee is $5.50, with that extra $1 charge for hairy beasts. The lake is north of Highway 12 in the easternmost part of the county. Follow the signs seven miles to the entrance. (209) 763-5178.

• **New Hogan Reservoir** 🐾🐾🐾 *See* ❽ *on page 194.*

It's cheaper (free, in fact) to visit here than Lake Camanche, and leashed dogs actually get to romp around on the trails. The terrain is about the same, with open land, rolling hills, rocks, dirt, and some oaks. Dogs can dip their paws in the lake, and they can even join you in your boat as the two of you pursue supper.

Water-skiers can make it noisy in the summer, but there are still plenty of places to escape most of the madness. The lake has 50 miles of shoreline, and partiers can't overtake every inch of it.

There are 182 campsites, all available on a first-come, first-served basis. Nightly rates range from $8 to $14. From Highway 26 in the Valley Springs area, you can't miss the signs for the lake. It's about three miles to the entrance. (209) 772-1343.

PLACES TO STAY

Lake Camanche: See Lake Camanche on page 198 for camping information.

New Hogan Reservoir: See New Hogan Reservoir above for camping information.

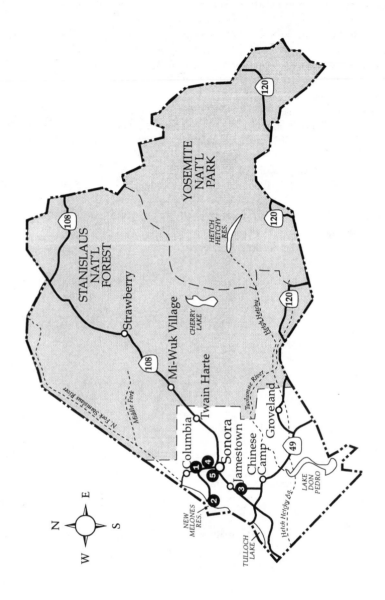

STANISLAUS NAT'L FOREST

YOSEMITE NAT'L PARK

HETCH HETCHY RES.

CHERRY LAKE

Strawberry

Mi-Wuk Village

Twain Harte

Columbia

Sonora

Jamestown

Chinese Camp

Groveland

NEW MELONES RES.

TULLOCH LAKE

LAKE DON PEDRO

N. Fork Stanislaus River

Middle Fork

Tuolumne River

Hetch Hetchy

Hetch Hetchy Rd.

108

108

120

120

120

49

N E S W

24
TUOLUMNE COUNTY

For any dogs who don't know how to pronounce the name of this county, think of what you'd say if someone asked you, "To whom should I give this huge, rare steak?" You'd probably pipe up and shout, "To all o' me!" or something like that. And that's close enough.

Tuolumne is a colorful Mother Lode county, with many exciting adventures awaiting dogs and their people. Be sure not to miss Jamestown or the Columbia State Historic Park. Dogs adore these places (during off-season when they're not so crowded).

NATIONAL FORESTS

See the National Forests and Wilderness Areas chapter starting on page 748 for important information and safety tips on visiting national forests with your dog.

•Stanislaus National Forest 🐾🐾🐾🐾🐾 🐕

There are plenty of places in this stunning forest where you can pull off along the northeast section of Highway 108 to hike or camp. See page 755 for more information.

NATIONAL PARKS

• **Yosemite National Park** 🐾½

Since a dog can barely even set paw inside this park (a major exception is the Redwoods Guest Cottages, described on page 223), we must give it a rather low rating. It's too bad because the park is so great for people. See page 222 for more information.

ARNOLD

This is a fun Old West town that shares its name with the pig on *Green Acres.* Joe Dog discovered that it's not mere coincidence. If you're good and hungry, visit the dog-friendly restaurants he scouted out and you'll discover why.

RESTAURANTS

Blue Coyote Cafe: Dogs feel a kinship with this place. Is it the water the servers give to dog visitors, or is it all in the name? Bring along your poochy dining companion and find out while eating great Southwest grub at the four outdoor tables. 1224 Oak Circle; (209) 795-2872.

Giant Burger: Forget about restaurants like Stars and Chez Panisse. Dogs like it plain and simple. And big. And beefy. Joe gives the food here his top rating: four paws and the big drool. Check it out with your dog at the 10 outdoor tables. 846 Highway 4; (209) 795-1594.

DIVERSIONS

Pick a pack for pooch adventures: See Diversions under the Sonora heading on page 207.

COLUMBIA

PARKS, BEACHES, AND RECREATION AREAS

• **Columbia State Historic Park** 🐾🐾🐾½ *See* ❶ *on page 200.*

This park is actually a ghost town from the Gold Rush. But it's preserved in such a manner that it still has a pulse. It's alive. You can get a haircut at the state's oldest barbershop, sip sarsaparilla at a saloon, and buy old-style dry goods at one of the 1850s stores.

Be sure to bring a friend if you want to enter these establishments, because dogs have to stay outside (and be leashed), and you shouldn't leave them tied up, even for a few minutes. Just take turns dogsitting.

But you don't have to go into the buildings to enjoy this town. The dogs and I like to saunter down the streets (no cars allowed!), kicking up dust as we amble along. We can stop and look inside these wonderful old buildings, but we get along fine without having to actually go inside. No shopping means no cash outflow. Since there's no admission fee at this "living museum," it's a very cheap date.

To give a dog a break from all the history here, go to the old schoolhouse and find the adjacent Karen Bakersville Smith Memorial Trail (named after a local teacher who died in a car crash). It's only six-tenths of a mile long, but it's a wonderful way to spy on nature as you hike through meadows and oak woodlands. So far, dogs are permitted, but if there are any problems, the rangers are ready to nail up the "No Dogs" signs.

Please don't bring a dog here during the summer, unless it's raining or at least threatening to. It gets torturously crowded. We last visited in late fall, when the weather was perfect and the park almost empty.

Stop by the park headquarters and pick up a brochure outlining a one-and-a-half-hour tour. From Highway 49, drive north on Parrott's Ferry Road/County Road E18. The entrance is in just over 1.5 miles, and it's on your right. (209) 532-4301 or (209) 532-0150.

RESTAURANTS

Columbia Frosty: This place only serves breakfast and lunch. Eat it in the company of your canine on the patio at the side of the restaurant. 22652 Parrott's Ferry Road; (209) 532-6773.

The Licked Skillet: Okay, we promise the name has nothing to do with the fact that this excellent restaurant welcomes dogs to dine at its outdoor tables. Dogs don't get to lick the skillets, but they do lick their chops over the unique cuisine and dog-friendly attitude here. "Dogs get water before their owners get a menu," says Peg, one of the dog-lovin' owners. The Licked Skillet is a favorite among locals, according to Tonja Peterson, who frequents the 35 outdoor tables with pooch Avery Mae as often as Avery Mae can convince her. The restaurant is open for lunch and dinner, and as with most other local eateries, the outdoor tables go south in the winter, so dogs are wise to come here in the warmer eight or nine months of the year. 11256 State Street; (209) 536-9599.

GROVELAND

PLACES TO STAY

Buck Meadows Lodge and Yosemite Westgate Motel: Rates are $50 to $90. Pooches pay a $10 fee per visit. 7647 Highway 120, Groveland, CA 95321; (209) 962-5281 or (800) 253-9673.

Groveland Hotel: The suites at this Gold Rush–era inn come with a fireplace and a Jacuzzi so that you can have an evening of romantic relaxation. The place was chosen as one of the "12 Best Country Inns" by *Country Inns* magazine. Rates are $105 to $185. A dog deposit is required. 18767 Main Street, Groveland, CA 95321; (209) 962-4000 or (800) 273-3314.

JAMESTOWN

Jamestown is one of Bill's favorite places to visit. During off-season, it's so uncrowded that he feels like one of the locals in this small Mother Lode town. That's when the town stops being quaint and becomes a real Old West hangout. Bill likes to sit on a bench outside one of the dusty buildings and listen to a couple of old natives tell their stories. But more than anything else, he enjoys wearing his rust-colored bandanna around his shiny black neck. He knows he looks devastating.

Dogs can really have fun here. Between panning for gold, riding in a horse-drawn carriage, and checking out some famous old locomotives, they'll have enough entertainment to last them until their next vacation.

PARKS, BEACHES, AND RECREATION AREAS

• **New Melones Reservoir** 🐾🐾🐾 *See* ❷ *on page 200.*

Since the bulk of the lake (and the best fishing) is on the Calaveras County side, you'll find its description on page 195.

• **Railtown 1897 State Historic Park** 🐾🐾🐾 *See* ❸ *on page 200.*

If you and your dog are train fans and movie buffs, prepare to be impressed. Remember the train in the movie *Back to the Future III*? How about the train in *Unforgiven, High Noon,* or the return of *Bonanza*? Get out your autograph book, because the vintage steamers at this park have acted in these and hundreds of other films, TV shows, and commercials.

Dogs can't go on rail excursions, but leashed pooches are allowed to walk around the grounds with you and check out the locomotives. They're also permitted to go on an intriguing 30-minute roundhouse tour offered during the warmer months. The fare is $2 for adult humans, $1 for child humans; dogs are free.

Be sure to bring a picnic lunch if you're with friends who are taking the train ride (given only during the summer, with prices of $6 for adults, $3 for kids ages 6 to 12). You and your dog can share a lunch in the shaded picnic area while your friends steam around Jamestown for an hour. When they're done, you'll have eaten all the good stuff and those fun-loving, windblown buddies of yours will have to settle for the squished sandwiches and generic sodas.

There's no entry fee. The train runs on weekends from April through October, and in November runs only on Saturdays. From Highway 49 traveling east, turn right on Fifth Avenue. Drive a few blocks and you're there. (209) 984-3958.

RESTAURANTS

Jimtown Frostie: Joan, the manager here, will be glad to give your pooch a drink of water and maybe even a meat patty or a dab of Frostie ice cream. Humans can eat here, too. Pooches and their people get to eat at the patio seating. The restaurant is located at the corner of Main Street and Highway 108; (209) 984-3444.

PLACES TO STAY

National Hotel: Want some luxury with your history? Try this enchanting place. Built in 1859, it's one of the oldest hotels in California to run continuously since it opened. Your dog can't wet his whistle at the old-fashioned saloon downstairs, but he'll probably be too busy admiring the simple antique decor in your room to notice. Unlike the old days (pre-1995), the hotel now provides private bathrooms. Rates are $80. 77 Main Street, Jamestown, CA 95327; (209) 984-3446 or (800) 894-3446.

DIVERSIONS

Get hot to trot: Tom Fraser's Carriage Tours provides a terrific way to experience Jamestown with your well-behaved pooch. You and your dog will sit side by side in an antique carriage while a beautiful horse pulls you along the historic streets. But when you talk with your dog after your trip, you'll realize that the two of you had completely different experiences.

What humans see: antique shops, wooden sidewalks, great Old West buildings, turn-of-the-century trains, and tourists taking pictures.

What dogs see: a horse's butt, a horse's butt, a horse's butt, a passing cat, and a horse's butt.

Co-owner Jan Fraser says she and her husband, Tom, love having quiet dogs as riders. "We've had Chihuahuas, poodles, collies, you name it. For most travelers, their pets are like their kids. How can we say no?"

The price is right. A 20-minute ride is $6 per adult, $5 per child. Dogs who can fit on the floor are free. Otherwise, they have to buy a seat and sit next to you. The carriages load at the lower end of town, across the street from Boomer's on Main Street. They run on weekends throughout the year, with additional hours during the summer. Special rides are available. Call (209) 984-3125.

Hit the Mother Lode: Cowabunga! No, er, Eureka! Aroooo! You and your dog will be hopping around like Yosemite Sam if you find a few specks of gold around here.

The folks at Gold Prospecting Expeditions say they've never met a dog who didn't like helping his owner pan for gold in the cool creeks and rivers here. You and your dog can take a walking tour guided by a prospector, then get down to the business of panning. You keep what you find—and the folks here say you'll always find something in their special section of the Mother Lode.

If your dog can pan like Twinkles, the company's resident poodle, you'll be rich. Twinkles sticks her head underwater in a panning trough and comes up with a gold nugget every time. Of course, she's been trained, and the nugget is always there, so don't be too disappointed if your dog doesn't scoop up the down payment for your new house.

For a real outback prospecting experience, you and your dog (as long as he's of calm disposition) can fly in a helicopter to some of the most remote areas of California's Gold Country. You can stay for just a day or camp for two weeks, panning and digging the whole time. The adventure isn't cheap, but if you're feeling lucky, it might be worth a try.

Prices range from $10 for an hour to thousands of dollars per week for the helicopter excursion. Gold Prospecting Expeditions is at 18170 Main Street, Jamestown, CA 95327; (209) 984-GOLD.

MI-WUK VILLAGE

PLACES TO STAY

Mi-Wuk Motor Lodge: There are VCRs in the country-style rooms, so if all the nature around here is just too natural for you, snuggle up with your dog in front of a campy old flick. Rates are $58 to $109. Pooches pay a $10 fee per visit. The street address is 24680 Highway 108, and the mailing address is P.O. Box 70, Mi-Wuk Village, CA 95346; (209) 586-3031.

SONORA

This is the county seat of Tuolumne County and it's a real charmer. A stroll through the colorful downtown area with your leashed dog is a fun way to feel out the town's history.

The early Gold Rush days here were times of bullfights, bear fights, and gold camp justice. The rough edges have changed form a little, but they've never completely disappeared. Witness the case of Ellie Nessler, convicted of killing the man accused of molesting her son. She shot him while he stood in court on trial. Locals were divided on the issue, but vigilante justice is a deep-rooted tradition here and she had many supporters. Nessler got out of jail in 1997, which made a lot of people around here mighty happy.

If you like an Old West town with an attitude, you'll enjoy Sonora.

PARKS, BEACHES, AND RECREATION AREAS

•**Coffill Park** 🐾½ *See* ➍ *on page 200.*

Dogs like the scenery here, but not the carpeting. This tiny park runs along an attractive creek, but there's no grass—just concrete. It's a convenient place to stop and smell the trees and sit for a bit while you're out on the town. It's between Washington and Green Streets, just north of Stockton Street on Sonora Creek. (209) 532-4541.

•**Woods Creek Rotary Park** 🐾🐾½ *See* ➎ *on page 200.*

Woods Creek runs through this pretty, shaded park. Dogs love to wet their paws in it on warm summer afternoons. Joe, the consummate landlubber, prefers to picnic at the tables set under shade trees. It's a great place to come to sample the tasty gourmet items you just bought downtown.

The park is just southwest of town, on Stockton Street and Woods Creek Drive (across from the Mother Lode Fairgrounds). (209) 532-4541.

RESTAURANTS

Caffeine Mary's: This sweet little joint is a combination bakery/cafe/bookstore/coffee shop. The little tables outside, recessed slightly from the sidewalk, are perfect for you and your dog. 52 South Washington Street; (209) 532-6261.

Cups: Thespian-leaning dogs love coming here with their people. Cups is not only a coffeehouse with really great java and sweet treats, it's also a playhouse. The theater is inside, and dogs need to stay at the outside tables, but some dogs love just being near the roar of greasepaint and the smell of the crowd. 208 South Green Street; (209) 532-2845.

Full of Beans: Enjoy java and baked goods at any of eight outdoor tables here. Full of Beans is located at the Timberhills Shopping Center, 1013 Mono Way; (209) 533-2486.

La Sierra Taqueria: They tell a tale here about the time a patron tied his dog up to one of the plastic tables outside and went in to the salsa bar after putting his food on the table. The loyal dog followed, and so did the table, and so did the food. The moral of the tale: Leave your dog in the hands of a friend if you need to go inside the restaurant. The food here is very good, but loses its appeal when it's splattered all over the ground. La Sierra Taqueria is located at the Junction Shopping Center on Highway 108, 13759-C Mono Way; (209) 532-1121.

PLACES TO STAY

Kennedy Meadows Resort: These cabins surround a scenic meadow, and the Stanislaus River flows by. It's a great escape from civilization. Rates are $52 to $105. The resort closes for winter in mid-October, so get there early. The folks here say there's no actual street name or address for the resort. Call for directions. P.O. Box 4010, Sonora, CA 95370; (209) 532-9632.

Miner's Motel: Small pooches only, please. Rates are $40 to $65. It's located at 18740 Highway 108, and the mailing address is P.O. Box 1, Sonora, CA 95370; (209) 532-7850 or (800) 451-4176.

Sonora Days Inn: Dogs can only stay in the motel section of this hotel. (Dogs aren't allowed in the hotel lobby, so they can't get to the hotel rooms beyond it.) Rates for the motel are $49 to $69. Dogs are $10 extra. 160 South Washington Street, Sonora, CA 95370; (209) 532-2400.

DIVERSIONS

Pick a pack for pooch adventures: When I met Tonja Peterson, co-owner of the Sierra Nevada Adventure Co., she was running around the winter woods on snowshoes with her dog Avery Mae at her side. (Avery was sans snowshoes. "Too awkward," claimed the rotty-Australian shepherd mix.) We got to talking about Peterson's terrific outdoor store, and it turns out it's more dog-friendly than even most pet stores we know. "All genders, shapes, and sizes of dogs are welcome. We'd rate it four paws for dogs," Peterson said, taking her cue from a terrific California dog guidebook she stocks.

So we checked it out, and sure enough, it's doggone great. Dogs who visit here will get water, a dog treat, and some serious ear rubs if the place isn't too busy. Dogs can also pick from lots of dog bowls, dog books, collars, leashes, and dog backpacks.

Peterson recently opened a new, larger branch of the store in Arnold, and she says it's just as dog-friendly. If Avery Mae isn't there, Al "the Pal," a sweet chocolate Lab, probably will be. The Arnold address is 2293 Highway 4; (209) 795-9310. The Sonora store is located at 173 South Washington Street; (209) 532-5621.

STRAWBERRY

RESTAURANTS

Strawberry Store: This is a cute old building painted a bright red/strawberry color. It's actually more of a store than a restaurant, but since there aren't too many places to eat around here with your dog (none, to be exact), we thought it just might do the trick when you have a hankering for a premade deli sandwich. There's a bench outside where you and your pooch can split your lunch. The place is located on Highway 108. There's no street address, but you won't miss it because it's one of only two businesses in these parts. (209) 965-3597.

PLACES TO STAY

The Rivers Resort: If you and your dog want to stay in cabins right on the Stanislaus River, rent one of the 10 very cozy cabins here. The cabins were recently upgraded (the place was formerly the Sparrow Resort), and they're better than ever. Humans drool over the large fireplaces in some cottages, and they love the quality wood interiors and the heated pool that's available in warmer months. Dogs go gaga over the fact that the national forest surrounds this resort. Joe loves to fall asleep to the sound of the river. If you don't want to get away from it all, fear not: There's cable TV.

Cottages range in size from one bedroom to four bedrooms, and rates are $85 to $185. Weekly rates are available. There's a $150 deposit for dogs. The deposit sounds like it smarts, but you can use your credit card. There's no street address, but the resort is one of the two businesses on Highway 108 in Strawberry. The mailing address is P.O. Box 81, Strawberry, CA 95375; (209) 965-3278 for information, or (800) 514-6777 for reservations.

TWAIN HARTE

Dogs enjoy strolling along the sidewalks of this charming little town, especially if they're of the literary persuasion. The town was named for writers Mark Twain and Bret Harte. It's a good thing that Aleksandr Solzhenitsyn and Michel Eyquem de Montaigne weren't big in the area when the place was named.

PLACES TO STAY

El Dorado Motel: Dogs are allowed here only in the winter months. Rates are $40 to $65, and dogs with long hair have to pay $5 to $6 extra. "The snow makes them all wet and really messy. The fee is just to keep the rooms clean," the manager told us. 22678 Black Hawk Drive, Twain Harte, CA 95383; (209) 586-4479.

25
MONO COUNTY

This is raw and rugged eastern Sierra country, where the cows graze amid such spectacular scenery that it's hard to believe they don't moo and ahh whenever we turn our backs.

When you contemplate the origins of the word "mono," you'll probably think of words like "alone," "one," or "single." Certainly they capture the feel of this unique land. But in this case, the meaning of the word isn't so romantic. Mono is the Yokut Indian word for "flies." Brine flies, abundant on the shores of salty Mono Lake, were an important source of protein for the Yokut, and they're still the most visible insect at Mono Lake. Fortunately, the flies don't bite, eat your picnic, or otherwise act tempestuously toward humans and their dogs.

In "Fly County," you can often just pull off the road into open public land and hike your heart out, especially in the county's northern reaches. As you drive along U.S. 395, you'll see so many signs for camping, fishing, and other outdoor recreation that you won't know where to turn first. This chapter describes a few of the more dog-friendly areas, but know that when you see signs for places like Convict Lake, Crowley Lake, and Bridgeport Lake, generally you and your leashed dog will be welcome.

A note to dogs: Don't get too excited when you see signs for the Dogtown State Historic Landmark on U.S. 395 just south of Willow Springs. It's interesting, but it's not what you think.

NATIONAL FORESTS

See the National Forests and Wilderness Areas chapter starting on page 748 for important information and safety tips on visiting national forests with your dog.

- **Inyo National Forest** 🐾🐾🐾🐾 🐕
  See page 750.
- **Toiyabe National Forest** 🐾🐾🐾🐾 🐕
  See page 755.

BODIE

PARKS, BEACHES, AND RECREATION AREAS

- **Bodie State Historic Park** 🐾🐾🐾 *See ❶ on page 210.*

This ghost town looks so much like *Gunsmoke*-land on a really bad day that it's hard to picture it as a thriving, raunchy, pulsating boomtown. But that's exactly what it was back in the 1870s during this area's gold rush. Dozens of saloons, a burgeoning red-light district, and murders nearly every day kept this lawless mining camp hopping.

These days, dogs can enjoy the 486 acres of this town-turned-historic park as long as they're law-abiding citizens on a leash. They're allowed to walk down the dusty streets with you and sniff at the 170 dilapidated buildings that remain, or they can kick up their heels in the more open areas of the park. Dogs seem to appreciate the wild and woolly luster that still shines through the educational veneer here.

From U.S. 395 just south of Willow Springs, take Highway 270/Bodie Road east about 13 miles. The last three miles are unpaved and can be impassable in winter. Fees are $5 per vehicle and $1 extra per dog. (760) 647-6445.

BRIDGEPORT

If you and your dog are film noir fans, you'll want to stop at this quiet little village and see if it looks familiar. Remember the movie *Out of the Past*, starring Robert Mitchum? Much of it was set right here in Bridgeport.

PARKS, BEACHES, AND RECREATION AREAS

- **Bridgeport Park** 🐾 *See ❷ on page 210.*

This tiny county park is just a bunch of picnic tables on grass in the midst of a few pieces of old mining equipment. It's right next to the Mono County Museum, in case you're with someone who wants a little culture.

From U.S. 395, go east on School Street and left on Middle Street. (760) 932-5248.

PLACES TO STAY

Best Western Ruby Inn: Stay here and you get a small area to walk your leashless pooch! You also get to stay in a smoking room, but at least you get to stay. Rates are $60 to $125. 33 Main Street, Bridgeport, CA 93517; (760) 932-7241.

Mono Village Fisherman's Resort and Family Vacation Hideaway: What this resort lacks in name brevity it makes up for in scenic beauty. Actually, it's the surrounding scenery that's exquisite, with Upper Twin Lake in the front yard and mountains and glorious trees everywhere else. The resort itself ranges from very tinny (several dozen RV sites) to very campy (many tent sites) to very rustic (many attractive log cabins). Dogs are relegated to the tent and RV sites.

Autumn here is especially beautiful. And if you're an angler, that's definitely the time to visit, since fishing is at its best then. The resort has a grocery store, cafe, cocktail lounge, and boathouse.

Sites are $10 to $16. There's no real street address, but the mailing address is Annett's Mono Village, Inc., P.O. Box 455, Bridgeport, CA 93517; (760) 932-7071.

Silver Maple Inn: Rates are $55 to $90. Dogs require a $20 deposit. 310 Main Street, Bridgeport, CA 93517; (760) 932-7383.

Walker River Lodge: This is a very dog-friendly motel. The kind owners here will show you a nearby little hike you can do with your leash-free pooch. The lodge is right on the Walker River, a big-time trout area. Rates are $60 to $120. 1 Main Street, Bridgeport, CA 93517; (760) 932-7021.

JUNE LAKE

PARKS, BEACHES, AND RECREATION AREAS

The June Lake Loop consists of four lakes west of U.S. 395. Dogs are permitted at all of them. Here we'll discuss only the two smaller lakes.

• **Gull Lake** 🐾 🐾 🐾 *See* ❸ *on page 210.*

As the smallest lake of the June Lake Loop chain, Gull Lake also tends to be the quietest. People are apt to miss this stunning 64-acre lake while on the prowl for its three bigger sisters. That's what dogs like about this place: Very few people get underfoot.

Nonetheless, pooches should be leashed here, and they're not supposed to swim, so watch those slippery water dogs. But they do have a good time watching you fish from shore for all those planted trout. They even seem to enjoy the scenery, or at least the smellery. The lake is set in what could be called "the Sierra Bowl," a dramatic, rocky expanse with all kinds of critters running around.

Camping is good here during the warmer months. There are 11 sites that go for $10 a night, first come, first served. From U.S. 395 about 13 miles north of Mammoth Lakes, exit at the June Lake junction and drive southwest about three miles to the lake. (760) 647-3000.

• **Silver Lake** 🐾 🐾 🐾 🐾 🐕 *See* ❹ *on page 210.*

Leashed dogs may wag a tail or two when you catch trout after trout here. This 80-acre lake is stocked with many thousands of rainbows each year. But what really sets dogs off is when you take them for a long hike up the magnificent trail that takes you far, far away from the bait store, the full-service resort, and the boat rental facility that make this lake seem a little less secluded than it is.

The trailhead is near the camping area ($10 per site, dogs must be leashed). Once you start hiking, you and your leash-free dog may never want to return. The trail actually can loop you into Yosemite National Park, so you have to watch how long you tread, because dogs are banned from Yosemite's trails. But an exciting and not too strenuous hike will take you along the Rush Creek drainage, past Gem Lake and Agnew Lake and into the pristine Ansel Adams Wilderness. Bring a big lunch and lots of water, and you'll have a vacation your dog will remember into her old age.

The lake is about halfway on the June Lake Loop, so you can exit U.S. 395 at the north or south end of the loop (Highway 158), depending on the direction you're traveling. The campground, which has about 63 sites, is open from May through September. All sites are first come, first served. (760) 647-3000.

PLACES TO STAY

Gull Lake: See Gull Lake on page 212 for camping information.

Gull Lake Lodge: You're surrounded by forest at this very dog-friendly lodge. Owner Vikki Magee loves dogs and has a great theory about traveling pooches: "No bad dogs make it as far as the car," she says. It's been her experience that dogs who get to vacation with their people must be pretty darned special. And she's right. "Besides," she says, "they don't steal towels."

Rates are $50 to $165, and that includes fish cleaning facilities. The higher-end lodgings are cottages with fireplaces and kitchens. Dogs are $6 extra. The lodge is between June and Gull Lakes. Some rooms have lake views. 132 Leonard Street, June Lake, CA 93529; (760) 648-7516.

June Lake Motel and Cabins: Rates for standard rooms are $46 to $60. Cabins go for $90. Dogs are $5 extra. Besides a sauna and indoor whirlpool, you'll find fish cleaning facilities. The motel is three miles west of U.S. 395 on the south June Lake Loop turnoff. 300 Boulder Avenue, June Lake, CA 93529; (760) 648-7547.

Silver Lake: See Silver Lake on page 212 for camping information.

LEE VINING

PARKS, BEACHES, AND RECREATION AREAS

•**Mono Lake** 🐾 🐾 🐾 1/2 *See* ❺ *on page 210.*

Spending the day at this strange and ancient lake is about the closest you and your dog will come to visiting another planet. You'll want to check your map and make sure you're still on Earth when you see the eerie volcanic formations, the old lake, and the tufa spires that look like giant oozy sand castles.

This 700,000-year-old lake covers 60 square miles, but it's just a shadow of its former self. Since Los Angeles started using the fresh streams that fill Mono Lake, the lake has dropped 40 feet and its salinity has doubled. These days, the lake is nearly three times as salty and 80 times as alkaline as seawater. The salinity increase in this already salty lake seems to be creating some problems for the local environment, and studies on its effects are ongoing. But on the upside, it does make for buoyant swimming.

The alkaline water isn't a new phenomenon. Mark Twain wrote of Mono: "Its sluggish waters are so strong with alkali that if you only dip the most hopelessly soiled garment into them once or twice, and wring it out, it will be found as clean as if it had been through the ablest of washerwoman's hands." You may be tempted to toss your dirty dog in for a little cleansing splash, but the water can be irritating to the eyes.

The land surrounding the lake is run by different agencies. Fortunately, these agencies all have the same rules, which makes it easy to traipse from one part of the lake to the other without getting busted for a dog violation. Dogs are permitted, but they have to be on a leash, even in the Mono Basin National Forest Scenic Area. It's that simple.

Drive on U.S. 395 to the Mono Lake Visitors Center in Lee Vining and pick up some brochures about the geology of this fascinating area. Then look for signs for areas like the Mono Lake Tufa State Reserve (there are areas on either side of the lake and the one on the south side is best) or the Mono Basin National Forest Scenic Area. Drive east until you're either in the middle of a dormant, pumice-covered volcano or standing on the shores of one of the oldest lakes in North America. It's ideal dog territory, with few souls venturing on the longer hikes.

The state reserve charges $2 per person or $5 per vehicle for day use. The national forest is free. Call the reserve at (760) 647-6331, or the national forest at (760) 647-3044.

RESTAURANTS

Lee Vining Market: Eat grocery-store cuisine with your dog at the benches outside this little market. 395 Main Street; (760) 647-6301.

PLACES TO STAY

Aspen Campground: A creek runs through this 56-site county-run campground, and if you're lucky, you can catch your supper of brookies and browns and cook 'em over the campfire. Aspen trees dot the grounds. There's a decent-sized meadow on the side.

Sites are $7 and are available on a first-come, first-served basis. From U.S. 395, take Highway 120 west for 4.7 miles. (760) 647-3044.

Lundy Canyon Campground: This county-run campground is set at 8,000 feet near Lundy Lake, just across the highway from Mono Lake. It's a barren, otherworldly dreamscape. Leashed dogs love it. They also seem to enjoy the county park where the campsites are located. But if you want to take your dog for a long and fascinating hike, just take a quick ride to nearby Mono Lake.

There are 60 sites, all first come, first served. Sites are $5. From U.S. 395 about five miles north of Lee Vining, look for the signs for the campground, which is on the west side of the highway. (760) 647-3044.

Murphey's Motel: Rates are $38 to $103. Dogs are $5 extra. The motel is directly on U.S. 395 in Lee Vining. You can't miss it. 51493 Highway 395, Lee Vining, CA 93541; (760) 647-6316.

MAMMOTH LAKES

PARKS, BEACHES, AND RECREATION AREAS

This charming resort town is a magical ski haven in the winter and an angler's dream in the summer. It's an excellent base for exploring the 200,000 surrounding acres known as Mammoth Lakes Recreational Area.

The lakes in this region are numerous and abound with great fishing and camping opportunities. The mountains and forests are rife with hiking and cross-country skiing areas for you and the pooch of your dreams. You can ski just about anywhere in the national forest, as long as you keep your dog off the groomed cross-country trails. And once you get away from people, you can unleash your obedient dog and bound through nature together.

• **Devil's Postpile National Monument** 🐾🐾🐾½ *See ❻ on page 210.*

Although Devil's Postpile is actually just over the border in Madera County, it is accessible only via its neighbor, Mammoth Lakes. If you're in the area with your dog, take advantage of this great exception to the national park system—dogs are allowed just about everywhere people can go, as long as they're leashed.

And what a place it is. If the devil ever did have a pile of posts, this would be it. The 60-foot wall of columnar basalt "posts" is truly awe-inspiring. Pick up a brochure and find out the fascinating geology behind these geometric (and geologic) wonders.

In addition to the postpile, this 800-acre park is also home to Rainbow Falls, where the Middle Fork of the San Joaquin River drops 101 feet over a cliff of volcanic lava. It's a remarkable sight.

Exit U.S. 395 at Mammoth Junction and drive west along Highway 203/Main Street through the town of Mammoth Lakes. Turn right at Minaret Summit/Minaret Road. Drive about seven miles to the park. There's a small entry fee. The road is impassable in the winter, so the park is closed during snowy months (which can sometimes last into June, so call first). During summer, you and your leashed dog can ride the shuttle bus from town to Devil's Postpile. The cost is $7 round-trip for adults. Dogs go free. Call the U.S. Forest Service at (760) 924-5500 for bus schedules and pickup locations. Phone (760) 934-2289 for Devil's Postpile information.

• **Horseshoe Lake** 🐾🐾🐾🐾 🐕 *See ❼ on page 210.*

Most of the lakes in this part of the eastern Sierra are developed and popular among humankind. But although Horseshoe Lake is just a stick's throw from civilization, it's a refreshing exception. Not only is it breathtaking, it's quiet.

You really can get away from folks here. In summer, it's not as heavily fished as other local lakes, partly because it's not stocked with trout. But if you visit with a dog, chances are you'll have more on your mind than fishing anyway. And that's where this lake is a little piece of dog heaven: While your dog has to be leashed around the lake, he's allowed to romp leashless once he hits the connecting trails.

At the north end of the lake, you'll find a trailhead that leads you through magnificent landscapes, all set around 9,000 feet. The air is so clean you can almost feel yourself getting healthier with each step. Joe thinks it's the cat's pajamas. Eventually, the trail runs into the Pacific Crest Trail, where you can choose to venture off on longer or shorter treks. Consult an Inyo National Forest ranger at (760) 934-2505 for maps and guidance.

To reach the lake, exit U.S. 395 at Mammoth Junction and drive west along Highway 203/Main Street, through the town of Mammoth Lakes. The road curves to the left and becomes Lake Mary Road. Follow it about seven miles. It loops by Lake Mary and eventually ends at Horseshoe Lake. (760) 924-5500.

• **Lake Mary** 🐾 🐾 🐾 🐾 🐕 *See* ❽ *on page 210.*

Dogs have to be leashed around developed and heavily used Lake Mary, but they can trot around leashless when they accompany you on the scenic trail that starts on the east side of the lake.

Lots of folks like to take their dog on an early morning walk on the trail, then turn around and fish for dinner. The trout are planted, and it's hard not to catch one while trolling, or even fishing from shore. Most dogs seem to enjoy watching people fish, even if nothing is being caught. Some people don't even mind just walking around the lake with a leashed dog. There's also a gold mine at the very end of Coldwater Campground, next to the trailhead parking. You'll see the signs.

Other folks come here just for the off-leash hiking. The trail takes you many miles away. If your dog is a water dog, she'll love it. You pass by several quiet little lakes and one big one on the way to the Pacific Crest Trail. Consult an Inyo National Forest ranger at (760) 873-2400 for maps and guidance.

From June to November, about 50 campsites are available here for $11 a night, first come, first served. Dogs must be leashed, but with the great views of the lake they get, they just don't seem to mind.

To reach the lake, exit U.S. 395 at Mammoth Junction and drive west along Highway 203/Main Street, through the town of Mammoth Lakes. The road curves to the left and becomes Lake Mary Road. Follow it about three miles to the lake. (760) 924-5500.

• **Mammoth Mountain** 🐾 🐾 🐾 ½ *See* ❾ *on page 210.*

See Diversions, page 219, for information on the exciting gondola ride you and your dog can take to get to some great hiking trails during the summer months. To get here, exit U.S. 395 at the Mammoth Junction exit and drive west along Highway 203/Main Street, through the town of Mammoth Lakes. Once past town, follow the signs to the mountain. (760) 934-2571.

• **Shady Rest Trail** 🐾 🐾 🐾 *See* ❿ *on page 210.*

This national forest trail is on the edge of the town of Mammoth Lakes, making it as convenient as it is splendid. Unfortunately, since the city officially runs this trail, leashes are the law.

During the summer, you and your pooch can walk or run on the six-mile forested trail that loops around Shady Rest Park (a Mammoth Lakes recreation park, where leashes are also the law).

In winter, it's a stunning place to take your dog on a little cross-country ski trip. Leashes can come in handy here. We've seen some people attach their dog to their belt with a leash while skiing. When there's a little uphill slope, guess who's the engine? Most dogs wouldn't appreciate this and are happier gamboling through the woods than playing mush dog.

From U.S. 395, exit at Mammoth Junction and drive west along Highway 203/Main Street until the U.S. Forest Service Visitors Center, which will be before town on your right. You can stop in here and ask for additional trail information or proceed west on Highway 203 another quarter of a mile to Old Sawmill Road. Turn right and follow the road to Shady Rest Park. You'll see parts of the trail weaving around the park's perimeter and even along the entry road. Call (760) 924-5500 for more information.

RESTAURANTS

Alpenrose: Your dog can be just on the other side of the rail on the Swiss-style patio here when you eat the delicious, homemade continental cuisine served by the Alpenrose's owners, a dog-friendly Swiss-German family. Try the Wiener schnitzel or the apple strudel. Just about everything is homemade. 343 Old Mammoth Road; (760) 934-3077.

Schat's Bakery: This is a great place to grab a coffee and warm pastry before a morning hike. Relax at the outdoor chairs here. 3305 Main Street; (760) 934-6055.

PLACES TO STAY

Austria Hof: This lodging on a mountain has one room where dogs are permitted to stay. Rates are $50 to $105. 924 Canyon Boulevard, Mammoth Lakes, CA 93546; (760) 934-2764.

Convict Lake Resort: Dogs love coming to this terrific resort. Joe Dog thinks it's because they feel so welcome here. Says the owner: "We love all pets, even ostriches and tarantulas." Sorry, Joe Dog, they even take cats.

Pets can stay at 23 rustic cabins (soon to be 35) with full kitchens. (Only a few are open during the winter.) They can go out on the lake in a boat, help fish for supper, watch you ride a horse, or just hike around the wilderness on the other side of the lake. The resort also has a wonderful restaurant, but you'll have to get take-out if you want your dog to partake.

Rates are $64 to $350. Route 1, Box 204, Mammoth Lakes, CA 93546; (760) 934-3800 or (800) 992-2260.

Crystal Crag Lodge: Stay at this charming mountain resort located on the shores of Lake Mary and you can wander around many acres of beautiful land with your leashed dog. But you'd better visit from May to mid-October, because the lodge is closed in the winter.

The rustic wood cabins are attractive and have full kitchens and baths. Most come with living rooms and fireplaces, too. Dogs like all that, but water dogs think it's truly the cat's meow that you can rent a small aluminum boat here and meander around the lake.

Rates are $55 to $205. Dogs are $7 extra. 307 Crystal Crag Drive, Mammoth Lakes, CA 93546; (760) 934-2436.

Econolodge Wildwood Inn: Rates are $49 to $99. The owners love pets, so you won't get one of those "oh, geez, another dog" stares. There's a fish cleaning station here, in case you have the hankering to clean a fish. They've also got a decent little continental breakfast. Traveling west on Highway 203, you'll find the inn three blocks into the main part of town. 3626 Main Street, Mammoth Lakes, CA 93546; (760) 934-6855.

Lake Mary: See Lake Mary on page 216 for camping information.

Motel 6: Rates are $40 to $50. This one looks more like a giant ski lodge than a roadside motel. One small dog per room is the rule here. 3372 Main Street, Mammoth Lakes, CA 93546; (760) 934-6660.

North Village Inn: Dogs enjoy staying at the cabins here, mostly because of the 10 acres they're set on. Pooches are permitted to stroll the attractive property on leash. Some cabins have kitchens. Joe says pass the bacon.

The cabins are open to dogs only in the non-ski season. Rates are $59 to $205. 103 Lake Mary Road, Mammoth Lakes, CA 93546; (760) 934-2525.

Old Shady Rest Campground: Believe it or not, you're pretty much in town when you camp here, though you'd never know it by the scenery. You're in the woods, without a trace of civilization. Dogs are permitted on leash. There are 52 sites. Fees are $10, first come, first served.

Sites are open year-round. From U.S. 395, drive west on Highway 203 for three miles to the Mammoth Visitor Center. Turn right and follow the signs to the campground. (760) 924-5500.

Royal Pines Resort: Rates are $60 to $89. Dogs are $5 extra, and they're allowed only in the housekeeping units. That's fine with all the dogs we know, because these units come complete with kitchenettes. And we all know what kitchenettes mean to dogs.

The resort is on Viewpoint Road, about one-half mile into town as you're traveling west on Highway 203. 3814 Viewpoint Road, Mammoth Lakes, CA 93546; (760) 934-2306.

Shilo Inn: Don't worry about your large dog being allowed to stay here—the manager prefers big dogs! All the rooms are mini-suites, and they're air-conditioned, which is a rare feature up here. It won't come in handy in the winter, but it can be a real blessing in August.

The dog-friendly owners ask to know ahead of time if you'll be bringing a dog so they can plan a room strategy (perhaps to avoid having a cat as your next-door neighbor). They also work with a nearby veterinarian who boards pets for people who will be skiing during the day and don't know what to do with the pooch. They'll be happy to give you the info you need.

Rates are $89 to $150. Dogs are $7 extra. The motel is a half block east of Old Mammoth Road, on Highway 203. 2963 Main Street, Mammoth Lakes, CA 93546; (760) 934-4500.

Sierra Nevada Rodeway Inn: Some rooms here have fireplaces and kitchens, for that home-away-from-home feeling. Most are just basic rooms. Joe Dog wants to thank his friend and neighbor Reggie Dog for the tip about this place. Rates are $54 to $129. 164 Old Mammoth Road, Mammoth Lakes, CA 93546; (760) 934-2515.

Thrift Lodge: This lodge operates two different properties where five housekeeping cabins, four apartments, and one regular motel room have been designated for dogs and their people. All are within a minute of the lodge's front desk, and all but the motel room have full kitchens. The place is so doggone dog-friendly that they even have designated dog-walking areas around the grounds. And the price is right: Rates are $59 to $95. Pooches require a $50 deposit. 6209 Minaret Road, Mammoth Lakes, CA 93546; (760) 934-2416.

Zwart House: The manager here is very wise. "Most dogs that travel are better behaved than children," she says. Rates at these homey one- and two-bedroom units are $36 to $100. Dogs are $5 extra. 76 Lupine Street, Mammoth Lakes, CA 93546; (760) 934-2217.

DIVERSIONS

Up, up, and away: If your dog gets white knuckles just looking out of your second-story window, it might be wise to forget about this lofty adventure. But if the idea of dangling 11,000 feet above sea level doesn't make you or your pooch break out in a sweat, you're bound to have an exciting time aboard the Mammoth Mountain Ski Area gondolas.

Actually, during your ascent from 9,000 feet to 11,000 feet, you'll glide only a few dozen feet above the ground. The spectacular views of the rugged surroundings just make it seem as though you're higher. While the ascent is a stimulating experience, it lasts only about 10 minutes. Your dog is almost certain to appreciate the descent more—you get to hike down the mountainside together, him on one end of the leash, you on the other. It can take several hours, if you're not in a rush.

We like to hike in early summer, when new life is abloom in this otherwise fairly barren land. As long as there's no skiing on the slopes, you can bring your dog. Some people even tote their dogs up during ski season and ski down the back of the mountain, but the practice can be dangerous and is highly discouraged by the people who run this place. Besides, it's tough to have a leashed dog while you're whooshing downhill.

Many dogs love every part of this adventure except for the grated stairs that lead to the gondolas. There's something about looking down and seeing nothing except air that makes even the bravest beast feel like he's on the bad end of a Road Runner cartoon. Fortunately for dogs and people of the vertigo-prone persuasion, there's an elevator.

The fee for adults is $10. Children are $5, and kids under six years go for free. Dogs of all ages go for free, too. To get here, exit U.S. 395 at the Mammoth Junction exit and drive west along Highway 203/Main Street, through the town of Mammoth Lakes. Once past town, follow the signs to the mountain. Call (760) 934-2571 or (888) 4-MAMMOTH for schedules and more information.

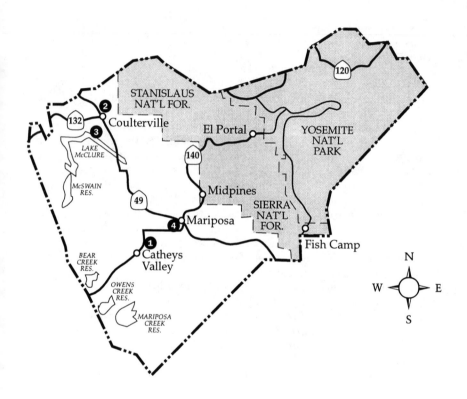

STANISLAUS
NAT'L FOR.

120

2

132

Coulterville

3

El Portal

YOSEMITE
NAT'L
PARK

LAKE
McCLURE

140

McSWAIN
RES.

Midpines

49

SIERRA
NAT'L
FOR.

4

Mariposa

Fish Camp

1

Catheys
Valley

BEAR
CREEK
RES.

OWENS
CREEK
RES.

MARIPOSA
CREEK
RES.

N

W   E

S

26
MARIPOSA COUNTY

It's bad enough that dogs don't have many places to hoof it or hang out in Yosemite National Park. (For a truly heavenly exception to this rule, see the Redwoods Guest Cottages, on page 223.) But to have to endure the attitude of a couple of administrators with this county parks system is enough to make a grown dog growl.

"Yep," said a razor-voiced woman on the other end of the phone. "We allow leashed dogs. But we don't like 'em." A voice in the background started cackling with sadistic laughter. "You tell her!" her cohort chortled.

"Nope, we don't like them at all." Click.

Don't pay any attention to those people, dogs. You've got the law on your side. It's a leash law, but just the same, it's the law. Exercise your right to exercise your legs. Don't let the snarling civil servants get you down.

NATIONAL FORESTS

See the National Forests and Wilderness Areas chapter starting on page 748 for important information and safety tips on visiting national forests with your dog. The following two national forests make up for Yosemite National Park's lack of canine hospitality.

• **Sierra National Forest** 🐾🐾🐾🐾 🐕
  See page 754.
• **Stanislaus National Forest** 🐾🐾🐾🐾 🐕
  See page 755.

NATIONAL PARKS

• Yosemite National Park 🐾 1/2

Ask just about anyone who's ever visited this park about what they've seen, and they'll gush about the impossibly beautiful geography, the dramatic waterfalls, the magnificent trails, the sheer cliffs, the pristine wildlife, and every other detail they can dredge up. It's not hyperbole. This fantastic park is bigger than the imagination, bigger than life. It inspires even the most reticent parkgoer to sing its praises.

Then ask the same question of people who've visited with dogs. They'll be able to tell you all about the lovely car campsites here. They can even expound on the glories of the commercialization of Yosemite Village, the clever way the parking lots are set up, and how toasty the pavement gets at 2 P.M. in August. If they're just back from vacation, their faces will show just what kind of adventure they had. It's pretty much the same disgusted, disheartened scowl their dog is wearing.

Dogs are not allowed on any trails, in meadows, or in the backcountry of Yosemite. About all they can do is camp at certain campgrounds and putter around Yosemite Village and the valley's paved paths as the two of you while away the hours until your human friends get back from a breathtaking hike. Actually, since this book's last edition, we've discovered that there are more of these paved paths in the valley than we knew of, so we've upgraded Yosemite's rating from its previous "fire hydrant" status. Dogs can also stay at the park's kennel from late May to mid-October. (They were closed for the 1997–98 season because of flood damage to the valley stables, since the kennel is open only when the stables are open. A reopening date hasn't been established.) We're not talking luxury suites here. We're talking your basic cagelike contraptions that make you feel incredibly guilty for leaving the little guy behind.

Some folks think they can get away with leaving their dog tied up to their campsite for a few hours while they go exploring. But remember, if the ranger doesn't catch up with you, there's always the chance that a mountain lion or other cunning critter might catch up with your tethered dog. "We call one of these camping areas Coyote Point," a park employee told me. "You'd be a fool to leave your dog behind even for a little bit."

One clever reader wrote to us and told us how she and her husband get away with taking their smallish dogs through Yosemite. They tote them along on little doggy trailers attached to their bikes. Sometimes they strap a dog carrier to their chests and away they go. It probably isn't legal, so I won't use their names. But their truck's license plate is so wonderfully appropriate to the theme of this book that I can't help but mention it: CAB4K9S. And it sure be. But not necessarily in Yosemite.

Unless you're as creative as these folks, Joe and I each give a thumbs-down to the idea of bringing your dog on a Yosemite vacation. That is, unless you spend your vacation at the beautiful Redwoods Guest Cottages, described on page 223.

But if you insist on roughing it, here are the campgrounds that permit pooches: In the valley, there's the Upper Pines Campground. Along Highway 120, you can stay at Hodgdon Meadow Campground, Crane Flat Campground (section A), White Wolf Campground (section C), Yosemite Creek Campground (front section), and the west end of the Tuolumne Meadows Campground. Along Glacier Point Road and Highway 41, you can stay at the Bridalveil Creek Campground (section A) and the Wawona Campground.

The kennel costs $8 per day, and space is limited. Dogs are required to have all their shots, and to be more than 10 pounds. (Sorry, teacup poodles!) Dogs are not boarded overnight.

The campsites cost $3 to $15. Some are first come, first served; others are by reservation only. Call (800) 436-7275 for reservation information, or (209) 372-0200 for park information.

PLACES TO STAY

The Redwoods Guest Cottages: This group of lovely, privately owned mountain homes is by far the best thing that's ever happened to dogs in Yosemite. The Redwoods is nestled in the forest at 4,000 feet, where the air is so clean you can smell it. The homes range in size from cozy one-bedroom cottages to big five-bedroom spreads. They're all different, but they're attractive and wooden, and most have decks and fireplaces.

General manager Joyce Koller is a very dog-friendly person. She's trying to get as many homes as possible to open their doors to dogs. So far, 15 of the Redwoods' 125 homes say yes. Some are really magical, with wide picture windows and huge stone fireplaces. Koller has an adorable Border collie, Jake, who loves life in Yosemite. She sent us a picture of him snuggled with his two panda dolls. It was hard to tell where the pandas began and the dog ended. He's a lucky dog indeed to live here.

Dogs who stay here get to peruse the surrounding area on leash. They can sniff at trees and cruise by streams. This is much more than they can do in the rest of the park. There's even a little market, the Pine Tree, where dogs can often be seen waiting for their people to finish shopping.

Homes rent for a minimum of two to three days. Rates are $82 to $414 a night. P.O. Box 2085, Wawona, Yosemite National Park, CA 95389; (209) 375-6666.

Yosemite National Park: See Yosemite National Park on page 222 for camping information.

CATHEYS VALLEY

PARKS, BEACHES, AND RECREATION AREAS

•**Catheys Valley County Park** 🐾 🐾 🐾 *See ❶ on page 220.*
Dogs like to gambol around the fenced-in ball field at this park. It's adjacent to some big, open cattle land, which makes a dog feel at home on the range. A few dogs have jumped over the fence in pursuit of a steak dinner, so make sure you hang on tight to that leash. If it's warm, other parts of this park have plenty of trees to shade you and your pal. We like to stop here for a picnic while traveling on Highway 140. It's on the south side of the highway at 2820 Highway 140. There's no cross street. (209) 966-2498.

COULTERVILLE

Dogs, listen up. Without your kind, this tiny Old West town may never have even made it onto the map. Here's why. Back in 1850, a certain George Coulter started a tent store here to keep roofs over the heads of the local gold miners. This fellow also built the first hotel, which helped attract a more civilized sort. But the place needed water. So Coulter convinced a couple of Newfoundland dogs to pump water from the well. The hotel is now home to the Northern Mariposa History Center. You'll have to stop in for a visit to learn the rest of this shaggy-dog tale.

PARKS, BEACHES, AND RECREATION AREAS

• **Coulterville County Park** 🐾 🐾 1/2 *See* ➋ *on page 220.*

This isn't a big park, but it's fenced on three sides, which is convenient if your dog's leash slips from your grip. Dogs like rolling in the grass and cooling off under the picnic tables. The park is conveniently located just off Highway 49, in the center of "town." Just pull off the highway and park, or take Highway 49 to Main Street, head east, and make an immediate left onto Park Lane. (209) 966-2498.

• **Lake McClure** 🐾 🐾 1/2 *See* ➌ *on page 220.*

With 7,100 surface acres of water, this beautiful lake is a water dog's dream. But it's not bad for landlubbers either. The lake is surrounded by the kind of perfect green land you only see around model-train sets and in picture puzzles your old aunt used to give you.

The lake has several recreation areas with decent places to walk a leashed dog and even better campsites. The 110 sites at the Horseshoe Bend Recreation Area at the northeast corner of the lake are filled with trees and provide plenty of privacy. During the off-season, you might even have the place to yourselves. The ranger here recommends walking your dog by the hang glider area when no one else is around. It's far from cars and has ample acreage.

The Bagby Recreation Area, on the Merced River section of the lake, has a pretty good trail along the river, across from the camping spots. The 25 campsites get more secluded the farther you drive down the winding road.

The day-use fee for the recreation areas is $5 per car. Campsites are $12 to $16. Reservations are required. Dogs are $2 extra, day or night. To get to the Horseshoe Bend Recreation Area from Highway 49 just south of Coulterville, go west on Highway 132 for about three miles. The entrance will be on your left. Call (800) 468-8889 for reservations. Call (209) 378-2521 for a brochure or directions to other parts of the lake.

PLACES TO STAY

Lake McClure: See Lake McClure above for camping information.

FISH CAMP

PLACES TO STAY

Tenaya Lodge at Yosemite: So what if Yosemite National Park, located just down the road (see page 222), is a dog's idea of a bad joke? This comfortable, large hotel will let them have the last laugh.

The four-diamond, four-paw Tenaya Lodge is spacious and luxurious, but do dogs care that their room comes with an honor bar? Not when they've got 1.3 million acres of Sierra National Forest awaiting them outside their door, with endless miles of trails through land some consider even more attractive than Yosemite. One great hike is about five miles round-trip and takes you and your pooch to a 20-foot waterfall. It's not Yosemite Falls, but it's not chopped liver either.

Cross-country ski lessons are offered when there's snow. The hotel also offers humans complimentary snowshoe hiking lessons. Tenaya even has indoor-outdoor pools and a fully equipped gym, complete with steam room and sauna. There's a $50 pooch fee per stay. Rooms are $69 to $239. 1122 Highway 41, Fish Camp, CA 93623; (209) 683-6555.

DIVERSIONS

Take a sentimental journey: If you're hankering to ride the old Logger Steam Train through some of Sierra National Forest's most magnificent scenery, you don't have to worry about waving good-bye to your dog. Leashed, calm dogs who can fit on your lap are welcome aboard the quaint old trains of the Sugar Pine Railroad.

We discovered on an earlier locomotive trip that Joe is not especially keen on the sound of a train's powerful blasts of steam. He cringes, tail down, until someone picks up his 70-pound body and holds him in a lap. He looks embarrassed afterward, but appears to have no regrets. At least he'd adhere to the lap rule here, if he ever decides to brave trains again.

If your dog is shy of loud noises, get as far back from the engine as possible, or simply take the railroad's "Model A"-powered trip. It's quieter, shorter (30 minutes as opposed to 45 minutes), and cheaper ($6.75 per adult, not $10.50) than the Logger train. But if your dog does accompany you on the "Model A," he's got to be on your lap. That could hurt with a mastiff.

The train station is located at 56001 Highway 41. It's about 12 miles past Oakhurst, two miles before the town of Fish Camp. And there's a terrific fringe benefit: It's right next to a couple of trailheads into dog-friendly Sierra National Forest. (209) 683-7273.

MARIPOSA

If you're on your way to Yosemite with your dog (not the kindest act in the world—see page 222), take time to stop at this historic town. It's the county seat, but it looks nothing like most governmental centers we've seen. It's full of historic Gold Rush buildings and antique shops. The restaurants aren't bad either.

PARKS, BEACHES, AND RECREATION AREAS

• **Mariposa County Park** 😺 😺 😺 *See* ❹ *on page 220.*

This tiered park is kind of like a wedding cake, with something delectable on every layer. Your dog will want to sink her teeth into it.

The top of the park is green and grassy, with picnic tables, a small playground, and excellent views of the town of Mariposa. A dirt road leads you to the lower levels, which have plenty of shade, picnic tables, and a decent walking path. Dogs must be leashed.

From Highway 49/140 going south, turn right on Sixth Street. In one block, jog right on Strong Street and make a quick left onto County Parks Road. (209) 966-2498.

RESTAURANTS

Frost Shop: Your dog may find canine company at the outdoor tables—plenty of dogs bring their people here for a bite of burger. In fact, photos of dog customers eating ice cream grace part of a wall. "Some of our best customers are dogs," says June Johnson, the owner. Dogs are treated to bowls of fresh water. 5087 Highway 140; (209) 966-5557.

PLACES TO STAY

The Guest House Inn: Rent this place and you're renting the entire three-bedroom house. The rate is $98, plus a pooch deposit. Or you can have the place for the week for $495. Such a deal for such a dog-friendly place! It's at 4962 Triangle Road, and the mailing address is P.O. Box 1848, Mariposa, CA 95338; (209) 742-6869.

Motherlode Lodge: Rates are $39 to $92. The physical address is 5051 Highway 140, and the mailing address is P.O. Box 986, Mariposa, CA 95338; (209) 966-2521 or (800) 398-9770.

MIDPINES

PLACES TO STAY

The Homestead Guest Ranch: When you stay here, the house is all yours. It comes with a fireplace, a barbecue, and a well-stocked kitchen. Rates are $95 per couple plus $35 for each additional person. This is a wonderful place to stay, and the owners are sweet, dog-loving folks. The ranch is on 13 acres of land located about a half mile off Highway 140. The mailing address is P.O. Box 113, Midpines, CA 95345; (209) 966-2820.

BAY AREA/DELTA COUNTIES

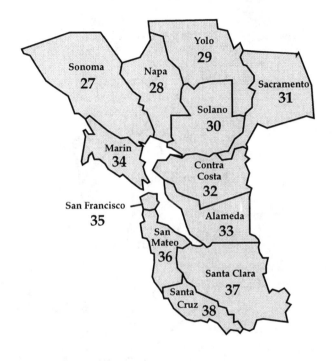

LAKE
SONOMA

32 Sea Ranch

3 Cloverdale

36 Timber Cove

37

128

1

Healdsburg

6 Windsor
Guerneville

101

8 Jenner

7

116

Occidental

Sebastopol

24-31

Santa
Rosa

12

Bodega Bay

1

Freestone

33

2

116

Rohnert
Park

4 **5** Glen Ellen

23

Cotati

9-22

Sonoma

34-35

Petaluma

116

12

121

N

37

W ✦ E

S

27
SONOMA COUNTY

The horticulturist Luther Burbank, who made his home in Santa Rosa and Sebastopol from 1875 to 1926, called Sonoma County "the chosen spot of all the Earth as far as nature is concerned." Practically anything will grow in Sonoma County. It's the Bay Area capital for trees, flowers, and vegetables, as well as goats, sheep, cattle, chickens, pigs, and probably a few farm animals that are just now being invented.

Unfortunately, dogs and farm animals don't mix. Some Sonoma sheep ranchers have been known to impose the ultimate penalty on loose dogs that they see near their livestock: They shoot them. They're not acting under the law of the Wild West, either. It's a county ordinance that dogs harassing livestock in unincorporated areas or on private property may be shot by the property owner.

But fear not. Sonoma County has many enchanting places where the only shot your dog will experience is a shot of adrenaline when he lays eyes on the stunning scenery and some mesmerizing, dog-friendly hangouts. Since the last edition of this book, the number of off-leash doggy areas in Sonoma County has gone up to 20. Oh joy, oh joy! The new leashless wonders are thanks to the towns of Petaluma, Santa Rosa, and Windsor. Most of these parks have very limited off-leash hours, but dogs are thrilled anyway. It's hard to find a Sonoma County dog whose tail isn't wagging a little faster these days.

BODEGA BAY

PARKS, BEACHES, AND RECREATION AREAS

• **Doran Beach Regional Park** 🐾🐾🐾 *See* ❶ *on page 228.*

This Sonoma County regional park offers leashed dogs access to marshland full of egrets, herons, and deer, as well as to the Pinnacle Gulch Trail. The plain but serviceable beach has almost no surf (which is great for dog swims), and there are picnic tables near the beach.

The fee for day use is $3. (It may soon increase.) Campsites are $14 ($12 for Sonoma County residents), plus $1 for each dog. The campground, which has 134 sites, is on a first-come, first-served basis. The park is on Highway 1, one mile south of Bodega Bay. (707) 875-3540.

• **Westside Regional Park** 🐾🐾 *See* ❷ *on page 228.*

This is an undistinguished but handy park and campground built on landfill right on the water, with picnic tables and barbecues. Spud Point Marina, just to the north, also allows leashed dogs.

The fee for day use is $3. (It may soon increase.) There are 47 campsites, costing $14 ($12 for Sonoma County residents), plus $1 for each dog. It's first come, first served. The park is on Westshore Road, a westward turn off Highway 1 in town. Call (707) 875-3540 for reservations or (707) 527-2041 for park info.

RESTAURANTS

The Boat House: This restaurant in downtown Bodega Bay will allow you to sit with your dog as you eat fish-and-chips, oysters, and calamari at one of the six unshaded tables on their patio. If fish isn't your dog's wish, he can order a burger. 1445 Highway 1; (707) 875-3495.

The Dog House: The name of the restaurant says it all. But if you need more, here are the words of one of the servers: "Dogs are treated better than people here." The Dog House is indeed a very dog-friendly place to dine. The food is unpretentious (hot dogs, burgers, etc.), and the servers love seeing a dog come to the eight outdoor tables. They often offer a bowl of water (and sometimes a snicky snack) before the pooch even gets a chance to peruse the menu. Joe gives it four paws for attitude. 537 Highway 1; (707) 875-2441.

Lucas Wharf: Your dog's nose will flair and drip with excitement as you dine at the outdoor tables here. That's partly because of the tasty seafood specials, but it's mostly because your dog will be getting high on sea smells at this place right on the water. Speaking of water, the folks here love dogs and will provide your pooch with water, should she need to wet her whistle. 595 Highway 1; (707) 875-3522.

PLACES TO STAY

Bodega Bay RV Park: If you have an RV and want to stay in this wonderful area, park 'er here. The managers will point you to some nearby property where you can run your good dog without a leash. Rates are $17 to $25. 2000 Highway 1, Bodega Bay, CA 94923; (707) 875-3701.

Bodega Coast Inn: Rates at this attractive former Holiday Inn are $99 to $298. Dogs are $15 extra. 521 Coast Highway/Highway 1, Bodega Bay, CA 94923; (707) 875-2217.

Doran Beach Regional Park: See Doran Beach Regional Park on page 230 for camping information.

Westside Regional Park: See Westside Regional Park on page 230 for camping information.

CLOVERDALE

PARKS, BEACHES, AND RECREATION AREAS

• **Lake Sonoma Recreation Area** 😺😺😺 *See* ❸ *on page 228.*

This is the only recreation site in the nine counties of the Bay Area run by the U.S. Army Corps of Engineers, and it's too bad. The Corps has a liberal attitude toward dogs, and this park is beautifully developed and managed, not to mention clean. It's also free. You must keep your dog on a six-foot leash, and he's not allowed on the swimming beach at the north end, but rangers told us there's no rule against dogs swimming anywhere else.

If you're the type who doesn't clean up after your dog, here's a warning: Change your act, or stay far from here. Rangers have been known to charge a cleanup fee for owners who ignore the deposits of their dogs.

A large lawn with picnic tables, some shaded, is located at the visitors center. You can rent a boat from the private concession on the lake, which allows leashed dogs on all boats. Follow signs from the visitors center. To reserve a boat, call (707) 433-2200. Waterskiing and camping are also popular here.

For a good dog hike, pick up a map at the visitors center and drive west on Dry Creek Road to the trailheads, which have their own parking lots. There are 40 miles of trails. Here are two of our favorites: There's a bit of shade at the Digger Pine Flat Trailhead. This smooth foot trail goes down to the lake through an unusual forest of digger pines, madrone, manzanita, and blooming desert brush. The buzz of motorboats on the lake blends with the hammering of woodpeckers. You get a good view of the lake fairly quickly. If you'd prefer less of a climb back to the trailhead, take the Little Flat Trail, which starts lower down.

Horses are allowed on these trails, but bikes aren't—a plus for your dog's safety. Unfortunately, it gets bone-dry here in summer, and poison oak is common.

Developed, primitive, and boat-in campsites are available. Liberty Glen Campground has 113 individual campsites. Sites are $8 to $14. To use the primitive sites (no water, but no fee either), you must get a permit from the visitors center. There are 15 secluded sites reachable only by boat. They're $4 to $8. All these sites are first come, first served. Dogs must be leashed or "restrained" in the campgrounds, which in this case means you can put them on a generous rope tether. The idea is to keep them from invading other campsites.

Take U.S. 101 to the Canyon Road exit. Go west to Dry Creek Road and turn right into the entrance. Take a right at the only fork. (707) 433-9483.

PLACES TO STAY

Lake Sonoma Recreation Area: See the Lake Sonoma Recreation Area on page 231 for camping information.

COTATI

Soon there may be a fenced dog park in this quaint town. At press time, it was under consideration by the city council. We think it's a grand idea. Call the city manager's office at (707) 792-4600 for updates.

RESTAURANTS

Johnny's Java: This coffeehouse is home to tasty baked goods. It's a convenient place to stop if you're on your way to or from Camp K-9 (see below). Dine with doggy at the four umbrella-topped tables on the patio. 8492 Gravenstein Highway; (707) 794-0168.

DIVERSIONS

Check out a canine country club: The smell of cow manure from nearby pastures is the first clue that your dog's going to dig Camp K-9. Then there are the chewed-up sneakers, the tipped-over fire hydrant, and the two chunky ducks who waddle by the dogs provocatively—on the other side of the fence.

This day camp for dogs is not exactly Club Med, and that's precisely why dogs enjoy their time here. The camp is set on two acres, with dogs spending most of the time in one of three fenced areas. Dogs can cavort around leashless, try their paws at a somewhat dilapidated agility course, or just spend the day dozing and watching fellow dogs.

Owner Randy Ashton says that while commuters are the biggest users of Camp K-9, people traveling to the nearby wine country find it a mighty pleasant and convenient place to drop off the pooch before hitting the wineries.

The camp is open from 7 A.M. to 7 P.M. Monday through Saturday. You're welcome to stay with your dog and hang out in the largest of the enclosures, or leave him for the day. It's $12 for a full day, $7 for a half day, or $3 an hour.

The address is 6915 Gravenstein Highway (Highway 116). From U.S. 101, take the Highway 116 West exit and travel west for about a mile. The camp will be on your right. (707) 795-5995.

DILLON BEACH

PLACES TO STAY

Lawson's Landing and Resort: When you camp here, you camp in a grassy meadow along the sand dunes. There are no set campsites, just the open meadow. That's great, because sometimes you can have the whole place to yourself. Other times you have to share the meadow with lots of other outdoorsy sorts of folks. Camping is $5 if you arrive before 8 P.M., $13 if you arrive after. Weekly rates are available. Please see Diversions, below, for a truly wonderful experience you and your dog can share while you're in the area. Lawson's Landing is easy to find once you're in Dillon Beach. The address is 137 Marine View Drive, P.O. Box 67, Dillon Beach, CA 94929; (707) 878-2443.

DIVERSIONS

Take a barge to a bivalve: This is one of the very coolest things a dog can do in California, especially if he digs boats and digs clams. You start at Lawson's Landing and Resort in Dillon Beach, where you can buy clamming devices like clam tubes or clam guns, if the ol' shovel and bucket method doesn't appeal to you. Then you and the pooch of your dreams board a barge for a ride out to a place they call Clam Island. During high tides the island disappears, so it's really more of a bar. The ride is great fun for dogs who like to sniff the briny breeze, but the highlight for many dogs is when you disembark on the mudflats of Clam Island. The smells send many a dog into the throes of ecstasy.

Clamming isn't as easy as it may sound. Take whatever help you can get from your dog. Some dogs bark at the small round holes that signify a clam could lurk below. Some even stomp their feet until they get a squirt of water, which definitely means a clam is in residence below. Some, like Joe, enjoy digging for clams, but that's really a no-no where the Department of Fish and Game is concerned. Regulations, regulations. That's okay with me, though, because the thought of eating clams makes me clammy all over. I just go along for the ride.

The best time to go clamming is during very low tides, especially in winter and spring. And that's convenient, because the barge runs only from February to June. You have to take your own boat over to Clam Island other times of year. Folks over 16 need a California fishing license. The fee for the Clam Ride (as it's known here) is $5 for adults, $4 for kids. Dogs go for free, but must be leashed. Lawson's Landing is easy to find once you're in Dillon Beach. The address is 137 Marine View Drive, P.O. Box 67, Dillon Beach, CA 94929; (707) 878-2443.

GLEN ELLEN

PARKS, BEACHES, AND RECREATION AREAS

•**Jack London State Historic Park** 🐾🐾🐾 *See* ➍ *on page 228.*

The extensive backcountry trails here are off-limits to dogs, but the parts of historic interest are not. You're free to take your dog (leashed) the half mile to Wolf House, visiting Jack London's grave en route, and around the stone house containing the museum of Londoniana (open 10 A.M. to 5 P.M., no pets inside). The trail is paved and smooth up to the museum, but then becomes dirt and narrow.

Oaks, pines, laurels, and madrones cast dappled light, and the ups and downs are gentle. Signs warn against poison oak and rattlesnakes. The ruins of the huge stone lodge that was London's dream Wolf House are impressive and sad. A fire of unknown origin destroyed it in 1913. London planned to rebuild it, but he died three years later.

Dogs are also allowed in the picnic areas by the parking lot and the museum. From Highway 12, follow signs to the park. Turn west on Arnold Drive, then west again on London Ranch Road. The fee is $6 for day use, $1 for dogs. (707) 938-5216.

•**Sonoma Valley Regional Park** 🐾🐾🐾 *See* ❺ *on page 228.*

This large, welcoming park has a paved, level trail that winds alongside a branch of Sonoma Creek. Better yet for dogs who like to roll, it sports many dirt trails that head off into the oak woodlands above. Varied grasses and wildflowers, madrones, and moss-hung oaks make this a scenic walk. Dogs like to chew some of the grasses, roll on the wildflowers (don't let them do this!), and do leg lifts on the madrones and oaks. They may enjoy it even more than you. If you start at the park entrance off Highway 12 and walk westward across the park to Glen Ellen for about a mile, you'll end up at Sonoma Creek and the old mill, with its huge working waterwheel.

There's some potentially terrific news for the future. The park is considering plans for a leash-free dog park! Private funding is needed to make this a reality. If you've got a few thousand clams burning a hole in your pocket, please give them a call.

The park is just south of Glen Ellen between Arnold Drive and Highway 12. The entrance is off Highway 12. The parking fee is $2. (707) 539-8092.

RESTAURANTS

Jack's Village Cafe: With gourmet/country dishes like local quail with chanterelles or wild mushroom risotto, a meal at Jack's is an exquisite dining experience for anyone. (Joe Dog thinks this sounds as if it were written by a chamber of commerce flunky. . . . He'd prefer to say the food here is snout lickin' good.) But dogs who get to come here feel especially lucky. Not only is the food drool-worthy, but so is the view from the restaurant's large patio. It's surrounded by fruit trees, an herb garden, and flowers, and it overlooks a creek. Joe thinks there's nothing as heavenly as coming here for breakfast on a cool autumn morning and ordering hot oatmeal or country-style French toast—making sure, of course, that you pass a little down to your friend who's giving you "the eye" from under the table.

The restaurant is at Jack London Village, at 14301 Arnold Drive, #23; (707) 939-6111.

PLACES TO STAY

The Big Dog Inn: The logo here is a giant Saint Bernard holding a glass of wine in one hand and resting his elbow on a wine barrel. It's as cute as the inn, and just as dog-friendly. The inn consists of a suite in the main house (where the owners live) and a guest cottage. Dogs are welcome in the cottage. It's an enchanting place, with a cathedral ceiling, country furnishings, a sitting room, a wood-burning stove, air-conditioning, a bath, and an efficiency kitchen.

When you arrive, you'll be greeted with a bottle of local wine, a basket of fresh fruit, and a cheese platter. Your stay also includes a tasty breakfast in the dining room. You and your leashed pooch are free to peruse the inn's six acres. The views of the surrounding Sonoma Valley are quite breathtaking in places. Humans can relax in the inn's swimming pool and spa, but dogs have to stay high and dry. (Never a problem for Joe "I Loathe Water" Dog.)

Dogs really dig it here, but not necessarily because of any of the inn's lovely accoutrements. They seem to know that the owners, Penny and Doug Mahon, are avid dog people. "We love dogs as guests. They're our favorites," says Penny. The Mahons have been breeding and showing the inn's namesakes, Saint Bernards, for more than 30 years. You'll likely find a few Big Dogs around during your visit, as well as one little dog, the resident Jack Russell terrier. He runs the place, of course.

There's one caveat to dogs being allowed here. When the Mahons have a new litter of pups, they have to be careful about pooch visitors. When you call for a brochure or to make a reservation, they'll let you know about the puppy situation. 15244 Arnold Drive, Glen Ellen, CA 95442; (707) 996-4319.

GUERNEVILLE

This wonderful resort community on the Russian River took an economic and aesthetic plunge with the recent floods, but it's recovered so well that it looks better than ever these days.

PARKS, BEACHES, AND RECREATION AREAS

• **Armstrong Redwoods State Reserve** 🐾🐾 *See* ❻ *on page 228.*

As is usual in state parks, you can take a dog only on paved roads and into picnic areas. But here you can give your dog and yourself an exceptional treat. The picnic grounds are a cool, hushed redwood cathedral. You can walk on Armstrong Woods Road, which winds along Fife Creek (usually lush, but dry in the heart of summer) all the way to the top of McCray Mountain, about three miles.

The drive is fairly terrifying, so you may prefer to walk anyway. Hikers, bicycles, and autos all share the road, so be very careful. Your dog must be leashed everywhere in the park. From Guerneville, go about 2.5 miles north on Armstrong Woods Road. The day-use fee is $5. Dogs are $1. (707) 869-2015 or (707) 865-2391.

• **Vacation Beach** 🐾🐾🐾🐾 🐕 *See* ❼ *on page 228.*

Vacation Beach is not really a beach, but an access point where the Russian River is dammed by two roads across it. It's one of several public spots where you and your dog can legally jump into the drink. Here, people picnic, swim, put in canoes, and let their dogs cool their paws. It's free and there are no posted leash rules, but watch out for cars going over the dam roads. No overnight camping is allowed.

From Highway 116 between Guerneville and Monte Rio, turn south at the unmarked road where you see Old Cazadero Road veering north. You can park at the approaches to the dams but not on the crossing itself. (707) 869-9000.

RESTAURANTS

Sweet's River Grill: You have to tie your dog to the other side of the gate bordering the patio, but it's not a problem. Your pooch can still sit right beside you and beg just as effectively. Dine on grilled seafood, steak, chops, you name it. 16251 Main Street; (707) 869-3383.

PLACES TO STAY

Creekside Inn & Resort: Dogs get to stay at two of several cottages and rooms at this fun inn near the Russian River. Bird dogs enjoy lounging in the Quail Cottage, a small, bright cottage with a fireplace. The Deck House, the other poochy haven, is a little larger, with a sunny deck.

The inn is dotted with several large redwoods. The property spans three acres, and dogs are welcome to cruise around on leash. Human guests may hang out in the inn's main dining room and lounge, both of which have fireplaces. Humans can also swim in the pool here. Dogs have to be content to do the dog paddle in the Russian River, not too far away.

Rates are $70 to $80. 16180 Neeley Road, P.O. Box 2185, Guerneville, CA 95446; (707) 869-3623 or (800) 776-6586.

Highlands Resort: If your dog has never been to a bar, ask to stay in the Highland's studio: The large room not only has a cozy fireplace and love seat, but it has its own wet bar. Joe says, "Make mine a mimosa." Teetotaling dogs might prefer the five larger cabins that allow dogs. The cabins have fireplaces, and some have kitchenettes, but no bar.

The Highlands is set on three wooded acres (which dogs can explore on leash), and has the feel of a country retreat. There's a swimming pool and outdoor hot tub—both clothing-optional. In the resort's brochure there's a bird's-eye-view picture of a fellow standing in the hot tub, with just a bit of bun showing. Joe blushed and came back for another look. The owner asked us to mention that people with diverse lifestyles feel right at home here.

Rates are $75 to $125. Dogs are $25 extra for the length of their stay. 14000 Woodland Drive, Guerneville, CA 95446; (707) 869-0333.

River's Retreat: Dogs are so happy when they stay at this little vacation rental just a block from the Russian River that they may refuse to leave. Marcia, the owner of the home, has three dogs, and she's set it up so you and yours feel right at home.

Your pooch gets dog treats when he comes here. And that's just the beginning. This two-bedroom house has a large yard, which is completely fenced. Dogs love to roam around, sniffing all the nooks and crannies. There's some shade back there, and good grass for rolling on. Better yet, there's a little fountain, which humans enjoy sitting around during the summer, and dogs love splashing in year-round.

The house is cozy and peaceful, with a small front porch, a wood stove, a full kitchen (dog-proof, says Marcia), two bedrooms, a living room (with two Labrador retriever pictures), an antique-furnished dining room (with dogsled art), and a large deck with a hot tub and barbecue/picnic area.

During your stay here, you might even get a visit from Hattie, a very friendly dog who lives across the street. Joe thinks she's foxy.

Rates are $150. If you stay for a week, the rate is $800—a significant discount. For privacy and safety sake, the address is given only to those renting the house. For more information or to rent the house, call Marcia at (510) 625-2844. (She lives in the East Bay, thus the different area code.)

Russian River Getaways: If you and your dog want a home away from home while you vacation in the Russian River area, you've hit the jackpot. Russian River Getaways has about 20 beautiful dog-friendly homes for rent on a nightly or weekly basis. The homes are generally quite upscale, but the prices are fairly down to earth.

What we like most about Russian River Getaways is its owner, Camille LeGrand. She loves dogs. Her dogs, Nicholas and Hugo, often come to work with her. "We don't care how beautiful the rental home, we think dogs should be allowed at all of them," she says. (They're not, but that's not Camille's fault.) When you get to her office to pick up the keys for your home, she'll point you in the direction of a couple of hush-hush off-leash spots, and will give your dog a treat or two. Now that's what we call one doggone good person.

Rates for the homes range from $115 to $290 nightly (the $290 home has five bedrooms, a fireplace, a lovely fenced yard with fruit trees, a 10-person hot tub on the deck, and canoes and kayaks for the river, which is one block away). Weekly rates are $650 to $1,740. Russian River Getaways has a very good Web site where you can check out the selection of homes before you decide which you like best; the address is Getaways@wclyx.com. For a brochure describing the homes, write Russian River Getaways at 16201 First Street, P.O. Box 1673, Guerneville, CA 95446, or phone (707) 869-4560 or (800) 433-6673.

Russian River Vacation Homes: Spend your Russian River–area vacation in your own charming private house. This is an ideal way to vacation with your pooch. Russian River Vacation Homes offers more than a dozen beautiful, quaint houses for pets and their people. From a one-bedroom rustic log cabin on the river to a three-bedroom riverside home complete with hot tub, you and your holiday hound will find the home of your dreams.

Joe's favorite is Larissa's House, a sweet one-bedroom home with a flowery, fenced-in yard on the river. Larissa, the owner, lives next door, and adores dogs. In fact, you pretty much have to have a dog to stay here. It's so doggone dog-friendly that the shower is designed so that you and your dog can shower at the same time. Joe is shy, so he doesn't care for this arrangement. If Larissa has time, she'll make sure your pooch has a welcoming bag of treats when she arrives. Dogs fall instantly in love when they meet Larissa, and the love-fest often continues year-round, because she sends them (note: *them*, not *you*) Christmas cards.

Another dog friend, Brandon, asked us to mention his favorite, the Raven House. It's a comfy, fairly quiet place with an Asian-Western style he says the owner improves on year after year. He especially likes all the fun walks he can take from here.

Larissa's House rents for $170 nightly or $600 per week. Rates at other houses range from $150 nightly or $550 per week to $275 per night or $1,400 per week. To see the various houses before you rent one, check out Russian River Vacation Homes' Web site: www.riverhomes.com. (A reader informed us of one potential dud, but that just may have been because of extra high expectations. Either way, it's good to see what you're renting before you rent it.) For a brochure describing all the dog-friendly properties, write Russian River Vacation Homes at 14080 Mill Street, P.O. Box 418, Guerneville, CA 95446, or phone (707) 869-9030, (800) 310-0804 (California only), or (800) 997-3312 (nationwide).

HEALDSBURG

RESTAURANTS

Costeaux French Bakery: Stroll around Healdsburg's good-looking town square, with its old buildings and benches for shady rest stops, and then drop in here for dinner or a wonderful pastry snack at an outdoor table. 417 Healdsburg Avenue; (707) 433-1913.

PLACES TO STAY

Best Western Dry Creek Inn: Rates are $69 to $94. Dogs are $10 extra. 198 Dry Creek Road, Healdsburg, CA 95448; (707) 433-0300.

Madrona Manor: So there we were, at a friend's wedding, surrounded by the luxurious elegance of this European-style inn. "I'm sure dogs are really welcome *here* . . . not," commented one tipsy wedding guest when he found out about my line of writing. I figured he was right, but decided to check, just in case this spectacular Victorian inn permitted pooches.

I came back to Sammy the Sipper with the great news: Dogs *are* allowed. He just about swallowed his martini olive whole. What I didn't tell him is that they're allowed at only one cottage. So your dog can't go with you to the mansion to inspect the handmade Persian carpets, and he can't dine at the inn's high-end restaurant. So what? He's allowed to peruse much of the manor's eight acres (on leash), and he can hang out with you at the enchanting, secluded Garden Cottage. It's the most private of the accommodations here, with its own gardens and sheltered deck. Inside, it's as attractive and unique as outside, with an antique water closet and marble fireplace. It's air conditioned, too, which isn't too common in this kind of place. But it's oh-so-necessary come summertime.

The rate for the cottage is $215, which includes a full breakfast. 1001 Westside Road, P.O. Box 818, Healdsburg, CA 95448; (707) 433-4231 or (800) 258-4003.

JENNER

PARKS, BEACHES, AND RECREATION AREAS

• **Sonoma Coast State Beaches** 🐾🐾🐾½ *See* ❽ *on page 228.*

A string of beautiful, clean beaches runs from Jenner south to Bodega Bay, and you can't go wrong from Goat Rock Beach south to Salmon Creek Beach: Gorgeous bluff views, stretches of brown sand, gnarled rocks, and grassy dunes welcome you. Always keep an eye on the surf and a leash on your dog.

Dogs are not allowed on any of the trails that run on the bluffs above the beaches, on Bodega Head, in the Willow Creek area east of Bridgehaven, or in the seal rookery upriver from Goat Rock Beach. (Watch for the warning sign.) No camping is permitted on any of the beaches, except Bodega Dunes and Wright's Beach, which have campgrounds. These two also charge a $5 day-use fee. Day use of all other beaches is free. For beach info, call (707) 875-3483.

The Bodega Dunes Campground has 98 developed sites, and Wright's Beach Campground has 30 developed sites. Sites at Bodega Dunes are $6 a night and sites at Wright's are $20. There's a $1 fee per dog. Both campgrounds are open year-round. Advance reservations are highly recommended in summer and early fall (you may reserve up to eight weeks in advance). Call Parknet for reservations at (800) 444-PARK. For general beach info, call (707) 875-3483.

RESTAURANTS
Seagull Deli: Don't look up when you eat at the outdoor tables here! Hah. It's an old joke, apparently, based on the deli's name. You and your dog can dine on creamy clam chowder while overlooking the mouth of the Russian River from one of the picnic tables. It's a tasty way to spend part of a crisp autumn afternoon. 10439 North Coast Highway (Highway 1); (707) 865-2594.

PLACES TO STAY
Bridgehaven Campground: Leashed dogs are welcome to visit or stay at this campground in the hamlet of Bridgehaven, where Highway 1 crosses the Russian River south of Jenner. For a day-use fee of $5, you and your dog can swim together. Campsites are $20. Dogs are free. There are 23 sites. The campground is open year-round. P.O. Box 59, Jenner, CA 95450; (707) 865-2473.

Sonoma Coast State Beaches: See Sonoma Coast State Beaches on page 238 for camping information.

OCCIDENTAL

PLACES TO STAY
Negri's Occidental Lodge: There's no official street address here, but it's in the middle of town—you can't miss it. Rates are $44 to $69. Dogs are $8 extra. P.O. Box 84, Occidental, CA 95465; (707) 874-3623.

PETALUMA

Petaluma is a captivating Sunday afternoon stroll, with its tree-lined streets and pocket parks for your dog's pleasure. Victorian buildings, old feed mills, and a riverfront that remains mostly original, but not dilapidated, complete the charming picture. And let's not forget an added canine bonus: Depending on the wind direction, you can often smell fresh cow manure wafting in from the surrounding hills. Dogs thrive on this.

Best of all, dogs get to run leashless during set (if early) hours in a whopping 12 parks! No wonder they call this place PET-aluma.

PARKS, BEACHES, AND RECREATION AREAS

Dogs who live in Petaluma are lucky dogs indeed. A few years back, the enlightened Parks and Recreation Department decided that dogs needed places to run off leash and gave dogs who are under voice control the okay to be leash-free in a dozen parks during certain hours. (Watch your off-leash hours like a hawk: The fine for a first offense is up to $100! Better to invest that money in a good watch.)

Now the city has one-upped itself, and dogs have their very own park, called Rocky Memorial Dog Park. Dogs are singing its praises ("Howlelujah," they're saying). Please see page 242 for more on Rocky Park.

• **Arroyo Park** 🐾🐾🐾 🐕 *See* ❾ *on page* 228.

Most of Arroyo Park is very well groomed, with golf course-like green grass and a perfectly paved walking path running through its three acres. However, it seems many dogs prefer the seedier side of the park—the weedier, uncut area on the right as you face the park. We hope that area remains like this for dogs who like to walk a little on the wild side.

Dogs are allowed off leash here from 6 A.M. to 9 A.M. weekdays and 6 A.M. to 8 A.M. weekends. It's just a bone's throw from Wiseman Airport Park (see page 244), though, which is a much safer place to run a dog, since you can get farther from the road. The park is at Garfield and Village East Drives. (707) 778-4380.

• **Bond Park** 🐾🐾🐾 🐕 *See* ❿ *on page* 228.

It's green here, so green that Joe couldn't help but run out of the car and throw himself down on the grass and start wriggling and writhing in ecstasy. I thought for sure he'd found something odious to roll in, but underneath him was just clean, green grass. He rolled for about 10 minutes, got up, and heaved himself down in another spot, rolling and groaning and making the children in the playground giggle. The park is pleasant, with some shade from medium-sized trees. With six acres, it's a good size for dogs. And it's set in a quiet area, on Banff Way just south of Maria Drive, so traffic is minimal. Off-leash hours are 6 A.M. to 9 A.M. Monday through Friday and 6 A.M. to 8 A.M. weekends. (707) 778-4380.

• **Del Oro Park** 🐾🐾🐾 🐕 *See* ⓫ *on page* 228.

Del Oro is very suburban. It's got a nice little play area for kids. It's got green grass. It's surrounded by not-too-old suburban homes. It's got soccer goal posts. When we last visited, there were even two Suburban sport utility vehicles parked in front.

Something not terribly suburban, a fire hydrant in one of the grassy areas, is probably the most coveted part of the park—at least for boy dogs. Well-behaved pooches can be off leash here from 6 A.M. to 9 A.M. weekdays and 6 A.M. to 8 A.M. weekends. The park is at Sartori Drive and Del Oro Circle. (707) 778-4380.

• **Glenbrook Park** 🐾🐾 🐕 *See* ⓬ *on page* 228.

Who'd believe it? When we last visited, a great blue heron landed in this narrow park, which is surrounded by newish homes. This was a wonderful sight, because the land around here looks like it's still in shock from all the recent development.

The park is nearly four acres, and is much longer than it is wide. It's directly across the street from Sunrise Park (see page 243), but it's a little quieter and more attractive, with some medium-sized trees here and there. Its off-leash hours are generous: from 6 A.M. to 9 A.M. and 5 P.M. to 10 P.M. daily. The park is at Maria Drive and Sunrise Parkway. (707) 778-4380.

• **Helen Putnam Regional Park** 🐾 🐾 ½ *See* ⓭ *on page 228.*

This county regional park is, and will remain, a minimally developed stretch of converted cow pasture with oak trees. A wide paved trail shared by hikers and bicyclists runs between the main entrance and the Victoria housing development (to enter from that end, go to the end of Oxford Court). Dogs must be leashed. There's no shade from the scrub oaks and it can get mighty windy. The paved trail has gentle ups and downs. Some other dirt trails give you steeper hill climbs. About a quarter of a mile in from the main entrance is an old cattle pond good for a dog swim (if the dog stays on a leash—quite a feat).

Parking is $2. Next to the lot is a kids' playground and a picnic gazebo, set by a creek that's only a gully in summer. Drive south on Western Avenue and turn left on Chileno Valley Road. After a half mile, you'll see the turnoff to the park. (707) 527-2041.

• **Lucchesi Park** 🐾 🐾 🐾 ½ 🐕 *See* ⓮ *on page 228.*

This is a well-kept, popular city park with a postmodern community center that impresses people, but doesn't stir dogs much. Dogs prefer strolling through empty sports fields, picnicking at shaded tables, lounging under the weepy willows, watching ducks and the spewing fountain at the large pond, and trotting along the paved paths here. No dog swimming is allowed in the pond, but that's a rule Joe "I Hate H$_2$O" Dog can live with just fine.

Dogs are allowed off leash here between 6 A.M. and 9 A.M. weekdays and 6 A.M. and 8 A.M. weekends. Be sure to keep dogs away from ducks and geese, who like to lounge beside their pond, because feathers should not fly as a result of the city's kindly off-leash allowances. The park is at North McDowell Boulevard and Madison Street. (707) 778-4386.

• **McNear Park** 🐾 🐾 🐾 🐕 *See* ⓯ *on page 228.*

McNear is an attractive seven-acre park, with green, green grass, plenty of shade, picnic tables, and a playground. But the part of the park dogs like best is the enclosed athletic field, where they're allowed to romp off leash from 6 A.M. to 9 A.M. Monday through Friday and from 6 A.M. to 8 A.M. Saturday and Sunday. The field is usually green and almost entirely fenced, but there are a couple of spots where a clever escape artist could slip out, so heads up. It's at F and Ninth Streets. (707) 778-4380.

• **Oak Hill Park** 🐾 🐾 🐾 🐾 🐕 *See* ⓰ *on page 228.*

Dogs love running up and down the gently rolling hills on this five-acre park set in the midst of beautiful old Victorian homes near downtown

Petaluma. Oak Hill Park is hilly and oaky (surprise!), qualities dogs enjoy. Some good-sized oaks make their home in various parts of the park, and Joe appreciates their shade-giving arms. At last visit, a sign warned of future construction, so some of the rustic nature of this park might be gone by the time you read this.

Dogs are permitted to run off leash in the park's lower section every single day, from 6 A.M. to 10 P.M. These are magnificent hours, matched only at Rocky Memorial Dog Park (see below). The park is at Howard and Oak Streets. (707) 778-4380.

• **Petaluma Adobe State Historic Park** 🐾🐾 *See* ⑰ *on page 228.*

Leashed dogs are welcome here, if they behave well around goats and such, and if you avoid the farm animals' courtyard. From the parking lot, walk across a wooden bridge over a wide, willow-lined creek (dry in summer) to the house, built in 1836 as headquarters for General Mariano Vallejo's 66,600-acre Rancho Petaluma. Clustered around the house are tempting displays of animal hides, saddles, and tallow makings, as well as sheep, chickens, and a donkey. Dogs must use their best manners. If you see them starting to think of lamb chops for dinner, make sure you hang on hard to that leash.

The park is southeast of Petaluma at Adobe Road and Casa Grande Road. From U.S. 101, you'll see an exit sign for the Petaluma Adobe. Admission is $2 for adults, $1 for children. (707) 762-4871.

• **Prince Park** 🐾🐾🐾🐾 🐕 *See* ⑱ *on page 228.*

Dogs are permitted off leash at this attractive 20-acre park during longer hours than they are at most other parks in the city, and they think this is just swell. On a recent visit, a springer-shepherd mix was running around drooling and panting and smiling like a dog in love. His person said when he comes here, he's ecstatic. "Willie loves the grass and the trees. I love the hours for off leash, and I love its safety from traffic," she said. (The park is set back quite far from street traffic.) Off-leash hours are 6 A.M. to 11 A.M. on weekdays and 6 A.M. to 8 A.M. on weekends. The park is across East Washington Street from the airport, just a little north of the airport sign. (707) 778-4380.

• **Rocky Memorial Dog Park** 🐾🐾🐾🐾 🐕 *See* ⑲ *on page 228.*

The scenery isn't great, and the land has nary a tree on it, but Joe couldn't help but give Rocky Memorial Dog Park his four-paw rating. "It's big, it smells good, and we don't need leashes," explains Joe.

This flat, barren nine-acre piece of land is the best thing that's happened to Petaluma's dogs since the park system began allowing them off leash at certain parks during limited hours a few years back. Rocky Park opened in early 1997 and has been drawing a good number of cavorting canines since. Dogs enjoy the smell that can pervade the land; it's beside a marshy area next to the Petaluma River. Fortunately, it's well fenced so dogs can't chase the marsh birds or roll in the marsh muck. The fencing keeps the dogs from escaping to all areas but the parking lot, which leads to the park entrance, which eventually leads a busy road. So if you have a pooch who's prone to running away, be aware the place is safe, but isn't foolproof.

Because it's so barren here, it can really roast on hot days. Be sure to bring water. A sign at the entrance says "No dogs in heat," and I thought it was nice of them to be so concerned about the temperature for dog walking. It took me a few seconds and an eye roll from my husband to realize the sign's true intent.

On our first visit, Joe searched in vain for something to lift a leg on. He found only some garbage cans and a few big weeds, and they were right next to the parking lot. The next visit he just succumbed to the lack of leg-lift targets and took to relieving his bladder like a girl dog. But not, of course, until looking around to make sure no one was watching.

Rocky Park was named after a big-hearted police dog who died at the too-young age of 10 during a narcotics search. It was kidney failure that got him, not the wrong end of a dealer's pistol. Rocky had helped seize a few million dollars of narcotics in his career, but his greatest act came in 1992 when he saved the life of his beloved handler one night. A felon had escaped and the officer chased him to a creek, where the felon got the upper hand and was holding the officer's head underwater. The officer managed to hit a remote control button that opened the windows of the patrol car and released Rocky, who'd seen his friend in trouble. Rocky bolted to the creek and got the upper paw. He saved his friend and helped bag the bad guy. "It was the beginning of the era of Rocky," said Officer Jeff Hasty, a dog handler with the Petaluma Police Department. At press time, a bust of Rocky was set to be mounted in front of the police department.

This is an easy park to visit if you're on U.S. 101 and your pooch is hankering to stretch his gams. Take the Highway 116 east (NOT west)/Lakeville exit and follow the street just over a half mile to Casa Grande Road, where you'll take a sharp right. Drive a few hundred feet past ugly storage bins and trucks and you'll soon hit the entrance to the park. Unlike most of the other city parks with off-leash times, this one has great hours: from 6 A.M. to 10 P.M. (707) 778-4380.

• **Sunrise Park** 🐾 1/2 🐕 *See* ⑳ *on page* 228.

If you're a real estate developer, there's a chance you might enjoy this park. It's very, very narrow, squeezed like an old tube of toothpaste by cookie cutter condos and townhouses. It's too close to traffic. It's not terribly attractive. But in its defense, it does have decent grassy areas and fun (for dogs) weedy patches. Another plus: Dogs are allowed to be off leash here between 6 A.M. and 9 A.M. and 5 P.M. to 10 P.M. every day. Those are some pretty long hours for a pretty slim park. It's at Marina Drive and Sunrise Parkway. (707) 778-4380.

• **Westridge Open Space** 🐾 🐾 🐾 🐕 *See* ㉑ *on page* 228.

Dogs get to peruse the east side of this three-acre park off leash from 6 A.M. to 9 A.M. every day. The park is long and narrow, with plenty of medium-sized trees, which turn a warm red in autumn. When we visited, a fluffy black cat teased Joe from the middle of the road. Joe warns his brethren to watch out for that guy, especially if your pooch is a chaser. The park is located on Westridge Drive, near its intersection with Westridge Place. (707) 778-4380.

•**Wiseman Airport Park** 🐾🐾🐾🐾 🐕 *See ㉒ on page 228.*

Plenty of pooches visit this park, and for good reason. Wiseman is 32 acres of well-kept playing fields, uncut grass, many shade trees, and comfortably wide walking paths. It's also a good place to watch little planes land and take off, because of its proximity to the airport. (They don't call it Airport Park for nothing.) Best of all, it's got a couple of safe areas where you can run your dog off leash during certain hours. From 6 A.M. to 9 A.M. weekdays and 6 A.M. to 8 A.M. weekends, dogs can go leashless from the south soccer field up to and including the north softball field. The best access is at St. Augustine Circle. (707) 778-4380.

RESTAURANTS

Apple Box: A store of antiques and housewares, this charmer also serves good desserts, teas, and coffee. There's a bookshop next door and 10 tables outside, right by the river. Joe's dog buddy Dabney loves the smell of sun on river water, mixed with baking cookies. 224 B Street; (707) 762-5222.

Aram's Cafe: Dine on really good Mediterranean and Armenian food at the five outdoor tables. Aram's is located in downtown Petaluma. 131 Kentucky Street; (707) 765-9775.

Rocket Cafe: On weekends, the dog-loving owners offer barbecue and live music. Other times, enjoy light meals at the outdoor tables. 100 Petaluma Boulevard, #104; (707) 763-2314.

PLACES TO STAY

Motel 6: Rates are $38 for the first adult, $7 for the second. One small pooch per room, please. 1368 North McDowell Boulevard, Petaluma, CA 94954; (707) 765-0333.

Quality Inn: Stay here and get a complimentary continental breakfast. The corporate rooms are on the more deluxe side. Some even have whirlpool baths. (No dog paddling, poochies!) Rates are $69 to $139. Dogs require a $20 deposit. 5100 Montero Way, Petaluma, CA 94954; (707) 664-1155.

DOGGY DAYS

Yikes! What a dog!: If your dog is so ugly that the fleas flee when they see his face, you'll want to know about this one. Petaluma's annual Ugly Dog Contest is a good time for you and your dog, ugly or not. (Beautiful dogs are welcome, so long as they don't mind losing.) It's held on the last day of the Sonoma-Marin Fair and it's open to any dog owner for a $3 entry fee. Water and shade are provided; bring your own pooper-scooper.

A winner is chosen in the Mutt and Pedigreed categories. These winners square off for the Ugly Dog of the Year award. Then there's the Ring of Champions division, in which past winners compete for the title of World's Ugliest Dog. Don't miss it. The event is held at the Sonoma-Marin Fairgrounds, usually on the third Sunday in June. Call (707) 763-0931 for this year's date.

ROHNERT PARK

PARKS, BEACHES, AND RECREATION AREAS

•**Crane Creek Regional Park** 🐾🐾 *See ㉓ on page 228.*

For years, this 128-acre patch of grazing land in the middle of nowhere has been undeveloped open space for your dog's pleasure. Recent improvements include an upgraded parking lot, the addition of picnic tables, and the widening of 2.6 miles of hiking trails. Unfortunately, the leash law is enforced here, and a sign tells you why: "Dogs Caught in Livestock May Be Shot." Carry water; you may get thirsty just trying to find the place in your car.

From Rohnert Park, drive east on the Rohnert Park Expressway to Petaluma Hill Road. Turn south on Petaluma Hill Road to Roberts Road, and go east for two miles on Roberts Road. You'll find the park shortly after Roberts turns into Pressley Road. A machine is there to collect a $2 parking fee from you. (707) 527-2041.

SANTA ROSA

PARKS, BEACHES, AND RECREATION AREAS

This sprawling city has gone to the dogs in the last few years, and dogs and their people couldn't be happier. It used to be that if you wanted to give your pooch a little off-leash exercise, you'd go out of town or sneak out to a park at night and hope no one was watching. But now the city has two very attractive off-leash dog runs (please see Doyle and Rincon Valley Parks), one in the works (see Northwest Community Park), and four parks that are serving as pilot locations for a trial off-leash program (please see Franklin, Doyle, Youth, and Southwest Parks). That sound you hear is the sound of tails thumping.

The dog parks are wonderful, but if you don't mind getting up early, the parks in the pilot program offer even more room and more doggy heaven scents. Dogs who visit those pilot parks are allowed to run off leash between 6 A.M. and 8 A.M. every day—and the hours are strictly enforced, so be sure to wind your watch. Dogs have to be under voice control, nonaggressive, spayed or neutered, and more than four months old. Of course, as is always the case wherever you go with your dog, you have to scoop the poop. "If our mower people go through and find a pile, we can close down the park to off-leash dogs," said Dan Neff, superintendent of park maintenance. "We don't want to, but that's the way it's got to be." There are stiff fines, from $35 to $500, for being a scofflaw, so be careful out there.

At press time, the experimental phase of this program was set to end in August 1998, but if all goes well, those four parks and more could have a more permanent off-leash setup. Call the parks department at (707) 543-3292 for updates. And be sure to say thanks if they give you good news.

• **Doyle Park** 🐾🐾🐾🐾 🐕 *See* ㉔ *on page 228.*

Doyle Park is a very stately place to take a pooch. A little stone bridge takes you over a stream and into the park's main entry area. The trees here have an elegant, deep-rooted look. The grass is like a cool, plush green carpet. At Doyle, even the squirrels don't look squirrely.

Dogs think it's all grand. But what they think is even better is the fact that they can run around all this splendor without a leash between 6 A.M. and 8 A.M., thanks to an experimental program run by the city's dog-friendly parks department. (If you're reading this after August 1998, please call the number below to make sure the city's experiment was successful and the leash-free hours still apply. See the introduction to this section, above, for more details about the pilot off-leash program.)

Dogs who aren't early birds don't have to sulk because of the hours: Doyle Park is graced with not only the pilot off-leash program, but it has its very own fenced doggy park. It's not as riveting as the rest of the park, but it's got water and some trees, and it's a very safe place to take even an escape artist. Unlike Rincon Park's dog run (see page 247), Doyle's dog run doesn't close during the winter rains. (Joe Dog wants to thank Silke Kuehl and her pooch for writing us and pointing us in the direction of this relative newcomer to the off-leash park world.)

In addition to the rules mentioned in the beginning of this section, there's one that's a little tough if you're a parent of a dog and a youngish child: No children under 10 years old are allowed in the dog run, whether accompanied by a parent or not. The park users devised this rule, which was apparently meant to protect kids from getting mowed over by herds of dogs, and also to protect herds of dogs from lawsuits.

For the main entrance, take Sonoma Avenue to Doyle Park Drive and turn south, driving a few hundred feet over insufferable speed bumps to the parking area. The dog run will be way over to the left. To park closer to the dog run, take Sonoma Avenue to Hoen Avenue and turn south. The parking lot is on the right, and the dog run is on the other side of the ball field. (707) 543-3292.

• **Franklin Park** 🐾🐾🐾 🐕 *See ㉕ on page 228.*

Franklin is the smallest of the four parks that allow dogs off leash between 6 A.M. and 8 A.M. (See the introduction to this section, page 245, for details about this wonderful experimental off-leash program. If you're reading this after August 1998, please call the number below to make sure the experiment was successful and the off-leash rule still applies.) It's green and slopey, with enough trees to make any boy dog happy. Be careful, because it's not as safe from traffic as some of the other parks. (But it's not exactly Indy 500 territory around here anyway.)

The park is at Franklin Avenue and Gay Street. (707) 543-3292.

• **Hood Mountain Regional Park** 🐾🐾½ *See ㉖ on page 228.*

Dogs and people love the trails in this park, but it's open only on weekends and holidays and closes every summer when fire danger gets high. It usually reopens only in late September. It can also close in winter because of mud slides. Make sure your dog wears a leash. If a sign appears at the Los Alamos Road turnoff saying that the park is closed, believe it.

To get to the only entrance, from Highway 12, turn east on Los Alamos Road (not Adobe Canyon Road, which leads only to Sugarloaf Ridge State Park, where dogs aren't allowed on trails). The road is long, winding, steep, and narrow for the last two miles. It's not for nervous drivers or carsick pooches, but it's a beautiful four-mile drive, with a good close-up of Hood Mountain's bare rock outcropping "hood."

A machine in the parking lot will ask you to pay $2. Call to make sure the park is open before driving here. A final note: Watch out for ticks. They're rampant. (707) 527-2041.

•**Northwest Community Park** 🐾🐾🐾🐾 🐕 *See* **㉗** *on page 228.*

At press time, the area for an off-leash dog park within the park was ready for fencing, awaiting the last few hundred dollars in donations. I'm going to go against my usual rule and describe a dog park before it's actually complete because, as park maintenance superintendent Dan Neff said, "It's definitely a go." By the time you read this, dogs should be tearing around having the time of their lives.

The dog run is a good size, about the size of Rincon's (see below), and will have some shade, water, and benches. If it's anything like Santa Rosa's other two dog parks, dogs are going to be lucky indeed to visit here. The dog area is located just northwest of the park's soccer fields. The park is located on Marlow Road, behind Comstock Junior High School, north of Guerneville Road. If you get a copy of this book hot off the press, you may want to call and make sure the fence is up before you venture over. (707) 543-3770.

•**Rincon Valley Community Park** 🐾🐾🐾🐾 🐕
See **㉘** *on page 228.*

The fenced dog park here is one of the most attractive we've ever seen. That's mostly because it has grass. Real grass. Not just a few green sprigs fighting their way through the tough dirt, but good ol' carpety grass. That's not because the dogs here pussyfoot around. In fact, dogs are so happy to be here that they tear around with great gusto. We're not exactly sure why there's so much grass, but we do know that the dog run closes during the rainy winter months, so that could have something to do with it.

A few trees grace the dog run area, and the views of the surrounding hills make it seem like it's in the middle of the countryside. As of this writing, it's actually on the edge of the countryside. By the next edition, it will probably be miles from the countryside, the way development encroaches around here.

The dogs who come to Rincon's dog run are a friendly lot, running to the fence and sniffing all newcomers, tails wagging exuberantly. The people who come here are much the same, except they chat rather than sniff. They're wonderful, outgoing, dog-loving folks—except for one persnickety woman who told me that I must not be in there with my child, who was blissing out on all the dogs. "Didn't you see the rules? No infants or children!" she snipped. "You could sue us if she got hurt." The woman suggested leaving Laura by herself in a stroller outside the gate, since you're not allowed to leave your dog alone in the dog run. Joe wanted to do a leg lift on the woman's ankle, but she left. I expected her to say "And your little dog, too!" and cackle as she flew off, but that's the stuff movies are made of.

Unfortunately it's true: No little kiddies under 10 allowed, even if they're with their parents. A parks department spokesman says the park users made up the rule. So apparently if you've got a kid and a dog, you'll have to hire a sitter in order to bring your dog here. Boo!

The park is on Montecito Boulevard, west of Calistoga Road. Don't forget that it's closed during the rainy months. (707) 524-5116.

• **Southwest Park** 🐾🐾🐾🐾 🐕 *See ㉙ on page 228.*

If your dog doesn't need a park in the hoity-toitiest part of town, this is a mighty convenient and friendly place to take him. First of all, it's relatively close to the freeway, so it's easy to get to if you're on the road. But better than that, it's big and green, with neatly paved paths that meander by cascading willows. It's also far enough from the road that the traffic danger is minimal. Why care about traffic? Because your dog can be off leash here from 6 A.M. to 8 A.M., thanks to an experimental program that's got dogs at its very heart. (If you're reading this after August 1998, please call the number below to make sure the experiment was successful and the off-leash rule still applies. See the introduction to this section, page 245, for more details about the pilot program.)

From U.S. 101, take the Hearn Avenue exit and drive west for nearly a mile. The park is on the left, across from Westland Drive. (707) 543-3292.

• **Spring Lake Regional Park** 🐾🐾🐾 *See ㉚ on page 228.*

In winter, this county park doesn't offer dogs much more than a leashed trot around the lake. But in summer, it's leafy and full of the sounds of kids yelling and thumping oars. It's more fun here for people than dogs, who must be leashed. This is a good spot for a picnic, roller skating, a parcourse workout, a boat ride, or human swimming (no dogs allowed in the swim area). The path around the lake is paved for skaters, strollers, and bicyclists, and there are short dirt paths off into the open oak and brush woods. You can fish from the banks, where they're cleared of tules and willows.

The parking fee is $3 in winter, $4 in summer; the large lot has some shady spots. Campsites are $14, plus $1 extra for a dog. Ten sites are reservable; 21 are first come, first served. Dogs must have proof of a rabies vaccination. The campground is open daily between May 1 and September 30, weekends and holidays only after September 30.

From Highway 12, on the Farmer's Lane portion in Santa Rosa, turn east on Hoen Avenue. Take Hoen four stoplights to Newanga Avenue. Turn left on Newanga, which goes straight to the entrance. (707) 539-8092.

• **Youth Community Park** 🐾🐾🐾🐾 🐕 *See ㉛ on page 228.*

If you like oak trees, come here. Big oaks hang out all over the park. Some really big, really old oaks even have their own fences, so no one can do leg lifts or initial carving on their trunks.

The main attraction for dogs is the big green meadowy lawn area. Pooches love rolling on it and cantering over it. Your dog can be off leash here from 6 A.M. to 8 A.M., thanks to an experimental dog-friendly pilot program. (If you're reading this after August 1998, please call the number below to make sure the experiment was successful and the off-leash rule still applies. See the introduction to this section, page 245, for more details about the pilot program.)

A word of warning: Skateboarders abound here. There's a little skateboard area in front of the park, and kids love skateboarding around the parking lot, too. Joe is fascinated with boarders, but some dogs cringe at the sound.

The park is in the far west reaches of the city, on the west side of Fulton Road, about a quarter of a mile south of Piner Road. (707) 543-3292

RESTAURANTS

Juice Shack: In the summer, come here with your hot pooch and cool off with a creamy smoothie or a fresh organic juice. In cooler months, you can enjoy hot juices here. Hmm. Joe Dog and I would rather go for the hot soup they serve, or the wrap sandwiches. Dine with your dog at the outdoor area under the big pine tree. 1810 Mendocino Avenue; (707) 528-6131.

PLACES TO STAY

Best Western Garden Inn: Dogs can stay in eight rooms here, but only one pooch per room, please. Rates are $65 to $99. Dogs are $10 extra. 1500 Santa Rosa Avenue, Santa Rosa, CA 95404; (707) 546-4031.

Best Western Hillside Inn: Small dogs only, please. Rates are $52 to $61. 2901 Fourth Street, Santa Rosa, CA 95409; (707) 546-9353.

Los Robles Lodge: Rates are $59 to $112. 925 Edwards Avenue, Santa Rosa, CA 95401; (707) 545-6330.

Santa Rosa Travelodge: Rates are $45 to $80. Small pets only, please. 1815 Santa Rosa Avenue, Santa Rosa, CA 95407; (707) 542-3472.

Spring Lake Regional Park: See Spring Lake Regional Park on page 248 for camping information.

SEA RANCH

PARKS, BEACHES, AND RECREATION AREAS

• **Sea Ranch Beach Trails** 🐾 🐾 ½ *See* ❷ *on page 228.*

Sea Ranch is a private development, but seven public foot trails cross the property leading to the beach, which is also public property. The smooth, wide dirt trails are managed by the Sonoma County Regional Parks, and they offer incomparable solitary walks through unspoiled grassy hills.

All the trails are clearly marked on Highway 1. Each trailhead has rest rooms and a box where you are asked to deposit $3 for parking. No motorcycles, bicycles, or horses are allowed. Keep your dog on leash.

Here are the distances to the beach, listing trails from north to south: Salal Trail, .6 miles; Bluff-Top Trail, 3.5 miles; Walk-On Beach Trail, .4 miles; Shell Beach Trail, .6 miles; Stengel Beach Trail, .2 miles; Pebble Beach Trail, .3 miles; Black Point Trail, .3 miles. Call (707) 785-2377 for more info.

PLACES TO STAY

The Welch House: If you find your dog wandering around this large, exquisite house with a big grin on his snout, do what Dorothy learned to do: Don't look any further than your own backyard for the source of his happiness. The backyard is expansive, the front yard is enclosed and faces the mighty Pacific, and in between is a magnificent, cedar-shingled, two-bedroom, two-bathroom house you can call home. "It's a wonderful place for people and dogs. I couldn't think of coming here and not taking a dog," says a longtime fan of the house.

With a house and area this glorious, it's hard to know where to start a description. In general, the place is top-drawer. "We like to keep it classed up," says dog-loving co-owner Trevor Paulson. "The nicer we make it, the better the dogs get."

The 30-foot-long living room has a huge, slate-faced fireplace and two window beds with views to drool about. The spacious kitchen is stocked with high-quality pots (Circulon, no less), pans, plates, flatware, and even champagne glasses. (You'll probably even find dog biscuits in here, too.) Each bedroom has a separate, completely fenced deck to foil escape pooches and add privacy. A private enclosed spa with an outdoor shower and an extremely comfortably furnished, walled 650-square-foot main/observation deck provides spectacular ocean, meadow, and forest views by day and, as the brochure says, "a celestial panoply of billions of stars" at night. "If it's a new moon, it blows your mind," says Trevor. Tugger and Penney, the sweet dogs owned by Trevor and the house's other co-owner, Dave Welch, helped make The Welch House as dog-friendly as it is. "Even though they're not here when you visit, their spirits are. Consider them your hosts," says Trevor.

From the property, you have access to the beach (with great seal- and whale-watching opportunities) and 10 miles of level hiking trails. The air here is sweet and salty at the same time.

The house is $200 a night and sleeps up to four people. There's a two-night minimum stay. Weekly and off-season specials are available. Dogs are $10 extra per visit. For understandable security reasons, the owners don't give out the address to anyone but guests. For reservations and information, call (707) 884-4235. That's the number for Beach Rentals, the agency the owners use to help them make arrangements for guests.

SEBASTOPOL

PARKS, BEACHES, AND RECREATION AREAS

• **Ragle Ranch Park** 🐾 🐾 🐾 1/2 *See* ㉝ *on page 228.*

This Sonoma County regional park, right in the town of Sebastopol, is surprisingly large and wild, once you pass the fields and picnic areas. Unlike most urban parks, it's not very crowded, except during ball games on weekends. Level hiking and equestrian trails wind alongside vineyards and apple orchards, which are in bloom beginning in early April. Waterfowl breed in marshy spots around the creek, so don't yield to the temptation to let your dog off the obligatory leash. The landscape is gently rolling, with reeds and willows lining the creek and oaks with mistletoe on the higher rises. Woo woo, it's kissy stuff.

The park is located at Healdsburg Avenue and Ragle Road. Admission is $2 per car. (707) 527-2041.

PLACES TO STAY

Becky's Guesthouse: This lovely house is tucked away from the road and comes complete with its own 10 acres of woods, yards, and a creek. Very well-behaved dogs may be leash-free when exploring the grounds with their people.

Dog-loving owner Becky Johnson greets guests each morning with dog-shaped toast (for canines) and human-shaped toast (for Homo sapiens).

That's just for starters. Humans then sit down to a delicious country-style breakfast, which tastes very appropriate in this restored farmhouse. Becky has so many doggy people stay here that she created a photo album of her canine guests. People love to paw through it. Be sure to bring your camera so you can send her a picture of you and yours.

This is Becky's home, but she devotes the back half of the house to guests. Entrances to the two bedrooms are private, and the rooms have private baths. Dogs and their guests love to relax on the fully fenced-in decks outside their rooms on sunny days.

The room rate is $85. The mailing address is 201 Wagnon Road, Sebastopol, CA 95412; (707) 823-2223.

DIVERSIONS
Sniff out the farm trail: If you're serious about buying homegrown produce and dairy products, or just like farms—and your dog wears a leash at all times and won't do leg lifts on the vegetables—pick up a Farm Trails map from Sonoma County Farmtrails, (707) 996-2154, or from the Chamber of Commerce, P.O. Box 178, Sebastopol, CA 95473; (707) 823-3032.

SONOMA

Downtown Sonoma is a treat for people, but dogs are banned from all the good spots—the State Historic Park areas of the mission, barracks, etc., and from the Sonoma Plaza, which is full of picnickers wolfing down fine wine and Sonoma Jack. But if you and your dog are there on a fine day, stroll to Depot Park (see below), just northwest of Sonoma Plaza, and follow a paved path in either direction from Depot Park for a mini-farm tour of the town.

PARKS, BEACHES, AND RECREATION AREAS
• **Depot Park** 🐾🐾🐾 *See* ❸❹ *on page 228.*

This fine park has a softball diamond, volleyball courts, a bocce court, picnic tables, a parcourse, a small childrens' playground, and fragrant eucalyptus trees for your dog. From here, you can take a paved biking and hiking trail, smooth enough for wheelchairs, in either direction. You have to leash, but you'll both enjoy the sights and smells.

The trail stretches almost the width of the town, from Fourth Street East westward to Highway 12 and into Maxwell Farms Regional Park (see below). Heading east, you can walk about half a mile from Depot Park, passing the Vella Cheese Factory, the Sebastiani Winery, and rows of sunflowers, patches of corn, and grapes in backyard farms. Westward the path stretches about one mile. You'll skirt the Mariano Vallejo Adobe and end up in Maxwell Farms park.

Depot Park is northwest of Sonoma Plaza. (707) 938-3681.

• **Maxwell Farms Regional Park** 🐾🐾½ *See* ❸❺ *on page 228.*

This park offers playing fields, picnic tables, a generous kids' playground, smooth paths, and a large undeveloped area where paths follow Sonoma Creek under huge laurels wound with wild grapevines. The creek is dry in summer, but leashed dogs like to sniff it anyway.

The entrance is off Verano Avenue, west of Highway 12. The day-use fee is $2. (707) 527-2041.

RESTAURANTS

The Coffee Garden: This is a peaceful haven for dogs and their people. The magnificent garden patio has a fountain that fascinates some dogs and makes others look like they need to head to the nearest tree fast. There's actually a big, 160-year-old fig tree in the middle of the patio area, but leg lifts are definitely *not* permitted.

The cafe is housed in the historic Captain Salvador Vallejo Adobe, which was built in the late 1830s. A brochure you can pick up at the cafe explains its history and suggests carefully examining its architecture for various details. Most dogs would rather not have to closely explore the unique adobe brick construction of the walls, as suggested by the brochure, unless there happened to be a little chicken salad splattered on it.

Brandon Dog, pooch extraordinaire of Forest Service spokesman extraordinaire Matt Mathes and his wife (also extraordinaire, says Matt), loves this place. When Brandon visited recently, a guitar player was strumming out some gentle melodies. "Brandon seemed to enjoy the guitar. But he was more interested in the food," says Matt.

The food here is light and very tasty. Try the smoked salmon sandwich or the zesty Chinese chicken sandwich. There's a good espresso menu and a small selection of beers and wines. The Coffee Garden is located on the Sonoma Plaza, at 415–421 First Street West; (707) 996-6645.

PLACES TO STAY

Best Western Sonoma Valley Inn: Rates are $79 to $199. Small dogs only, please, and they're $15 per night. 550 Second Street West, Sonoma, CA 95476; (707) 938-9200.

Sparrow's Nest: This quaint English country-style cottage is a big hit with dogs who like friendly digs. The owner, Kathleen Anderson, loves dogs. In fact, she has what she calls "a herd of pugs" (four, to be exact). When you arrive at the Sparrow's Nest, Kathleen, who lives in the other house on the one-acre property, will greet you with human cookies and greet your pooch with dog cookies. She'll even tell you about a couple of secret dog-walking spots nearby. And there's even a chance that she'll offer to baby-sit for your dog if you want to check out a local winery or two.

The cottage, surrounded by flowers, is as delightful as its owner. It's an airy 500 square feet, with one bedroom (complete with Laura Ashley bedding, so no dirty paws, please!), a living room with a sofa bed, a kitchenette, a bathroom, and a breakfast nook. If you want civilization, there's a phone, cable TV, and a VCR with complimentary videos. Kathleen always provides fresh flowers inside. For breakfast she'll either bring you a delectable continental breakfast of locally made bakery treats (yummm . . . mini quiches, when they're available) or she'll provide you with a certificate for breakfast at a nearby restaurant. Joe suggests eating in so your dog can catch your quiche droppings.

A fenced yard wraps around the cottage, and farther away on the property, ducks, geese, and a few chickens quack around like they own the place. Dogs love all this.

Rates are $85 to $115. The cottage is a mile from Sonoma's town square, at 424 Denmark Street, Sonoma, CA 95476; (707) 996-3750.

Stone Grove Inn: Dogs think they've died and gone to Greece when they stay at this rustic, charming inn. That's because owner Charles Papanteles has a flair for decorating with the old-world Mediterranean flair of his ancestors.

But what really makes Joe say "opa!" is that the inn is surrounded by acres of gorgeous meadows, pastures, and organic veggie gardens. There's plenty of room for walking (on leash). The stone cottage, where dogs are permitted (they aren't allowed in the red barn studio), is really made of stone, and it's small, private, and secluded. It had better be secluded, because it has a detached bathroom and an outdoor shower. We found this kind of fun, but if your bladder is the size of a peanut, this may not be the place for you. Bathrooms aside, the stone cottage, which is more than 100 years old, can be mighty cozy with the potbelly stove blazing.

Rates are $75 to $95. Dogs are $10 extra. The cottage is just a bone's throw from Sonoma's town square, at 240 Second Street, Sonoma, CA 95476; (707) 939-8249.

TIMBER COVE

PARKS, BEACHES, AND RECREATION AREAS

• **Salt Point State Park** 🐾🐾🐾 *See* ㊱ *on page 228.*

Dogs are allowed only on South Gerstle Cove Beach—south of the rocky tidepool area, which is an underwater reserve—and in the Gerstle Cove, Woodside, and Fisk Mill Cove picnic areas and campsites. Gerstle Cove picnic area is right above the portion of the beach where dogs are allowed, so that's your best bet. The surf is usually gentle here, but if in doubt, you can call for an ocean-conditions recording at (707) 847-3222. As far as walking around, dogs get to do it only on paved roads. They must be leashed everywhere.

The parking fee is $5. Dogs are $1 extra. Dogs are allowed at all campsites here except the walk-in and group sites. The park has about 30 tents in the upland portion of the park. East of Highway 1 are 80 family sites. Sites are $14 to $16 per night. The dog fee is $1. Between March 2 and November 30, reserve through Parknet, (800) 444-PARK. The rest of the year, it's first come, first served.

The park is about five miles north of Timber Cove and six miles south of Stewarts Point, off Highway 1. For park info, call (707) 847-3465.

• **Stillwater Cove Regional Park** 🐾🐾½ *See* ㊲ *on page 228.*

This is a tiny but delightful beach at the foot of spectacular pine-covered cliffs. Park in the small lot beside Highway 1, leash your dog, and walk down. There is a larger picnic area above the highway, where a $3 day-use fee is charged. From here, you have to cross the highway to get to the cove. Look both ways!

There are 23 campsites, available on a first-come, first-served basis. Sites are $14 per night for up to two vehicles ($12 for Sonoma County residents). Dogs are $1 extra. The turnout is about one mile north of Fort Ross State Park (where dogs are banned). (707) 847-3245.

PLACES TO STAY

Salt Point State Park: See Salt Point State Park on page 253 for camping information.

Stillwater Cove Regional Park: See Stillwater Cove Regional Park on page 253 for camping information.

WINDSOR

Until 1992, Windsor wasn't anything but an unincorporated county area. Then it became a town, thanks to the "d" word (development). Then, in 1997, it spawned its very first park, and with that park came a fenced-in dog park. Dogs think Windsor's movers and shakers are very smart people, indeed.

PARKS, BEACHES, AND RECREATION AREAS

•**Pleasant Oak Park** 🐾 🐾 🐕 *See* **38** *on page 228.*

You and your dog wouldn't want to travel far to come here—yet. There are plenty of bigger, prettier dog run areas in the county. But the fact is, dogs feel at home running around the park's fenced dog park. Even without trees. Even without water. They don't mind that it's pretty much just a dirt lot with a very high fence and a double gate system (good for escape artists). At least they get to run.

In fact, its relatively barren condition makes obedience a snap. "When I called my dogs, they came right away," said Leslie, the sweet mother of enchanting bassett hounds Annabelle and Max. Annabelle and Max were kind enough to check on the park for us before we had a chance to visit, and while their sojourn there wasn't a howlingly fun time, they did manage to make the best of half a torn-up ball they'd found.

The good news is that the park will be less austere in the future. On the park's wish list are trees, water, and maybe even some grass. Annabelle and Max may soon be able to drag their ears across some fresh turf, which would make them and their ear cleaner mighty happy.

The park is at Old Redwood Highway and Pleasant Avenue. (707) 838-1260.

28
NAPA COUNTY

Napa dogs don't whine. They wine. And since there are plenty of dog-friendly restaurants here, they often wine and dine.

This is the home of California's most famous wine-making valley, and dogs get to experience some of the fringe benefits of this productive area. A few attractive wineries invite well-behaved dogs to relax and sniff around with their owners, but most don't want to publicize their dog policy. When you do find a dog-friendly winery, don't let your dog do leg lifts on inappropriate items, because Bacchus will get you. And your little dog, too.

The county's parks come up a little on the dry side. With the county's lush, fertile, and inviting vineyards, it seems like there's so much land that dogs would be in heaven here. Not true.

Only nine public parks and a few miscellaneous sites in Napa County allow dogs. The city of Napa has four parks where dogs are allowed, and all four permit them off leash in certain sections. You may incur the grapes of your dog's wrath if you don't take her to visit one of these leash-free lands next time you're in town.

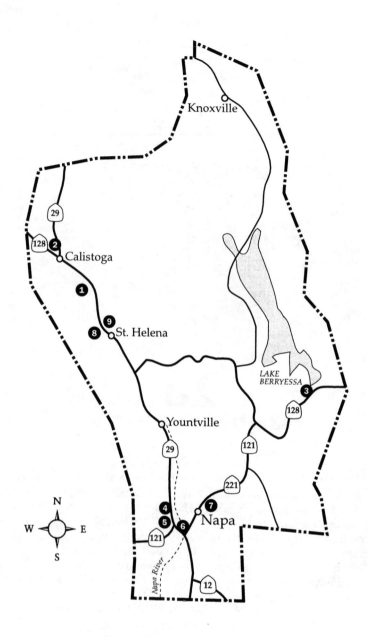

Knoxville

29

128 ❷ Calistoga

❶

❾
❽ St. Helena

LAKE
BERRYESSA

❸
128

Yountville

29

121

221

N
W   E   ❹ ❼ Napa
S   ❺ ❻

121

Napa River

12

CALISTOGA

PARKS, BEACHES, AND RECREATION AREAS

• **Bothe-Napa State Park** 🐾🐾 *See* ❶ *on page 256.*

Dogs are relegated to paved roads and campgrounds here, and it's a crime because of all the alluring trails. Hiking the highways can be fun, though. Joe seemed especially captivated by a man who was burning bacon over the campfire, his wife yelling that this was some vacation.

A wilderness haven this park is not, at least for you and your dog. Dogs must be leashed at all times. One of the two roads they're allowed on parallels Highway 29 and is so close you can see the drivers' eyes, often bloodshot from too much wine-tasting.

On the positive end, the roads are stunning in autumn when the leaves change color. And dogs are allowed to camp with you, on leash. Dogs are also allowed in some of the picnic areas just off the roads.

The day-use fee is $5. Dogs are an additional $1. There are 50 campsites. Fees are $15 to $16 a night, plus $1 extra for the dog. Call Parknet at (800) 444-PARK for reservations. The park is on Highway 29, halfway between St. Helena and Calistoga, just north of Bale Lane. The entrance is on the west side of the road. 3801 North St. Helena Highway (Highway 29). (707) 942-4575.

• **Pioneer Park** 🐾🐾 *See* ❷ *on page 256.*

This is a small park, but its location so close to the heart of Calistoga makes it a great place to stop for a relaxing picnic with your leashed pooch. The two-acre park has plenty of shade trees and enough open area so your canine won't feel claustrophobic.

Going north on Foothill Boulevard, turn right on Lincoln Avenue. In two blocks, turn left on Cedar Street. The park will be on your right within a block. (707) 942-2800.

RESTAURANTS

Home Plate: Far from the tourist parking woes in town, this inexpensive, unassuming short-order restaurant makes some of the best grilled cheese sandwiches that ever melted in a mouth. Dine at one of three big outdoor tables. 2448 Foothill Boulevard (Highway 128); (707) 942-5646.

Lord Derby Arms English Pub and Restaurant: You drink one of 11 imported beers offered on draft here, and your dog can drink a fine bowl of water supplied by the staff. "We're very dog-friendly here," one staffer told us. "Dogs are some of our best customers." The large outside deck, also known as the beer garden, has 10 shaded tables and is comfortable on all but the hottest of afternoons. Food is served until late at night, and you can choose from typical English pub grub like fish-and-chips or bangers and mash. 1923 Lake Street; (707) 942-9155.

PLACES TO STAY

Calistoga Ranch Campground RV Resort: There's a lake here where dogs love to swim, but otherwise you're asked to leash them on the hiking trails and in the camping areas. The owners keep guinea hens to chase the rattlesnakes away, and you don't want your puppy to tangle with either creature. There are 144 RV sites. Fees are $19 to $25 a night for up to four people. It's $1 extra for a dog. 580 Lommel Road, Calistoga, CA 94515; (707) 942-6565.

Hillcrest II Bed and Breakfast: On the outside it's a good-looking, large, modern house. But on the inside, it's filled with antiques and other family heirlooms of the locally famed Tubbs family. Debbie O'Gorman, owner of Hillcrest II, is the last of the Tubbs family to live in the Napa area, and she's tastefully stocked the house with items from the family mansion, which burned down in 1964. There's even an old Steinway grand piano waiting to be played in the sitting room (which also has a fireplace).

All this is well and good with dog guests, but what they really adore is that the house is set on 36 acres where they're allowed to romp without a leash if they're well behaved. This is a dog's dream come true, because there just aren't leash-free stomping grounds like these in Napa County, unless you own big property. Fisherfolks and their dogs love it here, too, because there's a fishing pond on the property and it's stocked with all kinds of fishies, including catfish and bluegill. The property is at the base of Mount St. Helena, and the house is on a hilltop (thus the name), so the views are breathtaking.

Humans enjoy using the 40-foot-long pool. Dogs enjoy dipping their paws in the pond. Humans can also use the kitchen and barbecue areas, which is convenient if you don't want to go out to eat every day. A delectable continental breakfast is served on weekends.

Debbie, who has two friendly dogs of her own, asks that you bring a bed for your dog, if he sleeps on the floor, or a blanket to place under him if he sleeps on human furniture.

Rates are $45 to $90. 3225 Lake County Highway, Calistoga, CA 94515; (707) 942-6334.

Meadowlark Country House: The simple elegance of this secluded 20-acre estate makes guests feel right at home. The house where dogs with people get to stay has a light and airy feel and attractive decor, but it's really the surrounding property that makes this place so special. Beware, though. Cats and guinea hens also make their home around the house, so if your dog is a chaser, hang on to that leash.

You and your leashed pooch can hike on the estate's trails, past pastured horses, ancient oaks, and fields replete with wildflowers (and meadowlarks, thus the name). It's quiet here—a perfect place for a hilltop picnic with the pooch. If it's warm, the humans in your party can cool their heels (and knees and shoulders) in the beautiful swimming pool, which is surrounded by a cobblestone walk. If all this isn't enough to fill your day, take a quick drive down the road and spend some time at the Petrified Forest (see Diversions, page 259).

Rates are $125 to $150. A delicious, large breakfast is included in the price. 601 Petrified Forest Road, Calistoga, CA 94515; (707) 942-5651 or (800) 942-5651.

Napa County Fairgrounds: A far cry from the great outdoors, this flat landscape with few trees is at least a good, fair-priced campground if all the inns and motels are booked. There are 50 sites, including some decent places to park your recreational vehicle. Sites are $10 to $18. Dogs (one per site) are $1 extra. 1435 Oak Street, Calistoga, CA 94515; (707) 942-5111.

Pink Mansion: This enchanting old place is an 1875 Victorian—very picturesque and very pink. The owners love dogs. "It's so stupid that so many hotels don't allow these wonderful animals. They add so much," says Jeff Seyfried, one of the owners. If you have a bird dog, think twice about staying here, since also in residence are some doves and a chicken. Water dogs will enjoy watching you splash around in the comfy heated indoor pool and adjacent hot tub, but they mustn't set paw in the water. Dogs are allowed in only one room here, so book ahead lest another dog beats you to the phone. Rates are $95 to $195. Pooches are $15 extra. 1415 Foothill Boulevard (Highway 128), Calistoga, CA 94515; (707) 942-0558.

Triple S Ranch: Once a working ranch, this hidden 11-acre spread in the hills above Calistoga still retains that old ranch feel. The nine rustic yet cozy cabins have only one large room each, so they feel kind of like bunkhouses. But each comes with a private bathroom, so you won't have to wander out to the outhouse in the middle of the night.

What really sets dogs' tails to wagging is that if they're obedient, they get to run around the ranch's property without a leash. That's right, a leash-free doggy haven. (Watch out for foxtails.) Don't be surprised if your dog doesn't want to leave this place. You'll probably be feeling much the same yourself. It's hard to kiss all this—and a pool, and a fun restaurant with some of the best onion rings around—good-bye.

Rates are $60. 4600 Mountain Home Ranch Road, Calistoga, CA 94515; (707) 942-6730.

Washington Street Lodging: Relax in any of several cabins, each with its own little kitchen. You're just a couple of blocks from Calistoga's main drag here. Joan, the animal-loving owner, has cats, but she says if they don't like your pooch, or vice versa, they'll make themselves scarce. She also has a happy basset hound who will probably become your fast friend when you visit.

Your stay here includes a continental breakfast and a doggy treat or two. Cabins are $90, and dogs are charged a $15 fee per visit. 1605 Washington Street, Calistoga, CA 94515; (707) 942-6968.

DIVERSIONS

The two places dogs can actually roam among the trees in this town happen to be at two private roadside attractions. Call them kitschy, call them tacky—they're more fun to explore than most public parks in this county.

Sniff out a petrified forest: You and your leashed dog can roam among trees entombed by a volcanic explosion 3.4 million years ago. During a summertime visit, Joe found out why they call it the Petrified Forest. For him, it had nothing to do with the fact that we were surrounded by trees of stone. The sign announced in big bold letters, "ONCE TOWERING REDWOODS— NOW THE ROCK OF AGES." But Joe didn't know the true meaning of petrified until we encountered—the elves.

They were the Elves of Ages, the ceramic kind you find on suburban lawns and know beyond a doubt they'll be discovered by archaeologists a million years from now, the ones with the leering grins and bewitching eyes that children find enchanting by day and have nightmares about at night. They appeared everywhere Joe looked—sitting beside giant ceramic storybooks, standing beside stony trees.

The elves were at eye level for an Airedale, and they were all staring at him. Every time he saw a new one, he backed away with his tail between his legs and twisted his head around to make sure it wasn't following him. I couldn't help wondering how Airedales have remained so popular for frontline duty during wars.

But then came the petrifying elf. He didn't look any different from the others. But as soon as Joe laid eyes on him and his donkey companion, his tail went down and he turned 90 degrees. For at least two minutes, he was too frightened to look at the elf, growling instead at a manzanita tree. When he peeked and the elf was still staring at him, he decided enough was enough and bolted—leash and all.

He was waiting by the wishing well when I finally caught up to him. He would have left the park if he could have negotiated the turnstile by himself.

The Petrified Forest is at 4100 Petrified Forest Road, off Highway 128. It's actually in the outskirts of Sonoma County, but its address is in Calistoga. The unpaved trail is a quarter-mile loop. Admission is $3 for adults. There are dozens of tables around the gift shop, so pack a picnic. The forest is open from 10 A.M. to 5:30 P.M. in summer, 10 A.M. to 4:30 P.M. in winter. (707) 942-6667.

See Old Faithful in your own backyard: You know you're in for a treat when a big sign greets you at the entry to Old Faithful Geyser: "Many Notable People Have Come to SEE HEAR AND LEARN the mysteries of this WONDER OF NATURE which captures the imagination. IT'S AMAZING."

And indeed, when dogs see the 350-degree-Fahrenheit plume of water gushing 50 to 70 feet into the air, they generally stare for a few seconds with their mouths agape. But the sight of tourists jumping in front of the geyser for a quick photo before the eruption subsides quickly bores them. Dogs then try to wander to the snack bar and persuade the person on the other end of the leash to buy a couple of hot dogs. But even more fascinating is the scent of goat and pig in nearby pens.

If your dog is the brave sort, don't hesitate to bring him to visit Clow, the fainting goat. Clow butts her head against her fence at first, but she's only playing. After a few minutes, she was calming Joe's fears by licking him on the nose. Soon he was in love. Valentino, the Vietnamese potbellied pig, is no longer here. (I hope he didn't go the way of so many of his oversized brethren.) Joe is relieved, since Valentino scared the heck out of him.

Old Faithful erupts every 40 minutes, and the eruptions last about two to three minutes. Picnic tables are plentiful, so bring a snack or buy one here between eruptions. A sign at the site warns that dogs aren't allowed in the geyser viewing area, but you can bring your dog—securely leashed—within a safe distance of the geyser and not get scolded or scalded.

The geyser and goats are between Highways 128 and 29 on Tubbs Lane and are open 9 A.M. to 6 P.M. in summer, 9 A.M. to 5 P.M. in winter. Admission is $6 for adults. (707) 942-6463.

LAKE BERRYESSA

PARKS, BEACHES, AND RECREATION AREAS

• **Lake Berryessa** 🐾🐾 *See* ❸ *on page 256.*

Lake Berryessa, the largest man-made lake in Northern California, offers 165 miles of shoreline for human and canine enjoyment. Most of the resort areas on the lake allow leashed dogs. Better yet, they allow them off leash to swim. The summer heat is stifling here, so your dog will want to take advantage of the water.

Most resorts rent fishing boats and allow dogs to go along on your angling adventure. The fishing is fantastic, especially for trout in the fall and black bass in the spring. It's cooler then, too, so you won't have to contend with so many water-skiers, and your dog won't roast.

If you just want to hike and swim for an afternoon, explore the Smittle Creek Trail. The entrance is just north of the lake's visitors center, on Knoxville Road. The trail takes you up and down the fingers of the lake. Dogs must be leashed, except when swimming.

To get to Lake Berryessa from the Rutherford area, take Highway 128 and turn left at the Lake Berryessa/Spanish Flat sign. It's a very curvy route, so take it easy if you or your dog tend toward car sickness. For more information about the lake, call the Bureau of Reclamation Visitor Information Center at (707) 966-2111. For questions about lakeside businesses, call the Lake Berryessa Chamber of Commerce at (800) 726-1256.

PLACES TO STAY

Here are some of the Lake Berryessa resorts that permit pooches. Prices and amenities vary depending on the season and the extent of the drought, so call the individual resorts for information.

Berryessa Marina Resort: Dogs are $1 extra per day. (707) 966-2161.

Rancho Monticello Resort: Dogs stay for free. (707) 966-2188.

Spanish Flat Resort: Dogs stay for free, but they aren't allowed on rental boats. (707) 966-7700.

Steele Park Resort: Dogs are allowed in the campground, but not in the motel. They're $1 extra. (800) 522-2123.

NAPA

The city of Napa has some 40 parks. Dogs are allowed in a whopping four, each of which has an off-leash section. You'll see dogs in some of the bigger parks, such as the Lake Hennessey Recreation Area, but they're not officially sanctioned, so we can't officially mention them.

PARKS, BEACHES, AND RECREATION AREAS

• **Alston Park** 🐾🐾🐾 🦮 *See* ❹ *on page 256.*

With 157 acres of rolling hills surrounded by vineyards, Alston Park seems to stretch out forever. The lower part of the land used to be a prune orchard, and these prunes are just about the only trees you'll find here.

From there on up, the park is wide-open land with a lone tree here and there. Without shade, dogs and people can fry on hot summer days. But the park is magical during early summer mornings or any cooler time of year.

Miles of trails take you and your dog to places far from the road and the sound of traffic. Dogs are supposed to be off leash only in the lower, flat section of the park. Signs mark the area. It's better than nothing, and it's reasonably safe from traffic. A water fountain and a water closet also grace the entrance.

From Highway 29, take Trower Avenue southwest to the end, at Dry Creek Road. The parking lot for the park is a short jog to your right on Dry Creek Road and across the street. It's open dawn to dusk. (707) 257-9529.

• **Century Oaks Park** 🌳 🐕 *See* ❺ *on page 256.*

This park is a cruel hoax on canines. Dogs are restricted to a dangerous dog run—a tiny postage stamp of an area without fences, just off a busy street. And as for the park's name, which promises granddaddy oak trees, we're talking saplings here—maybe a dozen in the whole dog run area. We don't know how many are in the rest of the park, because dogs aren't allowed there even on leash.

The dog run area (we suggest keeping all but the most highly trained dogs on leash here) is on Brown's Valley Road, just off Westview Drive. Park on Westview Drive and walk around the corner to the dog run. The short walk to the park, with its shade and shrubs, is more enjoyable than the park itself. It's open dawn to dusk. (707) 257-9529.

• **John F. Kennedy Memorial Park** 🐾 🐾 🐾 🐕 *See* ❻ *on page 256.*

Throw your dog's leash to the wind here and ramble along the Napa River. Dogs are allowed in the undeveloped areas near the park's boat marina. The only spot to avoid is a marshland that's more land than marsh during dry times.

Dogs enjoy chasing each other around the flat, grassy area beside the parking lot. There's also a dirt trail that runs along the river. You can take it from either side of the marina, although as of this writing, the signs designate only the south side as a dog-exercise area. The scenery isn't terrific—radio towers and construction cranes dot the horizon—but dogs without a sense of decor don't seem to mind.

Dogs like to amble by the river, which is down a fair incline from the trail. But be careful if you've got a water dog, because jet skiers and motorboaters have been known to mow over anything in their path. There's no drinking water in the dog area and it gets mighty hot in the summer, so bring your own.

Take Highway 221 to Streblow Drive, and follow the signs past the Napa Municipal Golf Course and Napa Valley College to the boat marina/launch area. Park in the lot and look for the trail by the river. The park is open dawn to dusk. (707) 257-9529.

• **Shurtleff Park** 🐾 🐾 🐾 🐕 *See* ❼ *on page 256.*

The farther away from the road you go, the better it is in this long, narrow park. It gets shadier and thicker with large firs and eucalyptus trees.

Dogs are allowed off leash as soon as you feel they're safe from the road. The park is almost entirely fenced, but there are a few escape hatches. Two are at the entrance and two others are along the side that lead you into the schoolyard of Phillips Elementary School. This isn't normally a problem, unless your dog runs into the day-care center at lunchtime, as Joe once did. A teacher escorted him out by the scruff of his neck before he could steal someone's peanut butter sandwich.

You'll find the park on Shelter Street at Shurtleff, beside Phillips Elementary School. It's open dawn to dusk. (707) 257-9529.

RESTAURANTS

Brown's Valley Yogurt and Espresso Bar: Cool off with a cold frozen one at the outside tables shaded by a wooden awning. 3265 Brown's Valley Road; (707) 252-4977.

Downtown Joe's: Joe Dog thinks the name of this place is first-rate. (Don't tell Joe, but it's named after chef-owner Joe Ruffino, not him.) This microbrewery is housed in a 100-year-old landmark building on the Napa River. Turns out he has good taste. Joe and Nisha loved it here. And here's a great deal for dogs: Last time we talked with dog-loving general manager Linck Bergen, he'd just bought some doggy water bowls and oodles of dog bones for his canine customers. Linck gets two paws up from Joe Dog.

Dogs get to sit with you at the edge of the area with outdoor tables (not in the covered section, though) or they can stretch out beside you on the comfy lawn. (Sadly, the sweet dog who originally told us about this place was subsequently treated very rudely by a waiter, and refuses to come back. When I brought it up to a manager, he said he would talk to his staff to make sure it didn't happen again. So you should be okay here, but I thought a heads-up wouldn't be a bad idea, just in case.)

You get to sip good beers made right on the premises. They even make a red ale called Tail Waggin' Ale. For a while, I thought Joe was foaming at the mouth with enthusiasm for the place, but I soon discovered he'd just dipped his snout into a near-empty, still-foamy glass of Tail Waggin' someone had left behind.

Foodwise, Downtown Joe's has something for every taste. Joe Dog likes to smell the porterhouse steaks, but he gets stuck with us ordering things like salads, fresh seafood (Tomales Bay oysters are always in season here), and pastas. 902 Main Street; (707) 258-2337.

Honey Treat Yogurt Shop: The nonfat frozen yogurt here will make you feel 10 pounds lighter and 10 degrees cooler after a long walk with the dog. Slurp it up at the outdoor tables. 1080 Coombs Street; (707) 255-6633.

Napa Valley Traditions: Enjoy fresh baked goods and cappuccino at four outside tables shaded by two trees and an awning. Your dog will find as much to enjoy here as you will—inside, they also sell dog biscuits and dog soap. 1202 Main Street; (707) 226-2044.

Racer's: General manager Linck Bergen wrote to tell us about his fun and unique dog-friendly restaurant. We raced on over to check it out, and it sure is a hoot. However, this may not be the restaurant for you if your dog has a passion for chasing cars; the theme here is racing cars. There's race car memorabilia everywhere, including a real live race car on the wall. And before you blame your chili-eating dog (the chili is super here) for certain strange noises, be aware that every so often racing sounds emanate from the speakers.

Of course, you'll be eating at the 25 tables in the outside area if you visit with your dog, so you may not get the full racing spirit. But you'll still have a good time sipping a "performance" microbrew and downing a burger or pizza. Thirsty dogs can always get a cool bowl of water here. 1201 Napa Street/Town Center; (707) 252-5475.

Rio Poco: Great burritos and easy take-out packages make eating on the outside bench a pleasure. Veteran's Park may beckon from across the street, but unfortunately you're not allowed in with your dog. 807 Main Street; (707) 253-8203.

PLACES TO STAY

Budget Inn: Rates are $40 to $85. Only one small pooch per room, and they're $10 extra. 3380 Solano Avenue, Napa, CA 94558; (707) 257-6111.

ST. HELENA

PARKS, BEACHES, AND RECREATION AREAS

• **Baldwin Park** 🐾 🐾 *See* ❽ *on page 256.*

Baldwin Park has everything you could want in a park, except size. But what it lacks in acreage, it makes up for in dog appeal. Set off a small road, it's almost entirely fenced and full of flowering trees, oaks, and big pines. A dirt path winds through green grass from one end of the park to the other, passing by a water fountain and a conveniently placed garbage can.

Unfortunately, dogs must be leashed, but it's still a pleasant place to stretch all your legs after a tour through the Wine Country. The park is on Spring Street between Stockton Street and North Crane Avenue and is open dawn to dusk. (707) 963-5706.

• **Lyman Park** 🐾 🐾 *See* ❾ *on page 256.*

You'll think you're on a movie set for some old-time village scene when you and your dog wander into this small, cozy park on historic Main Street. Leashes are mandatory, but the park has a gazebo, lots of trees and benches, a flower garden, and—best of all for dogs—an antique horse/dog water fountain. The top part is for horses, the lower bowl for dogs. Horses aren't allowed here anymore, so if your dog is huge, he might as well sip from the equine bowl.

The park is nestled snugly between the police station and a funeral home, at 1400 Main Street, and is open dawn to dusk. (707) 963-5706.

RESTAURANTS

Taylor's Refresher: The folks here are so doggone dog-friendly that you shouldn't drive by without stopping to pay homage to their kindly ways. Dogs have a choice of two items they can have for free: a Milkbone or a hot dog. Yes, a real live in-the-flesh (so to speak) hot dog. "I love seeing dogs munching their favorite treats here," says Sara Toogood, a manager who also house-sits all kinds of critters. Humans will enjoy ice cream, burgers, and other fun lunch items, but unlike dogs, they have to pay. 933 Main Street; (707) 963-3486.

Tomatina: The little sister of the more expensive and upscale Tra Vigne Ristorante (see below), Tomatina is just what the vet ordered if you have a pooch and a pedigreed palate, but a more paltry pocketbook. Lots of families come here. The pastas, pizzas, and salads are delicious. Munch with your dog at the four tables on the patio. 1016 Main Street; (707) 967-9999.

Tra Vigne Ristorante: This is one of the most attractive restaurants with some of the best food in the Bay Area. The wood-burning oven gives even the most simple pasta, pizza, and meat dishes a taste that's out of this world. Your dog can dine with you at the 20 tables in the large, garden-like lower courtyard. (The terrace is out because you have to go through the restaurant to get there, and that's a no-no.) The two of you are sure to drool over the gourmet cuisine. 1050 Charter Oak Avenue (you'll see the restaurant from Main Street, though); (707) 963-4444.

Valley Deli: Eat good deli food at a couple of sidewalk tables. 1138 Main Street; (707) 963-7710.

PLACES TO STAY

El Bonita Motel: This little motel provides decent lodging at very reasonable prices for this area. Rates are $75 to $219. Dogs are $5 extra. 195 Main Street, St. Helena, CA 94574; (707) 963-3216.

Harvest Inn: Dogs who stay in this Tudor-style lodging can wander the inn's 21 acres of gardens, vineyards, fields, and ponds (on leash). Rates are $149 to $399. Dogs are $20 extra daily. They prefer small dogs here. One Main Street, St. Helena, CA 94574; (707) 963-WINE.

DIVERSIONS

Grape Expectations: There are miles and miles of lush vineyards in Napa Valley and more than 70 wineries. But sadly, despite all the fine wine tours available, you'll be hard-pressed to introduce your dog to the joyous process of fermentation, since very few wineries permit pooches inside. However, many do have outdoor areas where you may be allowed to brunch with your pooch and have your own private wine tasting (provided your dog isn't planning on driving home).

Finding a dog-friendly winery can be hit or miss, so call ahead if you have a particular place in mind. For general info on Napa Valley, call (707) 226-7455. Here's one of the friendlier places that allows dogs to dine in the picnic area:

Cuvaison: You'll find three small picnic areas with a total of 11 outdoor tables here. Water is available. The person I spoke with even said, "Dogs are welcome in the tasting room if it's not too crowded." The winery is open 10 A.M. to 5 P.M. daily. 4550 Silverado Trail in Calistoga; (707) 942-6266.

YOUNTVILLE

Unlike the Yountville town government, which bans dogs from its parks, restaurateurs here have the right idea. Several exquisite restaurants welcome dogs to their patios, which are generally shaded and very accommodating to people and their canines. The only word of warning is to avoid these restaurants when they're packed with people from the tour buses that occasionally descend upon the town. It's just too crowded for dogs, who usually get tripped on and later photographed as tourist souvenirs.

RESTAURANTS

Compadres Mexican Bar & Grill: Tropical landscaping, intoxicating jasmine and honeysuckle, and umbrellas over tables make this one of the most pleasant restaurants for spending a few hours with your dog. Try the *pollo borracho*, a whole chicken cooked with white wine and tequila. 6539 Washington Street, at the Vintage 1870 complex; (707) 944-2406.

Napa Valley Grill: California cuisine reigns here, with fresh seafood as the focal point. Several outdoor tables with oversized umbrellas keep you and your dog cool. 6795 Washington Street; (707) 944-2330.

Piatti Restaurant: The atmosphere at the 10-table semienclosed patio is enchanting, and the food is just as wonderful. Choose from a couple of dozen house-made pastas, rotisserie-cooked chicken, fresh-caught fish, pizzas from a wood-burning oven, and many other delectable items. As long as it's not too crowded, your dog is welcome to dine at your side. 6480 Washington Street; (707) 944-2070.

Yountville Pastry Shop: Eat pastries, sandwiches, or pizza on the wooden outdoor patio. 6525 Washington Street, at the Vintage 1870 complex; (707) 944-2138.

PLACES TO STAY

Vintage Inn: Dogs who get to stay here are lucky dogs indeed. This inn ("inn" is an understated description of this place) puts dogs and their people in the lap of luxury, with a perfect blend of old-world charm and new-world design. The airy, beautiful, multilevel villas have fireplaces, and many have views of nearby vineyards. Dogs swoon over the grounds, which have pools, gardens, courtyards, and even a fountain. Rates are $150 to $300, and include a "California Champagne breakfast." Dogs pay a $25 fee per visit. 6541 Washington Street, Yountville, CA 94599; (707) 944-1112.

Bil Frank

29
YOLO COUNTY

The little towns along the winding Sacramento River haven't changed much since the early 1900s. That's good news for you, but it's not necessarily what your dog wants to hear. Restaurants with outdoor dining are rare, and dog-friendly parks are equally uncommon. You'll see mile after mile of wide-open land and dense forests, but most of it is privately owned and off-limits. For information on the one state wildlife area here (the Sacramento Bypass), call the California Department of Fish and Game at (530) 355-0978.

The Sacramento River is so integral to life here that many of the county's parks are formed around public boat ramps that charge nominal launching fees. If you have a dog who loves to go angling for salmon, stripers, or shad, this is a great place to bring her to show off your fishing skills.

Davis and Woodland are the only two cities with off-leash dog areas and a fair number of outdoor dining establishments. Some of the parks are close to major highways, so they're a blessing when your dog starts moaning and getting that bulgy-eyed look on a long trip.

DAVIS

This home to a University of California campus is a very friendly town, especially where dogs are concerned. There are three parks that have sections for leashless dogs. Joe and I didn't know about these parks the first

---

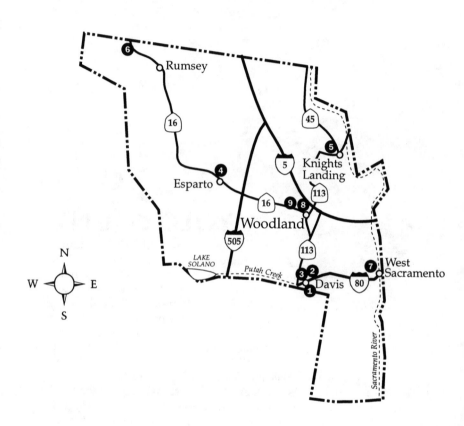

N

W · E

S

6

Rumsey

16

45

5

4

Esparto

5

Knights
Landing

16

113

9 8

Woodland

505

113

LAKE
SOLANO

Putah Creek

3 2

7 West
Sacramento

80

1 Davis

Sacramento River

few times we visited Davis, and we spent our time slinking leashlessly around the shadows of city parks where leashes are the law. Joe feels much better now that we've discovered these other parks and his scofflaw days are over.

PARKS, BEACHES, AND RECREATION AREAS

•**Pioneer Park** 😊 😊 ½ 🐕 *See* ❶ *on page 268.*

This park is good for kids, with playgrounds and basketball hoops, but the dog-exercise area is a little too close to the road for our comfort. It's also very small. If you have a very obedient dog who needs to stretch his legs off leash, but doesn't need to stretch them very far, this will do. It's clean, green, and has some shade. Fortunately it's on a quiet road, so the danger from cars is low.

Pioneer Park is convenient for dogs traveling through on the freeway. Heading east on Interstate 80, take the Mace Boulevard exit and go left on Chiles Road. Take a right on El Cemonte Avenue. Go left on Swingle Drive and you'll be at the park. The dog-walk area is just to the right, about halfway down the block on Hamel Street. (530) 757-5626.

•**Slide Hill Park** 😊 😊 😊 ½ 🐕 *See* ❷ *on page 268.*

The off-leash portion of this diverse community park is toward the back, protected from most traffic. It's also partly shaded and it has green grass, even in the middle of summer! What more could a city dog want? More room? Possibly, but this off-leash area is Davis' largest, so why be picky?

The park is also a great place to take kids. There are playgrounds and tennis courts, and there's even a decent-sized swimming pool in the front.

To get to the dog area, park in the lot at Temple Drive and walk into the park on the paved path, heading left past the tennis courts until you reach the back. The dog spot, under a small grove of trees, is marked by a garbage can and a sign. (530) 757-5626.

•**Sycamore Park** 😊 😊 😊 🐕 *See* ❸ *on page 268.*

If your dog won't be tempted to join in the fun and games of the playground on her right and the sports field on her left, the off-leash portion of this park will suit her just fine. It's green, grassy, and fairly safe from traffic.

Park along Sycamore Lane between Villanova and Bucknell Drives, not in the parking lot of West Davis Intermediate School. Go into the park's grassy field to the right of the school as you face it from Sycamore Lane. The dog-exercise area is to the left of the playground and is clearly marked. (530) 757-5626.

RESTAURANTS

Most of the city's best restaurants are downtown. Dog owners in Davis say that because so many students have let their dogs run loose around here, there's a kind of backlash going on against all dogs in the downtown area. We've never seen evidence of it, though.

The following restaurants are still dog-friendly. Be extra courteous and you can help resuscitate the sullied reputation of dogs here.

The Crepe Bistro: It's crepes, crepes, and more crepes at this small outdoor cafe in a gazebolike setting. And are they ever scrumptious. From the fruit-filled breakfast crepes to dinner crepes filled with beef bourguignonne, chicken, ham and cheese, and spinach, everything is first-rate. 234 E Street; (530) 753-2575.

London Fish 'n Chips: The fish-and-chips are a favorite of many a UC Davis student. Dine with your dog at the shaded outdoor tables. Joe the Anglophile Airedale says the chips dropped by fellow diners are jolly good. 129 E Street; (530) 753-7210.

Subway: Eat subs at a couple of outdoor tables. 130 G Street; (530) 756-1440.

PLACES TO STAY

Best Western University Lodge: When your dog needs to go see some-one graduate or consult with a professor on some "arcanine" matter, this motel one block off campus (and a few blocks from Central Park, a good spot for leashed dogs) is a convenient place to stay. Rates are $60 to $112. Dogs are $5 extra. 123 B Street, Davis, CA 95616; (530) 756-7890.

Econo Lodge: Rates are $54 to $65. Dogs are $5 extra. 221 D Street, Davis, CA 95616; (530) 756-1040.

Motel 6: Rates are $30 for the first adult, $6 for the second. This Motel 6, like most others, allows one small dog per room. 4835 Chiles Road, Davis, CA 95616; (530) 753-3777.

DOGGY DAYS

Party with your pooch: Dogs are always welcome on leash on the University of California campus. But on Picnic Day in mid-April, there's more than a mere welcome mat for them. There's a red carpet.

Dachshunds can run their stubby legs off at a race designed especially for them. If you've never seen these little hot dogs going all out against the clock, it's a sight you shouldn't miss. There's also a contest for Frisbee catchers, and even some sheepdog trials.

Besides dog events, 70,000 people attend the festivities and watch the extravagant opening parade, eat good food, listen to bands, and talk to university professors about their research at departmental demonstrations. (These are usually in the buildings, so dogs have to stay out.) (530) 752-2222 or (530) 752-1990.

ESPARTO

You could get your hopes up if you're hungry when entering the main street to this tiny old-time town. A sign bigger than most around here announces that the Dogtown Diner is dead ahead. When we arrived late one Monday afternoon, it was indeed dead. In fact, all three of the town's eateries were closed.

It turns out that even when they're open, only the Burger Barn (see below) has outdoor seating. About the only place to get hot food around here after 5 P.M. is at the Cache Creek Indian Bingo & Casino center, a few miles west on Highway 16. There are no outdoor tables, but if you're traveling with another human companion, one of you can walk the dog around the area outside the incongruously large building while the other goes inside and orders a three-piece fried chicken dinner with beans and mashed potatoes and gravy for $4.50. Be sure to order an extra mashed potato cup for your dog. While you're in there, you can take your change and try your luck at the video slot machines on the other side of bingoland. (Whatever you do, don't leave your dog alone in the car here. It is often mortally hot.)

PARKS, BEACHES, AND RECREATION AREAS
•**Esparto Community Park** 😊 😊 *See* ❹ *on page 268.*
A brochure announces that this four-acre park is "mainly used for passive recreation." That suits most dogs just fine, since they have to be on leash here anyway. It's a convenient stop on the long and scenic Highway 116.

The park, which is loaded with shade trees, is about five miles west of Interstate 505, on Highway 16. (530) 666-8115.

RESTAURANTS
Burger Barn: Eat big burgers at this eatery's lone, shaded picnic table. 17090 Yolo Avenue; (530) 787-3720.

KNIGHTS LANDING

PARKS, BEACHES, AND RECREATION AREAS
•**Knights Landing Boat Ramp** 😊 😊 *See* ❺ *on page 268.*
When you and your dog launch your boat here, you'll be gliding into movie history: In 1932, this once-bustling riverside community was the backdrop for the Mississippi River scenes in *Showboat.* Your dog may not be impressed, but it's something to think about when motoring out of Sycamore Slough into the Sacramento River.

The town is a mere shadow of what it once was, but it still retains that old-time river town feel. The three acres of trees and grassy glades that surround the boat ramp are open to you and your on-leash dog for such good old-fashioned activities as fishing from shore, swimming in the slough, and taking an easy stroll. There's even a dilapidated wood bridge to add to the Huck Finn ambience.

The entry fee is $5. Going north on Highway 113, make a left at Fourth Street in downtown Knights Landing. After you pass the first bridge, make your first left. It's a sharp one and easy to miss. (530) 666-8115.

RUMSEY

PARKS, BEACHES, AND RECREATION AREAS
•**Cache Creek Canyon Regional Park** 😊 😊 😊 *See* ❻ *on page 268.*
This 700-acre park is flat in the developed sections and very hilly when you get away from people. Couch-potato canines enjoy picnicking at any of three car-accessible sites, as well as "ruffing" it at the campground. More adventurous dogs prefer hiking over the creek and into the woods with their human friends on a self-guided nature walk.

We've found that some park hosts don't know about the trails, so it's best to get a map of the nature walk before you go. Write for one from the Yolo County Parks Division at 625 Court Street, Woodland, CA 95695.

Very feisty dogs may want to continue their treks onto federal land, where they're allowed to be off leash. More than 15,000 acres—some of it inaccessible because of the steep terrain—is out there for your leashless bliss. It can be tricky to find. Contact the Bureau of Land Management, Clear Lake Resource Area, 555 Leslie Street, Ukiah, CA 95482; (707) 462-3873.

Camping at Cache Creek Canyon Regional Park costs $12 to $15. Dogs are $2 extra. There are 45 sites, all first come, first served. The day-use fee is $5. The first of the three park turnoffs is about six miles west of Rumsey on Highway 16. All sites are on the south side of the road. (530) 666-8115.

PLACES TO STAY

Cache Creek Canyon Regional Park: See Cache Creek Canyon Regional Park above for camping information.

WEST SACRAMENTO

PARKS, BEACHES, AND RECREATION AREAS

• **Elkhorn Regional Park** 🐾½ *See* ❼ *on page 268.*

This is a lush 55-acre park along the Sacramento River. Sounds nice. But unless you and your leashed dog are willing to get out your sickles and blaze a trail through the thick bramble and trees that make up most of this park, you'll be relegated to a very small developed portion.

Joe and I arrived at the park just as some kids were coming out of the woods, yelling that they had been attacked by poison oak. Joe still wanted to check out the possibilities, but we remained on terra firma, near the shaded picnic tables at the top of the boat ramp.

The park is convenient to Interstate 5, and if you're passing through with your boat looking for a launch ramp, this is as good as any.

The day-use fee (including the boat ramp) is $5. From northbound Interstate 5 four miles north of West Sacramento, take the Elkhorn exit. Go right on Old River Road and follow it for about two miles. The park entrance is on the left, just after the railroad tracks. (530) 666-8115.

WOODLAND

This little city has churches and saloons in unusually high numbers. Though its an interesting phenomenon, neither should be vying for your dog's dollar. Dogs are better off investing their allowance in a permit to run leashless in the city's parks. For a mere $10, Woodland can be the Land of the Free for your dog. Call the Woodland Department of Parks and Recreation at (530) 661-5880 for details.

PARKS, BEACHES, AND RECREATION AREAS

The following two Woodland parks are rated based on their enjoyability with an off-leash permit from the city's Department of Parks and Recreation.

• **Crawford Park** 🐾🐾🐾🐾 🐕 (with permit) *See* ❽ *on page 268.*

You and your dog will enjoy the year-round green grass and the abundance of shade trees here. You can run the fitness course and play catch without being attached by a leash if you have a special permit. If you're at all worried about safety, try the side of the park bordered by a big wood fence.

This park is a great place to come to exercise your human and canine children at the same time. There's a pint-sized railroad village in the middle of the playground. Kids love it.

Exit Interstate 5 at East Street and go south for several blocks. Turn right on Gibson Road. After a few blocks, go left on College Street and you'll find the park at the corner of College Street and El Dorado Drive. (530) 661-5880.

•**Woodside Park** 🐾 🐾 🐾 ½ 🐕 (with permit) *See* **9** *on page 268.*

There's plenty of green, flat open space here for your dog's running pleasure. The park also has several shaded picnic tables for your dog's dining pleasure. Most pleasurable of all for your dog is the off-leash freedom he can experience if he goes out and buys a permit.

The park is on the corner of Cottonwood Street and El Dorado Drive, just six blocks west of Crawford Park (see above). (530) 661-5880.

RESTAURANTS

Depot Burgers: Dogs like to sit with you at the two umbrella-topped tables while you munch on hot dogs and hamburgers. 628 Main Street; (530) 661-2345.

The Grind: Eat tasty sandwiches under the shade of umbrellas or a roof overhang. 608 Main Street; (530) 666-3774.

PLACES TO STAY

Cinderella Motel: Dogs gloat at this little motel because they're the only pets allowed. Cats are just plain not welcome. Rates are $36 to $46. Dogs are $10 extra. 99 West Main Street, Woodland, CA 95695; (530) 662-1091.

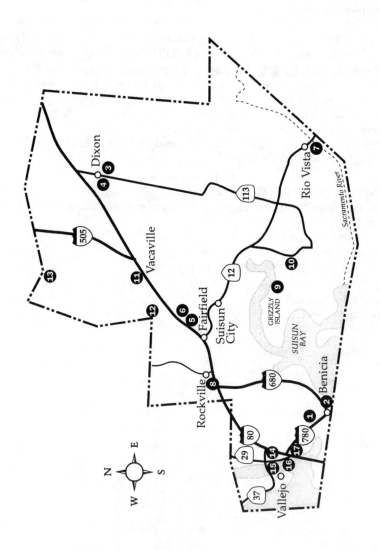

30
SOLANO COUNTY

Solano County is slowly going to the dogs. The Grizzly Island Wildlife Area (see page 280), in the thick of the Suisun Marsh, makes it absolutely worth the trip to Solano County. As long as you visit when dogs can be off leash, your pooch will think she's in heaven. Mud heaven. Bring a towel.

The best doggone news in Solano County is that there's now a dog park in Benicia (see below). It's one of the friendliest pooch parks we've seen. Brava, Benicia!

Two parks in Dixon allow off-leash dogs, but if your dog isn't at perfect heel when you're at either one, leash him fast, or you could find yourself paying a fine old fine.

BENICIA

Until 1997, dogs who lived in Benicia weren't exactly panting with joy. That's because the city's attractive parks, including one that looks like it's something out of Disneyland's Main Street USA, banned dogs. Dogs were pretty much relegated to sidewalks or the Point Benicia fishing pier area (see page 276). But that's all changed now, thanks to the Phenix Dog Park, described below.

PARKS, BEACHES, AND RECREATION AREAS
• **Phenix Dog Park** 🐾🐾🐾🐾 🐕 *See ❶ on page 274.*

Dogs here are rejoicing. They finally have a safe, attractive, easy-access park to call their own. Phenix Dog Park, named after a brave retired police dog, has everything a dog could want. It's got a little more than an acre of leash-free running room, and it's fenced, with water, picnic tables (which little dogs love to dodge under during chase games), pooper-scoopers, and

---

small trees that will be big one day. At press time, the ground was dirt, but by the summer of 1998, irrigation should be in and turf should be down. It'll be real purty then.

The folks here are also hoping to install an obstacle course soon. It will be good for training, but also fun for dogs who are chasing each other to use as part of their play,

And here's a first—this pooch park comes with its own barbecue grills! And you can use them! Of course, you have to be prepared to fend off burger-minded dogs, but if you don't mind, the park people don't mind either. I love this happy, relaxed attitude. Some dog parks I've visited won't even let you bring in a graham cracker for fear you'll be mauled. Those are generally the same parks that ban children. The attitude at Phenix toward children: "You have to allow kids. Kids need to have these friendly interactions with dogs," says Gretchen Burgess, who was behind the park's founding. I like this woman's attitude. If you want to help with park fund-raisers or help the park in other ways, you can reach Gretchen and the Benicia Canine Coalition at (707) 746-8405 or (707) 745-4600. The second number is the veterinary clinic where she works.

The park is located in the northwest corner of the 50-acre Benicia Community Park. Enter the parking lot at Rose and Kearny Drives and drive to the far west end. Then just follow the wide asphalt path with the painted paw prints (I love it!) to the dog park. Keep in mind that the rest of the park prohibits dogs, so don't let your dog talk you into visiting anywhere but the pooch park. If you enter the park at another location, the paw prints will still lead to Phenix. (707) 746-4285.

• **Point Benicia Fishing Pier Area** 🐾🐾 *See* ❷ *on page 274.*

Park and fish at this big drive-on pier at the end of First Street that juts into the Carquinez Strait. It's a popular spot among local anglers. If you're not up for fishing, bring a lunch from a nearby restaurant and park yourself on one of the benches near the old train station. You'll be amazed at the numbers of gulls vying for your crusts.

Dogs enjoy the smells of the strait. While the pier itself isn't conducive to dog exercise, there's an area of undeveloped land nearby where they can cut loose as much as their leashes will allow. There's been some talk of making this area more grassy. I hope this doesn't affect dog access.

This area also happens to be along the Waterfront Trail that winds through the city. The trail is a fun walk for you and your leashed dog, but make sure that when the trail passes through city parks, you and your dog take a detour.

The pier is at the southern end of First Street, just past A Street. (707) 746-4285.

RESTAURANTS

Java Point: You and the dog of your choice are sure to enjoy the soups, sandwiches, bagels, and jammin' good java served here. Dine at the umbrella-topped patio. 366 First Street; (707) 745-1449.

Pacifica Pizza: Choose from a large selection of pizzas to eat at tables shaded by umbrellas. 915 First Street; (707) 746-1790.

PLACES TO STAY

Best Western Heritage Inn: Rates are $65 to $75. Dogs require a $25 deposit. 1955 East Second Street, Benicia, CA 94510; (707) 746-0401.

BETHEL ISLAND
PLACES TO STAY

Sugar Barge RV Park & Marina: Got an RV? Got a dog? Got a boat? Then drive on over to the Sugar Barge and plug 'er in for a few days. Bethel Island, in the heart of the Sacramento–San Joaquin River Delta, is a fine place to visit if you want to sample the delta life with dog. The Sugar Barge has everything from a full-service marina to horseshoe pits. If you send away for a brochure, don't let yourself get too depressed about the photos of the near-empty store with the fluorescent lights or the completely empty, gray dining area with the fluorescent lights. Remember, it's an RV park, not the Ritz.

Rates are $23 to $28. 1440 Sugar Barge Road, Bethel Island, CA 94511; (800) 799-4100.

DIXON

Although it's no more stringent than most, the pooper-scooper law in Dixon has such a formidable name we had to pass it on. It's called the "Canine Defecation Ordinance." Yowza! It doesn't sound like anything *we* want to break.

Here's the good news: If your dog is super obedient and stays really close to you (actually, he'd need to stay at your heel), he can be off leash in the parks here!

PARKS, BEACHES, AND RECREATION AREAS

• **Hall Memorial Park** 🐾🐾 🐕 *See* ❸ *on page 274.*

If you have to conduct business with city government and you want your dog to conduct business, too, you couldn't have asked for a better location for a park. It's right behind City Hall.

There's not much in the way of shade here, but on cooler days this park proves a decent stroll for dogs, provided they're leashed or at very firm heel. The park also has a playground, a swimming pool, tennis courts, and picnic areas with barbecues, so it's even better for people.

The park is at Hall Park Drive and East Mayes Street. (707) 678-7000.

• **Northwest Park** 🐾🐾 🐕 *See* ❹ *on page 274.*

If your dog will stay very close at heel without a leash, she may go leashless at this grassy, 20-acre park. Otherwise, use your leash. With these fairly stringent rules, she probably wouldn't notice her freedom anyway.

The park is on West H and North Lincoln Streets. (707) 678-7000.

PLACES TO STAY

Best Western Inn: This is a convenient place to stay if you have to attend a packed University of California event and no rooms are available in Davis. It's just eight miles away, and a swift drive. They prefer to have small dogs here, but don't demand it. Rates are $60 to $75. Dogs pay a onetime fee of

$10. 1345 Commercial Way, Dixon, CA 95620; (707) 678-1400 or (800) 528-1234.

FAIRFIELD

PARKS, BEACHES, AND RECREATION AREAS

• **Dover Park** 🐾 🐾 *See* **5** *on page 274.*

The atmosphere here is right for relaxing. It's a fairly small park, but it has two ponds with lots of ducks, and big, shady willows, oaks, and firs. It's the place to go if you want to take a stroll with your leashed dog, then sit against a willow tree to read your favorite book.

On the other hand, if your dog doesn't feel like relaxing, this park can be a little too stimulating. Chaseable ducks abound, and the picnic areas are so popular that the smells just beckon dogs. We saw one unleashed mixed-breed fellow swipe a toddler's bag lunch and run away to eat it in peace. He came to the right place.

The park is located at Travis Boulevard and Flamingo Drive. (707) 428-7428.

• **Laurel Creek Park** 🐾 🐾 *See* **6** *on page 274.*

Remember the kind of park you used to play in as a kid—the big neighborhood park with a great playground where the ice-cream truck visited several times a day? This is it, only it's better, because there's some room for leashed dogs to roam.

The entire west side of this 40-acre park is open fields and undeveloped land. It's the right environment for running around with a dog but the wrong place for keeping cool on hot days since there's no shade.

The park is on Cement Hill Road at Peppertree Drive. (707) 428-7428.

RIO VISTA

Humphrey the humpback whale visited this Delta town, and so should your dog. For now, this is a real, dusty Old West town—not one of those cute villages loaded with boutiques and "shoppes." It's refreshing to find a town with more bait shops than banks. However, in the name of "progress," Rio Vista is soon slated to become home to some major housing developments and all the shopping centers and other unsightly amenities that go with them. Get here now, and take some photos on the old streets with your smiling dog. In a few years, they could be collector's items.

Rio Vista isn't bursting with dog amenities. In fact, it's really appropriate to visit with your dog only if you're on a fishing holiday. Then you and your pooch can slip your boat into the water and take off on the Delta for a few hours. Come back with your catch and eat dinner at the county park as the sun goes down on another Delta day.

PARKS, BEACHES, AND RECREATION AREAS

• **Sandy Beach County Park** 🐾 🐾 1/2 *See* **7** *on page 274.*

Take your dog to the very back of the park, and he can run around off leash and even do the dog paddle in the Sacramento River! It's not a huge area, but it's all you'll need to show your dog a good time. The closer day-use section is completely off-limits to dogs, so be sure you end up in the right area.

Your dog has another chance of getting wet if he follows you into the showers at the campground. Dogs are allowed at the campground. It's not terribly scenic and can get mighty dry at times, but hey, it's a place to stay on the river. There are 42 sites. Fees are $8 to $15 a night. Dogs are $1 extra. Half the sites are first come, first served. Reservations are recommended during summer.

Take Highway 12 all the way to Rio Vista; follow Main Street to Second Street, and go right. When the street bears left and becomes Beach Drive, the park is within a quarter mile. Bring proof of a rabies vaccination. (707) 374-2097.

RESTAURANTS

Janey's Delta Cafe: They've got every kind of fast food you could ever want here, and several picnic tables for your feast. Try the southern fried chicken, but watch that your leashed dog doesn't dispose of the bones for you. Janey's also has a variety of snout-lickin' good baked treats. 650 Highway 12; (707) 374-2020.

PLACES TO STAY

Sandy Beach County Park: See Sandy Beach County Park on page 278 for camping information.

DIVERSIONS

Roll on the river: Hire a houseboat. There's nothing like cruising around the Delta in your very own house. Your dog can feel right at home, and nothing makes her happier than having you home all the time. Just remember that, as on land, you have to walk your dog—only you have to dock to do it. Call the Rio Vista Chamber of Commerce at (707) 374-2700 for information on houseboat rentals in the Delta.

ROCKVILLE

PARKS, BEACHES, AND RECREATION AREAS

• **Rockville Hills Park** 🐾 🐾 🐾 *See* ❽ *on page 274.*

Hike, fish, and enjoy nature in this 800-acre park filled with trees and trails. The main trail is fairly steep and takes you to the top of the park, where you'll find two small ponds for fishing. After this hike on a summer afternoon, many dogs jump in when they reach the summit. A man told me that a small beagle once disappeared for several seconds and came up with a tiny fish flailing in her mouth. Could this be just another flagrant flailing fish story?

Once you enter the park, you're safe from traffic. But dogs are supposed to be leashed anyway, since the park is officially run by the city of Fairfield, which has a strict leash law. Check out the nature trail that a local Eagle Scout troop has created.

For the most vigorous workout, try the main trail. It's the one that bends slightly to the left and up a steep hill as you enter from the parking lot. The park is often desolate, so use judgment about hiking alone.

It's on Rockville Road, just west of Suisun Valley Road. (707) 428-7428.

SUISUN CITY

PARKS, BEACHES, AND RECREATION AREAS

•**Grizzly Island Wildlife Area** 🐾 🐾 🐾 🐾 🐕 *See* ❾ *on page 274.*

This is what dogs have been praying for since they started living in cities: 8,600 acres of wide-open land where they can run—leashless—among the sort of wildlife you see only in PBS specials.

This sprawling wetland, in the heart of the Suisun Marsh, is home to an amazing array of fauna, including tule elk, river otters, waterfowl of every type, jackrabbits, white pelicans, and peregrine falcons.

Of course, walking in marshy areas has its pros and cons. But you don't have to get muddy feet here; the landscapes are as varied as the animal life. Dry upland fields are plentiful. You can also canoe down a slough with your steady dog or hike on dozens of dirt trails. Many folks bring dogs here to train them for hunting, which brings us to the unfortunate subject of the park's schedule.

Because of hunting and bird-nesting seasons, Grizzly Island Wildlife Area is open for you and your dog only between mid-January and March 1, between July and early August, and for part of September. (Call for exact dates. These are approximate and are subject to change.)

If your dog helps you hunt for elk, ducks, or pheasant, she's allowed to join you during some of the hunting seasons. Department of Fish and Game staff also occasionally open small sections to people during the off-season, but it's unpredictable from one year to another when and if they'll do it. Even when the park is open, certain sections may be off-limits to dogs. Check with staff when you come in.

To get to the Grizzly Island Wildlife Area, exit Interstate 80 at Highway 12 heading toward Rio Vista. Turn onto Grizzly Island Road at the stoplight for the Sunset Shopping Center. Drive 10 miles, past farms, sloughs, and marshes, until you get to the headquarters. You'll have to check in here and pay a $2.50 fee. Then continue driving to the parking lot nearest the area that you want to explore (staff can advise you). Don't forget your binoculars. (707) 425-3828.

•**Rush Ranch Open Space** 🐾 🐾 🐾 ½ *See* ❿ *on page 274.*

From freshwater and saltwater marshes to rolling grass-covered hills and meadowlike pastures, this 2,070-acre open-space parcel is home to some wonderfully diverse landscapes.

Dogs are permitted on two of the three trails here. They're not allowed to peruse the Marsh Trail because of the fragile nature of the marsh. But the Suisun Hill Trail is a real hit among canines. That trail takes you into hills with killer views of the Suisun Marsh and the hills and mountains to the north. Rangers tell us that on a clear day, you can see the Sierra Nevada. Dogs are also allowed to amble along the South Pasture Trail, which is longer than the other trails and takes you farther from civilization.

Dogs are supposed to be leashed, partly because some of the land is still a working ranch. You don't want your dog tangling with a cow; they don't always make beautiful "moosic" together.

This is a special place. If you'd like to help support the educational and interpretive activities of the Rush Ranch Educational Council, call (707) 421-1351. From Highway 12, exit at Grizzly Island Road and drive south for a couple of miles.

RESTAURANTS

Valley Cafe: Your dog will have a hard time forgiving you if you're on your way to Lake Berryessa and you don't stop at this cute eatery. That's because the owner loves dogs and makes 'em feel right at home. On the porch is a jar of pooch treats that calls dogs from far and wide. If you cock your head just right, you can almost hear it in the breeze. "Oh dogggggyyyyy! Come eat us!!!! We're really nummmmmyyyyyy!!" Joe heard the cookie jar calling one fine summer afternoon, and he practically jumped into the driver's seat to steer the car into the parking area. Fortunately his foot doesn't reach the clutch.

By the way, humans enjoy the food here. It's tasty, with homemade soup and chili topping our list of favorites. Dine with your dog at the seven umbrella-covered tables outside. 4171 Suisun Valley Road; (707) 864-2507.

VACAVILLE

PARKS, BEACHES, AND RECREATION AREAS

• **Andrews Park** 😺 😺 *See* ⑪ *on page 274.*

If you need a shopping cart, try this park first. For some reason, the creek that cuts through the west end of the park contains more shopping carts than most supermarkets.

The chunk of park to the east of the creek is graced with gentle rolling hills, picnic areas, barbecues, deciduous trees, and a lawn as green and smooth as a golf course. But dogs must be leashed.

The west side of the creek is just a shady trail that officially stops at the first overpass and can get pretty seedy if you continue.

The best parking for the east side is on School Street, near Davis Street. For the west side of the creek, park in a lot at Kendal Street, off Dobbins Street. (707) 449-6276.

• **Lagoon Valley Regional Park** 😺 1/2 *See* ⑫ *on page 274.*

The hills you see in the background of this sprawling county park are off-limits to your dog. So are the two reservoirs. In fact, most of the park bans dogs. And you have to bring your dog's license and rabies certificate. All this fun stuff for only $3!

Dogs are allowed to walk by the reservoirs on leash, but that's legally as close as they can go. The section of park that you first enter is the only place dogs are allowed. There are a couple of open grassy areas and a trail that runs along one reservoir. We've seen people fishing with their dogs, which is the most fun you'll have together at this park. But there may be hope for dogs here in the future—the county is considering creating an off-leash area somewhere in the park! This would be a real boon for doggies.

Exit Interstate 80 at Cherry Glen Road and follow the signs to the park. The park is currently closed on Tuesday and Wednesday, but this may change, so call first. (707) 449-6276.

• **Lake Solano County Park** 🐾🐾 *See* **⓭** *on page 274.*

It's no picnic here for dog owners. In fact, dogs aren't allowed in the picnic/day-use area at all. The only way to visit this isolated county park with a dog is to use the camping area across the street. It costs $12 per vehicle on weekdays and $15 on weekends during peak season, $10 all week during off-peak season, and $1 per dog—fares higher than the day-use section.

But for dogs who love to swim, it's worth the price of admission. The big freshwater lake is an ideal respite on a hot summer day. Dogs are allowed off leash for swimming—and only for swimming. There are a couple of narrow trails along the shore, but they're very short.

The camping here is typical "pack 'em in" camping. The 90 sites are so close together you can hear your neighbors unzip their sleeping bags. But if you scout it out, you may be able to nab a site that has a little more privacy. There are even a few sites on the lake. Fees range from $8 to $15 a night.

Don't forget to bring proof of a rabies vaccination for your dog. This can be his certificate or just his up-to-date tag. The park is at Highway 128 and Pleasant Valley Road, about five miles west of Interstate 505. For park info or to make camping reservations, call (916) 795-2990 or (707) 421-7925.

PLACES TO STAY

Best Western Heritage Inn: Small to medium dogs are allowed here. Don't try to pass your Saint Bernard off as a lapdog, even if he is your lapdog. Rates are $52 to $57. Pooches require a $10 to $20 deposit. 1420 East Monte Vista Avenue, Vacaville, CA 95688; (707) 448-8453.

Gandydancer RV Park: The office here is made up of old cabooses. It's situated among groves of eucalyptus trees. Sites are $18. Dogs must be leashed. Take Interstate 80 to the Midway exit. 4933 Midway Road, Vacaville, CA 95688; (707) 446-7679.

Lake Solano County Park: See Lake Solano County Park above for camping information.

Motel 6: If you want to shop at the famous outlet mall in Vacaville and you're traveling with someone who will watch your pooch, this is a convenient place to stay—it's about 1,000 feet from the mall. Shop 'til you drop, then drag yourself back to your dog-friendly Motel 6. One smallish dog per room, please. Rates are $32 for the first adult, $6 for the second. 107 Lawrence Drive, Vacaville, CA 95687; (707) 447-5550.

VALLEJO

PARKS, BEACHES, AND RECREATION AREAS

Only one of Vallejo's city parks, Blue Rock Springs, bans dogs. Here's the best of the rest.

• **Dan Foley Park** 🐾🐾🐾 *See* **⓮** *on page 274.*

You won't often see this at Marine World-Africa USA—professional water-skiers practicing their acts over sloping jumps, then landing headfirst in the water when everything doesn't work out perfectly.

But you and your dog will be treated to this unpolished spectacle if you visit this park on the right day. The park is directly across Lake Chabot from Marine World, so you get to witness a good chunk of the goings-on there. Since dogs aren't allowed at Marine World, this is an ideal place to walk them if your kids are spending a few hours with more exotic animals. You still get to hear the sound of jazz bands and the roar of amazed crowds.

Dan Foley Park is so well maintained we initially were afraid it was a golf course. Willows and pines on rolling hills provide cooling shade, and there's usually a breeze from the lake. Leashed dogs are invited everywhere but the water. Even humans aren't supposed to swim in it. Picnic tables are located right across from the water-ski practice area, so if your dog wants entertainment with his sandwich, this is the place.

The park is on Camino Alto North just east of Tuolumne Street. There is a $2 parking fee. (707) 648-4600.

• **River Park** 🐾🐾🐾 *See* ⑮ *on page 274.*

With goldenrod as high as an elephant's eye and a preponderance of low brush, this waterfront park looks like a huge abandoned lot. That's actually one of its charms—you don't have to worry about your dog mowing over children in a playground or digging up a plug of green grass. The only parklike features here are a couple of benches along the Mare Island Strait.

A wide dirt path leads you toward the water and far from traffic danger. Unfortunately, the leash law is in effect here, and unless your dog is inclined to wade through several yards of mucky marsh to get to the water, he's not going to go swimming. It's still fun to walk along the water and look at the now-defunct Mare Island Naval Shipyard.

There are two entry points. If you're driving, use the south entrance on Wilson Avenue, just north of Hichborn Street, which has a small parking lot. Otherwise, you can enter at Wilson Avenue just across the street from Sims Avenue. (707) 648-4600.

• **The Wharf** 🐾🐾🐾 *See* ⑯ *on page 274.*

This is the place for hip Vallejo dogs, and it's not even an official park. The paved path along the Mare Island Strait looks toward the old Mare Island Naval Shipyard on the other side of the strait, providing a real nautical atmosphere.

It's also the perfect place to take your dog while you're waiting for your ship to come in, since this is where the Vallejo–San Francisco ferry stops.

There's a substantial strip of grass beside the path where dogs like to take frequent breaks. Here, they can socialize without getting under joggers' sneakers. Leashes are a must.

The wharf area covers almost the entire length of Mare Island Way, starting around the Vallejo Yacht Club. Your best bet is to park at the public parking area of the ferry terminal. (707) 648-4600.

• **Wilson/Lake Dalwigk Park** 🐾🐾½ *See* ⑰ *on page 274.*

What you've got here is a big neighborhood park that's mostly undeveloped, leaving lots of land for trotting around. A concrete walkway takes you by fields, big palm trees, and Lake Dalwigk, a small, fairly dirty body of water that can smell slightly of Porta Potti.

Cross over the lake on a small footbridge and your dog will be in a grassy section surrounded by bushes that shelter her from traffic, in case she happens to slip the leash. Be careful, though—it's so secluded that you may not want to go there alone.

The park is at Fifth and Lemon Streets. (707) 648-4600.

RESTAURANTS

Gumbah's Beef Sandwiches: Here's the beef. If your dog is your lunch partner, Gumbah's (pronounced *Goombah's*) meaty place is where he'll ask to go. Dine at the tables out front. 138 Tennessee Street; (707) 648-1100.

Sardine Can: Get a view of the strait while you eat some of the freshest seafood available. Dogs get great treatment here, including a big bowl of water. Dine at the two outdoor tables. It's at 0 (as in zero) Harbor Way; (707) 553-9492.

PLACES TO STAY

Holiday Inn–Marine World-Africa USA: While the kids are being entertained by dolphins and big cats at the nearby theme park, you and your small dog (the only pooches allowed) can curl up, read a book, and enjoy the peace. Rates are $90 to $175. Dogs are charged a $25 fee per visit. 1000 Fairgrounds Drive, Vallejo, CA 94590; (707) 644-1200.

Motel 6: This one's a mere two blocks from Marine World-Africa USA. Rates are $34 for the first adult, $6 for the second. Kids stay free with parents. This Motel 6, like just about every one, permits one small pooch per room. 458 Fairgrounds Drive, Vallejo, CA 94589; (707) 642-7781.

Quality Inn: Rates are $49 to $59. Depending on your dog's size, you could be charged a fee of $10 to $50 per stay. If you'll be spending only one night and have a Great Dane, consider another lodging. 44 Admiral Callaghan Lane, Vallejo, CA 94591; (707) 643-1061.

Ramada Inn: Rates are $75 to $125. Dogs are charged a $25 fee per visit. 1000 Admiral Callaghan Lane, Vallejo, CA 94591; (707) 643-2700.

DIVERSIONS

Seize the Bay: Lucky dogs! You get to take a ride to San Francisco on the Blue & Gold Fleet ferry. But you're going to have to turn to page 398 to read more about it.

31
SACRAMENTO COUNTY

Good news for Sacramento County dogs who don't believe off-leash parks really exist: They do, and now there's a poochy park in your county to prove it! (Finally.) Howe About Dogs Park in Sacramento is the first leash-free haven in the county, and it's mighty popular with the pooch set (see page 294).

The struggle for a leash-free dog park on three acres of land once occupied by Mather Air Force Base in Sacramento may be over in the near future. As soon as a vivacious grass-roots group called SCOOP (Sacramento Canine Owners for Off-Leash Parks) gets approved as a nonprofit organization, SCOOPees hope various construction companies will donate work or materials to make the park happen. They're also hoping to make part of Winn Park and a few other parks into off-leash dog heavens. For more on SCOOP, see the introduction to Sacramento on page 292.

The American River Parkway is one of the finest county park systems I've come across. This riverside greenbelt extends 23 miles from Discovery Regional Park to Folsom Lake, encompassing 20 recreation areas and 5,000 acres. A bike trail connects it all together. If your dog were a bike, you'd be all set.

Unfortunately, dogs aren't allowed on the bike trails here. They're also banned from the numerous horse trails. That leaves them with a few small hiking trails, plenty of open land, and the riverbank. It's not a bad fate, but it could be much better. Three of the American River Parkway recreation

---

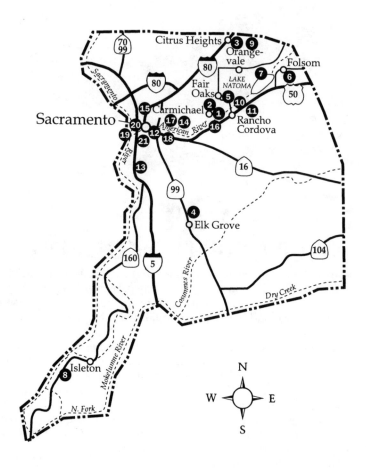

Citrus Heights

3 **9**

Orange-
vale

Folsom

70
99

80

LAKE
NATOMA

7

6

Fair
Oaks

50

2

5

10

Sacramento

15

Carmichael

1

20

17 14

American River

11

Rancho
Cordova

19

12

16

21

18

13

16

99

4

Elk Grove

160

5

Cosumnes River

104

Dry Creek

8 Isleton

Mokelumne River

N. Fork

N

W — E

S

areas are described in this chapter. For more information, call the county parks department at (916) 875-6961.

If you and your dog have a hankering to visit the state capitol building together, you'll get as close as the front door before you're ushered away. But it's more attractive from the outside anyway.

The park surrounding the capitol (called Capitol Park, strangely enough—see page 293) is an exquisite place, with hundreds of trees from around the world. If you're tired of high taxes and crooked politicians, you'll get vicarious pleasure watching your he-dog do leg lifts here.

Dogs who like alternative modes of transportation enjoy this county. Sacramento's historic district is the base for an enchanting horse-and-buggy ride that welcomes dogs (see Diversions, page 296). And in Folsom, it's "all aboard" for dogs who want to ride on an old-style miniature steam train (see Diversions, page 290). These entertaining asides don't make up for the lack of leash-free parks in Sacramento County, but chances are they'll bring a grin to your dog's snout.

CARMICHAEL

PARKS, BEACHES, AND RECREATION AREAS

• **Ancil Hoffman Park** 🐾 🐾 🐾 ½ *See* ❶ *on page 286.*

This 393-acre park is part of the grand American River Parkway. It has plenty of wooded areas for dogs who like to sniff trees and dozens of acres of open grassy land.

Our favorite part is toward the back of the park, near the picnic area. This section is full of shade trees and sports a wonderful dirt trail along the upper banks of the American River. It's also where you can easily access the river. When we visited, a few folks were picnicking at the tables above, but not a soul (canine or human) was down by the river. If you don't mind walking on small, smooth rocks, you can have a good riverside hike. Dogs are supposed to be leashed, but water dogs have no problem taking a short dip. And as with all county parks, dogs are not permitted on any bike or horse trails.

A $4 vehicle entry fee is usually charged. You can park at an outside street and walk in fee-free if you don't mind a bit of a hike. From Fair Oaks Boulevard, drive east on Kenneth Avenue a few blocks, south on California Avenue one block, then east again on Tarshes Drive, into the park. (916) 875-6961.

• **Carmichael Park** 🐾 🐾 *See* ❷ *on page 286.*

This is a flat park with some shade trees for those warmer days. It's a pretty good size for a morning stroll with your leashed beast. The park is at Fair Oaks Boulevard and Grant Avenue. (916) 485-5322.

CITRUS HEIGHTS

PARKS, BEACHES, AND RECREATION AREAS

• **Rusch Community Park** 🐾 🐾 ½ *See* ❸ *on page 286.*

When a park is made up mostly of ball fields, it doesn't bode well for dogs. But this park has some pretty, tree-filled land on the edges of its recreational sections. The ball fields themselves are enclosed, so if you have a dog who's an escape artist, it's a good place to exercise him.

A winding concrete path leads you around the park. Dogs must be leashed. Exit Interstate 80 at Antelope Road and drive east to Rosswood Drive. Turn left on Rosswood, and within a block, turn right on Rusch Drive. Park in the lot. (916) 725-1585.

ELK GROVE

PARKS, BEACHES, AND RECREATION AREAS

At press time, this 130-square-mile service area (it's not really a city) was in the process of building a new park, Laguna Community Park, located at the corner of Bruceville Road and Bighorn Boulevard. The great news is that the park will have a small fenced area for leash-free dogs! It's probably going to open before the year 2000. Dogs will be able to leap into the new millennium with tails wagging. Call (916) 685-3917 to check on the status of the poochy park.

• **Elk Grove County Park** 🐾🐾 *See* ❹ *on page 286.*

This 125-acre park is much better for people than for dogs. If you bring a dog, you'll have to avoid 12 busy ball fields, a pool, a horse arena, soccer fields, and a playground. What's left is a paved pathway that winds through green grassy areas. You and your dog can frolic on the grass or sit under a tree or near the little lake and read *The Call of the Wild* together. It's about as close to wilderness as you're going to get in this very developed park. Here's a real surprise: Dogs must be leashed.

The vehicle entry fee is $4, but if you walk in or get here before or after rangers are working the entry station, you can avoid that fee. The entry is on Elk Grove–Florin Road, just off Highway 99. (209) 875-6961.

FAIR OAKS

PARKS, BEACHES, AND RECREATION AREAS

• **Fair Oaks Park** 🐾🐾½ *See* ❺ *on page 286.*

Dogs run around here with Frisbees in their drooling mouths, but since they're supposed to be leashed, they can't go too far. The park has some rolling hills and trees. If you're going to be waiting for someone at the library located on the park grounds, it's a fine place to bring your dog.

The park entrance is on Fair Oaks Boulevard at Temple Park Drive. (916) 966-1036.

RESTAURANTS

Sunflower Drive-In Restaurant: We love this natural foods drive-in. So do many other people, judging by the crowds it attracts. You and your dog can eat a variety of healthful, tasty dishes at the two picnic tables here, but watch out for the chickens who like to hang out. If the tables aren't available, just walk next door to Village Park and eat at one of the picnic tables there. At least the chickens won't be henpecking you. 10344 Fair Oaks Boulevard; (916) 967-4331.

FOLSOM

Thanks in part to Johnny Cash, most folks who aren't from the area know of Folsom because of the imposing Folsom State Prison. But this is a charming Gold Rush town, which boasts in its motto that it's "Where the West Came and Stayed." A walk down historic Sutter Street will prove this slogan right. The wealth of antique shops, art galleries, and restaurants makes it a popular place for tourists.

PARKS, BEACHES, AND RECREATION AREAS

• **Folsom City Park** 🐾🐾 *See* ❻ *on page 286.*

If you and your dog are with a friend who's visiting the unusual gift shop (or an inmate) at the Folsom State Prison, this is the perfect place to wait. It's next door to the maximum security prison grounds. Even though your dog must be leashed, she'll feel free compared with the folks inside that gray granite structure.

The park is flat and grassy, with ball fields, playgrounds, picnic areas, and a zoo (which is not the most appealing place, if the sight of wild animals in small cages bothers you). Dogs can't go to the zoo, but they revel in sniffing the air that wafts out of it.

Dogs here get a real bonus—they get to ride a mini-steam train. If you have a train-loving pooch, see Diversions, page 290. The park is at East Natoma and Stafford Streets. (916) 355-7285.

• **Folsom Lake State Recreation Area** 🐾🐾🐾½ *See* ❼ *on page 286.*

The bulk of this 12,000-acre reservoir is located in Placer and El Dorado Counties, but its Folsom entrance is popular and easy to find. With four million visitors every year, this park is one of the busiest recreational lakes in the state park system.

Fortunately, that doesn't stop the rangers from permitting leashed pooches on the 80 miles of trails here. The farther you get from the water, the better, at least during crowded months. It can get really crazy around the lake. The operative word here is *party*. But the hiking and horse trails that meander through the recreation area should give you and your dog a little peace.

You'll wander through valley oaks, oracle oaks, digger pines, and toyon here. In the spring, wildflowers are everywhere. You'll see Indian paintbrush, California poppy, and countless other colorful varieties. It's the best time to visit this park, because it's usually not too crowded or hot.

Bring your binoculars. You and your keen-eyed dog may come across such winged beauties as quail, grebes, red-tailed hawks, and eagles. Many are visible from the lake's edge. Dogs aren't allowed on the swim beaches here, but with 75 miles of shoreline (when full), you're bound to find a few lakeside spots. You might even want to try your paw at fishing, which can be mighty good here.

The day-use fee is $5 to $6 per vehicle. Camping at one of the 182 sites costs $12 to $16. Dogs are $1 extra. Sites are available on a first-come, first-served basis, except in summer, when reservations are highly recommended. Call Parknet at (800) 444-PARK to reserve a site. There are many ways to access the park. To get to the park headquarters from the town of Folsom, go a couple of miles north on Folsom-Auburn Road. (916) 988-0205.

PLACES TO STAY

Folsom Lake State Recreation Area: See Folsom Lake State Recreation Area on page 289 for camping information.

DIVERSIONS

Vent some steam: The folks who run the miniature steam train at City Park boast that it's the only coal-fired locomotive that runs a regular schedule west of the Rockies. They're also proud that it may soon be the largest miniature railroad (is that like jumbo shrimp?) in the United States. The ride, now one mile long, could become a three-miler soon, if all goes as planned.

Regardless of all these records, dogs love this train. That's partly because Terry Gold, the train's engineer, loves dogs. "We've had Saint Bernards, Great Danes, all kinds of dogs," says Gold. "We've never had a problem. They have the best time. It's so much fun to watch their faces."

If the train looks familiar to you, you probably visited Berkeley's Tilden Regional Park between 1950 and 1970. It's the very same one-third-scale, narrow-gauge locomotive that was so popular there for two decades before Tilden's new train came along. The Folsom train was built in 1950 but was modeled after a train that ran around 1875.

Dogs and their people get to ride in the open-air cattle cars, gondolas, and hopper cars. The ride takes about 10 minutes and costs $1 per human. Dogs go free. The train runs Tuesday through Sunday. It's in City Park, at East Natoma and Stafford Streets. Call for a schedule. (916) 983-1873.

ISLETON

PARKS, BEACHES, AND RECREATION AREAS

•**Brannan Island State Recreation Area** 🐾 🐾 ½ *See* ❽ *on page 286.*
Most people come to this Delta haven to fish or windsurf. Those activities may not be among your dog's favorites, but even if your dog isn't the sporting sort, this park is pleasing enough. You and your dog can dip your paws in a cool slough, walk around open grassy land (on leash), or picnic in the shade of a eucalyptus. If you get tired, you can just saunter back to your tent and take a nap. It's a dog's life.

The day-use fee is $5. They have 102 campsites. Fees are $12 to $16. Dogs are $1 extra. Reservations are recommended in summer and on holiday weekends. From Highway 160 a few miles south of Isleton, go east at the signs for the park. Call Parknet at (800) 444-PARK to reserve a campsite. For park info, call (916) 777-6671.

PLACES TO STAY

Brannan Island State Recreation Area: See Brannan Island State Recreation Area above for camping information.

ORANGEVALE

PARKS, BEACHES, AND RECREATION AREAS

One of the movers and shakers in this city has been trying to get some land devoted to a dog park, where dogs can run leashless in an enclosed area. Last we'd heard, she'd given up for a while. But if you hear any rumblings about the issue, check with the parks department to find out what you can do to help. Such a park is long overdue in this county.

•**Orangevale Community Park** 🐾🐾🐾 *See ❾ on page 286.*

The northwest corner of this park looks more like it belongs in the northwest corner of the United States. It's wild and filled with trees and tiny dirt trails. It's not a huge area, but it's far enough from the more civilized parts of this park that you and your dog might actually feel as if you're in a rural setting (for at least 30 seconds, until the tennis courts or the street come into view).

Enter the park on Hazel Avenue. The parking lot entrance is south of Oak Avenue. (916) 989-0266.

RANCHO CORDOVA

PARKS, BEACHES, AND RECREATION AREAS

Rancho Cordova has 20 city parks, all of which permit leashed pooches. We list the best one below. For the last few years, dogs have been keeping their toes crossed about the possibility of having a little dog park to call their own in Rancho Cordova, So far, the city's decision-makers have just been discussing the idea. Nothing concrete (or grassy) yet. Dogs' toes are getting cramped. For information on the progress of the talks, or to find out how you can help the canine cause, call the city parks department at (916) 362-1841.

Meanwhile, the huge new Mather Regional Park (see below) is the newest dog-friendly county park around. And soon it too may become home to a large off-leash dog park. This is a historic time for dogs in these parts.

•**Hagan Community Park** 🐾🐾🐾½ *See ❿ on page 286.*

Leashed dogs adore visiting this grassy 61-acre park, which adjoins the American River Parkway. Dogs can get their paws wet in the river or they can stare longingly at the ducks in the park's serene pond.

Dogs have to stay away from the park's fun little petting zoo, which contains such cuties as goats, rabbits, chickens, a sheep, a pig, and a very friendly turkey. But they'll soon forget their disappointment when they learn that well-behaved pooches are permitted on the hand-built miniature train that travels on a quarter mile of track in the park. No fee is charged for the train ride, but donations are happily accepted. The good folks with the Sacramento Valley Live Steamers Club run the choo-choo and need the donations to keep the train chugging along. Call the number at the end of this listing for this year's train schedule.

A $2 vehicle entrance fee is in effect from early April through the end of October. From U.S. 50, exit at Mather Field Road and drive north a few blocks to Folsom Boulevard. Turn right at Folsom and in a few more blocks, head left on Coloma Road. In a few more blocks, go left on Chase Drive and follow it another nine blocks to the park. (916) 362-1841.

•**Mather Regional Park** 🐾🐾🐾 *See ⓫ on page 286.*

The community here is still reeling from the closure of Mather Air Force

Base, but there's a silver lining: The county recently opened a 1,440-acre park on part of the former base's site. For dogs, the cloud's lining could be gold. Plans for an off-leash dog run here may soon be a reality. See the information in the city of Sacramento section below to learn about the noble efforts of the Sacramento Canine Owners for Off-Leash Parks (SCOOP).

At this point, Mather Regional Park is pretty much undeveloped, with lots of knee-level weeds, dry grass, and no trees to speak of. Dogs like it this way. In the future, if the county can afford to develop the park, it could become the most heavily used park in the area. Fortunately, because much of the acreage is home to vernal pools and other fragile environments, up to a third of the land could be protected against development.

From U.S. 50, exit at Mather Field Road, drive south, and follow the signs to the golf course, which is adjacent to the park's main entrance. (916) 875-6961.

PLACES TO STAY

Comfort Inn: Rates are $49 to $85. A $100 pooch deposit is required. 3240 Mather Field Road, Rancho Cordova, CA 95670; (916) 363-3344.

Economy Inns of America: The rooms that are set aside for pets are on the ground floor, face the highway, and are for smokers. If your dog smokes and likes to watch traffic, you'll be all set. Oh, here's a new rule: Your dog has to be less than 20 pounds. This inn is located about a mile from the American River. Rates are $52 to $75. 12249 Folsom Boulevard, Rancho Cordova, CA 95670; (916) 351-1213.

SACRAMENTO

This is a capital place to have a dog who doesn't mind being on a leash. In addition to the 23-mile American River Parkway, which begins in Sacramento, the city has some real dog-pleasing parks of its own. In fact, the city now has its very own leash-free dog park, Howe About Dogs Park (see page 294). Pooches are pleased as punch.

The hard work of a group called SCOOP (Sacramento Canine Owners for Off-Leash Parks) continues. SCOOP has been trying for a few years now to create a dog park at Mather Regional Park (see page 291). The group finally won permission to build a dog park on a three-acre site there, and is awaiting nonprofit status so construction companies can donate goods and services. "It's been a long, long struggle, but I think it's finally within sight," says SCOOP's founder, Carol Michael.

SCOOP's mission is to eventually open five off-leash dog parks in the Sacramento area, including one at Winn Park. "Our population really warrants it," says Michael. "The response to our goal has been phenomenal. My phone rings off the hook all day." In the meantime, SCOOP has adopted Howe About Dogs Park for a while, helping with funding and upkeep. "It gives us something tangible to do," she says.

To join SCOOP or to find out how you can help (know anyone who's aching to donate three acres of chain-link fencing?), write to SCOOP at P.O. Box 19101, Sacramento, CA 95819-0101, or call Carol Michael at (916) 739-6415. Membership is $15 and comes with a subscription to SCOOP's quarterly newsletter and a poop-carrying pouch on which SCOOP's name is proudly emblazoned. Offer good while supplies last. (That sounds so official.)

PARKS, BEACHES, AND RECREATION AREAS

•**Capitol Park** 🐾 🐾 🐾 *See* **⑫** *on page 286.*

Your boy dog will be overwhelmed if you bring him here for the Capitol Park Tree Tour, a self-guided tour of this 40-acre park's magnificent assemblage of trees, which represent the continents and climates of the world. On the tour brochure, each tree is numbered and its scientific and common names are given. So when your leashed dog sniffs at or does a leg lift on a dawn redwood tree, you can impress him by saying, "That's quite a *Metasequoia glyptostroboides,* eh Spot?"

The park extends from the front of the state capitol building to several blocks behind it. It's a great excuse to get up close and personal with the capitol. Take a picnic and relax under the shade of a *Calocedrus decurrens* (incense cedar).

Warning: If your dog is anything like Joe, you may not want to bring him here. Squirrels are everywhere. Joe pulled my arm so hard I thought I wouldn't be able to drive home. And the squirrels are probably still talking about the loud howling shrieks that emanated from this refined-looking Airedale's face.

The park runs from the capitol back to 15th Street, between L and N Streets. Call (916) 324-0333 to receive a tree-tour brochure.

•**Chorley Park** 🐾 🐾 🐾 ½ *See* **⑬** *on page 286.*

If you and your dog are waiting to pick up a loved one at Sacramento's Executive Airport, a visit to this nearby park is a wonderful way for your dog to expend some energy so she won't maul the homecomer with jumps of adulation.

This park is a real find. At first it looks just like so many other neighborhood parks, with a small playground and a little grassy area. But as you walk in, you'll see that it has the potential to be Land of the Dogs. The back of the park is extremely wide, far from traffic, and fenced from the adjacent golf course. Tall firs provide some shade. During wet months, there's even a tiny creek back here.

Even when we've visited on beautiful Saturday mornings, the place has been empty. If it stays this way, it's actually a better place to visit than many of the sprawling county parks, which get heavier use and charge a fee. Dogs are supposed to be leashed here.

Exit Interstate 5 at Florin Road and drive east just a little more than a mile to 20th Street and turn left. Drive to the end and park on the street just outside the park. (916) 277-6060.

•**Del Paso Park** 🐾 🐾 🐾 *See* **⑭** *on page 286.*

This park is great if you have reason to walk your dog near the McClellan Air Force Base or the American River College. Leashed dogs like the horse trail that runs in the back of the park by Arcade Creek.

A couple of smaller dirt trails branch off from the main trail, and they're fun to try, especially if there are too many horses on the main path for your dog's taste (or if your dog likes the taste of horse manure). A shaded picnic area adds a different culinary dimension to the park.

Exit Interstate 80 at Watt Avenue and drive south to Auburn Boulevard. Turn left on Auburn Boulevard and drive a little less than a half mile to Bridge Road. Park past the ball field, and you'll see the trail. (916) 277-6060.

• **Discovery Regional Park** 🐾🐾🐾 *See ⓯ on page 286.*

Lots of leashed urban dogs stroll down here for their early evening walks, dragging their work-weary people behind them. The park has 275 acres of green open space, and although much of it is devoted to human activities like archery and softball, there's more than enough room for your average dog to take an average walk. It's nothing your dog will write home about, but since he can't write anyway, it's no fur off his back.

Unfortunately, because it's a county park, dogs are not permitted on the equestrian trails or the bike path here. That cuts down on easy walking. But the park is well manicured, so there aren't any bushes or dense tree groves to get in your way. You won't want to let that leash slip out of your hand, as roads wind throughout the park.

Water dogs enjoy Discovery Regional Park because it's at the confluence of the American and Sacramento Rivers. The banks are steep, so it's hard to reach out and touch the rivers. But they sure do look good.

Many people walk here with their dogs and avoid the $4 entry fee that is occasionally charged. If you're driving from the north end of the city, take Interstate 5 to the Garden Highway, drive east, and take the first road to the right, Discovery Park Road. (916) 875-6961.

• **Goethe Park** 🐾🐾🐾 *See ⓰ on page 286.*

This chunk of the American River Parkway has a dirt trail that runs along a segment of bank above the American River. It's one of the few trails here where dogs are actually permitted. All county parks ban dogs from bike trails and equestrian trails—and this one has both in abundance. In fact, it's not easy to get around here without them. You'll find some very well-shaded picnic areas here, but they don't make up for the lack of legally walkable places.

The vehicle fee is $4. You can park on the street a few blocks from the entrance and get in for free. Boat launching will cost you $8. Exit U.S. 50 at Bradshaw Road, head north, and follow the signs to the park. (916) 875-6961.

• **Howe About Dogs Park** 🐾🐾🐾 🐕 *See ⓱ on page 286.*

Sacramento dogs are delighted. In fact, some are doggone delirious. They finally have a leash-free haven to call their own! Howe About Dogs Park, located on Howe Avenue, thus the name (actually, it's a longer story, but you can ask the folks there), has trees, a picnic table, benches, and quite a bit of grass.

Unfortunately it's relatively small—a little over a quarter acre—and it's so popular with the pooches that it can be a bit of a zoo on weekends. Dogs wish it could be a little bigger. And guess what? They may soon get their wish. If the park can raise at least $7,000, it will have the money it takes to expand to an entire acre. The city has given the thumbs-up to the expansion, but not the money. There's a donation box at the park, or you can get in touch with SCOOP (see the introduction to the Sacramento section, on page 292, for more on SCOOP), which has adopted the park for a year or two.

The park is located within Howe Community Park, at Howe Avenue and Cottage Way (a few blocks north of Arden Way). (916) 277-6060.

• **McKinley Park** 🐾🐾½ *See* ⓲ *on page 286.*

You can tell lots of dogs visit here just by the signs everywhere. They shout at you to clean up after your dog.

The park has 38 acres of picnic tables, grassy fields, baseball diamonds, and tennis courts. It's at H Street and Alhambra Boulevard, just east of the business loop of Interstate 80. (916) 277-6060.

• **Miller Park/Sacramento Marina** 🐾🐾½ *See* ⓳ *on page 286.*

You and your leashed dog can stroll along a path overlooking the marina here or picnic under big shade trees while you watch the mighty Sacramento River flow by. You can dip your paws in or even do some casting for your supper. It's a very relaxing way to spend a dog-day afternoon.

Drive west to the end of Broadway (past all the lovely refinery tanks) and turn left on Marina View Drive. (916) 277-6060.

• **Southside Park** 🐾🐾½ *See* ⓴ *on page 286.*

Water dogs grimace here, but the truth is that the little lake is fenced off and shows no signs of being made accessible. About the only way to take a dip is with a fishing pole.

Landlubbing dogs think this is a decent park. There's plenty of shade, grass, and walkways to keep a leashed dog happy. There's even a fitness course so dogs can keep their youthful figures.

The park is about eight blocks south of the capitol, at T and Eighth Streets. (916) 277-6060.

• **William Land Park** 🐾🐾🐾 *See* ㉑ *on page 286.*

As you enter this 236-acre park, you may be struck by the thought that it looks just like a golf course. Now hold on to that thought and look around very carefully. See those shiny sticks glimmering in the background and those people in white-and-green outfits walking forward at a determined pace or standing around scratching their heads? Those are golfers. Joe, Nisha, and I learned this the hard way one day when we bounded out of our car and directly into the line of fire of a golfer quite some distance away. Nisha immediately tried to eat the ball. It was not a walk I care to remember, nor, I'm sure, was it a game the golfer remembers fondly.

The golf course is not fenced off from most of the rest of the park, so you really do have to be careful here. A safe, shaded section of the park is the north end. Since dogs must be leashed, it doesn't matter that a couple of little roads run fairly close. If you brought along the kids and someone to watch them, they can go explore the zoo and the amusement park located on the other side of the park.

You can access the park's north side by taking Riverside Boulevard (parallel to Interstate 5) to 12th Avenue and turning east. (916) 277-6060.

RESTAURANTS

A Shot of Class: Dine on fine continental cuisine at the outdoor tables, right in the heart of Sacramento. 1120 11th Street; (916) 447-5340.

Cafe Connection: This fine coffee cafe is located directly across the street from beautiful Capitol Park (see page 293). Dogs can watch you become caffeinated at the outdoor tables. 1007 L Street; (916) 447-8855.

Capitol Garage Coffee Company: Pooches and their human partners come here all the time to enjoy the ambience and great food. Ask Jim or George, the owners, about the dog-friendly bookstore nearby. 1427 L Street; (916) 444-3633.

New Helvetia Roasters and Bakers: Talk about dog-friendly! This place even has a dog biscuit dispenser. And your dog won't even have to have a dime or quarter to use it. (Okay, it's actually a basket, but they like calling it a dispenser here.) Dogs like to join their people when they dine outside in the little courtyard. Try the focaccia. 1215 19th Street; (916) 441-1106.

Vallejo's Mexican Cafe: The Mexican food here is tasty. Share it with your dog at the sidewalk tables. It's at the corner of O and 14th Streets. (916) 444-2837.

PLACES TO STAY

Beverly Garland Hotel: Rates are $74 to $89. Dogs require a $25 deposit. 1780 Tribute Road, Sacramento, CA 95815; (916) 929-7900.

Canterbury Inn: Rates are $45 to $69. Pooches require a $50 deposit. 1900 Canterbury Road, Sacramento, CA 95815; (916) 927-3492.

Doubletree Hotel: Small dogs are considered no problem at this hotel (formerly a Red Lion), but any dog larger than a cocker spaniel will have to have a chat with the manager to get permission to stay. Rates are $99 to $204. 2001 Point West Way, Sacramento, CA 95815; (916) 929-8855.

Howard Johnson Hotel: Rates are $60 to $80. Dogs are $10 extra. 3343 Bradshaw Road, Sacramento, CA 95827; (916) 366-1266.

Motel 6: Rates are $34 for the first adult, $6 for the second. Most Motel 6s permit one small pooch per room. 1415 30th Street, Sacramento, CA 95816; (916) 457-0777.

Radisson Hotel: "We're very dog-friendly here!" says a front desk person, and she's right. When we stayed here recently for a homeschooling conference, there were dogs walking up and down the lovely paths like they owned the place. The rooms here are pleasant and clean, and it's nice because although the hotel has lots of rooms, it's only two levels (it's very spread out). Some rooms provide a water dog with views of the ultimate temptation—a little lake on the hotel's property. But sorry, dogs. No dog paddling is allowed here, or in the hotel's pool. Rates are $119 to $139. Dogs require a $50 deposit. 500 Leisure Lane, Sacramento, CA 95815; (916) 922-2020.

Sacramento Hilton Inn: Rates at this attractive hotel are $86 to $146. There's a $25 pooch charge per visit, and a 25-pound size limit. That's about $1 per pound. 2200 Harvard Street, Sacramento, CA 95815; (916) 922-4700.

DIVERSIONS

A moveable beast: If you and your dog want to get a feel for Sacramento

---

before you start exploring on your own, Joe highly recommends a carriage ride through the charming old part of town.

The folks who run the Top Hand Ranch carriage company are more than happy to take you and your well-behaved dog on a carriage tour around the more quaint section of Sacramento. As long as your dog doesn't interfere with the horse who's pulling this old-style carriage, he'll be welcome on any of the rides offered by Top Hand Ranch.

You'll find the carriage somewhere on the streets of Old Sacramento just about every day and on weekend nights. The price for a 10- to 15-minute ride is $10 for a small family (including a dog). A river park ride is $35 and lasts about a half hour. For a higher fee, you can arrange to go just about anywhere in the carriage. The capitol building is a frequent request. That tour takes roughly one hour and will cost you about $50. Call (916) 655-3444 for locations and prices.

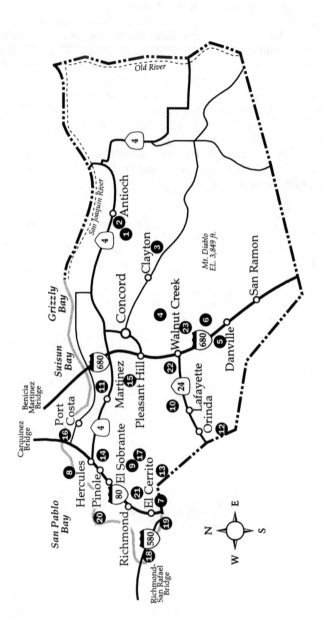

Old River

San Joaquin River

Grizzly Bay

Suisun Bay

San Pablo Bay

4

Antioch
1 2
1

Clayton
3

Concord

Mt. Diablo
El. 3,849 ft.

San Ramon

Walnut Creek
4
23 6
680 5
Danville

Benicia Martinez Bridge

680

Martinez
11
15
Pleasant Hill
22
10 24
Lafayette
Orinda
12

Port Costa

Carquinez Bridge

16
4

14
El Sobrante
9 17
El Cerrito
13

Hercules
8

Pinole
80 21
Richmond
7

20

19
580
18
Richmond-San Rafael Bridge

N
E
W
S

32
CONTRA COSTA COUNTY

Although much of Contra Costa County is considered a sleepy bedroom community for San Francisco, it's a rip-roaring frontierland of fun for dogs. From the renowned off-leash dog haven of Point Isabel Regional Shoreline (see page 309) to the leash-free inland nirvanas such as the Morgan Territory (see page 301), this county enables every dog to have her day, day after day.

For dogs who like long hikes through highly diverse lands, 10 long regional trails lace Lafayette, Walnut Creek, and the other urban areas of the Diablo Valley. There are 60 miles of trails in all, linking together a dozen towns and many beautiful parklands. Dogs must be leashed, but with all the horses and bikes that can visit here, it's a sensible rule.

The Briones to Diablo Regional Trail is one of the more popular trails. It's about 12 miles long and it snakes through some terrific parkland, including the off-leash wonderlands of the Acalanes Ridge Open Space Recreation Area (see page 311) and the Shell Ridge Open Space Recreation Area (see page 312). The trail, which is part paved/part dirt, starts at Briones Regional Park's Lafayette Ridge Staging Area, located on Pleasant Hill Road just north of Highway 24.

The Contra Costa Canal Regional Trail is a good one for dogs who like to look at water but not set foot in it. Joe loves this 12-mile trail that follows the off-limits canal. For information and a trail map of all 10 regional trails, call (510) 635-0135.

ANTIOCH

Antioch is pretty much a desert for dogs, but south of town are two charming spots of relief.

PARKS, BEACHES, AND RECREATION AREAS

• **Black Diamond Mines Regional Preserve** 🐾🐾🐾🐾 🐕
See ❶ on page 298.

Leash-free dogs, especially leash-free dogs of the male persuasion, think this park is an excellent place to visit. The coal miners who worked and lived here in the 1860s and 1870s planted a variety of drought-tolerant trees not usually found in the East Bay, including something called "trees of heaven." Dogs who sniff these trees seem to know why they're called trees of heaven. Their noses just can't get enough as they press them deep into the bark.

The hills of Black Diamond Mines are jumbled and ragged, looking a lot like the Sierra foothills. From the parking lot, it's a moderate climb to the Rose Hill Cemetery, where Protestant Welsh miners (the tombstones bear the names Davis, Evans, and Jenkins) buried victims of mine accidents and many of their children, who died of diphtheria, typhoid, and scarlet fever.

Plenty of tunnel openings and piles of tailings have been preserved by the park for walkers to examine. A brochure marks mine sites. You should be alert for rattlers during warm seasons, although any rattler not actually snoozing will probably get out of your way before you even know he's near.

You can walk into this East Bay regional preserve from the Contra Loma Regional Park just below it (see below). But from that direction, the trails are too hot and dry for a dog in summer. Instead, enter from the north by car via Somersville Road and park in the last lot, which has some shady trees.

From Highway 4 at Antioch, exit at Somersville Road and drive south to the park entrance. Keep driving for a bit more than one mile if you want to park in the lot farthest in. You'll pass wonderful old mining-era houses and barns, now used as park headquarters and offices. (510) 635-0135.

• **Contra Loma Regional Park** 🐾🐾 *See ❷ on page 298.*

This 776-acre park is so well hidden amid barren hills north of Black Diamond Mines that you might not ever know it was here. A few attractive trails, including a trail leading into Black Diamond Mines Regional Preserve (see previous listing), rise into the surrounding hills for you and your leash-free dog to explore.

Unfortunately, as in all regional parks, your dog may not accompany you in the swimming area. Nor can he take an informal swim himself in the fishing areas, since the park managers want to protect his feet from stray fishhooks. It's probably better not to bring your dog here on a hot day. Instead, save the trip for winter or spring, when the wildflowers burst open.

From Highway 4, take the Lone Tree Way exit. Go south on Lone Tree for a little more than a half mile, then turn right onto Bluerock Drive. Follow Bluerock along the park's east side to the entrance. The fee for parking is $3 or $4, depending on the season. The dog fee is $1. (510) 635-0135.

CLAYTON

PARKS, BEACHES, AND RECREATION AREAS

• **Morgan Territory Regional Preserve** 🐾🐾🐾🐾 🐕
See ❸ *on page 298.*

Morgan Territory, named after a farmer who owned the land long before it became part of the East Bay Regional Parks system, is as far away from the Bay Area as you can get while still being in the Bay Area. From its heights, on a rim above the Central Valley, you see the San Joaquin River, the Delta, the valley, and, on a clear day, the peaks of the Sierra. Eagles and hawks soar above as you and your leash-free pooch explore ancient twisted giant oaks and lichen-covered sandstone outcrops below. Morgan Territory is close to the end of the earth and well worth the journey.

As the crow flies, Morgan Territory is equidistant from Clayton, Danville, San Ramon, Livermore, Byron, and Brentwood. And "distant" is the key word.

This 2,164-acre preserve has miles of hiking and riding trails. If you don't want to climb much but want great views of the Central Valley, try the Blue Oak Trail, which starts at the entrance. You'll even see the "backside" of Mount Diablo. It's an unusual vantage point for Bay Area folks.

Most of the creeks are dry in the summer, though your dog can splash into cattle ponds, if he's so inclined. Watch for wicked foxtails in these grasses. These are the sticky wickets that help make veterinarians a well-off breed.

The easiest access is from Livermore in Alameda County. From Interstate 580, take the North Livermore Avenue exit and drive north on North Livermore Avenue. Shortly after the road curves left (west), turn right, onto Morgan Territory Road, and follow it 10.7 miles to the entrance. From the Walnut Creek/Concord area, take Clayton Road to Marsh Creek Road, then turn right onto Morgan Territory Road. The entrance is 9.4 miles from Marsh Creek Road. (510) 635-0135.

RESTAURANTS

Skipolini's Pizza: The folks here serve New York–style pizza, as well as salads and sandwiches. They welcome dogs at their outdoor tables. It's at Main Street and Diablo Road; (925) 672-5555.

CONCORD

PARKS, BEACHES, AND RECREATION AREAS

Most of Concord's parks are run-of-the-mill on-leash parks. But for a real treat, try this one:

- **Lime Ridge Open Space Recreation Area** 🐾🐾🐾🐾 🐕
  See ❹ *on page 298.*

This open space reserve is huge, sprawling across parts of both Walnut Creek and Concord. It's undeveloped and open to lucky leash-free dogs. You can sometimes find a creek, depending on the time of year and status of drought, and that's a real relief during the long, hot summers.

The only entry point from Concord is from the parking lot on Treat Boulevard west of Cowell Road. (925) 671-3270.

PLACES TO STAY

Holiday Inn Concord: Rates are $79 to $99. Dogs require a $50 deposit. 1050 Burnett Avenue, Concord, CA 94520; (925) 687-5500.

Sheraton Concord Hotel: "Smallish" dogs only at this attractive hotel, which features a 23,000-square-foot atrium (with a swimming pool . . . ahhhh . . . but not for dogs) and an exercise facility (also not for dogs, which is fine with Joe). Rates are $95 to $139. Dogs are $10 extra. 45 John Glenn Drive, Concord, CA 94520; (925) 825-7700.

DANVILLE

PARKS, BEACHES, AND RECREATION AREAS

- **Las Trampas Regional Wilderness** 🐾🐾🐾🐾 🐕
  See ❺ *on page 298.*

This regional wilderness is remarkable for its sense of isolation from the rest of the Bay Area. You can experience utter silence at this 3,298-acre park, and the views from the ridge tops are breathtaking.

Rocky Ridge Trail (from the parking lot at the end of Bollinger Canyon Road) takes you and your leash-free pooch on a fairly steep three-quarter-mile ascent to the top of the ridge, where you'll enter the East Bay Municipal Utility District watershed. Since dogs aren't allowed here and permits are even required for humans, it's better to head west on any of several trails climbing the sunny southern flanks of Las Trampas Ridge.

Creeks run low or dry during the summer, so bring plenty of water. Your dog should know how to behave around cattle, deer, and horses.

From Interstate 680 about six miles north of the intersection with Interstate 580, take the Bollinger Canyon Road exit and head north on Bollinger Canyon Road to the entrance. (Go past the entrance to Little Hills Ranch Recreation Area, where dogs aren't allowed.) (510) 635-0135.

- **Oak Hill Park** 🐾🐾🐾 *See* ❻ *on page 298.*

Here's a very clean, beautiful park run by the city of Danville. It's about as good as a park designed for people can get, offering picnic tables, a pond with ducks and geese and waterfalls, volleyball and tennis courts, and an unusually attractive children's play area with swings, a slide, and its own waterfall. The rest of the park is natural oak-studded hillside laced by an equestrian/hiking/exercise dirt trail, from which there is a fine view of Mount Diablo. Dogs will enjoy this path, but must remain on leash. No wading in the pond, either.

The park is at Stone Valley Road and Glenwood Court. (925) 820-6074.

PLACES TO STAY

Danville Inn: Rates are $60 to $90. 803 Camino Ramon, Danville, CA 94526; (925) 838-8080.

EL CERRITO

PARKS, BEACHES, AND RECREATION AREAS

•**Hillside Park** 🐾🐾🐾 🐕 *See ❼ on page 298.*

El Cerrito dogs have something to bark about: Hillside Park, an official off-leash dog run. It's not the prettiest park around; the southern end is mostly an eroded hillside of scrubby grass with power lines. But off Schmidt Lane is the much more attractive El Cerrito Foundation Memorial Grove. A bumpy dirt path leads up through coyote brush to eucalyptus groves at the hilltop, overlooking El Cerrito, the Golden Gate and Bay Bridges, and Mount Tamalpais. The trail doesn't go far into the open space.

Enter off Schmidt Lane, which runs north off San Pablo Avenue. (510) 215-4300.

EL SOBRANTE

PARKS, BEACHES, AND RECREATION AREAS

•**Sobrante Ridge Regional Preserve** 🐾🐾🐾🐾 🐕
See ❽ on page 298.

Dogs love visiting this quiet preserve, but Sobrante Ridge hasn't always been a place where animals smile. In the 1970s, the property belonged to Cutter Laboratories, which raised horses and cattle and used their blood to produce various vaccines. That breeze you may feel while visiting is just an equine and bovine sigh of relief that Cutter is outta here.

These days, Sobrante is a happy place, full of deer, coyotes, salamanders, and oodles of birds. Unless your dog is under perfect voice control, it's a good idea to use a leash here. From the Coach Way entrance, follow the dirt trail branching back to the left 100 feet from the entrance. This is the Sobrante Ridge Trail, which will take you through grass, dwarf manzanita, oaks, and coyote brush, up a half mile to views of both Mount Tam and the top of Mount Diablo. Branch off on the short loop, Broken Oaks Trail, for a picnic at one of the tables under cool oaks.

This 277-acre preserve is the habitat of the extremely rare Alameda manzanita. So that your dog knows what to watch out for, this manzanita is a gnarled, red-barked shrub that may have sprays of urn-shaped blossoms or clusters of red berries, depending on the time of year. The manzanitas cling to the hillsides. Don't let your boy dog do anything the manzanitas wouldn't want him to do.

From Interstate 80 in Richmond, exit at San Pablo Dam Road and drive south to Castro Ranch Road. Turn left on Castro Ranch, then left at Conestoga Way, going into the Carriage Hills housing development. Take another left on Carriage Drive and a right on Coach Way. Park at the end of Coach and walk into the preserve. (510) 635-0135.

HERCULES

PARKS, BEACHES, AND RECREATION AREAS

• **San Pablo Bay Shoreline Park** 🐾🐾🐾½ 🐕
See ❾ on page 298.

This tiny, undeveloped East Bay Regional Park shoreline is just right if you happen to be in Hercules exploring the old Santa Fe Railroad yard. A paved trail runs about one-eighth of a mile along the tracks. New housing developments and interesting restored Victorian railroad workers' housing surround a small but pretty area of grass, swamp, and eucalyptus trees. Best of all, you and your dog can check it all out without a leash.

If you follow Railroad Avenue to its end, across the line into Pinole, there's a very small and beautifully landscaped city park behind the wastewater treatment plant (which smells fresh as a rose). You must keep your dog on leash here.

From Interstate 80, exit at Pinole Valley Road and travel north. Pinole Valley Road becomes Tennent Avenue, then Railroad Avenue. Park somewhere around the Civic Arts Facility, a cluster of Victorian buildings in a grove of palms and eucalyptuses. Call (510) 724-9004 or (510) 635-0135.

LAFAYETTE

PARKS, BEACHES, AND RECREATION AREAS

• **Briones Regional Park** 🐾🐾🐾🐾 🐕 *See ❿ on page 298.*

From both main entrances to this park, you can walk one-quarter of a mile and be lost in sunny, rolling hills or cool oak woodlands. Unless you stick to the stream areas, it's not a good park for hot summer days. But with a good supply of your own water, you and your dog, who may run blissfully leashless, can walk gentle ups and downs all day on fire roads or foot trails.

The north entrance requires an immediate uphill climb into the hills, but you're rewarded with a quick view of Mount Diablo and the piping of ground squirrels, all of whom are long gone safely into their burrows by the time your dog realizes they might be fun to chase (much to Joe's chagrin). If your dog is a self-starter, this end of the park is fine for you. The Alhambra Creek Trail, which follows Alhambra Creek, does offer water in the rainy season. Stay away from the John Muir Nature Area (shaded on your brochure map), where dogs aren't allowed.

When we're feeling lazy, we prefer the south entrance at Bear Creek, just east of the inaccessible (to dogs) Briones Reservoir. Here you have an immediate choice of open hills or woodsy canyons, and the land is level for a few miles. The Homestead Valley Trail leads gently up and down through cool, sharp-scented bay and oak woodlands.

Watch for deer, horses, and cattle. Some dogs near and dear to me (they shall remain nameless, Joe and Bill) love rolling in fresh cow patties—an additional hazard of the beasts existing in close proximity.

From Highway 24, take the Orinda exit; go north on Camino Pablo, then right on Bear Creek Road to Briones Road, to the park entrance. The parking fee is $3 and the dog fee is $1. (510) 635-0135.

RESTAURANTS

Geppetto's Cafe: Gourmet coffee, gelati, and pastries may be enjoyed at sidewalk tables. Dogs are welcome. It's a good spot for a cool drink after a hot summer hike in Briones. 3563 Mount Diablo Boulevard; (925) 284-1261.

MARTINEZ

Martinez has a charming historic district right off the entrance to its regional shoreline park, so spend some time walking with your dog around the Amtrak station and antique shops. You'll see plenty of fellow strollers taking a break from the train.

PARKS, BEACHES, AND RECREATION AREAS

• **City of Martinez Hidden Lakes Open Space** 🐾🐾🐾
See ⓫ on page 298.

Although the city park called Hidden Valley Park doesn't allow dogs, the open space to the south of it does. It's crossed by one of the East Bay Regional Parks' trails (the California Riding and Hiking Trail) on its way from the Carquinez Strait Regional Shoreline to where it connects with the Contra Costa Canal Trail. Call (510) 635-0135 to order a map of the Contra Costa Regional Trails.

One entrance to Hidden Lakes is off Morello Avenue, where it intersects with Chilpancingo Parkway. (925) 313-0930.

ORINDA

PARKS, BEACHES, AND RECREATION AREAS

• **Robert Sibley Volcanic Regional Preserve** 🐾🐾🐾🐾 🐕
See ⓬ on page 298.

We're not exactly talking Mount St. Helens here, but this 371-acre park has some pretty interesting volcanic history. Geologically inclined dogs can wander leashless as you explore volcanic dikes, mudflows, lava flows, and other evidence of extinct volcanoes.

The preserve is actually closer to Oakland than Orinda, but it lies in Contra Costa County. From the entrance on Skyline Boulevard, you can get on the East Bay Skyline National Recreation Trail and walk north to Tilden Regional Park (see page 319) or south to Redwood Regional Park (see page 332). Or, for a shorter stroll, take the road to Round Top, the highest peak in the Berkeley Hills, made of volcanic debris left over from a 10-million-year-old volcano.

More attractive and less steep is the road to the quarries. It's partly paved and smooth enough for a wheelchair or stroller, but it becomes smooth dirt about halfway to the quarries. Both trails are labeled for geological features. (Pick up a brochure at the visitors center.) At the quarry pits, there's a good view of Mount Diablo. This is a dry, scrubby, cattle-grazed area, but in the rainy season your dog may be lucky enough to find swimming in a pit near the quarries. In the spring, look for poppies and lupines.

From Highway 24 east of the Caldecott Tunnel, exit on Fish Ranch Road, drive north to Grizzly Peak Boulevard, then take a left. Go south on Grizzly

Peak to the intersection with Skyline Boulevard. Go left on Skyline. The entrance is just to the east of the intersection. (510) 635-0135.

• **San Pablo Dam Reservoir** 🐾 🐾 🐾 ½ *See* 🔞 *on page 298.*

This reservoir is a top fishing spot in the Bay Area. It's stocked with more trout than any lake in California. That's great news for humans, but dogs could care less. They're not allowed to set paw in this magnificent body of water (and neither are people), so hanging out alongside a human angler is out of the question. You can't even take your pooch out on your own boat.

The paved and dirt trails around the reservoir are lovely and often empty once you and your leashed dog wind into the hills. The dirt trails get rougher as you leave the popular fishing areas. You'll have to ford some creek beds or streams, and there's too much poison oak for comfort if your dog doesn't step daintily right down the middle of the trail. The trails are wild and woodsy, though, and dogs recommend them highly.

The entrance fee is $5 for parking and $1 for dogs. You can buy a season ticket for $75 a car or $80 a boat. The lake itself is open from mid-February through mid-November.

From Interstate 80, exit at San Pablo Dam Road and drive east about six miles. From Highway 24, exit at Camino Pablo/San Pablo Dam Road and go north about 5.5 miles. (510) 223-1661.

RESTAURANTS

High Tech Burrito: The burritos and fajitas here are really, really good. The ingredients are fresh and combined in very interesting ways. Try the veggie burrito. It's *muy bien.* Dogs can dine with you (no spicy scraps, please!) at the many courtyard tables at Theatre Square. 2 Theatre Square; (925) 254-8884.

Pasta Cuisine: Of all the yummy pastas, soups, and salads served here, the one dish I've heard the most raves about is the special Caesar salad. It's made with smoked chicken and prawns. Joe drools just thinking about it. I get hives just thinking about it (allergic to shellfish). You can dine with doggy at the courtyard tables at Theatre Square. But beware: A server here tells us that patrons sometimes bring cats. If your dog thinks cats are entrées, keep your eyes peeled. 2 Theatre Square; (925) 254-5423.

PINOLE

PARKS, BEACHES, AND RECREATION AREAS

• **Pinole Valley Park** 🐾 🐾 🐾 *See* 🔞 *on page 298.*

This city park is fortunate enough to be contiguous with Sobrante Ridge Regional Preserve (see page 303). The paved bike path off to the right past the children's playground leads to Alhambra Creek—a good plunge for your dog, if he can negotiate the banks wearing a leash. The path then becomes a fire trail and ambles through brush, oaks, and nicely varied deciduous trees. This trail is quite wild and litter-free. It ends at an outlet on Alhambra Road.

The entrance is at Pinole Valley Road and Simas Avenue. (510) 724-9062.

PLACES TO STAY

Motel 6: Rates are $47 for the first adult and $6 for the second. This Motel

6, like most others, permits one small pooch per room. 1501 Fitzgerald Drive, Pinole, CA 94564; (510) 222-8174.

PLEASANT HILL

PARKS, BEACHES, AND RECREATION AREAS

• **Paso Nogal Park** 🐾🐾🐾🐾 🐕 *See* **⑮** *on page 298.*

This large park has smooth dirt trails along gentle oak-dotted slopes. Dogs must be on leash in the park, but locals use the lawn area as a leash-free dog run. Owners are expected to carry a leash, clean up after their dogs (there are no scoopers available), and cooperate with park rangers if there's a complaint. But "no complaint, no problem" is the operable phrase here.

The park is at Morello Avenue and Paso Nogal Road. (925) 682-0896.

PORT COSTA

Port Costa is a sleepy, picturesque town of Victorian cottages. In the nineteenth century, it was a booming wheat export dock. Of course, if your dog remembers Frank Norris' book *The Octopus*, he already knows this.

PARKS, BEACHES, AND RECREATION AREAS

• **Carquinez Strait Regional Shoreline** 🐾🐾🐾🐾 🐕
See **⑯** *on page 298.*

This regional shoreline, run by the East Bay Regional Parks, lies just east of Crockett. From the Bull Valley Staging Area, on Carquinez Scenic Drive, you can choose one of two leash-free hillside trails. The Carquinez Overlook Loop, to the right, gives better views of Port Costa, the Carquinez Bridge, and Benicia. We surprised a deer here sleeping in the shade of a clump of eucalyptus.

The eastern portion of the park, east of Port Costa, is contiguous with Martinez Regional Shoreline. But beware: You can't get there from here. (Carquinez Scenic Drive is closed at a spot between Port Costa and Martinez. You must turn south on twisty McEwen Road to Highway 4 instead.)

To get to the Carquinez Strait Regional Shoreline from Interstate 80, exit at Crockett and drive east on Pomona Street through town. Pomona turns into Carquinez Scenic Drive, from which you'll see the staging area. (510) 635-0135.

RICHMOND

Point Richmond, the Richmond neighborhood tucked between the Richmond–San Rafael Bridge and Miller-Knox Regional Shoreline, is a cheerful small-town hangout for you and your dog. Consider stopping by for a snack on your way to some of the magical, four-paw shoreline here.

Sit on a bench in the Point Richmond Triangle, the town center. You'll be surrounded by nicely preserved Victorian buildings, the Hotel Mac, and many delis and bakeries, some with outdoor tables. We were asked not to mention one by name because it welcomes cats as well as dogs. Grrrr. The Santa Fe Railroad rattles past periodically, blowing the first two notes of "Here Comes the Bride."

From Interstate 580, on the Richmond end of the Richmond–San Rafael Bridge, exit at Cutting Boulevard and drive west to town. Bear right on Richmond Avenue. The Triangle is at the intersection of Richmond and Washington Avenues and Park Place.

PARKS, BEACHES, AND RECREATION AREAS

•Kennedy Grove Regional Recreation Area 🐾🐾🐾
*See **⑰** on page 298.*

This is a large picnic and play area for folks who like softball, volleyball, and horseshoes. Dogs must be leashed. The best part of this park is that you can get to the Bay Area Ridge Trail from here from a gate to the right as you enter the park, or from a trailhead at the Senior Parking Area. You'll cross some East Bay Municipal Utility District land (no permits necessary in this section) and San Pablo Dam Road. The trail ascends and soon becomes the Eagle's Nest Trail. If you're really inspired and your pooch isn't pooped, you can then climb all the way to Inspiration Point in Tilden Regional Park (see page 319). Dogs like Joe firmly put their paw down when it comes to such rigorous tasks. He just sits there riveted to the ground like a fire hydrant. You can almost see him shaking his head "no way."

From Interstate 80, take the San Pablo Dam Road exit and go south; the entrance is a quarter-mile past the intersection of Castro Ranch Road. There's a $3 parking fee and $1 dog fee from April through October. (510) 635-0135.

•Miller-Knox Regional Shoreline 🐾🐾🐾🐾 🐕
*See **⑱** on page 298.*

Hooray! Wooooof! Yap! (The last utterance was from a dogette—the kind Joe likes to pretend is a cat.) Although your dog must be leashed in developed areas, she can run free on the hillside trails east of Dornan Drive in this 259-acre park.

West of Dornan is a generous expanse of grass, pine, and eucalyptus trees with picnic tables, a lagoon with egrets (so there's no swimming), and Keller Beach (dogs are prohibited). It's breezy here and prettier than most shoreline parks by virtue of its protecting gentle hills, whose trails offer terrific views of the Richmond–San Rafael Bridge, Mount Tamalpais, Angel Island, and San Francisco. Ground squirrels stand right by their holes and pipe their alarms. Although you can't bring your dog onto Keller Beach, there's a paved path above it along riprap shoreline, where your dog can reach the water if he's so inclined. In the picnic areas, watch for discarded chicken bones!

You can also tour the Richmond Yacht Harbor by continuing on Dornan Drive south to Brickyard Cove Road, a left turn past the railroad tracks. Or, from Garrard Boulevard, drive south till you see the Brickyard Cove housing development. The paved paths lining the harbor offer views of yachts, San Francisco, Oakland, and the Bay Bridge.

From either Interstate 80 or Interstate 580, exit at Cutting Boulevard and go west to Garrard Boulevard. Go left, pass through a tunnel, and park in one of two lots off Dornan Drive. (510) 635-0135.

• **Point Isabel Regional Shoreline** 🐾🐾🐾🐾 🐕

See ⑲ on page 298.

One exception to the East Bay Regional Parks' rule that dogs must be on leash in "developed" areas is Point Isabel Regional Shoreline. This is a decidedly unwild but terrific shoreline park with plenty of grass and paw-friendly paved paths. It's swarming with dogs. In a recent census by the park district, 558,930 people and 784,370 pooches visited in one year. Fortunately, people here are generally very responsible, and the park looks pretty good, despite being accosted by more than four million feet and paws annually. (Note: Pit bulls must be on leash here. Unfortunately, all pit bulls must pay the price for a few bad owners and their pit bulls.)

The large lawn area is designed for fetching, Frisbee throwing, and obedience training. People are often seen lobbing tennis balls for their expert retrievers or hollering, "Hey! Run! Go!" at a dog like Joe who can't catch anything except an occasional cold. The dog owners police themselves and their dogs very effectively.

And owners, as in most parks frequented by dogs, love to socialize. Even the shyest person will feel brave enough to start a conversation with another dog owner. It's one of life's mysteries.

There are benches, picnic tables, rest rooms, a water fountain for people and dogs, and many racks full of bags for scooping. A bulletin board posts lost-and-found dog notices, news of AARF (Area for Animals to Run Free) and its campaign for more open dog-run space, and membership information for the Point Isabel Dog Owners' Association (PIDO), which keeps the scooper dispensers full and otherwise looks out for dogs' interests in the park.

Cinder paths run along the riprap waterfront, where you can watch windsurfers against a backdrop of the Golden Gate and Bay Bridges, San Francisco, the Marin Headlands, and Mount Tamalpais. On a brisk day, a little surf even splashes against the rocks.

After a wet and wonderful walk, you may want to take your pooch to Mudpuppy's Tub and Scrub, which is located right here, for a little cleaning up (see Diversions, page 311). From Interstate 80 in Richmond, exit at Central Avenue and go west to the park entrance, next to the U.S. Postal Service Bulk Mail Center. To reach the front parking lot, pass Costco and turn right. (510) 635-0135.

• **Point Pinole Regional Shoreline** 🐾🐾🐾🐾 🐕

See ⑳ on page 298.

Of all the East Bay Regional Parks' shorelines, this is the farthest from civilization and its discontents, and thus the cleanest and least spoiled. It's also huge and a heavenly walk for dog or owner, with its views of Mount Tamalpais across San Pablo Bay, and its docks, salt marsh, beaches, eucalyptus groves, and expanses of wild grassland waving in the breeze. Some of the eucalyptus trees are so wind-carved they could be mistaken for cypresses.

The park has fine bike paths, and your dog should be leashed for safety on these, but he's free on the unpaved trails—even on the dirt paths through marshes, such as the Marsh Trail. Just make sure he stays on the trail and doesn't go into the marsh itself. Dogs may not go on the fishing pier or on the shuttle bus to the pier.

From Interstate 80, exit at Hilltop Drive, go west and take a right on San Pablo Avenue, then left on Atlas Road to the park entrance. There's a $3 parking fee and a $1 dog fee. (510) 635-0135.

•Wildcat Canyon Regional Park 🐾🐾🐾🐾 🐕
See ㉑ on page 298.

This is Tilden Regional Park's northern twin. Tilden (see page 319) has its attractive spots, but it's designed for people. Wildcat seems made for dogs, because not much goes on here. Dogs really dig this. Who needs all those human feet passing by anyway? (Unless, of course, they're tracking along *eau d' cow patty* or some other savory scent.) Best of all, you can leave your dog's leash tucked away in your pocket.

Large coast live oaks, madrones, bay laurels, and all kinds of chaparral thrive on the east side. And since the area was ranchland from the days of Spanish land grants and traces of house foundations remain, it isn't surprising that a lot of exotic plants flourish here alongside the expected ones. You'll find berries, nasturtiums, and cardoon thistle, which looks like an artichoke allowed to grow up. All kinds of grasses and wildflowers cover the western hillsides.

At the entrance parking lot is Wildcat Creek, which gets low but usually not entirely dry in summer. Then you can follow the Wildcat Creek Trail (actually an abandoned paved road); it travels gently uphill and then follows the southern ridge of the park. Or follow any of the nameless side trails, which are wonderfully wild and solitary. You can hear train whistles all the way up from Emeryville and the dull roar of civilization below, but somehow it doesn't bother you up here.

Other trails lead through groves of pines or follow Wildcat Creek. The park is roughly three miles long. If you come to the boundary with Tilden, remember that dogs aren't allowed in the nature area across the line. You can get on the East Bay Skyline National Recreation Trail (Nimitz Way), running along the park's north side. Don't branch off onto the Eagle's Nest Trail, however; it belongs to the East Bay Municipal Utility District, which requires a permit and frowns on dogs. But there's plenty of room here. You and your dog could spend several blissful days in Wildcat.

From Interstate 80, southbound, take the McBryde exit and turn left on McBryde Avenue to the park entrance. If you're northbound, take the Amador/Solano exit. Go three blocks north on Amador Street and turn right (east) on McBryde to the entrance. No fees are charged. (510) 635-0135.

DIVERSIONS

Drive your pooch to the pulpit: Want to take your dog to church? If you don't think he's ready to pray in a pew, you can bring him along to attend a service in the comfort of your car. Since 1975, the First Presbyterian Church of Richmond has offered a drive-in service in a shopping mall parking lot. Held at 8:30 A.M. every Sunday outside the Pinole Appian 80 shopping center, the ceremony attracts about 40 worshipers every week.

Reverend Don Mulford transmits the service over shortwave radio from a mobile pulpit, complete with a sermon and choral music. Church elders bring communion around to each car on a silver platter and parishioners honk and flash their headlights at the pastors to say "Amen." It's quite a scene—and afterward you can go shopping. Dogs are as welcome to attend as anyone. For more information, call (510) 234-0954.

Foof him up: Is your pooch starting to smell like a dog? If you go to Point Isabel (see page 309), you can give your dog both the walk of his life and a bath. Mudpuppy's Tub and Scrub, the park's very own dogwash, offers full- or self-service scrubbings in four elevated tubs—$15 for full service, $10 if you and your dog take charge of the tub. Not bad, considering it includes shampoo, drying, and someone else to clean the tub afterward. Owners Cynthia and Holly, and their mascot Hobie, provide a fun, clean atmosphere. Weekend reservations are a must. Mudpuppy's is next to the big parking lot at the front end of the park. (510) 559-8899.

SAN RAMON

PLACES TO STAY
San Ramon Marriott at Bishop Ranch: The folks who run this attractive hotel are very friendly to creatures of the doggy persuasion. Rates are $89 to $169. 2600 Bishop Drive, San Ramon, CA 94583; (925) 867-9200.

DIVERSIONS
Work up a lather: What kind of dog wags his tail about getting a bath? The kind of dog who visits ShamPooches. It's a dog-friendly environment, where you can wash your dirty dog for 45 minutes for $12. Special shampoos and dips are extra. 3151-1 Crow Canyon Place, at Crow Canyon Commons; (925) 806-0647.

WALNUT CREEK

Walnut Creek's big secret is its beautiful creeks and canals, former irrigation ditches that now adorn golf courses and housing developments. Walnut Creek, San Ramon Creek, the Contra Costa Canal, and the Ygnacio Canal all pass through town. Dogs must be leashed everywhere, except in the undeveloped areas of city-owned open spaces.

PARKS, BEACHES, AND RECREATION AREAS
• **Acalanes Ridge Open Space Recreation Area** 🐾🐾🐾🐾 🐕
  See ㉒ on page 298.
  In 1974, the city of Walnut Creek set aside a few open spaces for a limited-use "land bank." Dogs must be "under voice or sight command." (Translation: off leash if obedient.) Hoo boy! The trails are open to hikers, dogs, horses, and bicycles, however, so on a fine day, your dog may have some competition.

  Acalanes Ridge, close to Briones Regional Park (see page 304), is crossed by the Briones to Diablo Regional Trail. Like the others, it lacks water.

  A good entry point is from Camino Verde Circle, reached by driving south on Camino Verde from the intersection of Pleasant Hill and Geary Roads.

For information on any of the open spaces, call (925) 943-5899.

- **Shell Ridge Open Space Recreation Area** 🐾 🐾 🐾 🐾 🐕
  See ㉓ on page 298.

Dogs may run off leash everywhere but in the developed areas (parking lots, picnic grounds), but "must be under positive voice and sight command." The people who write these rules must be retired military document writers or part-time computer-manual writers.

Within the Shell Ridge Open Space is the Old Borges Ranch, a demonstration farm staffed irregularly by rangers. The ranch house is sometimes open on Sundays from noon to 4 P.M. Call first to check. For information or to make a reservation to visit, call (510) 943-5860.

You can enter by the Sugarloaf–Shell Ridge Trail at the north edge. From Interstate 680, take the Ignacio Valley Road exit, go east on Ignacio Valley Road to Walnut Avenue (not Boulevard), turn right and right again on Castle Rock Road. Go past the high school, turn right, and follow the signs. (925) 943-5899.

RESTAURANTS

Walnut Creek's "downtown," your respite from mallsville, is Main Street. Here, you'll find several welcoming outdoor restaurants, benches for just sitting, and good weather. A couple of our favorites follow.

Original Hot Dog Place: Every kind of hot dog is served in this tiny shop with a neat hot dog mural on the wall and a wooden Indian outside next to the tables. 1420 Lincoln Avenue at Main Street; (925) 256-7302.

Pascal French Oven: You and your dog will drool over the baked goodies. Waitresses often bring buckets of water out to dogs. 1372 North Main Street; (925) 932-6969.

PLACES TO STAY

Embassy Suites: This attractive hotel is eight stories high, with an atrium in the middle. Suites consist of a bedroom, living room, and galley kitchen. Couch-potato pooches enjoy the fact that there are two TVs per suite, each with cable and remote. Joe Dog has been known to change channels with the remote in his mouth once in a while, but since it usually ends up on something like channel 823, I can only guess this is an accident. Rates are $129 to $179. Dogs have to pay a $50 cleaning fee per visit, so make your stay at this lovely hotel a long one so it's worth the cost. 1345 Treat Boulevard, Walnut Creek, CA 94596; (925) 934-2500.

Holiday Inn: A few months before writing this, I got a letter from Daniel Fevre, general manager of this hotel. "My first question (when I took this job) was—you guessed it—'Do we take pets?' The answer was 'No.' My reply was 'We do now!' To test the program, I stayed with my two dogs (and one cat) for several days until the movers arrived, and the staff was great." He went on to tell me about how the hotel was also considering holding pet adoptions or pet education community events. He sounded like just the kind of hotelier this book loves.

When we finally called to get more information, we were told he was no longer with the hotel. But they still had Fevre's legacy—the dog-friendly policy—intact. What's really special about this place is its proximity to a hiking trail. They'll tell you about it at the front desk. Rates are $98 to $109. 2730 North Main Street, Walnut Creek, CA 94598; (925) 932-3332.

Walnut Creek Motor Lodge: Very small dogs only, please (15 pounds or under). Rates are $55 to $80. 1960 North Main Street, Walnut Creek, CA 94596; (925) 932-2811.

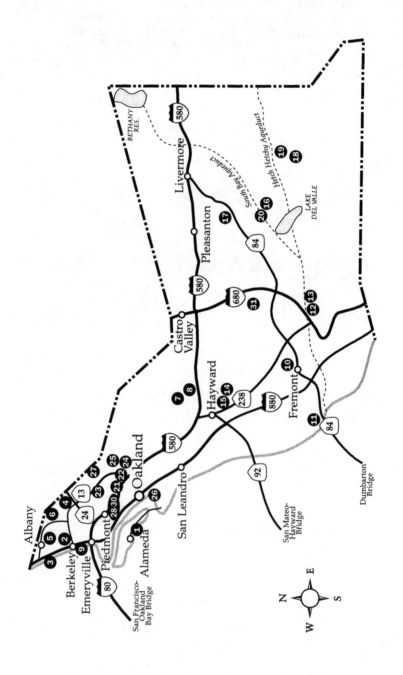

BETHANY RES.

580

Livermore

Pleasanton

South Bay Aqueduct

Hetch Hetchy Aqueduct

19 18

20 16

17

84

580

680

31

12 13

LAKE DEL VALLE

Castro Valley

Hayward

10

Fremont

7 8

15 14

238

880

11

84

Oakland

580

San Leandro

92

Dumbarton Bridge

San Mateo-Hayward Bridge

25 24

27

13 23 21 22

4 28 30

24 26

1

Albany

6

5 2

3 9

Berkeley

Emeryville

Piedmont

80

Alameda

San Francisco-Oakland Bay Bridge

N E S W

33
ALAMEDA COUNTY

From the hallowed hippie havens of Berkeley's Telegraph Avenue to the pleasing suburban pleasantries of Pleasanton, Alameda County is like California in miniature: It has nearly every level of population density and type, and nearly every temperate natural environment. Somehow, it all works.

Dogs dig it here, whether they're rasta dogs or shaved shih tzus. The county is like the creek it's named after—it's been lined with concrete, filled with trash, and dammed into oblivion, yet it still manages to gush joyfully onward. Some of the wildest country in the Bay Area is located in this county, full of hidden gems of nature. So many of these parks are off-leash havens that your dog may think he's dreaming.

The 12-mile Alameda Creek Regional Trail (see page 324) is a favorite among dogs. They can run off leash on most of the trail, but where signs say leashes are required, heed the message.

An even more invigorating trail is the East Bay Skyline National Recreation Trail. Well-behaved, leash-free dogs are welcome on the entire 31-mile length of this trail. Wowza wowza and howlelujah! The trail stretches from the northern end of Wildcat Canyon Regional Park in Contra Costa County

---

(see page 310) to the southern end of Anthony Chabot Regional Park (see page 323). Plenty of horses also use this trail, so if your dog is a hoof chaser, keep him leashed.

As if all this wasn't enough good news, your dog's hair will stand on end when he learns that unless he's a pit bull, he's allowed to run leashless on thousands of acres of parkland within the East Bay Regional Parks District. Some 50 parks and recreation areas and 20 regional trails—75,000 acres in all—fall under the district's jurisdiction. Pooper-scooper dispensers are installed at the most heavily used areas, such as Point Isabel Regional Shoreline (see page 309).

The only places where dogs must be leashed within the district's parks are in developed areas, parking lots, picnic sites, lawns, and in posted Nature Areas. They aren't permitted on beaches (Point Isabel Regional Shoreline is a major exception), wetlands, marshes, or in the Tilden Nature Area. In addition, at press time, the district was deciding whether dogs have to be leashed along Redwood Regional Park's Stream Trail (see page 332). Call (510) 635-0138 for more information on the East Bay Regional Park system.

A couple of bits of good news: The city of Oakland now has its very own pooch park. It opened in 1997, and at press time it wasn't a very good one, but it's headed for improvement. (Please see Hardy Dog Park, page 330.) Plus it seems to have inspired talk of other locations for pooch parks in the city. In addition, the Friends of Cesar Chavez Park, in Berkeley, has taken over what can seem like an impossible fight to convert 15 acres of this bayside park to an off-leash poochy paradise. It's a high-energy, dog-lovin', tail waggin' group that needs your help if you can lend a paw. See the introduction to Berkeley on page 317 for more on this group and its efforts.

Dogs who enjoy the great outdoors are truly in pooch heaven here, because this is the home base for the San Francisco Bay chapter of the Sierra Club. The club holds dozens of fun hikes for dogs each year, via its Canine Hike unit, and most of the hikes are in the East Bay. Dogs get to hike and play off leash, as long as they're well-behaved and under voice control. Hikes are of varying difficulties and lengths. Some involve easy swimming (I hear the water dogs drooling), some involve camping, some even involve meeting the love of your life (when Sierra Singles and their dogs come out to play). Get yourself an activities schedule at the chapter bookstore, or call and order one. They're $3.50 in person, $4.50 by mail. The schedule includes all the hikes, doggy and non-doggy, for the quarter. Schedules are available at the chapter bookstore, at 6014 College Avenue, Oakland, CA 94618. Call before you send a check, if ordering by mail, in case the price has changed; (510) 658-7470. You can call and order by credit card, too. This is money very well spent. The folks who participate in the canine hikes are almost as friendly and fun-loving as their dogs.

ALAMEDA

PARKS, BEACHES, AND RECREATION AREAS

• Washington Park 🐾 🐾 See ❶ on page 314.

Washington Park, next to Robert Crown Memorial State Beach (sorry, pooches, no can go), is Alameda's largest park. It has lots of great amenities for people, and leashed dogs enjoy the wide green expanses, the bike path, and the edge of the marsh here. Unfortunately for hungry dogs, pooches aren't permitted at the picnic areas.

From downtown, take Central Avenue toward Webster Street. The park is at the corner of Central and Eighth Street. For the beach, continue on Eighth Street. Call (510) 635-0135 for beach information or (510) 748-4565 for park information.

RESTAURANTS

The Good & Plenty Cafe & Deli: This wonderful cafe is a veritable Noah's Ark. Animals of all kinds come to the outdoor tables here with their people. It's not uncommon to see cats on laps and birds on shoulders. But dogs are by far the best—er, most common—critters who visit while their people dine on delicious deli food. Kira, a 100-pound malamute who moved here from Arizona to live on a boat, convinced her "dad" to write and tell us that the food servers "welcome pets with open arms and have been known to get suckered out of a snack or two by the appropriate big, brown-eyed doggy look . . . Kira gives this place a four-paw rating with no hesitation." The cafe is located near the Ballena Isle Marina, at 1132 Ballena Boulevard; (510) 769-2132.

DIVERSIONS

Seize the Bay: Water-loving dogs just about swoon when they learn they're allowed on the Blue & Gold Fleet's ferries that run between Oakland, Alameda, and San Francisco. Please turn to page 398 in the San Francisco chapter for more details.

ALBANY

RESTAURANTS

For a pleasant street with dog-friendly people and at least a couple of restaurants with outdoor tables, try Albany's Solano Avenue.

Barney's Gourmet Hamburgers: While its street address is in Berkeley, it's just over the border from Albany. Dogs drool while watching you eat gourmet burgers at the outdoor tables. 1591 Solano Avenue, Berkeley; (510) 526-8185.

Marco Polo's Deli Cafe: Dogs enjoy watching you eat tasty sandwiches at the outdoor tables here. 1158 Solano Avenue; (510) 524-5667.

BERKELEY

Berkeley, well known for its tolerance of eccentricity, is equally eccentric when it comes to dogs. Like most of Alameda County, it features strict leash laws: You break the law, you pay the price—which can be above $100 for the second offense.

But there is a unique loophole. If your dog is obedience-trained, Berkeley doesn't require him to be leashed. If an animal control officer sees you with your unleashed dog, you'll be asked to demonstrate that your dog is under absolute voice control. If the officer is not persuaded, you'll be cited and asked to appear in court with your dog, where you'll have another chance to prove it. (I can just picture Joe sitting, lying down, and rolling over in court. Well, maybe if a treat were involved. Nahhh.)

Whether they're all under absolute voice control or not, you'll see a lot more unleashed dogs in Berkeley than in any other Bay Area city. The University of California at Berkeley also has a leash law, but the campus is swarming with loose dogs, too. The only leashed animal you'll see is a local pet pig whose owner walks him there. Go figure.

Berkeley created the country's first official dog park, Ohlone Dog Park (see page 319). Still, it's been slow in approving a plan to allow dogs to run free on 15 of the 40 undeveloped acres of Cesar Chavez Park in the marina. A citizens' group that calls itself AARF (Area for Animals to Run Free) worked valiantly for five years to convert the space, but its efforts got swallowed by a bureaucratic sinkhole in 1993. A new, highly energetic group has emerged to continue the fight. They're called the Friends of Cesar Chavez Park—"The Friends" for short. At press time, they were still battling park naysayers who want this former landfill to remain as undoggy as possible. Foes include the Sierra Club and a blind woman. (Fortunately, the Girl Scouts and the Pope are staying out of this one.) Obviously The Friends needs as much help as it can get. It's a wonderful group, with terrific, responsible, environmentally concerned people, and the best regional dog newsletter— *The Berkeley Bark*—I've ever seen. For info on the group, its newsletter, or upcoming relevant city meetings, contact Claudia Kawczynska at Friends of Cesar Chavez Park, 2810 Eighth Street, Berkeley, CA 94710; (510) 704-0827.

PARKS, BEACHES, AND RECREATION AREAS

•**Aquatic Park** 🐾 🐾 ½ *See ❷ on page 314.*

Take advantage of this city park for a quick stroll by the water. Conveniently located off Interstate 80, it's fairly tranquil, even with the lagoon's powerboats and water-skiers whizzing by. The lagoon's banks are planted with a mixture of grass, willows, cypress, and eucalyptus. Boy dogs have lifted many a leg in homage here.

Thanks to its greenery, birds are plentiful. Dogs like to bird-watch from the paved paths and the parcourse. Leashed dogs enjoy splashing around the shallow, calm lagoon water.

From Interstate 80, take the Ashby exit and turn north on Bay Street. There's a small parking lot. If you come from the north side of the park, you can park at a couple of areas on Bolivar Drive, along the park's east side. (510) 644-6530.

•**Cesar Chavez Park** 🐾 🐾 🐾 *See ❸ on page 314.*

Someday, 15 of the 40 undeveloped acres of this 90-acre bayside park may become an off-leash pooch paradise. (Please see the introduction to Berkeley, above, for more on a group called Friends of Cesar Chavez Park and its efforts toward this commendable canine cause.) Meanwhile, you and your leashed dog can enjoy the grassy hills surrounded by the beautiful San Francisco Bay. Trails meander up and down the rolling hills and wind through a couple of quiet meadows.

The views of San Francisco, the Golden Gate Bridge, and the Bay Bridge are some of the best around. The park is equipped with plenty of pooper-scooper stations crammed with "Mutt Mitts." Use them. Impress those who could make this a leash-free mutt mecca. In fact, pick up an occasional "orphan" poop while you're at it, and the cards just may become stacked in favor of off-leash pooches. For more on how to help the park, contact Claudia Kawczynska at Friends of Cesar Chavez Park, 2810 Eighth Street, Berkeley, CA 94710; (510) 704-0827.

This is also a great place to fly a kite, and there are plenty of instructions posted on how to do it safely around here.

Take University Avenue west past the Interstate 80 interchange and follow the signs to the Berkeley marina and Cesar Chavez. (510) 644-6371.

• Claremont Canyon Regional Preserve 🐾🐾🐾🐾 🐕

See ❹ on page 314.

This large park is full of steep hillside trails that lead to crests with stunning views of the university and the surrounding hills and valleys. If your dog likes eucalyptus trees and doesn't like leashes, take him here. It's one of those tree-filled, leashes-optional parks.

From Highway 13 (Ashby Avenue), drive north on College Avenue. Turn right on Derby Street, past the Clark Kerr Campus. The trailhead is at the southeast corner of the school grounds, near the beginning of Stonewall Road. (510) 635-0135.

• Ohlone Dog Park 🐾🐾🐾 🐕   See ❺ on page 314.

Since 1979, when it opened as the first leash-free dog park in America, Ohlone has provided a model for other cities willing to experiment with the concept. Dogs across America revere Ohlone. It's kind of like the Mecca of mutts.

The park can get pretty beat up during winter, with mud overtaking everything, including the mulch and woodchips used to cover the mud. But even after years of unflagging popularity, the park is still in relatively good shape. This can be credited in large part to a conscientious park upkeep committee that keeps an eye on facilities and provides plastic bags for cleaning up after your dog. You'll find a water faucet, complete with a dog bowl set in concrete, and two picnic tables for owners who want to relax while their dogs socialize. The grass isn't always green here, but it's definitely better than what's on the other side of the fence.

The park is at Martin Luther King Jr. Way and Hearst Street. (510) 644-6530.

• Tilden Regional Park 🐾🐾🐾🐾 🐕   See ❻ on page 314.

Humans and dogs alike give Tilden a big thumbs-up (dewclaws-up). Leash-free dogs find the scents from its western ridge delectable and humans find the ridge's breathtaking views of the entire San Francisco Bay equally enticing.

Escapes from civilization are everywhere in this 2,078-acre park. Try the trails leading east from South Park Drive. They connect with the East Bay Skyline National Recreation Trail.

You can pick up the Arroyo Trail at the Big Springs sign and take it all the way to the ridgetop. There's a great stream at the trailhead that you can follow through laurel, pine, toyon, and scrub on your low-grade ascent. Your dog may want to take a dip in the stream for refreshment.

After the trail veers from the stream, it steepens and leads into cypress-studded meadows and eucalyptus groves. Eventually it feeds into the Skyline National Recreation Trail, also known as the Sea View Trail, offering vistas over the bay along the way.

Dogs aren't allowed in the large nature area at the northern end or in the Lake Anza swimming area. Leashes are required in all the developed areas, including picnic grounds and ball fields. Remember to watch your step in the areas frequented by dogs, as some owners neglect to clean up after their furry friends. There's nothing like stepping in a steaming pile of dog dung to put a damper on a day of exploring nature.

Speaking of steaming, be sure to check out Tilden's miniature steam train for a riveting good time. (See Diversions, page 321.)

From Highway 24, take the Fish Ranch Road exit north (at the eastern end of the Caldecott Tunnel). At the intersection of Fish Ranch, Grizzly Peak Boulevard, and Claremont Avenue, take a right on Grizzly Peak and continue north to South Park Drive. One more mile north brings you to Big Springs Trail. During peak season, continue on Grizzly Peak to the Shasta Gate. (510) 635-0135.

RESTAURANTS

Just north of University Avenue, a three-block stretch of Shattuck Avenue is home to several restaurants with outdoor seating. Here are a few:

Fontina Caffe Italiana: Dogs like dining with their people at the two umbrella-topped tables here. The food is snout-licking good. But what they like even better is that Fontina is right next door to the Shattuck Cat Clinic. Poor Joe Dog will never know the pleasures of Fontina, because he knows too well the pleasures of cats. 1730 Shattuck Avenue; (510) 649-8090.

The French Hotel Cafe: Someone sneaked Joe a saucer of espresso and he barked at feet for the rest of the day. It's the real stuff—good and strong. Sip it at the outside tables, but let your dog stick with water. 1540 Shattuck Avenue; (510) 548-9930.

Istanbul Grill: Mmm good! The food here is a delectable combination of Turkish, Mediterranean, and California cuisine. Dine with your dog at the outdoor tables. 1686 Shattuck Avenue; (510) 549-2316.

Elsewhere in Berkeley, you'll find many other outdoor options, including these:

Bongo Burger: There's only one regular ol' hamburger here. Other burgers include the Persian burger (marinated ground lamb) and the shish kebab burger (marinated chunks of beef). Joe and I highly recommend the Mediterranean plate, which involves things like falafel and hummus. There are three of these yummy places around Berkeley, but Joe's favorite for the flavor of the neighborhood is the one at 2154 Center Street; (510) 540-9014.

College Avenue Delicatessen: Dogs enjoy watching you eat standard deli fare at the outdoor tables here. 3185 College Avenue; (510) 655-8584.

La Mediterranée: This delicious and inexpensive Middle Eastern restaurant has built up quite a following; there's usually a line on weekends when Cal is mid-semester. The folks here will let your dog sit quietly at your feet at the outdoor tables, which have the added benefit of an outdoor heater on cool nights. You might want to tie your dog up on the sidewalk outside the fence separating the tables if it's especially crowded. 2936 College Avenue; (510) 540-7773.

NeFeli: The light Greek cuisine at NeFeli really hits the spot. Try the Athenian panini if you like your Greek sans meat. It's a real treat. Dogs get to join you at tables under the awning in front. 1854 Euclid Avenue; (510) 841-6374.

Noah's New York Bagels: Noah's has benches on the sidewalk, though no tables—but it's still a must-visit for you and your dog, if bagels and cream cheese are your yen. It's very popular on Sunday mornings. 3170 College Avenue; (510) 654-0944.

Peet's Coffee: Not only Peet's but the Bread Garden Bakery and various other cafes and shops encircle a sunny patio with benches. Nearly every morning, crowds of hungry bicyclists and amblers congregate to sit in the sun, argue (this is Berkeley), eat pastries, and sip Peet's coffee, which many call the best in the Bay Area. Dogs' noses don't stop quivering and they can often meet other frustrated dogs. 2916 Domingo Avenue off Ashby. Peet's: (510) 843-1434. Bread Garden: (510) 548-3122.

Rick & Ann's Restaurant: Dogs feel really at home here, because Rick and Ann and their staff love dogs. This is also a popular place among people. The food is delicious and unique. It may take you a while to choose something from the imaginative menu, but just about anything you select will be great. The restaurant is located next to Peet's (see above), at 2922 Domingo Avenue; (510) 486-8119.

Sea Breeze Market and Deli: Smack in the middle of the Interstate 80 interchange, you won't even notice the traffic as you and your dog bask at sunny picnic tables, where crab claws crunch underfoot and begging is outstanding. Dogs are perfectly welcome so long as they don't wander into the store itself. You can buy groceries, beer, wine, classy ice cream, or a meal from the deli: fresh fish-and-chips, calamari, prawns, scallops, chicken, and quiche. The deli serves croissants and coffee early; if you live in the East Bay, you can zip in for a quick croissant and a dog walk at Cesar Chavez Park (see page 318) before work. It's located at the foot of University Avenue, past the Interstate 80 entrance. 598 University Avenue; (510) 486-8119.

PLACES TO STAY

Golden Bear Motel: Rates are $45 to $65. Small dogs only, please, and they require a onetime $5 fee. 1620 San Pablo Avenue, Berkeley, CA 94702; (510) 525-6770.

DIVERSIONS

Ride a dog-sized train: If your dog's not an escape artist or the nervous type, he's welcome to ride with you on Tilden Regional Park's miniature train. The open-car train takes you for a 12-minute ride through woods and past stunning views of the surrounding area. Adventurous dogs like it when the train toots its whistle as it rumbles past a miniature water tower, a car barn, and other such train accessories. When Joe Dog appeared on *Bay Area Backroads* riding the train, he was fine until we hit the little tunnel—then he decided he wanted to go home. He's relieved that part ended up on the cutting-room floor.

The Redwood Valley Railway Company runs trains between 11 A.M. and 6 P.M. weekends and holidays only, except during spring and summer school vacations, when it runs weekdays, noon to 5 P.M. and weekends until 6 P.M. Tickets are $1.50; kids under two and dogs ride free. You must keep the dog on a tight leash and make sure he doesn't jump out. It's in the southeast corner of Tilden Regional Park. From the intersection of Grizzly Peak Boulevard and Lomas Cantadas, follow the signs. (510) 548-6100.

Flea to the Market: If your dog has the itch to shop, and promises not to do leg lifts on furniture even when it's outdoors, you can have a relaxed time at the Ashby Flea Market. Crowds will be tolerant, but keep him on a short leash and watch out for chicken bones and abandoned cotton candy. Joe's friend Dabney, for instance, is a dog who knows how to shop for scraps, nose to the ground for hours. He's been to his last flea market.

Good dogs love the easy camaraderie they'll find here. If it's hot, though, keep it short. This market is held every Saturday and Sunday at the Ashby BART station parking lot.

From Interstate 80, take the Ashby exit and drive about 1.5 miles east to the intersection of Adeline Street.

Go shopping in 1967: You and your dog can shop in the autumn of love when you stroll through the sidewalks of Telegraph Avenue near the UC Berkeley campus. Street vendors sell tie-dyed clothes, crystals, pottery, and T-shirts airbrushed with clouds. Street performers sing, juggle, beg for money, or do whatever else comes naturally. Incense and other herbaceous odors waft through the air, but dogs prefer the scents of all the non-deodorized humans.

Dogs who reminisce about the 1960s really dig it here. They're perceived as totally cool dudes and given major amounts of love from people who like to hug dogs hard. A palm reader made friends with Joe on a recent visit, but since Joe isn't a believer in soothsaying, he steadfastly refused to give her his paw. (Actually, he only gives a paw for food, not friendship. He's a very pragmatic Airedale.)

Some dogs—and humans—may find the weekend crowds a sensory overload. If your schedule allows, try a cool afternoon. From Interstate 80, take the Ashby exit, go about two miles east to Telegraph, and turn left (north). The street-merchant part begins around the intersection of Dwight Way. On weekends, parking is challenging.

Sniff out a good book: Dogs love Avenue Books, because the people at this bookstore love dogs. If they're not too busy, they'll make sure your dog gets a special doggy treat to munch on while you peruse the great selection of books. Joe thinks the pet section here is tops. "Dogs also like the nature section, but we try to be careful about that," joked one store manager. The store is in the Elmwood shopping district, at 2904 College Avenue, near the corner of Ashby Avenue; (510) 549-3532.

CASTRO VALLEY

PARKS, BEACHES, AND RECREATION AREAS

• **Anthony Chabot Regional Park** 🐾🐾🐾🐾 🐕 *See ❼ on page 314.*

You and your leash-free dog can throw your urban cares to the wind when you visit this 4,684-acre park filled with magnificent trails and enchanting woodlands. Except for the occasional sounds of gunfire, you'll scarcely believe you're in the hills east of metropolitan Oakland. But fear not—the guns you'll hear are merely being used for target practice at the park's marksmanship range.

The trails here are so secluded that if no one is firing a gun, the only sounds you may hear are those of your panting dog and the singing birds. Adventure-loving dogs like to take the Goldenrod Trail, starting at the southern terminus of Skyline Boulevard and Grass Valley Road. It connects with the East Bay Skyline National Recreation Trail, which winds through Grass Valley and climbs through eucalyptus forests. Lucky dogs can be off leash everywhere but in developed areas.

Campsites are $15 to $20. Dogs are $1 extra. Reserve by phoning (925) 373-0144. No reservations are taken between October 1 and March 31, when the 23 sites are first come, first served.

From the intersection of Redwood Road and Castro Valley Boulevard in Castro Valley, go north on Redwood about 4.5 miles to Marciel Gate. (The campground is about two miles inside the gate.) From Oakland at the intersection of Redwood Road and Skyline Boulevard, go about 6.5 miles east on Redwood to Marciel Gate. For general park info, call (510) 635-0135.

• **Cull Canyon Regional Recreation Area** 🐾🐾🐾½ 🐕
  See ❽ on page 314.

Dogs may be off leash up on the grassy slopes laced with eucalyptus stands, but they have to wear their leashes in the areas designed for human fun. It's not such a bad fate, considering that there are plenty of grassy slopes away from developed areas.

In summer, fishing and swimming are popular here. But pooches may not go near the swimming complex, which includes an attractive pavilion and sandy beach. Leashed dogs may visit picnic areas, the Cull Creek area, and the willow-lined reservoir that sports a wooden bridge and a handful of ducks and coots.

From Interstate 580, take the Center Street/Crow Canyon Road exit. Go left on Center Street and take a right on Castro Valley Boulevard. Follow it to Crow Canyon Road and take a left. Take another left on Cull Canyon Road. It's a half mile to the park entrance. (510) 635-0135.

PLACES TO STAY

Anthony Chabot Regional Park: See Anthony Chabot Regional Park above for camping information.

EMERYVILLE

PARKS, BEACHES, AND RECREATION AREAS

• **Emeryville Marina Park** 🐾🐾 *See ❾ on page 314.*

If you're a human, this is a fine park. If you're a leashed dog, it's just so-so. A concrete path follows the riprap shoreline past cypress trees and through manicured grass. A quick and scenic stroll down the north side will give you a fine view of the marina and a miniature bird refuge where egrets, sandpipers, blackbirds, and doves inhabit a tiny marsh. Dogs who like to bird-watch think it's cool here.

Dogs who like to fish don't have it so easy. Pooches aren't allowed on the fishing pier. But if you console them with an offer to picnic at tables with grand views of the Bay Bridge, they usually snap out of their funk.

From Interstate 80, take the Powell Street exit at Emeryville and go west on Powell to the end of the marina. There's lots of free parking. (510) 596-4340.

DIVERSIONS

Take your dog to daycare: Hey, dogs! If your person works and leaves you at home to chew up the shoes and stare at the walls, casually leave the book open to this page and your life might soon change. Most pooches who visit Every Dog Has Its Day Care have so much fun that they're drooling to come back day after day. Dogs get lots of room to run and play and hang out with others of their ilk all day. Just like kiddy day care, dogs also get quiet time if they need a snooze, and lots of toys to sink their teeth into. Unlike kiddy day care, they get individual laptime, which includes brushing, petting, and scratching by a dog-lovin' staffer. These activities might be frowned upon in kiddy day-care circles, but they're great for pooches.

The rate is $25 daily, or $450 per month (four free days). At least it's cheaper than kiddy day care, and you don't have to deal with nasty runny noses or chicken pox. 1306 65th Street, Emeryville, CA 94608; (510) 655-7821. The Web site is www.everydog.com.

FREMONT

PARKS, BEACHES, AND RECREATION AREAS

• **Alameda Creek Regional Trail** 🐾🐾🐾 🐕 *See ❿ on page 314.*

This 12.4-mile trail runs from the bayshore to the East Bay hills, and dogs can actually be off leash in many sections. But they may be disappointed when they discover that it's not as pristine a trail as the name might imply. First of all, the trail is paved. Second of all, the creek is paved. (You'll see what I mean.) But more important, the trail doesn't just pass through farmland and greenbelt areas. It also runs alongside railyards, industrial lots, and quarries. Junkyard dogs like it. Wilderness dogs just shrug their hairy shoulders. A scenic stretch of this paved trail is at the Niles Canyon end. Dogs find it especially interesting in winter after a storm, when there's actually water in the concrete-lined creek and ducks and coots splash around.

You may enter this trail at many points between the creek's mouth—in the salt flats of the bay by Coyote Hills Regional Park. The trail officially begins in Fremont's Niles district, at the intersection of Mission Boulevard (Highway 238) and Niles Canyon Road (Highway 84).

Although the East Bay Regional Parks District's usual liberal leash rules apply here, it has posted a good many areas with "leash up" symbols. If you see one, do so. On this trail, as on any you share with other hikers, horses, and bicycles, just use common sense. (510) 635-0135.

• **Coyote Hills Regional Park** 🐾🐾🐾 *See* ⓫ *on page 314.*

This park is a paradox. It's a working research project on Ohlone Indian history, a teeming wildlife sanctuary, and a family picnic and bicycling mecca—all rolled into 966 acres.

Dogs used to be able to run leashless in the small hills that give the park its name, but leashes are now the law. We understand. (Waaah.) Wildlife is abundant here. You'll see red-tailed hawks, vultures, and white-tailed kites that swoop down on unsuspecting squirrels. Joe hasn't ever seen one of these kite-gets-squirrel incidents, but since he's never even come close to capturing a squirrel, he'd give his canine teeth to witness such a spectacle.

The beautiful Bayview Trail climbs quickly up behind the visitors center. From the crest of Red Hill—green even in the dry season because its ground cover is drought-tolerant—you look down on varied colors of marsh grasses, waterfowl, and wading birds, and the shallow salt ponds in the bay. Most of the park is a fragile sanctuary, and dogs must stay on the little hills or at the picnic area by the visitors center.

Special doggy alert: We just got word that the park is offering guided dog walks once a month! Call the park for dates and times.

From Interstate 880, take the Decoto Road/Highway 84 exit in Fremont. Go west on Highway 84 to the Thornton Avenue/Paseo Padre Parkway exit. Go north on Paseo Padre about one mile to Patterson Ranch Road/Commerce. A left on Patterson Ranch Road brings you to the entrance. When the kiosk is staffed, the parking fee is $3. The dog fee is $1. For information on tours and activities, call (510) 795-9385. For general information, call (510) 635-0135.

• **Mission Peak Regional Preserve** 🐾🐾🐾🐾 🐕
See ⓬ *on page 314.*

Smart Fremont dwellers take their dogs to this 2,596-acre park. It's a huge expanse of grass, dotted with occasional oak groves and scrub. Unfortunately for humans who get short of breath, the foot trails head straight up. Trails to the top rise 2,500 feet in three miles. (Pant, pant.)

Leash-free dogs love this place. The entrance at Stanford Avenue offers a gentler climb than the entrance from the Ohlone College campus. You'll pass Caliente Creek if you take the Peak Meadow Trail, but in hot weather, there won't be much relief from the sun. Be sure to carry water for yourself and your dog. The main point of puffing up Mission Peak is the renowned view stretching from Mount Tamalpais to Mount Hamilton. (On very clear days, you can see to the Sierra's snowy crest.) Your dog may not care much for the scenery, but she'll probably appreciate the complete freedom of the expanse of pasture here.

From Interstate 680, take the southern Mission Boulevard exit in Fremont (there are two; the one you want is in the Warm Springs district). Go east on Mission to Stanford Avenue, turn right (east), and in less than a mile, you'll be at the entrance. (510) 635-0135.

• **Sunol Regional Wilderness** 🐾🐾🐾🐾 🐕 *See ⑬ on page 314.*

You and your leash-free dog will howl for joy when you visit this large and deserted wilderness treasure. It's like going to a national park without having to leave your poor pooch behind.

One of the best treats for canines and their companions is a hike along the Camp Ohlone Trail, which you reach via the main park entrance, on Geary Road. The trail takes you to an area called Little Yosemite. Like its namesake, Little Yosemite is magnificent. It's a steep-sided gorge with a creek at the bottom, lofty crags, and outcrops of greenstone and basalt that reveal a turbulent geological history. Its huge boulders throw Alameda Creek into gurgling eddies and falls. There's no swimming allowed here, much to Joe's relief.

You can return via the higher Canyon View Trail or head for several other destinations: wooded canyons, grassy slopes, peaks with peeks of Calaveras Reservoir or Mount Diablo. The park brochure offers useful descriptions of each trail. Dogs may run leashless on trails except for on the Backpack Loop.

Dogs are allowed only at the Family Campground site at headquarters and not at the backpacking campsites farther in. Sites are $11. The dog fee is $1. Dogs must be leashed in the campground or confined to your tent. (Anyone whose dog has ever chased off after a wild boar in the middle of the night understands the reason for this rule, and this park has plenty of boars.) Call (510) 636-1684 to reserve. Reserved sites are held until 5 P.M.

From Interstate 680, take the Calaveras Road exit, then go left (east) on Geary Road to the park entrance. The park may be closed or restricted during fire season, from June to October. (925) 862-2244.

PLACES TO STAY

Best Western Thunderbird Inn: Rates are $109 to $129. Dogs must pay a $50 fee per stay. 5400 Mowry Avenue, Fremont, CA 94538; (510) 792-4300.

Sunol Regional Wilderness: See the Sunol Regional Wilderness above for camping information.

HAYWARD

PARKS, BEACHES, AND RECREATION AREAS

Leashed pooches are permitted at five parks run by the Hayward Area Recreation and Park District: San Lorenzo Community Center and Park, San Felipe, East Avenue, Tennyson, and the Eden Greenway, which runs parallel to the BART tracks between Hesperian Boulevard and Whitman Street.

• **Garin Regional Park and Dry Creek Regional Park** 🐾🐾🐾🐾 🐕 *See ⑭ on page 314.*

Garin Regional Park is about one mile and one century away from one of the busiest streets in Hayward. It's a fascinating place for you and your dog to learn about Alameda County farming and ranching. The parking lot next to Garin Barn—an actual barn, blacksmith's shop, and tool shed that is also Garin's visitors center—is strewn with antique farm machinery.

A total of 20 miles of trails, looping among the sweeps of grassy hills, beckon you and your dog. Off-leash dogs are fine on the trails once you've left the visitors center. Dogs seem to like to think they're on their own farm here, looking for all the world like they're strutting down their very own property and watching out for evil feline intruders.

Dry Creek, which runs near the visitors center, was a delightful small torrent one day when we were there after a March storm. There isn't much shade on hot days, though. That's when you might want to try cooling your paws at tiny Jordan Pond. It's stocked with catfish, should your dog care to join you on his kind of fishing excursion.

From Highway 238 (Mission Boulevard), Tamarack Drive takes you quickly up the hill to Dry Creek Regional Park. Garin Avenue takes you to Garin, or you can enter Garin from the California State University, Hayward campus. The parking fee is $3 on weekends and holidays. Dogs are $1 extra. (510) 635-0135.

• **Hayward Memorial Park Hiking and Riding Trails** 🐾🐾🐾
See ⓯ on page 314.

For humans, Memorial Park offers all kinds of amenities, including an indoor pool, tennis courts, kids' swings and slides, picnic tables, a band shell, and even a slightly funky cage full of doves. But really, if you're a dog, the big question is "Who cares?"

The fun for dogs begins when you get on the Wally Wickander (poor guy) Memorial Trail and enter the greenbelt portion of the park, laced with dirt fire trails designed for hikers and horses. Dogs must remain leashed, but the trail is so beautiful that it doesn't seem to matter. It follows a steep-sided creek lined with a thick tangle of oak, laurel, maple, and lots of noisy birds. The trash pickup is a little lax, but if you're looking for solitude in a city park, you'll find it here.

You can enter through Hayward Memorial Park, at Mission Boulevard (Highway 238) just south of the intersection of Highway 92. You can also enter at the parking lots on East Avenue through East Avenue Park on the north end, or on Highland Boulevard through Old Highland Park on the south end. (510) 881-6715.

PLACES TO STAY

Motel 6: Rates are $32 for the first adult, $6 for the second. Small dogs only, please, and only one per room. 30155 Industrial Parkway Southwest, Hayward, CA 94544; (510) 489-8333.

Vagabond Inn: Rates are $65 to $75. Dogs are $5 extra. 20455 Hesperian Boulevard, Hayward, CA 94541; (510) 785-5480.

LIVERMORE

PARKS, BEACHES, AND RECREATION AREAS
• **Del Valle Regional Park** 🐾🐾🐾🐾 🐕 *See ⓰ on page 314.*

This popular reservoir is best known for swimming, boating, fishing, and camping. Like Anthony Chabot Regional Park (see page 323), it's primarily a manicured and popular human recreation area, with neat lawns and picnic tables (where dogs must be leashed).

But, glory be to dog, the park sports several unspoiled trails for leash-free hiking in the surrounding hills. And, unlike at Lake Chabot, here you're permitted to take a dog on a rented boat. Every dog can have his day here.

From this recreation area, you can enter the Ohlone Wilderness Trail—29 miles of gorgeous trail through four regional parks. (See Ohlone Regional Wilderness, below.)

The 150 sites at Family Camp allow dogs, but only on leash or confined to your tent. Sites are $15 to $18. Reserve by calling (925) 373-0144.

From Interstate 580, take North Livermore Avenue from downtown Livermore. It will become South Livermore Avenue, then Tesla Road. Take a right (south) on Mines Road, then turn right on Del Valle Road. The parking fee is $4, and $5 from March through October. The dog fee is $1. (510) 635-0135.

• **Livermore Canine Park** 🐾🐾🐾🐾 🐕 *See* **17** *on page 314.*

If it weren't for the efforts of local vet Martin Plone, Livermore wouldn't have this slice of dog paradise in Max Baer Park. After seeing leash-free dog parks in Marin, Dr. Plone asked himself, "Why don't we have one in Livermore?" Then he asked the city. In the spring of 1993, Livermore agreed to try it on a six-month trial basis, provided that the park be privately funded. Dr. Plone raised the needed cash from other local veterinarians, and it's been a smashing success ever since.

The half-acre, fenced-in park is level and grassy, with lots of shady trees. Inside the run are disposable scoopers, a water fountain and bowls, and chairs where people can hang out while their dogs romp. On summer evenings, as many as 25 to 30 dogs enjoy the park. "Everybody loves it," Plone says. "It's become a meeting place for people. While their dogs are playing, people form friendships." Jerry Ingledue, the city's parks superintendent, is just as pleased with response to the dog park. He has received more than 20 enthusiastic thank-you notes—more than a few co-signed with paw prints.

From Interstate 580 east, take the Portola exit. Go south on Murietta Boulevard. Turn right on Stanley Boulevard and follow it to Murdell Lane. Turn left on Murdell and go about two miles to the park. To get to the dog park area, park at the far end of the lot and follow the concrete path. (925) 373-5700.

• **Ohlone Regional Wilderness** 🐾🐾🐾🐾 🐕 *See* **18** *on page 314.*

The centerpiece of this magnificent parkland is the 3,817-foot Rose Peak—only 32 feet lower than Mount Diablo. Leash-free dogs are in heaven on earth as they explore the surrounding 6,758 acres of grassy ridges. Wildlife is abundant, so if your dog isn't obedient, it's best to keep her leashed. The tule elk appreciate it, and your dog will appreciate it, too, should you run into a mountain lion.

The regional parks system shares the wilderness with the San Francisco Water District, which wants to limit the human presence here. Dogs may not stay overnight in the campgrounds.

To enter this wild and breathtaking area east of Sunol Regional Wilderness, you must pick up a permit (which includes a detailed trail map and camping information) for $2 at East Bay Regional Parks headquarters or at the Del Valle, Coyote Hills, or Sunol kiosks. (510) 635-0135.

• **Ohlone Wilderness Trail** 🐾🐾🐾🐾 🐕 *See* **19** *on page 314.*

Some of the area's most remote and peaceful wilderness areas are accessible only by way of this 29-mile trail. The trail stretches from Mission Peak, east of Fremont, through Sunol Regional Wilderness and Ohlone Regional Wilderness to Del Valle Regional Park, south of Livermore. You and your occasionally leash-free dog (signs tell you when it's allowed) will hike through oak and bay woods and grassy uplands that are carpeted with wildflowers in spring.

You'll also see abundant wildlife—if you're quiet and lucky, you might even see an endangered bald eagle. If your dog can't take the pressure of merely watching as tule elk and deer pass by, you should keep him leashed.

A permit is required. Because of some restrictions, you won't be able to do all 29 miles at once with your dog. That's okay. In fact, that's probably just fine with your dog. (510) 635-0135.

•**Sycamore Grove Regional Park** 🐾 🐾 🐾 *See* ㉔ *on page 314.*

Sycamore Grove is an unusual and attractive streamside park. In rainy times, it can look semi-swampy, as most of the Central Valley used to look. In fact, it is Lake Del Valle's floodplain, and federal flood controllers occasionally send runoff into this park's stream, Arroyo Del Valle, when Lake Del Valle rises too high.

With its low hills, tall grass, and loud sounds of birds and squirrels, it's almost an African savanna. Blackbirds and swallows swoop over the stream and marshy spots, grabbing insects. Poppies are plentiful in spring. Kids, dogs, miniature horses, potbellied pigs, and llamas live in harmony here, mostly because everyone obeys the leash law. Water dogs and their kin love wading in the stream pools near the picnic tables. Follow the paths far enough and the place becomes satisfyingly wild.

The park is quite flat, perfect for dogs who don't do well in low gear. Take Interstate 580 to Livermore; exit to Portola Avenue. Go east to North Livermore Avenue and turn right. After 2.5 miles, North Livermore turns into Arroyo Road. Turn right on Wetmore Road. There's a $2 fee. (925) 373-5700.

PLACES TO STAY

Del Valle Regional Park: See Del Valle Regional Park on page 327 for camping information.

Residence Inn by Marriott: These are convenient little apartments/suites if you need more than just a room. Rates are $89 to $129, and there's a $75 fee per doggy visit, so you might want to stay a while. Dogs also have to pay $6 extra daily. 1000 Airway Boulevard, Livermore, CA 94550; (925) 373-1800.

OAKLAND

Oakland, the most urban city in the East Bay, is also blessed with a collection of generous and tolerant city parks. Unfortunately, what we call the "white gloves" part of Oakland—the parklands ringing Lake Merritt and the Oakland Museum—is off-limits to dogs. But read on. The city now has its very own leash-free dog park. See Hardy Dog Park, page 330.

PARKS, BEACHES, AND RECREATION AREAS

•**Dimond Park** 🐾 🐾 🐾 *See* ㉑ *on page 314.*

Dimond Park is a small jewel of a canyon, dense and wild in the midst of the city. Your leashed dog's eyes will sparkle when she sees this lush place.

The Dimond Canyon Hiking Trail begins to the east of El Centro Avenue. There's a small parking lot at El Centro where it bisects the park. A short foot trail goes off west of El Centro, ending quickly at the Dimond Recreation Center and an attractive jungle gym for children.

The main trail is wide and of smooth dirt. It starts on the east side and follows Sausal Creek about a quarter of a mile up the canyon. At that point, the trail becomes the creek bed, so you can continue only in dry season. But what a quarter mile! The deciduous tangle of trees and ivy makes the canyon into a hushed, cool bower, and the creek is wide and accessible to dogs longing for a splash. When the water level is high enough, there are falls and, except in the driest months, there's enough for a dog pool or two. After the trail goes into the creek bed, the going is a little rougher, but you can follow it all the way to the ridge at the eastern end.

From Interstate 580, take the Fruitvale Avenue exit north to the corner of Fruitvale and Lyman Road, the eastern entrance. Or, to park at the trailhead, take the Park Boulevard exit from Highway 13 and turn left (south) on El Centro Avenue. (510) 482-7831.

•**Hardy Dog Park** 🐾 🐾 ½ 🐕 *See ㉒ on page 314.*

This fenced, quarter-acre patch of packed dirt is the city's first leash-free dog park. We applaud Oakland for taking this step. (A city parks person tells me that this park has been such a success that it could pave the way for other such parks in Oakland.) Hardy Dog Park is not a great park, but at least it's a dog park. And from what I hear, it's going to get bigger and better in the not-too-distant future.

On the plus side, the park has easy freeway access and plenty of shade. On the minus side, the park is right under the freeway, which is what creates the shade. When no other dog people are here, it doesn't feel very safe. Signs at the entrance ask users not to talk loudly. I find that amusing, being that the din of Highway 24 and BART (which also runs overhead) can already create an aural overload.

The fence is very tall, foiling escape artists. There's water for doggy drinking, and a couple of plastic chairs for human sitting. I want to thank Fulton Dog, Mattie Dog, Chelsea Dog, and Isaac Dog for giving us the heads-up about this park. They like it because it's close to the Rockridge Market Center, where they can grab a baked good and a sandwich with their people.

To get to the park from Highway 24, take the Claremont exit and follow Claremont Avenue back under the freeway. The park is under the freeway, at Claremont and Hudson Street. (510) 238-3791.

•**Joaquin Miller Park** 🐾 🐾 🐾 *See ㉓ on page 314.*

This large, beautiful city park is nestled at the western edge of the huge Redwood Regional Park (see page 332). If it weren't for the Oakland city parks' rule that dogs must always be leashed, Joaquin Miller would be dog heaven.

Dogs can't enter some of the landscaped areas, such as around Woodminster Amphitheater. On the deliciously cool and damp creek trails below, however, you and your dog will feel like you own the place.

The West Ridge Trail, reachable from Skyline Boulevard, is popular with mountain bikers. It's waterless, but it's still a good run. The best trails can be entered from the ranger station off Joaquin Miller Road. The Sunset Trail descends about one-eighth of a mile to a cool, ferny stream winding through second- and third-growth redwoods, pines, oak, and laurel. It then ascends to a ridge overlooking cities and the bay. In spring, the ridge is peppered with wildflowers. Plenty of picnic tables and water fountains are scattered throughout the park.

From Highway 13 in Oakland, take the Joaquin Miller Road exit and go one-half mile east to the ranger station. (510) 238-7275.

• **Leona Heights Park** 🐾 🐾 🐾 1/2 *See* **24** *on page 314.*

This park is a miniature version of the incomparable Redwood Regional Park (see page 332), which is most dogs' idea of nirvana. Leona Heights would be among the best parks in the city, if not for Oakland's leash law. Few bikes can negotiate the trails here and few people know about the secluded areas of the park. You're likely to find yourselves on your own in this lush setting.

Park at the entrance on Mountain Boulevard. There are plenty of paths on both sides, but we recommend walking east on Oakleaf Street, past Leona Lodge. The street is actually the York Trail, which follows boulder-lined Horseshoe Creek, with falls and plentiful dog pools. The dirt path is passable for about a quarter mile, over wooden bridges and through glades of eucalyptus, ferns, oak, pines, redwoods, bay, and French broom. When you reach the stream crossing that's lacking a bridge, don't continue unless you're prepared to clamber, slide, and grab trees the rest of the way. Unfortunately, there's a distinct lack of trail maintenance here. Several spots on the York Trail are downright dangerous, and the lack of railings next to steep creek banks and slippery boulders rules out bringing any young kids along.

Take the Redwood Road exit from Highway 13 and go south on Mountain Boulevard. Park when you see the sign for Leona Lodge. There is also a fire trail starting behind Merritt College's recycling center—at the first parking lot on the right on Campus Drive (off Redwood Road). A new hiking trail leading down into the park from this lot will soon be open. (510) 238-6888.

• **Leona Heights Regional Open Space** 🐾 🐾 🐾 🐕
See **25** *on page 314.*

Unmarked on most maps, this open space stretches from Merritt College south to Oak Knoll, and from Interstate 580 east to Anthony Chabot Regional Park. Since it's part of the East Bay Regional Parks system, your dog need not be on leash. A bumpy fire trail goes from Merritt College downhill to the southern entrance, just north of Oak Knoll.

The best way to enter is to park at a lot off Canyon Oaks Drive, next to a condominium parking lot. Right at this entrance is a pond, but you won't see any more water as you ascend. It's a dry hike in warm weather.

The fire trail leads gently uphill all the way to Merritt, through coyote brush and oak woodland. In spring, it's full of wildflowers and abuzz with the loud hum of bees. Watch out for poison oak.

From Interstate 580, exit at Keller Avenue and drive east to Campus Drive. Take a left (north), then a left on Canyon Oaks Drive. (510) 635-0135.

- **Martin Luther King Jr. Regional Shoreline (formerly San Leandro Bay Regional Shoreline)** 🐾 🐾 ½ *See* ㉖ *on page 314.*

The Oakland shoreline doesn't have much to offer a dog besides this park, which is well maintained by the East Bay Regional Parks system. And it has a major flaw: The parks system classifies the whole thing as a developed area, so you must leash. The kind of fun a dog most wants—running full-out across grass or swimming in the bay—is illegal.

But you can have a genteel good time on a sunny day that's not too windy, ambling together along the extensive paved bayside trails. Amenities for people are plentiful: picnic tables, a few trees, fountains, a parcourse, a tiny beach, and a huge playing field.

There's a wooden walkway over some mudflats for watching shorebirds and terns fishing. For bird-watching, go at low tide. Keep your dog firmly leashed and held close to you and hike along the San Leandro Creek Channel to Arrowhead Marsh. If you enter from Doolittle Drive, walk along the Doolittle Trail. There's a small sandy beach here, but dogs aren't allowed to swim. (The usual East Bay Regional Parks rules apply: No dogs allowed on beaches.)

From Interstate 880, exit at Hegenberger Road in Oakland. Go west on Hegenberger and turn on Edgewater Drive, Pardee Drive, or Doolittle Drive. Parking is free at each of these entry points. (510) 635-0135.

- **Redwood Regional Park** 🐾 🐾 🐾 🐾 🦮 *See* ㉗ *on page 314.*

Although it's just a few miles over the ridge from downtown Oakland, Redwood Regional Park is about as far as you can get from urbanity while still within the scope of the Bay Area. Dogs who love nature at its best, and love it even more off leash, adore the 1,836-acre park. People who need to get far from the madding crowd also go gaga over the place.

The park is delectable year-round, but it's a particularly wonderful spot to visit when you need to cool off from hot summer weather. Much of the park is a majestic forest of 150-foot coast redwoods (known to those with scientific tongues as *Sequoia sempervirens*). The redwoods provide drippy cool shade most of the time, which is a real boon for dogs with hefty coats. Back in the mid-1800s, this area was heavily logged for building supplies for San Francisco, and it wasn't a pretty sight. But fortunately, sometimes progress progresses backward, and the fallen trees have some splendid replacements.

There's something for every dog's tastes here. In addition to the redwoods, the park is also home to pine, eucalyptus, madrone, flowering fruit trees, chaparral, and grasslands. Wild critters like the park, too, so leash up immediately if there's any hint of a deer, rabbit, or other woodland creatures around. Many dogs, even "good" dogs, aren't able to withstand the temptation to chase.

Mud is inevitable if you follow the Stream Trail, so be sure to keep a towel in the car. Water dogs may try to dip their paws in Redwood Creek, which runs through the park. But please don't let them. This is a very sensitive area. Rainbow trout spawn here after migrating from a reservoir downstream, and it's not an easy trip for them. If you and your dog need to splash around somewhere, try the ocean, the bay, or your bathtub. At press time, the East Bay Regional Parks District was looking at making dogs leash up along the Stream Trail to prevent any "foe paws." Please keep your eyes peeled for signage, in case this goes through.

No parking fee is charged at Skyline Gate at the north end (in Contra Costa County—the park straddles Contra Costa and Alameda Counties). Entering here also lets you avoid the tempting smells of picnic tables at the south end. The Stream Trail leads steadily downhill, then takes a steep plunge to the canyon bottom. It's uphill all the way back, but it's worth it. From Highway 13, exit at Joaquin Miller Road and head east to Skyline Boulevard. Turn left on Skyline and go four miles to the Skyline Gate.

If you prefer to go to the main entrance on Redwood Road, exit Highway 13 at Carson/Redwood Road and drive east on Redwood Road. Once you pass Skyline Boulevard, continue two miles on Redwood. The park and parking will be on your left. The Redwood Road entrance charges a $3 parking fee and a $1 dog fee. (510) 635-0135.

RESTAURANTS

Oakland's College Avenue, in the Rockridge district, has a tolerant family atmosphere. Lawyers with briefcases buy flowers on the way home from the BART station, and students flirt over ice cream. I've never seen anyone in this neighborhood who didn't love dogs. Even so, you should leash for safety on this busy street.

The avenue is known to be a food lover's paradise, and among the attractions are a string of restaurants with outdoor tables.

Cafe Rustica: The pizza here is elegant. Eat it at the outdoor tables with your drooling dog. 5422 College Avenue; (510) 654-1601.

Oliveto Cafe: This cafe and Peaberry's, next door, share a building with the Market Hall, God's own food emporium. The food's the best, but for a dog, the atmosphere is congested. It's not for nervous dogs. Oliveto serves very classy pizza, tapas, bar food, desserts, coffees, and drinks, but alcohol is not allowed at the sidewalk tables. 5655 College Avenue, just south of Rockridge BART; (510) 547-5356.

Peaberry's: Enjoy coffees, pastries, and desserts at the outdoor tables here. This is a favorite with BART commuters. 5655 College Avenue; (510) 653-0450.

Royal Coffee: This is a cheery and popular place with very good coffee (in the bean or in the cup), tea, and supplies. On weekend mornings, it's dog central. 307 63rd Street at College Avenue; (510) 653-5458.

Salty Dog: Located at the end of the pier in Jack London Square, this sandwich shop has four outside tables where you and your dog can chow down. The Salty Dog crew will even give your thirsty dog a bowl of water.

When asked what the specialties are, the owner said, "We make 25 different sandwiches and they're all special." On Sundays in the summer, after strolling through the farmers market, you might enjoy the barbecued burgers and spareribs while watching the sailboats cut across the estuary. 53 Jack London Square; (510) 452-2563.

PLACES TO STAY

Clarion Suites Lake Merritt Hotel: Dogs dig the lovely digs here. Some suites with kitchenettes are available. Rates are $109 to $149. Be sure to stay a while if you bring your dog, because there's a $75-per-visit pet fee, in addition to a $75 deposit. 1800 Madison Avenue, Oakland, CA 94612; (510) 832-2300.

Oakland Airport Hilton: They prefer the tinier pooches here. In fact, you'll need a ruler because the rule is that dogs must be no more than 12 inches high. Rates are $144 to $164. Dogs are $10 extra, and there's a $200 deposit. 1 Hegenberger Road, Oakland, CA 94614; (510) 635-5000.

DOGGY DAYS

Give your paw: The Oakland SPCA boasts one of the oldest dog walks in the country, with activities that include a two-mile run, a one-mile walk, an alumni parade (bring a hanky, this one's sweet), and various contests. The paper-retrieving contest is a fun one to watch, and has proven inspirational to more than one couch-potato dog (or at least his person). At last count, about 1,000 walkers and their dogs attended the event, usually held the first Sunday of October at the San Leandro Marina Par Course. Call (510) 569-2591 for details.

DIVERSIONS

Rent a flick together: The Video Room videotape rental store is so doggone dog-friendly that not only can pooches come in and help you choose a movie, they get a big dog biscuit just for accompanying you. If you have a choice between renting a video here or at a big chain store, give this medium-sized shop a shot. Your dog will be glad you did. 4364 Piedmont Avenue; (510) 655-6844.

Don't Eat the Furniture!: It's an admonition that has a familiar ring to dogs with splinters in their gums. It's also the name of an eclectic furniture/arts/pet supply store that welcomes well-behaved dogs. Actually, Don't Eat the Furniture! is just the first half of the name. The second half: For Pets and the People They Own. Aww.

You and your pooch can shop for unique furniture, including pieces made in Indonesia from "recycled" mahogany. Owner Rose Nied and her faithful briard, Lulu, have also filled the small store with hundreds of other unusual, high-quality items, such as gargoyles, cards, books, jewelry, and an interesting assortment of pet goodies. It's the perfect place to shop for someone who has everything (including your dog). 4024 Piedmont Avenue; (510) 601-PETS.

Seize the Bay: Ahoy doggies! Pooches who enjoy the bay are thrilled to learn that they're allowed on the Blue & Gold Fleet's ferries that run between Oakland, Alameda, and San Francisco. Please turn to page 398 in the San Francisco chapter for more details on this salty adventure.

PIEDMONT

Piedmont, the incorporated town in the midst of Oakland, is almost entirely residential and very proper and clean. This means you won't be able to find a stray scrap of paper to scoop with, so be prepared. Its quiet streets are delightful for walking, offering views from the hills.

Piedmont has no official park curfews. "We don't have the kind of parks people would be in after dark," says a woman at the city's recreation department, and it's true.

PARKS, BEACHES, AND RECREATION AREAS

• **Beach Park** 🐾🐾 🐕 *See* ㉘ *on page 314.*

It's not beachy here, and it's not parky either. But hey, it's off leash, so we have to give it a couple of paws. This is just a strip of pavement running down a narrow patch of grass about the length of one city block. There's some shade. The "park" is set along a hill, but it's too close to a couple of roads for true off-leash comfort—at least with a dog like Joe.

Beach Park is across from Beach School, at Linda and Lake Avenues. You'll see the little doggy signs. (510) 420-3070.

• **Dracena Park** 🐾🐾🐾🐾 🐕 *See* ㉙ *on page 314.*

Parts of this park are grassy, with tall shade trees here and there. But the part dogs long for is the off-leash section. It's a lovely area, with a paved path up and down a wooded, secluded hill. Tall firs and eucalyptus provide plenty of shade, and sometimes it's so quiet here you can hear several kinds of birds. The area isn't fenced, and at the top and bottom there's potential for escape artists to run into the road, so be careful and leash up at these points if you have any doggy doubts.

Pooper-scoopers are provided. Be sure to scoop the poop, because the fines are stiff—the equivalent of several 40-pound bags of dog food, or $200. The trail takes about 15 minutes round-trip, if you assume a very leisurely pace. We like to enter on Artuna Avenue at Ricardo Avenue, because it's safest from traffic and parking's plentiful on the park side of the street. But lots of folks enter at Blair and Dracena Avenues. (510) 420-3070.

• **Piedmont Park** 🐾🐾🐾🐾 🐕 *See* ㉚ *on page 314.*

The huge off-leash section of this beautiful park is one of the best examples of a leash-free dog area in the state. A few salmon-pink concrete pathways lead you and your happy dog alongside a gurgling stream and up and down the hills around the stream. It's absolutely gorgeous and serene back here. (On our last visit, a hummingbird greeted us at the entrance, and was back again when we left.) The park smells like heaven, with eucalyptus, redwood, acacia, pine, and deep, earthy scents wafting around everywhere. It reminds me of a serene Japanese garden, minus the Japanese plants.

The stream is fed year-round by a spring higher in the hills. This is pure bliss for dogs during the summer months. The trails for dogs and their people run on the cooler side anyway, with all the tall trees. Almost the entire leash-free section is set in a deep canyon, so it's very safe from traffic. A leisurely round-trip stroll will take you about an hour, if you want it to. Pooper-scoopers are supplied at a few strategically located stations along the paths. Use them. The fine for not scooping is about $200, and the police station flanks the park.

A hint if you want your walk to be as peaceful as possible: Don't come here during the school year around lunchtime or quittin' time for school. The high school at the top of a hill on the other side of the stream can spew forth some very loud students at those times. On one ill-timed visit, a couple of them were throwing glass bottles into the stream. Joe Dog almost got thwacked right in the ol' kisser.

Joe and I want to thank Lady Golden Rod and her person, Anna Castagnozzie Bush, for the tip that led us to this magnificent park. They thought this piece of dog heaven was too good to keep from other dogs.

To get to the leash-free section of this elegant park, come in through the main entrance at Highland and Magnolia Avenues. You'll see a willow tree just as you enter. Continue on the path past the willow tree and follow it down to the left side of the stream. You'll see signs for the dog area. Be sure to leash up in other parts of the park, should you explore beyond the stream area. (510) 420-3070.

PLEASANTON

PARKS, BEACHES, AND RECREATION AREAS

• **Pleasanton Ridge Regional Park** 😊 😊 😊 😊 🐕
   See ㉛ on page 314.

This fairly recent and beautiful addition to the East Bay Regional Parks system is an isolated treat. Dogs may run off leash on all the secluded trails here as soon as you leave the staging area.

You can access Pleasanton Ridge from either Foothill or Golden Eagle Roads. At the Foothill Staging Area, there are fine picnic sites at the trailhead. Climb up on the Oak Tree fire trail to the ridgeline, where a looping set of trails goes off to the right. The incline is gentle, through pasture (you share this park with cattle) dotted with oak and—careful—poison oak. Wildflowers riot in spring. It's a hot place in summer. At the bottom of the park, however, is a beautiful streamside stretch along Arroyo de la Laguna. There's no water above the entrance, so be sure to carry plenty.

From Interstate 680, take the Castlewood Drive exit and go left (west) on Foothill Road to the staging area. (510) 635-0135.

PLACES TO STAY

Crown Plaza: Rates are $60 to $135. Dogs require a $50 deposit. 11950 Dublin Canyon Road, Pleasanton, CA 94588; (925) 847-6000.

Doubletree Hotel: Rates are $60 to $100. Dogs are $15 extra. 5990 Stoneridge Mall Road, Pleasanton, CA 94588; (925) 463-3330.

SAN LEANDRO

DOGGY DAYS

Hustle your tail for a good cause: On the first Sunday of October, the Oakland Society for the Prevention of Cruelty to Animals holds a fundraising dog run. You and your dog can do a two-mile run or a scenic one-mile walk, watch the World Canine Frisbee Champs perform, or enter contests—goofy pet tricks, tail-wagging, that sort of thing. It's held in the San Leandro Marina. For this year's date and info on fees, call the Oakland SPCA at (510) 569-0702.

34
MARIN COUNTY

Long known as the home of hot tubs, back rubs, and ferny pubs, this comfortable, green county is also a heavenly place for the canines among us.

As you cross over the Golden Gate Bridge into this magical land, look to your left. See those hills overlooking the ocean and the bay? Dogs can explore many of the scenic trails here (see Marin Headlands Trails, page 359). Two magnificent beaches, run by the Golden Gate National Recreation Area, actually permit buck-naked (leashless) pooches. The GGNRA offers a helpful "Pet Trail Map." Phone (415) 556-0560.

In addition to those off-leash havens, Marin County operates 26 Open Space District lands. The landscapes include grassy expanses, wooded trails, redwood groves, marshes, and steep mountainsides. The idea is to set aside bits of land so that Marin never ends up looking like the Santa Clara Valley. The Open Space parks are free, completely undeveloped, and open 24 hours. Until 1995, dogs were permitted off leash just about everywhere on these lands. But now they can run leashless only on designated fire roads. They must be leashed on trails. It's still a pretty good deal, since most dogs don't mind the wide berth. For maps (they're $2 when ordered by mail), call (415) 499-6387.

Most dogs are surprised to discover that if they wear a leash, they're permitted to explore a bit of beautiful Mount Tamalpais (see Mount Tamalpais State Park, page 346, and Mount Tamalpais–Marin Municipal Water District Land, page 347).

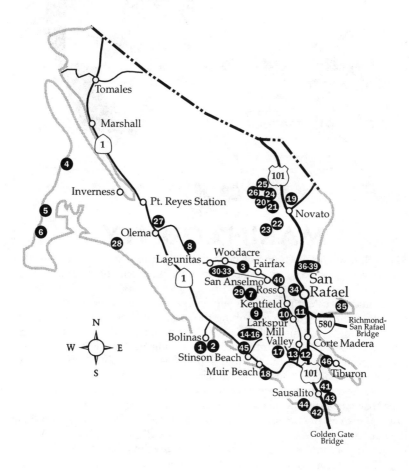

Tomales

Marshall

1

Inverness

Pt. Reyes Station

4

5

6

Olema

27

28

8

Lagunitas

1

Woodacre
Fairfax
30-33 3
San Anselmo 40
29 7 Ross
Kentfield
9
Larkspur
10 11
Mill
14-16 Valley
17 13 12
46
101
41
43
44
42

25
26 24
20 21
23 22

101

19

Novato

36-39

San
Rafael

34

35

580

Richmond-
San Rafael
Bridge

Corte Madera

Tiburon

Bolinas
1 2
Stinson Beach
Muir Beach 18

Sausalito

Golden Gate
Bridge

N
W E
S

Their mouths also tend to drop open when you mention they can visit parts of the 65,000-acre Point Reyes National Seashore. Because it's a delicate ecosystem and a national treasure, dogs are banned from campgrounds, most trails, and several beaches. Point Reyes National Seashore is home to 350 species of birds and 72 species of mammals (not including dogs). Where dogs are permitted, they must be on leash. It's a small price to pay to be able to peruse the place with the pooch at all. Kehoe Beach, Point Reyes Beach South, and Point Reyes Beach North (see page 341) are the seashore's most dog-friendly areas.

The Marin County ordinance doesn't specifically require dogs to be on leash. It states, "Dogs must be under the control of a responsible person at all times." But most towns—and even the parks within unincorporated areas—have their own leash laws that supersede this laid-back law. Bolinas is a refreshing exception (see below). If dogs could live in any town in Marin, this mellow hamlet would surely be their paws-down pick.

Dog-owning residents of Novato and San Rafael are about to make their communities even more dog-friendly than they are. At press time, each had just received word that their dream of a dog park was about to come true! See the introductions to these cities for more on their commendable efforts.

BOLINAS

Bolinas is famous for hiding from curious visitors—thereby drawing hordes of them. They keep coming, even though town citizens regularly take down the turnoff sign on Highway 1. So if you're coming from the east (San Francisco area), turn left at the unmarked road where Bolinas Lagoon ends. If you're coming from the west, turn right where the lagoon begins.

Sometimes it seems as if half the inhabitants of Bolinas are dogs, most of them black. They stand guard outside bars, curl at shop owners' feet, snooze in the middle of the road. There's no city hall in Bolinas, an unincorporated area, and no Chamber of Commerce. Dogs are always welcome here, but cars, horses, bicycles, and too many unleashed dogs compete for space. Be thoughtful and keep your pooch leashed in town.

PARKS, BEACHES, AND RECREATION AREAS

• **Agate Beach** 🐾🐾🐾🐾 🐕 *See* ❶ *on page 338.*

The county ordinance applies here: Dogs must be on leash or under voice control. There are lots of dogs on this narrow beach flanked by rock cliffs. Kelp bulbs pop satisfyingly underfoot. Watch that the high tide doesn't sneak up on you.

From the Olema-Bolinas Road (the Bolinas turnoff from Highway 1), turn west on Mesa Road, left on Overlook Drive, right on Elm Road, and drive all the way to the end. (415) 499-6387.

• **Bolinas Beach** 🐾🐾🐾½ 🐕 *See* ❷ *on page 338.*

At the end of the main street, Wharf Road, is a sand and pebble beach at the foot of a bluff. Dogs are free to run off leash. But watch for horses—with riders and without—thundering past without warning. It's animal anarchy here, and not the cleanest beach in Marin. We give it points for fun, though. (415) 499-6387.

RESTAURANTS

Bolinas Bay Bakery and Cafe: Eat pizza, salads, desserts, and baked goodies, and sip espresso on the outside benches with your dog. 20 Wharf Road; (415) 868-0211.

The Shop: This is a very dog-friendly spot for breakfast, lunch, and dinner, beer, wine, and ice cream. "Dogs are great," one enthusiastic waiter told Joe Dog. 46 Wharf Road; (415) 868-9984.

CORTE MADERA

Dogs are banned from all parks here. But mope not, pooches, because at least you get to munch on cafe cuisine.

RESTAURANTS

Book Passage Cafe: Whether your dog is illiterate or erudite, he's welcome to join you at the many shaded tables outside this incredible bookstore/cafe. You can dine on sandwiches, muffins, and a few assorted hot entrées, as well as tasty coffees and healthful smoothies. Dogs aren't allowed inside the bookstore, so if you want to peruse (and who wouldn't—the bookstore is one of the best we've seen), bring a friend and take turns dog-sitting. 51 Tamal Vista Boulevard; (415) 927-1503.

Twin Cities Market: Pick up a fresh deli sandwich (with your dog's favorite cold cuts, of course) and eat it with your pooch at the three tables outside. It's casual, but that's how most dogs like it. 118 Corte Madera Avenue; (415) 924-7372.

FAIRFAX

PARKS, BEACHES, AND RECREATION AREAS

• **Cascade Canyon Open Space Preserve** 🐾🐾🐾🐾 🐕
See ❸ on page 338.

As on all of Marin's open space lands, dogs can cavort about off leash on the fire roads. The fire road here is vehicle-free except for rangers. It's a pleasant walk that leads all the way into the Marin Municipal Water District lands of Mount Tamalpais. (Once you enter these, you must leash.)

These days, dogs must be leashed on all open space hiking trails. But the trails are so enticing that they're actually worth trying despite the new leash law. The main trail sticks close to San Anselmo Creek, which is reduced to a dry creek bed in summer. A no-bicycles trail branches off to the right and disappears into the creek; the left branch fords the creek. When the water's high, you may be stopped right here. But in summer, you can walk a long way. Side trails lead you into shady glens of laurel and other deciduous trees, but there's lots of poison oak, too.

The park is at the end of Cascade Drive. There's a Town of Fairfax sign saying "Elliott Nature Preserve," but it's official open space. Please don't park at the end of Cascade. Spread out so the folks who live at the end of Cascade don't get so inundated with dogs. Pooches have been a problem for some residents, whose beautiful flowers and lawns have succumbed to dog feet and pooch poop. Be courteous, and think how you'd feel if the shoe were on the other paw. (415) 499-6387.

INVERNESS

PARKS, BEACHES, AND RECREATION AREAS

• **Kehoe Beach** 🐾🐾🐾½ *See* ❹ *on page 338.*

This is our favorite of the Point Reyes National Seashore beaches that allow dogs, since it's both the most beautiful and the least accessible. The only parking is at roadside. You take a half-mile cinder path through wildflowers and thistles, with marsh on one side and hill on the other. In the morning, you may see some mule deer. Then, you come out on medium-brown sand that stretches forever. Since the water is shallow, the surf repeats its crests in multiple white rows, as in Hawaii. Behind you are limestone cliffs. Scattered rocks offer tidepools filled with mussels, crabs, anemones, barnacles, snails, and sea flora.

In such a paradise of shore life, the leash rule makes sense. The chief reasons for leashing dogs (or banning them altogether) at the Point Reyes National Seashore beaches are the harbor seals that haul out onto the beaches. They're in no position to get away fast from a charging dog. Snowy plovers, a threatened shorebird that nests on the ground, also appreciate your dog obeying the leash law.

From Inverness, follow Sir Francis Drake Boulevard to the fork; bear right on Pierce Point Road and go about four miles; park beside the road where you see the sign and walk about a half mile to the beach. (415) 663-1092.

• **Point Reyes Beach North** 🐾🐾🐾½ *See* ❺ *on page 338.*

Point Reyes Beach North is a generous, functional beach. There's no long trail from the parking lot, no special tidepools or rocks, just a long, clean, beautiful running beach for the two of you. Officially, however, dogs must be leashed.

From Inverness, take Sir Francis Drake Boulevard. Follow signs for the lighthouse. Go about 10 miles. The turnoff for the beach is well marked. (415) 663-1092.

• **Point Reyes Beach South** 🐾🐾🐾 *See* ❻ *on page 338.*

Point Reyes Beach South is a little narrower and steeper than Point Reyes Beach North, and it has a few interesting sandstone outcrops with wind-carved holes. It has a bit less of that wide-open feeling. Leash the dog.

Follow the directions for Point Reyes Beach North; it's the next beach southward. (415) 663-1092.

RESTAURANTS

The Gray Whale: The pizzas, pastas, and sandwiches here are hearty as a whale. The Gray Whale boasts "the best vegetarian pizza in three counties." That's bad news for dogs who like their pizza slathered with sausage. Dine with doggy at the large side patio. 12781 Sir Francis Drake Boulevard; (415) 669-1244.

The Inverness Store: Lots of dogs visit this little grocery store, which has been around for more than 80 years. The folks here are kind to doggies, and welcome them to munch a lunch at the picnic table at the dike here. They even invite dogs and their people to bring a blanket and make it a real picnic. (No ants, though.) 12784 Sir Francis Drake Boulevard; (415) 669-1041.

Manka's Inverness Lodge: This magnificent lodge is home to a mouth-watering restaurant, if wild game is the type of dish that makes your mouth water. (See Places to Stay below for more information.)

PLACES TO STAY

The Ark: Don't expect 40 days and 40 nights of rain during your stay at The Ark. But be assured that even if it's raining cats and dogs, you'll still have a wonderful time here. That's because this two-room cottage is cozy and charming, with vast skylights, a soaring ceiling, a nifty loft, and the down-home comfort of a wood stove. It's furnished with lovely wood pieces and locally handcrafted items. The Ark is far removed from the "hustle-bustle" of downtown Inverness, and is adjacent to a wildlife preserve, replete with trees. If you enjoy singing birds, open a window and let the songs stream in. Or walk outside to the beautiful, private area surrounding the cottage.

The Ark was built in 1971 by a class of UC Berkeley architecture students under the guidance of maverick architect Sim Van der Ryn. The class was called "Making a Place in the Country." If you took a class in the result of this project, it would probably be called "Making a Place in Your Heart." Your dog won't soon forget a vacation here, and neither will you. As long as your dog doesn't take a stab at the subjects of "Making a Hole in the Yard" or "Making Pee-Pee on the Floor," he'll be as welcome here as the humans in his party.

The Ark sleeps up to six people. Rates are $130 for two people, $10 per additional person. There's a $30 fee per visit for dogs. A healthful, delicious breakfast is $5 extra. 180 Highland Way, P.O. Box 273, Inverness, CA 94950; (415) 663-9338 or (800) 878-9338.

Manka's Inverness Lodge: Often, humans and their dogs spend the night here, eat breakfast, and decide never to return home. It's an old hunting lodge, surrounded by woods and the beaches and mudflats of Tomales Bay—and the owners love dogs. They have a sweet yellow Lab, who goes by the dignified name of Louie. Louie's fellow canines can stay in the cabins or the garden suite. Rates are $135 to $365. Dogs are $50 extra for the length of their stay, and only one pooch per stay, please.

The food here is exceptional. The lodge's restaurant was recently given a four-star rating by the *Marin Independent Journal.* The vegetarian dishes are exotic and mouthwatering. But it's all the wild game dishes that make dogs vote it a four-paw restaurant. If dogs accompany you for a meal at the outdoor tables here, they'll drool over every mouthful you eat. Monday nights are excellent nights to come for a bite, because the wild game dishes are a mere $5 to $10 each.

Look for the uphill turn off Sir Francis Drake Boulevard and take Argyle Way about 400 yards to the lodge. P.O. Box 1110, Inverness, CA 94937; (415) 669-1034.

Rosemary Cottage: If you have a romantic, nature-loving bone in your body, you'll love a getaway at this quaint, French-country cottage. It's set in a secluded spot, with a wall of windows looking out at the stunning forest scenery of the Point Reyes National Seashore. A deck overlooks a sweet-smelling herb garden. The inside of the cottages is cozy and beautifully crafted, with a full kitchen and many homey details. Snuggle up near the wood-burning stove on chilly evenings after a day of whale-watching and dog-walking at nearby beaches. Hearth-type dogs love it here.

Rates are $170 for up to two people. Dogs are $30 extra for the length of your stay, so Joe Dog recommends getting your money's worth and staying a few nights. Breakfast is optional, and is $5 extra. 75 Balboa Avenue, P.O. Box 273, Inverness, CA 94950; (415) 663-9338 or (800) 878-9338.

KENTFIELD

PARKS, BEACHES, AND RECREATION AREAS

• **Northridge/Baltimore Canyon Open Space Preserve** 🐾 🐾 🐾 🐾 🐕
See ⑦ on page 338.
From this spot, access is good for a lot of fire roads through the ridges connecting with Mount Tamalpais and water district lands. Leashes aren't required on the fire roads, but bikes are also allowed on these trails, so be careful. You'll be starting out fairly high on the slope. Dogs must be leashed on regular hiking trails.

Two access points are at the ends of Crown Road and Evergreen Drive. (415) 499-6387.

LAGUNITAS

PARKS, BEACHES, AND RECREATION AREAS

• **Samuel P. Taylor State Park** 🐾 🐾 🐾 *See ⑧ on page 338.*
An exception among the state parks: Dog access is generous. You can take a dog into the picnic areas, and that's worth doing here. The main picnic area right off Sir Francis Drake Boulevard is cool and often lively with the grinding call of jays. It's an easy place to bring out-of-state visitors who may just want to eat a sandwich, hug a redwood, and go home. There are hollow trees stretching 20 feet across that you can actually stand inside.

But best of all, you and your dog may spend a whole day on the wide fire trails—roughly 10 miles of them—clearly differentiated on the map you get at the entrance. Dogs may not go on the foot trails, but the fire trails are delightful enough. You can take the bicycle/horse trail from near the entrance along Papermill Creek, rising for four miles to Barnabe Peak, at 1,466 feet. Unfortunately, your dog must stay leashed, but you may actually appreciate that when you see the excellent artist's drawing of a poison oak cluster on the park's map—it's everywhere.

The park has 60 campsites. Sites are $12 to $16. Dogs are $1 extra. From April through October, call Parknet for reservations at (800) 444-PARK. The park's day-use fee is $5 for parking, $1 per dog. The entrance is on Sir Francis Drake Boulevard about two miles west of Lagunitas. (415) 488-9897.

RESTAURANTS

Lagunitas Grocery: Grab a sandwich at the deli inside and feast on it at the outdoor tables with your dog. 7890 Sir Francis Drake Boulevard; (415) 488-4844.

PLACES TO STAY

Samuel P. Taylor State Park: See Samuel P. Taylor State Park above for camping information.

LARKSPUR

PARKS, BEACHES, AND RECREATION AREAS

• **Blithedale Summit Open Space Preserve** 🐾🐾🐾🐾 🐕
See ❾ on page 338.

The access point at the end of Madrone Avenue—the north end of this open space—is a delightful walk in hot weather, through cool redwoods that let some light filter through. This isn't one of those really dark, drippy canyons; you're at a medium-high altitude on the slopes of Mount Tamalpais. The trail follows Larkspur Creek, which retains some pools in summer. Cross the footbridge and follow the slightly rough foot trail. Unfortunately, leashes are now the law on these trails. But you can let your dog off his leash once you hit the fire road.

The drive up narrow Madrone Avenue is an adventure in itself; redwoods grow right in the street. According to a sign at the entrance, the part of this space belonging to the city of Larkspur requires dogs to be leashed. (415) 499-6387.

• **Creekside Park** 🐾🐾½ See ❿ on page 338.

This is the small, attractive park where the multipurpose Bon Air Path starts. The 1.8-mile paved trail goes from Bon Air Road, following Corte Madera Creek, westward to the town of Ross and eastward to the Larkspur Landing shopping center, near the ferry terminal. There are lots of paths by Corte Madera Creek, as well as a kids' gym. You must leash your dog and be sure to keep him out of marshy areas. A bulletin board displays excellent bike trail maps and descriptions of local flora and fauna.

From Sir Francis Drake Boulevard, turn south on Bon Air Road; from Magnolia Drive, turn north. The park entrance is across from Marin General Hospital. You can get more information on the county's bike trails from the Bicycle Trails Council of Marin at (415) 456-7512. For more park information, call (415) 499-6387.

• **Piper Park (Canine Commons)** 🐾🐾🐾½ 🐕
See ⓫ on page 338.

Here's an ordinary people-style city park—athletic facilities, playground, picnic tables, community garden, the works—that has also included what your dog needs! It's got a small fenced area next to the community garden called Canine Commons, and it's just the ticket if your dog is a fetcher or an escape artist, hates the leash, or loves to meet other dogs. The drawback is its small size, a mere third of an acre—but we just got word that it's soon going to double in size! There's only one striving little tree. Still, it's better than nothing. Water, pooper-scoopers, and tennis balls are supplied.

The Larkspur City Recreation Department runs Piper Park. You can play or watch softball, volleyball, tennis, and even cricket. Outside Canine Commons, dogs must be leashed. The park is between Doherty Drive and Corte

Madera Creek. Canine Commons is at the west end of the park. (415) 927-5110.

RESTAURANTS

Bread & Chocolate Bakery: If you enjoy either of the two aforementioned goodies, this bakery is a must-visit. Eat these or many other delicious goodies at the outside tables with your pooch. (Remember that dogs and chocolate don't mix, though.) 1139 Magnolia Avenue; (415) 461-9154.

The Left Bank: Your dog doesn't have to be a poodle to enjoy dining at this terrific French restaurant. Because it's a French place, management knows that dogs and restaurants really do mix. But because they're in America, they have to abide by local health regulations and keep doggies from dining inside. That's okay, though, because there are plenty of outside tables. When it's crowded, managers ask that you tie your dog to the railing that surrounds the outdoor area. You can still dine right beside your pooch, but at least he won't trip a *garçon.* 507 Magnolia Avenue; (415) 927-3331.

Marin Brewing Company: They brew their own beer here, and it's really good. Swig some with your dog and your sandwich at the nine outdoor tables. 1809 Larkspur Circle; (415) 461-4677.

MARSHALL

DIVERSIONS

Mingle with the mollusks: Your dog doesn't have to be a water dog to appreciate the fascinating sights and scents at Abalone Acres. Abalone in many stages of their young lives grow in kelp-filled tanks here. You can look around the outdoor facility and buy small homegrown abalone for a decent price: four (or approximately one pound, including shell) for about $22. Next door is the Hog Island Oyster Company, where you can buy oysters and mussels alive, alive-o.

Abalone Acres is on Highway 1, along rural Marshall's "main drag." The mailing address is P.O. Box 837, Marshall, CA 94940; (415) 663-1384.

MILL VALLEY

PARKS, BEACHES, AND RECREATION AREAS

•**Bayfront Park** 🐾🐾🐾🐾 🐕 *See ⑫ on page 338.*

This good-looking park is well designed for every kind of family activity and for dogs. There's an exercise course, lawns are green and silky, and picnic areas are clean and attractive. The multiuse trails for bicycles, strollers, and whatnot may be used only by leashed dogs. (There are bikes galore.) But here's the canine payoff: It has a special dog run next to an estuary, where dogs are free to dip their paws.

The dog-use area starts where you see all the other dogs, and probably a sign or two by the time this edition hits the stores. Beware, owners of escape artists: The area is a big three acres, but it's not fenced. No scoops or water are furnished, but the Richardson Bay Estuary is right there to jump into.

At the end of the run there's even a marsh that dogs can explore, if you're willing to put a very mucky friend back into the car with you. Luckily, this marsh is all organic muck, free from the dangerous trash that fills many unprotected bay marshes.

For a dog park, this one offers an unparalleled view of Mount Tam. Horses and bikes pass by harmlessly on their own separate trail in the foreground, and mockingbirds sing in the bushes.

Until recently, there had been a heap o' controversy over whether this should continue to be a dog run area. Some people thought soccer players of the young human persuasion should have the area, and that dogs should have to be leashed. But hooray, the dogs won! The city council approved a permanent dog run here. That's thanks to the work of a magnificent, high-energy group called Park People & Dogs. If you want to find out how you can help Park People & Dogs in its continuing efforts to make this park dog heaven, call Barbara Berlenbach at (415) 388-0071.

The parking lot is on Sycamore Avenue, just after you cross Camino Alto, next to the wastewater treatment plant. Keep your dog leashed near the steep-sided sewage ponds; dogs have drowned in them. Also, be sure to keep your dog leashed until you've reached the grassy dog run area; There's a $50 ticket if you get caught unleashed. (415) 383-1370.

- **Camino Alto Open Space Preserve** 🐾🐾🐾½ 🐕
  See **13** *on page 338.*

In this accessible open space, your dog may run free on a wide fire trail along a ridge connecting with Mount Tamalpais. You'll walk through bay laurels, madrones, and chaparral, looking down on soaring vultures and the bay, Highway 1, the hills, and the headlands. A small imperfection is that you can hear the whoosh of traffic. Just pretend it's the wind. Dogs must be leashed on the regular hiking trails here. Park at the end of Escalon Drive, just west of Camino Alto. (415) 499-6387.

- **Mount Tamalpais State Park** 🐾🐾🐾 *See* **14** *on page 338.*

Generally, dogs are restricted to paved roads here. But dogs may stay in one of the campgrounds, and there are also a few spots near the summit where you can take your dog. The views from here are something you'll certainly appreciate on a clear day.

Stop for lunch at the Bootjack Picnic Area, west of the Mountain Home Inn on Panoramic Highway and about a quarter mile east of the turnoff to the summit, Pantoll Road. The tables are attractively sited on the hillside under oak trees. This picnic ground is an access point for the Bootjack Trail and Matt Davis Trail. The Matt Davis Trail is off-limits, but you and your dog may—howlelujah!—use the 100 feet of Bootjack Trail that leads you into Marin Municipal Water District land, where leashed dogs are allowed. (You must travel north on the Bootjack Trail, though, not south; it's all state park in that direction.)

Heading northward, you can hook up with the Old Stage Fire Road and the Old Railroad Grade Fire Road, which are water district roads going almost the whole distance to the summit. You can also enter the Old Stage Fire Road right across from the Pantoll Ranger Station, at the intersection of Panoramic Highway and Pantoll Road. Pooches have special permission to cross the 100 feet or so of state park trail approaching water district trail.

The Bootjack Picnic Area parking lot charges $5 to park. (Once you pay in any state park lot, your receipt is good for any other spot that you hit that day.) The park has 16 developed walk-in campsites that allow dogs. They're at the Pantoll Station Campground. Sites are $12 to $16, plus $1 for your dog. All sites are first come, first served. (415) 388-2070.

•**Mount Tamalpais Summit** 🐾🐾🐾 *See* ⓯ *on page 338.*

The summit of Mount Tam is worth the $5 fee that you're charged merely to drive here. But in addition to the magnificent views, you may also take your dog on one trail up here ($1 dog fee).

You'll find a small refreshment stand, rest rooms, a visitors center, and viewing platforms. On clear days, you can see nine counties, whether you want to or not. In summer, white fingers of fog obscure a good part of your view as they creep between the "knuckles" of Marin's ridges.

It's too bad if your leashed dog doesn't care about views. But he will take eagerly to the smoothly paved Verna Dunshee Trail, about one mile long, running almost level around the summit. About three-quarters of this trail is also wheelchair accessible.

From U.S. 101, take the Stinson Beach/Highway 1 exit. Follow Highway 1 to Panoramic Highway, which will be a right turn. Continue on Panoramic to the right turn off to Pantoll Road; Pantoll soon becomes East Ridgecrest Road and goes to the summit, then loops back for your trip down. (415) 388-2070.

•**Mount Tamalpais–Marin Municipal Water District Land** 🐾🐾🐾 *See* ⓰ *on page 338.*

Your very best bet for a dog walk high on the mountain is to find one of the water district fire roads near the summit. Your dog must be leashed, but at least she can go on the trails with you, and you both can experience the greenness of this wonderful mountain. At this elevation, the green comes from chaparral, pine, and madrone.

Just below the summit on East Ridgecrest Boulevard, watch for the water district's gate and sign. This is the Old Railroad Grade Fire Road, which descends 1,785 feet from the entry point just west of the summit. On the way it intersects with Old Stage Fire Road, then emerges at the Bootjack Picnic Area. En route, you'll cross three creeks. For obvious reasons, you'll be happier in warm weather taking this road down, not up; get someone to meet you in a car at the Bootjack picnic site.

Another spot to pick up a water district trail is off Panoramic Highway just west of the Mountain Home Inn. Look for the Marin Municipal Water District sign by the fire station. Park at the state park parking lot west of Mountain Home Inn and walk east along this fire road, called Gravity Car Road (though it's unmarked), through mixed pines, redwoods, fir, madrone, and scrub. Keep your eyes open for fast-moving mountain bikes. (415) 924-4600.

•**Old Mill Park** 🐾🐾🐾 *See* ⓱ *on page 338.*

Refresh your dog under cool redwoods right in the town of Mill Valley. The old mill, built in 1834, was recently restored. A wooden bridge over

Old Mill Creek leads to well-maintained paths that run along the creek. The creek is dog-accessible, though pooches are supposed to be leashed.

One picnic table here sits within the hugest "fairy ring" we've ever seen—40 feet across. Boy dogs like to imagine the size of the mother tree whose stump engendered this ring of saplings. The park is on Throckmorton Avenue at Olive Street, near the public library. (415) 383-1370.

RESTAURANTS

The Depot Cafe and Bookstore: This place is Mill Valley's town square and everybody's backyard. You and your dog may sit at cafe tables, benches, or picnic tables and snack or just bask in the sun—if you don't mind skateboarders, bikes, chess players, crying kids, telephones, Frisbees, hackeysack, and guitar music happening right next to you. These are Marin kids, the kind who will reach out to your dog's face without a moment's hesitation. Mellow is the watchword here. Both sun and shade are available, at least after mid-afternoon. It's on the Plaza; (415) 383-2665.

Perry's Deli: The house-made soups at Perry's are delicious on a cool afternoon, but Joe prefers his fellow diners to order roast turkey sandwiches so he can catch the "droppings." Dine outside under the awning. 246 East Blithedale Avenue; (415) 381-0407.

Piazza d'Angelo: This Italian lunch and dinner spot has 15 tables on two outside patios, one shaded, the other not. Dogs are welcome at either as long as it's not too busy. The premier dish for people here is the tortelloni della casa, and they'll even bring a bowl of agua for your dog. 22 Miller Avenue; (415) 388-2185.

PLACES TO STAY

Mount Tamalpais State Park: See Mount Tamalpais State Park on page 346 for camping information.

MUIR BEACH

PARKS, BEACHES, AND RECREATION AREAS

• Muir Beach 🐾🐾🐾🐾🐾 🐕 *See* ⑱ *on page 338.*

Muir Beach allows obedient, leash-free doggies these days! With so much of the Golden Gate National Recreation Area's lands being taken away from leashless dogs, this is a refreshing addition to this book. It's small, but a real gem, with rugged sand dunes spotted with plants, a parking lot and large picnic area, a small lagoon with tules, and its share of wind. Redwood Creek empties into the ocean here. Leashless dogs (under voice control, as leashless dog should always be) are permitted from the shoreline to the crest of the dunes. They must be leashed from the dune crest inland to Big Lagoon, and in parking lots and picnic areas.

You can reach Muir Beach the long way, hiking about five miles from the Marin Headlands Visitors Center (see Rodeo Beach, page 361), or the easy way, via Highway 1. From Highway 1, watch for the turnoff for the beach. (415) 388-2596.

NOVATO

Novato is one of the Marin cities whose dog ordinance is the county's:

Dogs must be on leash or under verbal command. Its city parks require leashes, though.

But that last rule will soon have an exception in the form of a leash-free dog park. After four years of hard work, a group called D.O.G.B.O.N.E. (Dog Owners Group Bettering Our Novato Environment) has succeeded in getting a terrific two-acre site for a dog park! It's in the San Marin area of Novato, a couple of lots past Morningstar Farms (the horse place) on the left side of North Novato Boulevard as you head toward Stafford Lake. Townies will know what I'm talking about. Others will get better directions in this book's next edition, when the park is a reality.

At press time, the group had just received the city's blessing, as well as a mandate to have the park ready to go in two years. The group now has to raise big bucks for grading the property, irrigating it, fencing it, and putting in a few doggy essentials. When the fencing goes up and a few dog things go in, the city says the park can open, even before all the other tasks are done. That means the park could be open as early as summer of 1998! To get an update or find out how you can help, call Lauren Cobb, founder of D.O.G.B.O.N.E., at (415) 898-5843, or write (donations are welcome) to D.O.G.B.O.N.E. at P.O. Box 359, Novato, CA 94948.

PARKS, BEACHES, AND RECREATION AREAS

• **Deer Island Open Space Preserve** 🐾🐾🐾🐾 🐕
   See ⓲ on page 338.

This preserve is called an island because it's a high point in the flood-plain of the Petaluma River, an oak-crowned hill surrounded by miles of dock and tules. You can easily imagine it surrounded by shallow-water Miwuk canoes slipping through rafts of ducks. The trail is a 1.8-mile loop of gentle ups and downs above ponds and marshy fields. There are some sturdy old oaks among the mixed deciduous groves, and lots of laurels. The trail is partly shaded and bans bikes. Dogs have to be leashed on the trails, but are permitted off leash on fire roads here.

From U.S. 101, exit at San Marin Drive/Atherton Avenue; drive east about 1.5 miles and take a right on Olive Avenue, then a left on Deer Island Lane. Park in a small lot at the trailhead, by a small engineering company building. (415) 499-6387.

• **Indian Tree Open Space Preserve** 🐾🐾🐾½ 🐕
   See ⓴ on page 338.

This open space and Verissimo Hills Open Space Preserve (see page 351) are good to know about because they're just east of Stafford Lake County Park. You needn't leash on fire roads here, but watch out for horses. Leashes are the law on the preserve's trails.

From U.S. 101, exit at San Marin Drive/Atherton Avenue; drive west on San Marin. After San Marin turns into Sutro Avenue, take a right onto Vine-yard Road. Park along the dirt county road that begins at the trailhead. (415) 499-6387.

• **Indian Valley Open Space Preserve** 🐾🐾🐾🐾 🐕
   See ㉑ on page 338.

Lots of dogs come here to trot around in leashless ecstasy on the fire road. On hiking trails, they have to trot around in leashed ecstasy. The hiking trail here is partly sunny, partly shaded by laurels, and much-revered by canines.

From U.S. 101, exit at DeLong Avenue and go west on DeLong, which becomes Diablo Avenue. Take a left on Hill Road and a right on Indian Valley Road. Drive all the way to the end; park on this road before you walk left at the spur road marked "Not a Through Street," just south of Old Ranch Road. Cross Arroyo Avichi Creek right at the entrance (dry in summer). (415) 499-6387.

• **Loma Verde Open Space Preserve** 🐾🐾🐾½ 🐕
See ㉒ on page 338.

There are two access points to this open space where dogs are allowed off leash on fire roads. One, south of the Marin Country Club, is a waterless, tree-covered hillside with a fire road. Bikes are allowed, so be sure to keep your leash-free dog under voice control. It's a good road if you like easily reachable high spots; there are fine views of San Pablo Bay. Exit U.S. 101 at Ignacio Boulevard. Go west to Fairway Drive and turn left (south), then left on Alameda de la Loma, then right on Pebble Beach Drive. Access is at the end of Pebble Beach.

The second access point is through the Posada West housing development. From Alameda del Prado, turn south on Posada del Sol. The trail opening is at the end of this street. (415) 499-6387.

• **Lucas Valley Open Space Preserve** 🐾🐾🐾🐾 🐕
See ㉓ on page 338.

This space of rolling, oak-dotted hills affords great views of Novato and Lucas Valley developments. There are a dozen access points, most from Lucas Valley and Marinwood.

One access point is reached by turning left (north) off Lucas Valley Road on Mount Shasta Drive, followed by a brief right turn on Vogelsang Drive. Park near this dead end and walk in. Keep in mind that all Marin open space preserves require pooches to be on leash except on fire roads. (415) 499-6387.

• **Miwuk Park** 🐾🐾🐾 *See ㉔ on page 338.*

This is one of the best city parks we've visited. Dogs must be on leash, but it offers a great combination of dog pleasures and human amenities. Paved paths, good for strollers, wind through pine trees. There are bocce ball courts, horseshoes, a kids' gym, and a lovely shaded picnic area with grills.

Outside the Museum of the American Indian, located in this park, is an intriguing display of California native plants that the coastal Miwuk used for food, clothing, and shelter.

Best of all for canines, Novato Creek flows deep and 30 to 40 feet wide—even in summer. A woman we encountered with a golden retriever told us that the muddy bottom can sometimes be soft and treacherous, so keep a close eye on your dog if he goes swimming. The park is at Novato Boulevard and San Miguel Drive. (415) 897-4323.

• **Mount Burdell Open Space Preserve** 🐾🐾🐾🐾 🐕
   See ㉕ on page 338.
   Mount Burdell is the largest of Marin's open space preserves. You'll share it with cattle, but there's plenty of room. There are 8 or 10 miles of cinder and dirt paths, including part of the Bay Area Ridge Trail, that wind through its oak-dotted grasslands. (Dogs have to be leashed on trails, but are permitted to run leashless on fire roads here.)
   A creek is located about one-eighth of a mile up the trail starting at San Andreas Drive, but it's dry in summer. In winter, you might find the preserve's Hidden Lake. In summer, there are lots of foxtails and fire danger is high. No fires are ever allowed. Camping is allowed by permit, but there are no facilities.
   From San Marin Drive, turn north on San Andreas Drive. Park on the street. (415) 499-6387.

• **Verissimo Hills Open Space Preserve** 🐾🐾🐾 🐕
   See ㉖ on page 338.
   The golden hills with clumps of oak have narrow foot trails only; bikes are prohibited. As you enter the area, you'll see a fork in the trail. Take the trail uphill to the left. This path features fine views of the hills as well as nearby residential areas. (Note that this open space preserve is co-managed by the Marin Municipal Water District, which means that if you're in doubt, leash. Be sure to close the gate to keep cattle inside.) Dogs are permitted off leash on fire roads only. Leashes are the law on regular trails.
   From U.S. 101, exit at San Marin Drive/Atherton Avenue; drive west on San Marin. Turn right (west) on Center Road. Go all the way to the end, where you can park. (415) 499-6387.

DOGGY DAYS

Enter him in the Olympics: Picture this: Your dog proudly marches up the Steps of Champions while Olympic music fills the air. An Olympic official says a few words of praise and hangs a bronze-ish, silver-ish, or even gold-ish Olympic medal around your dog's neck. The crowd cheers. It's a glorious moment.
   This is the stuff dog dreams may be made of (actually, we think they're made of chasing cats and eating steak and rolling in cow patties, but that's just one theory). Every spring, the Marin Humane Society makes this dream come true for hundreds of pooches at the Bay Area Canine Games, also known as the Doggy Olympics. And your dog doesn't have to be an athlete to compete. Sure, there are the usual physical challenges, like the 50-yard dash and the obstacle course. But the Olympics is also for the average dog in your life. Competitions like the Fastest Eater, Best Crooner, and Loudest Barker make the Olympics an event where just about any dog can have his day. If your dog puts his paw down when it comes to competing, bring him along as a spectator.
   The Olympics are held on the spacious grounds of the Marin Humane Society, at 171 Bel Marin Keys Boulevard, Novato, CA 94949. Write or call (415) 883-4621 for entry fees and details of this year's event. Proceeds benefit shelter animals.

OLEMA

PARKS, BEACHES, AND RECREATION AREAS

• **Bolinas Ridge Trail** 🐾🐾🐾 *See* ㉗ *on page 338.*

This Golden Gate National Recreation Area trail, part of the Bay Area Ridge Trail, is not for sissies—canine or human. It climbs steadily up for 11 miles from the Olema end, giving you gorgeous views of Tomales Bay, Bolinas, and the ocean, and ends up at the Bolinas-Fairfax Road below Alpine Lake.

You must keep your dog leashed. One good reason for this is that there are cattle roaming unfenced along the trail. And the trail is very popular with non-sissy mountain bikers. (The trail is wide, but made of dirt and rock.) From the western end, you'll walk through rolling grassland with cypress clumps. Rock outcrops sport crowns of poison oak, so watch it.

You may be able to cope with 11 miles of this, but remember your dog's bare pads and don't overdo it. Also, it isn't much fun for man or beast to walk 11 miles attached by a leash.

Unfortunately, only the Bolinas Ridge Trail is open to dogs; you can't take any of the spur trails going south.

The western end begins about one mile north of Olema on Sir Francis Drake Boulevard. There's roadside parking only. (415) 556-0560 or (415) 663-1092.

• **Limantour Beach** 🐾🐾🐾 *See* ㉘ *on page 338.*

This bountiful beach at Point Reyes National Seashore is most people's favorite, so it's often crowded. From the main parking lot, walk a quarter of a mile through tule marsh, grasses and brush, and scattered pines, past Limantour Estero. (Dogs are prohibited on the side trails.)

Rules for leashed dogs are clearly marked—a refreshing exception to the obscure and contradictory rules in so many parks. For example, approaching Limantour Beach on the path, you'll see a sign that says dogs are prohibited to your right, allowed to your left. This beach is plenty big, so it's an excellent arrangement that keeps dog owners and dog avoiders equally happy. You may walk with your dog to Santa Maria Beach.

From Highway 1, look for the turnoff to Bear Valley Road, which runs between Olema and Inverness Park. Take Bear Valley from either direction to Limantour Road; turn south on Limantour all the way to the beach. (415) 663-1092.

PLACES TO STAY

Olema Ranch Campground: It's hard to find a campground that's decent for both RVs and tent campers, so we were mighty pleased to find Olema Ranch. RV folks get all the hookups they need, and tenters get a choice of scenic meadow or forest campsites. Many sites come with water. The campground features amenities like a kitchen, laundry facilities, and a supply store, so we're not exactly talking the big wilderness adventure here. But still, it's a terrific spot to set up a tent with a dog who doesn't mind a little civilized camping.

Rates are $18 to $25. Dogs are $1 exra. 10155 Highway 1, P.O. Box 175, Olema, CA 94950; (415) 663-8001 or (800) 655-CAMP.

POINT REYES STATION

RESTAURANTS

Bovine Bakery: The bread here will make you drool, which will make your dog embarrassed. Dine on bread or pizza or "killer monster cookies" at the bench in front. 11315 Highway 1; (415) 663-9420.

Cafe Reyes: The patio on the cafe's side is big and very attractive, with excellent views of local scenery. Even dogs seem to enjoy its ambience. The food is great, too. Bring it to the seven umbrella-topped tables and wolf it down with your pooch at your side. The cuisine is best described as Tex-Mex with a California leaning. Try one of the Thai burritos for a true international experience. You can also get baked goodies and strong coffee, for those lazy, foggy days here. There's not really a street address. It's on Highway 1 and is big and wooden. You can't miss it. (415) 663-9493.

PLACES TO STAY

Jasmine Cottage and Gray's Retreat: These two glorious getaway cottages are the cat's meow for dogs and their people. Located on a serene stretch of rolling pastureland in Point Reyes Station, the cottages have a sweet country theme and seem perfectly at home in their surroundings. Dogs love it here, because the cottages are each adorned with their own private enclosed patio and garden. They're wonderful places to relax outside with your pooch.

The cottages also have fully equipped kitchens that come with a real bonus: a lovely picnic basket and all the gear that goes with it (excluding the food). Now there's no excuse for not taking your pooch on a picnic. In addition, each cottage has a fireplace, and the two share a secluded garden hot tub.

Jasmine Cottage is the smaller of the two romantic hideaways. It's sequestered in a country garden at the top of a hill and has small flower gardens, vegetable gardens, and even a flock of chickens, who provide guests with their morning eggs. (A full, simple breakfast is included in your stay at this cottage.) The chickens are in a protected area, but if your dog has a hankering for KFC, best keep her away. When we visited, Joe Dog went cuckoo over the cock-a-doodle-doos. We had to drag him kicking and screaming back inside the cottage for fear he would give a hen a heart attack.

Gray's Retreat is just as enchanting, but chicken-free and bigger. It's more geared toward families, since it sleeps up to six and comes with a high chair and a portable crib. Breakfast is not provided, but the kitchen is stocked with enough basic dry goods (including pancake mix) that with a few groceries, you can have yourself a feast.

If you'll be visiting with two pooches, you'll have to stay at Gray's Retreat. Jasmine Cottage permits only one pooch. Each dog pays a $15 fee for the length of her stay at either location. The cottage rate is $165 nightly for the first two people. Additional people are $15. The weekly rate is $990. The mailing address is P.O. Box 56, Point Reyes Station, CA 94956; (415) 663-1166.

DIVERSIONS

If only dogs could read: The Brown Study Bookshop sent me a letter that ended like this: "We welcome genteel canines, whether a reading rover or a browsing bowser—or just a patiently waiting companion. Se habla milkbone." So of course, next time we found ourselves pawing around for a good book, Joe hounded me to drive with him to this wonderful little bookstore. He immediately fell in love with the place. Dogs get lots of loving, some water, and a crunchy biscuit. I think he's trying to learn to read now. He used to chew books, now he's simply making dog-eared pages. Anything to go back.

This store really is a treat—for dogs and humans. There's a big selection of new and used books, with a strong outdoor book section. Combine a visit here with a hike and a lunch, and you've got yourselves a doggone great day. 11315 Highway 1; (415) 663-1633.

ROSS

PARKS, BEACHES, AND RECREATION AREAS

•**Natalie Coffin Greene Park** 🐾 🐾 🐾 *See* ㉙ *on page 338.*

Leashed dogs are welcome at this enchanted mixed forest of redwood and deciduous trees. The picnic area has an old-fashioned shelter built of logs and stone.

The park borders generic Marin Municipal Water District land, and from the park, you can pick up the wide cinder fire road leading to Phoenix Lake, a five-minute walk. Bikers, hikers, and leashed dogs are all welcome on this road, but the lake is a reservoir, so no body contact is allowed—for man or beast.

The road continues, depending how far you want to walk, to Lagunitas Lake, Bon Tempe Lake, Alpine Lake, and Kent Lake. (No body contact in any of them; sorry, dogs.) Combined, the water district offers 94 miles of road and 44 miles of trail in this area, meandering through hillsides, densely forested with pine, oak, madrone, and a variety of other trees. For a trail map, send a self-addressed, stamped envelope to Sky Oaks Ranger Station, P.O. Box 865, Fairfax, CA 94978, Attention: Trail Map.

At the corner of Sir Francis Drake Boulevard and Lagunitas Road, go west on Lagunitas all the way to the end, past the country club. You'll find a parking lot and some portable toilets. (415) 453-1453.

SAN ANSELMO

San Anselmo Avenue provides you and your mellow pooch with a laid-back stroll, and you can both cool your paws in San Anselmo Creek, which runs through town. Your well-behaved pooch can even be off leash, provided she's under voice control. There's a group called Friends of San Anselmo Dogs that's trying to get a permanent pooch park started at Red Hill Park, behind the Red Hill Shopping Center at the end of Shaw Drive. At press time, the dogs had only temporary status. By the next edition, we're hoping to find a four-paw dog park here. For more information on this noble effort, call (415) 258-4600.

PARKS, BEACHES, AND RECREATION AREAS

• **Creek Park** 🐾🐾🐾 *See* **30** *on page 338.*

San Anselmo Creek runs between Sir Francis Drake Boulevard—which has a wide variety of antique shops—and San Anselmo Avenue, the main shopping street. A bridge connects the two streets.

Creek Park is small, but handy and clean. It's next to a free public lot with some shady spaces. Along the creek banks on the Sir Francis Drake side are picnic tables on a lawn with beautiful willows and maples. Lots of people lounge on the grass. Wooden steps lead down to the water. There's plenty of shade in which to picnic or lie on the grass, while resting between shopping binges for antiques.

Turn into the parking lot from Sir Francis Drake Boulevard, near "The Hub" (intersection of Sir Francis Drake and Red Hill Avenue). (415) 258-4645.

• **Loma Alta Open Space Preserve** 🐾🐾🐾🐾 🐕
See **31** *on page 338.*

A little canyon amid bare hills, lined with oaks, bay laurel, and buckeye, this is an exceptional open space preserve. There's plenty of shade. The trail follows White Hill Creek, which is dry in the summer. Leashes are required on the trails, but obedient dogs can throw their leashes to the wind on the fire road.

You can park at the trailhead at the end of Glen Avenue, a turn north off Sir Francis Drake Boulevard. (415) 499-6387.

• **Memorial Park** 🐾🐾🐾🐾 🐕 *See* **32** *on page 338.*

This pleasant and popular city park has tennis courts, three baseball diamonds, and a children's play area. Next to the diamonds is a fenced dog-exercise area, where leash-free dogs romp joyfully, fetching, chasing Frisbees, or socializing. There's even a creek next to the dog run. A volunteer group, Memorial Park Dog Owners Association, publishes a newsletter and keeps an eye out for scooper-scofflaws. The park is off Sunnyhills Drive. (415) 258-4645.

• **Sorich Ranch Park** 🐾🐾🐾🐾 🐕 *See* **33** *on page 338.*

The biggest and by far the wildest city park in San Anselmo is Sorich Ranch Park, an undeveloped open space soaring up to a ridgetop from which you can see a distant make-believe San Francisco skyline across the bay. From the very top of the ridge, you also can see Mount Tamalpais and most of San Rafael, including the one-of-a-kind turquoise and salmon Marin County Civic Center, designed by Frank Lloyd Wright. (Some Marinites are glad there's only one.)

The entrance from the San Anselmo side is at the end of San Francisco Boulevard, and the path is pretty much straight up. But if you aren't up to a 10-minute puffing ascent, you can just stroll in the meadows at the bottom. No leash is required, and the park is uncrowded and often pleasantly breezy. There's no water available, and it can be scorching in summer. (415) 258-4645.

RESTAURANTS

Creekside Bistro: Dogs are welcome at the front patio, where they can dine on tasty bistro cuisine at an abundance of clean white metal tables. 626 San Anselmo Avenue; (415) 459-5708.

SAN RAFAEL

This charming town may soon go to the dogs, thanks to an enterprising organization called Field of Dogs. At press time, founder Mario Di Palma and his group had been working to open a dog park for more than five years. Most of the approvals had been granted at this time, but the group is still awaiting a final vote by the county board of supervisors. When the park is approved, it will be on an acre of land at the civic center. The park, which will be aptly named Field of Dogs (I love it) will be fenced, and have water, scoopers, shade trees, and trash cans. Joe Dog is keeping his paws crossed that Di Palma's dream comes true. So is Di Palma. "It's been a real battle," says Di Palma. For more information, or to make a donation for much needed park funding (the group has to raise the money for fencing and everything else itself), call Di Palma at (415) 454-4851.

Thanks to an enlightened high-tech company based here, San Rafael has already gone to the dogs in an unusual way: Autodesk, Inc., the world's fourth-biggest PC software company, permits employees to bring their dogs and other pets to work. Some 75 employees frequently show up at work with pooches in hand. It's apparently a real selling point when recruiting—and keeping—employees.

Sure, there are occasional problems when a dog hikes his leg on someone's chair or decides to gnaw on a computer cable, but generally pooches are seen as enjoyable additions to the company. We give Autodesk a four-paw rating, and hope other companies will follow its lead.

PARKS, BEACHES, AND RECREATION AREAS

• **Boyd Park** 🐾 🐾½ *See* ③④ *on page 338.*

This is not a very doggy park, until you drive past the Dollar mansion (now the Falkirk Community Cultural Center) into the hills on Robert Dollar Scenic Drive to the undeveloped portion. The only parking is at a turn-out off the drive, but at that spot, the drive becomes a dirt fire trail, closed to autos, that mounts the ridgecrest in a steady uphill climb through brush, oak, and madrone.

Leash your pup and start walking. You'll get a breathtaking view of the Richmond–San Rafael Bridge, the Bay Bridge, the Oakland skyline, and Mount Tam. Robert Dollar Scenic Drive begins at the end of Laurel Place. (415) 485-3333.

• **China Camp State Park** 🐾 🐾 🐾 *See* ③⑤ *on page 338.*

You shouldn't miss a drive through this lovely park, although it's not terribly hospitable to dogs except at Village Beach, the site of the 1890s Chinese fishing village for which the park is named. As you drive in, you'll see a rare piece of bay, marsh, and oak-covered hills as the Miwuks saw it. The hills, like islands, rise from salt marsh seas of pickleweed and cordgrass.

You'll see the "No Dogs" symbol at every trailhead, in case you're tempted. However, with your dog, you may visit any of three picnic grounds on the way, via North Point San Pedro Road. Buckeye Point and Weber Point both have tables in shade or sun overlooking San Pablo Bay, mudflats at low tide, and the hills beyond the bay. Bullhead Flat lets you get right next to the water, but there's no shade at the tables.

Watch for the sign to China Camp Village, a left turn into a lot, where there's some shade. You'll see the rickety old pier and the wood-and-tin village. Park, leash your dog, and walk down to the village and the beach. On weekdays, this park is much less crowded. There are more picnic tables overlooking the water by the parking lot, an interpretive exhibit (open from 10 A.M. to 5 P.M., and open to the air so that your dog can casually stroll in with you if it isn't crowded), and, on weekends, a refreshment stand serving shrimp, crab, and beer. You can eat at picnic tables right on the beach—small, but pleasantly sheltered by hillsides, with gentle surf.

Swimming is encouraged here, and it's often warm enough. Derelict fishing boats and shacks are preserved on the beach. You can walk all the way to a rocky point at the south end, but watch out for the luxuriant poison oak in the brush along the beach. You may occasionally find broken glass.

There are 31 primitive walk-in campsites here. As in all state parks, dogs must always be leashed or confined to your tent. Sites are $12 to $14. Dogs are $1 extra. Reserve through Parknet at (800) 444-PARK. From U.S. 101, take the North Point San Pedro Road exit and follow it all the way into the park. (Don't go near McNears Beach County Park just south of China Camp. Dogs are strictly forbidden.) (415) 456-0766.

•**John F. McInnis County Park** 🐾🐾🐾 🐕 *See* **36** *on page 338.*
This is an all-around, got-everything park for people. Among its riches are two softball fields, two soccer fields, tennis courts, a picnic area, a scale-model car track, a nine-hole golf course, miniature golf, batting cages, and a dirt creekside nature trail.

Best of all for trustworthy dogs, they can be off leash, so long as they're under verbal command and out of the golf course. This park isn't particularly pretty, but it's very utilitarian. From U.S. 101, exit at Smith Ranch Road. (415) 499-6387.

•**San Pedro Mountain Open Space Preserve** 🐾🐾🐾½ 🐕
See **37** *on page 338.*
A narrow footpath rises moderately but inexorably upwards through a madrone forest. But if you make it up far enough, you'll be rewarded with terrific views of the bay and Marin's peaks. Deer are plentiful, so it's kind to leash your dog if you don't trust him completely to stay by your side.

Park at the entrance at the end of Woodoaks Drive, a short street off North Point San Pedro Road just north of the Jewish Community Center of Marin. (415) 499-6387.

•**Santa Margarita Island Open Space Preserve** 🐾🐾🐾½
See **38** *on page 338.*
What a wonderful, secret place this is. Gallinas Creek, fortified by levees, is lined with rickety piers and small boats, like a bit of the Delta. You can

---

cross to a tiny island via a footbridge and climb the hill you'll find here, covered with oaks and boulders, or walk around the edge on a dirt path. Watch for poison oak on the hill. Though of course it isn't true, you can feel as if no one has been here before you except Coast Miwuks.

From North Point San Pedro Road, turn west on Meadow Drive. Where it ends, at the western end of Vendola Drive, is the footbridge. You can park on the street. Carry water if you plan to stay long. (415) 499-6387.

• **Santa Venetia Marsh Open Space Preserve** 🐾 🐾 🐾 ½
    See ㊲ on page 338.

Dogs are very lucky to be able to visit this saltwater marsh. Only leashed pooches on their best behavior should come here, because the preserve is home to two endangered species who don't need barking, chasing dogs to do them in.

Mmm, doggy, the scents can be mighty strong here sometimes. They're so doggone nose-flaring good your dog may not even notice he's wearing a leash. You may not feel the same about the odor, but hey, just keep saying to yourself "it's a natural smell."

It's cool and breezy here, but gentler than any San Francisco Bay shore park. The grasses and pickleweed make a pretty mixture of colors, and swallows dart above the ground hunting insects.

Vendola Drive has two distinct parts, and you can get to the marsh from the end of either. At the western end of the creekside segment of Vendola, at the corner of Meadow Drive, is a footbridge leading to Santa Margarita Island (see above). (415) 499-6387.

• **Terra Linda-Sleepy Hollow Divide Open Space Preserve** 🐾 🐾 🐾 ½
    🐕 *See ㊵ on page 338.*

There are many entrances to this ridgeline preserve, but generally the best are the highest on the ridge. We'll describe the one that starts you at a good high point, so that you don't have to climb. From the entrance at the end of Ridgewood Drive, you can walk into Sorich Ranch Park (see page 355).

From this ridge, you can see the city of San Rafael, Highway 101, the wonderful turquoise-roofed Marin County Civic Center, the bay, and the hills of Solano County. No leash is necessary on fire roads, unless you're worried about your dog tangling with deer. But pooches must be leashed on trails.

Park near the very end of Ridgewood Drive. The entrance is unmarked, and you have to step over a low locked gate. (415) 499-6387.

RESTAURANTS

Cento Stelle: We really enjoy eating at Cento Stelle, which in Italian means a hundred stars. Besides being in love with the name, we're also in love with the very good Italian food. Dine with dog at the four sidewalk tables. 901 Lincoln Avenue; (415) 485-4422.

Chinook Restaurant & Cafe: Dogs are thrilled to be able to join the humans who eat at this fine-dining establishment. The cuisine here is very California, very delicious. For the more casual mutt, there's also deli food. Dine at the six outdoor tables. 1130 Fourth Street; (415) 457-0566.

Erik's Drive-In: Formerly an A&W burger joint, Erik's maintains the drive-in burger tradition. Dogs whose manners require they eat in the car will appreciate this. But Erik's also has eight outdoor tables for dogs who dig dining al fresco. 836 Second Street; (415) 454-6605.

Phyllis' Giant Burgers: Dogs dig this drive-in burger joint. Order your meat-eater one of the giant burgers. Or if your pooch is in a no-beef mode, try a veggie burger. 2202 Fourth Street; (415) 456-0866.

Shaky Grounds: This restaurant's name reminds Joe too much of the Loma Prieta quake, so he has a hard time getting really relaxed here. Of course, the grounds probably refer to the coffee they serve, but that doesn't make Joe very relaxed either. Fortunately, you can also order pastries, smoothies, soups, salads, and sandwiches. Nothing melts Joe more than having a few sips of warm chicken soup from his porta-bowl. 1800 Fourth Street; (415) 256-2420.

Villa Romana: The Italian food here may not remind you of the Old Country, but it's a decent place for a pizza lunch with the pooch. Dine at the two sidewalk tables. 901 B Street; (415) 457-7404.

PLACES TO STAY

China Camp State Park: See China Camp State Park on page 356 for camping information.

Villa Inn: Rates are $60 to $83. Dogs require a $20 deposit. 1600 Lincoln Avenue, San Rafael, CA 94901; (415) 456-4975.

SAUSALITO

Even if you live here, you should play tourist and stroll around Sausalito's harbor in the brilliant sea light (or luminous sea fog). On weekends, it's especially pleasant early in the day, before the ferries disgorge their passengers. The city's attitude toward dogs is relaxed. It's the perfect place to stop and sniff around for awhile. Be sure to fortify yourselves with a big breakfast at one of Sausalito's many fine outdoor eateries (see page 361) before heading to the blustery Marin Headlands.

PARKS, BEACHES, AND RECREATION AREAS

• **Dunphy Park** 🐾 🐾 🐾 *See ⑪ on page 338.*

This is a small but accessible park by the bay, and it comes complete with grass, willows, picnic tables, and a volleyball court. Best of all, there's a small beach, and canine swimming is fine. You can watch sailing and windsurfing from here, too. Dogs officially must be on leash. The parking lot is at Bridgeway and Bee Streets. (415) 289-4125.

• **Marin Headlands Trails** 🐾 🐾 🐾 🐾 🦮 *See ⑫ on page 338.*

From Rodeo Beach (see page 361), you can circle the lagoon or head up into the hills, as long as your pooch is leashed. You're in for a gorgeous walk—or a gorgeous and challenging walk, depending on the weather. Look at a map of the Bay Area, and it will be obvious why the headlands' trees all grow at an eastward slant. In summer especially, cold ocean air funnels through the Golden Gate, sucked in by the Central Valley's heat—chilling the headlands and the inhabitants of western San Francisco with fog and wind. The Bay Area may be "air-conditioned by God," but the headlands sit right at the air inflow, and it's set on "high." Never come here without at least one jacket.

Your dog will love the wind. The combination of fishy breeze and aromatic brush from the hillsides sends many into olfactory ecstasy. What looks from a distance like green fuzz on these headlands is a profusion of wildflowers and low brush. Indian paintbrush, hemlock, sticky monkeyflower, ferns, dock, morning glory, blackberry, sage, and thousands more species grow here—even some stunted but effective poison oak on the windward sides. (On the lee of the hills, it's not stunted.) Groves of eucalyptus grow on the crests. You hear a lovely low rustle and roar of wind, surf, birds, and insects—and the squeak and groan of eucalyptuses rubbing against each other. Pinch some sage between your fingers and sniff; if you can ever leave California again after that, you're a strong person.

From the beach and lagoon, you can hike the circle formed by the Miwuk Trail starting at the eastern end of the lagoon, meeting the Wolf Ridge Trail, then meeting the Coastal Trail (à la the Pacific Coast Trail), back to where you started. Or you can pick up the Coastal Trail off Bunker Road near Rodeo Beach. There are trailhead signs.

Sights along these trails include World War II gun emplacements, the Golden Gate Bridge, and San Francisco. As the trail rises and falls, you will discover a blessing: You'll be intermittently sheltered from the wind, and in these pockets, if the sun warms your back, you'll think you've died and gone to heaven.

Dogs used to be able to run off leash on all these trails, but no longer. The Golden Gate National Recreation Area, which oversees this 12,000-acre chunk of heaven, has become stricter of late. The only trail where good dogs can be leashless is the Oakwood Valley Trail, on the left side of Tennessee Valley Road, a little bit before the Miwok Stables. Dogs can be off leash on the trail or adjacent to it, anywhere north of the small cattle pond. They have to be leashed south of the pond, and they're not permitted to do the dog paddle, backstroke, or any other swimming styles in the pond. The trail doesn't make for an arduous hike, but at least we can still take our dogs for some much-needed off-leash romping.

If you want to hike from Rodeo Beach to Muir Beach (see page 348), remember that dogs have to be leashed the entire way now. But the great thing is that you can travel nearly the whole width of the headlands with your dog. This is tick country, so search carefully when you get home. (415) 331-1540.

• **Remington Dog Park** 🐾🐾🐾🐾 🐕 *See ④③ on page 338.*

Your leash-free dog can exercise his paws while you both exercise your social skills at this delightful park. Remington Park is named after the dog whose owner, Dianne Chute, helped raise the money to put the park together a few years back. It's more than an acre, all fenced, on a grassy slope with trees. Dogs have the time of their lives tearing around chasing each other, and humans have a great time chatting. The park comes complete with an informative bulletin board, a leash rack, benches, scoopers, and water. There's even a tent you can hide under in foul weather! They make everything cozy here.

Best of all, on Friday evenings, about 100 human patrons and their dogs gather for cocktail hour, with wine, cheese, bread, and of course, doggy treats. It sounds very Marin, but it's really just very civilized. On a recent summer evening, the park was host to a Mexican happy hour. Margaritas, chips, and salsa made the atmosphere even more festive than the usual Friday night gathering. If Joe could talk, he would have said "Ole!" Or at least "Make mine without salt."

From the day it was finished, Remington and his dog friends have made terrific use of this place. "It's the social hub of Sausalito," says cartoonist Phil Frank, "where the elite with four feet meet." What a boon to freedom-loving Sausalito dogs, who otherwise must be leashed everywhere in town. D.O.G. (Dog Owners Group) of Sausalito maintains the park and publishes a newsletter. Write to D.O.G., 690 Butte Street, Sausalito, CA 94965, or call (415) 332-6086.

From U.S. 101, take the Sausalito/Marin City exit, driving west to Bridgeway. Turn right on Bridgeway and drive south the equivalent of a long city block. Turn right at Ebbtide Avenue and park in the large lot at the end of Ebbtide.

•**Rodeo Beach and Lagoon** 🐾🐾🐾🐾🐕 *See* 🚳 *on page 338.*

Rodeo Beach is small but majestic, made of the dark sand common in Marin. Large rocks on shore are covered with "whitewash," birders' polite name for guano. Voice-controlled dogs can go off leash from the shoreline to the crest of the dune. Water dogs enjoy this beach, but letting your dog swim in Marin County surf is always risky—currents are strong, and trying to rescue a dog who is being swept away is to risk your own life. Also, while on the beach, watch your dog like a hawk and don't turn your own back on the surf. Especially in winter, a "sneaker" wave can sweep you and your dog away.

Doggies must be leashed from the dune crest inland to Rodeo Lagoon, and of course in the parking lot and picnic areas. If your dog promises not to bark and disturb wildlife, he can join you, on leash, on an interesting walk around Rodeo Lagoon. The lagoon is lined with tules and pickleweed. Ocean water splashes into the lagoon in winter and rainfall swells it until it overflows, continually mixing salt and fresh water. Birds love this fecund lagoon. It can be almost too much for a bird dog to take. An attractive wooden walkway leads across the lagoon to the beach.

From the Marin Headlands Visitors Center, follow the signs west. (415) 331-1540.

RESTAURANTS

Just a few of Sausalito's pooch-friendly restaurants:

Gatsby's: They serve fresh California cuisine here, but if you want to get really decadent, try the Chicago-style deep-dish pizza. It's as close to the real thing as you can get way out west. Dogs can join you at the four sidewalk tables. 39 Caledonia Street; (415) 332-4500.

Tommy's Wok: This fun Chinese restaurant is located just a bone's throw from Remington Park (see page 360), so it's a great place to dine after your dog burns up all his energy. The food is delicious, leaning more toward Szechuan dishes, but accommodating Cantonese-loving palates as well. Dine with your good doggy at the four outdoor tables. 3001 Bridgeway; (415) 332-5814.

Winship's Restaurant: Dogs like coming to the two outdoor tables here for a big breakfast, but the fare later in the day is good, too. It's the usual tasty soup, salad, sandwich, pasta menu, but this stuff always tastes even better with your dog at your side. 670 Bridgeway; (415) 332-1454.

DIVERSIONS

Seize the Bay: Ahoy, dogs, if you love the Bay, then Carpe Diem and take a ride on the Blue & Gold Fleet's ferry. Lucky dogs get to go from Sausalito to San Francisco and Tiburon. Please see page 398 in the San Francisco chapter for more information.

STINSON BEACH

It's fun to poke around Stinson, which is swarming with surfers and tourists on beautiful days. There's a relaxed attitude toward dogs at the outdoor snack shop tables. Bolinas Lagoon, stretching along Highway 1 between Stinson Beach and Bolinas, is tempting but environmentally fragile, so you should picnic along the water only if your dog is controllable. You'll also be taking a chance with muddy paws in your car. Don't go near Audubon Canyon Ranch, where herons and egrets nest.

PARKS, BEACHES, AND RECREATION AREAS

• **Stinson Beach** 🐾 🐾 🐾 ½ *See* ㊺ *on page 338.*

Highway 1 to Stinson and Bolinas is worth the curves you'll negotiate. Don't be in a hurry. On sunny weekends, traffic will be heavy. Try it on a foggy day—it's otherworldly. Anyway, dogs often don't care whether or not the sun is shining.

Before setting out, we asked around. "Go to Stinson," said a friend. "There are dogs everywhere." "Dogs aren't allowed on Stinson Beach," said a Golden Gate National Recreation Area ranger. "Stinson is swarming with dogs," said another friend.

A kind woman in the Muir Woods bookstore solved the mystery. "No dogs on Stinson," she said sternly, "but there's this little part at the north end that isn't Stinson. We call it Dog Beach."

Indeed, the county-managed stretch where private houses are built at the north end does allow dogs on leash. This is itself a bit of a contradiction, because as you walk along with your obediently leashed dog, dogs who live in the houses lining the county stretch, and who don't have to wear leashes, come prancing out like the local law enforcement to check out the new kid. Leashed and leashless, dogs are indeed everywhere at Stinson. It's merry and there's plenty of room for them.

You and your dog will be equally happy on Stinson Beach, with its backdrop of low hills and lining of dunes. Keep the dog off the dunes where they're roped off, being "repaired" by the forces of nature. Dogs are allowed in Stinson Beach's picnic area by Eskoot Creek, a pretty setting redolent with tantalizing smells.

Take the beach turnoff from Highway 1. Turn right at the parking lot and park at the far north end. Walk right by the sign that says "No Pets on Beach"—you can't avoid it—and turn right. Where the houses start is the county beach. You'll see a sign dividing the two jurisdictions saying "End of Guarded Beach." (415) 868-0942.

TIBURON

The town of Tiburon is almost too Disneyland-perfect, with its green lawns and fountains, brick sidewalks, and lack of smells. On a sunny day you can't beat the clean, safe street atmosphere for eating and strolling. Dogs, of course, must be as polite and well behaved as their owners. Tiburon did a good job of planning for parking: There's almost none except for one large lot costing $2 just for the first hour, which means that cars aren't driving around searching for a spot. Just give up and park there.

The town has also arranged for fog banks to lie harmlessly to the west—usually over Sausalito. You and your dog can walk onto the ferry dock and watch boats of the Red & White Fleet come in and out, destination San Francisco or Angel Island. Dogs aren't allowed on Angel Island, but they can take pleasure with you sniffing the exciting scent of boat motor oil on the dock.

If you get a sudden impulse to take off for San Francisco, do it! One recreational secret of the Bay Area is that you may take your dog with you on the Red & White Fleet ferries, except to Angel Island or Alcatraz (see Diversions, page 398).

PARKS, BEACHES, AND RECREATION AREAS

• **Richardson Bay Park** 🐾 🐾 🐾 *See ㊻ on page 338.*

Generally known as the Tiburon Bike Path, this is a terrific multiuse park, unusual because it can be safely enjoyed by both bicyclists and dogs. It stretches two-thirds the length of Tiburon's peninsula and has parking at both ends. The larger lot is at the northern end. A dirt road, Brunini Way (no vehicles), leads into the park at the north end. You'll find a quiet, natural bay shoreline with a bit of marsh. There's some flotsam and jetsam, but only the highest quality, of course.

Keep walking and you'll enter McKegney Green, the wide bike path that runs for two miles along Tiburon Boulevard toward downtown. (It doesn't go all the way, though.) Your dog must be leashed. The path, marked for running trainers, swings past benches overlooking the bay and a kids' jungle gym.

Soon the path splits and goes past both sides of a stretch of soccer fields, fenced wildlife ponds (no dogs), and a parcourse. You can take your dog on either side, but be aware that bicyclists use both. You'll also share this path, on a fair weekend day, with roller skaters and parents pushing strollers. On the green are sunbathers and kite fliers.

The view: Mount Tamalpais and Belvedere, with the Bay Bridge, San Francisco, and the Golden Gate Bridge peeking out from behind it. Bring a jacket—it can be breezy here—and carry water for your dog if you're walking far. The only fountains are for people. Going toward town on Tiburon Boulevard, turn right at the sign that says Blackie's Pasture Road. It leads to the parking lot. (415) 435-7373.

RESTAURANTS

Paradise Hamburgers and Ice Cream: This place furnishes bike racks and lots of outdoor tables. There's always a Fido bowl of water outside the door. The owners adore dogs and occasionally give a pooch a special treat. 1694 Tiburon Boulevard; (415) 435-8823.

Tutto Mare: You and your well-behaved pooch will love it at this restaurant. If it's not too crowded, dogs can join you at the tables on the rear lower deck, right on the San Francisco Bay. (You can also dine at the front patio, but it's not as scenic.) The lower deck is shaded by the floor of the upper deck, so your pooch won't melt on a hot summer day. The food here is a tasty blend of Italian and California cuisine. The wood-fired pizzas are our favorite, but the grilled sea bass is also mouthwatering. It's tempting, but don't fill up on the delicious focaccia they serve with everything.

Dogs are often given bowls of water if they look thirsty. This is the restaurant Craig and our small wedding party, including the dogs, boated to after we got married on the bay. The dogs were more than welcome here, and Joe the landlubbing dog was more than happy to be on dry, solid land again. 9 Main Street; (415) 435-4747.

DIVERSIONS

Bless your dog: For Paws pet store holds a Blessing of the Animals ceremony on Memorial Day weekend. In past years, blessings have been bestowed by ordained Episcopalian priests; a woman once brought a bottle of water from the River Jordan. 90 Main Street. (415) 435-9522.

Disguise your dog: Many dogs actually seem to enjoy getting dressed up for the Doggy Costume Contest at For Paws pet store on the Sunday before Halloween. They prance around in little butterfly or ballerina costumes like everyone is staring at them. And of course, everyone is staring at them.

The competition is fierce for four costume awards; some 400 dogs attended last year, and owners work all year on their canine costumes. If your dog thinks dressing up is beneath her, there's a special Nude Beach area for water dogs and sophisticates—inflatable pools supplied with balls. In 1991, one of the judges was Grace Slick. So long as your dog likes crowds of other dogs looking silly, you shouldn't miss this. A $5 donation is suggested for the Marin Humane Society. 90 Main Street. (415) 435-9522.

Seize the Bay: Salty sea dogs love this: Poochies are welcome to ride on the Blue & Gold Fleet ferry between here and such dog-friendly destinations as Sausalito and San Francisco. Please turn to page 398 in the San Francisco chapter for more information on this briny adventure.

WOODACRE

PARKS, BEACHES, AND RECREATION AREAS

• **Gary Giacomini Open Space Preserve** 🐾🐾🐾🐾 🐕
  See **47** on page 338.

The most recent addition to Marin's open space lands is this 1,600-acre gem. The preserve stretches for seven miles along the southern edge of the San Geronimo Valley. Stands of old-growth redwoods shade the ferny lower regions of the park. The higher you go, the more grassy it gets. Dogs like Joe (i.e., male) prefer the trees, but they can get the best of both worlds by following one of the wide fire trails and sniffing out various areas along the way.

Pooches may go leashless on the fire roads, but not on the more narrow hiking trails. Come visit before the rest of the doggone world finds out about this hidden treasure.

From U.S. 101, take Sir Francis Drake Boulevard west to San Geronimo Valley Drive and turn left. You can park at the intersection of Redwood Canyon Drive, just west of Woodacre, and begin your hike at the nearby trailhead. This is a fun route to take with your dog, since it brings you from thick forest to the top of the ridge. (415) 499-6387.

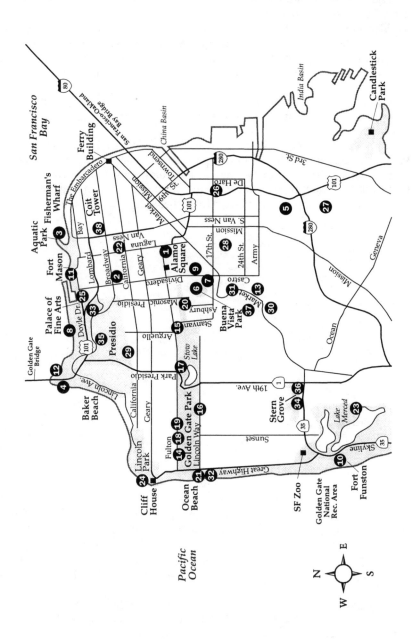

San Francisco Bay

Candlestick Park

India Basin

Ferry Building

Aquatic Park

Fisherman's Wharf

Coit Tower

Fort Mason

Palace of Fine Arts

Golden Gate Bridge

Presidio

Baker Beach

Alamo Square

Buena Vista Park

Stow Lake

Lincoln Park

Cliff House

Ocean Beach

Golden Gate Park

SF Zoo

Golden Gate National Rec. Area

Stern Grove

Fort Funston

Lake Merced

Pacific Ocean

N E S W

35
SAN FRANCISCO COUNTY

It's very likely that San Francisco is the most dog-friendly large city in the world. Sure, Parisians allow their poodles inside restaurants, but they don't have 18 parks and beaches where well-behaved dogs can run around in leash-free ecstasy. And no public transportation anywhere compares with San Francisco's, where pooches can ride cable cars, ferries, and buses. In addition, the finest hotels here permit pooches, as do some of the most popular tourist spots, including Fisherman's Wharf and Ghirardelli Square.

To top it all off, San Francisco is usually air-conditioned by the Big Dog in the Sky. So when temperatures are soaring around the rest of the area, it's often cool and foggy here.

But not everything is perfect in the City by the Bay. In fact, of late, many dog people have been howling mad over a few doggy digressions that have taken place here recently.

The Golden Gate National Recreation Area (GGNRA), which oversees a few pooch-friendly lands here, has closed off a two-mile strip of Ocean Beach to off-leash dogs (see Ocean Beach, page 380) and had made moves (and may once again) to reduce or eliminate Crissy Field's leash-free area (see page 371). A professional dog walker (who also happens to be an animal saint, according to many) is fighting the GGNRA in court over citations she got for walking dogs off leash in Presidio National Park (see page 382). A city supervisor is trying to dramatically increase dog patrols at parks to make sure dogs aren't off leash outside of designated areas. And at press time, dog people at Corona Heights Park/Red Rock Park (see page 370) were still fighting to maintain a leash-free area there.

Even with these problems, compared to most cities, San Francisco is still a blissful place to be a dog. And a few organizations have popped up in the last couple of years to make sure San Francisco keeps its Top Dog status. I'll mention organizations devoted to a specific park in the appropriate park's description.

An umbrella organization called the San Francisco Dog Owners Group (SFDOG) keeps track of all the dog park battles going on in the city (and occasionally in other parts of the Bay Area), and helps dog people network and support each other. The organization sponsors a fun monthly event called Critical Mutt, where dogs and their people get together and walk around to show their strength in numbers (à la bicyclists' Critical Mass). It's held on the last Saturday of every month at Crissy Field. SFDOG also puts out a newsletter that keeps people in touch with the issues. Membership is $10 (more if you feel like it, less if you can't afford it), and includes the newsletter. Write SFDOG, P.O. Box 31071, San Francisco, CA 94131, or call (415) 332-5800. Or you can check out SFDOG's Web page at www.sfdog.org.

SAN FRANCISCO

San Francisco is the only city in San Francisco County, but it's the only city this magical county needs.

PARKS, BEACHES, AND RECREATION AREAS

• **Alamo Square Park** 🐾 🐾 1/2 *See* ❶ *on page 366.*

A postcard comes to life in this park for you and your leashed dog. This is where the famed Painted Ladies hold court over the city. These six brightly colored Victorian homes are even better in person than they are on a postcard.

Walk up the east side of the park, near Steiner Street, to enjoy the view of the old houses with the modern city skyline in the background. Even if your dog doesn't care about architecture, she'll love the grassy hills that make up this park. There's plenty of room to roam and she'll find plenty of other dogs cavorting.

The park is bordered by Fulton, Hayes, Scott, and Steiner Streets. (415) 831-2700.

• **Alta Plaza Park** 🐾🐾🐾½ 🐕 *See* ❷ *on page 366.*

Smack in the middle of Pacific Heights, this park is where all the best breeds and most magnificent mutts gather daily. They flock to the hill on the north side of the park and conduct their dog business in the most discriminating fashion. It's not uncommon to see 25 dogs trotting around the park. Owners often address each other by their dogs' names—"Shane's mom! How *are* you?"

The park's off-leash run is actually on the other side of the playground and tennis courts, on the second level up from Clay Street. You can distinguish it by the two concrete trash cans that warn non-dog owners, "Dog Litter Only." Bushes line the paved walkway, and it's far enough from traffic that you don't have to worry about cars.

The park is bordered by Jackson, Clay, Steiner, and Scott Streets. (415) 831-2700.

• **Aquatic Park** 🐾🐾½ *See* ❸ *on page 366.*

You've got tourist friends in town and don't feel like taking them for the usual amble through Fisherman's Wharf? Here's a great plan that lets you be semi-sporting about the whole thing while you take your dog for a jaunt. Drop off your friends at Aquatic Park, point them toward the tourist attractions, and walk your dog right there.

Aquatic Park is just a few minutes from Ghirardelli Square, Fisherman's Wharf, a cable car line, and the Hyde Street Pier. It's also a decent place for a leashed dog to romp, with its large grassy field and plenty of pine trees, benches, and flowers. But stay away from the little beach—dogs aren't allowed. If you feel like shopping for T-shirts, jewelry, or arts and crafts, you can take your dog along Beach Street, where dozens of sidewalk vendors sell their wares (see page 399).

The park is on Beach Street between Hyde and Polk Streets. (415) 556-8371.

• **Baker Beach** 🐾🐾🐾🐾 🐕 *See* ❹ *on page 366.*

This beach brings your off-leash dog as close as she can get to the ocean side of the Golden Gate Bridge. And what a sight it is. Though in summer you shouldn't hold out much hope for a sunny day here, this sandy shoreline is ideal for a romp in the misty air. And dogs really appreciate Baker Beach in the summer. It's almost always cool and breezy.

If you like to sunbathe without a bathing suit and want to take your dog along, the very north end of the beach (closest to the bridge) is perfect. It's the only official nude beach in Northern California where dogs are welcome (as long as they're under voice control). But just make sure he doesn't get too up close and personal with your exposed co-bathers.

The south end is also intriguing, with trails meandering through wooded areas, and lots of picnic tables for leisurely lunches. Battery Chamberlain, with its 95,000-pound cannon aimed toward the sea, looms nearby.

From either direction, take Lincoln Boulevard to Bowley Street, then make the first turn into the two parking lots. The first one will put you closer to the off-leash area, which starts at the north end of the lot, closest to the Golden Gate Bridge. (415) 556-8371.

• Bernal Heights Park 🐾🐾🐾½ 🐕 *See* ❺ *on page 366.*

On a recent visit to this park, a dozen wolf-shepherds were the only dogs atop the amber hill. They ran and played in such pure wolf fashion that it was hard to believe they weren't the genuine item. The icy wind hit the power lines overhead and made a low, arctic whistle. The scene left an indelible impression that even in the middle of a city like San Francisco, the wild is just beneath the surface.

The rugged hills here are fairly rigorous for bipeds, but dogs have a magnificent time bolting up and down. Humans can enjoy the view of the Golden Gate and Bay Bridges. The vista makes up for the austere look of the treeless park. Dogs are allowed off leash on the hills bordered by Bernal Heights Boulevard. It can be very windy and cold, so bundle up.

Enter at Carver Street and Bernal Heights Boulevard, or keep going on Bernal Heights Boulevard until just past Anderson Street. (415) 831-2700.

• Buena Vista Park 🐾🐾🐾🐾 🐕 *See* ❻ *on page 366.*

The presence of vagrants who sometimes congregate at the front of the park has scared off lots of would-be park users, but it shouldn't. They're generally a friendly lot, posing no threat to folks exploring the park's upper limits with a dog.

This park is a real find for anyone living near the Haight-Ashbury district. Hike along the myriad dirt and paved trails winding through the hills, enveloped by eucalyptus and redwood trees. Some of the gutters are lined with pieces of tombstone from a nearby cemetery. The cemetery's occupants, who died in the 1800s, were moved to the oh-so-quiet town of Colma earlier this century. The gutters give the park a historical, haunted feeling.

From the top of the park, you can see the ocean, the bay, the Marin headlands, and both the Golden Gate and Bay Bridges. Birds sing everywhere, and there are lots of benches to rest on. Dogs are allowed off leash at the woodsy west side of the park, near Central Street.

A note: Sometimes people meet for assignations at the top of the park. If this bothers you or your dog, avoid this lovers' lane.

Enter at Buena Vista Avenue West and Central Street, or from Haight Street. (415) 831-2700.

• Corona Heights Park/Red Rock Park 🐾🐾🐾½ 🐕
See ❼ *on page 366.*

The rust-colored boulders atop this park cast long, surreal shadows at dawn. If you and your dog are early risers, it's worth the hike to the summit to witness this. And there's a fine view any time of day of downtown and the Castro district.

Unfortunately, dogs aren't allowed off leash on hikes up the hill. Until recently, the off-leash area was a roomy square of grass at the foot of the park. But now the off-leash space is in question. The city moved it (who knows why) to a smaller, less-attractive, foxtail-filled area at the side of the big hill here. At press time, the only thing in this area were fence posts that block neighbors' magnificent views. A group called Corona Heights Dog Owners Group (CHDOG) has stepped in to try to work with the city to get a better space. CHDOG is also taking up a few other issues with the city. To

---

check on the status of the leash-free area, call CHDOG president Neva Beach at (415) 863-4636. Or you can write to CHDOG at 183 Delmar Street, San Francisco, CA 94117.

Wherever the leash-free section ends up, your best bet is to park at Museum Way and Roosevelt Avenue. This is at least in the vicinity of any future leash-free area. After a bit of leashless playing (if we're lucky enough to have such an area by the time you read this), you can don a leash and take your pooch up the hill. Fences keep dogs and people from falling down the steep cliffs. Keep in mind that there's virtually no shade, so if you have a black rug of a dog, think twice about climbing the hill on hot, sunny days.

The park is at Museum Way and Roosevelt Avenue. (415) 831-2700.

• **Crissy Field** 🐾🐾🐾🐾 🐕 *See ❽ on page 366.*

There's nothing quite like Crissy Field at sunset: As the orange sun disappears behind the Golden Gate Bridge, you'll be viewing one of the most stunning blends of natural and man-made wonders in the world.

Crissy Field, part of the Golden Gate National Recreation Area, is a jewel of a park any time of day. Obedient, leash-free dogs can chase and cavort up and down the beach and jump into the bay whenever they feel like it. It's one of very few spots in the Bay Area where they are allowed to swim in the bay. This is a particularly good place to bring a dog who has no desire to brave the waves of the Pacific. The surf here doesn't pound—it merely laps.

As you walk westward, you'll see the Golden Gate Bridge before you, Alcatraz and bits of the city skyline behind you. Sailboats sometimes glide so close you can hear the sails flagging in the wind. There's a stretch of trees and picnic tables a few minutes into your walk, where you'll find water and a good place to relax while your dog investigates the scents. There's also a heavily used jogging and biking path parallel to the beach, but dogs should be leashed there. Dogs also need to be leashed a little bit before the old Coast Guard station. You'll see the signs. The area to the west has been designated as a protected area for birds.

Not long ago, park users had to battle the GGNRA to maintain the park's leash-free status. They won. But at press time, the GGNRA had announced a plan to dramatically alter the park to the tune of a $25 million restoration, which includes a 20-acre marsh. Dogs are still supposed to be able to run free here, but there's worry that any doggy–marsh animal conflict could put an end to that. Keep your paws crossed that this works out, and let's be careful out there.

Enter on Mason Street in the Marina district and drive past the warehouses. Go right on Mitchell Street and through a big, rough parking lot. If you go too far to the east, you'll run into a sea of windsurfers, so try starting your walk close to the western edge of the parking lot. The beach is bordered by delicate dunes that are undergoing restoration in many places, including the entrance, so keep canines off. (415) 556-8371.

• **Duboce Park** 🐾🐾 *See ❾ on page 366.*

If peering into people's windows is your dog's idea of fun, this urban park is his kind of place. A couple of large buildings have ground-floor windows that seem to fascinate dogs. Perhaps there's a cat colony inside.

Your dog will probably find other dogs to play with here. They're supposed to be leashed, since they're never more than a few fast steps from the nearest street. The park is grassy and has pines and a variety of smaller trees around some of its borders. There's also a children's playground at the west end.

The park is at Duboce Avenue between Steiner and Scott Streets. (415) 831-2700.

• **Fort Funston** 😊 😊 😊 ½ 🐕 *See ⑩ on page 366.*

If there were a heaven on Earth for dogs, this would be it. This scenic ocean park will make your jaw drop with awe the first (and second and third) time you see it. Trails wind through magnificent bluffs overlooking the mighty Pacific. Even on gloomy days, you're bound to find plenty of ecstatic dogs and their people cavorting around this elysian piece of nature and having a wonderful time.

Fort Funston provides the perfect mingling of environment and companionship. And dogs who are very obedient and promise not to chase horses or birds can experience it all sans leash. Unfortunately, because of people who don't clean up after their dogs and let them wreak havoc and tear up sensitive dune habitat, the Golden Gate National Recreation Area is occasionally forced to consider making Fort Funston a leashes-only park. That would be a mighty big doggy disaster, so be careful out there. (A wonderful organization, the Fort Funston Dog Walkers, works hard to keep Fort Funston dog heavenly. The group supplies pooper-scoopers and sponsors monthly cleanups and other events to help the park. If it weren't for this group, dogs would probably have to be leashed here. Membership is $10 annually, and includes an occasional newsletter. To find out more about the organization and how you can help, write or call Linda McKay, 241 Tocoloma Avenue, San Francisco, CA 94131; 415-468-1262.)

There are a few areas where you can start your walk, but the easiest access is from the main parking lot, next to the take-off cliff for hang gliders. Before you begin, walk your dog (still on leash, since it's a parking lot) to the watering hole—actually a bowl underneath a drinking fountain—and fill her up.

Now that you're all watered and ready for adventure, turn around and take the first trail to the north of the parking lot, the Sunset Trail. You'll meander through dunes and ice plant, encountering every kind of happy dog imaginable. You'll soon come to the main entrance to Battery Davis, which was built in 1939 to protect San Francisco from enemy ship bombardment. It was recently sealed shut because of some rotten sorts who hung out there, but you can still get the feel for the place.

Continue along on trails on either side of the battery. Both eventually end up in the same place. If you take the trail at the rear of the battery, you'll quickly be able to see the Golden Gate Bridge and the Cliff House. At that point, you'll also see a trail that takes you back into a mini-forest. Don't go all the way down, though, or you'll end up on the street.

You can get to the beach by following the narrow trails through the dunes shortly after the cypress groves. You'll notice that one trail takes you between two cliffs, where you won't be stepping on coastal dune plants. Take it all the way down to the beach. Depending on the tide, you can walk for miles or just a few feet.

You can go back the way you came, or walk along the ocean and take the steep trail back up to the main parking lot. (At press time, the stairs between the parking lot and the beach were closed because of weather damage, and there was no telling when they'd be fixed.) By this time, you and your dog will both be thirsting for that water fountain.

If you visit frequently, expand your explorations. Many trails wander throughout Fort Funston, and you and your dog will want to sniff out every inch of this place. (Be careful to avoid poison oak and areas marked as off-limits. A few spots have signs about staying out of dunes and away from bank swallow habitat. Please heed them. This is a delicate area.)

Because of the closure of a big chunk of Ocean Beach to off-leash dogs (see page 380), Fort Funston is getting very heavy use lately. On nice days, it can be impossible to find parking in the huge lot. "I just don't know if Fort Funston can support too many more people and dogs," said Fort Funston Dog Walkers organizer Linda McKay. And because of the larger number of dogs, skirmishes can ensue. Be sure that if you bring your dog here he gets along with other dogs. A man with a rottweiler recently had to carry his dog out because he was picking too many fights. (The dog, not the man.) McKay asks that people visit the park in the early morning if possible, so the park doesn't get overloaded in the afternoon.

To get to Fort Funston, follow the brown signs on the Great Highway. It's about one-half mile south of the turnoff to John Muir Drive. (If you get to the Daly City limits, you've gone too far south.) There's also some roadside parking near that intersection. Once on the main drive into the park, bear right (going left will take you to the interesting new Fort Funston Visitors Center, but dogs have no desire to visit, since they're not allowed). Continue past a little building with paintings of hang gliders, and drive into the main parking lot. (415) 556-8371.

• **Fort Mason** 🐾 🐾 🐾 *See* ⑪ *on page 366.*

This park, perched high above the bay, is full of surprises. Depending on the disposition of your dog, some of the surprises are great fun. One can be downright frightening.

The best stands right in the middle of the wide-open field that constitutes the main part of the park. It's a fire hydrant, and it sticks out like a sore yellow thumb from its flat green surroundings. Joyous male dogs bound up and pay it homage time and time again.

The object that seems to take dogs aback, although people find it riveting, is a gigantic bronze statue of Phillip Burton. Several feet taller and broader than life, with outstretched hand, it can send a dog fleeing as far as his mandatory leash will allow.

Lower Fort Mason is also interesting to investigate. You can walk alongside the piers and sniff the bay, or peer at the liberty ship *Jeremiah O'Brien*.

Enter the lower Fort Mason parking lot at Buchanan Street and take the stairs all the way up to upper Fort Mason. (Huff, puff.) Or park along Bay

Street or Laguna Street and walk in. (415) 556-0560.

• **Fort Point National Historical Site** 🐾🐾 *See* ⓬ *on page 366.*

Beneath the Golden Gate Bridge, this mid-nineteenth-century brick fortification stands as a reminder of the strategic military significance San Francisco once had. Now it serves as a tourist attraction and one of the best places to view the skyline, Alcatraz, and the bridge. It's also a magnificent spot for your dog to stand mesmerized by the crashing surf.

By itself, Fort Point doesn't offer much for dogs. They must be leashed and there's only a small patch of grass. We recommend Fort Point as the goal of a long hike that starts at Crissy Field (see page 371). After walking to the west side of Crissy Field, leash your dog when you get to the old Coast Guard station and follow the Golden Gate Promenade toward the bridge.

Along the way, you'll come to an old pier. There are actually two piers, but the one you're allowed on is closer to the bridge. Stroll to the end for a close-up view of sailboats being tossed about on the bay. When you finally reach Fort Point, it's a tradition among dog people to continue to the westernmost point and touch the fence. There's no telling why, but you may as well try it.

To get to Fort Point without a long hike, follow the signs from Lincoln Avenue as you approach the Golden Gate Bridge. (415) 556-8371.

• **Glen Canyon Park** 🐾🐾🐾 *See* ⓭ *on page 366.*

From the cypress forests to the streams and grassy hills, this park was made for you and your dog. The nature trail in the middle of the park follows a muddy creek and is so overgrown with brush and bramble that at times you nearly have to crawl. It's as though the trail were blazed for dogs. There are so many dragonflies of all colors and sizes near the creek, and so much lush vegetation, that you may wonder if you've stepped back to the age of the dinosaurs.

Park at Bosworth Street and O'Shaughnessy Boulevard and walk down a dirt trail past a recreation center, through the redwoods and loud birds. Stay away from the paved road—it can look deserted for hours on end, then a car suddenly whizzes by. Your dog is supposed to be leashed, but you should still be aware of the road. In a few minutes, you'll come to a long, low building. At this point, you can go left and up a hill for some secluded picnic spots or keep going and take the nature trail. When you finally emerge from the dragonflies and dense greenery, take any of several trails up the open, rolling hills and enjoy a panorama of the park.

At press time, a group called the Glen Park Dog Owners Group (GPDOG) was on the verge of getting the okay to have leash-free access in the canyon before 8 A.M. and after 5 P.M. If this happens, it will be a really terrific place to take a pooch.

The park is at Bosworth Street and O'Shaughnessy Boulevard. (415) 831-2700.

• **Golden Gate Park** 🐾🐾🐾

This famed city park provides much dog bliss, but only in the places where dogs are supposed to be leashed. Several areas are set aside for leashless dogs (see below), but dogs in the know like to avoid those places, for good reason. For information about any area in the park, call (415) 831-2700.

•**Golden Gate Park Dog Run** 🐾🐾🐾 🐕 See ⓮ *on page 366.*

This fenced-in dog exercise area has the dubious distinction of being right next to a field full of buffalo. Some dogs adore the location, especially when the wind is blowing in just the right direction. It's the only fenced-in dog run in the city, so it's really the only game in town for escape artists. But the park's fans aren't just dogs who walk on the wild side. All sizes and shapes of dogs come here for playtime. So many dogs use it that much of it is grassless and dusty.

If you're a new dog owner in the city, this is a good place to come and learn about the world of dogs. People here always talk with each other, and they're usually talking about dogs. There's a steady stream of dog advice on tap.

The place can sometimes get a little rough around the edges when the usual dog crowd isn't around. People who like their dogs tough will occasionally drop in and hang out with something to swig while their dogs strut around. It's not usually a problem, though, especially during the normal dog rush hours (before work and after work for 9-to-5ers, and all day on weekends).

We've found more amorous dogs here than in any other park, so if your dog isn't in the mood (or you don't want her to be), this isn't the place to take her. For some reason, Joe gets accosted by both boy and girl dogs at almost every visit, so it's not one of his favorite places. He's flattered, but he's not that kind of dog.

The Dog Run is at 38th Avenue and Fulton Street. Park on Fulton Street and walk in, or take 36th Avenue into the park and go right at the first paved road. Drive all the way to the end, and there it is.

•**Golden Gate Park (northeast corner)** 🐾 🐕 See ⓯ *on page 366.*

Then there are the narrow fields at the northeast corner of the park, up by the horseshoe courts. It's a strange little area with hills and dales and dirt paths. Homeless people live here, and some don't keep good house. You'll see the campfire remains, old sleeping bags, and trash of every type. It's best to avoid this place, except in the middle of the day.

Enter at Stanyan and Fulton Streets.

•**Golden Gate Park (south side)** 🐾🐾 🐕 See ⓰ *on page 366.*

The two other areas set aside for dogs are slivers along the south end of the park. One is between Fifth and Seventh Avenues and bounded on the north and south by Lincoln Way and Martin Luther King Jr. Drive. The other is on the south side of the polo field, between 34th and 38th Avenues and Middle and Martin Luther King Jr. Drives. Bring your dog to these sections if he's very good off leash. They're too close to busy traffic for less disciplined dogs.

•**Golden Gate Park (Stow Lake/Strawberry Hill)** 🐾🐾🐾
See ⓱ *on page 366.*

One of the "in" places in Golden Gate Park is the summit of the man-made mountain at Stow Lake. It's truly a sniffer's paradise. Dogs who like to look at ducks will also enjoy it. The path winds up Strawberry Hill to a breathtaking 360-degree view of the city. Unfortunately, dogs are not supposed to be off leash. It's best to avoid this walk on weekends, when bikers and hikers are everywhere.

Stow Lake is between 15th and 19th Avenues. From John F. Kennedy or Martin Luther King Jr. Drives, follow the Stow Lake signs.

•**Golden Gate Park (by the Polo Field)** 🐾🐾🐾 *See* ⑱ *on page 366.*
Dogs who prefer playing Frisbee (on leash) go to the meadow just east of the polo field. It's known for wide-open dells, good bushes, and plenty of gopher holes for old sports. Your best bet here is to go early in the morning.

•**Golden Gate Park (horse paths)** 🐾🐾🐾 *See* ⑲ *on page 366.*
Dogs who like to promenade—to see and be seen—take to the horse paths that radiate out from the stables. Or you can simply walk along the track that circles the field. One word of caution: The stables are rife with cats. Dogs need to know this. Leashes are mandatory, and remember, the mounted police station is uncomfortably close by.

•**Golden Gate Park (The Panhandle)** 🐾🐾🐾 *See* ⑳ *on page 366.*
That long, thin strip of park that extends eight blocks from the east end of the park to Baker Street is a great hangout for cool dogs. It's got a real Haight-Ashbury influence in parts, and although dogs must be leashed, they love to saunter around visiting other dogs wearing bandannas.

•**Golden Gate Park (Beach Chalet)** 🐾 *See* ㉑ *on page 366.*
Other lesser-known areas include the paths in back of the Beach Chalet—the soccer fields between the windmills near the ocean. The paths, which run along the edge of the fields, can be a little unsavory, but to leashed dogs, they're full of nothing but good smells. There's also the hilly, piney area up behind the archery field. We haven't heard of any accidental impalements up there, but be careful.

•**Lafayette Park** 🐾🐾🐕 *See* ㉒ *on page 366.*
This four-square-block park gets lots of dog traffic. For some reason, even though they have a legal grassy, off-leash section, dogs prefer to play on the paved paths in front of the playground. At least it's good for their nails.

The park is hilly and green and studded with palm trees, pines, and well-trimmed bushes. The official dog-run area is near Sacramento Street, between Octavia and Gough Streets. As you enter the park from the main Sacramento Street entrance, it's on your right. But most dogs gather atop the hill to the left, around two huge, smelly garbage cans.

The park is bounded by Laguna, Gough, Sacramento, and Washington Streets. (415) 831-2700.

•**Lake Merced** 🐾🐾½ *See* ㉓ *on page 366.*
As the city's largest body of water, Lake Merced is favored by Labrador retrievers, Irish setters, and the like. An ideal spot to explore is the footbridge area near the south end of the lake. There are a couple of sandy beaches there that are safe from traffic, but dogs are supposed to be leashed

---

anyway. Once you cross the bridge, you'll find an inviting area with lots of little trees.

You'll enter a small grassy section and come to a narrow dirt trail overlooking the lake's northeast bowl. We don't recommend letting dogs off the leash until you're at least a couple of hundred feet into the park, because menacing traffic is so close by. There are birds galore and purple wildflowers in spring. The park is a tease, though, because there's no way to get to the lake from here—it's down a very formidable slope covered with impenetrable brush.

The off-leash section of Lake Merced is at the north end, at Lake Merced Boulevard and Middlefield Drive. Park at Middlefield and Gellert Drives and cross Lake Merced Boulevard—very carefully. At times it's like a race car track. (415) 831-2700.

• **Land's End/Lincoln Park** 🐾🐾🐾½ *See* ㉔ *on page 366.*
This is probably the most spectacular park in San Francisco. You won't believe your eyes and your dog won't believe his nose. And neither of you will believe your ears—it's so far removed from traffic that all you hear are foghorns, the calls of birds, and the wind whistling through the pines and eucalyptus.

Unfortunately, leashes recently became the law at this Golden Gate National Recreation Area gem. Problems with mountain bikes and wildlife encounters led to the decision. But it's still a magnificent place to peruse with a pooch.

The towering cliffs, high above the crashing tide below, overlook virtually no civilization. For miles, all you can see is ocean, cliffs, trees, wildflowers, and boats. It looks more like Mendocino did 100 years ago—at least until you round one final bend and the Golden Gate Bridge jars your senses back to semi-urban reality.

If you want to venture the entire length of the dirt trail, keep two things in mind: Don't wear tight pants—you'll have to do some high stepping in some spots, and you don't want your legs packed into your Levi's—and don't bring a young puppy or an out-of-control dog. The cliffs here can be dangerous, especially where the trail becomes narrow.

There are many entrance points, but we like to start from the parking lot at the end of Camino del Mar. Go down the wooden steps to the wide dirt trail and turn right. As you hike, you'll come to occasional wood benches overlooking wildly beautiful seascapes. Take a moment to sit down. Your dog will appreciate the chance to contemplate the wondrous odors coming through her bulbous olfactory sensor.

As you continue, you'll pass a sign that makes its point efficiently and effectively: "Caution! Cliff and surf are extremely dangerous. People have been swept from the rocks and drowned." You'll have no problem if you proceed on the main trail and ignore the temptation to follow the dozens of tiny paths down the cliff face. (Naked men often hang out at a beach or two down there, so if your dog blushes easily, you'll have extra reason to stay on the wider paths.)

In a little while, you'll come to the second such sign. This time, instead of continuing on the main path (it gets extremely precarious, even for the most surefooted), take the trail to your right. It's a fairly hard slope, but it's safe and gets you where you want to go.

Rest at the bench halfway up, if you feel the need. The trail will soon bring you down and around to an incredible view. Keep going and turn around when you're ready to go home. Try not to end up on the golf course, though. Golfers don't appreciate canines at tee-off time.

A very convenient entry point is at the parking lot on Point Lobos (which is what Geary Street turns into toward the ocean) just above the Cliff House and Louie's. But we like to park in the lot at the end of Camino del Mar, a little street just above that lot. You'll pass a sign for Fort Miley on your right just after you enter Camino del Mar. Leashed dogs are allowed on this large patch of trees on a hill, and the views are stunning. It's a good place to visit to get away from the weekend crowds who can descend on Land's End. (415) 556-8371.

• **Marina Green** 🐾 🐾 ½ *See ㉕ on page 366.*

The clang of halyards against masts creates a magical symphony from the nearby marinas here on windy days. Your dog's first reaction may be a puzzled 30-degree head tilt.

Most of us know the Marina Green for its high-flying kites and hard-running joggers. But it's also a decent place to take your dog, as long as he's leashed. It's too close to the rush of cars on Marina Boulevard to be comfortable off leash, anyway.

The grass is always green here, as the park's name indicates. It's a treat for eyes overdosed on dry yellow grass and paws laden with foxtails. There's also an attractive heart parcourse and a great view of Alcatraz.

Enter on Marina Boulevard, anywhere between Scott and Buchanan Streets. (415) 556-0560.

• **McKinley Square** 🐾 🐾 🐕 *See ㉖ on page 366.*

The view from this little patch of land is, shall we say, interesting. You can see for miles and miles, and the view includes several other leash-free parks, such as Buena Vista, Corona Heights, Mission Dolores, and Bernal Heights Parks. But you can also see such lovely sights as Highway 101, with its cars rushing madcap-fashion just a couple of hundred feet down the hill from you. And if you ever craved a view of San Francisco General Hospital's most austere, Dickensian brick buildings, this is the place to come. If you had really long arms, you could almost reach out and touch them. Actually, depending on the direction of the wind, on some days *they* reach out and touch *you*—the steam from the hospital's huge chimneys has been known to slip right up to this hilltop park.

Dogs are permitted off leash in the back section of the park, between the playground and the community gardens. Signs will point you in the right direction. It's nothing beautiful, just a wide path with a little running room on a hillside dotted with brush and occasional trees.

The off-leash section is on 20th Street and San Bruno Avenue, just a few blocks from the heart of the Potrero Hill business district. (415) 831-2700.

• **McLaren Park** 🐾 🐾 🐾 🐕 *See ㉗ on page 366.*

You and your dog can enter this park anywhere and find a trail within seconds. The surprise is that most of the trails run through remote wooded areas and windswept hills with sweeping views.

It's an ideal place to visit if you're taking someone to play soccer or softball at the Crocker-Amazon Playground. They play, you walk up a hill behind the soccer fields and roam with your leashed dog. Better yet, drive to the northern part of the park, to the section bounded by John F. Shelley Drive. Dogs are allowed off leash here, where they're far enough from traffic. Certain parts can be crowded with schoolchildren or company picnickers or ne'er-do-wells, so watch where you wander.

There are many entry points, but we prefer Brazil Avenue, which turns into Mansell Street in the park. (415) 831-2700.

• **Mission Dolores Park** 🐾 🐾 🐕 *See* ㉘ *on page 366.*

You can get a little history lesson while walking your dog here. A statue of Miguel Hidalgo overlooks the park, and Mexico's liberty bell hangs at the Dolores Street entrance.

History may not impress your dog, but a wide-open space for running off leash will. It's behind the tennis courts.

There are two problems with this area, though. One: It's easy for your dog to run into the road. Even if she's the voice control type, she could find herself in Church Street traffic just by running a little too far to catch a ball. And two: You have to be on the lookout that your dog doesn't run over people who live in the park. Joe once slid into a sleeping homeless woman and scared her so badly she screamed and ran away.

Enter anywhere on Dolores or Church Streets, between 18th and 20th Streets. (415) 831-2700.

• **Mountain Lake Park** 🐾 🐾 🐾½ 🐕 *See* ㉙ *on page 366.*

In this sociable park, your dog can cavort with other dogs while you shoot the breeze with other dog people. The off-leash area is between two signs on the east side of the park. There's a bench for humans and a pretty good safety net of trees and grass between dogs and the outside world.

The favorite game among dogs here involves a big green bush. One dog usually starts running around it for no apparent reason. Circle after circle, he'll attract more and more dogs into chasing him until almost every dog is swirling around in a dizzying loop. Watch too closely and you can get seasick.

Dogs find the rest of the park mildly entertaining, although they have to be leashed. The lake that's the park's namesake is little more than a pond. Ducks and a couple of swans live here, and the temptation may be too much for your dog. We've seen dogs drag their owners ankle-deep into the muddy pond in pursuit of a duck dinner. The park is also home to an attractive playground and a decent heart parcourse.

To reach the dog-run area, enter on Eighth Avenue at Lake Street. (415) 831-2700.

• **Mount Davidson** 🐾 🐾 🐾 *See* ㉚ *on page 366.*

Hiking to the peak of this park can be a religious experience—literally. As you emerge from the tall pine and eucalyptus trees leading to the 927-

foot summit, a concrete structure looms in the distance. As you get closer you'll see that it's a gigantic cross, 103 feet tall. It's so huge, and in such a prominent spot—at the end of a long, wide path surrounded by trees—that it can be a startling sight. On his first encounter, Joe backed out of his collar and collided with a tree. Since leashes are the law here, we had to quickly put him back together.

In 1934, President Roosevelt became the first person to flick the switch and light the cross. It's visible for miles, especially vivid under its night-time floodlighting. On a night hike up Mount Davidson, you can follow the glow to the top. There was recently lots of controversy about keeping the cross (a religious symbol) in the park (a city-run property). That church and state mixing thing just wasn't making some folks happy. Thank God (so to speak), an Armenian group bought the property surrounding the cross. The cross, an intriguing landmark for generations—much more than a religious icon—will remain.

Since you enter the park at such a high altitude, it's only about a 10-minute pilgrimage to the peak. But you can make it a much longer walk by experimenting with different trails.

Enter at Dalewood Way and Lansdale Avenue. (415) 831-2700.

•**Noe Courts** 🐾 🐾 *See* ❸❶ *on page 366.*
This partially fenced park is very small and green, but it's at the center of a very large and red-hot battle. For years, dog people have let their pooches run around here off leash even though it isn't officially a leash-free park. Then some parents stepped in and started calling police because they said their tots were being mowed over by dogs running into the playground. Unfortunately what ensued was a kids-versus-dogs fight, with some dog people seeing parents as "evil dog haters" and some parents seeing dog people as inconsiderate menaces. Of course, there are many parents who are also dog people, and many in both camps who empathize with each other's plight.

A group of park users has formed the Noe Courts Coalition, with the goal of mixing kids and dogs safely in the same park. Among their proposals is to allow leash-free pooches before 9 A.M. and after 5 P.M. To check on the status of the park or find out how you can help make it a more dog-friendly spot, call (415) 675-0110. Or you can write for more info (or send donations) to the Noe Courts Coalition, P.O. Box 460520, Noe Valley Station, San Francisco, CA 94146-0520.

The park is on Douglass Street, between 24th and Elizabeth Streets. (415) 831-2700.

•**Ocean Beach** 🐾 🐾 🐾 🐾 🐕 *See* ❸❷ *on page 366.*
This broad, four-mile-long beach with a crashing surf isn't exactly Palm Beach. It's usually cold and windy and full of seaweed, jellyfish, jagged bits of shells, and less savory deposits from the Pacific. In other words, dogs think it's grand.

They used to think it was even better, since until recently, it was all a leash-free poochy paradise. But in 1997 the Golden Gate National Recreation Area (GGNRA) closed off a two-mile strip of beach to off-leash dogs.

GGNRA heads said they had to do this because a threatened bird, the western snowy plover, hangs out in the dunes and beach here. They said they'd determined dogs were hurting the plover population by walking in areas where they live and by chasing them. Dogs shouldn't chase any birds, and in my opinion the rangers should have come out and ticketed people whose dogs were bird chasers. But the GGNRA folks enacted this sweeping policy without giving dog people a chance to show responsibility. A group of bird-loving dog people, called Rovers for Plovers, wasn't able to make them budge. Rovers for Plovers believes that if the bird is really in decline (and they have great doubts about the method used to count the birds), there are many reasons, including bulldozing the dunes for sand control, and homeless people living in the dunes. To get in touch with Rovers for Plovers, call Jocelyn Kane at (415) 731-1885.

The sections where your dog can still be off leash are from stairwell 21 (a little north of Lincoln Way) north to the beach's northern end just below the Cliff House, and from Sloat Boulevard south (where it eventually becomes part of Fort Funston's beach area). Unfortunately, the northern end is the most crowded. Dogs like Joe may be tempted to eat picnics or do leg lifts on backpacks resting on the ground. And the southern end is narrow and not as accessible as other parts. The area between stairwell 21 and Sloat, which is where dogs would do best off leash, is now a leash zone. Be careful to use your leash here, because the rangers are out in force. I've seen them give many a ticket ($50 per dog), and I've seen the dog people give the rangers many a hard time. "I've been in law enforcement 25 years, and have dealt with all kinds of people, but the dog people are the toughest to deal with," said one GGNRA ranger/park policeman, who genuinely feels sympathetic for dog folks.

You can park along the ocean, between the Cliff House and Balboa Street. Walk south on the sidewalk until you hit the beach. Or park in the spaces between Fulton Street and Lincoln Way. There's also a parking lot at Sloat Boulevard and one a little south of Sloat. At press time, though, both of these were closed because of damage from erosion (they're up on the dunes, essentially, and the dunes done come down with all the rain). GGNRA folks weren't sure when this big problem would be fixed, so you might need to park elsewhere. (415) 556-8371.

• **Palace of Fine Arts** 🐾🐾🐾 *See* ㉝ *on page 366.*

The glory of ancient Rome embraces you even as you approach this relic of the 1915 Panama-Pacific Exposition. From the huge colonnaded rotunda to the serene reflecting pool, the place drips with Romanesque splendor.

The Palace is especially grand under its night lighting. It's also an ideal place to take your dog while the kids go to the Exploratorium, located inside. Walk around the paved path that winds through the grand columns and around the pond. But keep your eyes peeled for people feeding the multitudes of pigeons, ducks, and geese. Dogs like Joe love to break up the feeding frenzy with an abrupt tug on the mandatory leash. Feathers fly and dried bread scatters everywhere.

The best place to enter for the full Roman effect is on Baker Street, between North Point and Jefferson Streets. Dogs are not allowed inside the buildings, although Joe did sneak into the Exploratorium one fine afternoon. (It's a long story.) He got as far as the tornado demonstration machine when he was nabbed and whisked away. (415) 831-2700.

• **Pine Lake Park** 🐾🐾🐾 *See ❹ on page 366.*

Adjacent to its more famous cousin, Stern Grove (see page 383), Pine Lake Park can be even more fun for dogs because it has Laguna Puerca, a small lake at the west end of the park. Swimming isn't allowed, but there's always the muddy shore for wallowing.

The lake is in a valley at the bottom of steep slopes, so there's not much need to worry about traffic. Leashes are supposed to be on at all times, in any case. At the lake's east end, there's a big field where dogs can really cut loose—as far as leashes allow.

Enter at Crestlake Drive and Wawona Street and follow the paved path, which quickly turns into a dirt trail. (415) 831-2700.

• **Presidio National Park** 🐾🐾🐾🐾 🐕 *See ❺ on page 366.*

Dogs and their people like to pretend that the Presidio is their very own country estate, complete with acre after rolling acre (1,480 in all!) of secret pathways, open meadows, and dense groves of eucalyptus and pine. It's truly a magnificent spread.

The conversion of the land from the Army to National Park land hasn't changed the dog rules here. Pooches can breathe a sigh of relief, because they're still permitted (many were in doubt for a while). Not only are they permitted, but they're allowed off leash in a nice chunk of the park. A wide strip of land on the north side of West Pacific Avenue, from just west of Presidio Avenue all the way to Arguello Boulevard (but excluding the children's playground and ball fields), is the leash-free area. And it's an enchanting spot, made of big pines, little wildflowers, and long stretches of flat fields that blossom into rolling, densely shaded hills.

A controversy surrounding a professional dog walker who was issued tickets for walking dogs off leash in another part of the park was still brewing in court at press time. It's pitted dog people against the national park people. Again. This time it's especially contentious, since the dog walker, Michelle Parris, runs a dog rescue service with the money she makes walking dogs. They couldn't have picked on a worse person.

Now that the Presidio is a park, it's expected to draw more visitors than either Yosemite or Yellowstone National Parks. But there are still some out-of-the-way areas, such as the leash-free land, that even the most adventurous tourists will have a difficult time finding. A fun leashed tour starts when you park just north of the Arguello Boulevard entrance, at a roadside parking area on the west side of Arguello. Follow the path in and go down the hill as it gets wider. It will loop past wildflowers and seasonal sweet peas. Bear left at the first major fork and hike through a thick forest area, then bear right when that path gives you a choice. You'll hike up and down a gentle sequence of hills. Pull over and enjoy the larger hills to the west. Dogs thrill at speeding up and down them for no apparent reason. You'll run into a few more side trails along the way. Explore them as you wish, watching out for traffic on nearby roads.

In these hills, in the spring, you'll come across patches of bright yellow jonquils, many of them in formations resembling letters of the alphabet. An elderly British fellow who kept a good rapport with other dog owners used to plant them as a memorial to dogs who had gone to the Big Dog Run in the Sky. There's a "G" for a dog named George at the foot of the first large hill. The sweet old man, now deceased himself, liked to plant the flower bulbs in the spots favored by the deceased dogs. His spirit lives on with the dogs he memorialized in this piece of dog heaven on Earth. (415) 556-8371.

• **Stern Grove** 🐾🐾 🐕 *See ㊱ on page 366.*

Until the 1991 concert season, dogs were welcome at all Stern Grove music festivals. Unfortunately, complaints about hygiene and noise changed this policy. Though dogs aren't allowed at the concert meadow, as of this printing, they are still tolerated around the peripheral hills, on leash. Bring a picnic, a bottle of wine, a rawhide bone, and, of course, a pooper-scooper.

Stern Grove is a treasure of trees, hills, meadows, and birds. There's even a spot where dogs are allowed off leash. Unfortunately, it's one of the least attractive areas in the park—very close to the street—although trees act as an effective barrier. And if you perch on the inner edge, the dog-run area isn't a bad place to listen to a concert. The violins get a little tinny at that distance, but your dog won't care.

For the dog-run area, enter on Wawona Street between 21st and 23rd Avenues. (415) 831-2700.

• **Twin Peaks** 🐾🐾 *See ㊲ on page 366.*

So dogs aren't allowed at the Top of the Mark. So what. The view from up here will put all those "No Dogs Allowed" establishments to shame, and it's cheaper to entertain guests up here—it's free, in fact.

The summits of the twin peaks are higher than 900 feet. It's usually cold up here, so bundle up. You can drive to the northern peak and park in the lot. It's very touristy, and on this peak, signs tell you what you're looking at—Tiburon, Nob Hill, Mount Diablo, Japantown, and Mount Tamalpais. Your dog won't get much exercise, though, since all he can do is walk around the paved viewing area on leash. And frankly, Joe is bored by the marvelous vistas.

For your dog's sake, try exploring the other peak. It's a bare hill with wooden stairs up one side. While dogs must be on leash, it's not bad exercise. And the view—at almost 20 feet higher than the first peak—is magnificent. From here you can see other potential walks for you and your dog on the lower hills, where the views are almost as dynamic and the air is a little warmer. Be sure to keep him on leash, because the road is never far away.

The twin peaks are on Twin Peaks Boulevard, just north of Portola Drive. (415) 831-2700.

• **Washington Square** 🐾🐾 *See ㊳ on page 366.*

Grab a gelato, leash your dog, and relax in this park in the middle of North Beach. There are plenty of benches and enough trees to make your dog comfortable with his surroundings. The park is only about one block square, but it's great for a stroll when you're hitting the cafes of San

Francisco's Little Italy. And if you have a child with you, so much the better. There's a small playground that's popular with local parents.

Washington Square is right across from the ornate Saints Peter and Paul Catholic Church, and the Transamerica pyramid looks close enough to reach out and touch.

Enter the park at any of its four borders: Columbus, Union, Stockton, or Filbert Streets. Try not to drive to North Beach. Even during the day, parking's a bear. (415) 831-2700.

RESTAURANTS

Angelina's Caffe: Conveniently located one-half block from Cal's Discount Pet Supply, Angelina's is a good place for you and your dog to take a break from shopping. It's got everything from soup to pine nuts, plus a large variety of coffees. Enjoy them at one of six sidewalk tables. You can also stock on up on Italian souvenirs here, but watch out for the red, white, and green hats. 6000 California Street; (415) 221-7801.

Bepples Pie Shop: Joe thinks the cherry pie here is tops. He's right. Eat a piece at the little bench outside each of San Francisco's dog-friendly Bepples locations: 2142 Chestnut Street, (415) 931-6226, and 1934 Union Street, (415) 931-6225.

Blue Danube Coffee House: Have your cake and eat soup and sandwiches, too, at five tables outside this charming cafe. You can even indulge in a wide selection of beer or wine, but you'll have to drink alone if your dog is under 21. On sunny days, it may be hard to find an empty spot. 306 Clement Street; (415) 221-9041.

Brain Wash Cafe: The folks at this South of Market cafe-Laundromat are so doggone dog-friendly that they'll even let you . . . well, we'll let you find out. Dine at the outdoor tables with your pooch, and before you know it, you'll be ready to fold your clothes, gulp the last of your espresso, and head home. This is a really fun time for dogs who don't mind the whoosh of traffic from busy Folsom Street. 1122 Folsom Street; (415) 861-3663.

Cafe Francisco: Take your dog to one of the two outside tables at this North Beach-Fisherman's Wharf cafe, and dine on fresh Mediterranean food and good brunch cuisine. 2161 Powell Street; (415) 397-2602.

Caffe Centro: The bistro dinners are so good you'll wish you could afford to come here with your dog every night to dine at the eight outdoor tables. Try the seared tuna Nicoise or the saffron fettuccine with grilled prawns. You can also get gourmet breakfasts and lunches at this South of Market cafe. 102 South Park; (415) 882-1500

Caffe Freddy's: This is a real find in North Beach, especially if you want a touch of California influence to your Italian food. Pizzettas are the specialty here. A favorite has goat cheese and smoked salmon, but there are eight other kinds. And if you want to feel what it's like to drink from a bowl, order Freddy's special coffee-in-a-bowl. It's lip-licking good. 901 Columbus Avenue; (415) 922-0151.

The Cannery: This old Del Monte packing plant is home to three delightful restaurants with courtyard tables for you and your dog, and there's often entertainment here. The restaurants usually don't have courtyard service after dark because it's too cold, so call first to find out. The Cannery is at 2801 Leavenworth Street. Here are two of its dog-friendly restaurants:

• *Cafe Rigatoni:* Eat delicious Italian food outside with your dog. It's *benissimo.* (415) 771-5225.

• *Las Margaritas Restaurant:* Seven kinds of margaritas, mesquite-grilled shark, and a great view of the courtyard below make this one of the more popular Mexican restaurants this side of the Mission district. (415) 776-6996.

Crêpevine: Mmmm. MMMMMmmm. MMMMMM. That's the way Joe groans with desire when he comes here and looks at all the happy folks sitting at the outdoor tables dining on their steaming hot crepes. You can choose from a variety of delicious crepes or create your own concoction. Joe highly recommends the spinach-cheese-mushroom deal. Crêpevine has a cozy, bohemian feel, even outside. 624 Irving Street; (415) 681-5858.

Curbside Cafe: The servers here are very dog-friendly, and the continental cuisine is top-notch. Try not to let your dog block the sidewalk, since it's a tight squeeze here. 2417 California Street; (415) 929-9030.

Foggy's: If your dog is a poodle or Border collie or some other brilliant breed, she can sit at the wooden tables outside this Fisherman's Wharf coffeehouse and play chess with you. Dine on gourmet salads and sandwiches between your opening move and when your dog wins paws down. 540 North Point Street; (415) 474-2070.

42 Degrees: This sumptuous, unique restaurant has one of the most picturesque courtyard patios we've ever laid eyes on. Joe was overjoyed when we checked it out, because not only was it attractive, it was also popular with the pooches. "We get a lot of dog lovers here," a manager told us. I can see why. Dogs get water if they're thirsty, and if the restaurant has dog biscuits (and it usually does), they get those, too. Humans drool over 42 Degrees because of the amazing food. There are so many styles and choices of cuisine that the place can't be categorized. You can have French food, Italian food, Spanish food, Mideast food, and lots more. Everything here is top-notch. The outdoor seating is available only for lunch. 235 16th Street; (415) 777-5558.

Ghirardelli Square: What was once a chocolate factory is now one of the classiest tourist shopping centers in the country. More important than that, it's got a lot to offer residents and their dogs. Ghirardelli Square is at 900 North Point Street. Here are some restaurants with outdoor cafes:

• *Boudin Sourdough Bakery & Cafe:* Dine on pastries, croissants, cheesecake, or huge sandwiches as you gaze across Beach Street at the bay. (415) 928-7404.

• *Ghirardelli Fountain & Candy:* Here's where you can get some of that famous rich Ghirardelli ice cream with all the fixings. Just remember: The more your dog gets, the fewer sit-ups you have to do. Stay away from chocolate, though. It can be very bad for dogs. (415) 474-3938.

• *Ghirardelli's Too!:* This more healthful alternative to the previous entry offers nonfat yogurt desserts. (415) 474-1414.

Harry Denton's Bar & Grill: Your dog is a lucky dog to be able to hang out with you at this landmark San Francisco restaurant. The food has no pretenses. It's just extremely tasty and hearty with a San Francisco flair (no snide remarks, please). Your dog will be your best friend forever if you order Harry's famous pot roast. Dine with your pooch at the four tables in front. 161 Steuart Street; (415) 882-1333.

Horse Shoe Coffeehouse: Enjoy good coffee and pastries at a down-to-earth cafe with two sidewalk tables. 566 Haight Street; (415) 626-8852.

Hungry Joe's: Joe Dog loves this yummy greasy spoon–style restaurant every bit as much as the people who eat here seem to love him. "Oh, that's Joe? Is he hungry?" they'll say upon meeting him, and they'll then laugh at their humor and give him an onion ring, french fry, or lick of milk shake. The food is good, filling, and fits most budgets. Dine with your happy dog at Hungry Joe's two or three outdoor tables. 1748 Church Street; (415) 282-7333.

Il Fornaio: Your dog can't exactly sit right beside you at this splendid Cal-Ital restaurant, but she can sit quite close if you call ahead of time and tell them you'd like to bring your dog. If space permits, they'll reserve you a seat at the edge of the very popular patio, so you can be as near as possible to your pooch, who has to be tied to a tree or pole a few short arm's lengths away. If you bring your dog a couple of pieces of your delicious pasta or a bite of your chicken fresh from the wood-burning rotisserie, she probably won't mind the slight distance. The restaurant serves a good breakfast, too, and has tasty take-out pastries to boot, should you want to take your party elsewhere. 1265 Battery Street; (415) 986-0100. (Reminder: Call first!)

Java Beach: After a morning of combing Ocean Beach, you can catch some rays and eat some lunch on one of the benches outside this mellow soup, sandwich, and salad shop. 1396 La Playa at the Great Highway; (415) 665-5282.

Jayman's: If you're in the Castro with your dog and you're in the mood for a tall cool one, step up to the two sidewalk tables here and get yourselves a couple of frozen yogurts. 3600 16th Street; (415) 626-5410.

La Canasta: This Mexican take-out restaurant is where we get our favorite burritos. When Joe is with us, we like to sit on the bench outside while we wait—and often while we eat. 2219 Filbert Street; (415) 921-3003.

La Mediterranée: Dog owners are lucky—there are two of these top Mideast/Greek restaurants in the city; each puts tables outside in decent weather and has a dog-loving staff. Joe highly recommends the Mideast vegetarian plate, even for meat eaters. The restaurant at 2210 Fillmore Street, (415) 921-2956, has only a couple of tiny outdoor tables. (The area inside is fairly tiny, too.) The location at 288 Noe Street, (415) 431-7210, has several roomy sidewalk tables, some of which are covered by an awning.

Martha & Bros. Coffee Company: Strong coffee on a hard bench may not be an ideal way to start the day, but it will wake you up enough to take your dog for a long walk. 3868 24th Street; (415) 641-4433.

Mocca on Maiden Lane: Now your dog can dine in one of the most posh streets of the Union Square area. Just a bone's throw from the finest stores in San Francisco, Mocca is a European-style cafe famed for its many types of salads. Dine at the zillions of umbrella-topped tables right on the street, which is closed to traffic. 174 Maiden Lane; (415) 956-1188.

The Orbit Room: Situated between Hayes Valley and the Castro, this trendy spot serves sandwiches, bagels, salads, coffee drinks, and beer. There are two outdoor tables where dogs are welcome and glassed-in windows so you and your hip pooch can see the hipsters as they mix and mingle. And if you're in the mood to do your laundry between sips of Italian soda, you can take care of business at the Little Hollywood Laundrette next door. 1900 Market Street; (415) 252-9525.

Pier 39: If your dog doesn't mind flocks of tourists, there's a wide selection of decent eateries with outdoor tables for the two of you here. Your dog gets to smell the bay and sniff at the sea lions below. Pier 39 is off the Embarcadero, near Jefferson Street. These are some of the restaurants where you and your dog are allowed:

• *Burger Cafe:* Every burger imaginable is waiting for your dog to drool over. The mushroom cheeseburger is a big hit. (415) 986-5966.

• *Chowder's:* Fried seafood and several types of chowder make Pier 39 really feel like a pier. (415) 391-4737.

• *Eagle Cafe:* Eggs, potatoes, burgers, cheese—good heavy food for a cold day is yours for the asking. Management asks that you tie your dog to a pole near the tables, rather than have him underfoot. (415) 433-3689.

• *Le Carousel Patisserie:* The next best thing to being on the carousel at the end of the pier (sorry, no pooches on the painted ponies) is this restaurant with a carousel theme and painted ponies everywhere. It also has a large deli with a selection of cakes and pastries, and plenty of outdoor tables. (415) 433-4160.

• *Sal's Pizzeria:* You and your dog can get a real taste of San Francisco by biting into any of Sal's special pizzas. The 49er Special has sausage, pepperoni, onions, and mushrooms. The Earthquake, with sausage, salami, mushrooms, and tomatoes, was a hit with Joe. (415) 398-1198.

Polly Ann Ice Cream: Here, dogs are treated like people, in the best sense. Every dog gets a free mini-doggy cone. It's vanilla, it's creamy, and dogs think it's to die for. Even if you have several dogs, the owners welcome them all and dole out the goods with a smile. They're especially happy if you buy some ice cream for yourself, of course. The doggy cone tradition has been alive for more than 30 years. (Joe and Nisha's first date together was videotaped here as part of KRON-TV's delightful *Outdoor Journal* show. Little did they know . . .) 3142 Noriega Street; (415) 664-2472.

Pompei's Grotto: If your dog likes the smell of seafood, he probably won't mind joining you at an outdoor table at this famous restaurant on the main drag at Fisherman's Wharf. The fish is fresh and the pasta delicious. And if your dog is thirsty, one of the friendly servers will probably offer her a cup of water. 340 Jefferson Street; (415) 776-9265.

Real Food Deli: You'd think a place like this would have only the healthiest, most vegetarian cuisine. It does have gourmet natural food, like grilled tofu brochettes, but it also has decadent dishes, like prosciutto sandwiches. Desserts soar to the same extremes. Three outdoor tables make eating with your dog a pleasure. 2164 Polk Street; (415) 775-2805.

Rustico: This eatery in Potrero Hill features pizza, pasta, panini, soup, and salads. There are lots of outside tables. 300 DeHaro Street; (415) 252-0180.

Sally's Deli and Bakery: Right next door to Rustico (above), this spot serves brunch on the weekends in addition to breakfast and all kinds of salads and sandwiches during the week. 300 DeHaro Street; (415) 626-6006.

Simple Pleasures Cafe: This is a quaint cafe with a warm and cozy atmosphere, and food to match. You and your dog can sit at the outdoor tables and catch live folk and jazz music Wednesday through Saturday nights. It may be cold, so bring lots of money for hot chocolates. 3434 Balboa Street; (415) 387-4022.

South Park Cafe: Vive la France! You and your dog may think you're in the Left Bank of Paris when you come to the South Park Cafe. The three sidewalk tables look out at beautiful, small, sycamore-studded South Park, which is a great place to visit for a quick leg stretch after a meal here. And the food is *tres magnifique*, with such yummies as roasted duck breast with honey-lime sauce, crispy croque monsieur, and tarte au beurre noisette. Even if you can't pronounce half of the foods, you'll drool over them. Joe Dog liked the idea of ordering spicy blood sausage with mashed potatoes and carmelized apples, but I can't stomach the thought of sausages, much less bloody ones. 108 South Park Avenue; (415) 495-7275.

Suisse Italia: You and your hungry pooch can eat here and feel like you've gone far away from the Financial District without ever officially leaving at all. The half-dozen outdoor tables are under a canopy and look out on tree-filled Walton Square. The cuisine is a little European, a little Californian, and a lot good. 530 Davis Street; (415) 434-3800.

Tart to Tart: If you want to satisfy a sweet tooth (with your dog as accomplice), the outdoor tables are perfect for your desires. 641 Irving Street; (415) 753-0643.

Tassajara Bread Bakery: The goods here are as wholesome and natural as the bread Tassajara made famous. Although this Upper Haight cafe is usually crowded, there are plenty of outdoor tables. 1000 Cole Street; (415) 664-8947.

Toy Boat Dessert Cafe: You may not be able to say it 10 times fast, but you and your dog won't feel a need to speak when you're at the outside bench eating rich and creamy desserts. 401 Clement Street; (415) 751-7505.

Trio Cafe: Sandwiches, soups, and salads—the basics here are some of the best. Eat them at the shaded outdoor tables. 1870 Fillmore Street; (415) 563-2248.

PLACES TO STAY

Best Western Civic Center Motor Inn: This isn't in a great part of town, but you and your dog should feel safe outside—at least by day. Rates are $65 to $95. Dogs are $25 extra (per night, and in this neighborhood!). 364 Ninth Street, San Francisco, CA 94103; (415) 621-2826.

Campton Place: The European ambience and superb service make this a luxury hotel your dog will never forget. Your room comes with your choice of newspaper, a nightly turn-down service, a terry cloth robe, a hair dryer, and an in-room safe, to name a few of the unique extras. Pooches who weigh more than a large Thanksgiving turkey will pant with joy when they learn Campton Place has relaxed its size limitation for well-behaved pooches. It used to be that dogs over 25 pounds weren't permitted at this luxury hotel. But now, as long as your pooch "isn't really big," size won't be an issue, according to a dog-loving front-desk agent. And think of the fun your springer will have strolling through stately Union Square, only half a block away. Rates are $230 to $1,000. 340 Stockton Street, San Francisco, CA 94108; (415) 781-5555.

Clift Hotel: This first-rate, top-notch, crème-de-la-crème hotel is also one of the most dog-friendly hotels anywhere. When you call to make your reservation, ask for your pet to be put on the Very Important Pet list. Every VIP gets a basket of pet treats sent to his room on arrival. They don't even blink at dogs here. "We've had pigs, Bengal tigers, you name it, we've seen it," a concierge told us. Your dog can even get his own doggy bathrobe here. Dog walking is also available. And if you have a human child, the Clift has all kinds of goodies for them, as part of its Young Travelers Program.

The hotel itself is to die for. It was built in 1915, and, as its elegant brochure states, "embraces the grand traditions of the past while initiating unparalleled levels of service and comfort." Some members of the staff have been with the hotel for nearly a half century, if that tells you anything. The attention to detail is everywhere, from the way your bed is turned down at night to the way the picture-perfect Art Deco lounge is arranged. Rates are $255 to $655. Dogs are $40 extra per night. 495 Geary Street, San Francisco, CA 94102; (415) 775-4700.

Grosvenor House: Don't let the name fool you. This is a 200-room hotel, not a house. But the large, attractive rooms and suites are kind of like home, with most featuring cute little kitchens. The Grosvenor is on Nob Hill, an address that can impress. If you're thinking about staying here with your dog, though, you should know that you'll be charged a $175 pooch fee. That's a fee, not a deposit. Ouch! But if your stay is long enough, that doesn't sting quite as much. (By the way, to spare your dog the same embarrassment Joe Dog experienced when we visited here, you should know that the Grosvenor does not sound like it's spelled. The "s" is silent.) Rates are $99 to $189. 899 Pine Street, San Francisco, CA 94108; (415) 421-1899 or (800) 999-9189.

Hotel Nikko: Small dogs are welcome to spend the night with you at this lovely contemporary Japanese-style hotel three blocks west of Union Square. Rates are $175 to $2,500. 222 Mason Street, San Francisco, CA 94102; (415) 394-1111.

The Inn of San Francisco: This grand Victorian bed-and-breakfast was built in 1872, making it one of the oldest Victorians in the city. The style of Victorian is Italianate, for those of you who know your architecture. It's been fully and lovingly restored to its original grandeur, and as long as your dog promises not to poop in the beautiful English garden and to be a quiet guest, he's welcome here. Lucky dog! Classical music wafts through the inn's main area, mingling with the scent of roses. The woodwork is ornate, the carpets are oriental, and the fireplaces are marble. The 27 guest rooms are furnished with antiques and have marble sinks with polished brass fixtures. Most have private baths. The more deluxe rooms have featherbeds, and either a hot tub, spa, or fireplace. The flowery garden sports a gazebo, which is home to the inn's hot tub. A light but tasty breakfast buffet is served in the grand double parlors.

Rates are $85 to $235. The inn is located in the Mission District, where the sun shines more than anywhere else in San Francisco. The neighborhood here is not exactly Luxuryville, but you could do worse. 934 South Van Ness Avenue, San Francisco, CA 94110; (415) 641-0188 or (800) 359-0913.

Laurel Motor Inn: The owners love dogs, so many visiting dogs choose to stay here. It's conveniently located in a lovely neighborhood just far enough from downtown to be able to get great views of it from some of the rooms. It's also just a bone's throw from the magnificent Presidio National Park (see page 382). Rates are $80 to $104. 444 Presidio Avenue, San Francisco, CA 94115; (415) 567-8467.

Mansions Hotel: Step back in time in this elegant, mysterious old mansion, circa 1890. It's full of art treasures and beautifully attired mannequins. People tell tales of a resident ghost. The hotel has been described as "San Francisco's most San Francisco Hotel." The *San Francisco Examiner* said the Mansions is "elegance carried to the Nth degree." The *Wall Street Journal* says that "Upstairs, Downstairs is still a way of life at the Mansions Hotel." (The service is wonderful, something out of the past.) The hotel has five mini-museums, including the International Pig Museum and the Magic Museum. Dogs are allowed in only a few of the 21 opulent guest rooms, but at least they're allowed. Because the hotel itself is a work of art, bring only a very docile dog. Rates are $89 to $350. The price, amazingly enough, includes the Mansions' famous nightly magic show, complete with a performing ghost, and a delicious breakfast. (If you attend the magic show, be sure there's someone to watch your dog for you.) 2220 Sacramento Street, San Francisco, CA 94115; (415) 929-9444. The Mansions' Web site: www.themansions.com.

Ocean Park Motel: This Art Deco gem is San Francisco's very first motel. It was completed in 1937, one month before the Golden Gate Bridge. "When we took the place over (in 1977), Deco was pretty much a lost art," says owner Marc Duffett. "But my wife and I put everything into this place to preserve the Deco flair and at the same time make it homey."

Conveniently located just a long block from Ocean Beach (see page 380) and the San Francisco Zoo, this pleasant motel provides a quiet, safe atmosphere away from the hectic pace (and price) of downtown. You can hear the foghorns from the motel's relaxing hot tub. You can also hear the trolley cars, but it's not bad. And there's a special little play area for kids (the Duffetts have two and know the importance of playgrounds).

Joe and I stayed here with Laura (my human child) for a few days recently when our house was having the lead paint scraped from it, and we had a lovely time. Joe felt right at home after a couple of days, and I'm not sure he wanted to leave. He likes carpeting, something we lack in my house. Rates are $47 to $140. Two-room suites with three queen-sized beds and a kitchen are $100 to $140. Dogs are $5 extra. A few rooms don't have phones, so if you want a real break from the world, ask for one of these. 2690 46th Avenue, San Francisco, CA 94116; (415) 566-7020.

Pan Pacific Hotel: Before I begin, I want to let you know that only dogs under 25 pounds can stay here. Now I don't have to break your heart at the end of the description, should you have a Labrador retriever and a hankering for elegance.

The service at this downtown luxury hotel is impeccable. Your room is made up twice a day (more if you request), you have access to a free chauffeur-driven Rolls Royce, and there's even someone to draw a bath for you if you want. Speaking of baths, the bathrooms are delectable, with floor-to-ceiling marble, deep soaking tubs, and terry robes. The rooms are gorgeous, and come with such extras as in-room safes, voice mail, and in-room fax machines. The Pan Pacific also has a fitness center and a really good restaurant, but dogs will have to settle for their own version of this: a walk and a bowl of dog food in your room. Rooms are $199 to $1,700. Dogs pay a $50 fee per stay. 500 Post Street, San Francisco, CA 94102; (415) 771-8600 or (800) 327-8585.

San Francisco Marriott: The higher priced the room, the higher it will be in this towering pink downtown hotel (which many confuse with a giant Wurlitzer organ), so if your dog has vertigo, you'll save yourself some money. But the views from the top are magnificent. The city skyline, the bay, and the Bay Bridge are all in your scope. This modern hotel has 1,500 guest rooms and 136 suites, so there should be something here to suit every dog. For humans, there's a business center, an indoor pool, and a great health club with whirlpools, saunas, and a steam room. For dogs, there's you. Dogs have to sign a liability form, but there's no deposit. Rates are $149 to $225. 55 Fourth Street, San Francisco, CA 94103; (415) 896-1600 or (800) 228-9290.

San Francisco Marriott Fisherman's Wharf: Stay here and you and your pooch are just two blocks from all the T-shirt and souvenir shops that have taken over Fisherman's Wharf. Actually, some fishing boats still live at the Wharf, and some local crabs still frequent the restaurants, so it's not as commercialized as it looks at first (and second) glance. The rooms are decent, and your stay includes use of the hotel's health club and sauna. Rates are $149 to $300. 1250 Columbus Avenue, San Francisco, CA 94133; (415) 775-7555 or (800) 228-9290.

Sir Francis Drake Hotel: This famous Union Square hotel is a historic landmark, if your dog cares about such things. If there's someone in your party who can hang out with your pooch, check out Harry Denton's Starlight Room, a luxurious nightclub on top of the hotel. The views are truly to pant for.

Every one of the 412 rooms has voice mail, which is a big plus when your dog is expecting an important call. The cable car stops just a bone's throw away, so take your dog on a ride around this enchanting city. (See page 397, "Ride halfway to the stars," for more about dogs on cable cars.) Rates are $165 to $650. Dogs require a $100 deposit. 450 Powell Street, San Francisco, CA 94102; (415) 392-7755.

Travelodge by the Bay: Some rooms here have their own private patios. A few even have extra-length beds, should you find that you're tall. This motel (formerly the Rodeway Inn) is just three blocks from the part of Lombard Street that's known as "the crookedest street in the world." Rates are $65 to $135. Dogs require a $20 deposit. 1450 Lombard Street, San Francisco, CA 94123; (415) 673-0691.

The Westin St. Francis: At this luxurious Union Square hotel, "small, well-behaved dogs are as welcome as anybody," according to a manager. And "small" is not in the eye of the beholder. It's 15 pounds or under. That's about the size of Joe's head, so he won't be staying here any time soon. The cable car stops in front of this historic landmark, so there's no excuse for not taking your little dog on it. (See page 397, "Ride halfway to the stars," for more about dogs on cable cars.) The St. Francis also has a business center and a fitness center, for dogs with people on the go. Rates are $209 to $1,850 (super-duper suites are the pricey ones). 335 Powell Street, San Francisco, CA 94102; (415) 397-7000.

DOGGY DAYS

Celebrate a dog's life: At the San Francisco SPCA's Animal Wingding, you can also celebrate a cat's life, a llama's life, even an iguana's life. (If your dog goes for cats, though, you may want to keep him home so he doesn't put an end to those cat lives some are celebrating. The temptation is too much for poor Joe Dog, so he doesn't get to attend.) This huge, daylong street fair is the ultimate pet experience, with oodles of vendors, dozens of pet-related activities (including a pet star search), and the Parade of Life, a fun, colorful homage to the creatures who share our homes.

You can also take tours of the SPCA, and see its absolutely astounding, luxurious new dog and cat "apartments." The event takes place in early June in the streets around the SPCA, which is located at 2500 Alabama Street. This is not an event for dogs who are crowd-shy: Some 40,000 people attended the last Wingding. Hot dog! For more information, call (415) 554-3026 or (415) 554-3050.

Have a ball: The dog's version of the famous Black & White Ball is truly a spectacle to behold. At the Bark & Whine Ball, well-heeled dogs and their people shine. This is definitely one of those events to see and be seen. No one even shrugs when they see someone dancing with their dog. The ball features good music, passed hors d'oeuvres (dogs love this, but it's really for humans), and wine. It's held at the delightful Old Fed building. Tickets to this SPCA benefit (held in late February) are $75 per human. For more information, phone the SPCA at (415) 554-3050.

Show some poochy pride: Pet Pride Day, sponsored by the San Francisco Department of Animal Care and Control, is a day filled with pets on parade, pets in costumes (if the event falls near Halloween, the costumes get especially interesting), pets "pawditioning" for prizes, and many pet-oriented exhibits. Donations go directly to the department's adoption and outreach programs. Pet Pride Day is held in Golden Gate Park's Sharon Meadow the last Sunday in October. For more information, call (415) 554-9414.

Shake paws with Santa Claus: Whether your dog has been naughty or nice this year, he can have a one-on-one powwow with Santa Claus at the SPCA. In early November, pooches line up to see Santa and have their pictures taken with him. It's very cute. Better than watching the kids do it. Photos are $10, or two poses for $15. The SPCA is at 2500 Alabama Street. Call for this year's Santa date(s). (415) 554-3050.

Take your pooch out to a ball game: You won't strike out with your dog if you bring her to the Dog Days of Summer at Candlestick, er, 3-Com, er, soon-to-be Pac Bell Park. In fact, you'll score a home run. If you thought hot dogs and baseball go together, you should see just plain dog dogs and baseball. It's a match made in dog heaven!

At Dog Days of Summer, your pooch gets to accompany you to a baseball game on a set day in August. You'll sit together in "The Dog Zone" and watch the Giants pound the heck out of the visiting team (we hope). But that's not all. Before the game, you and your dog can take part in a poochy parade around the field! Not many dogs (or humans) can say they've cruised around a pro-ball park. There's also a dog costume contest, should your dog be feeling creative. Cost for the day is $9 per human. Dogs don't pay a dime. Two dollars from each ticket goes to the San Francisco SPCA. Dogs have to wear ID and rabies tags. For other rules and info, call (415) 330-2516. To order tickets, call (415) 467-8000.

DIVERSIONS

Be a stage parent: Anyone who watches KOFY-TV (aka "the WB-20") is familiar with the hairy beasts who sit in easy chairs every half hour for station identification. Maybe you've longed to launch your own dog into the living rooms of thousands of viewers, but never thought you had a chance.

The good news is that your dog doesn't need connections, an agent, or a Screen Actors Guild card to be a star. Just send KOFY-TV a photo of your dog, along with your daytime phone number. If they're interested, they'll call and set up a taping date. "They're always looking for unique breeds," advises Frank Pappas, aka the TV 20 Dog Guy, but any mutt with a lovable face can qualify.

An added benefit to being taped is that you can finally find out just what makes those TV dogs whirl their heads toward that TV set at the perfect moment. Write to KOFY-TV 20, Attention: Pets, 2500 Marin Street, San Francisco, CA 94124; (415) 826-8900.

Catch a rising star: If your pooch has his paws on the ground but his head in the stars, give the San Francisco Sidewalk Astronomers a call. Since 1986, once or twice a month, depending on what's happening in the sky, astronomer John Dodgson and friends have been setting up telescopes at city intersections (at such well-traveled areas as Ninth and Irving, and 24th and Noe) and hosting stargazing parties. Passersby can scan the universe through Dodgson's 18-inch telescope lens. (The telescope is so big it requires climbing up a six-foot ladder to peer through it.)

The group sets up at dusk, sometimes positioning telescopes on three different corners, and stays out for hours. On a given night, more than 100 people might check out the constellations. "If people want to walk by with their dogs, they're welcome to join in," Dodgson says. Best of all, it's free. To find out when and where the Sidewalk Astronomers will be stargazing next, call (415) 681-2565.

Celebrate great music and dance: Your dog's in for culture shock if you bring him to Golden Gate Park to catch top artists Saturday afternoons in the summer. Grab a picnic blanket, a leash, and lunch and head for the Golden Gate Park Music Concourse, in front of the Academy of Sciences. You'll see top dancers from around the world and hear some of the best jazz, classical, and ethnic music around. Just be considerate, and if your dog is the barking type, leave her at home. Admission is free. For more information, call (415) 831-2700.

From April through October on Sundays from noon to 3 P.M., the Golden Gate Band serenades parkgoers with a wide range of music. The band is a lively group with talent for both oompah rhythms and delicate tunes. For more information on the band, call (415) 831-2700.

Cruise the Castro: Your well-behaved dog is welcome to join you on a fascinating walking tour focusing on the gay and lesbian history of the Castro district. Tour leader Trevor Hailey will guide you and a small group to historically significant Castro settings while giving a superb narrative of how the Castro came to be what it is today. Trevor starts with the Lavender Cowboys of the 1849 Gold Rush and takes you through the impact of the 1906 earthquake, World War II, and the Summer of Love.

The only restriction on dogs who go on the Cruisin' the Castro tour is the brunch, which comes with the tour's $35 fee. Brunch is inside a restaurant, and pooches are not permitted. Trevor suggests, if possible, coming with a friend and taking turns eating brunch and walking the dog. You'll miss out on a little of the history Trevor relates at mealtime, but at least you won't miss out on the tasty brunch.

All tour takers, including dogs, get a miniature rainbow flag as part of the deal. Tours are given Tuesday through Saturday. For more information, write Trevor Hailey at Cruisin' the Castro, 375 Lexington Street, San Francisco, CA 94110, or call (415) 550-8110.

Explore a military pet cemetery: If only human cemeteries were so full of bright flowers (albeit many made of plastic or silk) and thoughtful epitaphs as this military pet cemetery located at the Presidio National Park (see page 382), death might not seem so somber. When you enter the little cemetery surrounded by a white picket fence, a sign tells you, "The love these animals gave will never be forgotten." You'll want to bring your leashed dog friend with you.

"Sarge," reads one simple epitaph. "Our pet George. George accepted us people," says another. Several markers bear only a large red heart, which means the pet was unknown but loved even after death. This is where cats, birds, dogs, and even Freddy Fish—whose grave is marked by a lone plastic rose—can live together in harmony. Take Lincoln Boulevard and turn north onto McDowell Avenue. The cemetery is just south of the corner of McDowell and Crissy Field Avenues. (415) 561-4516.

Find an apartment with your dog: With San Francisco's real estate market so tight (the estimated occupancy rate is 99.25 percent!), finding an apartment is grueling enough. Add a dog to the mix and you may as well move back to your hometown. But thanks to a wonderful new program of the San Francisco SPCA, dog people are finding it easier to rent apartments in the city these days. The Open Door Program helps landlords and potential tenants come together in several ways, including providing a listing of available pet-friendly housing, and giving renters tips on how to present their pooch in the right manner (making a doggy resume really helps). This is a hugely popular, free service, garnering 500 phone calls a month. There have been many terrific success stories. Maybe you'll be next. I sure wish they had this program when I was renting. For a complete packet of Open Door info, call (415) 554-3098.

Forget Greyhound; take a Tortoise: Traveling dogs delight in the knowledge that the Green Tortoise, last of the hippie bus companies that thrived in the 1970s, permits well-behaved pooches on its West Coast route. Green Tortoise buses are the ultimate way to travel by bus. Riders are generally a friendly, eclectic lot, which includes tots, retirees, yuppies, punksters, hippies, and students. At night, the whole bus converts to one big bed, with a few sort of private bunks. And if you cross into Oregon, you'll get treated to one of the best breakfasts (cooked by volunteers from the bus, under the guidance of a breakfast guru) and saunas and cold-creek dips of your life— all on the pastoral acreage of the owner of Green Tortoise.

All this makes up for one item that's lacking on Green Tortoise buses. I'll let driver Steve Spahr, a gentle bear of a man, tell you in his own words— the very words he bellowed to the riders on my first Green Tortoise trek: "There are no bathrooms. So we have a pee scale, from one to ten. Ten means your neighbors are scooting away from you as fast as they can. You gotta let me know when you hit five, okay?" If you communicate with the driver, you and your bladder should have no problem.

It's really easy to make buddies on the Green Tortoise. And with a dog in hand, you'll find folks even more friendly than usual. People traveling with dogs are on standby status until the bus driver makes sure your dog is clean, friendly, and fairly mellow and that no one on the bus has allergies or a big problem with pooches. Dogs pay full fare, and only one dog per bus is allowed. At night, your dog gets to sleep beside you, if he so desires and your neighbors don't mind. The bus stops pretty frequently, so be sure to take your dog out often so he can stretch his legs and get relief. After all, he can't tell the bus driver what number he's hitting on the "pee scale."

San Francisco is the main base for Green Tortoise, although you can go all the way from Los Angeles to Seattle with a dog. The ride from San Francisco to Seattle costs $59 one way and takes about 25 hours. From San Francisco to Los Angeles (a much less scenic, often less mellow ride), it's $35 one way and takes about 12 hours. A one-way ride from Los Angeles to Seattle costs $79. For more information, write the Green Tortoise at 494 Broadway, San Francisco, CA 94113, or phone (800) TORTOISE (that's 800-867-8647 for those of you who can't stand punching in letters on your phone) or (415) 956-7500.

Get it at Wilkes': Wilkes Bashford Co., one of the more upscale apparel and home stores on Union Square, is a joy for dogs who like shopping. Pooches of any size are welcome to peruse the store's beautiful merchandise (it's to drool for) as long as they're clean and don't do nasty things like leg lifts.

Wilkes Bashford, who happens to own Wilkes Bashford Co., adores dogs. He's been bringing his dogs to the store since 1968. Freddie, a longhaired dachshund given to Bashford by San Francisco mayor Willie Brown, goes to work with Bashford just about every day. And even when Bashford is out of town on business, Freddie makes his rounds at the store. Bashford's driver takes him there in the morning and drives him home in the afternoon.

"I'm a nut about dogs," says Bashford. "Dogs are a vital part of life." Bashford says people "are so surprised" when he invites them to come inside with a dog. "Sometimes they can't believe it. But there's never been a problem with a dog here. They've all been very well behaved."

Wilkes Bashford Co. is located at 375 Sutter Street. Phone (415) 986-4380 for store hours. And while you're at the store, be sure to check out the wonderful little pet section on the lower floor. A few of the items are truly works of art (look at the price tags).

Go organic: The California Harvest Ranch Market, known for its wide selection of fresh organic produce, has a healthy attitude toward dogs. The owners installed two clamps in the front just for dogs. The idea is to hook your dog's leash to the clamp and go shopping, knowing your dog is safe and secure. As always, though, don't leave him unchecked for long. They're open 9 A.M. to 11 P.M. 2285 Market Street; (415) 626-0805.

Help someone with AIDS: PAWS (Pets Are Wonderful Support) is dedicated to preserving the relationship of people with AIDS and their pets. If you've ever been comforted by your dog while ill, you've caught a glimpse of the importance of the work PAWS does. PAWS needs people to do office work, deliver pet food, and walk and care for pets. And if you have room for another dog in the house, PAWS usually has some special animals for adoption. Write them at 539 Castro Street, San Francisco, CA 94114, or call (415) 241-1460.

Hop on a bus: Dogs are allowed on Muni buses and cable cars anytime they're running. Only one dog is permitted per bus. Dogs must be on a short leash and muzzled, no matter how little or how sweet. Bus driver Tom Brown told us about the creative, but ineffective, ways some people muzzle their dogs. "This one man had a part pit-bull dog, and he put a little rubber band around its mouth," said Brown. "No way that dog was getting on my bus."

Dogs pay the same fare as owners. If the owner is a senior citizen, the dog pays senior citizen rates. Lap-sized dogs can stay on your lap, but all others are consigned to the floor. Keep your dog from getting underfoot and be sure he's well walked before he gets on. Call (415) 673-MUNI for more information.

Hurry to the surrey with the fringe on the top: Really cool dogs don't walk around Golden Gate Park with their people. They ride. And not in a car, but in a surrey. With a little pedal power and some good steering, you can cover plenty of ground in a relatively short time while your dog just sits there and does nothing but smile and sniff at the people you pass. Mike's Bikes & Blades, located at Stow Lake in the park, is happy to rent surreys to people with pets.

Small dogs seem to like riding in the basket in front of the surrey (with a sweater or coat under them so they don't get permanent basket marks on their buns), and medium-sized dogs do well sitting snugly on the seat beside their people. Big dogs might prefer to stick with walking, because even the large surreys aren't exactly gargantuan. Rates are $12 to $23 per hour, depending on the size of the surrey. Mike's Bikes & Blades can be reached at (415) 668-6699.

Nab it at Neiman's: Neiman Marcus, the exclusive, expensive department store with the historic atrium, is a very dog-friendly place. Who'd have guessed? One day as I was waiting outside to meet a friend, I saw two dogs and their people walk out with shopping bags. I thought the women must have been Neiman's aunts, but no. The dogs were not related to the store at all; when I asked the store's publicist, she told me that well-behaved, clean dogs are welcome here. Keep in mind that Neiman's is not for the light of wallet, but if you have a chunk of change you want to drop on some quality items, and you don't want to leave your dog behind when you do it, this is the perfect place to come. 150 Stockton Street; (415) 362-3900.

Ride halfway to the stars: As far as cable cars are concerned, opinions vary widely about whether dogs should ride inside or outside. Some drivers feel the outside is better because the cable noise isn't so amplified, and dogs don't get so nervous. Others say the outside is too dangerous—that a dog could panic and jump off.

If you do decide to do the full San Francisco experience and ride outside, have your dog sit on a bench, and hold her securely by the leash and by the body. The standing area is very narrow and precarious. And you never want to go on a crowded cable car with your dog, so stay away from the popular tourist areas during the peak seasons. (For rules, see "Hop on a bus," above.) For more information, call (415) 673-MUNI.

Joe was so terrified when he first boarded a cable car that he got in no trouble at all after barking at the bell. How much mischief could he get into hiding his head under my coat?

But after a while, with the coaxing of our personable California Street cable car drivers Louie and Dave, he started peeking out at the sights. As they regaled us with stories of dogs they'd known, and flea remedies that work, Joe loosened up. He got so relaxed by the middle of our trip that he fell off his seat as the cable car descended the steep hill in Chinatown. Fortunately, we were seated inside.

No one seemed to want to sit next to Joe. In fact, the deeper we rode into the Financial District and the more suits and ties we encountered, the more people avoided even looking at him. Joe got off at the end of the line with his feelings hurt, but his bravery intact.

Saunter across the Golden Gate: Like their people, dogs thrill to a jaunt across San Francisco's most famous landmark. The bridge spans 1.9 miles from the city to Marin County. It's open to pedestrians, both humans and dogs, from 5 A.M. to 9 P.M. daily. There's no fee.

The only thing that the Golden Gate Bridge Authority asks is that you pick up your dog's poop (they've had a problem with this of late) and that your dog wear a leash. You both probably will want to wear sweaters, too—it can be a little nippy when making your way across. But don't let that stop you. The spectacular views at daybreak and sunset make it all worthwhile. Take the last San Francisco exit before the bridge tollway. Free street parking is available on the west side of the bridge, next to the GGBA employee parking lot. For more info, call (415) 921-5858.

Say yippie for hippies: The Flower Power Haight Ashbury Walking Tour is a delight for humans and dogs, and you don't have to be flower children/puppies to enjoy it. This riveting tour guides you through the history of the Haight, from the Victorian era to the Human Be-in, the Digger feeds, the free Grateful Dead concerts, and of course, the Summer of Love. Dogs don't dig the history much, but they revel in the smell of old hippies who sit on the sidewalks.

Humans of all ages and leashed, well-behaved dogs are welcome. The price of the two-hour tour is $15. Dogs are free. For more information, write The Flower Power Haight Ashbury Walking Tour, 520 Shrader Street, #1, San Francisco, CA 94117, or phone (415) 221-8442.

Seize the Bay: Salty sea dogs wag their tails hard and fast when they learn that the Blue & Gold Fleet ferry system permits pooches on all its lines. This is great news, especially since the Blue & Gold Fleet recently took over the Red & White ferry service to Marin, and didn't end its dog-friendly policy. That means well-behaved, leashed dogs can go by ferry from San Francisco to all these destinations: Sausalito, Tiburon, Oakland, Alameda, and Vallejo. And they don't have to pay a dime. Two destinations are forbidden—Angel Island and Alcatraz, both state parks that don't allow dogs.

Most dogs really dig cruising on the bay. Their nostrils flare in ecstasy at the cool, fishy breeze, and they can look positively giddy upon disembarking. Unfortunately, Joe tends to turn a little green at the gills, even on relatively calm days. Craig and I got married on our boat in the bay, with Nisha and Joe at our side. Nisha had the time of her life. Joe looked like the poster boy for Dramamine. He has since put his paw down about riding on any boat, including the ferry.

Fares range from $4 to $7.50 one way for adults, depending on your des-

---

tination. Joe's favorite trip (when he was still tripping), from San Francisco to Sausalito, is $5.50 one way. Phone (415) 773-1188 for schedules and more information.

Send 'em to the sitter: Once you and your pooch walk through the bright purple door of the San Francisco SPCA's Doggy Daycare Center, you may never want to leave. Ecstatic dogs are everywhere. Water dogs cavort about in the wading pool. Ball dogs sniff through boxes of tennis balls until they select just the right one. Others chase each other around the big 1,400-square-foot room, test out agility equipment, nap on soft beds, and watch doggy videos on the 24-inch color TV. Some even use the "doggy toilet," a big bin of gravel with a real live shiny red fire hydrant.

Most of these dogs belong to owners who feel bad leaving them at home all day while they go to work. "This is a lot like a child day-care center, only I think the dogs have more fun," says Tory Weiser, center coordinator. Some "parents" even leave a bagged lunch in their pooch's very own cubbyhole.

But wait, that's not all! Dogs get two good long walks every day and can be given necessary basic training, too.

Pooches must be a least five months old to spend time here, and they have to have current vaccinations and a friendly demeanor. The cost is $20 daily for three to five days a week. For one or two days per week, the cost is $25 daily. Hours are 7 A.M. to 7 P.M. Monday through Friday. Doggy Daycare Center is located on the side of the SPCA building at 2500 16th Street; (415) 554-3079.

Shop on Beach Street: You can shop for baubles, bangles, and T-shirts with your leashed dog at any of dozens of little stands up and down this Fisherman's Wharf area street. You can even get your dog's caricature done by a local artist. Make sure to take him to nearby Aquatic Park (see page 369) while you're there, especially if he's sat patiently for the artist's rendition. The bulk of the stands on Beach Street are between Hyde and Polk Streets.

Wash that sand right outta her hair: The beauty of taking your dog to Bill's Doggie Bath-O-Mat is that you can bathe your dog without having to clean the tub afterward. (Or, worse yet, having to bathe in the tub yourself afterward!) Bill's is a no-nonsense kind of dog wash, with waist-high tubs and everything you need at your fingertips. The $10 fee includes use of shampoo, combs, brushes, towels, and a doggy blow-dryer. You even get to use a cute doggy apron. Such a deal! Bill, the owner, grooms dogs here, too. He's a nice guy who chats with his customers, gives good grooming advice if needed, and gives great little puppy calendars away in January. Bill's is at 3928 Irving Street; (415) 661-6950.

Wash your socks with your dog: A jug of wine, a loaf of bread, your dirty laundry, your dog, and you. Bring all this and feast at one of four tables outside Star Wash Laundry while your wash is in the rinse cycle. This is a very popular spot among dog owners with dirty clothes, and since the Laundromat owners adore dogs, chances are your pet won't be alone. It's especially enjoyable for your dog after a sprint in nearby Mission Dolores Park (see page 379). Don't forget water for your dog. 392 Dolores Street; (415) 431-2443.

Watch a big-screen flick: Picture this—you, your date, a romantic drive-in movie. The plot thickens, your date takes your hand, the lead characters start to kiss, lips locking. . . . You feel hot breath on your neck and turn in dreamy anticipation. And there, only millimeters from your face, is your dog's big black nose, sniffing away and asking for more popcorn.

Still, taking a dog to a drive-in theater can be fun. At the Geneva Drive-In Theater, a resident cat prowls around cars looking for a handout or a dog to tease. The Geneva is on Carter Street, off Geneva Avenue, next to the Cow Palace; (415) 587-2884.

36
SAN MATEO COUNTY

Joe and I were stuck in Redwood City on business all day. After a while, he began to glare at me. His brow wrinkled. His eyes got wide and seemed to float in extra liquid. Then he started groaning like a door in a bad horror movie. It was all too clear. This was a dog urgently in need of a park.

So we got in the car and drove until we found a little city park. I let Joe out and he bounded for a private spot behind a bush. But just as he was getting into position, a woman with a baby stroller bustled up. "No! Bad dog! No dogs allowed. Tell your mother that," she yelled and shot us an angry look.

Joe ran back to the car in a more cowardly manner than I care to admit, tail down, head low. Instead of arguing, we left. Besides, there was a big county park at the other end of Redwood City that looked even better.

Joe was so desperate that by the time we got there he was crossing his legs. But it seemed worth the wait. The park was big and grassy with lots of pine trees and bushes essential for Joe to do his thing. Birds and wildflowers were everywhere. It was one of the more alluring parks we'd ever seen.

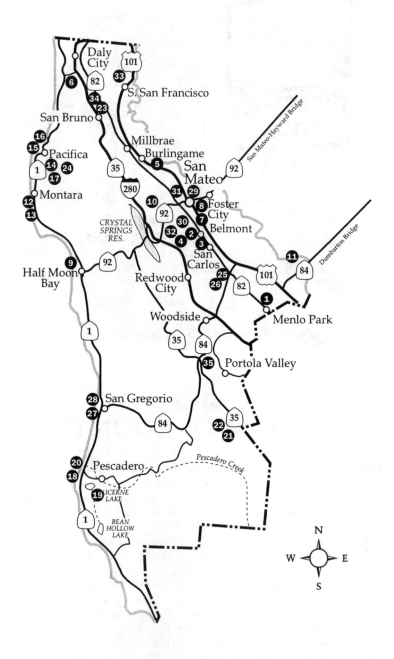

Daly City

101

82

33

S. San Francisco

6

34

123

San Bruno

16

15

Pacifica

1

14 24

17

Millbrae

Burlingame

5

San Mateo

92

35

Montara

280

31 29

12

10

Foster City

8

13

92

7

CRYSTAL SPRINGS RES.

30

Belmont

32

2

4

3

San Carlos

11

9

92

Redwood City

25

84

Half Moon Bay

26

82

1

Woodside

Menlo Park

1

35

84

35

Portola Valley

San Gregorio

28

27

22 35

84

21

20

Pescadero

Pescadero Creek

18

19 LUCERNE LAKE

1

BEAN HOLLOW LAKE

N

W E

S

San Mateo-Hayward Bridge

Dumbarton Bridge

But just as we entered, three words on a sign stopped us in our tracks. They were big, bold, and mean: **NO DOGS ALLOWED.** Joe lifted his leg on the sign and we were gone. Thus was our unsavory introduction to San Mateo County.

Once we started exploring San Mateo County in depth, we realized that it wasn't as unfriendly as it first seemed. There are many parks that allow dogs; six even allow them off leash. But some of the biggest and best have an outright ban on canines.

The worst offender is the county Department of Parks and Recreation. There are 15,000 acres of county parklands here, but none of the county's 70,000 licensed dogs may set paw in them. In past editions, I've written about groups that had formed to try to convince the county to open its gates to dogs, but all efforts have failed, and the county shows no signs of allowing dogs in its parks. If you have any friends in high places here, do what you can, but don't be surprised when the answer is NO.

Meanwhile, fortunately, there are some mighty dog-friendly places to visit throughout the county. The Midpeninsula Regional Open Space District has become one of dogs' best friends of late, with the addition in San Mateo County of two more preserves that allow dogs (bringing the total to four), including one that has a 16-acre off-leash area (see Pulgas Ridge, page 419). Be sure to follow extremely good doggy etiquette at all the district's preserves, because there are a lot of anti-doggers out there who would love to get the district to take away our privileges.

The district has unique rules about poop scooping and six-foot leashes. Scooping the poop is appreciated, but because of limited trash disposal sites, if you kick the poop off the trail, that's considered okay. (Helpful hint: Don't wear open-toed sandals.) And retractable leashes are allowed to go beyond the six-foot mark in many instances, which is a rare thing indeed. The exceptions: when you're within 100 feet of parking lots, roads, trailheads, picnic areas, and rest rooms, and when you're within 50 feet of other people or any body of water, including creeks. It's a great policy—one other park districts should follow, says Joe.

The district even offers very cool canine walks in conjunction with the Palo Alto Humane Society. The hikes, called Dog Days Hikes, are about two hours, and they're usually leisurely, although you can end up covering from three to five miles. It's a great way to meet dogs and their people. Pooperscoopers are provided, but you have to do the scooping. Bring a leash and water for your pooch. For more information, or to make reservations, call the district at (650) 691-1200, or the Palo Alto Humane Society at (650) 327-0631. (The Humane Society also offers easy hikes in other parklands about once a month. Call for a schedule.)

So hats off to the open space district. If the county park system would follow its lead, San Mateo could become a very doggone decent county.

A terrific group called Peninsula Access for Dogs (PAD) is trying to improve the park life of dogs all over the peninsula. For information, write to PAD at 809-B Cuesta Drive, Box 196, Mountain View, CA 94094, or check out PAD's Web site: www.rahul.net/pruski/pads.

ATHERTON

PARKS, BEACHES, AND RECREATION AREAS

• **Holbrook-Palmer Park** 🐾🐾

See ❶ *on page 402.*

Roses. Gazebos. Bathrooms that look like saunas. Trellises. Jasmine plots. Tennis courts. Buildings that belong in a country club. People in white linen love it here; dogs are often just plain intimidated. Joe didn't lift his leg once last time we visited.

"Don't put it in your book that we allow dogs," a woman with the Atherton Parks and Recreation Department told us. "We have too many weddings and banquets going on here, and the people don't want to be disturbed."

Don't forget a leash.

Holbrook-Palmer Park is located on Watkins Avenue, between El Camino Real and Middlefield Road. Leave your car at one of several lots in the park. (650) 688-6534.

BELMONT

PARKS, BEACHES, AND RECREATION AREAS

• **Cipriani Park Dog Exercise Area** 🐾🐾🐾🐾 🐕

See ❷ *on page 402.*

You want off leash? You want social? Then you want to come here. The folks at this two-acre, fenced-in dog run are so friendly that on your first visit you'll feel as though you've been a regular for many years. Of course, that would be impossible, because the dog run, the newest in the county, opened in 1993. But you get the idea.

People who come here love to celebrate dog birthdays with their park friends. And just about every Friday after work, they gather with refreshments and have a sort of happy hour. Or two. Or three. "You won't find cliques here. We're all in this dog world together, and we enjoy enjoying ourselves and watching our dogs have a great time," says Larry Miller, who heads the Belmont Bowser Club, the group that got this park going and maintains it with volunteer labor.

Dogs adore this grass- and wood-chip-carpeted park. A fire hydrant is the centerpiece and the totem for the boy dogs who come here. Tall pines provide shade, but dogs can frequently be found lounging under the two picnic tables. There are two water spigots for thirsty dogs and pooper-scoopers galore.

The park is located at 2525 Buena Vista Avenue, behind the Cipriani School. It's a little hard to find. From El Camino Real, go west on Ralston Avenue. In about 1.5 miles, you'll pass Alameda de las Pulgas. Drive about another three-quarters of a mile, and be on the lookout for Cipriani Boulevard. It's a small street you can easily miss. Turn right on Cipriani and follow it a few blocks to Buena Vista. Turn left on Buena Vista and park near the school. You won't see the dog run from the street, but if you walk west and enter through the main park entrance, you'll soon see it. Whatever you do, don't take your dog through the school's playground when kids are present. The school really frowns on this. (650) 595-7441.

•**Twin Pines Park** 🐾 🐾 🐾 *See ❸ on page 402.*

This park is a hidden treasure, nestled among eucalyptus trees just outside the business district of Belmont. You'd never guess the dog wonders that await within. Your dog may hardly notice she's leashed.

The main trail is paved and winds through sweet-smelling trees and brush. A clear stream runs below. In dry seasons, it's only about two feet deep, but in good years it swells to several feet. Dogs love to go down to the stream and wet their whistles. Past the picnic area are numerous small, quiet dirt trails that can take you up the woodsy hill or alongside the stream.

It's located at 1225 Ralston Avenue, behind the police department. (650) 595-7441.

•**Water Dog Lake Park** 🐾 🐾 🐾 *See ❹ on page 402.*

Dogs and their people seem magically drawn to this large, wooded park with a little lake in the middle. Maybe it's the way the moss drips off the trees at the bottom of this mountainous area, or the way the lake seems to create a refreshing breeze on the hottest days.

Or maybe it's got something to do with the name. We asked several dog owners how the park came to be called Water Dog Lake Park.

"I think the lake is kind of shaped like a dog. Actually, it's more like a kangaroo, isn't it?" said the proud owner of a beagle/terrier mix.

"It would be a good place to water your dog, if that were allowed," said a woman with a black Lab.

"When dogs and people were allowed to swim here, you couldn't get the Labs and all those water dogs out of this lake," explained a man with an Irish setter.

We hate to burst the romantic fantasy that a park as alluring as this one is named after man's best friend. But after some searching through historical records, we discovered the biting truth: Water Dog Lake Park was named after salamanders. A colloquial name for a salamander is "water dog," and apparently the little critters used to wriggle all over the place around here. We still think the park is great. Too bad dogs have to be leashed.

One other thing that we discovered about this park: If people would follow their dogs, perhaps a lot fewer would stumble onto the wrong trail. The one that goes up to the top of the park never comes near the lake and leads you more than a mile away from where you started. Joe tried tugging in the other direction, but I ignored him. We got a ride back to the entrance from a teenage boy who felt sorry for us.

Upon entering the park from the Lake Road entrance, take the wide path that goes straight in front of you. It will lead you down to the lake. Neither you nor your dog can go in the water, but you can have a great picnic there, or even go fishing off the little wooden pier.

If you start off taking the smaller trail that veers to the right, you'll get good exercise and a great view of the bay, but we don't recommend it, unless you enjoy getting lost and suffering heat fatigue in the summer. A final word of warning: Watch out for bikers. They're fast here.

Enter on Lake Road, just off Carlmont Drive. Try to come back to the same place. (650) 595-7441.

BURLINGAME

PARKS, BEACHES, AND RECREATION AREAS

At last check, Burlingame's movers and shakers were discussing the possibility of having a dog park somewhere in the city. Nothing was final, but at press time, it looked promising. If it happens, the sound of clapping paws should be resounding. Call (650) 696-7245 for an update.

• **Washington Park** 🐾 🐾 *See* ❺ *on page 402.*

This relatively small park has the look of an old college campus. Its trees are big and old and mostly deciduous, making autumn a particularly brilliant time. Bring a lunch and eat it on the thick, knotty old redwood picnic tables. They're something out of the Enchanted Forest. Joe is intrigued by the abundance of squirrels, but he doesn't get too far with his pursuits, since leashes are the law and the police station is around the corner.

The park is at 850 Burlingame Avenue below Carolan Avenue. (650) 696-7245.

RESTAURANTS

Cafe La Scala: The outdoor area at this exquisite Italian restaurant has dozens of tables, but it's still very romantic, with beautiful flowers, soft music, and pastoral murals. It's all very Florentine. Dogs need to sit at the edge of the patio area. In cooler months, the area is warmed by heat lamps. 1219 Burlingame Avenue; (650) 347-3035.

Caprice Restaurant and Cafe: The California cuisine here is very tasty, and the brunches are popular with dog owners. Dine at a half dozen shaded tables out front. 347 Primrose Road; (650) 375-8618.

PLACES TO STAY

San Francisco Airport Marriott: If you need to stay near the airport, and your dog appreciates good views of the San Francisco Bay and is under 30 pounds, you couldn't ask for a better hotel. Rates are $130 to $245. 1800 Old Bayshore Highway, Burlingame, CA 94010; (650) 692-9100.

Vagabond Inn: With prices like this, it's a wonder they still call it Vagabond Inn: Rates are $87 to $97. Dogs are $5 extra. 1640 Bayshore Highway, Burlingame, CA 94010; (650) 692-4040.

DOGGY DAYS

Turn your dog into a cat: Or try a rat. Or maybe even a ballerina. Your dog can be just about anything he doggone well pleases at the Peninsula Pet Masquerade. The daylong event is the toast of the Halloween season for pets (yes, that means cats, too) and their people. All participants, human or otherwise, should come in costume. Those registered for the costume contest will receive a fun trick-or-treat bag.

Admission is free to onlookers. Contestants pay $10 per entry ($25 for groups of three or more people or pets). All proceeds go to support the Peninsula Humane Society. The event is held on a Saturday near Halloween. In the past, it's been at the Hyatt Regency at 1333 Bayshore Highway.

Call the Peninsula Humane Society for this year's date and location. (650) 340-7022.

DIVERSIONS

Ask your dog for a date to a movie: It's greasy. It's kitschy. It's unique. (Witness the domed snack bar topped with very pink turrets.) But going to the Burlingame 4 Drive-In Theater is a great way to catch a movie and spare yourself the guilt of leaving your dog home alone. And it's cheap. Dogs are free—unless, like Joe, they have a hankering for popcorn. We saw a real classic here: *Don't Tell Mom the Babysitter's Dead.* Joe loved it. He couldn't take his eyes off the screen, except to lick the sound box.

(Oh, by the way, the theater is also for sale. Catch a flick while there are still flicks to catch.) Tickets are $5.75 for adults. Kids under 11 are free. So are dogs, old or young. 350 Beach Road; (650) 343-2213.

DALY CITY

We called the Daly City parks department to find out what its rule is regarding leashes. A helpful woman read the city ordinance: Animals must be "under control of owner by being saddled, harnessed, haltered, or leashed by a substantial chain, lead rope, or leash, which chain, lead rope, or leash shall be continuously held by some competent person capable of controlling such an animal."

So Joe wore a leash during our Daly City visits. But he put his paw down when it came to donning the saddle and halter.

PARKS, BEACHES, AND RECREATION AREAS

Here's one of the better Daly City parks where pooches are permitted. Many parks in Daly City don't allow dogs. If you're anywhere near the ocean, your best bet is to head to just the other side of the Daly City–San Francisco border and visit magnificent Fort Funston (see page 372).

• **Gellert Park** 🐾🐾 *See* ❻ *on page 402.*

The best feature of this flat, square park is that it's right behind the Serramonte Library. It's also conveniently located if you are going to pay homage to someone at the Chinese Cemetery, right across the street. The park is made up of a few sports fields—watch out for flying baseballs, soccer balls, and softballs. The park's trees, which surround two sides, aren't even accessible—they're on top of a very steep little ridge. Your dog may become frustrated, especially since he must wear a leash through all this.

The park is on Wembley Drive at Gellert Boulevard. (650) 991-8006.

FOSTER CITY

John Oliver, former mayor of Foster City, isn't the sort to beat around the bush. When he describes the older women who set out to improve the town by getting recreational vehicles off the streets and enforcing the leash law, he's not kind.

"They are the forces of darkness," he says. "They're a couple of little old ladies right from central casting for their nit-picking roles."

Oliver's feathers are ruffled for good reason. In 1988—a year after he stopped being mayor, and shortly after the "forces of darkness" started crusading for more dog patrols—a cop cited him for walking his little dog, Topper, off leash. The ticket was only $25. It was the principle that distressed him—not to mention the newspaper story. "Topper was an angel of a dog and in a totally empty park. Come on, let's get sensible here," he says.

This is the dog who used to break out of Oliver's truck and run into City Council chambers to find him during meetings. She's the same 20-pound mutt who stayed by Oliver's side during a recent bout of bad luck that forced them into homelessness. "She made life a lot easier when we were living in that truck," he says.

Oliver has always voted for leash laws, but he believes the real issue is control. "If you can control your dog in a safe area, and there's no one around to disturb, why not let her loose for a few minutes?" he asks. "It's a shame it has to cost you if you're caught."

Fortunately, two Foster City parks permit pooches off leash, far from Oliver's "forces of darkness."

PARKS, BEACHES, AND RECREATION AREAS

• **Boothbay Park** 🐾🐾🐾 🐕 *See ❼ on page 402.*

It's off with the leash once you find the right section of this park, which is the grassy area behind the tennis courts. It's surrounded on two sides by a tall wooden fence and is comfortably far from the road. This little corner of the park is nothing fancy, but it does allow dogs some freedom.

The park is at Boothbay Avenue and Edgewater Lane. (650) 345-5731.

• **Foster City Dog Exercise Area** 🐾🐾½ 🐕 *See ❽ on page 402.*

This fenced dog run has great potential, but it's a disappointment. Dogs are allowed off leash here, but as soon as they get down to having fun with each other, they kick up clouds of dust. The ground is pretty much packed dirt, with little bits of grass trying to push through.

The view isn't any more attractive, with power lines overhead, the back of City Hall in the foreground, and rows of look-alike town houses in the distance. What this place needs is a few good trees—and some water for the dogs.

There are two good points, though: The fences are very high, so if you have an escape artist for a dog, this place is about the safest around. And there are plenty of large trash cans—six, to be exact—and no shortage of pooper-scoopers.

It's at 600 Foster City Boulevard. Park in the lot behind City Hall. (650) 345-5731.

RESTAURANTS

Dogs dig dining at Foster City's lagoon-side restaurants. Here are a couple that welcome dogs:

O'Donegan's: Eat hearty burgers and other sandwiches with your pooch at any of 10 umbrella-shaded tables on O'Donegan's large wood deck. It overlooks the Foster City Lagoon, so if your dog is a water dog, she'll feel at home here. 929A Edgewater Boulevard; (650) 570-6099.

Papa's Cucina: Don't let the name fool you into thinking you're going to be rolling in meatballs and other Italian cuisine here. Papa's offers a few Italian dishes, but this is primarily a deli. It's a good one, too. Joe Dog recommends the Boston Philly cheese-steak sandwich. He once sniffed out a man eating one, and I doubt he's ever forgotten it. (Neither has the man, but that's another story.) Good dogs can dine with you on the attractive wood-planked deck. 929C Edgewater Boulevard; (650) 572-8268.

HALF MOON BAY

PARKS, BEACHES, AND RECREATION AREAS

• **Half Moon Bay State Beach** 🐾 🐾 🐾 ½ *See* ❾ *on page 402.*

This is the beach air-conditioned by the god of woolly sheepdogs. No matter how steaming hot it is elsewhere, you can almost always count on brisk weather here. It's cool and foggy in the summer, wet and windy in the winter, and moderate in the fall and spring.

The three-mile crescent of beach is actually made up of four beaches. From north to south, along Highway 1, they are Roosevelt Beach, Dunes Beach, Venice Beach, and Francis Beach. Leashed dogs are permitted on all four beaches (until mid-1994, they were banned from Francis Beach, but that ban has gone bye-bye!).

This isn't the place to come for a 15-minute romp: If you park in the park, it costs $5 per car and $1 per dog. The beaches are all clean and each is almost identical to the next, so your choice of beach should depend on which entry is most convenient. Rangers roam year-round. If you're thinking of breaking the leash law, this is a bad place to try it.

If you can ignore all the RVs and crowds of tents, the area above Francis Beach is a stunning camping spot. Perched on ice plant-covered dunes above the Pacific, it's one of the most accessible beach camping areas in the Bay Area. All of the 53 campsites are available on a first-come, first-served basis. Sites are $12 to $14. Dogs are $1 extra.

From Highway 1, follow the brown and white signs to the appropriate beach. (415) 330-6300.

RESTAURANTS

Cameron's Restaurant: Rich and creamy fountain treats are the specialty here, but burgers, pizza, and healthful salads are big sellers, too. Joe is particularly fond of smelling the aroma of fish-and-chips wafting off tables. Dine with your pooch at the big outdoor patio. 1410 South Cabrillo Highway; (650) 726-5705.

Moonside Bakery: All the delicious treats here are baked daily, except for the soup, which generally isn't baked. (But it's still made fresh daily.) This is truly an exceptional bakery, featuring all kinds of crusty breads and delectable sweets, but specializing in German baked goods. Dine with dog at the many attractive, wooden, umbrella-topped tables outside. 604 Main Street; (650) 726-9070.

Pasta Moon: This restaurant offers several sidewalk tables and every type of pasta imaginable. A *San Francisco Chronicle* food critic calls the house-made pastas here "addictive." Joe Dog suggests ordering the tagliatelle bathed in cream and surrounded by sliced sausage and prosciutto. It's a big plateful that you probably can't finish yourself, so your baleful-eyed canine might get lucky. 315 Main Street; (650) 726-5125.

PLACES TO STAY

Half Moon Bay State Beach: See Half Moon Bay State Beach on page 409 for camping information.

Holiday Inn Express: Just five blocks from Half Moon Bay State Beach, and a few blocks from downtown, this dog-friendly hotel is conveniently located for adventure-seeking pooches and their people. Rates are $79 to $139. Dogs are $10 extra. 230 Cabrillo Highway, Half Moon Bay, CA 94019; (650) 726-3400.

Ramada Limited: Rates are $60 to $115. Dogs are $10 extra. 3020 Highway 1, Half Moon Bay, CA 94019; (650) 726-9700.

The Zaballa House: This 1859 country Victorian is the oldest standing house in Half Moon Bay. Some of the nine quaint bedrooms have fireplaces and Jacuzzis. Breakfasts are fresh and out of this world. If you have any tendencies toward being a psychic, ask to stay in room 6. Many guests say they've felt a "presence" here, and the inn's owners are interested in just what that could be. It's not a bad presence, say those who have felt it, so don't let it spook you out of checking out this room.

The inn is not only dog-accepting, but dog-welcoming. There's the occasional pooch treat, and even a book with photos of all the pets who have been guests here. Dogs love to paw through it on foggy mornings. Be sure the folks here take your dog's picture, so other dogs and their humans can check him out.

Cats are occasionally guests, too, so if your dog likes cats for lunch, you may want to inquire as to their presence when you make your reservation.

Rates are $95 to $170. Dogs are $10 extra. They ask that you bring only one dog per room. 324 Main Street, Half Moon Bay, CA 94019; (650) 726-9123.

HILLSBOROUGH

• **Vista Park** 🐾 *See ⑩ on page 402.*

You can visit this park only if you live here, unless you choose to walk miles to get to it—there's no street parking for blocks, and no parking lot. And chances are that if you live in this town, your backyard is bigger anyway. There's a little section in the back with several tall eucalyptus trees that leashed neighborhood dogs call their own. It's good for sniffs when you can't get to a better park.

The park is at Vista and Culebra Roads. (650) 579-3800.

MENLO PARK

PARKS, BEACHES, AND RECREATION AREAS

• **Bayfront Park** 🐾🐾🐾 *See ⑪ on page 402.*

This place used to be a dump—literally. It was the regional landfill site until it reached capacity in 1984. Then the city sealed the huge mounds of

---

garbage under a two-foot clay barrier and covered it with four feet of soil, planted grass and trees, and *voilà*—instant 160-acre park!

Now it's a land of rolling hills with a distinctly Native American flavor. The packed dirt trails take you up to majestic views of the bay and surrounding marshes. There's no sign of garbage anywhere, unless you look down from the top of a hill and spot the methane extraction plant. Fortunately, very few vista points include that.

Our favorite part of the park is a trail studded with large, dark rocks arranged to form symbols, which in series make up a poem. The concept was inspired by Native American pictographs—a visual language system for recording daily events. At the trailhead, you'll find a sign quoting part of the poem and giving a map of the trail, showing the meaning of each rock arrangement as it corresponds to the poem.

Although leashes are required, dogs seem really fond of this park, sniffing everywhere, their tails wagging constantly. Perhaps they can sense the park's less picturesque days deep underground. Or they may be touched by the Native American magic that imbues these hills.

The park starts at the end of Marsh Road, just on the other side of the Bayfront Expressway. To get to the beginning of the rock poem trail, continue past the entrance on Marsh Road to the second parking lot on the right. (650) 858-3470.

RESTAURANTS

Garden Grill: This restaurant is among the finest dog-friendly restaurants in the state. It's so elegant you can eat like a king—an English king, to be precise. Dine in an old English garden under the canopy of an enormous 400-year-old oak tree. While Garden Grill specializes in traditional English dishes and a charming afternoon tea, it's especially proud of its medieval cuisine. Try the fourteenth-century soup, one of King Richard II's favorites. And your dog will salivate when your server brings you elk, venison, or squab with a hearty fruit and wine sauce. Unlike medieval tourist traps, Garden Grill encourages the use of fork and knife (Joe hasn't mastered this skill yet, but it's recommended for humans). There are 18 tables outside this English cottage restaurant. 1026 Alma Street; (650) 325-8981.

DIVERSIONS

Sniff out a good book: Your dog doesn't have to be Mr. Peabody to appreciate fine books. In fact, even if your dog doesn't know his assonance from his alliteration, he could have fun accompanying you to Kepler's Books. Kepler's, one of the largest and very best independent bookstores around, permits clean, leashed, well-behaved dogs to cruise the aisles with you. Common sense and good manners apply. Please, no leg lifts on the merchandise; Kepler's frowns on yellow journalism. And dogs who lean toward the literary are welcome. Those who jump on the literature are not. 1010 El Camino Real; (650) 324-4321.

MILLBRAE

Now that dogs aren't allowed on trails surrounding Crystal Springs Reservoir, they are howling. But they can still grab a bite and spend the night.

RESTAURANTS

Leonardo's Delicatessen: This truly Italian deli has plenty of outdoor tables, all comfortably far from sidewalk traffic. 540 Broadway Avenue; (650) 697-9779.

PLACES TO STAY

Clarion Hotel: Rates are $89 to $189. Dogs pay a $20 fee per visit. 401 East Millbrae Avenue, Millbrae, CA 94030; (650) 692-6363.

The Westin San Francisco Airport: If you're traveling by air, this is about the most convenient and luxurious place you and your dog can stay: It's only two minutes from the airport. Each of the 390 rooms is tastefully furnished and has two phones, a refreshment center, a coffeemaker, and voice mail. There's even a data port in every room, should your dog need to do some downloading. For humans, there's a fitness center and a yummy Mediterranean-style bistro. Rates are $120 to $310. 1 Old Bayshore Highway, Millbrae, CA 94030; (650) 692-3500 or (800) 228-3000.

MONTARA

PARKS, BEACHES, AND RECREATION AREAS

• **McNee Ranch State Park** 🐾 🐾 🐾 ½ *See* **⑫** *on page 402.*

State parks usually ban dogs completely, or at least from all but paved roadways. But McNee is a refreshing exception to the rule. At McNee, you can hike at the same level as the soaring gulls and watch the gem-blue ocean below. The higher you go up Montara Mountain, the more magnificent the view. Hardly a soul knows about this park, so if it's peace you want, it's peace you'll get.

And if it's a workout you want, you'll get that, too. Just strap on a day pack and bring lots of water for you and your dog. If you do the full hike, you'll ascend from sea level to 1,898 feet in a couple of hours. As you hike up and away from the ocean and the road, you lose all sounds of civilization, and Highway 1 fades into a thin ribbon and disappears below.

As soon as you go through the gate at the bottom of the park, follow the narrow trails to the left up the hills. You may be tempted to take the wide and winding paved road from the start, but to avoid any bikers, take the little trails. Besides, they lead to much better vistas.

Eventually, you'll come to a point where you have a choice of going left or right on a wider part of the trail. It's a choice between paradise and heaven. Left will lead you to a stunning view of the Golden Gate Bridge and the Farallon Islands. Right will bring you to the top of the ridge, where you see Mount Diablo and the rest of the San Francisco Bay.

This would be Joe's favorite park, but dogs are supposed to be leashed. Still, he always manages to slide down several steep grassy hills on his back, wriggling and moaning in ecstasy all the way.

It's easy to miss this park since there aren't any signs and there's no official parking lot. From Highway 1 in Montara, park at the far northern end of the Montara State Beach parking lot and walk across the road. Be careful as you walk along Highway 1, because there's hardly any room on the shoulder. You'll see a gate on a dirt road just north of you and a small state property sign. That's where you go in. A few cars can also park next to the gate on the sides of the dirt road. But don't block the gate or your car probably won't be there when you get back. (415) 330-6300.

• **Montara State Beach** 🐾 🐾 🐾 1/2 *See* ⓭ *on page 402.*

This long, wide beach has more nooks and crannies than your dog will be able to investigate. Around mid-beach, you'll find several little inlets carved into the mini-cliffs. Take your dog back there at low tide and you'll find all sorts of water, grass, mud, and beach flotsam. It's a good place for her to get her paws wet, while obeying the leash law.

The water at the inlets is as calm as pond water. This is where Joe first dared to walk in water. It was only a centimeter deep, but he licked his paws in triumph all the way home.

Off Highway 1, park in the little lot behind the Chart House restaurant. There's also a parking area on the north side of the beach, off Highway 1. (415) 330-6300.

PLACES TO STAY

Farallone Bed & Breakfast Inn: Each of the nine rooms in this homey Victorian inn has a private balcony and a small Jacuzzi. Some rooms have ocean views. A basic breakfast comes with your room. This place used to offer a really relaxing atmosphere with special treatment like afternoon tea and evening wine service, but under new management, it's back to the basics. Well, at least the room prices have dropped.

Rooms are $75 to $110. Dogs require a $25 deposit and are charged a $25 fee for the length of their stay. 1410 Main Street, Montara, CA 94037; (650) 728-8200 or (800) 350-9777.

MOSS BEACH
RESTAURANTS

Pony Espresso: Gallop on over, poochies! They give dogs treats here. So if the veggie pizza and the cozy coffees aren't enough to beckon your human, remind him about the treats and then pull hard on the leash. It's worth a try. Dine at the four outdoor tables in front and in back. 2350 Carlos Street; (650) 728-3540.

PACIFICA
PARKS, BEACHES, AND RECREATION AREAS

• **Milagra Ridge** 🐾 🐾 🐾 1/2 *See* ⓮ *on page 402.*

Follow the trail up to the top of the tallest hill and you'll end up with both an incredible view of the Pacific and a perfect plateau for a picnic. There are hillsides covered with ice plant and even a few Monterey pines along the way. Visit in the spring if you want to be wowed by wildflowers.

Despite the leash law, dogs really seem to enjoy this park. Make sure to keep them on the trail, as the environment here is fragile. And keep your eyes peeled for the Mission Blue butterfly. This park is one of its last habitats.

Milagra Ridge is especially magical at night. You've never seen the full moon until you've seen it from here.

Enter on Sharp Park Road in Pacifica, between Highway 1 and Skyline Boulevard. (415) 556-8371.

• **Pacifica State Beach** 🐾 🐾 *See* **⓯** *on page 402.*

This surfer's paradise has mixed messages for canines. First the bad news: Dogs must be leashed, picnickers abound, and the temptation to sneak a chicken leg can be too much for even the best dog. The beach isn't very wide, leaving little room for exploration.

Now the good news: The setting alone warrants a visit. With green rolling hills in the distance behind you and the pounding sea before you, you and your dog won't regret stopping here. On Highway 1, park between Crespi Drive and Linda Mar Boulevard. The beach is open sunrise to sunset. (415) 330-6300.

• **Sharp Park Beach** 🐾 🐾 ½ *See* **⓰** *on page 402.*

Don't make the mistake several people have told us they've made—get up at an ungodly hour, gather your fishing gear, and march out to the pier with your dog to catch your supper. Dogs aren't allowed on the pier, perhaps because they tend to eat the bait and the catch of the day. But you may take them to the beach 30 feet below, as long as they're leashed. It's a narrow beach, though, so make sure you go when the tide is out.

Enter at San Jose and Beach Boulevards, or Beach Boulevard at Clarendon Road. (650) 738-7380.

• **Sweeney Ridge** 🐾 🐾 🐾 *See* **⓱** *on page 402.*

See page 418 under San Bruno.

RESTAURANTS

Beach Cafe: After a walk on the chilly beach, there's nothing like a hot espresso and homemade croissant at the outdoor tables here. The owners have two Samoyeds, so it's a very dog-friendly place. It's so dog-friendly, in fact, that dogs who visit get a treat or two. Highway 1 at Rockaway Beach Avenue, next to Kentucky Fried Chicken; (650) 355-4532.

Sam's Deli: Sam's is a refreshing spot to hit after an afternoon at Pacifica State Beach. It has good sandwiches at low prices and two outdoor tables. It's at the Linda Mar Shopping Center, just behind the beach, on the same side as Denny's and the shoe stores, about halfway down the row of shops. 1261 Linda Mar Shopping Center; (650) 359-5330.

PESCADERO

PARKS, BEACHES, AND RECREATION AREAS

• **Bean Hollow State Beach** 🐾 🐾 🐾 ½ *See* **⓲** *on page 402.*

The rocky intertidal zone here is terrific for tidepooling, but only if you and your dog are surefooted. To get to the best tidepools, you must perform an amazing feat of team coordination—climbing down 70-million-year-old rock formations while attached to each other by leash. It's not that steep, just awkward. The pitted rocks can be slippery. This maneuver is not recommended for dogs who go deaf and senseless when the alluring ocean beckons them to swim. Besides, the surf can be treacherous in this area.

If you reach the tidepools, you're in for a real treat. But make sure your canine companion doesn't go fishing—we've seen a dog stick his entire head in a tidepool to capture a little crab. Fur and fangs aren't natural in the delicate balance of this wet habitat, so please keep dogs out of the tidepools. The mussels will thank you.

If you decide to play it safe and stay on flat land, you can still see the harbor seal rookery on the rocks below the coastal bluffs. Bring binoculars and you can really get a view of them up close and personal.

The beach is off Highway 1 at Bean Hollow Road. (415) 330-6300.

• **Butano State Park** 🐾🐾🐾½ *See* ⑲ *on page 402.*

Dogs are beside themselves when they learn that much of this 3,800-acre state park is open to them. State parks generally ban pooches from everything but paved roads and campgrounds. But Butano happens to have 11 miles of doggone good dirt fire roads, and leashed dogs are more than welcome to explore. (They're banned from hiking trails, though.) You may meet up with mountain bikers on the fire roads, so keep your eyes peeled and stay out of their path.

This park, nestled in the Santa Cruz Mountains, is resplendent with coastal scrub and redwoods. The ocean views from higher spots are breathtaking.

Dogs can even camp at the 39 sites here. Sites are $12 to $16. Dogs are $1 extra. The day-use fee is $5 if you park inside the park. Dogs are $1 extra. Butano is located five miles south of Pescadero, on Cloverdale Road, and off Highway 1 from Gazos Creek Road. (650) 879-2040 or 879-2044.

• **Pescadero State Beach** 🐾🐾🐾½ *See* ⑳ *on page 402.*

There are three entrances to this two-mile beach, and each one leads to a unique setting on the Pacific. The prime attractions at the southernmost entrance, on Highway 1 at Pescadero Road, are the small cliffs that hang over the crashing ocean. There are even a few picnic tables on the edges of the mini-cliffs for those who like lunch with a built-in thrill. Hold on to your leash!

The middle entrance, reached from the small parking lot, will lead you to a secluded and untamed rocky area. Take one of the less steep trails down and you'll find yourself in the middle of lots of rocks, rotting kelp, driftwood, and a few small tidepools. This is an eerie place to come on a very foggy day. Joe loves it here during pea-soupers.

Perch atop the vista point at this central entrance and you'll get a great view of the Pescadero Marsh Natural Preserve, just across Highway 1. You can't explore the preserve with your dog, a rule the birds and other critters who live there don't mind one bit.

The north entrance is the only one that charges a fee for use—$5 per car and $1 per dog. But many people park beside the road and walk over the sandy dunes to escape the cover charge. This is the most civilized—and mundane—entrance, with a wide beach and lots of kite fliers. Dogs must wear leashes on all parts of the beach.

The south entrance is at Pescadero Road and Highway 1. Follow the signs to the north for the other entrances. (415) 330-6300.

RESTAURANTS

Arcangeli Grocery Company: There's always fresh-baked bread here—still hot—waiting for you after a cold day at the beach. We like to buy a loaf of steaming herb-garlic bread and eat it at the picnic tables on the lawn in the back of the store. 287 Stage Road; (650) 879-0147.

PLACES TO STAY

Butano State Park: See Butano State Park on page 415 for camping information.

McKenzie House: The magnificent site of a single seaside cottage is about to become the magnificent site of several seaside cottages. They'll be New England in style (airy, spacious, and antique-filled) with fenced-in yards for your dog. The plan is for them to be staggered so guests will have privacy. At press time, the McKenzie House, which has long been a heavenly place to take a dog, had just received permits for the additional cottages. Even the original McKenzie house will be torn down to make way for these beauties. To get your name on a mailing list so you'll know when they're opening, call (408) 469-8300.

PORTOLA VALLEY

PARKS, BEACHES, AND RECREATION AREAS

• **Coal Creek Open Space Preserve** 🐾🐾🐾½ *See* ㉑ *on page 402.*

Joe loves visiting this 493-acre preserve in the winter months because of the little waterfalls that gurgle along a couple of creeks. In fact, year-round, this is one of the best of the Midpeninsula Regional Open Space District preserves for dogs, because it's generally cooler than most. The dense oak and madrone forests offer a real respite from the hot summer weather.

Banana slugs like this climate as much as dogs, so don't be surprised to see a few lurking on the trails. When Joe Dog happened upon a banana slug here, at first he looked disgusted. Then he barked at it a couple of times, and sat down and moaned at it when it didn't respond. I tugged hard on his leash to get him away, because I knew his next move would be to make a banana slug appetizer out of it.

If rolling meadows are more your dog's style, this preserve has those, too. The five miles of trails will take you through all kinds of landscapes. Let your dog choose his favorite, but make sure he's leashed.

The preserve has two entry points along Skyline Boulevard (Highway 35) in the southernmost part of the county (south of Portola Valley). One is about 1.2 miles north of Page Mill Road, at the Caltrans vista point, on the east side of the road. The other is at Skyline and Crazy Pete's Road, about two miles north of Page Mill Road, also on the east side of Skyline. This one has the closest access to the preserve, but there's only room for about three cars, and you'll need to walk down a fairly steep residential road to get to the trails. (650) 691-1200.

• **Windy Hill Open Space Preserve** 🐾🐾🐾 *See* ㉒ *on page 402.*

You can look out from the top of the first big hill you come to and see for miles all around—and though you're on the edge of the suburbs, you'll see hardly a house. This 1,130-acre preserve of the Midpeninsula Regional Open Space District has as many different terrains as it has views, including grassland ridges and lush wooded ravines with serene creeks and drippy redwoods.

There are more than three miles of trails that allow you and your leashed canine companion. But watch out for foxtails. The park is so dry that foxtails seem to proliferate all year.

Start at the Anniversary Trail, to the left of the entrance. The hike is a vigorous three-quarters of a mile uphill, and that may be enough, especially when it's baking. But you can continue down the other side of the hill and loop right, onto the Spring Ridge Trail. Near the end of this 2.5-mile path, you'll come to a wooded area with a small, very refreshing creek. This is a good place to sit a spell before heading back. These two trails are the only ones that permit pooches, so don't try your paw at any others.

Park at the lot on Highway 35 (Skyline Boulevard), 2.3 miles south of Highway 84 and five miles north of Alpine Road. You'll see the big sign for the preserve and three picnic tables. (650) 691-1200.

REDWOOD CITY

Dogs are not allowed in any of Redwood City's parks.

PLACES TO STAY

Good Nite Inn: If you and your small dog are on the road and just plain sick and tired of restaurant food, go to a grocery store, come here, and rev up your microwave. When you're done, put your leftovers in your minifridge. Then you can nuke them again for lunch tomorrow. Mmmm good. Not all the rooms come with these mini-kitchens, so if you want one, request it when you make your reservation. For some reason, you can stay only two nights here. Maybe they don't want to give the impression it's a doggy residential hotel. Rates are $43 to $60. 485 Veterans Boulevard, Redwood City, CA 94063; (650) 365-5500.

SAN BRUNO

PARKS, BEACHES, AND RECREATION AREAS

• **San Bruno Dog Exercise Area/Sandberg Field** 🐾🐾🐾🐾 🐕
See ㉓ on page 402.

This is a gem of a fenced-in park, where dogs can run their tails off—without a leash. The grass always seems to be green. There's plenty of water, pooper-scoopers galore, and benches for two-legged beasts. As an extra bonus, it has a great view of the bay. And for those who can't get enough of it while driving north on U.S. 101, there's an unparalleled view of that strange sign: "SOUTH SAN FRANCISCO—THE INDUSTRIAL CITY."

The park opened in 1989 after local dog trainer Mal Lightfoot was fined for walking his notoriously obedient dogs off leash. "I spend all my life training dogs to be good citizens, and I was treated like a criminal," says Lightfoot, who runs the San Bruno Dog Training School. "It was the last straw." It took him and dozens of other frustrated dog owners nearly two years of working with—and against—city officials to get the park of their dreams.

Some detailed directions are necessary for finding this out-of-the-way park, even for locals. From El Camino Real, take Sneath Lane west. Just past Interstate 280, turn right on Rollingwood Drive. Go right again at the first possible right, Crestwood Drive. Go left on Valleywood Drive and take a sharp right at Evergreen Drive. The park is in a few blocks, at Maywood and Evergreen Drives in back of the old Carl Sandburg School. Once at the school driveway, take the first road to the right and drive until you see the dog park. (650) 877-8868.

• **Sweeney Ridge** 🐾 🐾 🐾 ½ *See 24 on page 402.*

If your dog appreciates breathtaking vistas of the Bay Area, with a rainbow assortment of wildflowers in the foreground, this 1,000-acre park is a rare treat. But if your canine is like most, he can take or leave such a magnificent panorama.

Still, if you like stunning views and a vigorous uphill climb, take the Sneath Lane entrance. It may be toasty when you start, but bring a couple of thick wool sweaters if you plan to hike along the ridge—it's cold and often foggy up there. The furrier your dog, the more she'll take to the invigorating conditions.

The Skyline College entrance is ideal if you want a more moderate grade, but both trailheads will take you to the same place. The leash law here can come in handy if your dog is of the pulling mentality. Just say "mush" on those steep slopes.

From different parts of the ridge, you'll be able to see the ocean (and the Farallon Islands, on a good day), as well as Mount Tamalpais in Marin, Mount Diablo to the east, and Montara Mountain to the south. Judging by all the canines with flaring nostrils, the scents from all four directions must be as enticing as the views.

For the Sneath Lane entrance, take San Bruno's Sneath Lane all the way to the end. There's usually plenty of parking. The Skyline College entrance, off College Drive, is in the southeast corner of campus, near Lot 2. (415) 556-8371.

SAN CARLOS

PARKS, BEACHES, AND RECREATION AREAS

• **Heather Park** 🐾 🐾 🐾 ½ 🐕 *See 25 on page 402.*

This is one of the few fenced-in dog parks we've ever seen that comes complete with rolling hills, wildflowers, old gnarled trees, and singing birds. Your dog will have the time of his life here, bounding up and down hills or trotting down the winding paved path to the bottom of the park—sans leash. You may be tempted to take some of the tiny dirt trails up the steep hills, but they tend to end abruptly, leaving you and your dog teetering precariously. The only thing the park lacks is water, usually a given at dog parks.

If you have a dog who likes to wander, watch out: There are a couple of potential escape routes near the two gates at the far ends of the park. Apparently, some dog people have not been scooping the poop as they should be, and the city of San Carlos is trying to get them to clean up their act. The city is publicizing the problem to increase public awareness, and is also increasing enforcement. They sent us a fax with the poop on scooping.

Please, folks, it's not a fun job, but you've gotta do it.

The park is at Melendy and Portofino Drives. (650) 593-8011.

• **Pulgas Ridge Open Space Preserve** 🐾 🐾 🐾 🐾 🦮
   See ㉖ on page 402.

Dogs were happy when the Midpeninsula Regional Open Space District opened this 293-acre preserve to leashed pooches a few years back. But now that 16 acres in the middle of the preserve has been designated okay for leash-free dogs, dogs are downright delirious. In fact, Joe did a somersault when we checked out the leash-free area, but I think that was actually because he tripped on my foot.

The off-leash area is only for dogs under excellent voice control. That's always the case in off-leash, unenclosed areas, but it's particularly important here because of wildlife—and because of some vociferous folks who would love nothing better than to see leashes be mandatory here again. You know, *those* kind of people. The off-leash area is oak woodland and grassland, so dogs can explore a variety of landscapes. It's located in the middle of the preserve, and accessible via the Blue Oak Trail or the Cordilleras Trail.

Leashed dogs can explore the rest of this fairly flat, oak-chaparral area via three miles of trails that wind throughout. The best time to visit is in the spring, when the wildflowers come to life everywhere.

During your hike, you might see what you think looks like remnants of buildings. You'd be right. The preserve is on land that was once the site of the Hassler Health Home, a tuberculosis sanatorium owned by San Francisco. In the 1980s, the district bought the land and demolished the sanatorium, but you can still see rock retaining walls and steps here and there. Humans like this kind of trivia. Dogs could give a bark.

Exit Interstate 280 at Edgewood Road and drive east almost a mile. Turn left at Crestview Drive and make an immediate left onto Edmonds Road. You'll see signs for the preserve. There's limited roadside parking here, but it's usually enough. (650) 691-1200.

RESTAURANTS

Cafe La Tosca: Dogs sing the praises of this lovely Italian cafe. Dine on tasty pastas and a sumptuous risotto at the two outdoor tables. 777 Laurel Street; (650) 592-7749.

Coffee Club Two: Lots of dogs come here with their owners for a sip of coffee and a pastry on weekend mornings, sitting in any of several chairs outdoors. There's heavy socializing among dog people. 749 Laurel Street; (650) 592-9888.

SAN GREGORIO

PARKS, BEACHES, AND RECREATION AREAS

• **Pomponio State Beach** 🐾 🐾 *See ㉗ on page 402.*

This 1.5-mile beach is fine for sunbathing, but you can also go surf fishing for striped bass, search for driftwood, or walk to the south end of the beach and watch nesting ravens along the craggy bluffs. Dogs must be leashed, but they seem to feel right at home here. One of Joe's favorite pastimes is picking up long pieces of driftwood and "accidentally" tripping whoever is walking him as he trots merrily along. There's a $5 fee per car. Dogs are $1 extra.

The beach is on Highway 1, just south of San Gregorio State Beach. (415) 330-6464.

• **San Gregorio State Beach** 🐾 🐾 *See* **28** *on page 402.*

This place is usually a little too crowded with families for a comfortable dog walk—even a leashed one, which is the rule. It's sometimes just too difficult to negotiate through all the barbecuers, sunbathers, children, and sand castles. The beach is so popular in part because of a lagoon that often forms at the mouth of San Gregorio Creek. The still water is an ideal depth for children, but dogs tend to enjoy wading through, too. Watch out for crumbling cliffs above. And don't forget that if you park in the lot, there's a $5 entry fee, plus $1 per dog.

It's on Highway 1 just south of Highway 84. (415) 330-6464.

SAN MATEO

PARKS, BEACHES, AND RECREATION AREAS

• **Bayside-Joinville Park** 🐾 🐾 *See* **29** *on page 402.*

Human olfactory senses may be mildly offended by the scents in this park, but dogs seem to thrive on them. Depending on which way the wind is blowing, the odor is bound to hit you at some point. It's a stale smell, like a dishrag that's still in the sink a week after Thanksgiving. Sometimes it's even worse. The alleged culprit is an old compost site across the street, where Shoreline Park will be built in the future. When it's potent, Joe stands nose to the wind, tail trembling, glued in homage.

But the park has some notable qualities. It's just across the street from San Francisco Bay, it's on the Marina Lagoon (sorry, no swimming allowed), and it's well maintained.

The park has two sections. If you're the type who likes the bad news first, start at the Anchor Road entrance and take the path along the lagoon, over a guano-covered footbridge, past the big gray pump station, and onto a little dirt path on the edge of the lagoon. Then go left and take the second, cleaner footbridge over to the better half of the park. It's got a decent-sized field, young trees, and tennis courts. Or you can enter at Kehoe Avenue and Roberta Drive and reverse the path. (650) 377-4640.

• **Beresford Park** 🐾 🐾 *See* **30** *on page 402.*

The bulk of this park is made up of sports fields. But venture behind the garden center and you and your pooch can enjoy a pleasant little leashed romp on a large grassy field. A dozen or so adolescent pine trees are trying to grow despite dozens of daily assaults from male dogs. Several picnic tables and a children's play area near the field make this an adequate spot for a weekend afternoon with the family. People are friendly here—we were twice offered soda and beer by locals, who wanted Joe to "hang" with them.

The park is on Parkside Way at Alameda de las Pulgas. (650) 377-4640.

• **Central Park** 🐾 🐾 🐾 *See* **31** *on page 402.*

Bring plenty of quarters if you want to fully experience this strange park on the edge of downtown. It costs a quarter to park in the underground lot; a quarter to put your finger in the pulse machine; a quarter to watch the chicken lay a plastic prize egg; a quarter for the Pen Vendorama; it even costs a quarter for a cup of water at the refreshment stand, although smart shoppers know there's a water fountain within 20 feet.

As you enter the park from the Fifth Avenue side, you immediately encounter the concession stand and surrounding dispensers that rival any at state fairs. The stand has good ice cream and tolerable pizza.

The rest of the park is a lush, green, miniature version of Golden Gate Park. There's a Japanese garden, and although no dogs are allowed inside, the Japanese ambience spills outside. The days we've visited, there was always something going on at the outdoor stage in back of the recreation center. A couple of large meadows are bordered by big shady redwoods. There's even a pint-sized railroad that takes up part of a small field. Someone told us that dogs have been known to chase the cars as they chug along the track. Leashes are a must, a rule you'd be well advised to follow: The fine for loose dogs is not a quarter.

The park is on East Fifth Avenue at El Camino Real. (650) 377-4640.

• **Laurelwood Park** 🐾 🐾 🐾 *See* **32** *on page 402.*

A small, clear stream winds the length of this rural park in the suburbs. Joe won't have anything to do with the water and jumps from one side to the other without getting a toenail damp. But normal dogs delight in its fresh scents and enticing sounds. Follow the bike trail—heeding the leash law, as this is a popular spot for bikers—along the stream, and enjoy tree-covered hillsides in a virtually suburb-free environment. Only a few blocks from the Laurelwood Shopping Center, this park is an ideal getaway after a quick shopping trip. The kids can use the playground at the foot of the bike trail.

The park is at Glendora and Cedarwood Drives. (650) 377-4640.

RESTAURANTS

Borel's Deli: You have your choice of deli food or hot food here. "Order the baked, hot turkey. Get extra gravy. Then drop it so your dog can eat it," advises Joe. Dine with your pooch outside at two tables. 99 Bovet Road; (650) 573-7710.

Max's Bakery & Kitchen: You and your pooch can dine on good sweets and soups at several outdoor tables. 111 Fourth Avenue; (650) 344-1997.

The Patio Cafe: Many people bring their pooches here and eat at the outdoor area. They serve tasty hot meals, as well as many kinds of sandwiches. There's also a decent salad bar. 1 Lagoon Drive; (650) 595-0700.

PLACES TO STAY

Residence Inn by Marriott: There's a walking path not far from here, so it's a good place to stay with your pooch. Besides, it's a comfy lodging—not quite home, but it tries to come close. Rates are $159 to $179. Dogs are $10 extra, plus a $75 fee per visit. 2000 Winward Way, San Mateo, CA 94404; (650) 574-4700.

Villa Quality Hotel: Rates are $89 to $99. Dogs require a $50 deposit. 4000 South El Camino Real, San Mateo, CA 94403; (650) 341-0966.

DOGGY DAYS

Get Spooky: Every Halloween, a few dozen dogs (and cats, the party poopers) get dressed up in their favorite costumes and head for the costume contest at the pet supply store Togs for Dogs and Cats Too! The contest brings the usual jokers, princesses, and ghosts, but sometimes it attracts particularly creative dogs. One recent popular participant was a wolf-husky mix dressed in a sheep costume and a wool scarf. Get it? He was a wolf in sheep's clothing. Most dogs didn't understand the literary reference, but the humans got a kick out of it.

Any dog who shows up in costume gets a free bag of treats. The winner gets dog food for a year (unless the winner is a cat, but we don't like to think about those things).

The contest is usually held the Saturday before Halloween. If you don't happen to have a dog costume, Togs for Dogs stocks quite a supply. 24 West 41st Avenue; (650) 574-5364.

SOUTH SAN FRANCISCO

PARKS, BEACHES, AND RECREATION AREAS

• **Orange Memorial Park** 🐾 🐾 *See* ㉝ *on page 402.*
Hidden behind the park's large baseball field is a big square of land surrounded on all sides by tall trees. It's good for a quick on-leash romp. There seem to be all kinds of sniffs around the large weeping willow tree in the middle of the field.

It's on Orange Avenue at Tennis Drive. (650) 877-8560.

• **Westborough Park** 🐾 🐾 *See* ㉞ *on page 402.*
This is a hilly little park with many picnic tables, a tennis court, and a children's playground. Your best bet is to take the narrow, paved path along the back of the park. It's lined with trees and far from the madding baseball field below. Leashes are required.

It's on Westborough Avenue at Galway Drive, just west of Interstate 280. (650) 877-8560.

PLACES TO STAY

La Quinta Motor Inn: Rates are $85 to $109. 20 Airport Boulevard, South San Francisco, CA 94080; (650) 583-2223.

Ramada Inn San Francisco International: Rates at this attractive hotel are $89 to $189. Dogs have to be under 40 pounds to stay here, and they require a $100 deposit. 245 South Airport Boulevard, South San Francisco, CA 94080; (650) 589-7200.

WOODSIDE

PARKS, BEACHES, AND RECREATION AREAS

• **Thornewood Open Space Preserve** 🐾 🐾 🐾 *See* ㉟ *on page 402.*
This 141-acre preserve is a former estate, and the views of the valley

from parts of this land are magnificent. Dogs can peruse the preserve on leash. Thornewood is the smallest of the Midpeninsula Regional Open Space District's preserves, but dogs dig the one-mile trail that runs through the oak woodland, chaparral, and redwoods here.

Dogs have to stay away from Schilling Pond because swans call it home, and dogs and swans don't mix. In fact, although the pond is almost entirely surrounded by dense vegetation, rangers have spotted dogs swimming after these beautiful birds. If this happens very much, the entire preserve could be off-limits to all dogs, so let's be careful out there.

From Interstate 280, exit at Highway 84/Woodside Road and drive west into the hills, about five miles. The road will make several sharp turns, but keep following Highway 84. Go left at the narrow, signed driveway. It winds through the woods for a third of a mile before reaching the small parking lot on the west side of the driveway. (650) 691-1200.

RESTAURANTS

Alice's Restaurant: You can get almost anything you want at this restaurant, including a table for you and your dog on the large porch. Weekends here are packed with bikers, especially for Alice's colossal breakfasts. If your dog rides in your motorcycle sidecar, this is the place for you. It's at 17288 Skyline Boulevard, on the corner of Highways 35 and 84, just two miles north of Portola Valley's Windy Hill Open Space Preserve; (650) 851-0303.

King's Mountain Country Store: This store has everything from candles and books to dog food, crafts, and camping items. There's even a deli. Classical music plays almost all the time. You and your dog can grab a sandwich and sit at an outside table. 13100 Skyline Boulevard, adjacent to Purisima Creek Open Space Preserve (where no dogs are allowed); (650) 851-3852.

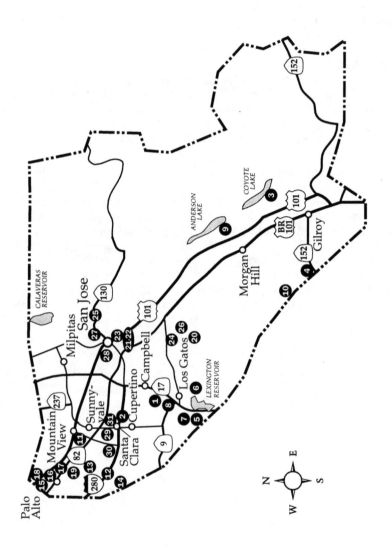

37
SANTA CLARA COUNTY

While some parts of Santa Clara County are quite scenic, dogs have to face the facts: The place still revolves around Silicon Valley, and it's not a pretty sight. Cookie-cutter duplexes and town houses abound. So do suburban-style office buildings, strip shopping centers, and low-lying metal warehouses. Even dogs with questionable taste wince.

But if you get your dog out of the more populated areas and into the quieter county parks, you'll scarcely know you're in the middle of a megabyting, microchipping mecca. Some of the larger, wilder county parks may put your dog back in touch with the wolf inside herself. One dog we met on a trail at Mount Madonna County Park was sitting and howling every few hundred feet. Her person said she was just happy to be there. Joe Dog thought maybe the dog was just saying "get this leash off me!"

Leashes are the law wherever dogs are allowed in county-run parks, with one sparkling new exception: the Shadowbluff Dog Run area at Coyote-Hellyer County Park (see page 439). Dogs are keeping their paws crossed that the county's movers and shakers see the dire need for more of these leash-free havens before the next edition of this book.

A few other off-leash parks keep dogs from going out of their minds. Palo Alto has three, and Sunnyvale and Santa Clara each have one. Mountain View has several that are open to leashless dogs who have special permits.

The Midpeninsula Regional Open Space District has become one of dogs' best friends of late, with the addition in Santa Clara County of one more preserve open to leashed dogs (see Sierra Azul, page 430). That makes three dog-friendly open space preserves in the county. The district has unique rules about poop scooping and six-foot leashes. See the introduction to the San Mateo County chapter on page 401 for more on these rules.

The district even offers very cool canine walks in conjunction with the Palo Alto Humane Society. The hikes, called Dog Days Walks & Hikes, are about two hours, and they're usually leisurely, although you can end up covering from three to five miles. It's a great way to meet dogs and their people. Pooper-scoopers are provided, but you have to do the scooping. Bring a leash and water for your pooch. For more information, or to make reservations, call the district at (650) 691-1200, or the Palo Alto Humane Society at (650) 327-0631. (The Humane Society also offers easy hikes in other parklands about once a month. Call for a schedule.)

An exceptional group called Peninsula Access for Dogs (PAD) is working to improve park life for dogs here. For information, write to PAD at 809-B Cuesta Drive, Box 196, Mountain View, CA 94094, or check out PAD's Web site: www.rahul.net/pruski/pads. So far they've been very effective in getting dogs into open space preserves here and in San Mateo County.

As if all this doggy good news weren't enough, Joe (aka "I adore manure") Dog wants to let you know that dogs are allowed at a glorious farm in Los Altos Hills (see Diversions, page 429). Joe becomes Old Farm Dog when we visit, especially when we're near the livestock. His whole demeanor, from his ecstatically sniffing schnoz to his competent swagger seems to say "I may be leashed, but at least I'm not fenced in." (The whole time he's thinking this, he's also praying a cow doesn't escape and find him at nearby Sunnyvale's fenced dog run.) Check it out if you and your pooch want to discover your agricultural roots.

CAMPBELL

PARKS, BEACHES, AND RECREATION AREAS

• **Los Gatos Creek County Park** 🐾 🐾 1/2 *See* ❶ *on page 424.*

Here your leashed dog can romp on grass, have a picnic with you in the shade of Los Gatos Creek's medium-sized trees, and watch ducks and geese in the percolation ponds of Los Gatos Creek, which are good for fishing. Dogs like Joe, who would ruffle duck and geese feathers with his barking, should be kept away from these critters. The Los Gatos Creek Trail runs through here, should you care to take a jaunt.

From Highway 17, exit at Camden Avenue; go west on San Tomas Expressway, south on Winchester Boulevard, and left on Hacienda Avenue to the park. A $4 parking fee is charged in summer and on weekends and holidays. (408) 356-2729.

RESTAURANTS

Orchard Valley Coffee: Enjoy coffee, snacks, and pastries, and nighttime live music, at one of five tables right on the sidewalk at this dog-friendly place. 349 East Campbell Avenue; (408) 374-2115.

PLACES TO STAY

Campbell Inn: Rates are $99 to $185. Dogs are $10 extra. 675 East Campbell Avenue, Campbell, CA 95008; (408) 374-4300.

Residence Inn by Marriott: This is a convenient, comfortable place to stay when traveling with a dog. Residence Inns only have suites and apartments, and they all come with kitchens. Rates are $149 to $189. Extended stays get a discounted rate. Dogs have to pay a $75 cleaning fee, plus $10 per night. 2761 South Bascom Avenue, Campbell, CA 95008; (408) 559-1551.

DIVERSIONS

You doity dog: Even if your dog hates a bath more than anything, he'll surely like it a bit better if it's you working him over and not some stranger. Shampoo Chez (pronounced "Shampoochers") is a wash-him-yourself dog grooming establishment with two branches in the Bay Area.

The current owners say they've hosted about a zillion self-service washes since they began. That's a lot of shampoo and fleas down the drain. A shampoo for any size dog is $10 for 30 minutes of wash time and an additional $1 for each five minutes after that. 523 East Campbell Avenue. (408) 379-WASH.

CUPERTINO

PARKS, BEACHES, AND RECREATION AREAS

• **Fremont Older Open Space Preserve** 🐾🐾🐾 *See* ❷ *on page 424.*

This 739-acre preserve smells sweet and clean, but that doesn't disappoint dogs. Pooches have enough trees and ground-level odors to keep them happily trotting along on their mandatory leashes.

Once you park in the small lot, you'll walk several hundred feet on a paved roadway, but be sure to turn right at the first sign for hikers. Otherwise you'll find yourself in the middle of a bicycle freeway. The narrow dirt trail to the right takes you on a three-mile loop through cool woodlands and rolling open hills up to Hunters Point via the Seven Springs Loop Trail. The view of Santa Clara Valley from the top of the 900-foot hill is incomparable. More trails may be open soon, so your dog's feet will be able to explore as never before.

Signs at the entrance warn of ticks, so be sure to give your dog (and yourself) a thorough inspection after your hike.

From U.S. 101 or Interstate 280, take Highway 85 (Saratoga-Sunnyvale Road) south to Prospect Road. Turn right and follow the road to the park entrance. (650) 691-1200.

GILROY

PARKS, BEACHES, AND RECREATION AREAS

• **Coyote Lake Park** 🐾🐾🐾 *See* ❸ *on page 424.*

This county park is full of wildlife no matter how high or low the lake. In fact, when we last visited, we saw foxes, wild turkeys, and a grazing deer— and there wasn't a drop of water in the reservoir. The reservoir had been bone dry for so long that it looked like an enormous open field. Brush and a few trees were starting to emerge from the hard, dry ground.

When it's in this drought condition, the lake bed is a favorite stomping ground for leashed canines—who are usually relegated to picnic areas, the campground, and the one-mile trail connecting them.

The campsites are roomy, and several are shaded by large oak trees. Others look out on the lake—or field, depending on the water level. We like to visit the nearby picnic areas after stopping at one of Gilroy's garlic stores for lunch supplies. Joe has a penchant for garlic-flavored pistachios.

There are 74 sites here, and they're $10, plus $1 for a dog. Phone (408) 358-3751 for reservations. The day-use fee is $4. From U.S. 101, exit at Leavesley Road and follow the signs to the park. (408) 842-7800.

• **Mount Madonna County Park** 🐾🐾🐾½ *See ❹ on page 424.*

This magnificent park is midway between Gilroy and Watsonville (in Santa Cruz County). No matter where you're coming from, it's worth the drive. The mountain, covered with mixed conifers, oak, madrone, and bay and sword ferns, is wonderfully quiet and cool—which is especially appreciated by San Jose dwellers, whose parks are almost never far from the roar of freeways. You may hear the screech of jays and little else.

Try driving on Valley View Road (to the right from the ranger station) to the Giant Twins Trail, where you can park in the shady campsite of the same name—at least when no one is camping there. (When we were there on a perfect Indian summer day in late September, the park was deserted.) Two huge old redwoods, green with lichen, give the trail its name. After half a mile, the trail becomes Sprig Lake Trail and continues for another two miles. Sprig Lake, really a pond, is empty in summer, but in spring it's stocked for children's fishing.

This walk isn't much of a strain. If you'd like more exercise, there are plenty of longer and steeper trails—18 miles in all, and as of this writing, your dog may enjoy every one of them. From the Redwood Trail or the Blackhawk Canyon Trail, you'll be rewarded with views of the Santa Clara Valley, the Salinas Valley, and Monterey Bay. For a walk almost completely around the park, try the Merry-Go-Round Trail.

The park's deer are only one of many reasons you should keep your dog securely leashed, tempting as it might be to let her off. "Dogs have instincts," a friendly ranger said.

Your dog might enjoy a camping vacation here. There are 113 large, private campsites available on a first-come, first-served basis. Sites are $10 to $20 per night, plus $1 for each dog. A $4 day-use fee is always charged on weekends and daily from Memorial Day through Labor Day.

From U.S. 101, exit at Highway 152 west to Gilroy. Continue on 152 (Hecker Pass Highway) through part of the park. The entrance is a right (north) turn at Pole Line Road. Call (408) 842-2341 for park and campground information.

PLACES TO STAY

Comfort Inn: Rates are $55 to $69. Pooches are $5 extra and can stay only at the management's discretion. 8292 Murray Avenue, Gilroy, CA 95020; (408) 848-3500.

Coyote Lake Park: See Coyote Lake Park on page 427 for camping information.

Leavesley Inn: Rates are $50 to $73. Dogs are charged a $10 fee per visit. 8430 Murray Avenue, Gilroy, CA 95020; (408) 847-5500.

Mount Madonna County Park: See Mount Madonna County Park on page 428 for camping information.

LOS ALTOS

Los Altos, like Saratoga and Los Gatos, is a clean town with civic pride, great for strolling. The hand-painted benches and spotless lawns look as if no dog has ever passed through, but in fact dogs are here in force. They're just mannerly.

RESTAURANTS

The Cookie Cafe & Bakery: Grab a cookie for each of you while exploring downtown. 133 Main Street; (415) 949-2521.

Italian Delicatessen: Drop by for great salami smells. Better yet, order one of the delicious specialty sandwiches and dine at the outdoor tables with your pooch. If you have a drop of Italian blood in you, The Godfather sandwich, which is loaded with mortadella, prosciutto, provolone, and lots of other great Italian ingredients, will make you drool. (But you can blame the drool on your dog.) 137 Main Street; (415) 948-6745.

Los Altos Bar & Grill: Here's a sports lover's eatery serving grilled meats, fish, pasta, and heavy-duty desserts (chocolate is the magic word) at five tables on the front patio. Last time we visited, two happy dogs were munching on bites of burgers at the feet of their people. 169 Main Street; (415) 948-4332.

DOGGY DAYS

Walk with the animals: Here's a tradition that has lasted for more than 48 years, and you can understand why. Any and all pets are welcome at the Los Altos Pet Parade, sponsored by the Kiwanis Club. Attending, many in costume, are llamas, horses, hamsters, cats, and dogs. One year Little Red Riding Hood came, with her dog as the Big Bad Wolf. "Everyone in town comes downtown early to get a seat," said a local restaurant owner. Held annually in May, the Saturday after Mother's Day. For information, call city hall at (650) 948-1491 for the number for the current Kiwanis contact.

LOS ALTOS HILLS

DIVERSIONS

Make Maggie an aggy: Dogs and farms belong together. Witness all the happy dogs in James Herriott's stories, or in the movie *Babe,* or in countless other works. "But," you say, "MY dog's a city/suburban dog. Alas, no farm life for her." Before you chuck your overalls, check out Hidden Villa Farm, where a dog (on leash) can sniff out all the earthy, cow patty delights of farm life.

This beautiful 1,600-acre organic farm and wilderness preserve is just what the doctor ordered for city-weary dogs and their people. Kids and adults can take part in all kinds of hands-on activities, but pooches have to pretty much stick to perusing the paths around the pastures and barns. They won't get to roll in any of the smells they revel in, but just getting to sniff the air and see the livestock usually makes their day, week, or year. Make sure you keep a good hold of her leash, and don't forget to scoop the poop (your dog's, not the sheep's, cow's, horse's, etc.).

Dogs aren't allowed on the wilderness trails that branch out from the farm center, and, like people, they're not allowed in the animal pens. 26870 Moody Road; (650) 949-8660.

LOS GATOS

Dogs like Los Gatos but think it needs a name change. Joe suggests "Los Perros."

PARKS, BEACHES, AND RECREATION AREAS

• **Lexington Reservoir County Park** 🐾 🐾 *See* ❺ *on page 424.*

When the reservoir is full, this park is full of life. Birds sing and the foliage is bright green. But in drought years, everything here—trees, grass, brush—is covered with silt. This death mask must frighten birds away to better nesting areas, because it's utterly silent, except for a few cars kicking up dust on a nearby road.

It can really bake during summer months, too. And since there's no swimming allowed, dogs get miserable fast. (To cool himself off here, Joe rolled on the dusty ground until his entire body was coated with ash-colored silt. He looked like some kind of moving statue on a mandatory leash.)

Exit Highway 17 at Montevina Road and drive east a quarter of a mile. You can stop at any of several parking areas along the road. There is no entrance fee, except for the Miller Picnic Site, where you'll pay $4. (408) 358-3741.

• **Sierra Azul Open Space Preserve (Kennedy-Limekiln area)** 🐾 🐾 🐾
See ❻ *on page 424.*

The wildlife at this 5,000-acre preserve has it pretty good. There's so much steep, rugged terrain and dense chaparral that humans and their leashed doggy interlopers are pretty much forced to stay on the trails, out of critters' ways. Unfortunately for dogs and their people, mountain bikes seem to be everywhere on these trails, and they can go really fast. So on weekends especially, keep your eyes and ears peeled and be ready to dodge the traffic.

This is not a park for the fair of paw. A hike to the 2,000-foot ridgetop can make even the most fit dog sweat. But the views from here or from the 1,700-foot Priest Rock are worth a little panting, at least on your part. Take it easy on your dog, though, and don't let him pant too much. It can get very, very hot here in the summer, and there's virtually no decent shade. The folks at the Midpeninsula Regional Open Space District beg you not to take your pooch here on summer afternoons.

Parking here is a real problem. More on that in the next paragraph, but if you visit on a busy day, have a contingency plan in case you don't get one of the coveted spaces. Also note that the two other sections of the Sierra Azul Preserve (Cathedral Oaks and Mount Umunhum) don't permit pooches.

From Highway 85, exit at Los Gatos Boulevard and drive west a little more than two miles. At Kennedy Road, turn left and follow the road about two more miles to the parking spot at the trailhead. There's currently room for only two cars here. This is utterly inadequate, and the district is working to do something about this. In the meantime, there's room for about seven cars across Kennedy, on Top of the Hill Road. Please be considerate of the residents here, and keep noise to a minimum and don't litter. (650) 691-1200.

• **St. Joseph's Hill Open Space Preserve** 🐾 🐾 🐾 1/2
  See ❼ on page 424.
  Want a quick escape from urbanity? Visit this scenic, 173-acre preserve with your leashed pooch. Dogs are allowed on all four miles of trails here, but beware, it can get steep. The trails wind through oak woodlands and open grassland, and at the top of the 1,250-foot St. Joseph's Hill, you'll get magnificent views of the surrounding parklands. Joe loves to sit here and let his nostrils flare.

  From Highway 17, take the Alma Bridge Road exit and go across the dam. Public parking is available at Lexington Reservoir County Park. The trail to St. Joseph's Hill starts opposite the boat launching area at the north end of the reservoir. (650) 691-1200.

• **Vasona Lake County Park** 🐾 🐾 🐾 *See ❽ on page 424.*
  This is a perfectly manicured park, with grass like that of a golf course. Dogs find it tailor-made for rolling, although they tend to get tangled in their leashes—which the county demands they wear here.

  Several pathways take you through this 151-acre park and down to the lake's edge. But no swimming is allowed. And dogs aren't allowed to visit the children's playground either. You can picnic in the shade of one of the large willows or lead your dog up to the groves of pines and firs for a relief session.

  From Highway 17, take Highway 9 (Saratoga-Los Gatos Road) west to University Avenue. Go right and continue to Blossom Hill Road. The park will be on your left. Enter at Garden Hill Drive. The parking fee is $4. (408) 356-2729.

RESTAURANTS

Classic Burgers of Los Gatos: This dog-friendly eatery has fine burgers. Dogs drool over them at the four tables on the patio. And they don't just serve hamburgers. "We have everything, even peanut butter and jelly," says one staffer. 15737 Los Gatos Boulevard; (408) 356-6910.

Dolce Spazio Gelato: On warm days, this is the place to come. The homemade gelato is creamy and delicious. When there's a chill in the air, try something from the cafe's espresso bar. The good-sized patio has heat lamps, which helps dogs and their people cozy up to a winter visit. 221 North Santa Cruz Avenue; (408) 395-1335.

MILPITAS

PLACES TO STAY

Best Western Brookside Inn: Rates are $79 to $129. Dogs are $10 extra, and it's requested that they not weigh more than 20 pounds. (Instead of putting your paunchy pooch on a crash diet, try Economy Inns.) 400 Valley Way, Milpitas, CA 95035; (408) 263-5566.

Economy Inns of America: Rates are $64 to $99. 270 South Abbott Avenue, Milpitas, CA 95035; (408) 946-8889.

MORGAN HILL

PARKS, BEACHES, AND RECREATION AREAS

• **Anderson Lake County Park** 🐾🐾½ *See ❾ on page 424.*

When there's enough water to keep the reservoir open to the public, dogs love to go along on fishing trips. But when it's low, dogs take solace in dipping their paws in the shady, secluded stream that runs between picnic areas. Call the rangers to find out if the reservoir is open, because if it isn't, it may not be worth a trip. You can't get anywhere near the lake if it's too low.

The only trail connects picnic areas, and it isn't even a half-mile long. There are plenty of picnic tables with lots of shade, but dogs tend to get bored unless hunks of hamburger happen to fall from the grills. The picnic areas can be rowdy, with lots of beer and loud music, so if your dog doesn't like rap, take him somewhere else.

From U.S. 101, follow Cochrane Road east to the park. (408) 779-3634.

• **Uvas Canyon County Park** 🐾🐾🐾½ *See ❿ on page 424.*

In the past, there was a lot of confusion about which trails in this park allowed dogs. Happily, the Santa Clara County parks department decided in 1992 to open all the trails to leashed dogs. You can get a map when you drive through the entrance kiosk.

This is a pretty, clean park of oak, madrone, and Douglas fir trees in cool canyons. The Uvas Creek Trail is a favorite trail. Dogs always appreciate a creek on a warm summer day, and this one doesn't dry up in hot weather. You might also try the wide, dirt Alec Canyon Trail, 1.5 miles long, within sight of Alec Creek, or the Nature Trail Loop, about one mile long, beside Swanson Creek. You may see some waterfalls in late winter and early spring.

Dogs are allowed in the campgrounds and picnic areas of Uvas Canyon. The park has 25 campsites, available on a first-come, first-served basis, for $10 a night. Dogs are $1 extra. The campground is open daily from April 15 to October 31, and Fridays and Saturdays from November through March. It's crowded on weekends during late spring and summer, so arrive early or camp during the week.

From U.S. 101, exit at Cochrane Road; go south on Business 101 to Watsonville Road, then right (west) on Watsonville to McKean-Uvas Road. Turn right on Uvas (past Uvas Reservoir) to Croy Road. Go left on Croy to the park. The last four miles on Croy are fairly tortuous. (408) 779-9232.

PLACES TO STAY

Best Western Country Inn: Rates are $65 to $85. Dogs are allowed in smoking rooms only. 16525 Condit Road, Morgan Hill, CA 95037; (408) 779-0447.

Uvas Canyon County Park: See Uvas Canyon County Park on page 432 for camping information.

MOUNTAIN VIEW

PARKS, BEACHES, AND RECREATION AREAS

At press time, the city was having workshops and public meetings about the possibility of a leash-free park here. (Currently the only way for a dog to be off leash is to get a training permit.) The city's community services department was doing most of the research on how dog parks work, so that's a sign that good things will soon happen here! For updates, call (650) 903-6331.

•**Rengstorff Park** 🐾 🐾 🐕 **(with permit)** *See ⑪ on page 424.*

This park is typically neat, green, and interesting for people, and it has another excellent feature: A sign reads "Dogs must be on leash (except by permit)." This means that you can get a permit from the city that allows you to train a dog off leash, with the understanding that he'll be under control. Be forewarned, though: If you don't bring the permit along with you when training, you will be ticketed.

Rengstorff Park is at Rengstorff Avenue between California Street and Central Expressway. Call for details on getting a permit. (650) 903-6331.

RESTAURANTS

Blue Sky Cafe: This is a popular neighborhood restaurant in a small house with outdoor tables. Ingredients are strictly fresh, with vegetarian dishes a specialty. Dogs are happy to know that meat is served, too. The owners will be glad to seat your dog on the sidewalk just next to the outside tables. 336 Bryant Street; (650) 961-2082.

PLACES TO STAY

Best Western Tropicana Lodge: Rates are $80 to $100. 1720 West El Camino Real, Mountain View, CA 94040; (650) 961-0220.

Residence Inn by Marriott: You and your dog will feel right at home at the suites at this attractive hotel. They have kitchens and lots of other extras you won't find in a regular hotel. But better than that is the very dog-friendly attitude here. "We take all pets, from snakes to rabbits. We see them as part of the family, and try to accommodate the owners' needs," one manager told us. The place even has a little fenced area for exercising dogs, and staff is happy to point you to nearby trails.

There's a $50 to $75 doggy fee per visit, so it's best to stay for a while to get the most bang for your buck. Dogs are $10 extra per night. Rates are $160 to $229. 1854 West El Camino Real, Mountain View, CA 94040; (650) 940-1300.

PALO ALTO

For dogs, this town is the county's garden spot. Here, you'll find lots of other dog lovers and well-behaved dogs, enticing city parks—all of which allow dogs—and no fewer than three leash-free dog runs. At the Baylands, you and your leashed dog can watch birds and get a good workout at the same time. And many student-oriented restaurants with outdoor seating welcome your dog. If you're lucky enough to have a Palo Alto address, or a friend with one, you may bring your dog to the glorious Foothills Park on weekdays.

The Palo Alto Humane Society offers a wonderful way to perambulate with your pooch. Twice a month, you can join dogs and their people for "Dog Days Walks & Hikes." The leashed hikes at some of the area's more scenic parks provide plenty of exercise for everyone, but beyond that, they're great fun. Joe, Nisha, and I met some enchanting dogs and people on a Dog Days Hike we took. Among them was a couple with five greyhounds and borzois. The man and woman met at Cipriani Park in Belmont (see page 404) with all their dogs, fell in love, married, and combined their doggy households to live—and scoop—happily every after.

The hikes are usually held on Saturday afternoons. Reservations are required. A $5 donation is requested, but members go for free. A little bag of doggy goodies, including a bandanna while supplies last, is included in the price. Contact the Humane Society at (650) 327-0631 for a schedule or for more information.

PARKS, BEACHES, AND RECREATION AREAS

• **Arastradero Preserve** 🐾 🐾 🐾½ See **12** on page 424.

With 613 acres of rolling savanna grassland and broadleaf evergreen forest, Arastradero Preserve is one of the more peaceful and attractive parks in the area. Dogs dig it, but they have to be leashed. It's a good rule, because mountain lions, rattlesnakes, poison oak, and coyotes can be part of the scene here. And so can bikers.

Anglers are right at home in the preserve. A hike to Arastradero Lake takes only about 20 minutes from the main parking lot, and the fishing can be very good. (Sorry, no swimming, boats, or flotation devices.)

There are 6.25 miles of hiking trails. Joe Dog enjoys the hilly 2.8-mile Acorn Trail when he's in the mood to pant. Bring plenty of water; it can get toasty here.

From Interstate 280, exit at Page Mill Road and go south. Turn right (west) on Arastradero Road (Refuge Road on some maps) and drive into the parking lot. (650) 329-2423.

• **Esther Clark Park** 🐾 🐾 🐾 See **13** on page 424.

This is a beautiful piece of undeveloped land with some dirt paths, right on the border of Los Altos Hills. There are no facilities but plenty of meadow and eucalyptus trees. A creek bed promises water in the wet season.

Where Old Adobe Road bends to the left and makes a cul-de-sac, the park is the undeveloped land on your right. (650) 329-2423.

• **Foothills Park** 🐾 🐾 🐾½ See **14** on page 424.

To use this park, privately owned by the city of Palo Alto, you must prove you're a resident or be the guest of one. Dogs are allowed only on weekdays (no holidays, though) and must be on leash, but they can go on all the trails.

The park has a large lake surrounded by unspoiled foothills, plus 15 miles of hiking trails of varying difficulty. At sundown, deer are plentiful. It's a beautiful sight, but be sure to keep tight hold of that leash. This park is heaven on Earth for dogs and people alike. If you don't already live in Palo Alto, it could make you consider moving.

To find Foothills Park from Interstate 280, exit at Page Mill Road and drive about 2.5 miles south. As usual, when you're searching for a really good Santa Clara County park, the road will become impossibly narrow and winding, and you'll think you're lost. But you aren't. The entry fee for Palo Alto residents is $2 per car, $1 for hikers and bicyclists. (650) 329-2423.

• **Greer Park** 🐾🐾🐾½ 🐕 *See* ⓯ *on page 424.*

This is one of Palo Alto's parks with an off-leash dog run, but it isn't the largest (see Mitchell Park, below). The park is green and pleasant, as are all the city's parks, but it's somewhat noisy because of nearby Bayshore Road. Dogs have to be leashed outside the dog run. There are athletic fields, picnic tables, and two playground areas. The dog run, near the Bayshore side, is small and treeless, but it's entirely fenced, if that's what your dog needs. Bring your own scoopers and water.

The park is at Amarillo Street and West Bayshore Road. The parking lot is off Bayshore, conveniently near the dog run. (650) 496-6950.

• **Hoover Park** 🐾🐾🐾 🐕 *See* ⓰ *on page 424.*

This park may be small, but dogs don't really care. It's home to a little-known dog run that's not as popular as the run at Mitchell Park (see below), but that's part of the charm. Dogs also dig the little stream that runs through the park.

The park is at Cowper Street between Colorado and Loma Verde Avenues. (650) 496-6950.

• **Mitchell Park** 🐾🐾🐾🐾 🐕 *See* ⓱ *on page 424.*

This generous, green park has some unusual amenities, including two human-sized chessboards and a roller-skating rink. The park is also a standout in the canine book: It has a four-paw dog run that's completely fenced and has a row of pine trees on one side, water dishes on the other, and scrappy tennis balls everywhere. When we last visited, there were a couple of beat-up old office-style chairs just waiting to be sat upon, knocked over, or at least marked by a leg-lifting varmint.

Sadly, there's been some controversy of late about the future of the dog run. It seems the run, which has been around since 1972, is irritating to some parents who feel it shouldn't be anywhere near children. At press time, it looked like the dog run would survive, but longtime users of the park say its future may be on shaky ground (and not because it's located near the San Andreas Fault).

The park itself has plenty of shade to delight a dog. Remember to leash outside the dog run. For kids, the playground area has sculptured bears for climbing and a wading pool (sorry, no dogs). The dog run is a short walk from the parking lot.

The park is on East Meadow Drive just south of Middlefield Road. (650) 496-6950.

• **Palo Alto Baylands** 🐾🐾🐾 *See* ⑱ *on page 424.*

This is the best-developed wetlands park in the Bay Area for adults, children, and dogs. It's laced with paved bike trails and levee trails. Along the pretty levee paths, benches face the mudflats. Don't forget your binoculars on a walk here. A cacophony of mewling gulls, mumbling pigeons, and clucking blackbirds fills the air. Small planes putt into the nearby airport, and your dog will love the fishy smells coming from the marshes. This seems to be a popular spot for dog exercise. Keep your pooch leashed and on the trails.

Dogs shouldn't go near the well-marked waterfowl nesting area, but they're welcome to watch children feed the noisy ducks and Canada geese in the duck pond, as long as they don't think about snacks *à l'orange.*

From U.S. 101, exit at Embarcadero Road East and go all the way to the end. At the entrance, turn left for the trails, ranger station, and duck pond. A right turn takes you to a recycling center. (650) 496-6997.

• **The Stanford Dish** 🐾🐾🐾 *See* ⑲ *on page 424.*

"The Stanford Dish" is not a park but Stanford University property surrounding the satellite dish used by the physics department. Stanford lets dog owners enjoy it, so long as dogs stay on leash and on the trails and their owners pick up after them. The hill is quite popular, with its grasslands reclaimed from cattle pasture and dotted with oaks. A reforestation project is under way, so in the future it will be even nicer. Cattle still graze on the Interstate 280 side, so there's good reason for the leash rule. A ranger patrols to enforce it.

You can park on campus across the street from the Tressider Student Union and walk up a path to Junipero Serra Boulevard. The dish property borders Junipero Serra. Don't park in the nearby residential areas. (650) 723-4311.

RESTAURANTS

Downtown Palo Alto is a walker-friendly and dog-adoring kind of place. It's full of benches and plazas for sitting, and quite a few restaurants will serve both of you out on the sidewalk or patio. Here are a few snout-licking options.

Boudin: Enjoy fine coffee and pastries here. There are about seven sidewalk tables subject to heavy foot traffic, but most of the feet will be of students who miss their dogs and want to stop and make a fuss over yours. 388 University Avenue; (650) 325-9353.

Fratelli Deli: Hungry for a quick salad, pasta, or sandwich? Pop over to Fratelli and grab a bite. Eat with your pooch at the two outdoor tables. 405 University Avenue; (650) 323-0423.

O'Connell's Eire House Restaurant and Bar: Top of the mornin' to you! Would you like a potato? Or how about one of 18 draft beers and a wee bit of Irish music to accompany it? Dogs and their people don't have to be Irish to enjoy the mood and the food at this clean, good-looking establishment (although we hear certain setters and wolfhounds get special treatment). Dine at any of several shaded outdoor tables. The restaurant is located in a pedestrian walkway between University and Hamilton Avenues and

Ramona and Bryant Streets; (650) 326-2000.

Rodger's Plaza Ramona: Snack on gourmet sandwiches and coffee. You're welcome at the relatively quiet sidewalk tables with your dog. It's on Ramona Street, off University Avenue; (650) 324-4228.

Taxi's Hamburger: Taxi's burgers are award winning (yes, there apparently are awards for hamburgers), and 100 percent beef. Just passing by makes dog drool. But you don't have to pass by. Dogs are welcome here. Many patrons of this upscale American-style grill order burgers for their dogs. When we ate here, a woman at the next table ordered a veggie sandwich and split it with her dog. Eventually, the dog got wind of what Joe was chowing down and went on a quest for meat. In the end, all she got was a piece of bun (the hamburger's, not Joe's). Dine at the dozen tables in the covered outdoor area. If your dog seems thirsty, they'll supply a bowl of water. 403 University Avenue; (650) 322-8294.

Torrefazione: All the coffees and pastries at this cafe are served in hand-painted Italian china. Dogs with a keen sense of aesthetics (such as Airedales, says Joe) appreciate this. Coffee fans love the whole-bean coffee, but I'm not even sure what that is. Doesn't sound like Taster's Choice to me, though. Sit outside the historic building that houses the cafe and dine with your dog at the two tables. 419 University Avenue; (650) 325-7731.

World Wrapps: The cooks here take anything that's delicious and slightly exotic and put it in wraps. To them, the world is a burrito, just waiting to be enveloped. We had a really good Thai wrap when we visited. Joe Dog wants to know when they're going to have a dog food wrap. The smoothies are tasty, too. Dine with doggy at the nine outdoor tables, some of which are shaded by trees. 201 University Avenue; (650) 327-9777.

PLACES TO STAY

Cardinal Hotel: Stay here and you're in the heart of downtown Palo Alto. Rates are $62 to $170. 235 Hamilton Avenue, Palo Alto, CA 94301; (650) 323-5101.

Holiday Inn—Palo Alto: Rates are $159 to $179. Dogs require a $50 deposit, and must be under 20 pounds. (That puts the itsy in itsy-bitsy.) 625 El Camino Real, Palo Alto, CA 94301; (650) 328-2800.

DOGGY DAYS

Jog that dog: The city of Palo Alto stages an annual Dog's Best Friend Run at the Palo Alto Baylands. The five-kilometer (3.1-mile) course, which you may run or walk with your leashed dog, begins and ends at the athletic center. Rules are as follows: You must have your dog on a regular six-foot leash, not a retractable one; you can't carry the dog; and she must cross the finish line before you do. (The idea of this last rule is to restrain hot-dog owners who drag their poor dogs across the finish line.) The record will show your dog's racing time, not yours. Nearly 600 dogs show up every year, yet the organizer, recreation supervisor Dave Brees, says he's never seen a dogfight in all the years he's hosted the race.

For your entry fee of $15, you get a T-shirt and the dog gets a bandanna and plenty of treats. Winners receive plaques and photos. The run takes place at the Palo Alto Baylands (see page 436) around the third week of April. Call (650) 329-2986 for this year's date.

DIVERSIONS

Shop with your best friend: You and your dog can drool over dresses and pant over pantsuits as you saunter down the corridors of the upscale Stanford Shopping Center. The huge open-air mall allows leashed, well-mannered dogs to window-shop with you and to join you for a snack at the outdoor tables here. But better yet, dogs are welcome in many of the mall's stores. We know of several that permit pooches, but since it's up to the store managers, and since managers move around a bit, we'll let you and your dog sniff out the dog-friendly places yourselves. Just poke your head in and ask a sales clerk if it's okay if your pooch comes in with you. Rest assured, this is a question they get all the time, so they won't be shocked.

The mall is on El Camino Real and University Avenue, next to Stanford University. (650) 617-8585.

SAN JOSE

We visited San Jose's downtown center hoping to find plenty of dog-friendly outdoor eateries and shopping malls, but we were disappointed. Only one mall—The Pavilion, next to the Fairmont Hotel, with an inviting array of shops and outdoor tables—looked as if it might allow dogs, but it didn't. The same went for outdoor restaurants. But a dog can drink from a fountain featuring wrought-iron fish in elegant St. James Square Park or gaze at 20 terrific pillars of water shooting from the fountain at Park Plaza. Keep your eye on the area if you have a boulevardier-type dog. Any day now, San Jose may change into his kind of place.

Dogs are welcome in most of the city's parks. Leashes are mandatory in all the parks, and there are no leash-free dog runs.

San Jose residents must enjoy most of their city parks—even the best ones—in the shadow of freeways (some literally) and under the buzz of airplanes landing at the central airport. This listing describes several of the larger, clean, green parks. Many others are undistinguished or full of litter. Call the parks department at (408) 277-4573 for more information.

PARKS, BEACHES, AND RECREATION AREAS

• **Almaden Quicksilver County Park** 🐾 🐾 🐾 ½ *See* ㉒ *on page 424.*

This rustic, 3,600-acre park allows dogs on about half of its 30 miles of trails. Some of these trails are popular for horseback riding, so watch out; although leashes are the law here, they don't always stop dogs who like to chase hooves.

In the spring, the hills explode with wildlife and wildflowers. Any of the trails will take you through a wonderland of colorful flowers and butterflies who like to tease safely leashed dogs. Speaking of insects, there's a downside to this park: Ticks seem to hang out here. "We got 20 off our dog, then three more when big welts developed," a poor San Jose resident writes. Keep your pooch in the center of trails, and the bloodsucking pests will have to go elsewhere for dinner.

Dogs are allowed on the Guadalupe Trail, the Hacienda Trail, portions of the Mine Hill Trail, the Mockingbird Picnic Area, the No Name Trail, and the Senator Mine Trail. Call the park for more information about the trails and the locations of their trailheads.

You can enter the park at several points. We prefer the main park entrance, where New Almaden Road turns into Alamitos Road, near Almaden Way. (408) 268-3883.

• **Coyote Creek Multiple-Use Trail** 🐾🐾🐾 *See ㉑ on page 424.*

When this trail is completely paved, it will furnish your dog with 13 miles of trail, if she doesn't mind sharing space with bicycles. Some pooper-scooper dispensers are being installed, too. You may take your dog, leashed, on any portion between the Hellyer County Park end and Parkway Lakes, a private fishing concession at the south end, close to Morgan Hill. (Your only reason to go there would be to pull in some of the club's stocked trout or to enter one of its fishing derbies.)

See the directions to Coyote-Hellyer County Park, below. (408) 255-0225.

• **Coyote-Hellyer County Park/Shadowbluff Dog Run** 🐾🐾🐾🐾 🐕 *See ㉒ on page 424.*

Dogs everywhere want to shake paws good and strong with the folks who worked to create the first county-run off-leash dog area, located in the east end of this 213-acre park. It took almost three years of public meetings to approve the Shadowbluff Dog Run, but patient pooches are getting their just rewards.

The dog run is one acre, enclosed by a four-foot-high chain-link fence. Dogs who have some steeplechase in them might be able to escape, but most dogs are very content to cavort around sans leash. The enclosure has just about anything a pooch could desire. There's shade from a few trees, water to slurp up, and lots of green grass. For humans, there are benches, pooper-scoopers, and garbage cans. Sounds like dogs get the better end of the deal.

Part of the reason the grass is so green is that the dog run is closed the first seven days of every month and each Monday for turf care. At those times, your best bet is to leash up and explore the rest of this park.

It's a generous, rustic park, popular with bicyclists. The best deal for dogs is the El Arroyo del Coyote Nature Trail, which by some miracle allows dogs. Walk to the left at the entrance kiosk and cross under Hellyer Avenue on the bike trail to find the entrance to the nature trail. Cross the creek on a pedestrian bridge to your right; once across, take the dirt path to your left. Bikes aren't allowed, making it all the better for dogs.

Willows and cottonwoods are luxuriant here, and in spring, poppies bloom. Eucalyptus groves provide occasional shade. Watch out for bees and poison oak. Otherwise, this is heavenly territory for your dog.

The park is very easy to access from U.S. 101. Exit U.S. 101 at Hellyer Avenue and follow prominent signs to the park. The dog area is about 100 yards past the entry kiosk. A parking fee of $4 is charged, and that can add up fast, since there's really no good parking nearby. So if you're planning to be a regular, your best bet would be to buy a $50 park pass for the year. It's a small investment to make for your dog's happiness. (408) 255-0225

• **Emma Prusch Park** 🐾🐾🐾 *See* ㉓ *on page 424.*

This park, one of San Jose's most attractive working farms, is a museum. Like a symbol of the county, it lies in the shadow of the intersection of three freeways. Yet it's a charming place and, surprisingly, it allows your leashed dog to wander around the farm with you so long as he stays out of the farm-animal areas. A smooth paved path, good for strollers and wheelchairs, winds among a Victorian farmhouse (which serves as the visitors center), a multicultural arts center, farm machinery, a barn, an orchard, and gardens. There are picnic tables on an expanse of lawn with trees.

During the summer and through October, a farmers market is held here every Saturday from 8:30 A.M. to 1 P.M. The city's K-9 Corps of trained police dogs occasionally shows off for children in the park, too. If you think your own dog won't be intimidated by dogs in uniform, call the park to find out when they'll be there.

The entrance is on South King Road, near the intersection of U.S. 101 and Interstate 680/280. (408) 277-4567.

• **Guadalupe Oak Grove Park** 🐾🐾🐾½ *See* ㉔ *on page 424.*

This park is a pleasant exception to most of the others in San Jose—it's undeveloped, beautiful, and doesn't allow bicycles—and sure enough, it may not be open to dogs forever. For years we've been hearing it may "soon" be declared an oak woodlands preserve. It hasn't been, so go and enjoy it.

Dirt trails wind through hills, alternately semi-open and covered with thick groves of oaks. Birds are plentiful and noisy. Be aware of high fire danger in the dry season, and don't even think of letting your dog off leash. The park's ranger loves dogs, but she'll ticket you, and she's heard all the excuses—from "He just slipped out of his collar for a moment . . ." to "I couldn't get my dog through the gate with his leash on . . ."

Guadalupe Oak Grove Park is at Golden Oak Way and Vargas Drive. (408) 277-4661.

• **Joseph D. Grant County Park** 🐾🐾🐾 *See* ㉕ *on page 424.*

Here's another huge, gorgeous, wild park that your dog can barely set foot in. Dogs are limited to the campgrounds, picnic areas, Edwards Field Hill, and the Edwards Trail. But if you don't mind a long, winding drive for one short—albeit satisfying—trail hike, by all means try this park. Stop in at the homey old ranch house that's now the visitors center for directions to the Edwards Trail, which isn't easy to find.

Or try these directions: On Mount Hamilton Road midway between the intersection with Quimby Road and the park border is a white barn on your right as you're heading out of the park. Just past the white barn is an unmarked pedestrian gate on the left, which is the trailhead. This trail is a fine walk through a deciduous forest.

There's a $4 parking fee. The park has 22 campsites, available first come, first served. Sites are $10 and dogs are $1 extra. The campground is open daily from April 1 to October 31 and open weekends in November and in March; it's closed from December to February.

To get to the park from Interstate 680, exit at the Capitol Expressway and drive south to Quimby Road. Turn left (east) on Quimby and wind tortuously to the park entrance. It's a long six miles and the road is often a one-lane cliffhanger. Alternatively, you can get to the park from Interstate 680 via Highway 130 (Mount Hamilton Road). It's similar, but at least it's a two-laner. (408) 274-6121.

• Los Alamitos-Calero Creek Park Chain 🐾🐾🐾
See ㉖ on page 424.
Six miles of multiuse trail, both dirt and paved, run along Los Alamitos Creek and Arroyo Calero from the southern end of Almaden Lake Park (which doesn't allow dogs) south to the western entrance of Santa Teresa County Park. San Jose dogs love these trails for their easy creek access and plenty of shade.

Two small adjacent city parks, Graystone Park and Carrabelle Park, have picnic tables and drinking fountains for a break, if you and your dog are making a trek of it. Keep your dog leashed and watch for bicycles and horses sharing the trail with you. You can park on a neighborhood street, but not along Camden Avenue.

From Camden Avenue at Villagewood Way or Queenswood Way, you can pick up a new segment of the Bay Area Ridge Trail that runs all the way to Santa Teresa County Park's western entrance, about 1.3 miles. Where the trail forks, take the westernmost fork—the trail paralleling Camden Avenue—westward across Harry Road and continuing to the county park.

The creek park chain runs parallel to the southern end of the Almaden Expressway. The trails run along the north side of Camden Avenue and along the east side of Queenswood Way. (408) 277-4573.

• Penitencia Creek County Park 🐾🐾🐾 See ㉗ on page 424.
This county park is largely a four-mile paved streamside trail designed for hikers, bicyclists, and roller skaters. Leashed dogs are welcome, and it usually isn't dangerously crowded. From the western end, at North King Road, you can connect with the Coyote Creek Multiple-Use Trail (see page 439). The Penitencia Creek Trail is paved from end to end, but not designed to go under roads like the better bicycle trails in Walnut Creek, for example. You will have to scramble your way across highways or around fenced portions. Or you'll be confronted with a locked gate protecting water district equipment.

At the Jackson Avenue end, large walnut trees line the creek and shelter some picnic tables. Rest rooms are scattered along the route.

There are parking lots on Penitencia Creek Road and on Jackson Avenue. This is the best portion of the trail for a dog, thanks to a dry lake bed. (408) 358-3741.

• Shadowbluff Dog Run 🐾🐾🐾🐾 🐕
See Coyote-Hellyer County Park, page 439.

• William Street Park 🐾🐾🐾 See ㉘ on page 424.
This park is a boy dog's dream come true. It's only about 12 acres, but it has 200 trees and 400 shrubs. On a recent visit, I think Joe sniffed out every one of them.

The trees make it a really pleasant, attractive place to visit, even in the armpits of summer. Head for the shade and let your happy, leashed pooch loll and roll in the green grass.

The park is at 16th Street and East William Street. (408) 277-4573.

RESTAURANTS

Bill's Cafe: You and your favorite dog can munch on simple cafe cuisine at this bistro with umbrella-topped tables. 1115 Willow Street; (408) 294-1125.

Grill Master: Frisky Dog and her human, Linda Bagnall, wrote us to rave about this super dog-friendly restaurant. "They treated Frisky like a Queen," they wrote. Well, after checking out the place for ourselves, Joe has news for Frisky. They don't treat all dogs like queens: They treat male dogs like kings. Grill Master not only has delicious kabobs and other grilled (and non-grilled) treats, it has some of the coolest managers and servers around, as far as dogs are concerned. When we visited, doggy Joe got a couple of dog biscuits and a bowl of water before I'd even decided which delectable dish to choose for lunch. Now that's doggone great service. Dine with your dog at the attractive patio tables. They're surrounded by trees, which makes it really inviting in the warmer months. 1408 South DeAnza Boulevard; (408) 725-0334.

PLACES TO STAY

Doubletree Hotel: Rates are $89 to $235. A $50 dog deposit is required. 2050 Gateway Place, San Jose, CA 95110; (408) 453-4000.

Homewood Suites: The suites here are comfy and much more like home than traditional hotels. Rates are $199. 10 West Trimble Road, San Jose, CA 95131; (408) 428-9900.

Joseph D. Grant County Park: See Joseph D. Grant County Park on page 440 for camping information.

Summerfield Suites Hotel: They only have suites here, which makes for a comfy stay. All suites are equipped with a kitchen. It's convenient for people traveling with pooches. Rates are $199 to $229. Dogs have to pay a $75 fee per visit, and they're $10 extra per day. 1602 Crane Court, San Jose, CA 95112; (408) 436-1600.

DOGGY DAYS

Bark in the Park: That's the name of a fun, incredibly popular dog day that takes place at a beautiful park (see William Street Park, page 441) every July. Bark in the park is also what your dog may do because he's so happy to be here. He'll be able to sniff out scads of doggy activities, like musical dog chairs, obstacle courses, and pooch "beauty" contests. There are vendors galore, selling all the things dogs love (including the *California Dog Lover's Companion*, plug, plug), and there's even a misting tent, complete with little wading pools, for dogs who need to cool their paws. The event is sponsored by the Beautification Committee of the Campus Community Association, a nonprofit neighborhood organization. For info about this year's event, call (408) 793-5125.

SANTA CLARA

PARKS, BEACHES, AND RECREATION AREAS

• **Central Park** 🐾 🐾 *See ㉙ on page 424.*

This Santa Clara city park, like most of the others, has a sign that reveals a certain slant: "No Dogs Allowed Except on Leash." If you can get past that, the park is big and has a wide assortment of trees. The creek here is large and deep, but dry in summer. A beautiful round picnic pavilion has tables fully shaded by wisteria vines, the most we've ever seen in one place.

The park is on Kiely Boulevard between Homestead Road and Benton Street. (408) 984-3223.

• **Santa Clara Dog Park** 🐾 🐾 🐾½ 🐕 *See ㉚ on page 424.*

It's not much, but this 200-by-200-foot fenced dog run is the only leash-free option in Santa Clara. Located on the grounds of what used to be Curtis Intermediate School, it's a flat stretch of grass bordered by stands of shady trees. Inside, you'll find water, pooper-scoopers, and benches to sit on. The park has been popular with dog owners since it opened in the fall of 1993, with up to 20 dogs using it at a time in the evenings. That's what you get for being the only game in town.

It's at the corner of Pomeroy Avenue and Lochinvar Street, near Lawrence Expressway and Homestead Road. (408) 984-3223.

PLACES TO STAY

Guest House Inn & Suites: Rates are $79 to $129. Dogs are $5 extra. 2930 El Camino Real, Santa Clara, CA 95051; (408) 241-3010.

The Vagabond Inn: Rates are $89 to $99. Dogs are $5 extra. 3580 El Camino Real, Santa Clara, CA 95051; (408) 241-0771.

DIVERSIONS

Go on a pilgrimage: Mission Santa Clara, on the Santa Clara University campus, allows leashed dogs on its grounds. You might make it part of your walk if you're exploring the campus. The building, dating from 1929, is a replica of one version of the old mission, which was first built in 1777 but was destroyed five times by earthquake, flood, and fire. Preserved fragments of the original mission and the old adobe Faculty Club are the oldest college buildings standing in the western United States. The mission is on campus, off El Camino Real. (408) 554-4023.

SARATOGA

RESTAURANTS

Bella Saratoga: The slogan of this Italian date spot is "It's Romantic," and it is, even at the front sidewalk tables next to a short stone wall right on the street. Dogs have to be tied up on the other side of the wall, but they're close enough for your handouts. If it's crowded, dogs aren't allowed, so be sure to visit during "off" times. Sit at one of the three tables by the wall. 14503 Big Basin Way; (408) 741-5115.

International Coffee Exchange: This very dog-friendly cafe serves the best mochas around. They're made with Ghirardelli chocolate and fresh, house-made whipped cream. The cafe also serves pastries and sandwiches, should you want a little nosh with your dog. The cafe's owners recently bought several large bowls for dog food (so you can share your lunch with your pal) and water. The smaller bowls they had before were pilfered one by one. Joe is very ashamed of the humans who did this, and says he's glad he's a dog. Drink and dine with doggy at the outdoor area's six umbrella-topped tables. 14471 Big Basin Way; (408) 741-1185.

Vienna Woods Restaurant and Deli: If you have an appetite for Austrian food, bring your dog here. You can get bratwurst, potato pancakes, and even apple strudel. The restaurant also serves sandwiches, quiches, lasagna, and other non-Austrian items. Dine with your pooch at the sheltered outdoor tables. 14567 Big Basin Way; (408) 867-2410.

SUNNYVALE

PARKS, BEACHES, AND RECREATION AREAS

• **Las Palmas Park** 🐾🐾🐾🐾 🐕 *See* ③ *on page 424.*

With its paved paths, green grass, and beautiful pond, this park used to be the best in town for a walk among rolling hills. Now it's really terrific, because of its recently opened dog run. The two-acre run has everything a dog could possibly desire—shade, water, pooper-scoopers, and even a fire hydrant. It's a kind of fenced-in nirvana. Dogs get deliriously happy when they visit. Some spend so much time rolling in the cool grass that they miss out on hanging with their fellow canines. But do they care? A look at their smiling snouts and flaring nostrils will answer that question.

A quick note about that fire hydrant. Enough dogs have run headlong into it that there was some thought about removing it. So far, it's still here. Doggies, keep your eyes open!

The park is at Danforth and Russet Drives. (408) 730-7350.

PLACES TO STAY

Summerfield Suites: There's supposed to be a 25-pound pooch limit, but so many of the employees here have and/or love dogs that this rule is often bent. The suites are large and very livable, with kitchens and most of the amenities of home. Rates are $94 to $199. There's a $75 pooch fee per visit (they're used to longish-term visitors), and dogs are $10 extra daily. 900 Hamlin Court, Sunnyvale, CA 94089, (408) 745-1515 or (800) 833-4353.

The Vagabond Inn: Rates are $65 to $75. Dogs are $5 extra. 816 Ahwanee Avenue, Sunnyvale, CA 94086; (408) 734-4607.

38
SANTA CRUZ COUNTY

Despite the leash that so obviously attaches Joe to me, my strange little Airedale pretends he's an orphan dog when he visits Santa Cruz County's beach towns. He puts on his best "I'm abandoned" face and gets pity from everyone he eyes. And at beaches, he eyes only girls in bikinis.

I don't know how he can tell a bikini from a one-piece, but when he spots someone walking around in a double-decker bathing suit, he stops in his tracks and sits while his eyes grow big and blank. Usually he'll hang his head low, all the time maintaining eye contact. When the object of his attention says "Awwwww," which she inevitably does, he gets up and smells her legs. If he likes her sunscreen, he tastes it. But alas, before he can sample more, he finds himself unceremoniously dragged away by his ruthless leash holder. His pitiable face freezes into a scowl—until his next paramour comes along.

If you have a beach-loving dog, Santa Cruz County is a great place to take him. The beaches here rarely get too warm, and while some are packed beyond belief (dogs are generally not allowed at the popular beaches), most are on the quieter side.

One of the best ways to get to the beach from mid-county is to take the turn-of-the-century steam train run by the Roaring Camp & Big Trees Railroad. The same company runs an 1880s narrow-gauge railroad through the redwoods. Both trips can be the thrill of a dog's life (see Diversions, page 450).

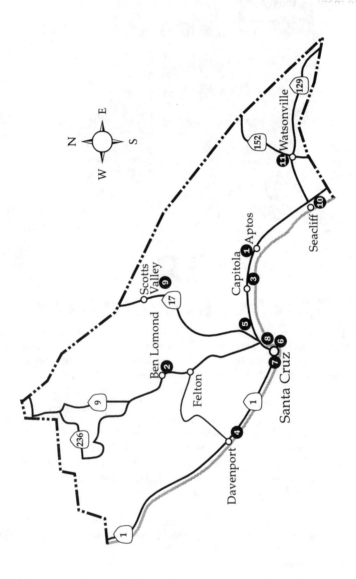

N
E
S
W

129
Watsonville
152
11
10 Seacliff
1 Aptos
Capitola
3
Scotts Valley **9**
17
5
8 **6**
Ben Lomond **7**
2
Felton
1
Santa Cruz
9
236
4
Davenport
1

Despite his penchant for beach bunnies, Joe's favorite beaches are the more desolate ones along the northernmost coast of Santa Cruz County. Only one (Bonny Dune Beach) is detailed later in this chapter because there are so many of them and they're relatively small, with parking only on the shoulder of the road. But they're wonderful for getting away from the crowds, especially if you're also looking at getting away from day-use fees.

These beaches run from Scott Creek in the north to Wilder Ranch State Park in the south. Davenport is the midpoint. Many of the beaches are hidden from Highway 1, so sometimes the only way to tell if there's a beach at all is to look for a few other cars parked on the roadside.

A word of warning about those big green patches you'll see when you look at a map of the county: They're mostly state parks and they ban dogs from doing everything but camping with you and hanging out on the paved portions of road (not a safe habit).

APTOS

If all suburbs could be like Aptos, this country would be a much better looking place. While Aptos is falling victim to the suburban sprawl of its neighbors to the north, it still retains a core of grace in its old village section. Check out the rustic Redwood Village, whose quaint stores were originally built in 1928 with redwood hewn from trees on the property.

While exploring Aptos, if you run into Loma Prieta Drive, don't sit around with your dog and wonder why someone would name a street after the deadly 1989 earthquake. This is the area of the epicenter of that quake, which measured 7.1 on the Richter scale. If your dog starts acting restless, you may want to move on. It could be fleas. It could be boredom. It could even be gas. But why take a chance? Actually, people around here say the pressure along the fault line was relieved by the quake, so there's probably little chance that another big one could be centered here again for a while.

If you do hear any rumbling, most likely it will be the sound of your empty stomach growling. That's a quaking that can be calmed easily by eating at a few Aptos restaurants that welcome dogs at their outside tables (see page 448).

PARKS, BEACHES, AND RECREATION AREAS

Don't be fooled by the map handed out by the Aptos Chamber of Commerce. That big patch of green that says Polo Grounds Regional Park is not a place where the public is welcome. In fact, it looks like a gigantic empty lot. The county says it's trying to figure out what to do with the land, but for now it's off-limits. If you're without a dog and are looking for a real patch of green, just move on to the gigantic Forest of Nisene Marks State Park, only a couple of miles away. Unfortunately, like most state parks, this one is so strict that a dog won't have much fun there. If you're with a dog, and that dog is desperate, try the Aptos Village Park.

• **Aptos Village Park** 🐾 🐾 *See* ❶ *on page 446.*

The grass here is perfectly manicured. The trees are perfectly shaped. The gazebo is perfect. The picnic tables are perfect. The playground is perfect. Even the people who use the park seem perfect. It's all a bit much for a dog who's just trying to go about the business of being a dog. About the only place where leashed dogs can let it all hang out in this park is on the nature trail.

The park is just off Soquel Drive, about 50 yards east of The Veranda restaurant. There's a road to the right that's unmarked except for the sign "Aptos Station." Go right and make an immediate left into the long and winding park driveway. (408) 688-5688.

RESTAURANTS

Cafe Sparrow: Eat your croissant sandwich on the bench in front of this little restaurant. 8042 Soquel Drive; (408) 688-6238.

Jorie's: This dog-lovin' deli serves big enough portions to satisfy even the heartiest appetite. We like the mashed potatoes with gravy. Dogs have been known to come away from here with very tasty treats. The folks here adore dogs. Dine at the outdoor tables topped with umbrellas. 7957 Soquel Drive; (408) 685-2627.

BEN LOMOND

PARKS, BEACHES, AND RECREATION AREAS

• **Quail Hollow Ranch** 🐾🐾🐾 *See* ❷ *on page 446.*

This 300-acre ranch-style park is the largest county park in Santa Cruz. It's also one of the least developed, making it a good area for a dog. There's plenty of wildlife around, so bring your binoculars and hold on tight to that leash. Deer and coyotes abound certain times of year. You'll also see a few quail, but don't get any ideas about dinner: No hunting is allowed.

From Highway 9, go east on Graham Hill Road and then north (left) on East Zayante Road. Turn left at Quail Hollow Road. The park is on the right. The official address is 800 Quail Hollow Road. (408) 462-8300.

CAPITOLA

This beautiful resort area's main beach, Capitola City Beach, is off-limits to dogs. But just down the road, New Brighton State Beach more than makes up for the loss.

If you feel like a beautiful stroll by Soquel Creek, take your leashed dog to the Esplanade, just off Opal Cliff Drive. It's the paved walk that usually has flowers at the entrance, east and inland of the Capitola Wharf (which also doesn't allow dogs).

PARKS, BEACHES, AND RECREATION AREAS

• **New Brighton State Beach** 🐾🐾🐾½ *See* ❸ *on page 446.*

Is your dog bored of the same old beach scene? Is she tired of sand and surf and surf and sand, bored of sitting around getting tan? Bring her here! There's much more to this place than beach. And it's a good thing, too, because dogs aren't allowed on the beach itself. (Actually, at press time, there was a trial period allowing leashed dogs on the beach. If it ends up being a permanent place for dogs, you'll see it in the next edition of this book.) The trails above the beach allow leashed dogs, and they love it.

Take your dog on the trail that leads up to big pines and eucalyptus trees. It starts to the left of the main beach entrance. If you walk along the forest/dune area, you'll be able to see Capitola as birds see it. Dogs like to sit up here and let their nostrils quiver over scents drifting in from around the world.

From Highway 1, take the New Brighton Beach exit west. Day-use fees are $6 per car, $1 per dog. You'll find 106 campsites set on bluffs and surrounded by trees. Rates are $14 to $18 per night, $1 extra for dogs. For campground reservations, phone Parknet at (800) 444-PARK. Call (408) 429-2850 for beach information.

RESTAURANTS

Caffe Lido: It's a kind of small outdoor area, but if you keep your dog from getting underfoot, you'll enjoy a relaxed California-Italian meal. 110 Monterey Avenue; (408) 475-6544.

Souza Cones Ice Cream & Candy: Dine on dripping waffle cones with your drooling dog at the outside bench here. If he's thirsty, they'll give you a bowl of water for him. 200 Monterey Avenue; (408) 475-9339.

PLACES TO STAY

New Brighton State Beach: See New Brighton State Beach above for camping information.

DAVENPORT

PARKS, BEACHES, AND RECREATION AREAS

• **Bonny Dune Beach** 🐾 🐾 🐾 *See* ➍ *on page 446.*

This beach is hidden from Highway 1 by bluffs, so few people know it exists. That's good news for dogs, even though they're still supposed to be leashed. Some days, you won't find a soul here. Other times, the crowd will consist of a couple dozen folks picnicking and strolling. Still other times (sunny, warm days, usually), the crowd will consist of quite a few naked people. Naked men, to be exact. If your dog is an incorrigible sniffer of private places, it's best to steer clear of here on pleasant days. (Joe flunked the sniff test on two other nudie beaches, so we visit here in fog only.)

See the introduction to this chapter for information on other small beaches along the north coast of Santa Cruz County. Bonny Dune Beach is at Highway 1 and Bonny Dune Road. There's a small dirt parking lot on the side of the road. (408) 462-8300.

RESTAURANTS

Whale City Bakery, Bar & Grill: This is a fun and convenient place to stop on a trip between San Francisco and some far-flung destination to the south. The name of this restaurant tells you just about everything you need to know about the cuisine. (Joe would like to add, however, that while the burgers here are to drool for, the fried calamari are truly a greaser-dog's dream come true.) Drink and dine at the tables out front, facing the ocean and Highway 1. They're wonderful in the cliffside fog or the bright sun. 490 Highway 1; (408) 423-9803.

FELTON

PLACES TO STAY

Henry Cowell Redwoods State Park: This being a state park, dogs aren't allowed to explore any of the magnificent trails here. They're restricted to pavement, the campgrounds, or the picnic area. That's rather limiting for dogs who love to run around the redwoods and the mountains. The 112 campsites are surrounded by the big old trees, if that's any comfort to your canine. Camping fees are $14 to $17. Dogs are $1 extra. From Felton, take Graham Hill Road southeast about two miles to the park. The entrance is on the right. Phone (408) 335-4598 for park information or call Parknet at (800) 444-PARK for campsite reservations.

DIVERSIONS

Choo on this: Riding on the antique Roaring Camp & Big Trees Narrow-Gauge Railroad through a redwood forest was one of Joe's favorite adventures ever—except whenever the engineer released loud bellows of steam. And whenever the railroad car moved.

Eventually he did get used to the chug-a-lug motion. Toward the end of the one and a half hours, he was thoroughly enjoying himself, nose in the air, sucking in the smells of the primeval redwood forest from our open train car. But he still wouldn't leave my lap.

Most dogs are ecstatic on the train. Nisha smiled the whole time and her tail never stopped wagging. When the steam let loose, she followed it with her eyes as if it were a beautiful white bird. She slept the rest of the day. Joe just stared blankly at the sky, trying to sort out what had happened to him.

The railroad company offers another trip, to the Santa Cruz city beach. But since dogs aren't allowed in that area, we recommend the excursion through the redwoods. Besides, halfway through the redwood trip, dogs and their people get to walk around the ancient forest a little before clambering back aboard.

At the end of either train journey, nothing beats spreading out a picnic at the old-fashioned depot's picnic tables. There's plenty of room for walking your leashed dog around the grounds. And humans have fun shopping at the antique general store. It's hard to leave the little shop without buying the kids a miniature train car, so if you don't want to spend extra money, you'd better not even go in.

Rates for the redwood trip are $13.50 for adults and $9.50 for children ages 3 to 12. Rates for the Santa Cruz beach excursion are $15 for adults and $11 for kids. Dogs get a free ride on both.

From Highway 1 in the Santa Cruz area, take Highway 17 north toward San Jose. Exit at the Scotts Valley/Big Basin exit, and drive west on Mount Hermon Road 3.5 miles to Graham Hill Road. Turn left onto Graham Hill Road. Roaring Camp is one-half mile ahead on the right. They often offer special trips, such as moonlight steam train parties and chuckwagon barbecue rides. Call for details and schedules. (408) 335-4484.

SANTA CRUZ

When I told Joe and Nisha we were going to visit Santa Cruz, they started whining and running around in circles. Joe began moaning what sounded like the word "cool." I figured somehow the dogs knew that this laid-back, liberal town had to be, like, *totally* relaxed about dogs.

I was wrong. Now that I look back on it, the dogs were probably whining with anxiety about driving for two hours to a place where they would not only have to stay on leash, but would be completely banned from certain beaches. Joe's "cool" moan was more likely a resounding "nooo!"

We'd been to Santa Cruz several times before and had survived just fine at some of the more remote beaches when we weren't aware of the rules. But now that we were trying to be law-abiding creatures, it was tough.

There are a couple of beaches that allow dogs off leash during limited hours. We're very grateful for those. But somehow we didn't think dogs would be outcasts at such hangouts as Santa Cruz Beach, the Boardwalk, and the Municipal Wharf.

If this were any other city, it wouldn't be such a disappointment. But this is Santa Cruz, land of the free, home of the unusual. The dogs had that "bummer" look the whole way back. Even their bandannas drooped.

PARKS, BEACHES, AND RECREATION AREAS

Two beaches and one field allow dogs off leash. Most city parks permit leashed dogs. San Lorenzo Park is a notable exception. So is Nearys Lagoon City Park, a popular wildlife sanctuary you may be tempted to visit with your canine friend. But since dogs aren't part of the natural scenery here, they're not allowed.

•**De La Veaga Park** 🐾🐾🐾 *See* ❺ *on page 446.*

When you get past all the golf courses here, this large park and its trails are remote and not widely used. That means party time, even for leashed dogs.

Many trails lead you through fields, into woods, and back through lush meadowland. Just watch out for flying arrows at the archery range on the east side of the park. If you like sitting down and resting every few hundred feet, this park provides benches. At the top of the park, you can see forever.

From Highway 1, exit at Morrissey Boulevard and go south for one block. Turn right at Fairmount Avenue. Within two blocks, go right on Brancifort Avenue. As you cross back over the highway and enter the park, the road turns into La Veaga Park Road. Bear right and then left. You'll pass through what will seem like an eternity of golf courses, then finally see your destination. (408) 429-3663.

•**Lighthouse Field State Beach (two sections)**

This beach area is divided into two parts, both of which allow dogs to run off leash during limited hours:

Lighthouse Field 🐾🐾½ 🐕 *See* ❻ *on page 446.*

Dogs can run off leash at this field from sunrise to 10 A.M. and 4 P.M. to sunset. It's a great dog privilege, but the field itself is no prize. It's not large enough for escape artist dogs to be safe from traffic, and there's barely any shade. But the view of the ocean is a winner. Unless your dog likes traipsing through eye-high dry grass, which is what this place has most of the year, you're better off taking him to West Lighthouse Beach on the other side of West Cliff Drive (see below).

Don't worry if signs tell you only that dogs must always be leashed, without mentioning the off-leash hours. The field is on the north side of West Cliff Drive, west of Point Santa Cruz. (408) 429-3777.

• **West Lighthouse Beach/It's Beach** 🐾 🐾 🐾 🐾 🐕
   See ❻ *on page 446.*

Dog dudes are allowed to run leashless from sunrise to 10 a.m. and 4 p.m. to sunset. The beach is narrow and not nearly as heavily used as Santa Cruz Beach. It's just below the famed Lighthouse Field State Beach Surf Museum, which houses the largest collection of surfing books on the West Coast. The beach is perfect if you want to hang out on the sand with your cool dog while a surfing dude friend checks out the museum. The beach is on the south side of West Cliff Drive, west of Point Santa Cruz and just west of the Surf Museum. (408) 429-3777.

• **Mitchell's Cove Beach** 🐾 🐾 🐾 🐾 🐕 *See* ❼ *on page 446.*

This is the place locals come with their dogs when they want to get away from the tourist scene. The beach is small, attractive, and conveniently located next to Lighthouse Field State Beach. But for some reason, hardly anyone uses it.

Dogs may run off leash from sunrise to 10 a.m. and 4 p.m. to sunset. The beach is between Almar and Woodrow Avenues, on the south side of West Cliff Drive. It's unmarked. (408) 429-3777.

• **Twin Lakes State Beach** 🐾 🐾 ½ *See* ❽ *on page 446.*

The beach here is wide and inviting for leashed dogs and their people. But unfortunately, even more inviting is a section that dogs should stay away from: Schwan Lagoon, a wildfowl refuge full of ducksch and geesch and, they say, even a few schwans.

Twin Lakes State Beach is on both sides of the Santa Cruz Small Craft Harbor, on East Cliff Drive and Seventh Avenue. (408) 429-2850.

RESTAURANTS

Santa Cruz has many, many restaurants with outdoor tables. Here's a sampling of the dog-friendly ones.

Aldo's Restaurant: Dogs who venture here get a big bowl of water if they're thirsty. "We're very dog-friendly around here," a manager told us. Dine on pastas, seafood dishes, and sandwiches on the deck over the water. 616 Atlantic Avenue; (408) 426-3736.

Cooper Street Cafe: The food at this European-style cafe is very tasty. Everything is house-made. Dine with your pooch at the umbrella-shaded tables on the large brick courtyard. If your dog looks thirsty, he'll probably be offered a big bowl of water. We like that. 725 Front Street; (408) 423-4925.

Emily's Bakery: Three reasons to visit here with your dog: 1) The baked goods hit the spot; 2) You and your dog can eat them at the big wooden deck alongside the bakery, overlooking a creek; 3) Emily loves dogs. So does her crew. If you're in the mood for fresh-baked bread or muffins, or a cup of joe, this is one of the best places to stop with your dog on a Highway 1 sojourn. 1129 Mission Street (Highway 1); (408) 429-9866.

Falafel Hut: I love the name of this place. Reminds me of a certain pizza chain, only with a wink and a Mideast flavor. The falafel here is very good, as is the hummus and tabouli. If your dog isn't into foreign foods, you can order her a burger. Dine with doggy at the two sidewalk tables. 308 Beach Street; (408) 423-0567.

Harbor Deli: The Mexican food and burgers are satisfying. 460 Seventh Avenue; (408) 479-1366.

Pleasure Pizza: Pop over here with your pooch for some primo pizza at Pleasure's outdoor tables. 4000 Portola Drive; (408) 475-4999.

Polar Bear Ice Cream: Dogs are welcome to eat with you under the awning in back of this ice creamery. 1224 Soquel Avenue; (408) 425-5188.

Tony & Alba's Pizza: Dogs like hanging out under the shade of a cool umbrella-covered table while you enjoy pizza and pasta. 817 Soquel Avenue; (408) 425-8669.

Walnut Avenue Cafe: You can sit next to your pooch at this cafe, but he must be tied to the other side of the railing. They serve a good breakfast. Joe once mooched some eggs Benedict from a toddler here. She started crying when he wouldn't eat the green garnishy thing that came with the eggs, so he ate that, too. Such a softy. 106 Walnut Avenue; (408) 457-2307.

Westside Coffee Co.: If you're in the mood for a light but tasty snack with your pooch, stop here and dine at the six tables nestled under an overhang. 849 Almar Street; (408) 427-1300.

PLACES TO STAY

Edgewater Beach Motel: No two rooms are alike at this attractive, dog-friendly haunt. Four of the rooms were built in 1886, although 1955 was the year a big chunk of the motel came into existence. You can get a room adorned with mahogany, redwood, or even a sunken fireplace, or a basic room with less character, but just as much comfort. (Face it. If you're traveling with your dog, you've probably got all the character you can handle anyway.)

Outside is a flower garden, a lawn area for kids, a picnic area with gas barbecues, and best for dogs, a big lot where they can do things doggies like to do. (Do clean up.) The lot is across the street from the wharf, where dogs are banned.

The owners love dogs and have three pooches themselves. "Pets make great guests. I'm more reluctant about having some people stay here than I am about dogs," says owner Win Alexander. Dog guests are supplied with a dog bowl and a dog sheet while they're here. Rates are $65 to $235. Dogs are $10 to $25 extra, depending on their size. 525 Second Street, Santa Cruz, CA 95060; (408) 423-0440.

Motel Continental: This one's about five blocks from the water. Rates are $45 to $280. Dogs are $10 extra. 414 Ocean Street, Santa Cruz, CA 95060; (408) 429-1221.

Ocean Pacific Lodge: You're just a couple of blocks from beach action when you stay here. This is a clean, decent-looking place, with mini fridges and nukers in all the rooms, which makes traveling with your canine troupe a bit easier. Humans enjoy the heated pool and continental breakfast. Rates are $59 to $139. Dogs are $10 extra. 120 Washington Street, Santa Cruz, CA 95060; (408) 457-1234 or (800) 995-0289.

Pacific Inn: The rooms all have little fridges, so you and your dog can have some cool midnight snacks. The motel also has a heated indoor pool, but no paw-dipping, please. Rates are $40 to $140. Dogs are $10 extra. 330 Ocean Street, Santa Cruz, CA 95060; (408) 425-3722.

Sunset Inn: Rates are $40 to $95. 2424 Mission Street, Santa Cruz, CA 95060; (408) 423-7000.

DOGGY DAYS

Enjoy the dog day of summer: Each August, the Santa Cruz SPCA holds a summertime festival called the Critter Carnival, complete with contests for the waggiest tail, the muttiest mutt, the best vocalist, the best celebrity look-alike, and the Queen Mutt. It's a terrific event, and it's especially fun for dogs who don't mind a little socializing. However, if your dog gets hungry looking at cats, canaries, and other critters, this might not be the place for him. Being The Critter Carnival, dogs and people aren't the only animals here. Call (408) 475-6454 for dates and details.

DIVERSIONS

Go to the movies: The Skyview Drive-In Theatre, like its cousin theater in Salinas, is one of those rare drive-in joints that dares to call itself a theatre. A tip for you and your doggy date: Put the speaker on the side of the car where the human will be sitting. Dogs have been known to knock off the speakers in a fit of boredom or lick them if they hear an appealing sound. 2260 Soquel Drive. (408) 475-3405.

SCOTTS VALLEY

PARKS, BEACHES, AND RECREATION AREAS

• **Lodato Park** 🐾🐾½ 🐕 See ❾ on page 446.

This 40-acre park is a decent size for your dog to get exercise, but where the workout really comes in is on the trails, which can be quite steep and rough. Dogs are allowed to roam off leash in this 40-acre site for now, but the city has big plans for the park. That means the brushy, ticky land will be cleaned up and improved, but it also means leashes will be mandatory. The park is on Green Hills Road, just east of Highway 17. (408) 438-3251.

RESTAURANTS

Rosie's Espresso Bar and Cafe: From Cajun food to pasta, pastries, muffins, and all sorts of sweet eats, the dining here is delectable. It's at Victor Square in Scotts Valley Junction; (408) 438-1735.

PLACES TO STAY

Best Western Inn: Small dogs and exemplary larger dogs are welcome. All pooches must stay in smoking rooms, so if you and Joe Camel don't see eye to eye, you may want to consider staying elsewhere. Room rates are $58 to $125. 6020 Scotts Valley Drive, Scotts Valley, CA 95066; (408) 438-6666 or (800) 528-1234.

Carbonero Creek RV Park: Dogs can only stay with you in an RV here, which is too bad—the tent sites come with water and electricity, which is nice for a dog who wants to shave or catch up on TV news. The rec room is one of the more attractive RV rec rooms we've run across, and the pool's not bad either. Certain dogs aren't allowed to stay here. Pit bulls are only one of the banned breeds. The others are dobies, rotties, German shepherds, chows, and Akitas. Hey, I don't make the rules, I just report 'em. Rates are $26. Dogs (those who make the cut) are $1 extra. 917 Disc Drive; (408) 438-1288 or (800) 546-1288.

SEACLIFF

At press time, Seacliff State Beach was allowing leashed dogs on the beach on a trial basis. We hope that by this book's next edition, dogs will be here on a more permanent basis. Until then, we're just listing the beach for its camping facilities (see Places to Stay, below). For an update on whether the beach is going to the dogs, call (408) 429-2850.

RESTAURANTS

Sno-White Drive-In: Dogs can sit with you at picnic tables as you dine together on calamari, burgers, and fries. 223 State Park Drive; (408) 688-4747.

PLACES TO STAY

Seacliff State Beach: If you, your RV, and your dog need a place to spend the night, try this scenic RV campground. While dogs are allowed to camp with you at the 26 sites in the area overlooking the ocean, they're not allowed on the beach below. (Actually, at press time, this rule had been temporarily changed. Please see the introduction to Seacliff, above, for details.) They're also banned from the concrete boat/fishing pier that juts into Monterey Bay. Sites are $28 to $29. Dogs are $1 extra. The campground is six miles south of Santa Cruz and then west on the Seacliff Beach exit. Call (408) 429-2850 for beach information or call Parknet at (800) 444-PARK for reservations.

SOQUEL

RESTAURANTS

Cafe Nimbus: The owner loves dogs and is happy to see good pooches dining with their people at the umbrella-shaded outdoor tables. The food is standard, tasty lunch fare. The baked goods hit the spot, too. 5736 Soquel Drive; (408) 475-1414.

WATSONVILLE

PARKS, BEACHES, AND RECREATION AREAS

• Palm Beach 🐾🐾🐾½ *See* ⑩ *on page 446.*

Dahling! What a mahvelous place! And not a sign of anyone rich and famous for miles!

This may not be the Palm Beach of Robin Leach fame, but it's a heavenly, remote place that has considerably more to offer down-to-earth dogs and their people. A trail takes you through a large eucalyptus grove where you and your dog can stop for a cool, relaxing picnic. Then it's onward to the large beach, where your dog has to remain leashed, but he can still have a jolly old time sniffing and walking and walking and sniffing. Even on perfect summer afternoons, this beach gets very little use, probably because of its location at the end of the county.

Fees are $3 per car and $1 per dog. Exit Highway 1 at Riverside Drive/Highway 129 and follow the signs to Beach Road, past huge farms. The beach is at the end of the road. (408) 429-2850.

• **Pinto Lake County Park** 🐾 🐾 1/2 *See* **⓫** *on page 446.*

If you and your dog like to fish on small lakes, have we got a small lake for you! There's a reason so many anglers, young and old, sit on their lounge chairs with their lunches by the lakeside: They're actually catching fish. The stories they tell aren't just fish stories. They're taking home bass, bluegill, catfish, crappie, and trout.

Even dogs have a decent day here when it's not too warm. They lay under the big trees watching their best friends land dinner. Sometimes they'll get their paws wet. When their owners walk them (on leash), there's enough space to stretch all their legs. And if it happens to be summer, they can stroll to the boathouse and drool over the candy, cookies, and bait.

Paddleboats and rowboats are available to humans for $5 an hour from June through August. It's perfect if the rest of the family wants to do something other than fish.

There's camping for RVs and trailers, but no tents are allowed. It costs $16 nightly for a complete motor-home hookup at the 28 sites here. Dogs are $1 extra. Day-use fees are $2 from May through October. There's no fee during the off-season. Driving from Santa Cruz, exit Highway 1 at Airport Boulevard. Make a left at Green Valley Road. The entrance is well marked. (408) 462-8333.

PLACES TO STAY

Motel 6: This one's only a couple of miles from Palm Beach. One small pooch per room is okay here. Rates are $36 to $45 for one adult, $4 for the second adult. The owners ask that you let them know ahead of time if you'll be bringing a dog. 125 Silver Leaf Drive, Watsonville, CA 95076; (408) 728-4144.

Pinto Lake County Park: See Pinto Lake County Park above for camping information.

Santa Cruz Resort KOA Kampground: Does your dog's idea of roughing it entail sleeping at the foot of your bed? The Kamping Kabins at this KOA resort are the answer to the prayers of dogs who wince at the notion of spending the night in a tent in the woods. The rustic log cabins have no bathrooms (they're nearby), but they do have plenty of space. You bring the linens and blankets, and the cabins supply the mattresses. One-room cabins sleep four; two-room cabins sleep six. There's some land around outside where you and your dog can stretch your gams.

The KOA is a family-oriented place, with a batting cage, volleyball courts, a hot tub, swimming pools, and horseshoes. Kamping Kabin rates are $49 to $59. Kids four to 17 years old are $2 extra. The KOA is located one mile from the coast, at 1186 San Andreas Road, Watsonville, CA 95076; (408) 722-0551.

Sunset State Beach: The main unit of Sunset State Beach allows dogs to camp, but doesn't allow them on the beach. Water-loving dogs should cruise down to Palm Beach (see page 455). This campground is a good one, though, with 90 sites set on a bluff over the Pacific. There's a decent amount of exercise area for your dog to survive without trying to sneak down to the beach.

Sites are $16 per night. Dogs are $1 extra. From Santa Cruz, exit Highway 1 at San Andreas Road and go right at Sunset Beach Road. For campsite reservations, call Parknet at (800) 444-PARK. For beach information, call (408) 724-1266.

CENTRAL AREA COUNTIES

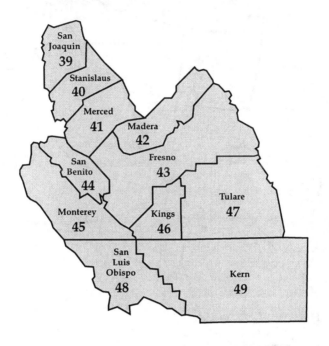

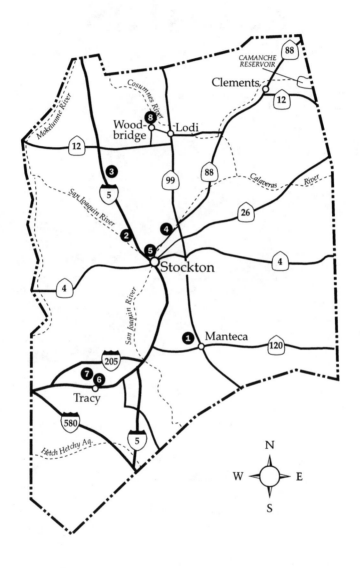

CAMANCHE RESERVOIR

88

Clements

12

Cosumnes River

Mokelumne River

Wood-bridge **8** Lodi

12

San Joaquin River

3

5

99

88

Calaveras River

26

2

4

5 Stockton

4

4

San Joaquin River

1 Manteca

120

205

7 **6**

Tracy

580

5

Hetch Hetchy Aq.

N
W • E
S

39
SAN JOAQUIN COUNTY

Chances are you won't be driving a few hundred miles just to vacation here with your dog. That's good. In fact, your dog is probably reading over your shoulder right now and slobbering in gratitude.

It's not that San Joaquin County is a terrible place for dogs. It certainly has its share of attractive parks. But since dogs aren't permitted off leash around here, and since this isn't exactly the wilderness capital of California, it's just not a great doggy destination.

Here's a good rule of thumb to remember if you don't want to come away with a ticket for a dog offense: Tempting as it may be, don't let your dog walk on the paths and trails in the county-run parks. It's an offense punishable by a few dollars out of your dog bone fund. It's a ridiculous rule. What would have happened to Toto if he hadn't been permitted to walk on the Yellow Brick Road?

BETHEL ISLAND
RESTAURANTS

Rusty Porthole: Picture this: steak, prime rib, chicken, french fries, your dog, you, the California Delta. What more could a dog desire? Dine with your happy pooch at the patio overlooking the water. If you come by boat, the parking's easy, with 200 feet of dock space. 3893 Willow Road; (510) 684-3607.

CLEMENTS

RESTAURANTS
A&W: You and your pooch can dine on good old A&W cuisine at the plentiful outdoor tables. It's conveniently located on Highway 88. 18737 Highway 88; (209) 759-3368.

LODI

Dogs are allowed in this city's parks, but only on the paved areas. Joe doesn't think the parks are even worth describing. With these kinds of rules, he prefers to stroll on the sidewalks. At least with garbage cans and cats, the scenery is more scintillating.

PLACES TO STAY
Best Western Royal Host Inn: Small pooches only, please. Rates are $50 to $60. There's a $20 cash deposit for dogs (or an open credit card deposit). 710 South Cherokee Lane, Lodi, CA 95240; (209) 369-8484.

MANTECA

PARKS, BEACHES, AND RECREATION AREAS
• **Northgate Park** 🐾🐾🐾½ *See* ❶ *on page 460.*
If your dog wants to meet the hounds of Manteca, come to Northgate Park, where Manteca dogs gather for long afternoons of leisure. The setting is grassy and fairly flat, with softball fields and picnic tables. It's not exactly Yosemite National Park, but dogs have more fun here.

Dogs are supposed to be leashed. The park is at Northgate Drive and Hoyt Lane. (209) 239-8470.

STOCKTON

PARKS, BEACHES, AND RECREATION AREAS
• **Louis Park** 🐾🐾🐾 *See* ❷ *on page 460.*
The address of this park is the intersection of the San Joaquin River and Smiths Canal. It's where the whole watery world converges—where freighters move their bulk alongside water-skiers, where tugboat captains wave to shoreline anglers.

You and your leashed dog will enjoy watching all the action from the comfort of this 70-acre park. It's slightly contoured, so some sections provide better views than others. Because the park was established in the 1920s, it has plenty of large trees for shade. Conifers, cottonwoods, native valley oaks, and broadleafs abound.

The park is also home to softball diamonds, tennis courts, a free boat ramp, and Pixie Woods, a children's play area complete with carousels and a miniature train. Louis Park is at the western end of Monte Diablo Avenue, at Occidental Avenue. (209) 937-8206.

• **Oak Grove Regional County Park** 🐾🐾🐾 *See* ❸ *on page 460.*
This 180-acre park has more than 1,500 oak trees. If you want shade, or your boy dog wants a target for leg lifts, you've come to the right place.

You can easily get around the park without use of the wonderful 1.5-mile nature trail, and it's a good thing, because dogs aren't allowed to set paw on it. As with all San Joaquin County parks, dogs aren't permitted on trails or paths. But this park has enough open land so it won't matter much except on muddy days.

Dogs must be leashed. There's a $2 vehicle entry fee on weekdays, $4 on weekends and holidays. (209) 953-8800.

• **Oak Park** 🐾🐾🐾 *See ❹ on page 460.*

This park is notorious for confusing people who are supposed to meet each other at Oak Grove Regional County Park, and vice versa. "I asked this girl I'd just met to meet me at Oak Park and she never showed up," teenage dog walker Frankie Ramirez told me. "She was new in town, so I had this idea and raced over to the Oak County Park, and there she was, waiting for me with her big dog. Now I love her and her dog, but these parks could have screwed up a great love story. Tell your readers to be careful out there." Awww. I couldn't have said it better myself.

Oak Park is just as pretty as the county park, but it's free. It's actually a large canopy valley oak grove, with hundreds of these lovelies packed into 60 acres. Leashed dogs love to hike on the shaded walkways through the park, sniffing the bark of these trees.

The park is also the home of the Stockton Ports, the farm team for the Milwaukee Brewers. Dogs aren't permitted at games, but they tilt their heads at the roar of greasy popcorn and the smell of the crowd. The park is between Alpine Avenue and Fulton Street, at Sutter Street. (209) 937-8206.

• **Victory Park** 🐾🐾🐾 *See ❺ on page 460.*

Local dogs come to mingle at this attractive park, which is full of large oaks and conifers. There's a paved walkway around the park's 27 acres. A hike around it makes for an excellent exercise routine.

Weekdays after work are the best times to visit if you want your leashed dog to hang out with other leashed dogs. Too bad the city couldn't set aside a couple of acres as a fenced-in dog exercise area so dogs could play as they really want to—sans leash.

The park is at Pershing Avenue and Picardy Drive. (209) 937-8206.

PLACES TO STAY

Best Western Charter Inn: Small dogs are fine at this motel, but large dogs need the approval of the manager. Rates are $54 to $72. Dogs require a $15 deposit. 550 West Charter Way, Stockton, CA 95206; (209) 948-0321.

La Quinta Inn: They prefer small to medium-sized dogs here. Rates are $65 to $84. Pooches have to pay a $25 fee. 2710 West March Lane, Stockton, CA 95219; (209) 952-7800.

Tiki Lagun Resort & Marina: This is kind of a fun place to come camping with your canine, especially if you're not into a big wilderness adventure. The 30 soft-grass campsites are set under tall shade trees, just a bone's throw from the Delta. Dogs dig it here. If you visit in an RV, there's a separate RV park, with 30 spaces and complete hookups. Compared to most RV/camp areas, it's small and secluded. Tiki Lagun even has launch ramps, should you bring a boat. Rates are $19 to $24. Dog are $2 extra. 12988 West McDonald Road, Stockton, CA 95206; (209) 941-8975 or (800) 338-7176.

DIVERSIONS

Doggy does Delta: There's really no better way to explore the Delta than on a houseboat. As your first mate steers the boat through the Delta's snaking waterways, you can prepare dinner, take a snooze on one of the boat's beds, catch some rays (and some fish), or just sit on the deck with your dog and sniff the brackish breeze. Just remember to park the boat occasionally (there's plenty of isolated, parkable land around) to let your pooch stretch his legs and tend to his business.

These floating houses are more like modest mobile homes than mansions. But dogs don't mind the aesthetics. It's the adventure, the togetherness, and the swimming (if they're of that persuasion) they adore.

A dog-friendly houseboat rental company, Herman and Helen's Marina, rents the boats by the weekend or week, depending on the time of year. Rates start at $410 for a weekend on a houseboat that sleeps six, and go up to $3,295 for a week on a houseboat that sleeps 10. For information, contact Herman and Helen's Marina, Venice Island Ferry, Stockton, CA 95219; (209) 951-4634 or (800) 676-4841. Another houseboat rental company, Seven Crown Resorts, will rent you and your dog and some friends a houseboat for $450 for three days/two nights to $1,700 for a week. Phone (800) 752-9669 for more information.

TRACY

PARKS, BEACHES, AND RECREATION AREAS

• **Lincoln Park** 🐾 🐾 *See* ❻ *on page 460.*

The trees are big and the walkways are flat here, just how lazy leashed dogs like it. The park is an old, attractive one in the downtown area.

It's at Eaton Avenue and East Street. (209) 831-4200.

• **Pescadero Park** 🐾 🐾 *See* ❼ *on page 460.*

If your leashed buddy likes to roll on the grass, he'll be happy to know that this grassy 15-acre park is ideal for canine rollers. It's not completely flat, because that isn't conducive to truly fine rolling. It's slightly contoured, making those upside-down wiggling maneuvers much more invigorating. And there aren't many trees to crash into should the roll get out of hand.

The park is at Kavanagh and Louise Avenues. (209) 831-4200.

RESTAURANTS

Banta Inn: Dogs are welcome at the patio tables while you dine on charbroiled sandwiches, steaks, and fish. 22563 South Seventh Street; (209) 835-1311.

WOODBRIDGE

PARKS, BEACHES, AND RECREATION AREAS

• **Woodbridge Regional Park** 🐾 🐾 🐾 *See* ❽ *on page 460.*

A quarter-mile stretch of the Mokelumne River is yours at this undeveloped riparian park. It's good for fishing or for dipping your paws on a warm day. It gets much less use than other county parks and it's free. Just keep your dog on a leash, and keep him off the trail here. It's the law. We don't like it, but what can you do?

The park is on East River Meadows Drive at the Mokelumne River, just north of Woodbridge Road. (209) 953-8800.

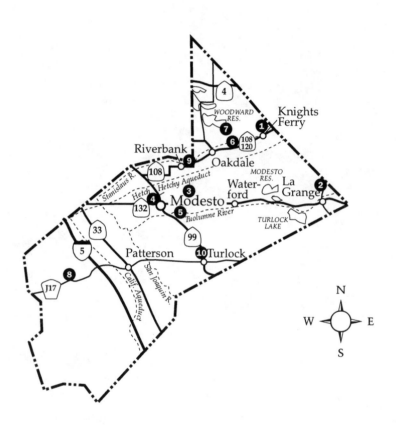

40
STANISLAUS COUNTY

Chambers of Commerce in these parts boast that "Summer Lasts Longer" here. Longer than what? When we asked, they weren't too sure. But when it's late September and your dog's tongue is unfurled just as long and bologna-like as it was in July, you may find the answer yourself: Summer lasts longer than hell here.

Fortunately, there are plenty of decent parks near the county's rivers. Dogs like to cool their fuzzy heels in the water.

Director George Lucas grew up here, surviving one sweltering summer after another. In his film *American Graffiti* (inspired by his younger years in Modesto, but not set there), a drive-in diner played a key role in the lives of his characters. It was a cool place to go on hot summer nights. If you and your dog want to dine alfresco here, you'll find a respectable number of outdoor restaurants. The most fitting is Modesto's very own A&W Root Beer drive-in restaurant, where carhops on roller skates will take your dog's order lickety split. Just don't let your dog do naughty things to any passing poodle skirts. See page 469.

KNIGHTS FERRY

PARKS, BEACHES, AND RECREATION AREAS

• **Knights Ferry Recreation Area** 🐾🐾🐾 *See* ❶ *on page 466.*

You and your leashed dog can swim, fish, hike, or just relax under a big oak tree at this popular riverside park. A historic covered bridge takes you from one side of the Stanislaus River to the other. You'll find picnic tables and room for a little walking on either side. It's crowded on weekends, but during weekdays, it's a relaxing getaway.

From Highway 108/120, head north on Kennedy Road to the river. (209) 881-3517.

LA GRANGE

PARKS, BEACHES, AND RECREATION AREAS

• **La Grange Regional Park** 🐾🐾🐾🐾½ *See* ❷ *on page 466.*

This 750-acre park has an undeveloped trail system that takes you along the Tuolumne River and through a delicate wilderness area. Woodpeckers, eagles, bobcats, deer, and all their friends make the park their home at different times of the year. Bring your binoculars and keep your dog leashed. (It's a real trick to bird-watch with a dog who's tugging on your arm to visit a nearby tree, but it can be done.)

The park is located in the historic town of La Grange, and contains ancient adobe buildings, an old jail, a schoolhouse, a cemetery, and an abandoned gold dredge. It makes for an interesting pit stop.

There are several parcels of La Grange Park. We like to start at the Basso Bridge Fishing Access. Exit Highway 132 at Lake Road and follow the signs. You'll be there in a snap. Park in the lot and head upriver. You can continue walking for a few miles and have a pleasant riverside hike. Or you can cross the street when you see a sign for the wilderness area and pay a visit to a more pristine setting. La Grange even offers camping. The sites are undeveloped and cost $12. (209) 525-4107.

PLACES TO STAY

La Grange Regional Park: See La Grange Regional Park above for camping information.

MODESTO

PARKS, BEACHES, AND RECREATION AREAS

• **Dry Creek Regional Park** 🐾🐾🐾 *See* ❸ *on page 466.*

A well-maintained bike/pedestrian trail leads you and the leashed dog in your life for more than three miles along the south side of Dry Creek. This park is actually a few parks strung together, so you'll find different terrain as you stroll merrily along. If your dog likes sniffing big trees or meditating at a riverside, he'll be happy here.

The park runs between La Loma Avenue and Claus Road. The section from El Vista Avenue east to Claus Road is not used much because it's very undeveloped. You may want to stick with the western part of the park. (209) 577-5344.

• **Roosevelt Park** 🐾🐾½ *See* ❹ *on page 466.*

Liquid ambers and horse chestnuts dot this pleasant neighborhood park. These colorful old trees provide a shaded setting for all the leashed dogs who visit. Roosevelt Park is known as one of the more popular places to take a dog around here, but when we visited, we didn't even see paw prints in the mud. Of course, it was pouring rain, so that may have had something to do with it.

The park is at Orangeburg and Bronson Avenues. (209) 577-5344.

• **Tuolumne River Regional Park** 🐾🐾🐾½ *See* ❺ *on page 466.*

It's rare to find a city park that's even a couple of miles long, but here's one that spans six miles. Dogs think it's the cat's meow.

It has just about everything a dog could want, except permission to run around off leash. It's mostly undeveloped, meaning few softball fields or playgrounds to get in the way of a dog's endeavors. It's on the banks of the Tuolumne River, so water-loving dogs can cool their paws where they're able to reach the river. And it has an appealing blend of wide-open meadows, oak knolls, and natural riparian land.

The park is on the north side of the Tuolumne River and runs from Ohio Avenue on the west to Mitchell Road on the east. It has a golf course where dogs are verboten. It's also broken up by the occasional road and some sections of parkland that aren't too appealing. Try the area east of Tioga Drive. (209) 577-5344.

RESTAURANTS

A&W Root Beer: It's not the same diner as the one in *American Graffiti*, but the carhops still come by on roller skates, and poodle skirts are still in. Come here on a summer afternoon and slurp down a root beer served in a frosted mug. Your dog can join you at the shaded patio. In the winter, the patio is heated. That's the time to try two piping-hot cheeseburgers, one for you, one for you-know-who. (Joe made me write that.) 1404 G Street; (209) 522-7700.

Mediterranean Market & Grill: Dine on tasty Italian food at one of the outdoor tables with your dog at your side. 1222 H Street; (209) 544-6433.

Piccadilly Deli: You and your dog will enjoy the deli fare, and you'll be grateful for the covered patio area during Modesto's long, hot summers. 941 10th Street; (209) 523-0748.

PLACES TO STAY

Best Western Town House Lodge: Rates are $49 to $58. A $25 pooch deposit is required. 909 16th Street, Modesto, CA 95354; (209) 524-7261 or (800) 772-7261.

Doubletree Hotel: This used to be one of the better Red Lions, but now it's an average Doubletree. Dogs who stay here have to sign a damage waiver. Rates are $89 to $120. 1150 Ninth Street, Modesto, CA 95354; (209) 526-6000.

OAKDALE

PARKS, BEACHES, AND RECREATION AREAS

• **Valley Oak Recreation Area** 🐾🐾🐾 *See* ❻ *on page 466.*

Some of the most pristine river woodland left in California lies along the Stanislaus River, and you should be able to see a sampling when you and your leashed dog visit this park. A hiking trail here offers a short tour of the lush river woodland. Moisture-loving trees such as cottonwoods, alders, and willows will keep you shaded while you dip your toes in the cool river.

This isn't a well-known park, so it doesn't get as crowded as some of the other riverside parks in the area. There are 16 boat-in campsites available for $6 to $8 per site. There is also one group site available (for a $36 to $38 fee). Reservations are required. From Highway 108/120, go north on County Road J9 and cross the river. Turn right at Rodden Road and follow it east to the park. (209) 881-3517.

• **Woodward Reservoir Regional Park** 🐾🐾🐾 *See* ❼ *on page 466.*
Although this is the largest county park in the system, dogs generally prefer Frank Raines Regional Park (see below). Raines Park is 1,800 acres smaller, but it's got a lot more of the natural stuff that some dogs need.

Woodward is more barren and yet much more developed. By virtue of its 3,800 acres of land (not including the 2,900-acre reservoir), it's a fine place to take the leashed dog in your life. If someone in your family has the urge to water-ski or fish, you and your dog can dip your paws in the reservoir and stroll around the park's rolling hills while you wait.

Since there are no official trails here, most people walk around on the small dirt roads. But when the park gets extremely crowded, as it's wont to do on some weekends, you and your dog won't feel safe on these roads. Stick to the meadowy sections of the park.

The day-use fee is $5 per vehicle. Camping fees range from $12 to $16 per site. Dogs are $2 extra day or night. There are 152 sites available on a first-come, first-served basis. If you want to launch your boat here, you'll pay an additional $5. From Highway 108/120, drive north on 26 Mile Road for about six miles to the park's entrance, which will be on your right. (209) 525-4107.

PLACES TO STAY

Valley Oak Recreation Area: See Valley Oak Recreation Area above for camping information.

Woodward Reservoir Regional Park: See Woodward Reservoir Regional Park above for camping information.

PATTERSON

PARKS, BEACHES, AND RECREATION AREAS

• **Frank Raines Regional Park** 🐾🐾🐾½ *See* ❽ *on page 466.*
This 2,000-acre county park is remote, mountainous, and full of wildlife you don't see much around these parts anymore. Leashed dogs love to hike among junipers, oaks, and digger pines on the many dirt trails that wind through the park.

Springtime is the best season for a visit. The wildflowers are fantastic and the creek looks splendid when it's full.

About 640 acres of parkland are set aside for off-highway vehicle use. There are signs to steer you away from this area, but if you hear a roar that's not your dog's stomach, hike to another area. You may have accidentally stumbled into OHV land. There are also 43 acres of lawn with barbecues, a baseball diamond, and a playground. Dogs actually seem to like this manicured section because of the enchanting little nature trail here.

Tempting as it may be to slip your dog's leash off in the backcountry, you really shouldn't. If I can't inspire you to listen to the law, perhaps the tarantulas, rattlesnakes, bobcats, and occasional mountain lions can.

Campsite fees range from $12 to $16. Dogs are $2 extra. There are 54 sites available on a first-come, first-served basis. From Interstate 5, exit at Del Puerto Canyon Road and head west. You'll reach the park in about 18 winding miles. Follow the signs. (209) 525-4107.

PLACES TO STAY
Frank Raines Regional Park: See Frank Raines Regional Park above for camping information.

RIVERBANK
PARKS, BEACHES, AND RECREATION AREAS
• **Jacob Meyers Park** 🐾 *See* ❾ *on page 466.*

At first glance (say at 7 A.M. on a fresh spring day), this is a lovely park, with lots of big trees and plenty of places to access the river. If you were so inclined, you and your leashed dog could go down to the Stanislaus River and dip your toes or fish for the catch of the day.

Unfortunately, many of the folks who hang out here go down to the river and do drugs and paint graffiti later in the day. It kind of puts a damper on the whole feel of the park.

If you're in town and your dog's gotta go, take Highway 108 to First Street and drive north to the park. If you're visiting later in the day, tell him to put on his best snarl. (209) 869-7101.

TURLOCK
PARKS, BEACHES, AND RECREATION AREAS
• **Donnelly Park** 🐾 🐾 ½ *See* ❿ *on page 466.*

One day, the adolescent trees here will be massive and shady, but for now, your dog will have to bring his own umbrella if he wants shelter from the sun. A pond takes up about half of the park. Ducks like it, and so do water dogs. But the latter aren't allowed.

The park is conveniently located in the middle of town. From Highway 99, exit at Fulkerth Road and drive east about 1.5 miles. (Fulkerth Road turns into Hawkeye Avenue, but keep going.) The park will be on your left, between Del's Lane and Donnelly Drive. (209) 668-5550.

PLACES TO STAY
Best Western Orchard Inn: Medium or small pooches are preferred here. If you're especially exhausted, you could even get a room with a Jacuzzi. Just don't let your dog try to rescue you from all those scary, dangerous bubbles. Rates are $48 to $63. There's also a $25 doggy deposit. 5025 North Golden State Boulevard, Turlock, CA 95382; (209) 667-2827.

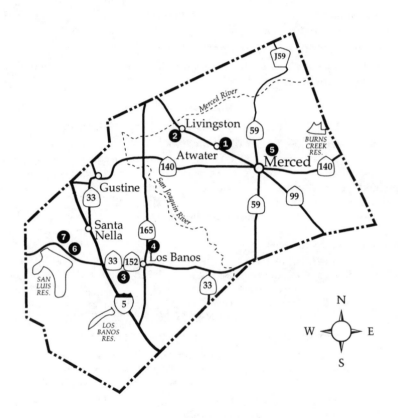

J59

Merced River

Livingston

2

1

59

Atwater

140

5

Merced

BURNS
CREEK
RES.

140

Gustine

San Joaquin River

99

33

59

Santa
Nella

165

7

4

6

33 152

Los Banos

3

SAN
LUIS
RES.

5

33

N

W — E

LOS
BANOS
RES.

S

41
MERCED COUNTY

The county parks here ban dogs. The national wildlife refuges ban dogs. Even some of the smaller cities ban dogs from their parks. It can make a dog howling mad.

But clench not thine paws, canines. Merced County is rescued from the recesses of rottendom by the state wildlife areas here. Most are huge and permit off-leash pooches for at least a few months of the year. Two of these areas, Los Banos and O'Neill Forebay, are discussed in this chapter. For information on the others, call (209) 826-0463.

ATWATER

PARKS, BEACHES, AND RECREATION AREAS

•**Ralston Park** 🐾🐾 *See* **❶** *on page 472.*

If you're window-shopping in the antique stores a few blocks away and need to rest your weary paws, Ralston Park is a decent place in which to sit a spell. It's got lots of lawn and plenty of trees for you and your leashed pal to snuggle up to and relax.

Ralston Park is located between Grove and Fir Avenues, on Third Street. (209) 357-6320.

RESTAURANTS

Out to Lunch: Owners Connie and George Corvelo love dogs. "The dogs who come here are more polite and well behaved than most children I know," says Connie. Dogs love sitting around the covered porch while their people eat tasty quiche or mouthwatering sandwiches. Try the zucchini bread sandwich with cream cheese and veggies. Got a sweet tooth? The Corvelos make their own cheesecake. Or order a slice of Kahlua cake. And stop drooling.

The Corvelos have played host to small doggy birthday parties. You provide the party hats and dog gifts, and they'll provide the roast beef sandwiches on paper plates (or whatever else your dog desires that's fairly healthful). It costs no more than the food you buy here, and they might even throw in a little scoop of vanilla ice cream for the partying pooches. 1301 Winton Way; (209) 357-1170.

GUSTINE

Dogs are banned from Gustine's parks. That smarts. But at least they can eat at one restaurant. It's not exactly Jeremiah Tower's Stars, but the food hits the spot when you and your dog get hungry on the road.

RESTAURANTS

Burger Hut: Eat cheeseburgers at the outside tables with your favorite pooch. 380 Fourth Street; (209) 854-6903.

LIVINGSTON

PARKS, BEACHES, AND RECREATION AREAS

• **Arakelian Park** 🐾1/2 *See* ❷ *on page* 472.

The trees here are young, and the picnic benches and playground equipment are new. It's an okay place to take a leashed dog, but when the trees grow big and muscular, it will be much better. It doesn't usually get crowded except on perfect weekends, so it's a pretty safe bet that if you want seclusion, you'll get at least a small dose of it.

The park is at the westernmost end of J Street, about a block west of Prusso Street. (209) 394-8041.

RESTAURANTS

Taco Bell: Dine with your dog at the outdoor tables here. 229 Simpson Avenue; (209) 394-4077.

LOS BANOS

PARKS, BEACHES, AND RECREATION AREAS

• **County Park** 🐾1/2 *See* ❸ *on page* 472.

If your dog is walking away from this book and scratching his fuzzy head in confusion, he has a right to. Just a few pages ago we mentioned that Merced County parks ban pooches, and now we're recommending one for a visit. Vot's goink on?

Fortunately, although the park is officially the county's, the city of Los Banos actually runs it and makes the rules. That means leashed dogs are welcome to explore the 11-acre park's proliferation of trees, which include pines, sycamores, and elms. It's not a large park, but it's the biggest one in the city.

The park is on the south side of Pacheco Boulevard, at Seventh Street. (209) 827-7000.

• **Los Banos Wildlife Area** 🐾🐾🐾🐾 🐕 *See* ❹ *on page 472.*

Dogs are allowed to roam leash-free here during certain times of the year, and the terrific news is that they don't have to be hunters' companions to do it. Unlike so many other state wildlife areas, even dogs who just like to walk around and watch the birds fly by are permitted to experience this leash-free bliss.

The wildlife area is 5,568 acres of flat, grassy land with intermittent marshlands and ponds. You and your dog can walk just about anywhere on the dirt roads and levees here. With more than 200 species of birds, plenty of reptiles (including the rare giant garter snake), and many mammals, you'll have plenty to watch. Bring your binoculars and a good pair of walking shoes. Don't forget a towel for your dog. It can get muddy.

Camping is available from mid-January to mid-September. While there are no developed campsites, the Department of Fish and Game can suggest areas where you might find a good primitive site. There's no fee for camping. The day-use fee is $2.50, but that's waived if you have a valid hunting, fishing, or trapping pass (eeks!) or a California Wildlands Pass.

From Highway 152, exit at Mercey Springs Road/Highway 165 and drive north for three miles to the wildlife area. Call first for a schedule of when it's open to leashless pooches, because dog visitation days are limited. You don't want to drive all the way here and find out that the entire wildlife area is closed for nesting season. Your dog will never forgive you—at least not until you take her to the nearest national forest. (209) 826-0463.

RESTAURANTS

Chubby's: This fun, '50s-style diner is ideal for travelers with dogs. It comes complete with a grassy area to walk your leashed dog. It also sports a faucet, where the owner's son likes to make sure thirsty dogs get plenty of water! The fare is your basic burgers and fries, and there's even music to relax you after a long drive. 1341 Pacheco Boulevard; (209) 826-8782.

Foster's Old-Fashioned Freeze: There are two picnic tables outside for you and your dog. 906 Pacheco Boulevard; (209) 826-4195.

PLACES TO STAY

Los Banos Wildlife Area: See Los Banos Wildlife Area above for camping information.

MERCED

Dogs of the male persuasion, rejoice! Merced is designated as a Tree City U.S.A. by the National Arbor Association. It's not exactly a forest, but the city does have an abundance of trees. It gives a dog plenty to sniff at, even if he's just accompanying you on a short walk.

PARKS, BEACHES, AND RECREATION AREAS

A Class-A bike path runs through town and passes many of the city's tree-shaded parks. You and your leashed dog are welcome to use the path, as long as you stay out of the way of things that could run you over. It's a great way to check out the various parks around the city.

If you get a chance, swing by the Courthouse Museum. It's a striking

---

Italian Renaissance–style structure with columns, sculpted window frames, and a magnificent cupola. Dogs can't hang out in the museum, but the park just outside is fine for leashed dogs.

• **Applegate Park** 🐾🐾🐾 *See* ❺ *on page 472.*

More than 60 varieties of trees grace this lovely 23-acre park that borders Bear Creek. Boy oh boy, do boy dogs adore Applegate Park! Kids like it, too. The park is home to a small zoo, as well as the Kiwanis Kiddieland mini-amusement park.

The city's 12-mile bike path runs through Applegate Park, so if you and your leashed dog want to saunter off to other parks, just follow the path to the next clump of greenery. Applegate is between M and R Streets, on the south side of Bear Creek. (209) 385-6855.

PLACES TO STAY

Motel 6: Merced has three Motel 6s. Rates at this centrally located one are $30 for the first adult, $6 for the second. They all allow one small pet per room. 1215 R Street, Merced, CA 95340; (209) 722-2737.

SANTA NELLA

This town is alive because of Interstate 5, which spews visitors into and out of town as quickly as they can get some gas and a bowl of Andersen's Split Pea Soup (which, in turn, can give folks enough of a different type of gas to last them clear to the Oregon border). If you want your pooch to have a sip of the delectable soup, go easy on it. Remember, you may be traveling in an enclosed vehicle together for many hours.

PARKS, BEACHES, AND RECREATION AREAS

• **O'Neill Forebay Wildlife Area** 🐾🐾🐾🐾 ✔
See ❻ *on page 472.*

If your dog's just aching to get out of the car and have a really good stretch, try this 700-acre grassland just to the west of Interstate 5. It's a terrific place if your obedient dog needs to run around without her leash for a while. (Dogs have to be leashed from April 1 to June 31, though.)

You'll find some marshy sections, but you'll be able to access most of the wildlife area by fire roads and levees. The wildlife viewing from here is wonderful.

But before you get your hopes up, call first and find out if the place is even open when you're planning to be here. At certain times of year, it's off-limits, even to leashed dogs. And you may not want to be hanging around during hunting season, unless you plan to hunt.

Exit Interstate 5 at Highway 33 and drive about two miles south to the entrance, which will be on your right. (209) 826-0463.

• **San Luis Reservoir State Recreation Area** 🐾🐾🐾
See ❼ *on page 472.*

The San Luis Reservoir is a water dog's dream. It's made up of three man-made lakes, and pooches currently have permission to do the dog paddle in all areas of the reservoir. In addition, part of the O'Neill Forebay (see above) is located within the recreation area's borders. While dogs aren't permitted on the beaches of the forebay, they can jump into the drink just about anywhere else there.

This park focuses on water activities, including fishing, swimming, and plenty of boating. It can get loud and crowded in the hot summer months, which always seem to attract fast boats. A better bet is in the spring, when it's cool and the fish are hungry. If you and the pooch are landlubbers at heart, you should probably find another park, since there's not much acreage outside of the picnic areas and campgrounds.

There are approximately 130 developed campsites and 400 primitive sites, many of which are along the water. Primitive sites are first come, first served and cost $7 to $10. Developed sites are $12 to $16. Dogs are $1 extra. Exit Interstate 5 at Highway 152 and drive west about four miles to the entrance road on the left. Call Parknet for reservations at (800) 444-PARK, or phone the park at (209) 826-1196 for more information.

PLACES TO STAY

Motel 6: Rates are $30 for the first adult, $6 for the second. One small pooch per room, please. 12733 South Highway 33, Santa Nella, CA 95322; (209) 826-6644.

Ramada Inn: Rates at this former Holiday Inn are $40 to $65. Dogs are $10 extra. 13070 Highway 33 South, Santa Nella, CA 95322; (209) 826-4444.

San Luis Reservoir State Recreation Area: See San Luis Reservoir State Recreation Area above for camping information.

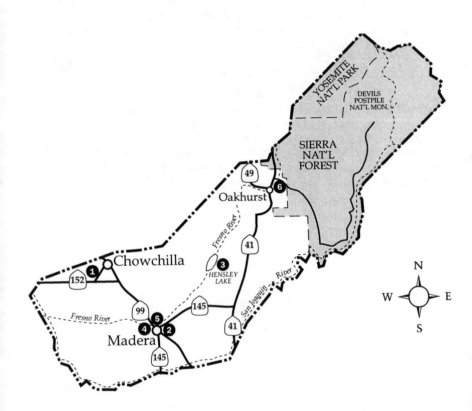

Bil Frank

42
MADERA COUNTY

A farm that looks like a pizza is one of the most dog-friendly places we've encountered in our travels through California. Dogs have to be leashed, but it's worth a stop to watch their jaws drop when the cows start mooing up-close and personal. See page 481.

Between the Pizza Farm, Sierra National Forest, and a couple of lakes where dogs can go leashless, Madera County is a hidden gem for dogs and their people. Okay, so it's more like a tourmaline than a diamond. It still outshines many of the nearby areas.

NATIONAL FORESTS

See the National Forests and Wilderness Areas chapter starting on page 748 for important information and safety tips on visiting national forests with your dog.

• **Sierra National Forest** 🐾🐾🐾🐾 🐕
See page 754.

NATIONAL MONUMENTS

• **Devil's Postpile National Monument** 🐾🐾🐾 ½
See page 215 in Mono County for a description of this park. You can't get there from here, even though the park is officially in Madera County.

NATIONAL PARKS

• **Yosemite National Park** 🐾½

See page 222 for the somewhat disheartening news about dogs in this otherwise amazing park.

CHOWCHILLA

PARKS, BEACHES, AND RECREATION AREAS

• **Sports and Leisure Community Park** 🐾🐾 *See* ❶ *on page 478.*

Dogs like the second half of this park's name better than the first. Besides, even sporting dogs are not allowed to play on the soccer and softball teams that often congregate here. If no sporting teams are using the park, you and your leashed pal will have 20 acres for your leisurely pursuits.

The park is at 15th Street and Ventura Avenue. (209) 665-8640.

PLACES TO STAY

Days Inn: Rates are $40 to $53. 220 East Robertson Boulevard, Chowchilla, CA 93610; (209) 665-4821.

MADERA

PARKS, BEACHES, AND RECREATION AREAS

As you'll note by the names of the three smaller parks, this is a very civic-minded area. Joe just wants to know where the Shriners' park is—and what about those Masons?

• **Courthouse Park** 🐾 *See* ❷ *on page 478.*

This is a perfect example of how well Madera's county parks masquerade as city parks. Courthouse Park is all of two acres and is just as flat, grassy, and square as any typical, tiny municipal park.

Despite its size, it's a pleasant place to visit. It's got some fairly large elms and there are picnic tables waiting for you and your leashed dog to visit with a lunch. It's a good spot for relaxing while waiting for a friend to check a book out of the nearby library, or to bail a buddy out of the nearby sheriff's headquarters.

The park is nestled between Yosemite Avenue and West Sixth Street, at Gateway Drive. (209) 675-7904.

• **Hensley Lake** 🐾🐾🐾🐾 🐕 *See* ❸ *on page 478.*

This 1,500-acre lake provides some choice fishing opportunities for you and your angling dog. With a launch fee of only $2, you can't lose, even if the bass aren't biting.

If you're the types who prefer to stick around terra firma, you'll be happy to know that the lake is surrounded by 1,500 acres of hilly land that you and your well-behaved dog can roam without a leash.

Visit in the springtime during the wildflower bloom if you really want a piece of paradise. If it's a tad warm, you'll find refreshing shade under the many oaks here. If it's still too warm for you, take a dip in the lake. Dogs are permitted to swim here, as long as they're not on the official beach areas. If you plan to go boating, the launch fee is only $2.

There are 68 campsites available on a first-come, first-served basis. Camping costs $8 to $12 per site. Dogs must be leashed at the campsites and other developed areas.

From Madera, drive northeast on Highway 145 for about six miles. Turn left on County Road 400 and drive 10 miles north to the lake. (209) 673-5151.

For information on Eastman Lake, located just northwest of Hensley Lake, call (209) 689-3255. The setting, prices, and rules are pretty much the same as Hensley's, but hydrilla weeds can prevent swimming.

•**Lions Town and Country Regional Park** 🐾🐾 ½
See ➍ *on page 478.*
There are lots of places to roam in this charming park. The rolling hills and shaded meadows make it a fine park for an afternoon walk with your leashed dog.

A little canal runs through the park. Arched wooden footbridges take you over the waterway to more romping room. As long as there's not a baseball game going on, you won't have to worry about crowds.

The park is in the southwest part of town, at Howard Road, just east of Granada Drive. (209) 661-5495.

•**Rotary Park** 🐾🐾 *See* ➎ *on page 478.*
If you're cruising along Highway 99 and your dog starts crossing his legs and humming an unintelligible tune while avoiding direct eye contact with the bottle of water you've wedged between the seats, pull over here. The park has plenty of trees and lots of grass, even for the most discriminating dog's needs.

If you have time, visit the dog-friendly Pizza Farm, located just across the highway in the Madera County Fairgrounds (see Diversions, below).

Exit Highway 99 at Cleveland Avenue and drive east about a block to Gateway Drive (just before the railroad tracks). Turn right. The park will be on your right almost immediately. Snap on that leash and trot, don't walk, to the nearest tree. (209) 661-5495.

RESTAURANTS
Eppie's: Dogs like to eat the good diner food at Eppie's outdoor tables. 1101 Country Club Drive; (209) 674-0368.

PLACES TO STAY
Best Western Madera Valley Inn: Rates are $56 to $85. 317 North G Street, Madera, CA 93637; (209) 673-5164.

Gateway Inn: Dogs are welcome to stay here "as long as they don't shed too much," says the manager. Joe Airedale, who is one of those non-shedding dogs, was happy to hear this. Rates are $32 to $59. 25327 Avenue 16, Madera, CA 93637; (209) 674-8817.

Hensley Lake: See Hensley Lake on page 480 for camping information.

DIVERSIONS
One half-acre pizza, please: Hold the anchovies! As long as your leashed dog doesn't poop on this gigantic pizza or try to terrorize the pepperoni pigs, she'll be mighty welcome at the Pizza Farm.

The point of the Pizza Farm is to show folks how integral farming is to the food we eat. The half-acre, circular Pizza Farm is divided into eight triangular "slices." Each slice contains something that's growing (or grazing for) the ingredients of a pizza. One slice has tomatoes. Another has cows who supply the milk for the cheese. Another has piggies for pepperoni. Other slices vary seasonally. Visiting all the slices is a fun, educational, and mouthwatering way to spend an hour or two.

The Pizza Farm is surrounded by a couple more acres of land, where your dog may stretch her legs and contemplate if she wants deep-dish or regular crust for dinner. You'll never look at a pizza the same way again. (Sorry, hungry dogs. You can't get pizza here, but the farm has a produce stand that might satisfy your pangs.)

The farm is open from March through October, seven days a week. The best time to visit is in the growing season, in late spring and summer. There's no fee. (It's the cheapest pizza you'll ever walk on.) It's located on the Madera County Fairgrounds. Exit Highway 99 at Cleveland Avenue and drive west. The farm/fairgrounds is on your left almost immediately. Call (209) 674-2391 for hours and more information.

OAKHURST

PARKS, BEACHES, AND RECREATION AREAS

• **Oakhurst Community Park** 🐾🐾½ *See* ⑥ *on page 478.*

This is a really green, meadowy park that you can get to by crossing over a wooden footbridge from the Chamber of Commerce parking lot. It's very convenient for people on the go with a dog who's got to go.

A little dirt path encircles the park. You can walk around the park a few times to stretch all of your legs, or relax in the gazebo or at a picnic table.

The park is just off Road 426 on Civic Circle. Follow the signs for the Chamber of Commerce. (209) 683-7766.

RESTAURANTS

Foster's Freeze Jr.: This place sees plenty of dogs during the tourist season. The deck has a few tables with umbrellas where you can have your choice of a wide variety of fast-food items. 40713 Highway 41; (209) 642-2600.

Subway Sandwiches and Salads: Eat subs at the outdoor tables here. 425A Stagecoach Road; (209) 683-3066.

PLACES TO STAY

Best Western Yosemite Gateway Inn: This inn is located 17 miles from the south gate of Yosemite. Rates are $52 to $115. 40530 Highway 41, Oakhurst, CA 93644; (209) 683-2378.

Pine Rose Inn: This bed-and-breakfast inn welcomes dogs as guests. "We love doggies and the people that come with them," says owner Anita Griffin. It's a beautiful place in a quiet mountain countryside setting just 12 miles from the south gate of Yosemite and two miles from Bass Lake. There's also plenty of hiking even closer to the inn. (Not that Yosemite is a hiking haven for dogs.)

Griffin has had some unusual guests. She once played hostess to a baby leopard who was so young his spots hadn't come out yet. A chimpanzee also made the inn his home for a few days while acting in a movie filmed in the area. "Obviously, good dogs are no problem at all," says Griffin.

You and your dog can stay in the main house or in one of five cottages. The rooms are full of country antiques, and some rooms even have fireplaces for those cold, wintry nights. A few rooms also have whirlpool tubs. This is the perfect place to get away from it all.

Rates are $39 to $99. Dogs are $5 extra and require a $50 deposit. The street address is 41703 Road 222. The mailing address is P.O. Box 2341, Oakhurst, CA 93644; (209) 642-2800.

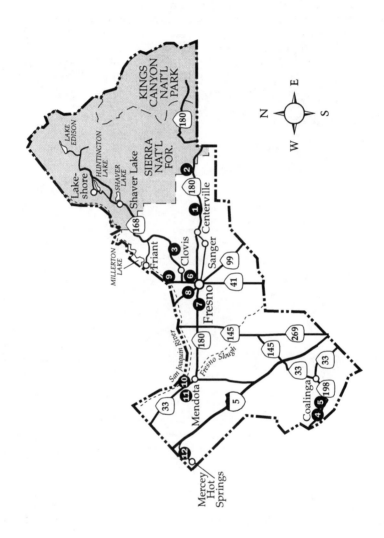

43
FRESNO COUNTY

At first glance, Fresno County seems like both an agricultural wonderland and a doggy wasteland. But your dog doesn't have to bite his toenails when he hears you're going to be spending some time exploring the area. The county has something for just about every dog's taste.

Rugged canines will enjoy the leashless freedom they'll experience in the national forest and the Bureau of Land Management areas. And those who prefer their toenails painted and their bouffants fluffed will enjoy the tinier, well-manicured city parks.

Dogs with a taste for olfactory offenses will appreciate visits to the pungent section near the zoo at Fresno's Roeding Park (see page 489) and to the stinky creek at Coalinga Mineral Springs (see page 487). You may not be crazy about the odors, but it's worth a few moments of holding your breath to see that enraptured expression on your dog's quivering snout.

NATIONAL FORESTS

See the National Forests and Wilderness Areas chapter starting on page 748 for important information and safety tips on visiting national forests with your dog.

•Sierra National Forest 🐾🐾🐾🐾 🐕

The cross-country skiing in some areas of this forest is first-rate. Leashless

---

dogs love to bound along beside you as you slice through the snow. See page 754 for more information.

NATIONAL PARKS

• **Kings Canyon National Park** 🔥
See page 527 for information on this not-so-dog-friendly park.

CENTERVILLE

PARKS, BEACHES, AND RECREATION AREAS

• **Avocado Lake County Park** 🐾🐾🐾 *See ❶ on page 484.*
Although there are no real trails around this 83-acre fishing lake, you and your dog can still manage to walk around just about the entire lake with little difficulty. That's because almost all 127 acres of county parkland surrounding the lake are more like lawns than wilderness.

It's a flat park, so if you don't like hills, you've got it made—in fact, you've got it made in the shade, because the park is full of trees. Just don't let your dog slip into the lake. Pooches aren't permitted, even if they wear a bathing cap.

From Centerville, exit Highway 180 at Piedra Road and follow it about five miles northeast to the lake. There's a $3 entry fee per car. (209) 488-3004.

• **Pine Flat Lake Recreation Area** 🐾🐾🐾 *See ❷ on page 484.*
Lakemeisters tell us there's about 120 acres of land for camping and hiking around Pine Flat Lake. But the lake itself is often extremely low—sometimes down to 10 percent of its capacity—because its water is being directed to farmland. When this happens, there's much more acreage for dogs and their leashed people to explore. But the loss of water isn't worth it. The lake is a sorry sight when it's in a depleted state.

But when it's full, it's a pleasure to hike around it. You'll amble through land dotted with digger pines, cottonwoods, oaks, and willows. The land is fairly flat and some of it is grassy. If you like to fish, you might try your luck on the spotted bass who hang out in the lake.

The day-use fee is $3. Campsites are $11. Call (209) 787-2589 for camping information. From Centerville, exit Highway 180 at Trimmer Springs Road and drive about 12 miles northeast to the lake. (209) 488-3004.

CLOVIS

PARKS, BEACHES, AND RECREATION AREAS

• **Letterman Park** 🐾🐾 *See ❸ on page 484.*
If you can't visit Johnny Carson Park in Burbank, why not give Letterman Park a try? So what if it's not named after TV's top late-night gap-toothed guy. Maybe someday it will be. Anyway, it's just as well, because he might not take kindly to his statue being on the receiving end of doggy leg lifts. Leashed dogs are welcome to poke around at this shady, eight-acre park. There's plenty of grass and a couple of small rolling hills.

The park is at Villa Avenue and West Ninth Street. (209) 297-2320.

RESTAURANTS

Deli Beans: If you're bringing your dog here, the manager prefers that you come after 2 P.M., when the place is less packed. You can eat sandwiches and slurp gourmet coffee on the patio. 2141 Shaw Avenue; (209) 323-8054.

COALINGA

PARKS, BEACHES, AND RECREATION AREAS

• **Coalinga Mineral Springs Recreation Area** 🐾🐾½
See ❹ on page 484.

Question: What smells like rotten eggs and attracts both man and beast? Answer: This park.

Leashed dogs love to come here because of the sulfur stench given off by the mineral-laden creek that runs through the park. Whenever Joe starts staring at the ground as if he's just had an epiphany, I know we're either getting near one of these sulfur heavens or approaching a piece of roadkill.

Humans enjoy this flat 35-acre park because it's full of pines and surrounded by mountains. There are warnings against drinking the stinky creek water, but a local woman in her 80s has been drinking it for decades and she looks mahhhvelous.

Camping here is very secluded, primitive, and cheap (free). It's used mostly by hunters during wild boar season. You have to bring your own water and get prior written permission from the county parks department. You could stay back in the campground for a few days and never see a soul.

The day-use fee is $3. From Coalinga, drive northwest on Highway 198 for about 18 miles and turn right on Coalinga Mineral Springs Road. Continue five more miles to the park. (209) 488-3004.

• **Coalinga Mineral Springs Scenic Trail** 🐾🐾🐾🐾 🐕
See ❺ on page 484.

Adjoining the county park (see above) are 9,000 acres of open land run by the dog-friendly Bureau of Land Management. If the 35-acre county park doesn't satisfy you or your dog, continue on to the adjacent BLM land and let the good times roll you through the grasslands. Just watch out for the occasional rocky outcropping.

The best part of this adventure is that if your dog is very obedient, you can let him run around leashless. But the 2.5-mile trail is also an equestrian trail, so if your dog thinks horses are giant dogs just waiting to be chased, keep him on his leash. Also be aware that deer live in the area surrounding the trail. If you aren't absolutely certain that your dog won't bound off after one, do everyone a favor and don't unleash him.

The hike is not for the fair of paw, since it can be steep. But if you and your dog are in good shape, it's worth the exertion. The trail leads you to Kreyenhagen Peak, where you'll have wonderful views of the southern Diablo Mountains. Come in the spring and watch the wildflowers go wild. In the warmer months, it can be mighty toasty and parched here.

We've heard that ticks can be a real problem at times. Call (408) 637-8183 for information, advice, and a schedule of when hunters might be shooting at the deer and other critters you and your dog are trying to avoid. The trail starts where the county park leaves off. See Coalinga Mineral Springs Recreation Area on page 487 for directions to the county park.

RESTAURANTS

Harris Ranch Restaurant: This enormous beef restaurant has outdoor tables where you can eat the food you ordered inside. Or if you prefer, you can bring a blanket, order your food inside, and bring it out for a cozy picnic on the lawn with your drooling dog. (You'd better order more than you can eat, because your dog will likely pull out all the stops for her begging routine.) Harris Ranch claims to be the largest beef company on the West Coast, so if you like red meat, you've struck gold. 24505 West Dorris Street; (209) 935-0717.

PLACES TO STAY

Coalinga Mineral Springs: See Coalinga Mineral Springs Recreation Area on page 487 for camping information.

The Inn at Harris Ranch: Ahh, Spanish-style architecture and the smell of broiling beef wafting into your room from the famed steak-o-rama next door. What more could a dog want? The only smell that could make this place more appealing to dogs is that of the Harris Ranch feedlot, but it's eight miles away. Unless the wind is just right, dogs are out of luck.

Rates are from $95 to $250. Dogs are $10 extra. It's just off Interstate 5, at the Highway 198/Hanford-Lemoore exit. The location is 24505 West Dorris Street, and the mailing address is Route 1, P.O. Box 777, Coalinga, CA 93210; (209) 935-0717.

FRESNO

In the midst of the region's raisin growers and cattle rustlers lies Fresno, the heart of the Central Valley. And like all hearts that are anatomically correct (not like the kind you get on a Valentine's Day card), it's functional and essential, but not too attractive.

Rest assured, there are some pretty good-looking parks in the midst of the malls and the cookie-cutter developments. If you have time to visit the charming Tower District, you may even start looking at Fresno in a different way. Or at least you'll start looking at Fresno.

PARKS, BEACHES, AND RECREATION AREAS

•**Einstein Park** 🐾🐾½ *See* ❻ *on page 484.*

There's a completely fenced-in section in the southwest part of this grassy park, and you don't have to be a genius to figure out why dogs and their people like it. We can say no more here. Go visit for yourself. Just a word of warning: There really is a leash law.

The park is at East Dakota Avenue, just west of North Millerbrook Avenue. (209) 498-1551.

•**Kearney Park** 🐾🐾🐾 *See* ❼ *on page 484.*

People who visit this tree-filled 225-acre park may well think that the man for whom this park is named was a philanthropic sweetheart. After all, his huge mansion is in the middle of the park, and the land for the park was essentially his yard, surrounded by thousands of acres of his farmland. Anyone who would give that kind of property to the city must be a kindly gent, right?

But according to Dave Caglia, head of parks and grounds operations for the county, English-born Martin Kearney was an ornery, racist farmer who acquired his land through crooked deals. He was jilted by the love of his life and became richer and more bitter over the years. The raisin mogul turned into a woman-hating recluse and built this mansion, complete with 18-inch-thick walls.

When he died in the early 1900s (on a transatlantic ocean crossing, no less), he left some of the land to the University of California. In 1949, the university gave it to the county. It was the start of the Fresno County Park System.

The old guy may have been mean, but he sure knew how to make a pretty park. It's very popular—too popular for a dog's taste, at times. Don't come here with your dog on beautiful weekend afternoons unless you want to share it with the masses.

The park is filled with 100-year-old trees, including maples, palms, oaks, and eucalyptus trees that are seven feet across and 200 feet tall! Boy dogs can barely contain themselves. But they can't go too wild, because leashes are the law here.

There's a $3 day-use fee. The park is on Kearney Boulevard, seven miles west of Fresno. (209) 488-3004.

•Roeding Park 🐾 🐾 🐾 See ❽ on page 484.

Before you and your dog look at your map and start drooling over this 157-acre chunk of land, you should know that it's much better for humans than for dogs. That's not to say dogs don't have a good time here. They have to be leashed, but they do enjoy the grass and trees in the sections where they're actually allowed.

But dogs are fairly restricted because of all the fun activities for humans. Between such dog-banning attractions as the Fresno Zoo, Storyland, Playland, and the park's numerous tennis courts and playgrounds, a dog could get to feeling like he's not a real person. But when he walks near the zoo and gets a whiff of the elephant and zebra poop, he'll be so enraptured that he'll probably forget all about his dejection.

There's a $1 parking fee from February through October. You can walk in free of charge. The rest of the year, there's no fee for parking. Exit Highway 99 at Belmont Avenue or Olive Avenue and drive east to the park's main entrance. (209) 498-1551.

•Woodward Park 🐾 🐾 🐾½ See ❾ on page 484.

At times, the line of cars trying to get into this park is so long that traffic in the area forms gridlock. It's obvious why the park is so popular. With 299 acres of grassy meadows, rolling hills, big trees, trails, streams, lakes, and ponds, Woodward Park provides a much-needed refuge from life in Fresnoland.

The park actually started out as a bird refuge. The sanctuary remains virtually untouched, but the surrounding parklands are burgeoning. It's not the kind of place your dog will want to visit on a weekend or just about any decent summer day. But if you pick the right time, you can pretty much have the run of the park. Early mornings are almost always a safe bet. Rainy days aren't bad either.

Dogs have to be leashed here, and they're not permitted in the Japanese garden. The parking fee from February through October is $2 per car, but you can walk in for free. The rest of the year, there's no charge. Driving north on Highway 41, exit at North Friant Road and drive northeast to East Audubon Drive. You'll be at the southeast corner of the park. Turn left and follow East Audubon Drive to the main entrance. (209) 498-1551.

RESTAURANTS

The City Cafe: Sometimes customers with canines order plain meat for their dogs while they dine on the tasty sandwiches served at the patio. Dogs also get a bowl of water here. 5048 North Blackstone Avenue, Suite 108; (209) 224-4399.

PLACES TO STAY

Best Western Tradewinds Motor Inn: Rates are $55 to $80. Pooches are $5 extra per day. 2141 North Parkway Drive, Fresno, CA 93705; (209) 237-1881.

Days Inn: At last check, leashed dogs were welcome to use the large, grassy area on the premises, as long as their human cleaned up after them. Rates are $35 to $64. Dogs are $5 extra. 1101 North Parkway Drive, Fresno, CA 93728; (209) 268-6211 or (800) 329-7466.

Executive Suites of Fresno: If you and your dog find yourself facing a long stay in Fresno, check out the pooch-friendly condos and apartments available through Executive Suites. Dallas Debatin, who manages the service, says he "would rather have dogs, cats, or snakes than smokers." Hiss, say the smokers (and the snakes), but howlelujah say the dogs. Rates are $550 to $1,250 per month. There's a $150 pooch deposit. There's no street address, since the suites are in various locations. P.O. Box 42, Fresno, CA 93707; (209) 237-7444.

Fresno Inn: Rates are $29 to $34. Dogs require a $25 deposit. 2345 North Parkway Drive, Fresno, CA 93705; (209) 268-0711 or (800) 621-0808.

Holiday Inn Centre Plaza: Rates are $84 to $110. 2233 Ventura Street, Fresno, CA 93721; (209) 268-1000.

Ramada Inn West: "Of course dogs are allowed. They are man's best friend!" exclaimed inn employee Richard, a dog owner himself. They don't have room, though, for "huge" dogs. Rates are $57 to $85. Dogs require a $20 deposit. 4278 West Ashlan Avenue, Fresno, CA 93722; (209) 275-2727.

FRIANT

PLACES TO STAY

Millerton Lake State Recreation Area: Since dogs aren't permitted on the trails, or in the lake (unless they're on a boat), about all you can do together is hang around one of the 138 campsites. Sites are $8 to $14. Dogs are $1 extra and should only camp here if someone will be with them if the rest of your party splits to do more interesting things. Call Parknet at (800) 444-PARK for reservations, or call the park at (209) 822-2332 for more info.

LAKESHORE

PLACES TO STAY

Lakeshore Resort: The managers at this 1920s-style mountain resort at Huntington Lake are a little gun-shy about allowing dogs. They've had people leave destructive pooches alone in the rooms only to find ruined furniture and torn-apart curtains and rugs. But more responsible dogs and their people might renew their faith in the canine species. And if you have a pupsitter and want to party, there's a saloon and dance hall on the premises.

Rates are $45 to $120. Dogs are $10 extra. During certain times of year, the managers may ask that you sign a pooch release. The street address is 61953 Huntington Lake Road, and the mailing address is P.O. Box 197, Lakeshore, CA 93634; (209) 893-3193.

MENDOTA

PARKS, BEACHES, AND RECREATION AREAS

• **Delta Mendota Canal Fishing Access** 🐾🐾🐾 *See ⑩ on page 484.*

If you and your favorite leashed dog don't mind whiling away the hours conversing with the fishies, you'll enjoy this 12-mile stretch along a farm-land irrigation canal.

The scenery wouldn't make a top-selling postcard. It's open land and the canal isn't pretty. But the fishing isn't bad, if you crave critters like cat-fish. Some folks bring a barbecue and make a day of it. Don't try this in the summer, though. There's no shade at all, and you can't cool off in the off-limits canal. Besides, the fishing isn't the greatest then anyway.

If you do plan to spend the day, be aware that there were no bathrooms here last time we checked. Park officials say every time they put some rest rooms out for public use, they get shot up and thrown in the canal. At $500 a pop, it adds up fast.

From Highway 33 just north of town, go east on Bass Road (just past the railroad tracks). In about 1.5 miles, you'll come to something called Mendota Pool Park. There are bathrooms there, should you plan ahead enough to need to use them before you fish. As you exit the park, you'll go up a little embankment. Turn left and you'll find the parking for the canal fishing. (209) 488-3004.

• **Mendota Wildlife Area** 🐾🐾🐾🐾 🐕 *See ⑪ on page 484.*

Your dog doesn't have to be a hunter in order to enjoy off-leash privi-leges at this 11,802-acre wildlife haven. As long as she's an obedient pooch, she can gambol at your side as you hike on trails and levees through the wetlands and grasslands here.

Bring your binoculars if you want to get up close and personal with the waterfowl and shorebirds who hang around the area. And watch out for skunks. We know one dog who got blasted here and has never quite smelled the same.

Follow the signs from Highway 180. Call (209) 655-4645 for a schedule of when the park is off-limits because of nesting seasons, and for information on hunting seasons.

MERCEY HOT SPRINGS

PARKS, BEACHES, AND RECREATION AREAS

• **Panoche Hills** 🐾🐾🐾🐾 🐕 *See* ⑫ *on page 484.*

Panoche has panache! These 30,000 acres of rolling hills and grasslands are heaven to dogs who need more than just your average community park to make them feel like real dogs. Because the Bureau of Land Management operates it, obedient dogs are allowed to run around leashless. Keep a close eye on your dog, though, because the hills are home to endangered species such as the San Joaquin kit fox and the blunt-nosed leopard lizard.

Hilltops, some of which are more than 2,500 feet tall, give you great views of the lush San Joaquin Valley and the dramatic Sierra Nevada. And if you visit in the spring (by far the best time of year to come), you'll be treated to a spectacular wildflower bloom. The hilltops are also excellent for setting up a telescope and watching other worlds go by. Bring a hearty dinner and a blanket for your dog, and you couldn't ask for a better viewing station.

The hills are near Mercey Hot Springs, off County Road J1. You'll see the signs. Call before you visit so you can find out about any hunting that might be going on and any closures due to fire danger. (408) 630-5000.

SANGER

PARKS, BEACHES, AND RECREATION AREAS

Dogs aren't allowed in Sanger parks—not unless you get written permission from the director of community services. Then you can let your dog saunter around on a leash that's up to eight feet long. That's a whole two feet longer than your standard leash law allows. Call (209) 876-6314 for more information.

• **Greenwood Park** 🐾🐾🐾 **(with permit)** *See* ⑬ *on page 484.*

Only dogs with written permission from the city can visit this green, grassy, somewhat hilly community park with picnic tables and plenty of trees. The park is at Fifth Street and Academy Avenue. (209) 876-6314.

SHAVER LAKE

PARKS, BEACHES, AND RECREATION AREAS

• **Shaver Lake** 🐾🐾🐾🐾 🐕 *See* ⑭ *on page 484.*

Although some of the land immediately surrounding this attractive lake is run by the county, even more of it is administered by the U.S. Forest Service. In fact, Sierra National Forest pretty much surrounds the lake. And you know what that means for dogs: No mandatory leashes on national forestland! (But be sure to leash up on county land.)

The lake is set at an elevation of 5,000 feet. There are 252 camping sites, ranging in fees from free to $22 per site and $2 for pooches. Reservations are highly recommended from mid-June to mid-September. From the town of Shaver Lake, follow Highway 168 north to the lake. (209) 841-3313.

PLACES TO STAY

Shaver Lake: See Shaver Lake above for camping information.

44
SAN BENITO COUNTY

If you look at a map of this county, you may wonder, "What's a dog to do here?" Joe looked as if he were being sent to purgatory when I told him we were going to visit San Benito County. He sat at the front door of the house and wouldn't budge. When I tried pulling him, he tugged back and slipped out of his collar. But since I have longer legs, a stronger body, and a box of desiccated liver treats, I won the battle. He gulped down the bait, frowned, and succumbed to his fate.

He must have remembered those vast stretches of privately owned nothingness we once drove across on the way from nowhere to not-much-of-anyplace-else. Even I wanted to be anywhere but there. But this time our visit was different. It wasn't heaven, but it wasn't hell either. At the end of our time in this county, even Joe had a smile on his boxy snout.

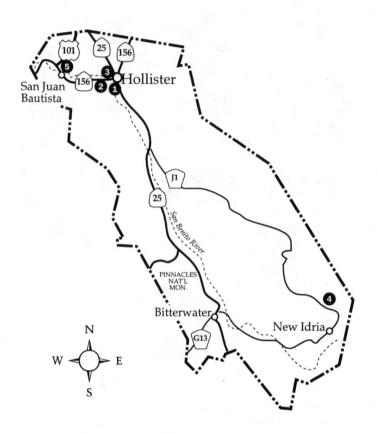

101

25 156

5

156 3

San Juan 2 1 Hollister
Bautista

J1

25

San Benito River

PINNACLES
NAT'L
MON.

Bitterwater 4

New Idria

G13

N

W E

S

BITTERWATER

PLACES TO STAY

Pinnacles National Monument: Dogs are permitted only in picnic areas, parking lots, paved roads, and the campground at this park, so they miss exploring all the fascinating pinnacle-shaped volcanic rock formations within. It's not much fun for your pooch, but if she's with someone who's not in the mood to hike around and explore the caves and trails here, the campgrounds aren't a bad place to hang out for a day.

There are 90 sites at the privately operated campground that you can get to from San Benito County. Campsites are $7. Dogs have to pay a $10 deposit. Reservations are required for groups of 10 or more. From Highway 25 about 13 miles north of Bitterwater (26 miles south of Hollister), take Highway 146 southwest to the park. The private campground phone number is (408) 389-4462. (A couple of people have told us that the managers of the private campground have been known to discourage dog visitors, so you may want to try the park's campground instead.) The park-operated campground costs $10 per night, but can be accessed only from its west side, on Highway 146. The east and west ends of Highway 146 don't connect, so you can't drive on it from one side of the park to the other. At press time, floods had closed this campground and its future was uncertain. Call before coming! The park number is (408) 389-4485.

HOLLISTER

PARKS, BEACHES, AND RECREATION AREAS

• **Dunne Park** 🐾🐾 *See* ❶ *on page 494.*

This downtown-area park is the city's oldest, and though it only covers about four acres, your leashed dog may feel like he's in a significantly larger space. Dogs of the leg-lifting persuasion enjoy the sycamore, olive, and bay trees throughout the park.

The park is at Sixth and West Streets. (408) 636-4370.

• **San Justo Reservoir County Park** 🐾🐾🐾 *See* ❷ *on page 494.*

You and your leashed dog are free to hike on the dirt trail/fire road that encircles this 580-acre park. Many folks like to come here to fish at the 200-acre reservoir, but dogs generally prefer to amble through the open land. It's not the most attractive place in the world, but it beats the backyard.

The day-use fee is $5 per vehicle. You can launch your boat from here for a mere $2 to $3. The park is west of town. Exit Highway 156 at Union Road and drive south. The park will be on your right in a little less than a mile. Hours are limited, so call (408) 638-3300 for a schedule.

• **Vista Park Hill** 🐾🐾🐾 *See* ❸ *on page 494.*

This hilltop park overlooks town and has plenty of undeveloped acres for your leashed dog to explore. In this case, though, undeveloped means dry grass, weeds, and, yes, foxtails in the wrong time of year. Be careful out there. You may want to stick with the green open spaces and the eucalyptus-lined walkways that are also in this park.

From Highway 156, go west on Hill Street for a long block to the park's entrance. This is also where the Bureau of Land Management's local office is located. It's a good place to stop in and pick up information on the nearby BLM lands (see Griswold Hills, below, for information on one of these off-leash areas). The city park department's phone number is (408) 636-4370.

RESTAURANTS

Hollister Coffee Roasting Company: You and your dog can sit at the sidewalk tables and enjoy fine coffee and pastries. 420 San Benito Street; (408) 636-0240.

NEW IDRIA

PARKS, BEACHES, AND RECREATION AREAS

• **Griswold Hills Recreation Area** 🐾 🐾 🐾 🐾 🐕
  See ❹ on page 494.

Some small city parks I've explored are run by departments that tell you the parks' acreage down to the hundredth of an acre. When you're dealing with parks that are 3.21 acres, you want to count every inch.

But then along comes the Bureau of Land Management. In its written material, it says Griswold Hills has "several thousand acres." We're not talking exact measurements here. But that's the charm of these off-leash BLM havens. Precision and rules are left at the gate (when there is a gate). Rules exist, but few restrict a well-behaved dog's good time.

This recreation area is made up of rugged canyons of scrub oak, juniper, and chaparral. Some trails take you up to ridgetops for good views of the surrounding valleys. Others take you to the riparian zone at Griswold Creek. Not many people know about this area, so if you and your dog need to get away from it all, there's a good chance you can.

The park isn't as big or as scenic as the BLM's nearby 50,000-acre Clear Creek Management Area. But we don't recommend that area for people who worry about things like asbestosis, mesothelioma, or cancer. Because of naturally occurring asbestos, you and your dog are supposed to wear protective clothing and respirators when setting paw on much of the land. It's not worth it.

The main entrance to Griswold Hills is located three miles south of Panoche Road on New Idria Road. Watch out for hunters during deer and quail seasons. Call (408) 630-5000 for hunting dates and more information on local BLM lands.

SAN JUAN BAUTISTA

Be sure to swing by the Mission San Juan Bautista when you visit this town, especially if you or your dog are fans of Alfred Hitchcock. The mission (the largest of the old California missions) starred in the Hitchcock classic *Vertigo.* It's worth a peek, but dogs have to stay firmly planted on the ground outside. Jimmy Stewart would have envied the stance.

If you're hungry, don't let all the restaurants with outdoor tables fool you. We couldn't find any eateries that would permit pooches. But as the pendulum swings, we don't expect that to last for long.

PARKS, BEACHES, AND RECREATION AREAS

• **San Juan Bautista State Historic Park** 🐾🐾½ *See* ❺ *on page 494.*

Leashed dogs who like local history are welcome to accompany you as you tour this small state park. You'll see buildings like the old Plaza Hotel, which was a popular stagecoach stop, and the Castro House, at one time the administrative headquarters of Mexican California. But since dogs must stay outside such buildings, they prefer to tour the livery stables, gardens, and orchards.

The park is on the plaza in the center of town. Admission is $2 per adult, $1 per child. Call (408) 623-4881.

PLACES TO STAY

San Juan Inn: If you and your pooch are looking for a quiet spot to spend the night, stay here. Rates are $42 to $65. Dogs require a $20 deposit. The inn is located at 410 Alameda Street, and the mailing address is P.O. Box 1080, San Juan Bautista, CA 95045; (408) 623-4380.

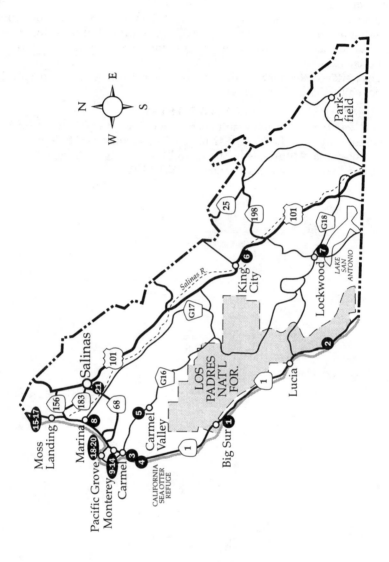

45
MONTEREY COUNTY

Native son John Steinbeck and his fearless blue poodle, Charley, visited here during their cross-country journey recorded in the 1961 classic, *Travels with Charley.* The Gentle Reader is never sure what Charley did while his master paid homage to old bars and old memories in Monterey and Salinas, but wherever Charley went in this county, he probably felt as accepted as his human friend. Monterey County is as warm and welcoming as an old Italian aunt.

The county is a wonderland for dogs and their drivers. People get part of the vast agricultural sweeps in the east part of the county and the rugged mountain coast along the mighty Pacific in the west. Dogs get the pungent odor of fresh fertilizer in the east and the tantalizing scents carried miles by the Pacific winds in the west.

The Carmel area is one of the most dog-friendly places on Earth. In fact, dogs are almost de rigueur here. Dog-loving restaurants and inns abound. There's even an art gallery that welcomes dogs by giving them biscuits in a crystal dish and letting them peruse the artwork. (See Galerie Blue Dog under Diversions, page 507.) And rumor has it that two dogs were recently married in Pebble Beach. Hey, I read it in a local magazine. It must be true!

If going leashless is your dog's fantasy, Carmel, Carmel Valley, and Pacific Grove are ideal stopping points. Their designated off-leash romping grounds are as picturesque as their cozy inns. And your dog would never forgive you if you forgot the northern segment of the magnificent Los Padres National Forest for a hearty leashless hike.

The area just got even more doggone great: There's now a dog tour agency that will take you and yours (and a few others and theirs) on a four-day walking holiday around Monterey and Carmel. You'll stay at pooch-friendly hotels, dine in dog-loving surroundings, and have a terrific time vacationing with your dog. You could arrange your own dog vacation and it would be cheaper, but Happy Dog Tours takes all the stress out of it and adds extras, like Doggie Bath Night. Linda Austin, who started the business, helped run a European dog tour recently, and it went so well that she figured, "Why not right in my own backyard?" Rates for single occupancy are $1,460. Two humans in a room pay $1,180 each. For more information, contact Happy Dog Tours, P.O. Box 568, Pacific Grove, CA 93950; (408) 647-1921. Their web address: www.happydogtours.com.

In addition, a less-expensive, two-hour walking tour welcomes dogs on its stroll through Carmel. Your dog will have a doggone great time, because part of the tour is devoted to the dogginess here. (See Diversions, page 507.)

NATIONAL FORESTS

See the National Forests and Wilderness Areas chapter starting on page 748 for important information and safety tips on visiting national forests with your dog.

• Los Padres National Forest 🐾 🐾 🐾 🐾 🐕

This spectacular, rugged terrain in the Big Sur area is great for an outing with a spectacular, rugged dog. Actually, even spectacular couch-potato dogs can enjoy some of the hikes here in the Ventana Wilderness. See page 751 for a description of Los Padres National Forest.

BIG SUR AREA

As the two-lane ribbon of Highway 1 winds 90 miles up and down what many think is the most spectacular coastal scenery in the world, your dog may be praying for the end of the trip—or at least wishing for a dose of Dramamine.

Carsick dogs are not uncommon as mountains shoot up 1,000 feet over the crashing Pacific, only to curve and slope down again, roller coaster fashion. It's a good idea to take your time and stop at as many vista points as you can along the road. Your dog will thank you for it, and you'll get to breathe the exhilarating Pacific air and study the rugged shoreline.

A must-stop vista point is at the Bixby Creek Bridge, 260 feet high and more than 700 feet long. There are pullouts on either side.

Whatever you do when you're making these stops along Big Sur, make sure your dog is securely leashed and in no danger of stepping too close to the edge of the world. There's usually not much room between Highway 1 and the hazardous cliffs.

PARKS, BEACHES, AND RECREATION AREAS

Unfortunately, there are plenty of state parks along the way, and few beaches. This isn't so bad for people without dogs, but canines are extremely restricted in state parks. Most allow dogs only where they allow cars: paved roads and drive-in campsites. It's not worth the price of admission, unless you're planning an overnight stay.

• **Pfeiffer Beach** 🐾 🐾 🐾 🐾 *See* ❶ *on page 498.*

You and your leashed dog will be stunned at the natural beauty of this white, sandy beach. Surrounded by sea caves, steep cliffs, and natural arches, you won't know what to marvel at first. Your dog will be so thrilled that he won't even notice he's leashed.

From the north, take the second right turn (Sycamore Canyon Road) off Highway 1 south of Big Sur State Park. It's a sharp turn. At the end of the narrow, two-mile road is a sandy trail under a canopy of cypress trees. It leads to the beach. (408) 385-5434.

• **Sand Dollar Picnic Area and Beach** 🐾 🐾 🐾 *See* ❷ *on page 498.*

Your dog will enjoy the romance of a picnic among the cypress trees here. After downing your French bread, Brie, and white wine, take one of the trails across the field and follow it down to the beach. Although dogs must be leashed, this is one of Joe's favorite spots. It's toward the southern end of Big Sur, so it's at a perfect place to take a break from driving.

The picnic area is about 11 miles south of Lucia, west of Highway 1. (408) 385-5454.

PLACES TO STAY

Here are just a few of the many private and public campgrounds along the Big Sur coast.

Big Sur Campground: If you're into family-oriented camping, this is your kind of place. This privately owned campground in the redwoods along the Big Sur River features basketball courts and a playground for the kids. Tent camps are $24 a site, and dogs are $3 extra. The more exclusive tent-cabins have queen-sized beds and cost $40 a night for two people; dogs are an additional $8. The campground is on Highway 1, about 24 miles south of Carmel. For reservations (and they'll take them up to a year in advance, so it's a good idea to make one), contact the campground at Highway 1, Big Sur, CA 93920; (408) 667-2322.

China Camp: It's fun to camp here if you're planning on hiking in the Ventana Wilderness (see page 751) but you're not quite sure about camping in the wilderness itself. A trail leads directly from the camp into the Ventana Wilderness. Dogs must be on leash at the campsite, but they can put their leashes in their doggy backpacks as soon as they're in the wilderness area.

Six sites are available on a first-come, first-served basis. There's no charge for the sites, but you can't get out of the red tape that easily: You need a wilderness permit to come here. Keep in mind that there's no piped-in water, so bring plenty, or be ready to filter any you find in streams along the way. The campground is inland, about 20 miles southwest of Carmel Valley, on Tassajara Road. Call the Los Padres National Forest main office at (408) 385-5434.

Kirk Creek Campground: You'll love the view from the bluffs above the beach here, and your dog will appreciate the cool Pacific breezes. You can bring your leashed dog down to the beach on a couple of steep trails, or you can take a trail from here that leads into the Ventana Wilderness. That's where your dog can legally remove his leash.

Kirk Creek has 33 campsites, costing $17. The campground is west of

Highway 1, about four miles south of Lucia. Call the Los Padres National Forest main office at (408) 385-5434.

Pfeiffer Big Sur State Park: Though this state park has 821 acres of redwoods, some near Big Sur River, dogs are permitted only in the camping area. It's not so bad—each of the 218 campsites has a picnic table where your dog can join you for gourmet outdoor cooking, or he can sleep under it when the shade of the redwoods isn't enough.

Sites are $14 to $23. Dogs are an extra dollar. The park is east of Highway 1, about 26 miles south of Carmel. Call park headquarters at (408) 667-2315 for information. For reservations, call Parknet at (800) 444-PARK.

Ventana Campground: This privately owned campground set in a redwood canyon is ideal for getting away from motor-home campers without getting too primitive. No reservations are necessary for the 70 campsites, but they are recommended for summer weekends. It's more rustic than many campgrounds you'll find around here, which is something Joe appreciates.

Sites are $25. Dogs are an extra $5. The campground is about 2.5 miles south of Pfeiffer Big Sur State Park. The mailing address is P.O. Box 206, Big Sur, CA 93920; (408) 667-2688.

CARMEL

Dogs feel more welcome in this picturesque village than almost anywhere in the world. Maybe there's an aura emanating from dog-lover Doris Day's Cypress Inn (see page 505) or the other gorgeous, super-dog-friendly inns here. Or perhaps it's the tantalizing dog burgers (that's burgers for dogs, lest a gruesome image flashed through your head) served at the wonderful Le Coq D'or (see page 504), or the water served to dogs in champagne buckets at the delightful Portabella restaurant (see page 504), or the dog biscuits offered to art-loving pooches at the Galerie Blue Dog. Or maybe it's the "doggy hitching posts" attached to shops around Ocean Avenue, Carmel's main street. The hook-and-snap devices make it possible for you to shop while your dog relaxes in the shade outside, without being forced to hear the incessant ringing of cash registers. Of course, that welcome feeling could well come from knowing that Carmel's city beach, one of the most enticing beaches in California, lets pooches run leashless (see Carmel City Beach, below).

Whatever the case, your dog can't help but be happy in Carmel, which in these busy times still shuns the idea of street addresses. You won't have a problem finding your destinations, though, because the village is small enough and the people are friendly enough that it's very hard to stay lost for long—especially with a dog on your side.

PARKS, BEACHES, AND RECREATION AREAS

•**Carmel City Beach** 🐾🐾🐾🐾 🐕 *See ❸ on page 498.*

The fine white sand crunches underfoot as you and your leash-free dog explore this pristine beach. It's the only beach for many, many miles that allows dogs off their leashes, so it's a real gem for dog travelers. Bordered by cypress trees and a walking trail, the beach is also popular among humans, especially on weekends. So if your dog is the type to mark beach blankets and eat things out of other peoples' picnic baskets, you may want to leash him until you find a less crowded part of the beach.

Pooper-scoopers are available at dispensers here, but it's a good idea to bring your own just in case doggy demand is high and they run out. From Highway 1, take the Ocean Avenue exit all the way to the end, where you'll find a large parking area that's not large enough on summer weekends. (At press time, this beach was a wreck because of El Niño storms. But it will have probably returned to its glory by the time you read this.) (408) 624-3543.

•**Carmel River State Beach** 🐾 🐾 🐾 *See ❹ on page 498.*

Dogs can enjoy this large stretch of beach as far as their leashes will allow. It's convenient if you're stuck south of Carmel, but most dogs prefer Carmel City Beach (see above) because of its leash-free policy.

The state beach is accessible from many points, including Ribera Road, off Highway 1. (408) 624-4909.

RESTAURANTS

Anton & Michel: Dine "fountainside" with your dog at the outdoor area of this yummy continental-style restaurant. The atmosphere is casual and elegant (these two adjectives pretty much define most of Carmel, by the way). The Italian and French food is delicious. Dogs get a big bowl of water here. The restaurant is at Mission Street and Seventh Avenue. (408) 624-2406.

Cafe Berlin: If you want German, this place has excellent German food. But it also cooks up lots of different European-style dishes, should you or your dog prefer something less, well, less German. It's on Junipero Street between Fifth and Sixth Avenues. (408) 626-8181.

Cafe Gringo: You and your dog will have a great time at this very dog-friendly, casual Mexican restaurant. Dogs get a bowl of water and dog biscuits on the house! Humans get a menu full of traditional Mexican dishes (burritos, et al) and nontraditional delights. (Try the chicken breast cooked with tequila under a brick. It melts in your mouth, and you can still drive.) Dine with your doggy at the outdoor tables. The restaurant is on San Carlos Street between Ocean and Seventh Avenues. (408) 626-8226.

Cafe Stravaganza: This is an excellent place to stop for a bite if you're on Highway 1 with a dog who is hungering for something different. The food here is eclectic, with everything from American comfort food to good Italian and Greek dishes. Try the primavera potatoes (garlic mashed potatoes topped with sautéed vegetables) for a taste that'll make you want seconds. Your dog might prod you to get the lamb marsala, too. We're told it's a winner. You and your dog can dine together at the outdoor tables. The cafe is at the Crossroads Shopping Center, at Highway 1 and Rio Road. (408) 625-3733.

Casanova Restaurant: Known around these parts as Carmel's most romantic restaurant, Casanova's is also surprisingly dog-friendly. It may take a little of the romance out of your evening when your dog starts grinding his chin into your date's lap in pursuit of a handout, but hey, it could also provide a much-needed icebreaker. Well-behaved pooches are welcome on the lovely front patio. The country French and Italian cuisine is superb. Casanova's is at Fifth Avenue between San Carlos and Mission Streets; (408) 625-0501.

Grasing's Coastal Cuisine: The seafood is so fresh here you'd swear it just jumped onto your plate from the ocean. The pastas and salads are tops, too. If your dog is thirsty, they'll make sure she gets a snootful of water. It's at Sixth Avenue and Mission Street. (408) 624-6562.

Le Coq D'or: This intimate, delightful European country-style restaurant that serves only dinner is a paws-down favorite among dogs: Pooches who come here get a burger to call their own. The dog-loving restaurant owner, Annelore, serves her own special dog burgers, which consist of ground beef, rice, and garlic, with a dash of salt and pepper. "They smell so good I could eat one myself," she says. The burger comes with a dog bowl filled with fresh water. The cost for all this: $0.00. "I do it because I love dogs and I think customers like seeing their dogs eat at a restaurant," says Annelore.

The people food here is out of this world. Try the coq au vin or the Alsatian onion tarte. We hear the sweetbreads are tasty, but you'll never get a firsthand review of them in this book unless Joe Dog takes over authorship. It's located on the east side of Mission Street, between Fourth and Fifth Avenues; (408) 626-9319.

Nico: You and your dog can get excellent burgers here. Nico also makes a couple of good sandwiches for non-meat eaters. Enjoy the bistro cuisine at the outdoor tables. The restaurant is at San Carlos Street and Ocean Avenue; (408) 624-6545.

Plaza Cafe and Grill: They've got everything a dog owner could want, from fresh fish to pizza. Dine at one of the many umbrella-shaded tables. You'll find it at Carmel Plaza, at the corner of Ocean Avenue and Junipero Street; (408) 624-4433.

Portabella: If you love delicious, unique French, Italian, and Spanish food, and if your dog loves being treated like the toast of the town, come to this elegant, yet casual, ristorante. Among the mouthwatering dishes are ravioli with pan-fried goat cheese and sun-dried tomatoes. It's truly to drool for. You can get all kinds of Mediterranean-style dishes and fresh seafood here, but you can also get ye ol' basic hamburger. Dogs think that's very cool. And they think it's even cooler that they're given water, and that the water comes not in a bowl but in a champagne bucket. It's enough to make even the most earthy mutt feel just a bit classy. Portabella is on Ocean Avenue between Lincoln and Monte Verde Streets; (408) 624-4395.

Sherlock Holmes Pub and Restaurant: Dogs enjoy being surrounded by such English goodies as fish-and-chips, bangers, English pies, and Yorkshire pudding while sitting at the patio here. If you and the pooch aren't Anglophiles, Sherlock Holmes also serves good hot turkey sandwiches, Reubens, fajitas, tacos, and even filet mignon. You'll find it at 3772 The Barnyard; (408) 625-0340.

PLACES TO STAY

Carmel Country Inn: If you and your dog feel like a cozy room in a quiet setting, you'll enjoy a stay at this pretty 12-room inn. Fresh flowers adorn the rooms, which have a serene country feel. Suites have a balcony, a sitting room, and a fireplace. The inn is set around a cheerful garden, which dogs love to sniff around. But no doggy business there, please!

Rates are $115 to $165. Dogs are $10 extra. The inn is at Third Avenue and Dolores Street, and the mailing address is P.O. Box 3756, Carmel, CA 93921; (408) 625-3263 or (800) 215-6343.

The Carmel Tradewinds Inn: The Tradewinds looks like a motel on the outside, but in your room you'll feel more like you're at a cozy country inn. That's because the rooms are airy, with vaulted ceilings, and many have a fireplace, a balcony, and ocean views. Unlike most Carmel lodgings, the Tradewinds is on a hill, which affords excellent views of the ocean. Humans get to enjoy use of an outdoor pool here, and there's a ton of parking—a real rarity in this town.

Dogs have to be under 50 pounds to stay here, and you must sign a pet agreement. Rates are $89 to $250. Dogs are $15 extra. The Tradewinds is on Mission Street at Third Avenue, and the mailing address is P.O. Box 3403, Carmel, CA 93921; (408) 624-2776 or (800) 624-6665.

Coachman's Inn: This 30-room motel is one of the least expensive lodgings in the area. Rates are $64 to $175. Dogs are $15 to $20 extra, depending on their size. It's on San Carlos Street at Seventh Avenue. The mailing address is P.O. Box C-1, Carmel, CA 93921.

Cypress Inn: Dogs get the royal treatment here, in part because actress and animal activist Doris Day owns this sumptuous hotel. The Mediterranean-style inn is very elegant, with fine oak floors and delicate antiques, but you never feel out of place with your dog. Day's staff makes sure your dog feels especially welcome, right down to offering pet beds and pet food for your four-legged friend. There's no doggy spa yet, but *que sera, sera.*

Rates are from $110 to $285. It's $17 extra for the first pooch and $10 for the second. The inn is at Lincoln Street and Seventh Avenue, and the mailing address is P.O. Box Y, Carmel, CA 93921; (408) 624-3871.

The Forest Lodge: You may feel as though you're in an enchanting forest cabin when you stay here, even though you're just a bone's throw from the center of Carmel. The Forest Lodge consists of four delightful wooden cottages surrounded by lovely gardens and an assortment of good-sized trees. The cottages range from small and cozy to large and, well, cozy. Two have wood-burning fireplaces, three have featherbeds, one has marble floors in the bathroom, and one even has a peek of the ocean.

The place is as dog-friendly as it is attractive. "Everyone on our street has at least two dogs. We're all dog lovers here," says Dee McGrath, the lodge's manager. To make matters even better for dogs, the Forest Lodge is seven short blocks from dog-friendly Carmel City Beach (see page 502).

Rates are $99 to $240 for up to two people. Extra people are $10 each. Dogs are $5 to $10 extra, depending on their size. The Forest Lodge is at Ocean Avenue and Torres Street, and the mailing address is P.O. Box 1316, Carmel, CA 93921; (408) 624-7023.

Quail Lodge Resort: This resort is exquisite. The cottages and two-story lodge buildings have a unique, warm design that's a beautiful blend of country and contemporary Asian. Some rooms have fireplaces. The spacious grounds are attractively landscaped and sport several little lakes/ponds. They also have tennis courts and a golf course, for the athlete in your life. You can walk your pooch around the grounds or head up the road to a less-landscaped area the resort owns. A staffer will point the way. Only one pooch is allowed per room, please. Pet sitting is available at $7 per hour, for a three-hour minimum. Rates are $250 to $550. 8205 Valley Greens Drive, Carmel, CA 93923; (408) 624-1581.

Sunset House: It's hard to know where to start a description of this attractive, romantic, extremely dog-and-people-friendly inn. First, since this is a dog book, let me introduce you to Maggy, a gorgeous husky-wolf mix. "She's part of the team here," says Dennis Pike, who owns the bed-and-breakfast with his wife, Camille. "She is so gentle, so kind. She loves our guests and gets along really well with other dogs. She likes other dogs as much as we do. Maggy gets more pictures taken of her than anyone I've ever seen."

Now let's talk about the Sunset House itself. (Details, details. With the dog-friendly attitude of the Pikes, many people I know would stay here if it looked like Skid Row.) The house was built in the 1960s to be a bed-and-breakfast inn, so all four of the rooms are large (600 square feet), with real brick wood-burning fireplaces and private bathrooms. The rooms are airy, yet cozy, and are furnished beautifully with a mixture of antiques and classic contemporary furniture. You and your dog can see the ocean from three rooms. The large windows you'll see it from are a whopping 4-by-12 feet. The inn is located in an attractive residential neighborhood, where it's a very, very quick walk to leash-free Carmel City Beach (see page 502) and the quaint shops of Carmel.

The Pikes know how to treat their guests. Every morning, a sumptuous breakfast of eight to 13 types of sliced fruit, warm baked goods, granola, and yogurt is brought to your room. If you prefer, you can dine in the comfy sitting room downstairs, but most guests, especially those with dogs, like the in-room option. The sitting area in front of your fireplace is perfect for sharing breakfast with someone special—and with your human companion, too.

In the evening, Dennis will give you a complimentary bottle of wine, champagne, or port, selected for you from his own collection of 1,300 bottles. "My biggest joy is giving it away," says Dennis. If Dennis gets to know you and your tastes well enough (if you become a regular), he'll even keep his eyes peeled for wines he knows you'll love when he's on wine-tasting sojourns. You'll be hard-pressed to find an innkeeper as caring and committed as this man. "This is my calling," he says, and he means it.

Rates are $130 to $190. Dogs are $10 extra. Big, hairy dogs may be charged an extra cleaning fee, so describe your pooch on the phone and you'll know if this applies to her. The Sunset House has a Web site: www.sunset-carmel.com. The inn is located on Camino Real, between Ocean and Seventh Avenues, and the mailing address is P.O. Box 1925, Carmel, CA 93921; (408) 624-4884.

Vagabond's House Inn: This is not a Vagabond Inn! Not by a looonnnng

---

shot. Your dog will drool over this inn's beautiful courtyard with its ancient oak tree, little waterfall, and magical garden. (You may drool, too, but don't let your dog catch you or you'll never hear the end of it.) The humans in your party will fall in love with this English Tudor country inn. It's located right in town, but you feel as though you're in merry old England here. When you sip the cream sherry that's brought to your room in the afternoon, you may think you've died and gone to the British Isles.

The rooms are furnished with antiques, and most have fireplaces and Ralph Lauren bedding. Yummy! In the morning, continental breakfast is brought to the room. And Sally, the dog-loving owner of the inn, is not one to forget your pooch: He gets his very own doggy biscuits with breakfast! (At least you won't have to share your pastries.)

Rates are $85 to $165. The inn is at Fourth Avenue and Dolores Street, P.O. Box 2747, Carmel, CA 92921; (408) 624-7738 or (800) 262-1262

Wayside Inn: Part inn, part motel, this is a charming old ivy-covered brick building well off the beaten path. What it lacks in divine exterior grace it makes up for inside, with comfortable country-style surroundings. Some rooms come with kitchenettes or fireplaces. Rates are $99 to $259. The inn is at Mission Street and Seventh Avenue, and the mailing address is P.O. Box 1900, Carmel, CA 93921; (408) 624-5336.

DIVERSIONS

Sniff out an art gallery: The Galerie Blue Dog is one of those places your dog just won't be able to believe he's allowed to set paw in. After all, it's one of four international homes of the art of George Rodrigue. The paintings start at $7,500, but hey, you can get a silk-screen print for as little as $750. One leg lift in the wrong place (some of the art is within aiming distance) and you've got yourself a wet masterpiece. (And yes, an excited pooch did make a little puddle here once, but no harm was done. Still, if you have any doubts about your dog, you may want to visit the beach instead.)

If any art gallery were to invite dogs in, it would be this one, and there are two reasons for this. One is that the gallery is devoted to Rodrigue's Blue Dog series. The blue dog (you may have seen the paintings in ads for Absolut Vodka, or in countless stories about Rodrigue) is the "ghost" of the artist's dog Tiffany, who watched him paint his Cajun people all her life. Tiffany's "ghost" is light blue with yellow eyes and a face that you can't get out of your head. There's a great story behind the evolution of this series, but I don't have space to tell it here. You'll learn about it when you visit the gallery.

The other reason your dog is welcome here is because gallery director Sandra Crake loves dogs. She has a crystal dish with dog biscuits ready for any dog who visits. At Christmas, she sometimes even bakes special biscuits for poochy visitors. The gallery is at Sixth Avenue and Dolores Street, and the mailing address is P.O. Box S-3214, Carmel, CA 93923; (408) 626-4444. You can check out the Web site at bluedog@mbay.net.

Take a walk on the dog side: You and your pooch can learn all about Carmel, its history, its art, and its dogs—yes, its dogs—on a very entertaining, educational stroll given by Carmel Walks. The walk lasts about two hours, and Gale, who runs the company, always includes a segment on Carmel's dogs. You'll go to a couple of dog-friendly haunts and you'll meet a couple of the town's famous pooches. Gale is a real dog lover; turns out Joe and I knew her Airedale Heidi way back when they lived in San Francisco! (Of course, being dog people, we don't remember each other, just each other's dogs.) Heidi is now in Airedale heaven, where the cats are always fat and the gophers always slow, but her spirit lives on through Gale's dog-friendly tours.

The tours are given five days a week, and they're $15 per human. Dogs go for free, but they must be leashed. Joe and I want to thank Wendy Ballard, publisher of the great *DogGone* newsletter, for tipping us off to this place before deadline! (For more on her newsletter, see page 19 in the book's introduction.) (408) 642-2700.

CARMEL VALLEY

Only 10 miles inland from Highway 1, this is one of the hidden jewels of the Central Coast. Carmel Valley boasts an average of 283 sunny days a year—quite a feat for any place so close to the ocean. The peaceful country setting isn't marred by the little Carmel Valley Village, the "city center" that's chockfull of outdoor cafes that put out the welcome mat for dogs.

Joe was disappointed to learn that when Charley and John Steinbeck reached Carmel Valley in their travels, the human half of the team wasn't happy. In *Travels with Charley*, Steinbeck wrote of a conversation he had with his old friend Johnny Garcia in a Monterey bar: "I went to the Carmel Valley where once we could shoot a thirty-thirty in any direction. Now you couldn't shoot a marble knuckles down without wounding a foreigner. And Johnny, I don't mind people, you know that. But these are rich people. They plant geraniums in big pots. Swimming pools where frogs and crayfish used to wait for us."

Joe, who hates swimming, agrees there are too many swimming pools here. But frogs and their friends still make Carmel Valley their home. You just have to visit Garland Ranch Regional Park (see below) to get a sampling of what was once wild and wonderful about the entire Carmel Valley area.

On your way here on Carmel Valley Road, you'll run across several small flower and vegetable farms, some of which occasionally allow dogs to tiptoe through the tulips with you. When you find one that appeals to you, stop in and check the rules. Many tend to be friendly to dogs who promise not to do leg lifts on their geraniums.

PARKS, BEACHES, AND RECREATION AREAS

• **Garland Ranch Regional Park** 🐾🐾🐾🐾 🐕 *See ❺ on page 498.*

This 4,500-acre park is heaven for any dog who has ever dreamed of living in the country. From the maple-filled canyons to the dense oak woodlands to the willow-covered banks of the Carmel River, you can find almost any environment you and your dog like.

Nine miles of trails can take you and your leash-free dog from just above sea level to 2,000 feet. The wildlife here is plentiful. At the visitors center, you can pick up trail maps as well as species lists of common birds, mammals, and plants to look for while on the trails. Make sure your dog is kind to nature and doesn't disturb the creatures of the woods. Your dog should also know that this is horse country, so if he's thinking of spooking any equines, he'd better be leashed.

While the park has its wild side, it also can be downright civilized. You'll find rest rooms and oodles of picnic tables near the visitors center.

Take Carmel Valley Road about 10 miles east from Highway 1. The park will be on your right. Park in one of the lots and follow any of the narrow trails over the Carmel River and to the visitors center, which is the convenient trailhead for all the park's trails. (408) 659-4488.

RESTAURANTS

Bon Appetit: Dine with your dog at tables with big umbrellas, where you can enjoy food with a Belgian-California flair. If your dog looks thirsty, they'll bring her a big bowl of cool water. 7 Delfino Place; (408) 659-3559.

Sweet Retreat: The ivy-laced rock wall outside this sweet eatery is the perfect backdrop for munching on the well-made cookies, pastries, and lunch items. Dine with your doggy on the partly shaded patio. 1 Delfino Place; (408) 659-0600.

Village Pizzeria: The pizza is snout-licking good here. Enjoy it with your dog at the pleasant outdoor tables. 10 Delfino Place; (408) 659-3112.

PLACES TO STAY

Valley Lodge: This quiet, secluded country inn is a great place for dogs to get away from city life. The redwood buildings and cottages, some with fireplaces, kitchenettes, and private decks, are the perfect place to relax after a long day of hiking at Garland Ranch Regional Park. Humans get to enjoy the lodge's heated pool, sauna, hot spa, and fitness center.

The place is as dog-friendly as it is beautiful. Its brochure features a picture of "Lucky, the Lodge Dog," and states in bold: "Children and dogs are welcome as long as the kids are on a leash and the dogs are at least 12." Hee hee. Rates are $99 to $269. Dogs are $10 extra. A hearty continental breakfast is included in the price. The lodge is located at Carmel Valley and Ford Roads. The mailing address is P.O. Box 93, Carmel Valley, CA 93924; (408) 659-2261 or (800) 641-4646.

KING CITY

This is a fine place to stop with your dog, but a word of warning: It's also a good place to get caught speeding. The California Highway Patrol seems omnipresent on this stretch of U.S. 101, so watch yourself. They don't take kindly to the old "my dog really has to go to the bathroom" excuse.

PARKS, BEACHES, AND RECREATION AREAS

• **San Lorenzo Regional Park** 🐾 🐾 🐾 *See* ❻ *on page 498.*

Conveniently located just off U.S. 101 almost midway between San Francisco and Los Angeles, this is a great park for your dog to get out and stretch his legs on a long journey. The park is home to the intriguing Agricultural and Rural Life Museum, which tells the story of Salinas Valley agriculture.

Although dogs aren't welcome in the buildings, humans are invited to enter a one-room schoolhouse and farmhouse.

If you want to make a night of it, you can camp at any of the park's 190 campsites. Reservations are only necessary for group sites, but are available for regular sites, too. Sites are $13 to $19. Dogs cost an extra dollar. Exit U.S. 101 at Broadway and follow the signs. (408) 385-5964.

PLACES TO STAY

Motel 6: Rates are $29 for the first adult, $6 for the second. One small pooch per room. 3 Broadway Circle, King City, CA 93930; (408) 385-5000.

San Lorenzo Regional Park: See San Lorenzo Regional Park above for camping information.

LOCKWOOD

PARKS, BEACHES, AND RECREATION AREAS

• **Lake San Antonio** 🐾🐾🐾 *See* ❼ *on page 498.*

Dogs who love water love this park because of its narrow, 16-mile-long reservoir. We've seen dogs on bass boats, dogs on houseboats, and dogs on rowboats, and they've all looked blissed out. Authorities here discourage dogs from jumping in the water. It's pretty tough for dogs to swim around here anyway, since they're required to be leashed.

On land, you'll find more than 600 campsites, plenty of playgrounds and picnic areas, and even a few hiking trails. The campsites are available on a first-come, first-served basis. The lake is usually very busy in the summer and very tranquil in the winter.

Remember, as always when you travel with your dog, to have him wear his rabies tag or to bring along other proof of his rabies vaccination. This is one of those places where they're going to ask to see it before letting him in.

The day-use fee is $6 per car. Camping fees are $16 to $22, and pets are $1 extra. From U.S. 101 in King City, take the Jolon Road exit. Jolon Road puts you onto County Road G14. Follow County Road G14 for 45 miles and then take either the North Shore or South Shore entrance into the park. (408) 755-4899.

PLACES TO STAY

Lake San Antonio: See Lake San Antonio above for camping information.

MARINA

PARKS, BEACHES, AND RECREATION AREAS

• **Marina State Beach** 🐾🐾🐾 *See* ❽ *on page 498.*

This is one of the largest state beaches on the Central Coast. Dogs have to be leashed, but they can still enjoy an exhilarating day here. It may be tempting to unleash your dog, but beware: The ranger's residence is always within eyeshot.

The main entrance is at the foot of Reservation Road, just off Highway 1. Park in the lot and walk down the 2,000-foot-long boardwalk to the beach.

(408) 384-7695.

PLACES TO STAY

Motel 6: Rates are $40 for the first adult, $6 for the second. One small pooch per room. 100 Reservation Road, Marina, CA 93933; (408) 384-1000.

MONTEREY

Although there's nowhere to legally let your dog off leash here, Monterey is still a grand stomping ground for dogs and their people. A few activities you can enjoy with your dog include taking in the sights of old/new Cannery Row, fishing off Municipal Wharf No. 2, and watching sea otters frolic about Monterey Bay.

Alas, dogs are not allowed on Fisherman's Wharf, home to some of the world's most dog-friendly scents. Joe visited a few times before we learned of the rule and he never got into trouble, except when he tried to eat the calamari out of somebody's carryout cup. And then there was the time he stuck his nose in a kid's cotton candy and set the kid to wailing so hard that her parents rushed to her thinking Joe had taken a bite out of her.

Another dog rule you should be aware of: Pooches aren't allowed to be tied up on public property. That means not even for a couple of minutes while you run inside a cafe to grab a cup of coffee. We learned about this law from an upset judge in the Sierra Nevada who had tied her dog Billy (a cocker–Lhasa apso mix) outside a restaurant while she went in to use the phone. When she came out, her dog was gone. In his place was a note to call the SPCA. Turns out a policeman had turned in Billy on the basis of this law. Getting Billy back proved to be a logistical nightmare, with events that included Billy's mom being sent to the County Corporation Yard, where she was promised Billy would be after she'd paid a fine (he wasn't).

When I called about the statute, a police officer told me it's in place for public safety and dog safety. I agree heartily that for a dog's sake, he shouldn't be tied up, especially anywhere you can't see him the few minutes you're shopping or noshing. Too many dogs have been stolen this way. Others have torn themselves loose and gotten lost. But I hope that in the future in Monterey, such situations are handled with a little more finesse than Billy's.

One last note. It's against this book's philosophy to include kennels, but in cases where people may be too tempted to leave a dog in the car or a hotel room, we bend the rule a little. I've seen too many dogs panting away in cars while their people are ogling the octopi and otters at the Monterey Bay Aquarium, so here goes the rule bending: The Casa De Amigos Animal Hotel, conveniently located just two blocks from the aquarium, is a decent place for your pooch to spend a few hours, if need be. The accommodations are nothing fancy (kennels and some indoor runs), but dogs are treated well and get three short walks a day. Rates are $10 to $13 for the day, depending on your dog's size. Be sure to call first, because it can get full fast. The "hotel" is at 715 Foam Street; (408) 373-0482.

PARKS, BEACHES, AND RECREATION AREAS

The only city park that allows dogs is El Estero Park. Keep that in mind while strolling past the small parks along the Recreation Trail. Leashed dogs are welcome on city beaches and county parks near Monterey.

• **El Estero Park** 🐾🐾🐾 *See* **9** *on page 498.*

Dogs are advised to stay away from this park's best feature, Dennis the Menace Playground (designed by the comic's creator, Hank Ketcham). But while the kids frolic on the playground's steam engine, roller slide, and giant swing ride, you and the dog can walk around El Estero Lake.

It's a fun walk for leashed dogs and their people. If you like bird-watching (and what dog doesn't?), you'll enjoy the ducks and migrating birds who hang out on the lake. Benches and picnic tables are scattered around this well-manicured park, so you can really make an afternoon of it.

If you're heading from Highway 1 to the Cannery Row area of Monterey, you'll run right into the park. Exit Highway 1 at the Central Monterey exit. Stay in the right lane and go right on Camino Aguajito. The park will be immediately on your left. You'll get to the best parking area by going left on Third Street. (408) 646-3866.

• **Jack's Peak Regional Park** 🐾🐾🐾½ *See* **10** *on page 498.*

Some of the most stunning views of the Monterey Bay, Carmel Valley, and Santa Lucia Mountain Range can be seen from 1,068-foot Jack's Peak, the highest point on the Monterey Peninsula. You and your leashed dog will love the cool Pacific Ocean breezes that sweep through the pine-covered ridges and cathedral-like forests.

On the 8.5 miles of intersecting trails (including a self-guided nature trail), you and your dog can make a day of it or just take in a little fresh air for a half hour. Joe enjoys the Pine Trail, which starts at the Jack's Peak parking area. This is also where you'll find one of the last three remaining native stands of Monterey pine in the world.

The best time to visit here is the spring, when the meadows are blanketed with wildflowers. But this park is worth a visit any time of year.

Fees are $2 Monday through Thursday and $3 Friday through Sunday. From Monterey, take Highway 68 east a couple of miles and go right on Olmstead Road. Then turn left on Jack's Peak Road and follow the signs to the park. (408) 755-4899.

• **Laguna Seca Recreation Area** 🐾🐾 *See* **11** *on page 498.*

Dogs may not jump for joy at the prospect of spending a couple of days at this county park, but if you're a sports car racing fan, you sure will. This is a race car enthusiast's heaven. Chances are good that almost any time of year you visit, you'll be able to see some kind of race car driving on the world-famous Laguna Seca Raceway in the middle of the park.

Joe was hoping to see Mario Andretti the last time we visited, but he had to settle for the Paul Newman Racing Team doing test laps. Many of the park's 180 camping sites for RVs or tents provide a prize-winning view of the track, where excitement-loving leashed dogs can also watch stock cars, motorcycles, and monster truck shows.

The park isn't known for its wild and scenic trails, but there are enough adequate spots on the oak-covered hills for a little exercise. There are also plenty of picnic tables for dining before or after the big race.

The day-use fee is $5 per car. There are 180 campsites available. Camping is $18 to $22, with dogs costing $1 extra. If no race is scheduled, reservations are required only five days in advance. If a race is scheduled, you must buy a race ticket to camp here. If your dog is gun-shy, you won't want to spend time here. One segment of the park is devoted to a rifle/pistol range.

Remember, as always when you travel with your dog, to have him wear his rabies tag or to bring along other proof of his rabies vaccination. This is one of those places where they're probably going to ask to see it before letting him in. From Monterey, follow Highway 68 about seven miles east to the signs for Laguna Seca Recreation Area, which is on the north side of the highway. For racetrack information and competition dates, call (408) 648-5111. You can phone the park at (408) 755-4899.

• **Macabee Beach** 🐾🐾 *See ⑫ on page 498.*

This is a very small beach, but it serves an important purpose: When the kids are holed up in the Monterey Bay Aquarium and you and your dog are taking in the sights of Cannery Row, the beach makes an excellent pit stop. Since your dog won't be able to smell the Cannery Row sardines of the early century, she'll be happy to sniff at some of the marine critters who call the Monterey Bay their home.

It's also a fun place for you and your leashed dog to get away from the throngs of weekend tourists and settle in for a picnic. But because it's so small, you wouldn't want to come here just for exercise.

The beach is between McClellan and Prescott Avenues, just off Cannery Row. (408) 646-3866.

• **Monterey State Beach** 🐾🐾½ *See ⑬ on page 498.*

This beach is actually in two segments, and neither is very large. We prefer to hit Marina State Beach (see page 510) if we have to find a beach in the area. It's much larger and usually less widely used.

But if you're strolling along the Recreation Trail (see below) and your dog needs to go roll in some sand, try the section on Del Monte Avenue, at the foot of Park Avenue. You can make your stroll and roll last longer by extending your walk to Monterey Beach Park, just east of the Municipal Wharf (see Diversions, page 515). This tiny beach also requires that your dog wear a leash. (408) 649-2836.

• **Recreation Trail** 🐾🐾🐾 *See ⑭ on page 498.*

Stretching five miles from Lover's Point in Pacific Grove (no dogs allowed in the little Lover's Point Park) past Cannery Row and into Seaside, this paved bike and walking path is a great way to see Monterey.

You and your leashed dog can get your fill of sight-seeing and exercise here. You can sit on one of the many benches that dot the trail and watch some of the world's most fascinating marine life. Joe likes to check out the mama otters wrapping their babes in kelp before they swim off to forage for food. He could stare for hours at the bobbing babes, but fortunately, the mothers return pretty quickly.

You can start the trail anywhere, but many folks like to start at Fisherman's

Wharf. Although dogs aren't allowed on the wharf, this is where smaller dogs get to embark on one of the funnest adventures known to canines: riding on a bike, while you pedal. (See Diversions, page 515.)

RESTAURANTS

Bagel Bakery: Dogs love eating at the outdoor tables here. That's because they get to dine on "bagel bones"—twice-baked bagels that are very hard and made primarily for dogs (although people with sharp teeth enjoy them, too). Humans, and dogs like Joe ("make mine goopy") Dog, may prefer the omelette-on-a-bagel dish or any of a variety of bagel sandwiches. There are two locations in Monterey: 201 Lighthouse Avenue, (408) 649-1714; and 452 Alvarado Street, (408) 372-5242.

Tarpy's Roadhouse: When you and your good dog dine at the courtyard tables at this turn-of-the-century roadhouse, you'll know why this is such a popular place. The wonderful food, understated elegance, and beautiful gardens make it special indeed.

If you're a fan of grilled food, your mouth will water over any food that comes from Tarpy's wood-burning grill. Try the grilled turkey breast with roasted garlic mashed potatoes. Joe Dog gets weak in the knees even thinking about it. Tarpy's is located right next door to the dog-friendly Monterey Stone Chapel (see Diversions, page 515), which makes Tarpy's a perfect place to visit after saying your nuptials there. 2999 Monterey Salinas Highway; (408) 647-1444.

PLACES TO STAY

Bay Park Hotel: Plenty of trees surround this lodging, so dogs who like shade or leg lifts enjoy a stay here. Rates are $99 to $160. Dogs are $5 extra. 1425 Munras Avenue, Monterey, CA 93940; (408) 649-1020 or (800) 338-3564.

Cypress Garden Motel: Dogs are allowed as long as they're smaller than the guests. You're relegated to smoking rooms when you stay here with a dog, but what the hack, er, what the heck. Rates are $69 to $119. 1150 Munras Avenue, Monterey, CA 93940; (408) 373-2761.

El Adobe Inn: Rates are $89 to $119. 936 Munras Avenue, Monterey, CA 93940; (408) 372-5409 or (800) 433-4732.

Laguna Seca Recreation Area: See Laguna Seca Recreation Area on page 512 for camping information.

Monterey Bay Lodge: Dogs like staying here because it's relatively close to Monterey Bay (less than two blocks). They can wake up and sniff the crabby breezes. Rates are $49 to $139. Dogs are $10 extra, and there's a limit of two pets per room. 55 Camino Aguajito Road, Monterey, CA 93940; (408) 372-8057 or (800) 558-1900.

Monterey Beach Hotel–Best Western: This is one of Joe's favorites. From his first-floor room (dogs are restricted to ground level) he can see the beach, gulls walking around, and girls in bikinis. But what he likes even more is the easy access to Monterey State Beach (see page 513). Rates are $69 to $189. There's a $25-per-visit pooch fee. 2600 Dunes Drive, Monterey, CA 93940; (408) 394-3321.

Monterey Marriott: Dogs are welcome at this attractive hotel for an extra $10 nightly. Room rates range from $99 to $235. Some rooms and suites have views of Monterey Bay. 350 Calle Principal, Monterey, CA 93940; (408) 649-4234.

Motel 6: This is one of the most expensive Motel 6s we've ever seen, but the location near the heart of Monterey (albeit on cheapy motel row) makes it worth the price. Rates are $55 for the first adult, $6 for the second (but slightly cheaper on weekdays). One small pet per room. 2124 North Fremont Street, Monterey, CA 93940; (408) 646-8585.

Victorian Inn: If you're willing to pay a onetime doggy fee of $25 and a $100 deposit, this beautifully furnished Victorian-style inn is as relaxing as it is attractive. Dogs love to curl up in front of the marble fireplaces here. Rates are $89 to $199. 487 Foam Street, Monterey, CA 93940; (408) 373-8000 or (800) 232-4141.

DIVERSIONS

Fish for your supper: The Municipal Wharf No. 2, built in 1926, is one of the best places in the Monterey Bay for landlubbers and their dogs to nail perch and other catches of the day. It's also ideal for watching commercial fishing boats unload their bounties—everything from anchovies to salmon. The wharf is at the foot of Figueroa Street. (408) 646-3950.

Take someone furry on a surrey: Chicks and ducks and geese better scurry when you take your dog on a bicycle-powered surrey from Bay Bikes, located on the famous Cannery Row. The surreys come complete with a fringe at the top. And so what if the dashboard isn't genuine leather? These surreys have baskets in the front, perfect for small- or medium-sized dogs. You and a friend can pedal up and down Monterey's scenic Recreation Trail (see page 513) while your dog just sits back and takes in the scents and sights. Folks who know recommend bringing a jacket or something soft and comfy for your dog to sit on. Wire baskets and dog tushies just don't mix.

Large surreys fit six adults and two children and cost $25 per hour. Smaller surreys fit fewer people, but they're only $15 per hour. 640 Wave Street (under the carousel); (408) 646-9090.

Tie the knot, bring Spot: If, while saying your wedding vows at the enchanting Monterey Stone Chapel, you begin to feel someone's cold nose nuzzling your ankle, don't blame a fresh guest or an eager spouse. It's just your dog. Probably.

The Monterey Stone Chapel is a terrific place to get hitched with your favorite pooch at your side. Owner Patt O'Brien loves dogs, especially dogs who don't mistake the green carpeting in the chapel for grass. The only dog who ever did that was her three-pound Yorky, and he did it when he was only a puppy. When something that small does his business, you almost need a magnifying glass to clean it up.

O'Brien has been through it all with dogs at weddings. One time, a dapper Lab in a bow tie threw up all over his master's shiny shoes in the middle of the ceremony. But most of O'Brien's dog weddings go without a hitch (so to speak).

The chapel itself is a real looker. Unlike so many of its brethren, it's completely un-kitschy, with a big stone fireplace, white lace curtains, and handmade wrought iron candelabras. If you prefer to hold your ceremony outside, the setting in front of the chapel is a photographer's dream, complete with a little lake, redwoods (a boy dog's dream), and a wrought iron archway. O'Brien can even set up your ceremony at one of many breathtaking outdoor coastal locations. Her business is called A By-the-Sea Wedding, and once you check out her favorite spots, you'll know why. Another real plus about getting hitched here: The terrific Tarpy's Roadhouse (see page 514) is located right next door. It's a superb place to unwind after tying the knot.

The price is right, too. O'Brien will marry you with your dogs and up to 10 friends at your side outside the chapel for $150. The price goes up slightly for more guests if the wedding is in the chapel. For an additional $64, she can supply you with the required license so you can get married as quickly as California law allows—and in some cases, that means lickety-split.

For more information, write to O'Brien at A By-the-Sea Wedding, 2999 Monterey-Salinas Highway, Suite 3, Monterey, CA 93940, or call (408) 375-8574.

MOSS LANDING

PARKS, BEACHES, AND RECREATION AREAS

• **Moss Landing State Beach** 🐾🐾½ *See ⑮ on page 498.*

This is one of the busier state beaches in the area, but dogs still like getting out of the car to stretch their legs here. Leashed pooches can explore the low sand dunes and the attractive beach. If you like to watch surfers or surf anglers, you'll get an eyeful here. Joe once caught a surfer dude changing behind a towel. In fact, Joe visited him under his towel. The visit lasted only a few seconds before Joe was politely shooed away.

From Highway 1, take Jetty Road west to the beach. (408) 384-7695.

• **Salinas River State Beach** 🐾🐾🐾 *See ⑯ on page 498.*

With 246 acres of sand and steep dunes, this is our favorite beach of the three in the Moss Landing area. Because the beach is so large, the beachgoers are more spread out, so it rarely seems crowded. This beach is renowned for its excellent clamming and fishing. Leashed dogs enjoy a good romp here.

You'll find easy access at the end of Portrero Road, off Highway 1. (408) 384-7695.

• **Zmudowski State Beach** 🐾🐾🐾 *See ⑰ on page 498.*

Leashed pooches can peruse the dune trails and the secluded, sandy beach here, but they need to stay away from the Pajaro River Estuary. You may run into some horses during your visit here, but they're allowed only near the waterline, so at least their turf is limited. Strong rip currents make doing the dog paddle a bad idea. It's best to save the water sports for the bathtub.

Just in case you tell any locals what beach you'll be visiting, we thought you might like to know the right way to pronounce it. Don't say Zmudowski the way it looks like you should say it, or they'll immediately brand you an out-of-towner. The beach's name is pronounced "Mud-ow-skee." So now you know-skee.

The beach is located just south of the Pajaro River. From Highway 1, take

Struve Road and turn west to Giberson Road. You'll see signs for the beach. (408) 384-7695.

RESTAURANTS

Maloney's Restaurant: The owner here loves dogs, so pooches and their people are welcome to dine at the 20 outdoor tables overlooking the ocean. Dogs enjoy the fresh and fishy breezes blowing in from the Pacific, and you'll enjoy the fresh fishies served at Maloney's. There's not really a street address, but it's easy to find. It's located at Highway 1 and the bridge in Moss Landing. (408) 724-9371.

Moss Landing Cafe: If you or your dog like your seafood casual, grab a bite here. The fish sandwiches are yummy, as are the other seafood dishes. Try the deep-fried artichoke if you don't mind a little heart-unhealthy cuisine. It's to die for . . . almost. 421 Moss Landing Road; (408) 633-3355.

PACIFIC GROVE

This quaint town on the rocky coast is a good place to get away from the crowds that can sometimes smother you and your dog during the peak tourist season in its neighboring city, Monterey. And if you like Monarch butterflies, Pacific Grove is your kind of town: It's known as "Butterfly City, USA" because of the millions of Monarch butterflies who winter here every year.

PARKS, BEACHES, AND RECREATION AREAS

• **Asilomar State Beach** 🐾🐾🐾 *See ⑱ on page 498.*

The beach here is great fun for leashed dogs. Not only do they get to romp on prime beach land, but they also can watch whales in the fall and winter and see what real tidepooling is all about year-round.

Tucked in and around this rugged shoreline are a vast variety of marine critters representative of the Central Coast. I've seen dogs try to eat the contents of tidepools—a dining activity that should be strictly forbidden. And for your dog's safety, don't take him on slippery rocks or let him get too close to the surf, where there can be hazardous rip currents.

Park along the shore on Sunset Drive, across from the infamous Asilomar Conference Grounds. For sandy beach, park along the south end of Sunset Drive. (408) 372-8016.

• **George Washington Park** 🐾🐾🐾 🐕 *See ⑲ on page 498.*

If you're dining at any of Pacific Grove's many outdoor eateries in the village center and your dog starts crossing his legs, have no fear, this park is near. And better yet, part of the park is devoted to off-leash dogs during certain times of the day.

Dogs may run leashless from sunrise to 9 A.M. and from 4 P.M. to sunset. During winter, those hours can be a little restrictive, but it's better than nothing.

The segment of the park for leash-free canines is bounded by Short Street, Melrose Avenue, Alder Street, and Pine Avenue. Dogs are allowed on leash in the entire park at any time during the day. (408) 648-3100.

• **Lynn "Rip" Van Winkle Open Space** 🐾🐾🐾🐾 🐕
See ⑳ on page 498.

This scrub oak haven near Pebble Beach is large enough so that even dogs who tend to wander out of sight aren't in much danger of wandering into the road. Dogs may be leashless from sunrise to 9 A.M. and 4 P.M. to sunset.

You'll find many a dog and many a dog person here during the off-leash hours. They tend to congregate near the park's entrance, but if your dog would prefer walking to talking, there are plenty of trails leading through the twisted scrub oaks and the small clear areas of the park.

The entrance can be hard to find. Follow the non-toll portion of Seventeen Mile Drive south and go left on Sunset Drive, then right on Congress Avenue. Pass Forest Grove Elementary School on your left. Within a few hundred yards, you'll see a dirt parking area on your right. There's no sign, but this is the main entrance to the open space. (408) 648-3100.

RESTAURANTS

Bagel Bakery: It's bagels, bagels, bagels at this dog-friendly eatery. Get some bagel bones (twice-baked, extra hard bagels) for your dog while you nosh on a bagel sandwich, a bagel with shmear, or a plain old naked bagel. Dine together at the outdoor tables. 1132 Forest Avenue; (408) 649-6272.

Fandango: They love dogs at this romantic Mediterranean country-style restaurant. Dine with your favorite pooch at the quiet tables on the front patio. Try the paella. 223 17th Street; (408) 372-3456.

Fishwife Seafood Restaurant at Asilomar Beach: Dogs like to grab a quick bowl of soup with their people at the bench outside. 1996 1/2 Sunset Drive; (408) 375-7107.

Rocky Coast Ice Cream Company: Share a cold, creamy cone while chilling with your pooch at the little benches out front. 708 Lighthouse Avenue; (408) 373-0587.

PLACES TO STAY

Andril Fireplace Cottages: In these homey cottages, it's easy to get away from it all or to be on top of it all: All the separate cottages in this quiet area have cable TV, with VCRs for the asking. They also have wood-burning fireplaces, perfect for snuggling up with a human friend and a dog friend after a long day exploring the nearby beach. Rates are $64 to $165. Dogs are $5 extra. 569 Asilomar Boulevard, Pacific Grove, CA 93950; (408) 375-0994.

Best Western Lighthouse Lodge & Suites: You want cottages, a pool, a Jacuzzi, and tasty continental breakfasts? This is the place for you and your dog. Rates are $89 to $149. Dogs are $10 extra. 1150 Lighthouse Avenue, Pacific Grove, CA 93950; (408) 372-0503.

Olympia Motor Lodge: Dogs are allowed here only from November through March. Then you and your dog can sit on your private balcony and contemplate life while staring at the ocean. Rates are $64 to $120. There's a $20 pooch fee per visit. 1140 Lighthouse Avenue, Pacific Grove, CA 93950; (408) 373-2777.

DIVERSIONS

Out, damned spot: At the Best Friends pet wash, scrubbing your dog need not be a dramatic production. For $12 to $15, your dog walks up some steps to a waist-level bathtub, and dirt and grime are history. You can blow-dry him to look good enough for even the fanciest Monterey Peninsula event. The pet wash is in a convenient location for travelers with dirty dogs, just blocks from the beach. 167 Central Avenue; (408) 375-2477.

PEBBLE BEACH

PLACES TO STAY

The Lodge at Pebble Beach: Jack Lemmon brings his poodle here. Joe Pesci brings his pooch here, too. This magnificent lodge, adjacent to the Pebble Beach Golf Links, is as dog-friendly as it is distinguished.

The place is beautiful on the outside and like home (if your home is gorgeous and has spectacular views) on the inside. Most rooms have a fireplace, and all are lovely, with a wet bar, an honor-stocked fridge, and a patio or deck with to-drool-for views. In your bathroom you'll find an extra phone and a plush terry robe.

All this is fine with dogs, but what they really love about The Lodge is that it's a dog-adoring place. "We love doggies!" says the concierge, and she means it. They stock treats at several strategically located points in the lobby, including the concierge desk, the bell desk, and the front desk. And even better than this, dogs get to explore the large, wooded area surrounding the inn. If they're really well-behaved, you can let them be leashless! The paths here are splendid. Be forewarned, though, that you might be sharing the paths with horses, so if your dog is a chaser, keep that leash on.

Rates are $350 to $1,600. The lodge is on Seventeen Mile Drive. When you call for reservations, you can get directions. The address is simply Seventeen Mile Drive, Pebble Beach, CA 93953; (408) 624-3811 or (800) 654-9300.

SALINAS

The "Salad Bowl of the World" is one of Joe's favorite places to visit on a Sunday drive. Most other city dogs we've talked to agree that it's a grand olfactory experience. When Joe smells the chicken manure spread across great fields of green and sees horses readying for the rodeo, his nostrils shiver and his eyes bug out. Afterward, he's always exhausted.

PARKS, BEACHES, AND RECREATION AREAS

• **Toro Regional Park** 🐾🐾🐾 *See* ㉑ *on page 498.*

This is the only park in the Salinas area where you and your dog can really take a hike. More than 4,500 acres of wilderness await leashed pooches. About 12 miles of hiking and horse trails are etched into the rolling foothills of Mount Toro. As you climb, you'll occasionally be rewarded with shade from oak trees. It can be very hot in the summer, so be sure to bring extra water for you and your dog.

The views up high are spectacular. You can see both the Salinas Valley and the Monterey Bay, depending on where you hike. The park also features a self-guided nature trail adjacent to a gentle creek, as well as many picnic sites and play areas in the flat green valley near the parking lots.

Remember, as always when you travel with your dog, to have him wear his rabies tag or to bring along other proof of his rabies vaccination. This is one of those places where they're going to ask to see it before letting him in. From Salinas, follow Highway 68 west about five miles to the signs for the park. The park's entrance is just a few hundred yards from the highway. Fees are $3 per car Monday through Thursday and $5 Friday through Sunday. (408) 755-4899.

PLACES TO STAY

The lodgings that accommodate dogs here may not be fancy, but they're excellent places to relax and watch bad TV with your dog after a day of traveling.

Motel 6: There are two of these motels in Salinas where dogs are welcome. They both allow one small pooch per room. Rates are $30 to $35 for the first adult, $6 for the second. One motel is at 1010 Fairview Avenue, Salinas, CA 93905; (408) 758-2122. The other is at 1257 De La Torre Boulevard, Salinas, CA 93905; (408) 757-3077.

Vagabond Inn: Close to U.S. 101, this is where Joe and I once stayed and encountered at least five other dogs who were also guests. There's a $5 charge for dogs. Rates are $51 to $65. 131 Kern Street, Salinas, CA 93905; (408) 758-4693.

DIVERSIONS

Get thee to a flick: The Skyview Drive-In Theatre is one of the few drive-in theaters that dares to call itself a theatre. It must be the tasty popcorn they serve here, because they sure don't show Ingmar Bergman flicks. Good, non-barking, non-howling dogs are welcome. The theater is open Friday, Saturday, and Sunday nights. It's located at North Sanborn Road and Garner Avenue. (408) 424-6510.

46
KINGS COUNTY

This is farm country, the kind of land that drives dogs crazy around the time the fertilizer's being spread. But despite all the open fields and rural surroundings, it's tough to find a place to take a dog for a good time. Dogs would love to roll in the cow patties, but between your objections, the farmers' objections, and that killer look on Bessie's face, they quickly realize it's not the best idea in the world.

Ironically, the most appealing areas for dogs are in the small cities, especially Lemoore and historic Hanford. Off-leash parks are nonexistent, but pooches still manage to stretch their legs a little.

CORCORAN

You'll see plenty of dogs here, but they're usually in the backs of big pickup trucks parked at local bars and convenience stores. The dogs like to bark, especially at each other.

To want to drive all the way out here with your dog, you probably have to have a loved one at the maximum security Corcoran State Prison. Dogs aren't allowed to visit any of the prison's 5,500 inmates, so they'll be sorely disappointed if that's the only reason they came with you.

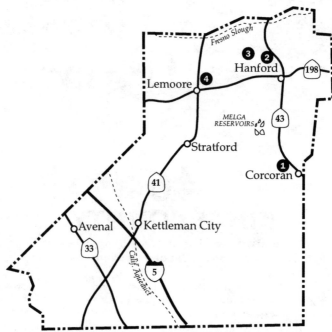

PARKS, BEACHES, AND RECREATION AREAS
•**Community Park** 🐾🐾 *See* **❶** *on page 522.*

This is exactly what it sounds like—a park for the community, featuring picnic tables, ball fields, and children's playgrounds. It's the only game in town if your dog needs to relieve her bladder, and it can be quite crowded with local kids. The park is at Dairy and Patterson Avenues. (209) 992-4514.

HANFORD

Anyone looking for a set for *The Music Man?* You couldn't find a more perfect one than the turn-of-the-century town square in the middle of the old part of Hanford. It's got all the charm and permanence of River City, Iowa, and you won't have to put up with a freckle-faced kid with a bad lisp. The city has some of the grandest old buildings in California. Most of them are in or around Civic Center Park, where your leashed dog can enjoy green grass and big, stately trees (see below).

Dogs also seem to enjoy walking down China Alley, the center of an area that in its heyday boasted one of the largest populations of Chinese immigrants in the United States. The Taoist Temple, built in 1893, still retains its position as the centerpiece of China Alley. It's now a theater, and dogs have to stay outside, but it's still amazing to see something like this in the middle of the San Joaquin Valley.

If you stray out of the old core of town, you'll be transported to Wal-Mart world—not a pretty sight. A hefty chunk of Hanford is a fairly major suburban-style shopping area, complete with the biggest chains and fast-food restaurants. Dogs highly recommend staying in the historic district, especially since their kind isn't always appreciated in department stores.

PARKS, BEACHES, AND RECREATION AREAS
•**Civic Center Park** 🐾🐾🐾 *See* **❷** *on page 522.*

If you were to find yourself in the middle of a park with huge shade trees, flowers, an antique carousel, a fire engine from 1911, and a neoclassical courthouse building, in what year do you think you'd be? 1920? 1930? It's hard to believe, but this old charmer exists today.

It must be something about the clock on the front of the Civic Auditorium across the street. The impressive classical revival building's big clock actually works. The whole thing is reminiscent of *Back to the Future*—clock, columns, and all. But the title of this ideal town square would have to be *Back to the Past.*

The place is very friendly to leashed dogs. The courthouse has been converted into quaint shops and offices. There's even a deli with outdoor tables (see Port of Subs on page 524).

Exit Highway 198 at 11th Avenue, drive north a few blocks, and go right on Seventh Street. The park is at Irwin and Seventh Streets. (209) 585-2500.

•**Hidden Valley Park** 🐾🐾🐾 *See* **❸** *on page 522.*

At first, this extremely well manicured park with low rolling hills seems like a golf course. Everything is so beautifully landscaped that it's hard to believe people and dogs can play anything but 18 holes here. Willow trees abound, and there's even a pond and a gazebo for that old-time flavor this town cultivates.

Leashed dogs are welcome at this six-block-long park. But beware: The grass is so low that if you don't clean up after your dog, the stuff will stick out like a mountain. Exit Highway 198 at 11th Avenue and drive north about two miles. The park is on your left. For good parking lots, turn left at West Cortner Street. (209) 585-2500.

RESTAURANTS
Port of Subs: Munch good deli food outside with your pooch. 729 West Lacey Boulevard; (209) 582-7651.

KETTLEMAN CITY
PLACES TO STAY
Super 8 Motel: This is a convenient stop a half block east of Interstate 5. Rates are $42 to $50. There's a $50 deposit for dogs. 33415 Powers Drive, Kettleman City, CA 93239; (209) 386-9530.

LEMOORE
Besides the gigantic Harris Ranch (a must-smell for dogs, described on page 488), Lemoore is the first civilization you come to driving east on Highway 198 from Interstate 5. It's got a cute town center, lined with trees and antique stores.

PARKS, BEACHES, AND RECREATION AREAS
Unfortunately, the large Heritage Park was still in the development stage as the third edition of this book went to press, so we couldn't rate it. The park was scheduled to be ready for leashed dogs sometime in mid-1994, then mid-1996. Joe's hoping for the new millennium. Park officials tell us you can still bring a leashed pooch to the area while things are in flux.

It's on the corner of Hanford-Armona Road and Avocado Drive. To find out the status of Heritage Park, phone (209) 924-6767.

•**City Park** 🐾🐾 *See ❹ on page 522.*

This square-block park is usually green and grassy, which makes it ideal for dogs who like to roll. Willows and palms abound, so even in the heat of summer, you and your dog can survive. Kids like it here because of the special playground.

Take the Lemoore/Fresno exit (Highway 41) from Highway 198 and go north to West Bush Street. Go right on West Bush Street and drive for about 12 blocks. The park is on your left. (209) 924-6767.

47
TULARE COUNTY

Some people come here from other parts of the state and call this place "Tool-air" County. Others call it "Tool-ahh-ray." Don't do dat! You'll be pegged as an outsider immediately and your dog's credentials as a real dog will be questioned. When you're trying to remember how to say the name of this place, just think about the personality of a late-night CNN talk show host. If you say he's just too, too, "*Too-larry*" (King), you'll fit right in.

Don't worry if you don't find your thrills in the civilized parts of Tulare. About one-third of the county belongs to the U.S. Forest Service, the Bureau of Land Management, and the California Department of Forestry. In dog-speak, that translates to "Look, ma, no leash!"

The BLM's dog-friendly Chimney Peak Recreation Area is split between Tulare County and its southern neighbor, Kern County. While Tulare County contains the best portion of the recreation area, it's more easily reached from Kern County. Please see page 559 in Kern County for a description.

NATIONAL FORESTS

See the National Forests and0 Wilderness Areas chapter starting on page 748 for important information and safety tips on visiting national forests with your dog.

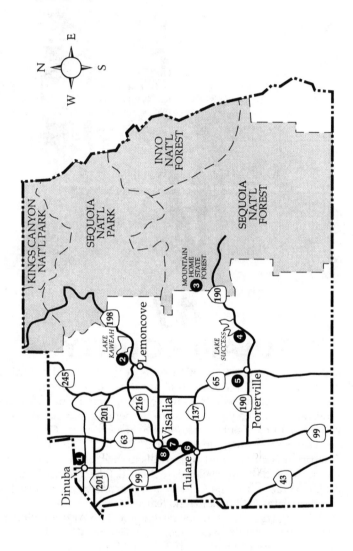

- **Inyo National Forest** 😊😊😊😊 🐾
  See page 750.
- **Sequoia National Forest** 😊😊😊😊 🐾
  See page 753 for more information on this remarkable land of big trees.

NATIONAL PARKS

- **Sequoia and Kings Canyon National Parks** 🔥

If you were a chocoholic, your idea of hell would probably include being chained to the middle of a small island surrounded by a sea of unreachable, creamy Ghirardelli, Godiva, and Guittard chocolates. If you were an ice skater, purgatory might include being relegated to gravel driveways for the rest of your life, never being able to set a blade on the ice that's all around you. And if you were a dog, your idea of hell would probably involve a visit to these two exquisite national parks.

Sequoia National Park contains the thickest concentration (and the biggest individual specimens) of giant sequoia trees in the world. And while Kings Canyon doesn't have the huge trees, it's wild and untamed, just begging to be sniffed at by an inquisitive dog snout. Dogs, however, must be cloistered in the car-camping areas and the little villages here, far from the trails and the madding trees. This is bad news. This makes boy dogs moan. This is hell.

The day-use fee is $10 per car. Fees for sites where dogs can camp are $5 to $12. There are approximately 1,300 sites available on a first-come, first-served basis. The parks are connected and stretch for almost 60 miles from north to south. Because of their sizes, we can't provide specific directions here. Call the parks at (209) 565-3134 for information on what areas might be best for you and your traveling dog. And if no one in your traveling party is going to be around to hang out with your dog while you explore the parks, leave him home with a friend. Too many dogs get stuck in cars here, and that can be dangerous as well as a crashing bore.

DINUBA

PARKS, BEACHES, AND RECREATION AREAS

- **Rose Ann Vuich Park** 😊😊 *See* ❶ *on page 526.*

Leashed dogs are welcome to stroll through this grassy, tree-filled park. It's in the middle of town, so if you've got business to attend to, you can take your dog here for some doggy business afterward.

The park is at East El Monte Way at McKinley Avenue. (209) 591-5921.

LEMONCOVE

PARKS, BEACHES, AND RECREATION AREAS

- **Lake Kaweah Recreation Area** 😊😊😊 *See* ❷ *on page 526.*

A few dirt trails will lead you and your favorite dog around various parts of the lake. These trails are not for the soft of paw, though. This is foothill country, and it can be rough going, with some trails taking you over rocks and through steep turns.

The lake itself is adequate for dipping your paws. Since dogs have to be leashed, they can't turn into fuzzy little Mark Spitzes here, but just a dip'll do them good.

Summer is the worst time to visit the lake. The fishing is cold and the temperatures are hot. Joe likes winter best. The farther he can get from scorching weather, the better.

Campsites are $14 per night, and you'll find a decent trail running right through the campground. There are 80 sites available on a first-come, first-served basis. The lake is on Highway 198, just north of Lemoncove. (209) 597-2301.

PLACES TO STAY

Lake Kaweah Recreation Area: See Lake Kaweah Recreation Area above for camping information.

MOUNTAIN HOME

PARKS, BEACHES, AND RECREATION AREAS

• **Mountain Home State Forest** 🐾🐾🐾🐾 🐕 *See* ❸ *on page 526*

If you and your leash-free pooch want to see the seventh-largest tree in the world, you'd better make nice with the rangers here. The tree isn't on any maps, and rangers prefer to point it out only to the folks they like.

If the ranger just doesn't dig you or your dog enough to let you check out that tree, don't worry. There are plenty of other trees to make up for your loss. The forest's 4,800 acres are filled with trails that take you past other giant sequoias in addition to ponderosa pines, sugar pines, cedars, and firs.

Some of the rangers aren't keen on the forest's leash-free policy, and they recommend it only for the best-trained dogs. They say they've seen too many dogs get lost or chase down critters that are best left alone. But chances are if you and your dog aren't used to elevations around 6,500 feet, neither of you will be in the mood to run far. In the words of one ranger: "People just suck for oxygen until they get accustomed to the air up here."

Campsites are free, but dogs must be leashed. Sites are available from June through October and are on a first-come, first-served basis. From Highway 190 in Springville, drive north on Balch Park Drive for three miles and then head east on Bear Creek Road for 15 to 21 miles, depending on your destination within the forest. Mobile homes should take an alternate route, continuing up Balch Park Drive for about 30 more miles to the park. Be sure to get a trail map and some ranger advice before venturing into the forest. (209) 539-2855.

PLACES TO STAY

Mountain Home State Forest: See Mountain Home State Forest above for camping information.

PORTERVILLE

PARKS, BEACHES, AND RECREATION AREAS

• **Lake Success Recreation Area** 🐾🐾🐾 *See* ❹ *on page 526.*

The nature trails and wildlife areas around this water-ski haven make life more than tolerable for dogs and their tranquillity-seeking people. Dogs do best here in the non-summer months, when temperatures are cooler and loud boats are rarer. If you visit in the spring, you might have a shot at some good bass fishing.

When the water in the lake is down, there's even more land for hiking. It's pretty much open foothill land, but your dog won't complain if you make sure he doesn't get too warm.

Camping is available on a first-come, first-served basis for fees ranging from free to $14 per site. From Porterville, drive eight miles east on Highway 190 to the lake. (209) 784-0215.

• **Veterans Park** 🐾🐾🐾 *See* **5** *on page 526.*

This L-shaped park has a nature trail that leashed dogs are welcome to sniff out. It runs the length of the park, so you get to hike a total of almost two miles in one direction. You'll walk by cottonwoods and huge oaks. If you get tired, you can relax at the picnic tables or under the shade trees here.

The really interesting part of this park is the big HU1B dust-off helicopter that's mounted about 20 feet up in the air on the park's north side. It's in a landing position, and it's meant to symbolize the end of the Vietnam War.

This town was hard-hit by the war. A local veteran told me that the Porterville area is home to the highest number of men per capita killed in Vietnam. In addition to the chopper, the memorial is encircled by several young redwood trees—one per local hero killed in the war. This end of the park is at Henderson Avenue and Newcomb Street. (209) 782-7536.

PLACES TO STAY

Lake Success Recreation Area: See Lake Success Recreation Area above for camping information.

Paul Bunyan Lodge: Your dog doesn't have to be a big ox to stay at this 100-room lodge, but if he is, it's not a problem—dogs of all sizes are more than welcome. "The Paul Bunyan can't very well turn down a big dog, can it?" said the front desk person when we asked. The lodge has plenty of recreation available, from tennis courts for humans to space for your dog to romp outside. Rates are $32 to $38. There's a $10 pooch fee per visit, and a $50 pooch deposit. 940 West Morton Street, Porterville, CA 93257; (209) 784-3150.

TULARE

PARKS, BEACHES, AND RECREATION AREAS

• **Live Oak Park** 🐾🐾½ *See* **6** *on page 526.*

If you happen to be passing through town and stopping at the carryout Foster's Freeze down the street, be sure to visit this green park with your leashed canine companion (and your ice-cream cones).

After that ice-cream cone, you and your dog may want to take a siesta under a shade tree. Then, when your snacks are digested, try out the fitness course here. It's not grueling, so it's a pleasant way to work off those free-floating fat calories.

The park is close to Highway 99. Take the Tulare Avenue exit east a few blocks and turn left on Laspina Street. In a few more blocks, you'll be at the park. It's right beside the Live Oak Middle School. (209) 685-2380.

PLACES TO STAY

Best Western: Rates are $44 to $85. Dogs are usually free, but during dog shows, when plenty of pooches stay here, dogs pay a $10 fee per visit. 1051 North Blackstone Avenue, Tulare, CA 93274; (209) 688-7537.

Friendship Inn: Rates are $30 to $48. Pooches require a $20 deposit. 26442 Highway 99, Tulare, CA 93274; (209) 688-0501.

Inns of America: There's a little lot just a bone's throw away where you can walk your leashed pooch. The rate here is $37. 1183 Blackstone Street, Tulare, CA 93274; (209) 686-0985.

VISALIA

PARKS, BEACHES, AND RECREATION AREAS

• **Blaine Park** 🐾 🐾 1/2 *See* ❼ *on page 526.*

This is a very attractive park in a lovely neighborhood. There are enough trees, ball fields, and picnic tables for even the most suburban of dogs.

The park is on the west side of South Court Street, just a few blocks north of Caldwell Avenue. (209) 738-3365.

• **Plaza Park** 🐾 🐾 1/2 *See* ❽ *on page 526.*

If you and your dog are staying at the Holiday Inn across the street, you couldn't ask for a more conveniently located park. Although the park is full of activities for humans, there's lots of room for leashed dogs to hike on the trail, relax under a big shade tree, or watch kids fish in the little pond.

The crowd here can swell on weekends and during softball and baseball games, but it's generally less packed than the city's other large park. It's located west of town, at Highway 198 and Road 80, just east of Highway 99. (209) 738-3365.

RESTAURANTS

Java Jungle: They've had dogs "act like apes" here, say the managers. But as long as your pooch behaves with the decorum befitting a high-class canine, she's welcome. Eat bagel sandwiches and pie and sip coffee on the lovely tiled patio. 208 West Main Street; (209) 732-5282.

Meritage: Eat eggs, pancakes, sandwiches, and burgers with your dog friend at the outdoor tables here. 120 West Main Street; (209) 739-0708.

PLACES TO STAY

Best Western Visalia Inn Motel: Rates are $58 to $66. Small pooches only, please, and they're $4 extra. 623 West Main Street, Visalia, CA 93291; (209) 732-4561.

Holiday Inn Plaza Park: They prefer small pooches here, but they're willing to consider others. Rates are $79 to $99. 9000 West Airport Drive, Visalia, CA 93277; (209) 651-5000 or (800) 465-4329.

48

SAN LUIS OBISPO COUNTY

Home of Hearst Castle, spectacular beaches, quaint seaside hamlets, and the mighty Pismo clam, this county is one of the state's most popular getaways. Dogs appreciate the olfactory beauty—the fishy piers, the farm-fresh soil, the suntan lotion—as much as their drivers enjoy the scenery and the history.

Dog activities are numerous. Your dog can dine with you at countless restaurants with outdoor tables. She can trot alongside you at most of the county's beaches. She can camp with you, fish with you, and tour wineries with you. (Check out our favorite, Dover Canyon Winery, page 551, for some "Dog Gone Good Wine," as its motto goes.) She can even be the flower dog if you get married in a chapel in a teeny town appropriately named Harmony (see page 539).

Two of the county's most popular attractions don't allow dogs. Hearst Castle unfortunately doesn't offer a tour of the grounds from the outside, so your dog can't go anywhere near this architectural wonder (see the section on Cambria, page 536, for help with this problem). And dogs are banned from the city of San Luis Obispo's spectacular Thursday night farmers market. This is one giant street party with some of the best food and freshest produce available in these parts. If you do go without your dog, don't try to appease her with fresh flowers from the farmers market. Bring her part of your leftover burger from one of the barbecue grills here and she just might let you back in the house again.

NATIONAL FORESTS

See the National Forests and Wilderness Areas chapter starting on page 748 for important information and safety tips on visiting national forests with your dog.

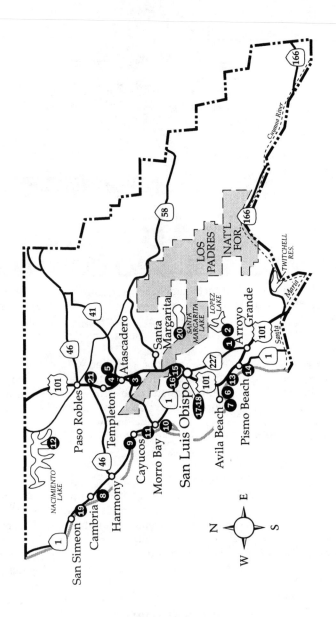

166

Cuyama River

58

166

TWITCHELL RES.

LOS PADRES NAT'L FOR.

Santa Maria

41

Santa Margarita

SANTA MARGARITA LAKE

LOPEZ LAKE

20

Arroyo Grande

1 2

101

46

101

Atascadero

227

101

101

1

5

21

4

3

16 15

14

17-18

13

Paso Robles

Templeton

1

10

6 7

Pismo Beach

NACIMIENTO LAKE

12

Cayucos

11

Morro Bay

San Luis Obispo

Avila Beach

46

9

8

Harmony

19

Cambria

1

San Simeon

N W E S

• **Los Padres National Forest** 🐾🐾🐾🐾 🐕

Both the Santa Lucia Wilderness and the Manchesna Mountain Wilderness, east of the city of San Luis Obispo, are ideal for dogs who like their wilderness spelled with a capital W. See page 751.

ARROYO GRANDE

PARKS, BEACHES, AND RECREATION AREAS

• **Biddle Regional Park** 🐾🐾½ *See* ❶ *on page 532.*

Cows graze in the pastures adjacent to this secluded county park. That's all you have to tell your dog to get her excited about a visit. To avoid the crowds who can occasionally descend here (and to avoid the weekend entry fee), the best time to come is on weekdays. Between the draw of the softball fields, the group picnic areas, and the shaded creek, this quiet park can be too popular for your leashed dog to feel comfortable just being a dog.

Remember, as always when you travel with your dog, to have him wear his rabies tag or to bring along other proof of his rabies vaccination. This is one of those places where they're going to ask to see it before letting him in.

An entrance fee of $1 per car and $1.50 per dog is charged on Saturdays, Sundays, and holidays in the summer only. Exit U.S. 101 at Grand Avenue and travel northeast, following the signs to Lopez Lake. You'll find Biddle Regional Park on the right a couple of miles before the lake. (805) 781-5930.

• **Lopez Lake Recreation Area** 🐾🐾 *See* ❷ *on page 532.*

The rules at this county-run park are just like those at state parks: Dogs are not allowed anywhere but at campsites and paved areas. It's a restrictive, frustrating place for dogs. All the trailheads are marked by something that looks like a horse with a slash through it. Rangers swear it's a dog, though a big one. But if you sneak your dog onto a trail and get caught, don't try the old "I thought it meant 'No Great Danes'" excuse. They've heard it before and it didn't work then either.

The 940-acre lake is off-limits to dogs, unless they fish in your boat with you. In fact, most of the 4,200-acre park bans dogs. Plenty of dogs do camp here, though, at any of the 359 sites set in oak woodlands. Reservations are recommended. Leashes are mandatory, and dogs are supposed to sleep in your tent or camper at night. There's a resident bear here and plenty of deer.

The entrance fee is $5 per car, $2 per dog. Campsites are $13 to $21. Call (805) 489-8019 for reservations. As always, be prepared with proof of your dog's rabies vaccination. You'll probably need it here. Exit U.S. 101 at Grand Avenue and travel northeast, following the signs to Lopez Lake. (805) 489-2095.

RESTAURANTS

Burnardo'z Candy Kitchen & Ice Cream Parlor: Sweet tooth hounding you? Savor these treats with your dog at the outdoor benches. 114 West Branch Street; (805) 481-2041.

Vic's Hamburger Haven: You don't have to eat beef to eat here. They've got veggie burgers that even dogs seem to enjoy. 803 Grand Avenue; (805) 473-1727.

PLACES TO STAY

Econo Lodge: Rates are $45 to $125. 611 El Camino Real, Arroyo Grande, CA 93420; (805) 489-9300.

Lopez Lake Recreation Area: See Lopez Lake Recreation Area on page 533 for camping information.

ATASCADERO

PARKS, BEACHES, AND RECREATION AREAS

• **Atascadero Lake Park** 🐾 🐾½ *See* ❸ *on page 532.*

Great blue herons, ducks of every shape, bluebirds, and even red-tailed hawks are just a few of the birds you may see during a visit to this large city park. Dogs have to be on leash to explore the lake and surrounding lawns and picnic areas, but they seem to enjoy themselves despite the constraints.

This is *the* place to take your dog in Atascadero. While they aren't allowed to swim or rent a paddleboat, they revel in life's simple pleasures, like sniffing each other end to end.

The Charles Paddock Zoo is next door. Instead of those typical zoo odors, this place smells like fresh jasmine when you walk by. It's good if you're trying to fool your dog into thinking you just dropped off the kids at some botanical garden and not at the home of wild and smelly animals.

From U.S. 101, take Santa Rosa Road west for three long blocks. The park is on your right, between Mountain View Drive and Morro Road. For the best parking, turn right on Morro Road and make another right into the park. (805) 461-5001.

• **Sunken Gardens Park** 🐾 🐾½ *See* ❹ *on page 532.*

Pat St. Clair of the Atascadero Chamber of Commerce is proud of how friendly her city is to animals. In fact, she says, this lush strip of green with fountains and statues in front of the grand old city administration building is where some of the strangest-looking creatures go for walks.

One day she saw a pig wandering around, who she assumed was an escapee from a nearby farm. "It's a beautiful park. I thought he had good taste," she says. But on inquiring, it turned out that the pig was someone's pet. He was off his leash and having a grand old time rooting around. Since then, the pig has become a regular, scaring dogs away, or at least making them freeze in their tracks with curiosity. Dogs, unlike Mr. Piggy, are supposed to be leashed.

From U.S. 101, exit at Traffic Way and go northeast for a block. Turn right on El Camino Real. The park will be on your left in four blocks, at West Mall Street. (805) 461-5001.

• **Traffic Way Park** 🐾 🐾 *See* ❺ *on page 532.*

The only reason to come to this park is if you have to play softball or walk the dog. The park is made up of two ball fields. Since each is very well fenced, even at the entrances, dogs who tend to run away are safe here. Of course, they're supposed to be leashed anyway, but dogs can do the darndest things if a cat beckons from down the street.

Exit U.S. 101 at Traffic Way and drive northeast for about six blocks. The park is on your right. (805) 461-5001.

PLACES TO STAY

Motel 6: Rates are $28 for one adult, $6 for the second adult. This Motel 6, like most others, allows one small pooch per room. 9400 El Camino Real, Atascadero, CA 93422; (805) 466-6701.

AVILA BEACH

This small coastal community is about the farthest north you'll find the Southern California beach lifestyle. And if you hear three siren blasts, prepare to have the beaches to yourself—the Diablo Canyon Nuclear Plant, which sits on a fault six miles north of town, just may have had a little boo-boo.

PARKS, BEACHES, AND RECREATION AREAS

• **Avila Beach** 😊 😊 *See ❻ on page 532.*

If you have images of strolling down the beach paw-in-hand with your dog all day long, change that image. Or at least change the hours. Dogs are permitted here, but only before 10 A.M. and after 5 P.M. You can understand the restrictions if you come here in the summer, when the place looks like Son of Jones Beach.

Dogs must be leashed. The beach runs along Front Street in the main part of Avila Beach. (805) 595-5400.

• **Olde Port Beach** 😊 😊 😊 *See ❼ on page 532.*

Dogs, get your hankies ready. This used to be the only off-leash beach in this part of California. But leashes are now the law. (Sniff, honk.) That's a shame, because the beach is secluded, with nary a soul around.

It's still a much better beach for dogs than Avila Beach (see above). The name itself is picturesque, and so is the beach, looking out as it does on fishing boats moored offshore. If you have any salt in your blood, you'll enjoy the view from here. The occasional jet skier can mar the tranquillity, but if you visit in the cooler months, the jet skiers are usually off doing more quiet activities.

From Highway 1/U.S. 101, take the Avila Beach exit west. Once in town, continue west, on Harford Drive. The beach is on your left. If you reach the Port San Luis Pier (not the modern, very long Union Oil Pier you'll come to first, but the woody old one in the harbor), you've gone too far. It's not so bad, though. You can either turn right around and find the beach or hang out at the pier and harbor area for a while. Dogs are fond of those fishy breezes and you'll enjoy looking at the old boats. (805) 595-5400.

PLACES TO STAY

Avila Hot Springs Spa & RV Resort: If you want to treat yourself like a king or queen, stay here. You won't be able to sleep at the spa's luxurious suites or rooms because you're traveling with your pooch, but you may camp here. Tents and RVs are welcome, as are the dogs who stay in them. Granted, it's not very regal to stay in a tent or a traveling tin box, but that's okay, because the real royal treatment here is given in the spa. The massages and mineral baths are out of this world. Avila Hot Springs is famous for its spa treatments. Take turns with your human friend walking your dog friend around the beautiful grounds (on leash) so you can each get massages without having to leave your pooch alone. Sorry, but no dog massages are given at this time. There's also a swimming pool and a hot mineral pool here, but dogs aren't allowed in those either.

Camping is $18 to $28. Call for spa prices—they're reasonable. 250 Avila Beach Drive; (805) 595-2359 or (800) 332-2359.

CAMBRIA

A stroll through this charming village can be fun for you and your dog, but Cambria serves a more important purpose: It's the home of the Tail Wag's Inn, a quality kennel where you can board your dog for part of a day while you visit Hearst Castle about nine miles north in San Simeon.

Laura, the owner of this kennel, heard of too many dogs who had been left unattended in sweltering cars as their caretakers sauntered around the magnificent castle for hours. So she created a relatively inexpensive, yet luxurious package to encourage people not to risk the lives of their dogs. For $10 (she hasn't upped the price for more than a decade), your kenneled dog gets a "continental breakfast" of dog treats, takes at least two good walks, and drinks Crystal Springs bottled water. Hey, what the heck, if you're spending the day among opulence, why shouldn't your pup? And the walks aren't just to the corner and back. Laura takes the dogs' needs to heart, and strolls them to a nearby grassy area with a creek, trees, "and god knows, lots of smells," she says.

The Tail Wag's Inn is a boarding kennel (overnight boarding is the mainstay), but it's the kind of kennel a dog doesn't seem to mind. One regular boarder escaped from her house during a thunderstorm and her owner was frantically looking everywhere for her. Where did she run? To the Tail Wag's Inn, in fact, to the kennel she normally uses. "She was just there barking at her kennel as if to say, okay, let me in, and where's my blanket and some food?" says Laura.

Day-boarding dogs can arrive from 8 A.M. to 1 P.M. and have to leave by 5 P.M. Reservations are required. This is important, because some folks have thought they could just drive here and drop off their pooch. They've been mighty disappointed when they've had to forgo their trip to Hearst Castle because there was no room at the inn. In addition, your dog's shot record is also required. The kennel is at the Village Service Center, 2419-A Village Lane. Call (805) 927-1589 for reservations or more information.

PARKS, BEACHES, AND RECREATION AREAS

• **Moonstone Beach/Shamel County Park** 🐾 🐾 🐾 ½

See ⑧ on page 532.

This is a perfect place to take your dog for a little exercise while visiting this beautiful town. The beach here is long and wide, except during high tide, when it can break up into shorter, narrow beaches. Better look at a tide table if you're planning a long walk; otherwise you might literally be stuck between a rock and a hard place until the tide goes back out.

If you're lucky, you and your dog can sniff out some pearly moonstones (thus the beach's name) and even bits of jade, but they're getting harder and harder to find. Your dog will be more interested in sniffing out adventures on this terrific stretch of sand.

If you're staying at a motel on Moonstone Beach Drive, just walk a few hundred feet and you're here. If you want to start your walk in a pretty little park, go to Shamel County Park, located where Windsor Boulevard (on the ocean side of Highway 1) makes a 90-degree turn. It's a small park, with a swimming pool and picnic tables. Santa Rosa Creek runs through it, too. Follow your leashed dog's nose to the beach, just a long stick's throw away. (805) 781-5200.

RESTAURANTS

West End Bar & Grille: The food here is just the kind you'd hope to find at a seaside town like this. I grew up with this kind of stuff, and call it coastal comfort food. It's your basic fish-and-chips/burgers/grilled cheese cuisine with great steamers and award-winning chili. There's a picnic area next to the restaurant where you can dine with your doggy. 774 Main Street; (805) 927-5521.

PLACES TO STAY

Cambria Pines Lodge: You and your dog get to stay at one of two cabins here that permit pooches. They're the oldest cabins on the property (built in the 1940s), and pretty basic, but dogs don't care. They're just happy they get to snooze in the same room as you. Your stay here comes with a full breakfast in the lodge. The cabins are $65. 2905 Burton Drive, Cambria, CA 93428; (805) 927-4200 or (800) 445-6868.

Cambria Shores Inn: This little inn is built in a horseshoe shape around a quiet lawn area. Dogs can sniff the grass there, but doggy business should be taken elsewhere. Dogs and their people love to look out on the ocean from their rooms. There's easy beach access from here. If you're weary from trying to find dog-friendly restaurants on the road, the Cambria Shores Inn will give you a little break: Breakfast is brought to your room. 6276 Moonstone Beach Drive, Cambria, CA 93428; (805) 927-8644 or (800) 433-9179.

Mariner's Inn: The owners here like dogs; they have a 132-pound boy rottweiler who's the sweetest thing around. Some of the rooms have ocean views. Rates are $55 to $210. Dogs are $10 extra. 6180 Moonstone Beach Drive, Cambria, CA 93428; (805) 927-4624 or (800) 344-0407.

CAYUCOS

A funkier coastal community would be hard to find. Cayucos, about eight miles north of Morro Bay, provides a great escape from summer crowds. Even on holiday weekends, the place doesn't get packed. The Old West stores and saloons are a real find, but if you'd rather fish than shop and drink, try the old pier on Cayucos State Beach. It was built in 1875, and those in charge figure a few dogs aren't going to hurt it now. Besides, the fishing is great, and what dog wouldn't enjoy watching you reel in a mackerel or a salmon?

PARKS, BEACHES, AND RECREATION AREAS

• **Cayucos State Beach** 🐾🐾🐾½ *See* ❾ *on page 532*

This beach is wide and wonderful. Dogs have to be leashed, but they can still enjoy a long walk here. Since there are a couple of good greasy-spoon take-out joints nearby, we like to order lunch and bring it to the beach, where dogs pray hard that you'll drop a french fry in the sand.

The south end of the beach has fewer people and more seaweed—the stuff of fine dog outings. From Highway 1, go southwest on Cayucos Drive and turn left at Ocean Drive. You can enter almost anywhere between Cayucos Road and E Street, west of Ocean Drive. (805) 549-3312.

PLACES TO STAY

Dolphin Inn: Frankly, I'd stay here just for the name, but the inn has other attractive features, like its proximity to the water and a continental breakfast that comes with your room. Rates are $45 to $65. Dogs are $5 extra. 399 South Ocean Avenue, Cayucos, CA 93430; (805) 995-3810.

Estero Bay Motel: Located just a half block from the ocean, this U-shaped motel is a fine place to spend the night with your dog. We like the owner's explanation for the motel's dog-friendly policy: "There are a lot of nice older women who have dogs they just can't part with. We want to help them stay together." Awwww. Rates are $45 to $110. There's a $10-per-stay charge for dogs. 25 South Ocean Avenue, Cayucos, CA 93430; (805) 995-3614 or (800) 736-1292.

Shoreline Inn: If your dog longs for sand between his toes, stay here. This attractive inn is a few long steps from the beach, where leashed pooches are allowed. All rooms have a view of the strand, surf, and ocean. The rooms are typical motel-style, but the suites are really lovely. They're light and airy, and all feature private balconies and TVs with extended cable channels. Our favorite two suites have fridges and fireplaces. All rooms and suites come with video cassette players, which is a real plus when traveling with kids. Rates are $60 to $105. Dogs are $10 extra. 1 North Ocean Avenue, Box 376, Cayucos, CA 93430; (805) 995-3681.

HARMONY

"Living in Harmony" was a classic episode of Patrick McGoohan's science fiction TV series, *The Prisoner*. But here in this two-acre dairy town-turned-artist's colony several miles south of Cambria, all 18 residents live in Harmony and there's nothing odd about it. They thrive on being off the beaten track.

Word is that William Randolph Hearst liked to stop by a creamery here to swig down a glass of fresh buttermilk and buy a couple of wheels of cheese. He certainly knew a good thing when he saw it.

And there's good news for dogs: People in these parts are as dog-friendly as they come. If your dog is of the well-behaved ilk, she might be invited into some of the businesses here. Be aware that this is an equal-opportunity town and felines frequent just about every nook.

Sadly, at press time, all this harmony was in jeopardy because of a Beverly Hills businessman who bought the three acres that encompass the center of

Harmony. The landlord, Samson Mehdizadeh, essentially bought Harmony. That's bad enough, but at the time he was also trying to close escrow on 700 acres adjacent to that property. His dream for the acreage: To make it into a sprawling "peace village," which would house families from around the globe. That doesn't sound like a terrible thing, but read on.

He wants to build lots of housing, a tram system, a "hall of nations," restaurants, a mobile home park, a petting zoo, and a kosher slaughterhouse. Yes, a kosher slaughterhouse in Harmony.

According to the *San Francisco Chronicle*, the slaughterhouse will be a model for others that can be franchised to state prisons. "When some people are unfulfilled in their need to handle blood, they can become murderers. The kosher preparation of livestock takes away the desire to commit violence," Mehdizadeh told the *Chronicle*. Oh. Well, then, judging by the reactions of the locals to some run-ins they say they've already had with Mehdizadeh, he'd better open a kosher slaughterhouse for residents of Harmony quick, or he'll really be heading for the hills.

For now, visit with your dog and keep your fingers and paws crossed that Mehdizadeh decides to really give peace a chance and leave Harmony alone.

RESTAURANTS

Old Harmony Pasta Factory: They make their own pasta here, and boy is it delicious. If you want an amazing dessert, try the apple ravioli. It's stuffed with apples, cheese, and cinnamon and is topped with fresh whipped cream. It's to drool for.

The patio features umbrella-covered tables, heat lamps, and cats. This is something your dog should know, because if he can't keep harmony with the kitties here, he won't be a welcome guest. 2 Old Creamery Road; (805) 927-5882.

DIVERSIONS

Get me to the church on leash: Folks around here say that if you wed in the town of Harmony, your lives together will be blessed with harmony. Fortunately, your dog can be part of the ceremony at the Harmony Wedding Chapel, so you should never again have a problem with him barking or chasing the cat, if all this harmony stuff is true.

This unique chapel was built as a cold storage facility in 1914. The door is the bottom of a huge wine cask and the walls are two feet thick. Inside, the pews are oak, the floors are pine, and the walls are whitewashed. With all this plus stained glass windows, the chapel seems like a shrunk-down mission. There's not a hint of froufrou anywhere, unless your dog decides to wear a ruffled shirt under his tuxedo.

The owner loves dogs, so your pooch shouldn't be at all apprehensive about being best beast or flower hound. Weddings, including the minister's fee, run between $200 and $300. It's worth the price: "People like getting married here. At least they start their marriages in Harmony," winks Rev. Denise Mikkelson. For more information, contact Mikkelson at P.O. Box 1523, Morro Bay, CA 93443. There is no street address, but you'll find the chapel in the northeast corner of Harmony, behind a restaurant. (805) 772-4000.

MORRO BAY

The landmark Morro Rock draws more visitors to this seaside community than its beaches and quaint stores. This 576-foot-tall, 50-acre-wide extinct volcano peak juts into the Pacific and beckons anyone who gets a glimpse. In fact, in 1512 it attracted explorer Juan Rodriguez Cabrillo, who named the rock, which has become a landmark for ocean navigators and tourists.

The best area to take a dog to see the rock is along the left-hand edge of the rock as you face the ocean. There's a small, fairly secluded beach here, which makes for a pleasant walk with a leashed dog. Dogs have a number of reactions to Morro Rock. Most ignore it. Some give it only a sideways glance. But others stare at it, sniffing the air in fascination. Maybe they smell the scents of the eons. Or maybe they're just contemplating what a challenge it would be to leave their own unique mark on such a gigantic chunk of rock. By the way, the rock is now *Joe's* rock, because last time we visited, he, you know, did a little leg lift near the base of it. He trotted back to the car so proudly, knowing that he'd acquired something special with that last wee wee. (Don't tell him if your dog has done the same since then, okay?)

Morro Bay is one of the few remaining sleepy seaside hamlets that hasn't succumbed to rampant development. Yet. Unfortunately, a mammoth, upscale "planned community," stretching six miles along the coast from Morro Rock to Cayucos, may soon pollute the aesthetics (as well as the ocean) of this serene town. A lot of locals are fighting it to the death. But just in case the big bucks win, get here with your dog before it turns into Suburbia by the Sea.

PARKS, BEACHES, AND RECREATION AREAS

• **Coleman City Park** 🐾 🐾 ½ *See* ❿ *on page 532.*

This is the park to visit if you forgot your sunscreen. At the right time of day, the shadow of Morro Rock will loom over you and protect you from those wrinkling rays.

Walking through the dunes here while under the spell of the volcanic mound can be a hypnotic experience. Don't let the otherworldly quality of it all make you forget that your dog is supposed to be leashed.

The park is to the north of Morro Rock. For easy access to both Coleman City Park and the southern portion of Morro Strand State Beach, park in the Morro Rock lot, after Embarcadero turns into Coleman Drive. There's another lot for the park on the north side of Coleman Drive just before the rock. (805) 772-6200.

• **Morro Strand State Beach** 🐾 🐾 🐾 ½ *See* ⓫ *on page 532.*

This three-mile beach doesn't get heavy use, so it's a good place to take your leashed dog in this popular tourist haven. Dunes aren't abundant, but there are enough to keep your walks interesting.

The beach is an especially appealing stop for Highway 1 travelers because it comes complete with a 104-site campground. The campground is nothing fancy or rustic. It's actually a converted day-use parking lot. But it's right over the beach, so if sounds of crashing surf send you to sleep, you'll get your eight hours here.

Camping costs $14 to $16. Dogs are $1 extra. There's no day-use fee. The beach is west of Highway 1 between Atascadero Road and Yerba Buena Avenue. For camping reservations, call Parknet at (800) 444-PARK. For beach information, phone (805) 772-8812.

RESTAURANTS

Dorn's Original Breakers Cafe: The specials here include clam chowder, fresh seafood, and New York steaks. Dogs are allowed only at the two tables in front of the restaurant, not on the spacious deck in back. 801 Market Avenue; (805) 772-4415.

Foster's Freeze: If you're in the mood for a cold, creamy cone or sundae, trot on over here and dig in with your dog at the outdoor table. 801 Piney Way; (805) 772-8373.

PLACES TO STAY

Adventure Inn: Eighty-five pound German shepherd Jasmine and her person, Carolyn Green, wrote to tell us they had a fun time staying at this motel, so we checked it out. Thanks for the tip, Jasmine and mom. When Jasmine stayed here, the policy was that only small dogs were allowed. But they allowed Jasmine, and now other big dogs are welcome. Maybe good-dog Jasmine set the precedent.

This place faces the waterfront, and has terrific views of Morro Rock, a view the Adventure Inn claims is the best view in Morro Bay. The rooms are small, but there's a pool and an attractive sunning area with a hot tub. Rooms have fridges, and come with a continental breakfast. Rates are $59 to $159. Dogs are $10 extra. 1150 Embarcadero, Morro Bay, CA 93442; (805) 772-5607 or (800) 799-5607.

Best Western El Rancho: Rates are $50 to $90. Dogs pay a onetime $10 fee—"to cover the bug bomb," the manager told us. Joe says "Nuke 'em!" (But he doesn't care for toxic substances, so he's in a bit of a quandary about the whole thing.) 2460 Main Street, Morro Bay, CA 93442; (805) 772-2212.

Gold Coast: Small dogs only, please. Rates are $35 to $110. Dogs are $5 extra, and require a $30 deposit. 670 Main Street, Morro Bay, CA 93442; (805) 772-7740.

Morro Bay State Park: This verdant state park overlooking Morro Bay has 135 campsites set in pine woodlands. Dogs are banned from the park's trails and from every other natural wonder. Campsites and paved roads are their only stomping grounds. Sites are $14 to $20. Dogs are $1 extra. Take Highway 1 to the south end of Morro Bay and follow the signs to the park. This campground gets crowded, so call Parknet at (800) 444-PARK for reservations. Phone (805) 772-7434 for park information.

Morro Dunes Travel Trailer Park & Resort Campground: I'm not sure the name of this place is long enough. Anyway, there's plenty of space for recreational vehicles and tents here, and the view of Morro Rock is pretty good from some areas. But what dogs like best is that Morro Dunes has its very own little dog run in back, for dogs who need to exercise off leash. It makes it worth staying here, even if you're a tenter who balks at life among the trailers. Rates are $17 to $25. Dogs are $1 extra. 1700 Embarcadero, Morro Bay, CA 93442; (805) 772-2722.

Morro Strand State Beach: See Morro Strand State Beach on page 540 for camping information.

Motel 6: Rates are $30 to $40 for one adult, $6 for the second adult. Like most other Motel 6s, this one allows one small pooch per room. 298 Atascadero Road, Morro Bay, CA 93442; (805) 772-5641.

Sunset Travelodge: Rates are $45 to $195. Dogs are $10 extra. 1080 Market Avenue, Morro Bay, CA 93442; (805) 772-1259.

DIVERSIONS

Knight to King-Dog 3: Did you ever wonder what it would be like to play chess with your dog? Ponder no more. At the giant chessboard just a block from the bay, you, your friends, and even your dog can play chess—literally. You can be king, if you want. Your stepmother can be a pawn. Your dog can occasionally sub for people getting tired of standing around acting like a bunch of bishops. One man, a local named Bob, told me his dog plays queen, so she gets a lot of action and doesn't become bored. He gives her a treat every time she captures a piece or checks the king. But Queen Janey, his cocker spaniel, is not brilliant enough to figure out the moves for herself, so Bob guides her along.

Fill in the empty squares, or all the squares for that matter, with the giant pieces you can borrow from the city. If you bring your dog along for a short game, make sure it's cool enough and she moves around as much as Queen Janey. To reserve the giant chess pieces, call (805) 772-6278.

Don't you hurry in that furry surrey: Dogs seem to be highly entertained watching their caretakers push the pedals in these fringed surreys/bikes. Dogs can afford to be entertained, since all they have to do is sit down in the front basket and watch. They don't have to lift a paw. Just bring them a blanket to cushion the hard basket and make sure they're secured so they can't zip out after a passing kitty.

Small dogs are most comfortable. Large dogs just don't fit. "Any dog is better than a lot of the teenage boys we get here," a surrey rental agent told me as he watched a surrey full of teens swerve down the road. Surrey rental fees range from $10 an hour for the small ones to $20 an hour for the large sizes. The Morro Bay Surrey Company is located at 850 Embarcadero. There is no phone. Kites Galore, which also rent surreys, is located at 108 Front Street; (805) 772-8322.

PASO ROBLES

PARKS, BEACHES, AND RECREATION AREAS

Dogs are not allowed at any Paso Robles city park unless there's an event that includes them (training or a show, to be more specific). Let's hear it, dogs: Hissssss. Booooooo.

Fortunately, Lake Nacimiento (see below) is around to help dogs get over their disappointment. It's not very close and there is a fee, but it's pooch-friendly.

• **Lake Nacimiento** 🐾🐾½ See ⑫ on page 532.
While this oak-lined lake has 165 miles of shoreline, only the portion run

by Lake Nacimiento Resort is open to the public. And with the resort's limited dog areas, that means just a so-so vacation for canines. Dogs are allowed on leash in the meadows and picnic areas. They're also allowed to camp with you at any of the resort's 350 sites. But unless your dog enjoys helping you fish for white bass and smallmouth bass from your boat, a visit here probably won't be the highlight of her year.

The day-use fee is $10 per car. Campsites are $22 a night. Dogs are $5 extra, day or night. Reservations are needed for RV sites. From U.S. 101, exit at Highway 46 and go west at the off-ramp. Follow this road, known for most of its span as Nacimiento Lake Road, for eight miles. When you get to County Road G-14, make a hard right and drive another eight miles. The resort is on the left. (805) 238-3256.

RESTAURANTS

A&W: If you're on the road and want to stop for some quick eats with your pooch, this is a fine place to grab a bite, if you don't mind burger cuisine. The shakes here are as close to "real" as any fast-food shake can get. Dine with doggy at the outdoor tables. 2110 Spring Street; (805) 238-0360.

Bakery Works Cafe: This used to be a fun place to come with a dog, because dogs and their people could dine under the umbrella-topped outdoor tables. But the mean ol' health department recently issued the cafe a citation for allowing pooches, so now dogs have to be tied up on the other side of the picket fence. That's not as bad as it sounds, because all you have to do to be virtually right beside your dog is get a table by the fence. You can just reach over and pet him. Bakery Works serves three meals a day, plus Sunday brunch. 1646 Spring Street; (805) 239-1070.

Deli Squeeze: The name of this eatery may conjure up images of someone juicing a ham sandwich, but fear not—they serve juices and sandwiches here, but they're not related. There's also an espresso bar. Share a meal with your dog at the outdoor tables. 545 Spring Street; (805) 238-3795.

DK's Donuts: Eat your way out of your New Year's resolution at the sidewalk tables. Your dog can be at your side to witness the downing of the doughnuts. 1740 Spring Street; (805) 238-9371.

Good Ol' Burgers: Dogs and their people have to sit at the farthest possible rugged wood tables, but that's okay. You can smell the charbroiled beef from hundreds of yards away. 1145 24th Street; (805) 238-0655.

Skinny Dippers Frozen Yogurt & Fruit Shakes: Dog heaven! Everyone here seems to love dogs, so everyone with a dog comes here. You can often see 4-H'ers hanging out at the benches with their pooches. The manager trains dogs, and the place is close to a park that allows dogs. 1131 Creston Road; (805) 238-3477.

PLACES TO STAY

Budget Inn: There's a big open area here for walking dogs. Just make sure you do your part and clean up. Rates are $32 to $120. 3745 Spring Street, Paso Robles, CA 93446; (805) 239-3030.

Lake Nacimiento Resort: See Lake Nacimiento on page 542 for camping information.

Motel 6: Rates are $33 for the first adult, $6 for the second. This Motel 6, like most others, permits one small pooch per room. 1134 Black Oak Drive, Paso Robles, CA 93446; (805) 239-9090.

Travelodge: Rates are $40 to $80. They used to advertise that only small dogs were allowed, but now "we're more dog-friendly. As long as your dog's not an elephant," he's allowed, says the manager. Dogs are $5 extra. 2701 Spring Street, Paso Robles, CA 93446; (805) 238-0078.

DIVERSIONS

A loaf of bread, a glass of wine, and thee dog: When you think of Wine Country, Paso Robles may not be the first place that comes to mind. But there are some fine wineries east of town, and a few allow your dog to hang out with you at their serene picnic areas while you sip your newly bought wine. Eberle Winery and Meridian Vineyards, both east of town on Highway 46, welcome dogs in their picnic areas. Eberle has the added advantage of a water spigot handy dandy for your dog. Call Eberle at (805) 238-9607. Meridian's number is (805) 237-6000. For a super dog-friendly winery, see Dover Canyon Winery on page 551.

PISMO BEACH

The Chumash Indians, who lived here for at least 9,000 years, referred to this area as the place to find *pismu,* or tar. History has changed this once-pristine land to a busy seaside community, but your dog might show you that there's one thing that hasn't changed: This is still the place to find tar. Joe found it all over his paws when he was exploring one of the beaches. Later, despite cleaning his feet, I found it all over the inside of the truck. Even the dry cleaner found it—he found it amusing that the jacket I'd left inside the truck was covered with indelible paw prints.

This never happened again, and it has never happened to any other dogs we talked to on the beaches, so fear not. Pismo Beach is a good place for you and your dog to share some quality time. Most of the beaches here allow leashed dogs, who can be champion partners in clamming for the famous Pismo clams. They don't need a fishing license, but you will.

Pismo Beach is usually cool and foggy. It's ideal if you have a dog who melts in the heat. When we drive to Southern California, this is a must-stop area for Joe. Although there are no leash-free areas, he always appreciates land that is naturally air-conditioned.

PARKS, BEACHES, AND RECREATION AREAS

City parks here don't allow dogs. The 1,250-foot pier in the middle of the beach area also bans them. But there are a couple of beaches that more than make up for these places.

•**Oceano Dunes/Pismo State Beach** 🐾 🐾 🐾1/2 *See* ⑬ *on page 532.*

It's hard to tell what dogs enjoy more here—exploring the long, wide beach or wandering through the great dunes above. Your leashed dog can get all the exercise he needs by trotting down the miles of trails on the unspoiled dunes. If he likes cold ocean spray, take him down to the beach for a romp among the gulls.

Camping is available at a couple of sections of the beach. Fees are $6 for the on-beach camping area south of the Grand Avenue entrance (four-wheel-drive vehicles are recommended) and $14 to $24 for camping among the trees at the Pismo State Beach North Beach Campground. Dogs are $1 extra. There are a total of 225 campsites. For more info, call (805) 549-3312. Call Parknet for reservations at (800) 444-PARK.

To avoid the $4 day-use fee at the Grand Avenue entrance, drive west from Highway 1 and park on Grand Avenue before the ranger kiosk. Once at the beach, head north. Walking south will put you in the middle of a busy off-highway vehicle area—not the best place for a dog; (805) 473-7230.

• **Pismo Beach City Beach** 🐾 🐾 🐾 *See* ⓮ *on page 532.*

Does your dog like watching people in bathing suits play volleyball? Does she enjoy sniffing at bodies slathered with coconut oil? If so, this beach is for her. It's rarely so crowded that it's uncomfortable, but it's rarely so uncrowded that it's a bore for a social butterfly dog.

The farther north you walk, the fewer people you'll encounter. Dogs have to be leashed everywhere, though. But this shouldn't stop the digging breeds from helping you uncover prize Pismo clams (fishing licenses are required for the human half of the team). We once saw a dog who would thrust his entire snout into the wet sand and come up with a clam every time. His owner didn't even have to use his clam fork.

One of the many access points is west of Highway 1, at the foot of Main Avenue near the recreation pier. (805) 773-4658.

RESTAURANTS

Old West Cinnamon Rolls: This little cafe has some of the best cinnamon rolls we've ever laid teeth on. They're hot, sticky, and absolutely decadent. Enjoy them at the front bench with your pooch at your side. 861 Dolliver Street; (805) 773-1428.

The Scoop Ice Cream Parlor: When you say "The Scoop" to most dog people, they tend to think of the plastic bags, newspapers, or little shovels they use for scooping the, well, you get the picture. But this ice-cream parlor is so good that "The Scoop" might hold a whole new meaning to you after you visit with your pooch. Hang out, cone in hand, canine at feet, at the outdoor seating. 607 Dolliver Street; (805) 773-4253.

PLACES TO STAY

Motel 6: Rates are $28 to $40 for one adult and $4 for the second adult. This Motel 6, like most others, allows one small dog per room. 860 Fourth Street, Pismo Beach, CA 93449; (805) 773-2665.

Oceano Dunes/Pismo State Beach: See Oceano Dunes/Pismo State Beach on page 544 for camping information.

Oxford Suites: From the attractive lobby with the tiled fountain and big fireplace to the guest suites, which include a work table (should you actually want to work while in Pismo Beach), sofa, microwave, and fridge, this place is a comfy home away from home. It's ideal for traveling with a dog, because you can do some kind of cooking here. Oxford Suites looks motel-ish from the outside, but once inside it doesn't really feel that way. Your stay here includes a full breakfast buffet and an evening reception with beverages and light hors d'oeuvres. There's even a year-round pool, but dogs have to keep their paws on terra firma. Rates are $69 to $99. Dogs are charged a $10 fee per visit. 651 Five Cities Drive, Pismo Beach, CA 93449; (805) 773-3773 or (800) 982-7848.

Sandcastle Inn: This one's on the beach. Even dogs enjoy an ocean view. Rates are $79 to $140. Dogs are $10 extra. 100 Stimson Avenue, Pismo Beach, CA 93449; (805) 773-2422.

Spyglass Inn: This is a great place for the family, from the breakfast to the pool to the miniature golf course. Many of the rooms have ocean views. The managers don't like gigantic dogs as guests, but they're pretty generous about the size of the pooches they'll accept. Rates are $75 to $149. Dogs are $10 extra. 270 Spyglass Drive, Pismo Beach, CA 93449; (805) 773-4855.

SAN LUIS OBISPO

This city is the big jewel of the Central Coast. Some of the smaller gems like Pismo Beach and Morro Bay can be more lustrous for dogs, but there's so much history here, and so much to do, that you're both bound to enjoy your visit.

If the past interests you at all, be sure to stop at the Chamber of Commerce and pick up a Heritage Walks pamphlet showing the fascinating buildings where much of California's history was shaped. Dogs may yawn as they trot by some of the ice-cream-colored Victorians and whitewashed adobes, but when they arrive at Mission Plaza, the good times roll.

The plaza is the heart of the city and the home of Mission San Luis Obispo de Tolosa, built in 1772. Dogs aren't allowed inside, but it's the world outside that will interest them more anyway. That's where the beautiful Mission Plaza tantalizes with scents and sounds dogs love. A brick path follows a cool stream nestled in conifers full of songbirds and takes you by a few delicious-smelling restaurants with tables on the wood patios overlooking the stream (see the Restaurants section starting on page 547).

But beware: The reason dogs like it here so much isn't necessarily for the food or ambience. They're wild about all the four-legged creatures who slink around here meowing for handouts of food and attention. If you have a cat-crazed canine, either avoid this area or keep a very tight hold on her leash.

PARKS, BEACHES, AND RECREATION AREAS

• **Cuesta Canyon County Park** 🐾 🐾 ½ *See* ⑮ *on page 532.*

This park would be a peaceful place to visit, if not for the constant barking of dogs at the adjacent veterinary hospital and the nonstop drone of nearby U.S. 101. Even with these distractions, the atmosphere isn't bad. Between the cool creek, the singing birds, and the large trees, Cuesta Canyon County Park is a decent place to take a dog in need of a short romp. The playing field area in the back of the park is almost completely fenced and well protected from the freeway.

The park is conveniently located near California Polytechnic State University. Exit U.S. 101 at Grand Street and go east immediately onto Loomis Street. Follow Loomis Street as it runs parallel to U.S. 101. The road ends in the park's parking lot. (805) 781-5930.

• **El Chorro Regional Park** 🐾 🐾 🐾 1/2 *See* **16** *on page 532.*

For some reason, very few people visit this 1,730-acre park, except on holidays and some summer weekends. You'll rarely find others on the four miles of trail here, but you may well run into deer, so keep your dog leashed.

It's not even that common to see people using the many group picnic areas. There are 48 developed campsites, all with full hookups. A fee of $1.50 per dog is charged only on weekends and holidays. Sites are $18 to $21. Exit U.S. 101 at Santa Rosa Street/Highway 1 and drive northeast about seven miles. The park is on the right. (805) 781-5219.

• **Laguna Lake Park** 🐾 🐾 🐾 1/2 *See* **17** *on page 532.*

Early morning is the best time to visit this beautiful, large city park shaded by willows, pines, and eucalyptuses. That's when it's the coolest and most peaceful. The moist morning air and the smell of pine, clean earth, and fresh lake water intermingle and make for a relaxing outing for you and your fine furry friend.

During days when the park is a little crowded (it rarely gets this way), there are still plenty of spots for you and your dog to escape from the masses. If you follow the Fitness Trail and bear right after Fitness Stop Number 8, you'll come to secluded fields abutting a marshy part of the lake. If you're not doing the Fitness Trail, you'll find this quiet area by walking to the other side of the long line of eucalyptus trees past the gazebo.

From U.S. 101, take the Los Osos Valley Road exit northwest for several blocks and turn right on Madonna Road. In a few blocks, go left on Dalido Drive and park at any of the several lots in the park. (805) 781-7100.

• **Santa Rosa Park** 🐾 1/2 *See* **18** *on page 532.*

With its playgrounds, ball fields, and basketball courts, this park is great for kids. But dogs are relegated to the section in the back of the park, where tall trees and a little grass make a so-so rest area.

From U.S. 101, go north on Santa Rosa Street/Highway 1. For the part of the park dogs can visit, turn right at Montalban Street in about three blocks. The entrance is on your left. (805) 781-7100.

RESTAURANTS

Cisco's Restaurant: This is by far the most beautiful patio restaurant in this part of California. It even has great sandwiches and live music every day. Dogs feel relaxed and not at all cramped. Enter from the Mission Plaza side and try to get a table overlooking the creek. 778 Higuera Street; (805) 543-5555.

Cold Store Creamery: I love the name of this place. It sounds so sweet and smooth and old fashioned. Turns out the ice cream here is just as good as the name. Share some with your dog at the three outdoor tables; 860 Higuera Street; (805) 545-0926.

Country Yogurt Culture: Enter from the Mission Plaza side and you and your dog can enjoy creekside tables and eight flavors of award-winning yogurt. The friendly service makes dogs feel right at home. 746 Higuera Street; (805) 544-9007.

Old Country Deli: A lot of people come here and give their dogs a bone as they eat the fresh barbecued meat the staff cooks out front. That's often not a good idea, but it's especially bad if you don't clean up after your dog eats. The owners still allow pooches, but they won't if people don't mind the mess their pets make. 600 Marsh Street; (805) 541-2968.

Rudolph's Coffee & Tea Company: Enjoy a spot of tea, coffee, or hot chocolate while your dog guards your muffin for you. 670 Higuera Street; (805) 543-4902.

San Luis Fish & Barbeque: If you and Tex feel like good ol' barbecued anything, this is the place to get it. Slurp it down at the tables out front. 474 Marsh Street; (805) 541-4191.

San Luis Obispo Donuts: Open 'round the clock. You can sit at the umbrella-covered tables and eat doughnuts, pastries, and even egg rolls as your dog looks on. 1057 Monterey Street; (805) 544-8580.

Uptown Espresso: Sip yours with your dog and a fresh bagel at your side on the large patio here. 1065 Higuera Street; (805) 783-1300.

PLACES TO STAY

Best Western Royal Oak Motor Hotel: This is a terrific place to stay if your dog wants to stretch his legs. It's a quick walk to beautiful Laguna Lake Park (see page 547). When you're done walking, you can wash your sweaty clothes at the motel's laundry facility. Rates are $59 to $115. Dogs are charged a $10 fee per visit. 214 Madonna Road, San Luis Obispo, CA 93405; (805) 544-4410.

Campus Motel: They want only small dogs here. Rates are $44 to $148. Dogs are $7 extra. 404 Santa Rosa Street, San Luis Obispo, CA 93405; (805) 544-0881.

Days Inn: Cuesta Canyon County Park (see page 546) isn't far away, so this is a good place to stay if you and your dog need some fresh air and exercise. Only small dogs can stay here, which we think is a shame. Rates are $49 to $109. Dogs are $10 extra per day and require a $50 deposit. 2050 Garfield Street, San Luis Obispo, CA 93405; (805) 549-9911.

El Chorro Regional Park: See El Chorro Regional Park on page 547 for camping information.

Heritage Inn Bed & Breakfast: Very well-behaved dogs who promise not to rile the owner's cat can stay with you on weekdays at this lovely, antique-furnished Victorian house. Advance arrangements are essential. The owner, Georgia, just recently started permitting pooches, and she's understandably careful about which dogs get to stay here. Joe would definitely not be a welcome guest because of his tendency to try to make cats into eats.

Dogs who get to stay are lucky indeed. The inn, while not in a rural area, is in a natural creekside setting. Pooches who do the dog paddle love it. Rates are $85 to $120 and include a full breakfast and a wine and cheese hour in the afternoon. Dogs require a $25 security deposit. 978 Olive Street, San Luis Obispo, CA 93405; (805) 544-7440.

Howard Johnson Lodge: Dogs like all the open space around this mountainous locale. Boy dogs are especially fond of the trees out back. Rates are $59 to $89. Dogs are $10 extra. 1585 Calle Joaquin, San Luis Obispo, CA 93401; (805) 544-5300.

Motel 6: There's a big field in back where dogs are allowed at least for now. One small pooch per room. Rates are $35 for one adult, $6 for the second adult. 1625 Calle Joaquin, San Luis Obispo, CA 93401; (805) 541-6992.

Sands Suites & Motel: The Sands is a good place to stay if you need to do your laundry (or your dog's) after a few days on the road. It's got a little laundry facility if you've got the quarters. Rates (for rooms, not laundry) are $59 to $99. Dogs pay a $5 fee per visit. 1930 Monterey Street, San Luis Obispo, CA 93401; (805) 544-0500.

San Luis Obispo Coast Hostel: Joe Dog thinks it's very, very cool that dogs are allowed to stay at this hostel. It's not often that pooches get to go hosteling. Dogs can't sleep in the dorms, but there are three private rooms where they can bed down for the night. "Just no barking, please!" said the desk monitor. They've apparently had a problem with this in the past, so make sure your doggy's lips are sealed. Also, unfortunately, a medium-sized dog is the biggest dog they want here. But as Joe always says, medium is in the eyes of the beholder.

The hostel is located next to a train station, but the choo choo shouldn't bother your pooch or you. Rates for the private rooms (for up to two people) are $30 to $34. 1617 Santa Rosa Street, San Luis Obispo, CA 93401; (805) 544-4678.

Vagabond Inn: Rates are $44 to $81. Small to medium dogs are preferred, and they're $5 extra. 210 Madonna Road, San Luis Obispo, CA 93401; (805) 544-4710 or (800) 522-1555.

DIVERSIONS

Catch a fur flick: The Sunset Drive-In Theater allows quiet dogs for no extra charge. Some pooches really enjoy a movie starring a dog, so be sure to bring your best friend if you notice one playing. Rates are $4 per human adult. Kids under 12 are free. 255 Elks Lane; (805) 544-4475.

SAN SIMEON

Dogs aren't trusted anywhere near the gilded towers of William Randolph Hearst's castle, so if you're thinking of visiting while your dog is with you, forget it. He'll have to wait in the car for at least three hours while you tour the castle, and that's a very bad idea.

But that doesn't mean you have to forgo this spectacular attraction. The Tail Wag's Inn, about nine miles south in Cambria, will board your dog for as long as your tour takes. With all the frills they provide your pet, she may come back thinking she should be living in Hearst Castle (see page 536 for details).

PARKS, BEACHES, AND RECREATION AREAS

• **San Simeon State Beach** 🐾 🐾 🐾 *See* ⑲ *on page 532.*

This rocky beach stretches for two miles between Cambria and San Simeon. Beachcombing and tidepooling can be first-rate, depending on the tide.

The beach is very popular because of its proximity to Hearst Castle. Even more popular here is the developed San Simeon Creek Campground and the more primitive Washburn Creek Campground. There's nothing quite like setting up a tent among 200 other tents just after you've visited Hearst's 38 lavish bedrooms. Sweet dreams!

Campsites range from $7 to $17. Dogs are $1 extra. The beach and campgrounds are about six miles south of Hearst Castle, along Highway 1. For reservations (essential during the summer), call Parknet at (800) 444-PARK. For beach information, phone (805) 927-2035.

PLACES TO STAY

Best Western Cavalier Oceanfront Resort: This is San Simeon's only oceanfront motel, and it's one of the most attractive and well-run Best Westerns we've ever checked out. (But don't let its brochure get your hopes up: The picture on the cover is not of the Best Western. It's Hearst Castle.) Many of the 90 rooms have a wood-burning fireplace, a stocked mini-bar, close-up ocean views, and a private patio. There's even room service, so you and your dog can dine together in the comfort of your own seaside abode. The humans in your party can keep in shape in the fitness room or at the two outdoor pools here (with ocean views to drool for). And if you stay here, you and your leashed pooch will have access to the long beach that backs up to the lodging.

Many people are tempted to leave their dogs in their rooms when they go explore magnificent Hearst Castle, but this is a big no-no. The Cavalier makes it easy for you to do the right thing: It has the phone number for a mighty nice kennel, the Tail Wag's Inn (see page 536), programmed into the room phones. (Be forewarned, though: At busy times, you need to make reservations well ahead of your visit.)

Dogs can't stay in nonsmoking rooms. (If you're going to use the fireplace, who's going to notice the lingering scent of cigarette smoke anyway?) Rates are $69 to $179. 9415 Hearst Drive, San Simeon, CA 93452; (805) 927-4688 or (800) 826-8163.

Motel 6: Until recently, this was a Holiday Inn, so it's a cut above many other Motel 6s. Rates are $33 for one adult, $6 for the second adult. This Motel 6, like most Motel 6s, allows one small pooch per room. 9070 Castillo Drive, San Simeon, CA 93452; (805) 541-6992.

San Simeon State Beach: See San Simeon State Beach above for camping information.

Silver Surf Motel: The cover of the brochure for the Silver Surf has a picture of a magnificent mansion-like building with a cherub statue pointing to it. "Stay at Silver Surf Motel" it declares. And you thought Hearst Castle was gorgeous. Oh, wait, that is Hearst Castle on the cover. Ohhh, the brochure also says "Visit Hearst Castle." Alas. The Silver Surf isn't exactly Hearst Castle, but then again, what is? This motel is pretty darned decent, with 72 rooms in a peaceful garden setting with plenty of trees to sniff, and a really attractive indoor pool and spa. Some rooms even have ocean views and fireplaces. Not bad for a motel, eh?

We really admire the Silver Surf's management, because instead of closing the motel's doors to dogs, as managers once considered doing (primarily because people were leaving dogs alone in their room when they visited Hearst Castle), they now have you sign a pet agreement stating things like you won't leave your dog alone in the room. (See the Tail Wag's Inn, page 536, for a way to visit the castle and make your dog comfortable at the same time.) Rates are $39 to $99. Dogs are $5 extra. 9390 Castillo Drive, San Simeon, CA 93452; (805) 927-4661 or (800) 621-3999.

SANTA MARGARITA

PARKS, BEACHES, AND RECREATION AREAS

• **Santa Margarita Recreation Area** 🐾🐾🐾 *See ⓴ on page 532.*

You and your dog don't have to like swimming or fishing to enjoy this park centered around Santa Margarita Lake. If hiking is more your style, try the 10 miles of trails that weave through the area. Keep your dog leashed and watch out for horses.

For the rest of the family, there are playgrounds, horseshoe pits, and a swimming pool. And if you just can't help throwing a line in the water, you may well land supper.

The entry fee is $5 per car and $2 per dog. But there's plenty of parking just outside the park, if you want to avoid the vehicle fee. The park even has camping, for $13 per site. From U.S. 101, take the Highway 58 exit and drive east about four miles. Follow the signs the rest of the way. (805) 438-5485.

PLACES TO STAY

KOA at Santa Margarita Lake: You and your dog can camp at the 110 sites a quarter-mile from the lake, then fish for catfish, trout, bass, or crappie (pronounced "croppy," in case angling isn't your cup of fish). Rates are $19 to $25. 4765 Santa Margarita Lake Road, Santa Margarita, CA 93453; (805) 438-5618.

Santa Margarita Recreation Area: See Santa Margarita Recreation Area above for camping information.

TEMPLETON

PARKS, BEACHES, AND RECREATION AREAS

• **Templeton Park** 🐾🐾🐾 *See ㉑ on page 532.*

This is among the most peaceful neighborhood parks we've visited. You could daydream the day away here under the huge shade trees, or kick back in the gazebo and read your favorite old book with another dog-eared friend (leashed). There's an old Southern Pacific railroad car on one corner and a fairly well fenced ball field on the other.

The park is between Crocker Street and Old County Road and Fifth and Sixth Streets. (805) 781-5930.

DIVERSIONS

Wine not?: Dover Canyon Winery is probably the most dog-friendly winery we've ever been to. Its label features a richly colored painting of a dog's face. Its motto is "Dog Gone Good Wine." Its general manager, Amy, has two boxers and says, "We prefer dogs to most children here." If you had any trepidation about visiting a winery with your dog, that last sentence should put you at ease.

Well-behaved, leashed poochies are welcome to join you for a picnic on the grounds. This is a small winery, so no tours are given, but there's a tasting room (with the painting of the dog from the label hanging in it) and a little gift shop (where you can buy, among other things, wineglasses with paw prints). Buy a bottle of one of Dover's delicious reds and share some Brie and bread with your dog outside. The winery is located on Bethel Road. You'll see the signs. (805) 434-0319.

49
KERN COUNTY

This large southern San Joaquin Valley county is a diverse land o' plenty. There are plenty o' farms, plenty o' deserts, plenty o' mountains, and plenty o' windmills—5,000 to be exact, enough to make Don Quixote quiver.

The county also has plenty of fertilizer, and that fact will jump right out at you as you cruise down certain roads during certain fertilizer seasons. Bring a gas mask or forever hold your breath. When we drove through one fine October afternoon, the humans in the car turned green from the extra ripe cow patty smell. Joe Dog just sat there mesmerized, with a big smile on his snout.

NATIONAL FORESTS

See the National Forests and Wilderness Areas chapter starting on page 748 for important information and safety tips on visiting national forests with your dog.

• Los Padres National Forest 🐾🐾🐾🐾 🐕

A sliver of this huge national forest pokes into the southwest edge of Kern County. See page 751.

• Sequoia National Forest 🐾🐾🐾🐾 🐕

Only little segments of this grand forest dribble into Kern County from Tulare County. See page 753.

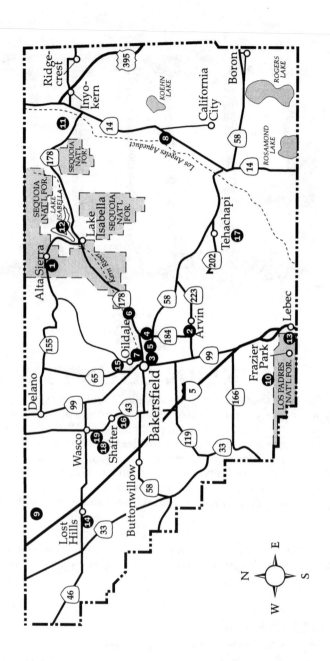

ALTA SIERRA

PARKS, BEACHES, AND RECREATION AREAS

• **Greenhorn Mountain County Park** 🐾🐾🐾½ *See* ❶ *on page 554.*

This rugged park is surrounded by extraordinary Sequoia National Forest land. While the park itself is a speck compared with the forest, it resembles the wooded wonderland in every other way except one: Dogs must be leashed. Joe likes the place, but it's really easy to drive down the road a bit and start on a real wilderness hike in the national forest.

Greenhorn is slightly more civilized, if that's what your dog prefers. It's got a playground and a picnic area. But most of the undeveloped forest areas at Greenhorn are as wild as the surrounding national forestland. Its 160 acres are set at 6,000 feet. Trails run through thick cedar and white fir forests.

The park is on Highway 155, about six miles west of Lake Isabella. (805) 868-7000.

ARVIN

PARKS, BEACHES, AND RECREATION AREAS

• **DiGiorgio Park** 🐾🐾 *See* ❷ *on page 554.*

Up until about 15 years ago, this 18-acre park was packed with trees. Then along came a big windstorm and blew about half of them to smithereens.

But fear not, dogs of the male persuasion: There are still plenty of trees here to claim as your own. There's also a ball field, a pool, and a playground. The rest is flat and grassy. From Highway 233 (Bear Mountain Boulevard), go south on Meyer Street for four blocks. The park is at Haven Drive and Meyer Street. (805) 868-7000.

BAKERSFIELD

This is the country music capital of California. You'll know it when you turn on your car radio. Find yourself a good country station, and as you cruise past oil derricks and the surrounding agricultural land, you'll feel right at home.

Bakersfield also happens to be the hub of the southern San Joaquin Valley. It doesn't draw many tourists, but whether you live here or just do business here (with your pooch, of course), you'll find enough decently dog-friendly parks to make your friendly dog happy.

PARKS, BEACHES, AND RECREATION AREAS

• **Bakersfield Beach Park** 🐾🐾🐾 *See* ❸ *on page 554.*

The grass is often so green and so short that you feel as if you're walking on crunchy AstroTurf here. This 27-acre park by the often-dry Kern River has ball fields, horseshoe pits, picnic tables, and a playground, but where's the beach? It's there if you look hard, but it's difficult to recognize a beach when it doesn't touch some sort of water. Since dogs have to be leashed, they don't miss the river much during drought years.

The park is at 24th and Oak Streets. (805) 326-3117.

• **Central Park** 🐾½ *See* ❹ *on page 554.*

"Stay out, stay alive," reads a sign next to the creek that runs through this 11-acre park. Even dogs who can't read will heed this advice: The creek is completely fenced off. It's not a pretty sight, but the parkees who put up the sign probably know what they're talking about. The park is flat and grassy, with plenty of trees, a playground, and loads of picnic tables. It's located in the heart of the city's antique shopping district, at 19th and R Streets. (805) 326-3117.

• **Jastro Park** 🐾 *See* ❺ *on page 554.*

This nine-acre park has shade, manicured lawns, and picnic tables to recommend it. Other than that, dogs don't care much for the other features like tennis and basketball courts and a swimming pool. It's at Truxton Avenue and Myrtle Street. (805) 326-3117.

• **Hart Park** 🐾🐾🐾 *See* ❻ *on page 554.*
This park is actually part of the larger Kern River County Park. See below.

• **Kern River County Park** 🐾🐾🐾 *See* ❻ *on page 554.*

Hart Park and Lake Ming make up the bulk of this 1,400-acre park. Hart Park, in a setting that's part golf course and part lunar landscape, is by far the better one for dogs. The bare rock mountain on one edge of the park gives way to huge green meadows, with shaded paths running throughout. And if you're a food hound, you'll be happy to know you and your leashed dog are never more than a one-minute walk from a picnic table.

Down the road a bit is a huge soccer area. When no one's around, it's a terrific place to trot about with your pooch.

The easternmost section of the park is Lake Ming, a 100-acre lake with tolerable fishing in the cooler months and nothing in summer. At last look, only two tiny sections were open to anglers. Because of a parasite that can cause swimmer's itch, swimming and wading are often banned here. In all, it's not exactly a water dog's dream.

The 57 first-come, first-served campsites here are set in a remote, lush section of the Lake Ming area. Unlike the dry, dusty feel of most of the lake's shoreline, the camping here is a riparian escape. Site are $8 to $12. Dogs are $2 extra.

From Panorama Drive in north Bakersfield, drive east to Alfred Harrell Highway and follow it as it curves by the Kern River. Eventually the road will lead you through the gates of the park. Follow the signs to the areas that most interest you and your dog. (805) 868-7000.

• **Panorama Park** 🐾 *See* ❼ *on page 554.*

If a park is going to have the guts to call itself "Panorama" Park, it had better supply a pretty decent view. Not so here. There's a view, all right, but it's not the kind you photograph, enlarge, and hang on your living room wall as evidence of your enviable summer vacation.

The vista includes oil tanks, a refinery, smokestacks, and freeways. Somehow, the few pastured horses by the river lose their rustic charm amid these surroundings.

The park is fairly narrow and follows the road closely. About all you and your leashed dog can do here is walk down the paved path, sit on the benches, and admire the industrial scenery. The park is set along Panorama Drive from Union Avenue to Bucknell Street. The best parking is at the foot of River Boulevard. (805) 868-7000.

PLACES TO STAY

Bakersfield has so many dog-friendly lodgings that it puts many larger cities to shame. We'll mention just a fistful of them here.

Best Western Hill House: "Not too big" dogs are welcome, says the manager. Rates are $55 to $72. Dogs are $5 extra. 700 Truxton Avenue, Bakersfield, CA 93301; (805) 327-4064.

Doubletree Hotel: This is one of the better Bakersfield accommodations. Rates are $69 to $150. Dogs are $15 extra. 3100 Camino del Rio Court, Bakersfield, CA 93308; (805) 323-7111.

Kern River County Park: See Kern River County Park on page 556 for camping information.

La Quinta Motor Inn: Dogs under 35 pounds may sleep here. Rates are $55 to $65. Dogs are $8 extra. 3232 Riverside Drive, Bakersfield, CA 93308; (805) 325-7400.

Motel 6: There are four Motel 6s in Bakersfield, all of which accept one small dog per room. This is an amazing per capita number. Lappish-sized dogs who don't need the lap of luxury will enjoy a night or two here. Call the national reservations number at (800) 466-8356 for the location nearest your destination.

Oxford Inn: Bakersfield Beach Park is only about a mile from here. Rates are $39 to $49. Pooches are charged $10 per visit. Efficiencies are available. 4500 Pierce Road, Bakersfield, CA 93308; (805) 324-5555.

Residence Inn by Marriott: This is a convenient place to stay when traveling with a pooch. The rooms are all suites and apartments, and they all have full kitchens, so you don't have to worry about finding a pooch-friendly restaurant in these parts. They even provide dogs with their own pooper-scooper and dog dish. Rates are $70 to $125. The long-term rate is less. Dogs require a $40 to $60 cleaning fee per visit and pay $6 extra per night. 4241 Chester Lane, Bakersfield, CA 93309; (805) 321-9800.

BORON

Don't be surprised if your dog starts looking inquisitively at the empty sky here. Chances are that within a few moments the sky won't look so empty. This is the home of the Edwards Air Force Base, and they fly some mighty odd-looking experimental aircraft up yonder. Dogs usually seem to notice well before their people.

DIVERSIONS

Call out the 20-mule team: If your dog has fond memories of those puppyhood days when you sprinkled 20 Mule Team Borax on the rug almost daily to get out those "oops" odors, a trip to the 20 Mule Team Museum will be a journey down olfactory memory lane.

The town of Boron is the home of U.S. Borax, whose open pit mine is one of the major sources of borate in the world. The museum pays homage to the days when 20-mule teams hauled 36-ton wagonloads of borax across 180 miles of desert to waiting railroad cars in Mojave. On the museum's grounds, you'll find the oldest house in Death Valley, built in 1883 by a borax miner. Other features of the rather small museum include an early Boron beauty shop and tons of mining equipment.

Your dog is free to join you at the outdoor displays, and if the caretaker likes your dog (she says all a dog usually has to do is smile at her and she's hooked), your pooch can go inside the museum with you and look at the exhibits and the movies of the early days of borax mining. They haven't had any leg-lifting types of accidents yet, and although they've got access to tons of borax deodorizer, they'd prefer not to have to use it. In other words, if there's even a remote possibility of a squat or leg lift, don't bring your dog inside.

There's no fee, just a requested donation. From Highway 58, take the Boron Avenue off-ramp and drive south about 1.5 miles. (760) 762-5810.

CALIFORNIA CITY

PARKS, BEACHES, AND RECREATION AREAS

No California City parks permit pooches, and the Bureau of Land Management would sure appreciate it if you wouldn't take your dog to the Desert Tortoise Natural Area here. Even leashed dogs can pose a threat to the tortoise population.

• **Red Rock Canyon State Park** 🐾🐾🐾½ *See* ❽ *on page 554.*

This magnificent park is known as "the Grand Canyon of the West," and lives up to the hype. The best time to be at this 10,384-acre park is at sunrise or at sunset. The low-lying sun dances with the red and white cliffs, and the results are magical. Dogs aren't permitted on the trails, but they can go along the small roads and seek out some of the stunning paleontological sites with you. Leashes are a must.

If you want to continue your education about borax (see Diversions, on page 557), you'll be happy to know that this was a watering hole for the 20-mule team freight wagons on their grueling journey hauling the stuff.

The day-use fee is $5. There are 50 camping sites available on a first-come, first-served basis for $10 per night. Dogs are $1 extra day or night. The park is located 25 miles northeast of the town of Mojave, on Highway 14. (805) 942-0662.

PLACES TO STAY

Red Rock Canyon State Park: See Red Rock Canyon State Park above for camping information.

DELANO

PARKS, BEACHES, AND RECREATION AREAS

• **Kern National Wildlife Refuge** 🐾🐾🐾🐾 🐕
See ❾ *on page 554.*

If your dog hunts waterfowl, she'll find this 10,618-acre refuge a four-paw destination. If your dog isn't a hunter, as long as she doesn't chase or harass wildlife, she's welcome, too. (Just be careful during hunting seasons.) There's a great auto tour route that goes around the natural valley grasslands and marsh areas. Wildlife watching is excellent. There are at least 200 species of birds here during the year, along with all sorts of other critters. You may see snowy egrets, ring-billed gulls, warblers, peregrine falcons, endangered San Joaquin kit foxes, and leopard lizards. If you're walking around the refuge, be sure your dog is leashed when near the wildlife. In more open spaces, dogs under voice control can be leashless.

From Interstate 5 around the town of Lost Hills, take Highway 46 five miles east to Corcoran Road and turn north. Drive 10.6 miles and you'll be at the refuge. (805) 725-2767.

FRAZIER PARK

The dusty little streets of this community near the interstate hide a fairly dog-friendly park. If your dog is crossing his legs on a long journey down the highway, it's not a bad place to stop.

PARKS, BEACHES, AND RECREATION AREAS

• Frazier Mountain Park 🐾🐾🐾 See ⑩ on page 554.

This 26-acre park is almost entirely fenced, but dogs are supposed to be leashed anyway. In addition to a grassy picnic area and a little pond, sections of the park have shrubs, shady oaks, and scrubby fields. Dogs love the fact that it's not a perfectly manicured work of art.

Exit Interstate 5 at the Frazier Park exit and drive east about 3.5 miles. Turn left at the post office (Monterey Trail) and make an immediate right onto Park Trail Drive. Park on the street. (805) 868-7000.

INYOKERN

Friends who visited from New York could only call this town "Inyoface." It was amusing for at least a few seconds the first time they said it. But dogs find high amusement at the Chimney Peak Recreation Area, which lets them run around off leash and get rid of all that pent-up canine energy.

PARKS, BEACHES, AND RECREATION AREAS

• Chimney Peak Recreation Area 🐾🐾🐾🐾 🐕
See ⑪ on page 554.

This large swath of land is not the Mojave Desert and it's not the Sierra Nevada. It's somewhere in between—a transition zone with less severe temperatures and an unusual mix of vegetation.

You and your well-mannered mutt will enjoy hiking through pinyon and juniper woodlands, digger pines, sage, and desert needlegrass without the bondage of a leash. In the spring, wildflowers explode with color and the place comes to life.

Speaking of coming to life, a brochure produced by the Bureau of Land Management describes another aspect of nature here: "Highlighting the wildlife attractions of the area are mule deer, black bear, mountain lion, bobcat . . ."

When I read this to Joe, he agreed that it might be best to keep him on a leash around here. Three out of those four critters make him a little antsy. If you have a pooch who's less than perfect, as Joe is wont to be sometimes, it's best to keep him on a leash and not take a chance with lions and bobcats and bears. There's no scarecrow here to help your Toto out of a difficult situation.

The trails here join up with the surrounding dog-friendly national forest land, making this piece of dog heaven seem utterly vast. While there's plenty of good BLM turf in Kern County, the best portion of the Chimney Peak Recreation Area is in Tulare County to the north. You can get there by taking Highway 178 to Canebrake Road and heading north. You may stop on the Kern side of the border if you wish, but the Tulare side has the good campgrounds and trails. (805) 391-6000.

LAKE ISABELLA

PARKS, BEACHES, AND RECREATION AREAS

• **Lake Isabella** 🐾🐾🐾 *See* **⑫** *on page 554.*

If what you want is a long hike with your leash-free dog, don't expect to find it right here. The land is surrounded by Sequoia National Forest, but there really aren't any trails around the lake. Just a short drive up the road, you'll find all the nude dog hiking you could imagine. Ask a ranger for directions to the national forest trails.

You can walk around some of the lake with your dog, but he must be leashed. With 38 miles of shoreline, this is the largest freshwater lake in Southern California, and it's worth taking a look around. The bird-watching is hot here, and so is the fishing for such goodies as largemouth bass.

There are nearly 800 campsites. Some sites are available on a first-come, first-served basis. Reservations are recommended for holiday weekends; call (800) 280-CAMP. Campsites are $12 to $14; there are four no-fee primitive sites available. Some offer blissful seclusion. The lake is located at Highways 155 and 178. From Bakersfield, head east on Highway 178 for about 30 miles. Call the ranger office for directions to your particular destination within the lake area. (760) 379-5646.

PLACES TO STAY

Lake Isabella: See Lake Isabella above for camping information.

LEBEC

PARKS, BEACHES, AND RECREATION AREAS

• **Fort Tejon State Historic Park** 🐾🐾🐾½ *See* **⑬** *on page 554.*

The U.S. Army's First Dragoons established a camp here in 1854. Their mission was to protect white settlers and Native Americans in the Tejon Reservation from raids by other Indian groups, including the Paiutes, Chemehuevi, and Mojave.

The buildings here are all restored versions of structures that were the backbone of the fort back then. There's even a miniature museum to get you up to date with the past.

Dogs like it here, but their pleasure has little to do with the buildings and lots to do with the land. There's plenty of land to peruse, on leash of course. If you get away from the main features of the fort and walk toward the backcountry (past the outhouses), you're in for a treat. Large valley oaks, blue oaks, black willows, and cottonwoods are plentiful here, and critters like deer, rabbits, quail, and several kinds of hummingbirds call the park home.

Admission is $2 for adults and $1 for kids and dogs. Exit Interstate 5 at the Fort Tejon exit and follow the signs. It's just west of the freeway. (805) 248-6692.

LOST HILLS

PARKS, BEACHES, AND RECREATION AREAS

• **Lost Hills Park** 🐾 🐾 *See* ⓮ *on page 554.*

There's nothing lost about this park. In fact, it's about as found as they come. A popular weekend haunt for locals, the park has barbecues, ball fields, playgrounds, and acres of well-maintained grass. It's not exactly a doggy delight, but a dog could do a lot worse. Leashes are the law.

The park is at the corner of Highway 46 and Lost Hills Road (only a few blocks southwest of the airport). (805) 868-7000.

OILDALE

If you like oil (the dark, inedible kind), you'll love this town. Grasshopper-like oil derricks are everywhere. Tanks, too. It's an interesting place to visit if you happen to be sick of forests and other forms of pristine landscapes.

PARK, BEACHES & RECREATION AREAS

• **Standard Park** 🐾½ *See* ⓯ *on page 554.*

Old railroad cars and oil tanks clutter the area just to the east of the park. There's no mistaking where you are: You're in Oildale, land of much oil and many places named after the oil companies that have a stake in the town.

Standard Park is a flat 15-acre park edged with trees. If your leashed dog needs to get out of the car, it's a tolerable place for a little stretching and a few leg lifts. The park is a block south of Norris Road, just east of North Chester Avenue. (805) 392-2000.

RIDGECREST

PLACES TO STAY

Heritage Inn: About a third of the 125 units here are efficiencies. Bring your own utensils and you'll be all set out here in this remote city. Rates are $65 to $90. 1050 North Norma Street, Ridgecrest, CA 93555; (760) 446-6543.

Heritage Suites: This one is just around the corner from the Heritage Inn, and it offers kitchens with most units. Rates are $75 to $90. 919 North Heritage Drive, Ridgecrest, CA 93555; (760) 446-7951.

SHAFTER

Shafter is surrounded by agricultural land, but its promotional brochure shows nothing but pictures of industrial parks and a nearby airport. A dog haven it is not.

PARKS, BEACHES, AND RECREATION AREAS

• **Richland School Park** 🐾 *See* **16** *on page 554.*

The park is just roomy enough for your leashed dog to have a good stretch. Try one of the open fields. The park is at Atlantic Avenue and Valley Street. (805) 746-6361.

TEHACHAPI

The Tehachapi area is home to thousands of windmills that supply more than one billion kilowatt-hours of electricity per year. Next time you're driving through some of the back roads with your dog, pull over and turn off your engine for a minute. The humming turbines provide an eerie contrast to the silence of the surrounding desert. Joe loves the strange noises and tilts his head every which way to try to figure out who's making them. When he rules out the other passengers and the nearby rocks, he stares at me with an accusing look on his furrowed brow.

PARKS, BEACHES, AND RECREATION AREAS

• **Tehachapi Mountain Park** 🐾🐾🐾½ *See* **17** *on page 554.*

We love coming to this 490-acre park in late autumn, when there's a little nip in the pure, pine-scented air. With elevations of up to 7,000 feet and dozens of types of pines, firs, and oaks, this park provides a stunning contrast to the desert surroundings.

Bill and Joe slid around on their butts last time we visited, because there was a good layer of slick snow in the upper reaches of the park. They had a great time slipping, sliding, and sniffing the mountain sage that was poking out of the snow. Leashes are the law here, but you can still have a terrific time exploring this beautiful park via the trails that run throughout. And you may never run into another soul.

The camping is some of the best we've seen in any county park. Many of the 61 sites are 200 feet away from each other. Tall trees add a little more privacy. Sites are $8 to $10 and are available on a first-come, first-served basis. Pooches are $2 extra.

From Highway 58, exit onto Highway 202 and drive south, continuing straight onto Tucker Road when Highway 202 veers west. In about another mile, at Highline Road, turn right, drive about 1.5 miles to Water Canyon Road, and turn left. The park is another 2.2 miles. (805) 868-7000.

PLACES TO STAY

Best Western Mountain Inn: Rates are $49 to $55, and they ask for advance notice if you're coming with a pooch. 416 West Tehachapi Boulevard, Tehachapi, CA 93561; (805) 822-5591.

Tehachapi Mountain Park: See Tehachapi Mountain Park above for camping information.

WASCO

PARKS, BEACHES, AND RECREATION AREAS

• **Barker Park** 🐾 *See* **⑱** *on page 554.*

We thought maybe, just maybe, this park was named for all the leash-free dogs who frequent it. But no one was barking for joy here. Leashes are the law at this eight-acre park. It has a small grassy area with some trees, but most of the park is filled with non-dog amenities, like swimming pools and playgrounds. The park is at Poso and Poplar Streets. (805) 758-3081.

• **Westside Park** 🐾 🐾½ *See* **⑲** *on page 554.*

Park staff labored hard to get some little hills built into this 17-acre park. "We didn't want it to be flat and boring like the rest of the landscape," a city worker told me. In addition to some contours, the park has many different adolescent trees, including rose hill ash trees, elms, oaks, and even some redwoods.

The park is in the west end of town, just west of Beckes Street, at Parkside Drive. (805) 758-3081.

RESTAURANTS

Teresa's Taco Villa: Get a taco for you, grab a burger for your best bud, and dine together at the outdoor tables. 441 F Street; (805) 758-2027.

SOUTH COAST COUNTIES

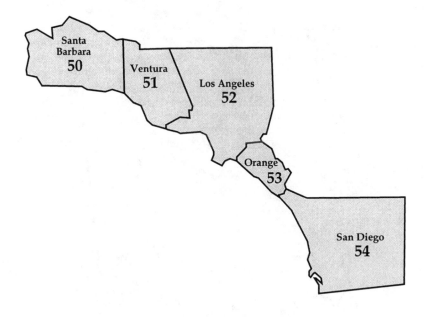

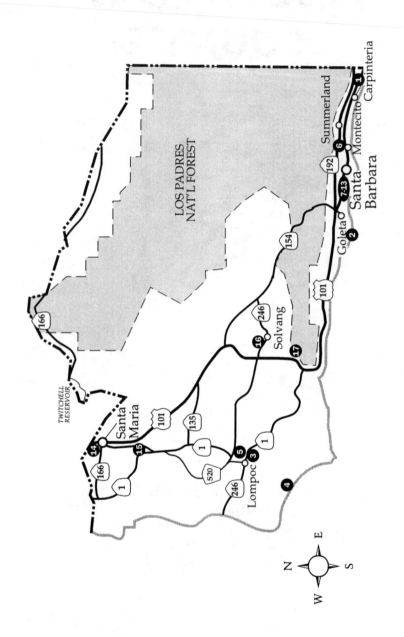

LOS PADRES NAT'L FOREST

Summerland

Carpinteria

Montecito

Santa Barbara

Goleta

Solvang

Santa Maria

Lompoc

TWITCHELL RESERVOIR

1

192

6

7-53

2

154

101

246

16

17

166

101

135

1

1

S20

5

3

246

14

15

166

1

4

N
E
S
W

50
SANTA BARBARA COUNTY

If you're like most folks, when you hear the words "Santa Barbara," you probably think of a sun-drenched vacation paradise on the central California coast. Images of whitewashed, Spanish-style buildings, palm-lined beaches, and big green resorts representing big green bucks may flash through your head. You can almost smell the suntan lotion and feel the warm sand caressing your body.

On the other hand, if you're a dog, when you think of Santa Barbara County, you'll likely think of a leash that never comes off on beaches that are to drool for. Images of "No Dogs" signs on the most glorious beaches will flash through your furry head. You may even try to convey to your owner, "Hey, I've got a great idea. Let's go to San Francisco!"

But there's some terrific news for pooches and their people in this new edition of the book: There are now two parks where your dog can be off leash! And one is so close to the ocean you won't even care about setting paw on the beach. Both are in the city of Santa Barbara. See Douglas Family Preserve and Las Positas Friendship Park on page 573 for more on these. The city and the county are also having powwows to see if they can come up with more areas for dog parks. A group called Dog PAC of Santa Barbara is behind this all the way. Call Dog PAC at (805) 563-2773 for more information or to see how you can lend a paw to the cause. Or you can write to Dog PAC, P.O. Box 3716, Santa Barbara, CA 93130. (This group actually does more than seek leash-free parks. Dog PAC folks are working on canine welfare legislation, among other things.)

In addition to sniffing out the two new dog parks, dogs can have fun in lots of ways here. Many Santa Barbara restaurants welcome dogs to dine at their outside tables. A few beaches permit dogs on leash, and some of the inland areas, such as Solvang, make dogs feel right at home. Enchanting, pooch-friendly lodgings abound throughout the county, so your pooch can spend her nights having happy dreams. And let's not forget the magnificent Los Padres National Forest. Until very recently, it was the only public land in the county where dogs could be their doggy selves and cavort around off leash.

NATIONAL FORESTS

See the National Forests and Wilderness Areas chapter starting on page 748 for important information and safety tips on visiting national forests with your dog.

•Los Padres National Forest 🐾🐾🐾🐾 🐕

Sections of the forest are near the Santa Barbara coast. The off-leash trails provide a much-needed breather from the strict leash rules around this county. See page 751.

CARPINTERIA

PARKS, BEACHES, AND RECREATION AREAS

The part of the city beach where dogs are permitted is fairly difficult to access, and it pretty much bans dogs during the harbor seal birthing season in the spring. It's much easier to go to the Rincon Beach County Park (see below), but if you really want to hit the small strip of city beach that permits dogs, call (805) 684-5405 and find out its status.

•Rincon Beach County Park 🐾🐾🐾 *See ❶ on page 566.*

A wooden stairway takes you from a green blufftop picnic area down to the sandy beach. It's not a huge beach, but the Beach Boys sang about it and surfer dudes love it.

The bluff provides an excellent view of the ocean. Even though nude bathing is illegal, naked people flock here. Just cover your dog's eyes as you pass by the fleshy masses. (The nudists really appreciate it if your dog obeys the leash law.)

The park is at Bates Road and U.S. 101, at the south end of Carpinteria. (805) 684-5405.

RESTAURANTS

The Coffee Grinder: This is an attractive place, with wooden outdoor tables for your dog's dining enjoyment. 910 Linden Avenue; (805) 684-5503.

Padaro Beach Grill: A German shepherd named Bo Jackson came across this incredibly dog-friendly place and insisted that his translator, Hiroko Komori, tell us about it. Every pooch who visits gets a big Milk-Bone. There's also always a water bowl waiting for your dog's thirsty snout. The restaurant is on a half acre of lawn that goes right down to the beach. The healthful human food here is really good, but who cares about that? (That was Bo speaking through Hiroko.) 3765 Santa Claus Lane; (805) 566-0566.

The Spot: This eatery down by the beach is known for its great hamburgers and Mexican food. Your pooch can keep you company on the patio. 389 Linden Avenue; (805) 684-7120.

Toyland: You can't miss this store/restaurant. It's the one with the giant Santa Claus on top, staring longingly at U.S. 101. Do your Christmas shopping at this oceanfront toy store, and then have your dog join you at the outdoor table for a date shake or hot chocolate and a piece of pumpkin bread. If you have kids, they can ride the rocking horse and elephant for a mere quarter while your dog watches and pulls on the leash, hoping for a chance to tame these mechanical beasts. 3821 Santa Claus Lane; (805) 684-3515.

PLACES TO STAY

Best Western Carpinteria Inn: Joe and I stayed here once while I was covering the aftermath of the big Santa Barbara blaze a few years back. We met this wonderful old woman who frequented the inn for long spells. She had us in for tea and biscuits, which made Joe's English heritage come bubbling up to the surface. He drank his water right out of a teacup, and when it was time to leave, he offered our hostess a gracious paw. Rates at this charming inn are $89 to $135, and there's a $40 dog deposit. 4558 Carpinteria Avenue, Carpinteria, CA 93013; (805) 684-0473.

Carpinteria State Beach: Camp along the Pacific Ocean at one of the 262 beachfront sites here. Dogs love it, but don't let them get any ideas about running around on the beach. They're banned. Sites are $14 to $29. Dogs are $1 extra. From U.S. 101, take the Casitas Pass exit and drive west about a mile to the campground. Call (805) 684-2811 for information, or call Parknet at (800) 444-PARK for reservations.

GOLETA

PARKS, BEACHES, AND RECREATION AREAS

• **Goleta Beach County Park** 😺 😺 😺 *See ❷ on page 566.*

Leashed dogs enjoy strolling down the beach at this county park. You and your pooch can enjoy a relaxing picnic under pine and palm trees in the small park area, then go get your paws wet as you saunter down the beach together. We prefer the section of beach near the Goleta Slough, which is wilder and more primitive.

From U.S. 101, go west on Highway 217. Just before you get to the University of California, turn left onto Sandspit Road and follow it to the beach. (805) 568-2461 or (805) 967-1300.

LOMPOC

It may be the home of a notorious federal penitentiary, but because of a few pooch-permitting parks, dogs don't feel imprisoned here.

PARKS, BEACHES, AND RECREATION AREAS

• **Beattie Park** 🐾 🐾½ *See* ❸ *on page 566.*

If you get away from the playing fields and basketball courts, you and your leashed dog can experience a decent degree of solitude here. Follow the fitness course for a little extra calorie-burning activity or just hike up one of the mild-mannered hills.

Exit Highway 1 at Seventh Street and drive south a few blocks to Olive Avenue. Turn right, drive two blocks to Fifth Street, and turn left into the park. The speed bumps on the way in get to be very annoying, so the sooner you park, the better. (805) 736-6565.

• **Jalama Beach Park** 🐾 🐾 🐾½ *See* ❹ *on page 566.*

The park may be only 24 acres, but there are so many ways to enjoy nature here that it seems much larger. Bring your binoculars and you won't regret it. Gray whale watching is excellent in February and March and from September through November. Bird-watching is hot year-round, but springtime attracts many rare birds.

Joe's favorite activity is rockhounding, but he probably just likes the name. The beachcombing is great here, and since the park is within the Pacific Missile Range of the Vandenberg Air Force Base, you never know what you'll find. Wildlife watching and surf fishing are also first-rate. As long as your dog is on a leash and not harming the environment, she can accompany you anywhere here.

There's also camping at 110 campsites, some right by the beach. Sites are $14 to $18. Dogs are $1 extra. All sites are first come, first served. The beach is 15 miles off Highway 1, at the end of Jalama Road. The Jalama Road exit is about four miles south of the main part of Lompoc. (805) 934-6123.

• **La Purisima Mission State Historic Park** 🐾 🐾 🐾½
See ❺ *on page 566.*

This is a truly amazing place to bring a dog. Not only can they hike with you along 14 miles of trails here, they're actually allowed *inside* the restored mission. They have to promise not to do leg lifts, bark, throw up, or any of those other activities that are not suited to the indoors. And they have to be on a leash at all times.

The original La Purisima Mission was founded in 1787, but an earthquake destroyed it in 1812. The mission was eventually picked up and moved across the Santa Ynez River to its present spot. During the 1930s, many of the mission's adobe buildings were restored. It was the largest mission restoration in California.

It's a treat to be able to take a dog inside such a historic place. But frankly, most dogs would rather be outside exploring this 967-acre park in their own doggy fashion.

The entrance fee is $5 per vehicle and it's good for up to nine people (and a dog). From Highway 1 in Lompoc, turn east on Purisima Road. The park entrance will be on your left in a couple of miles. (805) 733-3713.

PLACES TO STAY

Best Western Vandenberg: Beattie Park is just three blocks away from this motel. Rates are $50 to $65. Dogs pay a $20 fee per visit. 940 East Ocean Avenue, Lompoc, CA 93436; (805) 735-7731.

Jalama Beach Park: See Jalama Beach Park on page 570 for camping information.

Quality Inn & Executive Suites: If you want a view of the Lompoc Airport, you've got it from the parking lot here. Joy of joys. Rates are $69 to $99. Dogs are $25 extra (per day!). 1621 North H Street, Lompoc, CA 93436; (805) 735-8555.

Redwood Motor Lodge: Rates are $32 to $60. Dogs are $10 extra. 1200 North H Street, Lompoc, CA 93436; (805) 735-3737.

Tally Ho Motor Inn: Rates are $40 to $55. Dogs pay a $10 fee per visit. 1020 East Ocean Avenue, Lompoc, CA 93436; (805) 735-6444.

MONTECITO

PARKS, BEACHES, AND RECREATION AREAS

• **Manning County Park** 🐾🐾🐾 *See* ❻ *on page 566.*

It's beautiful here—lush and heavenly. This isn't a huge park, but with its narrow, ivy-covered walkways and ultra-green lawns and foliage, you may want to make a day of it. Bring your leashed dog, a picnic, and a book, and enjoy this verdant wonderland to its fullest. A heads-up: The ranger lives on the premises. If you're going to break a leash law, don't do it here.

Exit U.S. 101 at San Ysidro Road and drive north for almost a mile. The park will be just after the school, on your left. (805) 568-2461.

PLACES TO STAY

San Ysidro Ranch: A word to the pooches who plan to come here: You lucky dogs! This top-notch 540-acre resort (where Laurence Olivier and Vivien Leigh wed and Jackie and John F. Kennedy honeymooned) is treat enough. But dogs who stay here get the truly royal treatment, also known as the Privileged Pet Program. The Ranch has been offering the program to pooches for a century. Here's how it goes:

Upon registering at the Pet Register and wolfing down some tasty peanut butter biscuits, the guest dog goes to his cottage and finds his name and his accompanying human's name on a wood-burned sign outside his cottage door. (To him, the sign looks like something to chew on, but it's the thought that counts.) Inside, he'll be greeted by a basketful of VIP goodies, including a personalized bowl filled with squeak toys, rawhides, cookies, and a two-liter bottle of Pawier water. His bed is soft and comfortable and shaped like a steak.

A pet menu offers dining items, including biscuits, canned dog food, and even New York ground sirloin. "Shoes are available at market price," the VIP literature reads, and we're not sure if there's a wink behind that offer or not. We weren't about to find out, since their shoes probably come from I. Magnin, not Payless Shoe Source, which is Joe's usual style.

Dogs must stay in one of the Ranch's 21 freestanding cottages. Rates are $325 to $3,000. Dogs pay $75 per visit. Dog menu items are extra. You must let the staff know ahead of time that you'll be coming with your pooch so appropriate arrangements can be made. 900 San Ysidro Lane, Montecito, CA 93108; (805) 969-5046.

SANTA BARBARA

Great news for dogs: You now have two parks where you can be leashless here! Suddenly the idea of vacationing in Santa Barbara seems pretty cool, doesn't it? One park, the Douglas Family Preserve (see page 573), was allowing off-leash dogs on a trial basis at press time, but the hope is that dogs pass the trial and get it as a permanent chunk of Dog Heaven. There's a great deal of controversy surrounding dogs here. To help with the fight, call Dog PAC of Santa Barbara, at (805) 563-2773. The other park, Las Positas Friendship Park (see page 573), is privately run, but the city somehow has its hand in it. Fortunately, thanks to some wrangling by dog people, the park is now able to legally say yes to leash-free dogs.

Dogs are not allowed on any city beaches in this exquisite community, but if they visit Douglas Family Preserve, they'll come so close to the ocean that it almost makes up for the beach ban. Dogs can also stroll very close to the beach on a wonderful walkway that runs the entire beach length along Cabrillo Boulevard. On Sundays and holidays, the Santa Barbara Arts and Crafts Show makes its home under the grand palm trees here. It's a great opportunity to go shopping and take your dog along for advice on issues like which scarf would look best on Aunt Minnie.

An interesting way to spend a dog day is to walk around the historic sections of the city. While pooches aren't permitted inside buildings like Mission Santa Barbara or the city's historic adobes, they love having their pictures taken outside so their friends at home can envy their worldly ways.

Although you'll see pooper-scoopers beckoning you toward Mission Historical Park's rose garden across the street from the famed mission, the folks in the parks department beg you not to take your dog there. "We don't need any more foot traffic than we already have, especially foot traffic that has to go to the bathroom," says a parks supervisor. Looks like he wants us to take our business elsewhere.

On a sad note, Rosa, the cheery Airedale member of the city's five-member Animal Control Team, left this world at the too-young age of seven. Cancer got her. The humans on her team miss her a great deal, as do the folks she used to meet "on the job." But on a happier note, Pam Christian, Rosa's kindly person, can now be seen on the beat with a German shepherd she adopted after he was hit by a car and no one came to claim him. His name is Boon. He's the "tail-free" shepherd you might see walking down the street. (His tail had to be amputated as a result of the accident. Pam named him Boon because he looked like a baboon.)

PARKS, BEACHES, AND RECREATION AREAS

• **Alice Keck Park Memorial Gardens** 🐾 🐾½ *See* ❼ *on page 566.*

There's an abundance of natural sniffables here for dogs and their human friends. This one-square-block park is a fragrant, voluptuous garden, complete with flowering trees, a pond, a gazebo, and a stunning procession of brilliant flowers. Leashed dogs like it here, but most would rather be able to inspect a good, fresh cow patty than a dahlia.

The park is at Arrellaga Street and Carmelita Avenue, four blocks away from the courthouse. (805) 564-5433.

• **Arroyo Burro County Beach** 🐾🐾🐾 *See* **8** *on page* **566.**

Watch people with parachutes jump off a cliff above the back parking lot, or better yet, walk your leashed dog on the beach. Around this city, the latter is about as daring as parachuting. But it's actually legal to take your dog on the beach here, since it's a county beach and the only one in the city where dogs are officially permitted.

Even though the beach here isn't very wide, it's good just to be able to take your dog for a sandy stroll. The beach is on Marina Cliff Drive, just west of Las Positas Road. (805) 568-2461.

• **Douglas Family Preserve** 🐾🐾🐾🐾 🐕 *See* **9** *on page* **566.**

This is one terrific chunk of leash-free land—at least at press time. (See the information in the next paragraph about the park's fragile status.) It's about 70 acres, and it's on a magnificent bluff overlooking the Pacific. Dogs drool over this place, and rightly so. The ocean breeze is cool, relaxing, and must contain some pretty fascinating scents, judging by the looks on dogs' faces as they sniff it in rapture. The park has great unpaved trails for perusing the preserve. It also has quite a few oaks, cypress, and pines. To the north of the park is oak woodland, to the south is coastal sage scrub. An estuary and wetlands are below. Way below. Two-hundred feet down the bluff, to be exact. Dogs have to stay away from there, because that's where some protected species hang out. There's really no access anyway, so it's almost a moot point.

The sole problem with this park is that it's this heavenly only on a trial basis. Leashes could become the rule again if things don't go in favor of dogs. A management plan for the park is supposed to be finished in early 1999, and it will probably decide the fate of dogs here. There's a lot of optimism about the future of pooches in some circles, but it's still a very controversial subject in the city. A highly motivated group of dog people, called Dog PAC, is doing everything it can to better dogs' chances. To find out how you can help, call (805) 563-2773.

Before you visit for the first time, you should call the parks department at (805) 564-5433 or Dog PAC for an update on dog status. You can enter the park at Medcliff Drive, Borton Drive, or Mesa School Lane. Right now, there's only street parking. Please be considerate of the neighbors on your way to the park.

• **Las Positas Friendship Park** 🐾🐾🐾🐾 🐕 *See* **10** *on page* **566.**

In previous editions, I didn't rate this park very highly. That's because dogs were supposed to be leashed here. But now, this park is a super place to take a dog. What a difference a lack of a leash and an excellent new hiking trail make! The park is home to many ball fields, which, if you visit when they're not being used, are great places to ramble with your dog. (But, as you should always do, clean up after your dog! There's nothing like a little poop on a playing field to foster ill will toward dogs.)

The Sierra Club Trail, built by Sierra Club volunteers, offers a one-mile loop or a 1.5-mile round-trip to Jesuit Hill. (The Jesuit Hill hike is very steep, and not a good hike for most dogs.) The views of the Santa Barbara coast from much of the trail are to drool for.

This hilly, 136-acre park (which is doubling in size soon!) is a fine example of the way parks might go in this era of park de-funding; the park is privately operated and funded, yet open to the public. It seems almost everything here is sponsored, from picnic tables to a massive oak tree. (Mercedes-Benz got that one.) But that's okay with dogs, who are glad to have the government's hand out of their piece of Dog Heaven. Anyway, anyone who sponsors a tree is okay by Joe.

From U.S. 101, exit at Las Positas Road and drive south about 1.2 miles to the park's entrance, which will be on your left. (805) 569-5611.

• **Plaza Del Mar Park** 🐾½ *See* ⓫ *on page 566.*

This flat park is about a block from the beach, but it's nothing spectacular. It's a fairly good size, with enough grass and trees to please a leashed dog. Unfortunately, lots of people just hang out here, so the navigating can be difficult.

The park is on Cabrillo Boulevard at Castillo Street. (805) 564-5433.

• **Santa Barbara Botanic Garden** 🐾🐾🐾½ *See* ⓬ *on page 566.*

As soon as you park your car, you'll be enveloped in the magical scents of lush vegetation and fresh earth. Dogs prefer to smell the compost heaps here, but what else would you expect?

This botanic wonderland is a rarity. Places like this usually exclude dogs without a second thought. But here, they actually like dogs. In fact, there's even a philanthropic doggy donor, a poodle named Sophie. This environmentally conscious gal has a bouffant hairdo and the distinction of being the garden's only canine member.

You and your leashed dog are welcome to explore this 65-acre garden on the 5.5 miles of trails that take you through the meadows, canyons, and ridges here. The garden features more than 1,000 species of rare and indigenous California plants. The entry fee for adults is $3.

Exit U.S. 101 at Mission Street and drive northeast. The road curves to the left after about 10 blocks (its name becomes Mission Canyon Drive). Continue to Foothill Road, bear right, and then take a quick left on the continuation of Mission Canyon Drive. The park will be on your left in about a half mile. (805) 563-2521.

• **Shoreline Park** 🐾🐾 *See* ⓭ *on page 566.*

Lots of dogs come here for their daily walks. Leashed dogs are allowed on the green area (not the beach). They walk the path, roll on the grass, and smell the ocean and the scent of the offshore oil rigs that dot the coast.

The park is on Shoreline Drive, between San Clemente Street and San Rafael Avenue, just south of Leadbetter Beach. (805) 564-5433.

RESTAURANTS

Acapulco Mexican Restaurant and Cantina: This place sports an enchanting plaza setting with huge umbrellas and a fountain in the center. Your dog is welcome, as long as you sit at the outer perimeter of the patio, where he won't accidentally step in front of a busy waiter. 1114 State Street; (805) 963-3469.

Andersen's Danish Bakery and Restaurant: They adore dogs here and will offer pooches a bowl of water if they look a little dry around the gills. You and your pooch can sit under an umbrella at the edge of this patio and enjoy each other's company while dining on wonderful Scandinavian cuisine. 1106 State Street; (805) 962-5085.

Earthling Bookshop: This delightful place offers a huge variety of coffee and espresso drinks, along with good grub like quiche, lasagna, burritos, and salads. The folks here get a lot of customers with dogs on their patio, and they find it especially endearing when customers come in with little dogs' faces peeking out of backpacks. 1137 State Street; (805) 965-0926.

Fatburger: Come and savor a chubby burger with your drooling dog at one of the outdoor tables. 718 State Street; (805) 962-8955.

Hot Spots: Though your pooch may shy away if you tell her the name of this deli/coffee bar, you can assure her it's safe. Lots of dogs have come here with no adverse effects. 36 State Street; (805) 963-4233.

Pierre La Fond Deli: You and your dog can sit at the sidewalk tables and watch the intriguing streets of Santa Barbara. 516 State Street; (805) 962-1455.

Santa Barbara Coffee Roasting Company: If you can find an empty table outside, you and your dog are welcome to relax and socialize at this hopping cafe. 321 Motor Way; (805) 962-0320.

Santa Barbara Nutrition Center: Enjoy health food and delicious smoothies at the sidewalk tables. 15 East Figueroa; (805) 962-3766.

PLACES TO STAY

Cachuma Lake Campgrounds: Although Cachuma Lake has 42 miles of shoreline and numerous trails, dogs who visit here are stuck in the campgrounds. Dogs are banned from trails, and pooches and people aren't permitted to swim in the lake. Dogs can't be within 50 feet of the lake, and they're not even allowed to accompany their people on a boat here. Bummerooo, say the dogs.

Fortunately, there are plenty of campsites here—500 to be exact. You won't be roughing it, but at least you'll be with your dog. Sites are $14 to $18. Dogs are $2 extra. All are available on a first-come, first-served basis. The day-use fee is $5. From Santa Barbara, take the San Marcos Pass exit (Highway 154) off U.S. 101 and drive about 20 miles to the entrance. (805) 688-4658.

Fess Parker's Red Lion Resort: This lovely, sprawling resort is across from the beach, but unfortunately, it's a beach you can't visit with your dog friend. Try the path that runs along the beach's edge, if being near the water is your wish. Otherwise, the lovely 25-acre resort has ample room for romping with your leashed friend. Dogs stay in the ground-floor rooms. Rates are $269 to $349. 633 East Cabrillo Boulevard, Santa Barbara, CA 93103; (805) 564-4333.

Four Seasons Biltmore: This elegant oceanfront resort is renowned for its impeccable style, and its gracious, dog-friendly policy is the epitome of that style. Upon check-in, dogs get a complimentary dog bowl, a toy, and some tasty snacks. Dog-walking is available, but who'd want someone else to walk their dog with nearby parks and the beautiful grounds of the Biltmore beckoning?

The Biltmore is made up of a gorgeous, top-drawer hotel surrounded by 30 private cottages that are to die for. People with pooches have to stay at the cottages. If your budget is plump, it's well worth the stay. Cottage rates are $405 to $435. 1260 Channel Drive, Santa Barbara, CA 93108; (805) 969-2261.

Ivanhoe Inn Bed & Breakfast: Regarding dogs as guests, one of the owners of this stylish bed-and-breakfast has some choice words: "They're my favorite." The Ivanhoe is so dog-friendly there's even a little gallery of pictures of dog guests (sent in by happy dog people after their stay). Be sure to bring your camera so your favorite pooch can be immortalized here.

The inn has a range of rooms, from basic but beautiful to suites with a kitchen. Dogs can play with you in the yard, but be sure to clean up if they do any doggy business there. Rates are $95 to $195. 1406 Castillo Street, Santa Barbara, CA 93101; (805) 963-8832.

The Mary May Inn: This Queen Anne-style Victorian inn shows that yes, you can have elegance and dogs in the same setting. The Mary May, built around 1880, is full of examples of fine craftsmanship of days gone by, and dogs who stay here seem to respect that. In fact, dog people have to sign a pet release to ensure that their dogs will be on their best behavior here.

The 12 rooms at the beautifully restored Mary May (which is actually made up of two adjacent properties) are romantic and unique. Some rooms have canopied beds, wood-burning fireplaces, or whirlpool tubs. All rooms have a private bath—something not often found in inns of this era. Your stay here includes a big, delicious breakfast as well as a cozy afternoon tea by the inn's main fireplace. Rates are $100 to $180. Dogs are $10 extra. 111 West Valerio Street, Santa Barbara, CA 93101; (805) 569-3398.

Motel 6: Rates are $47 for the first adult, $6 for the second. This Motel 6, like most others, allows one small pooch per room. 3505 State Street, Santa Barbara, CA 93108; (805) 687-5400.

Pacifica Suites: If you and your dog need more room than just a room, check out the luxurious Pacifica Suites. The Pacifica is an all-suites hotel, so no matter which room you stay in, you'll have a bedroom and a living room. Each room has a phone and a TV (this is convenient if *Lassie* is on at the same time as *Melrose Place*). Suites also have stereo cassette players, VCRs, fridges, and microwaves. These extras make a real difference when traveling with a dog.

A complimentary, full breakfast comes with the room, so don't worry about cooking your eggs in the nuker. People love the pool and spa, and leashed dogs dig walking around the Pacifica's grounds. The hotel is nestled in a peaceful grove of exotic plants and trees and century-old gardens. Sniff out the area via a meandering pathway. The hotel is located right next to the Sexton House, a beautifully restored architectural landmark from the 1880s.

Small to medium dogs are preferred, but we've heard about some exceptions. Dogs and their people have to stay in the first-floor smoking suites. Rates are $135 to $165. 5490 Hollister Avenue, Santa Barbara, CA 93111; (805) 683-6722 or (800) 338-6722.

Sandy Beach Inn: Dogs like staying here because it's so close to the beach. Unfortunately, dogs aren't allowed to set paw on the beach, but they can stroll on the adjacent walkway. The staff here is very dog-friendly, and may whisper some of their favorite hush-hush dog spots to you. Rooms at the inn run from basic motel style to comfy suites with fireplaces. There's a heated pool for humans. Rates are $55 to $265. Dogs require a $15 deposit. 122 West Cabrillo Boulevard, Santa Barbara, CA 93101; (805) 963-0405 or (800) 662-1451.

DOGGY DAYS

Big Dog Parade: The Big Dog Parade really *is* a big dog parade. The most recent parade had about 1,000 dogs in it, and 10,000 spectators. Move over, Macy's! Dogs get dressed up in all kinds of outfits, and some go in their birthday suits. Prizes are awarded for the best of parade, most humorous, etc. A block party after the parade has music, food, kids' rides, doggy demos, and lots more.

The parade starts at De La Guerra Plaza and goes down State Street. There's no cost to enter, but the Big Dog Foundation (makers of all those Saint Bernard-clad clothes and doodads you've seen lately), which sponsors the event, asks for a donation. Every bit of the donations goes to nonprofit animal welfare groups. The parade is held the first Saturday of June. For info on this year's event, or to get an entry form, write, visit, or call Big Dog Sportswear (Attention: Parade Entries, if you write), 121 Gray Avenue, Santa Barbara, CA 93101; (805) 963-8727.

DIVERSIONS

Buy the book: Pacific Traveler's Supply, a terrific little store with all the travel books and goodies you'll ever need, is very dog-friendly. You and your clean, travel-happy pooch can sniff through an assortment of globes, compasses, backpacks, money belts, and travel guides. "We love dogs and encourage their participation in making vacation choices (as long as their opinion isn't permanent)," a manager writes. 12 West Anapamu Street; (805) 963-4438.

Hi ho, surrey, away!: Get your canine companion to hop up into your lap or onto the seat beside you, and drive away in your very own surrey with the fringe on the top. Don't you hurry, though, because there are plenty of dog-friendly spots where you can rent one of these pedal-powered vehicles.

One of our favorites is Beach Rentals, at 8 West Cabrillo Avenue. They want you to hang on to your dog, and for good reason: Cats and hamburgers are common sights on the oceanfront paths you're likely to use. Small surreys (for three adults and two small kids/one hefty dog) are $12 an hour. Large surreys are $22. Good news: The second hour for either size surrey is free. (805) 966-2282.

SANTA MARIA
PARKS, BEACHES, AND RECREATION AREAS
• **Preisker Park** 🐾🐾 *See* ⓮ *on page 566.*

If you're traveling south on U.S. 101 and you've promised your pooch that you'd stop at the very first park you find when you cross the border from San Luis Obispo County into Santa Barbara County, this is it.

This park is right on the border. It's flat, with lush grass and plenty of places to barbecue those burgers you've been keeping in your cooler. (Joe asked me to say that last part.) It can get crowded with locals who sometimes hang out here all day, but since dogs must be leashed anyway, there's little danger of your dog crashing someone else's picnic.

Driving south from the northern edge of the county, exit U.S. 101 at Highway 135. Drive southwest and take your first right, Preisker Lane. You'll be at the park within a few blocks. (805) 925-0951.

• **Waller County Park** 🐾🐾🐾 *See* ⓯ *on page 566.*

This park is conveniently located next to the Santa Maria Public Airport. Parts of it look like a golf course, parts look like a miniature forest. Paths take you and your leashed dog past duck ponds and through quiet picnic areas.

We prefer to enter on the Waller Lane side. From Highway 135, take Waller Lane west about a half block, park on the street, and walk in. (805) 934-6211.

PLACES TO STAY
Comfort Inn: Waller County Park (see above) is fairly close to this motel. Rates are $45 to $55. Pooches are $10 extra. Since only two rooms allow dogs, it's very wise to call ahead. 210 South Nicholson Avenue, Santa Maria, CA 93454; (805) 922-5891.

Hunter's Inn: Poodle-sized dogs (unfortunately, we're not talking standard-sized poodles) and smaller are okay. Rates are $42 to $75. Dogs are $5 extra. 1514 South Broadway, Santa Maria, CA 93454; (805) 922-2123.

SOLVANG

Solvang is a sweet Danish village, with architecture as authentically Danish as its baked goods. The place was settled in 1911 by Danish folks who missed their homeland. They bought property and perpetuated all the Danish customs they could.

After an article about the small community appeared in the *Saturday Evening Post* in 1947, entrepreneurs rushed in from all over the country and created something of a Danish theme park atmosphere here. Still, the town retains its core of true Danish charm.

PARKS, BEACHES, AND RECREATION AREAS
• **Hans Christian Andersen Park** 🐾🐾🐾 *See* ⓰ *on page 566.*

When you tell a dog that he's going to get to visit a park that's half developed and half rough, you know which half he's going to want to explore. This 52-acre park has a good undeveloped section for dogs who could care less about refinement.

The area is full of brush, but there are enough trees and navigable walking areas for any dog to have a good time, even on the mandatory leash. If some human in your group insists on hanging out at the developed section of the park, your dog will get along just fine.

From Highway 246, take Atterdag Road north. The arched gateway to the park is about three blocks on the left. (805) 568-2461.

• **Nojoqui Falls County Park** 🐾 🐾 🐾 ½ *See* ⓱ *on page 566.*

In non-drought springtimes, you'll be wowed by the Nojoqui (pronounced "Nah-ho-wee") Waterfall, which plunges 100 feet. The rest of the year, you and your dog will still be in awe.

People often compare this 88-acre park with Yosemite National Park. It's kind of a miniature version, complete with thick forests and mini-mountains (also known as hills). Unlike Yosemite, dogs are allowed to explore the area. They have to be on leash, but they don't seem to mind.

From Solvang, go south on Alisal Road about 10 miles. After about six miles, the road will veer sharply to the right. Follow it for four more miles, and the park will be on your left. If you're on U.S. 101 south of Buellton, you can exit at the signed marker for the park and follow the signs for about two miles. The park will be on your right. (805) 568-2461.

RESTAURANTS

Sally's Front Yard: This place has been a friend to dogs for years. In fact, Sally, the owner, told me that Ronald Reagan's Secret Service agents used to sit outside with their dogs. It makes one wonder just how well-disguised these sunglass-clad gents were. At least they had good taste. This is a fun little restaurant for dogs and their people. 475 First Street; (805) 688-7674.

The Touch: You and your pooch can share breakfast until 4 P.M. (try the Belgian waffles). Then, at dinnertime, The Touch becomes a Chinese food restaurant. Bizarre, but true. As long as it's not too crowded, your dog is welcome here. If it's busy, the owners suggest tying your pooch to a big shady tree that's within close eyeshot while you dine. The address is the same as Sally's Front Yard: 475 First Street; (805) 686-0222.

PLACES TO STAY

Hamlet Motel: Only small dogs are allowed here. Rates are $55 to $95. Dogs are $10 extra. 1532 Mission Drive, Solvang, CA 93463; (805) 688-4413.

Kronborg Best Western: If your dog is under 20 pounds, she can stay here. Rates are $50 to $95. Dogs are $10 extra. 1440 Mission Drive, Solvang, CA 93463; (805) 688-2383.

Meadowlark Motel: Rates are $40 to $80. 2644 Mission Drive, Solvang, CA 93463; (805) 688-4631.

Viking Motel: You'd think a place with the name "Viking" would allow big, brawny dogs. Even dogs with horns. But alas, only small poochettes are allowed here. Rates are $33 to $78. The motel sometimes charges a pooch fee. 1506 Mission Drive, Solvang, CA 93463; (805) 688-1337.

SUMMERLAND
RESTAURANTS

Summerland Beach Cafe: Dogs are allowed to dine on tasty food at the brick patio here. A dog-loving waiter told me the outside area "is big enough for all kinds of dogs." 2924 Lillie Avenue; (805) 969-1019.

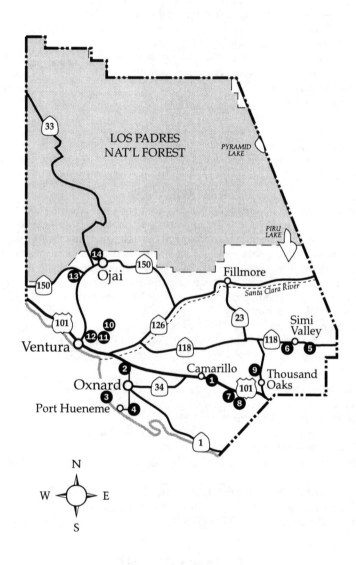

LOS PADRES
NAT'L FOREST

PYRAMID LAKE

PIRU LAKE

33

14

150

13 Ojai

150

Fillmore

Santa Clara River

101

10

126

23

Simi Valley

12 11

118

118

6 5

Ventura

2

Camarillo

1

9

Thousand Oaks

Oxnard

34

101

3

7

8

Port Hueneme

4

1

N
W · E
S

51

VENTURA COUNTY

This diverse coastal county is not a place to bring a dog who is seriously obsessed with swimming. Most beaches along the 42 miles of coastline here ban dogs, although some allow them in their camping or picnicking areas.

Even the big and bassy Lake Casitas makes sure dogs stay more than 50 feet from the lake's edge. We've seen water dogs tremble with genetic anticipation as they try to pull their owners close enough to dip a paw. A ranger told us about a dog who got so frustrated at not being able to swim that when he got back to the motel that night, he ran straight past the manager and into the swimming pool.

Try not to let your dog visit Dog Hell here. You enter Dog Hell when you drive miles and miles to get to a county park, only to find Sir Ranger shaking his head at you, hands on hips, ready to do battle. County parks ban dogs from every inch of their terrain except campgrounds, which are generally not the most scenic spots in the world.

NATIONAL FORESTS

See the National Forests and Wilderness Areas chapter starting on page 748 for important information and safety tips on visiting national forests with your dog.

- **Los Padres National Forest** 🐾🐾🐾🐾 🐕
See page 751.

CAMARILLO

PARKS, BEACHES, AND RECREATION AREAS

- **Community Center Park** 🐾 *See ❶ on page 580.*
There's a decent-sized open green area here and a few trees, but this park isn't anything your leashed dog will brag about to his buddies.

Exit U.S. 101 at Carmen Drive and go north several blocks. At Burnley Street, go right and park in the lot. (805) 482-1996.

FILLMORE

RESTAURANTS

Margaret's Cocina Drive-In: The dog-friendly people here will give a thirsty canine customer a big bowl of water while she joins you for a bite on the patio. 446 Ventura Street; (805) 524-3638.

OXNARD

PARKS, BEACHES, AND RECREATION AREAS

I had a scintillating conversation with a parks department employee about the subject of dog doo-doo. He quoted from the scriptures (city code): "It says right here—'No person shall permit any dog to defecate on public property . . . without the consent of the person owning it.' That's the law."

"Okay, so you have to fax the parks commissioners, tell them your dog ate a whopper of a supper last night, and that you might be needing the use of their parks the next morning?" asked I. It took him a few minutes before he figured out that maybe there was more to this law than meets the eye. "Oh, right here it says that if you clean it up right away, you don't have to get permission," said he. "Whew!" said I. "Whew!" breathed Joe.

Another city law says that you must always carry a pooper-scooper when with your dog. If you don't have one on hand, you could be fined. But what if your dog already did his business and you threw it out? "You'd better carry a spare just for show," another city employee told me.

The biggest park in the city, College Park, doesn't permit pooches because it's actually a county park. But with the new leash-free area that's supposed to open at the Oxnard State Beach (see below), who needs it anyway?

• **Orchard Park** 🐾🐾 *See* ❷ *on page 580.*

It's not a large park, but it's attractive for its size. Even dogs seem to think the park is okay, but only early in the morning when less traffic is whizzing by. And there are plenty of trees.

The park is at Edelweiss Street and Erica Place, a few blocks west of Highway 1 and north of Gonzales Road. (805) 385-7950.

• **Oxnard State Beach** 🐾🐾🐾½ *See* ❸ *on page 580.*

Alas, a long stretch of this beach was supposed to have been open to off-leash dogs by now, but it looks like that's not going to happen. The city of Oxnard actually runs this state beach, and for the last few years, a city resolution allowing pooches off leash in a segment of beach had been awaiting final approval. Now that whole movement seems to have gone out with the tide. Dogs are disappointed.

This park is less developed than many other beaches in the area. It covers about 62 acres and features dune trails and a picnic area. Dogs really dig it here, even though they have to be attached to people.

The parking fee is $3 for the day, or 50 cents per hour. The beach is west of Harbor Boulevard, between Beach Way and Falkirk Avenue. (805) 385-7950.

RESTAURANTS

Fisherman's Wharf: This is a thoroughly charming, dog-friendly collection of old-fashioned shops and good restaurants. Little benches abound, but many of the restaurants have their own outdoor seating. We see at least a couple of dogs here each time we visit and we figure they're dogs of the nautical persuasion. They're in great shape, but their leashes seem to be boating line and their owners have tan, leathery skin and a hint of salt on the hair. Here's a fun spot to check out with your pooch:

•*Marine Ice Cream & Candy:* Share a treat with your best friend at the table near this shop. 2741 South Victoria Avenue; (805) 985-5532.

Popeye's Famous Fried Chicken and Biscuits: Eat at the outdoor tables here. (There's no spinach on the menu, in case your dog was wondering.) 1900 North Ventura Road; (805) 983-3928.

PLACES TO STAY

Residence Inn by Marriott: This is a convenient place to park it when traveling with a pooch. All the rooms are studios or apartments and all come with full kitchens. Rates are $89 to $159 and include a continental breakfast and complimentary afternoon beverages. Dogs pay a $100 fee for the length of their stay (dogs usually stay a while here to make it worth their money), and they're $5 extra per night. 2101 West Vineyard Avenue, Oxnard, CA 93030; (805) 988-0130.

Vagabond Inn: Rates are $48 to $64. Dogs are $5 extra. 1245 North Oxnard Boulevard, Oxnard, CA 93030; (805) 983-0251.

PORT HUENEME

PARKS, BEACHES, AND RECREATION AREAS

Dogs are not allowed at this Navy city's beaches, but they can peruse the parks here.

•**Moranda/Bubbling Springs Park** 🐾🐾½ *See* ❹ *on page 580.*

A stream runs through much of this park, and in the summer, dogs love to dip their hot little toes in it to cool off. The park is actually two connected parks. Most of the Bubbling Springs Park, to the north, is a greenbelt area. Moranda Park is a chunk of green with trees, green grass, shaded picnic areas, and playgrounds.

Many people and their leashed dogs hike from one end of the adjoining parks to the other. Going north to south (toward the beach), you can begin your walk at Bard Road and Park Avenue and follow the park as it winds south, crossing a few streets along the way. Your hike will end around Seawind Way. (805) 986-6542.

PLACES TO STAY

Point Mugu State Park Campgrounds: Dogs aren't permitted on the magical trails in this spectacular park, even with a leash. "They're a hazard to wildlife and other park visitors," a young ranger told me in a monotone, robotic voice. Creepy! But there are a few paved roads you can walk them on, if tar's your cup of tea.

At least dogs are allowed to help you pitch a tent at one of their 131 campsites. Rates are $14 to $16. Dogs are $1 extra. The park is about nine miles south of Port Hueneme Road, on Highway 1. For park info, call (818) 880-0350. Call Parknet at (800) 444-PARK to reserve a site.

SIMI VALLEY

PARKS, BEACHES, AND RECREATION AREAS

•**Rancho Santa Susana Community Park** 🐾🐾 *See* ❺ *on page 580.*

Now *this* is suburbia. Parents in Volvo station wagons pull into the parking lot and out of the car pop a few little soccer demons raring to clobber whatever team they happen to be opposing. Neighbors greet each other with compliments about how fine their lawns look this year. Women push strollers up and down the walkway. Then they push them up and down again.

But when the talcum powder has cleared and it's just you and your leashed dog, you can actually have a decent time here. Between strolling on the path, checking out the bushes, and running on the playing fields, your dog might even enjoy himself. The park is at Stearns Street and Los Angeles Avenue. (805) 584-4400.

•**Rancho Simi Community Park** 🐾🐾½ *See* ❻ *on page 580.*

This park is pretty much one big field of green turf with some trees and shaded picnic tables. It's quite an attractive, decent-sized area for a community park. Despite a few sports courts and a playground, you can usually find some seclusion here. Just go to the back section of the park. You'll know it when you see it.

Dogs would like to tear around chasing Frisbees and softballs, but alas, they have to be leashed. The park is on Royal Avenue, about a block east of Erringer Road. (805) 584-4400.

RESTAURANTS

Rasta Pasta and Salads: You'll enjoy eating healthful foods at the outdoor tables with your pooch at your side. 464 Madera Road; (805) 520-4649.

PLACES TO STAY

Oak County Park Campground: This county campground is located directly below some railroad tracks in what looks like a dirt parking lot with a few trees. It's not what you'd call a hot spot for getting back to nature.

There are 55 sites. Rates are $5 per person for tent sites. RV sites are $12 to $15 per RV. Dogs are $1 extra, and they're not allowed on the park's trails or anywhere but the campground. About halfway between Moorpark and Simi Valley on Highway 118, exit onto Los Angeles Avenue and drive southeast about 1.5 miles. The park entrance will be on your left, directly across from a really big, ugly contractor's storage facility. (805) 654-3644.

THOUSAND OAKS

PARKS, BEACHES, AND RECREATION AREAS

Zounds! The Thousand Oaks area is home to 13,000 acres of open space you can peruse with a leashed dog. Most of these areas are difficult to access, but if you can find them, they're well worth the visit. We describe a couple of open space areas below. The Conejo Open Space Conservation Agency, which oversees these areas, can provide you with a general map and directions to other open space parks. The number is (805) 495-6471.

The city is even considering starting a leash-free park within one of its many parks. (Leashed dogs are also allowed at all city parks.) At press time, nothing had been settled, but keep your ears peeled for good news. The Thousand Oaks area is also home to some of the Santa Monica Mountains National Recreation Area (see page 594). Dogs dig Thousand Oaks. As one very helpful local reader, Carolyn Greene, put it: "Although I enjoy living here myself, it's even better for dogs." Her beautiful 85-pound German shepherd, Jasmine, couldn't agree more.

• **Borchard Community Park** 🐾🐾½ See ❼ on page 580.

Pooches prefer this park's pretty paved path to plenty of places in the proximity. Say that 10 times fast and you'll have something to occupy your time as you stroll through this attractive green park. There's not too much else here to occupy your attention, but boy dogs will give their attention to the many trees.

From U.S. 101, exit at Borchard Road/Rancho Conejo Road and follow Borchard Road southwest about a mile. The park will be on your right, at Reino Road. (805) 495-6471.

• **Los Robles Open Space** 🐾🐾🐾½ See ❽ on page 580.

If it's trails you want, it's trails you'll get at this terrific swatch of open space land run by the Conejo Open Space Conservation Agency (COSCA). The total trail system here is 15 miles! That's a lot of trail for you and your leashed, outdoors-loving pooch to peruse. Some of the trails are killer, with very steep grades, so avoid these for the sake of your dog's paws. The trail system is going to be a real wonder one day—there are plans to join the trails in Los Robles with trails in the Santa Monica Mountains National Recreation Area (see page 594) to form a 40-mile trail system from Malibu to Point Mugu.

Before I continue, I promised COSCA coordinator Mark Towne that I'd make a plea for dogs to be leashed here. Since he said it so well, I'll put it in his words: "We have a lot of problems with dogs off leash. It impacts the wildlife, and it could impact the dogs, too," he said. "We've had dogs chasing rabbits, ground squirrels, and other wildlife. For a dog's sake, leashes are important because there are rattlesnakes and ticks." Got it? It's tempting, but leashes are the law here, and apparently for good reason.

The trails at Los Robles are actually wide fire access roads, winding through chaparral country and coast live oaks. They're very well marked. If you start at the parking area at the end of Moorpark Road, you can connect to the Los Robles Trail. Take the trail west to the Spring Canyon Trail and follow it to Lynn Oaks Park and back for an easy three-mile round-trip hike. If you're in the mood for food, pack a lunch and take the Los Robles Trail due south (from Moorpark) for about a mile. You'll come to a pleasant little picnic area where you and your leashed beast can have a feast. If you continue on that trail, it gets extremely steep, with lots of switchbacks and mountain bikes careening blindly down. The views become splendid, but it's not worth it unless you're very tough of paw.

Dogs who like nature love the half-mile Oak Creek Canyon Loop. This is a self-serve nature trail detailing the plant life indigenous to the area. You can get here by hiking from the Moorpark entrance, but you can also drive to this trail by following Green Meadow Avenue to the end.

JoAnna Downey, and her gorgeous George Dog, checked out this park for me on a recent visit and provided me with great info on the park. I don't usually rely on others to visit parks for me, but JoAnna and George are highly qualified dog park explorers: They're the co-authors of the wonderful *Boston Dog Lover's Companion*, one in the series of Dog Lover's Companions. Joe Dog and I give them a big thank-you for hoofing it over here for us. If you're ever in the Boston area with your dog, buy their book.

From U.S. 101, take Moorpark Road south to the end (about a mile). The parking lot is on the right. (805) 495-6471.

• **Wildwood Park** 🐾 🐾 🐾 1/2 *See* ❾ *on page 580.*

It's not every day you and your dog get to hike to a 60-foot waterfall, so take advantage of this amazing 1,700-acre park, run by the Conejo Open Space Conservation Agency. Joe likes to walk to the waterfall and stand there in awe that such waterworks can actually exist in what is otherwise dry land.

Several trails wind through the coastal sage and xeric scrub-covered hills that make up most of the park. In the spring, the wildflowers go wild in a burst of intoxicating color and scent.

You'll have to keep your dog leashed as you hike the many miles of trails. The wildlife appreciates it. After all, there's not much habitat around here for these animals anymore. If you need more convincing, see the plea made by a park official in the Los Robles Open Space description on page 585.

From U.S. 101, exit at Thousand Oaks Freeway/Highway 23 and drive north about 2.5 miles to Avenida de los Arboles. Turn left and follow the road all the way to the end (about three miles). The parking area is on the left, next to the entry kiosk that holds maps and brochures of the park. (805) 495-6471.

RESTAURANTS

Jamba Juice: You and your thirsty dog can down all kinds of tasty, healthful concoctions here. (Joe recommends avoiding the green ones, though.) Share your fruit shake at one of many tables at the plaza. (Jamba Juice shares its tables with the likes of Starbucks and Noah's Bagels, so there's something for every taste here.) 33 North Moorpark Road; (805) 449-1300.

PLACES TO STAY

Best Western Oaks Lodge: You have to sign a doggy agreement to stay here, but there's nothing unreasonable in it. No huge dogs are welcome, though. Rates are $52 to $61. Dogs are $5 extra. 12 Conejo Boulevard, Thousand Oaks, CA 91360; (805) 495-7011 or (800) 528-1234.

Thousand Oaks Inn: Stay here and you're next to Border's Books, which is great for literary dogs. You'll also get use of the hotel's free video library, which is great for couch potato dogs. Your room comes with complimentary passes to a local workout joint, as well as a continental breakfast. Rates are $79 to $110. There's a $50 pooch fee per visit. 75 West Thousand Oaks Boulevard, Thousand Oaks, CA 91360; (805) 497-3701 or (800) 600-6878.

VENTURA

This seaside community has a wealth of parks for you and your leashed friend to sniff out. It's also home to the ninth—and last—mission founded by Father Junipero Serra. Dogs can't go inside, but they're more than happy to smile at the camera for an exterior shot.

PARKS, BEACHES, AND RECREATION AREAS

• **Arroyo Verde Park** 🐾🐾½ *See* ⑩ *on page 580.*

Most of this 129-acre park is on rugged land that's pretty much impassable by anyone but the critters of nature. There's a trail that takes you from the 14-acre open grass area into a tiny bit of the wilder area, but you'll barely get your paws moving when the trail loops you right back down the hill.

This is a better park for kids than for dogs (who must be leashed). The civilized segment has a nature center, a playground, a wading pool, and Fort Keller—a children's play fort. There's not even a fire hydrant for our four-legged friends.

There's a $1 fee per vehicle on Sundays and holidays. It's probably not worth it to take your dog on these days anyway, because it can be jampacked. Exit U.S. 101 at Victoria Avenue and drive north on Victoria for about two miles. Where it ends, turn left on Foothill Road. In about two-thirds of a mile, the park will be on your right, at the corner of Foothill and Day Roads. (805) 652-4550.

• **Camino Real Park** 🐾🐾½ *See* ⑪ *on page 580.*

When this 38-acre park isn't being used for ball games, it's a fine place to take a leashed pooch. The fields are really large, beckoning you and the leashed dog of your choice to run and jump and act like a couple of pups together.

The park has a refreshing eucalyptus smell. Enjoy the trees from the paved path that winds through much of the park. The park is at Dean Drive at Varsity Street, just a few blocks south of Ventura College. (805) 652-4550.

• **Grant Memorial Park** 🐾🐾🐾 *See* ⑫ *on page 580.*

In 1782, Father Junipero Serra raised a wooden cross on the mountain overlooking his newly built Mission San Buenaventura. That mountain is now part of this 107-acre park. A cross still sticks out of the top of the park, and if you go anywhere near it, you'll find wonderful views of the city, the Pacific, and the Channel Islands.

Surrounding the cross is a little grassy area where you can unwind, take in the views, or eat a picnic. But if you want to be kind to your dog, before you sit down to ooh and ahh at the scenery, turn around. On the other side of the parking lot you'll see a dirt trail heading up the adjacent hill. It's not shady, so your leashed dog won't be able to ooh and ahh at the trees, but it's a great way for you to get away from the park's never-ending trickle of visitors.

From Cedar Street (two blocks east of Ventura Avenue), turn east on Ferro Drive and follow it to the top of the park. (805) 652-4550.

• **Lake Casitas Recreation Area** 🐾🐾🐾 *See* ⑬ *on page 580.*

Don't bring a water dog here. She'll just stare at the water and weep. Dogs have to be kept 50 feet away from the lake, meaning they can't even go on a boat with you. With 50,000 people who rely on this lake for water, it's understandable that they wouldn't want a bunch of flea-bitten beasts floating around in their drink. But that's a hard one to explain to a quivering, frothing Labrador retriever. Actually, people aren't permitted to swim here either, but that news probably won't do much to console your dog-paddling pooch.

Once you enter this 6,200-acre park, your best bet is to bear to the right and follow the road to a dense, lush, oaky campground. Park wherever you can and walk with your leashed dog as far back as possible. You'll find some short trails winding through this part of the park and some excellent places to relax and get away from the bulk of the people who visit here. (They're all at the water, like most normal folks.)

The day-use fee is $6. Dogs are $1. There are 480 campsites, with rates ranging from $12 to $39. Camping dogs cost $2. Reservations are not necessary. From the heart of Ventura, drive 11 miles north on Highway 33. Turn left on Highway 150 and drive about four miles to the main entrance. (805) 649-2233.

• **Ojai Valley Trail** 🐾 🐾 🐾 *See ⑭ on page 580.*

You and your leashed dog may have to share this nine-mile trail with a few fast bicycles, but don't let that stop you. It's a great way to see the valley east of Lake Casitas.

The trail will take you through little forested areas and quiet neighborhoods, past rolling hills and Christmas tree farms. For the fair of foot, there are plenty of shaded, tranquil resting spots along the way.

Even if you walk only one segment of the trail, it's worth the trip. When the trail first opened, dogs were banned, but the rule was so difficult to enforce that eventually pooches were given the okay. Take advantage of this! Rejoice! Take a hike!

The trail runs parallel to Highway 33. We like to start at Foster County Park (see page 589). It's the trail's staging area. But keep in mind that dogs are allowed at this park only at the trailhead and the campsites. Exit Highway 33 at Casitas Vista Road and follow the signs. As you head northeast on the trail, you can also access it from points such as San Antonio Creek, Santa Ana Boulevard, Barbara Street, and Baldwin Avenue. (805) 654-3951.

RESTAURANTS

Beachside Pizzeria: This place has wood tables by the beach. You and your dog can enjoy the waves and eat gourmet pizza. Try the pesto and garlic varieties, but only if your dog doesn't have a hot date afterward. 1141 Seaward Street; (805) 648-7858.

Cafe Voltaire: This cute little cafe has a courtyard where you and your dog can dine on croissant sandwiches and other cafe-style food. The folks who work here are doggone dog-friendly. Joe fell in love with a waiter who offered him water, but the waiter had to tell Joe he was already spoken for (he has his own dog). Joe stopped rolling on his back whenever the waiter appeared thereafter. 34 North Palm Street; (805) 641-1743.

Classic Carrot Cafe: Although there are two patios at this natural foods cafe, you and your dog can only dine out front, since the back patio has no outdoor access. But that's not a problem, because the sidewalk seating area is a fine place to dine on all the delicious, healthful foods here. Homemade soups, killer burritos, and hot sandwiches are popular lunch items. 1847 East Main Street; (805) 643-0406.

The Coastal Cone Company: Dine on frosty treats at one of three patio tables. 1583 Spinnaker Drive; (805) 658-2837.

Duke's Griddle 'n Grill: Your dog just might get a special treat from a waiter while you dine on the good grilled grub served at the outdoor tables here. 1124 South Seaward Avenue; (805) 653-0707.

Taco Jalisco: Despite its name, burritos are really the specialty here. Eat with your dog at the outdoor tables. 2292 East Main Street; (805) 643-2820.

Top Hat Burger Palace: You don't have to be of royal blood to enjoy this fast-food palace. All of the seating is outdoors; you just go to an order window to get your food and then dine in leisure with your mutt. 299 East Main Street; (805) 643-9696.

PLACES TO STAY

Doubletree Hotel at Ventura: This hotel is a mere block from the state beach, where pooches are not permitted (alas). Rates are $85 to $200. Dogs are charged a $15 fee per visit. 2055 Harbor Boulevard, Ventura, CA 93001; (805) 643-6000.

Faria County Park Campground: You're so close to the water here (you're actually at the ocean's edge), yet so very far away. Dogs aren't allowed on the beach, and that can be a bummer with a capital B. There are 42 sites, with fees ranging from $17 to $20. Dogs are $1 extra. From the main part of Ventura, drive seven miles northwest on U.S. 101. For park info or campsite reservations, call (805) 654-3951.

Foster County Park Campground: Some of the sites here are near oaks, but that's about the best thing we can say about this place, except that the park is the staging area for the Ojai Valley Trail (see page 588). Dogs are banned from the day-use area of the park. The 48 sites here are $8 to $11. (805) 654-3951.

Lake Casitas Recreation Area: See Lake Casitas Recreation Area on page 587 for camping information.

La Quinta Inn: This inn has had all sorts of nonhuman visitors—even birds and rabbits. Dogs are welcome here, as long as you don't have more than two per room. Rates are $56 to $65. 5818 Valentine Road, Ventura, CA 93003; (805) 658-6200.

McGrath State Beach Campsites: Your dog can't go on the beach with you here, but the camping area is pretty enough that it's not such a bad fate to hang out here together and read a good book. There are 174 sites. Rates are $14 to $16. Dogs are $2 extra. From U.S. 101, take the Seaward Avenue/ Harbor Boulevard exit and drive four miles west on Harbor Boulevard to the beach. For reservations, phone Parknet at (800) 444-PARK. For park info, call (805) 899-1400.

Motel 6: Rates are $33 for the first adult, $6 for the second, and we're told these rates will be going up in the near future. You can bring one small pooch here. 2145 East Harbor Boulevard, Ventura, CA 93001; (805) 643-5100.

Vagabond Inn: Rates are $63 to $80. (That's a hefty price for vagabonds.) Dogs are $5 extra. 756 East Thompson Boulevard, Ventura, CA 93001; (805) 648-5371.

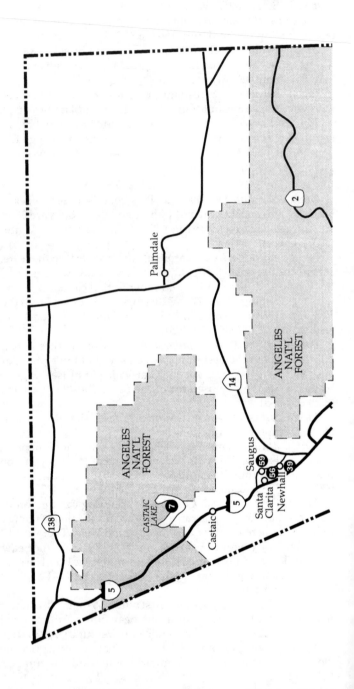

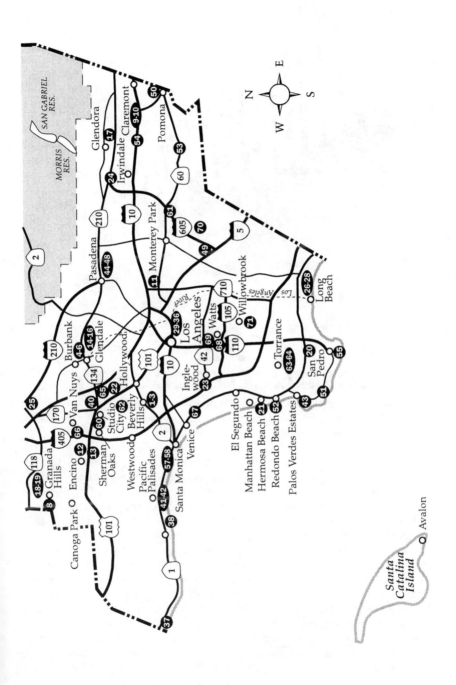

52
LOS ANGELES COUNTY

Slowly but surely, Los Angeles County is going to the dogs, in the best sense of the phrase. This is a very good thing, if you're a dog or just someone who knows a dog.

Los Angeles still isn't Dog Heaven, but it's come a long way since the first edition of this book a few years back. The introduction to L.A. County in that edition started like this: "If you took all the 'No Dogs Allowed' signs in this county, put them side by side, and strung wire around them, you'd have a hell of a fenced-in dog-exercise area. The county could sure use it. There just aren't enough places to let your dog frolic off leash here." In fact, back then there were only a couple of leash-free areas in the whole county. Today, there are 10—and counting! (The community of Cheviot Hills, for instance, is trying to get a pooch park of its own.) Go ahead, wag your tail, pant, let it all hang out. Look for the running dog symbol (🐕) in the pages that follow, and take your dog to a doggone great place.

The Los Angeles County Parks system is a good one, with dozens of large parks dotting the county. Most allow leashed pooches. Of course, not everything's to a dog's liking here. Dogs are still banned from all beaches except one, in the Malibu area. Until recently, they were allowed at four beaches around Malibu, but pooch privileges have been revoked because people didn't like them on the beach. The rest of the county's 74 miles of shoreline are off-limits, verboten, badlands. Too bad the county or some of the cities here can't follow the lead of San Francisco or San Diego and open some of the less-used beach areas to leash-free dog traffic. The leash-free part of this dream may never happen because almost all of this county's beaches draw large crowds, but at least leashed pooches should be allowed to sniff out L.A.'s footprints in the sand.

The show must go on.

One of the best deals going for L.A.'s well-behaved dogs is the Sierra Club's K9 Committee, which encourages dogs on outings. Its stated purpose is "to explore and enjoy the trails and remote areas of the great outdoors with our canine friends and promote responsible dog ownership and behavior in pursuit of these goals." Outings include hikes in pristine national forestland, camping trips, and full-moon doggy hikes. "It's admirable to see a Pomeranian do a 10- to 12-mile hike cross-country, agilely dodging chollas (most of the time), fending off ticks, bounding over boulders in order to contemplate the fantastic views from the summit," writes Julie Rush, the K9 Committee's chair of safety and outings. For information on the K9 Committee and its entertaining newsletter, *Waggin' Trails*, contact the Angeles chapter of the Sierra Club at (213) 387-4287.

Another terrific group to consider joining for awe-inspiring (and sometimes sweat-inspiring) hikes is the California Canine Hikers. These fun folks hold about 50 hikes per year. For more information, write the CCH at 2154 Woodlyn Road, Pasadena, CA 91104-3333. There's a Web page, but its address is a bit long for the likes of this book. Try a Web search instead.

Back in civilization, you can take a train ride with your dog at Griffith Park (see Diversions, page 615) and even take your extremely well-behaved poochum-woochums shopping at certain exclusive Beverly Hills stores (see Diversions, page 597). Some fine hotels permit pooches, including the exclusive Chateau Marmont (see page 610).

Dogs can compare paw prints with the prints of Hollywood's biggest stars at Mann's Chinese Theatre (see Diversions, page 611). If you want a little exercise with your stargazing, pick up a map of the stars' homes and take a little walk around town. It's an extremely hackneyed, sometimes rude pastime, but most of the homes on these tours have long since changed hands, so you're often just staring at a home where the star lived many moons ago. Anyway, it's a great excuse to walk your dog.

Anthony Shipp, a Beverly Hills veterinarian to the stars, says celebrities often feel that their dogs are the only ones who really love them for who they are. "So many people like them only for what they can get from them, or for the dazzle," says Shipp, who has ministered to the dogs of Frank Sinatra, Kirk Douglas, Peter Falk, and even Richard Simmons, to drop a few names. (He recounts how, many years ago, he helped Sinatra's and Douglas' disinterested dogs to mate, but the dogs would do it only after they put on a tape of the crooner's hits. "It seems even dogs get romantic to Sinatra's voice," he says.)

Chances are good that you'll see a star or two just by going to some of the cafes and restaurants that permit dogs at their outdoor tables. Joe and I aren't stargazers by nature, but when he saw Goldie Hawn saunter out of a Beverly Hills cafe that we were just about to walk into, he couldn't stop staring. It was embarrassing, even for him, but he just couldn't take his eyes off her. And when she glanced down at him and smiled, he melted. His mouth opened and he stared straight ahead, stunned. She walked on with her friend, never knowing the impression she had made on one lovestruck Airedale.

Joe and I usually prefer to stargaze in the direction of the heavens, in an open field on a clear night. Joe's favorite star (excluding Goldie Hawn) is the brilliant Sirius, part of the constellation Canis Major. If you or your dog enjoy dabbling in astronomy, the Los Angeles Astronomical Society may have some activities of interest (see Diversions, page 620).

This chapter separates some of the districts in the city of Los Angeles into their own sections. For instance, instead of listing Hollywood under "Los Angeles," it has its own heading. The city is too huge to lump all its districts together.

NATIONAL FORESTS

See the National Forests and Wilderness Areas chapter starting on page 748 for important information and safety tips on visiting national forests with your dog.

• **Angeles National Forest** 🐾🐾🐾🐾 🐕
See page 749.

NATIONAL RECREATION AREAS

• **Santa Monica Mountains National Recreation Area** 🐾🐾🐾½
Attention smog-coated dogs and city-weary people: You can breathe a sigh of relief. Nature is only a stick's throw away from the crowded freeways and urban sprawl of one of the largest cities in the world.

Contrary to what some local dog people have heard, leashed dogs really *are* allowed to explore portions of this 65,000-acre wonderland of mountains, canyons, woods, and fern glens. This national recreation area is a patchwork of county, state, and federal lands located throughout the Santa Monica Mountains. While dogs are banned from trails on all state lands and from all but a few Malibu-area beaches (see page 620) within the recreation area, they're welcome at 26 of the parks here.

The following are dog-friendly parks, from A to Z: Arroyo Sequit, Calabasas Peak, Castro Crest, Charmlee County Natural Area, Cheeseboro Canyon, Circle X Ranch, Coldwater Canyon, Corral Canyon, Franklin Canyon Ranch, Fryman Canyon, Laurel Canyon (includes an off-leash dog park, described on page 634), Paramount Ranch, Peter Strauss Ranch, Rancho Sierra Vista/Satwiwa, Red Rock Canyon, Rocky Oaks, Runyun Canyon, San Vicente Mountain, Serrania Canyon, Solstice Canyon, Stuart Ranch, Tapia, Temescal Gateway, Wilacre, Wildwood Regional, and Zuma Canyon.

The parks are too numerous to describe in detail in this book, but the Mountain Parks Information Service provides a free map showing all the parks, delineating which permit dogs. You can also get free brochures of many of the dog-friendly parks, which show trailheads and give descriptions and directions. They're essential for planning any enchanting back-to-nature outing with your dog. Call (800) 533-PARK to get your maps and brochures. For the National Park Service Visitors Center, call (818) 597-9192.

Spring is a terrific time to explore these lands. Wildflowers blossom white, yellow, orange, blue, red, and every other color your dog might not be able to see if he's as color-blind as scientists claim. Birds sing their hearts out. The grasslands, normally a dead tan-brown color, get as green as green gets.

BEVERLY HILLS

As Joe, Bill, and I rattled around this opulent city in our 14-year-old pickup truck on a recent research trip, we were the objects of unmasked curiosity and a smidgen of concern. Joe's head stuck out one side of the camper top in back, Bill's hung out the other, and the truck had hiccups at the time and was making obscene noises.

Park rangers and cops paid my little Beverly Hillbillies mobile a visit three times as we stopped at park after park. "Just want to make sure you're not lost, Miss," was the general theme of their very cordial way of evaluating our menace potential.

PARKS, BEACHES, AND RECREATION AREAS

Dogs aren't allowed in the stunningly beautiful Greystone Park. But then again, neither are cameras or picnics, so canines shouldn't feel too offended.

As for the rest of the parks, a woman at the parks department here had to double-check the dog rules with a supervisor when we called to update the book. When she came back to the phone, she had this answer: "I'm told we prefer the wind-up type, but we'll take the live ones." We give four paws for self-effacing humor in the land of 90210.

• **Beverly Gardens Park** 🐾🐾½ See ❶ on pages 590–591.
Stretching from Wilshire Boulevard to Doheny Drive, this narrow, 20-block-long park is great for dogs on the go. It runs along the north side of Santa Monica Boulevard, so if you and your dog are trying to sprint from one end of town to the other, you couldn't ask for a greener way to go.

The strip of park has a path, so you're not relegated to the sidewalk. But since it does parallel the busy boulevard, it's not without its share of exhaust fumes and honking Mercedes. Dogs must be leashed. (310) 285-2541.

• **La Cienega Park** 🐾½ See ❷ on pages 590–591.
If your pooch wants to fraternize with the cream of the Beverly Hills canine corps, there are fancier places to take her. But this is a passable neighborhood park with fenced-in ball fields and a playground. If the ball fields are in use, there's not much room for you and your leashed dog to roam, but you can always find a strip of grass.

The bulk of the park is on the east side of La Cienega Boulevard, between Gregory Way and Schumacher Drive. A smaller segment of the park is on the west side of La Cienega Boulevard. (310) 285-2541.

• **Will Rogers Memorial Park** 🐾🐾½ See ❸ on pages 590–591.
Dogs and their elegantly clad people come to this lush park to lounge

the afternoon away. Dogs have to be leashed here, and it's not a large park, but it is verdant and rich with the colorful sights and sounds of Beverly Hills. When Joe, Bill, and I visited, we witnessed a tiny bit of a dog being led out of a Rolls by a chauffeur who had the same air of noble servitude as if he were escorting the queen of England. He walked the little thing around once and said "Now, Emily." The dog did her little business on command. The chauffeur scooped and they sped off, no doubt to more pressing engagements.

The Will Rogers Memorial Park is a triangular chunk of fine real estate at the corner of Canon and Beverly Drives and Sunset Boulevard, right across from the Beverly Hills Hotel. (310) 285-2541.

RESTAURANTS

Bistro K: If you enjoy fun and fascinating combinations of food, this is the place for you. Try the scallop-ginger-pheasant dish for something truly unique. Dine at the attractive outdoor area with your pooch. 267 South Beverly Drive; (310) 276-1558.

California Pizza Kitchen: Your dog can dine outside with you here, but she has to be tied up on the other side of the wrought iron fence. 207 South Beverly Drive; (310) 275-1101.

Il Tramezzino: The eggplant parmesan here is *delicioso.* Eat it at one of the umbrella-topped tables. 460 North Canon Drive; (310) 273-0501.

Jacopo's Pizzeria: Besides pizza, you can get chicken, seafood, and pasta at the outdoor tables here. 490 North Beverly Drive; (310) 858-6446.

Mulberry Street Pizzeria: Dine on truly delectable pizza with your dog at your side at any of several outdoor tables. 347 North Canon Drive; (310) 247-8100.

Subway: Yes, Virginia, there is a Subway in Beverly Hills. It seems even people whose zip code is 90210 appreciate a good ham and cheese sub with all the fixings. But they have to bring their own Grey Poupon. 279 South Beverly Drive; (310) 278-7827.

PLACES TO STAY

Beverly Hilton: If elegant hotels like this have few qualms about allowing dogs to spend the night, shouldn't others follow suit? Just sign a doggy damage waiver and the room is yours. Rates are $190 to $305. 9876 Wilshire Boulevard, Beverly Hills, CA 90210; (310) 274-7777.

L'Ermitage: If you can afford the first-class European elegance of this exclusive and very private hotel, you won't regret a night or two here. You and your small dog (the only kind of dog who can stay here) will be pampered beyond belief. A chauffeur comes with your stay, so you and the pooch (who will be treated like anything but a pooch) can hitch a ride to nearby locales. A wonderful array of goodies awaits you daily and nightly in your suite. The marble bathrooms alone come complete with a steam room, phones, a TV, and a plush robe. All this and more can be yours for $380 to $3,000. Dogs are charged a $100 fee for the length of their stay. 9291 Burton Way, Beverly Hills, CA 90210; (310) 278-3344.

Regent Beverly Wilshire: This hotel puts the "E" in elegance, the "L" in luxury, and the "!" in dog-friendly! First, since your dog is probably reading over your shoulder by now, let's talk about what's in store for him here. Upon arrival, your pooch will be presented with a silver tray containing two ceramic bowls. One has Milk-Bones and is accented by a sprig of fresh mint, the other bowl is for the bottle of Evian water your dog gets. Also on the tray are two white linen napkins, a rubber squeeze toy, and a vase with a long-stemmed rose. Your dog will also get a special pillow for napping. And all this is free! In addition, for a fee, the hotel provides dog sitting and dog walking. They'll even arrange for a vet or a groomer to come to your room, should you need one. Special gourmet meat selections are also at your dog's pawtips.

Oh yeah, the hotel. Well, it's in the heart of Beverly Hills, at Wilshire Boulevard and Rodeo Drive, and it's exquisite. It's a historic hotel, built in 1928, and has 275 luxurious guest rooms, including 69 suites. All the rooms have a marble bathroom with deep-soaking bathtub, fully stocked private bars with fridges, fresh flowers, terry robes, a private safe, foam and down pillows, 100 percent cotton linens, an in-room fax, twice-daily maid service, and so on. You get the picture. There's even a heated outdoor pool, but no dog paddling pooches, please.

The hotel is probably best known in recent years as the setting for the hit Disney movie *Pretty Woman*. The more intimate scenes between Richard Gere and Julia Roberts took place in the hotel's Presidential Suite. For a mere $5,000 per night, you and your dog (and your human guests) can stay here, too. For the price, you get 4,000 square feet of space with gobs of rooms, two fireplaces, and lots of special touches (not the kind of touches in *Pretty Woman*, though). Some notables who *really* stayed in the Presidential Suite are Elvis Presley, the Dalai Lama, King Hussein and Queen Noor, Prince Andrew, Andrew Lloyd Webber, Elton John, and Mick Jagger.

If you want something a little simpler (read cheaper), you can stay in a gorgeous room for as little as $335. The average room rate runs about $400. 9500 Wilshire Boulevard, Beverly Hills, CA 90212; (310) 275-5200 or (800) 545-5000.

DIVERSIONS

Charge it with your wee doggy: If you can easily carry your well-behaved pooch under your arm, many top Beverly Hills shops will welcome your business (but not your dog's business, if you know what I mean—walk your dog first). "We have one customer who leaves her tiny dog with the doorman while she shops around, but most just carry their dogs around with them as they pick out what they want," said Ed Bodde, former vice president and general manager of Saks Fifth Avenue on Wilshire. Bodde has moved on to another store, but his replacement says he's happy to keep the pooch-friendly policy.

The Beverly Hills I. Magnin has a general store policy against pooches, but security guards and regular dog-carrying customers tell us that if you can tote your dog, you're in. I couldn't try this with 70-pound groaning Joe, so you'll have to find out for yourself if they're as dog-friendly as local shoppers say.

Several small boutiques also allow the occasional pooch, but they asked not to be mentioned for fear of being besieged with giant dogs and dogs with bad bathroom habits.

One place you'll have to avoid with your dog is Neiman-Marcus. A dog in another Neiman store recently bit a customer, and the Beverly Hills store has had to go along with a company policy banning all dogs. But they're discreet. Says a smooth-voiced representative: "We hand them a form that explains the situation, and they're usually very understanding. It can be a real disappointment."

I. Magnin is at 9634 Wilshire Boulevard; (310) 271-2131. Saks' address is 9600 Wilshire Boulevard; (310) 275-4211.

BRENTWOOD

RESTAURANTS

Belwood Bakery: You and your pooch can dine on tasty baked goods and sandwiches at the three outdoor tables here. 11625 Barrington Court; (310) 471-6855.

BURBANK

PARKS, BEACHES, AND RECREATION AREAS

•**Izay Park** 😊 😊 *See* ❹ *on pages 590–591.*

Here it is: Not huge, but not tiny, a few ball fields, lots of grass and trees surrounding much of the park. We can't say much more, except that you must leash your dog. The park is at Glenoaks Boulevard between Andover and Amherst Drives. (818) 238-5378.

•**Johnny Carson Park** 😊 😊 ½ *See* ❺ *on pages 590–591.*

Remember all of Johnny Carson's lines about "beautiful downtown Burbank"? Since the former *Tonight Show* host did his best to put Burbank on the map, the city decided to do the same for him. Just across from the NBC studios where he hosted his show year after year, there's a decent little park named after him.

The park, which used to be called Buena Vista Park, is a great place to visit with your dog if you're dropping off a friend at NBC or at the nearby Disney studios. It's well shaded and has many picnic tables and a footbridge that leads you to a fitness course. With Highway 134 roaring so close, it's not quiet, but who comes to this part of Burbank for tranquillity?

A word of warning: Don't let your male dog lift his leg on the stone "sign" with Johnny Carson's mug engraved on it. We met a man who apparently sits on the grass all day watching for such indiscretions. He came running up to Joe after the dog did a quick leg lift. I thought perhaps he knew Joe or was running up to say Joe was a fine dog, but something about the way he was screaming "No, no pee on this! Bad dog!" led me to believe he had another mission.

Exit Interstate 5 at Alameda Avenue and drive southwest for about 20 blocks. At Bob Hope Drive, turn left. The park will be on your left in about a block. (818) 238-5378.

•**Wildwood Canyon Park** 🐾🐾🐾½ *See* ❻ *on pages 590–591.*

The only way Joe would like this big park better than he already does would be if he could go leashless. It's beautifully manicured and surrounded by miles of forest. If he's in the mood to roll on the grass and enjoy a picnic near regal stone archways, we stay in the developed part of the park. If he's raring to explore nature and admire trees in his unique way, we take the myriad trails leading out from various points around the park.

His favorite kind of day involves a long hike through the hills, followed by a a leisurely picnic at the serene, secluded, shaded picnic spots that dot the main area. You can't help but feel pampered in this lush park: It's run with such class that even the portable toilets are disguised to look distinguished.

Coming north on Interstate 5, take the Olive Avenue exit and head northeast. Turn left at Sunset Canyon Drive. In six blocks, turn right on Harvard Drive, which will take you into the park. Make sure you bear right once you come to a fork in the road, or you'll end up on the adjacent golf course. (818) 238-5378.

RESTAURANTS

Chez Nous: If you like California-continental cuisine, you'll enjoy dining under the canopies with your pooch. 10550 Riverside Drive; (818) 760-0288.

El Mexicano: Your Chihuahua might beg you for a piece of your delicious burrito, but don't succumb to that hang-*perro* look. Joe Dog snuck a bite of my spicy burrito when I wasn't looking, and within an hour, he was pulling me toward the nearest park as fast as his hairy legs could take him. 3121 West Olive Street; (818) 567-0177.

Juicy Harveys: "We love dogs here. Bring 'em down," one enthusiastic Harvey-ite told us. The AstroTurf here looks awfully realistic, so watch your dog closely lest he think it's a miniature park. 3203 West Alameda Avenue; (818) 846-9033.

Priscilla's: If you and your pooch want to feel really welcome at a restaurant, come here. "We *love* dogs and would let them inside if we were allowed," says a manager. "We give them water, a little milk, whatever they want." You'll like the relaxed atmosphere on the patio with umbrella-shaded tables, as well as the gourmet coffees and tasty light fare. 4150 Riverside Drive; (818) 843-5707.

Toluca Garden: This is a good Chinese restaurant where you and the dog can dine at umbrella-topped outdoor tables. 10000 Riverside Drive; (818) 980-3492.

PLACES TO STAY

Burbank Airport Hilton: Rates are $129 to $179. Dog people have to sign a release for their furry traveling companions. 2500 Hollywood Way, Burbank, CA 91505; (818) 843-6000.

Holiday Inn: Rates are $109 to $119. Dogs can stay on the second floor. 150 East Angeleno Avenue, Burbank, CA 91510; (818) 841-4770.

DIVERSIONS

Coif your canine: If you want some good, clean fun with your dog, visit

U Wash Doggy, a self-service dog wash. There are five of them in Los Angeles County. See Diversions in Encino on page 605 for details on the dog wash. This one's at 1056 West Alameda Avenue; (818) 864-9600.

CASTAIC

PARKS, BEACHES, AND RECREATION AREAS

• **Castaic Lake** 🐾 🐾 🐾 *See* ❼ *on pages 590–591.*

At 9,000 acres, this is the largest of Los Angeles County's recreation areas. But before your dog starts drooling with excitement, you should be warned that there's not much for a dog to do around here.

Hiking trails are virtually nonexistent. Dogs must be leashed everywhere. They're never allowed in either the large Castaic Lake or the 180-acre Afterbay Lagoon, no matter how many trout or bass they see. (But humans can once again go swimming at the lake now that a bacteria problem is gone.)

Because there are no trails around Castaic Lake, it's pretty much impossible to hike its perimeter. The Afterbay Lagoon is a good sight easier for a dog jaunt, since it's developed. It has plenty of grassy areas, some trees, picnic tables, and a couple of playgrounds.

If you and your dog aren't anglers, but you're with someone who is, it's a fine place to spend the day. But it's not the kind of destination you'd want to visit just to walk your dog.

There's a $6 fee per car. The fee is waived during weekdays from November through February. Boat launching is an additional $6. The lake's 40 campsites are new and cost $12 nightly. From Interstate 5, exit at Lake Hughes Road and follow it to the lake. (805) 257-4050.

PLACES TO STAY

Castaic Lake: See Castaic Lake above for camping information.

Comfort Inn: The lake is down the road a bit. Rates are $55 to $75. Dogs can stay only in smoking rooms. 31558 Castaic Road, Castaic, CA 91384; (805) 295-1100 or (800) 228-5150.

CATALINA

Contrary to popular belief, dogs are allowed on enchanting Santa Catalina Island. But with the exception of a 10-by-10-foot patch of dog-dedicated dirt on the way from the ferry to town, dogs are not allowed at any parks, beaches, or along Crescent Avenue, the main drag here. It got even tougher for dogs recently, when Pebbly Beach, the only beach that allowed dogs, was annexed by the Catalina city of Avalon (as opposed to L.A. County). Dogs are now banned there, too. As if that's not bad enough, if you're caught without a pooper-scooper in your possession (regardless of whether you've already used it and won't be needing one), you can be fined.

Add to this scenario the fact that no hotels, motels, or campgrounds permit dogs, making it pretty tough to spend the night together, and you'll see just what a challenge it can be to visit here with a dog.

For years, the no-dogs-at-hotels situation has made minor criminals out of dog-loving folks, forcing them to sneak their pooches into their rooms when eyes were diverted. When they were caught, their dogs would usually be banished to the car, or worse yet, the whole party had to return to the mainland on the next ferry.

But fortunately, the president of the Avalon Humane Society opened the Avalon Boarding Service. At least dogs can now spend the night in their own accommodations. While it's not the same as snoozing the night away by your side, at least you know that first thing in the morning, you can arrange to pick up your dog and spend the whole day with him. Owner Neva Jennings knows dogs, loves dogs, and will treat your pooch kindly and warmly. Even the most skittish dogs tend to feel content at her side.

Jennings says she's "very elastic" about pick-up and drop-off times, and she'll meet you somewhere other than the kennels if it's easier for you. She'll even just board your pooch for the day, if that's all you need. Dog boarding starts at $15 a day, which includes high-quality pooch food and some exercise. Contact Jennings at (310) 510-0852 or (310) 510-2221, or write her at P.O. Box 701, Avalon, CA 90704.

PARKS, BEACHES, AND RECREATION AREAS

If you don't know where to go, this place can be hell for a dog. It seems like every time you find a decent spot of green or beach, you also spot a "No Dogs Allowed" sign or a ranger with his hands on his hips and a frown on his lips. Pebbly Beach was the only beach of respite, but now that, too, says no to dogs.

The interior of the island is run by the Santa Catalina Island Conservancy and Los Angeles County. You'll need to get a permit to hike in these rugged areas. Call (310) 510-1421 for a permit and dog info. Dogs aren't allowed anywhere near the campgrounds.

RESTAURANTS

Casino Dock Cafe: This is the only public place on the island that welcomes dogs! Joe still can't believe it. Dine outside, overlooking Avalon Bay, at the base of the casino. The cuisine is of the burger-seafood-chicken variety. 2 Casino Way; (310) 510-2755.

DIVERSIONS

Nautical dog! Nautical dog!: Unless you have your own boat or care to hire a helicopter to sweep you to the island, you're going to have to rely on passenger ships to take you to Santa Catalina Island. Although dogs must be leashed and muzzled, most seem to enjoy the scenes, smells, and sounds they experience aboard these big boats. If lodgings in Catalina were as dog-friendly as the cruise services, dogs would give a Catalina Island vacation a four-paws stamp of approval.

Two Los Angeles-area lines offer dogs ship-to-shore hospitality. The Catalina Express is the fastest passenger boat to the island's only real town, Avalon. The excursion takes a little more than an hour. If it's foggy, however, the trip can last a long time, so the short cruise time is not a guarantee. Our last excursion to Catalina on this line took well over two hours because of the drippy September morning fog. Fortunately, it was a pretty flat day and no one on the boat, not even Joe Dog, got green at the gills. Trips leave from San Pedro and Long Beach and cost $36 round-trip per adult. Call (310) 519-1212 for more information. Catalina Cruises offers a more leisurely experience, with cocktails and snacks available during the nearly two-hour trip from Long Beach. Adults are $25 round-trip. Call (800) 228-2546.

Dogs go free on all excursions. Reservations are highly recommended, and usually essential. If anyone in your party (dogs included) is prone to seasickness, it may be wise to choose the faster of the boats. Every minute you spend with a green countenance and trembling gut can seem like an hour, and the Express boat will shave at least 50 of those eternal minutes off your trip. Unless, of course, it's foggy.

CENTURY CITY

PLACES TO STAY

Century Plaza Hotel & Tower: Wow! This is some fancy joint. (That's what dogs say when they find out they're allowed here.) Only dogs smaller than a cocker spaniel can stay, though. The hotel is right across the street from the ABC Entertainment Center, which won't matter to your dog since dogs aren't the kind of guests ABC seeks. Rates are $135 to $285. 2025 Avenue of the Stars, Century City, CA 90067; (310) 277-2000.

CHATSWORTH

PARKS, BEACHES, AND RECREATION AREAS

• **Chatsworth Park South** 🐾 🐾 🐾 ½ *See* ❽ *on pages 590–591.*

Joe and Bill had a rollicking good time roaming and rolling in this very spacious park one sunny afternoon. Other dogs were having the same grand old time, and when they joined together, it was a major pooch party.

The park's 81 acres provide lots of leg room for dogs, but the creatures are supposed to be leashed. An elysian green meadow stretches as far as you care to run with your dog. If tiptoeing through the grass isn't your idea of a good time, you can walk along the park's wide dirt hiking trail.

The craggy mountains towering north of the park make for an impressive backdrop. Enough trees grace the park that you can lounge in the shade while you admire the scenery and the friendly dogs who frequent the place.

Exit Highway 118 at Topanga Canyon Boulevard and drive south for almost 1.5 miles to Devonshire Street. Turn right and drive a few blocks into the park. (818) 341-6595.

PLACES TO STAY

Summerfield Suites Hotel: The suites are big and their fireplaces are awfully inviting. Rates are $90 to $139. Dogs are $10 extra nightly, on top of a $75 to $100 cleaning fee. 21902 Lassen Street, Chatsworth, CA 91311; (818) 773-0707.

CITY OF COMMERCE

What a quaint, cozy name for a city. Not. Well, at least if you need to do business here, and you're lucky enough to have your dog with you, you'll have one great place to stay.

PLACES TO STAY

Ramada Inn: "We're very pet-friendly," boasted one of the managers of this hotel. At a typical Ramada, that usually means dogs are allowed. Period. But at this Ramada, it means dogs are as welcome as their humans. For an extra $12 per day, dogs get their very own doggy bed and enough rawhide chews to make their jaws look like Arnold Schwarzenegger's biceps. This is wonderful news for dogs on the go.

Speaking of dogs on the go, there's even a dog exercise area for leashed pooches in the back of the hotel.

The hotel asks that only small- to medium-sized dogs stay here, but we're told the rule can be bent for some big dogs. Rates are $51 to $70. 7272 Gage Avenue, City of Commerce, CA 90040; (310) 806-4777 or (800) 547-4777.

CLAREMONT

Claremont has recently become a very dog-friendly place to be. Not only is there a fairly new leash-free dog park (see Pooch Park below), but now there's also a huge park where leashed dogs love to roam (see Claremont Hills Wilderness Park below). All this, and Claremont is the home of famed rapper Snoop Doggy Dog. Just thought your own doggy dog would like to know.

PARKS, BEACHES, AND RECREATION AREAS

• **Claremont Hills Wilderness Park** 🐾 🐾 🐾 ½ *See ❾ on pages 590–591.*

The city recently obtained a beautiful 1,200-acre chunk of land and turned it into a beautiful 1,200-acre chunk of park. Pooches can peruse this delightful acquisition, as long as they're on leash.

Claremont Hills is a hilly park (duh), with several miles of trails and fire roads leading through open land dotted with oaks and scrub. A creek runs through during non-drought years. The park has cool, shaded canyons as well as terrific vistas of the surrounding valleys. Enter at the very south end of Mills Avenue. (909) 399-5490.

• **Pooch Park** 🐾 🐾 🐾 🐾 🐕 *See ❿ on pages 590–591.*

Dogs are so happy to come here you can sometimes hear them baying from blocks away. Since it opened in 1996, Pooch Park has become the most popular park in Claremont, at least according to Ralph Dog and Zippity Dog, who are frequent visitors and can be trusted implicitly.

This 1.25-acre park is completely fenced, so dogs can run around to their heart's delight. It's a long park, which is great for dogs who want to work up a full head of steam before having to turn around and run in another direction.

Pooches love the green grass and the old trees that grace a couple of sides of the park. There are benches galore for people, and a water fountain for pooches and their people. Two fire hydrants sit in the middle of the park and garner adulation from male dogs.

Pooch Park is located within College Park, on College Avenue, just south of First Street and the Metrolink station. (909) 399-5490.

PLACES TO STAY

Howard Johnson: Rates are $45 to $65. Dogs are $10 extra. 721 Indian Hills Boulevard, Claremont, CA 91711; (909) 626-2431 or (800) 654-2000.

EAST LOS ANGELES

PARKS, BEACHES, AND RECREATION AREAS

• **Belvedere Regional Community Park** 🐾🐾½

See ⓫ on pages 590–591.

Although Highway 60 bisects this county park, it's still a decent place to take a leashed dog for a romp. In fact, the freeway's proximity makes it attractive to dogs on the go who find they have to go.

Just exit Highway 60 at Atlantic, go north a block, and turn west on First Street. Proceed on First Street about 10 blocks. The north half of the park will be on your right. Park in the lot and enjoy acres of green grass and a few trees. (213) 260-2342.

ENCINO

PARKS, BEACHES, AND RECREATION AREAS

Hooray! Encino is now home to a mighty dog-friendly park. In fact, it's a dog park. (See Sepulveda Basin Off-Leash Dog Park below) This is great news! Tails are wagging fast around here.

• **Balboa Park and Lake Balboa** 🐾🐾🐾 *See ⓬ on pages 590–591.*

Balboa Park is completely recreation-oriented, which is good news for leashed dogs, for once. Pooches are allowed on the many playing fields that make up this large city park. And they're welcome on the big empty fields where no sports are played. If your dog likes to hike on forested trails, this place won't be his idea of heaven, since there are none. But if he enjoys a good roll in the grass, take him here at once. If no one is playing soccer or softball, he's in for a real treat.

Lake Balboa, located across Balboa Boulevard from the park, is another story. It's officially considered part of the park, although people here seem to think of it as its own entity. Leashed dogs and the people they're attached to find it a more pleasant place, with a wide 1.3-mile walking path around the lake's edge. "It's more fun than a regular leash park," writes reader Sheryl Smith, mother of Gracie Dog. "There's an occasional fish flopping around to bark at, that some fisherman has just landed, and there are ducks and white and blue herons. . . . There must be lots of good smells there, because Gracie's nose is always to the ground there." If you ever run into Sheryl and Gracie, ask them about their collection of dog license tags from around the world. Their incredible collection numbers about 1,000, and some of the designs should be museum pieces.

Exit U.S. 101 at Balboa Boulevard, drive a couple of blocks north, and you'll be at Balboa Park's entrance. (818) 756-9642.

• **Sepulveda Basin Off-Leash Dog Park** 🐾🐾🐾🐾 🐕

See ⓭ on pages 590–591.

It's big, it's fairly grassy, it's completely fenced, and it has four boy dog toilets (okay, fire hydrants). What more could a dog want? Water? It's here at four mud-free drinking stations. Dog toilets? Check out the fire hydrants. Shade? There are enough small shade trees for comfort during the summer months. If those won't do, there are plenty of picnic tables. Dog friends? They're everywhere. Sirloin strip? Okay, the park doesn't have *everything*.

Sepulveda Basin Off-Leash Dog Park, one of the most recent dog parks to open in the state, is a heavenly place to visit if you're a dog who longs to be off leash, or if you're a dog person who longs to see your dog off leash. There's been a dire need for a park like this in the valley for a long time. Gracie Dog and her wonderful person, Sheryl, gave us the heads-up on this park when it first opened. They wrote and told us that at the leash-cutting ceremony, dozens of dogs ran through the gate barking and sprinting and having the time of their lives on the field. To this day, dozens (and on weekends, hundreds) of dogs a day frequent the park. But with five acres to run around on, it rarely seems too crowded. "It's been successful beyond our wildest dreams," says Ken Novak, a manager with the city of Los Angeles Recreation and Parks Department.

Every dog has his day here—even the tiniest of the species. Your small dog need not worry about getting trounced upon by an ungainly 125-pound pooch because within the park there's a small, fenced area for wee dogs who prefer not to mingle with the big mutts. Of course, itsy-bitsy dogs who think they're great big brutes are welcome to hang out with the big boys.

The park is good for escape artist dogs, because it has double gates and adequately high fencing. What's great about the fencing is that it's green, so it matches the park. Ivy has been planted at its base, so in a few years, if all goes well, the fence will look like a wall of ivy. Male dogs will love this. And outside the fence, there's a little more acreage for leashed dogs who want to lounge around on the grass and/or have a picnic with their people pals. What a peachy idea!

The park is at the corner of White Oak Avenue and Victory Boulevard. (818) 785-5798.

DIVERSIONS

Wash your dog: Sure, there's the tub method of scrubbing your dog, but you have to deal with hoisting your dog in and out, and there are all those wet and smelly stray hairs to confront afterward. (Even if you think you've cleaned out every hair, they always float up to haunt you during your next bath.) There's always the garden hose method, but it's cold and the water has a way of dribbling onto your shoes (and if your dog maneuvers just right, into your face). But if you take your dog to U Wash Doggy, your pooch-bathing troubles will be down the drain. The tubs are waist high, you don't have to clean them afterward (much less bathe in them), and shampoo, brushes, and combs are provided. The cost: $10 to $14, depending on your dog's size. There are five U Wash Doggy locations in Los Angeles County. This one's at 17336 Ventura Boulevard; (818) 906-7200.

GLENDALE

PARKS, BEACHES, AND RECREATION AREAS

• Brand Park 🐾 🐾 🐾 ½ *See* 🄬 *on pages 590–591.*

If you feel as if you're on the estate of William Randolph Hearst when visiting this green and verdant park, you're not far off. It's actually the former property of the late real estate tycoon Leslie C. Brand, aka "The Father of Glendale."

Upon entering the park, you'll be greeted by a great white Moorish/Indian-style mansion. The mansion is now a library, surrounded by lush, shaded land. You and your leashed dog can pass an afternoon in perfect serenity here. Go ahead, pretend it's your estate. Relax, read, sniff the flowers, and have a little picnic.

If you prefer a little exercise with your lounging, there's a fire road that takes you through the park and up to a ridge with a great view. This hike is not for the fair of foot: It's almost a six-mile round-trip and, to put it mildly, it's not flat. But it's one of the more enjoyable hikes we found in the Los Angeles area. And if you want to keep going, there are ways to access the thousands of acres of open space that lie outside the park's perimeter. Unfortunately, the leash law applies in this area, too.

Exit Interstate 5 on Western Avenue and go northeast about 1.5 miles. The road will take you to the park's magnificent library entrance. (818) 548-2000.

• **Dunsmore Park** 🐾 🐾 ½ *See* ⓯ *on pages 590–591.*

If, after a hike at the dusty, rugged George Deukmejian Wilderness Park (see below), you and your pooch are longing for mowed green grass, come here. It's only 10 blocks away and has many signs of civilization, including water fountains, shaded picnic areas, a large playground, and a fenced-in ball field.

The directions are the same as they are for George Deukmejian Wilderness Park, but you'll drive only four blocks north of Foothill Boulevard on Dunsmore Avenue. (818) 548-2000.

• **George Deukmejian Wilderness Park** 🐾 🐾 🐾 ½
See ⓰ *on pages 590–591.*

When we first heard the name of this park, we thought someone was making a joke. The words "George Deukmejian" and the word "wilderness" were often used in the same sentence when he was governor, but more like: "That *George Deukmejian*, he should have been more concerned about *wilderness*."

A couple of locals told us that back in the late '80s, the Duke was actually against setting aside this large parcel of land for a park. But he was finally sold on it when a clever environmentalist came up with the idea to name the park after him. Whether this is true or just a semi-urban myth, dogs can be grateful to the governor for making room for this 700-acre square of land.

This isn't what you'd call a breathtaking park. It can be very dry and dusty, with only an occasional tree to provide relief from the sun in these chaparral-covered hills. But the dogs we've seen cavorting around the park really love it here. They seem to smile as they accompany their leashed people up and down the canyon.

Maybe they're smiling because of the lack of people or the abundance of singing birds. Maybe it's the scents of strange fauna on the couple of miles of dirt road here. Or perhaps they know that if they walk far enough, they'll be in Angeles National Forest, where they can run around in leashless ecstasy. (It will be 100 percent easier to get there once some trails connecting the two areas are completed.) Whatever the case, this is a park that you might not find aesthetically pleasing, but your dog will.

Exit U.S. 101 on Pennsylvania Avenue. Go north a few blocks and turn left at Foothill Boulevard. Drive northwest about six blocks, then turn right on Dunsmore Avenue. The road will lead you into the park in about a mile, where you'll bear right after the sign for the park and drive up a narrow paved road to a dirt parking lot next to a horse corral. The wide, gated road just above the lot is where you'll start your hike. (818) 548-2000.

RESTAURANTS

Hot Wings Cafe: This little restaurant has a shaded outdoor area and a loyal following of dog-toting patrons. 314 North Brand Boulevard; (818) 247-4445.

La Fontana Italian Kitchen: You and your dog will be surrounded by an impressive wrought iron fence as you dine at one of their umbrella-topped tables. 933 North Brand Boulevard; (818) 247-6256.

PLACES TO STAY

Days Inn: Rates are $58 to $74. Small pooches only, please. 450 West Pioneer Street, Glendale, CA 91203; (818) 956-0202.

Vagabond Inn: Rates are $60 to $75. Dogs are $5 extra and are relegated to smoking rooms. 120 West Colorado Street, Glendale, CA 91204; (818) 240-1700.

DOGGY DAYS

Catch your dog kissing Santa Claus: Dogs who have the holiday spirit adore the poochy Christmas party hosted by the Glendale Humane Society each December. In exchange for a small (or, if you prefer, large) donation, your dog gets to hang out with other happy dogs, eat tasty treats, and pay a visit to Santa. He can even have his picture taken with the big man. The money goes to food and vet care for the Humane Society's pets. The Humane Society is located at 717 West Ivy Street. Call (818) 242-1128 for details.

GLENDORA

PARKS, BEACHES, AND RECREATION AREAS

Only one park allows dogs, but it's a doozy.

• **Big Dalton Canyon Wilderness Park** 🐾 🐾 🐾 ½
See ⑰ on pages 590–591.

This is among our favorite non-national forest parks in this part of Los Angeles County. It's so remote, so wild, and so unused that you'll barely believe you're in a major metropolis. Big Dalton Canyon Wilderness Park is for people who don't want perfectly mowed park meadows, strict rules, tennis courts, and droning freeways. The only hitch in this otherwise wild park is that dogs are supposed to be leashed.

The deeper you venture into the park, the farther you'll get from any signs of civilization. You can pull over at any of a few tiny (one- to two-car) parking areas near various trailheads. Since the park is part of a canyon, the trails won't always be easy, but they're rarely too rugged. The park is made up almost entirely of forestland, so you usually won't have to worry about the sun melting you.

What's especially wonderful about this park is that it extends into Angeles National Forest, a four-paw piece of Dog Heaven (see page 749). This particular section of the forest is the 27-square-mile San Dimas Experimental Forest, where watersheds from two acres to 9,000 acres are used to test land-management measures to increase water yield.

As usual in this area, be aware that mountain lions live and dine here. When we last visited, there were several signs posted for a poor lost dachshund who may have run into a hungry feline.

A quick heads-up: A ranger here told us that there was a bad incident involving a dog recently (but he didn't go into details), and said there's a chance the dog-friendly policy here could change. You may want to call before you visit, just in case.

This park takes some patience to find, but it's well worth it. Exit Interstate 210 at Auto Centre Drive and follow the signs toward Glendora for a few blocks. Go right on Lone Hill Avenue. At Alosta Avenue, turn left. In just under a mile, turn right on Loraine Avenue. In about 20 blocks, go right on Sierra Madre Avenue. Drive about eight blocks to Glendora Mountain Road and go left. Finally, turn right at Big Dalton Canyon Road, which will take you into the park. Park officials say there's a possibility that the county will soon start charging a user fee for the trails it maintains. Call (626) 914-8228 to find out the latest.

GRANADA HILLS

PARKS, BEACHES, AND RECREATION AREAS

• **Moonshine Canyon Park** 🐾 🐾 🐾½ See ⑱ on pages 590–591.

Our favorite part of this fairly narrow, twisty park is to the north of Highway 118. Within about two-thirds of a mile of the highway, you'll start to see the park and entries into it on your left.

Pull over and park on the road. (You'll see the parking possibilities on the southbound side of the street.) Enter the park at the trailheads that jut out of the edge of the canyon. You'll make a quick descent into the canyon bottom. Once there, it's best to go left on the trail. Going right will take you to a few dicey spots full of abandoned washing machines and cars, then to a busy road. The trail to the left, however, takes you alongside a creek, past brushy hills and the occasional songbird.

The hike is fairly secluded, with only an occasional glimpse of a house on a ridge. This is good and bad. It's good if you and your dog need to get away from civilization and see hardly a soul on the trail. It's not so good if you're worried about who might be lurking in the bushes. Remember: At all large urban parks, it's better to hike with a human companion than alone with your pooch. If you feel at all unsure about the safety of the park, go with someone else or don't go at all.

Exit Highway 118 at Tampa Avenue. If you drive south, the park will be immediately on your right. It stretches to the south along Tampa Avenue for another mile. If you drive north on Tampa Avenue, the road doesn't come very close to the park until after the golf course. The park will be on your left. (818) 363-3556.

• **O'Melveny Park** 🐾🐾🐾½ *See* ⑲ *on pages 590–591.*

This 672-acre park offers so many great hiking opportunities that your dog won't know which trail to try first.

Joe would like to suggest a fairly flat two-mile hike that takes you along a tree-lined creek at the bottom of the canyon here. It's often pretty green, and the creek actually has water in it, so it's not like so many dry L.A. County canyon parks.

Joe likes this park because he knows he's going to get a picnic after his leisurely hike. The picnic tables are plentiful, and they're at the beginning/end of this particular hike, so he knows if we don't eat upon entering, we'll definitely have a bite before leaving.

Exit Interstate 5 at Balboa Boulevard and drive south about a mile to Orozco Street. Turn right and drive to the parking lot for the picnic area. The trail starts at the north end of the picnic area. For info on tougher hikes in this park, call (818) 363-3556.

HARBOR CITY

PARKS, BEACHES, AND RECREATION AREAS

• **Harbor Regional Park** 🐾🐾 *See* ⑳ *on pages 590–591.*

This 210-acre park between Harbor City and Wilmington is right beside a huge oil refinery. Yum, yum. The air is often an otherworldly hue. It's not the most appetizing place, but you can manage to stomach a picnic here. To the park's credit, there's a good-sized lake along the east end. It may not be a prime fishing spot, but at least it's good old H_2O.

The best thing about this park is its proximity to Interstate 110. If you have a dog who's in dire need during a Sunday drive, a jaunt to this park won't take you far off course. Exit Interstate 110 at Highway 1/Pacific Coast Highway and drive west a short half mile. The entrance is on your left. (310) 548-7515.

HERMOSA BEACH

PARKS, BEACHES, AND RECREATION AREAS

Dogs aren't allowed at any of Hermosa Beach's beaches.

• **Hermosa Valley Greenbelt** 🐾🐾½ *See* ㉑ *on pages 590–591.*

This long, narrow strip of green runs 30 blocks—the entire length of the city. It's got a pleasant soft dirt/chipped bark path down the middle, which leashed dogs really enjoy treading on. It's shaded in parts and can be fairly quiet, considering that it's sandwiched by two roads. But it's quite narrow, not ideal for a dog who likes to do heavy-duty exploring.

You can enter the park almost anywhere along Ardmore Avenue or Valley Street. The park continues north into Manhattan Beach (see Manhattan

Beach Parkway Park, page 621). (310) 318-0280.

RESTAURANTS

Le Petite Cafe: "We are very happy to tell you we are very dog-friendly," announced the manager when last we spoke. Dogs can join you at the outdoor eating bar, where you can get a great omelette or a beefy burger. 190 Hermosa Avenue; (310) 379-1400.

Martha's 22nd Street Grill: They'll often let your dog sit beside you at the outside tables here, but if it's crowded, you'll be asked to tie your dog up to one of the poles on the side. The food is really good—and good for you, too. The menu includes apple pancakes, Monte Cristo sandwiches, and veggie burgers. 25 22nd Street; (310) 376-7786.

HOLLYWOOD

Tinseltown just isn't what it used to be. The wealth of Art Deco architecture and grandiose theaters has faded. The half-mile Hollywood Walk of Fame is home to the homeless (although there are plans in the works to improve the area). But it's still worth visiting, for the myth and lure of Hollywood will never completely fade. (If you visit toward dusk, you may be glad you brought your dog.) Meanwhile, if you can foot the bill, a stay in the fabulous Chateau Marmont (below) might restore a little of the old glow of Hollywood for you and your dog.

PARKS, BEACHES, AND RECREATION AREAS

• **Runyon Canyon Park** 🐾🐾🐾🐾 🐕 *See* **22** *on pages 590–591.*

Dogs are allowed to be their leash-free selves at this 125-acre undeveloped park. It's full of overgrown weeds and brush, but dogs don't care. In fact, they like it this way. Besides, there are plenty of trees to keep their interest while they walk up and down the hilly paths here.

And while it happened a long time ago, Joe thought you might want to know a little Hollywood lore a park ranger told us: This is the very same park where Errol Flynn was caught with a minor, causing a major public scandal. (Was this at the same time he was making the film *Assault of the Rebel Girls?*)

The park is on Fuller Avenue, north of Franklin Place. (213) 485-5572.

PLACES TO STAY

Chateau Marmont Hotel: This is that grand, white, castle-like building that makes you do a double take as you're driving on Sunset. Yes, dogs really are allowed to stay in this legendary Hollywood hideaway. Joe Dog was on his best behavior when we checked it out, walking rather regally and not even stopping to scratch his ears.

The chateau, which opened in 1929, is modeled after an elegant Loire Valley castle. You'll hear a lot of French around here. Actually, the staffers speak several languages, including "discreet." That last language has helped make the chateau very popular with Hollywood's icons over the decades.

Huge suites and romantic bungalows offer privacy, and many are set among lush, peaceful gardens. There's something for nearly every robust budget, from a 400-square-foot bedroom ($205) to a two-bedroom penthouse suite with two bathrooms, a dressing area, a large living room with hardwood floor and working fireplace, a full kitchen, a formal dining room, and a 1,250-square-foot private terrace with great views of Hollywood ($1,800). I think that's the room Joe wanted, but we ended up elsewhere. (The Motel 6 in Long Beach, to be exact. Hey, you can't tell one place from the other when the lights are out. Well, not when there's no moon and you're sleeping. Deeply.)

Dogs pay a $100 pooch fee per visit. 8221 Sunset Boulevard, Hollywood, CA 90046; (213) 656-1010 or (800) 242-8328.

Hollywood Celebrity Hotel: Huge dogs are welcome. The owners love dogs. In fact, you may run into the hotel's resident pooch and get licked to death. Rates are $55 to $89. There's a $50 pooch deposit. 1775 Orchid Avenue, Hollywood, CA 90028; (213) 850-6464.

DIVERSIONS

Compare paw prints: On a recent visit to the forecourt of Mann's Chinese Theatre, Joe found out his paws are as big as the heels of Gene Autry's boots. Since he's an old Western movie buff (we've caught him watching Westerns on TV when he's alone), it was doubtless a thrill for him to see that he could, if necessary, walk a mile in Autry's boots. You and your dog can spend part of a fun-filled Hollywood afternoon measuring your feet and paws against the footprints of the stars. Be sure to bring a camera. Everyone else will have one, and your dog is likely to have his mug snapped more than once. (213) 464-8111.

Walk on the stars: When you're done comparing shoe sizes with the stars at the Chinese Theatre, take your feet for a stroll down the Hollywood Walk of Fame. It's on Hollywood Boulevard, between Gower Street and Sycamore Avenue, and along Vine Street, from Sunset Boulevard to Yucca Street. More than 2,500 celebs are immortalized with stars planted into the sidewalk featuring their names. The walk is free, but be prepared for a barrage of homeless people and scam artists with their hands out. (213) 469-8311.

INGLEWOOD

PARKS, BEACHES, AND RECREATION AREAS

•**Edward Vincent Jr. Park** 🐾🐾🐾 *See* ㉓ *on pages 590–591.*

With 55 acres of hills, meadows, and trees, this park is large enough for a good walk with your good leashed dog, but not so big that you're going to get lost. The path through the park is wide, so you, your dog, and a passerby all won't be squished together as you mosey along.

The best place to park is along Warren Lane, near Centinela Avenue. (310) 412-5370.

IRWINDALE

PARKS, BEACHES, AND RECREATION AREAS

•**Santa Fe Dam Recreation Area** 🐾🐾🐾 *See* ㉔ *on pages 590–591.*

When you're approaching this large county park, you'll find it hard to believe anything but industry could exist here. The area is utterly fraught with unsightly evidence of rampant "progress."

But in the middle of it all is a big patch of green doing its best to fend off the onslaught of civilization. It's not the most attractive park in the world, but it's a commendable attempt.

The park's Santa Fe Reservoir is a decent place to share a picnic with your dog. You can also fish for trout or launch a boat here for a relaxing morning on the water. You won't exactly feel like you're in the middle of Wisconsin, but it's better than some water holes we've seen down here. If you want to know what's going on with the fish, call the 24-hour fishing hot line at (626) 334-0713.

The best time you can have with your dog at this park is if you take a hike on the nature trail. Signs and pamphlets point out the flora and fauna you'll come across in the 1,000-acre nature area. The trail provides a good hike, but it's not without its sad side: As if the surrounding scenery were not enough of a reminder, signs tell you how humans have destroyed the habitat. Do your part to protect it, and make sure your dog is leashed and doesn't disturb the birds and beasts here.

There's a $6 fee per vehicle, which you can avoid by parking on a nearby street. (If you have the $6, keep in mind that the county park system is financially devastated and can use every penny to keep parks running.) Exit Interstate 210 at Irwindale Avenue and go south about 1.5 miles. Turn right at Arrow Highway, and within a few blocks turn right again at the signs for the park. To get to the nature trail, bear to the right after the entry kiosk and follow the signs. (626) 962-5070.

LAKEVIEW TERRACE

PARKS, BEACHES, AND RECREATION AREAS

• **Hansen Dam Recreation Area** 🐾 🐾 🐾 ½ *See* ㉕ *on pages 590–591.*

This is 1,400 acres of hills, trees, shrubs, and grassy meadows. A lake used to be the center of attention here, but it's gone for a while during a long process of reclamation. The lake will probably be its old self again by 1999. Until then, try the equestrian trails or the bike path. Leashed dogs seem to prefer the horse trails. They just smell better, and they may find an occasional munchy along the way (but try as your dog might, don't let him nibble these morsels).

From Interstate 210, exit at Osborne Street and follow the signs for a couple of blocks. (626) 899-4537.

LONG BEACH

The downtown area used to be a pit stop (as in "the pits") for off-duty Navy folks. Porn shops, prostitutes, and sleazy saloons were the big draw.

But in the last decade, the city has stripped these seedy-if-colorful images from its repertoire and become kind of a classy joint. At least parts of it have. Other sections are still dilapidated and somewhat shoddy. Fortunately, the waterfront really shines. These days, the worst problem is the smog, which can be a choking green haze some hot afternoons.

The best attraction here for dogs has nothing to do with the upgraded downtown or waterfront. It's a dog-exercise area where dogs are free to run around *sans* leash (see Recreation Park, below). It's the only park for many, many miles where you don't have to sneak to let your dog get the kind of exercise she craves.

PARKS, BEACHES, AND RECREATION AREAS

Dogs aren't allowed at any Long Beach beaches.

•**El Dorado Regional Park** 🐾🐾🐾½ *See ㉖ on pages 590–591.*

You and your dog can fish in the lakes here, watch dozens of ducks waddle around, stroll down shaded winding paths, or frolic together on the park's numerous huge fields of green.

Pooches have to be leashed, so it's not quite as dog heavenly as it could be. But you don't find too many 450-acre parks in these parts, so your pooch will be pleased as punch to visit here.

Fees are $3 per vehicle on weekdays, $5 on weekends and holidays, but free street parking is available on some of the side streets. Exit Interstate 605 at Spring Street and drive west about a quarter mile to the park's entrance, which will be on your right. The nature study area of the park, where dogs aren't allowed, will be on your left. (562) 570-3100.

•**Recreation Park** 🐾🐾🐾🐾 🐕 *See ㉗ on pages 590–591.*

Pooches passing through or living in Long Beach are extremely lucky dogs. The city has one of the best dog runs around. It's an incredibly fun, attractive park for leashless dogs and their people.

The fenced-in park has about two acres worth of grass with a few big old shade trees, a couple of picnic tables, and running water for running dogs. Dogs tremble with excitement as they approach. It's wonderful to watch their joy as they bound from one end of the park to the other, somersaulting and crashing into each other with gleeful abandon.

If all this giddiness makes your tiny dog tremble with fear instead of excitement, he's in luck. The park's most recent addition is a fenced enclosure for small dogs. Most small dogs think they're big dogs and don't seem to realize they come up to the ankles of some dogs who visit here, so they don't need this enclosure. But for those tiny pooches who are a little more cognizant of their situation, this "park within a park" is just what the vet ordered. Miriam Yarden, a pet psychologist and the dynamic force behind this park's founding, is greatly responsible for this petite-pooch paradise. Three yips and a yap for Miriam.

If you have a herding dog, you may witness an interesting phenomenon: A golf course abuts two sides of the dog park, and collies and others of their ilk routinely run after the little golf carts that pass by, perhaps trying to get them back to their herd. It's amusing, and the cart drivers don't seem to mind since a fence separates them from the well-intentioned dogs.

Exit Interstate 405 at Bellflower Boulevard and drive south about two miles to Seventh Street. Turn right and drive about another mile to the sign for the park's maintenance yard and dog park. Turn right again and park in the lot next to the dog run. Dogs are allowed in other parts of Recreation Park, but they must be leashed. (562) 570-3100.

• **Shoreline Park** 🐾 🐾 🐾 *See ㉘ on pages 590–591.*
If your dog appreciates a good view, this park's for her. More likely, she'll appreciate the potent smells to be found here.

Eyes and noses have a feast at this 40-acre shoreline park. Among the sights you can see clearly, if the smog isn't like pea soup, are Shoreline Village, the marina, and the *Queen Mary*. Among the smells dogs can snort are tracks from other dogs who frequent the park, fish being caught in the lagoon, and enticing food from nearby restaurants.

The only trees here are palms, so there's little shade on hot days. If you're going to have a picnic at the many tables, make sure you pick a cool day.

From downtown Long Beach, take Pine Street to its southernmost end and turn right. (Note: At press time, it was possible that the park would be temporarily closed in the near future for construction of an aquarium. Please call before visiting to check on the park's status.) (562) 570-1581.

RESTAURANTS
Dogs are banned from the charming Shoreline Village shops and restaurants. Too bad, because it's the perfect atmosphere for well-behaved pooches and their people. Unfortunately, Long Beach just isn't long on dog-friendly restaurants. Here's one for the hungry pooch in your life:

Johnny Rockets: If you and your dog are fans of the '50s, you'll feel right at home at the outside tables here. Try the chocolate malted. It's really decadent. 245 Pine Avenue; (562) 983-1332.

PLACES TO STAY
Guest House Hotel: This one's close to Cal State Long Beach. Rates are $59 to $149. Small dogs only, please. 5325 East Pacific Coast Highway, Long Beach, CA 90804; (562) 597-1341.

Long Beach Hilton at the World Trade Center: This is a beautiful hotel in a jazzy location. Unfortunately, only very small dogs (under 20 pounds) can stay here. Rates are $109 to $225. Two World Trade Center, Long Beach, CA 90831; (562) 983-3400.

Motel 6: Rates are $47 for one adult, $6 for a second adult. One small pooch per room. 5665 East Seventh Street, Long Beach, CA 90804; (562) 597-1311.

DIVERSIONS
Cruise to Catalina with your canine: You and your pooch can board a fast (about 75 minutes) ferry to Catalina from Long Beach. There's nothing like a little sea spray in the face to make you wake up and realize what a good traveling buddy you have. See the Diversions section under Catalina for details about the ferry service (page 601).

LOS ANGELES
Many communities within the city have their own listings. See individual headings if you don't find what you need here.

PARKS, BEACHES, AND RECREATION AREAS
• **Elysian Park** 🐾 🐾 🐾 ½ *See ㉙ on pages 590–591.*
The views of Dodger Stadium and downtown Los Angeles don't get much

better than from this 585-acre park. The hills here often rise above the smog, and the Los Angeles skyline actually looks attractive from a couple of high-altitude picnic spots.

Angel's Point is a must-see for leashed dogs and baseball fans. Dogs like the breezes that blow in from the different sections of the city. Ball fans enjoy being able to peer into a little segment of Dodger Stadium. The park is conveniently nestled between Interstate 5, U.S. 101, and Interstate 110. To get to Angel's Point and the many roads and trails beyond, exit Interstate 5 at Stadium Way and follow the signs to the park. Once you're in the park, take your first left, Elysian Park Drive. If you're on your way to drop off friends at a Dodger game and your dog needs a quick walk, take your first right after you enter the park. It's a very green, tree-laden area that won't take you far off track from your destination. (213) 485-5054.

• **Ernest E. Debs Park** 😊 😊 😊 *See* **30** *on pages 590–591.*

There's something for almost every dog at this large park. Adventurous leashed dogs can accompany you along the fire roads here, while pooches who prefer to lounge around can stretch out on the manicured grass. And those who prefer to eat with you can do so with gusto at the dozens of picnic tables in the civilized part of the park.

The park is located between the communities of Lincoln Heights and Highland Park. The best way to enjoy any of this difficult-to-access park is to take the entrance just south of Terrill Avenue, off Monterey Road. Be forewarned: The speed bumps will drive you crazy. (213) 485-5054.

• **Griffith Park** 😊 😊 😊 ½ *See* **31** *on pages 590–591.*

If only this 4,017-acre park had an off-leash trail, or at least a few acres for a fenced-in dog exercise spot, it would be a four-paw chunk of Dog Heaven. But alas, much of the acreage is taken up by such non-dog attractions as the city's zoo, an observatory and planetarium, a bird sanctuary, an outdoor theater, an equestrian center, golf courses, tennis courts, a swimming pool, a transportation museum, and a Western heritage museum.

Fortunately, two-thirds of the park is wild and wonderful, straddling the eastern end of the Santa Monica Mountains. You can explore the undeveloped sections of park via more than 57 miles of trails! This is the U.S.A.'s largest municipal park, and it can be a quite an attractive place considering it's in the middle of three major freeways in the city that puts the "m" in metropolis. About 100 tree species thrive here, including oaks, pines, and even redwoods. Birds are abundant, which makes sense when you consider their alternatives in the urban realities beyond the park's perimeter.

With all the trails here (few are very developed), you have myriad choices about what kind of hiking you and your dog can do. Here are two suggestions to get you started:

1) Get a map before you arrive, so you'll have time to plan out your trek. Call the ranger headquarters at (213) 665-5188 and they'll send you a free map showing all the trails.

2) Be careful. Because of the remoteness of some of the trail areas, they've become dumping grounds for bodies. And we're not talking bodies of literature, bodies of evidence, or even pigeon and squirrel bodies. Even with

your dog at your side, you may not want to venture too far by yourself.

One fun hike you can take is the one that winds you as close as is legally possible to the infamous "HOLLYWOOD" sign. From central Hollywood (Franklin Avenue and Beachwood Drive), go north on Beachwood Drive about 1.5 miles. At the street's northernmost end, it will come together with Hollyridge Drive. Park around here, and after walking about a block, you'll come to a wide trail on your left. It's not marked, but it will take you about 1.5 miles up Mount Lee, where you'll be stopped by an ungracious fence. The fence is there at least in part because of the radio tower at the hilltop. (Maybe they also don't want dogs doing leg lifts on this oft-molested sign.)

One of the most entertaining activities you and your dog can share at Griffith Park is a train ride. (See Diversions, page 620.)

U.S. 101, Interstate 5, and Highway 134 surround the park. A popular entry is off Interstate 5 at Los Feliz Boulevard. (213) 665-5188.

• **Hancock Park** 🐾 🐾 *See* **32** *on pages 590–591.*

Take your dog to a tar pit that once trapped scads of Ice Age animals! What fun! The tar still bubbles up from its pondlike setting, but fear not: It's well fenced, so even the most ardent water dogs will be safe from the alluring mire. You can see how animals were drawn here thinking it was a place to splash around and guzzle some liquid refreshments. A few replicas of mammoths charging into the tar pit now add a prehistoric air to the park.

The park itself has enough green grass for a pleasant stroll, but it's not big enough for a major exercise experience. There's a snack bar near the tar pit, but hanging around here probably won't give you an appetite, since on a hot day, it can smell like roofing tar.

Hancock Park is located alongside the George C. Page Museum, which houses skeletons and re-creations of formidable prehistoric animals trapped in the Rancho La Brea Tar Pits during the Ice Age. The Los Angeles County Museum of Art flanks the park's other side, so the park is convenient if you have to drop off a culturally minded friend.

The park is located between Sixth Street and Wilshire Boulevard and Curson Avenue and Ogden Drive. Your best bet for free parking is along Sixth Street. The park is "owned" by one government entity and operated by another, and no one seems to want to take phone calls for it. In fact, last time we talked to them, no one even knew the park existed. Scary! Well, here's the number for the L.A. County Department of Parks and Recreation, which at one point was aware of this park's existence: (213) 738-2961.

• **Kenneth Hahn State Recreation Area** 🐾 🐾 🐾 ½
See **33** *on pages 590–591.*

Here's a Los Angeles–area park where the birds singing in the trees are actually louder than the drone of the freeways! The hilly section of this large park is a fascinating place to visit. Not only can you and your leashed dog do some intense hiking, you can also experience the world-uniting feel of the Olympics.

In 1932, the area was the site of the 10th Olympics. Then in 1984, Los Angeles again hosted the Olympics, drawing athletes from 140 nations. To serve as a continual (and growing) reminder of the events, 140 trees have been planted together on the hills where the 1932 events occurred. Each tree represents a nation that took part in the 23rd Olympics.

Watching their young leaves blowing in the breeze is enough to send patriotic shivers up your spine. It's also enough to make most male dogs stretch their leashes to pay their kind of homage to these saplings. But they can't. The trees are fenced in until they are big enough to withstand such assaults.

But there are many other trees to sniff in this large park. Several trails branch out from the parking lot at the Olympic Forest. Most take you up the hill, but you can also hike down by the lake and stream in the adjoining section of park.

Fees are $3 per vehicle on weekends and holidays. Driving north on La Cienega Boulevard in the Ladera Heights neighborhood north of Inglewood, you'll pass an oil drilling site, then come to signs for the park. Although it's a state park, it's operated by Los Angeles County. (213) 298-3660.

• **Lincoln Park and Recreation Center** 🐾🐾🐾 *See ❸ on pages 590–591.*

There's plenty of shade here, so it's great for leashed dogs in the summer. And there's a really funky Egyptian-themed playground for kids, so the young ones like it year-round. The 46-acre park is centered around a small lake, where neighborhood folks come with their fishing rods and a lunch and spend the day. The park is also home to the fascinating Plaza de la Raza.

Exit Interstate 10 at Soto Street and drive north to Valley Boulevard. Turn left and then go right at the next intersection. There's usually plenty of street parking. (213) 237-1726.

• **Pan Pacific Regional Park** 🐾🐾 *See ❸ on pages 590–591.*

Set next to CBS Television City and the Farmers Market, this park is in a fun, central location. It's a long, narrow park that stretches between Beverly Boulevard and Third Street at Curson Avenue, on the former site of the exquisite 1930s Pan Pacific building (which an arsonist burned down in 1989). It's primarily made up of playing fields, but a paved path winds through the other sections of the park. There's not much shade, so it can be relentlessly hot on summer days.

At the Beverly Boulevard end of the park is a memorial to victims of the Holocaust. If you approach it from the opposite side, it's a very moving, powerful monument. (213) 485-5054.

• **Silver Lake Park** 🐾🐾🐾½ 🐕 *See ❸ on pages 590–591.*

Joe's jaw dropped when he learned about Silver Lake's recently opened dog park. It's hard to believe, but right in the middle of what has traditionally been the Land o' Leashes (that is, in the metro region of the city rec and parks department) lies this small, fenced, leash-free mecca.

The trees here are relatively wee, but dogs still are relatively happy weeing on them. Someday when the trees get big and strong, they won't mind so much. The park also has water for pooches and people. The benches here make for more comfy human visits, and also make a great place to sit down and talk to a new human acquaintance. (The park draws lots of singles from the surrounding community. We've heard there have been some matches made in heaven here.)

The park is on Silver Lake Boulevard, just south of Silver Lake and a bit north of Sunset Boulevard. (213) 485-3287.

RESTAURANTS

A Votre Sante: This is among our favorite California restaurants. The outdoor area is lovely, they like dogs, and the food is healthful and very delicious. 345 North La Brea Avenue; (213) 857-0412.

Melrose Baking Company: If you want great baked goods at a fun outdoor setting, don't skip this place. 7356 Melrose Avenue; (213) 651-3165.

Melrose Place: Graf, a sweet collie-shepherd mix, wrote to us via his person, Donald Gilbert Christian, to tell us about this terrific restaurant he sniffed out. "It's . . . one of the nicest restaurants in the Los Angeles area," he wrote. And indeed it is wonderful. The food is excellent—kind of nouvelle California with a healthful Japanese touch. And the atmosphere is just as delectable, with a good-looking covered patio that can seat 40 people and a few good dogs. Regular dogs get offered a bowl of water. Graf himself is a regular, who can be found many Saturday evenings happily ensconced under Donald's table. He's the big black dog with the smile on his snout. 650 North La Cienega Boulevard; (310) 657-2227.

Nature Club Cafe: We adore this cafe with great vegetarian food. It's on a lively and lovely part of Melrose, but the atmosphere at the outdoor tables is mellow. Lots of folks bring their dogs. 7174 Melrose Avenue; (213) 931-8994.

Stir Crazy: They love dogs at this coffee shop. "We don't discriminate against anyone," one of the managers told us. 6917 Melrose Avenue; (213) 934-4656.

PLACES TO STAY

Please see other cities and communities (like Beverly Hills or West Hollywood) for nearby hotels.

Beverly Hills Plaza Hotel: This is certainly an attractive hotel, but only dogs who weigh less than your typical Thanksgiving turkey are allowed to stay here. (The weight limit is 15 pounds.) There's a $100 fee for these petite pooches and a $500 deposit, so bring the bankroll or the credit card if you decide to stay here. Rates are $155 to $285. 10300 Wilshire Boulevard, Los Angeles, CA 90024; (310) 275-5575.

Century Wilshire Hotel: Here's another fine hotel on the downtown Wilshire strip that permits only the most diminutive doggies. It's a good place to stay if you had your heart set on the Beverly Hills Plaza Hotel (see above) but your dog exceeds the size limit by five pounds. Dogs here can be up to a whopping 20 pounds. Such discrimination in such an open-minded city . . . Tsk, tsk. Some suites with kitchens are available. Room rates are $75 to $225 and include a continental breakfast. There's a $150 fee (yes, fee, not deposit) for dogs. For a 15-pound dog, that comes out to $10 per pound, if you want to look at things that way. 10776 Wilshire Boulevard, Los Angeles, CA 90024; (310) 474-4506 or (800) 421-7223.

Checkers Hotel: This downtown hotel is really special, but dogs don't get to swim in the rooftop pool, despite the fact that the hotel was named after Richard Nixon's pooch (who was small, as all dogs who stay here are supposed to be). Rooms are $189 to $229. Suites range up to $1,000. Dogs are charged a onetime $25 fee. 535 South Grand Avenue, Los Angeles, CA 90071; (213) 624-0000.

Continental Plaza: This one's near the airport, which is convenient for traveling pooches. Rates are $65 to $105. There's a $75 deposit for dogs, who also have to pay $10 extra nightly. 9750 Airport Boulevard, Los Angeles, CA 90045; (310) 645-4600 or (800) 529-4683.

Holiday Inn—City Center: Pooches under 30 pounds are okay here, as long as they pay a $30 deposit. Rates are $90 to $130. 1020 South Figueroa Street, Los Angeles, CA 90017; (213) 748-1291.

Hotel Bel-Air: This is not your typical Los Angeles hotel. It's more like a hotel you'd see in paradise. Before you continue reading, it's only fair to give you the room/suite rates up front: The range is from $350 to $2,500 nightly. Dogs are $250 extra for the length of your stay. If you're still reading and haven't turned to the nearest Motel 6 listing, you'll be pleased to know that dogs are allowed to roam almost everywhere on the gorgeous, lush 11.5-acre garden setting that enfolds the captivating rooms and suites. You won't have to go to a park to exercise your pooch. "We've had some wonderful dogs stay with us. We like to make everyone feel right at home, humans or not," says one of the managers here. Many of the suites and rooms offer fireplaces and hot tubs, but there are so many distinct decors that you should call ahead and discuss your options with the very personable hotel staff. 701 Stone Canyon Road, Los Angeles, CA 90077; (310) 472-1211 or (800) 648-4097.

Hotel Sofitel Ma Maison: Oui, French poodles do feel at home here. In fact, most dogs do, thanks to the dog-friendly attitude of the management. "We love dogs here," more than one dog-happy manager has told us. This big, attractive hotel is near the best of Beverly Hills. Rates are $209 to $500. 8555 Beverly Boulevard, Los Angeles, CA 90048; (310) 278-5444.

Vagabond Inn Figueroa: Rates are $62 to $84. Dogs are $5 extra. 3101 South Figueroa Street, Los Angeles, CA 90007; (213) 746-1531.

DIVERSIONS

Bless your beast: Maybe your dog rummages through rubbish and maybe he chews your shoes, but you've probably still got a few thousand reasons to be grateful for his companionship. You may bless your dog every day, but why not let a pro do it? Whatever your religious persuasion, you can get your pooch blessed at a couple of ceremonies around town.

The smaller of the celebrations is at the St. Francis of Assisi Church at 1523 Golden Gate Avenue. It's held in early October, around St. Francis Day The ceremony is inside the church, so you may not want to bring your cows or your non-house-trained dogs. Call (213) 664-1305 for the exact time and date.

The big animal blessing bash is held in February or March, sometime during Holy Week. It's downtown but outside, so horses and other giant four-footed critters can accompany you and your dog. This blessing is held right across from Our Lady Queen of the Angels Church at 535 North Main

Street. Call (213) 629-3101 for more information.

Choo on this: From your seat aboard one of Griffith Park's miniature trains, you and your dog will see goats, horses, llamas, pigs, and a little Native American town. Your dog's ears will flap with wonder as the open-air train chugs gently along. The ride lasts only about eight minutes, but the price is right: Dogs go for free. Kids are $1.25 and adults are $1.75. (That's less than one-fourth the price of a movie—and your seat moves!) The train departs dozens of times every day from the section of Griffith Park around Los Feliz Boulevard and Riverside Drive. Call (213) 664-6788 for more information.

Take a trip on a tortoise: You and your dog can embark on a couple of fun journeys aboard the infamous "hippie" bus, the Green Tortoise. Please see the "Forget Greyhound; take a Tortoise" listing on page 395 of the San Francisco chapter for more on this adventure.

You can't be Sirius: But you can look at this bright "dog star" and millions of other heavenly bodies when you attend a Los Angeles Astronomical Society star party. Well-behaved, non-klutzy canines are welcome to join you when you observe the universe with other astronomy buffs a few times a year at the Griffith Observatory hill.

If your dog is an angel, but shares certain characteristics with Gerald Ford and Chevy Chase, don't bring him. Telescopes on tripods can tip over easily, and dogs who go bump in the night don't go over well here. These nice folks who share their expensive equipment with the public deserve the utmost in consideration. If they ask you to take your pooch home and come back, for any reason, please respect their wishes. (213) 664-1191.

MALIBU

This mountainous, oceanfront community is L.A.'s final frontier. Too remote for some, too expensive for others, it's one of the more natural and untouched areas in the county. Malibu's combined incorporated and unincorporated areas cover about 45,000 acres and are 27 miles long and up to eight miles wide. Only 27,000 people live here. Compared with the typical Los Angeles ratio of people to acres, this seems like the countryside.

PARKS, BEACHES, AND RECREATION AREAS

Many of the Santa Monica Mountains National Recreation Area parks are located here. See page 594 for information on these wonderful natural areas you and your leashed dog can explore together. Malibu is also home to the only beach in L.A. County where pooches are permitted. In the past, dogs were allowed at a total of four state beaches here, but alas, we're down to only one. Please respect the privilege and tread lightly.

• **Leo Carrillo State Beach** 🐾 🐾 🐾 *See* ⑰ *on pages 590–591.*

Leashed dogs are allowed to trot around a portion of this 6,600-foot-long beach that straddles Los Angeles and Ventura Counties. Dogs can sniff around the beach north of Lifeguard Tower 1 and south of Lifeguard Tower 3. Ask a ranger about this area's location when you pay your $6 parking fee (plus $1 for the dog).

Dogs may also camp at one of the 136 sites here. Dogs prefer the campsites by the beach, but they go fast, so reserve ahead. Sites are $17 to $18. Dogs are $1 extra. Call Parknet at (800) 444-PARK for reservations or (805) 986-8591 for beach info. The beach entrance is on the 36000 block of Pacific Coast Highway, just south of the county border.

RESTAURANTS

Johnnie's New York Pizza: Small dogs are preferred here, but if you've got an angelic larger pooch, you can bring him to eat with you at the outdoor tables if it's not too crowded and it's okay with your neighbors. 22333 West Pacific Coast Highway; (310) 456-1717.

PLACES TO STAY

Leo Carrillo State Beach: See Leo Carrillo State Beach on page 620 for camping information.

MANHATTAN BEACH

Dogs and people usually take an automatic liking to this seaside town. It's a friendly place, with people who stop you in the street to talk about how much they like your dog. This is not that common in these parts, so enjoy it. Unfortunately, the friendly attitude doesn't extend to the city's beaches or parks. Only one allows pooches.

PARKS, BEACHES, AND RECREATION AREAS

•**Manhattan Beach Parkway Park** 🐾🐾1/2 *See* ③ *on pages 590–591.*

This is a jolly green continuation of Hermosa Beach's Hermosa Valley Greenbelt (see page 609). It's skinny and dozens of blocks long, and it's the only public green in town that allows dogs. Leashes are a must.

The park runs along Ardmore Valley Avenue for much of its length. (310) 545-5621.

RESTAURANTS

El Sombrero: They make a mean burrito here. Try one at the sidewalk benches. 1005 Manhattan Avenue; (310) 374-1366.

PLACES TO STAY

Dockweiler Beach RV Park: Got an RV and an urge to cozy up to the ocean? Stay at one of the 118 sites here for a couple of nights. Pets must be leashed, and they can't officially go to the nearby beach. Rates are $15 to $25. Call Parknet at (800) 444-PARK.

From Interstate 405 about 12 miles south of Santa Monica, exit at Imperial West Highway and drive four miles west to Vista del Mar. That's where you'll find the park. Call (310) 322-4951 or (213) 738-2961 for more information.

Residence Inn by Marriott: You and your dog can get a roomy apartment-style suite here. Some come with fireplaces, and all come with a kitchen, which is a mighty convenient feature when traveling with a pooch. Rates are $90 to $200. There's a $75 cleaning fee for dogs, who must also pay $8 extra for each night they stay. 1700 North Sepulveda Boulevard, Manhattan Beach, CA 90266; (310) 546-7627.

MARINA DEL REY

RESTAURANTS

The Cow's End: This is a fun coffeehouse where you can sip your stuff under a canopy. They're so doggone friendly here that your dog may even be offered a tasty dog biscuit if he plays his cards right. 34 Washington Boulevard; (310) 574-1080.

Normandie Bakery & Cafe: The baked goods here are to drool for, as is the French-style food. Dine with doggy at an umbrella-topped table on the big patio. 123 Washington Boulevard; (310) 822-5379.

NEWHALL

PARKS, BEACHES, AND RECREATION AREAS

• **William S. Hart Regional Park** 🐾 🐾 🐾 1/2 *See* 39 *on pages 590–591.*

If you and your dog are fans of the Old West, you must amble on down here. Coming to this park is like getting a personal invitation to the house and ranch of the silent Western movie hero William S. Hart. Unfortunately, Hart isn't around anymore to give you a personal tour, but feel free to peruse the property via a couple of trails. If you get a hankering to check out his hacienda, you can leave your dog at the shaded picnic area with your traveling pardner and take a guided tour.

Dogs have to be leashed at the park. Hart, a cowboy himself, might not have liked that rule, but it's a small price to pay to enjoy the hospitality of the ghost of these here hills. Besides, the property houses a little zoo with farm animals and a compost demonstration site. You don't want your pooch meddling with either.

Exit Highway 14 at San Fernando Road and follow the signs west to the park. (805) 259-0855.

NORTH HOLLYWOOD

PARKS, BEACHES, AND RECREATION AREAS

• **North Hollywood Park and Recreation Center** 🐾 🐾 🐾
See 40 *on pages 590–591.*

Not many parks have giant blue stars on their fences, but after all, this *is* Hollywood's neighbor. The part of the park south of Magnolia Boulevard is the best area for dogs. It's really big—one grand swath of meadow with a large area shaded by tall old trees. There's even a jogging trail around the park.

The southern section of the park is such a generous size that it would be the perfect place for an off-leash dog exercise area, but alas, dogs must be on leash here. Exit Highway 170 at Magnolia Boulevard. Go east a block, then turn right on Tujunga Avenue. The park is immediately on your right. (818) 763-7651.

PACIFIC PALISADES

PARKS, BEACHES, AND RECREATION AREAS

• **Temescal Canyon Park** 🐾 🐾 1/2 *See* 41 *on pages 590–591.*

This park is nearly a mile long, running from Bowdoin Street to the Pacific Coast Highway. It's narrow in places, and at times it seems to disappear, but the bulk of the park is wide enough so that if you want to pull off the path and picnic in the shade, there's plenty of room.

It's a fun walk. We see people running their dogs from the top of the hill down to the ocean. It's green and tranquil, despite the fact that it's bisected by Temescal Canyon Road. (310) 454-1412.

•**Will Rogers State Historic Park** 🐾🐾🐾 *See* ㊷ *on pages 590–591.*

"It's great to be great, but it's greater to be human," said humorist and actor Will Rogers, who made his home here during the 1920s and 1930s. Dogs may not exactly agree with this sentiment, but they do appreciate being able to peruse this 186-acre park.

Leashed dogs may explore along the trails that wind past a polo field, a roping ring, and Rogers' ranch house. Dogs can't go into the ranch house and should stay away from the stables and from the polo fields on weekends, when polo matches are held.

A major warning: Heed the leash law. Rattlesnakes abound in the far reaches of the park, and nosy dogs who are allowed to romp off leash find them fairly frequently. Rangers here say about one dog a month gets bitten in the summer. Half survive it. Half don't. The trail here is wide, and if you stay toward the middle, you'll have no problems.

There's a $6 parking fee, with dogs costing $1 extra. The park is located at 14235 Sunset Boulevard. (310) 454-8212.

RESTAURANTS

Palisades Bakery: Choose from a variety of foods here, from burgers to Chinese food to Indian specialties. Eat at umbrella-covered tables with your pooch. 15231½ La Cruz Drive; (310) 459-6160.

PALOS VERDES ESTATES

PARKS, BEACHES, AND RECREATION AREAS

•**Malaga Park** 🐾 *See* ㊸ *on pages 590–591.*

We mention this tiny park only because it's so close to a really lovely European-style part of this luxurious city. You and your leashed dog can catch a refreshing ocean breeze at Malaga Park, since it's high on a hill. Dogs like to relax on the small plot of lush grass and contemplate what it would be like if their backyard looked like this. People enjoy sitting on the stone benches and contemplating the same thing. In the spring, a little garden comes alive with color. Make sure your leashed dog doesn't think the park is larger than it is and accidentally wander into the flower beds.

From Palos Verdes Drive going west, go right on Via Corta. Park on the street. The park is immediately on your left. Don't blink or you'll miss it. (310) 378-0383.

RESTAURANTS

Rive Gauche: Elegance is the operative word at this four-star French restaurant. Yet the managers gladly permit pooches to dine with you at the patio tables. "We're very dog friendly here," they say. Some patrons have been bringing their dogs here for years, much as they would if this restaurant were in France. One regular told us that sometimes her dog manages to mooch a little something from her waiter. But I don't think that's the norm here. Still, maybe your dog will get lucky.

There's now a canopy over the patio, so you and your *chien* can dine without the sun smacking you in the eyeballs. 320 Tejon Place; (310) 378-0267.

PASADENA

PARKS, BEACHES, AND RECREATION AREAS

Pasadena residents have been fighting to get a much-needed off-leash park or dog-run area for years. As of this book's press time, the battle was still being waged.

Meanwhile, there's an encouraging exception to the leash law. At Brookside, Central, and Victory Parks, dogs may be off leash for training purposes only. And we're not talking about training your dog to hike off leash or chase tennis balls. The training clause is for specific feats that don't cover a lot of ground, such as teaching your dog to come when called, to stay, and to heel.

Armed with this knowledge, a lot more people might decide their dogs need to brush up on their training. But be careful out there; park rangers know the difference between truly training your dog and walking around the park reading the newspaper with your dog. Training hours at the three parks are 7 A.M. to 10 P.M. Monday through Friday and 7 A.M. to 10 A.M. Saturday and Sunday. Dogs are not permitted at playgrounds or reserved picnic areas. For more information, phone (626) 794-0581.

• **Brookside Park** 🐾🐾🐾½ 🐕 **(for restricted training purposes)**
See **44** *on pages 590–591.*
Note: See the introduction to the Pasadena parks section for details on the off-leash training hours and rules here.

Brookside Park, home of the Rose Bowl, is a beautiful place, with roses hither and thither. The park has a playground, ball fields, trees, and acres of green grass. When there are no major games going on, it's a quiet park. There's even a trail you and your leashed pooch can take to get farther away from the madding crowd, in case you happen to be accompanying someone who has only one Rose Bowl ticket.

Exit Interstate 210 at Seco Street and follow the signs to the Rose Bowl. As you approach the Rose Bowl stadium, look for a big green meadow on your left. It's part of this large park complex. (626) 794-0581.

• **Central Park** 🐾🐾½ 🐕 **(for restricted training purposes)**
See **45** *on pages 590–591.*
Note: See the introduction to the Pasadena parks section for details on the off-leash training hours and rules here.

Visiting Old Town Pasadena? Bring your leashed dog here for a little siesta between your cafe-hopping adventures. The park has several tall old trees that boy dogs are wild about, and plenty of other good dog amenities like big grassy areas, a shaded paved path, and lawn bowling. (Okay, they can't bowl, but they enjoy watching for a few seconds.) The park is at Del Mar Boulevard and Fair Oaks Avenue. (626) 794-0581.

• **Eaton Canyon County Park** 😺 😺 😺 ½ *See* **46** *on pages 590–591.*

Sadly, this was one of the worst-hit areas during the 1993 fires. The enchanting old Nature Center building was leveled (although it is scheduled to reopen in August of '98). The rest of the 184-acre park is recuperating, bringing new life to chaparral, coastal sage scrub, and oak woodlands. It's fascinating to visit periodically to watch how a natural area recovers from devastation. Dogs must be leashed—an especially important rule during the healing process here. (626) 398-5420.

• **Lower Arroyo Park** 😺 😺 😺 ½ *See* **47** *on pages 590–591.*

The dirt trails at this park go and go and go until you and your dog are so pooped you can't go anymore. Wander through the bottom of the canyon, safe from cars, free from the sounds of civilization. The canyon bottom is pretty wide, so you'll have your choice of paths. It's really important to keep your dog leashed here, because the park is home to wild animals, and some dogs have been harassing them out of their homes, according to park watchers.

If landlubbing activities like hiking fatigue you, try perfecting your casting skills at the casting pool located next to the parking lot. Take advantage of this park, because the adjoining Arroyo Seco Park in South Pasadena doesn't even allow a dog to set paw inside it.

Take Interstate 210 to its southernmost end. At its termination point, it becomes St. John Avenue. Go two blocks on St. John Avenue and turn right on California Boulevard. In about four blocks, the park will be directly in front of you. Turn right on Arroyo Boulevard and drive a couple of blocks. On your left, you'll find a driveway to the parking lot. (626) 794-0581.

• **Victory Park** 😺 😺 ½ 🐕 **(for restricted training purposes)** *See* **48** *on pages 590–591.*

Note: See the introduction to the Pasadena parks section for details on the off-leash training hours and rules here.

Leashed dogs who enjoy watching people play softball like coming to this 25-acre park. It sports three softball diamonds and a baseball diamond, in addition to some open land and tree-studded picnic areas. Dogs who aren't sports fans can walk with you on the asphalt path that runs through the park.

The park is at Paloma Street and Alda Dena Drive. (626) 794-0581.

PLACES TO STAY

Holiday Inn: This one's a cut above some of the other Holiday Inns in the county, but they'll only take small to medium dogs. Rates are $99 to $164. There's a $50 dog deposit. 303 East Cordova Street, Pasadena, CA 91101; (626) 449-4000.

Millard Campground: This tiny five-tent site is the perfect getaway just north of town. Since it's in Angeles National Forest, your dog is welcome. And outside the campground, he can go off leash on the many first-rate trails here. The beauty of this camping area is that you don't have to make a reservation, and it's free.

Exit Interstate 210 at Lake Avenue and drive north to Loma Alta Drive. Go left on Loma Alta Drive. Follow the signs to the campground. (626) 574-5200.

Vagabond Inn: Rates are $53 to $68. Dogs are $5 extra. 1203 East Colorado Boulevard, Pasadena, CA 91106; (626) 449-3170.

PICO RIVERA

PARKS, BEACHES, AND RECREATION AREAS

• **Pico Park** 🐾 🐾 *See* **49** *on pages 590–591.*

This is your typical, respectable-sized neighborhood park. It's grassy, with picnic tables, a playground, ball fields, and quite a few trees. It's not Dog Heaven, but it's large enough for leashed dogs to at least stretch their hairy legs.

From Interstate 605, take the Beverly Boulevard exit west across the San Gabriel River. The park will be on your left within a few blocks. (562) 942-2000.

POMONA

PARKS, BEACHES, AND RECREATION AREAS

• **Ganesha Park** 🐾 🐾 🐾 *See* **50** *on pages 590–591.*

If you don't feel like paying $6 to get into the nearby Frank G. Bonelli Regional Park (see page 628), try this fee-free park. It's a popular place, but most visitors congregate around the swimming pool, tennis courts, and playground. Leashed dogs can zip around the rest of the park without much fear of crashing into hordes of people. The grassy, rolling hills and flat meadows are perfect for a good romp.

The park is at White Avenue, just north of Interstate 10 and south of the Los Angeles County Fairplex. (909) 620-2321.

PLACES TO STAY

Motel 6: Rates are $35 for one adult, $6 for the second adult. One small dog per room. 2470 South Garey Avenue, Pomona, CA 91766; (909) 591-1871.

Sheraton Suites Fairplex: "The bigger the dog, the better," a staffer here told us. That's the attitude we like to see. If you and your dog are going to be spending some time at the adjacent Fairplex Exhibition Center, this might be the place to stay. It's pretty exotic for this area. Rates are $105 to $115. There's a $75 deposit required for dogs, who also get charged $10 extra nightly. 600 West McKinley Avenue, Pomona, CA 91768; (909) 622-2220.

Shilo Inn Hotel: Rates are $59 to $129. Dogs are $7 extra. They don't want huge pooches. 3200 Temple Avenue, Pomona, CA 91768; (909) 598-0073.

RANCHO PALOS VERDES

PARKS, BEACHES, AND RECREATION AREAS

• **Ladera Linda Community Center** 🐾 🐾 ½ *See* **51** *on pages 590–591.*

This isn't the biggest park in Rancho Palos Verdes, but since it doesn't get nearly as much use as many others, it's one of the better places to take a dog. It covers about 33 acres, much of it devoted to playing fields and open space.

From Palos Verdes Drive in the Portuguese Bend area, go north on Forrestal Drive. The park will be on your left in a few blocks. (310) 541-4566.

REDONDO BEACH

PARKS, BEACHES, AND RECREATION AREAS

Dogs are banned from all city parks, beaches, and open space lands, with one very special exception.

• **Redondo Beach Dog Park** 🐾🐾🐾🐾🐾 🐕 *See ❺❷ on pages 590–591.*

A few years ago, dogs were thrilled to have a 2.5-acre leash-free, fenced park to call their very own, even though there was no shade and much of the park ran under big power lines. After all, before that, dogs couldn't even set paw in any local parks. But now that the park has been expanded and gussied up a bit, dogs are positively ecstatic.

The park is now six big acres. It's divided into three parts—two big parks that switch off being open to give the grass a chance to grow, and one smaller park for small dogs. The park also has about 30 new trees. The trees are currently too small to give shade, but at least they give hope for shade in the near future.

The power lines over a swatch of the park don't do much for the place aesthetically, but dogs don't care. There's doggy drinking water, cool green grass, good sniffs, and lots of other dogs to pal around with. In fact, a survey recently showed that the dog park was the busiest park in the city, with about 1,500 visitors on some of the busy weekends. "The great thing is that it never really seems crowded," says Cindy Szerlip, one of the park's founders.

Driving north on Highway 1, go right on Beryl Street. In about 10 blocks you'll come to Flagler Lane. Go left and take the second entrance into the park. (310) 318-0610.

RESTAURANTS

Surf-Break: Okay, dogs and dog people, you've struck gold here! This family-owned business is so dog-friendly that dogs have been known to run away from home to come here. They supply pooches with water, and will always give a dog a biscuit or two from their bottomless jar of dog treats. Dogs and their people are some of their best customers. Oh, by the way, the home-style food here is really good and the outdoor seating is enjoyable. 1700 South Catalina Avenue; (310) 540-5652.

ROWLAND HEIGHTS

PARKS, BEACHES, AND RECREATION AREAS

• **Schabarum Regional Park** 🐾🐾🐾½ *See ❺❸ on pages 590–591.*

Your dog will enjoy rolling on the many acres of well-manicured grass here almost as much as he enjoys sniffing the hundreds of trees for the history of dogs who have visited before him. You can explore this park via a fitness trail or a winding paved path, or just traipse through the meadows. Dogs need to be leashed. It's a good idea here, because there's a horseback riding school on the premises. While dogs can be awestruck by what they think are the gods of dogs, they can also decide these dog gods look like fun things to chase.

We like driving to the end of the park, near Picnic Area No. 8. When it's a fairly crowded day, this is where you're bound to find the fewest people.

If you find street parking or arrive early enough, you won't have to pay the $3 fee that's charged on weekends. But don't grumble if you pay—the county needs every penny it can get to maintain these parks. Exit Highway 60 at Azusa Avenue and head south. Turn left on Colima. The park will be immediately on your right. (818) 854-5560.

SAN DIMAS

PARKS, BEACHES, AND RECREATION AREAS

• **Frank G. Bonelli Regional Park** 🐾 🐾 🐾 1/2 *See* 54 *on pages 590–591.*

The good rating we're giving this park has nothing to do with friendliness. Park officials (the ones in the office, not out and about in the park) were so rude that we almost decided not to include this place in the book. If you can avoid it, don't go to the visitors center. At least don't go there and let them know you have a dog.

After they let us into the park (free on weekdays, $6 on weekends), we drove past the entry kiosk and a tree immediately came crashing down. It would have landed right on the car, but I was able to swerve. The dogs ended up squished together in the corner, but at least they weren't squished to the floor by a lumberjack's mistake.

When we were done dealing with the humans here, it became obvious that this really is a great place to take a dog. Some 14 miles of trails can easily make you forget about any churlish people you may have encountered earlier. The trails are rugged and geared toward equestrians, so be sure to keep that leash on your dog. You can hike up grassy hills and scrubby, weedy areas to majestic views of the region. The best spot we found to start one of these hikes was right across from the entrance to the east picnic valley. It's perfect; after a rigorous hike, you can hang out at a shaded picnic table and enjoy a little wine/water and cheese with your dog.

Puddingstone Reservoir is the centerpiece of the park, and the bass and trout fishing here is rumored to be pretty hot. But dogs aren't allowed to swim in it. Too bad, because it's a whopping 250 acres when full. When we visited, humans weren't even allowed to swim in the lake because of bacteria. But you can still pull a bunch of fish out and eat them for dinner.

The park is right next to Raging Waters, so it's a convenient place to take your dog if you don't feel like going home after you've dropped off the kids at that exhilarating attraction. From Interstate 210, exit at Raging Waters Drive/Via Verde and follow the signs east into the park. (909) 599-8411.

SAN PEDRO

The smog here can turn the sky such a grim color that you can't imagine how so many tourists frequent the place. But you and your dog can survive nicely and even enjoy this city if you stick close to the waterfront. Los Angeles Harbor is a working harbor, where you can see tankers, container vessels, cruise ships, and pleasure craft going about their business.

PARKS, BEACHES, AND RECREATION AREAS

Angel's Gate Park looks huge and green on the map, but don't let cartographers fool you. Except for an area around the Korean Friendship Bell, the place is almost entirely off-limits to hikers, since it's got roads and barracks-like buildings almost everywhere. Your best bet is to try Fermin Park, on the ocean just below Angel's Gate Park.

• **Fermin Park** 🐾 🐾½ *See* 55 *on pages 590–591.*

Lined with palm trees, this long, green park would be attractive enough inland, but since it's on the ocean, it's especially appealing. Dogs have to be leashed, which is only appropriate since the park is narrow and close to the road. But they still have a fun time sniffing the sea breezes and rolling on the lush lawns here.

The park is on Paseo del Mar, just west of Gaffey Street. It's a convenient place to visit if you're taking your dog to Ports O' Call (see below) or any of the other Port of Los Angeles attractions. (310) 548-7671.

RESTAURANTS

Ports O' Call: This enchanting shopping and eating area is modeled after a New England–style seaside village. It's located at the harbor, and full of crafts shops and small boutiques, some of which allow perfect pooches to browse with you. But more important, it's home to many restaurants that welcome dogs at their outside tables. For details, call (310) 831-0287.

Sacred Grounds: In case you end up downtown, here's one dog-friendly downtown eatery. Desserts, pastries, and robust coffees are the specialties. Eat, drink, and be merry at the sidewalk tables. 399 West Sixth Street; (310) 514-0800.

PLACES TO STAY

Vagabond Inn: Rates are $50 to $60. Dogs are $5 extra. 215 South Gaffey Street, San Pedro, CA 90731; (310) 831-8911.

DIVERSIONS

Set sail for a faraway isle: Okay, the island isn't *that* far away. It's Catalina. San Pedro is a point of embarkation for one of the ferry lines to Catalina. It's a fun excursion to take with a sea-loving pooch. See the description of the various ferry services to the island on page 601.

SANTA CLARITA

PARKS, BEACHES, AND RECREATION AREAS

• **Santa Clarita Woodlands Park** 🐾 🐾 🐾½ *See* 56 *on pages 590–591.*

Come here on a spring day and you and your leashed dog will swear you're nowhere near Los Angeles County. That's because this park is huge, with deep green (okay, seasonally green) hills of oaks and grasslands, hidden meadows, and a long, gurgling stream banked with lush flora. We enjoy hiking here in the rain. After a long day in the valley, it's a refreshing way to wash away the dirt and stress of urban life.

The park, with its miles of trails and splendid views of the surrounding canyons and forests, opened to the public in 1997 after more than 100 years in the hands of the oil industry. It was actually the oil industry that kept this large swatch of land from succumbing to the rampant development of neighboring communities. Fortunately, the Santa Monica Mountains Conservancy got hold of the property before developers could. The result awaits the pitter-patter of your dog's paws.

I've listed the park under Santa Clarita because it's the closest real city to the park. But technically, the park is located on the outskirts of Mentryville, a town with a population of two. Yes, two. And those two people live together. Mentryville is a ghost of what it once was—a semi-booming oil town. It's fun to take a stroll through and check out the surviving buildings. Also be sure to check out the site of the first commercially successful oil well in the West, about a half mile up the road.

Exit Interstate 5 at Calgrove Boulevard and drive west a short jog to The Old Road, where you'll drive south until you see signs for the park, where you'll head west again. The main entrance is at Ed Davis Park. Call the conservancy at (310) 589-3200 or Ed Davis Park at (805) 255-2974 for more information.

DIVERSIONS

Scrub-a-dub-dog: If you want some good clean fun with your dog, visit U Wash Doggy, a self-service dog wash. There are five of them in Los Angeles County. See Diversions in Encino (page 605) for details on the dog wash. This one's at 23013 Soledad Canyon Road; (805) 255-9600.

SANTA MONICA

Until not all that long ago, no dogs were allowed in any Santa Monica parks— enough to make a grown dog grimace. Several citizen groups had been organized to change the archaic law in the last couple of decades, but no one succeeded until a coalition organized by resident Karen Brooks hit City Hall.

Brooks is a longtime Santa Monica dog owner who has always managed to rack up tickets for dog violations. "I couldn't keep my dogs on leash and out of the parks. It's cruel," she says. So almost every day, she and about 30 other local dog people would meet at one of the parks and let their pooches play off leash. "When authorities came around, we'd all scramble and run. Sometimes a few would get caught. They'd call police backups, threaten to impound your dog. It was like living like a criminal."

One day, she tired of her subversive lifestyle and started the Santa Monica Dog Owners Group (Santa Monica DOG). She figured that since Santa Monica has 5,000 registered dogs (and countless unregistered ones), the political clout of their owners alone would turn a few heads at City Hall. Their plans and pleadings didn't work initially, but they kept fighting. They brought in the press and state senators, and eventually they managed to crack through the bureaucracy.

The result is a tough, but infinitely better, set of dog rules: Anyone can take a leashed dog to any Santa Monica city park. If you don't have a pooper-scooper implement showing, you can automatically be fined. (Bring extra bags just in case the cop comes after your dog goes.) And if your dog poops and you don't scoop, you can be nailed for more than $200 for the first offense.

Letting your dog off leash also qualifies you for a whopping fine. But if your dog is a registered Santa Monica pooch, and if you go to Pacific Park or Joslyn Park, you'll be allowed to let your dog go leashless. Out-of-towners won't have that luxury.

Local dog owners say they're grateful for the chance to be able to let their dogs be dogs. "A lot of people were fighting this, but the dogs finally won," says a victorious Brooks.

The two off-leash parks here have become so crowded since opening that Brooks and other Santa Monica DOG members are scouting out a location for a third off-leash park. For updates or more information on how to join Santa Monica DOG, call (310) 392-3583.

PARKS, BEACHES, AND RECREATION AREAS

Leashed dogs are permitted in all city parks. Here are the two that currently permit licensed city dogs to be off leash.

• **Joslyn Park** 🐾🐾🐾½ 🐕 *See ⑤⑦ on pages 590–591.*
The park may be small, but it's beautiful. It's set on a grassy hill with a few trees and has great views of the city. And better yet, it's completely enclosed, so those lucky pooches who get to go leashless are safe from traffic.

Licensed Santa Monica dogs may run leashless from 6 A.M. to 9 A.M. and 6 P.M. to 10 P.M.; they must stay away from the playground and recreation area. All other dogs must be leashed. The park is at Seventh Street and Kensington Road. (310) 393-9975.

• **Pacific Park** 🐾🐾🐾 🐕 *See ⑤⑧ on pages 590–591.*
This small, completely enclosed dog park, located right next to a kennel, won't provide your pooch with endless miles of leash-free exercise, but it will provide her with endless leash-free socializing. If your dog is a social pooch, she'll probably get all the exercise she needs here while engaging in faux wrestling matches and chase games. The park has everything a dog needs, including water, a little shade, occasional grass, and benches to chase each other under.

Licensed Santa Monica dogs may run leashless in the enclosed section west of the tennis courts from 6 A.M. to 9 A.M. and 6 P.M. to 10 P.M. All other pooches have to be leashed. The park is at Marine and 16th Streets. (310) 393-9975.

RESTAURANTS

If we listed all, or even most, of the restaurants in the popular eating parts of Santa Monica, we'd run out of pages in the book. So here are just a few.

Main Street Restaurants: These places are in a quieter setting than the restaurants in the Third Street Promenade. Unfortunately, we've found that most of the more upscale eateries won't allow dogs to dine with you outside. Here's a sampling of the mellower places:

• *Joe's Diner:* Joe likes this one. He thinks the name is in good taste, but thinks the good old-fashioned American cuisine is even tastier. Eat at one of two outdoor tables. 2917 Main Street; (310) 396-8804.

• *Starbucks Coffee Company:* Sip a cup of java at the tables out front while your dog gets that Maxwell House expression on his face. You'll recognize it. It's that "Ahh-I'm-so-content-with-the-world-because-I'm-smelling-good-coffee" look. 2671 Main Street; (310) 392-3559.

Newsroom Espresso Cafe: Dine with your dog at the many umbrella-topped outdoor tables here. A must-try dish, even if you're not a vegetarian, is the Ultimate Maui Veggie Burger. 530 Wilshire Boulevard; (310) 319-9100.

Third Street Promenade: Some of Santa Monica's most unusual and trendy restaurants reside on Third Street between Wilshire and Broadway, and most have outdoor areas. That doesn't necessarily mean your dog is welcome at all of them, but your chances are better than walking down a row of restaurants in Tahoe in January. You may want to watch your food, though, because a few of the homeless have been known to sneak up and grab it out from under you. Here are two restaurants that welcome dogs:

• *Chillers:* Besides their icy drinks, they serve mouthwatering salads, chicken, and steaks. Dine with your dog tied up on the other side of the patio railing. 1446 Third Street; (310) 394-1993.

• *Sunset Bar & Grill:* Eat continental cuisine on their happening patio with your happy pooch. Actually, your happy pooch has to be tied to the other side of the rail, but she'll still be well within petting (and mooching) distance. 1240 Third Street; (310) 395-7012.

PLACES TO STAY

Holiday Inn: Small dogs only, please. This Holiday Inn is located near the Santa Monica Pier, just a couple of blocks from the Third Street Promenade (see above). Rates are $149 to $189. There's a $100 fee for your dog's stay. 120 Colorado Boulevard, Santa Monica, CA 90401; (310) 451-0676.

Loews Santa Monica Beach Hotel: Haul out the credit cards: Rates are $220 to $735 per night, and there's a $250 to $500 doggy deposit required (the price depends on the room). This is a great place for people, but dogs don't take well to steam rooms and health clubs. They don't seem to mind the elegant atmosphere, though. 1700 Ocean Avenue, Santa Monica, CA 90401; (310) 458-6700.

SAUGUS

PARKS, BEACHES, AND RECREATION AREAS

• **Vasquez Rocks Natural Area Park** 🐾 🐾 🐾 1/2 *See* ⑤⑨ *on pages 590–591.*

This is Los Angeles County? It looks more like another planet. The slanted, jagged rocks and hidden caves are among the state's most famous geological wonders. They're so unusually beautiful that film crews routinely use them as a backdrop. When you call the park, chances are the answering machine will tell you how to get permission to make movies here. It's probably not the kind of information you and your dog need to know, but that's entertainment.

This smog-free 745-acre park, located in the high desert near Agua Dulce, also features Tataviam Indian archaeological sites. Many trails branch off through chaparral and riparian plant communities. Make sure you bring drinking water; there's none in the park and you can work up a mighty thirst.

Dogs must be leashed, but back in the days of the bandit Tiburicio Vasquez, there were no such rules. If there had been, Vasquez, the park's namesake, would have found a way to break them. In the mid-1800s, Vasquez was a sort of Robin Hood character, robbing from the wealthy and giving the money to poor Mexicans. He used the caves and rocks as a hideaway from the sheriff's posses and vigilantes who were always on his trail. When you visit the park, stop at the entry kiosk and read about Vasquez' dramatic final days here. Then take your dog for a hike on the very trails Vasquez may have fled on, and let your imagination take you back to the days of the Wild West.

There's a $3 fee per vehicle. Exit Highway 14 at Agua Dulce Canyon Road and follow the signs to the park. (805) 268-0840.

SHERMAN OAKS

PARKS, BEACHES, AND RECREATION AREAS

•Van Nuys–Sherman Oaks Park and Recreation Center 🐾🐾½
See 60 on pages 590–591.

The backdrop is ugly, scattered as it is with little apartment buildings. But the park itself is one huge, green, grassy field, with a great fitness course. You'll have no excuse not to exercise here, but dogs have to be leashed.

Take the Van Nuys Boulevard exit from U.S. 101 and drive north to Hartsook Street. The park will be on your right. (818) 783-5121.

SOUTH EL MONTE

PARKS, BEACHES, AND RECREATION AREAS

•Whittier Narrows Regional Park 🐾🐾🐾½ *See 61 on pages 590–591.*

Is your pooch picky about parks? This one is bound to please: There's something for almost every dog in this very large chunk of county land. For dogs who like to hang out near lakes, the park is home to the Legg Lakes. These are actually three ponds connected together. The fishing for trout is about as good as it gets in the middle of a major metropolitan area. The section of the park with the lake also has a long path around it for dogs who prefer not to get grass on their paws.

For dogs who like to explore nature, try the self-guiding nature trail at the Whittier Narrows Nature Center. Starting at the visitors center, get a pamphlet explaining the various phenomena you might encounter on the half-mile nature trail. Make sure your leashed dog doesn't disturb this precious little piece of nature. There's a chicken who sometimes runs around the parking lot, so beware in case your dog plans to be self-sufficient for dinner.

And for chow hounds, a very big area east of Santa Anita Boulevard is devoted almost entirely to picnic tables. When it's not crowded, it's a great place to run around with your dog. Although dogs are supposed to be leashed, it's nice to know that two sides of this large section are fenced.

There's actually a small segment of the park where dogs are allowed off leash for sport training. Call the park to find out the details.

From Highway 60, exit at Rosemead Boulevard, go south to Durfee Boulevard, and turn left. The Legg Lakes part of the park is in about three-quarters of a mile, and the parking lot is on the left. On summer weekends there can be a $3 fee per car, but there's plenty of free street parking if you drive a little farther and go left on Santa Anita Avenue. This is also the place to park if you want to take your dog to the very large picnic section of the park. For the nature trail, continue on Durfee past Santa Anita Avenue and follow the signs to the visitors center. The park also extends north of Highway 60, both to the east and west of Rosemead Boulevard. (626) 575-5526.

STUDIO CITY

PARKS, BEACHES, AND RECREATION AREAS

• **Laurel Canyon Park** 😊 😊 😊 😊 🐾 *See ㉒ on pages 590–591.*

Yee haw! Dogs, throw off your leashes and come here to be all the dog you can be! This is the biggest of the off-leash dog runs in Los Angeles County, and many consider it the best. It's nearly 20 acres, and there are sufficient trees and picnic tables to make everyone comfortable.

If you and your dog like to socialize, you couldn't ask for a better place. Canine rush hour (around 5 P.M., depending on the time of year) is a real scene. On a typical dog day afternoon, you'll find more than 100 dogs running like mad, sniffing each other in unmentionable places and pushing their noses to the ground in search of unusual odors. Their owners, meanwhile, chitchat about this and that (often, "this" being their dog and "that" being your dog).

People flock here from all over Los Angeles and the San Fernando Valley. There's plenty of water, plenty of pooper-scoopers, plenty of fence, and, most importantly, plenty of good dog fun. And for people who like to watch the stars, we hear that celebrities sometimes frequent the place on weekends.

Dogs are allowed during limited hours, from 6 A.M. to 10 A.M. and 3 P.M. to dusk. Get here early so you can nab a parking space. The park is on Mulholland Drive, about a quarter-mile west of Laurel Canyon Boulevard. From Laurel Canyon Boulevard, go west on Mulholland and take the first left. The road winds down a hill and into the parking lot. (818) 756-8189.

RESTAURANTS

Jumpin' Java: Don't let the name fool you. There's more than just coffee

---

for your canine here. You can get breakfast, lunch, and dinner, too. The Mediterranean-style cuisine makes for tasty, light eating. Dine with your dog at the covered patio with six tables. 11919 Ventura Boulevard; (818) 980-4249.

Studio Yogurt: If the cool, creamy, refreshing frozen yogurt they serve here is beyond your caloric capacity, order one of their fat-free or sugar-free treats. They taste every bit as good. Your dog won't complain either. Dip your spoon with your dog at the covered patio. 12050 Ventura Boulevard; (818) 508-7811.

DIVERSIONS

Lather up: If you want some good, clean fun with your dog, visit U Wash Doggy, a self-service dog wash. There are five of them in Los Angeles County. See Diversions in Encino (see page 605) for details on the dog wash. This one's at 11392 Ventura Boulevard; (818) 762-8300.

TORRANCE

PARKS, BEACHES, AND RECREATION AREAS

• **Columbia Park** 🐾 🐾 1/2 *See ㊽ on pages 590–591.*

The park may be under many power lines, but it has the most amusing dog-rule signs we've seen. Joe didn't even try to lift his leg on them. If other cities would approach the pooper-scooper issue like this, it would make the task much more pleasant. Stop by and check them out. When you do, you may as well run around the huge swaths of grass with your leashed dog.

Exit Interstate 405 at Crenshaw Boulevard and drive south about 15 blocks. Go right at 190th Street and right again into the park. (310) 618-2930.

• **Miramar Park** 🐾 1/2 *See ㊾ on pages 590–591.*

Is your dog thirsty? This tiny, grassy park overlooking the ocean provides the best dog-watering hole in the county. Fido Fountain was built in 1990 because dogs were drinking from the human water fountain and many humans were complaining. "The large dogs jump up as their masters turn on the water for them," wrote one resident. "Very upsetting to me, and others, if they knew they were drinking after dogs. I myself love my dog, but I do not eat or drink after my own dog."

Fortunately, City Hall didn't allow such letters to result in more regulations against dogs. The city just went ahead and built a dog-sized fountain right beside the other drinking fountain. Then the tables were turned: Sand-covered humans started rinsing off their feet in the Fido Fountain. So the city built a miniature headstone reading "Fido Fountain—Dogs only, please." It did the trick. Now human feet and dog lips rarely come together at Miramar Park.

The park is at the northern border of the city, just south of Redondo Beach on Paseo de La Playa. (310) 618-2930.

UNIVERSAL CITY

If you go to the exciting Universal Studios tour/theme park here, your pooch will be pleased to know that she can accompany you at least part of the way.

Universal Studios has a kennel, which dogs of visitors get to use for free. Bring a blanket and her favorite toy so you won't feel terribly guilty knowing she's not with you as you fly the friendly skies with E.T. or get jostled around a bit by King Kong. The climate-controlled kennel is unattended, but locked. You can visit your dog any time, though, by getting a key-bearing information booth employee to accompany you.

To use the kennel, bring your leashed dog to the information booth just before the main entrance. (818) 622-3801.

PARKS, BEACHES, AND RECREATION AREAS
• **South Weddington Park** 🐾🐾½ *See* 65 *on pages 590–591.*

Golf, anyone? This park is so green and trim that you can't help but think of Arnold Palmer. Joe likes it because of its proximity to Universal Studios—it's right across the street. He enjoys the kennels there (see above for details), because he knows a cat could end up spending the day just down the row from him.

The park is bordered by a couple of small side roads, so it's fairly safe from traffic. But since dogs are supposed to be leashed, that's not something you have to worry about.

Heading south on Lankersheim Boulevard, go right on Bluffside Drive (directly across from the north gate of Universal Studios). (818) 756-8188.

VAN NUYS
PARKS, BEACHES, AND RECREATION AREAS
• **Woodley Park** 🐾🐾🐾 *See* 66 *on pages 590–591.*

If you like your parks big and grassy, check out this one. Dogs really enjoy it here. There's ample shade, plenty of picnic areas, and a fitness course to keep you and the pooch in good condition. Unfortunately, there's also an unattractive water reclamation plant on the north side of the park, but they have to put them somewhere.

The park is located between Interstate 405 and U.S. 101. Take the Burbank Boulevard exit from Interstate 405 and drive west into the park. Turn right on Woodley Avenue and drive past signs for the Japanese garden. The meadow area will be on your right. (818) 756-8891.

VENICE
Looking around Venice these days, you can see barely a hint of the dream of Abbot Kinney, the city's founder. In 1900, he began creating a city that was a near duplicate of Italy's Venice, complete with canals, Italian architecture, and imported singing gondoliers. He had hoped to create a cultural renaissance in America.

If he could see the scantily clad roller skaters, the punkers with earrings in every conceivable body part, the homeless, and the body builders and religious zealots in action, old Mr. Kinney would shudder. But despite the wayward ways of those inhabiting his dream, the place has a wild charm, a playland quality. And what really counts is that dogs think Venice is cool.

There are plenty of dogs here. As of this writing, they're not allowed on the beach, but there's a big battle being waged about that. One dog battle has been won, though, and it's great news for dogs in need of off-leash exercise. At press time, a new dog park, the Westminster Dog Park, had just had its groundbreaking ceremony. By the time you read this, dogs should be running themselves silly there. For information on how you can help with this dog park or with the beach battle or potential future dog parks (three new Venice locations are being drooled over by dogs and their people), contact a group called FREEPLAY. It stands for Friendly, Responsible, Environmentally Evolved Pet Lover's Alliance—Yes. That's kind of catchy. (310) 314-9600. FREEPLAY's Web page is www.freeplay.org.

PARKS, BEACHES, AND RECREATION AREAS

•Westminster Dog Park 🐾🐾🐾🐾 🐕 *See ⑰ on pages 590–591.*

At press time, the park was poised to become a reality. The many political and other hurdles had been cleared, the ground had been broken, and the money pretty much raised. I'm taking a chance and writing about the park as if it exists because by the time you read this, it should, and I'd hate to have dogs wait until the next edition of this book before finding out about the place. But please call first before making a long sojourn here, just in case there was a surprise last-minute stumbling block.

The dog park will be a little more than an acre within very tiny Westminster Park. It will have plenty of shade and a few benches, and there are high hopes for some kind of water fountain for dogs.

Small dogs will have a choice of running with the big boys or playing in their very own smaller fenced-in dog run area. Most tiny canines we know would opt for the chance to be as big as they feel, and not be set apart as a little dog. But it's a great feature for dogs in need of some protection from giant paws.

At press time, the park was set to open by August 1998, as long as everything goes according to plan. Again, be sure to call first. Your best bet is to phone the energetic group FREEPLAY, which was instrumental in starting this park, at (310) 314-9600. You can also check out their Web site at www.freeplay.org. The park is at Pacific and Westminster Avenues. The regional park office phone is (310) 837-8116.

RESTAURANTS

In addition to these restaurants, little eateries abound along Ocean Front Walk (see Diversions, page 638). Just grab a chair and table from the communal sidewalk restaurant furniture and enjoy one of the most scenic and unusual lunches you've ever experienced.

Figtree Cafe: The food here is fantastic and eclectic. You may eat at the patio as long as you tie your dog to the other side of the rail. She'll still be at your side, but there will be a couple of bars between you. 429 Ocean Front Walk; (310) 392-4937.

Siamese Garden: Eat good Thai food at an umbrella-topped table with your fuzzy-headed beast. 301 Washington Street; (310) 821-0098.

DIVERSIONS

Do it all at the Dogromat: All the Milk-Bones your dog can eat and a bath to boot. That's the way life is at the Dogromat, one of the most engaging self-service "dog laundromats" in the West. Just as Mary Poppins sang the virtues of a spoonful of sugar helping the medicine go down, a Dogromat owner chimes about the role of treats/bribes in helping bathtime be fun time. "They can work absolute wonders for a reluctant dog," she says. It's the little details like these that make this place supercalifragilistic-expealidocious.

Even dogs who hate baths don't mind coming here. There's something in the air that says, "It's okay. Thousands of dogs before you have been bathed here and survived, and you're next, and you won't melt." Humans like it even better than dogs. It's so much easier to bathe a dog here than at home, primarily because the tubs are waist high and everything you need is at your fingertips. Other benefits include ready advice from the staff (which is made up of grooming professionals), socializing in a dog-friendly atmosphere, and letting flea carcasses wash down someone else's drain.

You'll also find some fine, natural dog products here. And Dogromat plays host to an intriguing seminar series. Pet chiropractors, pet psychics, and pet herbalists have been among the lecturers.

The *Los Angeles Times* wrote that "What Chuck E. Cheese is to children, this place is to dogs." And your dog won't have greasy pizza drippings all over his clothes when he leaves. Dogromat rates are based on the size and hair type of your pooch. The average is $10. Dogromat is located at 12926 Venice Boulevard; (310) 306-8885.

Stroll to a different drummer: Since Venice's parks are so tiny, most dog owners like to take their dogs for a jaunt along Ocean Front Walk, between Rose Avenue and Venice Boulevard. This is about as close to the beach as dogs are allowed, and for many, it's close enough. This is where you can consult a psychic; have your cards read by a tarot dealer; listen to street musicians; buy incense, T-shirts, or sunglasses; and watch skaters skate and lovers love.

It's also where Joe almost met the Big Dog in the Sky. He was trotting merrily along sniffing the air for all the great, cheap places to eat along the walk, when suddenly a hand appeared on the path before him. It wouldn't have been a big deal, except the hand wasn't attached to a body. It was writhing and doing sickening somersaults. He trembled and ran backwards right into a juggler. He stood there wrapped around the juggler's leg until the hand crawled away, back to the pile of motionless rubber hands from which it had strayed. He gave a shudder, unwrapped himself, and marched onward, never glancing back.

All was well until a G.I. Joe–type mechanical doll crawled in front of us, blasting his semiautomatic weapon. Joe (that is, the Joe without the camouflage attire) gave me that "Can we go home now?" look, and we did.

WATTS
PARKS, BEACHES, AND RECREATION AREAS
• **Will Rogers Community Regional Park** 🐾🐾½
See ⓬ *on pages 590–591.*

Perhaps because it's not in as luxurious a setting as Beverly Hills' Will Rogers Memorial Park, your dog may feel more like he can be himself here. The park sports a couple of large shaded areas, a big green field for romping (on leash), a gazebo, and a fenced-in ball field.

The oodles of picnic tables attract crowds on the weekends, so it might be a good idea to bring your pooch here Monday through Friday, unless you're planning to bring him to a picnic. The park is between Century Boulevard and 103rd Street, at Success Avenue. (213) 357-3032.

WEST HOLLYWOOD
RESTAURANTS
Comedy Store: Have a drink on a Friday or Saturday night with your best bud at the comedy palace of Los Angeles. As you sip your screwdriver and eat your little pizzas at the outdoor bar, you and your pooch can watch for your favorite comic. If you arrive early enough, you can have a bite with your dog, drive her home, and come back in time for one of the shows. 8433 West Sunset Boulevard; (213) 650-6268.

Greenwich Village Pizza: Eat delicious New York–style pizza with your pooch at the shaded tables. 8937 Santa Monica Boulevard; (213) 272-8646.

Le Petit Four: The food here is exquisite and the outdoor setting is very precious. Only the most exemplary dogs may dine with you, and even then, they may have to be tied close by. 8654 Sunset Boulevard; (310) 652-3863.

Normandie Bakery & Cafe: If you and your dog dig delicious pastries and breads, this is a great place to get them. It's also a fine place to pick up a full breakfast or lunch. Dine at the many outdoor tables. 8375 Santa Monica Boulevard; (213) 360-0622.

Rage: It's all the rage to eat the continental cuisine with your dog at the shaded tables out front. 8911 Santa Monica Boulevard; (310) 652-7055.

Tango Grill: Chicken and steak are the specialties here, and they're pretty tasty, too. Dine outside with the dog of your choice. 8807 Santa Monica Boulevard; (310) 659-3663.

PLACES TO STAY
Le Montrose Suite/Hotel Gran Luxe: This attractive French-influenced hotel is homey, cozy, and nestled in a lovely neighborhood. All rooms have fireplaces and some have kitchenettes. Rates are $190 to $475. Dogs usually require a $250 deposit. 900 Hammond Street, West Hollywood, CA 90069; (310) 855-1115 or (800) 776-0666.

DIVERSIONS
Lather, rinse, and repeat: If you want some good, clean fun with your dog, visit U Wash Doggy, a self-service dog wash. There are five of them in Los Angeles County. See Diversions in Encino (see page 605) for details on the dog wash. This one's at 8731 Santa Monica Boulevard; (310) 360-0300.

WESTWOOD

This lively University of California community is a fun place to have a dog. People around here genuinely like them.

PARKS, BEACHES, AND RECREATION AREAS

•**Westwood Park** 🐾🐾½ *See* ㊴ *on pages 590–591.*

For a flat, squarish park, this isn't a bad place for a leashed dog. Long dirt paths wind their way through very green grass, past modern sculptures and many shaded picnic tables.

Exit Interstate 405 at the Wilshire exit heading toward Westwood. Take your first right (on Veteran Avenue). The park will be on your right shortly after the federal building. Another section of the park is on Sepulveda Boulevard, just north of Ohio Avenue. (310) 473-3610.

RESTAURANTS

Piccolo Mondo: Dogs love to join their people for a luscious Italian lunch at the outdoor tables. 10917 Lindbrook Drive; (310) 824-0240.

Stan's Corner Donut Shop: Lots of local cops hang out here, so it's got to be good. If you're in the mood for Indian food or a hot dog, Stan's serves them, too. Stan says, "I love dogs. I have a little French blood in me!" And dogs love the outdoor tables on this sunny corner. 10948 Weyburn Avenue; (310) 208-8660.

PLACES TO STAY

Beverly Hills Ritz: I've been dogless when I've stayed here, and it's a good thing: There's a $500 deposit required when you stay with a pooch. If Joe had visited during his furniture-gnawing days, it would have been like watching 25 huge bags of dog food fly out the window. The place is charming, though, and it's got all the fine touches of an elegant European getaway. Rates are $155 to $385. 10300 Wilshire Boulevard, Westwood, CA 90024; (310) 275-5575.

DOGGY DAYS

Walk and clown around: The Friends of Animals' Dog Walkathon is one of the best dog activities in Southern California. You and your pooch can walk a two-mile or five-mile course, and when you return to the starting point, clowns, balloons, and free human and doggy treats will be there to greet you. The money raised goes to help the homeless and abandoned animals being cared for by the organization. It's a very good cause. Grab a dog and walk your "a-thons" off.

The walk and party usually start at the federal building's parking lot, at Wilshire Boulevard and Veteran Avenue. The event is held in the spring or summer. Call (310) 479-5089 for details.

WHITTIER

PARKS, BEACHES, AND RECREATION AREAS

Dogs are banned at all but one Whittier city park.

•**Hellman Park** 🐾🐾🐾 *See* ㊵ *on pages 590–591.*

We tried to visit a couple of times (before the big fire of '93), but the park was closed due to fire hazards, so we couldn't really get in to take a good look. But from what we could see, dogs would have a fun time frolicking around here. It's hilly and rough, with 200 acres of trees and shrubs and even some grass to roll on.

City park folks tell us the park may close from May to December because of potential fires, so you and your leashed dog are very limited in your walking days here. Remember what Sinatra crooned: "It's a long, long time from May to December." It may even be closed at other times of the year. Be prepared to walk elsewhere.

The park is located at the northernmost end of Greenleaf Avenue. Call (562) 464-3375 about its status.

WILLOWBROOK

PARKS, BEACHES, AND RECREATION AREAS

•**Willowbrook State Recreation Area** 🐾🐾🐾 *See* **71** *on pages 590–591.*

The hills are so gently rolling at this large, grassy park that it looks like a huge bedsheet being shaken out by the Jolly Green Giant. There's a little lake in the middle and plenty of picnic tables. The trees here are adolescents, but they provide adequate shade on warm summer days. Leashed dogs like to roam from tree to tree trying to figure out who's been there before them.

You can park anywhere along 120th Street or in the park's main lot at 120th Street near Wadsworth Avenue. Although it's a state park, it's operated by Los Angeles County. (213) 586-6543.

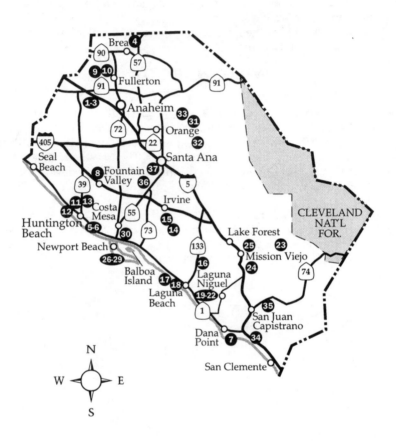

Brea 4
90
57
9 10
91 Fullerton
1-3
Anaheim
72 33 31
Orange
22 32
405 Santa Ana
Seal
Beach 8 Fountain 37
Valley 36
39 5
11 13 Irvine
12 Costa
Mesa 55 15
Huntington 5-6 14
Beach 30 73 Lake Forest
Newport Beach 133 25 23
26-29 Mission Viejo
Balboa 16 24
Island 17 Laguna 74
18 Niguel
Laguna 19-22
Beach 1 35
San Juan
Dana Capistrano
Point 7 34

San Clemente

CLEVELAND
NAT'L
FOR.

N
W ✦ E
S

53
ORANGE COUNTY

This is the amusement capital of America, and that's not an amusing thought to dogs. They're banned from such first-rate attractions as Disneyland and Knott's Berry Farm. But the county is also home to some dog-friendly places that just might put a grin on your pooch's rubbery lips and make a stay well worth his time.

The scent of money is unmistakable here—the land is some of the most expensive in the country. That ends up being a boon for dogs, since the communities can afford to support hundreds of parks.

Dogs are allowed at all county-run parks except wilderness parks. The only beaches that permit pooches are those of Huntington Beach, Newport Beach, and Laguna Beach, and dogs are very restricted as far as times they can visit the parks or sections they can use. See the headings for these cities for details.

If you and your dog are salty sea dogs, make a beeline to Newport Beach's Balboa Pavilion. You can sail away with two boat companies here. You won't go far—the shorter trip lasts three minutes, while the longer trip goes around the harbor for a couple of hours. But you will have a splashingly smashing good time. See Diversions, page 661.

The truly great news is that there are two new leash-free fenced dog parks in the county (see Central Park in Huntington Beach and Pooch Park in Laguna Niguel), bringing Orange County's total to four leash-free areas, not including the Cleveland National Forest. (The other two dog parks are in Costa Mesa and Laguna Beach. See pages 646 and 654.) This is a big increase from a few years ago, when the number of leash-free parks was zip. A romp in one of these parks and then lunch at the dog-oriented Park Bench Cafe (see page 652) in Huntington Beach is enough to put a smile on the snout of even the most dour of dogs.

NATIONAL FORESTS

See the National Forests and Wilderness Areas chapter starting on page 748 for important information and safety tips on visiting national forests with your dog.

• **Cleveland National Forest** 🐾🐾🐾🐾 🐕
See page 749.

ANAHEIM

Anaheim is the home of Disneyland and just a few miles from Knott's Berry Farm, Movieland Wax Museum, Medieval Times Dinner Tournament, and Wild Bill's Western Dinner Extravaganza.

These attractions may be fun and laughs for humans. But they don't exactly make a dog howl with joy. "Who cares?" say the dogs. If humans were banned, you'd feel the same way.

If someone in your party is sick of Disneyland and has just come along for the ride, he can take the dog around while you play. There are several parks that make life a little easier for the canines among us.

Otherwise, if you go to Disneyland and don't have a dogsitter, you can bring your dog to the Disneyland Kennel Club for the day. Rates are $10 per day (no dogs overnight). Bring your dog's favorite toy or blanket. (The Kennel Club supplies food and water, but you can bring your own food if you prefer.) You can take a break from Fantasyland, Tomorrowland, or any of the other incredible lands and take your pooch for a leashed walk in the kennel's tiny exercise area whenever you want. For details, call (714) 999-4565 and ask for the kennel.

PARKS, BEACHES, AND RECREATION AREAS

• **Boysen Park** 🐾🐾½ *See* ❶ *on page 642.*
Not only is this park attractive and green, it's also fairly close to Disneyland. Leashed dogs enjoy romping in the short grass, lounging under a big shade tree, and watching the kids ride in the faux rockets in the creative playground here.

From Harbor Boulevard around Disneyland, go north several blocks and turn right on Vermont Avenue. The park will be on your right in about 1.5 miles. You can park on the street, or turn right on State College Boulevard and make a quick right onto Wagner Avenue, which will take you to the parking lot. (714) 254-5191.

• **Pearson Park** 🐾🐾 *See* ❷ *on page 642.*
This park is a straight shot north from Disneyland. Besides all the recreational facilities, which include tennis courts and a pool, there are plenty of trees and a ducky little pond. Leashed dogs like walking in the green, grassy fields here.

From Disneyland, continue north on Harbor Boulevard for a little more than 1.5 miles. The park will be on your right, at Cypress Street. If it's too crowded here, drive up the street another six blocks and take your dog to La Palma Park, a triangular park with a winding path and palm trees. (714) 254-5191.

• **Yorba Regional Park** 🐾🐾🐾 *See* ❸ *on page 642.*

If you like suburban-style parks, this one's for you. There are tot lots, ball fields, and plenty of picnic areas in this 166-acre park. You can also fish at the little lakes and connecting streams or ride your bike or hike around the trails here.

The park can get very crowded, so try to visit on a weekday. Dogs must be leashed. The parking fee is $2 per car. From Highway 91 in the far east reaches of Anaheim, exit at Weir Canyon Road/Yorba Linda Boulevard, drive north to La Palma Avenue, and follow the signs. (714) 970-1460.

PLACES TO STAY

A minuscule percentage of Anaheim's zillion or so hotels permit pooches. A big reason is that folks often leave them behind when they go off for a day at Disneyland or Knott's Berry Farm. Do not do this! If no one is going to be around to hang out with the dog, either leave him at home or find a suitable local kennel. Dogs left unattended in strange places can get scared and anxious. It's not good for them, the hotel room, or the housekeeper. Disneyland's kennel is a pretty good deal if you're doing the Disney scene. See page 644 for details.

Anaheim Hilton and Towers: This luxurious hotel takes small pooches only. Rates are $150 to $230. 777 Convention Way, Anaheim, CA 92802; (714) 750-4321.

Anaheim Marriott Hotel: Rates are $89 to $195. Small pooches only, please. 700 West Convention Way, Anaheim, CA 92802; (714) 750-8000.

Best Western Raffles Inn & Suites: Rates are $59 to $79. Dogs are $10 extra. 2040 South Harbor Boulevard, Anaheim, CA 92802; (714) 750-6100.

Canyon RV Park: This is a really attractive park, with 700 acres of wilderness and 117 campsites. But you and your dog can only come to the park if you camp. Observe the leash law here, as they've lost a couple dogs to coyotes in the past. Sites are $17.50 to $22.50. Dogs are $1 extra. Reservations are required from mid-May through October. From Highway 91 in the eastern part of Anaheim, exit at Gypsum Canyon Road and follow the signs to the park. Since it borders the highway, it's just a couple of minutes until you're there. To reserve a campsite, call (714) 637-0210.

Motel 6: This one's about a block away from Disneyland. Rates are $39 for one adult, $6 for the next. As long as your dog isn't a rottie or a pit bull, he can stay here. (What would "Good Dog Carl" say about this?) 100 West Freedman Way, Anaheim, CA 92801; (714) 520-9696.

Quality Hotel & Conference Center: Rates are $139 to $159. 616 Convention Way, Anaheim, CA 92802; (714) 750-3131.

Red Roof Inn: Rates are $40 to $75. Small dogs only, please. 1251 North Harbor Avenue, Anaheim, CA 92801; (714) 635-6461.

BALBOA ISLAND

This small Newport Harbor island is a bayfront wonderland. You can drive here from the mainland, but dogs prefer to take the ferry from Newport Beach (see Diversions, page 661). The island isn't exactly replete with big parks, but dogs enjoy a stroll down Bayfront, to the Grand Canal and back. When you've worked up a big hunger, head for the dog-friendly Park Avenue Cafe, not far away.

RESTAURANTS

The Main Squeeze: This juice bar has a bench out front where you and the pooch can share a drink. 211 Marine Avenue; (714) 673-3060.

Park Avenue Cafe: Dogs are welcome to dine at one of the two tree-shaded patios with you, and boy do they like it here. It may have something to do with the thick steaks, steaming racks of lamb and other assorted goodies. (Just a hunch.) Troovee Dog and his wonderful pal Mary Bavry gave us the heads-up about this great place. A woof and a wag to them. They highly recommend the Ferryboat sandwich. 501 Park Avenue; (714) 673-3830.

BREA

PARKS, BEACHES, AND RECREATION AREAS

•**Carbon Canyon Regional Park** 🐾🐾🐾 *See* ❹ *on page 642.*

This 124-acre park is nestled among the rolling foothills of the Chino Hill Range. It has the usual recreational facilities, including tennis courts, ball fields, and tot lots. But by far the favorite attraction for dogs and their people is a 10-acre grove of coastal redwoods located near the Carbon Canyon Dam.

Joe thinks I should mention that dogs can also check out the pepper trees, sycamores, eucalyptuses, and Canary Island pines. But be careful not to let the trails lead you into the adjacent Chino Hills State Park. Pooches are not permitted in most places there.

The entry fee here is $2 per car on weekdays, $4 on weekends, $5 on major holidays. Exit Highway 57 at Lambert Road and drive four miles east (Lambert becomes Carbon Canyon Road). The park entrance is one mile east of Valencia Avenue. (714) 996-5252.

PLACES TO STAY

Hyland Motel: Small, well-trained dogs are welcome here. Rates are $40 to $45. 727 South Brea Boulevard, Brea, CA 92621; (714) 990-6867.

CORONA DEL MAR

Please see Newport Beach, starting on page 658, for Corona del Mar info.

COSTA MESA

PARKS, BEACHES, AND RECREATION AREAS

•**Bark Park/Tewinkle Park Dog Run** 🐾🐾🐾🐾 🐕
See ❺ *on page 642.*

I met a woman who has trained her dog, Nadine, to go to the bathroom on command. The magic word: "Tinkle." It's not dignified, but it works just about every time. When she first took her dog to Tewinkle Park, a few people were talking about "Tewinkle," and sure enough, Nadine went tinkle just about every time.

Dogs can tinkle in Tewinkle, but they can also do plenty of other fun things. Now that this 50-acre park has three acres fenced for dogs, they can cavort about the dog run sans leash for hours on end. The park was opened in 1994 and is a terrific addition to Costa Mesa. It's located at Arlington Drive and Newport Boulevard. (714) 754-5300.

• **Fairview Park** 🐾 🐾 🐾 *See* ❻ *on page 642.*

The pooper-scoopers here are handsome, and the city offers them free to all dog owners. But if you need a better reason to visit the park with your pooch, try this one: It's a big, mostly undeveloped park, with dirt trails that wind through grassy, weedy areas. Your dog will have a good time sniffing around. The farther back you go, the less likely you are to run into other people.

Very exciting breaking news: At press time, the city was considering making part of this expansive park into a dog park. This would be the best news for Costa Mesa canines since Bark Park's creation. For updates, call the number below.

Traveling north on Placentia Avenue, the entry road is on your left. (714) 754-5300.

RESTAURANTS

Cornerstone Cafe: You and your dog can order breakfast, lunch, or dinner here and chow down together at the three outdoor tables. 1907 Harbor Boulevard; (714) 646-5776.

Diedrich Coffee: This is a happening place for dogs. "We get lots of good dogs. They're the best," one server said. On pleasant days, the big windows here are wide open, so if you don't want to find an outdoor seat for you and your pooch, you (the human) can sit inside by a window and pat your outside dog on the head. (It helps if you order him a really buttery pastry.) 474 East 17th Street; (714) 646-0323.

Gypsy Den: Located at the wonderfully different Lab Anti-Mall (see page 648), the Gypsy Den serves up some great veggie food as well as "light carnivorous cuisine," as one employee puts it. Dine with your dog at the many outdoor tables, which come with heat lamps when needed. 2930 North Bristol Street; (714) 549-7012.

Rock-n-Java: The coffee here really rocks. Sip some with your dog at your side at the outdoor tables. 1749 Newport Boulevard; (714) 650-4430.

PLACES TO STAY

La Quinta Motor Inn: Rates are $59 to $64. Small dogs only, please. 1515 South Coast Drive, Costa Mesa, CA 92626; (714) 957-5841.

Ramada Limited: Stay here and you get a complimentary continental breakfast, a free *USA Today* (my alma mater), a heated pool and spa, a fitness room, and a pleasant guest room. This is all fine and dandy with your dog (at least the muffins at breakfast are of some interest), but what dogs really enjoy about this place is that there's a Trader Joe's adjacent to it. If you can't figure out why your dog might be pawing you to go in Trader Joe's direction, I'll give you a hint: Dog treats are delicious and plentiful at TJ's, and inexpensive too. Grab a bag of rawhides or a box of peanut butter biscuits, and your stay at this hotel will be one your dog will look back on fondly.

Dogs are supposed to be 25 pounds or less to stay here. Rates are $79 to $109. 1680 Superior Avenue, Costa Mesa, CA 92627; (714) 645-2221 or (800) 345-0825.

Vagabond Inn: Rates are $49 to $60. Dogs are $5 extra. 3205 Harbor Boulevard, Costa Mesa, CA 92626; (714) 557-8360.

The Westin South Coast Plaza Hotel: This is a fine place to take a small, well-bred mutt. Rates are $119 to $169. 686 Anton Boulevard, Costa Mesa, CA 92626; (714) 540-2500.

DIVERSIONS

Go "anti" shopping: Dogs are welcome to cruise around with you as you peruse the Lab Anti-Mall. The Lab is kind of the flipside of malls. It's mellow. It's artsy. It's a dog's kind of place. "You're never going to see as many people with tattoos and pierced body parts as you'll see here," says Mary Bavry, who shops at the Lab with Gratsie, her people-loving terrier/basset who has some significant eyebrows to punctuate his charismatic personality. "But dogs sure do feel welcome."

The stores are not what you'd find at the Fashion Island mall (see page 661 for a description). The Lab has bead stores, art galleries, a big courtyard with an outdoor pool table, and a Tower Records Alternative store, which isn't exactly stocked with John Denver hits. Many stores will let your pooch inside to shop with you. The Gypsy Den cafe (see page 647) permits pooches at its outside table.

The Lab Anti-Mall is located at 2930 North Bristol Street, about a half-mile from Tewinkle Park (see page 646). (714) 966-6660.

DANA POINT

PARKS, BEACHES, AND RECREATION AREAS

Dogs are not allowed in any beaches here or at any Dana Point city park. The city's adventure-loving namesake, Richard Henry Dana, Jr., who wrote the high seas novel *Two Years Before the Mast*, probably wouldn't have liked Dana Point's attitude. But he's been dead for more than a century, so there's little he can do about it.

•**Lantern Bay Park** 🐾 🐾 🐾 *See* ❼ *on page 642.*

Since this is a county park, pooches are permitted. It's a beautiful stretch of grass and trees set high above the ocean. Paved walkways meander throughout and there are picnic tables galore. Leashed dogs love to sniff the sea breezes and watch the gulls.

From Highway 1, turn toward the beach on Harbor Drive and make a right onto Lantern Street. (714) 771-6731.

RESTAURANTS

Yama Teppan: Dine in comfort on Japanese delights. This place will keep you and your pooch warm in the winter and cool in the summer with its heat lamps and umbrellas. 24961 Dana Point Harbor Drive; (714) 240-6610.

PLACES TO STAY

Doheney State Beach: Dogs can't go on the long sandy beach here, but if you camp with them at one of the 122 sites, they can hang out on the grassy area of the park. Some campsites border the beach. Rates are $14 to $23. Dogs are $1 extra. From Highway 1, turn toward the beach on Harbor Drive and make a left onto Lantern Street. Call (714) 496-6172 for information, or call Parknet for reservations at (800) 444-PARK.

FOUNTAIN VALLEY

PARKS, BEACHES, AND RECREATION AREAS

• **Mile Square Regional Park** 😺😺😺 *See ❽ on page 642.*

The park has many miles of scenic trails that leashed dogs love to explore. The trails go through 200 acres of grass, trees, and picnic areas. If your pooch is a sports enthusiast, take her to the fishing lakes, soccer fields, or ball fields. She's even permitted to watch from a suitable distance as folks in the large hobby area play with model rockets, remote-control airplanes, and model cars.

This is a welcome expanse of green for folks in the dense residential developments that surround the park. The parking fee is $2 per vehicle on weekdays, $4 on weekends, $5 on major holidays. At press time, there was a pending fee increase, so don't be surprised if it costs you more than a two spot. The park is at Edinger Avenue and Euclid Street. There are entrances on both sides. (714) 962-5549.

FULLERTON

PARKS, BEACHES, AND RECREATION AREAS

Most Fullerton parks don't permit pooches. Here are a couple that do, plus a dog-friendly county park. Unfortunately, as of press time, a recent, hard-fought bid by local dog people to start an off-leash dog park has fallen flat. Apparently the city couldn't find any land where nearby residents would tolerate a fenced-in dog enclosure. This is very sad for local dogs, indeed.

• **Brea Dam Recreation Area** 😺😺😺 *See ❾ on page 642.*

Dogs love to cool their heels in the stream that winds through this 250-acre park. While there are plenty of trails throughout the park, not one runs by the stream for any significant length. But it's fairly open land with only occasional thick brush, so it's not too tough to get around.

For dogs who like trees (and what canine isn't an arborist at heart?), you'll find oaks and California peppers galore. Joe likes to picnic under a shady oak and sleep on his back, all four legs pointed straight up to the sky.

Enter at the Fullerton Tennis Center area, at Harbor Boulevard and Valencia Mesa Drive. (714) 738-6300.

• **Craig Regional Park** 😺😺😺 *See ❿ on page 642.*

This natural haven's undulating tiers of green slopes create an island of tranquillity right next to the bordering Highway 57. A nature trail leads for 2.2 miles through the hills and flats of the park. Pick up a brochure at the ranger kiosk and learn about the multitude of plant and animal life that hides from civilization here.

For the humans in your crew, there are facilities for basketball, softball, volleyball, and racquetball. You can picnic with your pooch or have your dog help you watch your kids at the playground.

The parking fee is $2 per car on weekdays, $4 on weekends, $5 on major holidays. At press time, a fee increase was pending. The entrance is on State College Boulevard, just south of Highway 90. (714) 990-0271.

PLACES TO STAY

Fullerton Marriott Hotel: If you and your pooch need to stay near California State, this is the place for you. Rates are $59 to $114. 2701 East Nutwood Avenue, Fullerton, CA 92631; (714) 738-7800.

HUNTINGTON BEACH

Hey, dog dude! This is the surfing capital of the Orange coast. Dogs are allowed at only a small section of the beach here, and they have to be leashed, but at least they get to get their paws wet. (A group of doggone great beach lovers is trying to better dogs' plight at Dog Beach. See Dog Beach, page 651, for more on this effort and how you can help.)

The best news for dogs is Central Park's four-paw, off-leash dog park. See below. Dogs are proclaiming it a howling success.

PARKS, BEACHES, AND RECREATION AREAS

Dogs are banned from the Huntington State Beach and from most of the city beach. They're not even permitted on the paved path that parallels the beach. But there are still plenty of places for a pooch to play.

•**Central Park** 🐾 🐾 🐾 🐾 🐕 *See* ⓫ *on page 642.*

This huge city park has everything a dog could want. Hills, meadows, foresty areas, lakes, and trails are everywhere. You can walk on the paths that wind through the park and suddenly come upon an enchanting grassy knoll hidden behind a circle of trees, or find yourself in the middle of an intriguing nature observation area.

Best of all, Central Park now has a fenced-in dog park! Pooches can let down their hair and run around like the dogs they were meant to be—happy and leash-free, sniffing anywhere they want to sniff without their people getting embarrassed. The dog park is two acres, with mulch ground cover (for mud-free romping), fledgling trees, running water, benches for people, pooper-scooper dispensers (they go through 52,000 scoopers a year!), and even an ocean breeze. You can see the ocean from parts of the park.

Small dogs love it here, because they have their own little fenced area. Of course, most small dogs think they're really huge dogs, so they don't need their own park. But for the more timid tiny pooch, this "park within a park within a park" offers a feeling of security.

At press time, Patti Goff, one of the park's movers and shakers, was planning a "walk of fame" for the park. The sidewalk from the parking lot to the park's front gate will be covered with 12-inch-square cement pieces on which dogs can impress their own paw prints and people can write something about their dog. It's a fund-raising effort for the park, with squares going for $25 each. With more than 800 squares, it should net some good money for the park's needs. It will also be something that even people without dogs can enjoy. Kind of a Mann's Chinese Theatre of the canine world.

The dog park is located in the west side of the park, on Edwards Street, a little north of Ellis Avenue and south of Slater Avenue. Call the Huntington Beach Dog Park hotline for info on dog park activities: (714) 536-5672.

As for the rest of the 350-acre Central Park, unless you visit the park on a sunny weekend day, it isn't hard to find a peaceful place where you can be away from people and just have a restful picnic with your favorite person, your favorite book, and your favorite dog.

The park is divided in half by Golden West Road. It's almost as if there are two separate parks. Each half even has a truly wonderful restaurant chock-full of outdoor tables (see Alice's Breakfast in the Park and the amazing Park Bench Cafe, a must-visit for dogs, described on page 652). You can enter the east half of the park by heading east on the entry road, just across from Rio Vista Drive. The west half is accessible by driving west on Ellis Avenue. (714) 848-0690.

• **Dog Beach** 🐾 🐾 🐾 *See* ⓬ *on page 642.*

Wow, a place called Dog Beach right here in Orange County? Don't get excited! Stop panting! This portion of the Huntington City Beach isn't a leashless dog heaven. Dogs must remain fully clothed here, leashes and all.

The beach probably got this somewhat optimistic name from people who were enthusiastic that dogs could even set paw on a beach. After all, if you're coming south from Los Angeles County, where dogs are banned on all beaches, this is the first beach you'll come to where they're permitted.

The section of beach that allows dogs is the area from Golden West Street north to Seapoint Avenue (just south of Bolsa Chica State Beach, where pooches aren't permitted on the beach at all). The beach in the north part is plenty wide, but in the southern part you may want to check your tide tables —a very high tide can cover the entire sandy beach area here, leaving virtually no dry space between the breakwater and the ocean. Don't get caught between a rock and a wet place! The phone number for more beach info is (714) 536-5281.

As recently as early 1998, dogs were in danger of losing their pooch privileges here, because too many owners seemed to think their dogs had *poop* privileges. The poop on the beach was getting out of hand. The problem was actually that it was never getting *into* hand, or at least into pooper-scoopers. When the city made noises about banning dogs here, a group of responsible, energetic dog people got together and formed the Preservation Society of Huntington Dog Beach. Their motto: "To preserve, protect and pick up."

Their clean-up rallies and increased signage, as well as casual spot patrols for scofflaws, have started bringing dogs back into good graces with the city. But the battle is far from over: At this point, the city countil is voting about the beach's future on an anual basis. At press time, the dogs won by one vote. Whew.

If dog people keep up the good work, maybe one day the beach will be designated as a permanent dog area. At a recent rally, more than 700 people came to help scoop the poop. Newspapers and TV stations got the scoop and gave the group lots of coverage. "All my life I've done important things and haven't had a lot of public notice," says society chairman Martin Senat, a dapper English gent. "All of a sudden I'm picking up dog feces and the world is watching."

Senat and his group have now increased their ambitions. They want to make Dog Beach a leash-free beach. That would be an amazing feat, one that would make a lot of tails wag. They're using San Diego's Dog Beach (see page 680) as a model. To find out what you can do to help with this or other society efforts, call (714) 841-8644.

• **Farquhar Park** 🐾 🐾 *See* ⓭ *on page 642.*

This is a beautiful park that's just north of the dog-friendly strip of restaurants on Main Street. It's not very big, but the lush green grass and thickets of healthy palm trees create a charming place for even the most discriminating dog to lift a leg.

The park is on Main and 11th Streets. (714) 536-5486.

RESTAURANTS

Alice's Breakfast in the Park: Many folks bring their dogs to this enchanting restaurant during a Sunday morning stroll. It's located in the western half of Central Park, and has plenty of outdoor tables. The cinnamon rolls are great. 6622 Lakeview Drive; (714) 848-0690.

Breadcrumb Sugar Shack: This place serves breakfast and lunch, and the patio sees its share of canine companions. 215 Main Street; (714) 960-5051.

Midnight Espresso: Find yourself needing energy to keep up with your dog? Stop here and sip strong coffee on the patio. 2110 Main Street; (714) 960-5858.

Park Bench Cafe: This extremely dog-friendly eatery warrants a write-up in the *Los Angeles Times*. It deserves to be featured on *NBC Nightly News*. The BBC could even do a nice piece on it. In fact, these news organizations and many others have been drooling over this place since owner Mike Bartusick created a dog menu and added some picnic tables just for dogs and their people in 1994.

Now dogs can drool just like the media, thanks to some snout-watering culinary treats for dogs only. The motto here is "Every Dog has his Day at the Park Bench Cafe." On weekends, the place is jammed with dogs having their days. "It's crazy busy," says Bartusick. "I love it." Now that Central Park has its very own leash-free pooch park, the place is hopping as it never hopped before.

The Canine Cuisine menu items include the Hot Diggity Dog (a plain, all-beef hot dog, *sans* bun, cut up in doggy bite sizes), the Wrangler Roundup (a juicy lean turkey burger patty, again bun-free), and Anabelle's Treat (four chopped strips of bacon). As you can see, the dog menu is much like the human menu, only with the focus more on meat, less on accessories. Prices range from 75 cents for a scoop of dog kibble to $2.25 for the Wrangler. For dessert, order your dog a Chilly Paws (a scoop of vanilla ice cream) for $1.25. All pooch items are served on disposable dishes, so don't worry about finding dog slobber on your plate when you're downing your own food here.

Bartusick recently started offering Poochie Parties, with dog biscuit appetizers, each dog's choice of entrée from the Canine Cuisine menu, and Chilly Paws ice cream. Balloons and party hats are included, as is a "Bone Appetit" T-shirt for the birthday dog's person. The price for all this is $39.95 for up to six dogs. Additional dogs are $4.95 each. Cakes made with such goodies as liver (I won't be sneaking a finger of frosting on that one) are available for $24.95, but you have to order it two weeks in advance.

The Park Bench Cafe, located in the shade of pine trees at the edge of Central Park (see page 650), has been a dog-friendly eatery for years. Thirsty canine cruisers were invariably offered a big bowl of water when their people stopped by for a bite during a long walk through this beautiful park. Bartusick saw that many of the people were also ordering food items for their pooches. "Eventually I thought, why not have a menu where dogs are as welcome as people?" he says. "It's very California, but hey, what's wrong with that?"

The cafe is conveniently located at the entrance to the east side of Central Park. 17732 Golden West Street; (714) 842-0775.

PLACES TO STAY

Bolsa Chica State Beach campsites: Your dog can come mighty close to the beach here if she joins you for a night of camping at one of their 60 sites. Fees are $14. Dogs are $1 extra. The camping area turns into a parking lot by day, so don't be expecting to lounge around.

There's a small paved trail where you and your dog can go for a stroll. Sorry, pooches, but you can't set a paw on the beach itself. Fortunately, just down the sand a bit is Dog Beach (see page 651).

The state beach is on Highway 1, about three miles north of the main section of Huntington Beach. For information, call (714) 846-3460. For reservations, call Parknet at (800) 444-PARK.

IRVINE

PARKS, BEACHES, AND RECREATION AREAS

• **Turtle Rock Park** 😺😺 *See* **⑭** *on page 642.*

During the week, this 20-acre park gets little use. That's what makes it so comfortable for dogs. Leashed pooches can walk around the hills and the flats of the park with little danger of getting hit by a foul ball.

The park is on Turtle Rock Drive at Sunnyhill, between the suburbs and the San Joaquin Hills. (714) 724-6000.

• **William R. Mason Regional Park** 😺😺😺½ *See* **⑮** *on page 642.*

If you're a local University of California dog and you need to get away from campus for a few hours, tell your owner about this county park. Three miles of hiking and biking trails wind through the park's eastern wilderness. It's a great escape from the urban realities lurking just outside the park's perimeters.

The park has the usual human recreational facilities, as well as one unusual one: a Frisbee golf course. It's a good thing dogs have to be leashed, or it would be pure, unbridled, ecstatic mayhem among the retrieving pooches here.

Here's some exciting news: The county has given the city of Irvine the okay to install a fenced-in dog exercise area on about two acres of land here. If the city goes through with its tentative plan to install the dog run, it will be the best thing to happen to Irvine dogs and their families since *US News & World Report* cited the city as one of the 10 best places to live in the United States. If you know any of the decision-makers here, you may want to do a little lobbying.

The parking fee is $2 per car on weekdays, $4 on weekends, $5 on major holidays. You don't have to pay a thing if you walk in. The park is at University and Culver Drives. (714) 854-2491.

PLACES TO STAY

Irvine Marriott Hotel: This fancy hotel permits pups of every poundage. Rates are $80 to $160. 18000 Von Karman Avenue, Irvine, CA 92715; (714) 553-0100.

La Quinta Inn: Some of the rooms here are architecturally fascinating—one of the buildings used to be a lima bean silo! You must see this place for yourself. Rates are $62 to $77. 14972 Sand Canyon Avenue, Irvine, CA 92718; (714) 551-0909.

LAGUNA BEACH

Exclusive but friendly, Laguna Beach has an unmistakable Mediterranean feel, thanks to the mild seaside climate and all the fine art galleries and outdoor cafes. Dogs are happy here, especially because of a fine off-leash dog run. (See Bark Park, below.)

PARKS, BEACHES, AND RECREATION AREAS

• **Bark Park/Laguna Beach Dog Run** 🐾🐾🐾🐾 🐕
   See **16** *on page 642.*

People come from many miles away to take their dogs to this fenced-in dog-exercise area in the canyon. During dog rush hour, it's not uncommon to see a couple dozen leashless, grinning dogs running and tumbling around in great joy.

Although there's no shade, there's plenty of doggy drinking water. Picnic tables add a dimension of comfort for the park's humans.

The park has to close periodically because of the danger of mudslides, so if you're traveling a long way to get here, you may want to call the city first to check on the situation. In addition, we've heard that there was quite the problem with poop not long ago. The city had to come in and haul it out in huge barrels. Park people have apparently been doing a better job of scooping since that ugly day.

From Highway 1, go north on Broadway/Laguna Canyon Road. The park will be on your right in 2.6 miles, just before the GTE building. (714) 497-0706.

• **Heisler Park** 🐾🐾 *See* **17** *on page 642.*

The landscaping is lovely and the view is just as good. This small, palm-filled park sits on a bluff just above Picnic Beach. Dogs must be leashed, but they enjoy cruising around here during the times they're restricted from the beaches.

The park runs from Canyon Drive to Broadway/Laguna Canyon Road, just west of Cliff Drive. (714) 497-0706.

• **Laguna Beach Beaches** 🐾 🐾 🐾 *See* ⓲ *on page 642.*

Leashed dogs can peruse the beaches, but from June 1 to mid-September, their visiting times are limited. During that period, pooches aren't allowed on the beach from 8 A.M. to 6 P.M.

Main Beach is a long, sandy beach that has a playground and basketball courts. A good entry point is just south of the Heisler Park area (see above). If you want to get away from people, you may be better off at any of the pocket beaches that dot the city's coast. There are also several small, rocky pocket beaches you can reach via walkways off Cliff Drive. (714) 497-0706.

RESTAURANTS

A la Carte: You and your dog are welcome to dine on the patio of this pink restaurant. With 16 different entrées (not to mention numerous salads and desserts), it's likely that no one will go away hungry. 1915 South Coast Highway; (714) 497-4927.

Cafe Zinc: This place is just one outdoor table after another. At times, reports cafe regular Mary Bavry, "there's a dog at every table." Don't trip, and try the apple spice muffins. 350 Ocean Avenue; (714) 494-6302.

The Cottage Restaurant: As long as you and the pooch sit on the outer rim of the patio, the folks here will be happy to see you. 308 North Coast Highway; (714) 494-3023.

The Heidelberg Pastry Bistro: Besides tasty pastries, you and your best furry friend can dine on all sorts of traditional European foods amid the trees at the outdoor area. 1100 South Coast Highway; (714) 497-4594.

Subway: There are plenty of benches for you and the hungry pooch. 1350 South Coast Highway; (714) 376-1995.

242 Cafe: Wow, dogs! Check out this dog-friendly cafe. It features a dog station just for you, complete with water bowls and tasty dog bones. The food for humans is good, too, but really now—who cares? 242 North Coast Highway; (714) 494-2444.

PLACES TO STAY

The Carriage House: Only the most well-behaved dogs are welcome here, and only if you call ahead of time and get the okay. After all, it's not every day a dog gets to stay in a 1920s bed-and-breakfast that's a historic landmark. Rates are $95 to $150. Dogs are $5 extra. 1322 Catalina Street, Laguna Beach, CA 92651; (714) 494-8945.

Casa Laguna Inn: The Casa Laguna is an enchanting, romantic Spanish-style bed-and-breakfast that overlooks the mighty Pacific Ocean. Its 15 rooms, four suites, Mission House, and charming cottage are set on a terraced hillside. Surrounding the lodgings are luscious tropical gardens that include such goodies as banana and avocado trees and bougainvillea. Well-behaved dogs and their people love to relax on the aviary patio, beneath a family of glorious queen palms.

There are many little nooks and gardens to discover at the Casa Laguna, and your dog will enjoy helping you find them all. As the day ends, watch the sun set over Catalina Island.

Rates are $69 to $225 and include an extensive buffet breakfast and afternoon wine with hors d'oeuvres. Dogs are $5 extra. 2510 South Coast Highway, Laguna Beach, CA 92651; (714) 494-2996 or (800) 233-0449.

Vacation Village: Dogs love staying here, because they're allowed on the beach, which is right behind the hotel. Leashed pooches can peruse the beach here anytime it's open to dogs (see Laguna Beach beaches, page 655, for dog-okay times). Humans like the fact that there's full-beach service, complete with towels and lounge chairs. Usually, however, sunbathing and dogs don't mix. The hotel's restricted dog times (they're not allowed in July or August) certainly decrease the temptation to get tan with your dog.

If you (the human in your party) want to swim but find the surf a bit rough, the hotel has two pools for your paddling pleasure.

Rates are $67 to $206. There's a $10 pooch fee per visit. 647 South Coast Highway, Laguna Beach, CA 92651; (714) 494-8566 or (800) 843-6895.

LAGUNA NIGUEL

Three cheers and a woof for Laguna Niguel! Read about Pooch Park (page 657) and you'll know why tails are wagging fast here.

PARKS, BEACHES, AND RECREATION AREAS

• **Aliso/Wood Canyons Regional Park** 🐾🐾🐾½
See ⑲ on page 642.

Since dogs aren't permitted in county wilderness areas, they're banned from the Wood Canyon section of this 2,500-acre park. But because Aliso Canyon isn't considered wilderness, leashed dogs are welcome. The good news is that about two-thirds of the acreage is in Aliso Canyon. The 13-mile-long Aliso Creek Trail takes you and your pooch through some very scenic areas, but unless you're both in extraordinary shape, you won't want to tackle the whole thing.

The "eh" news is that Aliso Canyon is brushy and scrubby, with none of the wonderful trees that grace Wood Canyon. One school of thought behind the contrasting landscapes is that back around 1776, when Father Junipero Serra was building missions, his men may have denuded this canyon to create the San Juan Capistrano Mission. The county is considering reforesting the canyon, but it's an expensive task.

The parking fee is $2 per car on weekdays, $4 on weekends, $5 on major holidays. There's an entrance to the park off Alicia Parkway, just west of town. Call (714) 831-2790 for directions to specific parts of the park.

• **Crown Valley Community Park** 🐾🐾🐾 *See ⑳ on page 642.*

It's so peaceful here that it's hard to believe you're in a community park. The park is fairly large, with green hills, lots of trees, and trails that wind through all this splendor. You and your leashed dog will enjoy the tranquillity here.

The park is on the west side of Crown Valley Parkway, just north of Niguel Road. (714) 362-4300.

• **Laguna Niguel Regional Park** 🐾🐾🐾 *See* ㉑ *on page 642.*

A big chunk of the accessible land here is devoted to a lake where you and your leashed dog can fish for rainbow trout from shore. It's a fun pastime, but dogs can get bored just watching you cast and reel in all day.

If your dog needs a hiking break, the equestrian trail here isn't a bad place for a walk. Parts of it are too close to La Paz Road for traffic-free ambience, but other sections (especially the trail far west of the lake) are more secluded. You'll be shaded by eucalyptus trees and acacias as you hike up and down the rolling hills.

From Crown Valley Parkway, turn northwest on La Paz Road and follow the signs to the entrance. The parking fee is $2 per car on weekdays, $4 on weekends, $5 on major holidays. If you walk in, it's free. (714) 831-2791.

• **Pooch Park** 🐾🐾🐾½ 🐕 *See* ㉒ *on page 642.*

It's only a bit over one acre, and it has only three small trees, but to dogs who long to run unfettered by a leash, this fenced park is poochy paradise.

Pooch Park, which opened in November 1997, is gobs of fun for dogs on the go. It's grassy, it's at the top of a canyon, and it's got the coolest dog-watering area yet. If your dog is Lassie, or a Lassie wanna-be, she can press a lever with her paw and drink the water as it streams several inches into the air. Or she can let the water fill a strategically placed water bowl. Of course, if she's like Joe, she can accidentally step on the paw-activated fountain, get splashed in the face, and have the heebie-jeebies for the rest of the afternoon. (Most dogs are not like Joe.)

At press time, a brass fire hydrant was scheduled to be installed to take the "male dog" pressure off the young trees here.

The park is located on the west side of Street of the Golden Lantern, between Beacon Hill Way and Chapparosa Park Road (closer to Beacon Hill Way). (714) 362-4337.

MISSION VIEJO

PARKS, BEACHES, AND RECREATION AREAS

• **O'Neill Regional Park** 🐾🐾🐾½ *See* ㉓ *on page 642.*

So close to suburbia, and yet so far, this is the paws-down favorite Orange County park for dogs who like wilderness. Dogs are not permitted in the county's true wilderness parks, but for some reason, this 1,700-acre piece of lush land doesn't fall into that category.

Dogs love to hike along the six and a half miles of trails that go past streamside oak and sycamore woodlands. They have to be leashed, which is something the mountain lions here don't appreciate. Besides the woodlands, you can peruse grassy meadows and shrub-covered hillsides. And if you're in a hungry mood, the area near the entryway has plenty of picnic tables. You supply the food and the park will supply the ambience.

Camping is available along the creek and in the higher elevation Mesa Camp area. There are 90 campsites, all first come, first served. Fees are $12.

Camping pooches are $1 extra. If you're just here for the day, you'll be charged a parking fee of $2 per car on weekdays, $4 on weekends, $5 on major holidays.

Follow El Toro Road (in the city's northernmost reaches) northeast. It eventually turns into Live Oak Canyon Road and veers to the south. About three miles past where the road changes names, you'll come to the park's main entrance. It's just south of the Rama Krishna Monastery, on the right side of the road. (714) 858-9365.

• **Oso Viejo Park** 🐾 🐾 ½ *See ㉔ on page 642.*

It can get mighty crowded here on days when the sports fields are jammed with ball players. But you can almost always find an escape by heading to the creek that runs along the northwest side of the park. There, you'll find some trees, shrubs, and enough room for you and your dog to sit down and read a good book. Make sure to keep your dog on leash, because rattle-snakes and mountain lions have been seen here.

The park is on La Paz Road at Oso Viejo, just east of Marguerite Drive. (714) 470-3000.

• **Wilderness Glen Park** 🐾 🐾 🐾 *See ㉕ on page 642.*

At certain times of year, a creek rushes through this narrow, two-mile-long wooded park and provides a refreshing escape from the surrounding suburbs. This is a hidden, unmarked park that most people just drive past without realizing it's there. It's in a narrow canyon, surrounded by lush foliage. A trail follows the creek, so you and your leashed dog can have a waterside sojourn. You can even dip all your feet in the water to cool off on a warm afternoon.

The park is bordered by Los Alisos Boulevard on the east side. You can enter the park at many points by turning left on any street that runs into the park. Our favorite is Via Noveno. Park around Atomo Drive and walk down the wooden stairs into the park. (714) 470-3000.

PLACES TO STAY

O'Neill Regional Park: See O'Neill Regional Park on page 657 for camping information.

NEWPORT BEACH

If your dog enjoys the water-dog lifestyle, he's sure to love Newport Beach. Between the beaches, bays, and boats (see Diversions, page 661), many watery adventures await any dog who doesn't get seasick while watching you fill the bathtub.

The city encompasses several communities, including Balboa Island, Corona del Mar, and Mariners Mile. Balboa Island has its own heading in this chapter (see page 645).

This is where my superb correspondents Troovee Dog and Mary Bavry live. If you should meet them at a cafe, be sure to give Troovee Dog a scratch on the head. He's done a lot of paw work searching for places to include in this book. (He's a little guy, kind of grayish, kind of brownish, kind of terrierish. He'll have a smile on his snout for being with such a kind and dog-devoted person.)

PARKS, BEACHES, AND RECREATION AREAS

• **Balboa Beach** 🐾🐾🐾 *See* ㉖ *on page 642.*

Balboa Beach is wide and sandy enough for a dog to forget that it's a dog's life. The only reminders here are the mandatory leash attire and the restricted dog-access hours.

Dogs aren't permitted on the beach at all from June 15 to September 15, and the rest of the year they can only go to the beach before 9 A.M. and after 5 P.M.

The beach runs from around Main Street to the West Jetty area. You can enter the beach at the ends of many of the streets here. (714) 644-3047.

• **Corona del Mar State Beach** 🐾🐾🐾 *See* ㉗ *on page 642.*

Fear not! Although this is a state beach, dogs are permitted during certain times of year. That's because the city of Newport Beach maintains it and makes most of the rules. Dogs aren't allowed on the beach at all from June 15 to September 15, and the rest of the year they're only permitted before 9 A.M. and after 5 P.M.

If you happen to be east of the eastern jetty at the entrance to Newport Harbor, you'll be happy to know that this large and popular beach permits pooches during the off-season. The beach starts at the eastern jetty at the entrance to Newport Harbor. (714) 644-3047.

• **Newport Beach** 🐾🐾🐾 *See* ㉘ *on page 642.*

This beach starts out quite narrow at the northern border of Newport Beach and widens as it continues south to around Main Street. You'll have fun watching the surfers surf and the sun worshipers worship.

The only problem is that during the times when dogs are allowed, there's not a whole lot of sun to worship. Dogs aren't permitted on the beach at all from June 15 to September 15, and the rest of the year they can only go to the beach before 9 A.M. and after 5 P.M. They always have to be leashed.

Joe enjoys hanging out by the pier area and grabbing a bite from the nearby restaurants. Your dog will, too. (714) 644-3047.

• **Peninsula Park** 🐾 *See* ㉙ *on page 642.*

What? It's summer, you're near the beach, and your leashed dog needs to go for a walk? If she can't hold it until fall, when the beaches here permit pooches, a visit to this square-block park is a tolerable solution.

The park is west of Ocean Front Avenue, just south of the Balboa Pier. It's flat and grassy, with a band shell, baseball diamonds, a playground, and picnic tables. There's not much shade, but the ocean breeze usually cools things off enough. (714) 644-3062.

• **Upper Newport Bay Regional Park** 🐾🐾🐾½ *See* ㉚ *on page 642.*

The Upper Newport Bay is surrounded by shopping centers and suburban sprawl. But fortunately, this large park preserves the remaining sanctity of the once-pristine bayside.

The myriad dirt trails in this open, hilly area provide you and your leashed dog with a great way to get around. Dog footprints are embedded in the trails—evidence of happy pooches on muddy days.

The park is made up of tall grasses and twiggy weeds. No trees get in the way of the bird-watching here. Bring your binoculars and try to ignore the tall office buildings in the distance.

You can also do some excellent, up-close bird-watching from Back Bay Road, on the east side of the bay. But it's easier to get to the regional park section, and it's less stress for the birds if you keep your dog far from them. The poor birds have enough on their minds with the onward march of malls and suburban subdivisions.

Traveling north on Irvine Avenue, turn right on University Drive. About the equivalent of a block down the road, turn around and park on the other side of the street (there's no parking on the south side) and walk back across the street and to the park entrance. (714) 644-3151.

RESTAURANTS

Alta Coffee: The large gazebo outside the restaurant is a terrific place for you and your pooch to sip the great coffee and dine on the cafe's tasty soups, pastas, and pastries. In fact, the gazebo is packed with lucky dogs every weekend, according to a manager. We've also heard it's a great place to sniff out potential romance (with your dog first introducing you to someone else's dog, and then, of course, the dog's person). 506 31st Street; (714) 675-0233.

Bruegger's Bagel Bakery: If you don't have a dog, you may feel positively naked here. This terrific bagelry is so doggone dog-friendly that on weekends, you can find up to a couple dozen dogs at a time hanging out on and around Bruegger's wraparound porch. Dogs love it here, not only because they get to chat with each other and socialize with other humans, but because Bruegger's treats dogs like kings: Dogs who visit get a free bagel! And not even a day-old bagel. A fresh one. The bagels are delicious, so your dog will be a lucky dog indeed if he gets to accompany you here. George Dog and his person JoAnna Downey told us about this place. A big thanks to them! (George Dog is the one with the poppy seeds stuck between his teeth.) Dogs also get fresh water. This is a four-paw, must-visit destination. 2743 East Pacific Coast Highway; (714) 723-4485.

Newport Beach Brewing Co.: You and your dog are welcome to dine on delicious food and drink house-made brewskis at the huge outdoor area here. The restaurant, located in the historic cannery area, is very attractive, but dogs care much more about the food, which includes woodfire pizzas, tender lamb dishes, unique pastas, and good ol' burgers (Joe's favorite). 2920 Newport Boulevard; (714) 675-8449.

Sabatino's Sicilian Restaurant: The Sicilian cuisine here is *fantastico.* Joe highly recommends the sausages, although the lasagna is to drool for, too. Dogs get to dine very close to you, but they have to be tied on the other side of the shrubbery "railing." If your dog's snout looks dry, they'll likely offer him a bowl of cool water. 251 Shipyard Way; (714) 723-0621.

PLACES TO STAY

Marriott Suites Hotel: Our intrepid correspondent Troovee Dog and his mom, Mary Bavry, wrote to tell us that the bay views from one side of this hotel are terrific. And indeed they are. The hotel is right across the street from the Back Bay area, where you can walk your pooch right next to the water. All the rooms are suites (no kitchens, though), so there's plenty of room for dogs of the big galoot ilk. The suite rate is $159. 500 Bayview Circle, Newport Beach, CA 92660; (714) 854-4500.

DIVERSIONS

Go island shopping: Dogs are a normal part of the scene at Fashion Island, Newport Beach's huge open-air shopping mall. There's plenty of walking room and even some grassy areas where your dog can rest her weary paws. Some stores permit pooches inside, but since they do it on a case-by-case basis, we'll let you explore for yourself. And there's plenty of exploring to do: The mall is home to 200 stores. One woman I met attaches a small purse to her large dog's collar. "That way I think twice before I buy," she says. "Besides, it's safer on him than on me."

As an added bonus, the mall is just a bone's throw away from Upper Newport Bay Regional Park (see page 659, a great place to drop after you shop. Fashion Island is on the Pacific Coast Highway (Highway 1), between Jamboree Road and MacArthur Boulevard (Veterans Memorial Highway). (714) 721-2000.

Pooches make great passengers: The historic Balboa Pavilion/Balboa Fun Zone is where you and your dog can embark on nautical adventures on two unique boat lines. This is one of our favorite places to go with pooches because they're so welcome on these vessels. It's easy for your dog to feel like one of the family here. Best of all, pooches go for free on both excursions.

The smaller of these boats is the Balboa Island Ferry, which is open-hulled and fits only three cars and a few passengers at a time. The trip to lovely Balboa Island (see page 645) takes only a few minutes, but it's a good way to test if your dog is up for a longer journey on the other dog-friendly boat line here. Fees range from 35 cents for a walk-on passenger to $1 for a car and passenger. The ferries run every few minutes during daylight hours.

Dogs with a more nautical bent can join you for a howling good time on a cruise of Newport Harbor—one of the nation's finest yacht harbors. The Showboat Cruise offers a couple of grand tours. On one, you'll see the homes and yachts of celebrities and learn the history of the area. On the other tour, you'll cruise up to the haunts of the vocal, local sea lions. "The sea lions are fascinated by the dogs, and the dogs are fascinated by the sea lions," says Captain Mike. "It's quite a sight." Each tour is 45 minutes long and costs $6 per adult and $2 per child. Or take a 90-minute tour that combines both of the shorter jaunts. It costs $9 per adult and $2 per child. Call (714) 673-0240.

Unfortunately, dogs are not allowed on the *Catalina Flyer*, which motors with amazing speed over to beautiful Catalina Island. But if you're interested in hitting the island with your pooch, see page 601 for info on how to get there and what you'll find once you're there.

Before or after either of the two dog-friendly boat trips, make sure you check out the Balboa Pavilion area. Dogs love to watch the merry-go-round go round and the Ferris wheel whirl. It's also a great place for watching the famed Christmas Boat Parade of Lights. The pavilion is located two blocks north of Balboa Boulevard, at the north end of Main Street.

ORANGE

PARKS, BEACHES, AND RECREATION AREAS

No dogs are permitted in any City of Orange parks.

• **Irvine Regional Park** 🐾🐾🐾½ *See* ㉛ *on page 642.*

This 447-acre park is home to the Orange County Zoo, but since dogs aren't allowed at the zoo, they don't care much for it. They prefer to hike along the miles of equestrian and nature trails that run through chaparral and forests of huge oaks and sycamores.

There's something for everyone here. You can rent a horse, a pony, a bicycle, or a paddleboat. You can walk by the creek, eat lunch at shaded picnic tables, play softball, throw horseshoes, or just do nothing and take a snooze with your dog under a big old tree. Dogs usually opt for the hike, the snooze, or both.

The parking fee is $2 per car weekdays, $4 on weekends, $5 on major holidays. If you walk in, there is no fee. From Highway 55, take the Chapman exit and head east for about five miles to the park entrance. (714) 633-8074.

• **Peters Canyon Regional Park** 🐾🐾🐾½ *See* ㉜ *on p. 642.*

Dogs love this park, and for good reason: It has 358 acres of coastal sage scrub, freshwater marshes, and grasslands. Trees such as willows and black cottonwoods line the 55-acre reservoir (no dogs in water here!) and the creek (again, no paws, please). Our favorite trail, the Peters Canyon Creek Nature Trail, takes you and your leashed dog along the creek through lush groves of trees. Joe Dog thinks this is peachy.

We got word about this park through Honey Dog and her person, Sandy Koizumi. Thanks for the tip! We checked out the park and agree that it's terrific. But I almost decided not to include it in the book because some things a park ranger told me. He said too many people allow their pooches off leash here, and that this is jeopardizing the already fragile environment, in addition to the future of dogs in the park. "Peters Canyon is a biological hot pot, an area of exceptional biodiversity in a rapidly urbanizing landscape. Studies of at-large dogs in protected areas attest to increased reproductive failure, stress and mortality in breeding avifauna." (Joe Dog looked up this word, and it means birds). "At least two documented nest failures last spring were directly attributed to at-large dogs here."

I finally decided to include this park in the book because I believe it's better that people know the risks and keep their dogs leashed than if they proceed blindly and hurt the environment and eventually get dogs banned from the park. If there are some folks out there who want to form an informal "watchdog" group to let folks know about leashes, that might be just what the park ranger ordered.

If all this doesn't convince you to leash up here, maybe this will: Wildlife abounds here. Included in the mix: mountain lions, rattlesnakes, bobcats, and coyotes. There's poison oak, too. So grab a leash, head for the hills, stick to the trails, and everyone will be happy. End of lecture.

The park is in the far east end of Orange. From Newport Boulevard (a few blocks south of Chapman Avenue), drive east on Canyon View Avenue to the park entrance on the right. The parking fee is $2 per car on weekdays, $4 on weekends, $5 on major holidays; (714) 538-4400.

• **Santiago Oaks Regional Park** 🐾 🐾 🐾 1/2 *See* **33** *on page 642.*

This 350-acre wildlife reserve is dominated by majestic coast live oaks and California sycamores. Santiago Creek, the main tributary of the Santa Ana River in Orange County, runs through much of this park.

Dogs love it here, but they have to be leashed. Boy dogs seem to have a special fondness for the park, no doubt because there are thousands of ornamental trees on the north side of the creek.

Bring your binoculars. The wildlife watching is terrific. More than 130 species of birds have been observed here. Coyotes, bobcats, and mountain lions have also been known to frequent the park. If you need any extra inspiration to keep your dog leashed, that should do the trick.

The parking fee is $2 per car on weekdays, $4 on weekends, $5 on major holidays. From Highway 55, take the Katella Avenue exit east about 4.5 miles to Windes Drive (Katella Avenue eventually becomes Santiago Canyon Road). Turn left on Windes Drive and follow its angular turns as it leads you north to the park entrance. (714) 538-4400.

RESTAURANTS
Pickle's: This deli serves great sandwiches and fries at its outdoor tables. 312 South Main Street; (714) 978-6071.

SAN CLEMENTE
Dogs are not permitted at any of the city's parks or beaches or at the county beach. Fortunately for San Clemente dogs, the pooch restrictions may be eased in the future. Unfortunately, "future" means different things to different people. "I couldn't count on it happening real soon," said one parks department official last time we checked. "We have absolutely no idea when it could be." If you're feeling optimistic or antsy, call (714) 361-8264 for an update.

RESTAURANTS
Beach Garden Cafe: The views from the outdoor tables are gorgeous, and the breakfast and lunch fare is just as delectable. 618 1/2 Avenida Victoria; (714) 498-8145.

Louise's: You and your dog can share a refreshing snack outside this yogurt/juice bar. 1624 North El Camino Real; (714) 361-1825.

PLACES TO STAY
Holiday Inn San Clemente: If you're lucky, you might get a room with an ocean view here. Rates are $70 to $99. There's a $10 charge per visit for your dog. 111 South Avenida de Estrella, San Clemente, CA 92672; (714) 361-3000.

SAN JUAN CAPISTRANO
The rebuilt version of the mission that was constructed by Father Junipero Serra in 1776 attracts some 300,000 visitors annually. Around March 19 every year, the swallows arrive from Argentina to nest in the valley. They used to flock to the mission, but with recent noisy renovations and hordes

of visitors, they've taken to other parts of the valley. "They've gone to the suburbs, just like humans," says one docent.

Dogs aren't allowed on the grounds of the mission, but you can watch this annual migration from just about anywhere in town. It's not as dramatic as Alfred Hitchcock's *The Birds*, but it's still a great way to pass a lazy afternoon in one of the parks here.

PARKS, BEACHES, AND RECREATION AREAS

• **Acu Park** 😺😺½ *See* ③④ *on page 642.*

This park is about 11 blocks long, but only a couple of blocks wide. When the park isn't packed with people, you and your leashed pooch can cruise through the soccer fields, play in the open areas, or picnic at the many tables here. Trees surround the park, but there's not much shade in the heart of the park.

The park is between Connemara Drive and Camino Las Ramblas and Kinkerry and Pescador Lanes. (714) 493-5911.

• **C. Russell Cook Park** 😺😺😺 *See* ③⑤ *on page 642.*

Big old trees line the perimeter of this park, where you and your leashed dog may choose to amble along the shaded path near the creek bed.

If your dogs likes his paws to hit green grass with every step, you can hang out on the greenbelt area. You'll find ball fields and playgrounds here, but you'll also find some open areas where you can get away from other folks.

The park is on Calle Arroyo and stretches for several blocks between Calle del Campo and Avenida Siega. (714) 493-5911.

RESTAURANTS

Cedar Creek Inn: You and your history-loving dog can dine at the lovely, big, tree-shaded patio that faces the Mission San Juan Capistrano. The fresh fish is delicious, as are the house-made desserts. 26860 Ortega Highway; (714) 240-2229.

PLACES TO STAY

Best Western Capistrano Inn: Small dogs only, please. The hotel offers a complimentary breakfast to humans on weekdays. (Actually, it's a breakfast voucher for Denny's.) Rates are $71 to $95. 27174 Ortega Highway, San Juan Capistrano, CA 92675; (714) 493-5661.

SANTA ANA

It's refreshing to see that a few farm fields still thrive in the midst of this governmental center of Orange County. The downtown area is a charmer, but there's not much for a dog to do, unless he feels like soaking up history on a walking tour of the renovated district. Call the Orange County Historical Society at (714) 543-8282 for information.

PARKS, BEACHES, AND RECREATION AREAS

• **Centennial Regional Park** 😺😺😺 *See* ③⑥ *on page 642.*

If you want a real treat, get here early on a cool morning and watch the steam from the park's lake rising up through the surrounding willows. As the sun's rays turn the vapors a golden-orange hue, you'll swear you've never seen such a beautiful sight.

The sign on the lake says "No Swimming," but the ducks just don't listen. You and your leashed dog should stay high and dry, though, no matter how tempting a little wade would be on a hot summer afternoon.

The park has many big green fields, most of which are sports fields. But if you visit during a non-athletic time, you'll just about have the whole place to yourself. Walkways run throughout the park, so you and your dog can cover lots of ground with ease.

A word of warning: We recently heard from faithful correspondent Mary Bavry that the park is strewn with broken crack pipes, smashed bottles, used condoms, and discarded needles. A humane society fund-raiser had to be cancelled because of the horrible mess. A call to the park department leads me to believe that things have improved, and that vigilance is the watchword. However, vigilance can slip, so keep your eyes open and look before you let your dog leap out of the car. On good faith that the park department will keep the situation in check, I'm keeping the three-paw rating.

The park's main entrance is at Centennial Park and Mohawk Drives. (714) 571-4200.

•**Prentice Park** 🐾 🐾 🐾 *See* **37** *on page 642.*
While your kids are visiting the adjacent Santa Ana Zoo, you and your leashed dog are free to wander around the attractive parkland surrounding it. Dogs like the grass and picnic tables, but they're often so intoxicated by the ripe animal odors emanating from the zoo that they notice little else.

Exit Interstate 5 at the First/Fourth Avenue exit and follow the signs to the zoo. It's at Chestnut Avenue, a few blocks east of Grand Avenue. (714) 571-4200.

RESTAURANTS
Red Robin Burger and Spirits Emporium: This restaurant serves big burgers and lots of other tasty dishes at its sidewalk tables. 1307 Sunflower Avenue; (714) 432-1111.

PLACES TO STAY
Motel 6: Rates are $34 for the first adult, $6 for the second. One smallish pooch per room. 1623 East First Street, Santa Ana, CA 92701; (714) 558-0500.

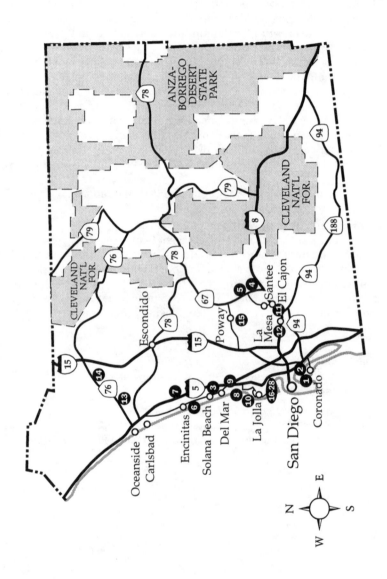

ANZA-
BORREGO
DESERT
STATE
PARK

CLEVELAND
NAT'L FOR.

CLEVELAND
NAT'L FOR.

Escondido

Poway

Santee
El Cajon
La Mesa

Oceanside
Carlsbad

Encinitas
Solana Beach
Del Mar
La Jolla
San Diego
Coronado

N
E
S
W

54
SAN DIEGO COUNTY

Look at a map of the county and you'll see green blotches everywhere. But don't be fooled. Most of these verdant expanses are golf courses. Golf is the game of choice here, and since dogs don't play golf very well (their hair gets in their eyes), you can ignore all those areas.

But fear not. San Diego County isn't such a tough place for dogs. Most county-run parks permit them, although they're banned from trails. And there are now six beaches and parks (not including Cleveland National Forest) where dogs are allowed to run in leash-free ecstasy. The most recent addition to these havens is a fun, fenced dog park in Poway, described on page 678.

The majority of the eastern half of the county is taken up by Anza-Borrego Desert State Park and Cleveland National Forest. The forest is heavenly for dogs (see page 749). The 600,000-acre desert park, on the other hand, is a doggy drag. Pooches are permitted only in campgrounds and on roads. Granted, there are some dirt roads that aren't used much, but it's just not the same as hiking the trails here. And dogs are banned from walking on the desert itself.

Speaking of deserts, the coastal area from Oceanside all the way down to

Cardiff is a virtual desert for dogs. They don't get to go near the water at all because beaches in this stretch ban the beasts.

Fortunately, once you get down to the Del Mar area, little bits of Dog Heaven pop up fairly frequently. You'll really hit paydirt (paysand?) when you venture onto San Diego's Dog Beach (see page 680). Many adventures await you, including a wonderful new restaurant devoted to dogs—and other pets (see The Original Paw Pleasers, page 688).

NATIONAL FORESTS

See the National Forests and Wilderness Areas chapter starting on page 748 for important information and safety tips on visiting national forests with your dog.

• **Cleveland National Forest** 🐾🐾🐾🐾 🏃
See page 749.

CARLSBAD

Dogs aren't allowed in any city parks or beaches here. Joe thinks we should pronounce this city with the emphasis on the second syllable: Carls*bad*.

RESTAURANTS

Jay's Gourmet Restaurant: The locals know about this place and drool over it, and now you know, too. So drool! The pastas, pizzas, and Italian-style seafood are delicious. The attitude here is dog-friendly, with pooches who dine at the four outdoor tables getting lots of oohs and ahhhs from the staff. 2975 Carlsbad Boulevard; (760) 720-9688.

La Costa Coffee Roasting Company: As long as they don't go hopping onto the furniture, dogs are fine here. The staff will even give your dog a "glass" of water. And since the patio is in a mall, you could go shopping if you have a pooch-sitter along with you. 6965 El Camino Real; (760) 438-8160.

Spirito's: If you're in the mood for Italian food, this patio is for you (and your dog). They even have handmade ravioli. Joe likes the frozen kind better, but only if they're still frozen when he eats them. 300 Carlsbad Village Drive; (760) 720-1132.

PLACES TO STAY

Inns of America: This place overlooks the freeway, but the price is right. Rates are $51 to $61. 751 Raintree Drive, Carlsbad, CA 92009; (760) 931-1185.

South Carlsbad State Beach: Dogs aren't allowed on the beach here, but they're welcome to camp with you, even at the oceanside campground. There are 224 sites, with nightly fees ranging from $14 to $21. Dogs are $1 extra. For reservations, call Parknet at (800) 444-PARK. For campground information, call (760) 438-3143.

CORONADO

Folks traveling with dogs aren't allowed to take the ferry to this island-like destination across the San Diego Bay. But a graceful 2.2-mile bridge will get you there just as fast—which is the speed your dog will want to go when she learns she can run off leash at one of the beaches here.

PARKS, BEACHES, AND RECREATION AREAS

• **Coronado City Beach/Dog Beach** 😀 😀 😀 😀 🐕

See ❶ on page 666.

The westernmost part of this beach is a nude beach for dogs, where they can strip off their leashes and revel in their birthday furs. And since few people know about it, even the shyest dog will feel at home running around flaunting her more natural self.

As long as your dog is under voice control, she can be leashless at a small segment of this little beach. Your dog has only a few hundred feet of shoreline to run along, but the area between the beach border and the water is fairly wide.

The off-leash section is marked by signs and runs along Ocean Boulevard from around the foot of Sunset Park (on Ocean Drive) to the border of the U.S. Naval Station. You'll see the doggy litter bags. From the bridge, continue straight. In a few blocks, turn left on Orange Avenue and drive through town all the way down to the traffic circle. Go around the circle to Loma Avenue and follow it south about a block to Ocean Boulevard. Drive northwest a few blocks and park on the street around Sunset Park. (619) 522-7380.

• **Coronado Tidelands Regional Park** 😀 😀 😀 *See ❷ on page 666.*

Located on San Diego Bay just north of the toll plaza, this is the largest of Coronado's parks and it's got a little of everything. From manicured golf-course-like lawns to playing fields, walking paths, and terrific views of San Diego, the park suits the needs of just about any dog. There's even a small beach here. Dogs must be leashed, though, so there's no swimming back to San Diego!

After crossing the bridge, take your first right onto Glorietta Boulevard. Go right again into the park on Mullinix Drive. (619) 435-4179.

RESTAURANTS

Bay Books Cafe: Besides coffees, teas, and pastries, this place sells books. Make sure you have a pooch-sitter along to hang out at the outdoor tables with your dog while you scope out the selections inside. 1029 Orange Avenue; (619) 435-0070.

Cafe 1134: Pooches are welcome to keep you company at these outdoor tables while you dine on sandwiches and coffee. 1134 Orange Avenue; (619) 437-1134.

Coronado Bakery: Besides the usual cakes and muffins, this place serves cappuccino and other specialty coffee drinks. You and your dog are welcome to partake in these treats at the outdoor seating. 1206 Orange Avenue; (619) 435-9272.

Dairy Queen: Your pooch will beg you to take him to this DQ—they'll give him a free vanilla soft-serve while you dine at the outdoor tables! 926 Orange Avenue; (619) 437-4183.

Deli by the Bay: Stop and smell the cool ocean breezes with your dog as you eat on the patio. The deli has tasty soups, sandwiches, and salads. 1201 First Street; (619) 437-1006.

Primavera Pastry Cafe: This bakery/cafe serves a mean breakfast and a meaner lunch. Sit outside with your pooch and try their delectable waffles or grilled sandwiches. 956 Orange Avenue; (619) 435-4191.

Viva Nova: The folks at this restaurant love dogs. The vegetarian cuisine includes hot soups and chili, which you can eat at the outdoor tables. There's also a juice bar and a health food store that stocks all-natural pet supplies. 1138 Orange Avenue; (619) 435-2124.

PLACES TO STAY

Loews Coronado Bay Resort: This is quite a resort, and management says that if your dog isn't "monster sized," she's welcome here. If you feel like getting some exercise, you can take your leashed dog with you to the jogging area just outside the hotel gate. The bay views are beautiful here. Rates are $235 to $595. 4000 Coronado Bay Road, Coronado, CA 92118; (619) 424-4000 or (800) 81-LOEWS.

DEL MAR

This stylish but sweet coastal community has wonderful, dog-friendly restaurants and a four-paw beach.

PARKS, BEACHES, AND RECREATION AREAS

• **Del Mar City Beach** 🐾🐾🐾🐾 🐕 *See ❸ on page 666.*

Okay, dogs, if you're reading this in the summer, don't get your hopes up. You can't be off your leashes anywhere on public land from June through September. But for the rest of the year, the north end of this beach is your kind of place—off leash and rugged.

Here's the breakdown of the rules for the different segments of beach:

The part of the beach most dogs like to know about is the north section. Dogs congregate at the northernmost end, near the bluffs. It's not a long segment, but it's wide and very far from the road. Dogs have so much fun here that they usually collapse in ecstatic exhaustion when they get back to the car.

Leashes are the law from June through September, but the rest of the year, your well-behaved dog can go sans leash. The entire off-leash area runs from 29th Street north to the Solano border. The best way to access it from Interstate 5 is to exit at Via de la Valle and drive west to Camino del Mar, where you'll go south for just about a block before you should start looking for street parking. It's across from the Del Mar Racetrack.

The middle section of the beach, from 17th Street to 29th Street, prohibits dogs from June through September. During the rest of the year, they can visit with a leash.

Dogs who visit the south portion of the beach, from Sixth Street up to 17th Street, can visit year-round, as long as they wear a leash.

A current dog license is required. And because too few people are cleaning up after their dogs, it may soon become mandatory to carry a pooper-scooper in plain view. That way, you're telling the world (and any poop patrol police who pass by) "My dog doesn't need a toilet. He has *me*." Call (619) 755-1556 for updates.

RESTAURANTS

Garden Taste: This scenic little sidewalk cafe facing the beach offers fresh, tasty organic vegetarian food. What could be healthier? ("A rare T-bone steak," says Joe. Such sarcasm.) 1555 Camino del Mar; (619) 793-1500.

Poseidon: You lucky dog! This restaurant is on the beach in Del Mar. You'll have to tie your pooch to the railing just outside the eating area, but you can pick a table where he'll still be right beside you. The seafood here is fresh, but dogs prefer to drool over the juicy steaks. And if you're in the mood for breakfast on the beach, get it here. 1670 Coast Boulevard; (619) 755-9345.

DOGGY DAYS

Party with pugs: You've never seen so many pug mugs as you'll see if you go to the Pug Rescue of San Diego County's annual Pug Party. Sam Donaldson called the Pug Party ". . . the premier west coast pug event." There are pug costume contests, kissing contests, and lots of speakers and food vendors. Joe Dog wants to see a pug pub next time. They could sell pug mugs so pugs could chug. At a recent Pug Party, 1,500 people and 600 pugs showed up. Dogs of all shapes and breeds are welcome, but it's just not the same when you show up with a poodle.

The Pug Party is held the first Sunday in May at the Del Mar Fairgrounds. For more information, contact Pug Rescue at P.O. Box 710277, San Diego, CA 92171; (619) 685-3580.

Walk with llamas, ponies, and birds: Wow, it sounds kind of like a canine dream. Each October for the last few years more than 2,000 people have brought animals of every shape, type, and model to take part in the Helen Woodward Animal Center's Pacific Classic Walk for Animals. (Well, every kind but cats. They're not banned, they just have smart owners.) It's a fun and relatively calm four-mile walk along the beach. Keep your camera poised for the moment your dog sees his first llama. That shocked, dropped-jaw look is definitely worth a photo.

The money raised by this event goes to the center's programs that help people and pets in need. In addition to a large animal adoption facility, the center has several therapeutic pet encounter programs for injured or ill people.

The center is also the home of Club Pet, a premier boarding facility that gives your dog huge doses of love. The staff even plays soft music all night so your pooch gets maximum relaxation. If you need to board your dog, the place comes with high recommendations, and the money goes to a good cause. Call (619) 756-4117 for details and event information.

EL CAJON

PARKS, BEACHES, AND RECREATION AREAS

•**Lake Jennings County Park** 🐾🐾🐾 *See* ❹ *on page 666.*

Since this is a county park, dogs aren't allowed to hike on the miles of trails that unfold along the chaparral-covered hills here. But there's plenty of open land, and as long as your dog doesn't set foot on the trails, she's free to enjoy it.

Lake Jennings holds three billion gallons of water for use by local residents. All this water harbors a tantalizing variety of fish, including largemouth bass, rainbow trout, and bluegill. Most dogs enjoy the ease of lolling around (on leash) while their angling companions cast around for supper.

There are 96 campsites. Nightly fees range from $12 to $16. Dogs are $1 extra. From Interstate 8 about four miles northeast of central El Cajon, exit at Lake Jennings Park Road and drive north one mile to the park entrance. Call (619) 694-3049 for park information or (619) 565-3600 for camping reservations.

• **Louis A. Stelzer Regional Park** 🐾 🐾 🐾 *See* ❺ *on page 666.*

You and your favorite leashed pooch can walk in dreamy seclusion on most winter weekdays here. A series of small meadows and a mile-long stretch of riparian woodland beg to be visited. Unfortunately, dogs and their people must stay off the trails here (county park rules), but there's plenty of room elsewhere in this 314-acre park. With a little ingenuity, you can even make it to Stelzer Ridge, where you'll get spectacular views of the surrounding land.

If civilization is more your style, you can picnic under big, shady trees while the kids frolic at the two playgrounds. Louis A. Stelzer, who donated his ranch to create this park, specified in his will that he wanted the park to be developed for disadvantaged and disabled children. The results are commendable.

From Highway 67, exit at Mapleview Street and drive east about a half mile to Ashwood Street. Turn left and follow it for a couple of miles as it changes its name to Wildcat Canyon Road and leads you into the park. (619) 694-3049.

PLACES TO STAY

Lake Jennings County Park: See Lake Jennings County Park on page 671 for camping information.

ENCINITAS

Although this is the home of Paramahansa Yogananda's gold-domed Self Realization Fellowship Center, and although the city calls itself "the flower capital of the world," not everything is bright and beautiful here: Dogs are banned from the city's municipal beaches (including Swami's Beach!).

The beach that does allow dogs is a state beach in the charming Cardiff-by-the-Sea district of Encinitas (see below).

Fortunately, most of the city's parks allow dogs. We visited the biggest and most beautiful, Quail Botanical Gardens, only to find out that dogs aren't allowed there. But there's still plenty of green space in town.

PARKS, BEACHES, AND RECREATION AREAS

• **Cardiff State Beach** 🐾 🐾 🐾 *See* ❻ *on page 666.*

We last visited here during the highest tide of the year. Joe looked at me as if I were crazy for bringing him to a beach that was all ocean and no sand. He slowly shook his head, glared at me, and pulled me back to the car.

But normally there really *is* sand here, and quite a bit of it, too. It's a good place to bring a leashed dog, especially since it's the last beach area that allows dogs for many, many miles as you drive north.

If you're going to park your car here, it's $4. But you can walk in for free. The beach is on Old Highway 101, directly west of the San Elijo Lagoon, in Cardiff-by-the-Sea. (760) 753-5091.

• **Pacific Scene Recreation Trail** 🐾🐾🐾 *See ❼ on page 666.*

You and your leashed dog can walk almost two miles one way on this rugged trail. The trail goes through both chaparral land and a lush riparian creekside area. The Escondido Creek runs the entire length of the trail.

Eventually, city officials are hopeful that the trail will be connected with another trail, so the round-trip won't entail turning around and walking the same path back. You may encounter some horses on the trail, but they're generally not going to be going very fast on this terrain.

Enter at Lone Jack Road and Camino del Rancho. (760) 633-2740.

RESTAURANTS

Sakura Bana: If you're in the mood for sushi, teriyaki, or tempura, the patio portion of this restaurant will suit you and your pooch just fine. 1031 First Street; (760) 942-6414.

PLACES TO STAY

San Elijo State Beach Campgrounds: Dogs are banned from all but a smidgen of the cobblestoned beach here, but they can camp right above it on the bluffs. There are 171 sites, and they cost $17 to $23. Dogs are $1 extra. Reservations are required from Memorial Day to Labor Day, and the campgrounds are closed December through February. The part of the beach that permits leashed pooches is at the south end, south of lifeguard tower 7. It's only about 50 feet of running room, but it's better than nothing.

The entrance is on Old Highway 101, north of Chesterfield Drive, in Cardiff-by-the-Sea. For campsite reservations, call Parknet at (800) 444-PARK. For beach information, call (760) 753-5091.

ESCONDIDO

Dogs are banned from this city's parks. The only exception is an undeveloped service road in a portion of Kit Carson Park, but it's generally just used by very local neighbors. Even the large Dixon Lake Recreation Area bans dogs, since it's operated by Escondido.

But a trip to the beautiful, if odd land of the Lawrence Welk Resort (see page 674) is certain to cure any dog of the parkless blues. Be sure to take your dog's picture with the infamous statue of the maestro himself.

RESTAURANTS

The Metaphor: Thirsty dog? This pooch-friendly cafe comes complete with water bowls for pooches who need quenching. You can also order anything from pastries to pasta. Dine at the outdoor benches here. 258 East Second Avenue; (760) 489-8890.

PLACES TO STAY

All Seasons RV Park & Campground: If you get lucky, you can stay at a lakeside RV site with your pooch. Tent campers can set up camp in a separate area with grass and shade. If fishing is your angle, you'll be happy here; there's free fishing in a stocked, five-acre lake. But you won't be having a fish fry with your dog, because the fishing's all catch-and-release. They just keep getting bigger that way. (The fish, not the dogs.) Rates are $12 to $32. 30012 Highway 395, Escondido, CA 92026; (760) 749-2982.

Econolodge: Rates are $30 for the first adult, $6 for the second. Small dogs only, please, and they're $10 extra. 509 West Washington Avenue, Escondido, CA 92025; (619) 743-6669.

Lawrence Welk Resort: A one-uh or a two-uh of you-uh can bring your favorite dog to the resort built by the king of tiny bubbles. Dogs are allowed at one-uh of the buildings here, and it just happens to overlook the expansive golf course. That means your dog will have plenty of entertainment while you and someone special are eating breakfast in bed.

The resort is on 1,000 acres—much of which is a golf course. But there's still plenty of room to romp with a leashed dog. Rates are $110 to $210. 8860 Lawrence Welk Drive, Escondido, CA 92026; (760) 749-3000.

LA JOLLA

Back in the 1950s, Raymond Chandler wrote that La Jolla is "a nice place . . . for old people and their parents." He could have added two more categories to his description and it would have been more accurate. Something like: La Jolla is "a nice place for old people, their parents, young people, and dogs."

Dogs, young folks, old folks, and older folks adore strolling along the seven miles of cliff-lined seacoast here. And they all equally love the impressive restaurant scene.

Unfortunately, your pooch won't be able to visit the parks and beaches of this stunning coastline from 9 A.M. to 6 P.M., but few dogs mind a nighttime stroll above the pounding Pacific. Luckily, cool cafes and elegant eateries abound. Many of them allow dogs to hang out with you as you dine at their outdoor tables.

La Jolla means "the jewel" in Spanish. The name couldn't be more appropriate for this pristine, sparkling village. That's why, although it's actually part of the city of San Diego, it's being given its own listing here. It's kind of like Monaco—a ravishing principality unto itself.

PARKS, BEACHES, AND RECREATION AREAS

• **La Jolla Shores Beach** 🐾 🐾 🐾 *See* ⑧ *on page 666.*

Just down the road from the famous Scripps Institution of Oceanography, this beach provides some breathtaking views of the La Jolla coast. But if you're visiting in the dark winter months, you might not get to see the views if you're with a dog. Dogs are banned year-round from 9 A.M. to 6 P.M. During their visiting hours, they must wear the mandatory leash.

The beach here is wide and lined with palms. Since you can't come here before 6 P.M. anyway, try to visit at sunset, when the gulls circle the bright gold sky and the orange waves crash on the distant cliffs. It's a stunning sight.

The beach is located just west of Camino del Oro in the northern part of La Jolla. (619) 221-8901.

• **Mount Soledad Park** 🐾 *See* ❾ *on page 666.*

If you've never been to La Jolla, this is the ideal starting place for your visit. Unlike other city parks, this one allows dogs during daylight hours, so get on up here and take a gander. The views of San Diego and the La Jolla coast are phenomenal. Spending a few minutes at the top of the hill is a great way to get your bearings.

That's about all you can do at the top of the hill. The park looks quite large on the map, but most of the land is made up of impassable cliffs. The flat, walkable area on the hilltop is actually rather small. Unless you own a teacup poodle, your leashed dog won't feel exercised after a visit to this park. But boy will he know his geography.

From the south part of the La Jolla coast, take Nautilus Street east about two miles to South Street. Turn left and then make a right onto Soledad Road, in a couple of blocks. You'll know you're here when you see the large white cross that is visible from many areas of San Diego. It's a memorial to the war dead, and every Easter, it's the site of a magical sunrise service. (619) 552-1658.

• **Point La Jolla Cliffs and Beaches** 🐾🐾🐾 *See* ❿ *on page 666.*

This is another one of those 9-to-6ers famous in the San Diego area. Dogs can visit the cliffs and beaches here only before 9 A.M. or after 6 P.M. Get out those infrared goggles and have a great time with your leashed pooch. Okay, a flashlight would be more appropriate, but the goggles would make a better statement.

What's great about this area is that there's access to the beach, via stairs that take you down the cliffs, and there's also a grassy little park at the top of the cliffs. It's extremely beautiful and dramatic here. During the right tides, tidepooling is magnificent. Just make sure your dog doesn't stick his snout in the tidepools. The critters who call them home need all the peace they can get.

Enter on Coast Boulevard around Girard Avenue, and when you're done, go grab a bite to eat in any of the nearby mouthwatering restaurants. (619) 221-8901.

RESTAURANTS

La Jolla is a terrific place to grab a bite to eat with your dog. Many restaurants have lovely outdoor areas, and most of those happily permit pooches.

Froglander's Yogurt: The dog-loving owner here will gladly give your canine companion a free yogurt sample. 915 Pearl Street; (619) 459-3764.

Girard Gourmet: Enjoy the beautiful blue skies while Girard's serves you gourmet food at the outdoor tables. 7837 Girard Avenue; (619) 454-3321.

Il Forno: If you're in the mood for delectable Italian food, your pooch and you will love this place. 909 Prospect Street; (619) 459-5010.

La Terrazza: Trees and grass surround you and your dog as you dine on fine Italian food on the patio tables. 8008 Girard Avenue; (619) 459-9750.

The Living Room: Dogs can accompany you at the tables on the sidewalk. Enjoy soups, sandwiches, salads, and pastries. 1010 Prospect Street; (619) 459-1187.

Sammy's California Woodfired Pizza: The folks here love dogs, and dogs love the folks here, so everyone's happy. You'll drool for the incredible pizzas. Try the barbecued chicken pizza. It's out of this world, if you can stomach the idea of something other than pepperoni on your pizza. Dine at the outdoor tables with your favorite doggy. 702 Pearl Street; (619) 456-5222.

Shelby's: Feel a cold coming on? Or just want some warm and cozy soup? This soup restaurant's for you. When the weather is nice, ornate tables are set up on the patio outside where you can sit with your dog. 6737 La Jolla Boulevard; (619) 456-6660.

PLACES TO STAY

La Jolla Holiday Inn Express: This hotel is just a block from the beach. Rates are $99 to $129. Dogs are $10 extra. 6705 La Jolla Boulevard, La Jolla, CA 92037; (619) 454-7101.

Residence Inn by Marriott: This is a lovely place for humans and their hairy sidekicks. Stay at studios or penthouse suites. All rooms come with kitchens and range from $99 to $189. There's a $100 pooch cleaning fee per visit. (The pooch fee cleans the room after your visit, not your dog.) In addition, dogs are $10 extra per night. 8901 Gilman Drive, La Jolla, CA 92037; (619) 587-1770.

LA MESA

PARKS, BEACHES, AND RECREATION AREAS

• **Harry Griffen Park** 🐾 🐾 🐾 *See* ⓫ *on page 666.*

This grassy, 53-acre park is home to a pleasant little reservoir and some good fields for a leashed dog's enjoyment. For even better exercise, try the jogging path here. Dogs like it almost as much as they like the shaded picnic area.

The park is in the easternmost portion of the city, on the border of El Cajon. The main entrance is on Milden Street, in back of Grossmont High School. (619) 694-3094.

• **Lake Murray** 🐾 🐾 1/2 *See* ⓬ *on page 666.*

If you have a water-loving pooch, think twice about visiting this park. Dogs have to stay at least 50 feet away from the lake's edge. That's tough when you're fishing with your dog. To make things a little easier on the angling front, call (619) 465-3474 for the lake's ever-helpful Fishline.

Fortunately for dogs, paved and dirt paths circle the lake, so there's more for them to do than just sit around and drool at the water. For instance, they can walk around and drool at the water.

The park's setting is not what you'd want to see on a postcard, but scenery isn't everything. The place is kind of barren, with few trees but plenty of grass and dirt areas to exercise a leashed dog.

The park is officially run by San Diego water entities, but most people think it's in La Mesa, so that's why we're listing it here. Exit Interstate 8 at Lake Murray Boulevard and drive northeast for about one mile. Turn left at Kiowa Drive. The street will take you into the park. (619) 668-2050.

RESTAURANTS

Caruso's: Dogs often frequent the patio. The place is casual, serving light breakfast and dinner fare. 8201 La Mesa Boulevard; (619) 460-4800.

Por Favor Mexican Restaurant: You and your pooch can enjoy a Mexican meal at the outdoor tables here. They ask that when it's crowded, you tie your dog to the other side of the fence. You can still pet him, but he won't be tripping up the waiters. 8302 La Mesa Boulevard; (619) 698-5950.

OCEANSIDE

Dogs are banned from the city's beaches, as well as the Oceanside Pier. Bummer, doggy surfer dudes.

•**Buddy Todd Memorial Park** 🐾 🐾 🐾 *See* ⑬ *on page 666.*

This is a really green, fairly quiet park that's far enough off the beaten path to dissuade most visitors. Dogs should be happy here—they're allowed to have 24 additional inches on their leashes, making for a grand total of eight feet!

There are plenty of pines here, plus fun little trails on the hilly part of the park. Kids love it, too, because the playgrounds have a train theme.

From Interstate 5, exit at Highway 76 and drive east about 1.5 miles to Butler Street. Go right and follow it as it curves; then turn left onto Barnwell, left again on Mesa, and then left into the park. (760) 966-4500.

•**Guajome Regional Park** 🐾 🐾 🐾 *See* ⑭ *on page 666.*

Bring your binoculars and settle in for a day of bird-watching and hiking in one of the richest riparian areas in the county. Spring-fed lakes and a marsh are the centerpieces of this 569-acre park.

It's a little tricky to get around this place with a dog, because while there are miles of hiking trails, dogs aren't allowed on any of them. That's the general rule in San Diego County's parks and it's a doggy drag. But you can fish with your dog or picnic in the grassy hilltops here.

Humans like visiting the historic 22-room adobe ranch house on the park's eastern boundary. About 150 years ago, when this land was part of a vast Mexican land grant and the hub of the area's cultural life, the ranch house was the centerpiece of social activity.

Thirty-five campsites are available at $14 per site. Dogs are $1 extra. All but one site is reservable. From Interstate 5, take Mission Avenue east seven miles to Guajome Lakes Road, then south to the park's entrance. Call (619) 694-3049 for park information or (619) 565-3600 for camping reservations.

RESTAURANTS

Amedeo's Italian Cafe: Dogs are welcome to join you on the patio at this upscale Italian restaurant. 2780 State Street; (760) 729-8799.

Armenian Cafe: Have a craving for Armenian food? Bring the pooch onto the deck and dig into a delicious meal. Besides lip-smacking good food, the place exudes doggy love. "We love dogs a lot," says a canine-crazy worker. 3126 Carlsbad Boulevard; (760) 720-2233.

Beach Break Cafe: You and your dog can enjoy each other's company at the tables outside this daytime cafe. 1902 South Hill Street; (760) 439-6355.

PLACES TO STAY

Day's Inn: If the dog who wants to dream here is big, she's out of luck. But medium-sized dogs are allowed. Rates are $47 to $60. Dogs are $7 extra. 1501 Carmelo Drive, Oceanside, CA 92054; (619) 722-7661.

Guajome Regional Park: See Guajome Regional Park on page 677 for camping information.

POWAY

PARKS, BEACHES, AND RECREATION AREAS

• Poway Dog Park 🐾🐾🐾🐾 🐕 *See ⑮ on page 666.*

A visit to Poway Dog Park is like a stint on *Let's Make a Deal.* Dogs get to choose between door number one, door number two, or door number three. But unlike the old Monte Hall game show, no matter which door your dog chooses, she'll always be a winner. (No booby prizes of canned spinach here.) Poway Dog Park has three separate fenced areas for leash-free dogs, and they're all doggone great. Your dog can visit any or all of them in a given day. If the sniffs are boring in one area, try another. If there's a cute dog your pooch wants to meet in another fenced area, open the door for her mystery date and let the good times roll.

Each section of this nearly two-acre park is a poochie wonderland, with dog water fountains and even a fire hydrant for your dog's pee-rusal. There's some shade, but on hot days dogs could use a little more. At press time, there was a fund-raising drive to put in lights, which will brighten the lives of many an after-work park user.

Exit Interstate 15 at Poway Road and drive east about four miles. Turn right on Bowron Road. Park in the lot at the end of the road. Walk past the soccer and baseball fields to the pooch park, which is behind the swimming pool and baseball fields in Poway Community Park. (619) 679-4342.

RESTAURANTS

Papachino's: Daisy Dog and Sheila Dog told us about this fun Italian restaurant (via their interpreter, Lani Butcher Smith), and we're sure glad they did. The servers are as dog-friendly as can be, giving thirsty pooches like Joe their own bowl of water. If your dog is really good, why not get him a side order of meatballs. Mama mia, you'll make your dog's day. 13425 Poway Road; (619) 748-7100.

DIVERSIONS

Wash those fleas right out of her hair: Ever notice how your dog's wet, dirty hair sticks to your tub when you're done bathing her? (Bathing yourself in the same tub is never quite the same after seeing the grime that comes off your dog, is it?) How about how your back feels after hoisting her in and out and bending over for a half hour or more? Would you like to use someone else's tub? Preferably a tub at waist level? Then pay a visit to Lucky Dog Pet Wash, where shampoo and towels are provided, and where you never, ever have to bathe in the same tub as your dog. This self-serve pooch wash has some really friendly attendants. Come here after a messy, slobbery run at the Poway Dog Park (see above). Rates are $6 to $12. Blow drying is $2 extra. 13248 Poway Road, Suite B; (619) 486-8056.

RANCHO SANTA FE

PLACES TO STAY

The Inn at Rancho Santa Fe: Dogs and their people love it at "the inn," as everyone seems to call it. Set on 22 acres of lawns, gardens, and tree-dotted expanses, this is a very peaceful place to stay with a pooch.

The inn consists of 104 rooms, most of them in the form of cottages. Half have wood-burning fireplaces, most have private patios or balconies, and some come with kitchens. Most of the cottages have four rooms, which is a comfortable size when you're traveling with a pooch.

Rates are $100 to $580. 5951 Linea del Cielo, Rancho Santa Fe, CA 92067; You have your choice of phone numbers: (800) 843-4661, (800) 843-2928, or (619) 756-1131.

SAN DIEGO

Every dog-owning San Diego resident should be given a pair of infrared scopes when they license their pooches at City Hall. Since so many city parks and beaches have a tough rule banning dogs between 9 A.M. and 6 P.M., sometimes the only time to walk a dog around here is at night. Being able to have those Desert Storm–type glasses that let you see into the night would be a great boon.

San Diego is laid-back and exciting. You and your dog can stroll through the old Gaslamp district, eating up the local history as well as the good food served at a few dog-friendly eateries. You can visit La Jolla's pristine shores (see page 674) for breathtaking scenery and clean-breathing air. You can even walk on historic land where California actually started (see Presidio Park, page 684). If that's not stimulating enough, you can stroll down action-packed beaches together at sunset (see page 683, Mission Beach/Pacific Beach).

Unfortunately, dogs are banned from beautiful Seaport Village. The restaurants and shops are wonderful, but liability problems prevent the managers of this renovated waterfront area from allowing pooches. Joe secretly suspects it's because of the shop called Whiskers, which touts itself as "the ultimate cat shop," but I think he's being paranoid.

PARKS, BEACHES, AND RECREATION AREAS

• **Balboa Park** 🐾🐾🐾🐾 🐕 *See ⑯ on page 666.*

This luxurious semitropical park is one of California's best urban parks for people. Attractions include the San Diego Zoo, an enormous planetarium, several theaters, and a few world-class museums. But with the recent addition of three off-leash areas for dogs, Balboa Park is now one of the best urban parks for pooches, too.

Dogs used to be relegated to the lush, green center and dirt paths on the east and west sides of this 1,200-acre park. Leashes were—and still are—a necessity in those areas. Dogs who wanted more freedom were out of luck until a kindly park official thought it might be nice to give them a chance to cavort about sans leash in a small area. The dogs all thought this was a mighty good idea, and they've been so well behaved that the park has now doubled their stomping grounds. For a while, there had actually been three leash-free areas, but one didn't work out well.

The two dog runs aren't fenced, but they're well marked with signs. The more popular dog area is Morley Field Dog Park, which is actually the smaller of the two. It's lined by a grove of eucalyptus trees, so there's plenty of shade on hot days. You'll almost always find gaggles of pooches gallivanting about in high spirits. You can get to Morley Field from Morley Field Drive, off Florida Drive, in the northeast portion of the park (southwest of the tennis courts). The larger of the areas is Nate's Point, on the west side of the park off Balboa Drive, just south of the Laurel Street Bridge. It's a picturesque place (nice for pooches with a sense of aesthetic beauty), with views of the famous old California Tower, Coronado, and even part of Mexico.

To get to the park from Interstate 5, exit at Park Boulevard and head north. Call the Balboa Park Visitors Center for more information and maps. (619) 239-0512

• **Black Mountain Open Space** 🐾 🐾 🐾 ½ *See* **17** *on page 666.*

It's utterly quiet here. So quiet you can hear your dog breathe when he's sitting still. So quiet you'll swear you hear his fleas gnashing their teeth. And except when people are shooting bullets through the signs that say "No Liquor" and "No Firearms," it's almost always this silent.

A few miles of trails run through this mountainous, shrubby, completely undeveloped 200-acre park. It's not exactly Mount Whitney, but from the top of Black Mountain (elevation 1,552 feet), you can get some good views of the surrounding hills and peaks.

The trek here looks complicated, but it's not bad. Exit Interstate 15 at Rancho Peñasquitos Boulevard/Mountain Road and drive west about two miles to Black Mountain Road. Turn right and drive north about 2.5 miles, where the road will come to an abrupt end. Just before it does, turn right on the dirt road there. Follow the winding road up the mountain and eventually you'll come to a sharp right, where the road becomes paved. The road ends in a small parking lot. From here, you can see the start of the trail. (619) 685-1351.

• **Dog Beach** 🐾 🐾 🐾 🐾 🐕 *See* **18** *on page 666.*

"Welcome to Dog Beach!" the sign announces at just about the same place that your dog charges out of the car to meet with all his best buddies. Dogs truly do feel welcome here. They're free to run off leash and to get down to the business of being a dog. As long as they listen when you call and don't get into trouble, they can hang out leashless all day. Many dog people bring a folding chair so they can relax while their dog experiences heaven on Earth.

We've seen several folks visit here because, although they don't have a dog, they get great joy out of watching the footloose creatures tearing around. "They have such innocent happiness when they run about and play so gleefully," said dogless dog lover Maxine Chambers one gray morning. "It makes my day."

There are more dog footprints in the sand than human footprints, and not just because dogs have more feet. People come from many miles around, sometimes bringing their friends' dogs and their neighbors' dogs to participate in the whirlwind of excitement.

Dogs are allowed off leash at the north end of the beach, which is wide enough to be very safe from traffic. It's marked by signs. If you wander onto the other part of the beach, make sure you do so before 9 A.M. or after 6 P.M., and be sure to leash your dog.

Exit Interstate 5 at Interstate 8. Drive west and follow the signs to Sunset Cliffs Boulevard. After several blocks, bear right at Voltaire Street. Follow Voltaire Street to its end and the entrance to Dog Beach. (619) 221-8901.

• **Embarcadero Marina Park** 🐾🐾🐾 *See ⓳ on page 666.*

This park is like a big green thumb jutting into the San Diego Bay. It's a terrific place for a little walk with your leashed dog. Dogs and their people enjoy watching the seabirds glide around the fresh air over impressive views of the city and Coronado.

The big bummer here is that dogs are not allowed to visit Seaport Village, a major dining and shopping attraction located right next to the park. Hey, who needs to spend money anyway? Take Kettner Boulevard (it runs parallel to Pacific Highway, one block to the east) to its southernmost end. (619) 686-6225.

• **Fiesta Island** 🐾🐾🐾🐾 🐕 *See ⓴ on page 666.*

Hey, dogs! You're going to find out just why they call this 1.5-mile-long island Fiesta Island. You can have a fabulous fiesta, then take a soothing siesta—and you can do it all off leash.

Yes, pooches, you can meet with friends, swim in the bay, chase your shadow, and catch a stick without ever wearing that pesky old leash. As long as you listen to your people and don't cause any problems, this island is all yours. There's no development (as of this printing, anyway, although there's plenty of talk about it)—just dirt and sand and a little grass.

If you aren't very good at listening to your owners, ask them to take you to the far side of the island, where fewer cars cruise by. The perimeter of the island is a beach, and unfortunately, the road runs right behind the beach. It doesn't give water dogs a whole lot of room to run around, but it's enough for most.

If you choose to stay on the beach, you can avoid annoying little jet skiers by staying away from the watercraft recreation sections of water, which are clearly marked. The interior of the island is made up of fields of dirt. Since this is a bigger area, you'll be farther from traffic here.

The views of downtown San Diego and Mission Bay Park are really spectacular from the south side of the island. Cameras come in mighty handy here. (Fiesta Island is actually part of Mission Bay Park, but the rules are so different that I prefer to discuss them separately. See page 682 for Mission Bay Park information.)

From Interstate 5, take the Sea World Drive/Tecolote Road exit southeast to Fiesta Island Road, which is your first right. The road will take you onto the island. (619) 221-8901.

• **Kate O. Sessions Park** 🐾🐾🐾 *See* ㉑ *on page 666.*

This is another of those San Diego parks that looks so much like a golf course that it fools people. In fact, this park even has a sign: "Golf practice prohibited!" The other major rule up here is that dogs must be leashed.

Kate O. Sessions Park is very green, very hilly, very peaceful, and very charming. Not that dogs care, but the views of the city are terrific from up here.

The park is located between Pacific Beach and the Muirlands districts of town, on Soledad Road at Park Drive. (619) 581-9924.

• **Los Peñasquitos Canyon Preserve** 🐾🐾🐾½ *See* ㉒ *on page 666.*

You may have to say good-bye to this gem any minute now, dogs. This sprawling, 4,100-acre preserve in the Mira Mesa area is an intoxicating place for a leashed dog to hike. The trails are long and the preserve is full of fascinating plants and animals.

That's just why county officials are working to ban dogs. However, since the park is co-managed by the city, there may be a minor scuffle that could delay or prevent this doggy demise.

For at least the last few years, there have been three confusing signs here. One said that dogs have to be on a six-foot leash. Another said dogs have to be on an eight-foot leash. The third had a picture of a dog with a slash through it, meaning no dogs are allowed at all. "It's rather embarrassing," says one county official, who attributes the sign confusion to city-versus-county rules. And at press time, the park was closed because of flooding, so no dogs or people were allowed anyway.

The preserve is in the Mira Mesa area. If you're there, and it's not flooded, and you really want to walk your dog, call (619) 484-7504 (the county ranger) to check on the status of the anti-dog ruling. If it's still open to dogs, you can get there by exiting Interstate 15 at Mercy Road and driving west. As soon as you pass Black Mountain Road, you'll be in the park. Park in the lot at the end of the road.

• **Marian Bear Memorial Park** 🐾🐾🐾½ *See* ㉓ *on page 666.*

A stream flows through much of the length of this long and narrow park, and it's easy to access from the dirt trail that parallels it. As long as there are no trees and bushes preventing you and your leashed pooch from reaching the stream without getting all scraped up, you can veer between the trail and the stream all afternoon.

Despite this 466-acre park's proximity to Highway 52, dogs seem to like it here. There are all kinds of good smells and sights along the path. But keep your eyes peeled. Your dog may get a few sights he didn't bargain for if you visit at the wrong time: Signs warn against "lewd acts." Gosh . . . and just when Joe was going to lift his leg.

Exit Highway 52 at Regents/Clairemont Mesa Boulevard, drive south very briefly, and the park will be on your right. Once in the park, you can head left or right. Joe recommends going to the right, but that's just one Airedale's opinion. (619) 581-9924.

• **Mission Bay Park** 🐾🐾🐾½ *See* ㉔ *on page 666.*

Dogs are not allowed here from 9 A.M. to 6 P.M., making for some rather tight daylight hours in the winter. But when it's light enough to see, you can't help but enjoy yourself here. This is one of the nation's largest and most beautiful aquatic parks.

It's so big (4,600 acres, including the bay), with so many more entry points than signs, that you may make the same mistake many others have when seeing the park for the first time: "I thought it was a bloody golf course! Gawd! Okay, Ginger, let's go for a walk," said Henry Miles, a British chap in his 70s. He was walking Ginger for his sister, who had told him about Mission Bay Park and how to get there. But when he saw the perfect grass, the gently rolling hills, and the sand, he figured he'd gotten the directions wrong. "They've got a lot of golf courses here, you know. Gawd, even their parks look like them. Ginger looks relieved, eh?"

I ran into Miles at the section of park near the San Diego Visitors Information Center. That portion is particularly reminiscent of a golf course—in fact, it's just around the bend from a golf course that's a dead ringer for the park.

If you're on Interstate 5 and your pooch wants to exercise while you get tourist information, exit at the Clairemont Drive/Visitors Center turnoff and follow the signs to the visitors center. Keep in mind that the visitors center and the pooch-walking hours rarely coincide, so it helps if you have a friend who can get the necessary tourist information while you walk your dog. You can park in the parking lot for only an hour, so if you're planning on a longer stay, there's street parking a little farther south.

The zillions of other access points are located north of the San Diego River and south of Pacific Beach Drive. The east-west boundaries are East Mission Bay Drive (which parallels Interstate 5) and Mission Boulevard (which runs a block east of the Pacific). For information on dog-friendly Fiesta Island, which is actually part of this park's territory, see page 681. (619) 221-8901.

• **Mission Beach/Pacific Beach** 🐾🐾🐾½ *See* ㉕ *on page 666.*

The great thing about strolling down these two contiguous beaches with a dog is that no one seems to care if you don't have bulging biceps or a bikini-perfect body. Having a dog eliminates the need for physical prowess here. And on beaches that have built a worldwide reputation on how dazzling its bathers look, that's a mighty big plus.

On the downside, dogs are allowed to accompany you here only before 9 A.M. and after 6 P.M. The same hours hold for the paved promenade that runs behind the beaches. It's an understandable law during crowded summer days, but it would be a real boon for dogs if that rule could be eliminated during the winter months. Since the poor pooches have to be leashed anyway, what's the harm? (Joe made me write that.)

To make the best of these restricted hours, try a visit to beautiful Belmont Park. The big attraction at this old-style amusement park is a restored 1925 roller coaster, the Giant Dipper. In addition, there's a quaint old carousel and a historic indoor swimming pool. Dogs are required to be leashed and remain with all four feet planted firmly on the ground, but they can still have a good time watching the kids have fun. The park area is also home to dozens of shops and restaurants. It's located at West Mission Bay Drive and Mission Boulevard. Its back faces Mission Beach. Call (619) 491-2988 for Belmont Park hours and information.

Pacific Beach is north of Mission Beach. It starts around Tourmaline Street. The beach hooks up with Mission Beach and is one long, never-ending strip all the way down to the Mission Bay Channel. (619) 221-8901.

• **Mission Trails Regional Park** 🐾🐾🐾 *See* ㉖ *on page 666.*

This is a really big chunk of green—5,109 acres, to be exact. Actually, it's a good deal greener on a map than it is in reality. Several miles of dirt trails wind through low brush and boulders, all in a rather desolate setting. Because this park is managed by the city (although owned by the county), dogs are permitted on the trails.

They love to bound up and down hill after hill with you tagging along behind them. There's a leash law here, so make sure that if they're bounding, you're bounding, too.

One good destination for your leaps and bounds is the Old Mission Dam Historical Site. Native Americans built it many decades back and it's still in good working order.

Good news for pooches: Dog-friendly rangers now give informative guided nature hikes for dogs and their people every other month. The hikes are not for the soft of paw or the fair of foot, but they're not usually terribly difficult, and we hear they're great fun. Call (619) 668-3275 for more information.

Exit Interstate 8 at Mission Gorge Road (one of the exits for the San Diego-Jack Murphy Stadium) and drive northeast past all the gas stations and fast-food marts. In about four miles, turn left on Father Junipero Serra Trail and you're in the park. Or if you want, you can park on Mission Gorge Road, at the trailhead off Jackson Road, just before you get to Father Junipero Serra Trail. (619) 668-3275.

• **Presidio Park** 🐾🐾🐾½ *See* ㉗ *on page 666.*

This is where California began. The hill here is known as the "Plymouth Rock of the West." Dogs are stepping on very historic land when they walk here. Back in 1769, Father Junipero Serra dedicated his first of many California missions on this very same hill.

The mission has since moved, but a fascinating museum is a major draw here. Dogs don't have great interest in the Spanish furniture and historic documents in the museum, though, and they're not permitted inside anyway. They prefer the many wide dirt trails that run around the hill.

The trails are on rolling hills, shaded by plenty of trees. The views from here are incredible. On a clear day, you can see all of the city. Someone marching with a telescope said he could check out the beach scene from here, but Joe and I didn't confirm that.

From Interstate 8, take the Taylor Street exit west. Go left at Presidio Drive, which will take you up to the park. You can park at the museum and get a map of the park. There's also a lower parking lot that has easy trail access. Call (619) 297-3258 for the history of the area and general park information.

• **Tecolote Canyon Natural Park** 🐾🐾🐾½ *See* ㉘ *on page 666.*

There's a brand-new, nine-acre nature center just as you enter one end of this huge canyon. Dogs love looking at the whale skeleton that was found here, and they even seem to like listening to rangers chat about the geologic wonders and natural history of the place. But they'd give it all up to go on a hike down this rugged eight-mile canyon.

The trails don't go all the way through the canyon in one neat sweep. If you dare to do the entire hike, you'll have to negotiate a golf course, some fairly rough terrain, and a couple of roads. But once you reach the northern Clairemont area of the park, you're in for some real beauty. Tecolote Creek is particularly refreshing here, and the scrub doesn't look as scrubby as it does elsewhere. There are even some shaded little ponds where you still might be able to find some crawdads.

From Interstate 5, take the Sea World Drive/Tecolote Drive exit (just north of the intersection with Interstate 5) and drive east. You'll be dumped off almost immediately into the recreation center/nature center area. (619) 581-9930.

A word of warning: Rangers here beg folks not to let their dogs off leash. They say there's a real danger that Africanized honey bees could be here soon, and the insects can be deadly. In two other U.S. cities, dogs rummaging through bushes have been killed by these bees, which defend a quarter-mile radius much faster than you or your dog can run. The bees won't attack out of the blue, so just hiking and minding your own beeswax probably won't get you in any trouble. It's only when you start poking around their hives that they get upset, rangers say.

If you won't listen to the bees, then watch the birdie: Rangers are supposed to take photographs of people with off-leash dogs. The photos can be used as evidence against you if you try to argue with the ranger's word.

RESTAURANTS

Cheese Shop: "We're one of the cool shops," says one waiter. And he's right—while dining with your dog under umbrella-topped tables outside, the two of you can enjoy mouthwatering cheese samplers and delicious sandwiches. If your dog is a cheese nut (like Joe's good friend Grinny, aka "Cheesehead"), she'll find it an ecstatic experience just to sit and sniff the Brie. 401 G Street; (619) 232-2303.

K-9 Country Club: This is a doggone fun, casual place to take a pooch. The name alone beckons, but since the owner loves dogs, this deli/cafe has pictures of dogs and sells all kinds of hot dogs, further adding to the poochy ambience. You and your dog can get sandwiches, gourmet coffees, and, of course, hot dogs. Dine together at the outdoor tables. 202 C Street; (619) 239-0304.

The Original Paw Pleasers: Please see "Dine in a dog (and cat and bunny) restaurant," in the Diversions section, page 688, for more information on this doggone great eatery.

Point Loma Seafood: You want a dog-friendly restaurant? Romp on over to Point Loma Seafood, where the dog-loving attitude is as yummy as the seafood. You and your dog can share a bayside table and the stuff memories are made of (that is, french fries). While you dine on such goodies as a shrimp sandwich or crab Louie, your dog will be eating and drinking his own restaurant food: free biscuits and fresh water. The only thing Joe Dog winced at here was the pickled squid cocktail. As it passed by our table, en route to some less fortunate soul, he sniffed the air and backed up as far as his leash would allow. I always said he had good taste. 2805 Emerson Street; (619) 223-1109.

Thidwick Books: Please see the "Grab a bite and a book" listing under Diversions, page 688, for more information on this wonderful bookstore/cafe.

Trattoria La Strada: Enjoy a delicious meal outside with your pooch at this classy Gaslamp district restaurant. If you like Northern Italian cuisine, or just plain pizza, you'll love it here. 702 Fifth Avenue; (619) 239-3400.

Zen Bakery: This health-minded bakery is conveniently located just down the street from Dog Beach (see page 680). Come here after some fun in the sun, and down a whole-grain muffin and a smoothie with your pooch at the couple of tables out front. 4920 Voltaire Street; (619) 221-1220.

PLACES TO STAY

Beach Haven Inn: Dogs have to be itsy-bitsy angels on their best behavior to stay here—25 pounds is the limit and they have to be "well behaved and well trained." The hotel is in the Pacific Beach area. Rates are $60 to $130. 4740 Mission Boulevard, San Diego, CA 92109; (619) 272-3812.

Campland on the Bay: Dogs can stay at one of the 240 sites in a special (less landscaped) section of this 42-acre park on Mission Bay. They probably won't notice the reduced scenic value, though, if you take them to Dog Beach, which is only two miles away (see page 680). Rates run anywhere from $23 to $67, depending on the time of year and how rustic you want your site to be. Dogs cost an additional $3 in winter and $4 in summer. Reservations are recommended in the summer. 2211 Pacific Beach Drive, San Diego, CA 92109; (619) 581-4260 or (800) 422-9386.

Crown Point View Suite-Hotel: If you want to feel right at home while staying in a dog-friendly part of town, try the apartments/hotel rooms here. Crown Point is a mere five-minute walk from Mission Bay Park (see page 682). Rates are $75 to $125, and there's a minimum five-day stay. Dogs are $50 to $100 extra for the duration of the stay. The fee depends on the size of the dog. 4088 Crown Point Drive, San Diego, CA 92109; (619) 272-0676.

De Anza Harbor Resort: If you have an RV and want to set up camp in San Diego, De Anza is the answer. It's near the bay, with some great views from a few of the sites. Rates are $27 to $72 (yes, $72, but that's the peak-season rate for sites with killer views and all the amenities an RVer could want). Dogs are $2 extra. 2727 De Anza Road, San Diego, CA 92109; (800) 924-PLAY.

Holiday Inn on the Bay: As long as you're willing to sign a contract stating you will accept responsibility for any damage your dog may do and you won't leave him alone in your room, you and your dog are welcome here. But don't try to sneak and leave the pooch alone—they'll call the pound folks, who will arrive pretty quickly since they're located just across the street. How convenient. Rates are $179 to $199. 1355 North Harbor Drive, San Diego, CA 92101; (619) 232-3861.

Marriott San Diego Marina: Wow! This is an impressive place, right next to Seaport Village (which bans pooches). Oh well, dogs love the harbor views. Two dogs reside here permanently, so it's definitely a dog-friendly lodging. The hotel can provide you with everything from children's programs to scuba diving instruction. Rates are $214 to $275. 333 West Harbor Drive, San Diego, CA 92101; (619) 234-1500.

Residence Inn by Marriott: Stay at studios, apartments, or penthouse suites at this attractive lodging designed for travelers who want more than a bed in their hotel room. All rooms come with kitchens. Rate are $99 to $150. Extended stays get discounted rates. Dogs are charged a $50 fee and $6 per night. 5400 Kearny Mesa Road, San Diego, CA 92111; (619) 278-2100.

San Diego Hilton Beach and Tennis Resort: You and your dog can stay in some very attractive digs here. It's been re-created as a colorful Mediterranean village. All rooms feature a private terrace or patio, two phones, voice mail, a fridge, a mini bar, a coffeemaker, and a TV with gobs of stations. (Joe is tapping my knee and asking when we can move in.) Not only that, it's right across from Mission Bay Park (see page 682), which is a terrific place to take a dog if you can time it within the very restricted doggy hours. Rates are $150 to $600. Dogs are charged a $50 fee. 1775 East Mission Bay Drive, San Diego, CA 92109; (619) 276-4010.

San Diego Marriott Mission Valley: This one's just a ball's throw from the San Diego-Jack Murphy Stadium, not that it matters to your dog. Rates are $109 to $155. There's a $250 dog deposit, and a $50 nonrefundable post-dog-visit room cleaning fee. 8757 Rio San Diego Drive, San Diego, CA 92108; (619) 692-3800.

San Diego Princess Resort: Stay here and you're staying in beautiful Mission Bay Park. This resort on lush Vacation Island, just minutes from the off-leash dog havens of Dog Beach and Fiesta Island (see pages 680 and 681), will have your medium or small dog wagging her tail all day. There's so much to do here that you wouldn't even know where to start. Rates for the cabana-style rooms are $120 to $365. There are no deposits for dogs, but you must sign a pet agreement. 1404 West Vacation Road, San Diego, CA 92109; (619) 274-4630.

U.S. Grant Hotel: Tired of being turned down by fine hotels that cater only to small dogs? You and your dog of any size will feel mighty welcome here. I promise. After all, this is the same hotel that recently had a gorilla stay in one of its rooms. And we read about a movie star orangutan who stayed here not long ago. In fact, the beautiful, classic Victorian-style U.S. Grant Hotel has gained an international reputation for being superbly friendly to beast and man.

Starlet animals stay here on a fairly regular basis, and you never know who you'll see walking through the lobby. Actually, all dogs are given the star treatment. Any dog who stays here becomes part of the hotel's "Pampered Pet Program," which doesn't cost their humans a dime. Dogs get their very own doggy bed, a water dish, and a biscuit on their pillow at night.

The bellman will even take your dog for a walk, should you not feel like doing it yourself.

Dogs and their people feel positively presidential here. It's not every day your dog gets to spend the night in a hotel once owned by a U.S. president (Ulysses S. Grant opened the hotel in 1910). A few presidents have visited here, including Woodrow Wilson and Franklin Delano Roosevelt. The 280-room hotel has recently been restored (to the tune of $80 million) to be even more elegant than ever. The U.S. Grant is a Grand Heritage Hotel, known around the globe for top-quality hotels. Rates are $150 to $310. 326 Broadway, San Diego, CA 92101; (619) 232-3121 or (800) 237-5029.

Vagabond Inn: This one's in the Mission Valley area. Rates are $59 to $74. Dogs are $10 extra. 625 Hotel Circle South, San Diego, CA 92108; (619) 297-1691.

DIVERSIONS

Dine in a dog (and cat and bunny) restaurant: Dogs, sit down. I've got great news for you: There's now a restaurant/bakery dedicated exclusively to pets! You can actually go *inside* this one! The Original Paw Pleasers is a beautiful little restaurant with gorgeous murals of a park scene of happy dogs and cats. It's a cozy, uplifting place, with oak cabinets and even a "tree." (Okay, it's a post disguised as a tree, but it looks enough like a tree that your boy dog might be tempted . . . Don't let him!) And the food is to die for—if you're a pet. If you're a human, you can use coupons they have in conjunction with eateries nearby and grab yourself a bite to bring here so you can eat beside your dog. Some of the more popular items are "dogolate" chip cookies and "bark-la-va." There's also yogurt with doggy toppings, and a doggy Sunday brunch. Owners Sharon and Loree will even custom-make birthday cakes for your dog.

I rarely mention other animals in this book, but this is too good to ignore. Cats can come here and get a tuna or liver cake with faux cream frosting, or a tuna muffin with a delicious non-dairy whipped topping. Mmm, good! Birds and bunnies can order such yummies as vegetable salads. By the way, if your dog thinks cats and bunnies are part of the menu, make sure there are none inside before you venture in.

The restaurant also sells lots of gift items for pets and their people. It's located in an upscale shopping center in the Hillcrest area of San Diego. This is a must-visit on any dog's list. 1220 Cleveland Avenue; (619) 293-PAWS.

Grab a bite and a book: Thidwick Books, in the Mission Hills area of San Diego, is such a dog-friendly bookstore and cafe that dogs have been known to run in, dragging their poor, hapless human behind them. Tails wag hard and fast here, mostly because store owner Leagrey Dimond adores dogs and keeps a jar of dog biscuits on the counter. She also makes sure thirsty dogs who dine at the outdoor tables with their people get a bowl of fresh water. Well-read humans wag their tails because this is such a good bookstore. You won't find computer books here, just lots of really good literature. (Oh, Thidwick's also sells *The California Dog Lover's Companion.* "Obviously a quality establishment," says Joe Dog.) *Sunset* magazine recently rated

Thidwick's as the best small bookstore in town. 1612 West Lewis; (619) 291-4532.

Wash that sand right outta his hair: After a long jaunt on Dog Beach (see page 680), come to the Dog Beach Dog Wash, a wonderful place to keep your pooch looking like he just strolled out of a dog-food commercial. If location is everything, this business has it all. It's only two blocks from Dog Beach. The owners say that some folks bring their dogs here almost every time they visit the beach. It's a great way to get rid of all that sand and dog slobber before getting back in your car.

For only $6.50, you can give your dog the works in any of five waist-high tubs. It's $3 extra for a blow-dry, and $3 extra for the automated pet dryer, known here as the "box dryer." A new feature is the "clipper vac," which lets you clip your own dog without sending hair all over the world. That's $5 for 20 minutes. 4933 Voltaire Street, Suite C; (916) 523-1700.

SOLANA BEACH

Dogs aren't allowed at the city's beaches, but since you're so close to beautiful, off-leash Del Mar City Beach, there's little reason to visit anyway.

RESTAURANTS

Loco Wraps: Eat just about anything you can wrap in a tortilla-ish shell here. It's good, it's healthful, and best of all for dogs, it can be very messy. Dine with your pooch at the outdoor tables. If you're thirsty, you'll be able to get a good smoothie here, too. And if your dog is thirsty, he'll be able to get a bowl of cool water. 125 North U.S. 101; (619) 481-9800.

SOUTH INLAND COUNTIES

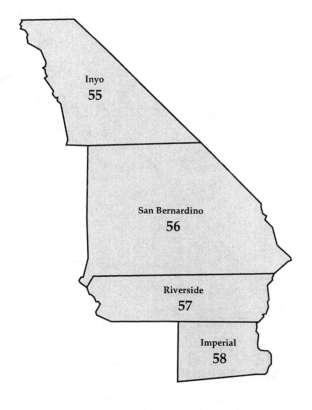

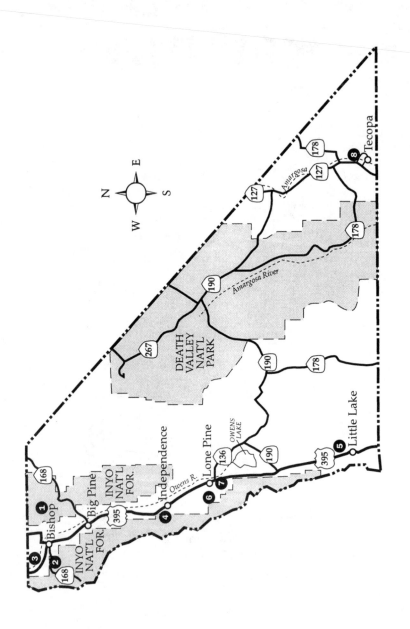

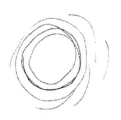

GULP!

55
INYO COUNTY

The elevation: As low as 282 feet below sea level.

Some of the hot spots to visit: Funeral Mountains. Chloride City. Death Valley. Furnace Creek.

It may sound like pure hell, but a visit to this county during the cooler months of the year actually might be one of the most interesting adventures you and your dog share in California.

Inyo County has an incredible variety of landscapes. The desert contains the lowest land in the United States, at 282 feet below sea level. The adjacent Sierra Nevada and the silver, knifelike pinnacles of towering Mount Whitney make a strong contrast. In fact, Mount Whitney, with its peak at 14,494 feet, is the highest point in the contiguous United States. Because its sheer eastern wall rises out of the low desert landscape of the Owens Valley, the effect is especially dramatic.

But Mount Whitney is a place you just want to observe with your dog. First of all, while many areas of Inyo National Forest are enchanting places to take a dog, this climb is very difficult, and no pooch should be asked to perform such feats. But even more importantly, dogs aren't allowed anywhere near the mountain's peak. It happens to be in Sequoia National Park, which pretty much bans dogs. Rangers tell me that a few avid, sicko climb-

---

ers have left their dogs behind (tied up) at the national forest border when they discovered no dogs were allowed at the peak. Stick with the lower elevations here.

In spring, wildflowers are everywhere. The sight of towering mountains against flowering desert makes dogs sniff the air in heavenly awe.

The canine and human folks who inhabit these areas are every bit as colorful as the desert springtime. During my research, I received a letter from Martha Watkins of the Death Valley Chamber of Commerce. It could have been from Mark Twain.

She wrote, "The only mayors of Shoshone and Tecopa have been dogs. B.J. was the mayor of Tecopa for many years. He was a small wirehaired terrier mix who really had a way with (human) women. I had the dubious distinction of running him over. My name was mud for a long time. No dog since B.J. has reached his stature.

"Shoshone's mayor is a small wiener-and-Doberman mix named Lifter. You can guess where his name came from. He's very macho."

Watkins still occasionally gets the evil eye from women who were seduced by B.J.'s scruffy looks. She told me that the late mayor lived with one of "our very hard-rock miners. Talk about a big wheel. B.J. would get up in the morning and sit by the side of the road until someone gave him a ride into town. He'd hang out at the bar all day. If he saw a girl with bare shoulders sitting in a booth by herself, he'd jump in the adjoining booth and start kissing her shoulders."

B.J.'s charms won him the unofficial vote as mayor of this small Death Valley town. Alas, he met Death Valley face-to-face under Watkins' tire on his barhopping rounds one fateful day. But his spirit still lives on in this dog-lovin' land.

Warning: Don't bring your dog to the desert areas of the county in the summer or early fall. Dogs who aren't accustomed to the heat may not survive the average daily temperatures of 116 degrees Fahrenheit, not to mention the perilously hot ground. It's not much fun for most humans, either.

NATIONAL FORESTS

See the National Forests and Wilderness Areas chapter starting on page 748 for important information and safety tips on visiting national forests with your dog.

•Inyo National Forest 🐾 🐾 🐾 🐾 🐕

Dogs love the 28,000-acre Ancient Bristlecone Pine Forest, part of this national forest northeast of Big Pine. The gnarled pines that look like living driftwood are thought to be the world's oldest living trees—and probably the oldest living things on Earth! Tell your boy dog to be respectful of these aged arboreal wonders. Temperatures here are cooler than in much of the surrounding area because of the 10,000-foot elevation.

See page 750 for more information on Inyo National Forest.

NATIONAL PARKS

•Death Valley National Park 🐾 🐾 🐾 ½

What's in a name? When I first thought about taking Joe to Death Valley,

I pictured him ending up as a pile of bones in the sand while coyotes bayed and vultures licked their beaks. Taking a dog to Death Valley seemed like something Cruella de Vil would do.

But not so! As long as you stay away during the grueling months before, during, and after summer (from April through September), you and your dog could have some of your best adventures ever. Dogs must be leashed, but it's for their own good. There are some hungry coyotes here, and the heat of the sun can surprise you even during the cooler months. It's best to have your pooch close at hand.

This 3.2 million-acre park is new in name only. It encompasses the former Death Valley National Monument, Eureka Sand Dunes National Natural Landmark, and several other federally run natural areas. In 1994, the Desert Protection Act merged these areas into one big, full-fledged national park. In most areas, that doesn't affect dog rules. But where dogs were once permitted to run around off leash at Bureau of Land Management lands here, they have to obey the new leash rules. And sadly, at the Eureka Sand Dunes area, whose centerpiece is a 700-foot-high mountain of sand, dogs can no longer cavort about on the dunes at all. It's a howling shame.

Fortunately, although dogs aren't permitted on trails at Death Valley, there are so few trails that it won't matter to you. What matters is that they're allowed to hike at your side on the more than 500 miles of roadway that stretch from one landscape to another within Death Valley. Most of these roads are unpaved and barely get used by vehicles, so chances are you can get plenty of pure desert solitude with pure desert air.

Keep in mind that dogs also aren't supposed to wander far off the road into backcountry. About 100 yards is the limit. Remember that with air as clean and land as flat as this, rangers are omnipresent. Watch yourselves, because they are sure to be watching as well.

You'll see some of the most fascinating geologic formations on Earth here. Of course, most of the time it won't look like you're even on Earth, but don't let that bother you. The park's otherworldly nature is one of its charms. Much of the park is below sea level. The lowest point in the United States is here, in Badwater Basin. Within the park are elevations from 282 feet below sea level to 11,049 feet above sea level. Betwixt and between, you'll find vast salt flats, endless sand ridges, huge rocks, and twisting mountainsides.

When you get to the visitors center, pick up brochures on the history and geology of the place and decide which parts of Death Valley you and your dog would enjoy most. The park has nine campgrounds, three of which are open all year. There are more than 1,500 campsites available on a first-come, first-served basis. Fees range from free to $16. Rangers say more campsites (from the former Bureau of Land Management lands) will eventually be added to the list.

The entry fee for the park is $10 per carload, good for visits of up to a week. Being that the park is bigger than the state of Connecticut, there are many spots where you can enter it. To get to the main visitors center from U.S. 395, take either Highway 136 or Highway 190 east. Highway 136 will join up with Highway 190. From U.S. 395, the drive is a little more than 100 miles. Follow Highway 190 through all its confusing turns and you can't miss it. Even in the cooler months of the year, it's a good idea to bring extra water, just in case you break down and the temperature decides to do one of its soaring routines. (760) 786-2331.

BIG PINE

PARKS, BEACHES, AND RECREATION AREAS

• **Ancient Bristlecone Pine Forest** 🐾🐾🐾🐾 🐕
See ❶ on page 692.

This remarkable area is located in Inyo National Forest, about 25 miles northeast of Big Pine. See page 750 for a description.

Dogs can be off leash as long as they're not on trails, picnic areas, or campgrounds. It sounds like a lot of places, and it is. But there's still plenty of room to roam.

Campsites range in price from free to $12. Winter usually makes the roads getting here impassable, but the forest is accessible from early June to late October. From U.S. 395 in Big Pine, take Highway 168 east about 15 miles to White Mountain Road. Turn left, and in another 10 miles you'll come to the south end of the forest. (760) 873-2400.

PLACES TO STAY

Ancient Bristlecone Pine Forest: See Ancient Bristlecone Pine Forest above for camping information.

Big Pine Motel: Your dog can't weigh more than 35 pounds if he's going to stay here. Rates are $35 to $38. Dogs are $4 extra. 370 South Main Street, Big Pine, CA 93513; (760) 938-2282.

BISHOP

Set between the state's two highest mountain ranges, Bishop has become the hub of this recreational wonderland. It's a small, laid-back town with only one thing that peeves pooches: Dogs are banned from the only city park here.

PARKS, BEACHES, AND RECREATION AREAS

• **Izaak Walton County Park** 🐾🐾🐾 See ❷ on page 692.

Do you like clear mountain creeks and wooden footbridges that take you over them? Does your dog like to go for short walks on a leash after a long drive on a highway? Come to this special little park to stretch all your car-cramped legs.

It's a really pretty park with green grass most of the year and plenty of trees for shade. There's a narrow trail cutting through brush to the back of the park, which is brambly, but fenced and safe from traffic.

This park is where I first discovered that Bill liked to "eat" fast-flowing ribbons of water. He stuck his snout in the creek and grabbed mouthful after mouthful of the evasive stuff for 20 minutes, but he stopped and looked downright embarrassed when a stranger said nice and loud, "That your dog? He sure is weird."

From U.S. 395 in the middle of town, go west on West Line Street for about 2.5 miles. The park will be on your left. (760) 878-0272.

• **Pleasant Valley County Park** 🐾🐾🐾 *See* ❸ *on page 692.*

This park has the long, narrow Pleasant Valley Reservoir as its center-piece. The reservoir is created by the Owens River, and fishing here is pretty hot (thanks in part to planted trout). Leashed dogs are allowed to cheer at your side as you catch supper from shore.

For dogs who aren't fishing fans, try the hiking trail located on the reservoir's east side. The big rocky bluffs here are interesting, but the surrounding mountains topped with snow year-round are really impressive. However, dogs don't seem to care much for the visuals. Something about this place keeps their flaring nostrils pressed firmly to the ground. Since leashes are the law, you may feel some tugging when your dog decides to try to track one of these enticing smells.

There are 200 campsites, but they're pretty far from the lake. Sites are $6. Reservations are not necessary. Take U.S. 395 about seven miles north of Bishop, then turn north on Pleasant Valley Road and drive about 1.5 miles to the lake. (760) 878-0272.

RESTAURANTS

Erick Schat's Bakery: This has been the home of the Original Sheepherder Bread since 1938. Stop with your dog in the summertime and break some of this bread at the outdoor tables. 763 North Main Street; (760) 873-7156.

Manor Market: This grocery store is home to some pretty good grub, including hot chicken and soup. There are a few outdoor tables in the warmer months. 3100 West Line Street; (760) 873-4296.

PLACES TO STAY

Comfort Inn: This isn't just your average Comfort Inn. It's a mighty dog-friendly Comfort Inn. Hannah Dog (a husky-shepherd mix) and her folks were nice enough to write to let me know that the owner adores dogs, and that she "cheerfully takes dogs of all sizes." I called the owner to confirm, and indeed she's a doggy person. "Sure, we take all good dogs," she said. "We've even had Saint Bernards." The place even has a fish-cleaning station. I guess the owner likes fish, too. Rates are $64 to $92. 805 North Main Street, Bishop, CA 93514; (760) 873-4284 or (800) 576-4080.

Millpond Recreation Area: Dogs with human children in the family enjoy spending the night here, because little humans are allowed in the adjacent park. (Dogs aren't allowed there, though.) There's a playground, sports fields, tennis courts, a pond, and horseshoe pits. The campground itself is comfortable, but not too exciting. There are 60 sites available. Dogs must be leashed. Fees are $12 to $15.

From U.S. 395 about six miles north of town, take Ed Powers Road south. Go the equivalent of about three city blocks, and turn west on Sawmill Road. In about a half mile, you'll be at the park. The campground is open from March through November. (760) 873-5342.

Pleasant Valley County Park: See Pleasant Valley County Park above for camping information.

Rodeway Inn: No huge dogs, please. Rates are $45 to $75. 150 East Elm Street, Bishop, CA 93514; (760) 873-3564.

Sierra Foothills Motel: They used to ban dogs larger than small- to-medium-sizers, but now all good dogs are allowed. And they used to charge extra for them, but now they're free. We like this dog-friendly turn. Rates are $60 to $96. 535 South Main Street, Bishop, CA 93514; (760) 872-1386.

Thunderbird Motel: Rates are $36 to $44. Dogs are $4 extra. 190 West Pine Street, Bishop, CA 93514; (760) 873-4215.

Vagabond Inn: This one comes with its own fish-cleaning facilities and a freezer. If you and your dog have a successful day angling, this might be the place for you. Rates are $44 to $75. Pooches are $5 extra. 1030 North Main Street, Bishop, CA 93514; (760) 873-6351.

DEATH VALLEY

PLACES TO STAY

Stove Pipe Wells Village: Set on 100 acres of Death Valley National Park (see page 694), this sprawling, rustic resort is mighty dog-friendly. Maggie the Wonder Dog, the canine companion of San Francisco's Kim Wonderly, wrote to us to tell us she gives it two paws up. You and your leashed dog are free to peruse the village's 100 acres and beyond. The lodging is a mere 10-minute walk from the most-photographed sand dunes in the world—if you love *Lawrence of Arabia,* you can pull a Peter O'Toole here and run around in your white robe. Rates for the hotel/motel are $53 to $76. Dogs require a $20 deposit, and your room may be checked for doggy damage before you leave. There's no street address. For information, write Stove Pipe Wells Village, Death Valley, CA 92328; (760) 786-2387.

INDEPENDENCE

PARKS, BEACHES, AND RECREATION AREAS

• **Dehy County Park** 🐾 🐾 🐾 *See ➍ on page 692.*

A river doesn't run through this park, but a creek sure does. Besides the usual picnic tables and shade trees, the park is home to an attractive old locomotive. But the best feature of this county park is that it's directly off U.S. 395, so weary travelers don't have to go far out of their way. It's at the very north end of Independence, at West Wall Street. (760) 878-0272.

LITTLE LAKE

PARKS, BEACHES, AND RECREATION AREAS

• **Fossil Falls** 🐾 🐾 🐾 ½ 🐕 *See ➎ on page 692.*

Before you read any further, heed this warning: Although dogs may run off leash here, you may want to leash yours when you're anywhere near the park's main feature—the 80-foot-deep chasm that was once a waterfall. It's probably a good idea to keep an eye on the kids here, too.

Pick up a brochure and you'll learn all about the intriguing history and geology behind what caused the fossilized falls to form. Dogs don't usually give a hoot for such subjects, but they do seem interested in the bumpy lava covering the ground on your way from the parking lot to the falls. Joe tries to dig at it, but we discourage this behavior. It's not every day a volcano leaves behind such amazing tracks.

From about three miles north of Little Lake on U.S. 395, turn east onto Cinder Cone Road (watch for the cinder cone) and follow it to the park. The parking lot is about 1.5 miles from the highway. Your drive will take you through a large volcanic field, which is almost as interesting as the fossilized falls themselves. (760) 384-5400.

LONE PINE

This is a one-stoplight town—the gateway to Mount Whitney. As Marilyn, an enthusiastic native who works at the Chamber of Commerce put it: "We've got a real pretty town, real Western."

And real Westerns are what they've been shooting here for decades. See the Alabama Hills description below for details on the showbiz history of this area. This place is a must-visit location for dogs and their people.

PARKS, BEACHES, AND RECREATION AREAS

• **Alabama Hills** 🐾🐾🐾🐾 🐕 *See ❻ on page 692.*

Pardner, if you like those Western films and TV shows, you're gonna love this place. For more than 70 years, Hollywood has used Lone Pine's unique scenery in almost 300 films and countless TV shows.

This is where the *Lone Ranger* ambush was first filmed, where Roy Rogers found Trigger, and *Bonanza* became a bonanza. Giants like Gene Autry, Roy Rogers, Hopalong Cassidy, Humphrey Bogart, Cary Grant, Gregory Peck, Spencer Tracy, and Clint Eastwood did their big scenes here. In fact, this is where Roy Rogers and Robert Mitchum filmed their first features.

Put a bandanna on your four-legged varmint and have a rip-roaring time exploring the rock formations, canyons, and barren flats that are the real stars here. Some photo markers are placed in the area showing which famous scenes were shot where. It's a real education for you and your dog. Be really careful where and if you allow your dog to be leashless, because dogs and the cars that wind around the park don't mix.

From U.S. 395, take the Whitney Portal Road about 2.5 miles west of Lone Pine and you'll find yourself on Movie Road. That's where your trek through movieland begins. Don't forget to bring a camera. (760) 872-4881.

• **Diaz Lake** 🐾🐾½ *See ❼ on page 692.*

This small lake is set under the watchful eye of the Sierra Nevada and Mount Whitney, and it really bustles in the summer. Leashed dogs can hike around the 86-acre lake with you and hang out while you catch bass, bluegill, or trout.

Camping here costs $7. It's a convenient place to spend the night, since it's just off U.S. 395, two miles south of Lone Pine. (760) 878-0272.

RESTAURANTS

Frosty Stop: You can have your hamburgers and eat ice cream, too, at the outdoor tables here. 701 South Main Street; (760) 876-5000.

PLACES TO STAY

Diaz Lake: See Diaz Lake on page 699 for camping information.

Dow Villa Motel: Dogs can stay in smoking rooms only, but the managers like dogs and will make them feel at home. Rates are $70 to $85. 310 South Main Street, Lone Pine, CA 93545; (760) 876-5521.

National 9 Trails Motel: Small pets only, please. Rates are $36 to $59. Dogs are $5 extra. 633 South Main Street, Lone Pine, CA 93545; (760) 876-5555.

DIVERSIONS

Git in line, lil' doggy: Leashed dogs are welcome to attend all the outdoor segments of the three-day Lone Pine Film Festival celebrating the myriad Western flicks shot in the nearby Alabama Hills (see page 699). Some of the most famous old cowboys and cowgals gather during this three-day festival, which is held on the second weekend of October, to talk with fans and even reenact a scene or two. If your dog is lucky, maybe he'll get to shake paws with one of the greats. Call (760) 876-4314 for information on this year's event.

TECOPA

The population is 300, which is a big number when you get this deep into the desert. The neighboring community of Shoshone has a whopping 30 residents. See page 694 for the tale of the mutty mayors of these tiny towns.

PARKS, BEACHES, AND RECREATION AREAS

• **Tecopa Hot Springs County Park** 🐾 🐾 🐾 *See* **8** *on page 692.*

The Paiute Indians used to bring their lame and sick ancestors to bathe in the hot mineral springs here, and now people from all over the world come for a soak. The 107-degree waters are supposed to help alleviate the pain of arthritis, rheumatism, and other bodily woes.

While dogs can't take a dip, they are allowed to roam the 40-acre park with you. Switch off hanging out with the dog with a friend as you take turns rejuvenating yourselves in the baths.

Most of the park is taken up by a large, 300-site campground. Sites are $6.50 to $8 per night. Many are available on a first-come, first-served basis, but you can also make reservations if that makes you feel better about driving all the way out here. The bathing is free. Make sure you don't come with your dog in the hot months. The temperature can climb to 118 degrees Fahrenheit some summer months, and that's hotter than the mineral baths.

From Death Valley Junction (Highways 190 and 127), follow the road about 36 miles to the park. (760) 852-4264.

PLACES TO STAY

Tecopa Hot Springs County Park: See Tecopa Hot Springs County Park above for camping information.

56
SAN BERNARDINO COUNTY

This is the Texas of California. It's just plain big. In fact, it's the biggest county in the nation, weighing in at more than 20,000 square miles.

That means you'll find a lot of variety here. This is where dogs can do just about everything they ever imagined a dog could do. They can ride the rail through a ghost town, roam around off leash on millions of acres of land, herd goats in Chino, take a horse-and-buggy ride in Big Bear, and even visit Santa and his elves in a beautiful place called Skyforest.

Try to visit the San Bernardino Mountains at sunset, when occasionally they play an optical trick. A few of the mountains will turn purplish pink, while others stay the same sandy brown and forest green. Then everything fades into a surreal orange mist. For people, it's a stunning sight. If dogs really do have black-and-white vision, they're probably not quite so thrilled.

NATIONAL FORESTS

See the National Forests and Wilderness Areas chapter starting on page 748 for important information and safety tips on visiting national forests with your dog.

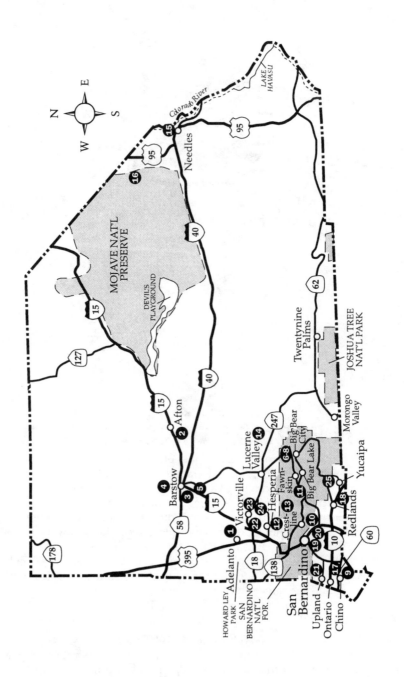

•San Bernardino National Forest 🐾🐾🐾🐾 🐕

Much of the southwest corner of San Bernardino County is San Bernardino National Forest land. So far, dogs are allowed off leash in most parts of the forest, except for several times when they meet up with state parks. (Dogs aren't even allowed there on leash.) Unfortunately, local national forest rangers are facing the question of whether off-leash rules are appropriate in the forest. Complaints about dogs running up to frightened humans or fighting with each other have led to this dilemma. So make absolutely certain your dog is Mr., Mrs., or Ms. Obedience before taking off that leash.

On the way up to Big Bear Lake via Highway 38, you'll find numerous forest trailheads and picnic areas that make great rest stops on a long journey. See Big Bear Lake on page 707 for more on this popular resort area. For general information on San Bernardino National Forest, turn to page 753.

NATIONAL PARKS

•Joshua Tree National Park 🐾🐾🐾

Although most of this 794,000-acre park is in Riverside County, Twentynine Palms is where you'll find the visitors center and the gateways to some of the most beautiful areas in the park.

This is amazing land, with striking granite formations rising around dramatic desert plants and wildlife. In spring, it becomes a showcase of brilliant wildflowers. The giant Joshua tree plants are in the higher western half, and they're definitely worth a visit.

Dogs can be walked on paved and dirt roads, but not on hiking trails. They're permitted to wander on leash up to 100 yards from the road, and there are plenty of small dirt roads where you'll be far from most traffic. Leashes are the law here, but they're also a very good idea because of critters like mountain lions and bobcats. A bigger danger than those cats is actually the cactus. Dogs sometimes rub up against the prickly plants or try to bite them and end up with a major problem. One last warning: The ground here can get really toasty—sometimes too toasty for your dog's paws. If you wouldn't want to walk barefoot here, neither would your dog. Rangers report several cases of paw pad injury each year because of the hot ground. Come when it's cooler and you'll be better off.

There's a $10 entrance fee, and if you want to camp without water, you can camp for free. Otherwise, sites are $8 to $10. There are 492 sites available on a first-come, first-served basis. However, the 100 sites at Black Rock Canyon require reservations. Always bring lots of water on your hikes here, and make sure your dog gets her fill. It doesn't usually get nearly as hot as in other parts of the desert, but you don't want to take a chance. From Interstate 10, exit at Highway 62 and drive northeast for about 39 miles to the town of Twentynine Palms. The visitors center is on Utah Trail, just south of the highway about a mile east of town. (760) 367-7511.

ADELANTO

A lot of people drive past this little town on U.S. 395 and never stop. But have we ever got a convenient, dog-friendly place for your pooch to stretch his gams, should they need stretching:

PARKS, BEACHES, AND RECREATION AREAS

• **Howard Ley Park** 🐾🐾½ *See* ❶ *on page 702.*

U.S. 395 can be a beautiful but lonely road down in these parts. When you're traveling with a dog, it can be tough when he starts crossing his legs and getting that "I gotta go" look. But you're in luck if he needs a rest stop in this area: The town of Adelanto has a rest stop tailor-made for your leashed pooch. Howard Ley Park is a half acre of well-kept grass, shade trees, shrubs, and flowers. You have to keep your dog off the grass, but that's okay, because there's a wide lane on the side of the park where dogs know they're welcome: It's called "Pet Area Lane," as two cute street signs will attest. "Three-Dog Dave," a volunteer pet therapist with the Riverside Humane Society, was kind enough to send me wonderful pix of the park and tell me how it spells relief for his dogs en route to and from the Eastern Sierra. His dogs are not alone. "It's a regular stop area for people with pets," says a city official in the know. "We like that we can help."

The park is very conveniently located. From U.S. 395, take Air Base Road east (there will be a four-way stop sign at this intersection) just a smidgen. The park is on the north side of Air Base Road, across from the High Desert Casino and right next to a Circle K convenience store. (760) 246-2300.

AFTON

PARKS, BEACHES, AND RECREATION AREAS

• **Afton Canyon Natural Area** 🐾🐾🐾🐾 🐕 *See* ❷ *on page 702.*

Wow! Woof! How does 42,000 acres of mostly off-leash land sound to you and your canine companion? If you don't demand lush green meadows to be part of your elysian ideal, this can be heaven on Earth.

Afton Canyon is one of only three places where the Mojave River flows above ground year-round, so not only has it attracted visitors throughout history, it's also a water dog's delight. If you don't expect fine fishing here, no one will be disappointed.

Keep in mind that hundreds of bird, mammal, and reptile species call Afton Canyon their home, or at least their migratory hotel. It's a great place for wildlife watching, but unless you can trust your dog to stay at your side, you should keep her leashed when anywhere near these creatures.

Camping here isn't the prettiest, but it's comforting to know you're just a stone's throw from another day of off-leash adventures. Sites are $4, and dogs must be leashed in the campground. There are about a dozen sites available on a first-come, first-served basis.

Afton is about 40 miles east of Barstow. From Interstate 15, exit at Afton Canyon Road and drive three miles south to the park. (760) 252-6060.

PLACES TO STAY

Afton Canyon Natural Area: See Afton Canyon Natural Area above for camping information.

ANGELUS OAKS

PLACES TO STAY

The Lodge at Angelus Oaks: One day I got a letter written in silver ink and very big, childish handwriting, and signed with paw prints by Jake Dog and Sadie Dog. They were writing to tell me about this wonderful place, which they call "a hidden secret."

Jake and Sadie are very smart dogs, indeed, because The Lodge is one terrific place to stay with a dog. The Lodge is made up of several homey wooden cabins and is set on some prime acreage in the San Bernardino National Forest. It was built in the early 1900s as a stagecoach stop for pooped-out travelers, and it really hasn't changed much since. Each of the 12 cabins has a kitchen, bathroom with shower, and one or two bedrooms. The main lodge/office is very cozy, with a stone fireplace, a library, and an antique billiards table. But what dogs dig most about The Lodge is that it has lots of fun things to do outside. There's a snow play area (in winter) and a horseshoe pit and other fun non-snow recreational opportunities. Best of all, the San Bernardino National Forest is everywhere. Some prime trails start just a short car ride away.

Rates are $50 to $85. Dogs are $5 extra. 37825 Highway 38, Angelus Oaks, CA 92305; (909) 794-9523. The Lodge has a Web site: www.at-la.com/lao.

BARSTOW

This is a mighty dog-friendly town. In fact, it's just the place for a bruised canine ego to go after stepping on one too many threadbare doggy welcome mats. The folks here generally like dogs at least as much as they like people.

PARKS, BEACHES, AND RECREATION AREAS

• **Foglesong Park** 🐾 🐾 ½ *See* ❸ *on page 702.*

This is a decent-sized city park with plenty of shade for those searing summer days. The kids will like the playground, and the dogs are sure to enjoy the open grassy fields. Enter at Avenue G, just north of Nancy Street. (760) 252-4800.

• **Rainbow Basin Natural Area** 🐾 🐾 🐾 🐾 ➤ *See* ❹ *on page 702.*

If you or your dog like bones, faults, sediment deposits, or leash-free walks, don't miss this geological and anthropological wonder. Fossils of ancient animals are everywhere in the colorful sedimentary layers of the canyon walls (once a lake). Mastodons, camels, three-toed horses, rhinos, and dog-bears are among the animals whose remains have been discovered here. As you hike around, you'll be able to see insect fossils that are among the best-preserved in the world. You and your dog need to keep your paws off these fossils so they remain undisturbed for others to enjoy them.

The geology of the place is also fascinating. Rainbow Basin's sediment deposits are textbook examples of folds, faults, and other disturbances of the earth's crust. If you're studying geology in school, this is the place to visit if you want to get the big picture.

Unfortunately, your dog probably doesn't give a hoot about bones she can't eat and sediment she can't wallow in. She knows what's important— being able to be at your side, off leash, while you peruse the area. The Bureau of Land Management, which operates the park, has some of the most lenient, dog-friendly rules in the state for obedient pooches.

The best place to take an off-leash dog is any flat area where she won't have much chance of disturbing this national natural landmark. There are no developed paths or trails, but since the place is nearly devoid of trees and thick underbrush, it's easy to navigate a course almost anywhere here. Be aware that you may run across desert kit foxes and bobcats. If you can't control your dog with critters like these around, keep her leashed. And make sure she goes nowhere near desert tortoises, the California state reptile (bet your dog didn't know that). Tortoises are easily traumatized, and contact with people or dogs could lead to their death.

For your pet's sake, don't visit in the summer. Our favorite time to hike here is in late autumn, when it's crisp but not freezing. Leashed dogs are allowed to camp with you at the 31-site Owl Canyon Campground. The fee is $4 per vehicle. No reservations are necessary.

From Highway 58 in Barstow, drive 5.5 miles north on Fort Irwin Road and turn left on Fossil Bed Road. It's a rough dirt road, and it will seem like an eternity of bouncing before you reach your destination, but it's actually just three miles. (760) 252-6060.

• **Stoddard Valley Open Area** 🐾🐾🐾🐾 🐕 *See ❺ on page 702.*

Is your dog tired of those five-acre parks where leashes are a must? Does she long for wide-open desert ranges where she can tear around without a care in the world (except rattlesnakes and their friends)?

This 52,000-acre parcel of land just southeast of Barstow could be the answer to her poochie prayers. Not only are there mountains and endless open areas, there are also plenty of fascinating rock formations for you and your dog to explore.

To enter at the northern end, where there's a campground, exit Interstate 15 at Sidewinder Road and drive the only way the road takes you. The campground has no developed sites, and no reservations or permits are required. The public land here is interspersed with private land, but Bureau of Land Management folks say unless an area is fenced off, posted, or developed, it's probably okay for hiking. (760) 252-6060.

RESTAURANTS
Foster's Freeze: 1580 West Main Street; (760) 256-8842.

PLACES TO STAY
There's no shortage of dog-friendly lodgings in Barstow.

Barstow Inn: Dogs are welcome in the first-floor rooms here. Rates are $25 to $35. 1261 East Main Street, Barstow, CA 92311; (760) 256-7581.

Best Motel: Rates are $28 to $36. 1281 East Main Street, Barstow, CA 92311; (760) 256-6836.

Calico Ghost Town Camping and Cabins: See Diversions on page 707.

Desert Inn Motel: Rates are $28 to $38. There's a $20 dog deposit. 1100 East Main Street, Barstow, CA 92311; (760) 256-2146.

Econo Lodge: Rates are $30 to $55. A $5 deposit is required for dogs. 1230 East Main Street, Barstow, CA 92311; (760) 256-2133.

Gateway Motel: Dogs are permitted in smoking rooms only, which is very convenient if your pooch happens to smoke. Rates are $20 to $32. 1630 East Main Street, Barstow, CA 92311; (760) 256-8931.

Quality Inn: The folks here really like dogs. But because of guests' allergies, you'll have to stay in a room designated for smokers. Rates are $49 to $64. 1520 East Main Street, Barstow, CA 92311; (760) 256-6891.

Rainbow Basin Natural Area: See Rainbow Basin Natural Area on page 705 for camping information.

Stoddard Valley Open Area: See Stoddard Valley Open Area on page 706 for camping information.

DIVERSIONS

Go west, young pup: How many dogs can say they watched an Old West shoot-out on a dusty saloon-packed street? How many can tell their buddies they rode aboard a narrow-gauge railroad through a silver mining boomtown/ghost town? And how many can brag that they got to see a piano player striking up old haunting tunes?

Your leashed dog can be that lucky dog, if you take him on a visit to Calico Ghost Town. It's a campy, kitschy, but thoroughly entertaining town-turned-park. Calico thrived during the 1880s silver boom, and you can still roam around the tunnels of silver mines and stroll along the wooden sidewalks of Main Street. Some of the proprietors of the old-timey stores will probably even let your pooch go shopping with you.

If you're a real fan of this era, why not spend the night? Camping costs $18 to $22. There are about 260 campsites available here. Reservations are recommended in the spring and fall. Better yet, if your dog doesn't do tents, rent one of the six cabins in the ghost town. They're not haunted, but the price is so low you'll howl for joy: $28 for up to four people. A $25 deposit is required.

Admission to Calico Ghost Town Regional Park is $6 for adults, $3 for children. Train rides are $2.25 for adults, $1.25 for children. Dawgs go free. From Barstow, drive about six miles east on Interstate 15, and exit at Calico Ghost Town/Ghost Town Road. Drive north for three miles. When you see a yellow wagon, you'll know you're there. (760) 254-2122.

BIG BEAR LAKE

This lakeside mountain resort community isn't exactly Lake Tahoe, but that's part of its charm. It's generally more rustic, more natural, and far less crowded. The crisp, clean alpine air is a godsend any time of year.

The town's old-fashioned honesty and lack of smooth public relations pros is evident as soon as you approach the old village section. There, you'll see a road sign for skiing, with an arrow pointing to the left. Immediately below that is a sign for the hospital, with an arrow pointing to the right. It's not a joke.

Several dogs we know dream of going along on their owners' annual cross-country ski trip through San Bernardino National Forest. Before Joe can join them, he has to learn that he can walk in the snow, not just roll on top of it.

This is a very dog-friendly community, complete with incomparable off-leash hikes, great restaurants, and hotels where dogs are as welcome as their chauffeurs. Check out the old Big Bear Lake village. It gives a new meaning to old-style charm.

PARKS, BEACHES, AND RECREATION AREAS

Although this book doesn't normally go into detail on specific trails in national forests, we're mentioning a few here because they're so integral to your pooch having a doggone good time in the Big Bear Lake area.

•**Cougar Crest Trail** 🐾🐾🐾🐾 🐕 *See* ❻ *on page 702.*

This two-mile trail goes through a mixed conifer section of San Bernardino National Forest. It's full of juniper, Jeffrey pine, and pinyon. Obedient dogs are welcome to peruse the area sans leash, but keep in mind that this off-leash rule might be reconsidered by the authorities.

We like it best here in late autumn, when a dusting of snow rests on the pine needles and the air is crisp. We've never run into another person on the trail during this time of year. Cougar Crest Trail eventually connects with the Pacific Crest Trail, which traverses 39 miles of the Big Bear area. The scenery here is outstanding.

From the Big Bear Lake village, cross the lake at the Stanfield Cutoff and turn left on Highway 38. As you drive west, the trail is just over a half mile west of the ranger station, on the right side of the road. There's plenty of parking. (909) 866-3437.

•**Pedal Path** 🐾🐾🐾½ *See* ❼ *on page 702.*

Here's one way to hike the Big Bear Lake area without roughing it too much. This six-mile paved path allows you and your leashed, lake-loving dog to hike along the scenic north shore of Big Bear Lake.

Sometimes bikers think they own the trail (it *is* called Pedal Path, not Four-Paw Path, after all), so make sure your dog is close to you. The trail starts at the north end of the Stanfield Cutoff. (909) 866-3437.

•**Woodland Trail** 🐾🐾🐾🐾 🐕 *See* ❽ *on page 702.*

This 1.5-mile nature trail in San Bernardino National Forest has 20 stops where you and your well-behaved, leashless dog may learn about the flora and fauna of this mountainous region. It's especially glorious in an early-morning mist.

The trail rarely gets crowded. If you encounter more than a few people, be courteous and keep your dog leashed. Rangers are reconsidering the off-leash rule for the forest, so good pooch public relations are essential. On last call, one ranger told us dogs had to be leashed. Another said good dogs can be leashless. Joe said he feels a close kinship with the second ranger.

From the Big Bear Lake village, cross the lake at the Stanfield Cutoff and turn left on Highway 38. Shortly after you turn, the trail will be on your right. (909) 866-3437.

RESTAURANTS

Many of the restaurants listed below are in the old-style Alpine village in the heart of Big Bear Lake. Whenever you visit here, you'll feel like it's Christmas.

Belotti's: The pizza is really tasty, and the fresh-baked goods will send you running to the nearest aerobics class. 41248 Big Bear Boulevard; (909) 866-9686.

The Log Cabin: You can eat on the deck here, which is three feet above the lawn, where your dog has to be tied. You can tie your dog securely under a shady tree and hover above her as you eat the German-American food here or sip any of the 10 beers they have on tap. 39976 Big Bear Boulevard; (909) 866-3667.

Mozart's Restaurant: This place looks like a huge alpine cottage, with a big wooden deck where dogs may watch their people dine. 40701 Village Drive; (909) 866-9497.

Paoli's Country Kitchen: The Italian food is really tasty. Your dog gets to hang out with you as you dine on the patio. 40821 Pennsylvania Avenue; (909) 866-2020.

Pine Knot Coffee & Bakery: Mmm. Come here on a cool autumn afternoon and try the hot pot pies or mulligan stew while sitting on the small deck. 535 Pine Knot Avenue; (909) 866-3537.

PLACES TO STAY

Big Bear Lake is one of the best places in the entire state to spend the night with your dog. There are so many lodgings that accept dogs that you'll have a hard time choosing. Here are just a few. For a more complete list, call the Big Bear Chamber of Commerce at (909) 866-4608 and ask for their Lodging Guide. Be sure you request the one that lists whether pets are allowed.

Bear Claw Cabins: These homey cabins are a quarter of a mile from the lake and skiing. Rates are $55 to $99, and dogs can stay in all rooms except the ones with Jacuzzis. 586 Main Street, Big Bear Lake, CA 92315; (909) 866-7633.

Big Pine Flat Campground: This is one of the more out-of-the-way campgrounds in the Big Bear area. You and your dog can hike around the area and be fully enveloped by ravishing Mama Nature. Or you can drive a few miles and be in the heart of Big Bear Lake. There are 20 sites available on a first-come, first-served basis. The campground closes in winter. Sites are $15. From Fawnskin, follow Rim of the World Drive (its name will change) for seven miles to Big Pine Flat Station. The campground is on your right. (909) 866-3437.

Cozy Hollow Lodge: This lodge deserves its name, since most cottages have fireplaces. It's a great place to stay after a long day on the slopes. In summer, a stream runs through the woods behind the lodge. Rates are $59 to $159. There's a $50 deposit for dogs and an additional $5 fee for each pooch. 40409 Big Bear Boulevard, Big Bear Lake, CA 92315; (909) 866-8886.

Eagle's Nest Bed & Breakfast: This romantic getaway is furnished with country antiques. The cottages have fireplaces. Dogs love it here. Rates are $85 to $150. There's a $50 deposit for dogs. 41675 Big Bear Boulevard, Big Bear Lake, CA 92315; (909) 866-6465.

Frontier Lodge: There's a big covered wagon in front of these cabins, so dogs who like the Old West feel right at home. Rates are $65 to $290. Dogs are $10 extra. 40472 Big Bear Boulevard, Big Bear Lake, CA 92315; (800) 457-6401.

Grey Squirrel Resort: These charming cottages are a half block from the lake, on 4.5 acres. Several of the cottages have fireplaces. For those achy muscles fraught with post-skiing-stress-disorder, the resort has a heated pool, which is enclosed in the winter (but pooches can't paddle here). Rates are $75 to $155. There's a $100 deposit for pets and an additional $10 fee per pooch. The cabins are on Highway 18, just west of town. The mailing address is P.O. Box 5404, Big Bear Lake, CA 92315; (909) 866-4335.

Happy Bear Village: All the cottages here have fireplaces. Dogs enjoy the large grassy areas that come complete with picnic tables and barbecues. Rates are $60 to $130. There's a $100 deposit for dogs, and an additional $10 per pooch. 40154 Big Bear Boulevard, Big Bear Lake, CA 92315; (909) 866-2350 or (909) 866-6816.

Quail Cove: These cozy cottages are in a wooded, parklike setting by the water. Rates are $79 to $189. Dogs are $5 extra. 39117 North Shore Drive, Big Bear Lake, CA 92315; (909) 866-5957.

Serrano Campground: If you like rustic campsites and good hot showers, this San Bernardino National Forest campground is worth the $15 to $24 fee. The 132 sites are close to Big Bear Lake and the solar observatory (which is open to the public during certain days in the summer). The campground is on the north side of the lake, about two miles east of Fawnskin. It's very close to the Cougar Crest Trail (see page 708). Call (800) 280-CAMP for reservations or (909) 866-3437 for more information. The campground is closed in the winter.

Shore Acres Lodge: This one's on the lake and has its own boat dock. They prefer small dogs here, but will go for larger ones if they're well behaved. Rates are $65 to $145. Dogs are $5 extra. 40090 Lakeview Drive, Big Bear Lake, CA 92315; (800) 524-6600.

Smoke Tree Lodge: Rates at this charming inn are $60 to $130. Dogs require a $100 deposit and a fee of $10 extra. 40154 Big Bear Boulevard, Big Bear Lake, CA 92315; (909) 866-6816.

Snuggle Creek Lodge: It's a short walk to the lake from here. Dogs are permitted only in the cottages, not the lodge. No puppies, please. Rates are $69 to $149. Pooches are $10 extra. 40440 Big Bear Boulevard, Big Bear Lake, CA 92315; (909) 866-2555.

Timberline Lodge: This one is close to the village, but set in a little forest area. Rates are $71 to $200. Dogs are $10 extra. 39921 Big Bear Boulevard, Big Bear Lake, CA 92315; (909) 866-4141.

DIVERSIONS

Wag in the wagon: So you're in beautiful Big Bear Lake village with your dog. You see a gent with a huge beard, shiny top hat, and fancy coat standing beside his English draft horse and antique carriage, waiting for a passenger. "Gee, honey, too bad we have Rex with us," you say to your loved one as Rex gives you the evil eye. "That horse-and-buggy ride sure looks like a good time."

Say no more. As long as Victoria Park Carriages owner and driver Michael Homan thinks Rex is cool (and not too huge), you'll all be able to take a spin through town. His horses don't mind well-behaved dogs, but some dogs don't take well to the horses, so make sure you've got your pooch under control before even approaching Homan.

If you catch Homan at his carriage stand, on Village Drive across from Chad's Place, a half-hour tour will run you about $30 per couple at night, $25 in the daytime. Mini rides are a mere $15 to $20. Or you can reserve the carriage, which holds up to six people, for about $100 an hour. Homan also runs a hayride that can take up to 25 people. Dogs really enjoy this back-to-the-farm setup. Victoria Park Carriages runs year-round. You can find Homan at his stand most weekends and holidays. Call (909) 584-2277 for more information.

Get hitched, with your dog's help: The Hitching Post Wedding Chapel is a dog's kind of marriage sanctuary. It's got a mountain/western theme and no overly frilly froufrou.

Owner Rob Hastings says he's played host to canine ring bearers and canine best men. Once he even helped a dog sign a marriage certificate (not the license, though). "We just put his paw on the ink pad, then stamped the certificate. He was a smart dog, but his penmanship wasn't good enough to sign his name," says Hastings.

Hastings asks that dogs attend only midweek weddings. On busy days like Saturday, he doesn't have enough time to vacuum up dog hairs, and a few people visiting after dogs participated have complained about their allergies flaring up.

The fee for getting hitched here is $75 and includes the chapel and a donation for the minister. Licenses are extra. For more information, call (909) 584-1030 or write them at P.O. Box 6489, Big Bear Lake, CA 92315.

CHINO

PARKS, BEACHES, AND RECREATION AREAS

• **Prado Regional Park/Prado Recreation, Inc.** 🐾🐾🐾🐾 🐕
See ❾ on page 702.

This 2,200-acre park is actually in two sections. There's the regular old regional park, with lakes, huge manicured fields, and playgrounds, and the dog park, with 1,100 acres of land for dogs to go leashless.

The regular old park charges $5 per vehicle on weekdays, $6 on weekends, and $1 per dog. Dogs must be on leash. A day here makes for a pleasant family outing. Camping can be fun, too. Sites are $15.

The dog training park will cost you $9 per person or per couple per day (up to two dogs are included in the fee). Camping anywhere on the 1,100 acres costs $5.50. But don't get the idea that this place is just a heavenly area where your dog can run like a crazy California canine. This is a dog training area, and we're generally not talking about the old sit-stay stuff. We're talking hunting and herding. We're talking dogs who work for a living.

Prado Recreation is not for vegetarians or anti-hunting folks. Chances are good that you'll see some dead birds here. You'll even see the people shooting and the dogs retrieving what they've shot. As we drove through, we saw Labs and springers everywhere obeying hand signals in ponds and fields where there were bound to be birds.

People laughed at poor old Joe Airedale as we cruised through. "Ha ha ha" was all we could hear as they pointed at his dumbfounded, curly head.

Somehow they could tell that his retrieval instincts stop where his nose starts. He was embarrassed, but he continued to stick his out the window anyway.

Dogs who herd really can go to town here. On a mist-shrouded field, we saw an elderly gent walking with a long wooden staff. He would quietly whistle or give subtle hand signals to two very intense Border collies who were keeping a couple of big goats in line. It was as if we'd been transported across the Atlantic. Aye, rarely have we seen a more lovely dog scene.

You'll need to bring along proof of your pooch's rabies vaccine to either part of the park. The regular section of Prado Regional Park is located about seven miles south of Highway 60, on the left side of Euclid Avenue. Call (909) 597-4260 for information or camping reservations. To get to the dog section, take the first left after Prado Regional Park. You'll be on a very bumpy dirt road for what may seem like a long time, but eventually you'll come to the park's office. Call the Prado Kennel at (909) 597-6366 for more information.

PLACES TO STAY

Prado Regional Park: See Prado Regional Park on page 711 for camping information.

CRESTLINE

PARKS, BEACHES, AND RECREATION AREAS

•**Lake Gregory** 😺😺😺½ *See* ⑩ *on page 702.*

Here's a county park the way we like to see them: free. It's rare, but it happens. Lake Gregory is an 86-acre lake in a park that has only about 20 acres of dry land. But the land is lush and forested, with ponderosa pines, sugar pines, and cedar trees everywhere.

A 2.75-mile path (complete with fitness stops) takes you around the lake, but alas, dogs aren't allowed in the water. They must be leashed at all times.

From Highway 18, take the Crestline exit, which turns into Lake Drive. Follow the road into the park. For the hiking path, start at the south shore. (909) 338-2233.

FAWNSKIN

PARKS, BEACHES, AND RECREATION AREAS

•**Dana Point Park** 😺😺😺 *See* ⑪ *on page 702.*

Swimming dogs adore this county park. It's located along the north side of Big Bear Lake's Grout Bay, so it's somewhat off the beaten track. It's a fairly small park, but it has some romping room for leashed dogs, as well as a picnic area for hungry dogs and their people. Bird-watching is one of the big activities here, so be sure to bring your binoculars. From November to March, you might see bald eagles roosting and feeding.

The park is located just off the main part of this charming old village, on the south side of Highway 38. (909) 866-0130.

HESPERIA

PARKS, BEACHES, AND RECREATION AREAS

• **Hesperia Lake Park** 🐾🐾🐾 *See* **⑫** *on page 702.*

Most people visit this 200-acre park to nab a trout or catfish out of the seven-acre lake. But since dogs aren't allowed on the lake bank, or in the lake, it's probably not the activity of choice if you're looking for something you can do with your pooch at your side.

The park has plenty of trees for shade and leg lifts, plus sports fields and playgrounds for the humans in the family. Look for the small waterfall, which feeds a meandering rock-lined stream that eventually leads to the lake. It's a great spot to stop for a picnic.

While there's no day-use fee, you'll be charged $5 to fish. Camping is $12 to $15, and dogs are $2 extra. The 86 campsites are set near the lake. The campsites are available on a first-come, first-served basis. Although there's a sign for this park from the Bear Valley Cutoff exit of Interstate 15, don't be fooled into thinking it's just off the highway, especially if your dog is getting that glazed look that tells you he can wait no longer. The park is actually several miles southeast of the exit. The route is complicated, but the signage is excellent, so follow the brown signs all the way. (760) 244-5951.

• **Silverwood Lake State Recreation Area** 🐾🐾🐾½
See **⑬** *on page 702.*

Water-loving dogs, brace yourselves for bad news: You have to stay high and dry here. You can't go to the beaches at this 1,000-surface-acre lake. In fact, you're not even allowed in the lake in the most remote areas.

While people can swim, fish, water-ski, and sail on the lake, dogs must be content just to watch. Fortunately for dogs and their landlubbing human companions, this 2,500-acre park has 13 miles of paved hiking/biking trails. You'll go through high chaparral country here, with all the bushes and trees a boy dog could ever dream of claiming for himself. And if that's not enough, you can head over to the national forestland on the lake's east side and hike forever.

Dogs must be leashed at Silverwood Lake. There are coyotes and bobcats and bears, oh my. Camping costs $17 to $18 a night. There are 134 sites available on a first-come, first-served basis. (Reservations are required in the summer.) Call Parknet at (800) 444-PARK for reservations. The day-use fee for the park is $6 per vehicle. Dogs are charged $1 extra for day use and camping, so make sure yours brings his allowance. From the Crestline area, 10 miles north of San Bernardino, take Interstate 15 to Highway 138 and drive east about 11 miles on Highway 138 to the park. (760) 389-2281.

PLACES TO STAY

Days Inn Suites: Rates are $49 to $89. Dogs require a $10 deposit. 14865 Bear Valley Road, Hesperia, CA 92345; (760) 948-0600.

Hesperia Lake Park: See Hesperia Lake Park above for camping information.

Mojave River Forks Regional Park: Last time we visited, you had to camp here to have access to the park's 1,100 acres. No more day users were allowed, the ranger told us, but we've been given a heads-up that day users may soon be permitted again, for a fee of $5. Call before planning a day trip.

There are 84 campsites and four group areas available. Reservations are recommended. Sites are $13 to $19. Dogs are $2 extra. If you camp here, you can hike, explore the often-dry Mojave River, and have access to the nearby Pacific Crest Trail. Be sure not to miss the Santa Fe Mormon Trail, complete with ruins. The park is on Highway 173 between Silverwood Lake and Hesperia. (760) 389-2322.

Silverwood Lake State Recreation Area: See Silverwood Lake State Recreation Area on page 713 for camping information.

LAKE ARROWHEAD

This attractive resort village in the mountains of the San Bernardino National Forest has plenty for a dog to do. Dogs can lounge in lodges. They can hike the hillsides.

The Arrowhead district of the national forest has some terrific trails ranging in elevation from 3,000 to 7,000 feet. Pooches are welcome to join you on a day hike or an overnighter. Contact the ranger station at (909) 337-2444 for trail maps and advice on which hikes and campsites are better suited for your skill level and the time of year you'll be visiting. We've listed one of the more popular campgrounds below, but there are plenty of smaller hike-in sites as well.

The lake itself is managed by an exclusive homeowners association, so public lake access is rather limited.

PLACES TO STAY

Arrowhead Tree Top Lodge: "We love dogs," says a kindly employee who works for the local humane society. Your dog might even be lucky enough to get a dog biscuit here.

Some of the rooms at this attractive lodge have kitchens and fireplaces, for that homey touch. The lodge is on five acres with a nature trail and creeks. Dogs dig that. It's a short walk to the village and to the lake from here. Rates are $59 to $157. Dogs are $8 extra. 27992 Rainbow Drive, Lake Arrowhead, CA 92352; (909) 337-2311 or (800) 358-TREE.

Dogwood Campground: This isn't one of the more secluded or rustic campgrounds in the area, but I mention it here because it's conveniently located one mile from the lake, and because Joe Dog insisted I list it due to its name. Dogwood is a privately operated national forest campground with 93 sites and all the amenities a camper could need, and then some ("then some" refers to things like laundry facilities). The camp is set along the lake's outlet.

The campground is open from May through mid-October. Sites are $12 to $18. Dogwood is located at Highway 18's Blue Jay turnoff. For information, call (909) 337-2444. For reservations, call (800) 280-CAMP.

Prophets' Paradise Bed & Breakfast: This bed-and-breakfast is a real charmer. You and your dog will drool over the cozy antique-filled living room, which is especially inviting in winter when the fireplace is roaring. Take a dog here at Christmas for the best present you could give him. (And speaking of Christmas, the "Prophet" in Prophets' Paradise is the last name of the innkeepers, not anything prophetic.)

The bed-and-breakfast is a five-level, 5,000-square-foot house on a hillside. Each room has its own floor. It's wonderfully private for a B & B. The pet rooms have decks and outside entrances. Rates are $90 to $160. 26845 Modoc Lane, Lake Arrowhead, CA 92352; (909) 336-1969 or (800) 987-2231.

LUCERNE VALLEY

PARKS, BEACHES, AND RECREATION AREAS

• **Johnson Valley Open Area** 🐾🐾🐾🐾 🐕 *See* ⓱ *on page 702.*

If city life has your dog tied in knots, a visit to the Johnson Valley Open Area is bound to unkink him. There's nothing like 250,000 acres of leashless terrain—including mountains, scrubby desert, dry lakes, sand dunes, and rock formations—to take the "d" out of "doldrums" and put it back in "dog."

While you may not run into any other people during your visit, keep in mind that much of this land is okay for off-highway vehicles to cruise. If you hear one of these loud beasts coming, make sure your dog is close by. Some dog owners like to put something bright orange on their dog just in case. You'll also want to be aware that coyotes are not unheard of around here. Don't let your dog wander far from you.

There are many access points to this huge acreage. One good bet is to exit Highway 247 at Bessimer Mine Road and drive north a few miles. Big signs will show you the way. The public land here is interspersed with private land, but Bureau of Land Management folks say unless an area is fenced off, posted, or developed, it's probably okay for hiking. (760) 252-6000.

NEEDLES

Named for the sharp peaks at the southern end of the valley, this Colorado River town is surrounded by some of the most fascinating desert landscapes in the world.

If all the wide-open territory near Needles makes you and your dog feel like insignificant specks in the universe, try a side trip to London Bridge, just down the road a bit in Lake Havasu City, Arizona. This is the same London Bridge that was sinking into the Thames River in 1962, until developers of this town bought it for $2.5 million and shipped it to the U.S. granite block by granite block. Your dog can go back home and tell all his buddies that he visited London Bridge, and they'll be impressed (most of them think it's still in London). English springer spaniels get a misty, faraway look when they come here.

PARKS, BEACHES, AND RECREATION AREAS

• **Moabi Regional Park/Park Moabi** 🐾🐾🐾 *See* ⓯ *on page 702.*

If your dog likes the water, tell her that the Colorado River runs through this park. If she's a landlubber, let her know that most of the park is lawns and desert land. There's something for most tastes at this 1,025-acre county park. Unfortunately, it's the most expensive park in the county. With a $6-per-vehicle day-use fee and $12 to $20 for camping (the pricier sites are on the river), you're not looking at cheap outdoor fun. There are 45 campsites. And it's not always the quietest place in the world. Anglers can become frustrated with all the jet skiers and fast boats that cruise around here. To have the run of the lake, you can try renting a houseboat from the park's marina. It's loads of fun, and all your dog has to do to go for a swim is hop out the back door.

The park is at the intersection of Interstate 40 and Park Moabi Road. (760) 326-3831.

• **Mojave National Preserve** 🐾 🐾 🐾 1/2 *See* ⑯ *on page 702.*

The next time your dog gives you one of those sideways glances that says "I gotta get outta the city," you might want to consider spending a few days exploring a desert environment that seems to go on forever. It actually does go on forever, or at least for 1.5 million acres to the west and north of Needles, whichever comes first.

Within this gigantic swath of land are volcanic cinder cones, booming sand dunes, old mines, new mines, mysterious petroglyphs, and dramatic cliffs. If you're a newcomer to desert life, you'll find the wildflowers, cacti, and yucca fascinating.

Dogs must be leashed here, now that the once leash-free land has been transferred from the dog-loving Bureau of Land Management to the National Park Service. Fortunately the Park Service designated it as a preserve rather than a park, so dogs are still allowed in many areas. They can join you for a jaunt along any of the many miles of old mining roads, but they're not permitted on the trails. And they're not allowed in the designated wilderness area unless they're hunting with you, and then they may hunt off leash. (Hunting just doesn't work well with leashes.)

Keep in mind that nearly 300 species of animals live here, including coyotes and Mojave green rattlesnakes. Since these rattlers are more aggressive than most other rattlers, and since dogs have been known to be a coyote delicacy, it's extra inspiration to keep your dog close at paw.

Camping ranges from no cost for wilderness camping to $10 for regular sites. Dogs must be leashed at the campgrounds. There are 65 campsites available on a first-come, first-served basis. The preserve can be entered at several points along Interstate 40, and several points along Interstate 15. Call (760) 733-4040 to find out which entrance would best suit your travel plans.

RESTAURANTS

Burger Hut: Sure, you can get their traditional beef burgers, but vegetarians will be happy to know that they also serve a mean veggie burger here. 701 Broadway; (760) 326-2342.

Jack-in-the-Box: It's so refreshing to find a dog-friendly link in a restaurant chain. This one allows pooches to dine at the 12 outdoor tables, and they'll even supply your dog with water if you tell them he's thirsty. 221 J Street; (760) 326-4746.

PLACES TO STAY

Best Motel: Rates are $20 to $35. 1900 West Broadway, Needles, CA 92363; (760) 326-3824.

Best Western Colorado River Inn: As long as you don't bring your dog in the office when you check in or out, you and your pooch are welcome here. Rates are $60 to $65. Pooches pay a $10 deposit. 2271 West Broadway, Needles, CA 92363; (760) 326-4552.

Moabi Regional Park: See Moabi Regional Park on page 715 for camping informatiojn.

Mojave National Preserve: See Mojave National Preserve on page 716 for camping information.

River Valley Motor Lodge: If your dog is small and has short hair, the management here will be mighty accommodating. Otherwise, you'll find there's no room at the inn. Rates are $21 to $40. A $10 pooch deposit is required. 1707 West Broadway, Needles, CA 92363; (760) 326-3839.

ONTARIO

PARKS, BEACHES, AND RECREATION AREAS

• **John Galvin Park** 🐾 🐾 ½ *See ⑰ on page 702.*

Lazy leashed dogs like this park. The big old trees seem like they were made for shading dogs whose main focus is sleeping. For a perfectly lazy afternoon outing, bring a book, lean against a tree, and revel in the sound of your snoring pooch. An open field in one section of this municipal park provides just enough room to roam should your mellow dog choose not to snooze.

Leashed dogs are permitted in all of Ontario's parks, should you care to check out some others. For John Galvin, exit Interstate 10 at Fourth Street and go west a couple of blocks. The park will be on your left. (909) 391-2513.

RESTAURANTS

Joey's Pizza: Joe Dog likes it here. But he seems to believe that since the restaurant bears his name, he should be entitled to an occasional bite of pizza. I don't generally succumb to his pleading eyes until I'm down to the crust. And if there's even a hint of bell pepper on it, he spits it out with a horrified grimace (just like my husband). 790 North Archibald Avenue; (909) 944-6701.

PLACES TO STAY

Country Suites by Carlson: Rates are $69 to $109. Dogs are $50 extra for the length of their stay. 231 North Vineyard Avenue, Ontario, CA 91764; (909) 983-8484.

Doubletree Hotel: Rates are $69 to $131. Dogs require a $50 deposit and are $10 extra. 222 North Vineyard Avenue, Ontario, CA 91764; (909) 983-0909.

Holiday Inn Airport: This is the best hotel for dogs who have to stay near the airport. Not only do you get a continental breakfast, but all the rooms are actually suites, complete with kitchenettes. And guess what else? Fire hydrants are pretty prominent outside the hotel. It's a boy dog's dream. People prefer the Jacuzzis, which grace half the rooms. Rates are $79 to $110. There's a $50 dog deposit. 3400 Shelby Street, Ontario, CA 91764; (909) 466-9600.

REDLANDS

Parts of this lush, resort-like town provide a breath of fresh air from smog-ridden and traffic-filled Southern California.

PARKS, BEACHES, AND RECREATION AREAS

• **Prospect Park** 🐾🐾🐾½ *See* ⑱ *on page 702.*

You'll be surrounded by exquisite views, towering palms, multitudes of orange trees, and flowers everywhere at this enchanting, verdant park. Prospect Park is out of a fairy tale. It's one big hill, with delicate wooden seats overlooking the surrounding orchards. At the top, you'll find an open-air theater, some peacocks, and a resident cat, so be sure to follow the rules and leash your dog.

This one's well worth the short trek from Interstate 10. For the most scenic ride, exit the freeway at Orange Street and drive south, through the quaint downtown area. In about seven blocks, bear right at Cajon Street. The park is on your right in about one mile. Park on Cajon Street just after Highland Avenue (just past the orange grove and before the picnic area on your right). Walk back several feet to the wide paved path and embark on your wondrous journey. (909) 798-7509.

RESTAURANTS

Cafe Society: Dogs are welcome to help you dine on good sandwiches and tasty bakery items at the sidewalk and patio tables. 308 West State Street, #1A; (909) 798-5578.

Rama Garden Thai Restaurant: The big dog rule here is that pooches should not walk in the restaurant's waterfall. Joe Dog, the water-hating Airedale in my life, doesn't mind this restriction at all. The place can get crowded, and if it does, management may ask you and your dog to come back another time. 309 West State Street; (909) 798-7747.

RUNNING SPRINGS

PLACES TO STAY

Giant Oaks Motel & Cabins: All cabins have a kitchen and a fireplace. There's plenty of land nearby where you can take your pooch for a good stroll. The lodging is down the road from Lake Arrowhead. Rates are $59 to $149. Dogs require a $20 deposit and are $10 extra. 32180 Hilltop Boulevard, Running Springs, CA 92382; (909) 867-2231 or (800) 786-1689.

SAN BERNARDINO

PARKS, BEACHES, AND RECREATION AREAS

• **Glen Helen Regional Park** 🐾🐾🐾½ *See* ⑲ *on page 702.*

This 1,425-acre park features two lakes that are regularly stocked with such goodies as trout and catfish. But if your dog doesn't like to fish, she's sure to enjoy such goodies as an ecology trail and lots of grassy little hills that await your leashed dog's happy feet.

Rangers tell us that some dogs seem to get a kick out of watching kids zoom down the 300-foot, two-part water slide at the swim complex in the park's southeast corner. Dogs aren't allowed there, but the park has plenty of viewing spots for pooches and their people.

With all these activities, Glen Helen Regional Park is a great place for your dog to take the family. You can even camp here. There are 50 sites available on a first-come, first-served basis. The fee is $10, and dogs are $1 extra. The day-use fee here is $5, and $1 per dog. Fishing is $5 per person over six years old. Exit Interstate 215 at Devore Road (just south of the Interstate 15/215 junction) and follow the signs about 1.5 miles to the park. (909) 880-2522.

•**Perris Hill Park** 😺😺😺 *See* **⑳** *on page 702.*

This park makes dogs happy, in part because there's dense shade almost everywhere. The trees providing this comfort are generally very big and very old. Although dogs must be leashed, they have smiles on their snouts when they gather during dog rush hour, around 5 P.M. or so.

The park is at Highland and Valencia Avenues. (909) 384-5233.

PLACES TO STAY

Best Western Sands Motel: This Best Western has a doggy delight out back, in the form of a small, fenced-in, leash-free "pet rest stop." It's about 30 by 50 feet. Rates are $40 to $50. Dogs are $10 extra and require a $50 deposit. 606 North H Street, San Bernardino, CA 92410; (909) 889-8391.

Glen Helen Regional Park: See Glen Helen Regional Park on page 718 for camping information.

La Quinta Motor Inn: Dogs are allowed to stay in this motel's smoking rooms. Fortunately, there's a little grassy area outside where they can get some fresh air. Rates are $61 to $66. 205 East Hospitality Lane, San Bernardino, CA 92408; (909) 888-7571.

Motel 6: Rates are $33 for the first adult, $6 for the second. This Motel 6, like almost every Motel 6, permits one small pooch per room. 1960 Ostrems Way, San Bernardino, CA 92407; (909) 887-8191.

TWENTYNINE PALMS

PARKS, BEACHES, AND RECREATION AREAS

•**Joshua Tree National Park** 😺😺😺½

This town houses the headquarters and a good-sized swatch of this stunning park. See page 703 for details.

RESTAURANTS

Fosters Freeze: Eating the cold, creamy treats here is the perfect way to end a day of exploring Joshua Tree National Park (see page 703). Joe gives the vanilla shake two paws up. 73629 Two Mile Road; (760) 367-9303.

PLACES TO STAY

Knott's Sky Park: This small, shaded park is popular among RV campers. There are 40 RV campsites and many tent sites. Rates are $7.50 to $17. It's at El Sol Avenue, just off Twentynine Palms Highway/Highway 62. Call (760) 367-9669 for reservations.

29 Palms Inn: Set on 70 acres of beautiful desert, this rustic resort is just what the vet ordered for you and your pooch. It's a stress-free environment, with a peaceful spring-fed shaded pond for toe-dipping, a pool (with a cute little bar) and hot tubs for lounging, hammocks galore, phone-free bungalows and adobe cottages, and a view of the heavens you don't want to miss. You can get a massage in your room, on your sun patio, or even in the great outdoors. The cooks at the delightful restaurant here can pack a picnic lunch that you and your dog will drool for. Take it on a hike in Joshua Tree National Park, whose entrance is just down the road (see page 703).

The cottage and cabins are unique, with a down-home, Old West, nouvelle-desert feel. Some have a fireplace and a kitchen. They all have evaporative coolers for hot summer days and heaters for cool winter nights. They also have cable TV, but the TVs are small and most are black and white. The resort's brochure says this is to help guests focus on more important things, but Joe Dog thinks it's because televisions are expensive. I love the lack of big Sonys, though, and I believe the brochure. Besides, snazzy new TVs just wouldn't fit in.

A woman I met on a plane gave me the heads-up about this magical place. Meg Renfrew, thank you. Rates are $63 to $225. There's a $10 dog fee per visit. 73950 Inn Avenue, Twentynine Palms, CA 92277; (760) 367-3505. The inn also has a Web site: www.cyberspike.com/29palmsinn.

TWIN PEAKS

PLACES TO STAY

Arrowhead Pine Rose Cabins: This five-acre property is located three miles from Lake Arrowhead. Dogs like the fact that they can walk around the spacious land here and check out all the sweet-smelling pines. About half of the 15 cabins permit pooches. Some cabins have back patios where your dog can relax in a quasi-outdoor atmosphere without escaping.

Pet blankets are provided. If your dog makes himself at home on human furniture, please cover it with the blanket. Rates are $49 to $350. Dogs are $5 extra, and there's a $100 pooch deposit. 25994 Highway 189, Twin Peaks, CA 92391; (909) 337-2341 or (800) 429-PINE.

UPLAND

PARKS, BEACHES, AND RECREATION AREAS

• **Upland Memorial Park** 😺 😺 *See* ㉑ *on page 702.*

You feel as if you're in a royal garden at this peaceful city park. The front of the park is almost entirely shaded by large old trees. A colorful rose garden is the centerpiece. That's a nice touch for dogs who like to stop and sniff the flowers (but don't let them do leg lifts on them). The back of the park used to have an off-leash section, but now it's next to a new road, so leashes are a must.

The park is conveniently located for road-weary dogs whose owners get their kicks on Route 66. It's at the junction of Route 66 (Foothill Boulevard) and 11th Avenue. (909) 931-4280.

VICTORVILLE

PARKS, BEACHES, AND RECREATION AREAS

• **Center Street Park** 🐾 🐾 ½ *See* ㉒ *on page 702.*

While it's only a couple of blocks long, this park is Victorville's most attractive municipal park. It's full of trees, so there's plenty of shade and plenty of places for your leashed dog to sniff. And it's usually quiet, except when there's a ball game going on at one of the playing fields here.

Exit Interstate 15 at Mojave Drive and go east a little more than a mile to Hesperia Road. The park is on your right. (760) 955-5257.

• **Eva Dell Park** 🐾 *See* ㉓ *on page 702.*

This park is literally on the other side of the tracks. Just a couple of blocks from the railroad tracks, it's not in the most desirable part of town. Nor is it the most desirable park. It's got a rough, dusty feel. But if you find yourself in this part of town with a pooch who's got to go, the fenced-in ball fields aren't bad. Keep in mind that dogs are supposed to be leashed.

Eva Dell Park is just above the Mojave River (tough access, though). Take D Street to Sixth Street and drive northeast, following the signs to the park. (760) 955-5257.

• **Mojave Narrows Regional Park** 🐾 🐾 🐾 *See* ㉔ *on page 702.*

This 840-acre park is by far the largest park in the area. It's kind of triangular, bordered on the left by railroad tracks and on the right by the Mojave River. The rangers tell that to people hiking with dogs, lest they get a little lost in their eagerness to get back to nature.

There are plenty of fields here, but the best place for walking around with your leashed dog is the more forested part of the park. If you're an angler with a dog who likes to cheer you on as you cast for supper, you'll be happy to know there's fishing year-round for $4 per day.

Camping costs $10 to $15. Dogs are $1 extra. There are approximately 65 campsites available. Reservations are recommended, and there's a $2 reservation fee. The park's day-use fee is $5 per vehicle, $1 per dog. From Interstate 15, take the Bear Valley Cutoff exit and drive east for five miles. When you come to the railroad track overpass, turn left at Ridgecrest Road. Drive three miles north to the park. (760) 245-2226.

PLACES TO STAY

Budget Inn: Rates are $30 to $45. Small pets only, please, and there's a $10 to $20 deposit for them. 14153 Kentwood Boulevard, Victorville, CA 92392; (760) 241-8010.

Mojave Narrows Regional Park: See Mojave Narrows Regional Park on above for camping information.

Red Roof Inn: This motel is conveniently close to Mojave Narrows Regional Park. Rates are $36 to $65. 13409 Mariposa Road, Victorville, CA 92392; (760) 241-1577.

YUCAIPA

PARKS, BEACHES, AND RECREATION AREAS

• **Yucaipa Regional Park** 🐾 🐾 🐾 ½ *See* ㉕ *on page 702.*

This picturesque park is surrounded by the San Bernardino Mountains and Mount San Gorgonio. But dogs who visit here have more important things on their mind than pretty scenery. First of all, they're not relegated to the usual six-foot leash—their leashes can be 10 feet long! Joy of joys. Then there's the size of this park—it's 885 acres, with enough grassy fields to tire even the friskiest hound dog.

Water-loving dogs enjoy accompanying their people to the three trout-stocked lakes, and water-loving kids get a kick out of the 350-foot water slides at the swim lagoon (no dogs allowed on the slides because they're too hairy). Several campsites are available near the lake, so if you're in the mood for a little camping with your angling, you couldn't ask for a much more convenient location. Sites are $11 to $17. There are about 35 campsites here. Reservations are recommended.

The day-use fee is $5 per vehicle on weekdays, $6 on weekends. Dogs are $1 extra. Fishing permits are $5 daily for anyone over eight years old.

From Interstate 10, take the Yucaipa exit and follow the brown signs for "Regional Park." It's about five miles from the freeway. (909) 790-3127.

PLACES TO STAY

Yucaipa Regional Park: See Yucaipa Regional Park above for camping information.

57
RIVERSIDE COUNTY

Dogs are dancing with happiness in Riverside County these days, because they finally have a dog park to call their very own. It's in the city of Riverside, and it's only an acre, but it's beautiful and it's theirs. (See Carlson Park Dog Park, page 736.) They can throw their leashes to the wind and cavort about in true doggy glee. Until recently, dogs weren't even allowed to set paw in a Riverside park, and now they've got Carlson *and* they're permitted in all of the city's parks. This is positive pooch progress. And at press time we got the great news that beautiful Palm Springs will finally be getting its very own dog park! (Please see the Palm Springs section, page 730, for more on this exciting development.) Dogs are no longer going to have to take to the desert to have a good time around here.

Actually, a trip to the desert during the more temperate months isn't a bad idea at all. In fact, dogs think it's a four-paws notion. But if it's hot or even warm outside, please forget it. The sand can be scorching even if the air isn't, and can poach a pooch's paws.

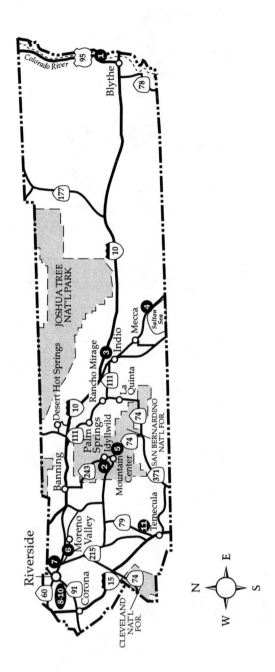

The Bureau of Land Management oversees millions of acres of desert and mountain land out here, and dogs applaud the great job the agency does. On almost all the BLM land (except places like nature preserves), pooches are permitted to go leashless.

Our favorite BLM land in Riverside County is the Santa Rosa Mountains National Scenic Area. It's rugged, desolate, and utterly pristine. It's also so sweeping that giving general directions is futile. It spans much of the area of the central county from Interstate 10 south to the north border of the Anza-Borrego State Desert. Call the BLM's Palm Springs district office at (760) 251-4800 for specifics.

County parks welcome leashed dogs, but be forewarned: Most of these parks charge $4 per vehicle plus $2 per pooch. That adds up if you use the parks for your daily dog walks. You can often park on the street outside the entrance and avoid the $4 fee, but you can't get out of the $2 canine charge.

NATIONAL FORESTS
See the National Forests and Wilderness Areas chapter starting on page 748 for important information and safety tips on visiting national forests with your dog.

- **Cleveland National Forest** 🐾🐾🐾🐾 🐕 See page 749.
- **San Bernardino National Forest** 🐾🐾🐾🐾 🐕 See page 753.

NATIONAL PARKS
- **Joshua Tree National Park** 🐾🐾🐾½
Although the bulk of this huge desert park is in Riverside County, the large visitors center area with easily accessible hikes is north of the border, in San Bernardino County. Please see page 703 for details.

BLYTHE
If you're traveling from the east on Interstate 10 and vow that you'll stop in the first California town you hit, get ready to brake. Blythe isn't an exciting town, but it's a welcome sight if you've traveled across the country with the Golden State as your goal.

PARKS, BEACHES, AND RECREATION AREAS
- **Mayflower Park** 🐾🐾🐾 See ❶ on page 724.
This park covers only 24 acres, but because it backs up on the refreshing Colorado River, it seems much bigger. The folks here are pretty laid-back about dogs when it's not crowded. Pooches should be leashed, but you can still let them do a little wading in the water. Just watch out for those pesky boats.

Mayflower Park is an excellent place to stop if you've been driving all day and feel like fishing for stripers or catfish, cooking your catch for dinner, and then camping by the river.

The day-use parking fee is $4, plus $2 extra for dogs. Camping costs $15 to $16, with dogs costing $2 extra. There are 180 sites available. The park is six miles northeast of Blythe, just north of Sixth Avenue and Colorado River Road. Call Parknet at (800) 234-PARK for camping reservations. For park info, call (760) 922-4665.

PLACES TO STAY

Best Western Sahara Motel: Rates are $49 to $64. 825 West Hobsonway, Blythe, CA 92225; (760) 922-7105.

Comfort Inn: Rates are $38 to $62. Small pooches are preferred. 903 West Hobsonway, Blythe, CA 92225; (760) 922-4146.

Hidden Beaches: This is one of the many camping resorts along the Colorado River. Sites are $17 per day, and pooches cost $1 extra. There are 92 sites available. Reservations are recommended in the summer. 6951 Sixth Avenue, Blythe, CA 92225; (760) 922-7276.

Lost Lake Resort: Campsites are $10 to $15 per day. There are 106 sites available. A reservation with payment in advance is required. It's located 31 miles north of Blythe on U.S. 395. The mailing address is P.O. Box 6046, Blythe, CA 92225; (760) 664-4413.

Mayflower Park: See Mayflower Park on page 725 for information.

McIntyre Park: Dogs can stay here only in the winter, from November through March. The camping fee is $16 to $20 per car. There are sites to accommodate approximately 700 people. We're not exactly talking intimate. Sites are available on a first-come, first-served basis. 8750 East 26th Avenue, Blythe, CA 92225; (760) 922-8205.

DESERT HOT SPRINGS

This little community is known for its naturally hot mineral water—it doesn't smell like rotten eggs! Folks with aches and pains come to soak in pools and tubs full of the stuff, and they swear by it. Dogs do some swearing of their own around here, but for a different reason: Pooches aren't permitted in any city parks.

PLACES TO STAY

Kismet Lodge: I love the name of this place. Reminds me of the enchanting musical about fate. The owner says lots of people like the name—so much so that one man stopped his Mercedes in the middle of the road here and wanted to buy the place. She didn't sell. She likes it too much here.

The motel has 10 rooms, all with views of the nearby mountains. Most have kitchens. There's a fireplace in the lobby for chilly winter evenings. Most folks come here for the naturally hot mineral pool and Jacuzzi. If you have environmental allergies, this is a good place to stay; the owner has them, too, and uses natural cleaning products, bans smoking (or tries to, but she says this is a tough one), and discourages perfumes. Rates are $45 to $65. 13-340 Mountain View Road, Desert Hot Springs, CA 92240; (760) 329-6451.

Sky Valley Park: If you have an RV and a hankering to soak in water that's good for you, come here. Sky Valley Park has nine naturally heated mineral Jacuzzis, as well as four large swimming pools. The RV resort is set on 160 acres, with eight fishing ponds and lots of grassy areas and palm trees for leashed pooches to sniff out. It's also surrounded by the desert, so you can get a taste of the area's natural environment, too. If you're bored traveling around in your RV, the park also offers 10 shuffleboard courts; horseshoes; a huge clubhouse; a hobby court with lapidary, stained glass, and ceramic equipment; and tennis courts. Sky Valley Park has a sister RV park where only seniors are permitted, but all ages are welcome here. Rates are $28 to $31. 74-711 Dillon Road, Desert Hot Springs, CA 92241; (800) 800-9218.

Stardust Spa Motel: A large spa that can seat 20 people is the focal point of this little motel. There's also a small heated pool. Some rooms have fridges, others have kitchens. This is mighty convenient when traveling with a pooch. When you call to get information or make reservations, ask them to send you a copy of a fun little article about Desert Hot Springs and the Stardust. Rates are $46 to $55. 66-634 Fifth Street, Desert Hot Springs, CA 92240; (760) 329-5443.

IDYLLWILD

PARKS, BEACHES, AND RECREATION AREAS

•**Idyllwild County Park** 🐾🐾🐾½ *See* ❷ *on page* 724.

In the morning, the cool mountain air is delicately scented with fresh pines, and you may find yourself so invigorated that you actually want to get out of your tent and start the day early.

This is an attractive park, with scenic self-guided nature trails for you and your leashed pooch to peruse. Better yet, there's easy access to the wonderful, off-leash trails of San Bernardino National Forest (see page 753). But you must check with a ranger before venturing out, because you could easily find yourself in the middle of Mount San Jacinto State Park—a major no-no for four-legged beasts of the domestic persuasion.

The drive-in day-use fee is $4. Dogs are $2 extra. Campsites cost $15, with dogs being charged the usual $2 county fee. There are 96 campsites available from the first weekend in April to the last weekend in October (sometimes into November). In winter, six sites are available on a first-come, first-served basis. The park is one mile north of Idyllwild, at the end of County Park Road; (909) 659-2656. For reservations call (800) 234-PARK.

PLACES TO STAY

Idyllwild County Park: See Idyllwild County Park above for camping information.

INDIO

It may look flat and boring, but this dry old town has the distinction of being the king of the only region in the United States that grows dates. And we're not talking a few trees—we're talking 4,000 acres' worth, making a semi-oasis out of an otherwise blah, depressing area.

If you thought you and your dog had absolutely no reason to visit here, think again. One look at the date-oriented diversion described below, and you may decide to come here next weekend.

PARKS, BEACHES, AND RECREATION AREAS

•**Miles Avenue Park** 🐾½ *See* ❸ *on page* 724.

If you're dropping someone off at the adjacent Coachella Valley Museum and Cultural Center, your dog might appreciate a little pause at this grassy, meadowy park. It looks like a golf course, but miraculously enough in this golf-inundated land, it's not. There are some deciduous trees, as well as palms, for the benefit of the boy dogs in the crowd.

The park is on Deglet Noor Street and Miles Avenue, about three blocks north of Highway 111. (760) 347-8522.

RESTAURANTS

Andy's Restaurant: The outdoor seating area is not huge, but that won't make your dog drool any less over the burgers, pastrami, and hot dogs you can eat here. Breakfast is also available. 83-699 Indio Boulevard; (760) 347-1794.

Shield's Date Gardens: See Diversions, below.

PLACES TO STAY

Best Western Date Tree Motor Hotel: Rates are $54 to $78. Pooches require a $50 deposit. 81-909 Indio Boulevard, Indio, CA 92201; (760) 347-3421.

Holiday Inn Express: Rates are $52 to $99. A $20 deposit is required for your dog. 84-096 Indio Springs Drive, Indio, CA 92201; (760) 342-6344.

Royal Plaza Inn: You'll get a heated pool and a spa when you stay here, but no pooches in the agua, please. Rates are $44 to $95. 82-347 Highway 111, Indio, CA 92201; (760) 347-0911.

DIVERSIONS

Date your dog: Blech! The thought sends shivers up the spine, until you realize that to date your dog in these parts merely means to take him on a date date. You know, inundate him with dates. Still not clear?

Fadi Saab, general manager of Shield's Date Gardens, explains: "Order a date shake and walk around our 30 acres of date trees, so your dog can stretch his tired legs. We love dogs here, almost as much as we love dates."

While you're at Shield's Date Gardens, be sure to step inside (leave your pooch outside in the shade with a friend and take turns dog-sitting) and watch the ongoing slide show entitled "The Romance and Sex Life of the Date." The date trees might rate it "X," but humans definitely give it a "G." (That stands for General Audiences or, in this case, Good Gawd!)

Shield's Date Gardens is at 80-225 Route 111; (760) 347-0996.

LA QUINTA

PLACES TO STAY

La Quinta Resort & Club: First, for all of you who have stayed at the La Quinta motel chain with your dog, this isn't one of those motels. Not by a long shot. This La Quinta is the mother of all La Quintas. This internationally famous resort is probably the most legendary of all the posh getaways in the Palm Springs area. The town of La Quinta was named after it, if that tells you anything. Built in 1926, it's the area's oldest resort. It quickly became a favorite retreat for the stars of the Golden Era of Hollywood. (La Quinta was also the inspiration behind Frank Capra's *It Happened One Night.* Rent it before you visit, if you really want to feel the history of the place.)

Before you read on, you should know that if your dog is more than 28 pounds, he can't accompany you here. Joe Dog cried in his kibble when he learned about this rule. (Why 28, he moaned, why not 68?) I thought I'd spare you and yours the same disappointment and tell you up front, and not down below. Actually, according to some unidentified sources, bigger dogs have been known to be allowed here. It may be worth a try, if your heart is set on this wonderland and your dog weighs more than his bag of dog food.

Everything here is top drawer. The 640 guest casitas, each a Spanish-style cottage, are beautifully furnished and offer real privacy and peace. Many have wood-burning fireplaces. The landscaping is lush, with gorgeous flowers and palms everywhere. The restaurants are magnificent (some allow doggies at their patios) and the shops at La Quinta's plaza are some of the finest around. Even the beauty parlor is special—a fun Art Deco style. For humans, there are 25 swimming pools, 38 hot spas, 30 tennis courts, and 72 famous holes of championship golf. You can get a massage in the sun, work out in the fitness center, and do a zillion other wonderful things. (The resort supplies you with a brochure titled "50 Fun Things to Do at the La Quinta Resort & Club," in case you need more ideas.) For dogs, there are a few little areas to ramble leash-free on the surrounding 45 acres, but you'll have to ask about those because we're not supposed to tell you where they are.

Rates are $129 to $3,000. Dogs are $25 extra per day. 49-499 Eisenhower Drive, P.O. Box 69, La Quinta, CA 92253; (760) 564-4111 or (800) 598-3828.

MECCA

PARKS, BEACHES, AND RECREATION AREAS

• **Salton Sea State Recreation Area** 🐾🐾🐾½ *See* ❹ *on page 724.*

If you ever wanted to explore the Salton Sea (see the introduction to the Imperial County chapter on page 739 for information on this strange and wonderful body of water), this is a great place to start your observations. The park has 16 miles of shoreline, including five beaches. Dogs must wear the mandatory leash attire, but they manage to have a fabulous time anyway.

Unfortunately, dogs are not allowed on the trails that connect a couple of these areas together, but you can transport your pooch from one area to another by car. You should try to spend at least one night. Three of the beaches are primitive and they have campsites right at the seaside. While dogs must be leashed, they still love dunking their paws in the very buoyant water.

The day-use fee is $5. Camping costs $7 to $16. Dogs are $1 extra, day or night. There are 149 developed sites available on a first-come, first-served basis. Dogs generally prefer the cheaper, more primitive sites. About half of the park is in Imperial County. If you're approaching the lake from the southeast side, see page 741 for directions. Otherwise, take Highway 111 southeast of Mecca about 10 miles, and you'll find the park headquarters and visitors center on the west side of the highway. (760) 393-3052.

PLACES TO STAY

Salton Sea State Recreation Area: See the Salton Sea State Recreation Area above for camping information.

MOUNTAIN CENTER

While in town, stop by the Living Free animal sanctuary and see just how beautiful and livable an animal rescue facility can be. Living Free occupies 160 acres of scenic mountain country at the edge of the San Bernardino National Forest. You and your dog can visit together, and while you're on tour finding out about the many wonderful programs here, your dog will be cared for in a special pen. Your dog is guaranteed tender loving care while you learn about ways to help other animals get the same kind of love. For more information, call (909) 659-4684.

• **Hurkey Creek Park** 🐾 🐾 🐾 1/2 *See* ❺ *on page 724.*

At an elevation of about 4,500 feet and surrounded by 7,000-foot-high peaks, this meadow-like park stays cool even in the summer. Hurkey Creek flows through here, attracting lots of critters, so be sure your dog is leashed.

There are a couple of hiking trails here and dogs love them. They'd really like to be able to sneak into the adjacent San Jacinto Wilderness, but it's one of the few national forest wilderness areas that doesn't permit pooches (because of its intermingling with a state park that bans dogs).

The day-use parking fee is $4. Pooches are $2 extra. Camping is $15, with dogs paying $2 for the privilege. The park is four miles south of Mountain Center off Highway 74. There are 100 campsites available. For camping reservations, call Parknet at (800) 234-PARK. The park phone number is (909) 659-2050.

PLACES TO STAY

Hurkey Creek Park: See Hurkey Creek Park above for camping information.

PALM SPRINGS

First, the warning, straight from the typewriter of Esther M.W. Petersen, of the Palm Springs Animal Shelter: "Our area can be quite warm (HOT!!!!) all year-round, so please, Please, *please* be sure to warn travelers about the dangers . . . . Our visitors don't seem to realize how hot it is. With our low humidity, it doesn't feel as hot as it really is, and pets can't handle the hot cement sidewalks, hot desert sand, and hot asphalt without getting burned pads."

Petersen knows her stuff. She has seen too many dogs whimper their last breaths because of heatstroke and other heat-related horrors. The municipal code forbids dogs to be left unattended in enclosed vehicles, no matter what time of year. The law is a good one. Since it was enacted in 1988, not a single pet has been lost to this disastrous practice.

Believe it or not, the entire posh desert playground city of Palm Springs is a wildlife preserve. You can routinely spot coyotes, bobcats, raccoons, snakes, lizards, and migratory birds around town. Occasionally, mountain lions and badgers have been sighted. Make sure your dog is leashed and that you hold the leash securely at all times.

For many, many years, dogs were not allowed to set paw in any of the parks. But as of autumn of 1998, the city will at last be opening its very own dog park! For more on this, see the Parks section on page 731. Palm Springs

---

is also home to a few natural areas around town where you can take your pooch for a good walk. In addition, you can also take your dog to some fun, if unnatural, places.

Many Palm Springs restaurants permit dogs to dine outside with you. And many of the shops on Palm Canyon Drive (north and south) let pets shop with their people. They don't want to be mentioned for fear of being inundated with leg-lifters. But if someone beckons you and your dog inside while you're window shopping, you'll know which ones we're talking about. Petersen, of the animal shelter, tells me that one store has a resident potbellied pig, so if your dog likes his ham rare, beware.

PARKS, BEACHES, AND RECREATION AREAS

Dogs of Palm Springs are panting, but not because of the heat (they all live in air-conditioned quarters, after all). They're panting in anticipation of finally being permitted in a Palm Springs park. And this isn't just any old park. This is a park of their very own–the Palm Springs Dog Park. This is very exciting to pooches and their people, because dogs haven't been able to set paw in any of the city's parks for eons, at least. The 1.6-acre park promises to be a real work of art, complete with an iron fence and gate designed by a local artist. (How many dog park fences have dog paws and faces carved into them?) It's going to be located behind City Hall and is set to open in October 1998, if all goes according to plan. Call Jan Truscott, of the dog park subcommittee, at (760) 322-8362 to get an update on its status or to find out how you can help. If you want to feel the desert in your paws when you and your dog go out for a walk, you'll be happy to know that Palm Springs is surrounded by land run by the Bureau of Land Management. Call (760) 251-4800 for information on fun places to hike during the cooler months.

Dog owners in town frequently use the many local "wash" areas (dry streambeds) to run on leash with their dogs. You'll see them on the outskirts of town and beyond, but with the new park opening, you might not see them as much as you used to.

You can also take your leashed pooch to a nearby hiking area for an interesting desert romp. The Carl Lykken Hiking Trail starts at the extreme west end of Ramon Road. Don't forget your water. Unfortunately, our other favorite area for dogs, the 27,000-acre Indian Canyons, no longer allows dogs because of some very bad incidents with pit bulls and their people.

RESTAURANTS

Palm Springs is full of fine restaurants with outdoor areas where dogs are welcome.

Blue Coyote Grill: You and your dog can't exactly eat together here, since she must remain tied up just outside the railing while you sit just inside it. But she'll still be close enough to drool over the Southwestern delights on your dish. 445 North Palm Canyon Drive; (760) 327-1196.

Carlo's Italian Deli & Restaurant: The outdoor area here is well suited for dogs and their people. 119 South Indian Canyon Drive; (760) 325-5571.

Harry's Hoffbrau: With so much outdoor seating, there's bound to be space for you and your pooch. This cafeteria-style place serves all kinds of dishes, including sandwiches and stews. 205 South Palm Canyon Drive; (760) 320-2911.

Lalajava: The coffee and light cuisine is good, but better yet, customers' dogs get a nice, cool bowl of water. 332 North Palm Canyon Drive; (760) 325-3354.

Nate's Deli & Restaurant: Lots of dogs come here to dine under the umbrellas. Maybe they know that the owner's daughter is the secretary of the local bull terrier club and that the folks here love dogs. Corned beef is the specialty, and there's also a full bar. 100 South Indian Canyon Drive; (760) 325-3506.

Peabody's: You won't find Mr. Peabody here, but all other dogs, brainy or not, are welcome to dine with you on the patio. 134 South Palm Canyon Drive; (760) 322-1877.

PLACES TO STAY

Palm Springs has plenty of quality canine accommodations. If you're in the mood for a condo, contact Desert Condo Rentals at (800) 248-2529. The folks there might be able to set up you and your dog in a home away from home.

Casa Cody Country Inn: Dogs love this quaint, quiet historic country inn almost as much as their peace-seeking people do. Past canine visitors have caused some problems because irresponsible owners have left them alone in the room. Don't even think of doing this. Rates are $49 to $199. Dogs are $10 extra for the length of your stay. 175 South Cahuilla Road, Palm Springs, CA 92262; (760) 320-9346.

Doubletree Resort: This attractive hotel is set on a golf course. Some of the rooms have great views. Small dogs only, please. Rates are $89 to $119. Dogs require a $100 deposit. 67-967 Vista Chino, Palm Springs, CA 92234; (760) 322-7000 or (800) 637-0577.

Estrella Inn: Bing Crosby slept here, and so can you and your lucky dog. The resort is truly to croon for. The oversized guest rooms, two-room suites, and private bungalows are simply, yet beautifully, furnished. With an updated 1930s ambience and truly friendly, happy-to-be-here service, you feel like you're back in the Golden Age of Hollywood.

Dogs have to be small or "smallish" to stay here. Thirty pounds is usually the limit. They get to stay in the rooms and bungalows with tile floors. These rooms are very attractive, and some dogs have a great time running and sliding on the smooth surface. (This is not encouraged, of course.) Some rooms have fireplaces, some have old-fashioned, thick wood furniture (which is the perfect contrast to the airy, adobe-like feel of the place), and all get a big "paws up" from pooches who stay here. From a dog's point of view, however, it's really the outside grounds that make this inn so special. Towering palms, bountiful fruit trees, and lush flowers abound on three acres. For the humans, there are three pools and two spas. Ahh.

Rates are $99 to $350. Dogs are $20 extra. 415 South Belardo Road, Palm Springs, CA 92262; (760) 320-4117 or (800) 237-3687.

Ingleside Inn: You and your lucky pooch can sleep where the likes of Greta Garbo, Salvador Dalí, and Howard Hughes have spent the night. This gorgeous mountainside inn feels like your own private estate, from the jasmine-covered veranda to the antique-furnished rooms. Very small dogs (under 10 pounds) are welcome with prior approval.

If your dog is any bigger than the average cat, he won't be able to stay here with you. But don't worry. The folks who run this place want your pooch to be as happy as possible, so they've made a special arrangement with the exclusive Desert View Pet Resort in Rancho Mirage. The Pet Resort will pick up your pooch in a dog limousine and transport him to a world of canine opulence. See page 735 for details on the Pet Resort. Rates for the Ingleside Inn are $95 to $600. 200 West Ramon Road, Palm Springs, CA 92264; (760) 325-0046.

Musicland Hotel: "Any pooch under 200 pounds is okay," says a dog-friendly staffer. Rates are $29 to $89. The doggy deposit is $25 to $50. 1342 South Palm Canyon Drive, Palm Springs, CA 92264; (760) 325-1326.

Palm Springs Hilton Resort: "We are delighted to have dogs as guests. They find it very entertaining here," a vivacious, dog-loving staffer tells us. "That's why all the rooms have balconies. Dogs like to look out and see what's going on." From one side of this very comfortable, attractive hotel, dogs can look out at the mountains. From the other, they can look down at the swimming pool. Joe says "gimme the pool." (While he hates swimming, he has a weird thing for women in bikinis.) Ask the concierge about nearby places to walk with your dog. "Lots of folks bring their pets here, and we've got some great places for them to walk," another staffer said. Rates are $59 to $365. Dogs require a $300 deposit. 400 East Tahquitz, Palm Springs, CA 92262; (760) 320-6868 or (800) 522-6900.

Place in the Sun: This is a fun place to stay if you like your motel room or larger bungalow surrounded by palms and backed by mountains. The two-bedroom bungalows (the largest accommodations) have a patio and fireplace, as well as a full kitchen. The surrounding greenery is pretty, and the rooms themselves are standard motel fare, but decent enough. Unfortunately, only dogs weighing 20 pounds or less can stay here. Rates are $39 to $159. Dogs are $10 extra. 754 San Lorenzo Road, Palm Springs, CA 92264; (760) 325-0254.

Quality Inn Resort: Rates are $49 to $189. 1269 East Palm Canyon Drive, Palm Springs, CA 92264; (760) 323-2775 or (800) 221-2222.

Royal Sun Inn: There's a little area across the street to walk your leashed dog. Rates are $99. Dogs are $10 extra. 1700 South Palm Canyon Drive, Palm Springs, CA 92264; (760) 327-1564 or (800) 619-4786.

DIVERSIONS

My fair laddy: On Thursday evenings from 6 P.M. to 10 P.M., well-behaved, leashed pooches may accompany you to glamorous Palm Canyon Drive, where an old-fashioned street fair will charm the spots off your dog. Musicians, food, arts and crafts vendors, and a certified farmers market make this street even more charming than it normally is. The fair takes place between Tahquitz Canyon Drive and Baristo Road. Parking is best behind the Desert Inn Fashion Plaza. Call (800) 34-SPRINGS for more information.

PERRIS

Dogs love Perris in the springtime. Dogs love Perris in the fall. Dogs love Perris in the winter, when it drizzles. Dogs *don't* love Perris in the summer, when it sizzles. Other than summertime, Perris is a favorite place for dogs. Not, as with the Paris song, because their love is near, but because the Orange Empire Railway Museum is here. See Diversions below for more on this great dog getaway.

PARKS, BEACHES, AND RECREATION AREAS

• **Lake Perris State Recreation Area** 🐾 🐾 🐾 *See* ❻ *on page 724.*

When people talk about this park, they generally focus on the lake. Comments I got when I asked friends about the park included the following: "You can catch some world-class fish there." "We had a great time swimming at the beach." And "I like to stand on the edge and watch for birds."

Great. Well, dogs, if you're into any of the above activities, forget it. You can't go near the lake, much less in it or on it. In fact, pooches have to stay at least 50 feet from the lake's edge. But fortunately, you are allowed to wear a leash and hike the trails here. You'll be in sage scrub countryside, and there's not much shade, so go somewhere else if it's a hot day.

The day-use fee is $6 per vehicle and $1 per pooch. Camping costs $8 to $16. Dogs are $1 extra. There are 167 sites for tents only and 265 sites for RVs. Reserve through Parknet at (800) 444-PARK. From Highway 60, exit at Moreno Beach Drive and drive south a little more than three miles to the park. (909) 940-5603.

PLACES TO STAY

Lake Perris State Recreation Area: See Lake Perris State Recreation Area above for camping information.

DIVERSIONS

Chug it out with your dog: Dogs and railroads go together like love and marriage—or even better, in some cases. The Orange Empire Railway Museum is a great place to take a pooch. Joe Dog and I want to thank reader Marsden Chew MacRae for opening our eyes to this fun place. "On one memorable day, my golden retriever and I rode every single running exhibit, including the steam engine," writes Marsden Chew MacRae. (I use his three names again because he has such a great name.) "I also noted a rail fan with an attending German shepherd, who was much better trained than my dog and could actually get on and off without being lifted! Many dogs find the steps confusing and can't or won't navigate them, so bringing a dog small enough to lift might be important." That's some good advice from a man who knows his railroads. (He's traveled to many of the state's railroads with his faithful pooch.)

Leashed, well-behaved dogs can visit the museum's collection of streetcars, trolleys, a steam engine, and several diesels. They're not allowed in the buildings, but that's okay because the trains are much cooler. Speaking of cooler, it can get really hot here in summer, and this place can roast, so it's a good idea to bring your pooch here during other times of year.

Trolleys and trains operate Saturdays and Sundays and major holidays from 11 A.M. to 5 P.M. Special events are held throughout the year. Call or write for details. 2201 South A Street, P.O. Box 548, Perris, CA 92572-0548; (760) 657-2605.

RANCHO MIRAGE

This exclusive desert community is home to one of a dog's best friends, the Desert View Pet Resort. It's a terrific place for your pooch to repose while you bask in the glory of the local arid opulence. In addition to good food and lots of love, dogs get at least two off-leash playtimes daily in an enclosed grassy yard.

And if you have special instructions for the care of your dearly beloved, almost anything goes. "We have one dog who only eats waffles, so we make them and he loves them," says employee Jim Prindle. "One woman has a dog who has to have a special day bed, a night bed, and he'll only eat out of his crystal bowl. She also likes his bum to be wiped with baby powder after he does his thing. We get unusual requests, but we understand how important it is for owners to know their pet is happy." Rates are $17 daily. A "dog limousine" is available for pickup and delivery. Rates range from $15 to $200, depending on how far your dog needs to travel. The Pet Resort is at 71-075 Highway 111; (760) 341-1166.

PLACES TO STAY

Marriott's Rancho Las Palmas Resort: You and your petite dog can hang out on several acres of gorgeous land here, or just enjoy the surroundings from your balcony. Rates are $69 to $279. 41-000 Bob Hope Drive, Rancho Mirage, CA 92270; (760) 568-2727.

The Westin Mission Hills Resort: You and your small or medium-sized dog (that's all they take) can pretend you're in Morocco during your stay at this luxurious resort hotel. The Moroccan-style architecture fits in beautifully with the many acres that surround the hotel. Rates are $169 to $300. Dogettes require a $100 deposit. 71-333 Dinah Shore Drive, Rancho Mirage, CA 92270; (760) 328-5955.

RIVERSIDE

Until recently, dogs were banned from all city parks in Riverside. We used to say "boooo" to Riverside's policy. But after a bit of pressure from some dog people, leashed dogs are welcome in all city parks. Plus the city even has a brand-new off-leash dog park! (See Carlson Park Dog Park, on page 736). Now we say "yahoo." (Okay, Joe says "Arrooo," but I know what he means.) Way to go, Riverside!

Meanwhile, if your dog loves trees (Joe's ears just perked up), a jaunt along beautiful Victoria Avenue is a must. The seven-mile-long historic avenue is lined with more than 4,000 trees of 95 species. Male dogs think they've died and gone to heaven when they stroll down the avenue's walking path, past tree after tree after tree. To get a brochure that will help you identify the trees you and your dog admire here, call the visitors center at (909) 684-INFO.

PARKS, BEACHES, AND RECREATION AREAS

• **Box Springs Mountain Park** 🐾🐾🐾 *See* ❼ *on page 724.*

I'm not sure how this place got its name, but I found that, like a box spring, it's not all that comfortable by itself. You need a little padding to enjoy it. Lots of people bring their horses here, but a dog will do. When you decide to take a break from hiking the many trails, you can lie down and rest against your reposing pooch.

This hilly park has little shade, so it may not be an ideal place to take a dog (don't take her if it's hot). But there aren't many options in this city.

Driving east on Highway 60, exit at Pigeon Pass Road (about five miles east of town) and drive north to the park. (909) 275-4310.

• **Carlson Park Dog Park** 🐾🐾🐾🐾 🐕 *See* ❽ *on page 724.*

It's been years in the making, but it's finally here—the first off-leash dog park in all of Riverside County. It's in a really pretty spot, at the base of Mount Rubidoux (see below), along the Santa Ana River. The dog park is completely fenced and about one acre in size, with green grass and big shady trees. Dogs really dig it here. Joe Dog has come to call it "Dog's Green Acre."

I first learned about the plans for this park a couple of years ago, when I got a letter from David Hepperly, also known as "Three-Dog Dave." He became one of my best doggone correspondents, letting me know the progress of the park month after month as he and others involved in a group called Dog People worked with the city to make the park happen. The park's future was touch-and-go at times, but he and his three dogs always had faith that pooches would prevail. He was right, thank dog. For more information on the magnificent group called Dog People, phone founder Bruce Rubin at (909) 682-6438.

The park is one mile west of downtown Riverside, on the east bank of the Santa Ana River, at Mission Inn Avenue near the bridge. (909) 715-3440.

• **Mount Rubidoux** 🐾🐾🐾½ *See* ❾ *on page 724.*

The views from the top of this isolated granite outcrop are well worth the hike to get here. From its 1,364-foot elevation, you and your dog will see the surrounding mountains, the Santa Ana River, the city of Riverside, and probably a few other happy, peppy, leashed pooches.

There's not a lot of shade on the way up, so make sure you go when it's not hot. You and your dog should be in good shape to make this hike. If you have any doubts, go to Carlson Park (see above) and let your dog off leash to romp at a more leisurely pace.

A bit of history, courtesy of Patty Tambe of the city's parks department: In 1907, one of the park's founders put a cross at the hill's summit. The first Easter sunrise service here was held two years later, and that service is said to have inspired a cycle of outdoor Easter services across the country. Apparently, this was the granddaddy of these Easter events. So now you know. It's kind of fun to think about while you're at the summit.

The most convenient entrance to Mount Rubidoux is at the small parking lot at Carlson Park. (See above for directions.) (909) 715-3440.

• **Rancho Jurupa Regional Park** 🐾🐾🐾½ *See* ❿ *on page 724.*

This huge county park encompasses a few others, including the Hidden Valley Wildlife Area. Stretching east to west for almost 10 miles, it more than makes up for all those smaller city parks that say "no way" to dogs.

Depending on which section you visit, you and your leashed dog can see lots of wildlife, fish for your supper, hike through fields and woods, or relax on the manicured grass of a shaded picnic area. Since our tastes are sometimes dictated by money, we like to go where we can avoid driving in and paying the $2 per person and $2 per pooch fee—especially if we just need to stretch our legs. We've found a wonderful spot next to the park's nature center, where many interesting hikes originate.

To reach this fee-free area, exit Highway 60 at Rubidoux Boulevard, drive southwest a few blocks, and turn right on Mission Boulevard. In about six blocks, turn left on Riverview Drive/Limonite Avenue. In just a little more than a half mile, there should be a sign for a county park. That's where Riverview Drive veers to the left (Limonite will continue straight). Follow Riverview for about another 1.5 miles. It will be smaller and more rural than the previous road. The park will be on your left. Park in the lot near the nature center. Look for a trail and have yourselves a great hike.

If camping is your bag, you'll have to go to the fee area at Rancho Jurupa. From Highway 60, exit at Rubidoux Boulevard and drive south to Mission Boulevard. Turn left and drive about a half mile to Crestmore Boulevard. Follow Crestmore as it curves around the north side of the park. In about 1.5 miles, you'll be at the gate. Sites are $16. Dogs are $2 extra. There are approximately 70 sites available. For camping information, call Rancho Jurupa at (909) 684-7032. For camping reservations, call Parknet at (800) 234-PARK.

RESTAURANTS

Check out the attractive pedestrian mall along Main Street for some doggone friendly eateries and some interesting history. These restaurants are a bone's throw from the Mission Inn, the city's premier historic and architectural landmark, located at 3696 Main Street. You can't go inside with your dog, but you can gawk from the outside.

42nd Street Bagels: "We're dog-friendly here," one of the servers told us. "We really like dogs." Dogs do feel welcome. The people are friendly, but I think it's the cream cheese that makes dogs feel particularly at home. Slather a bagel with shmear and share it with your dog at the outdoor tables. 3737 Main Street; (909) 274-9445.

Mission Inn Coffee Co.: The coffee here is delicious, as are the tasty pastries and the sandwiches. Dine at the outdoor tables with your favorite dog. 3600 Main Street; (909) 341-6789.

Simple Simon's: This bakery and cafe in the old mission district is a great place to lunch with your pooch. There's plenty of outdoor seating. 3639 Main Street; (909) 369-6030.

PLACES TO STAY

Dynasty Suites: This lodging is not overly enthusiastic about housing dogs and generally won't give an okay over the phone. But if you arrive and look very polite and responsible, and your small dog gives them one of her "I'll love you forever" looks, you're in. Rates are $46 to $90. Pooches are $10 extra. 3735 Iowa Avenue, Riverside, CA 92507; (909) 369-8200.

Holiday Inn Express: You'll get a continental breakfast when you stay here. Rates are $59 to $149. Dogs require a $10 deposit. 11043 Magnolia Avenue, Riverside, CA 92506; (909) 688-5000 or (800) 465-4329.

Motel 6: Rates are $32 for the first person, $6 extra for the second person. One small pooch per room here. 1260 University Avenue, Riverside, CA 92507; (909) 784-2131.

Rancho Jarupa Regional Park: See Rancho Jarupa Regional Park on page 736 for camping information.

TEMECULA

PARKS, BEACHES, AND RECREATION AREAS

•**Lake Skinner County Park** 😊 😊 😊 ½ *See* ⑪ *on page 724.*

So what if your dog can't swim in the lake or even hang out in your boat with you? Of the 6,040 acres of park, the lake makes up only about 1,200 acres. That means several thousand acres of hilly chaparral country are all yours. Leashed pooches are permitted to peruse the trails and run around the open turf areas.

During the rainy season, the trails may be closed. Call before you visit. The day-use fee is $2 per adult and $1 per child. Campsites are $12 to $18. Dogs are $2 extra. There are approximately 265 campsites. From Interstate 15, take the Rancho California Avenue exit northeast and drive about nine miles to the park. Call Parknet for camping reservations at (800) 234-PARK. For park information, call (909) 926-1541.

PLACES TO STAY

Lake Skinner County Park: See Lake Skinner County Park above for camping information.

58
IMPERIAL COUNTY

Although this county is home to the Imperial Valley, one of the richest farming areas in the world, it's much more than just an agricultural wonderland. In fact, when you wander into the most dog-friendly areas, you'll wonder how land around here could be used for anything but sandboxes.

Some 1.5 million acres of desert here is run by the Bureau of Land Management—those dog-friendly folks who rarely demand a leash. The dune areas are fascinating, and your dog will love racing up and down the sandy expanses.

Nearby is the strange and salty Salton Sea. At 36 miles long and 15 miles wide, it's one of the world's largest inland bodies of salt water. Although officially considered a lake, it's got most of the qualities of a sea, including the fact that from most of its shoreline, you can look across and see vast, astounding nothingness.

The sea is situated at 234 feet below sea level (the "normal" sea level, that is), directly atop the San Andreas Fault. Millions of years ago, the valley region here was filled with lakes and streams. But the lakes dried up as seismic activity caused the mountains to the west to grow, cutting off the moist, cool air from the ocean.

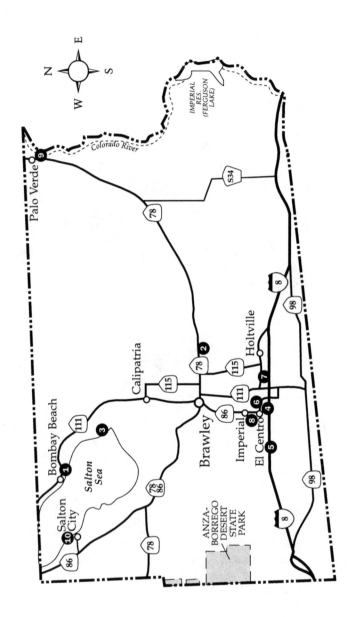

IMPERIAL RES. (FERGUSON LAKE)

Colorado River

Palo Verde

S34

78

8

98

Holtville

Calipatria

78

115

115

7

111

115

111

6

Bombay Beach

111

86

4

Brawley

8

Salton Sea

Imperial

5

El Centro

78
86

98

ANZA-BORREGO DESERT STATE PARK

Salton City

10

86

78

8

Then in 1905, the Colorado River flooded in Mexico and caused a two-year flood through the brand-new Imperial Valley irrigation system. It sparked the rebirth of the lake known as the Salton Sea.

Mixed with minerals left by earlier seas, as well as present-day evaporation and fertilizer runoff, the water is 10 percent saltier than an ocean. Dogs like to float around in it, but watch out for their eyes.

And if you smell a really foul stench while you're here, you may be tempted to drive away as fast as your four wheels will take you. The occasionally malodorous air is caused by an algae bloom and resulting fish die-off, and the operative expression here is "Peeuuuw!" But before you zip away, stop for a moment and let your dog take a few good, deep breaths of this wretched stink. She'll be on an olfactory high for the rest of the day.

BOMBAY BEACH

PARKS, BEACHES, AND RECREATION AREAS

• **Salton Sea State Recreation Area** 🐾🐾🐾½ *See* ❶ *on page 740.*

Since most people visit the north end of this 16-mile-long park that sits on the northeast portion of the Salton Sea, you'll find its description in the Riverside County chapter, on page 729. But if you have a hankering to discover the Imperial County portion of the park, take Highway 111 to any of several entrances, including the popular Bombay Beach area. (619) 393-3052.

PLACES TO STAY

Salton Sea State Recreation Area: See page 729 in the Riverside County chapter for camping information.

BRAWLEY

PARKS, BEACHES, AND RECREATION AREAS

• **Imperial Sand Dunes** 🐾🐾🐾🐾 🐕 *See* ❷ *on page 740.*

Before going on about how enthralling this enormous, off-leash desert sandbox is, I want to play back something local Bureau of Land Management staffer Roseann Madrigal told me.

"Too often we get calls from someone who starts out crying, and when we ask what's wrong, they say they lost their poor dog in the desert," she said. "We hate those kind of calls. It's so sad. People let their pets wander too far sometimes, and they get disoriented and lost. Out here, there's not a good chance for survival, even when it's not extremely hot. We try to help them find their dog, but this is a big place. You feel so helpless.

"Please tell your readers not to let their dog go far, and always have an eye on him. If they can't, then just keep him leashed," she said.

Got it? This applies to any off-leash area discussed in this book, but out here in the desert, follow Madrigal's words like the gospel. She's fielded many of these distraught phone calls and she knows what she's talking about.

Now the good stuff. The Bureau of Land Management oversees 1.5 million acres in Imperial County. Much of the acreage is within this vast dune system, full of wind-sculpted crests and ripples that extend for more than 40 miles. The Imperial Dunes (also known as the Algodones Dunes) rise up to 300 feet, and they're great fun to hike on or around with your leash-free pooch.

Two-thirds of the dune area north of Highway 78 is closed to vehicles, so it's an ideal place for a dog hike. This is also where you may spot all sorts of desert wildflowers. An added bonus: You can set up your tent just about anywhere in the area, and there's no fee.

The BLM ranger station is a good place to start your adventure. No permit is necessary. From central Brawley, drive east on Highway 78 about 19 miles to Gecko Road. Turn right, and the ranger station is about a mile down the road. (619) 337-4400.

PLACES TO STAY

Imperial Sand Dunes: See Imperial Sand Dunes on page 741 for camping information.

Town House Lodge: All rooms come with a microwave and a refrigerator, so if you and your dog want to eat in, this is a good choice. Rates are $49 to $54. 135 Main Street, Brawley, CA 92227; (619) 344-5120.

CALIPATRIA

PARKS, BEACHES, AND RECREATION AREAS

• **Red Hill Marina County Park** 🐾🐾🐾 See ❸ on page 740.

This peninsular park jutting into the southeast corner of the Salton Sea feels more like an island. The terrain is early moonscape and the 240-acre park is pretty much one big hill. You and your dog can see all the way to the Mexican border from here!

Dogs must be leashed, but at least they're allowed. They're banned from the neighboring Salton Sea National Wildlife Refuge.

The day-use fee is $2. Campsites are $7 to $12. There are 400 campsites available. No reservations are necessary. From Highway 111 just north of Calipatria, go west on Schrimpf Road, which is a graded dirt road. In about five miles, you'll be at the park. (619) 348-2310.

PLACES TO STAY

Red Hill Marina County Park: See Red Hill Marina County Park above for camping information.

EL CENTRO

PARKS, BEACHES, AND RECREATION AREAS

• **Bucklin Park** 🐾🐾½ See ❹ on page 740.

It's like a golf course here, complete with ultra-green, ultra-short turf, the occasional palm tree, and a little pond. It's a lovely place to take a Sunday afternoon stroll with your favorite leashed pooch.

The park is at Eighth Street and Ross Avenue. (619) 352-2111.

• **Sunbeam Lake County Park** 🐾🐾🐾 See ❺ on page 740.

This county park is filled with big old eucalyptus trees. That's not normally a selling point, but boy dogs who are tired of lifting their legs on desert boulders around this area seem to appreciate any kind of tree.

Sunbeam Lake itself is a fun fishing and swimming hole. Dogs must be leashed, so swimming is a bit restricted. The trails in this 140-acre park provide a fun walk for you and the leashed pooch.

It'll cost you $2 to use this park during the day and $7 to $12 to camp here. There are 309 sites for RVs only. Reservations are suggested during the spring and summer. Call (619) 352-7154. The park is seven miles west of El Centro. Exit Interstate 8 at Drew Road and drive about a half mile north. (619) 339-4384.

• **Swarthout Park** 🐾🐾 *See* ❻ *on page 740.*

The bulk of this park is made up of ball fields, but there's some unclaimed grassy turf, too. Leashed dogs enjoy trotting around with you. If they happen to slip out of your grip for a minute, it could be worse. The park is well fenced, with only a couple of escape hatches.

From Highway 86, go east on Euclid Avenue. The park will be on your left, at Cross Street. Park in the lot. (619) 337-4557.

PLACES TO STAY

Brunner's Motel: Rates are $46 to $75. 215 North Imperial Avenue, El Centro, CA 92243; (619) 352-6431.

El Dorado Motel: In the mornings, you get sweet rolls, fruit, coffee, and juice at this very animal-friendly joint. There's even a special grassy area just for your dog's relief. "We like dogs, cats, fish, and birds," says Virginia, one of the El Dorado's receptionists. "They're always better behaved than certain people." They'll even throw in a free movie when you visit. Rates are $32 to $45. 1464 Adams Avenue, El Centro, CA 92243; (619) 352-7333.

Sands Motel: Small pets only, please. Rates are $30 to $45. A $10 pooch deposit is required. 611 North Imperial Avenue, El Centro, CA 92243; (619) 352-0715.

Sunbeam Lake County Park: See Sunbeam Lake County Park on page 742 for camping information.

HOLTVILLE

PARKS, BEACHES, AND RECREATION AREAS

• **Heber Dunes County Park** 🐾🐾🐾½ *See* ❼ *on page 740.*

Dunes, native vegetation, and former farmland make up this 300-acre park. Leashed dogs love a good romp down the trails. The picnic spots are worthy of lunch, but better yet is the camping. Unlike many of the county's other parks, it's free, as is admission to the park. Dogs on a tight budget are sure to appreciate this.

From Highway 111, take Heber Road east about 6.5 miles to the short road that leads to the park. (619) 339-4384.

PLACES TO STAY

Barbara Worth Country Club & Hotel: Rates are $50 to $64. 2050 Country Club Drive, Holtville, CA 92250; (619) 356-2806.

Heber Dunes County Park: See Heber Dunes County Park on page 743 for camping information.

IMPERIAL

PARKS, BEACHES, AND RECREATION AREAS

•**Eager Park** 🐾 *See* ❽ *on page 740.*

Stop here if your dog is longing to get out of the car or house and doesn't mind visiting a postage stamp-sized park. There are a few small trees and a small playground. Maybe the park should be reserved for Chihuahuas and Pekingese pooches, or at least dogs with small expectations. Dogs must be leashed.

From Highway 86, go west on 10th Street and left on H Street. (619) 355-4371.

PALO VERDE

PARKS, BEACHES, AND RECREATION AREAS

•**Palo Verde County Park** 🐾 🐾 1/2 *See* ❾ *on page 740.*

While this is only a 10-acre park, its location at the border of Arizona directly off Highway 78 makes it a popular stopping point for dogs and their human chauffeurs.

The park is set on a backwater of the Colorado River. It's a refreshing place to spend an hour, a day, or a night. Camping and day-use fees are nonexistent and no permits are required. The fishing's pretty decent, too, in case you're hankering to angle.

From Interstate 10 in the Blythe area (Riverside County), exit at Highway 78 and drive south, following the occasional westward jogs in the highway. After about 18 miles, you'll cross into Imperial County. The park is another 2.5 miles down the road, just off the highway. (619) 339-4384.

PLACES TO STAY

Palo Verde County Park: See Palo Verde County Park above for camping information.

SALTON CITY

If you happen to have a tape of the *Twilight Zone* theme in your car, pop it in as you approach this land that time forgot.

After you notice the bright blue Salton Sea in the background, you'll become aware of lots and lots of lots. Empty ones. Many miles of curved, suburban-style roads wind in and out of this flat waterfront community, but no one is home. There should be thousands of houses on these paved grids, but there's only a smattering. It's as if Rod Serling went all out and made one of his eerie dollhouse-scale sets life-size.

What actually happened was an optimistic real estate sellout in the 1950s and '60s. An extensive road system was developed and some 20,000 lots were sold. But the folks who bought them generally just kept their investment without plopping down so much as a mobile home. So the roads essentially lead to nowhere. When you get lost on them, don't panic. Just remember that Rod Serling isn't around anymore, so this really couldn't be as strange as it seems, and you really couldn't be in the Twilight Zone. Could you?

PARKS, BEACHES, AND RECREATION AREAS

•**Martin Flora Park** 🐾1/2 *See* ➓ *on page 740.*

Although the Salton City area is full of empty shoreline, community service folks ask that you stick to the public parks with your dog. This isn't such a bad place to take a leashed pooch. It looks a little like a gravel parking lot, but never mind that. The Salton Sea is right here and so are plenty of picnic tables. The park is an unusual place to stop for lunch.

From Highway 86, turn northeast on North Marina Drive and follow it past all the empty streets. As the road approaches the sea, it will curve to the right. In a few blocks, you'll come to Sea Port Avenue. Go left, and follow it a few more blocks to the park. Make sure you can figure out how to get back to Highway 86 before you leave, because many people have become mighty lost here, and there aren't many homes where you can stop and ask for help. (619) 393-3052.

APPENDICES

NATIONAL FORESTS AND WILDERNESS AREAS

Dogs of California, rejoice! If you really want to stretch those gams, the U.S. Department of Agriculture's Forest Service has a real treat for you. Instead of a walk in your friendly neighborhood park, how does an exhilarating, off-leash hike sound? You'll have your choice of 20 million acres of national forests (an astounding 20 percent of California) spread over a fascinating variety of terrain.

Most dogs call the forests "Dog Heaven." Those who don't speak English just pant with joy. There's something for every dog's tastes in national forests. Desert dogs are as happy as dogs who like dank redwood forests. Most national forests have no entry fees, few leash rules, and plenty of free camping. And they all have some of the most beautiful land in California.

If your dog is obedient enough to come when she's called, and you trust her not to wander off in pursuit of deer or other wildlife, she's more than welcome to be off leash in most of the forest areas. In the descriptions that follow, I mention the exceptions to the off-leash policies that I'm aware of, but there may well be more. And since rules change frequently, you should call before you visit. Be aware that the frontline personnel at the forests might tell you that dogs must be on leash, but they're not always right. Ask for a supervisor or ranger if you have reason to think the leash laws are more lax.

Always carry a leash with you, just in case. It's a good idea to leash your dog on the trail when you see other hikers, or at least to pull your dog to the side so they can pass by. "Believe it or not, not everyone loves dogs," says Matt Mathes, a dog-loving, very helpful representative of the Forest Service. Dogs must be leashed in developed campgrounds (which usually charge a small fee) and in developed recreation areas. But most areas of the forests are set up so that you can plop down a tent just about anywhere you please (for free). When you find that perfect, cool stream with a flat, soft area on the bank, your dog doesn't have to be leashed. But it's a bad idea to leave your dog leashless and outside your tent at night. (See page 12 for more on camping safety.)

In each listing, I've noted any wilderness areas that fall within the forest I'm describing. Many require permits for hiking and camping. Contact a ranger to find out about the rules in a particular wilderness area. (Sometimes wilderness areas spread out to two or more forests, so don't be baffled if you see the same name more than once. Joe hasn't been pawing around with my computer keyboard again.)

For a free guide to all of California's wilderness areas, write the U.S.D.A. Forest Service, Public Affairs Office, 630 Sansome Street, San Francisco, CA 94111, or call (415) 705-2874. Maps of specific national forests and wilderness areas are available for $3 to $6 each. (At REI, they're double the price.) Call or write for a list. You can also write to this address for a list of all the Forest Service offices in the state. This list can come in handy when you have a dog, because you can call the office nearest your travel destination and ask if there are any exceptions to the leash-free policy in the part of the forest you'll be visiting. It's also a good list to have to find out if your forest destination is charging a small fee for use. Only a few forest areas are charging fees at this point (and they're nominal), and at least 80 percent of the fee goes back into upkeep and improvements of those forests.

Now for the obligatory poop paragraph. As far as bathroom etiquette goes, it's not necessary to pack out the poop. If you don't mind it squishing along in your backpack, that's great. But if you bury it, as you should bury your own, that's okay. Leave the forest as you found it. And please don't let your dog go to the bathroom near a stream. It can be a health hazard to anyone drinking the water later.

And dogs, if you come to really love your national forests, tell your people that because of severely reduced budgets, trail maintenance is suffering. Tell them that the trails could sure use a hand. Tell them that rangers would be thrilled to have teams of dog owners working together to help keep up the trails they use. Your people can contact a ranger to see how they can volunteer.

What follows is a very brief description of each forest. Again, be sure to contact a ranger before setting out so you can check on changed rules and portions of forests or trails that might be closed.

ANGELES NATIONAL FOREST

This 693,000-acre forest covers about one-quarter of Los Angeles County and most of the San Gabriel Mountains. With more than 620 miles of trails, the forest provides an essential recreational outlet for millions of Southern Californians and their city-weary dogs.

Highlights include waterfalls, out-of-the-way canyons and streams, wildflower-covered slopes, and thousands of acres of bighorn sheep territory. (Leash your dog if you go sheep-watching.)

The Cucamonga, San Gabriel, and Sheep Mountain Wilderness Areas are all part of Angeles National Forest.

For more information, contact Forest Headquarters, 701 North Santa Anita Avenue, Arcadia, CA 91006; (626) 574-5200.

CLEVELAND NATIONAL FOREST

Cleveland National Forest takes you and your *perro* within five miles of the Mexican border. This 566,000-acre chaparral- and conifer-covered land has 331 miles of trails, including a section of the Pacific Crest Trail that runs between the Anza-Borrego Desert and Mexico.

Because of high fire danger, due in part to strong Santa Ana winds, rangers prefer that campers stay at developed sites.

The Agua Tibia, Hauser, Pine Creek, and San Mateo Canyon Wilderness Areas are within the forest.

For more information, contact Forest Headquarters, 10845 Rancho Bernardo Road, Rancho Bernardo, CA 92127-2107; (619) 674-2901.

ELDORADO NATIONAL FOREST

You and your dog can hike from gentle oak foothills all the way up to the 10,000-foot crest of the Sierra Nevada (although that's recommended only for the most athletic of pooches) on hundreds of miles of trails here.

Alpine meadows, rivers, streams, and glacial lakes are among the refreshing landscapes you'll come across in this forest, which encompasses 884,000 acres. More than 320 species of birds, mammals, and reptiles make their home in the forest. Beware: The black bears here are known to enjoy goodies like freeze-dried fettuccine Alfredo and doughnuts.

The Desolation and Mokelumne Wilderness Areas are within the forest. Dogs must be leashed in the Carson Pass area of the Mokelumne Wilderness and in all of the Desolation Wilderness. "A few people cause the problems by being irresponsible about their dogs, and everyone gets hit with stricter rules," a forest spokesperson said. The official map of the forest also states that dogs must be leashed on trails, but a ranger told me that as long as the dog is under voice control, off leash is okay.

For more information, contact Forest Headquarters, 100 Forni Road, Placerville, CA 95667; (530) 622-5061.

INYO NATIONAL FOREST

This 1.8 million-acre forest stretches 165 miles from eerie, salty Mono Lake south past Owens Lake. It borders Mount Whitney, the highest peak in the lower 48 states, and is home to hundreds of waterfalls and glacial lakes. A whopping 1,200 miles of trails meander throughout the forest.

The Ancient Bristlecone Pine Forest is set within Inyo's borders. The thick, twisted trees of this astounding forest are the oldest living things on Earth—some date back to 2000 B.C. Guy dogs should treat them with the reverence such trees deserve.

In addition, Inyo comprises the Ansel Adams, Golden Trout, Hoover, John Muir (584,000 acres!), and South Sierra Wilderness Areas. Many trails in Inyo lead into trails at Sequoia National Park and Yosemite National Park. Make sure you look carefully at your trail map so you don't stumble inadvertently from Dog Heaven into Dog Heck.

For more information, contact Forest Headquarters, 873 North Main Street, Bishop, CA 93514; (760) 873-2400.

KLAMATH NATIONAL FOREST

Tired of traffic, loud neighbors, and people snarling at your dog? Come here! (But don't tell anyone else about it.) This lovely 1.7 million-acre forest is one of the least-used of California's national forests.

With 1,160 miles of trails running through wildflower-filled meadows, you and your dog will have no problem finding an escape route from civilization. Ponderosa pines, incense cedars, and dozens of other species of trees help make every inhalation a breath of fresh air.

The fast-moving Klamath River is a terrific place for anglers with dogs. Some of the nearby trails also make it a perfect location for a refreshing riverside hike.

The Marble Mountain, Red Buttes, Russian, Siskiyou, and Trinity Alps Wilderness Areas are all part of this forest.

For more information, contact Forest Headquarters, 1312 Fairlane Road, Yreka, CA 96097; (530) 842-6131.

LAKE TAHOE BASIN MANAGEMENT UNIT

The bulk of this 205,000-acre unit of national forest is on the southern half of beautiful Lake Tahoe. Because it gets such heavy use, dogs are required to be leashed at all times.

Pooches and their people enjoy the underground viewing area of the stream profile chamber at the Lake Tahoe Visitors Center. Water dogs also like frolicking around Fallen Leaf Lake and Echo Lake, especially when Lake Tahoe is just too crowded. Both offer excellent trailheads into the Desolation Wilderness.

In addition to the Desolation Wilderness, the Mount Rose Wilderness is part of this forest. As in the rest of the forest, dogs must be leashed.

For more information, contact Forest Headquarters, 870 Emerald Bay Road, Suite 1, South Lake Tahoe, CA 96150; (530) 573-2600.

LASSEN NATIONAL FOREST

Beautiful Lassen National Forest has so many fascinating volcanic features that it more than makes up for Lassen Volcanic National Park's ban on dogs in any interesting areas (unless you consider parking lots intriguing).

This 1.4 million-acre forest completely surrounds that restrictive national park, so you and your pooch have to be very careful about where you tread. But wherever you tread will be breathtaking. Try a 1,300-foot lava tube, or take an educational 1.5-mile hike among volcanic craters and lava domes on the Spattercone Trail. If that's not enough, you can walk along some 300 miles of trails within the forest.

The Caribou, Ishi, and Thousand Lakes Wilderness Areas are located here.

For more information, contact Forest Headquarters, 55 South Sacramento Street, Susanville, CA 96130; (530) 257-2151.

LOS PADRES NATIONAL FOREST

Ranging in elevations from sea level at Big Sur to nearly 9,000 feet at the crest of Mount Pinos, this spectacular forest is one of the most rugged and beautiful in the West.

It's also the second-largest forest in California, with much of its 1.9 million acres encompassing the Big Sur area. Some of the forest's trails crisscross cool streams, where you can set up a tent and sleep deeply as the sound of the rushing water blocks out those oh-so-appealing sounds of your dog chewing and scratching himself.

The Dick Smith, Machesna Mountain, San Rafael, Santa Lucia, and Ventana Wilderness Areas are all part of the forest. Joe loves hiking in the Ventana Wilderness on easy trails shaded by coast redwood and the spire-like Santa Lucia fir.

For more information, contact Forest Headquarters, 6144 Calle Real, Goleta, CA 93117; (805) 683-6711.

MENDOCINO NATIONAL FOREST

Many Bay Area residents come to this million-acre forest for quick day or weekend trips. This is the only one of California's national forests that is not crossed by a paved road or highway, so if you're looking to escape the world of wheels, you'll find your peace here.

The forest's 615 miles of trails provide dramatic vistas of forested mountains and rugged river canyons. And if you like wildflowers, you'll be in horticultural heaven here. Blue lupine, orange poppies, bush lilac, and redbud are among the wildflowers that add brilliance to the meadows during spring and early summer.

If your dog has a penchant for trees, you'll find huge stands of conifers as well as dogwoods (Joe likes these), beech trees, and oaks.

There's some disagreement about the off-leash rules here. Some rangers say dogs should be leashless only in wilderness areas, while others say they can be leashless anywhere but developed campgrounds. The rules on the official forest map ask that dogs be "on leash in campgrounds, picnic areas, and trails." We tell it like we see it, and we see confusion. It's probably best to ask the ranger when you call with other questions.

The Snow Mountain and Yolla Bolly-Middle Eel Wilderness Areas are within the forest.

For more information, contact Forest Headquarters, 420 East Laurel Street, Willows, CA 95998; (530) 934-3316.

MODOC NATIONAL FOREST

If you and your dog feel like getting away from civilization, this 1.9 million-acre forest in the far northeast reaches of the state will whisk you away from the modern world and into an unusually peaceful setting. This is where the wild horses and the antelope play, unfettered by crowds that can make parts of some other national forests seem more like national parks.

The spartan chaparral- and juniper-covered Modoc Plateau and the surrounding evergreen lands are home to more than 300 species of wildlife. Bald eagles are known to inhabit the area, so if you bring your binoculars, you won't regret the extra baggage. (Let your dog carry them in her backpack.) About 120 miles of trails wind throughout the forest.

The forest lies in an area once occupied by the Modoc, Achomawi, and Northern Paiute Indian tribes. Petroglyphs and pictographs from these tribes, which may have started inhabiting the area 10,000 years ago, are common in portions of the forest.

The South Warner Wilderness Area is also located here.

For more information, contact Forest Headquarters, 441 North Main Street, Alturas, CA 96101; (530) 233-5811.

PLUMAS NATIONAL FOREST

Canine hikers and other outdoors enthusiasts are attracted year-round to this magical forest's streams, lakes, deep canyons, and lush mountain valleys. The forest has more than 1,000 miles of sparkling rivers and streams, along with some 100 lakes.

You and your dog can hike, fish, pan for gold, cross-country ski, swim, and relax in the serenity of this 1.2 million-acre forest. A terrific adventure for able-bodied creatures is a two-hour hike through the woods to reach Feather Falls. This 640-foot waterfall is the sixth highest in the nation, and it's well worth the effort to traverse the sometimes steep terrain leading you there.

The Bucks Lake Wilderness Area is within Plumas National Forest.

For more information, contact Forest Headquarters, P.O. Box 11500, 159 Lawrence Street, Quincy, CA 95971; (530) 283-2050.

SAN BERNARDINO NATIONAL FOREST

This forest is home to famed Big Bear Lake and Lake Arrowhead, popular Southern California resorts. It comprises 810,000 acres of land that range from thick pine woods to rocky, cactus-filled desert.

A favorite activity here is cross-country skiing. Leashless dogs love to lope beside their skiing people in the winter. About 700 miles of trails are open to hikers and skiers.

Because of recent complaints about dogs, they could soon have to be leashed throughout the forest. Check with a ranger before setting out. And dogs are not permitted in much of the San Jacinto Wilderness because it runs into Mount San Jacinto State Park (which bans dogs from its trails and backcountry).

The Cucamonga, San Gorgonio, San Jacinto, and Santa Rosa Wilderness Areas are part of the forest.

For more information, contact Forest Headquarters, 1824 Commercenter Circle, San Bernardino, CA 92408; (909) 383-5588.

SEQUOIA NATIONAL FOREST

Giant sequoias, among the world's largest trees, grow in more than 35 magnificent groves on Sequoia National Forest's lower slopes. The famed Boole Tree, at 90 feet in circumference and 269 feet tall, is the largest tree in any national forest. (Talk about boy dog heaven.) The park encompasses 1.1 million acres and has 830 miles of trails.

Portions of the Kern River Canyon are closed to dogs, and it may be just as well if you happen to have a dog who thinks he's Mark Spitz: An average of seven people drown each year in a section of the Kern River that runs through this region. But the water that makes the river flow fast also contributes to an abundance of wildflowers and lush mountain meadows.

The forest is also home to the Domeland, Golden Trout, Jennie Lakes, Monarch, and Southern Sierra Wilderness Areas.

For more information, contact Forest Headquarters, 900 West Grand Avenue, Porterville, CA 93257; (209) 784-1500.

SHASTA-TRINITY NATIONAL FOREST

Magnificent, massive Mount Shasta is the most striking of many visual highlights within this 2.1 million-acre forest. Dogs can explore the less steep parts of this 17-mile-wide, 14,162-foot-high mountain, but the forest has a whopping 1,500 miles of other, more appropriate trails to try.

This is the largest of the California-based national forests. Anglers and their dogs adore the gigantic Shasta and Trinity Lakes. Shasta Lake, when full, has 370 miles of shoreline—more than San Francisco Bay. A trip to Trinity Lake is like a trip to the Swiss Alps, with the magnificent Trinity Alps towering in the background.

Dog-owning cross-country skiers, wildlife watchers, and hikers love this land. While the area is spectacular year-round, I find it particularly breathtaking in autumn, when the deep oranges and reds of the quaking aspen stand in stark contrast to the snowcapped peak of Mount Shasta.

The Castle Crags, Chanchelulla, Mount Shasta, Trinity Alps, and Yolla Bolly-Middle Eel Wilderness Areas are all part of the forest.

For more information, contact Forest Headquarters, 2400 Washington Avenue, Redding, CA 96001; (530) 246-5222.

SIERRA NATIONAL FOREST

Dogs, go ahead and thumb your snouts at Yosemite National Park to the north. Do the same to Sequoia and Kings Canyon National Parks to the south. They may not want you, but this forest is almost as spectacular and it welcomes your kind.

Sierra National Forest encompasses more than 1.3 million acres, with elevations between 900 feet and 13,157 feet. There's abundant fish and wildlife here, with oak-covered foothills, heavily forested slopes, more than 400 lakes, and the stark and stunning alpine landscape of the high Sierra. Explore it via 1,100 miles of trails.

The Ansel Adams, Dinkey Lakes, John Muir, Kaiser, and Monarch Wilderness Areas are located here.

For more information, contact Forest Headquarters, 1600 Tollhouse Road, Clovis, CA 93612; (209) 297-0706.

SIX RIVERS NATIONAL FOREST

Six major rivers (surprise!) are among the 1,500 miles of water in the forest. If you have a water dog who promises not to get in over her head if the water's too fast, these rivers beckon. You'll have your choice of exploring the Eel, Klamath, Mad, Smith, Trinity, and Van Duzen Rivers.

This long, narrow forest encompasses one million acres of Douglas firs, incense cedars, ponderosa pines, and dozens of other types of trees. The wildlife viewing is excellent here. From hummingbirds to black bears, the forest has it all. (Just a reminder: Don't let your dog get near a bear. If you don't trust your dog to come as soon as you call her in any situation, keep her leashed.)

The North Fork, Siskiyou, Trinity Alps, and Yolla Bolly-Middle Eel Wilderness Areas are part of this forest.

For more information, contact Forest Headquarters, 1330 Bayshore Way, Eureka, CA 95501; (707) 442-1721.

STANISLAUS NATIONAL FOREST

You and your dog can hike on 660 miles of trails that take you over volcanic ridges, through lush alpine meadows, and under tall pines and cedars. This million-acre forest is an enchanting place to take your dog for a day of cross-country skiing. Lake Alpine is a major attraction, but as with all recreation areas within these forests, dogs must be leashed. The official national forest map of Stanislaus requests that dogs be leashed everywhere, but rangers told me the official rule for most of the forest calls for voice control only.

The Carson-Iceberg, Emigrant, and Mokelumne Wilderness Areas are located here.

For more information, contact Forest Headquarters, 19777 Greenley Road, Sonora, CA 95370; (209) 532-3671.

TAHOE NATIONAL FOREST

Lake Tahoe, the blue jewel of the Sierra, makes up this forest's southeast boundary. A hike on even a small portion of the forest's 600 miles of trail will take you and your dog through a vast variety of vegetation, including mountain chaparral, mixed conifers, alpine plants, lodgepole pine, and pinyon-juniper. Dogs and their people enjoy a good hike along the North Fork of the American River.

While dogs are not welcome at the many downhill ski resorts within the forest, they like to romp beside their cross-country skiing human companions on the many miles of groomed roads and Nordic trails.

The Granite Chief Wilderness Area is located at the headwaters of the American River. Dogs are prohibited in the northwest portion of this wilderness from May 15 to July 15 because of deer fawning.

For more information, contact Forest Headquarters, Highway 49 and Coyote Street, Nevada City, CA 95959; (530) 265-4531.

TOIYABE NATIONAL FOREST

Although most of this 3.5 million-acre forest is spread throughout Nevada, a portion of it crosses into California. You and your dog can peruse thundering waterfalls, clear streams, glacial lakes, and alpine meadows. You can also ooh and ahh and woof at a bunch of 10,000-foot peaks in the portion of the Toiyabe near Lake Tahoe.

This is the largest national forest in the lower 48, but the section in California is relatively small. Still, it includes hundreds of miles of trails and the Hoover and Carson-Iceberg Wilderness Areas.

For more information, contact Forest Headquarters, 1200 Franklin Way, Sparks, NV 89431; (702) 355-5301.

THE GOLDEN BONE AWARDS

With this edition of *The California Dog Lover's Companion*, we're proud to unleash the Golden Bone Awards. These awards go to those inns, stores, restaurants, and other special businesses that roll out the welcome mat for dogs in a particularly wonderful way, taking dog-friendliness to new heights. The dogs of California applaud every one of these winners.

In the lodgings category, most of the Golden Bone winners offer dogs tasty treats and lots of scratches and pats. Some provide unbelievable doggy extras. (The Regent Beverly Wilshire, for instance, supplies dogs with biscuits on a silver tray, bottled water, two white linen napkins, a rubber toy, a special pillow for napping, and a vase with a long-stemmed rose. The hotel also offers dog-sitting, dog-grooming, and doggy menu items for an extra fee.) We've also included a few winners on the basis of magnificent leash-free land they're set on, coupled with a very dog-friendly attitude.

In the restaurant category, every winner gives dogs a treat of some kind. Most give biscuits, but a couple give ice cream, one doles out hot dogs, and one even cooks burgers for dogs. The two marked with a paw (🐾) are actually doggy restaurants, specializing in canine cuisine. This book is replete with kindly restaurants that give your dog a bowl of water, but for purposes of brevity, we couldn't include them as Golden Bone recipients. The only exception is one elegant place, Portabella, in Carmel, where dogs get water in a champagne bucket. It's so Carmel we couldn't exclude it.

Some winners, like those in the transportation category, get a Golden Bone award simply because they allow dogs at all.

If you know of a business you think deserves a highly valued Golden Bone Award, call our California Dog Lover's Companion Hotline at (707) 773-4264 and tell us about it. Or you can write us at 340 Bodega Avenue, Petaluma, CA 94952. Our e-mail address is foghorn@well.com. If your tip makes it into the next edition of this book, whether or not it wins a Golden Bone, we'll mention you and your dog as the tipsters in the description of the place you recommended. It's our way of saying woof, er, thanks.

And now, the envelope please.

NORTHERN CALIFORNIA

LODGINGS

Becky's Guesthouse, Sebastopol
Clift Hotel, San Francisco
Edgewater Resort, Kelseyville
Gray Eagle Lodge, Blairsden
Hillcrest II Bed & Breakfast, Calistoga
Lake Oroville Bed and Breakfast, Berry Creek
Larissa's House, Guerneville
Redwood Guest Cottages, Yosemite
River's Retreat, Guerneville
Rollins Lakeside Inn, Chicago Park
Rustic Cottages, Tahoe City
Saundra Dyer's Resort, Downieville
Sheep Dung Estates, Yorkville
Sparrow's Nest, Sonoma
Stanford Inn by the Sea, Mendocino
Tenaya Lodge, Fish Camp
Triple S Ranch, Calistoga
Washington Street Lodging, Calistoga
The Welch House, Sea Ranch
Zaballa House, Half Moon Bay

RESTAURANTS

Beach Cafe, Pacifica
The Dog House, Bodega Bay
Downtown Joe's, Napa
42 Degrees, San Francisco
Good and Plenty Cafe, Alameda
Grill Master, San Jose
The Hitchin' Post, Lewiston
Java Point, Gualala
Mendocino Cafe, Mendocino
Mother Barclay's Cafe, Squaw Valley
Naughty Dawg, Tahoe City

New Helvetia Roasters and Bakers, Sacramento
Oy Vey Cafe, Chico
Paradise Hamburers and Ice Cream, Tiburon
Polly Ann Ice Cream, San Francisco
Pony Espresso, Moss Beach
Racer's, Napa
Shubert's Ice Cream, Chico
Taylor's Refresher, Napa
Valley Cafe, Suisun City

STORES

Avenue Books, Berkeley
Brown Study Book Shop, Point Reyes Station
Don't Eat the Furniture, Oakland
Kepler's Books, Menlo Park
Neiman Marcus, San Francisco
Sierra Nevada Adventure Company (Sonora and Arnold)
The Video Room, Oakland
Wilkes Bashford Clothiers, San Francisco

TRANSPORTATION

Antler's Resort (houseboats), Lake Shasta
Blue & Gold Fleet ferries, based in San Francisco
Blue Goose Steam Train, Yreka
Cedar Stock Resort (houseboats), Trinity Center
The Clam Barge, Dillon Beach
Folsom Miniature Steam Train, Folsom
Green Tortoise Bus, based in San Francisco
Holiday Harbor (houseboats), Lake Shasta
Jones Valley Resort (houseboats), Lake Shasta
Mammoth Mountain Ski Area gondolas, Mammoth Lakes

Mikes Bikes & Blades (surreys),
San Francisco
Muni buses, San Francisco
Nevada City Carriage Company,
Nevada City
Sacramento Valley Live Steamers
Club, Rancho Cordova
San Francisco's cable cars
Seven Crown Resorts (house-
boats), Lake Shasta, Stockton
Skunk Train, Fort Bragg
Squaw Valley Ski Resort
gondolas, Squaw Valley
Sugar Pine Railroad, Fish Camp
Tilden Park Miniature Steam
Train, Berkeley
Tom Fraser's Carriage Tours,
Jamestown

WALKIES

Cruisin' the Castro, San
Francisco

Flower Power Haight Ashbury
Walking Tour, San Francisco
Midpeninsula Regional Open
Space District's Dog Days
Hikes, based in Los Altos
Palo Alto Humane Society's Dog
Days Walks & Hikes
Sierra Club Canine Hikes, San
Francisco Bay Area, based in
Oakland

PROFESSIONAL SPORTS TEAM

San Francisco Giants, for the Dog
Days of Summer

MOVIES

Burlingame 4 Drive-In Theater,
Burlingame
Geneva Drive-In Theater, San
Francisco

FARM

Hidden Villa Farm, Los Altos Hills

EMPLOYER

Autodesk

CENTRAL CALIFORNIA

LODGINGS

Cypress Inn, Carmel
Four Seasons Biltmore, Santa
Barbara
Ivanhoe Bed & Breakfast, Santa
Barbara
The Lodge at Pebble Beach
San Ysidro Ranch, Montecito
The Sunset House, Carmel
Vagabond's House Inn, Carmel

RESTAURANTS

Cafe Gringo, Carmel
Chubby's, Los Banos
Jorie's, Aptos
Le Coq D'or, Carmel
Out to Lunch, Atwater
Padaro Beach Grill, Carpinteria
Portabella, Carmel

ART GALLERY

Galerie Blue Dog, Carmel

TRANSPORTATION

Bay Bikes (surreys), Monterey
Beach Rentals (surreys), Santa
Barbara
Herman and Helen's Marina
(houseboats), Stockton
Kites Galore (surreys), Morro Bay
Morro Bay Surrey Company,
Morro Bay
Roaring Camp & Big Trees
Narrow-Gauge Railroad,
Felton

WALKY

Carmel Walks, Carmel

DOG TOUR

Happy Dog Tours, Pacific Grove

WINERY

Several California wineries allow dogs, but this one takes the biscuit:
Dover Canyon Winery, Templeton

MOVIES

Skyview Drive-In Theatre, Salinas
Skyview Drive-In Theatre, Santa Cruz
Sunset Drive-In Theater, San Luis Obispo

FARM

Pizza Farm, Madera

SOUTHERN CALIFORNIA

LODGINGS

Arrowhead Tree Top Lodge, Lake Arrowhead
Hotel Bel-Air, Los Angeles
The Lodge at Angelus Oaks, Angelus Oaks
Ramada Inn, City of Commerce
Regent Beverly Wilshire, Beverly Hills
U.S. Grant Hotel, San Diego

RESTAURANTS

Bruegger's Bagel Bakery, Newport Beach
Froglander's Yogurt, La Jolla
🐾 The Original Paw Pleasers, San Diego
🐾 Park Bench Cafe, Huntington Beach
Priscilla's, Burbank
Rive Gauche, Palos Verdes Estates
Surf-Break, Redondo Beach

STORES

I. Magnin, Beverly Hills
Pacific Traveler's Supply, Santa Barbara
Thidwick Books, San Diego

TRANSPORTATION

Balboa Island Ferry, Newport Beach
Calico Ghost Town Narrow Gauge Railroad, Barstow
Catalina Cruises, Catalina
Catalina Express, Catalina
Griffith Park miniature steam train, Los Angeles
Orange Empire Railway Museum, Perris
Showboat Cruise, Newport Beach
Victoria Park Carriages, Big Bear Lake

WALKIES

California Canine Hikers, Pasadena
Sierra Club Canine Committee hikes, Los Angeles

HOW TO START YOUR OWN DOG PARK

Ahh, the typical dog-walking routine: Get the leash, walk around the neighborhood, try not to let your dog lift a leg on Mrs. Crimson's prize-winning roses, breathe in some car fumes, clean the poop off Mr. Smith's sidewalk, get cornered by the neighborhood busybody, and finally go back home, where your dog looks at you with those Peggy Lee "Is That All There Is?" eyes.

From your dog's point of view, the experience is probably even less scintillating. It's sidewalk, sidewalk everywhere, and the incessant pulling of that darned leash.

If you're lucky, your dog walk takes place in a park, but it's likely there's still that leash to contend with. And if you think you don't like it, consider your dog. Chances are his dream is to be able to run around in a park buck naked (that's dogese for leash-free), feeling the wind running through his fur while joyously frolicking with other dogs, rolling in the grass without getting tangled in a leash, and playing ball with abandon.

"Saying dogs can get enough exercise on leash is like saying humans can get enough exercise walking to work," says Ian Dunbar, the veterinarian and animal behaviorist who developed Sirius Puppy Training, the first temperament training course for puppies done entirely off leash. "It's a quality of life issue."

When I wrote the first edition of *The California Dog Lover's Companion* in 1993, the idea of a dog park was still relatively new. "Dog what?" was the frequent response to my questions of park and recreation folks. Of course, being California, we already had much more public leash-free land than most other states, thanks to entities like the Forest Service, the Bureau of Land Management, the Golden Gate National Recreation Area, the East Bay Regional Parks District, and a smattering of other leash-free districts. If you can get land like this to open up to you (as a group called Dog PAC of Santa Barbara recently did), you've got an automatic poochy paradise. But in many urban and suburban areas, the only chance a dog has to run leash-free is in a park dedicated to dogs and their people. These dog parks are usually fenced (but some of the most wonderful, like Piedmont Park in Piedmont, are not), and have amenities like pooper-scoopers, benches, and trees.

Back in this book's infancy, there were only a half-dozen of these dog-dedicated parks around the state. Today, there are more than 30, and the number is growing, even as I write this. (That breeze you feel is the wagging of California dog tails!)

California dog people have become much more politically active in the last few years. As people began hearing about dog parks here and there, they'd start hankering for one in their own neck of the suburbs, and they'd work their tails off trying to get one. Some ran into so many brick walls that they gave up. Others persevered through hellish odds. Still others had great success quickly. (The record speed for a dog park approval is in Roseville, where it took less than four months from approaching the city to final approval!)

What follows in the next few pages are tips to help make your quest for a dog park as painless as possible. The one thing everyone I talked with for this chapter agreed on is that the more you know about other dog parks, and the more input you get from those who have been there and done that, the better your chances of success. I can't go into as much detail as I'd like in such limited space, so at the end of the chapter I list some contacts that will provide you with so much great information that your city will be hard-pressed to turn you down.

Ken Novak, a manager with the city of Los Angeles Recreation and Parks Department, which has become increasingly dog-friendly of late, has this to say to other cities about dog parks: "If you build it, they will come. Believe me."

Dogspeed to you.

GET INSPIRED

To have the commitment it takes to start a dog park these days, it helps to have a passion for the subject. Are you fed up with dogs being looked upon as a bane in your community? Are you tired of sneaking your dog off leash in a hidden corner of a park late at night? Do you feel strongly about your dog's need to have leash-free exercise?

"What it takes sometimes is someone who's angry, someone who gets a ticket for trying to exercise her dogs properly and has nowhere else to turn," says Dianne Chute, founder of the Remington Dog Park in Sausalito. She knows of what she speaks. She got a ticket for having her dogs off leash in a remote Sausalito park at 6:45 A.M. A year later, she got herself a dog park.

THEN GET ORGANIZED

Most people who've started a dog park say they couldn't have done it without a core group of organizers. If you don't already know people who feel as strongly as you do about starting a dog park, put up notices in local pet stores or even at kiosks at a park you and your dog frequent. Try to get about five or six people who are willing to work hard and persevere. Ideally, someone in your group will know his or her way around city or county government. Another important person to have in your group is a lawyer. You can give yourselves a name, if you want. Many such groups use the term "friends of" the so-and-so park. And, as luck would have it, "Dog Owners Group" has the handy acronym of DOG, which several groups have been quick to adopt and attach to the name of their city.

You don't have to work in a group, though, if this doesn't appeal to you. Some successful dog park founders have thrived on working alone. "You have more latitude and no one to disagree with you," says Miriam Yarden, an animal psychologist who almost single-handedly organized the creation of a dog park in Long Beach's Recreation Park.

SET REASONABLE GOALS

Don't think you're going to accomplish everything in a few weeks. "It's not an easy process," says Mary Braunworth, a director of the Los Angeles Recreation and Parks Department. "Working with city governments, getting funding, everything that goes along with starting a dog park takes time."

Whether working with a group or by yourself, it's a good idea to set goals. "We met in the library each month and determined monthly goals. It really helped keep things moving along," says Bruce Rubin, who organized a group called Dog People, which won a battle for a leash-free park in the city of Riverside.

LOCATION, LOCATION, LOCATION

Some dog park founders only had to make a general plea for a park, and the city did the work of finding an appropriate site. But most say it's best to determine at least a couple of potential locations before approaching your city.

When looking for a site for a dog park, keep in mind that these parks can be anywhere from a quarter of an acre (which is a bit on the small side) to several acres. Those without fences can be even bigger. Ideal sites have grass, shade, and easy access by car. It's usually best if they're already part of an existing park. It's even better if dog people are already using it as an unofficial off-leash area. But sometimes the only way to get a dog park is to take land that has little other use. In Petaluma, the nine-acre Rocky Memorial Dog Park is built on a former dump. Oakland's Hardy Dog Park is directly under a freeway. Roseville's Marco Dog Park is in a flood-control area that is under three feet of water in winter.

Sometimes land that has little other use also happens to be in an existing park. That can be a real boon. "When we got this park, we got dirt. It was like the dust bowl," says Patti Goff, of the now beautiful Huntington Beach Dog Park. "I felt like we were in *The Grapes of Wrath*. But we were so grateful for anything, and we knew we could make it work."

Keep in mind that if there are neighbors near your park site, you may hear from them. Dog parks and neighbors can get along well if there's adherence to no-barking rules and poop scooping. But some dog park organizers have found nearby neighbors to be an impossible obstacle. "You wouldn't believe the 'nimby' (not in my backyard) attitude of so many people here," says Mario Di Palma, founder of San Rafael's Field of Dogs group, which has worked for more than five years to find a location for a dog park. At press time, Field of Dogs was about to get final approval for a park far from the madding suburban crowds.

RULES, RULES, RULES

Like it or not, you'll have to come up with a list of rules for your dog park. You can get ideas from other parks. Some have just a few basic rules, requiring that you clean up after your dog and don't bring in young puppies or aggressive dogs or females in heat. Others have lists so long that your puppy will be full grown by the time you get done reading them. Some of these rules include banning children and banning food and drink. Being able to present a list of rules to the city will help your group seem like the responsible dog owners you are. (But don't go over-board. I don't like the rule banning kids one bit.)

While you're on the subject of rules, you should also discuss ways to enforce them, and how you'll do upkeep at the park. Sometimes a city will mow and water (but no city I'm aware of picks up the poop), and sometimes it's all up to the park users.

FOCUS ON A VISION

Dog parks not only come in all shapes and sizes, and with different rules, but what's in them also varies from one park to another. Some are full of fun things for dogs and their people. They have everything from fire hydrants to bulletin boards to doggy/human water fountains to lights for night visits. The ground cover is perfectly manicured grass. A few are utterly glorious, designed so there's safety without fences. (Pied-mont Park, page 335, is a good example of this.) Others are lucky to even have a fence around some dirt. When drawing up a proposal for your park, it's helpful to have an idea of where you want to go with it. Dare to dream, because you may be able to get quite a few items donated. Which brings us to the next subject, the unavoidable issue of money.

FIGURE OUT FUNDING

Dog parks don't come cheap. If you're lucky enough to be given a part of a preexisting park that already has trees, grass, and parking, your initial costs will be relatively minor. Depending on the type of fencing you choose and the size of your park, you might be able to start with as little as $5,000.

But the bigger the dog park, the more expensive it will be. Not only is there the fencing to consider, there's the upkeep as well. And if you start in territory that's very primitive, you'll also have to face the costs of grading the land, planting grass or some kind of ground cover, irriga-tion, and developing parking. The Sepulveda Basin Off-Leash Dog Park, in Encino, opened recently to the tune of $250,000 (on land that had been given up on for development).

Some cities are willing to paw the entire bill. But those cities are rare indeed. Several dog park people recommend against even asking. "It's a bad move to ask most cities to finance the park. I gave them my word that it wouldn't cost them a nickel," says Long Beach's Miriam Yarden. Other cities agree to help maintain the park, and may chip in for a few basic items. But these days, most cities are putting the bulk of the finan-cial responsibility on the dog people. And dog people are meeting the challenge beautifully. I'm really impressed with the range of ways dog parks have been able to come up with money for things they need.

Some are able to become nonprofit organizations and get big-ticket items, like fencing and trees, donated. Some seek out obscure grants. Some look for public-private partnerships. The Sepulveda park is a great example of a public-private partnership that's thriving—Friskies donated $50,000 to the cause, and got its name on brochures and signage.

I've rarely seen such creative fund-raising as I've seen for dog parks. There are some awfully imaginative, energetic dog people out there. (Keep in mind that even after the park is up and running, there are costs that have to be met.) Some examples of fund-raising successes:

•Miriam Yarden deciphered the signatures on her petitions, sent out fund-raising letters to everyone who signed, and raised the $5,000 it took to open the Long Beach dog park within three months.

•The dog park in Long Beach now offers memberships for $25 per year to help defray the $5,000 yearly upkeep bill. You don't have to be a member to use the park, but member benefits include a vote on dog park issues, a bandanna, and a newsletter.

•The folks at Huntington Beach are putting together a Doggy Walk of Fame. For $25 per one-foot square of concrete, a dog person can immortalize his dog's paws or his dog's name, or scrawl a doggy-related sentiment. It will take 834 such squares to make a walkway from the parking lot to the dog park. The overhead is minimal, since many of the goods and services are being donated. The net profit could be as high as $20,000, which will go toward goodies like lighting. At press time, squares were flying off the shelves.

•At Howe About Dogs Park, in Sacramento, there's a similar fund-raising event going on. The park people are selling bricks for $25 each, which includes the name of the buyer's dog being stamped into it. They'll go to make a brick walkway. The park folks also make about $1,000 a year selling dog cookies at Christmas.

•Some dog parks have installed parking meters around entrances so that people with spare change can donate it to the park. At Huntington Beach Dog Park, the meters are generating $250 a month.

•Poway Dog Park people sponsored Dog Days, with dog games and vendors, in order to help raise money for lights. The Redondo Beach Dog Park has held similar events, including the Houndtown Fairs.

•A gate at the Redondo Beach Dog Park is covered with "bones" with names of people who bought them. (The money, of course, went to the park.) The "bones" are rawhide, brass, silver, and gold. It's the same idea as the plaques you see at parks or in museums.

•Sausalito's Remington Dog Park people have leaned toward the culinary in their fund-raising efforts. They've had lasagna dinners at a yacht club, sold ice cream at a vintage boat show, and sold hot dogs for dogs in a donated booth at a street fair. Non-food money-raisers include selling oodles of sweatshirts, T-shirts, and sweatpants with their logo (done by none other than our own illustrious illustrator, Phil Frank).

GO WITH YOUR CITY'S FLOW

Every city and county has its own unique way of driving you crazy with rules of hierarchy, order, and the like. Find out how your city works when it comes to making changes in parks. Do you have to approach the animal care and control people first to change the leash ordinance? Or should you first go before the park and recreation department, or before an advisory board of the city council? This is where having someone in your group who knows local government comes in mighty handy. If you're flying blind, and you're making no headway with phone calls to various departments, try hooking up with a sympathetic, knowledgeable person at your local SPCA. They often know how to handle the city on matters of pets, and can have valuable contacts in local government.

Lauren Cobb, of the group D.O.G.B.O.N.E., which recently got the green light for a dog park in Novato after four years of wrangling, recommends starting at the top regardless of protocol. "Don't start at lower levels. We wasted years there. Go to the city council and let it work down from there." She says approval of their park would have taken as little as a year if they'd done it this way.

PETITIONS PAY OFF

One of the best things you can do at a big public meeting with your city's decision-makers is to present them with as many petitions as you can. "I walked into chambers with a wheelbarrow full of petitions," says Long Beach's Yarden. "Politicians listen to petitions. These are their voters speaking."

Your petition should state the objective of having a park where dogs can exercise leash-free. Wording can vary greatly. The lawyer in your group (if you're lucky enough to have a lawyer) can be a real help here. If you're set on a location, make sure you include it. Otherwise, it can be a general plea for a dog park.

DO YOUR RESEARCH

When you come to your city's decision-makers armed with revised ordinances from other cities with dog parks, rules from other dog parks, and pictures and videos of other dog parks, you've got half the battle won. Says Patty Tambe, administrative analyst with the city of Riverside: "It makes it much easier for the city when you don't have to start looking at the project from scratch, like you're the first city ever to do it." She says Riverside's Dog People "did a great job doing their homework, and that definitely helped them."

The resource list at the end of this chapter will provide you with some good research tools. To get videos and photos of other parks, you'll probably have to visit them yourself (at least until there's some kind of a lending library established for this sort of thing). Finding leash-free parks is easy, because you have a copy of this book in your hand. Leaf through it and look for the running dog (🐕) symbol, which means the park doesn't require leashes. If the park sounds like one that might help your cause, it might be worth a visit with your cameras. Pictures/videos are truly worth thousands of words when it comes to dog parks.

"Having a videotape of another dog park was a stroke of genius," says Long Beach's Yarden, whose advice has helped countless other dog parks get started across the U.S. and Canada since starting the park in Long Beach. "All the councilmen were mesmerized by the video. They were staring it at completely absorbed and enchanted. They approved the park then and there with a unanimous 'woof.' "

(I think it would be fun to play the *Born Free* theme while showing the video. It couldn't hurt, unless a council member was once attacked by a lion.)

PACK 'EM IN

When the big meetings start happening, get as many people as possible to come in support of the dog park. "I went out and got lots of signatures on a petition, and it didn't matter much to our commissioners. But when they actually saw all the people behind the park, suddenly things changed," says Gretchen Burgess, the main founder of Phenix Dog Park in Benicia.

Have supporters wear bright-colored tags or labels saying something like "I'm for the dog park." It makes for a brilliant display. It's the kind of stuff the media eat up as well.

CALL IN THE MEDIA

A little good press can go a long way toward getting the right people to take notice of your group. "The council wouldn't even listen to us until we started getting publicity," says Karen Brooks, founder of Santa Monica Dog Owners Group, which helped open all the city's parks to leashed dogs, and two parks to leash-free dogs. "Things turned around after an article in the *Los Angeles Times*."

Brooks suggests writing an article or press release about your dog park situation and submitting it to local newspapers, TV stations, and radio stations. "Keep it positive," she says. Name-calling and overly negative statements don't work as well.

If you have influential dog people in your community, try to enlist their support as well, says Brooks. Santa Monica DOG rallied some actors to write letters to politicians, which seemed to help, she says.

EMPHASIZE PEOPLE, NOT POOCHES

Most decision-makers in the public sector have to consider the humans they serve, not their dogs. So approach it from their angle.

"Stress that these are people parks," says Rick Johnson, associate executive director of the Marin Humane Society. Johnson has given talks about the benefits of dog parks at national meetings of park and recreation heads. "Talk less about the benefits for the dogs (they don't care) and more about the fact that you deserve a place to recreate in a park setting like the many kid programs and athletic programs."

Johnson has done an extensive survey that shows that dog people use dog parks more than any other park user group uses "human" parks. "They're out there twice a day, just about every day. How many other park users can say the same thing?" His survey also shows that the average dog park user is 40 to 60 years old, and that two-thirds of dog park users are women. "We have a whole user group here that doesn't normally use most of what parks have to offer in the way of organized sports and such. It's a compelling argument, because the goal is for all populations to be served."

(Johnson continues to add to his survey. To get a copy of the survey, write to him at the Marin Humane Society, 171 Bel Marin Keys Boulevard, Novato, CA 94949.)

Other human-oriented benefits of having a dog park are that it will help curtail off-leash scofflaws in other parks, and it will ease up on the dog poop problem at other parks.

MAKE NICE TO YOUR POLITICIANS

One thing that can help you over dog park hurdles more than any other is to get some friends in relatively high places. (As high as your city council, anyway, or at least the people who influence your council.) Take it from the experts:

• "You have to kiss up to a lot of politicians to make it work," says Huntington Beach Dog Park's Patti Goff.

• "If you can rally politically powerful people, like those who give money to politicians, it's a big help," says Field of Dogs' Mario Di Palma.

• "I sold everything except my soul. It's so against me to suck up to politicians. But if I hadn't, this park might not be here," says Long Beach's Miriam Yarden.

You may be lucky enough that you don't have to resort to playing the political game, but if you do, at least you know you won't be alone.

ALLAY THEIR FEARS

Chances are good that there will be some people who are certain that dogs will suddenly start running in packs around the neighborhood once you let them have some freedom. Still others will reckon the noise will drive down their property values, and the stench will hammer them further. This is where having a solid set of rules, and people to help enforce them, comes in.

Your city may still be afraid of being sued. Insurance is an issue some parks and cities have had to deal with. Many dog parks are able to work out something with indemnification, and with a law stating that every person is responsible for her own dog's actions. It's also possible for your dog group to buy its own liability insurance with the city named as co-insurer, but this is expensive. A small book could be written about this subject. (Not by me. I'm lucky to have car insurance.) The listings at the end of the chapter will help provide you with some places to go for more help.

PERSIST FOR YOUR POOCH

It can get mighty tough out there when you're in the middle of getting a dog park approved. It truly can be a dog-eat-dog world. The obstacles may seem insurmountable at times. Organizations and people you might have once considered allies, or at least nice folks, can become your foes. In Berkeley, for instance, the fight for Cesar Chavez Park to become a leash-free haven has met with strong resistance from the Sierra Club and a blind woman. These are not a dog lover's everyday opponents.

When times are tough, and you're heading to your umpteenth boring meeting with city officials, and facing stumbling blocks at every turn, it helps to look down toward the ground, because there you'll find the reason you're going through all this trouble. Pet her, give her a hug, have a talk with her if you need to. Then take a deep breath and step into the battle zone again. Remember, Rome wasn't built in a day. And if it helps, think about Poway's dog park, which took about nine years from start to finish. Yours couldn't possibly take that long. Could it?

Almost without exception, every person involved with starting a dog park says it was worth the trouble. "The people and the dogs are nuts for the park. I look around at all the dogs having a great time, and I realize if I hadn't been just a total pain in the butt, this wouldn't have happened," says Renee St. Denis, founder of Roseville's Marco Dog Park.

HELPFUL RESOURCES

The people, brochures, info packets, and Web sites on the next few pages are just some of the many places you can turn to for help with your dog park.

THE WRITTEN WORD

SCOOP, Sacramento Canine Owners for Off-Leash Parks, has a very helpful, very huge, packet of information available for $10. It includes articles about the value of dog parks, a sample petition for starting a dog park, several SCOOP newsletters, survey results, a sample dog park proposal, examples of park rules, and dozens of other goodies you'll find invaluable. Call SCOOP before sending a check to make sure the price hasn't gone up; (916) 739-6415. The address is P.O. Box 19101, Sacramento, CA 95819-0101. SCOOP also provides a brochure on dog parks. It's yours if you send a stamped, self-addressed envelope with your request.

The Marin Humane Society has a brochure that lists community benefits of dog parks, things an ideal dog park should include, people etiquette, and other useful info. It also includes phone numbers of Marin County dog park groups. The brochure is actually titled "Marin County Dog Parks." Write to Rick Johnson, associate executive director of the society, for a copy. The address is 171 Bel Marin Keys Boulevard, Novato, CA 94949. When you write, ask him for a copy of his dog park survey, so you can take part in a doggone important piece of research.

The city of Claremont can provide you with a packet of documentation of how the city's Pooch Park came into existence. It includes a well-researched sheet of info from dog people on why Claremont needed a dog park, a city analysis of the park's potential, the city's ordinance change, and a few articles on the park. For a copy of the packet, write to Dick Guthrie, Director of Human Services, Human Services Department, 840 North Indian Hill Boulevard, Claremont, CA 91711. Or call him at (909) 399-5493.

The city of Poway also has a small packet available on starting a dog park. Call its Community Services Department (Chris is very helpful) at

(619) 679-4343 to get yours. Or you can write to Poway Community Services Department, P.O. Box 789, Poway, CA 92074.

THE SPOKEN/E-MAILED WORD

Rick Johnson, associate executive director of the Marin Humane Society, goes around the country speaking to large groups of park and rec people about the benefits of dog parks. If you still have questions after reading his brochure, mentioned on page 768, you can call him at (415) 883-4621 extension 260.

Mary Lee Batcheller is with Friends of Claremont Pooch Park, (909) 626-5744. She's a very friendly woman who can help you with general questions.

If you leave a message on the Huntington Beach Dog Park hotline, someone will get back to you. When they do, you should call them back so they're not footing the bill for the call; (714) 536-5672. Or send e-mail to jovamor@aol.com or BarkusMaximus@Juno.com. These folks have plenty of experience with every aspect of starting and maintaining a dog park.

Claudia Kawczynska, editor of a fabulous publication called *The Berkeley Bark,* has lots of experience trying to start a leash-free park against all odds. She's part of a group that's still trying, and can offer valuable advice; (510) 704-0827. Her publication may go national. If so, it's a wonderful source of dog info, and worth a subscription.

Miriam Yarden, who started the dog park at Long Beach's Recreation Park, is one of the most dynamic, quotable, helpful people I've ever talked with about dog parks or anything else. (She's an animal psychologist who teaches at universities and ministers to pets of the stars, although she's very hush-hush about the stars part of her work.) Since starting the Long Beach park, she's been instrumental in helping people all over the U.S. and Canada start their own parks. You can phone her at (562) 428-1824. (Please call her back if she ends up returning your call so she doesn't have to be charged for a long-distance call.) You can also fax her at (562) 428-8855.

Karen Brooks is the enterprising founder of the Santa Monica Dog Owners Group, which organized nothing short of a doggy revolution in Santa Monica several years ago. She can provide you with sage, time-tested advice; (310) 392-3583.

Bruce Rubin, who helped start Riverside's dog park, has good advice on how to plot your course. He can be reached via e-mail at brubin@genesisnetwork.net.

Gretchen Burgess, who worked for years to get a park in Benicia, can offer some really helpful hints on everything from wooing your city to making a park into dog heaven. Plus, in my opinion, her dog group has some of the most wonderfully mellow rules around. (But they do keep the park safe.)

A group called Dog PAC of Santa Barbara recently got a couple of magnificent, large parks to permit dogs. The parks are not dedicated to dogs, but I include the group here because their victories are so fresh and their parks are the kind of places dogs dream about being allowed in off leash (as are places like Fort Funston, in San Francisco, and many of the East Bay Regional Parks in the Bay Area). Call Dog PAC at (805) 563-2773 or write to Dog PAC at P.O. Box 3716, Santa Barbara, CA 93130. (Dog PAC folks are also producing a video on leash-free dog behavior!)

Sandi Brown, a personable pet therapist who also spends 25 hours a day working on Santa Rosa's dog parks, is happy to field questions via e-mail: Foxtail7@aol.com.

Lauren Cobb, founder of the group D.O.G.B.O.N.E., has good advice on how to pull a dog park together. At press time, her group had just received the final okay from the city of Novato for a two-acre park. Contact her at P.O. Box 359, Novato, CA 94948; (415) 898-5843.

Sandie Rhodes, president of the Friends of the Redondo Beach Dog Park, also has terrific suggestions and can answer questions via e-mail. Her address is sandieroad@aol.com.

Mario Di Palma's group, Field of Dogs, is on the verge of getting the final okay for a dog park that's been in the works for more than five years. He's been through it all, and you can profit from his wisdom if you have a few questions; (415) 454-4851.

THE WEBBED WORD

The Dog Park Reporter is an excellent Web site that deals with how to start dog parks and then goes on to discuss numerous examples of dog parks. It also provides links to other dog park pages: www.mindspring.com/~patmar/index.html.

A group called FREEPLAY (Friendly, Responsible, Environmentally Evolved Pet Lover's Alliance–Yes) has an informative Web site on its brand-new dog park in Venice Beach: www.freeplay.org.

Remington Dog Park has an excellent Web site that features a brief history of the park, fund-raising efforts, and a detailed park description: www.dogpark-sausalito.com.

The Marin Humane Society's brochure listing dog park benefits, etc., can also be found on the society's Web page: www.marin-humane.org.

A Web site called Chowder's page lists suggestions for starting your own dog park, in addition to showing the joys of an off-leash dog park: www.sonic.net/~bgould/

Phenix Dog Park, in Benicia, has a site with pictures of their piece of dog heaven and the history of the park. It might provide you with some ideas for your own park. You'll find links for the site at www.benicia_veterinary.com.

Index

ABOUT THE AUTHOR

Joe Dog (top of opposite page) has traveled throughout the state to check out some of the most dog-friendly parks, beaches, lodgings, and restaurants in the world. As part of his research, he's ridden on ferries, horse-drawn carriages, and steam trains. He's visited drive-in movies, marched in numerous dog parades, and inspected his share of kitschy tourist attractions. His favorite saying: "Ahh, it's a dog's life."

Since Joe is an Airedale without a driver's license, **Maria Goodavage** (top of opposite page), author of *The Bay Area Dog Lover's Companion,* and Northern California correspondent for *USA Today* from 1989 until she had a human child in 1996, goes along as chauffeur. "Maria is of invaluable assistance in interpreting my reactions for human consumption," says Joe. "She does a four-paw job."

Joe lives with Maria, her husband, Craig Hanson, and their daughter, Laura Hanson, in a house two blocks from the beach in San Francisco.

ACKNOWLEDGMENTS

Thanks and arf . . .

To my fantastic husband, Craig Hanson, who worked his tail off helping with research for this edition. (He's the one whose ears are still flattened from all the phone calls he made.) He's a doggone great man. I rate him four paws.

And to the dozens of wonderful dog and human readers who sent in suggestions about their own favorite haunts. California will be all the more dog-friendly thanks to these intrepid travelers. Joe Dog and I are especially grateful to the terrific tips from Orange County's Troovee Dog and his dynamic person, Mary Bavry, and to "Three-Dog Dave" Hepperly, who kept us updated on how beautifully Riverside was going to the dogs. Joe Dog and I would also like to thank Sheryl Smith and her cute dog Gracie for all the wonderful letters they sent us.

I would like to give special thanks to Nisha Dog (bottom left of opposite page) and Bill Dog (bottom right of opposite page), who were a tremendous part of this book but have since moved on.

Maria Goodavage with Joe Dog

Nisha Dog

Bill Dog

CREDITS

Editors	Jean Linsteadt
	Karin Mullen
Production Manager	Kyle Morgan
Production Assistants	Jean-Vi Lenthe
	Jan Shade
	Mark Aver
Research	Craig Hanson
Acquisitions Editor	Judith Pynn
Cover and Interior Illustrations	Phil Frank
Author Photo	Linda Sue Scott

FOGHORN ⋈ OUTDOORS

Founded in 1985, Foghorn Press has quickly become one of the country's premier publishers of outdoor recreation guidebooks. Through its unique Books Building Community program, Foghorn Press supports community environmental issues, such as park, trail, and water ecosystem preservation.

Foghorn Press books are available throughout the United States in bookstores and some outdoor retailers. If you cannot find the title you are looking for, visit Foghorn's Web site at www.foghorn.com or call 1-800-FOGHORN.

The Dog Lover's Series

- *The Bay Area Dog Lover's Companion* (352 pp) $17.95—New 3rd edition
- *The Florida Dog Lover's Companion* (602 pp) $20.95—New 2nd edition
- *The Texas Dog Lover's Companion* (602 pp) $20.95—New!
- *The Seattle Dog Lover's Companion* (256 pp) $17.95
- *The Boston Dog Lover's Companion* (416 pp) $17.95
- *The Atlanta Dog Lover's Companion* (288 pp) $17.95
- *The Washington D.C. Dog Lover's Companion* (288 pp) $17.95—New!

The Complete Guide Series

- *California Camping* (768 pp) $20.95—New 10th anniversary edition
- *California Hiking* (688 pp) $20.95
- *California Waterfalls* (408 pp) $17.95
- *California Fishing* (768 pp) $20.95
- *California Golf* (864 pp) $20.95—New 7th edition
- *California Beaches* (640 pp) $19.95
- *California Boating and Water Sports* (608 pp) $19.95
- *Pacific Northwest Camping* (656 pp) $20.95—New 6th edition
- *Pacific Northwest Hiking* (648 pp) $20.95
- *Washington Fishing* (480 pp) $20.95—New 2nd edition
- *Tahoe* (678 pp) $20.95—New 2nd edition
- *New England Hiking* (416 pp) $18.95
- *New England Camping* (520 pp) $19.95
- *Utah and Nevada Camping* (384 pp) $18.95
- *Southwest Camping* (544 pp) $17.95
- *Baja Camping* (288 pp) $14.95—New 2nd edition
- *Florida Camping* (672 pp) $20.95—New!

A book's page length and availability are subject to change.

For more information, call 1-800-FOGHORN,
e-mail: foghorn@well.com, or write to:
Foghorn Press
340 Bodega Avenue
Petaluma, CA 94952

BARKER'S INDEX

52,000:

The number of pooper-scoopers stocked at the Huntington Beach Dog Park annually

Best quote about dog doody duty:

"Here I've been doing important things all my life, and suddenly I'm getting on TV and in newspapers all over the place for picking up dog feces." Martin Senat, chair of the Huntington Dog Beach Preservation Society

Park where you're most likely to catch a scooping star:

Laurel Canyon Park, in the Studio City area

The concierge desk, the bellman's desk, and the front desk:

Where your dog will find pooch treats at The Lodge at Pebble Beach

Inn where you and your dog will most feel like mystery mavens:

The Blair House, in Mendocino, home of *Murder, She Wrote*

Where you can be a gorilla or a dog or a cat and still get the royal treatment:

The U.S. Grant Hotel, in San Diego

Where several presidents have stayed and received the royal treatment:

The U.S. Grant Hotel, in San Diego

What Elvis Presley, King Hussein, Ringo Starr, Queen Margrethe of Denmark, Andrew Lloyd Webber, and hundreds of dogs have in common:

They've all stayed at the **Regent Beverly Wilshire.** (So can your dog.)

$7,500:

Least expensive painting for sale in Carmel's dog-friendly Galerie Blue Dog

1:

Number of dogs who have done a leg lift in the Galerie Blue Dog

Wilkes Bashford:

Favorite store of San Francisco mayor Willie Brown

Wilkes Bashford:

Favorite store of discriminating San Francisco dogs

Beach where it's harder these days to be a dog:

Ocean Beach, in San Francisco, with a new leash law on two miles of beach

Beach where it's harder these days to be a U.S. park ranger:

Ocean Beach, in San Francisco. "I've been doing law enforcement all my life and never have I had such a hard time as dealing with dog people. They're tough." Anonymous park ranger.

Dog park with the most shade and best freeway access:

The quarter-acre **Hardy Dog Park,** in Oakland

Reason Hardy Dog Park has the most shade and best freeway access:

It's under the freeway.

Number of feet of water Roseville's dog park is under during winter:

3

Dog-to-duck ratio of Roseville dog park users in winter:

0:1,000

Harmony:

Dog-loving town where a Beverly Hills businessman wants to build a Kosher slaughterhouse in the name of peace